KAMEN RIDER

50TH ANNIVERSARY EDITION

story & art by
SHOTARO ISHINOMORI

Translation by
KUMAR SIVASUBRAMANIAN

◀ CONTENTS ▶

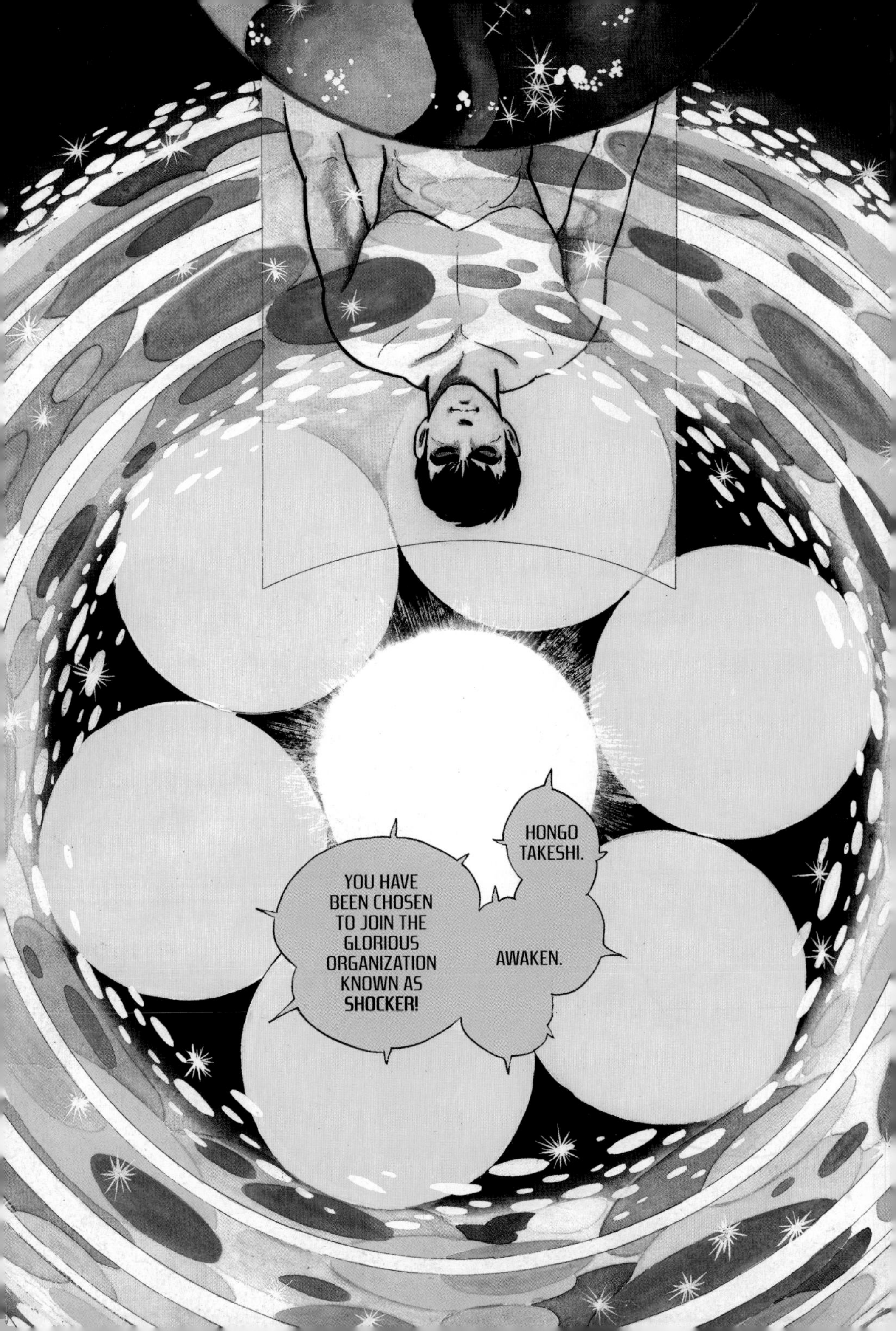
HONGO TAKESHI.
AWAKEN.
YOU HAVE BEEN CHOSEN TO JOIN THE GLORIOUS ORGANIZATION KNOWN AS SHOCKER!

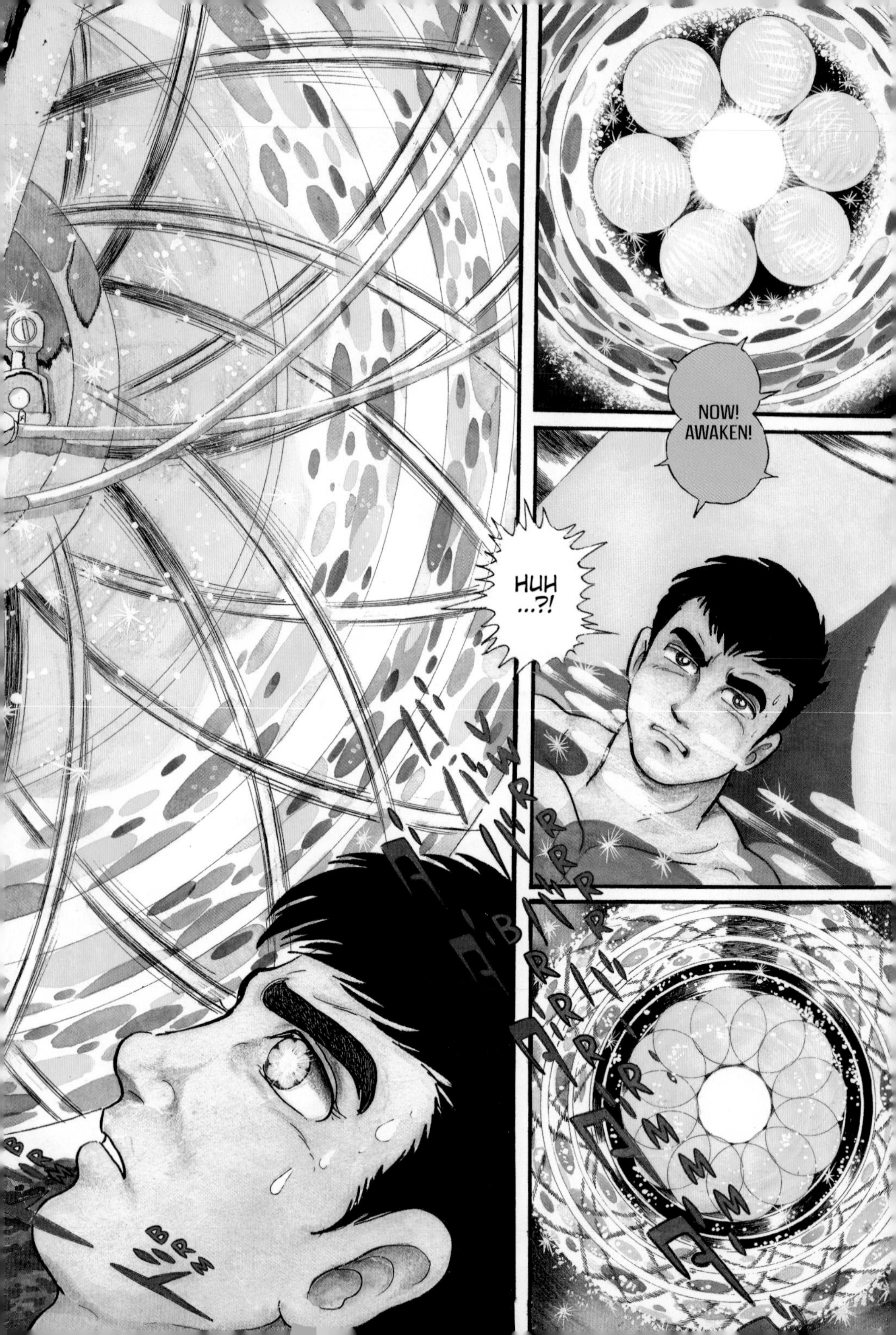
NOW! AWAKEN!
HUH ...?!
VWRRRRRR
BRRRRRMMMM
BRRM
BRRM

PART 1: The Uncanny Man-Spider

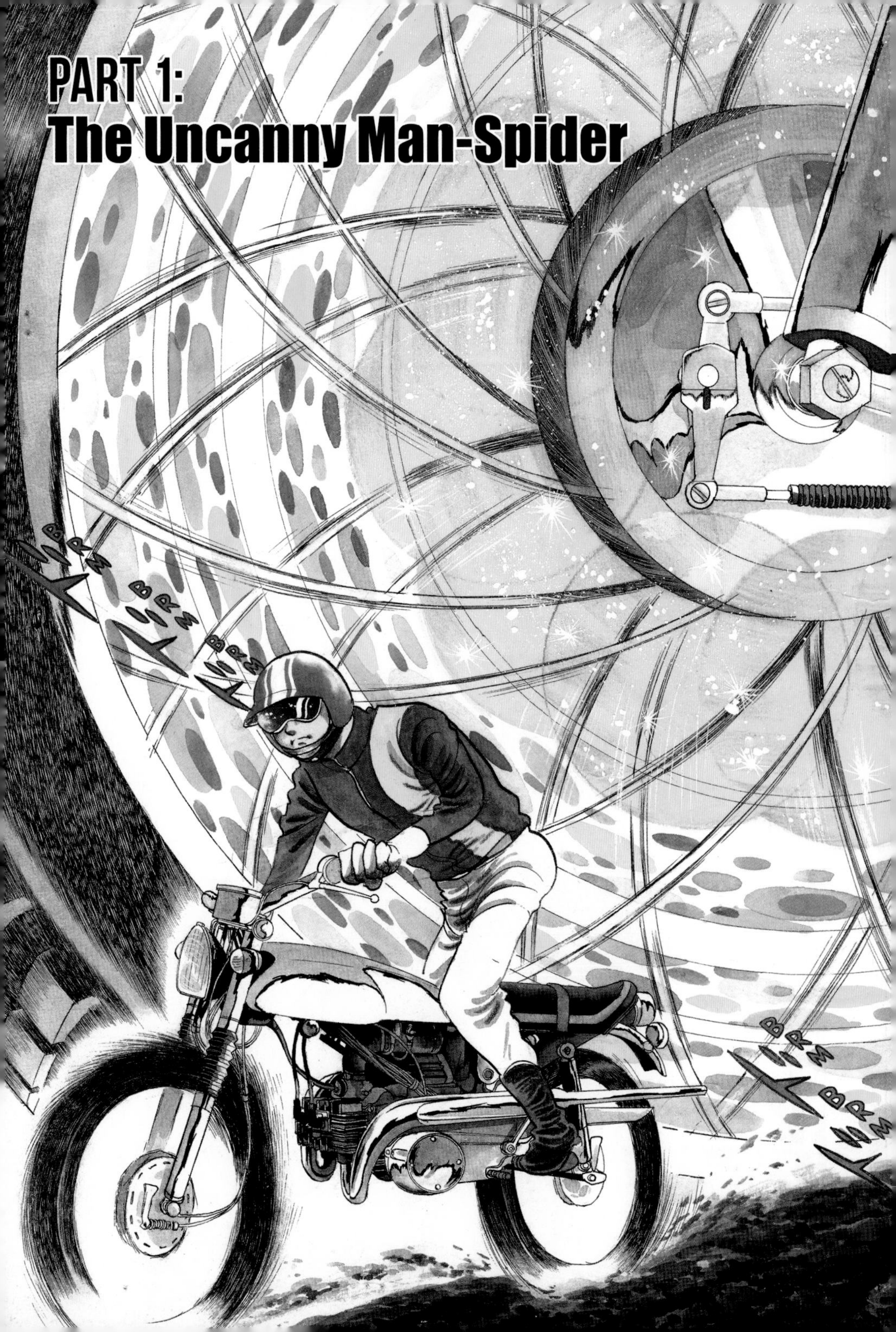
BRRM
BRRM
BRRM
BRRM
BRRM

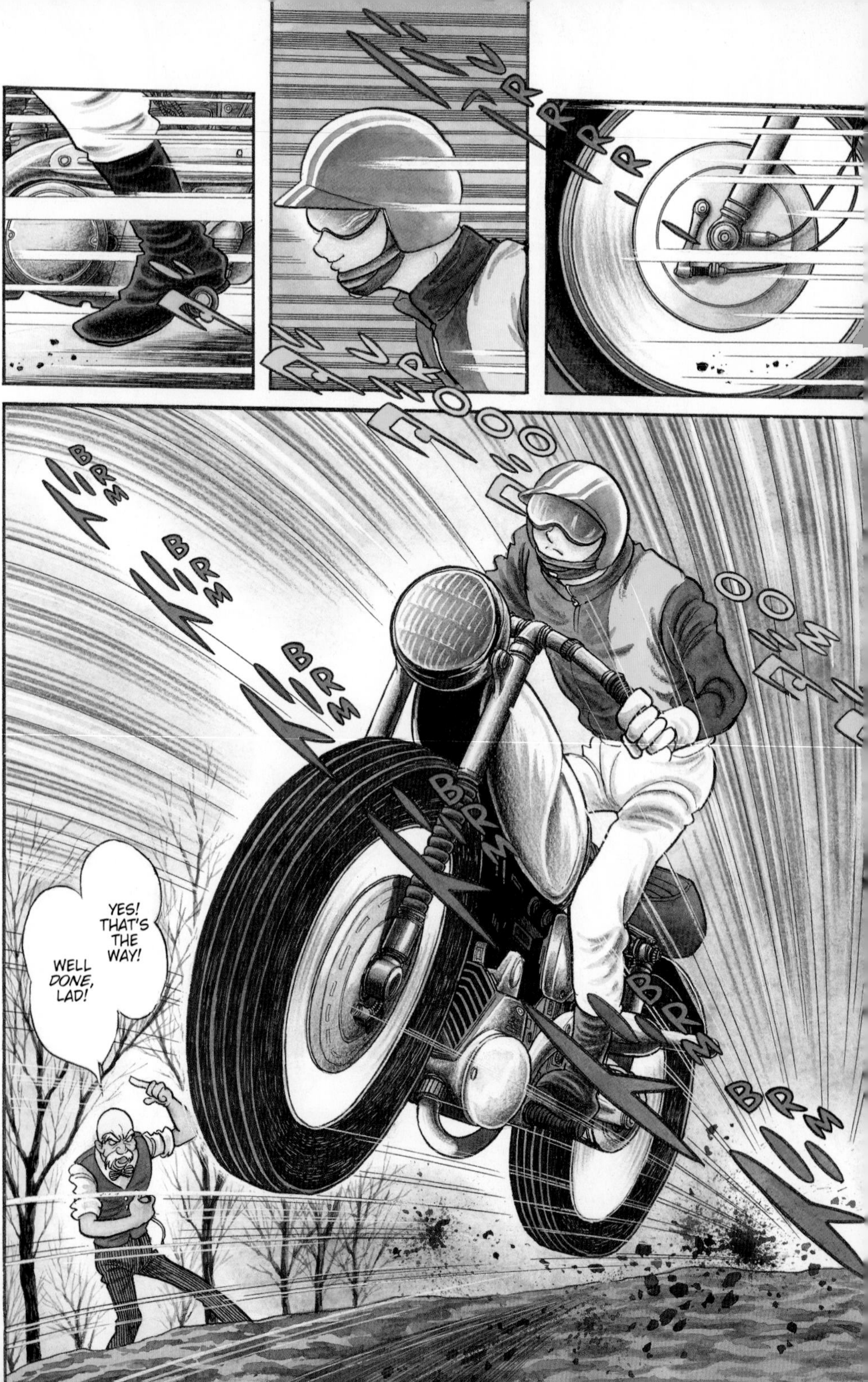
VRRRR
VROOOO
BRRM
BRRM
BRRM
OOM
BRRM
BRRM
BRRM
YES! THAT'S THE WAY!
WELL DONE, LAD!

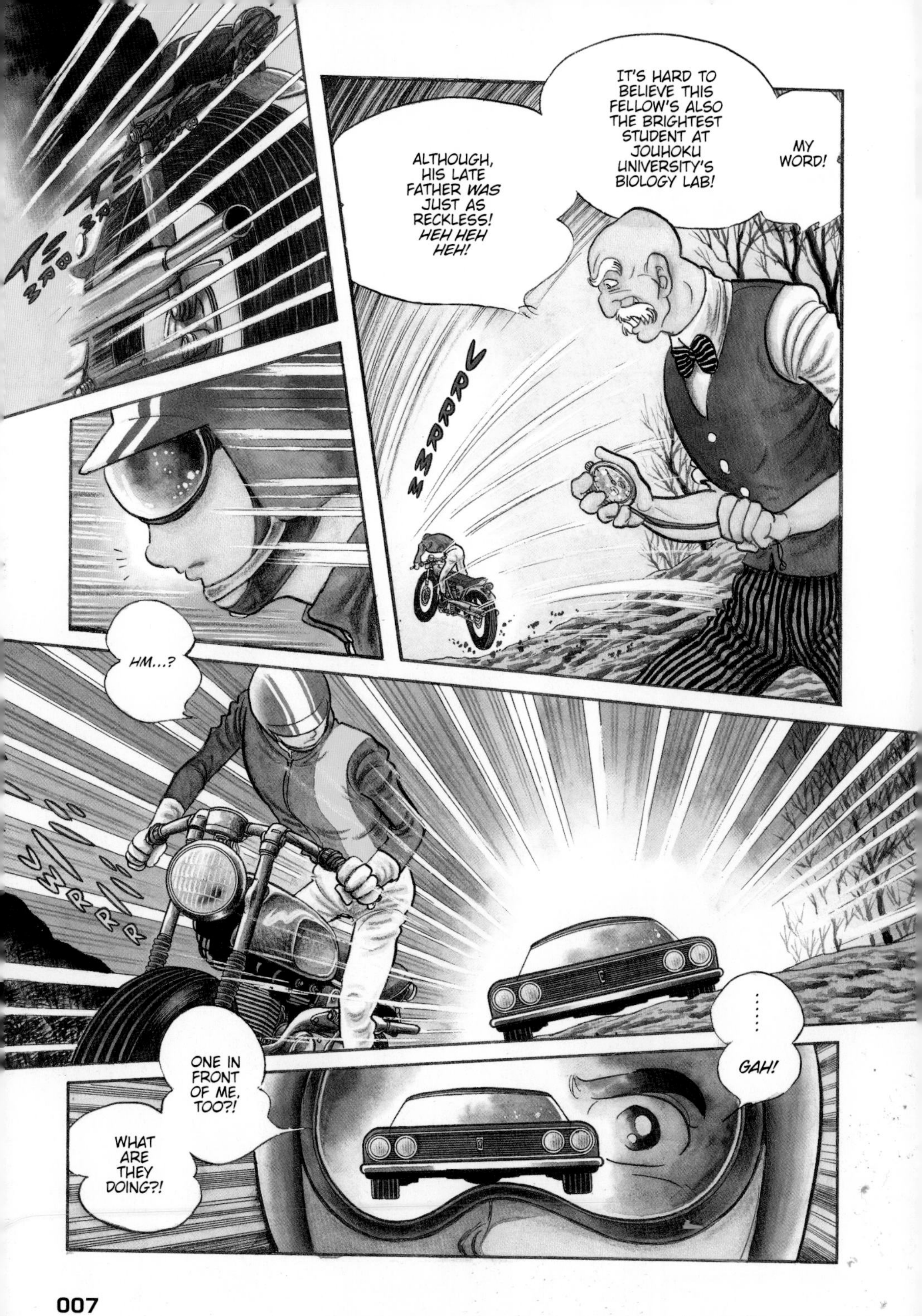
MY WORD!
IT'S HARD TO BELIEVE THIS FELLOW'S ALSO THE BRIGHTEST STUDENT AT JOUHOKU UNIVERSITY'S BIOLOGY LAB!
ALTHOUGH, HIS LATE FATHER *WAS* JUST AS RECKLESS! *HEH HEH HEH!*
VRRRRMMM
......
HM...?
GAH!
ONE IN FRONT OF ME, TOO?!
WHAT ARE THEY DOING?!

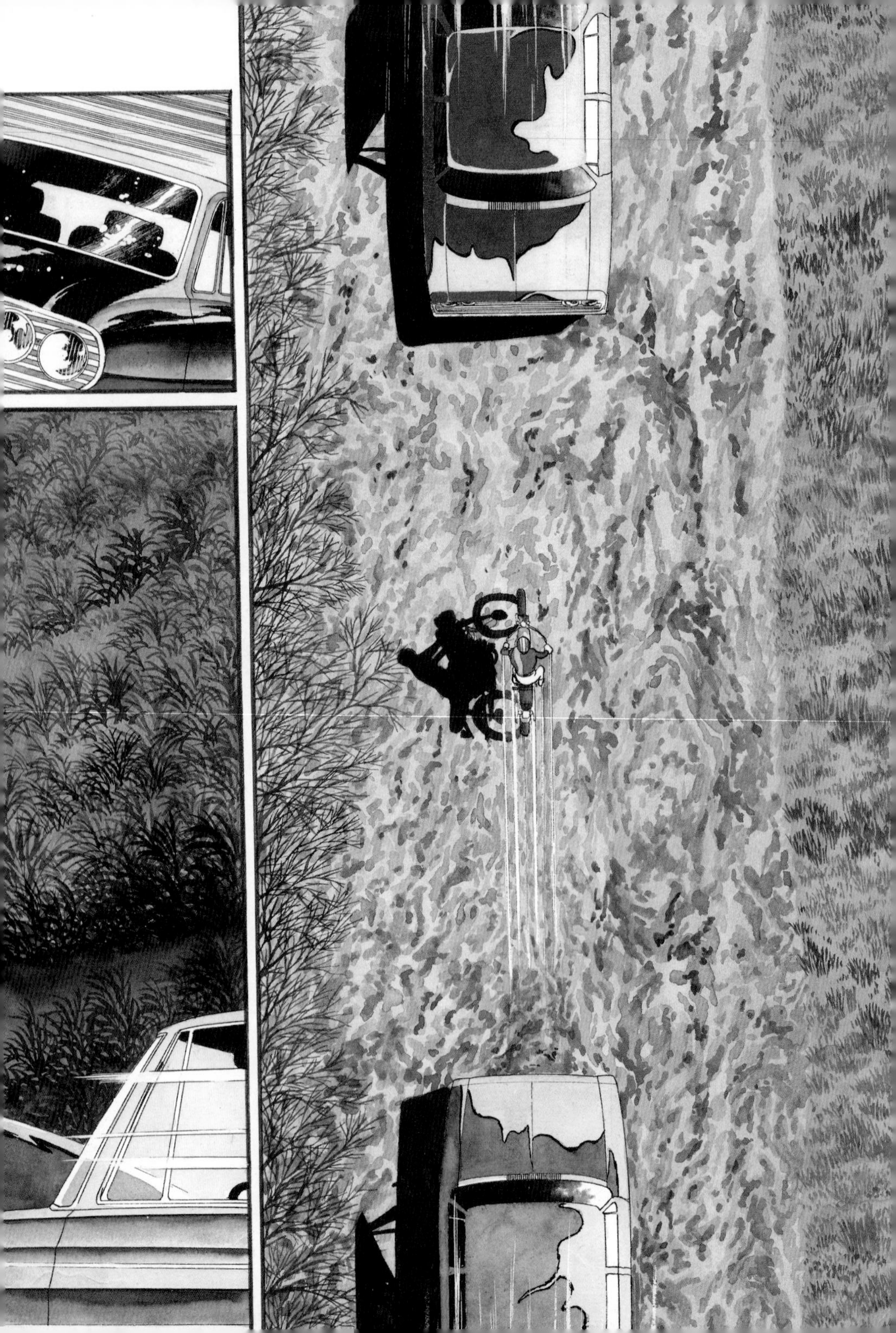

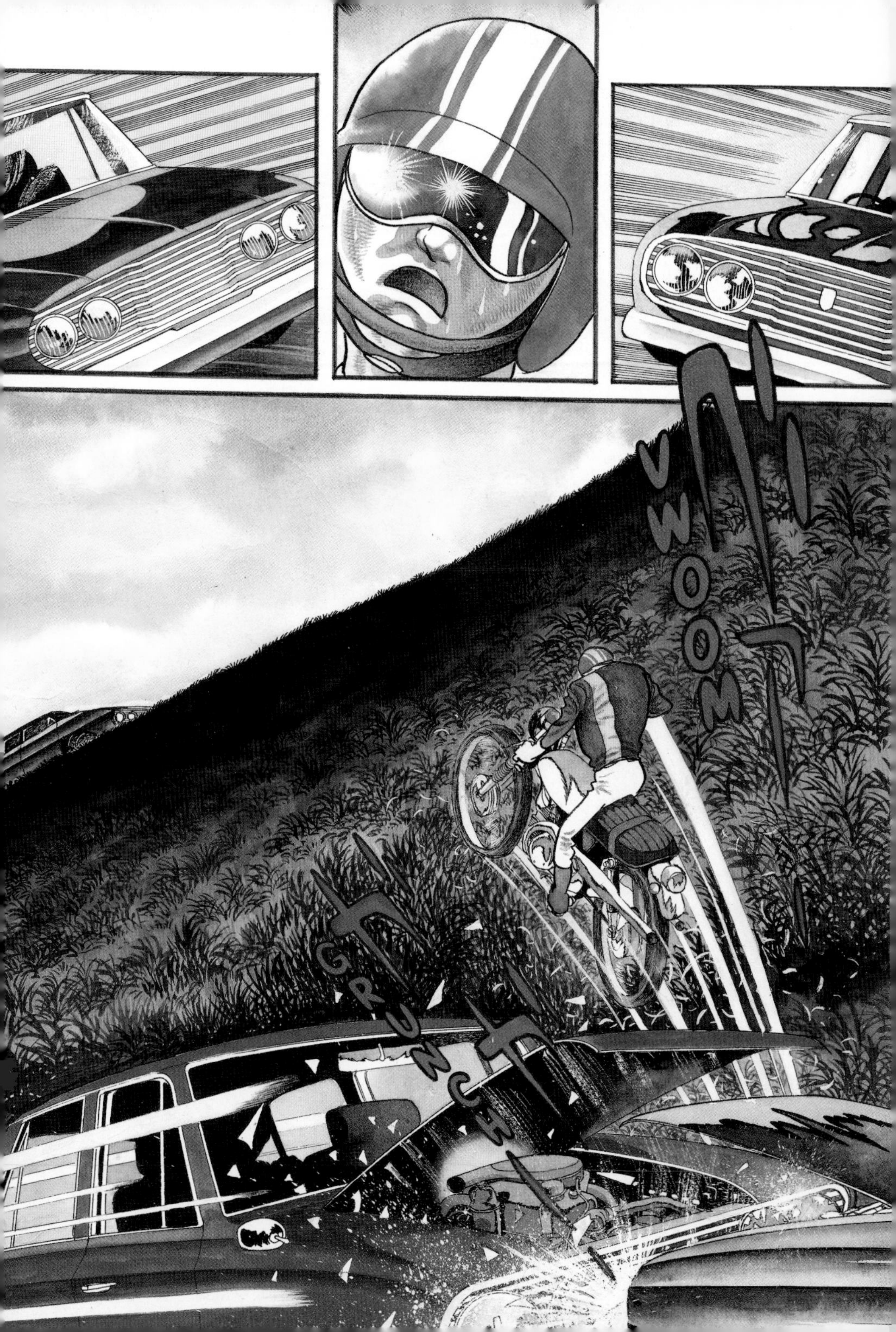
VWOOM
GRUNCH

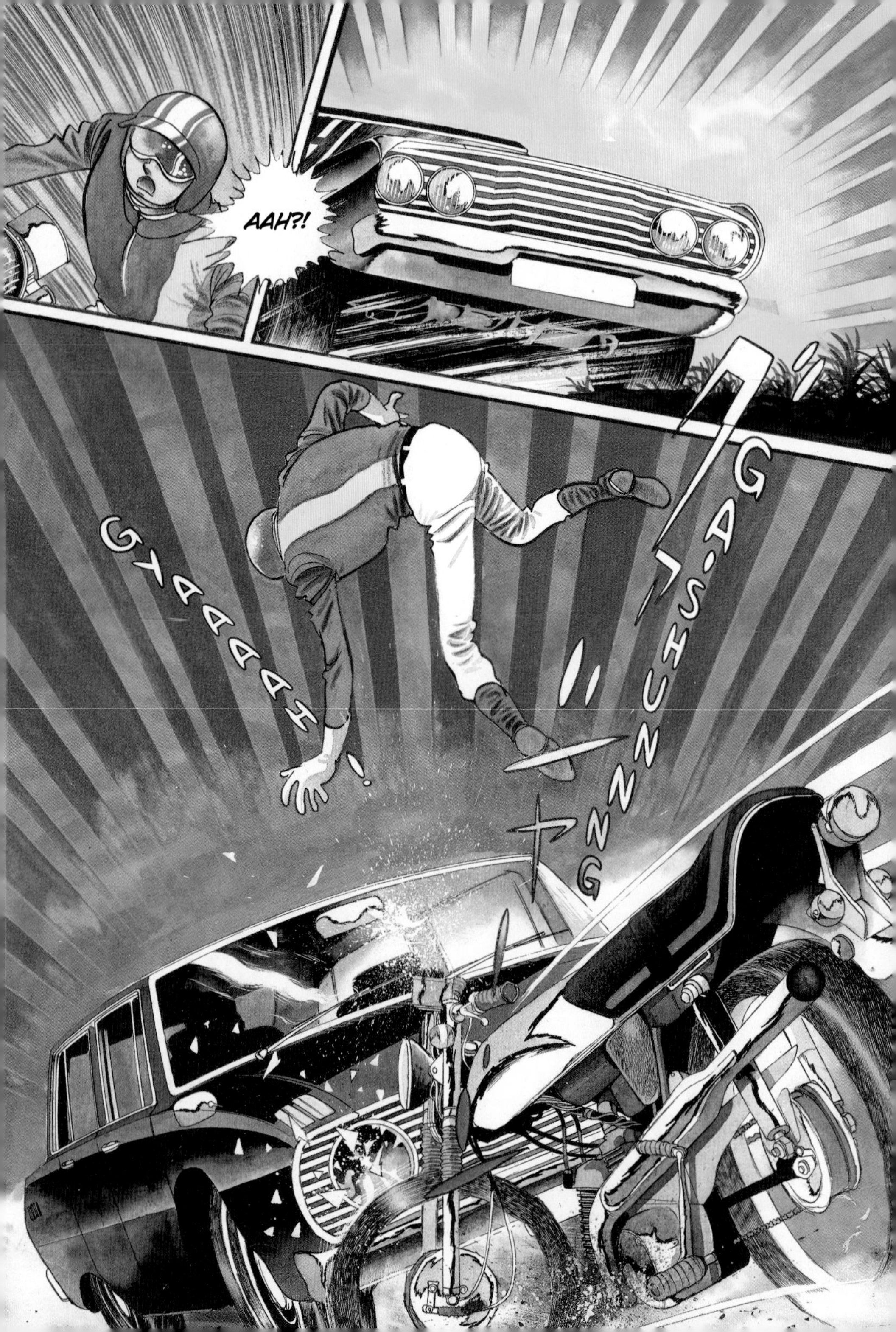
AAH?!
GA-SHUNNNNG
GYAAAAH!

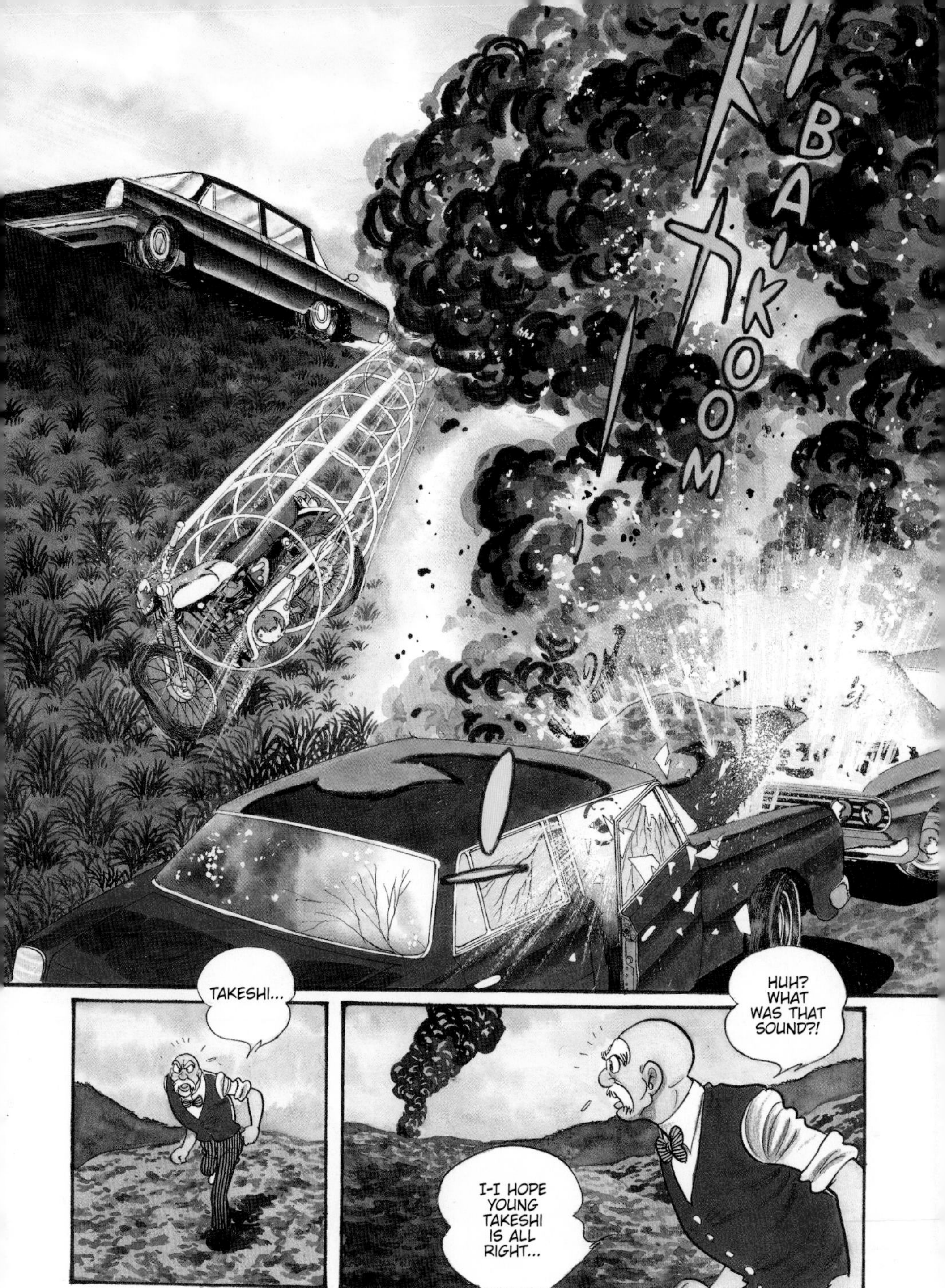
BA-KOOOM
HUH? WHAT WAS THAT SOUND?!
I-I HOPE YOUNG TAKESHI IS ALL RIGHT...
TAKESHI...

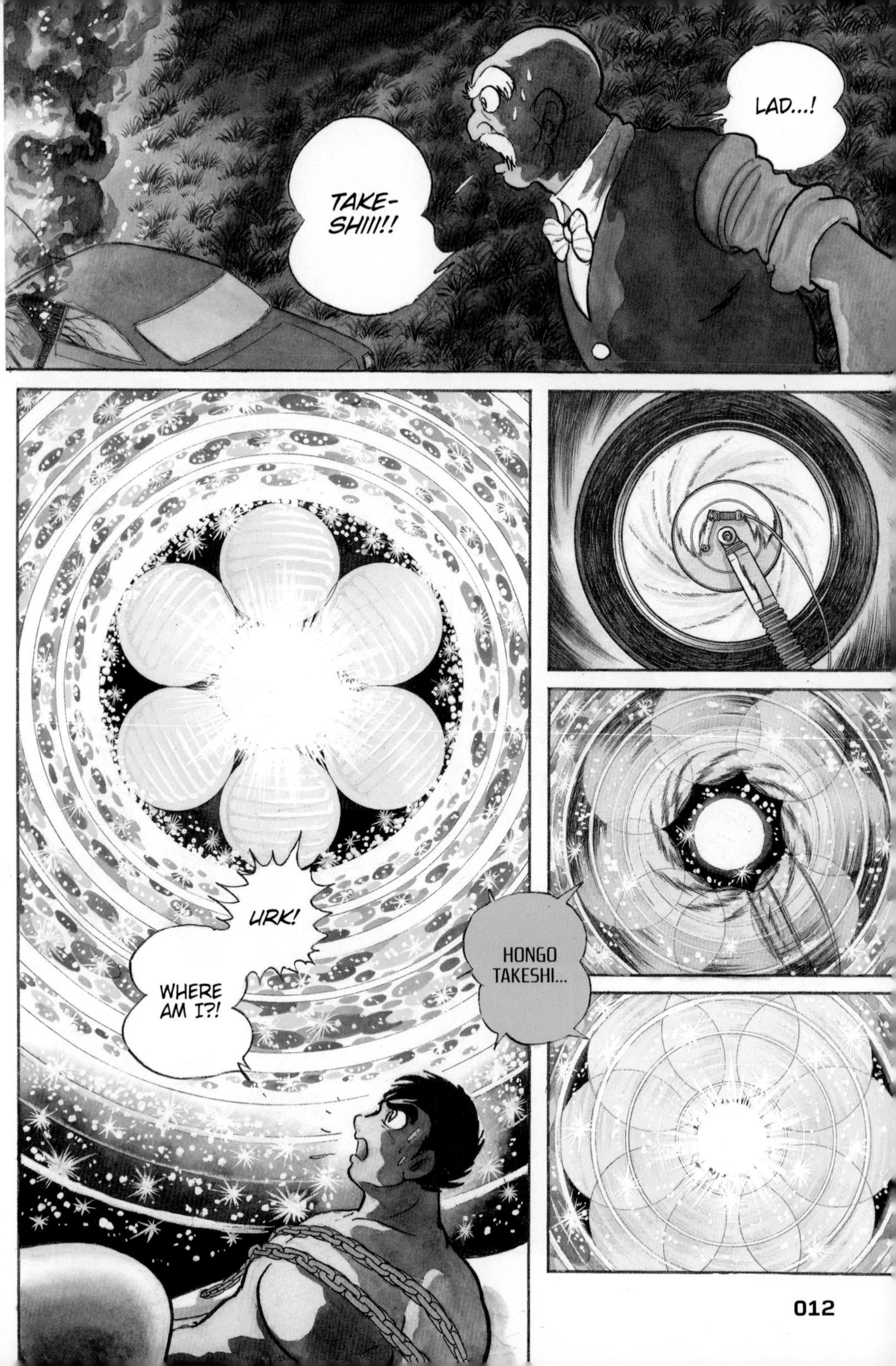
LAD...!
TAKE-SHIIII!!
HONGO TAKESHI...
URK!
WHERE AM I?!

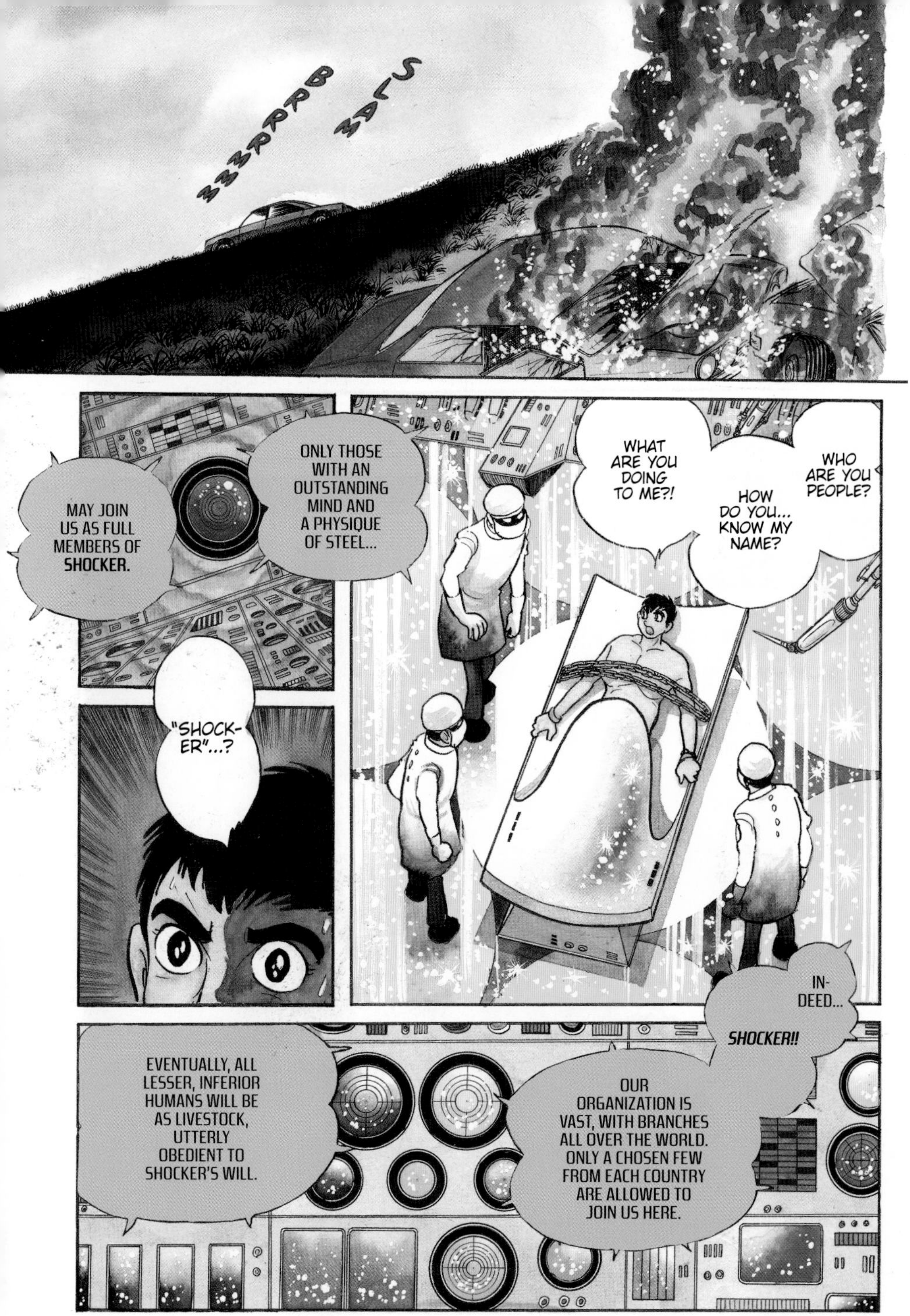
WHO ARE YOU PEOPLE?
WHAT ARE YOU DOING TO ME?!
HOW DO YOU... KNOW MY NAME?
ONLY THOSE WITH AN OUTSTANDING MIND AND A PHYSIQUE OF STEEL...
MAY JOIN US AS FULL MEMBERS OF **SHOCKER.**
"SHOCK-ER"...?
IN-DEED... ***SHOCKER!!***
OUR ORGANIZATION IS VAST, WITH BRANCHES ALL OVER THE WORLD. ONLY A CHOSEN FEW FROM EACH COUNTRY ARE ALLOWED TO JOIN US HERE.
EVENTUALLY, ALL LESSER, INFERIOR HUMANS WILL BE AS LIVESTOCK, UTTERLY OBEDIENT TO SHOCKER'S WILL.

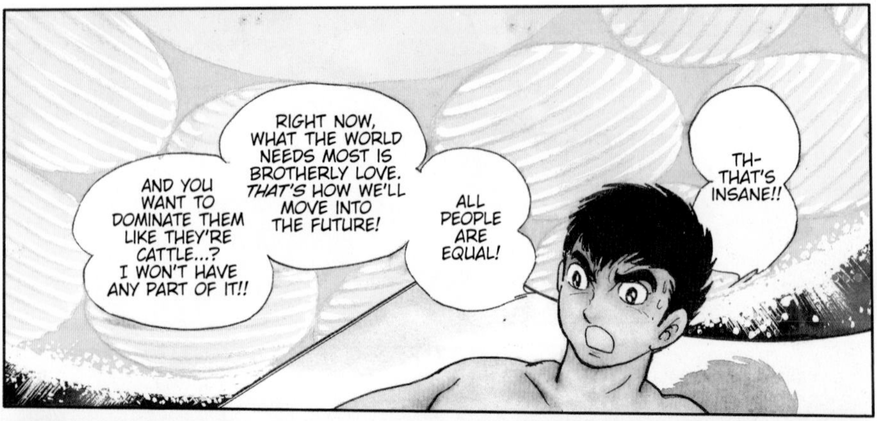
TH- THAT'S INSANE!!
ALL PEOPLE ARE EQUAL!
RIGHT NOW, WHAT THE WORLD NEEDS MOST IS BROTHERLY LOVE. *THAT'S* HOW WE'LL MOVE INTO THE FUTURE!
AND YOU WANT TO DOMINATE THEM LIKE THEY'RE CATTLE...? I WON'T HAVE ANY PART OF IT!!

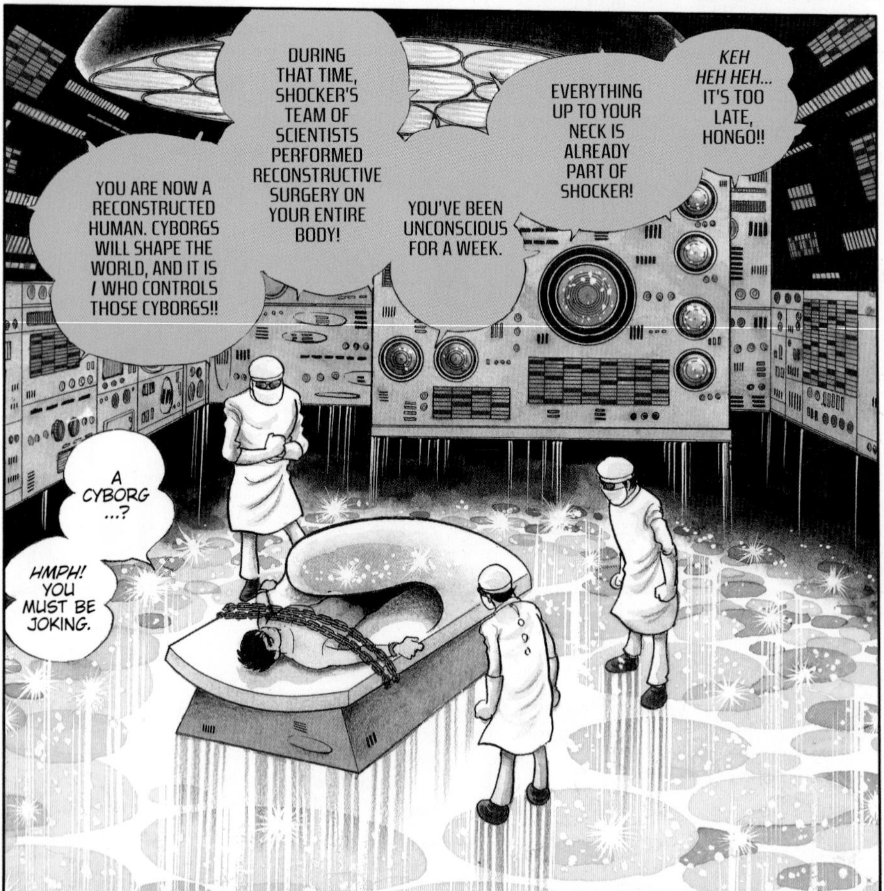
KEH HEH HEH... IT'S TOO LATE, HONGO!!
EVERYTHING UP TO YOUR NECK IS ALREADY PART OF SHOCKER!
YOU'VE BEEN UNCONSCIOUS FOR A WEEK.
DURING THAT TIME, SHOCKER'S TEAM OF SCIENTISTS PERFORMED RECONSTRUCTIVE SURGERY ON YOUR ENTIRE BODY!
YOU ARE NOW A RECONSTRUCTED HUMAN. CYBORGS WILL SHAPE THE WORLD, AND IT IS *I* WHO CONTROLS THOSE CYBORGS!!
A CYBORG ...?
HMPH! YOU MUST BE JOKING.

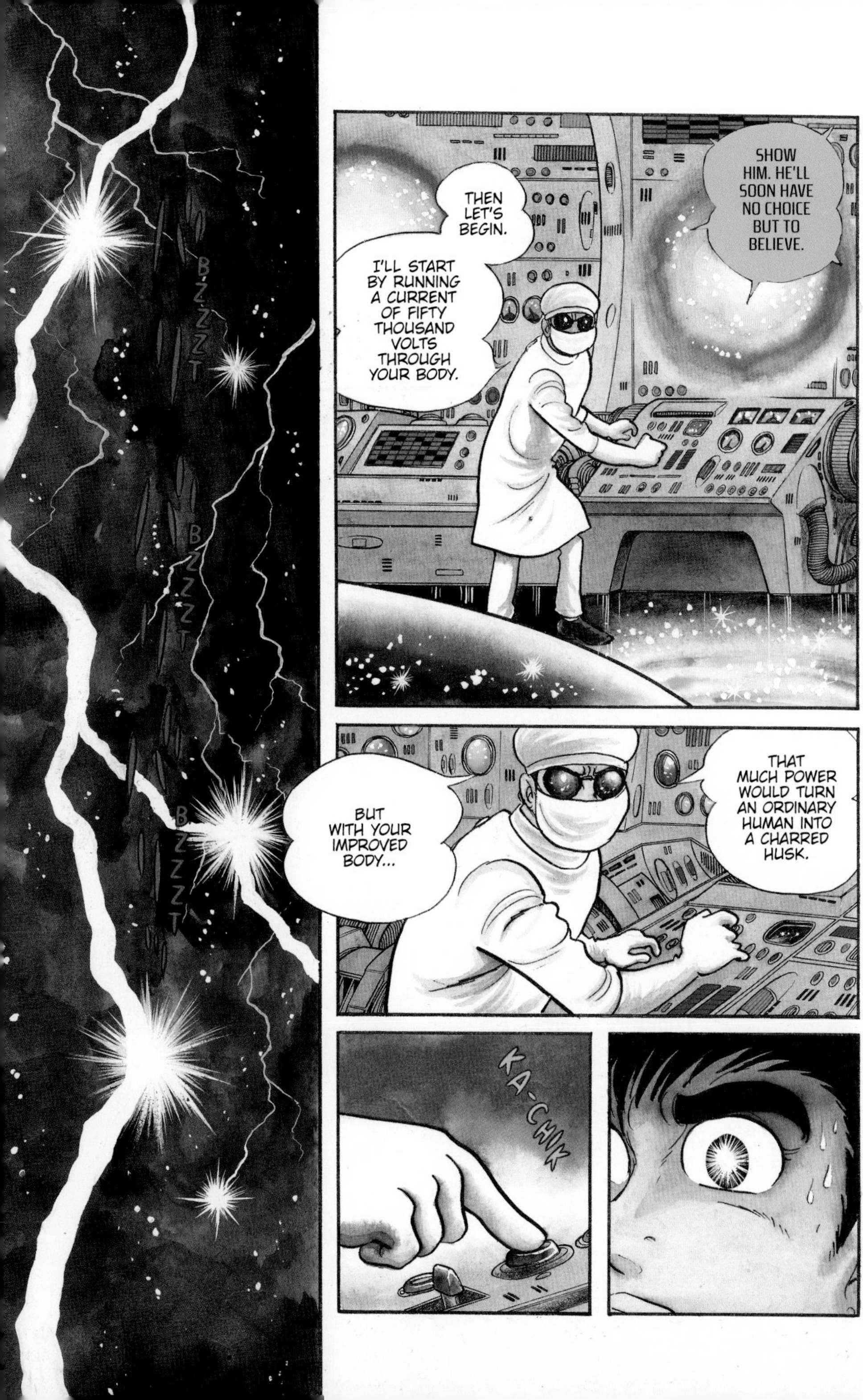
SHOW HIM. HE'LL SOON HAVE NO CHOICE BUT TO BELIEVE.
THEN LET'S BEGIN.
I'LL START BY RUNNING A CURRENT OF FIFTY THOUSAND VOLTS THROUGH YOUR BODY.
THAT MUCH POWER WOULD TURN AN ORDINARY HUMAN INTO A CHARRED HUSK.
BUT WITH YOUR IMPROVED BODY...
KA-CHIK
BZZZT
BZZZT
BZZZT

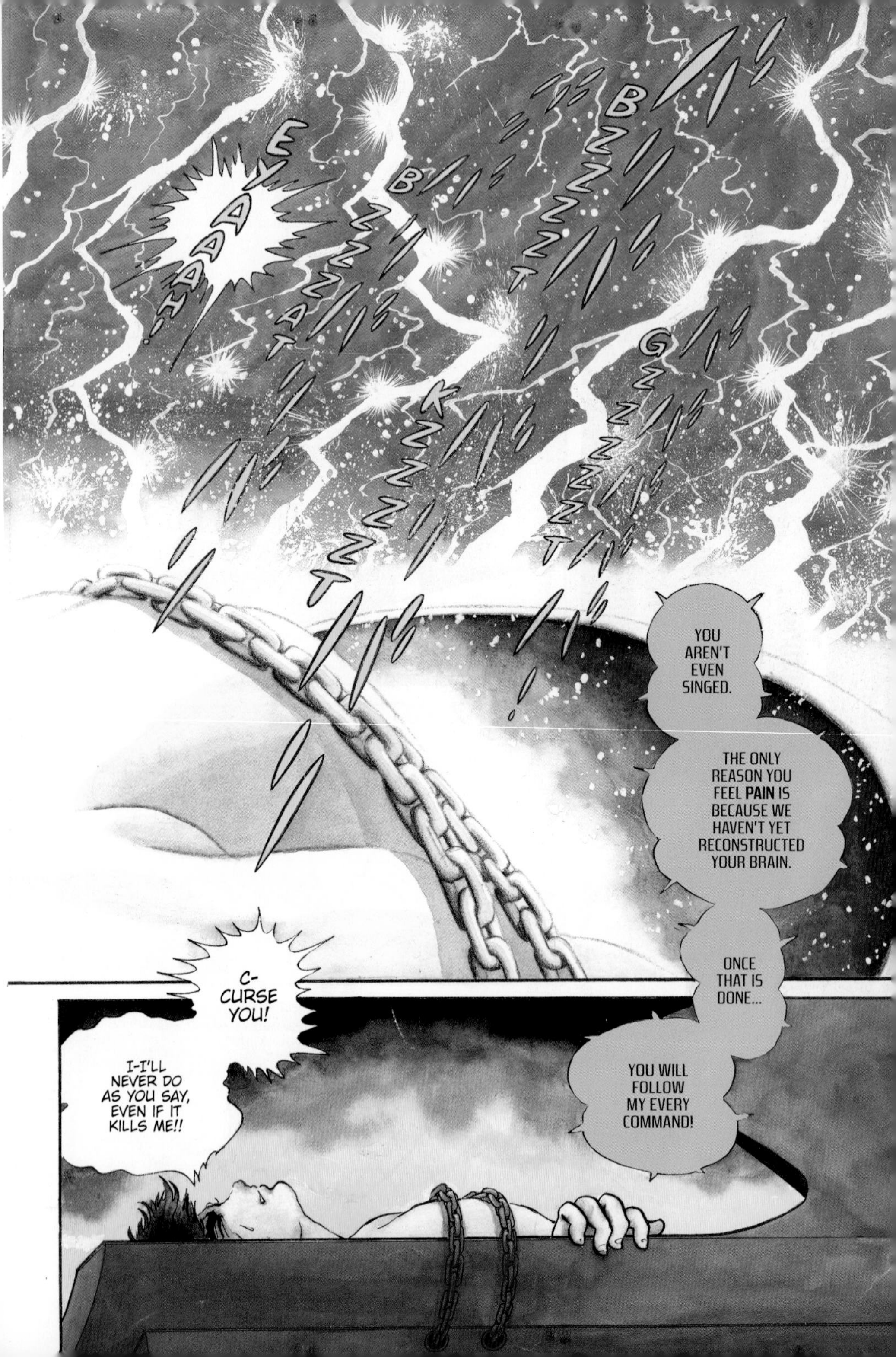
BZZZZZZT
GZZZZZZZT
BZZZZAT
KZZZZZZT
EYAAAH!
YOU AREN'T EVEN SINGED.
THE ONLY REASON YOU FEEL **PAIN** IS BECAUSE WE HAVEN'T YET RECONSTRUCTED YOUR BRAIN.
ONCE THAT IS DONE...
YOU WILL FOLLOW MY EVERY COMMAND!
C-CURSE YOU!
I-I'LL NEVER DO AS YOU SAY, EVEN IF IT KILLS ME!!

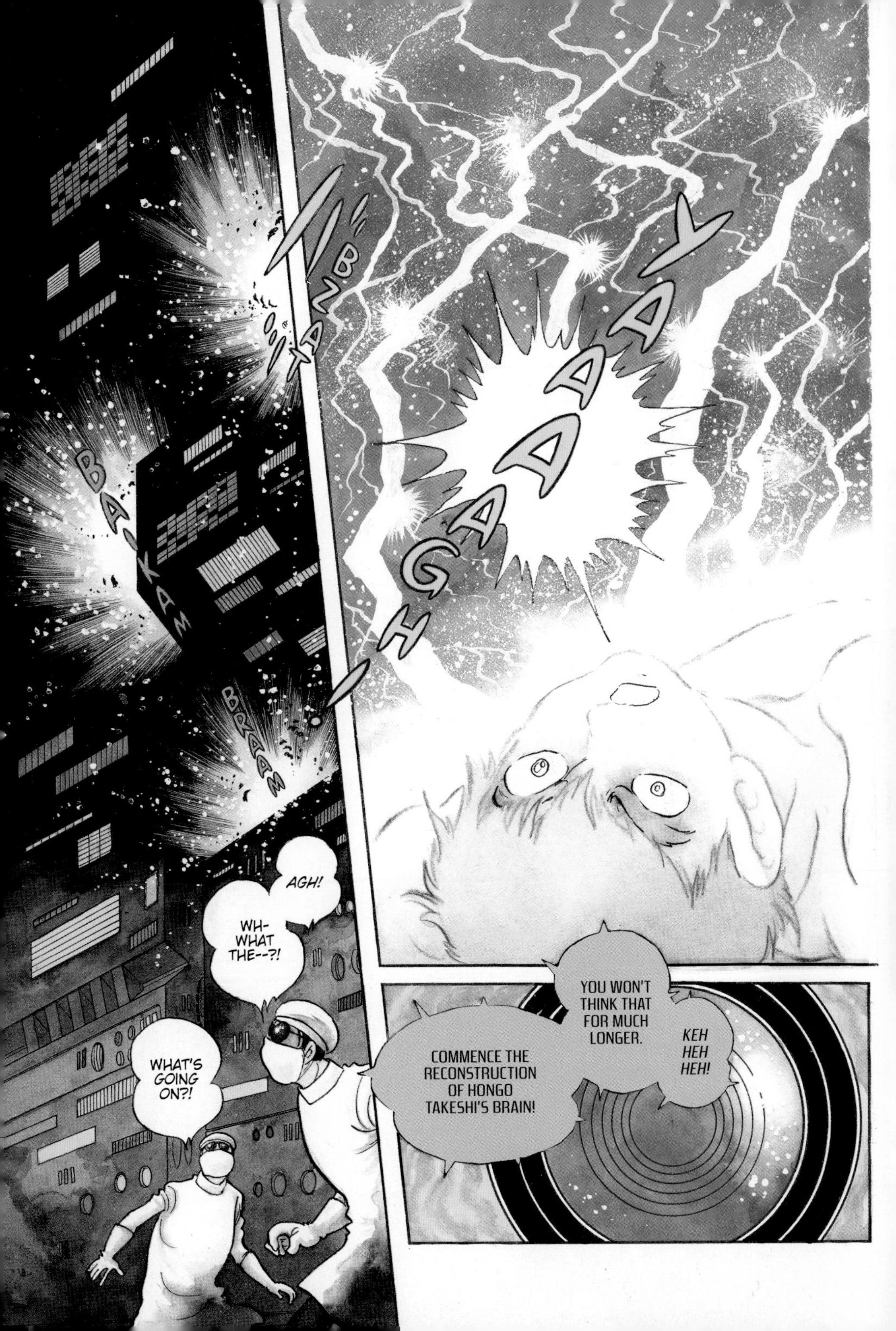
YAAAAGH!
YOU WON'T THINK THAT FOR MUCH LONGER.
KEH HEH HEH!
COMMENCE THE RECONSTRUCTION OF HONGO TAKESHI'S BRAIN!
BZAT
BA-KAM
BRAAM
AGH!
WH-WHAT THE--?!
WHAT'S GOING ON?!

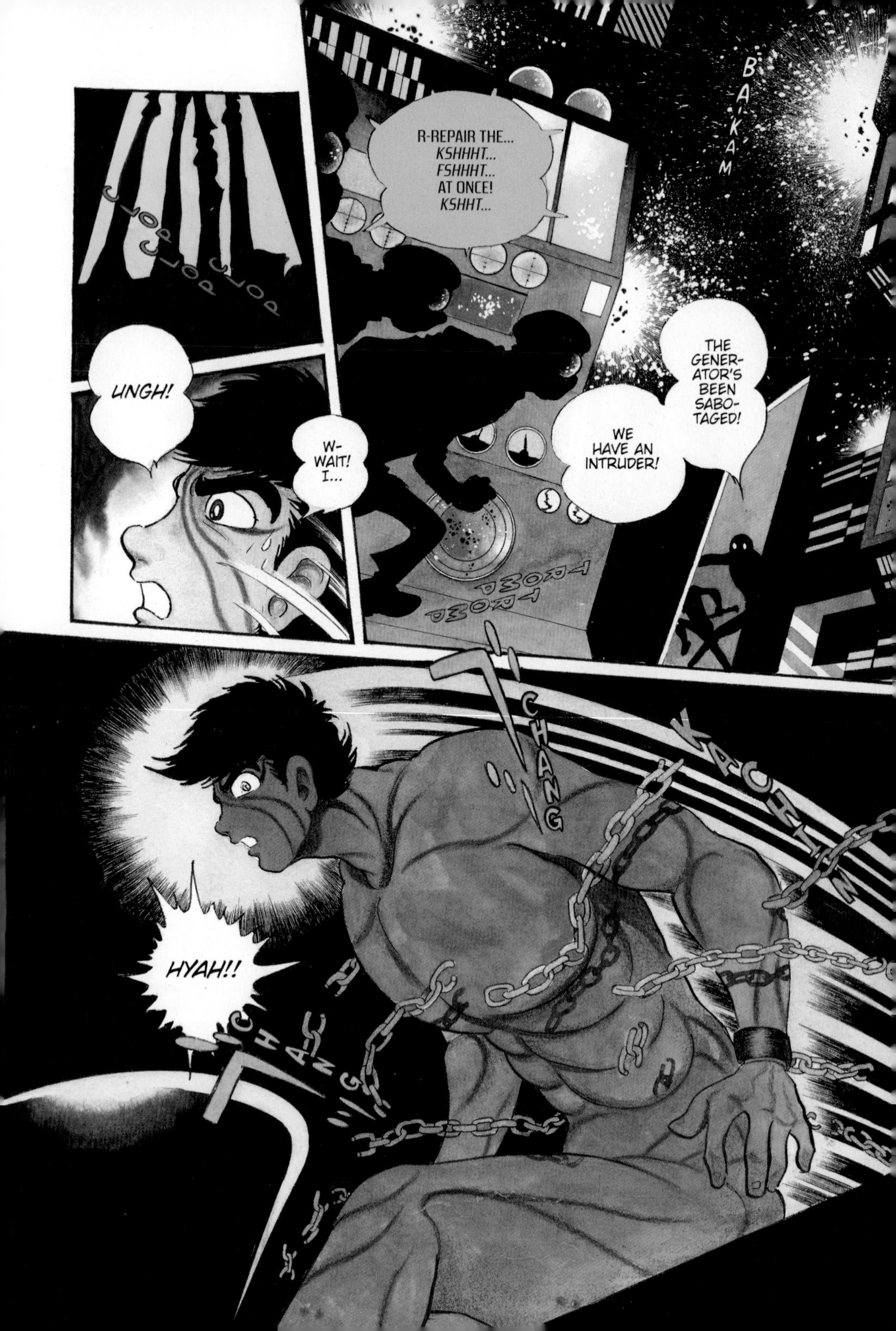
BAKAM
THE GENER-ATOR'S BEEN SABO-TAGED!
WE HAVE AN INTRUDER!
R-REPAIR THE... KSHHHT... FSHHHT... AT ONCE! KSHHT...
TROMP TROMP
CLOP CLOP CLOP
UNGH!
W-WAIT! I...
CHANG
KACHIN
HYAH!!
CHANG

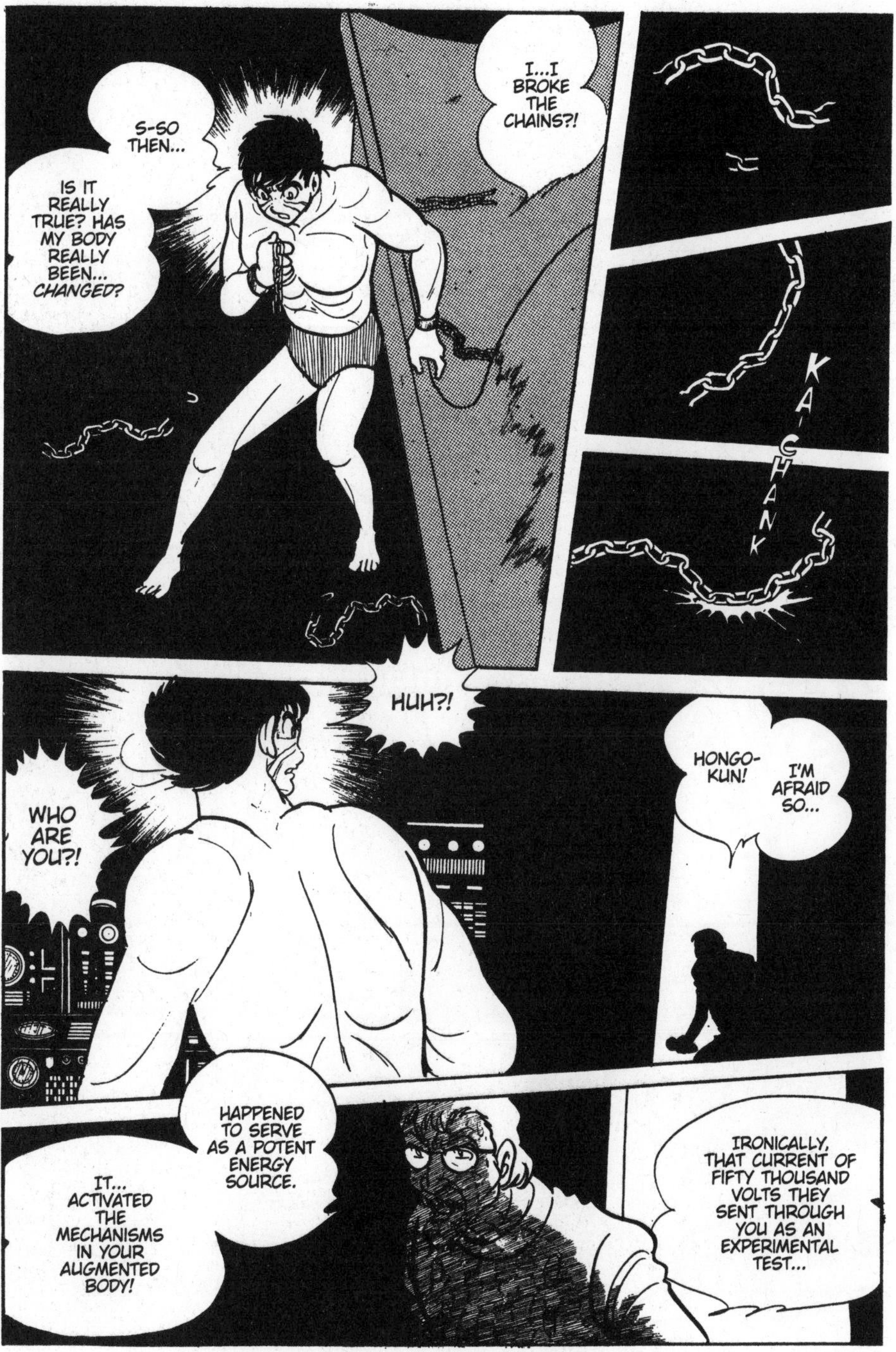
KA-CHANK
I...I BROKE THE CHAINS?!
S-SO THEN...
IS IT REALLY TRUE? HAS MY BODY REALLY BEEN... CHANGED?
HONGO-KUN!
I'M AFRAID SO...
HUH?!
WHO ARE YOU?!
IRONICALLY, THAT CURRENT OF FIFTY THOUSAND VOLTS THEY SENT THROUGH YOU AS AN EXPERIMENTAL TEST...
HAPPENED TO SERVE AS A POTENT ENERGY SOURCE.
IT... ACTIVATED THE MECHANISMS IN YOUR AUGMENTED BODY!

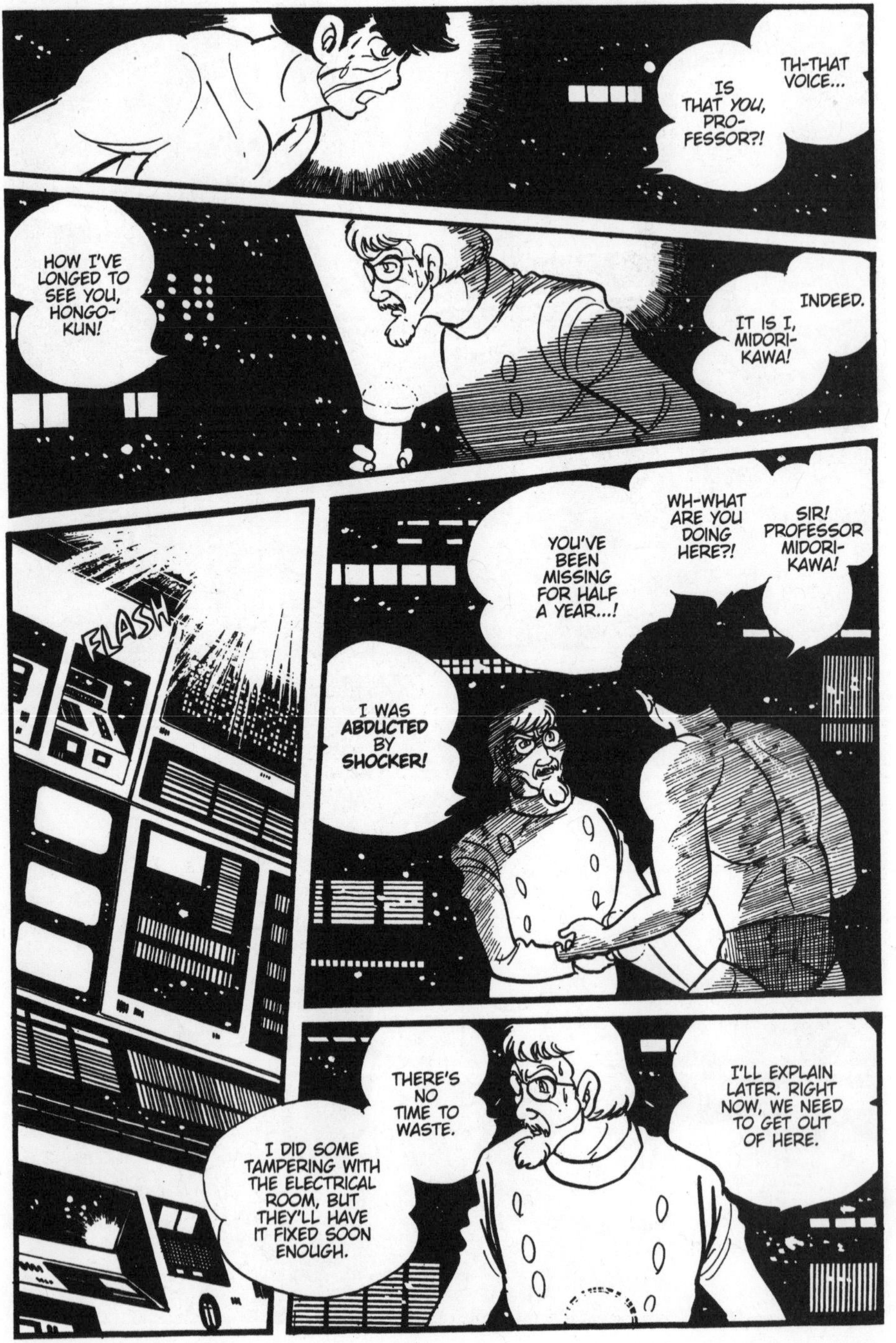
TH-THAT VOICE... IS THAT *YOU*, PRO-FESSOR?!
INDEED. IT IS I, MIDORI-KAWA!
HOW I'VE LONGED TO SEE YOU, HONGO-KUN!
SIR! PROFESSOR MIDORI-KAWA! WH-WHAT ARE YOU DOING HERE?! YOU'VE BEEN MISSING FOR HALF A YEAR...!
I WAS **ABDUCTED** BY **SHOCKER!**
I'LL EXPLAIN LATER. RIGHT NOW, WE NEED TO GET OUT OF HERE.
THERE'S NO TIME TO WASTE.
I DID SOME TAMPERING WITH THE ELECTRICAL ROOM, BUT THEY'LL HAVE IT FIXED SOON ENOUGH.
FLASH

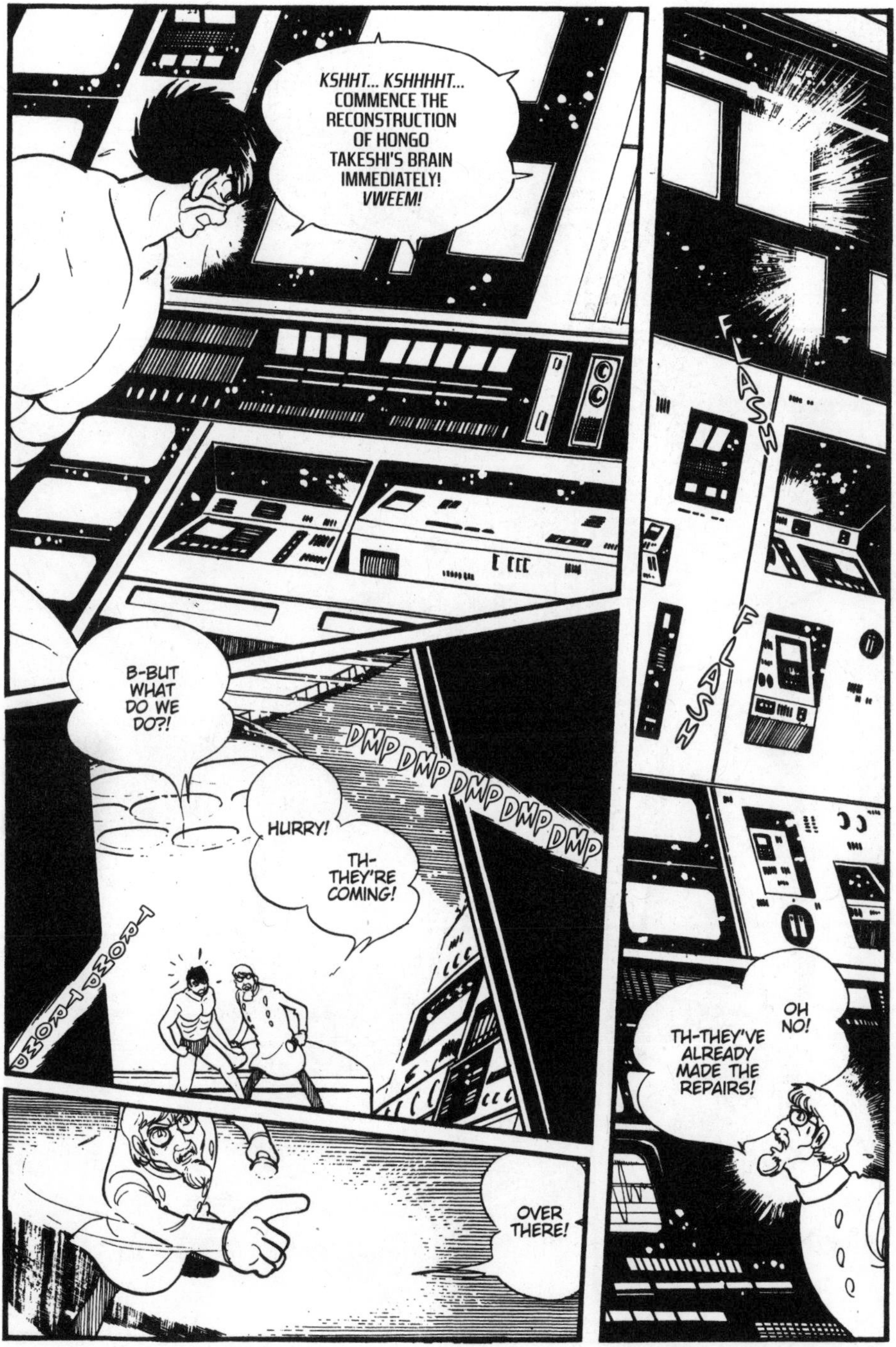
FLASH
FLASH
KSHHT... KSHHHHT... COMMENCE THE RECONSTRUCTION OF HONGO TAKESHI'S BRAIN IMMEDIATELY! VWEEM!
B-BUT WHAT DO WE DO?!
HURRY!
TH- THEY'RE COMING!
DMP DMP DMP DMP DMP
TROMP-TROMP
OH NO!
TH-THEY'VE ALREADY MADE THE REPAIRS!
OVER THERE!

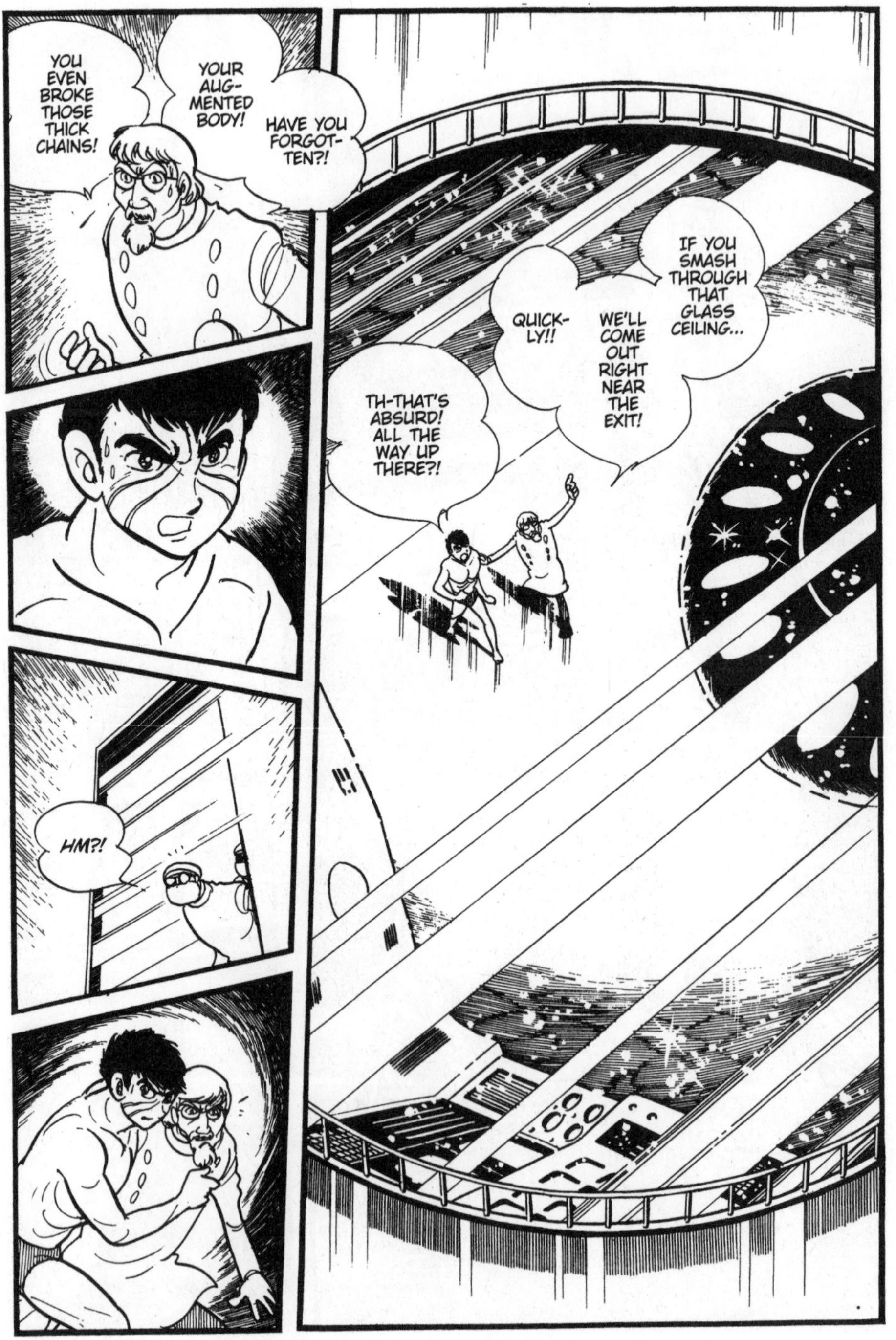
IF YOU SMASH THROUGH THAT GLASS CEILING...
WE'LL COME OUT RIGHT NEAR THE EXIT!
QUICKLY!!
TH-THAT'S ABSURD! ALL THE WAY UP THERE?!
HAVE YOU FORGOTTEN?!
YOUR AUGMENTED BODY!
YOU EVEN BROKE THOSE THICK CHAINS!
HM?!

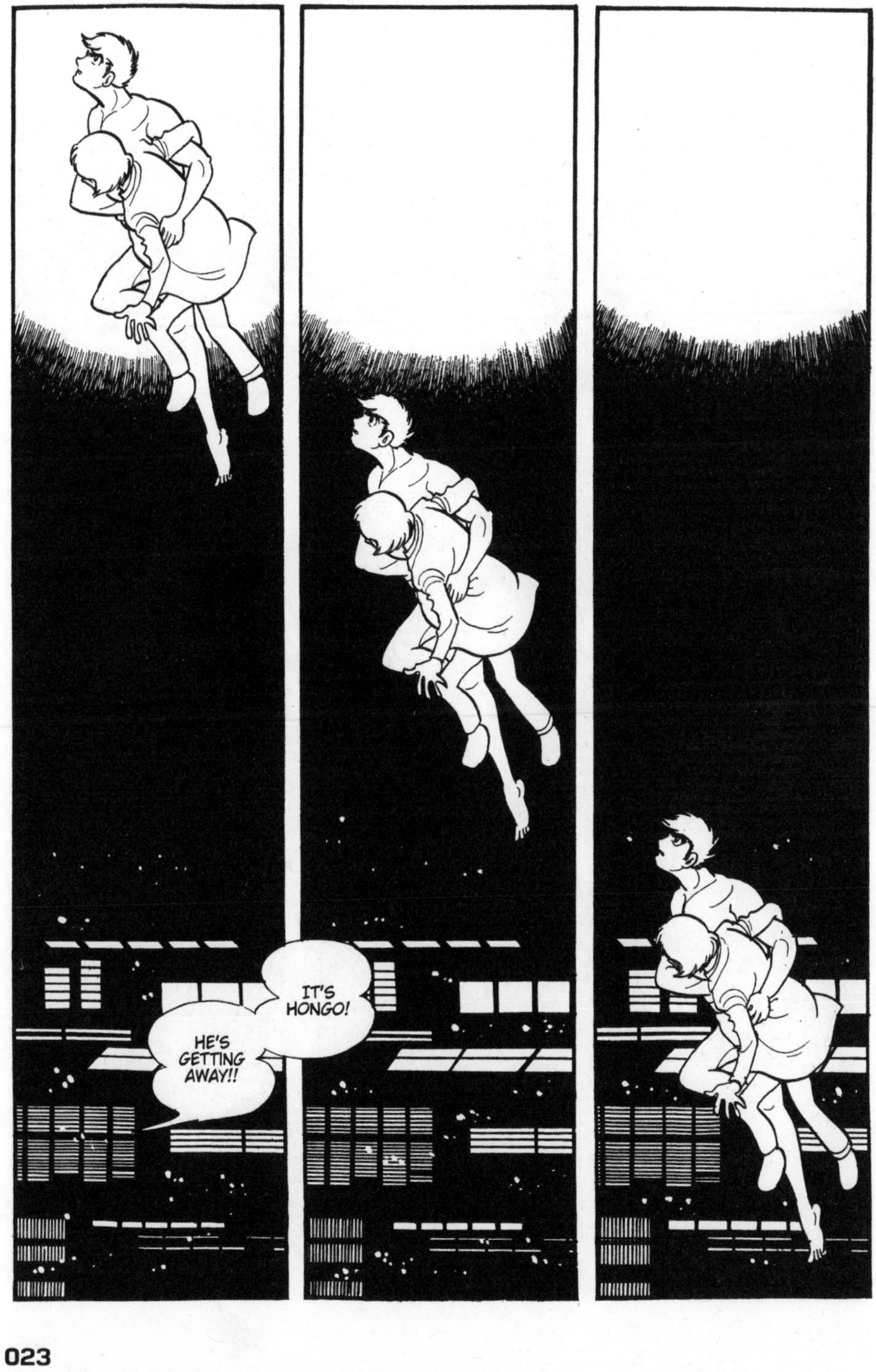
IT'S HONGO!
HE'S GETTING AWAY!!

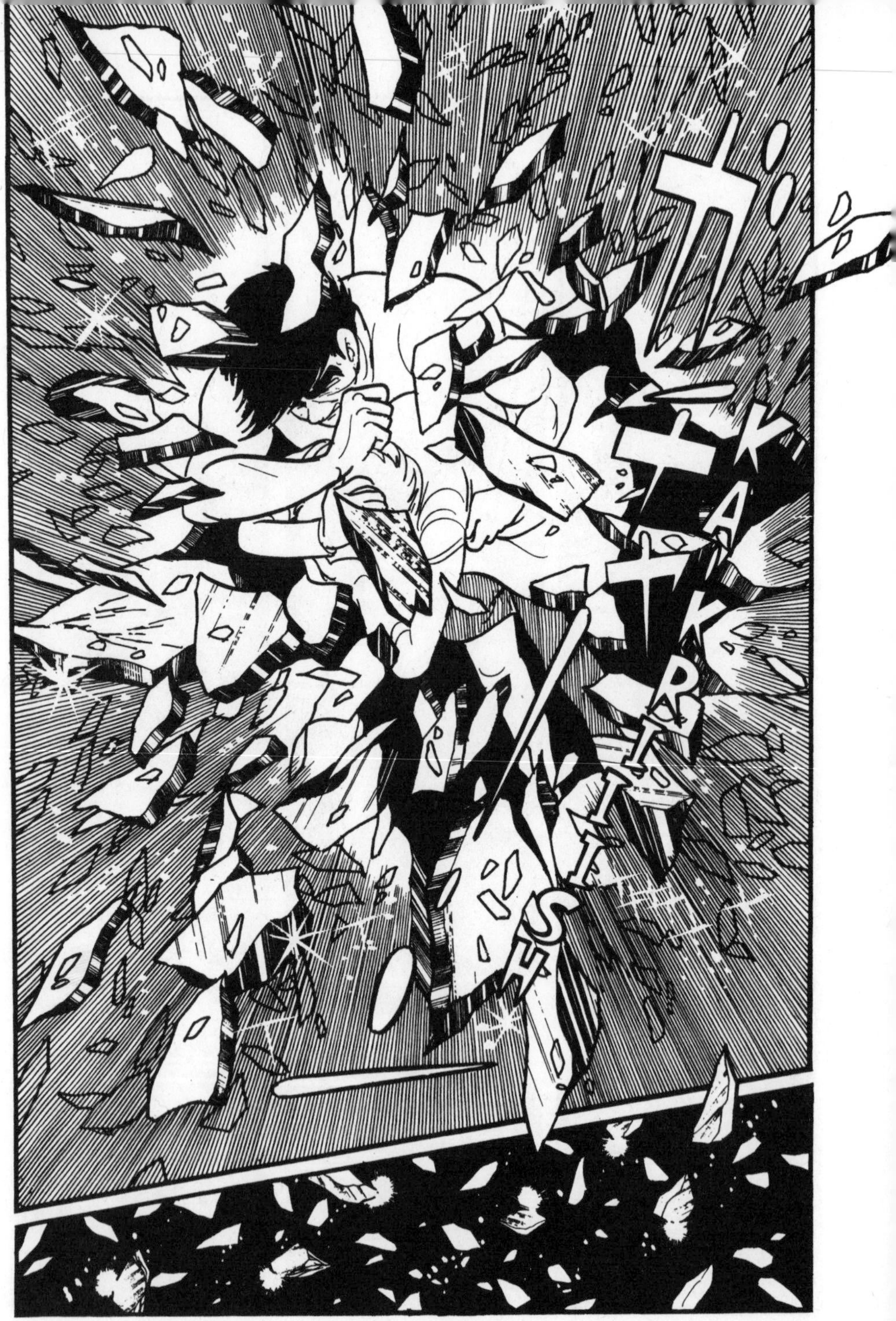
KAKRIIISH

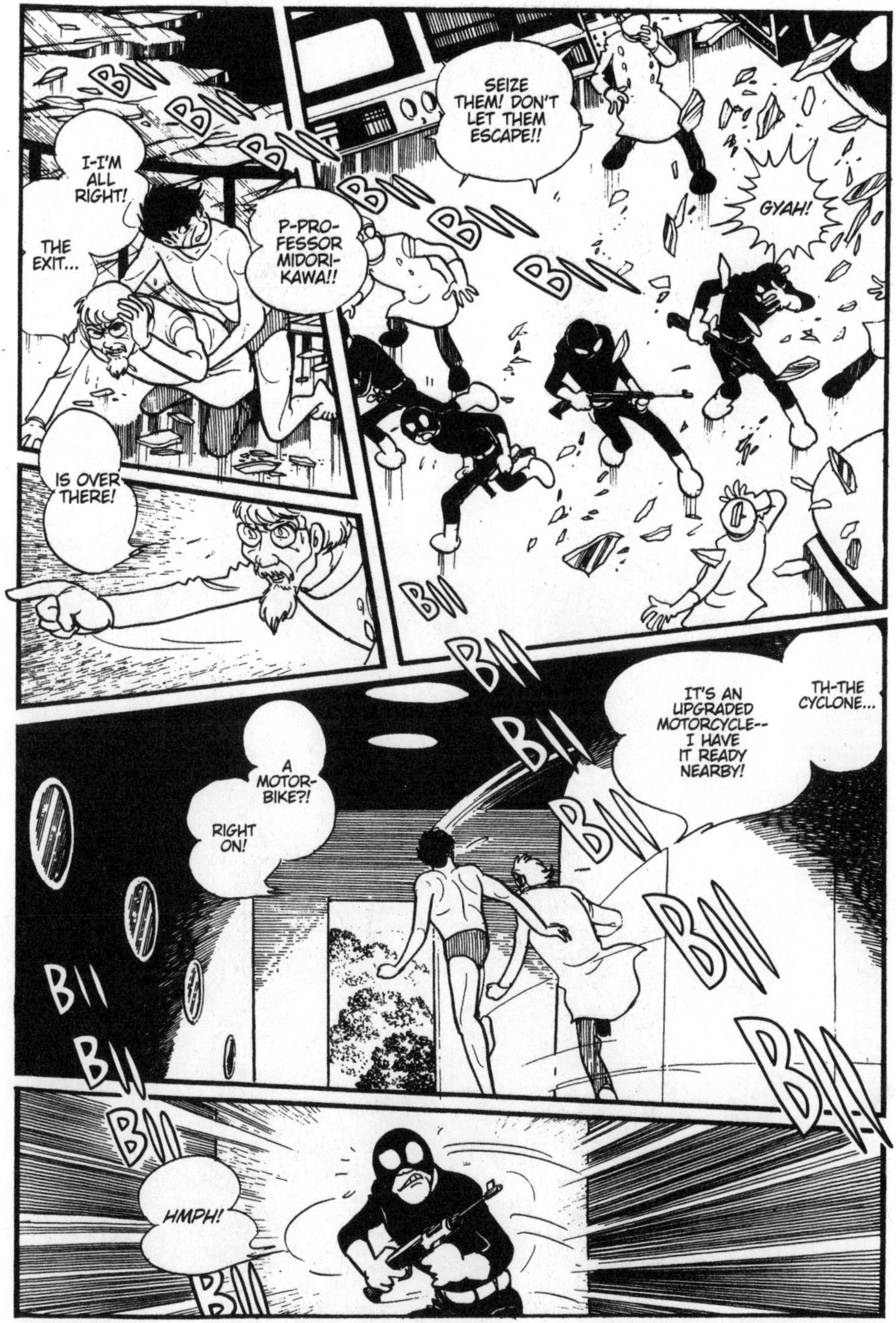
SEIZE THEM! DON'T LET THEM ESCAPE!!
GYAH!
BII
BII
BII
P-PROFESSOR MIDORIKAWA!!
I-I'M ALL RIGHT!
THE EXIT...
IS OVER THERE!
TH-THE CYCLONE...
IT'S AN UPGRADED MOTORCYCLE-- I HAVE IT READY NEARBY!
A MOTORBIKE?!
RIGHT ON!
BIIII
HMPH!

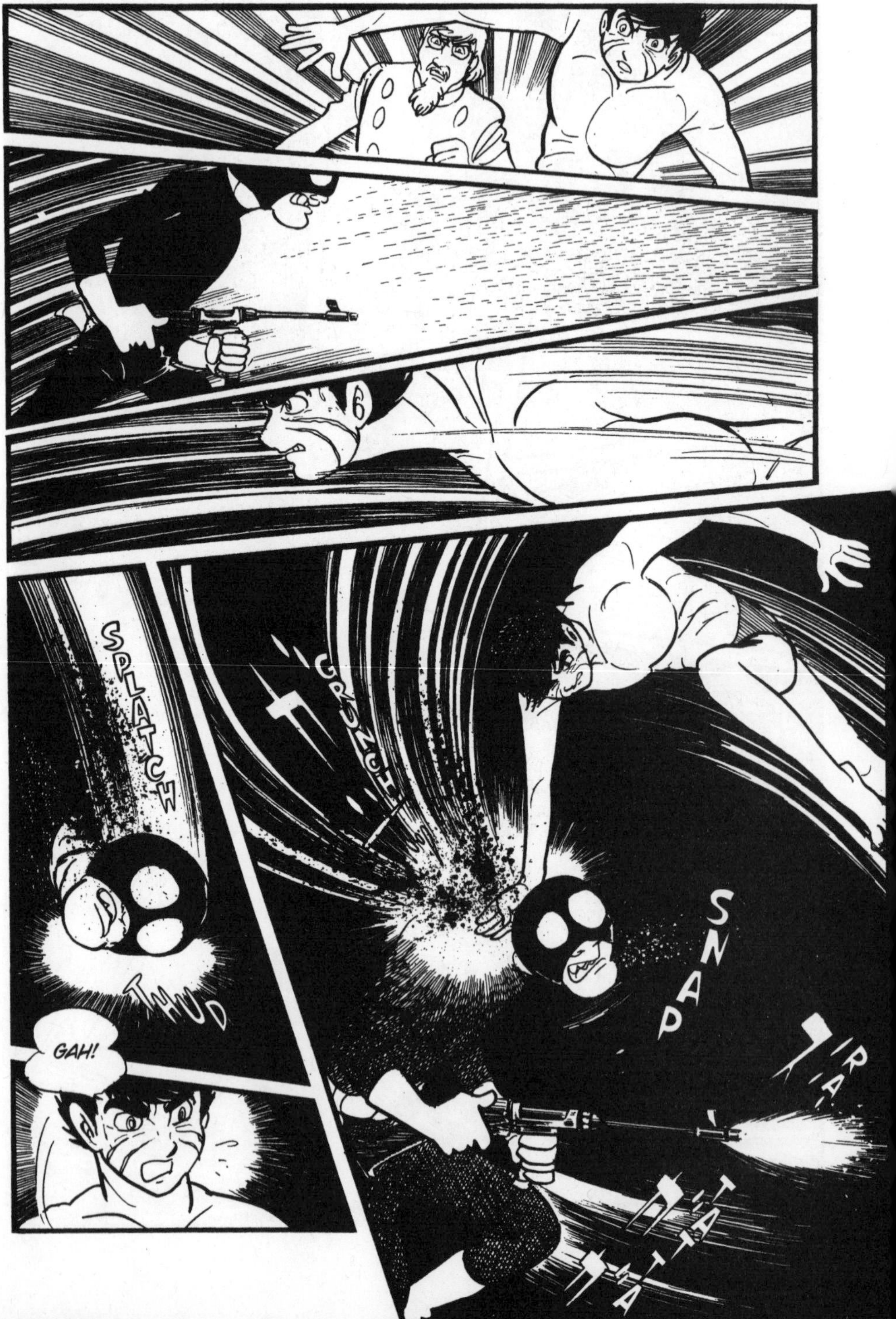
SNAP
RA
TATTA
GRUNCH
SPLATCH
THUD
GAH!

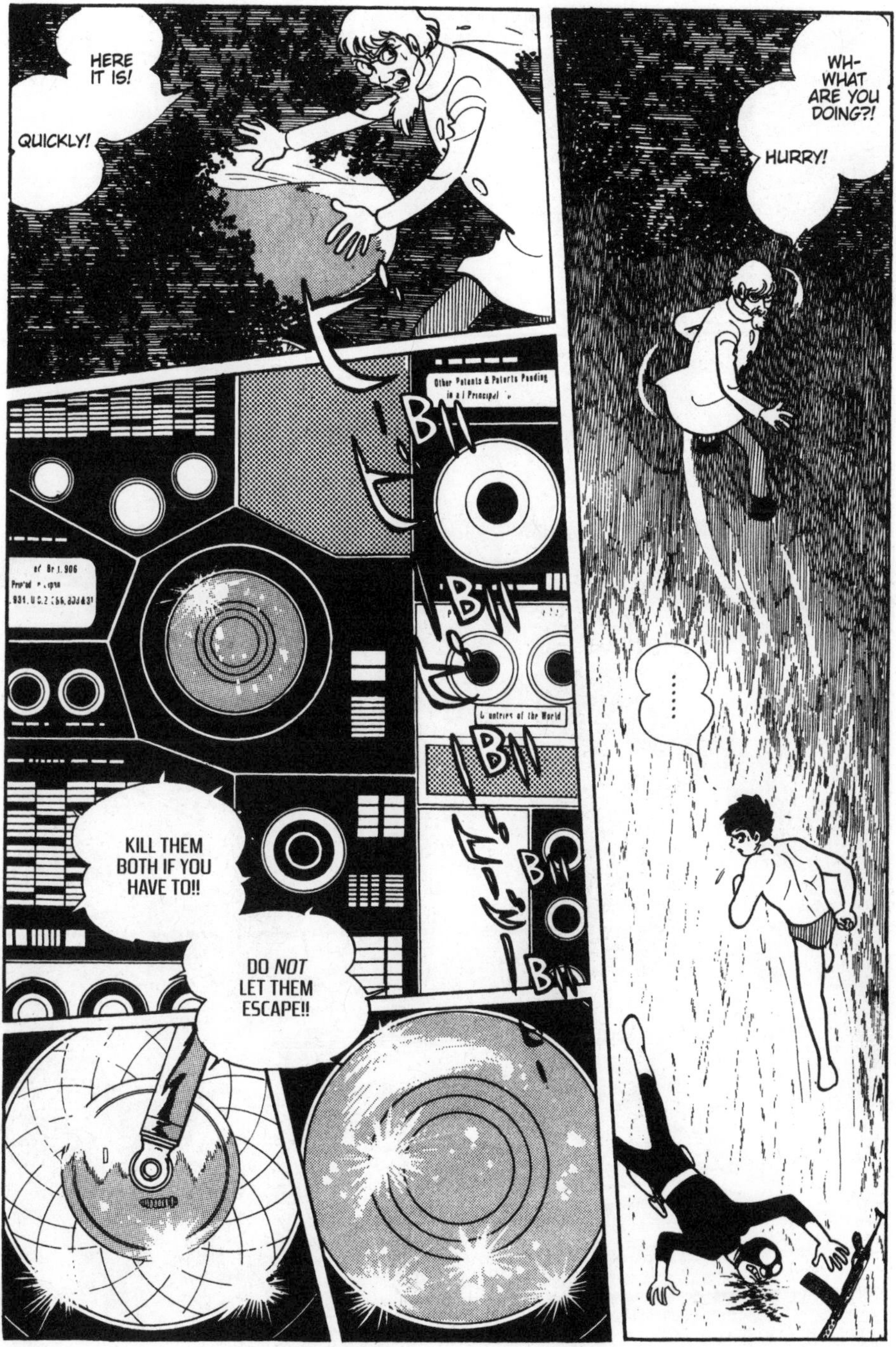
WH- WHAT ARE YOU DOING?!
HURRY!
......
HERE IT IS!
QUICKLY!
B
B
B
B
B
KILL THEM BOTH IF YOU HAVE TO!!
DO *NOT* LET THEM ESCAPE!!

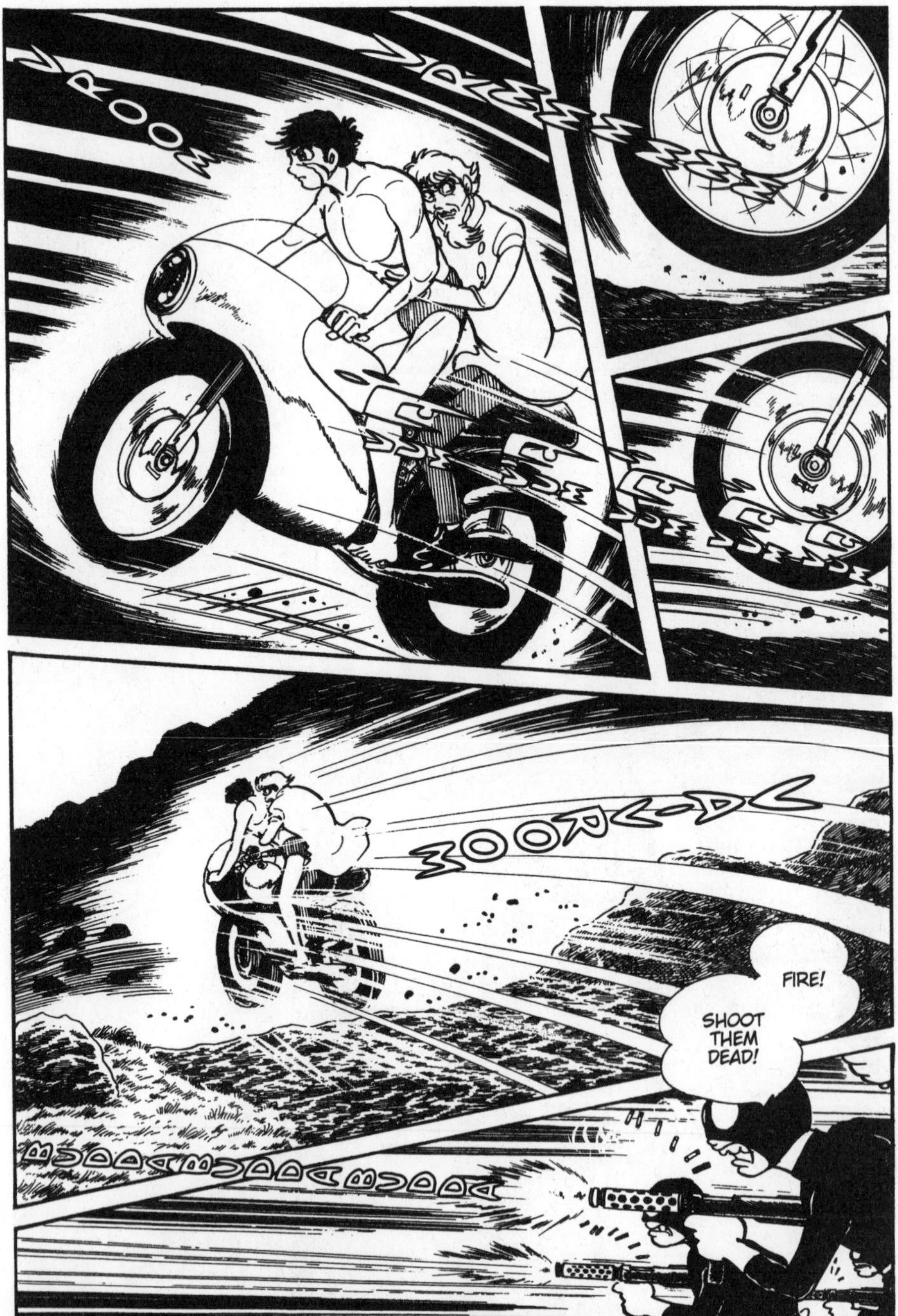

VROOM
FIRE!
SHOOT THEM DEAD!

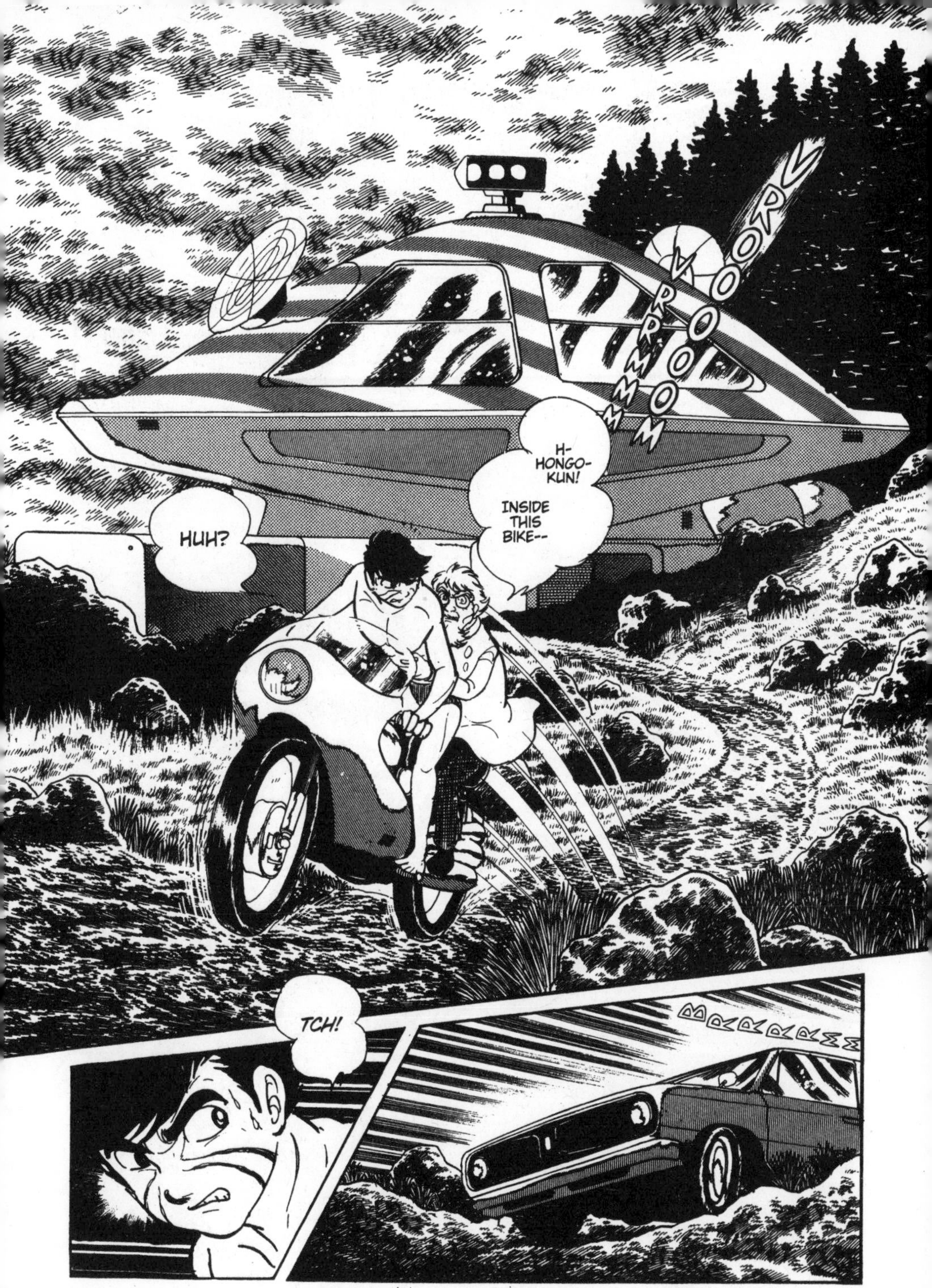
VROOOOOM
VRRMMMM
H-HONGO-KUN!
INSIDE THIS BIKE--
HUH?
BRRRREE
TCH!

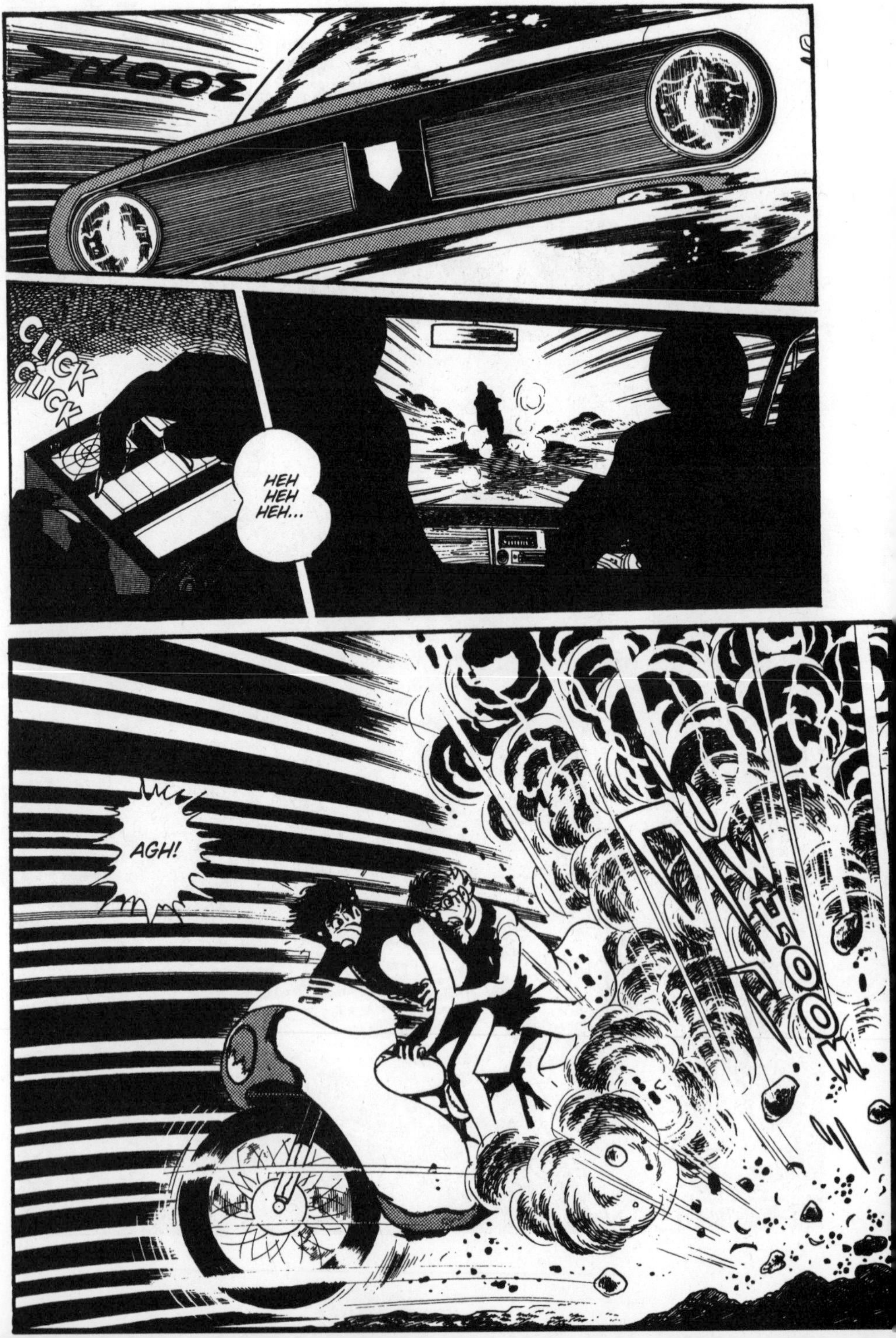
ZOOM
CLICK CLICK
HEH HEH HEH...
WHOOM
AGH!

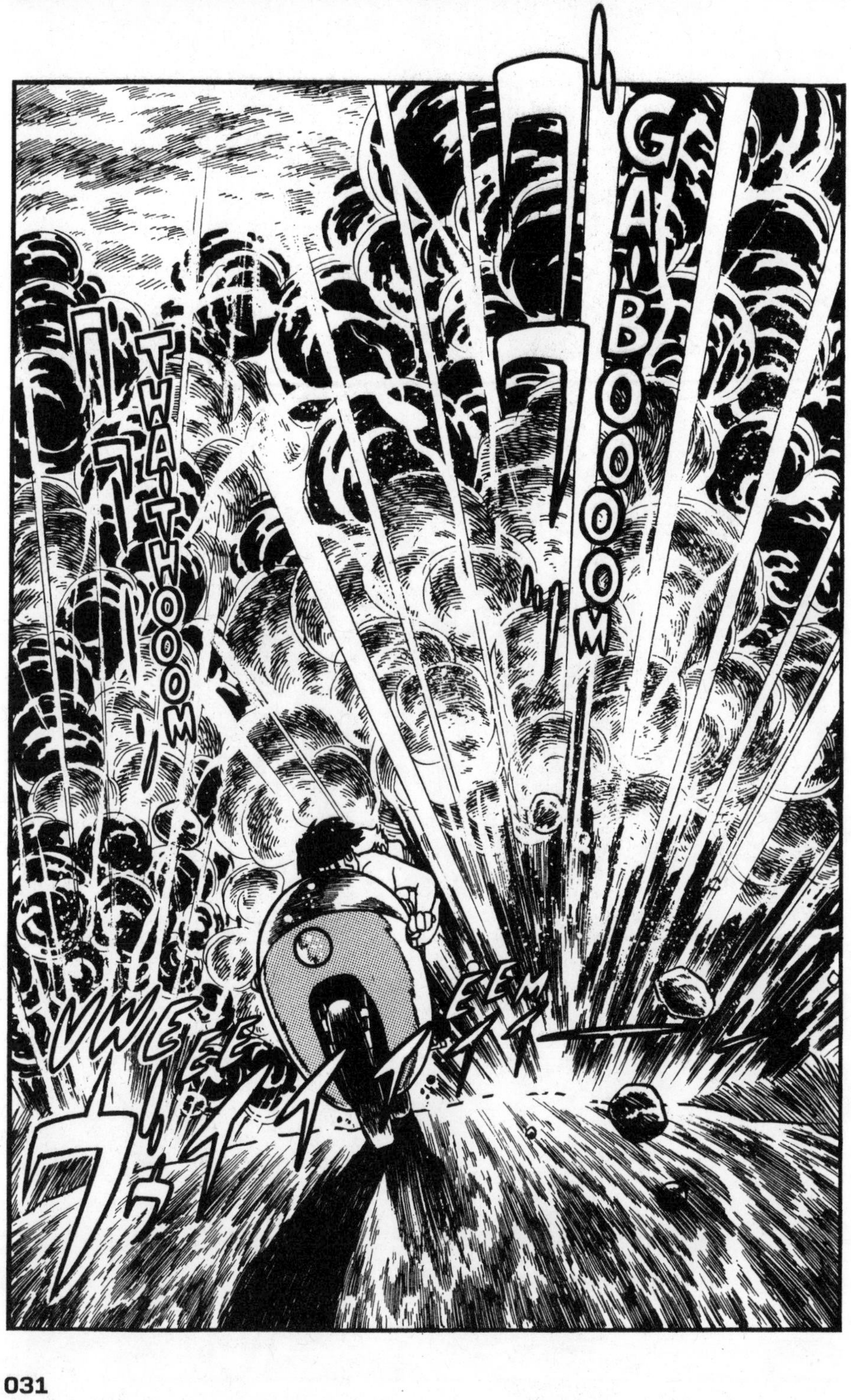
GABOOOOOM
THATHOOOOM
VWEEEEEM

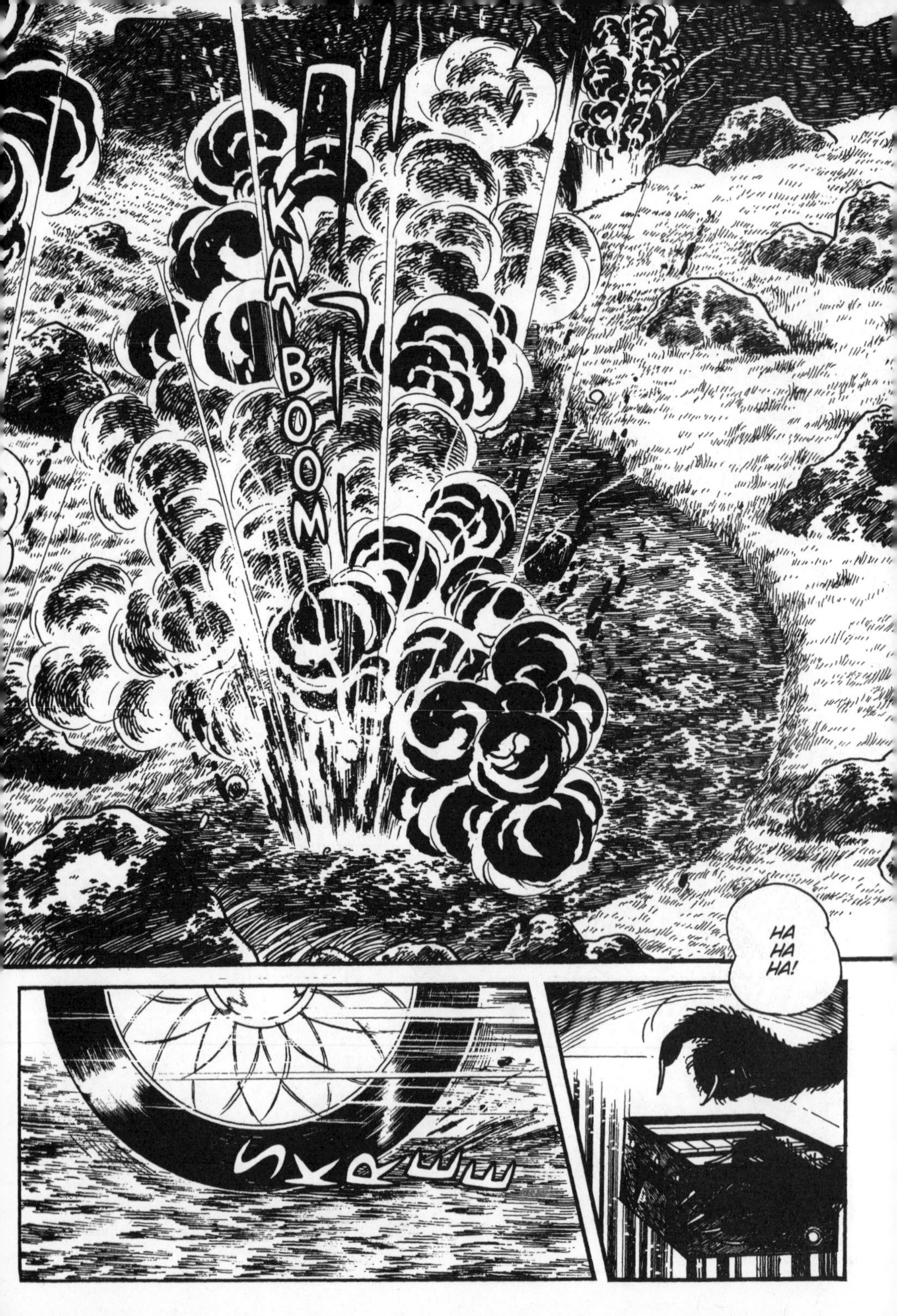
KA-BOOM
HA HA HA!
SKREE

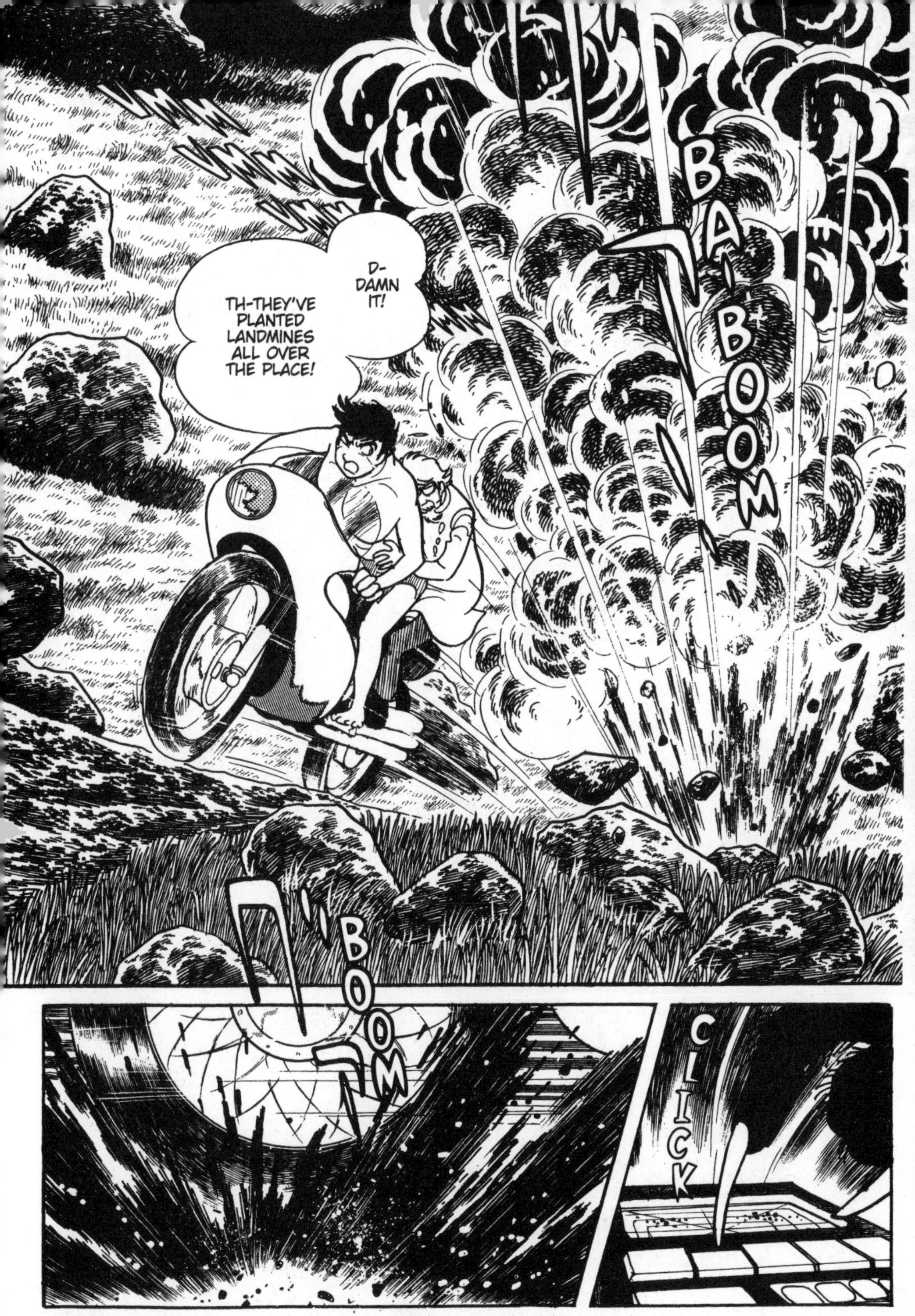
BA-BOOM
D-DAMN IT!
TH-THEY'VE PLANTED LANDMINES ALL OVER THE PLACE!
CLICK
BOOM

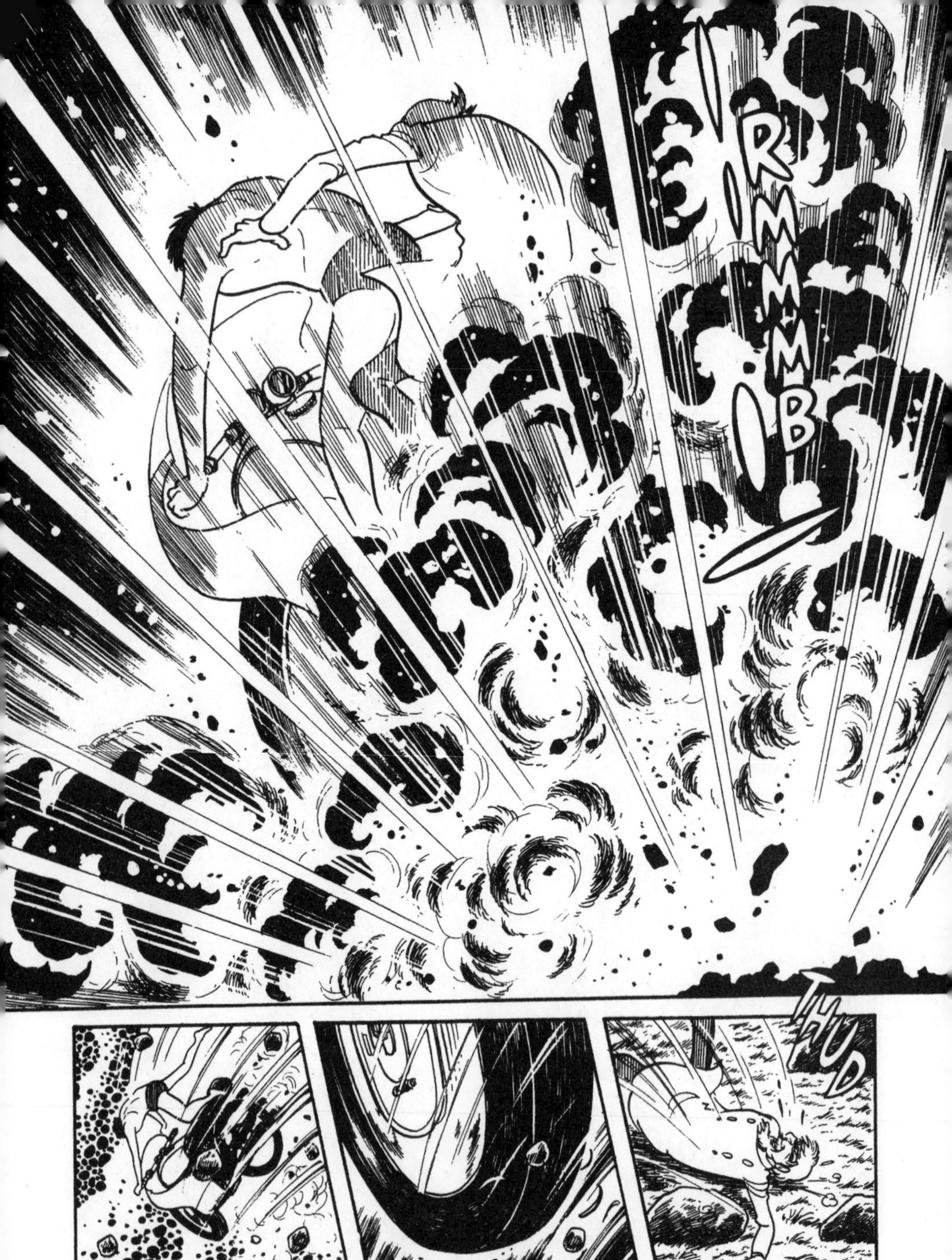
RMMMB
THUD

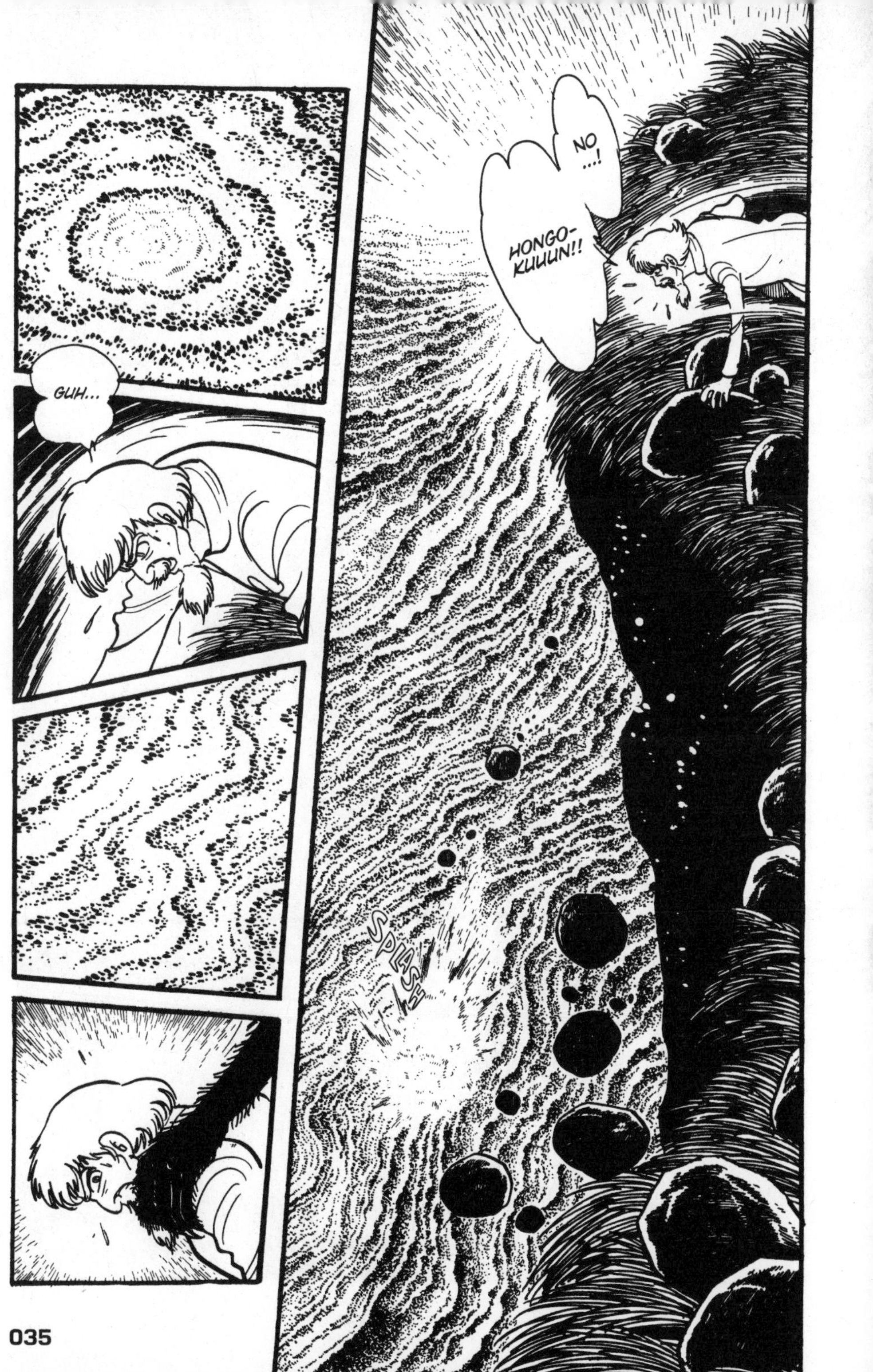
NO ...!
HONGO-KUUUN!!
SPLASH
GUH...

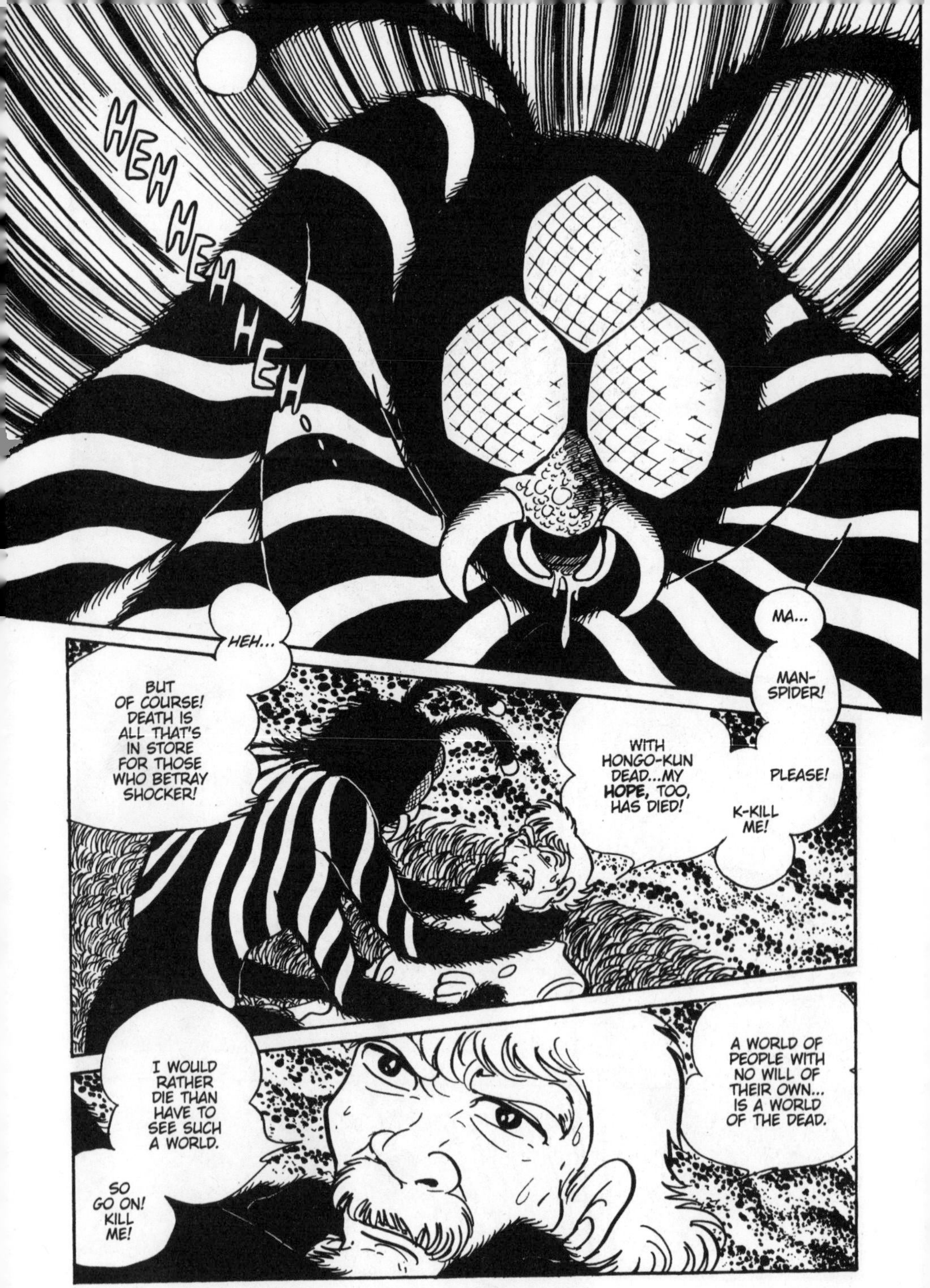
HEH HEH HEH HEH...
MA...
MAN-SPIDER!
HEH...
PLEASE!
K-KILL ME!
WITH HONGO-KUN DEAD...MY **HOPE**, TOO, HAS DIED!
BUT OF COURSE! DEATH IS ALL THAT'S IN STORE FOR THOSE WHO BETRAY SHOCKER!
A WORLD OF PEOPLE WITH NO WILL OF THEIR OWN... IS A WORLD OF THE DEAD.
I WOULD RATHER DIE THAN HAVE TO SEE SUCH A WORLD.
SO GO ON! KILL ME!

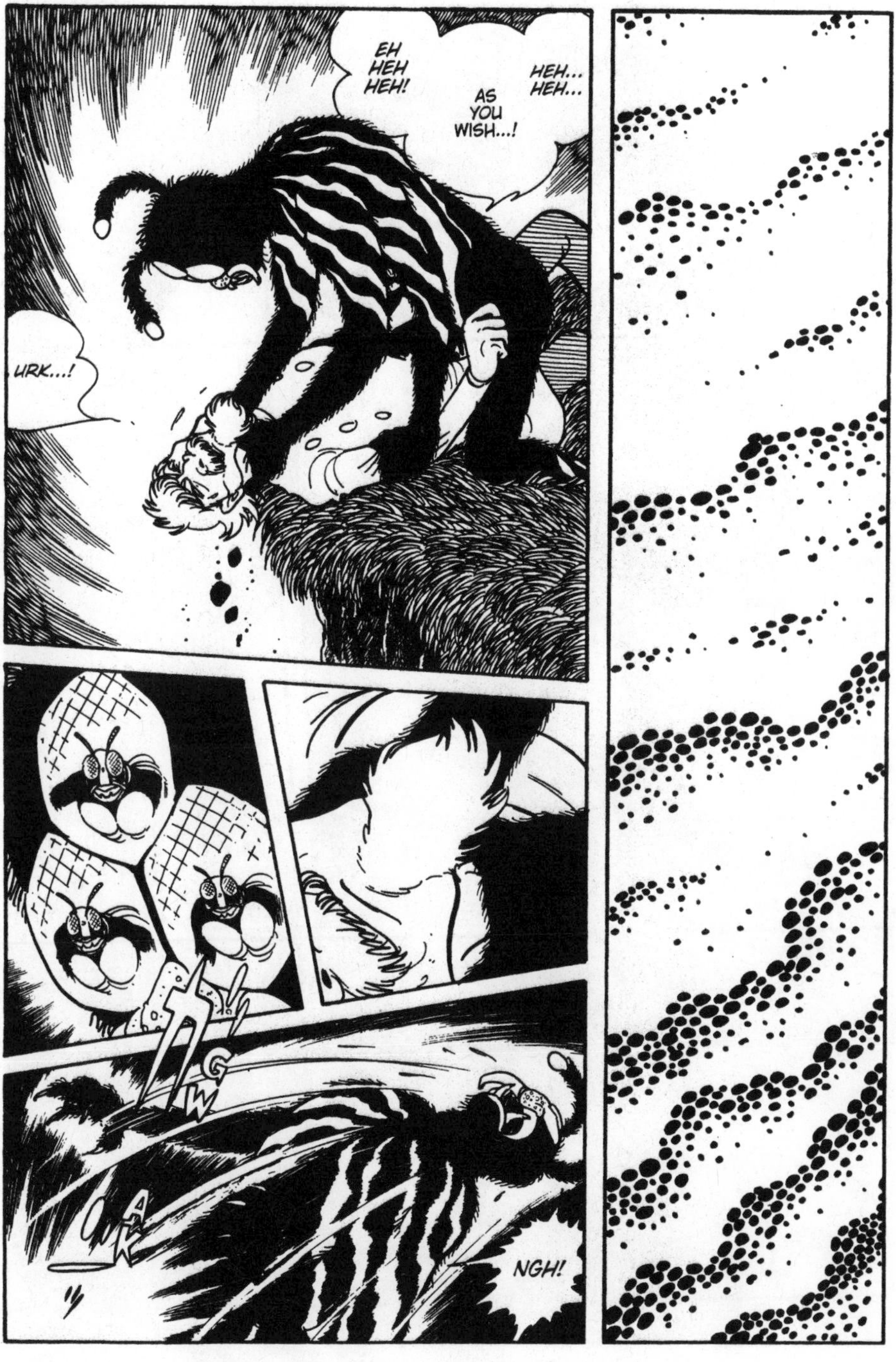
HEH... HEH...
AS YOU WISH...!
EH HEH HEH!
URK...!
NGH!

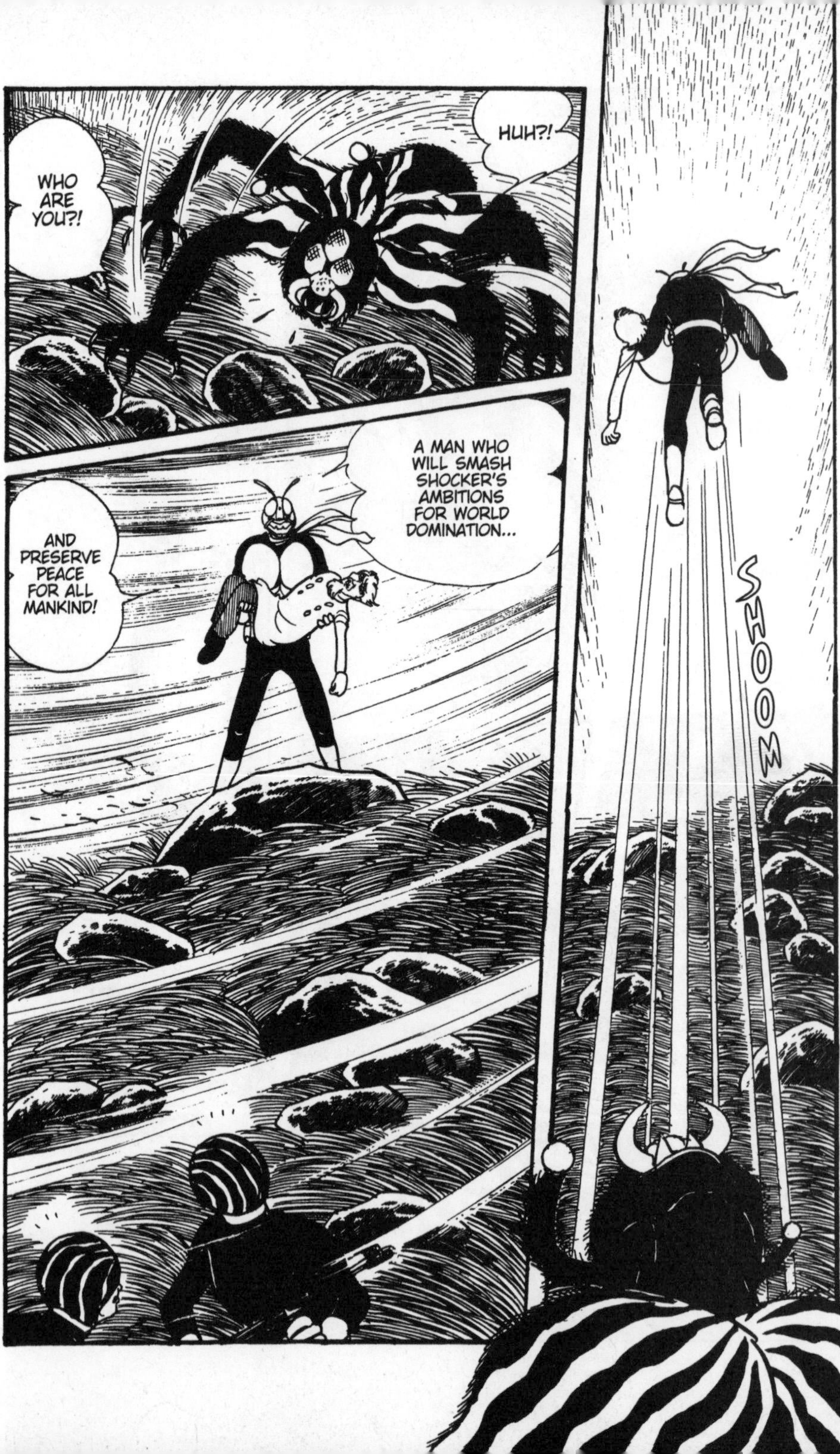
SHOOM
HUH?!
WHO ARE YOU?!
A MAN WHO WILL SMASH SHOCKER'S AMBITIONS FOR WORLD DOMINATION...
AND PRESERVE PEACE FOR ALL MANKIND!

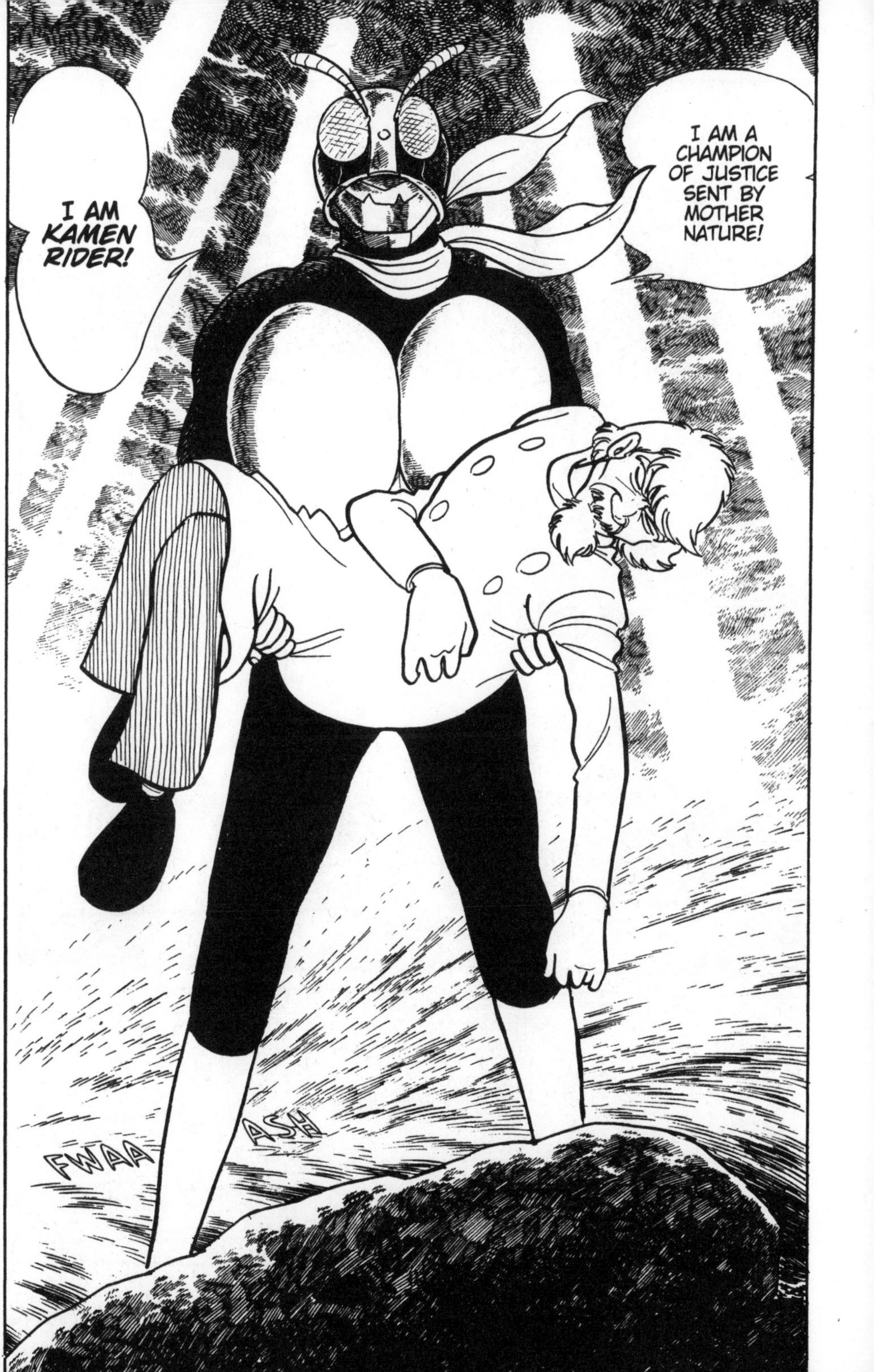
I AM A CHAMPION OF JUSTICE SENT BY MOTHER NATURE!
I AM KAMEN RIDER!
FWAA
ASH

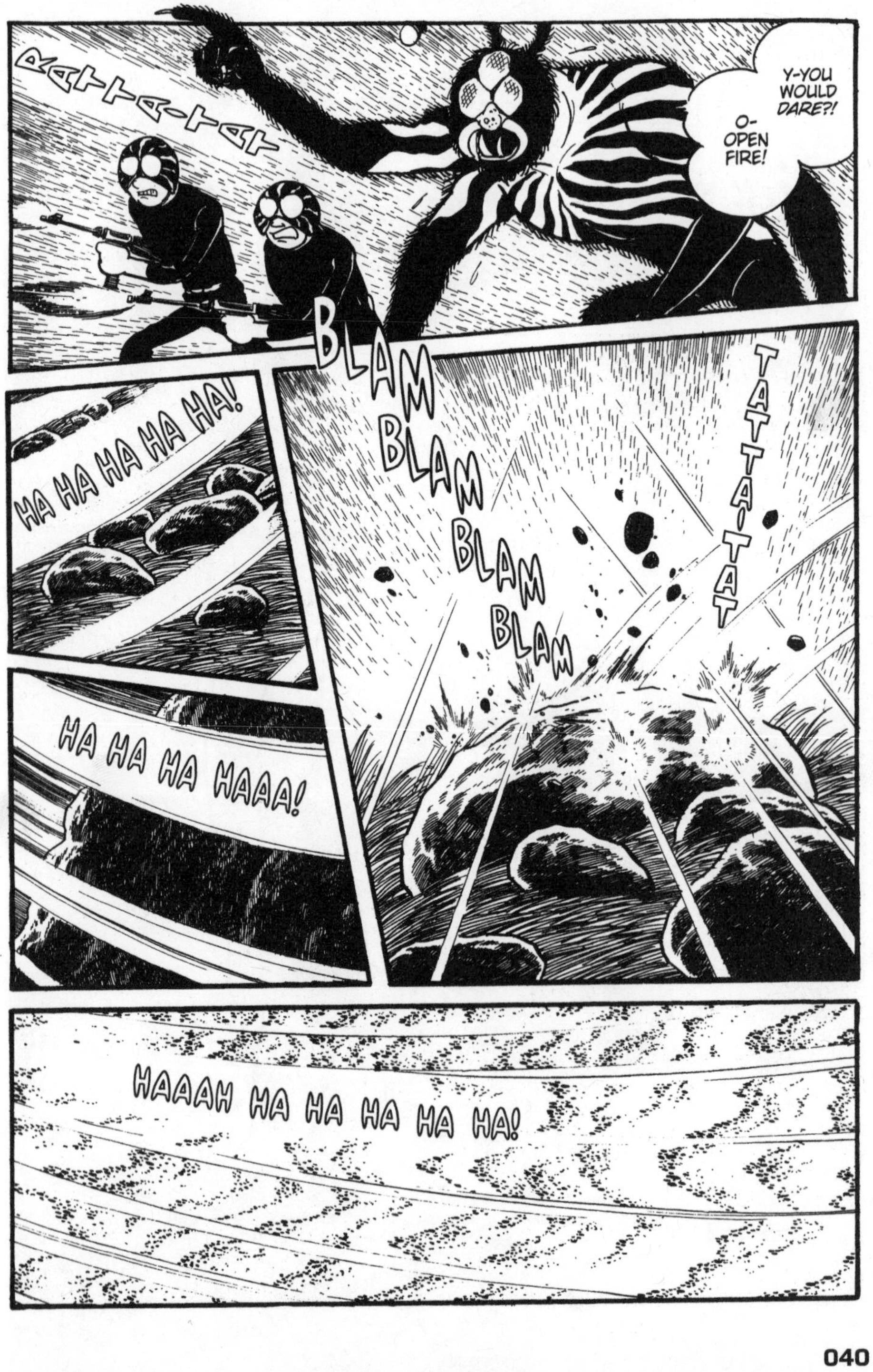
Y-YOU WOULD DARE?!
O-OPEN FIRE!
RATTA-TAT
BLAM BLAM BLAM BLAM
TATTATAT
HA HA HA HA HA!
HA HA HA HAAA!
HAAAH HA HA HA HA HA!

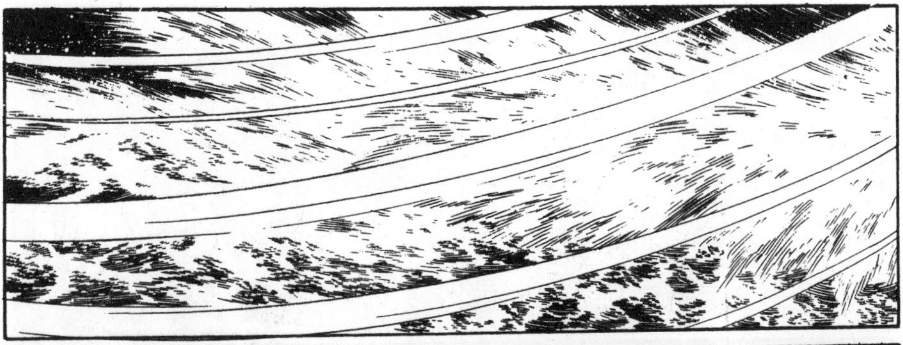

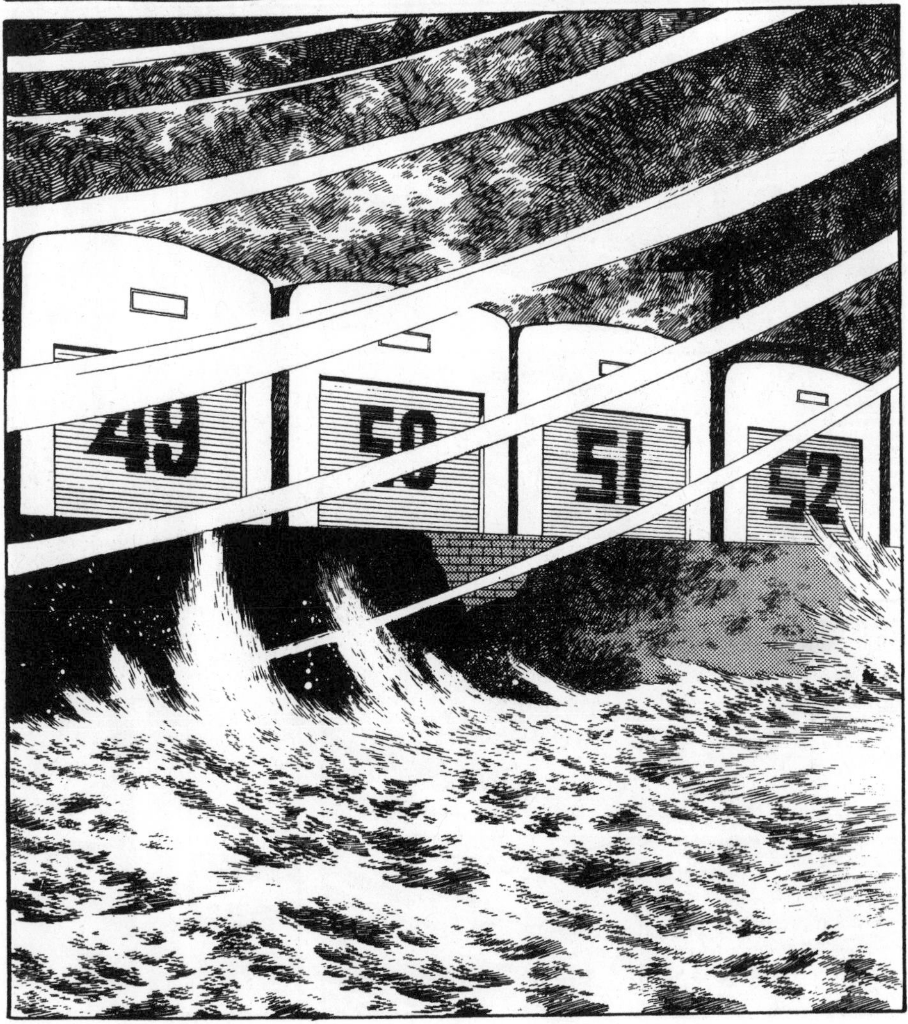
49
50
51
52

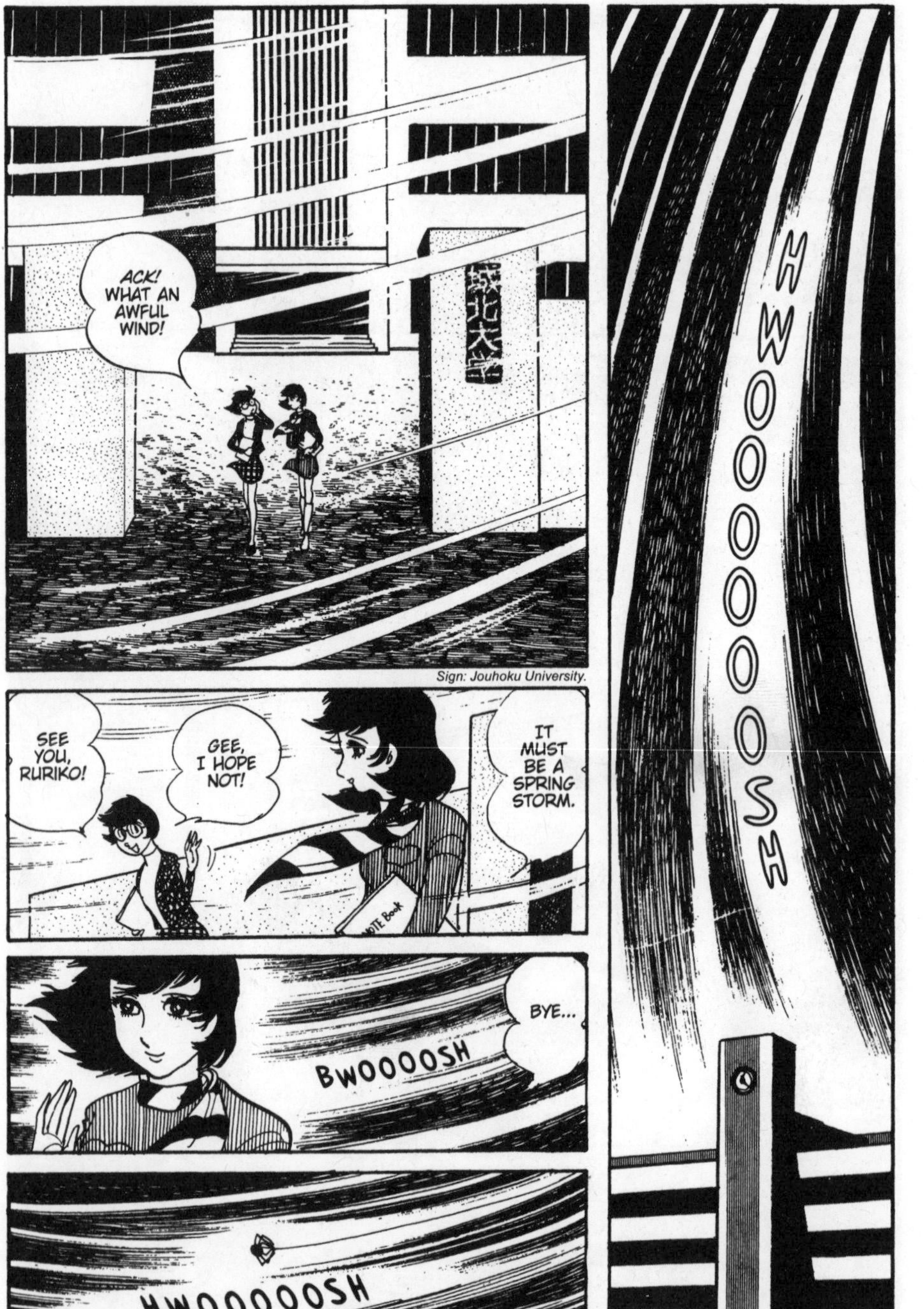
HWOOOOOOSH
ACK! WHAT AN AWFUL WIND!
IT MUST BE A SPRING STORM.
GEE, I HOPE NOT!
SEE YOU, RURIKO!
NOTE Book
BYE...
BWOOOOSH
HWOOOOOSH

Sign: Jouhoku University.

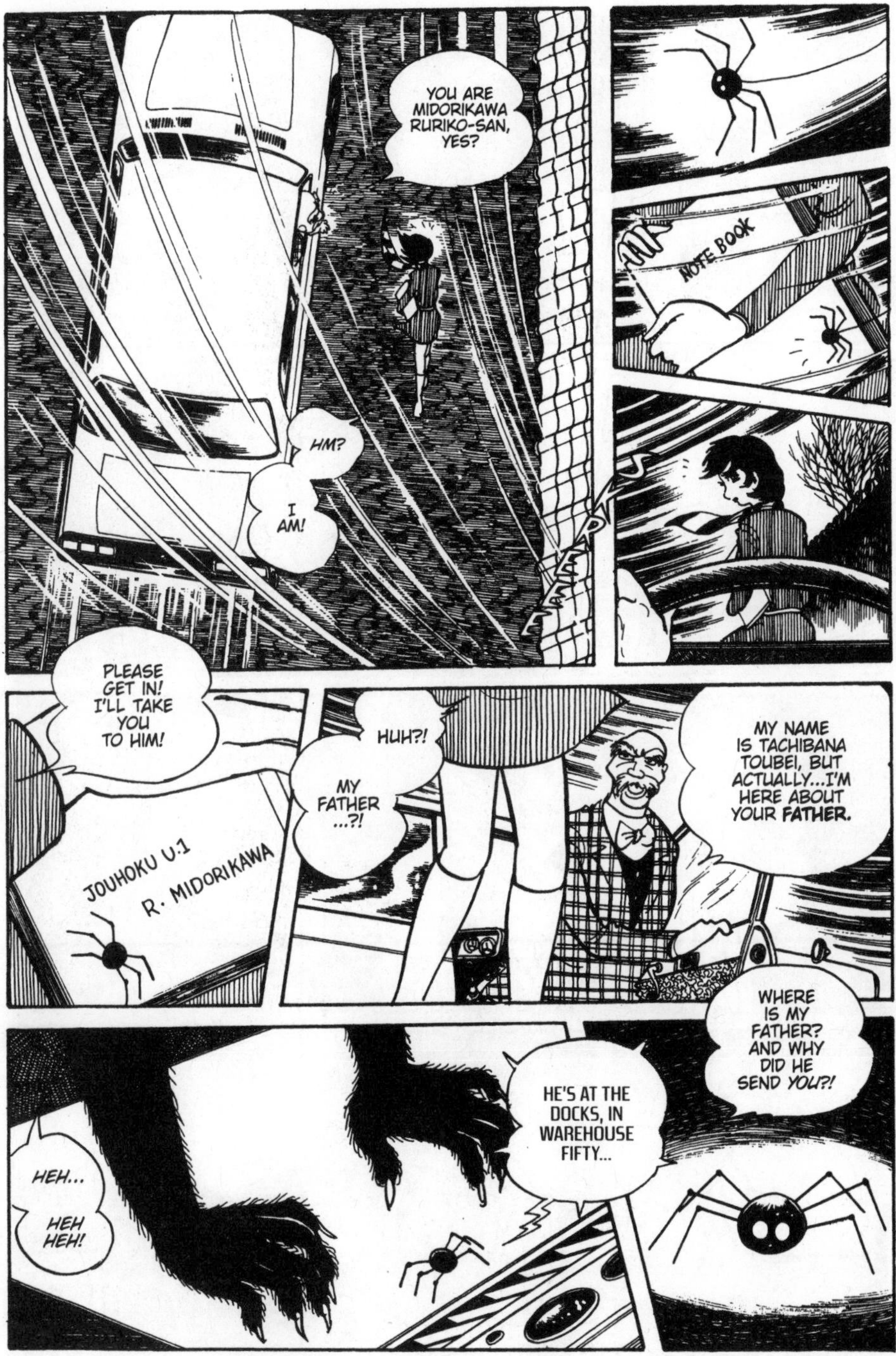
NOTE BOOK
YOU ARE MIDORIKAWA RURIKO-SAN, YES?
HM?
I AM!
MY NAME IS TACHIBANA TOUBEI, BUT ACTUALLY...I'M HERE ABOUT YOUR **FATHER.**
HUH?!
MY FATHER ...?!
PLEASE GET IN! I'LL TAKE YOU TO HIM!
JOUHOKU U.1
R. MIDORIKAWA
WHERE IS MY FATHER? AND WHY DID HE SEND *YOU*?!
HE'S AT THE DOCKS, IN WAREHOUSE FIFTY...
HEH...
HEH HEH!

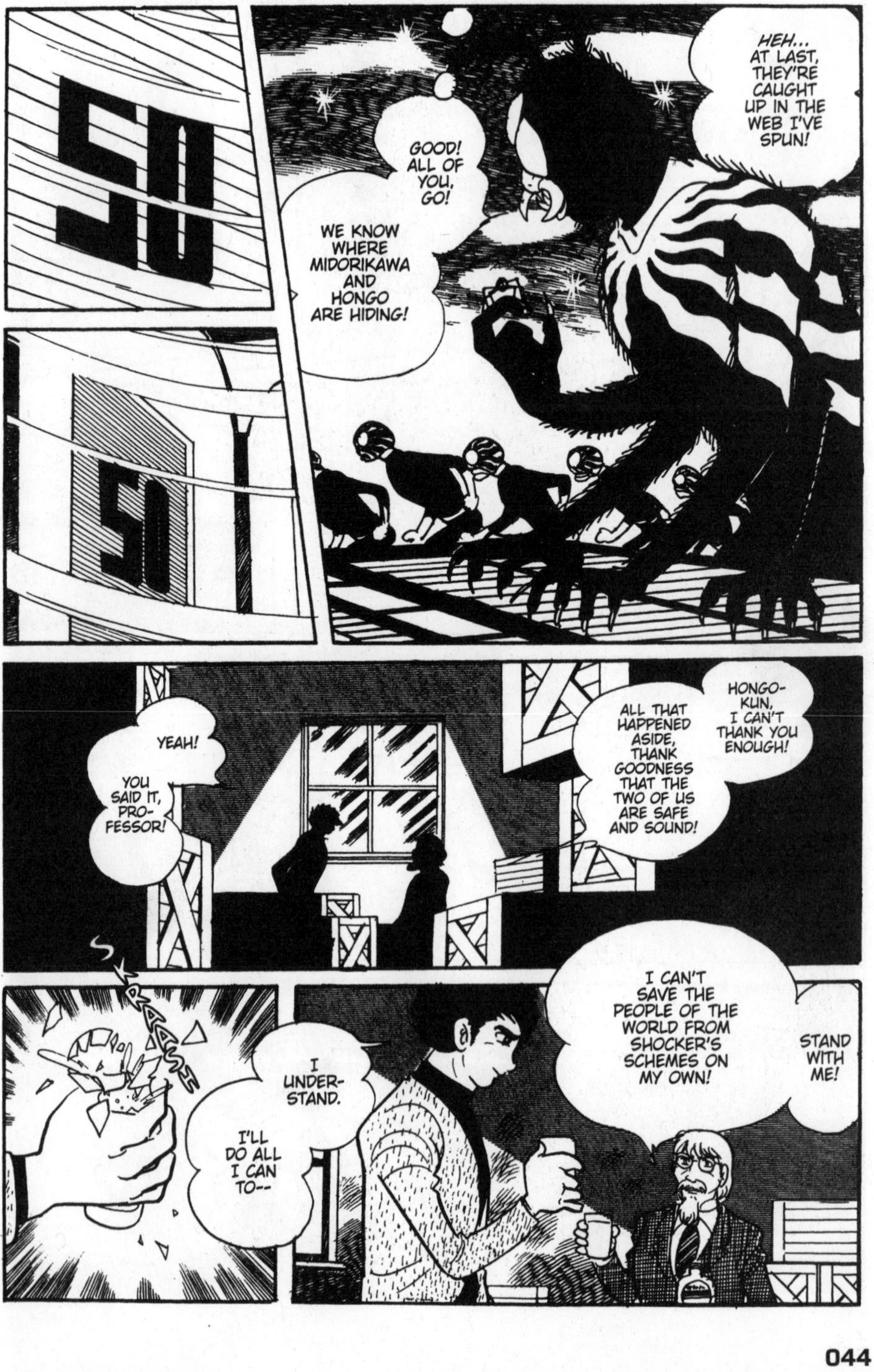
HEH... AT LAST, THEY'RE CAUGHT UP IN THE WEB I'VE SPUN!
GOOD! ALL OF YOU, GO!
WE KNOW WHERE MIDORIKAWA AND HONGO ARE HIDING!
HONGO-KUN, I CAN'T THANK YOU ENOUGH!
ALL THAT HAPPENED ASIDE, THANK GOODNESS THAT THE TWO OF US ARE SAFE AND SOUND!
YEAH!
YOU SAID IT, PRO-FESSOR!
STAND WITH ME!
I CAN'T SAVE THE PEOPLE OF THE WORLD FROM SHOCKER'S SCHEMES ON MY OWN!
I UNDER-STAND.
I'LL DO ALL I CAN TO--
SKRAASH

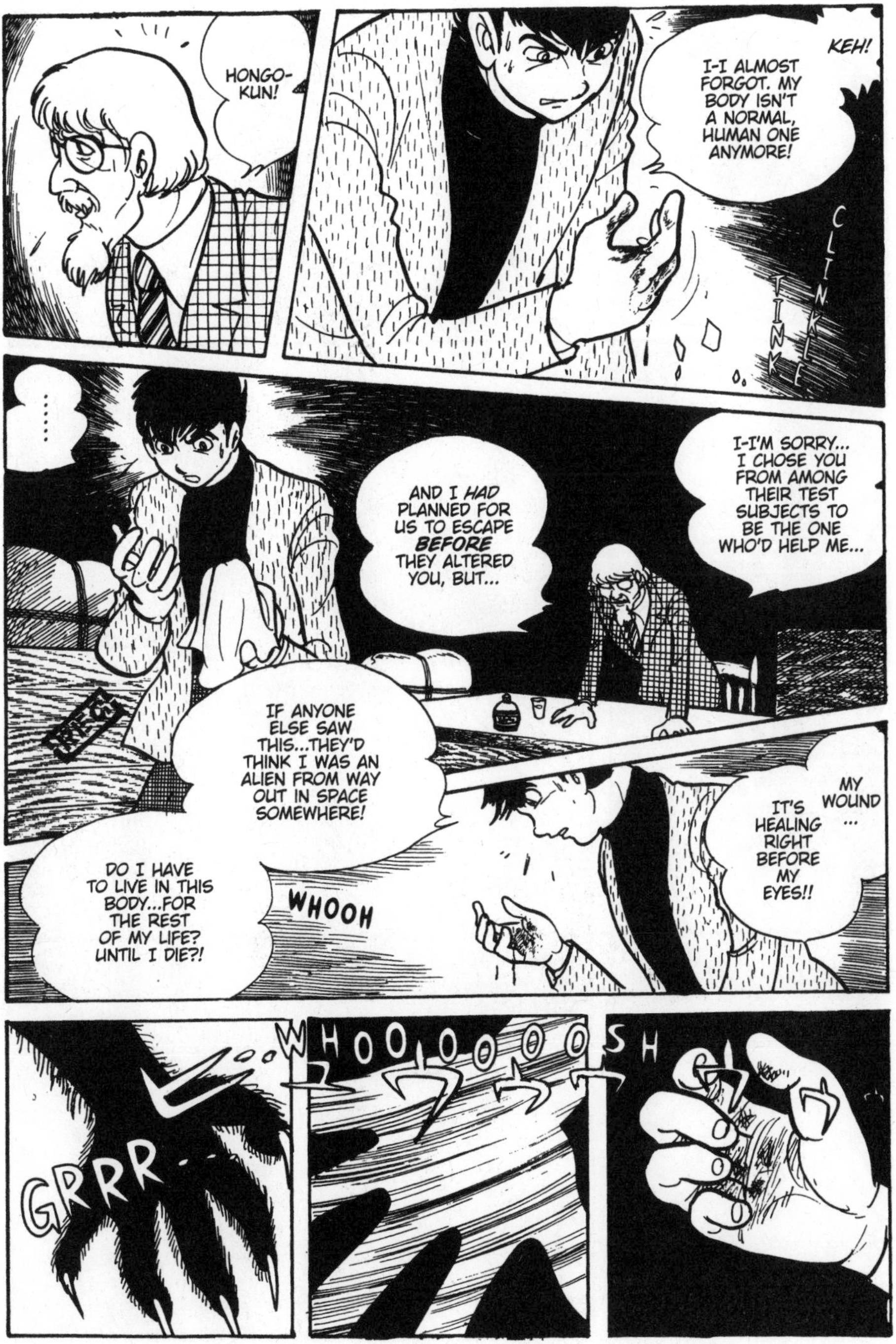
KEH!
I-I ALMOST FORGOT. MY BODY ISN'T A NORMAL, HUMAN ONE ANYMORE!
CLINK
TINKLE
HONGO-KUN!
I-I'M SORRY... I CHOSE YOU FROM AMONG THEIR TEST SUBJECTS TO BE THE ONE WHO'D HELP ME...
AND I *HAD* PLANNED FOR US TO ESCAPE ***BEFORE*** THEY ALTERED YOU, BUT...
......
MY WOUND...
IT'S HEALING RIGHT BEFORE MY EYES!!
IF ANYONE ELSE SAW THIS...THEY'D THINK I WAS AN ALIEN FROM WAY OUT IN SPACE SOMEWHERE!
WHOOH
DO I HAVE TO LIVE IN THIS BODY...FOR THE REST OF MY LIFE? UNTIL I DIE?!
WHOOOOOOSH
GRRR

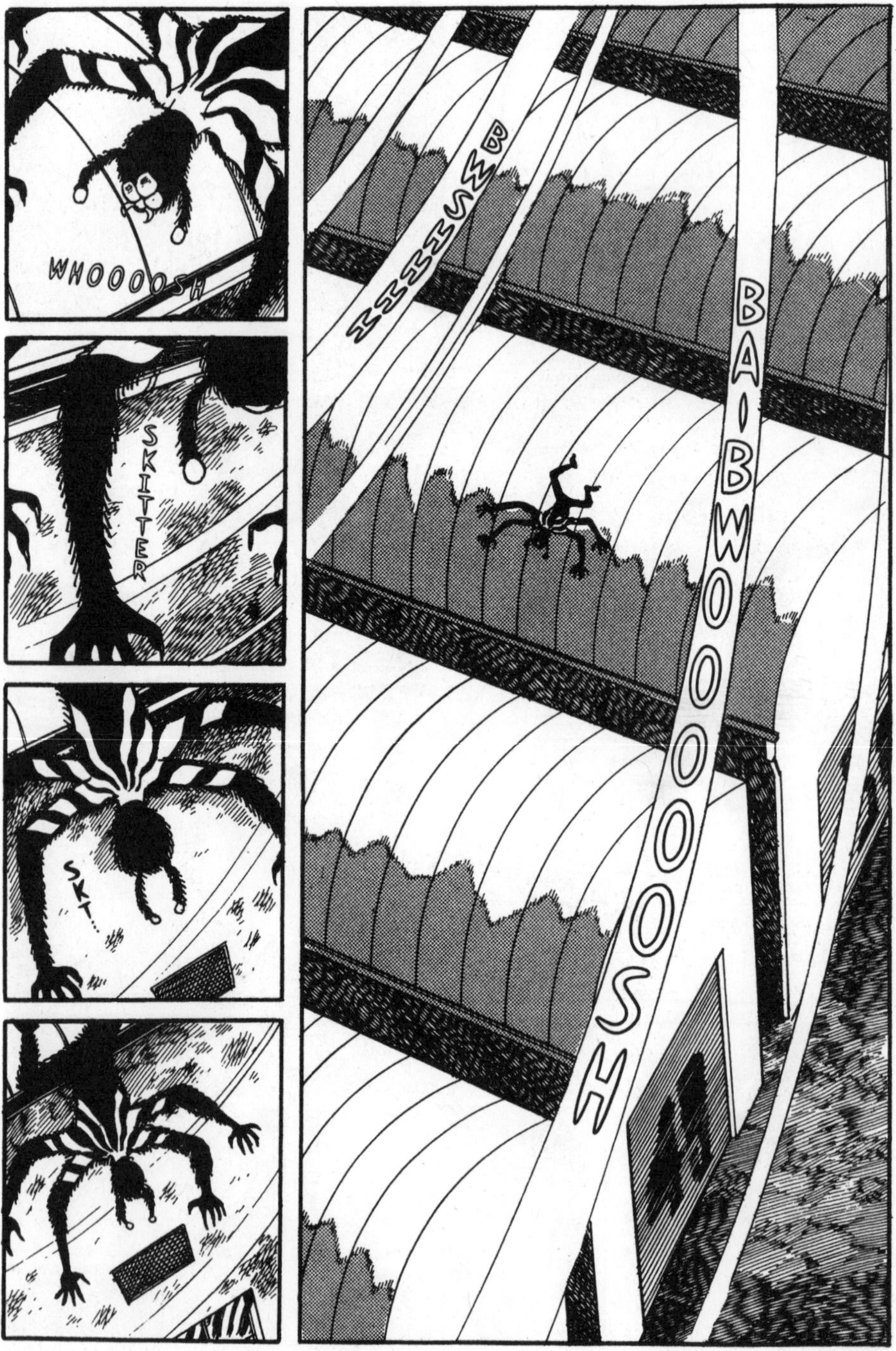
BWSHHHHHH
BAIBWOOOOOSH
WHOOOOSH
SKITTER
SKT...

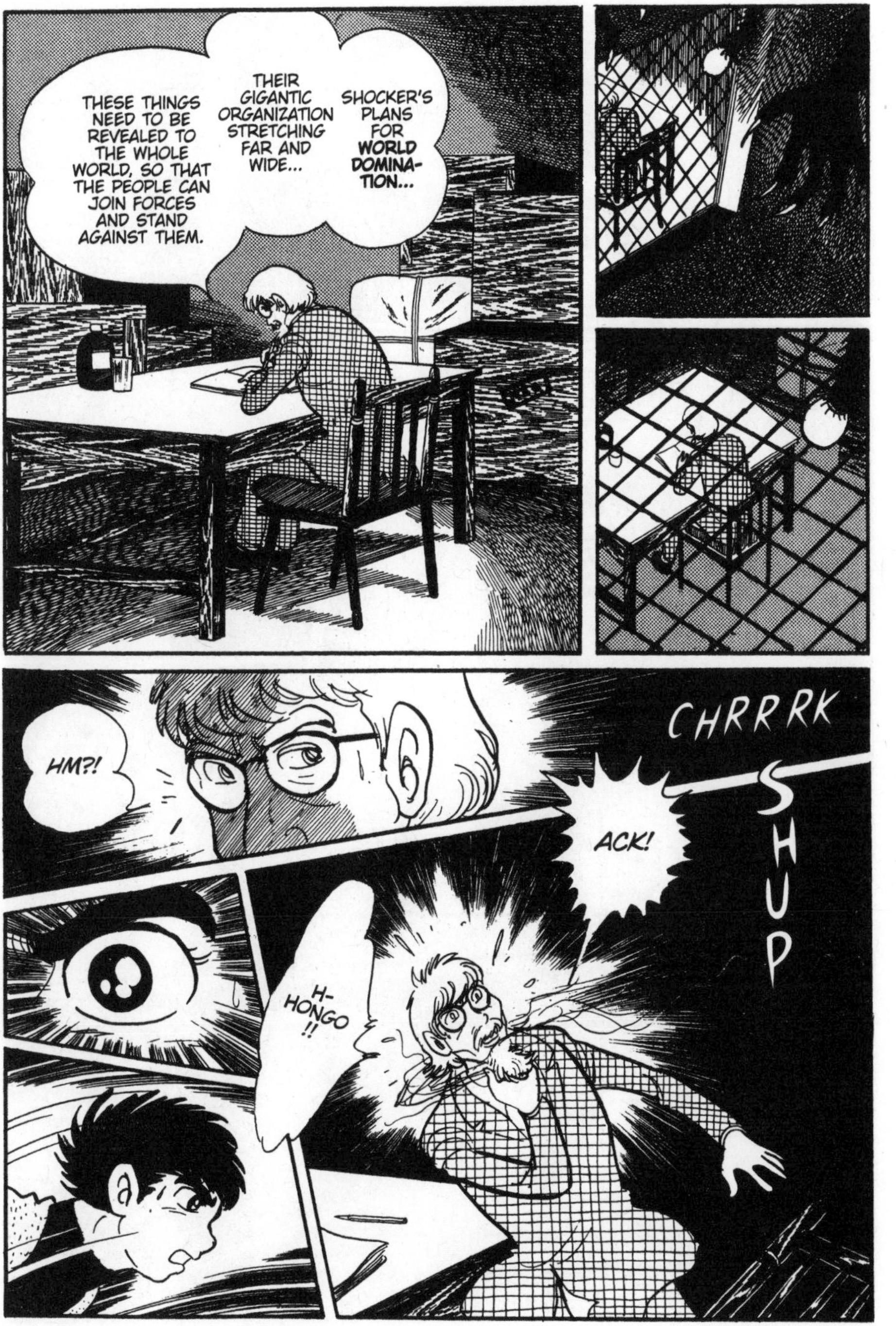
SHOCKER'S PLANS FOR **WORLD DOMINATION...**
THEIR GIGANTIC ORGANIZATION STRETCHING FAR AND WIDE...
THESE THINGS NEED TO BE REVEALED TO THE WHOLE WORLD, SO THAT THE PEOPLE CAN JOIN FORCES AND STAND AGAINST THEM.
HM?!
CHRRRK
SHUP
ACK!
H-HONGO!!

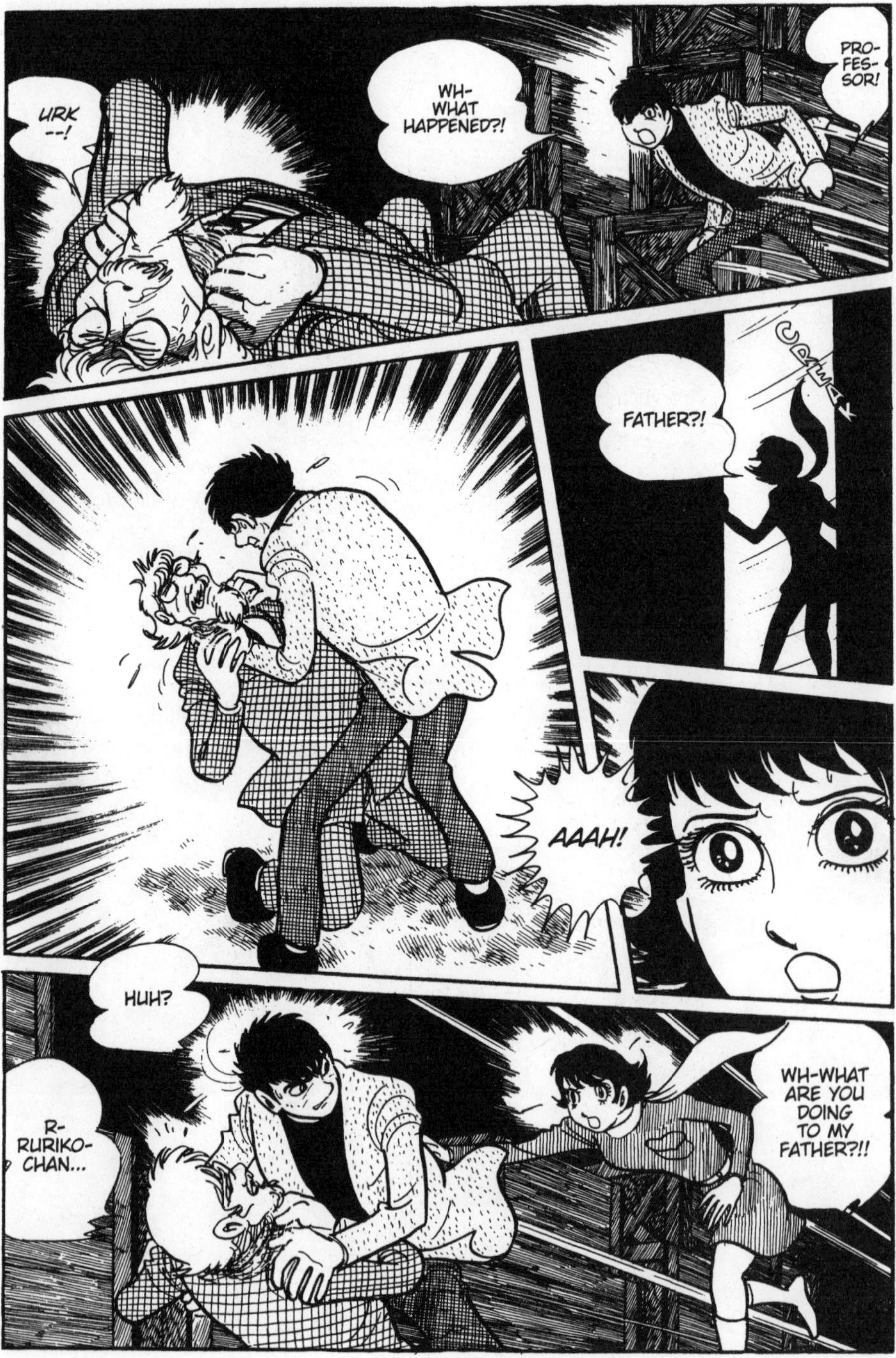
PRO-FES-SOR!
WH-WHAT HAPPENED?!
URK --!
CRWAK
FATHER?!
AAAH!
WH-WHAT ARE YOU DOING TO MY FATHER?!!
HUH?
R-RURIKO-CHAN...

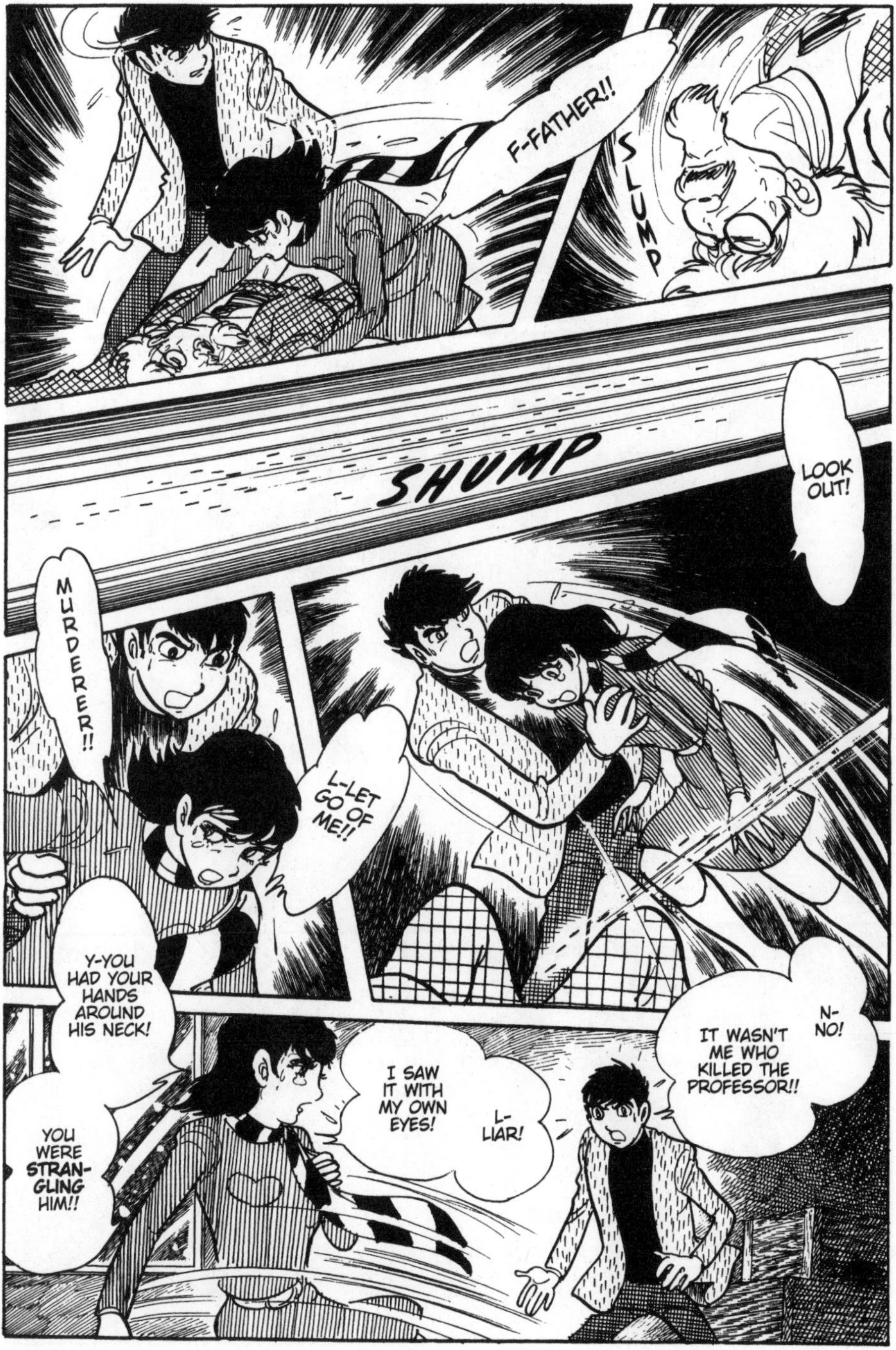
SLUMP
F-FATHER!!
SHUMP
LOOK OUT!
MURDERER!!
L-LET GO OF ME!!
N-NO!
IT WASN'T ME WHO KILLED THE PROFESSOR!!
L-LIAR!
I SAW IT WITH MY OWN EYES!
Y-YOU HAD YOUR HANDS AROUND HIS NECK!
YOU WERE STRANG-LING HIM!!

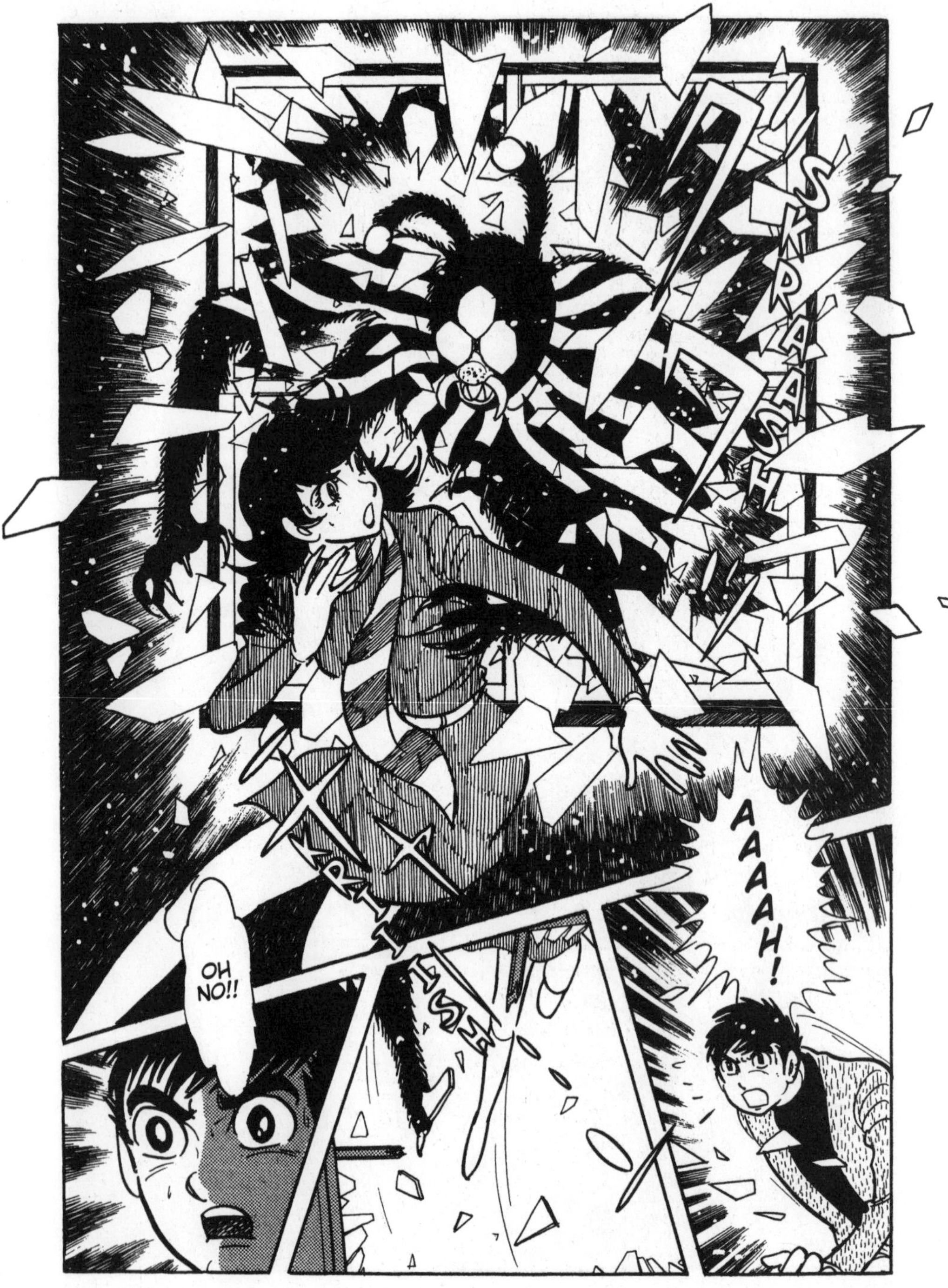
SKRAASH!!
KRITTSH
AAAAH!
OH NO!!

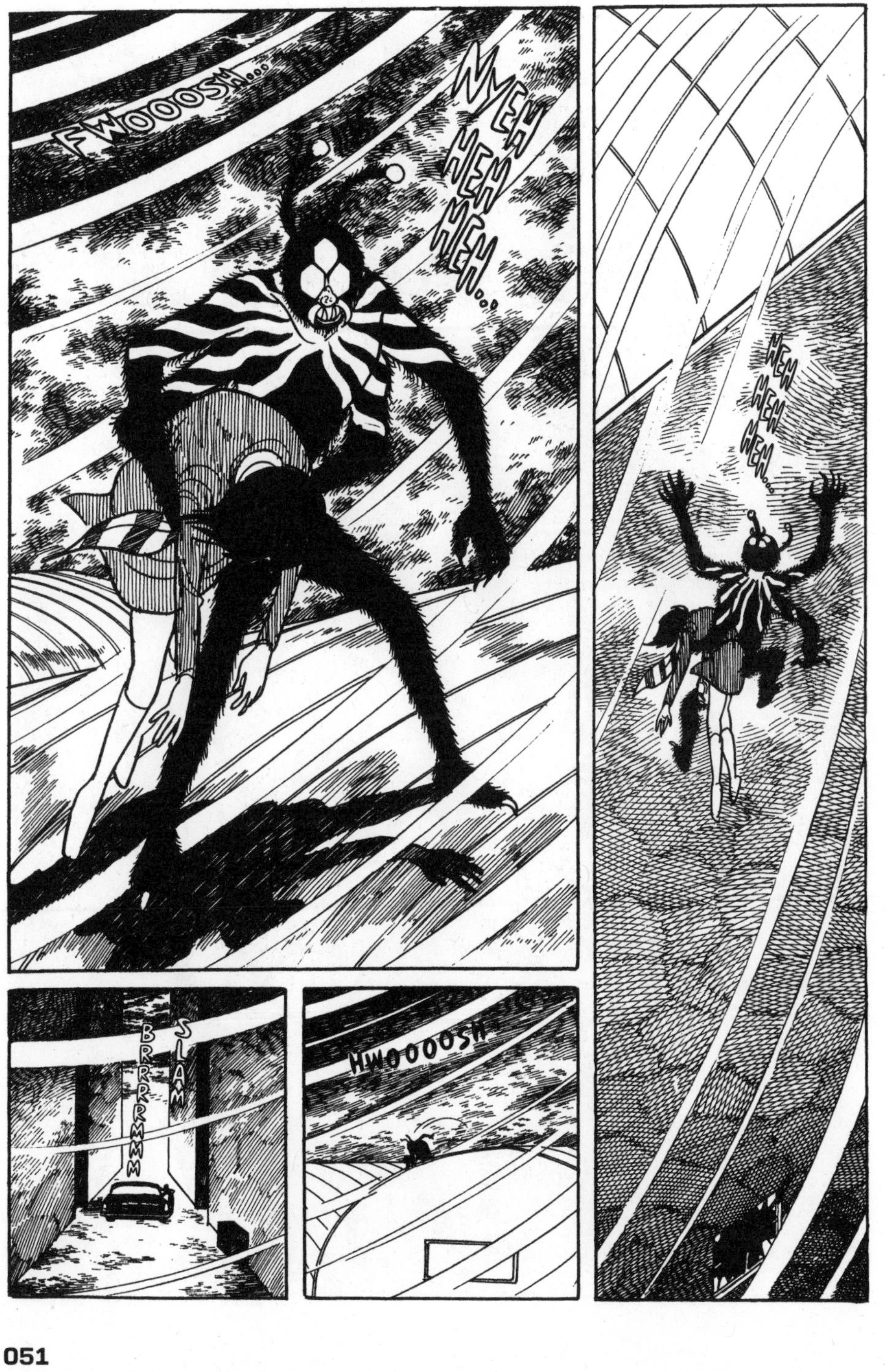
HEH HEH HEH HEH...
NYEH HEH HEH HEH...
FWOOOSH...
HWOOOOSH
SLAM
BRRRRMMM

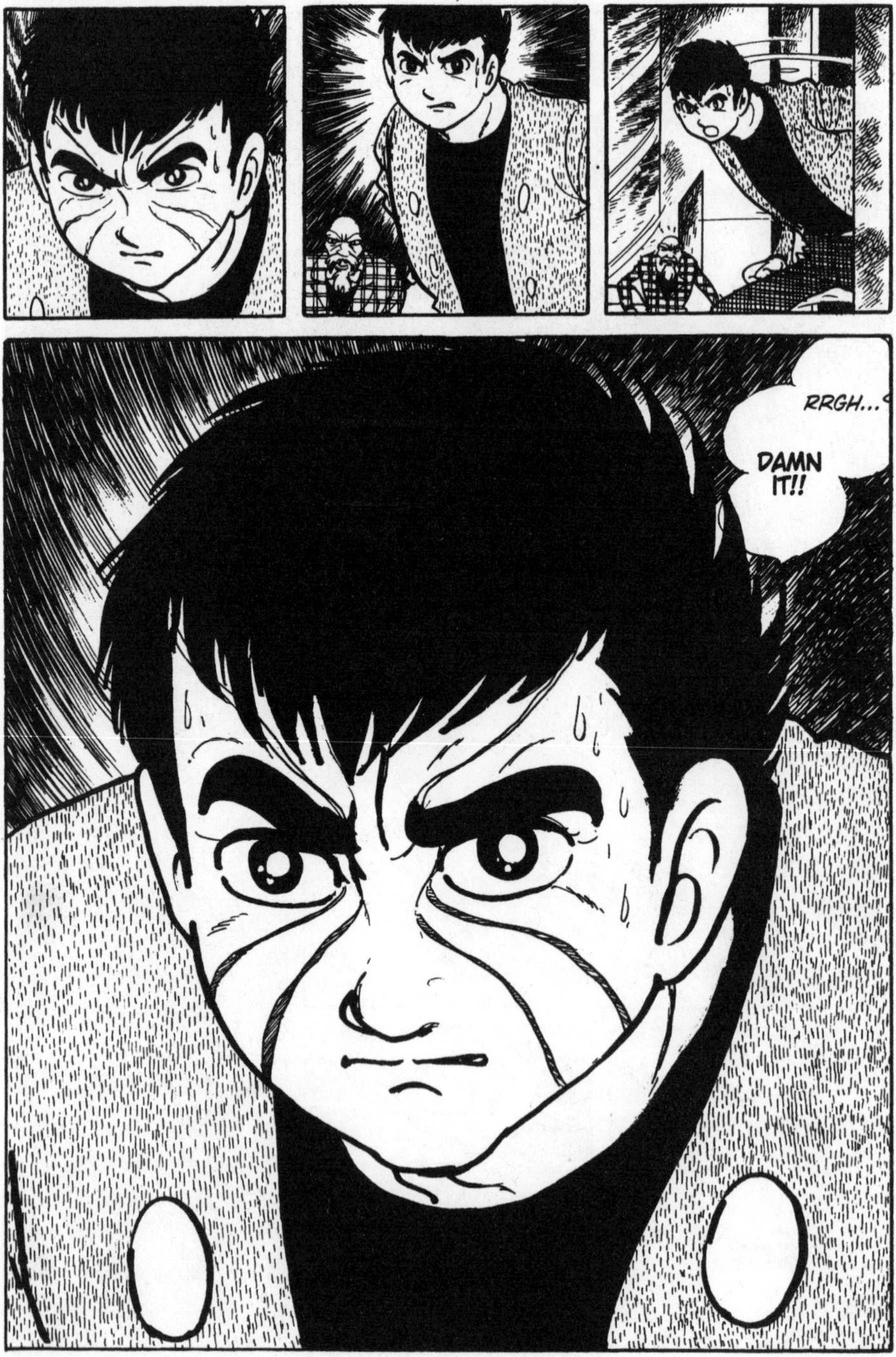
RRGH...
DAMN IT!!

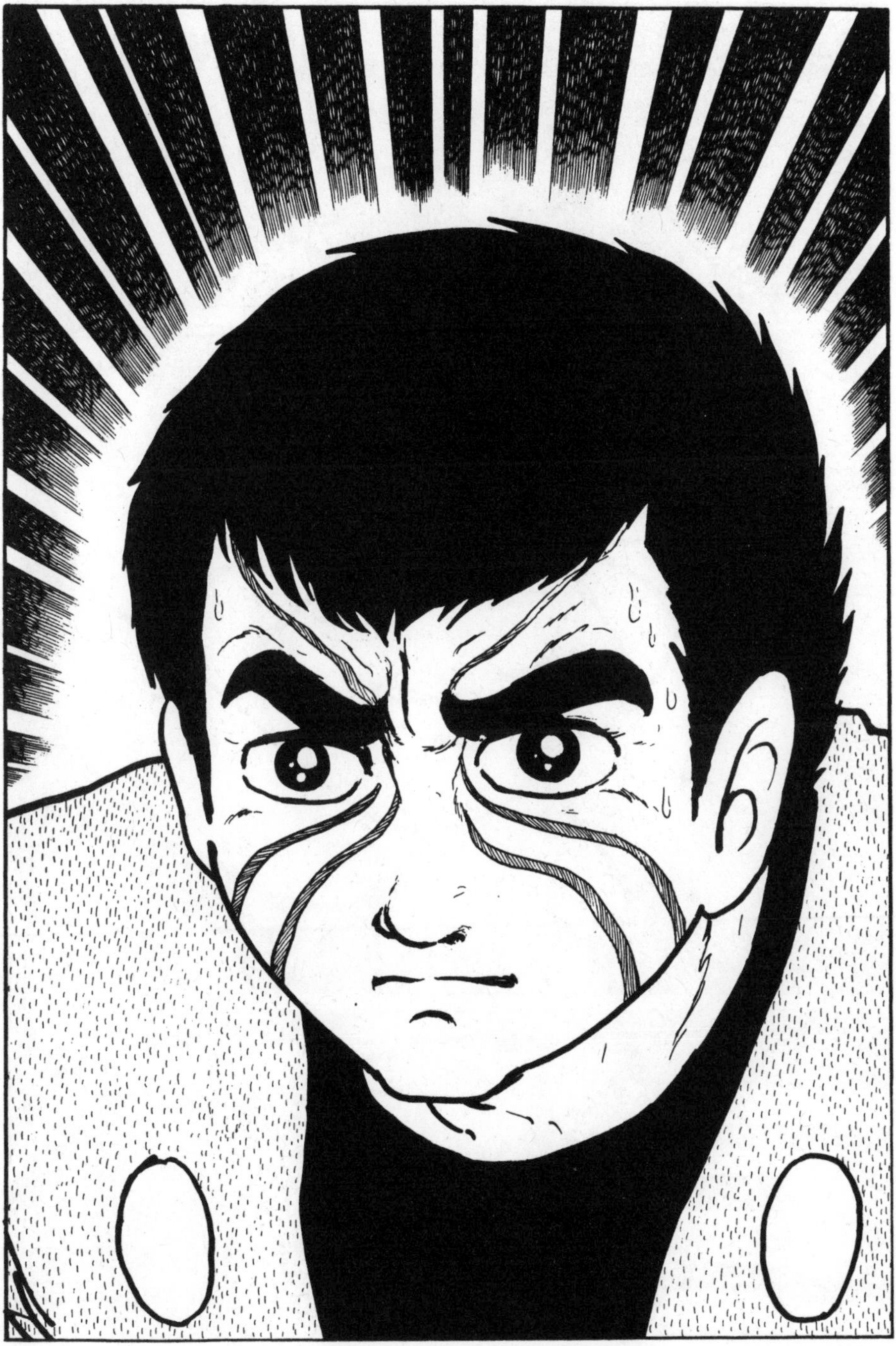

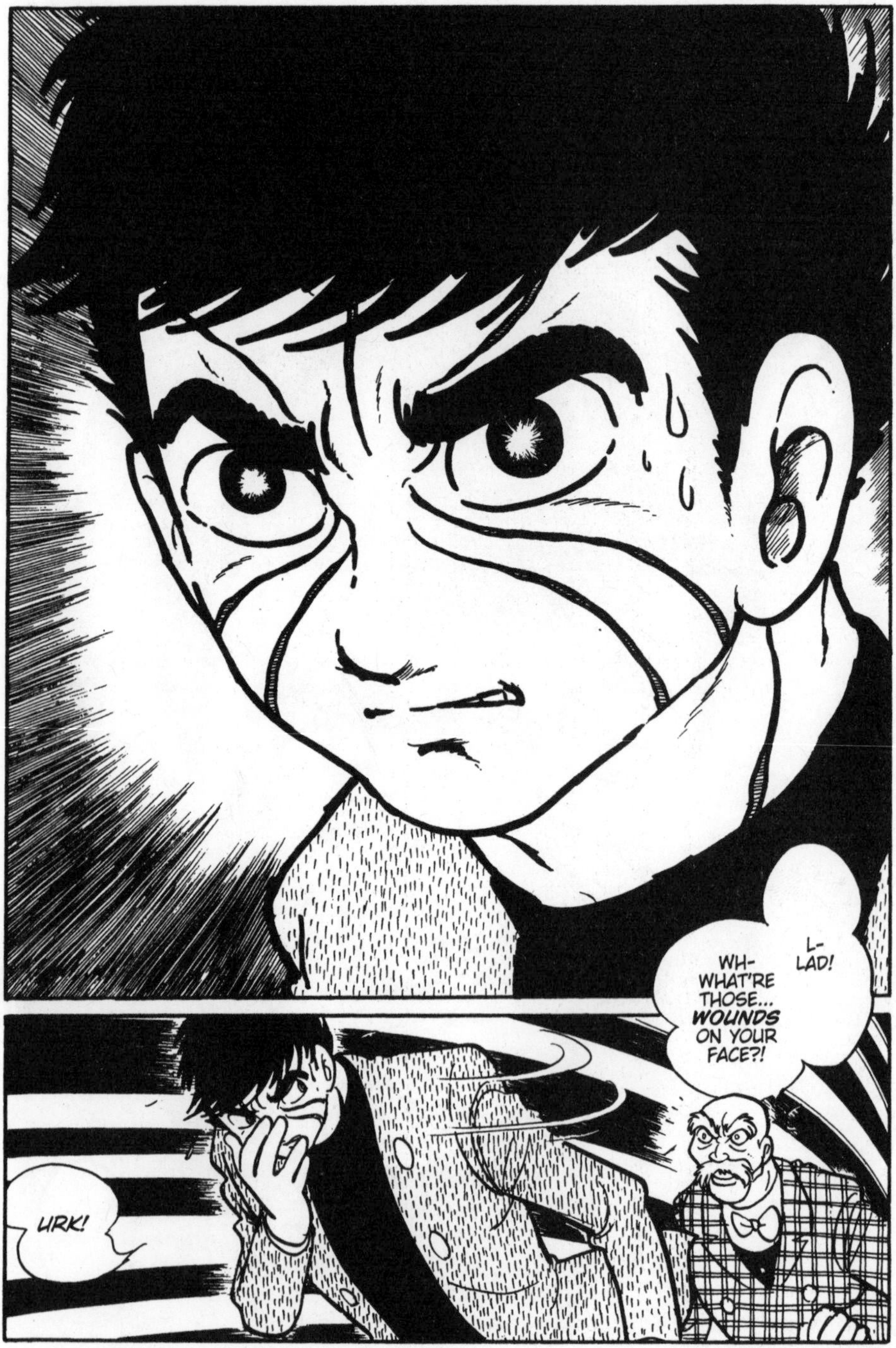
L-
LAD!
WH-
WHAT'RE
THOSE...
WOUNDS
ON YOUR
FACE?!
URK!

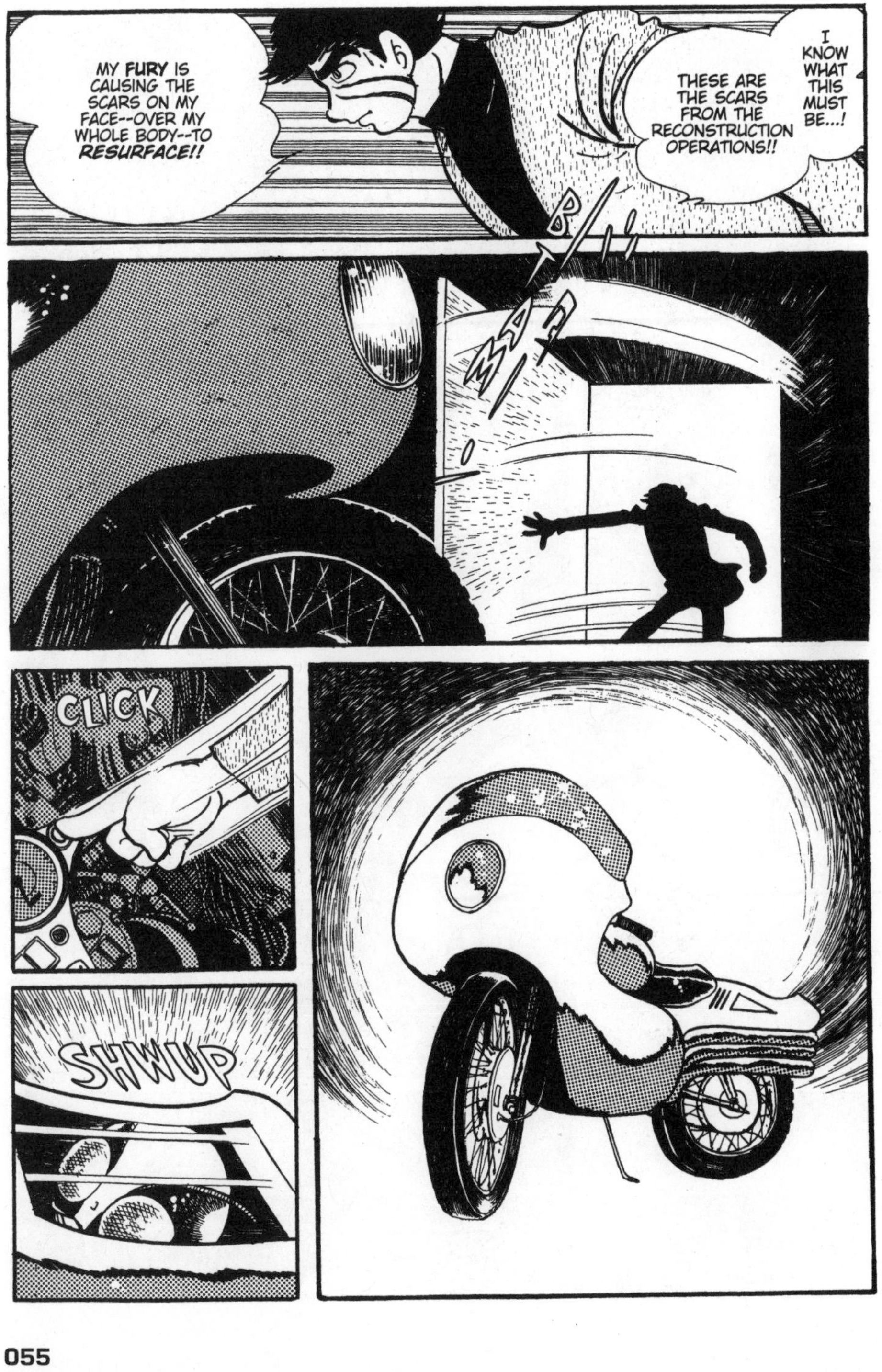
I KNOW WHAT THIS MUST BE...!
THESE ARE THE SCARS FROM THE RECONSTRUCTION OPERATIONS!!
MY FURY IS CAUSING THE SCARS ON MY FACE--OVER MY WHOLE BODY--TO RESURFACE!!
CLICK
SHWUP

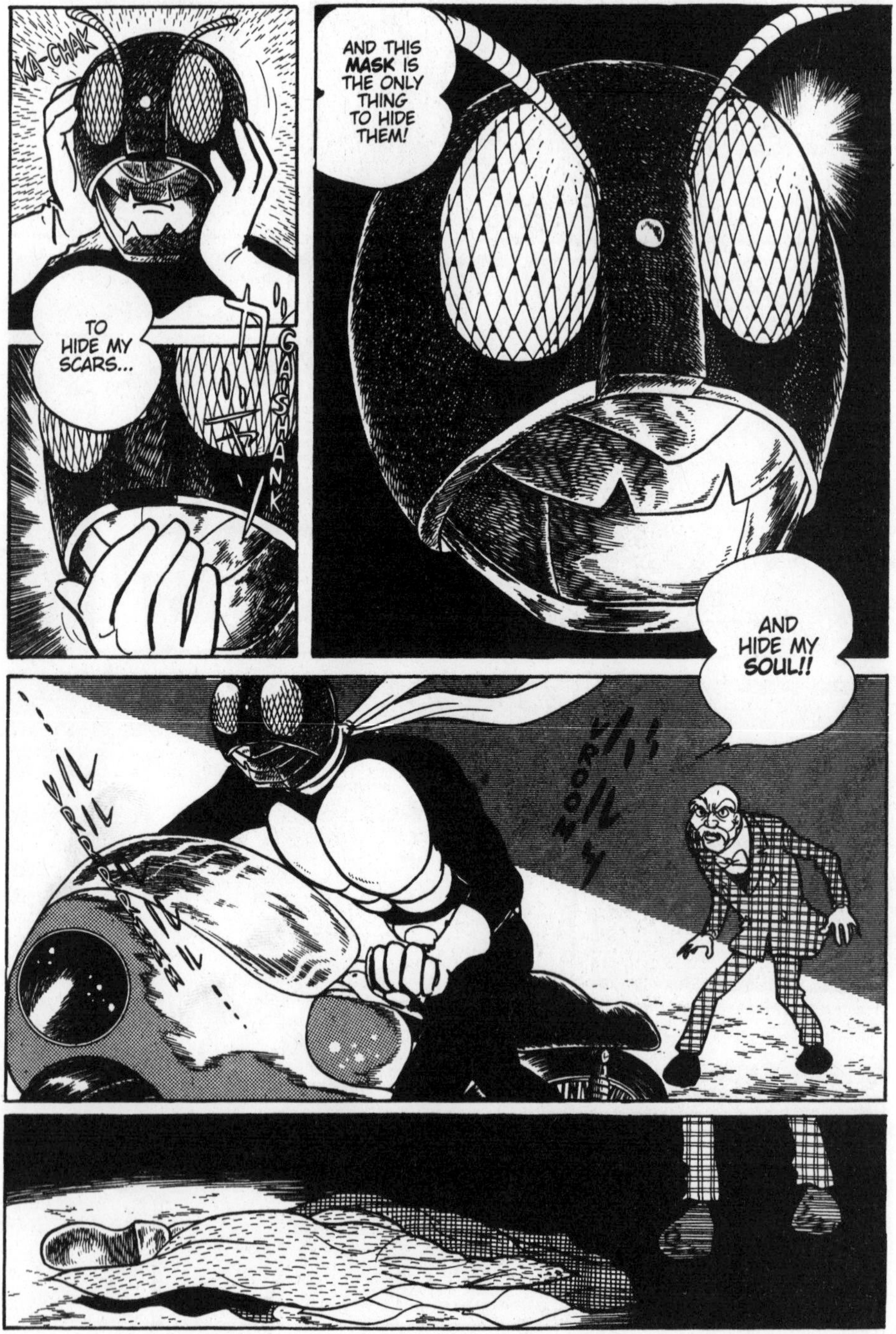
AND THIS MASK IS THE ONLY THING TO HIDE THEM!
KA-CHAK
TO HIDE MY SCARS...
GASHANK
AND HIDE MY SOUL!!
VROOM

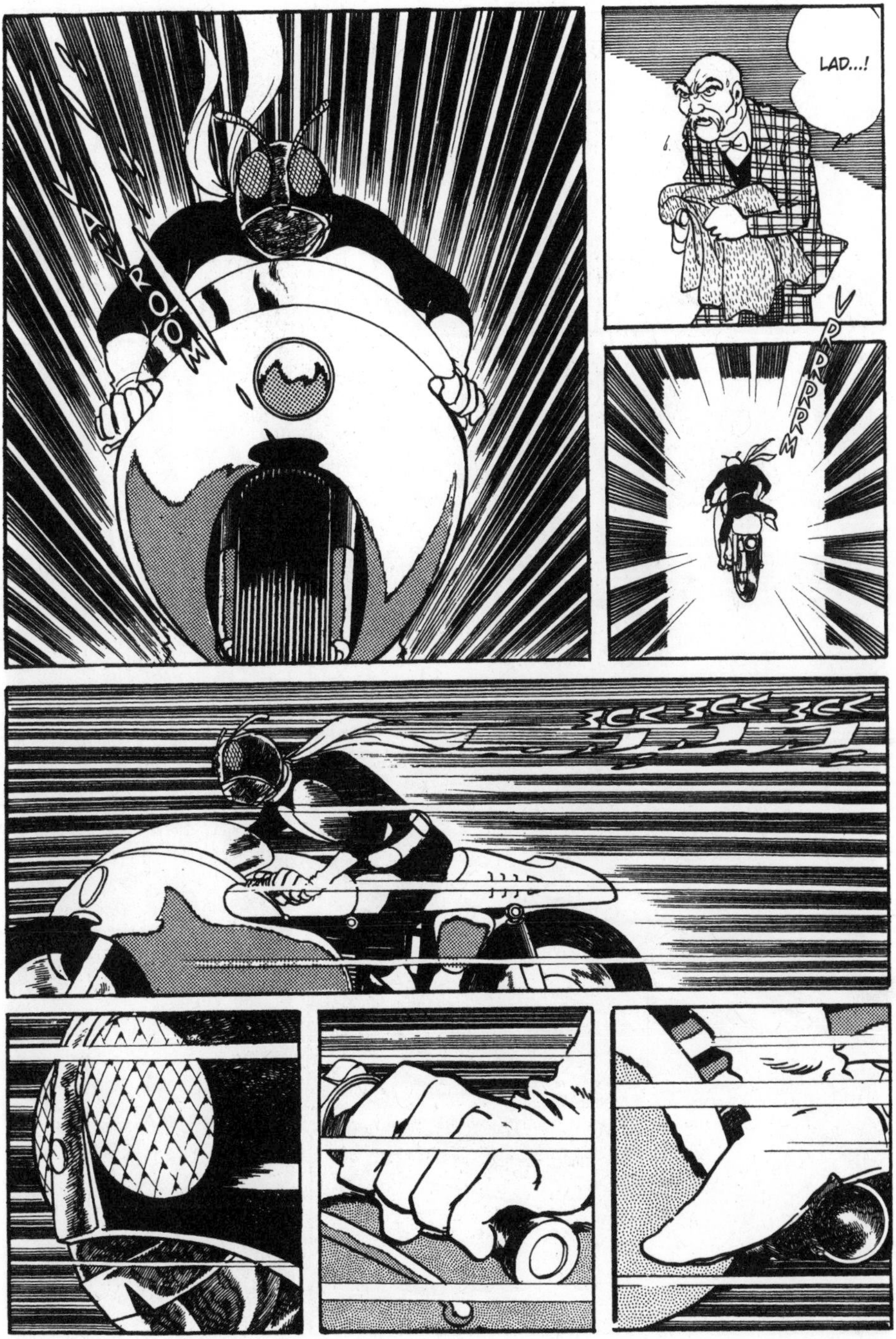
LAD...!
VRRRRRM
VAVROOM

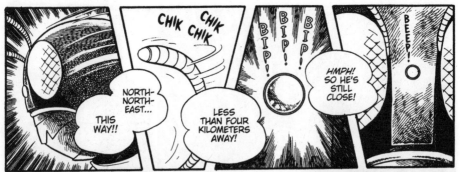

BEEP!
HMPH! SO HE'S STILL CLOSE!
BIP! BIP! BIP!
LESS THAN FOUR KILOMETERS AWAY!
CHIK CHIK CHIK
NORTH-NORTHEAST...
THIS WAY!!
VAVVRMMMM
KSHAK
KSHAK
SHAK

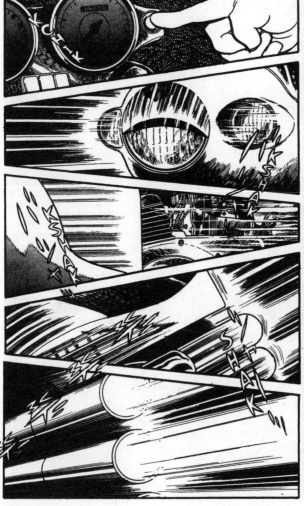

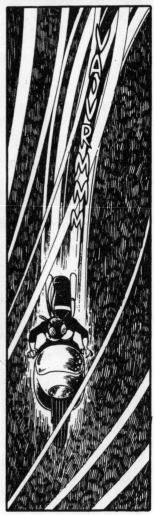

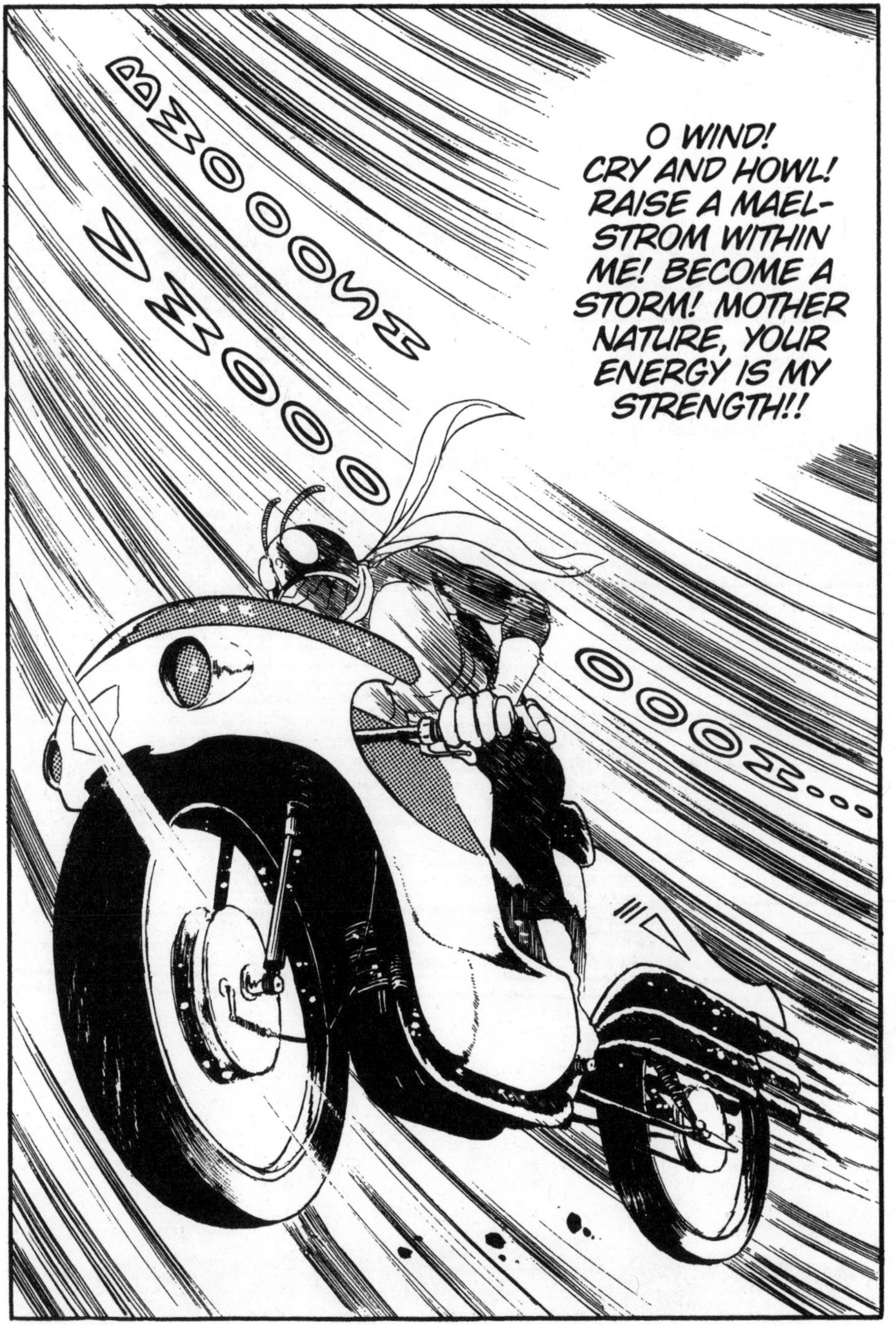
O WIND! CRY AND HOWL! RAISE A MAEL-STROM WITHIN ME! BECOME A STORM! MOTHER NATURE, YOUR ENERGY IS MY STRENGTH!!
BWOOOOSH
VWOOOO
OOOOOSH...

BWOOOOOOSH

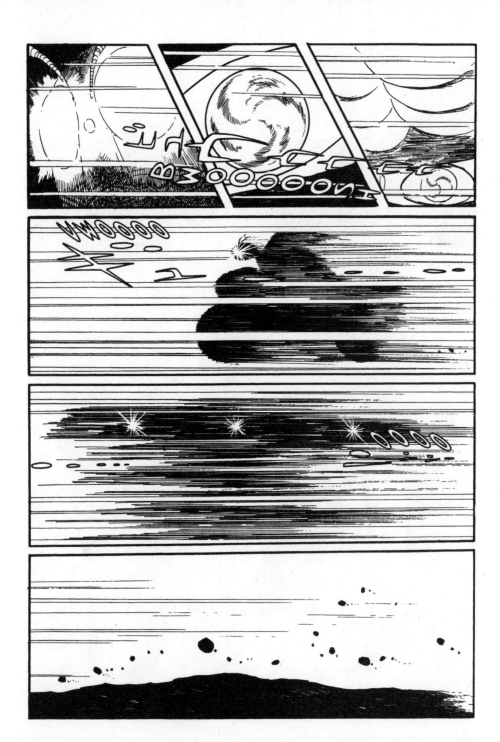

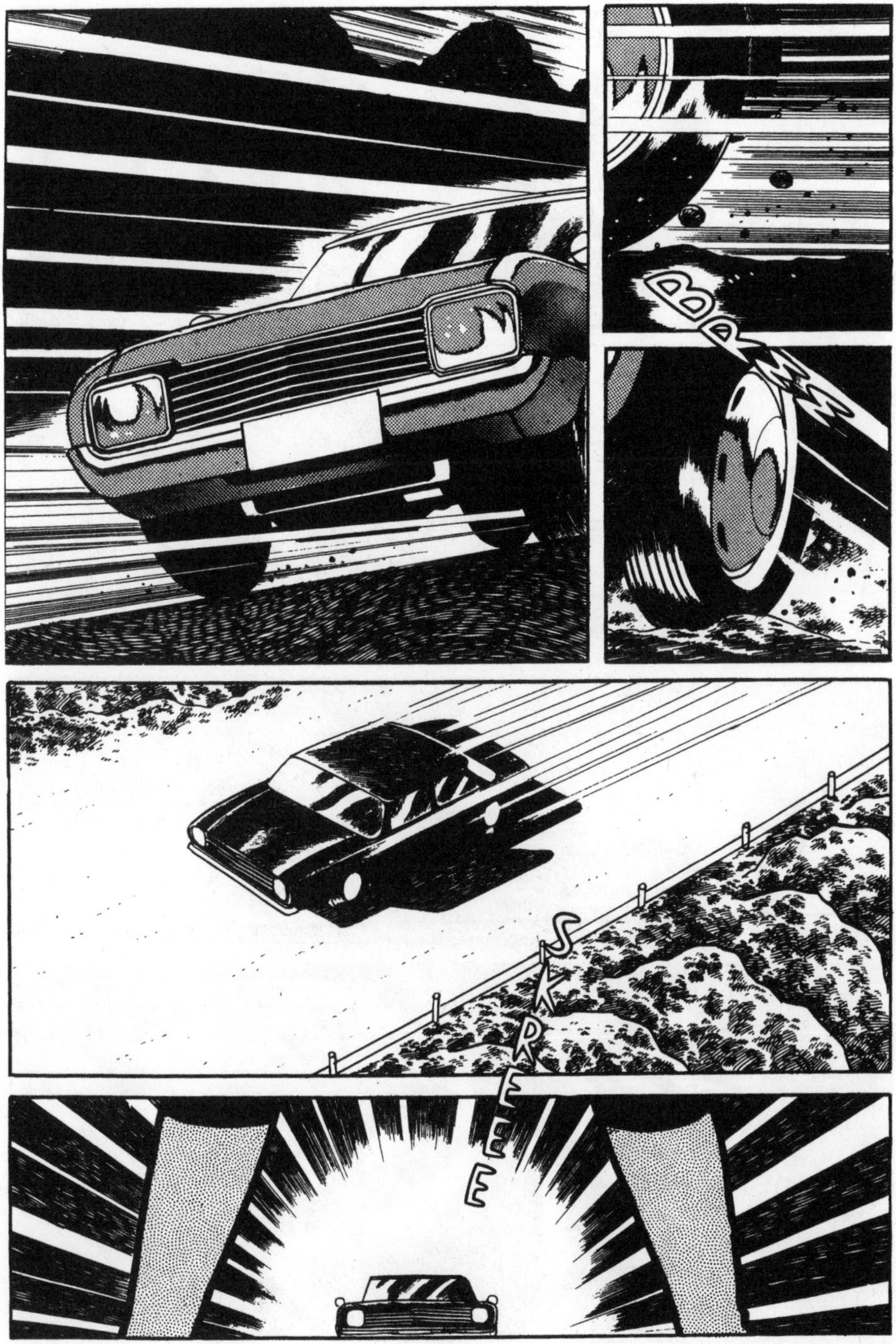
BRMM
SKREEEE

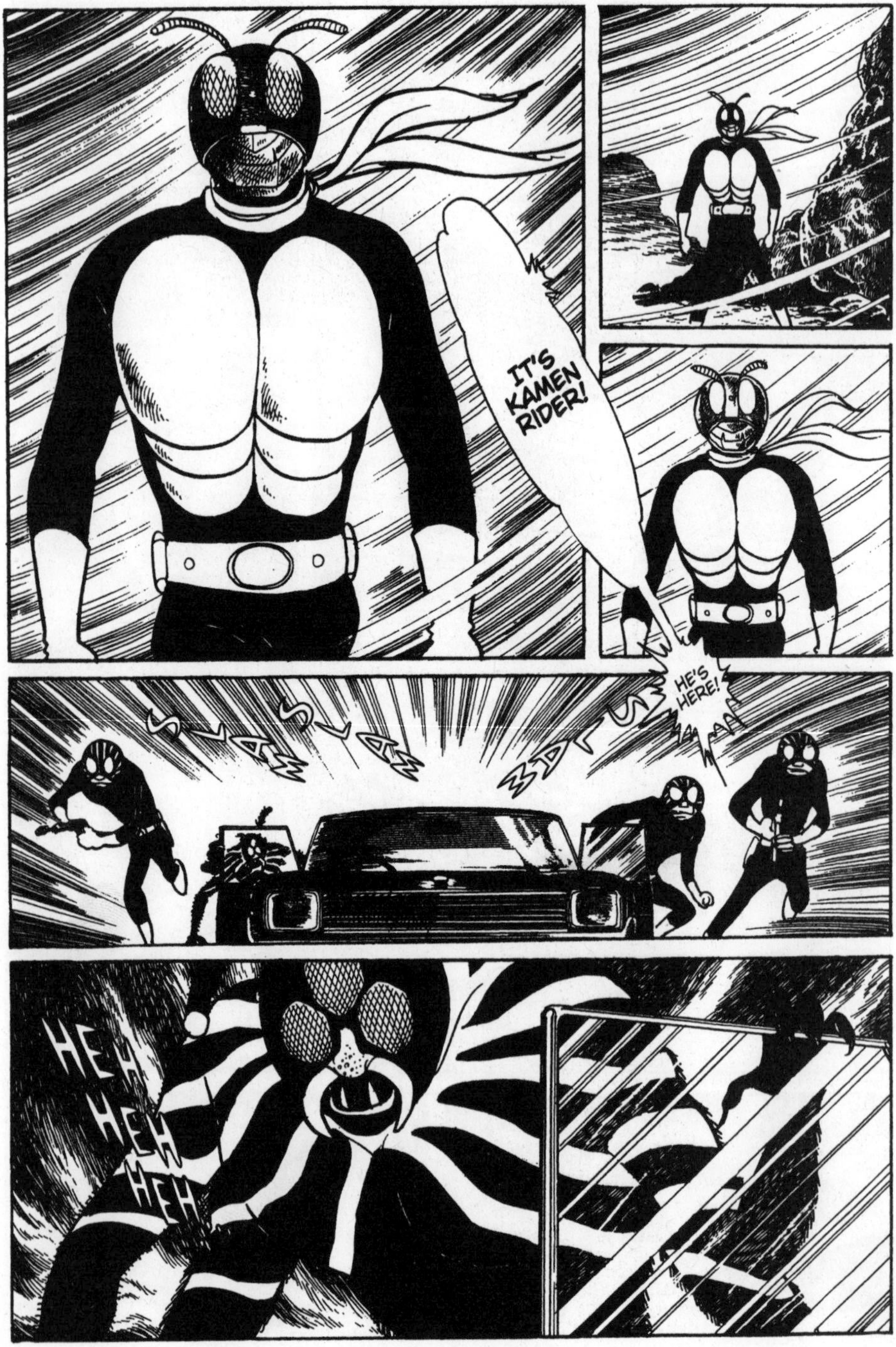
IT'S KAMEN RIDER!
HE'S HERE!
SLAM
SLAM
SLAM
HEH HEH HEH

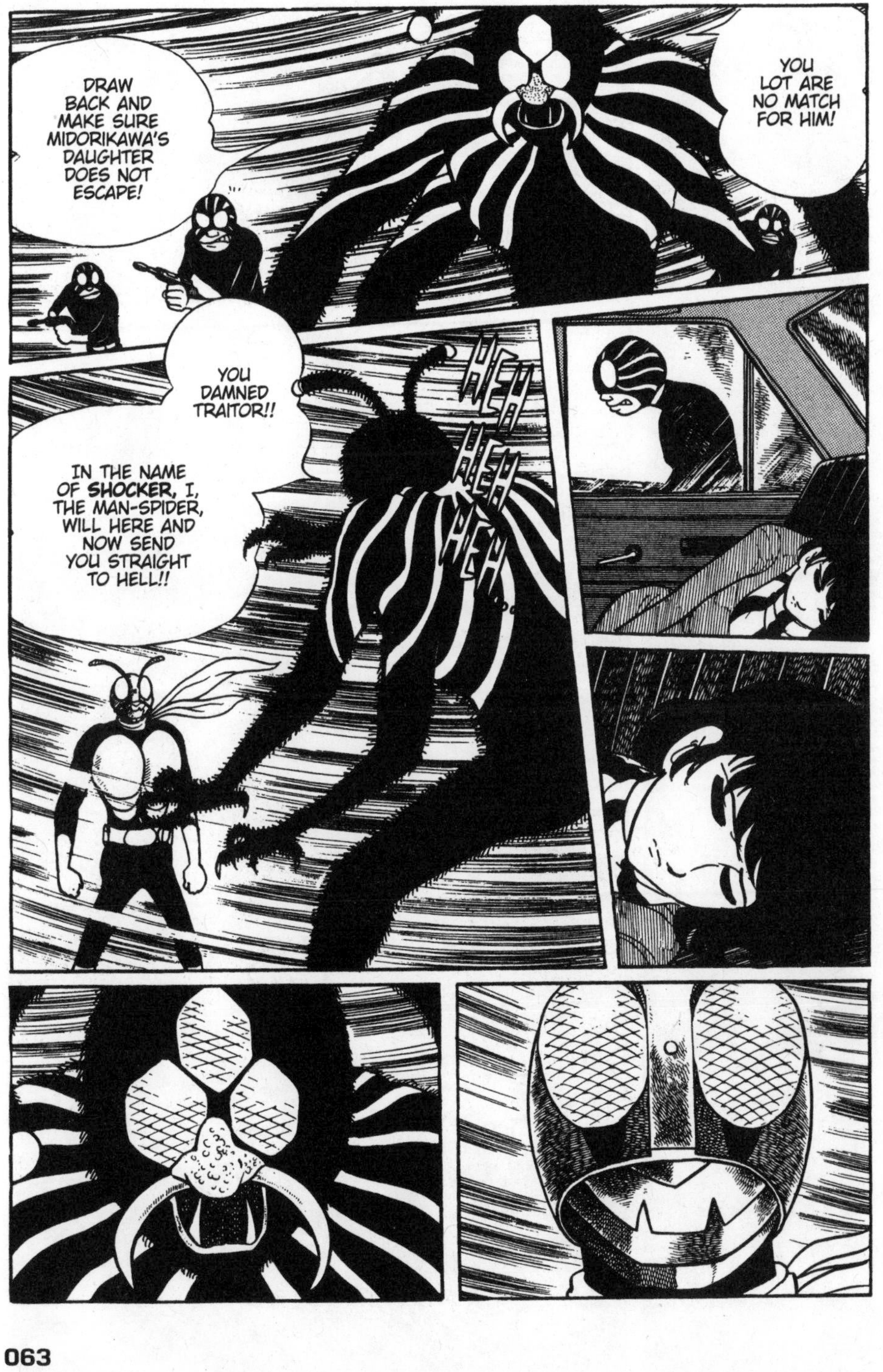
YOU LOT ARE NO MATCH FOR HIM!
DRAW BACK AND MAKE SURE MIDORIKAWA'S DAUGHTER DOES NOT ESCAPE!
YOU DAMNED TRAITOR!!
HEH HEH HEH...
IN THE NAME OF **SHOCKER,** I, THE MAN-SPIDER, WILL HERE AND NOW SEND YOU STRAIGHT TO HELL!!

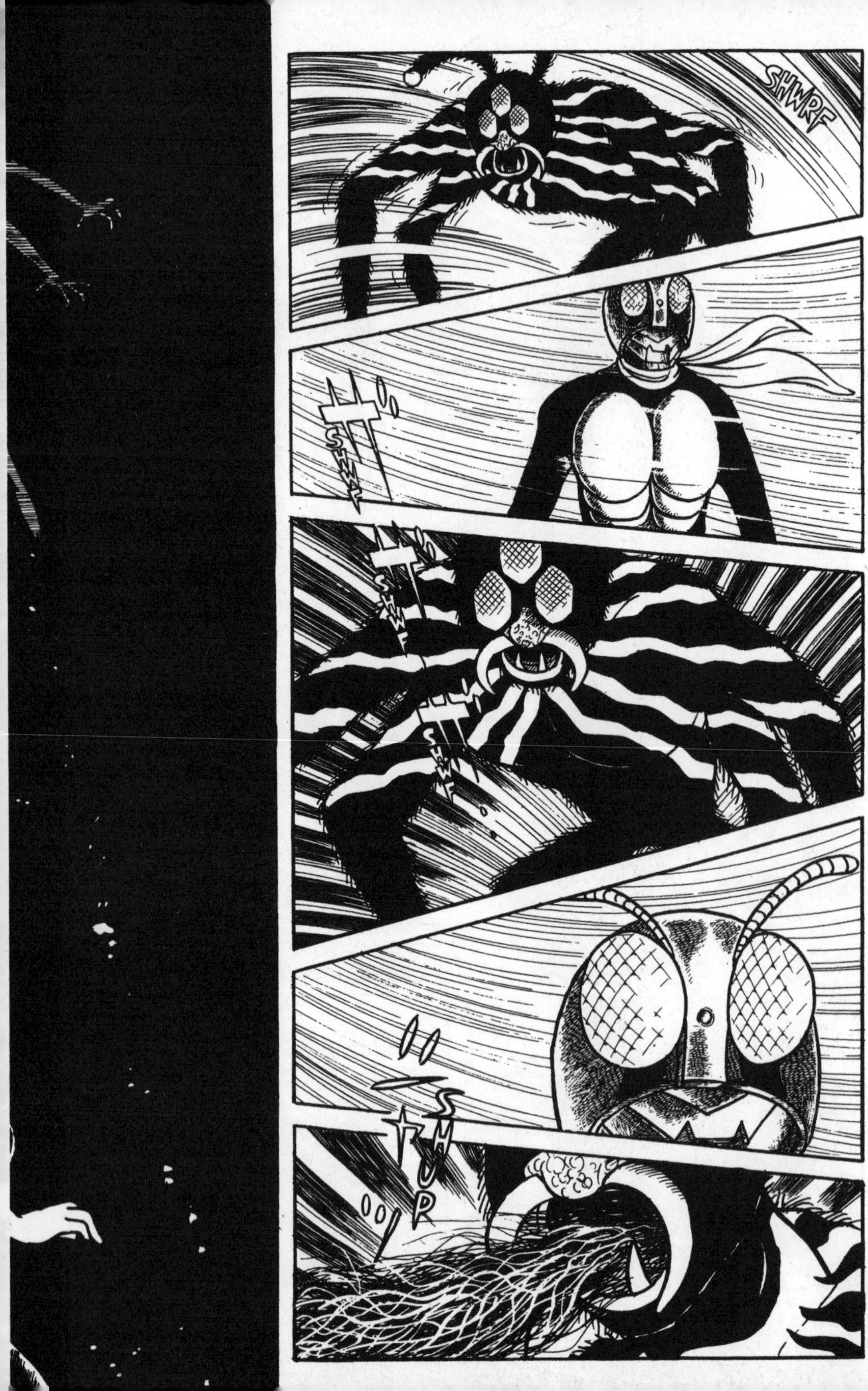
SHWRF
SHWF
SHWF
SHWF
SHUP

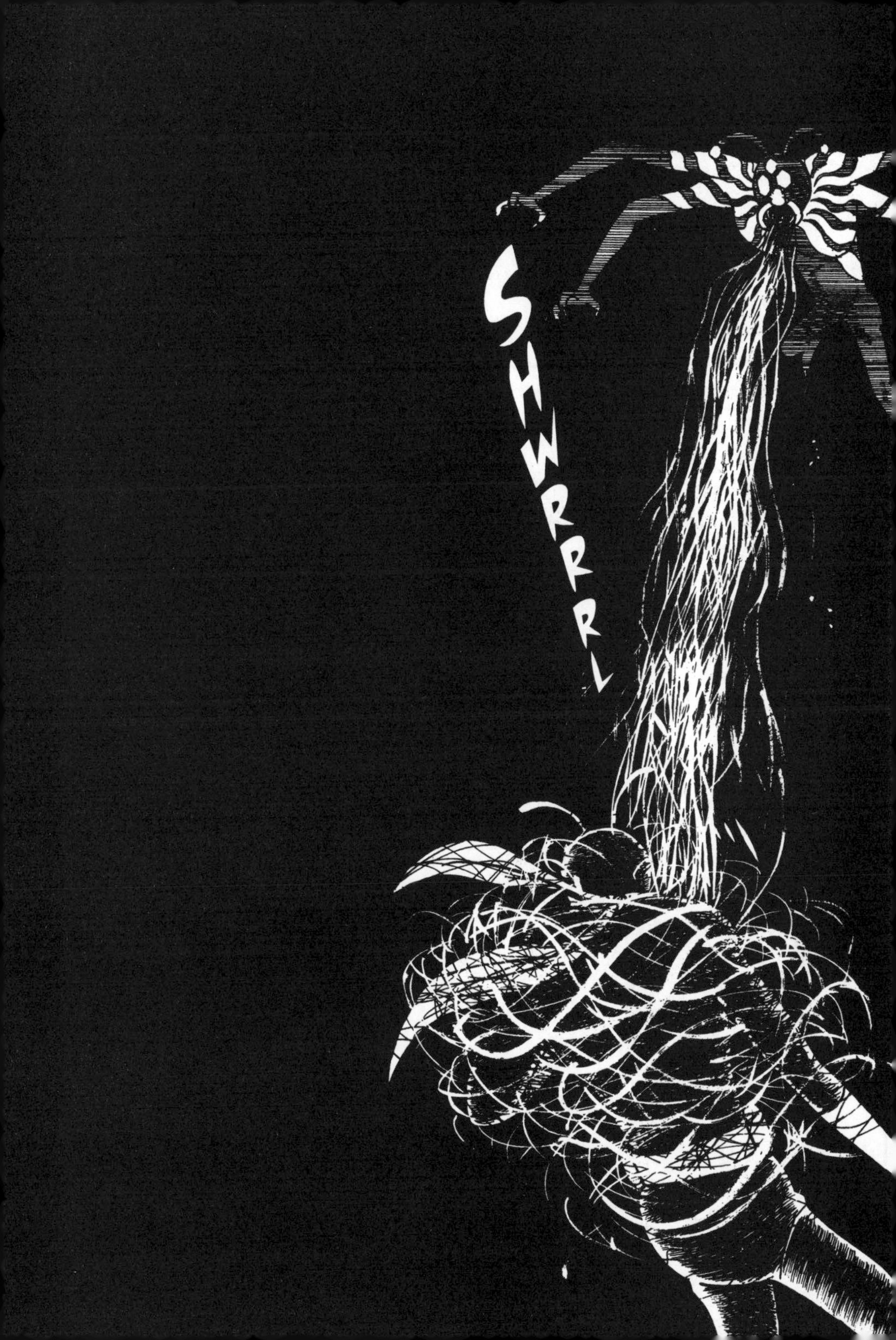
SHWRRRL

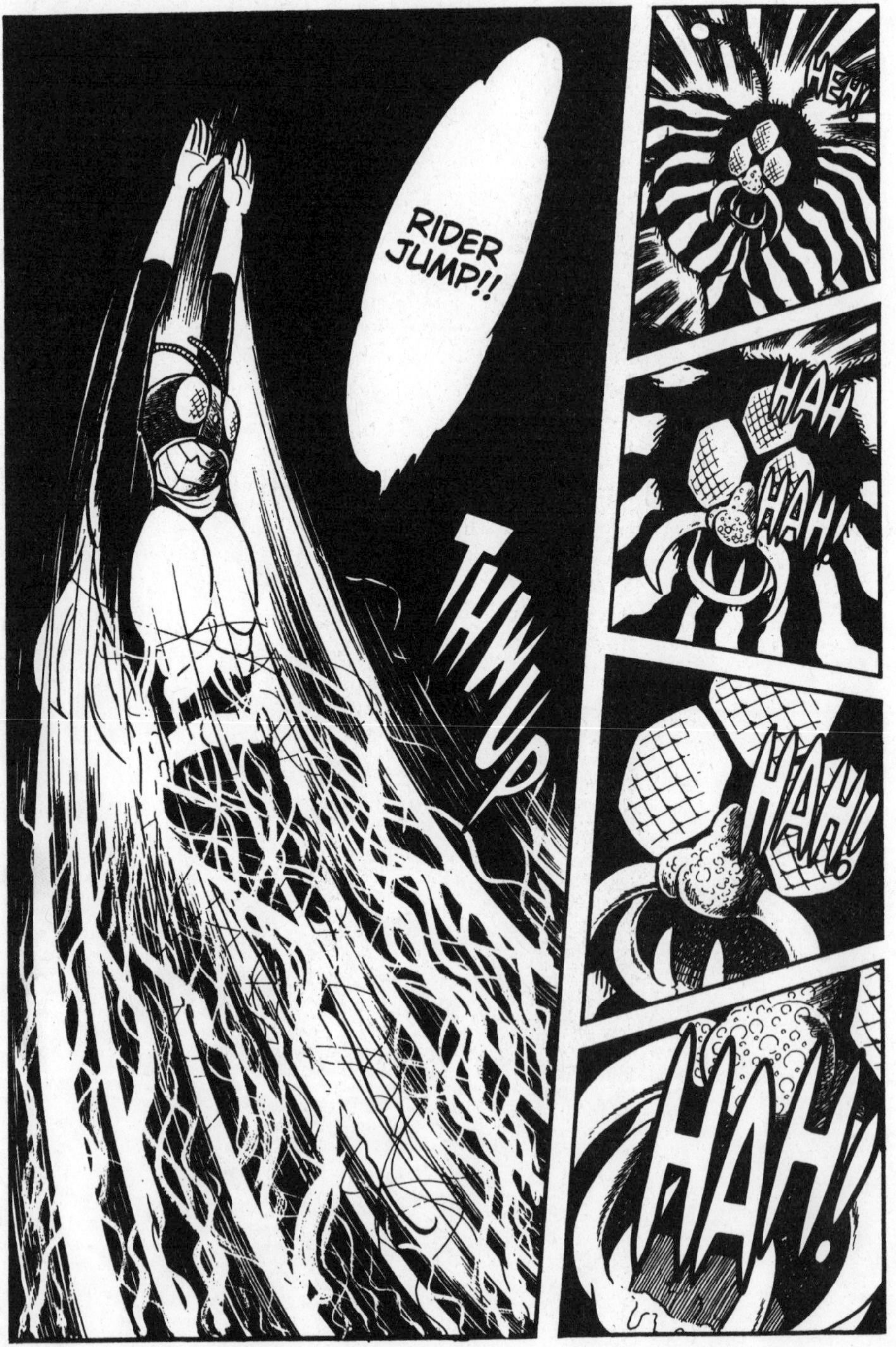
HEH!
HAH
HAH!
HAH!!
HAH!
RIDER JUMP!!
THWUP

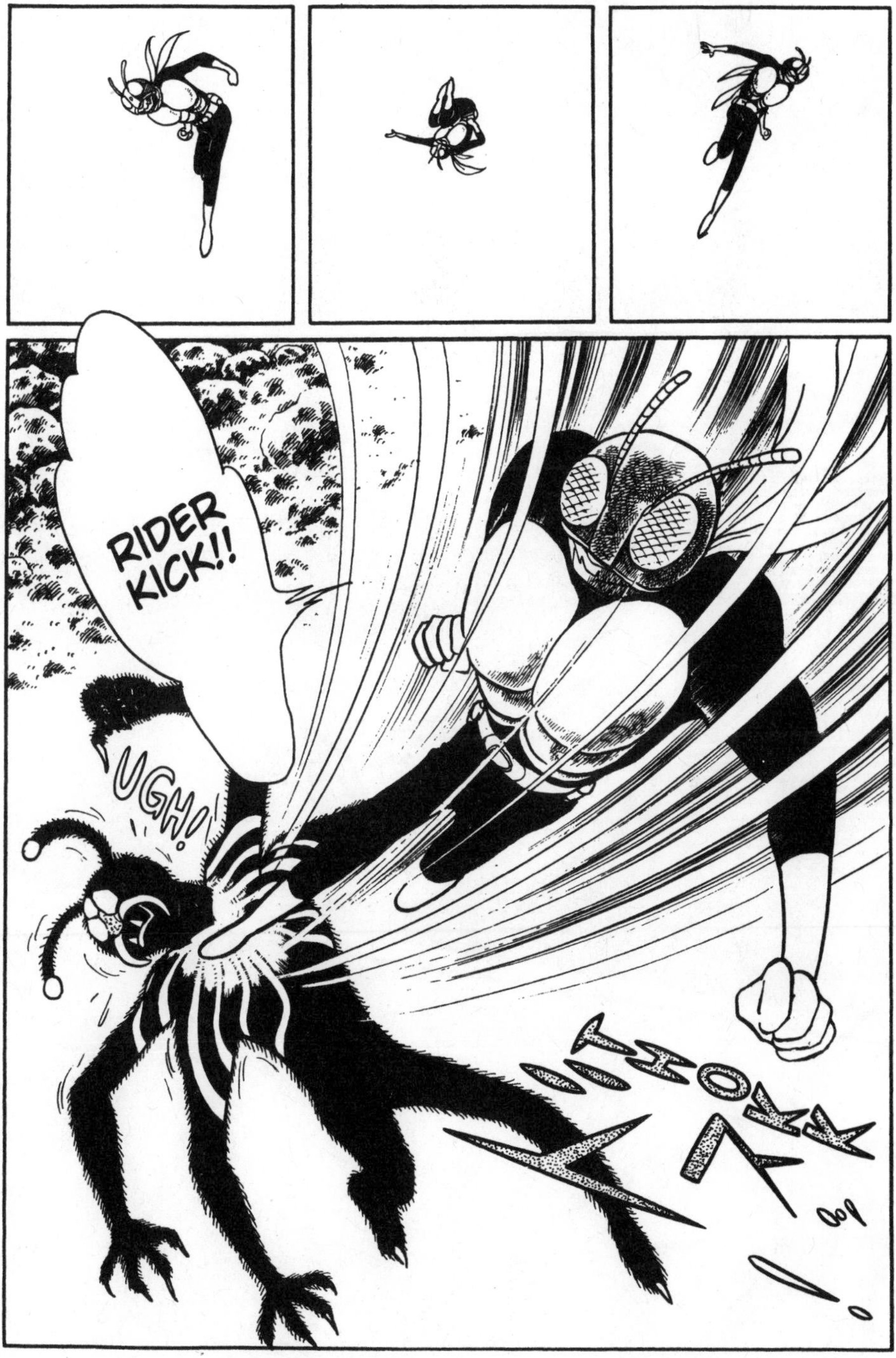
RIDER KICK!!
UGH!

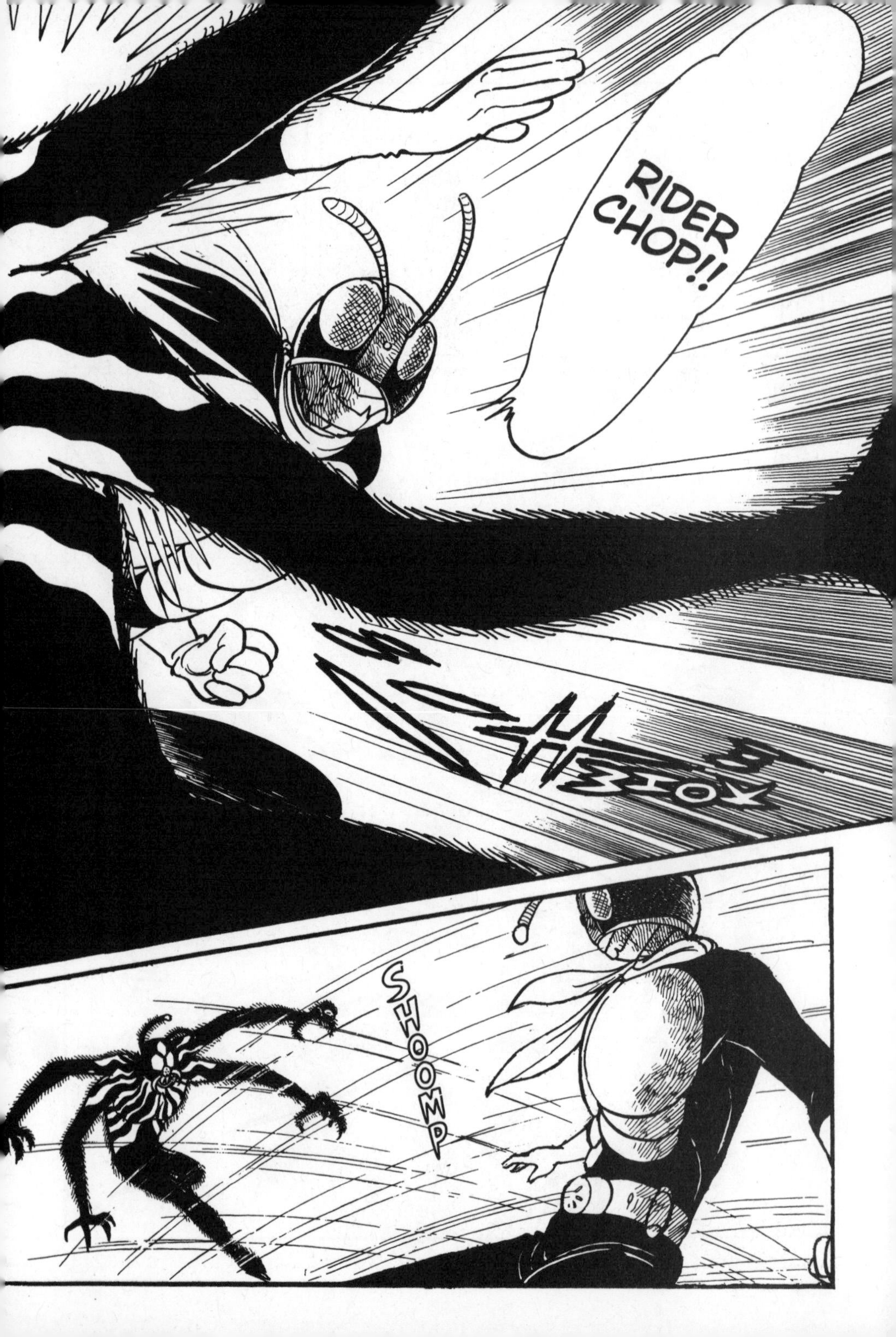
RIDER CHOP!!
SHOOMP

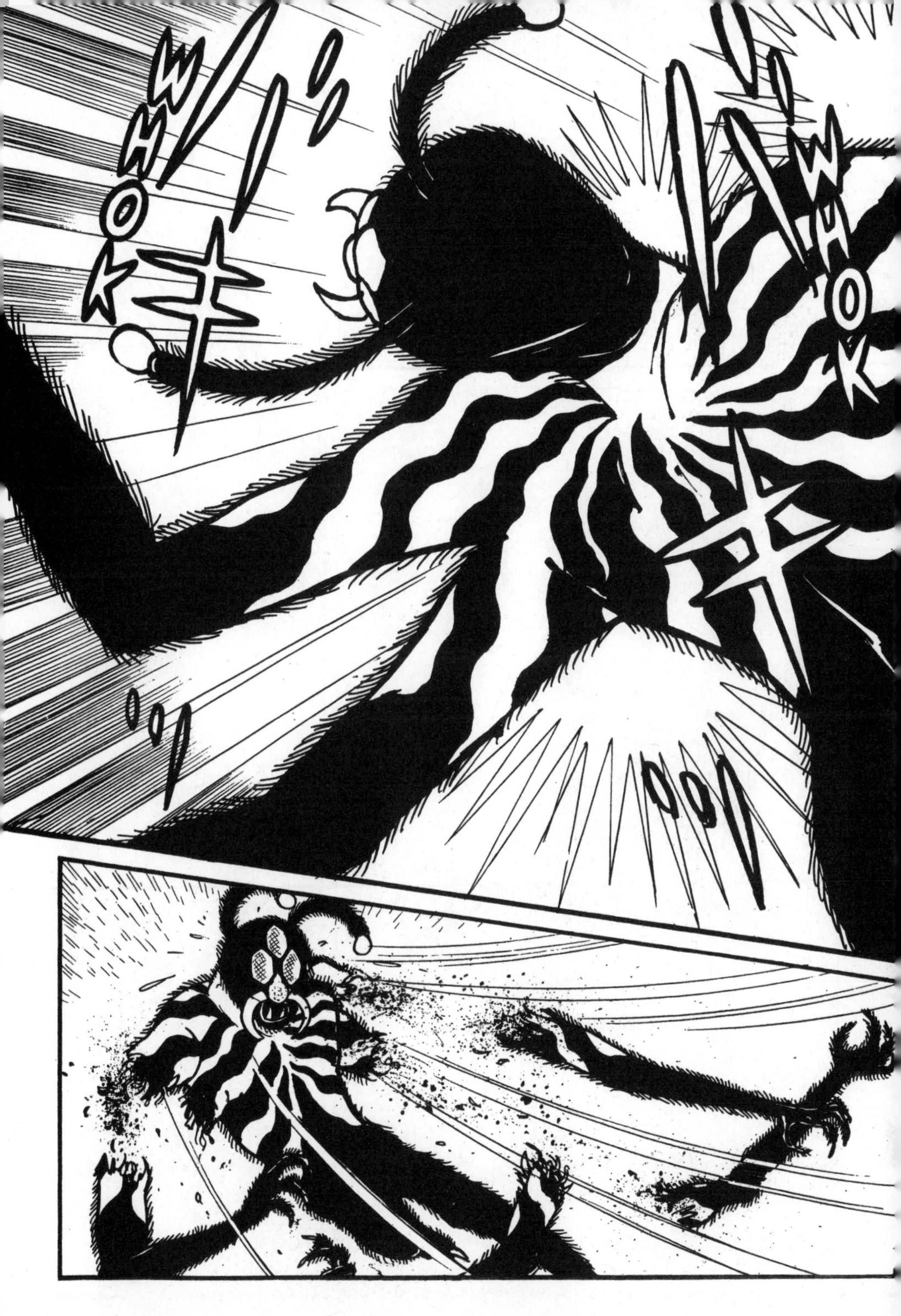
WHOK
WHOK

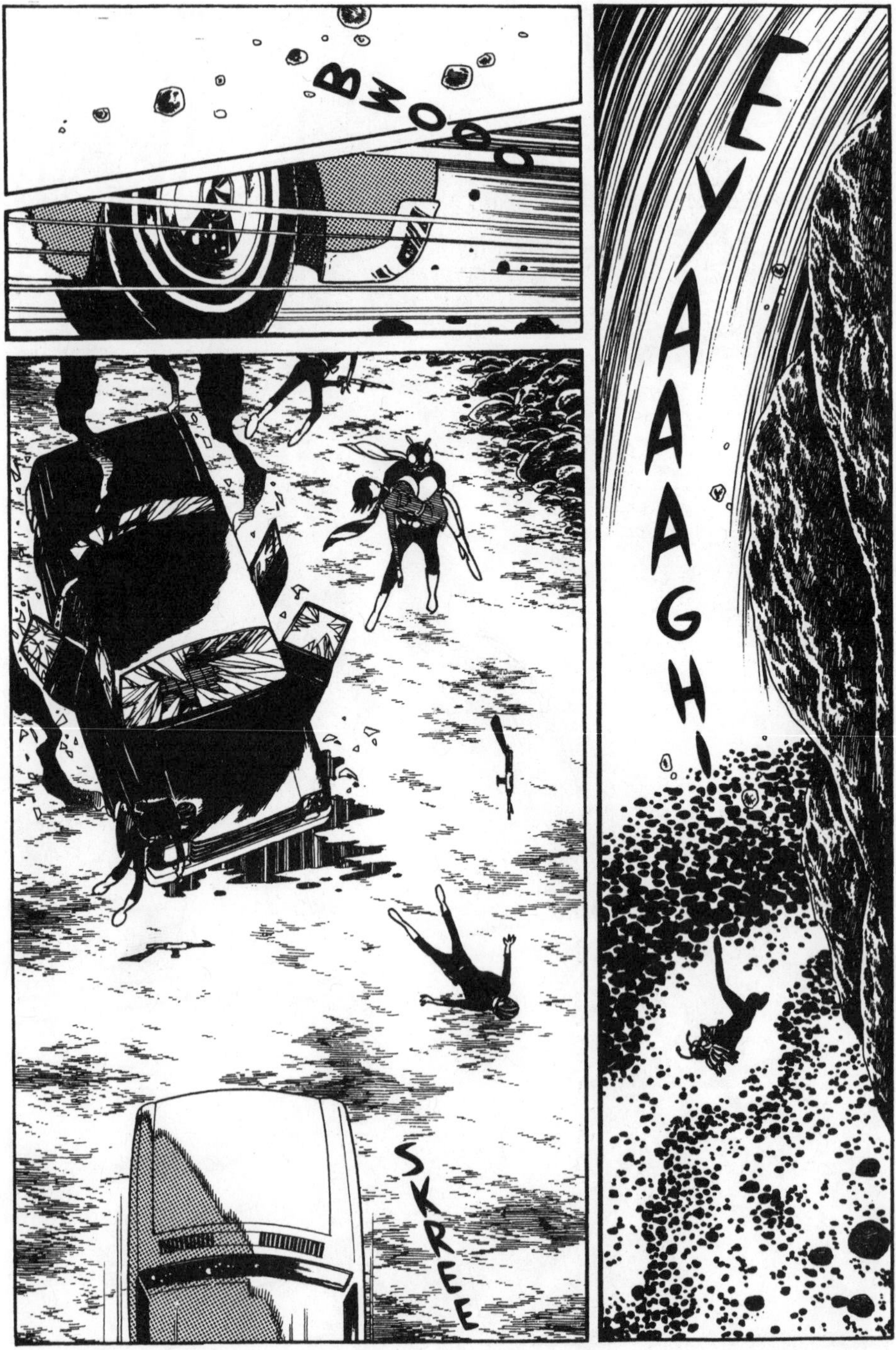
EYAAAGH!
BWOOO
SKREE

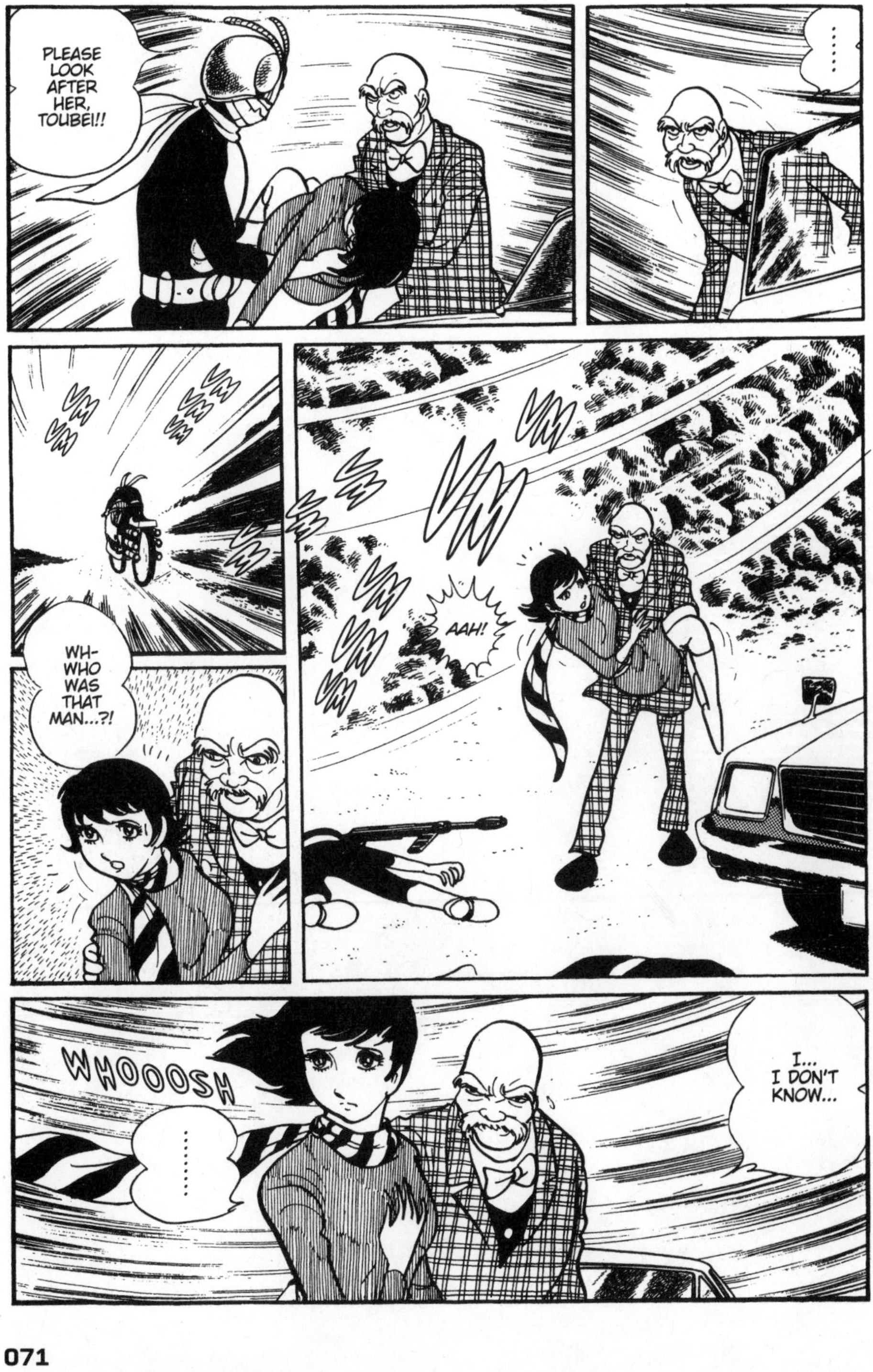
......
PLEASE LOOK AFTER HER, TOUBEI!!
AAH!
WH-WHO WAS THAT MAN...?!
I... I DON'T KNOW...
WHOOOSH
......

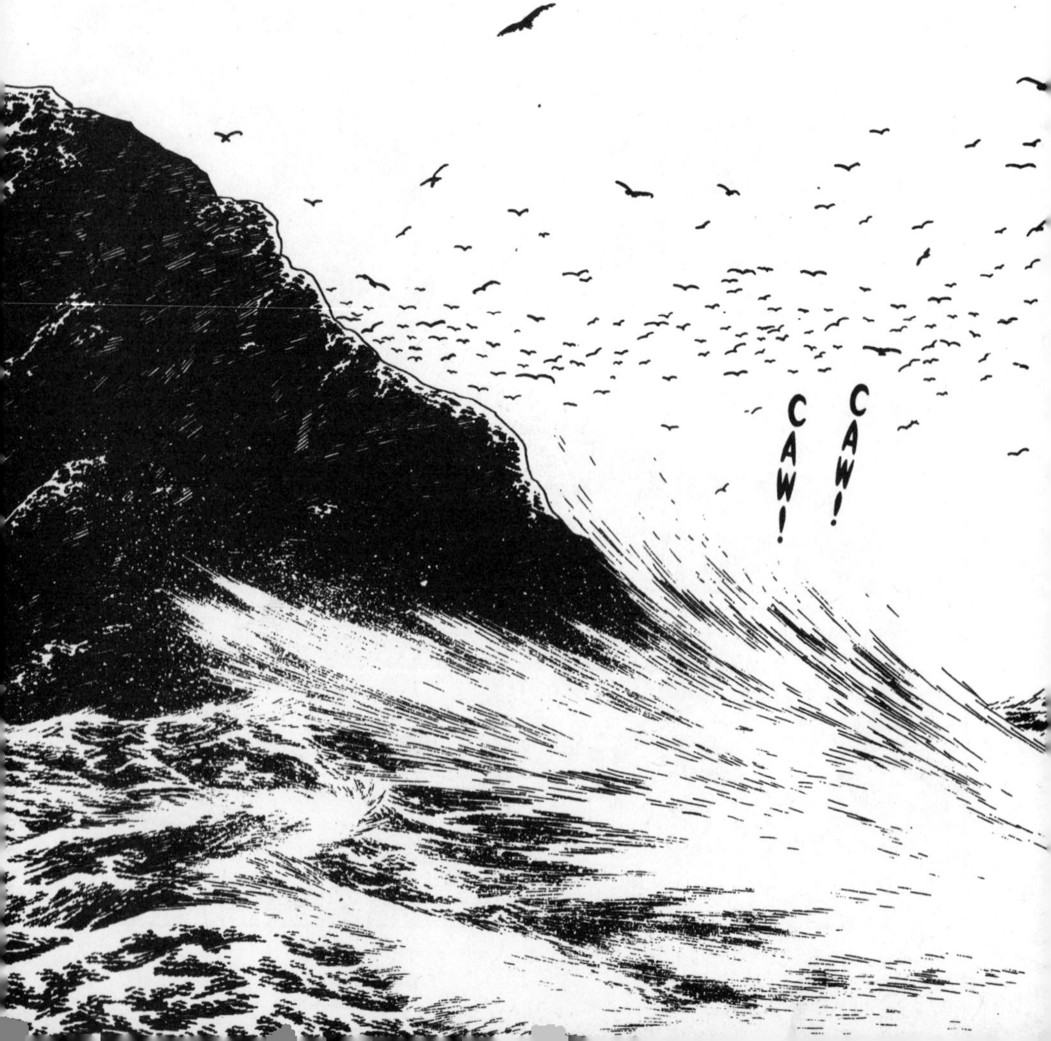
CAW!
CAW!

PART 2:
The Flying Man-Bat

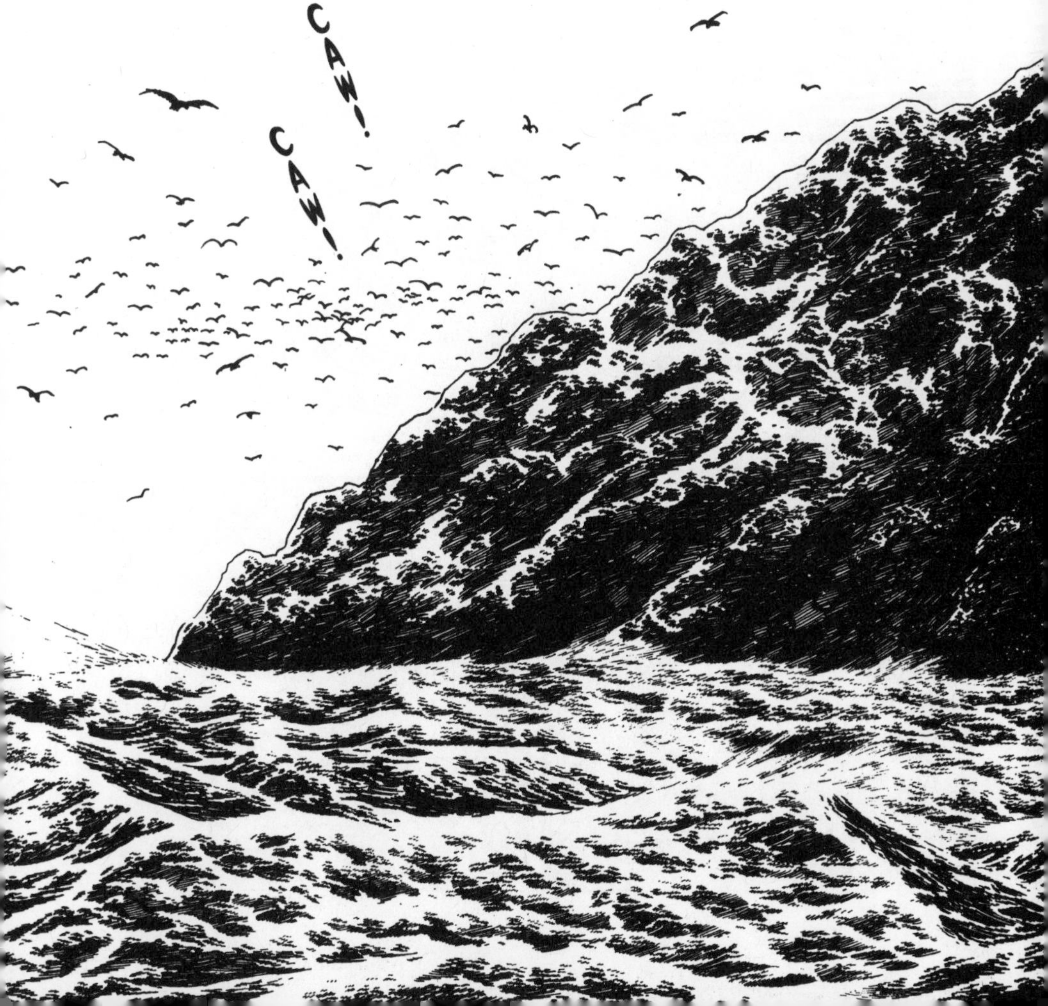
CAW!
CAW!

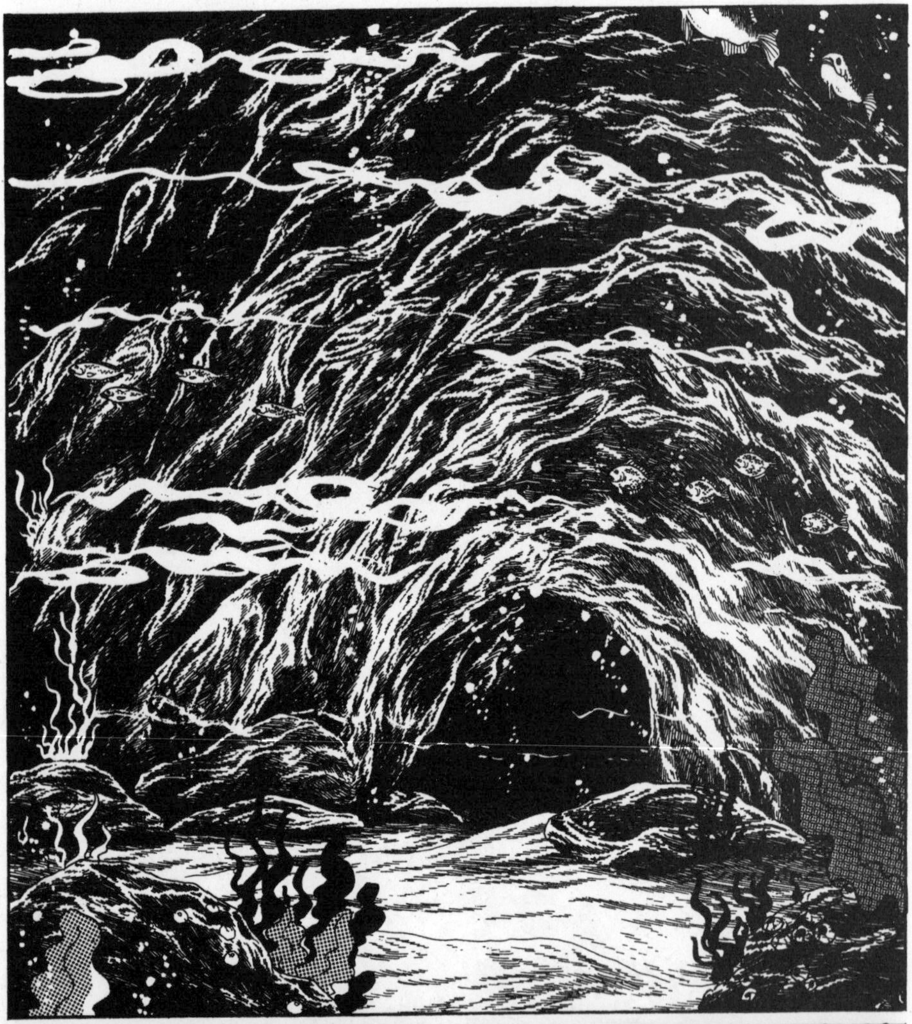
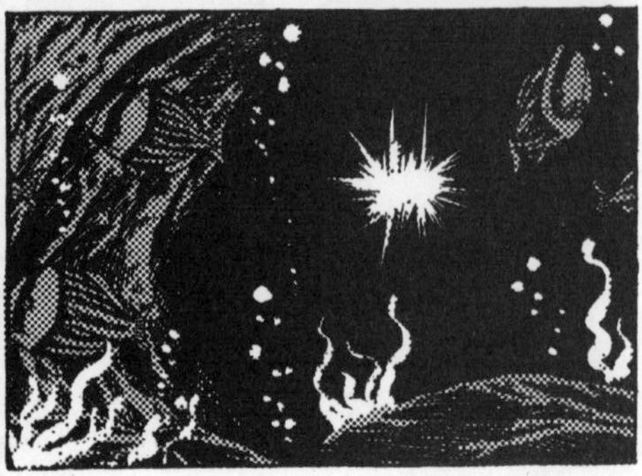
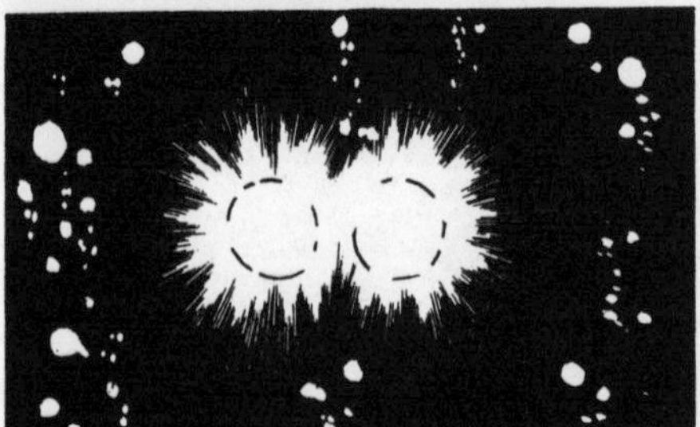

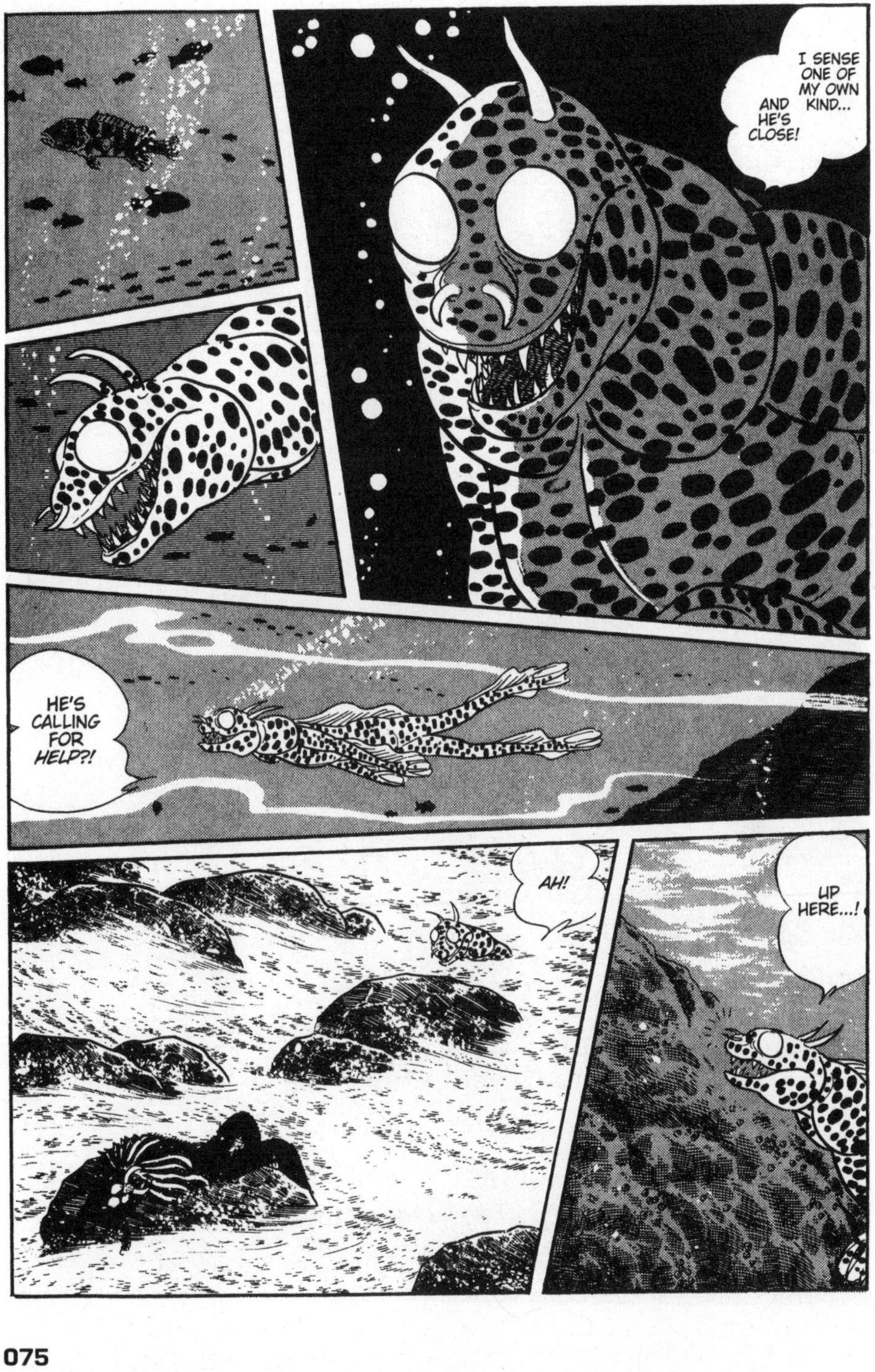
I SENSE ONE OF MY OWN KIND... AND HE'S CLOSE!
HE'S CALLING FOR HELP?!
UP HERE...!
AH!

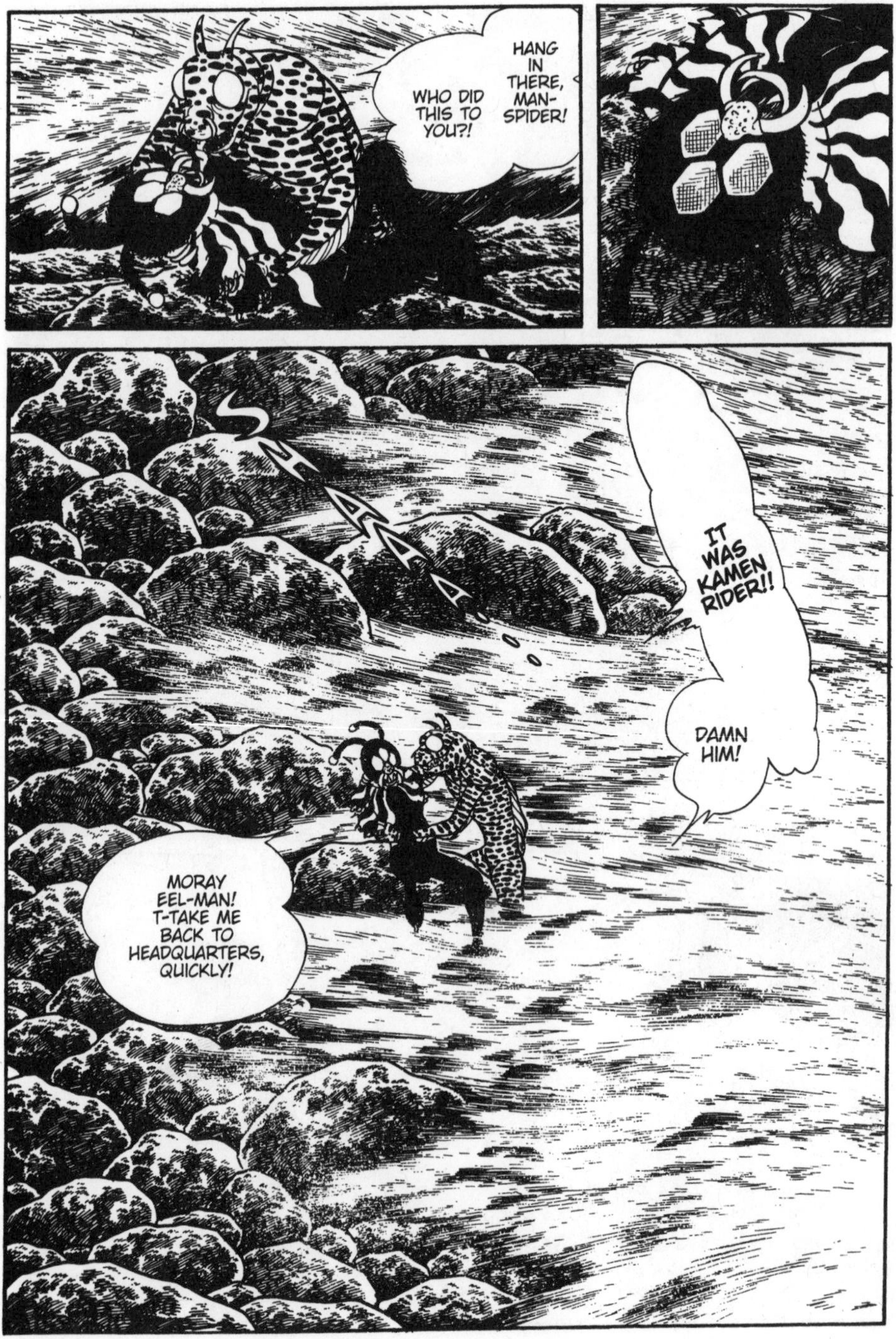
HANG IN THERE, MAN-SPIDER!
WHO DID THIS TO YOU?!
IT WAS KAMEN RIDER!!
DAMN HIM!
MORAY EEL-MAN! T-TAKE ME BACK TO HEADQUARTERS, QUICKLY!

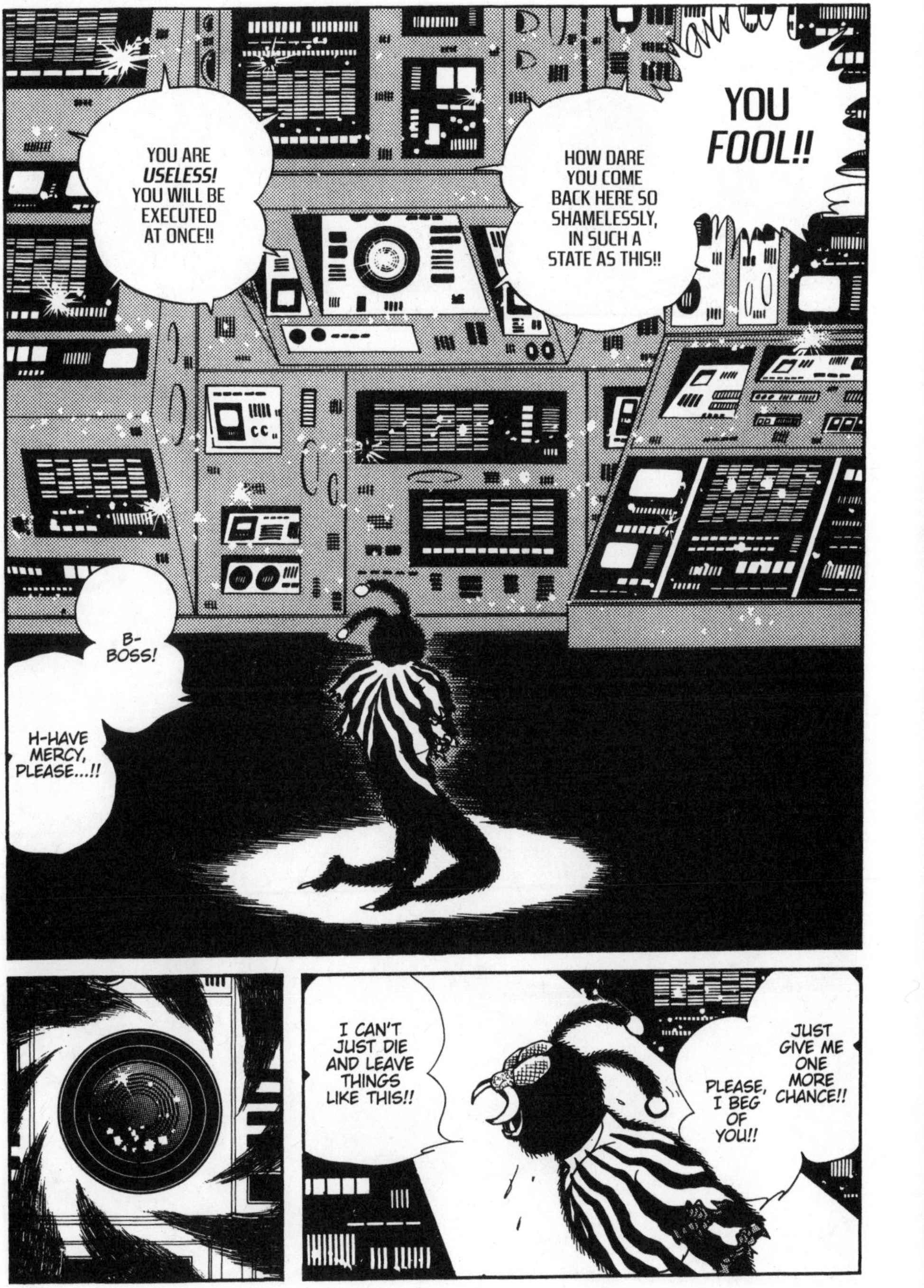
YOU *FOOL!!*
HOW DARE YOU COME BACK HERE SO SHAMELESSLY, IN SUCH A STATE AS THIS!!
YOU ARE *USELESS!* YOU WILL BE EXECUTED AT ONCE!!
B-BOSS!
H-HAVE MERCY, PLEASE...!!
JUST GIVE ME ONE MORE CHANCE!!
PLEASE, I BEG OF YOU!!
I CAN'T JUST DIE AND LEAVE THINGS LIKE THIS!!

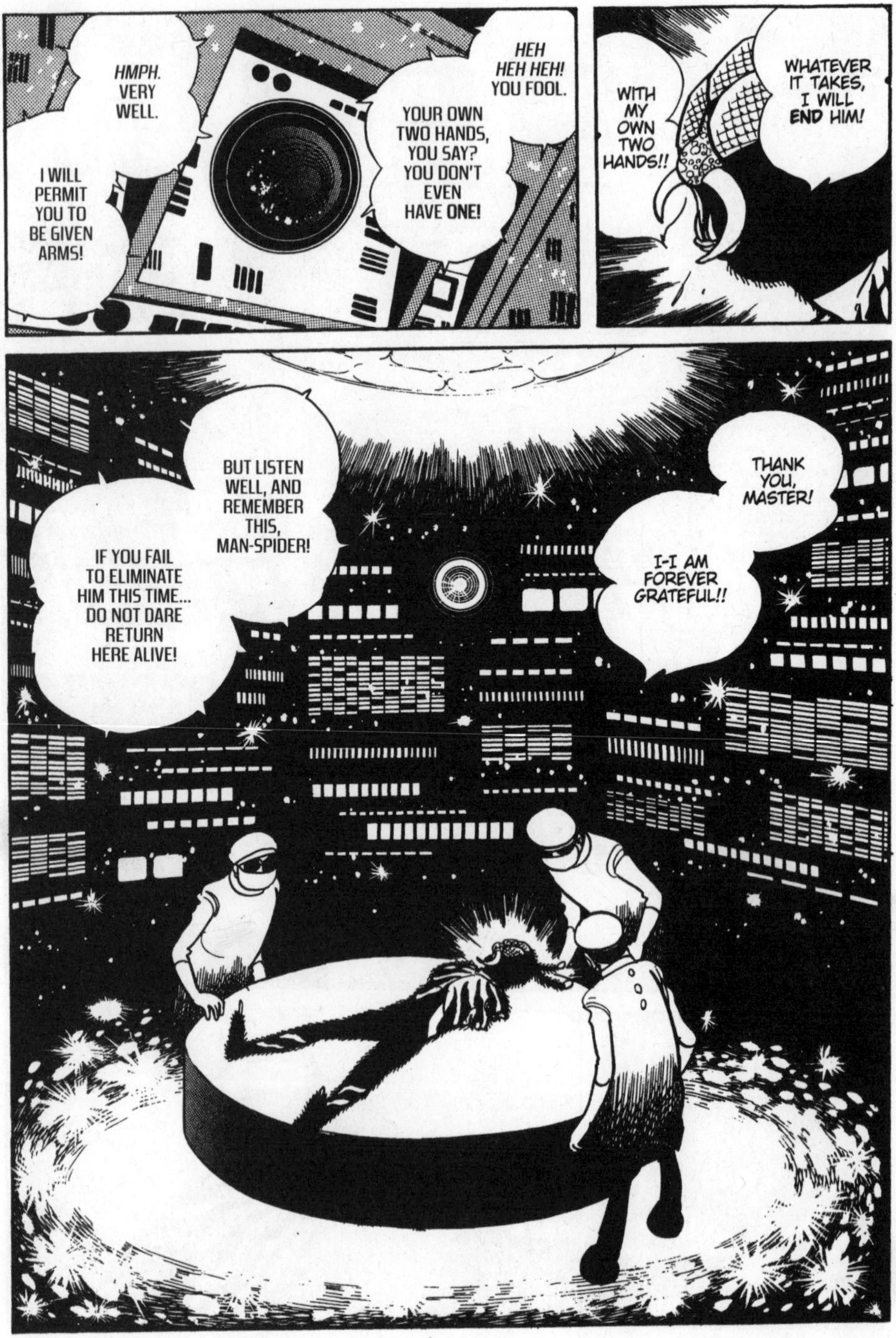
WHATEVER IT TAKES, I WILL END HIM!
WITH MY OWN TWO HANDS!!
HEH HEH HEH! YOU FOOL.
YOUR OWN TWO HANDS, YOU SAY? YOU DON'T EVEN HAVE ONE!
HMPH. VERY WELL.
I WILL PERMIT YOU TO BE GIVEN ARMS!
BUT LISTEN WELL, AND REMEMBER THIS, MAN-SPIDER!
IF YOU FAIL TO ELIMINATE HIM THIS TIME... DO NOT DARE RETURN HERE ALIVE!
THANK YOU, MASTER!
I-I AM FOREVER GRATEFUL!!

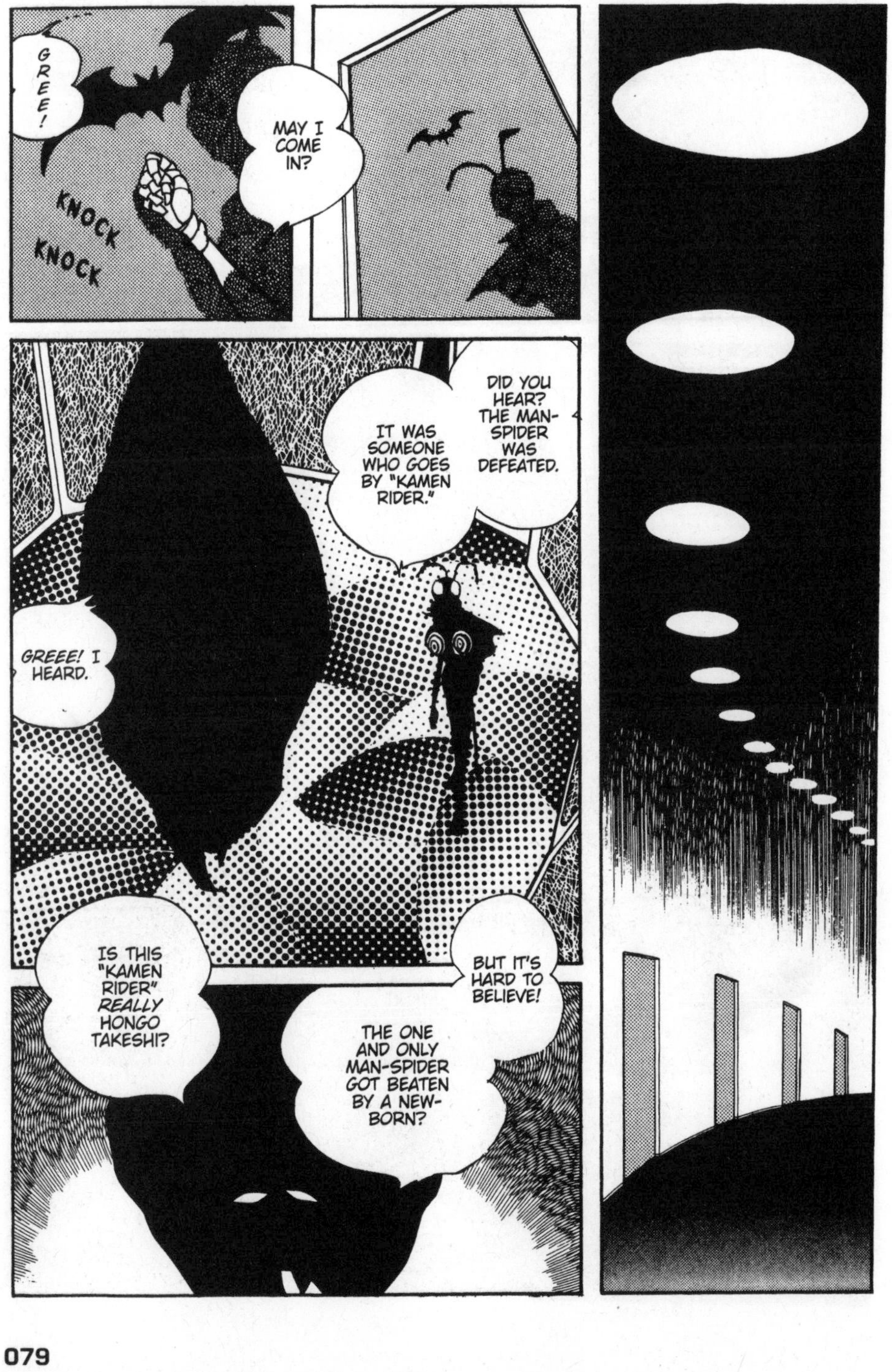
MAY I COME IN?
GREE!
KNOCK KNOCK
DID YOU HEAR? THE MAN-SPIDER WAS DEFEATED.
IT WAS SOMEONE WHO GOES BY "KAMEN RIDER."
GREEE! I HEARD.
BUT IT'S HARD TO BELIEVE!
THE ONE AND ONLY MAN-SPIDER GOT BEATEN BY A NEW-BORN?
IS THIS "KAMEN RIDER" *REALLY* HONGO TAKESHI?

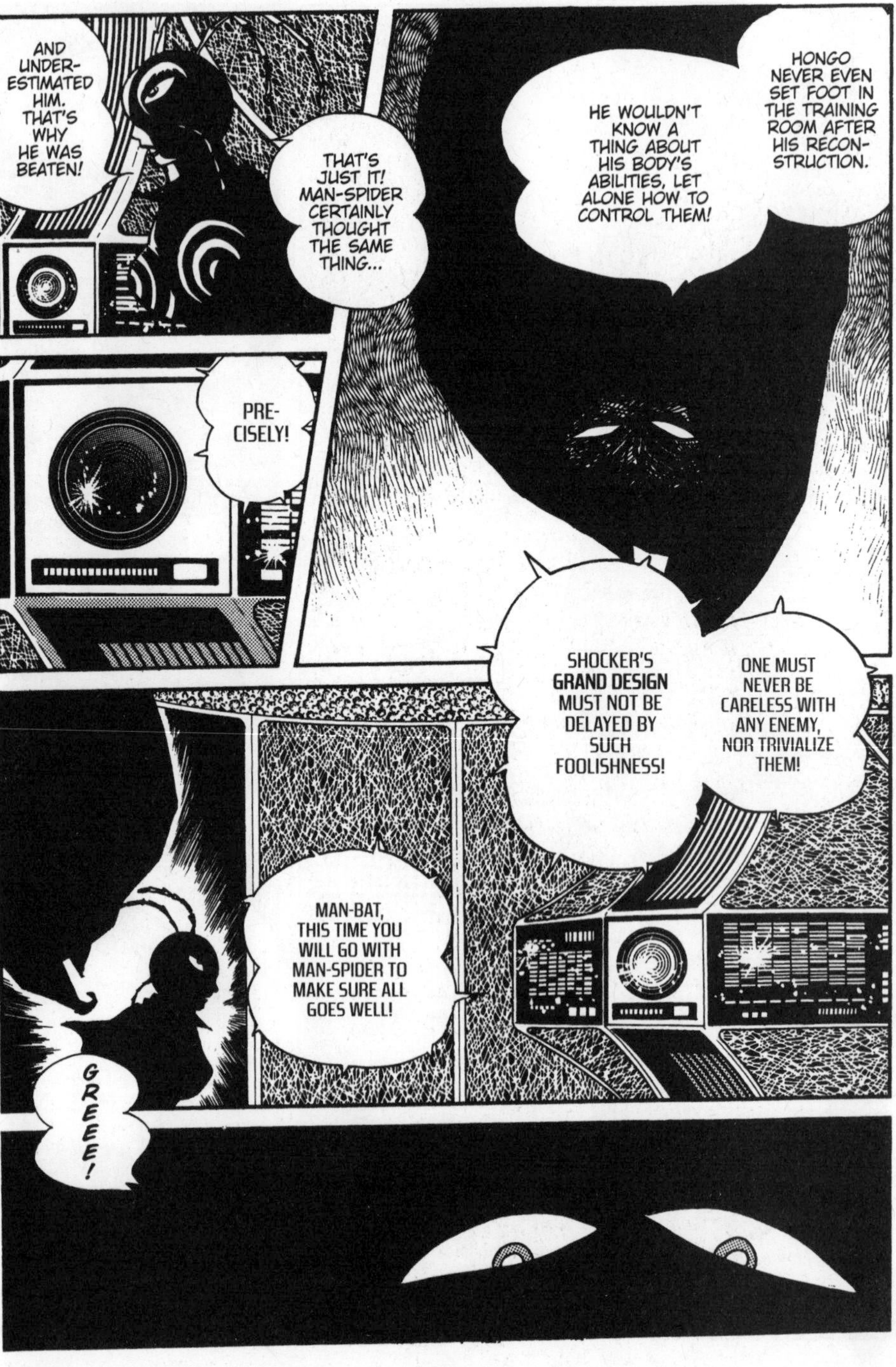
HONGO NEVER EVEN SET FOOT IN THE TRAINING ROOM AFTER HIS RECON-STRUCTION.
HE WOULDN'T KNOW A THING ABOUT HIS BODY'S ABILITIES, LET ALONE HOW TO CONTROL THEM!
THAT'S JUST IT! MAN-SPIDER CERTAINLY THOUGHT THE SAME THING...
AND UNDER-ESTIMATED HIM. THAT'S WHY HE WAS BEATEN!
PRE-CISELY!
ONE MUST NEVER BE CARELESS WITH ANY ENEMY, NOR TRIVIALIZE THEM!
SHOCKER'S **GRAND DESIGN** MUST NOT BE DELAYED BY SUCH FOOLISHNESS!
MAN-BAT, THIS TIME YOU WILL GO WITH MAN-SPIDER TO MAKE SURE ALL GOES WELL!
GREEE!

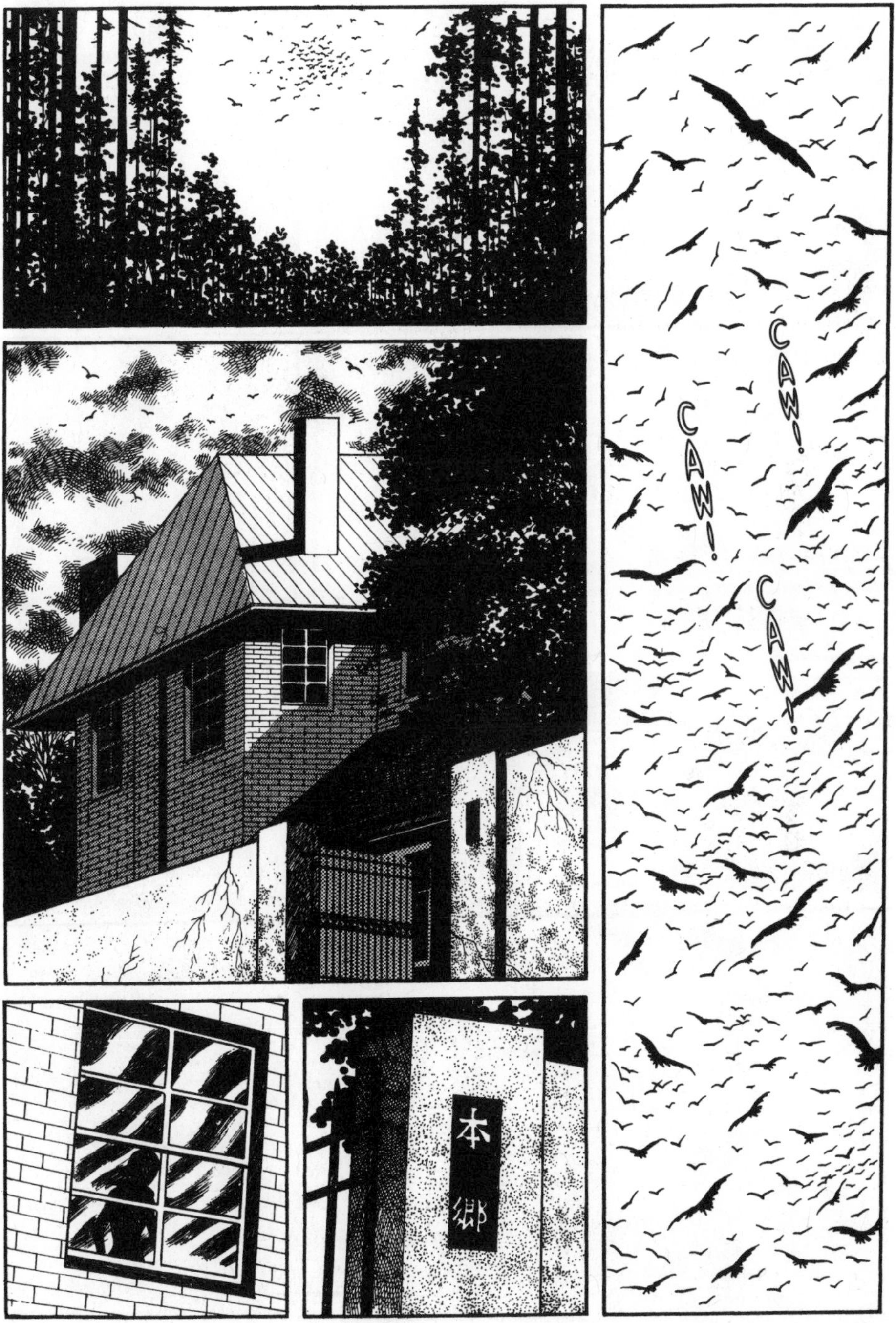
CAW!
CAW!
CAW!
本郷

Sign: Hongo Residence.

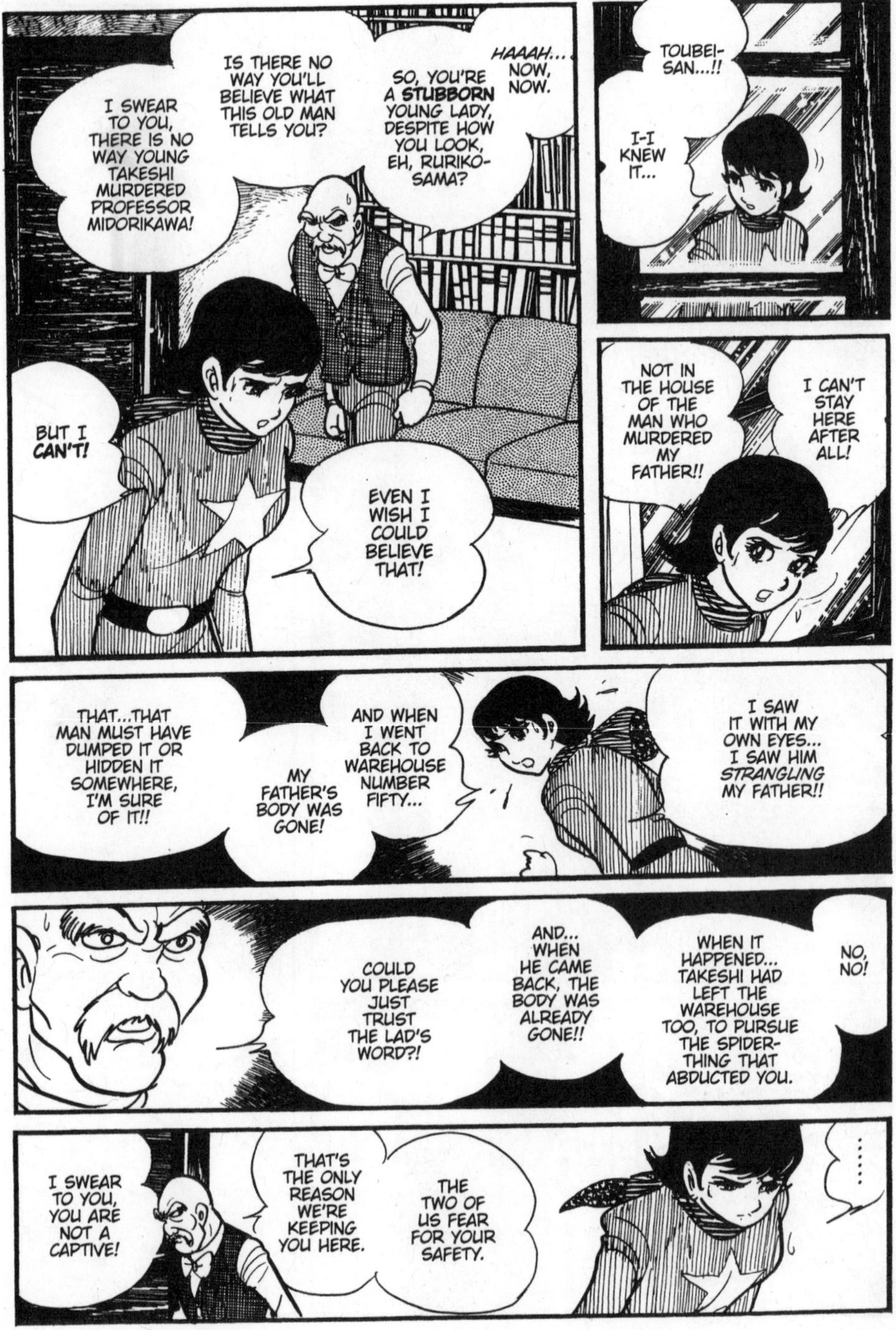

TOUBEI-SAN...!!
I-I KNEW IT...
I CAN'T STAY HERE AFTER ALL!
NOT IN THE HOUSE OF THE MAN WHO MURDERED MY FATHER!!
HAAAH... NOW, NOW.
SO, YOU'RE A STUBBORN YOUNG LADY, DESPITE HOW YOU LOOK, EH, RURIKO-SAMA?
IS THERE NO WAY YOU'LL BELIEVE WHAT THIS OLD MAN TELLS YOU?
I SWEAR TO YOU, THERE IS NO WAY YOUNG TAKESHI MURDERED PROFESSOR MIDORIKAWA!
EVEN I WISH I COULD BELIEVE THAT!
BUT I CAN'T!
I SAW IT WITH MY OWN EYES... I SAW HIM STRANGLING MY FATHER!!
AND WHEN I WENT BACK TO WAREHOUSE NUMBER FIFTY...
MY FATHER'S BODY WAS GONE!
THAT...THAT MAN MUST HAVE DUMPED IT OR HIDDEN IT SOMEWHERE, I'M SURE OF IT!!
NO, NO!
WHEN IT HAPPENED... TAKESHI HAD LEFT THE WAREHOUSE TOO, TO PURSUE THE SPIDER-THING THAT ABDUCTED YOU.
AND... WHEN HE CAME BACK, THE BODY WAS ALREADY GONE!!
COULD YOU PLEASE JUST TRUST THE LAD'S WORD?!
......
THE TWO OF US FEAR FOR YOUR SAFETY.
THAT'S THE ONLY REASON WE'RE KEEPING YOU HERE.
I SWEAR TO YOU, YOU ARE NOT A CAPTIVE!

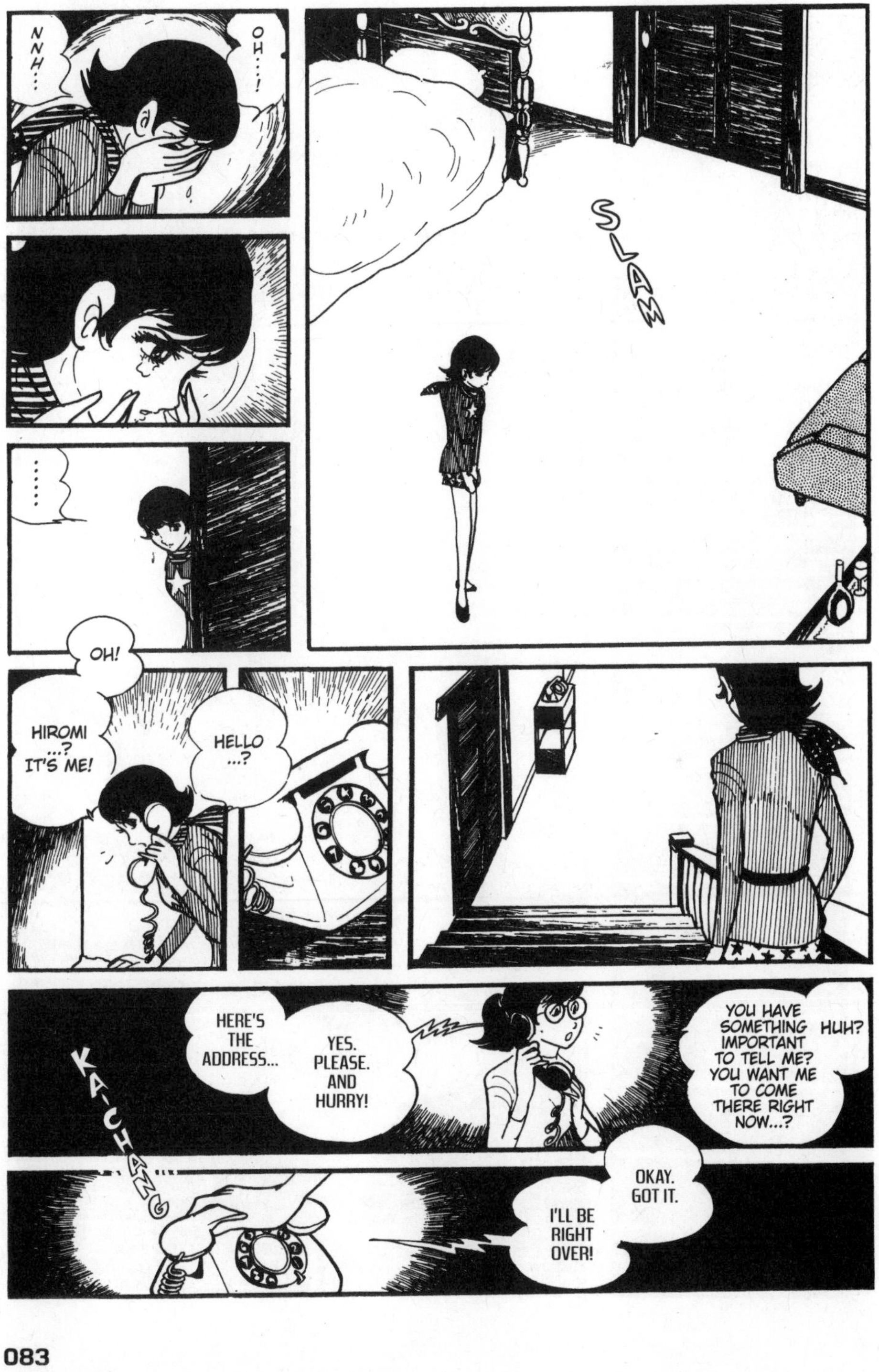
SLAM
OH...!
NNH...
......
HELLO ...?
OH!
HIROMI ...? IT'S ME!
HUH?
YOU HAVE SOMETHING IMPORTANT TO TELL ME? YOU WANT ME TO COME THERE RIGHT NOW...?
YES. PLEASE. AND HURRY!
HERE'S THE ADDRESS...
KA-CHANG
OKAY. GOT IT.
I'LL BE RIGHT OVER!

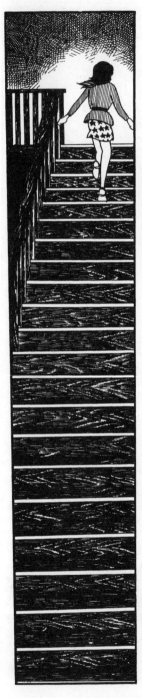

WHO WERE YOU CALLING...?

DON'T WORRY! I WON'T CALL THE POLICE YET!

NOT UNTIL I HAVE PROOF YOU MURDERED MY FATHER!

AND WHOEVER I CALL, I DON'T ANSWER TO YOU!

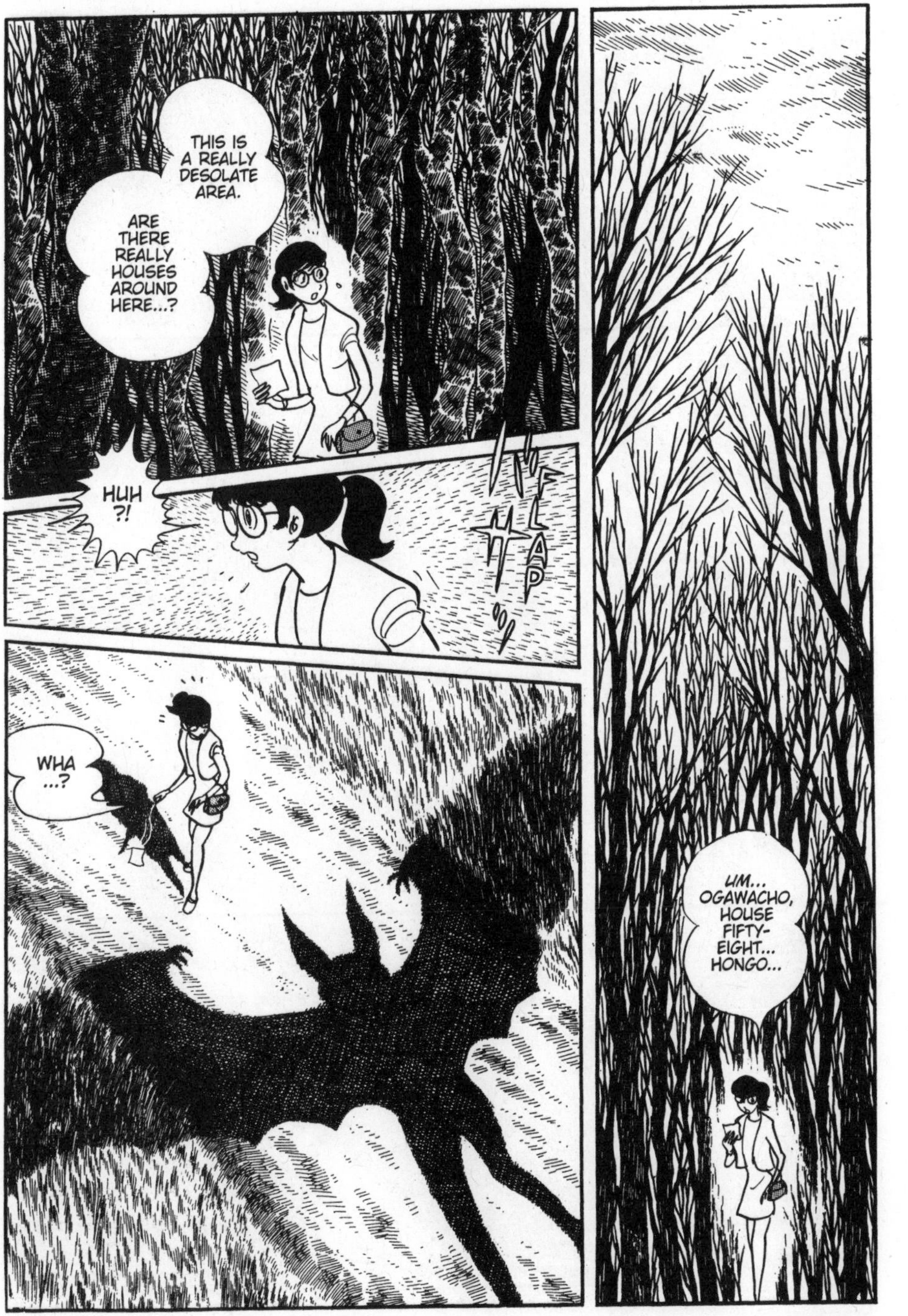
UM... OGAWACHO, HOUSE FIFTY-EIGHT... HONGO...
THIS IS A REALLY DESOLATE AREA.
ARE THERE REALLY HOUSES AROUND HERE...?
HUH ?!
FLAP
WHA ...?

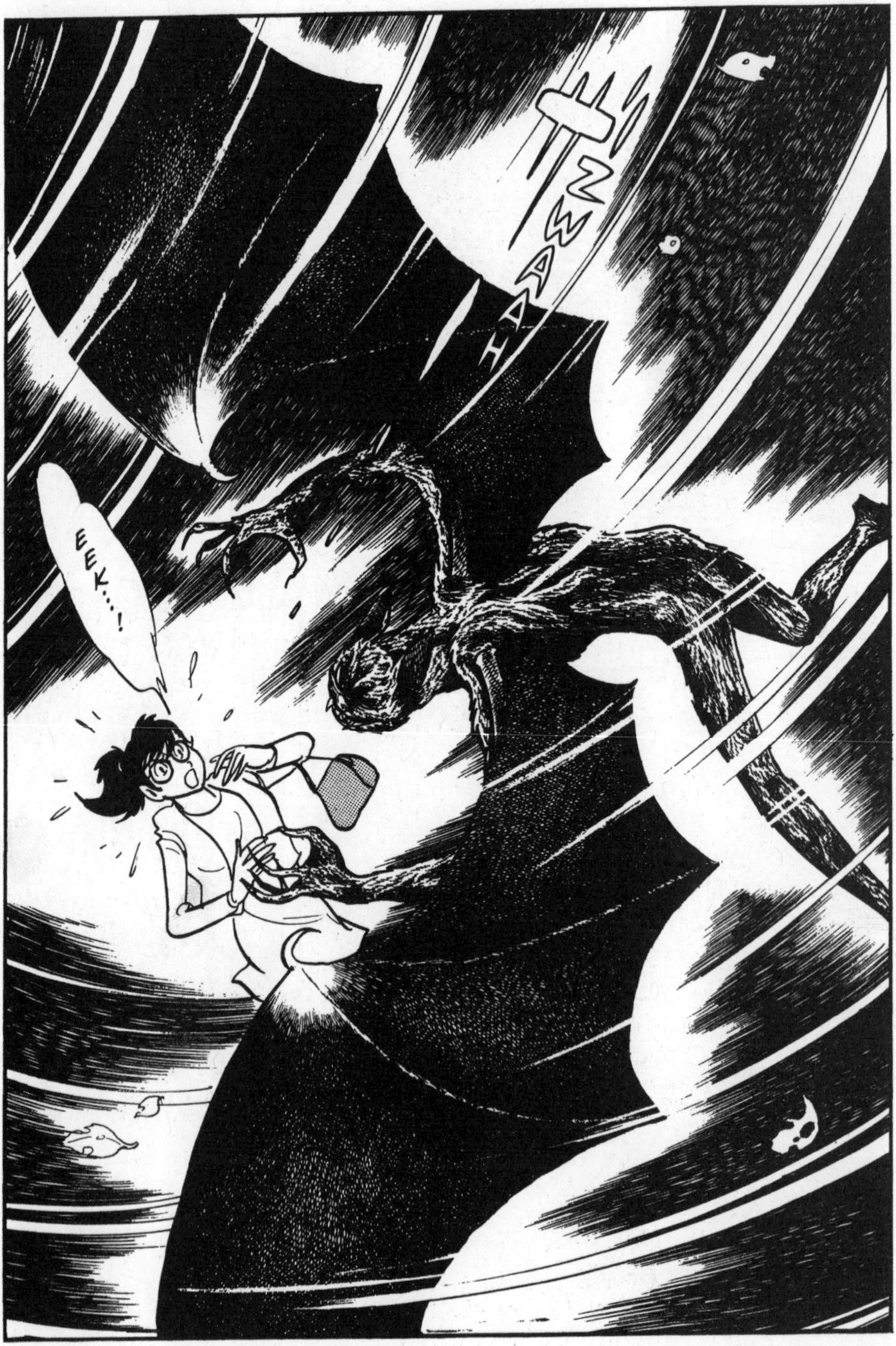
ZWAAAH
EEK...!

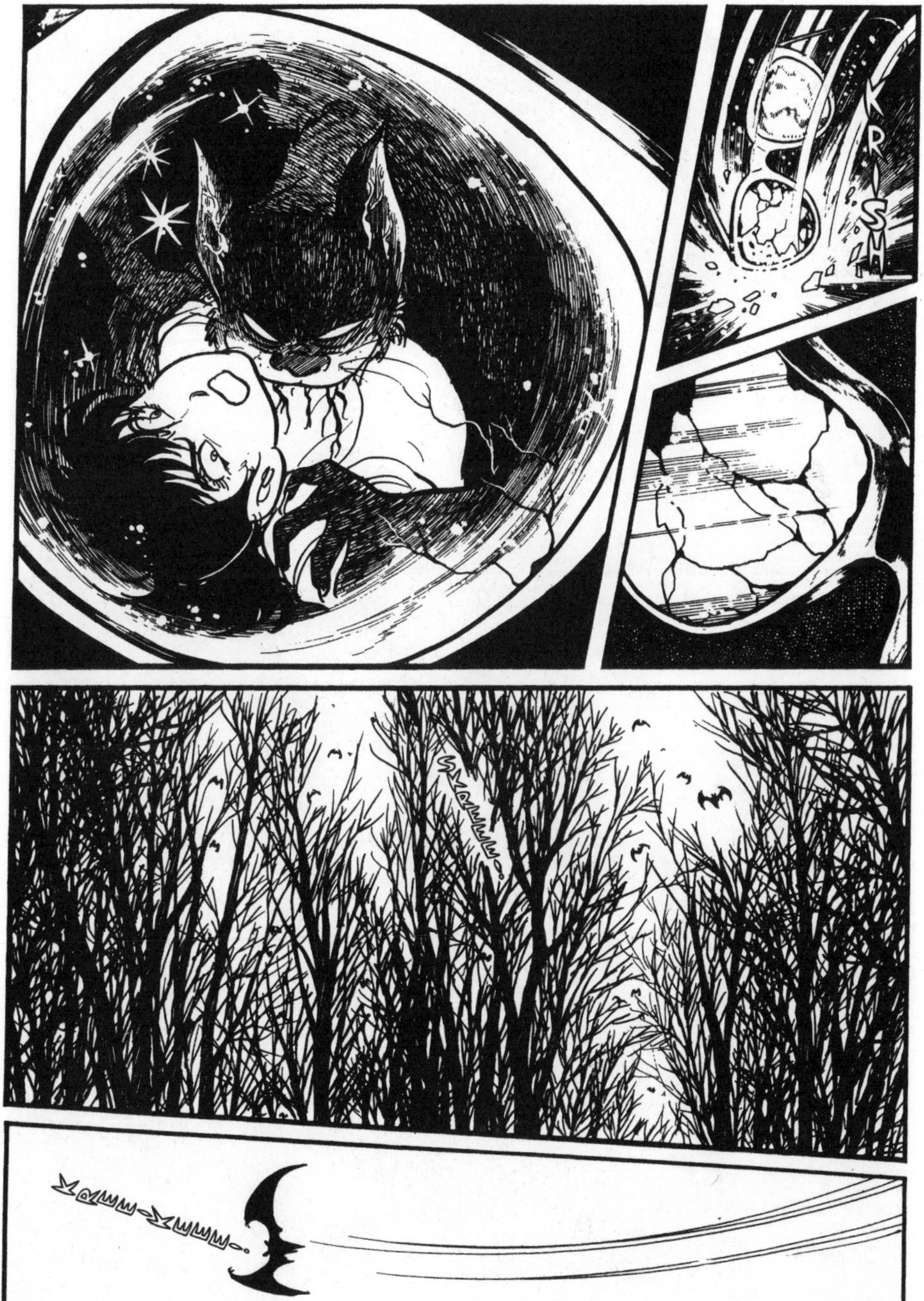
KRISHH
SKREEEE!
KREE-KEEEE!

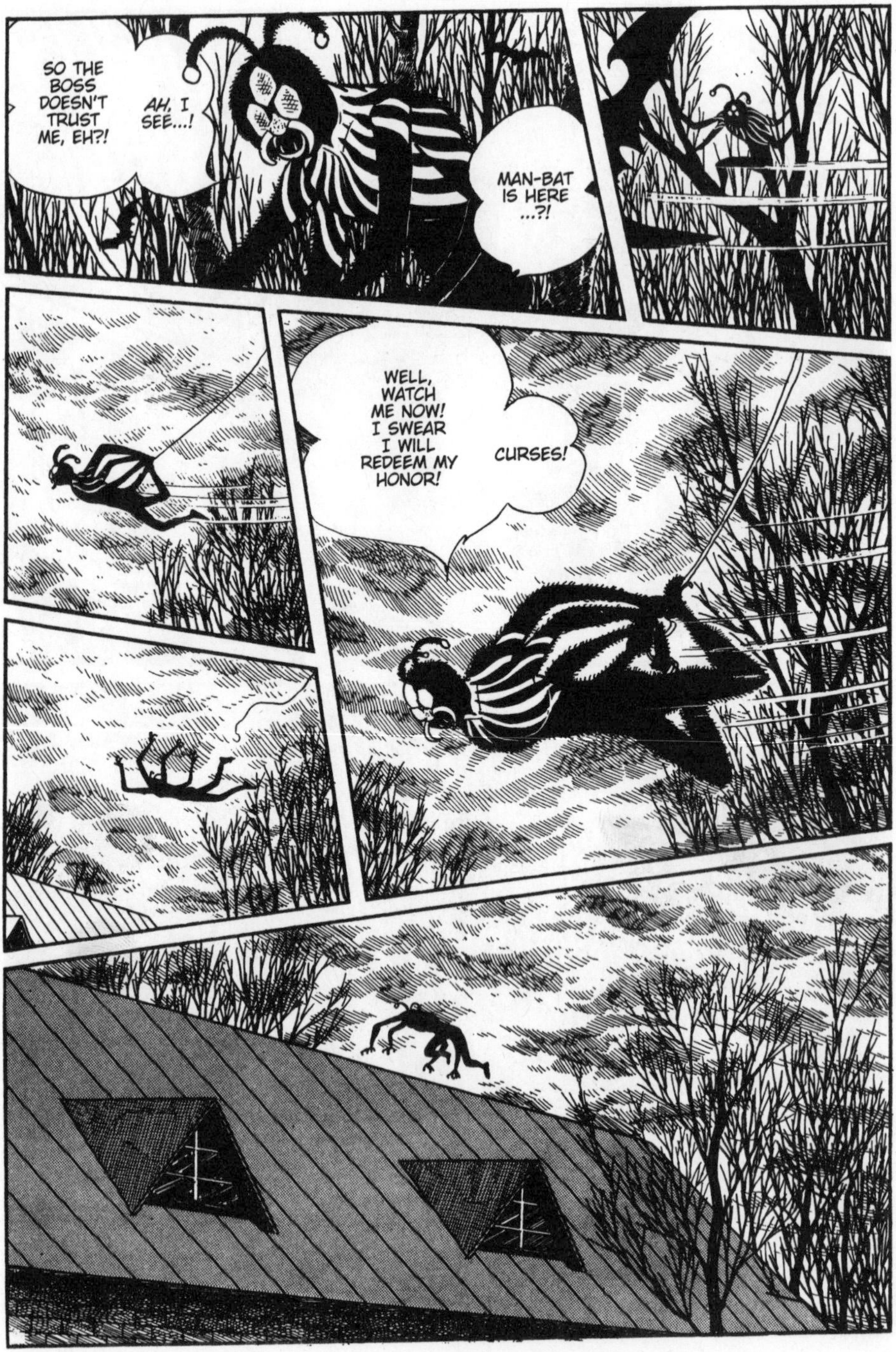
MAN-BAT IS HERE ...?!
AH, I SEE...!
SO THE BOSS DOESN'T TRUST ME, EH?!
CURSES!
WELL, WATCH ME NOW! I SWEAR I WILL REDEEM MY HONOR!

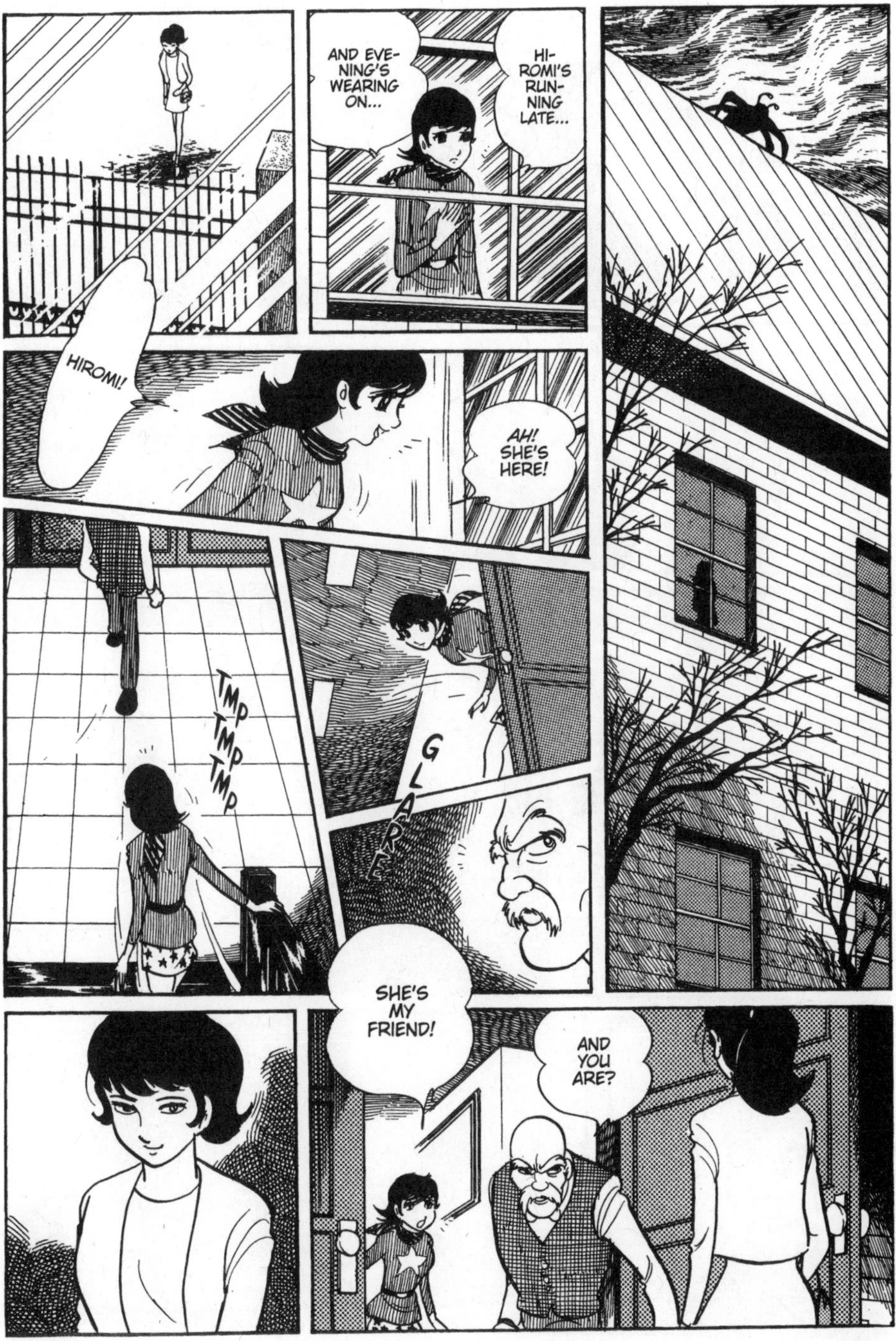
HI-ROMI'S RUN-NING LATE...
AND EVE-NING'S WEARING ON...
AH! SHE'S HERE!
HIROMI!
GLARE
TMP TMP TMP
AND YOU ARE?
SHE'S MY FRIEND!

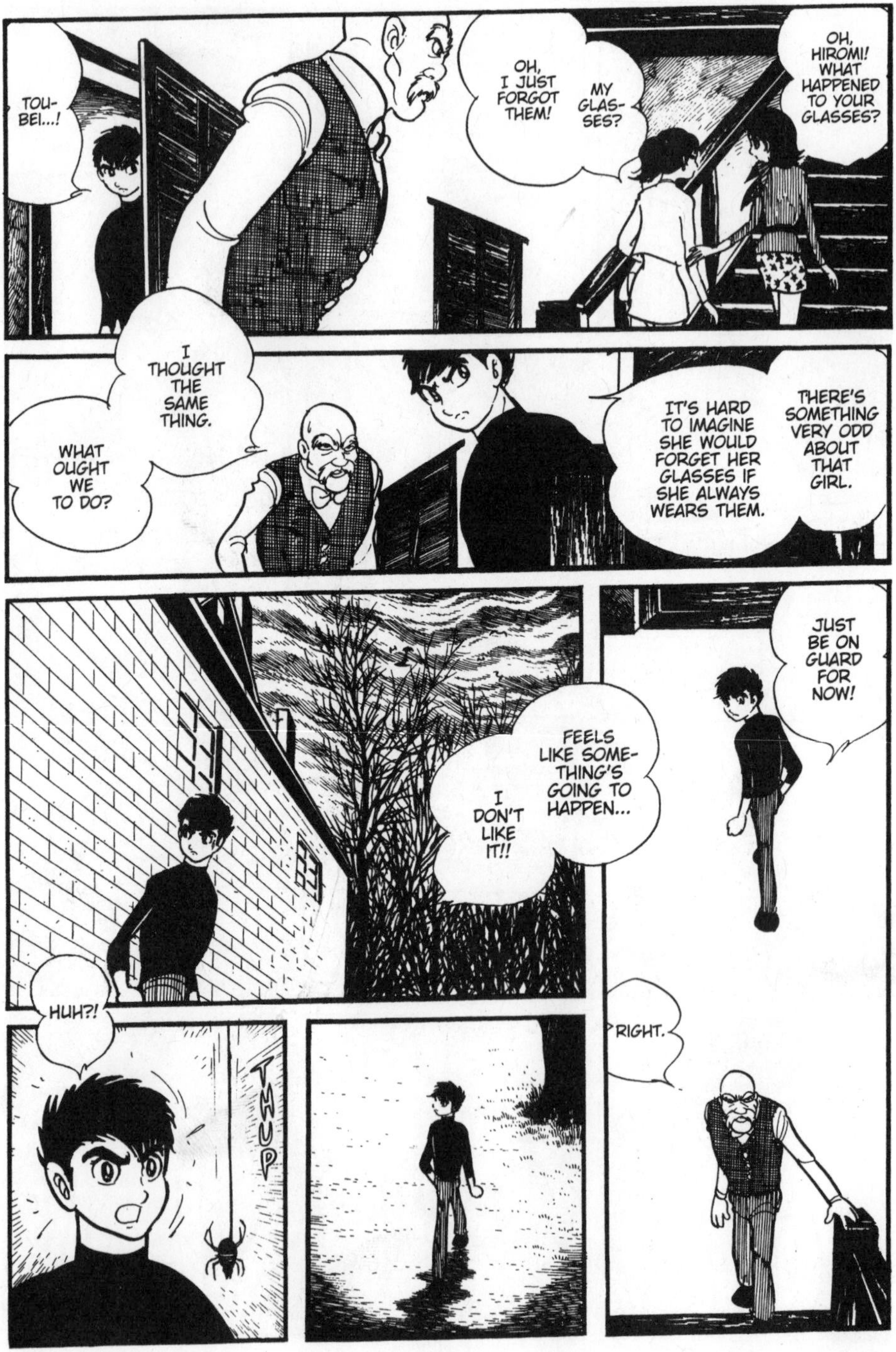
OH, HIROMI! WHAT HAPPENED TO YOUR GLASSES?
MY GLASSES?
OH, I JUST FORGOT THEM!
TOU-BEI...!
THERE'S SOMETHING VERY ODD ABOUT THAT GIRL.
IT'S HARD TO IMAGINE SHE WOULD FORGET HER GLASSES IF SHE ALWAYS WEARS THEM.
I THOUGHT THE SAME THING.
WHAT OUGHT WE TO DO?
JUST BE ON GUARD FOR NOW!
RIGHT.
FEELS LIKE SOMETHING'S GOING TO HAPPEN...
I DON'T LIKE IT!!
HUH?!
THUP

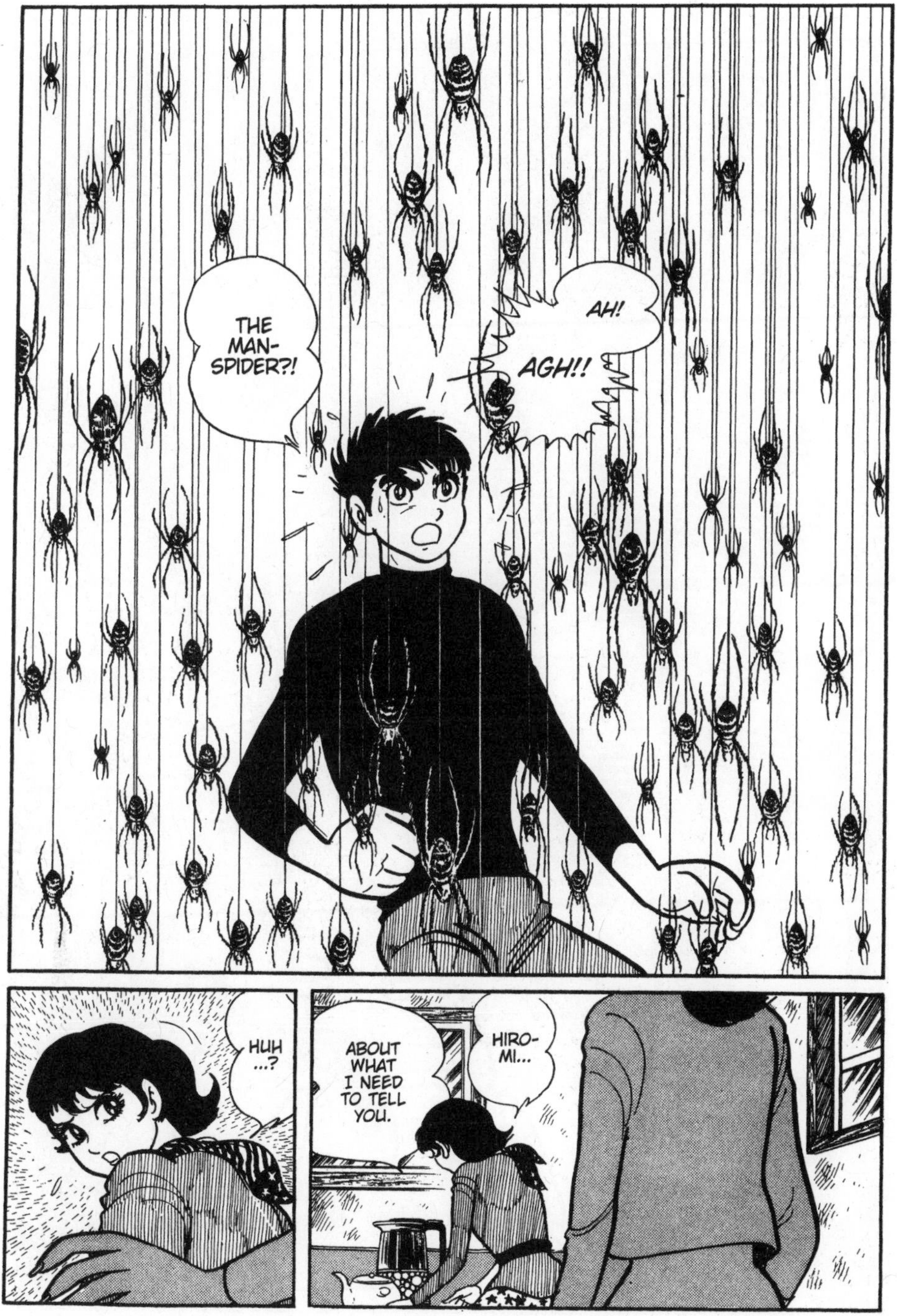
AH!
AGH!!
THE MAN-SPIDER?!
HIRO-MI...
ABOUT WHAT I NEED TO TELL YOU.
HUH ...?

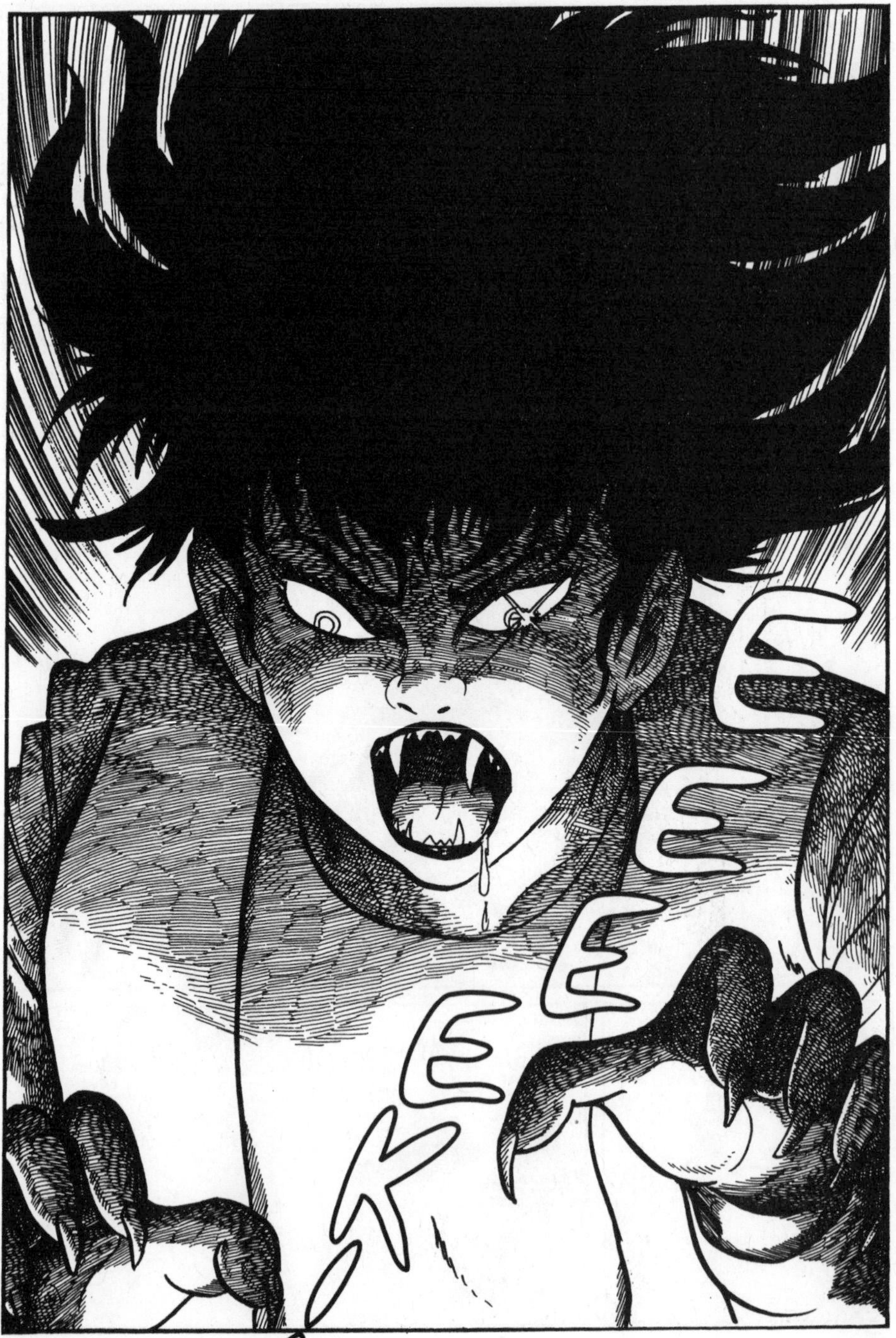
KEEEEE!

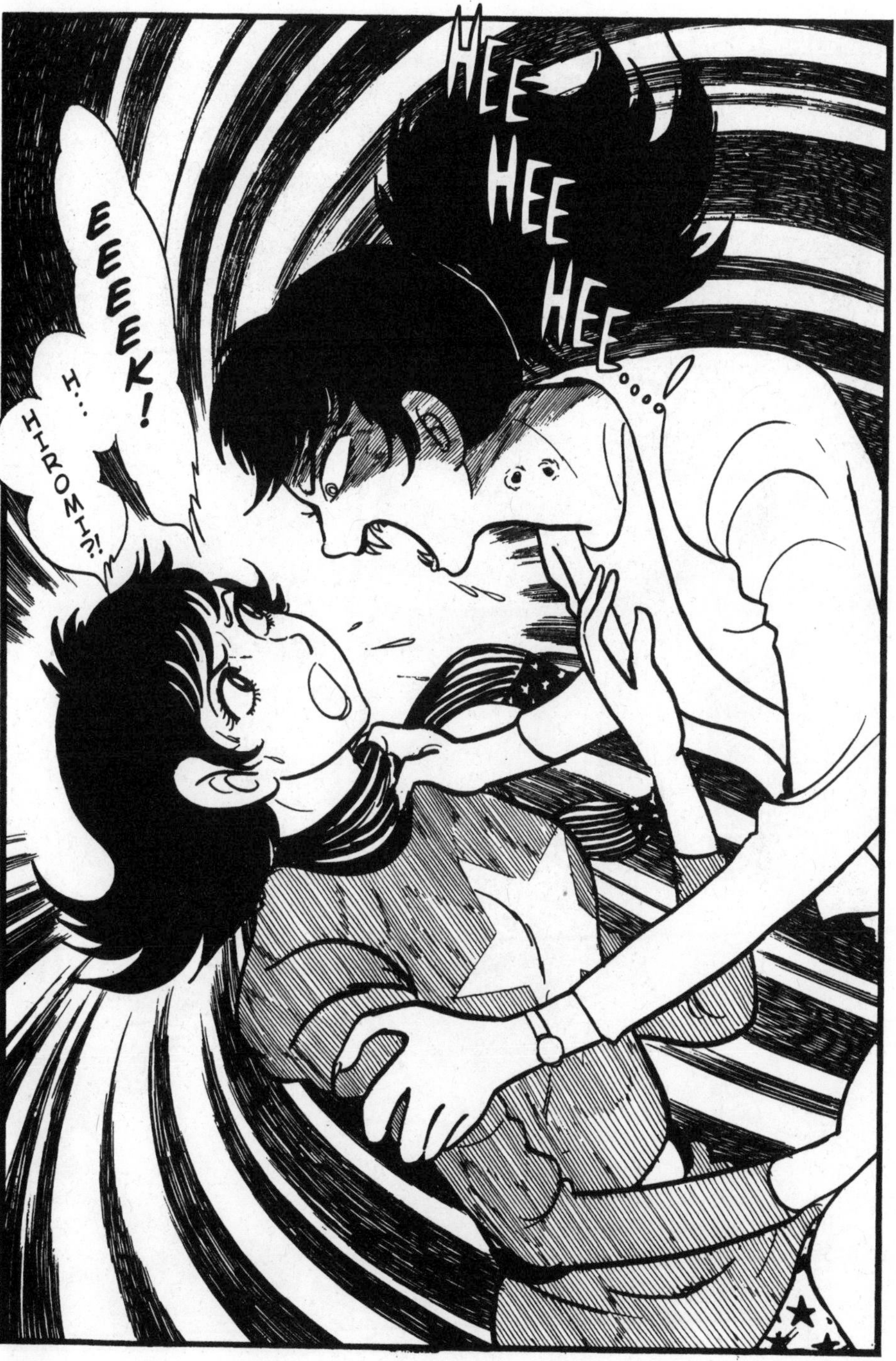
HEE HEE HEE HEE...!
EEEEEK!
H... HIROMI?!

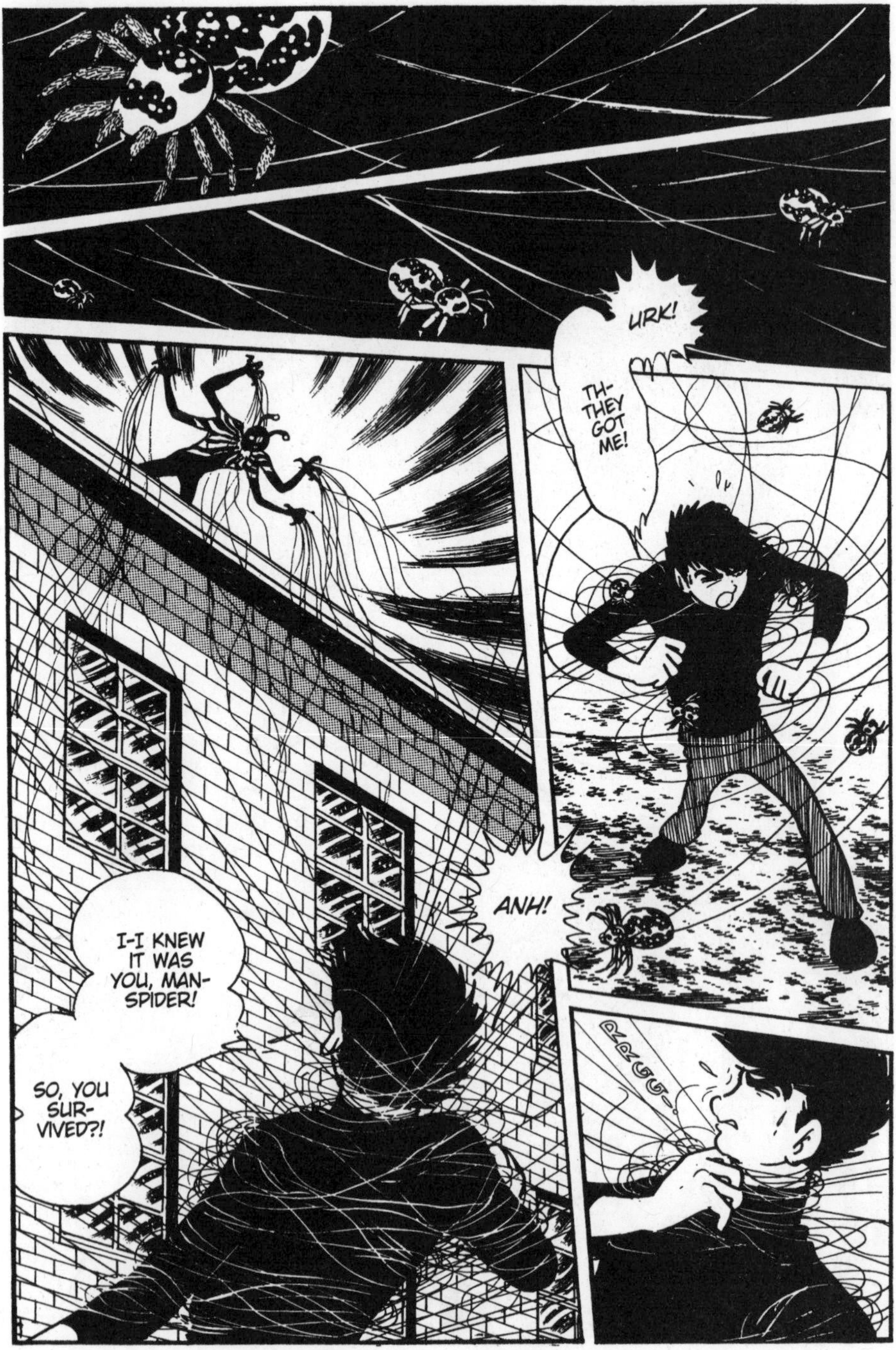
URK!
TH-THEY GOT ME!
ANH!
RRGG-!
I-I KNEW IT WAS YOU, MAN-SPIDER!
SO, YOU SUR-VIVED?!

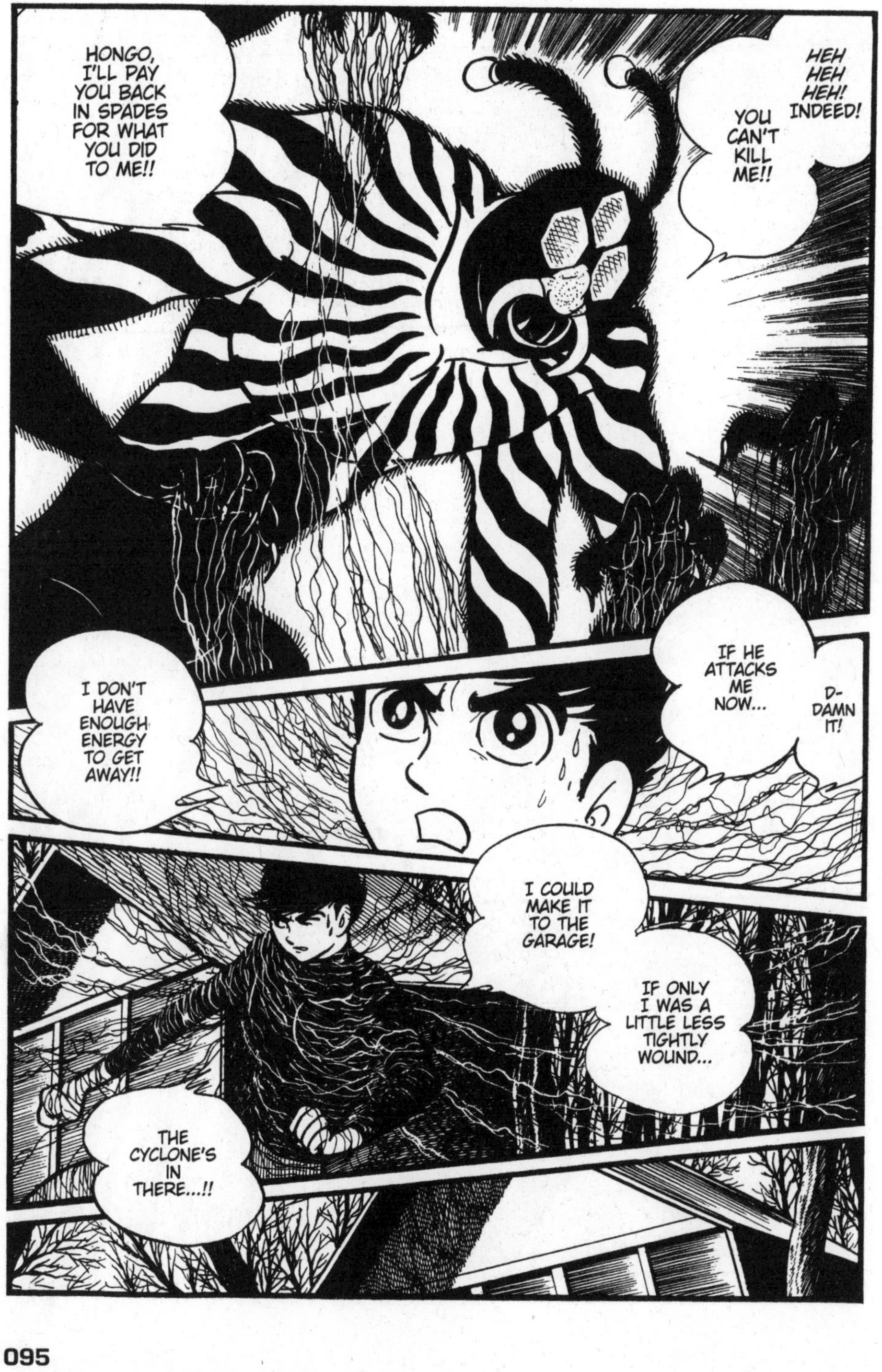
HEH HEH HEH! INDEED!
YOU CAN'T KILL ME!!
HONGO, I'LL PAY YOU BACK IN SPADES FOR WHAT YOU DID TO ME!!
D-DAMN IT!
IF HE ATTACKS ME NOW...
I DON'T HAVE ENOUGH ENERGY TO GET AWAY!!
I COULD MAKE IT TO THE GARAGE!
IF ONLY I WAS A LITTLE LESS TIGHTLY WOUND...
THE CYCLONE'S IN THERE...!!

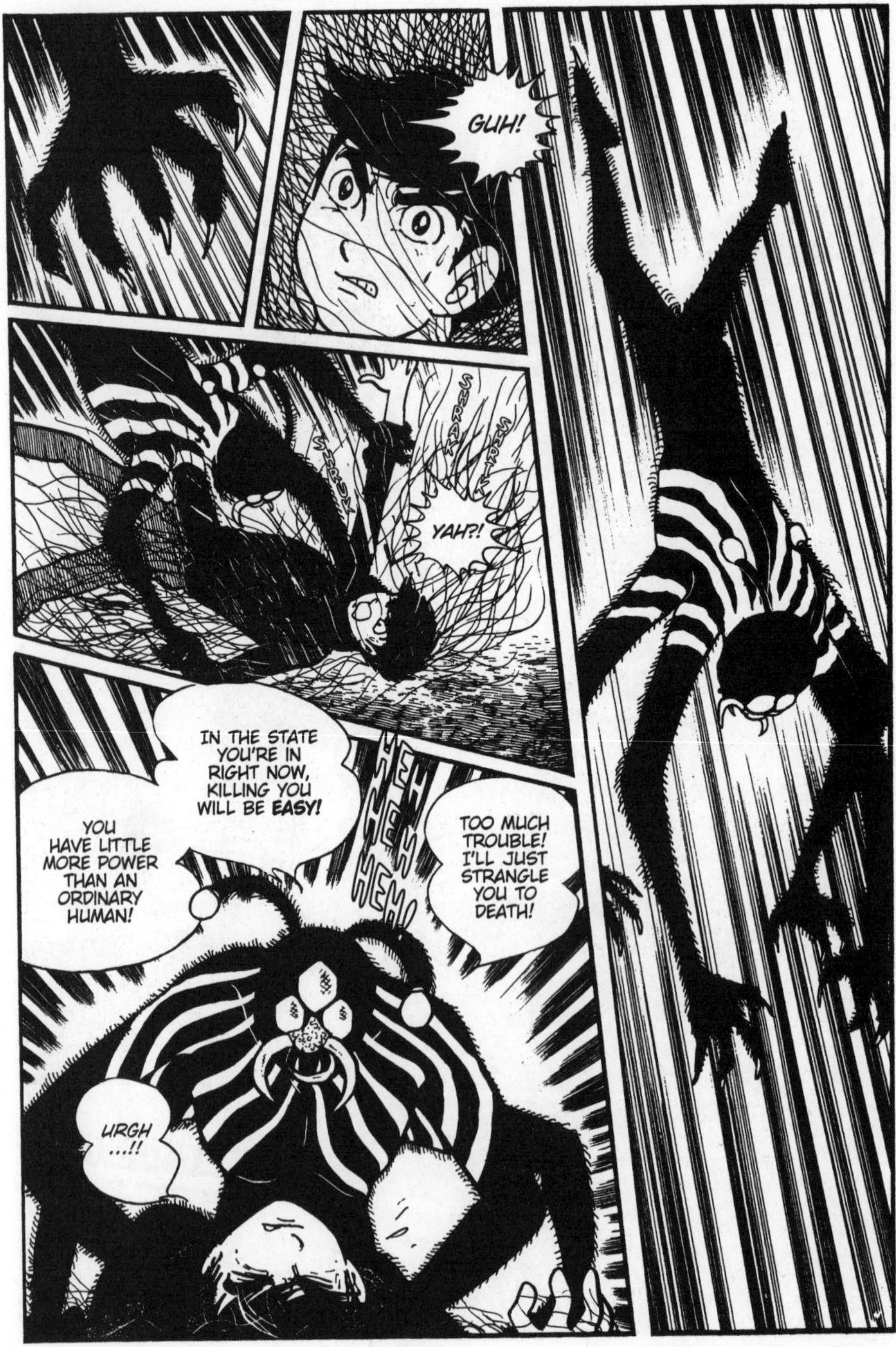
GUH!
SHRIK
SHRAK
SHRUK
YAH?!
TOO MUCH TROUBLE! I'LL JUST STRANGLE YOU TO DEATH!
HEH HEH HEH
IN THE STATE YOU'RE IN RIGHT NOW, KILLING YOU WILL BE **EASY!**
YOU HAVE LITTLE MORE POWER THAN AN ORDINARY HUMAN!
URGH ...!!

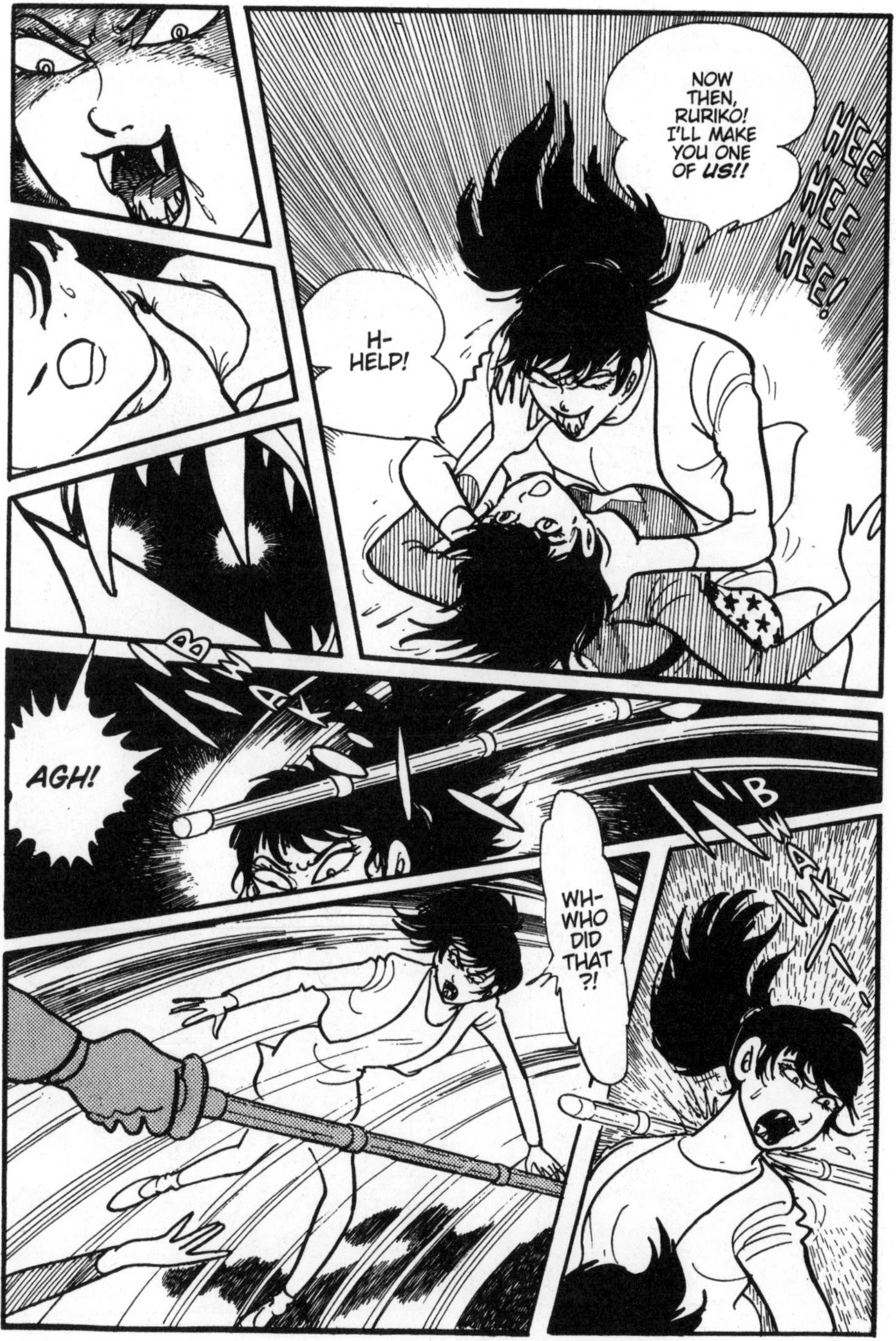
NOW THEN, RURIKO! I'LL MAKE YOU ONE OF ***US!!***
HEE HEE HEE!
H-HELP!
BWAK
AGH!
BWAK
WH-WHO DID THAT?!

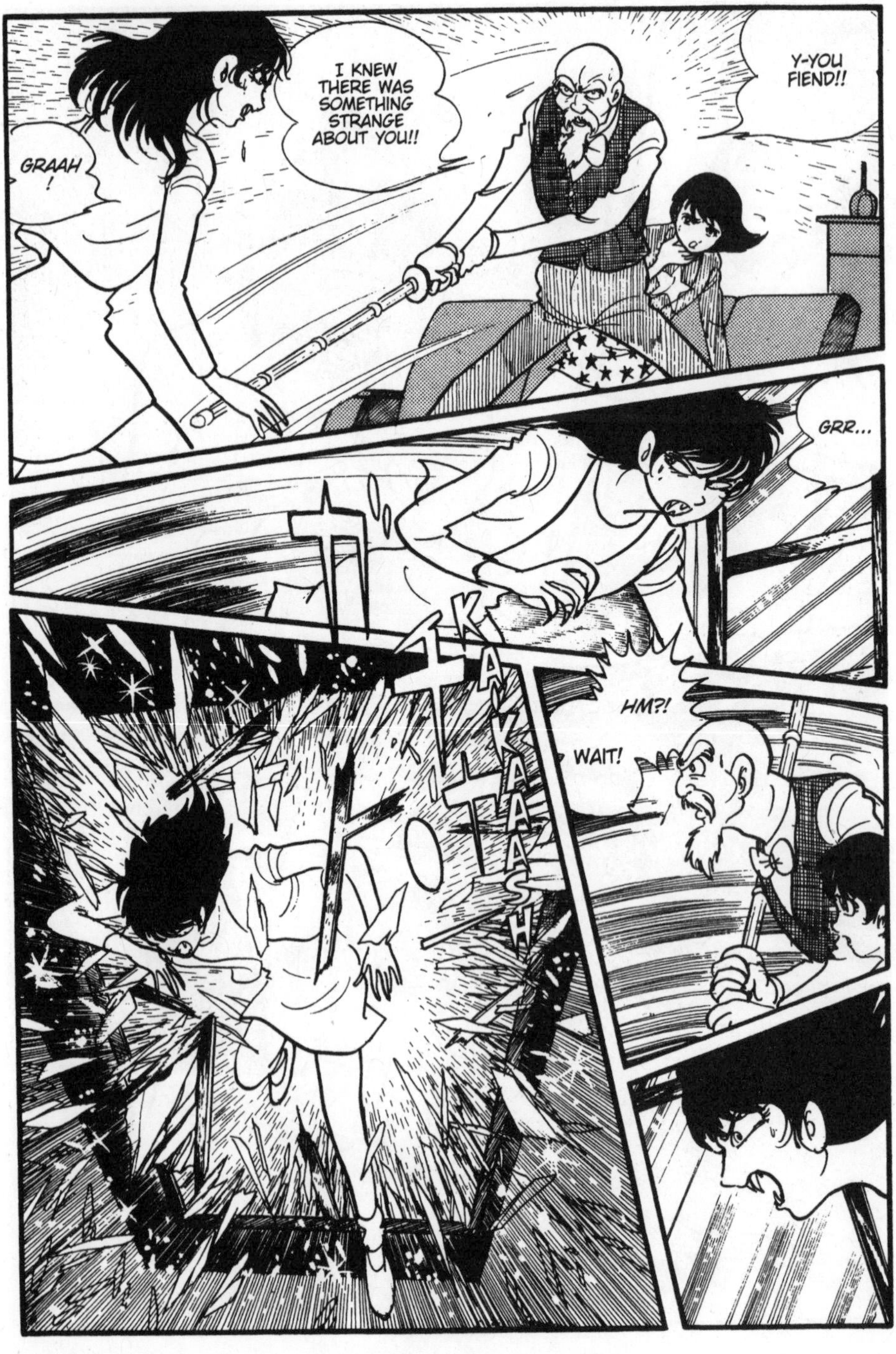

Y-YOU FIEND!!
I KNEW THERE WAS SOMETHING STRANGE ABOUT YOU!!
GRAAH!
GRR...
KAKAAAASH
HM?!
WAIT!

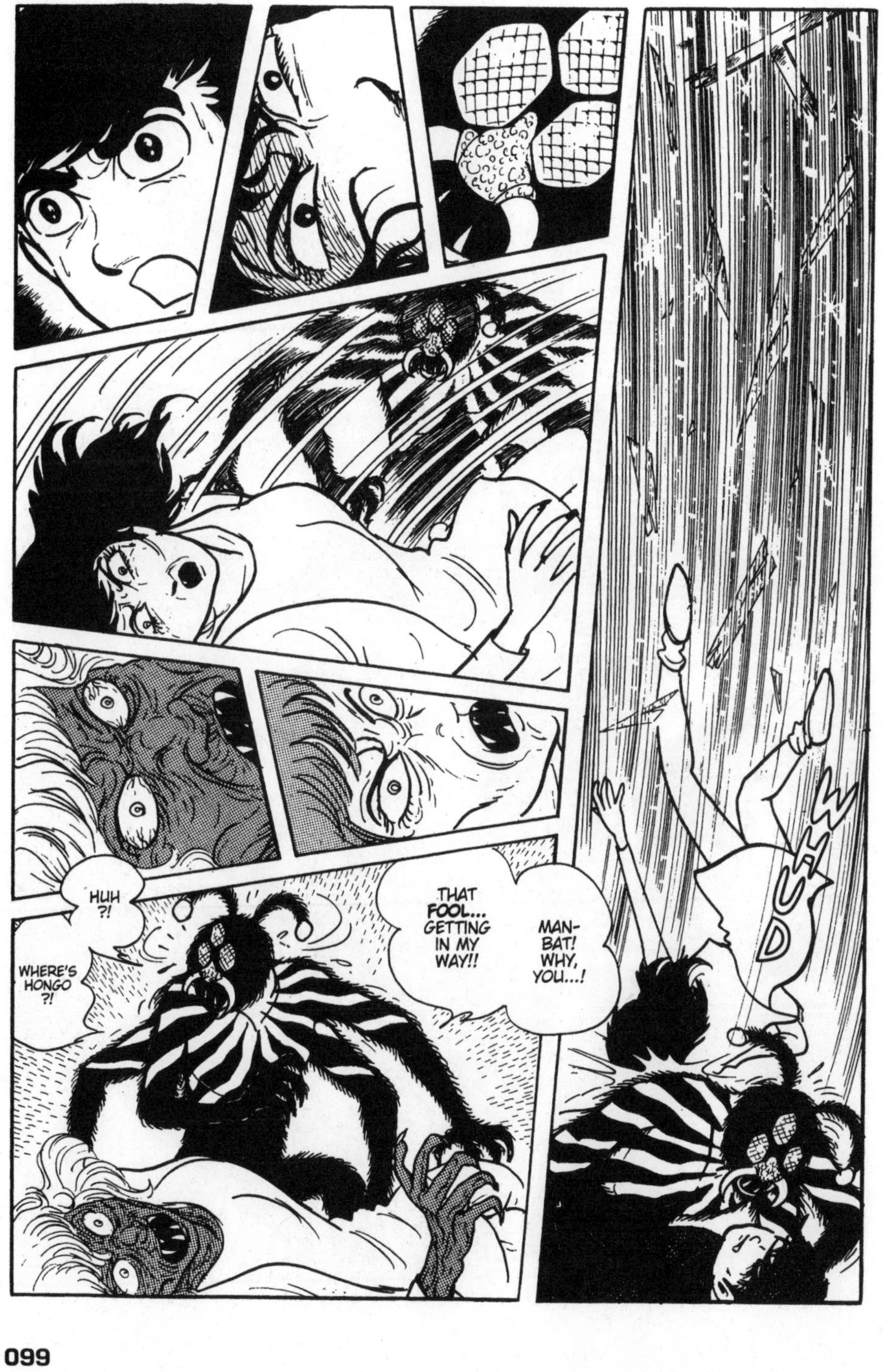
WHUD
MAN-BAT! WHY, YOU...!
THAT FOOL... GETTING IN MY WAY!!
HUH ?!
WHERE'S HONGO ?!

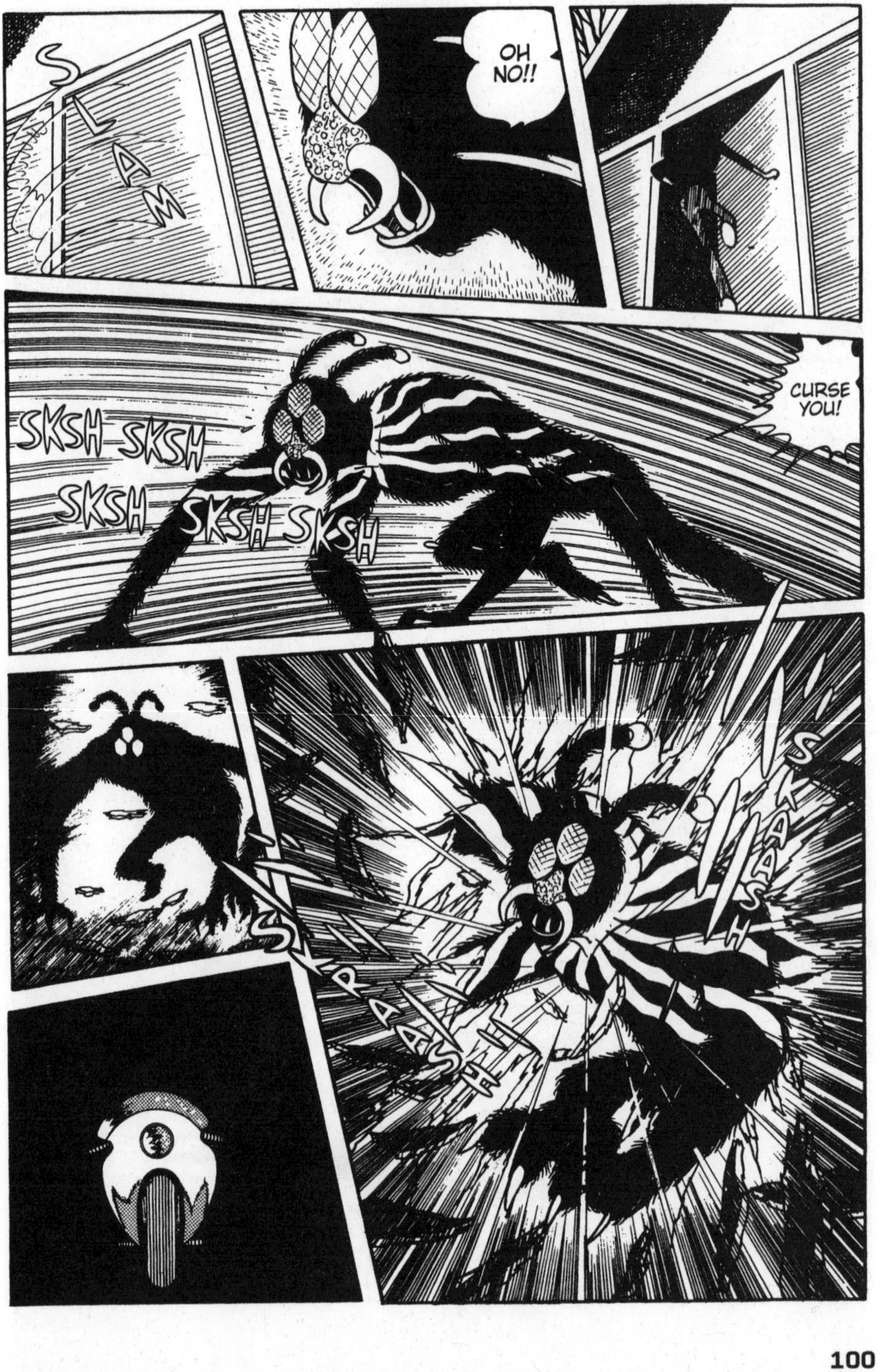

OH NO!!
SLAM
CURSE YOU!
SKSH SKSH SKSH SKSH SKSH
SKAASH
SKRAAASH

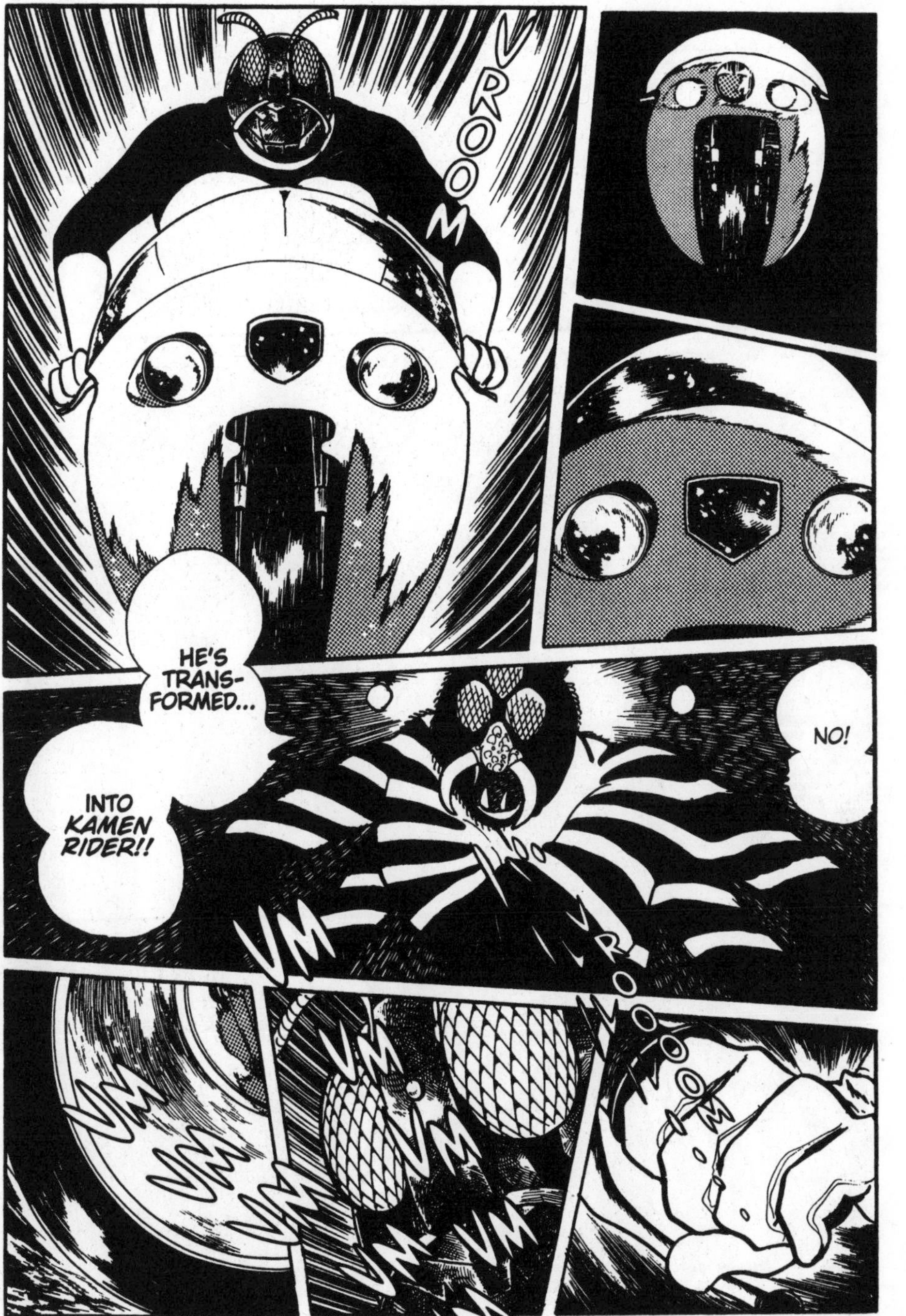
VROOOM
NO!
HE'S TRANS-FORMED...
INTO KAMEN RIDER!!
VROOOM
VM
VROOOOM
VM VM VM VM
VM VM VM VM

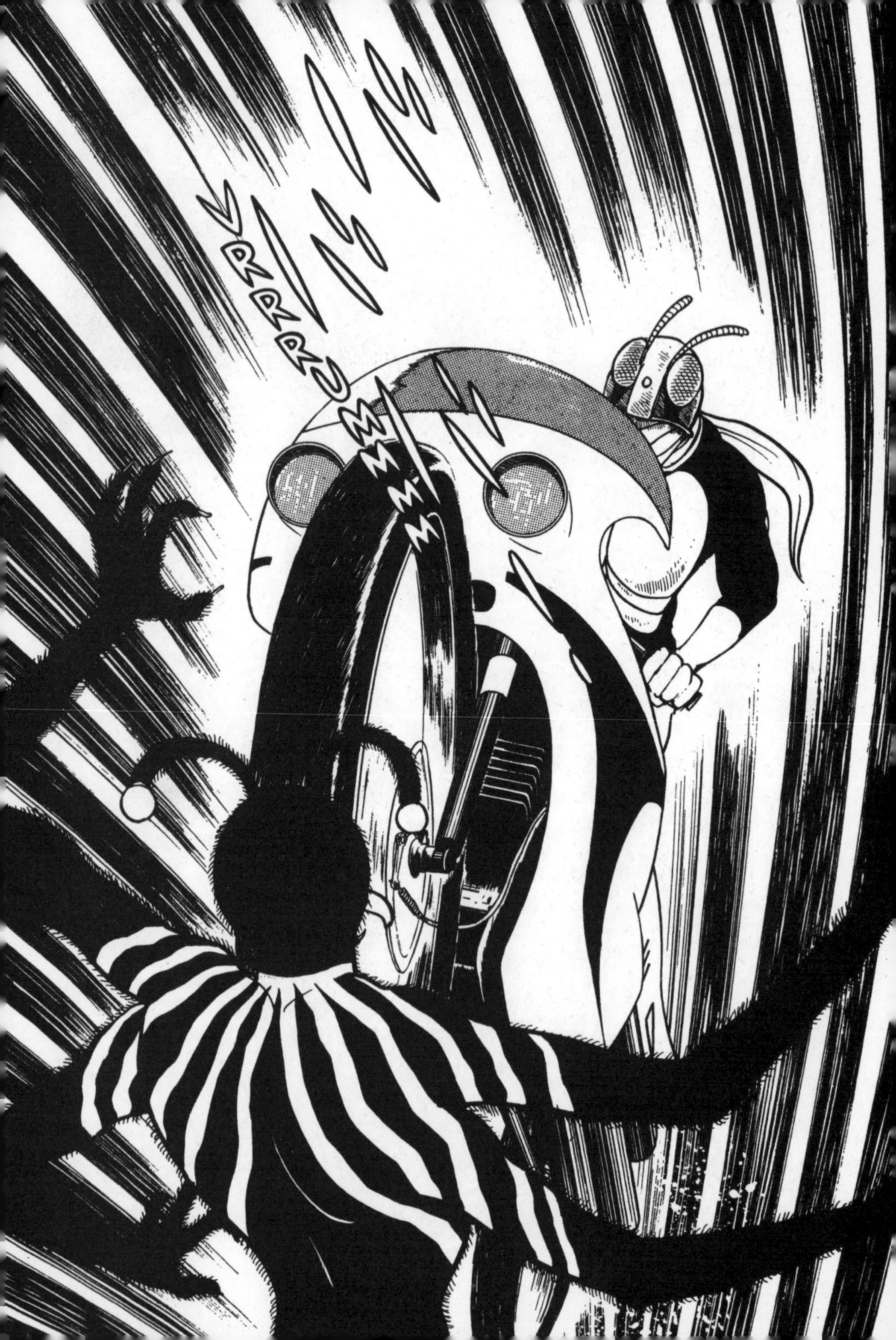
VRRRUMMMM

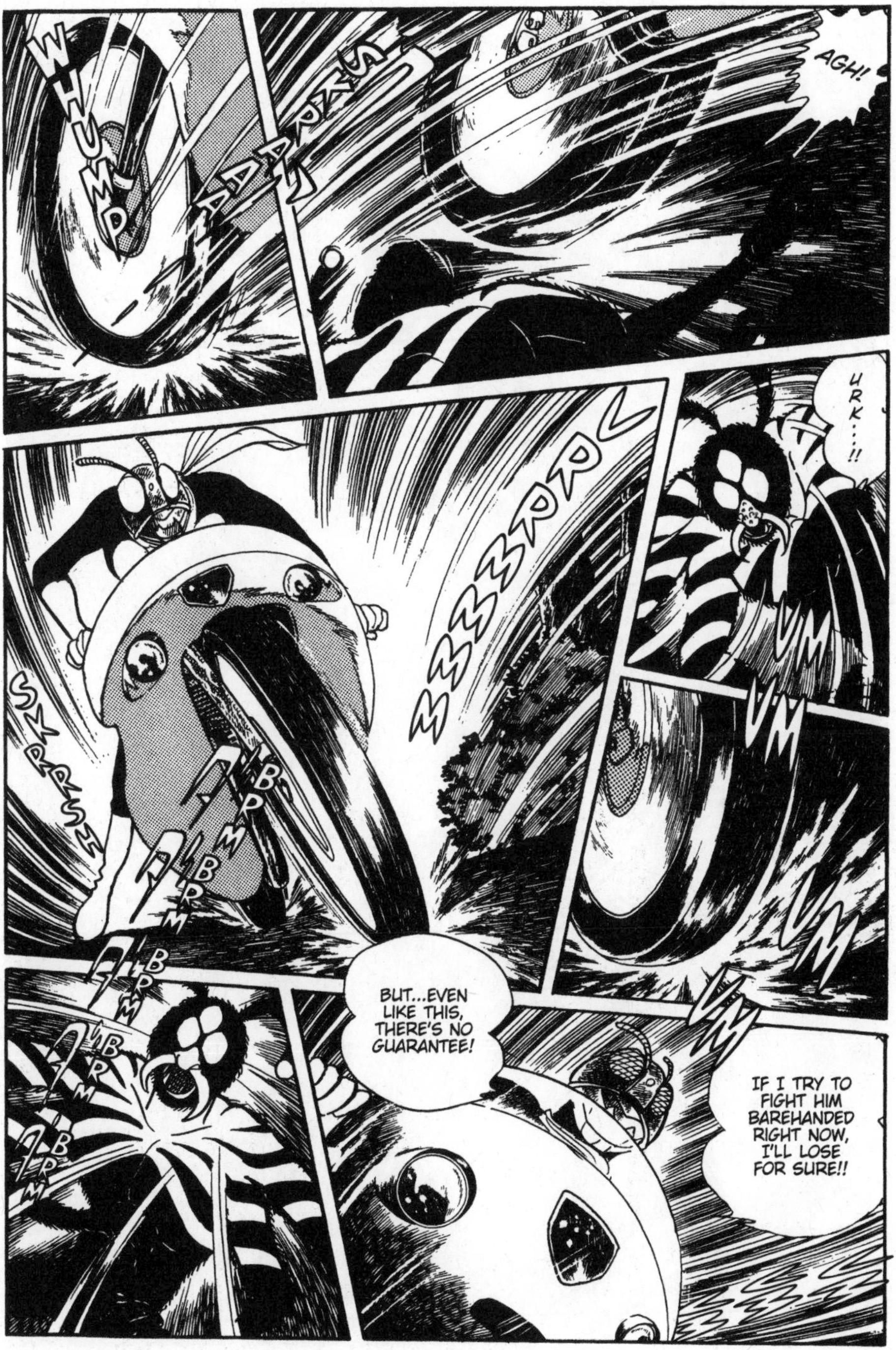
AGH!
SKRAAAA
WHUMP
URK...!!
VM
VM
BBBBBRRRL
SKRRRSH
BRM
BRM
BRM
BRM
BRM
VM
VM
IF I TRY TO FIGHT HIM BAREHANDED RIGHT NOW, I'LL LOSE FOR SURE!!
BUT...EVEN LIKE THIS, THERE'S NO GUARANTEE!

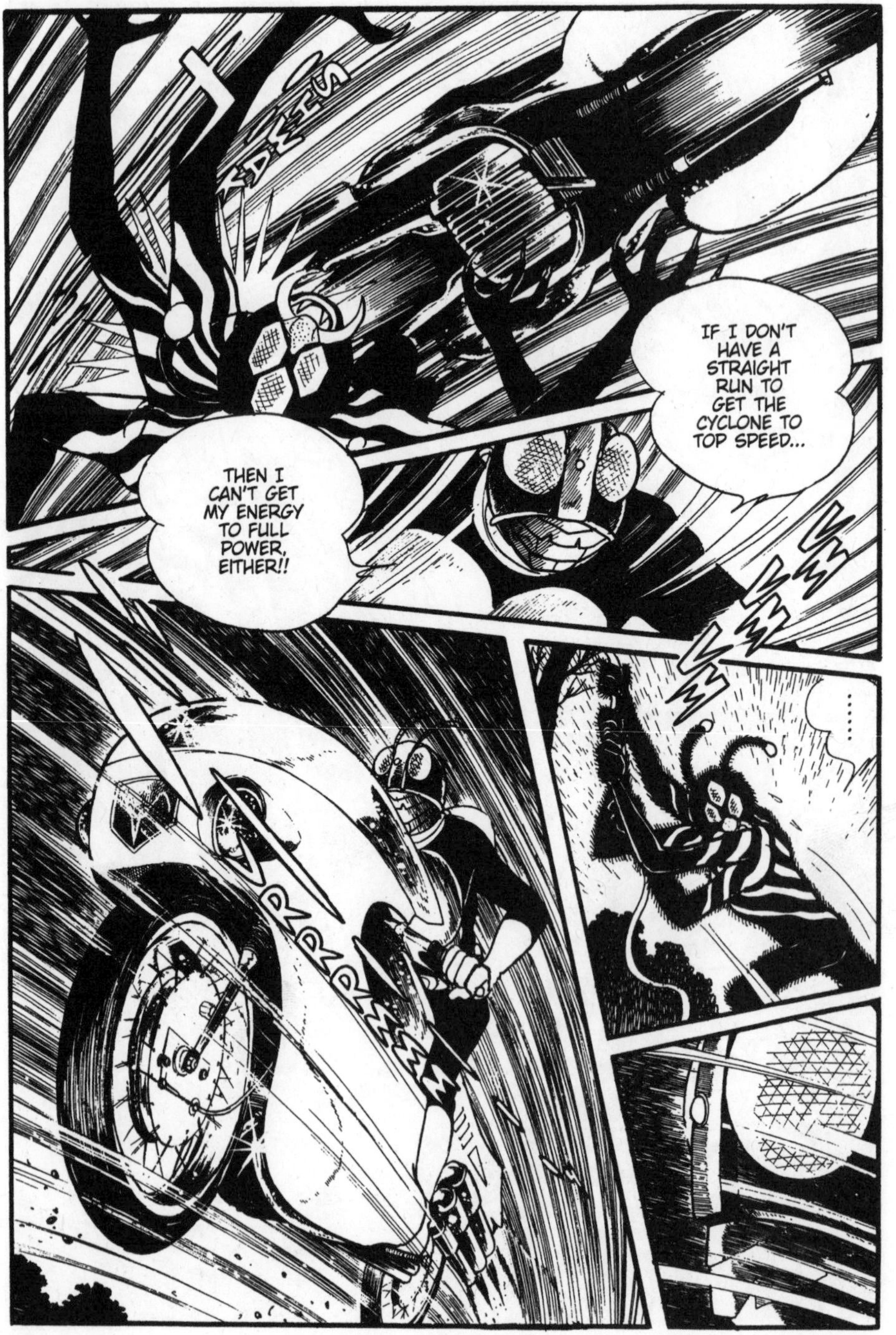
IF I DON'T HAVE A STRAIGHT RUN TO GET THE CYCLONE TO TOP SPEED...
THEN I CAN'T GET MY ENERGY TO FULL POWER, EITHER!!
......

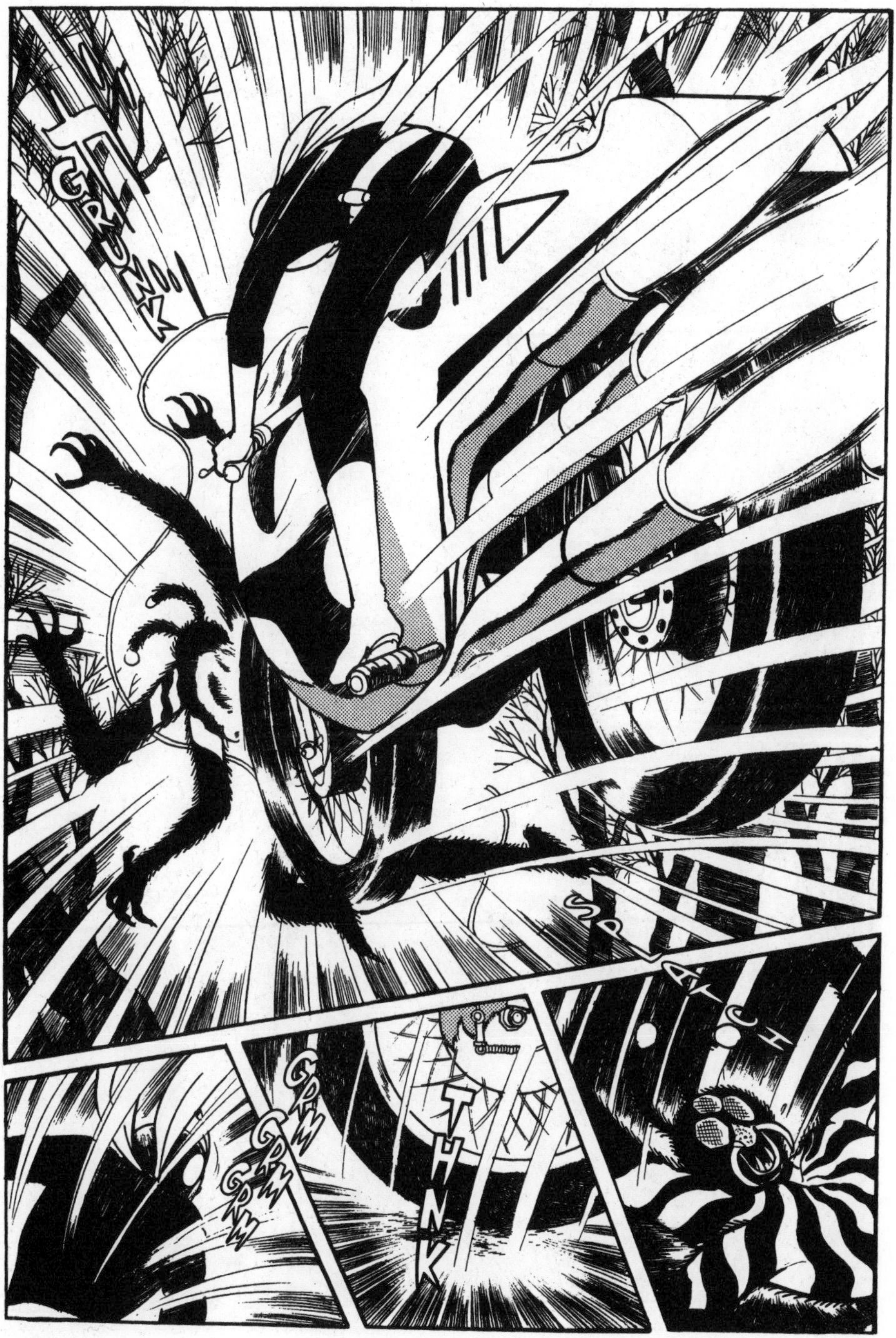
GRUNK
SPLATCH
THUNK
GRM GRM GRM

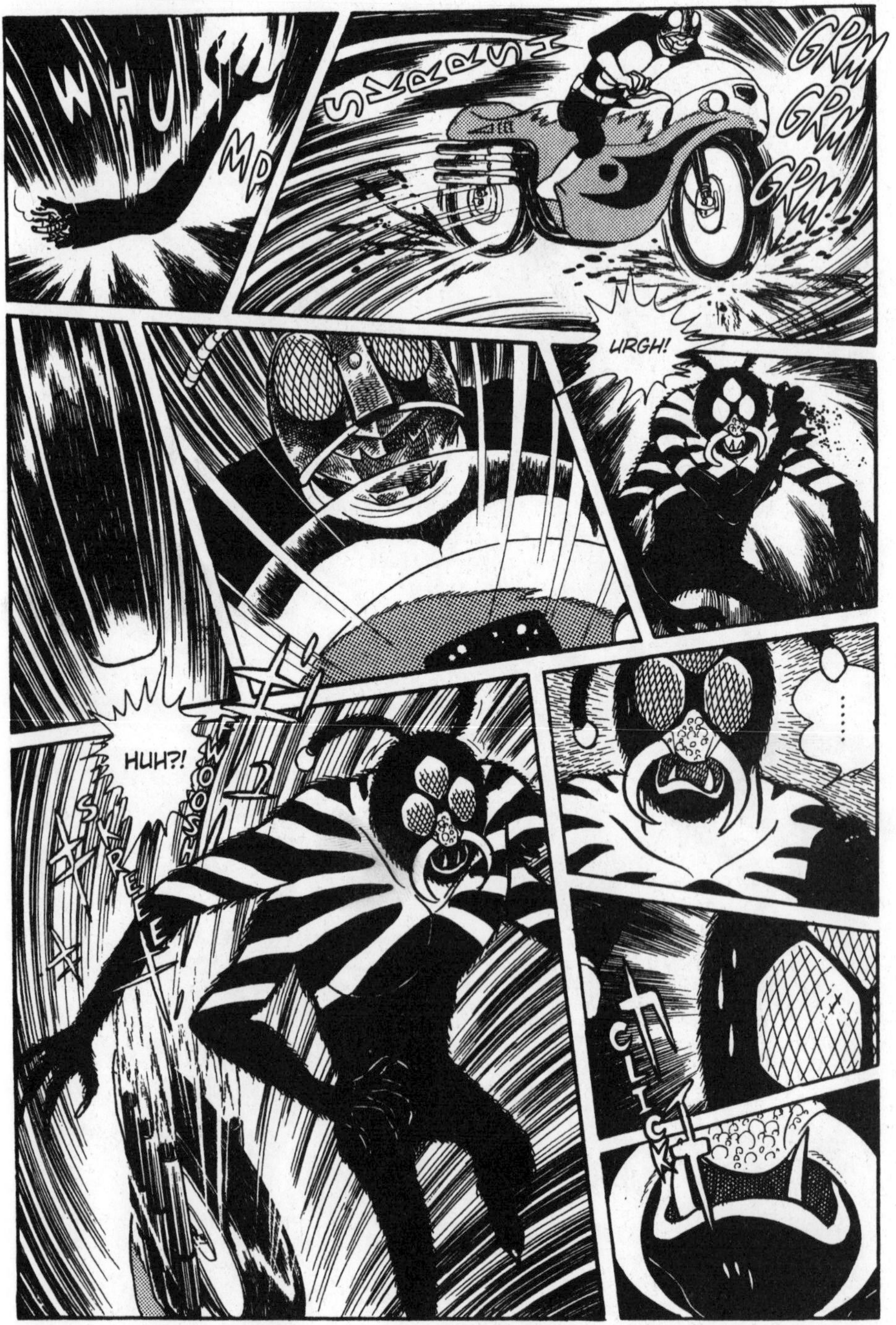
SKRRUSH
GRM GRM GRM
WHUMP
URGH!
HUH?!
WOOSH
SKREEE
......
CLICK

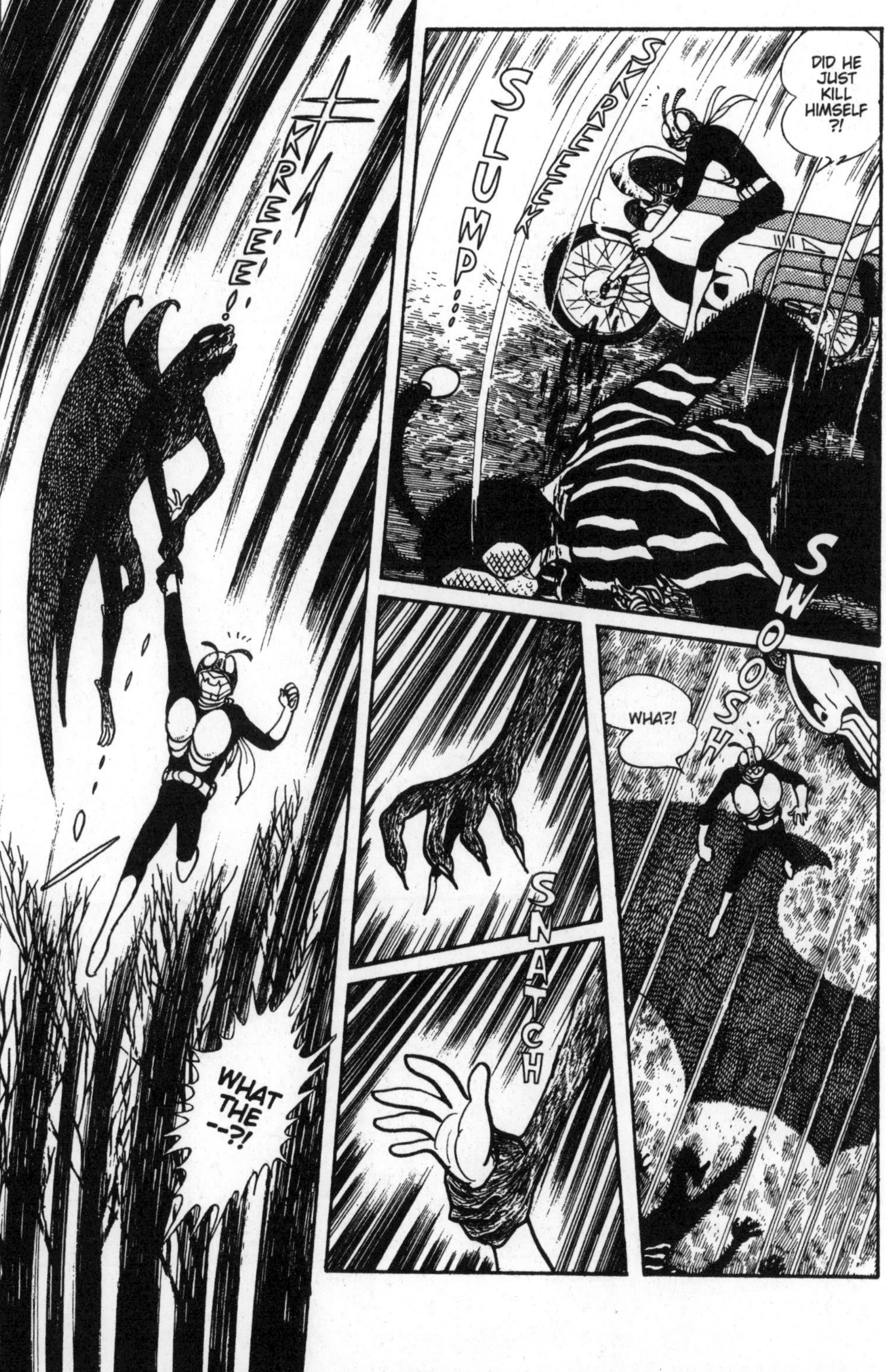
SKREEEEK
SLUMP...
DID HE JUST KILL HIMSELF ?!
SWOOSH
WHA?!
SNATCH
SKREEEE...!
WHAT THE --?!

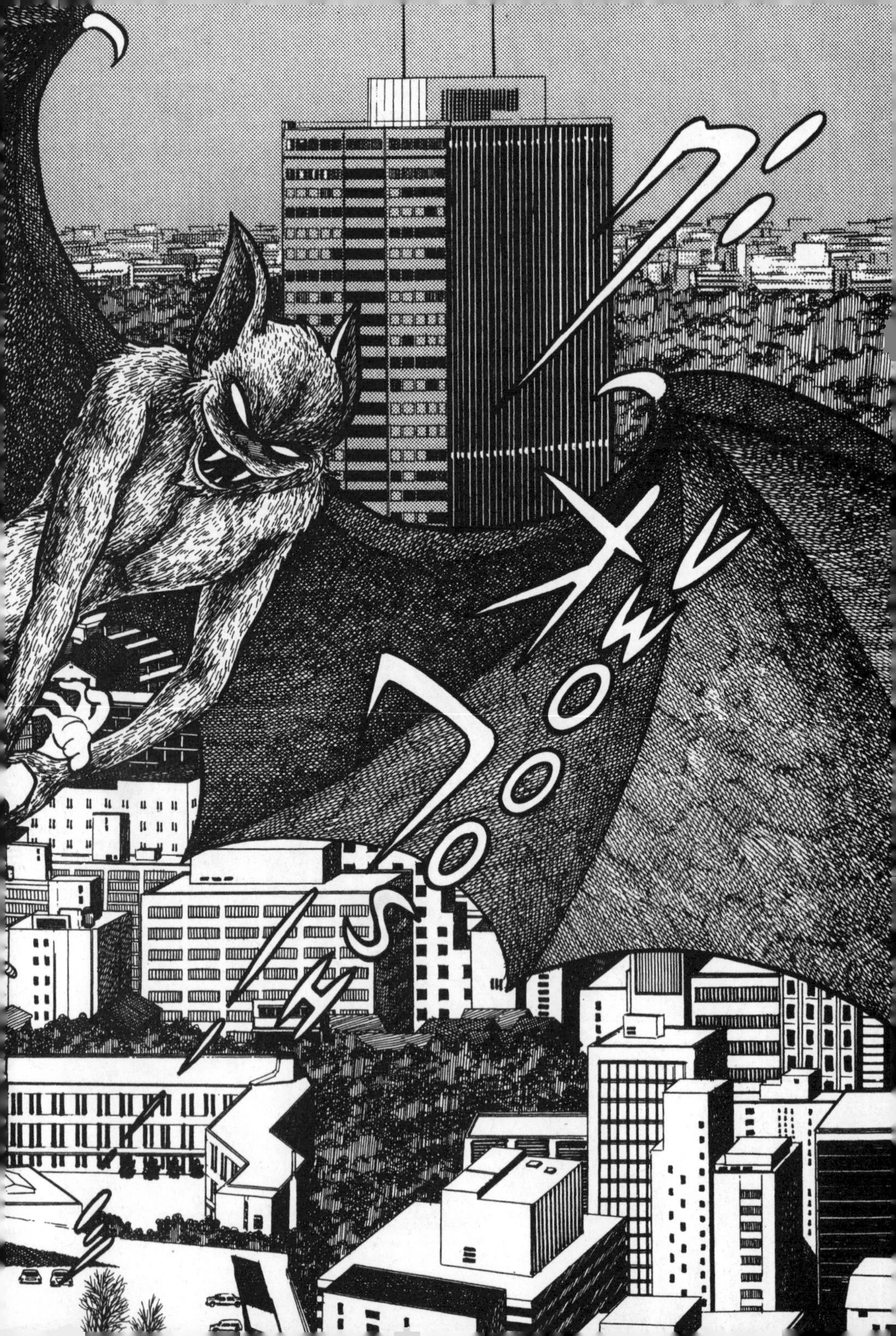
WOOOSH

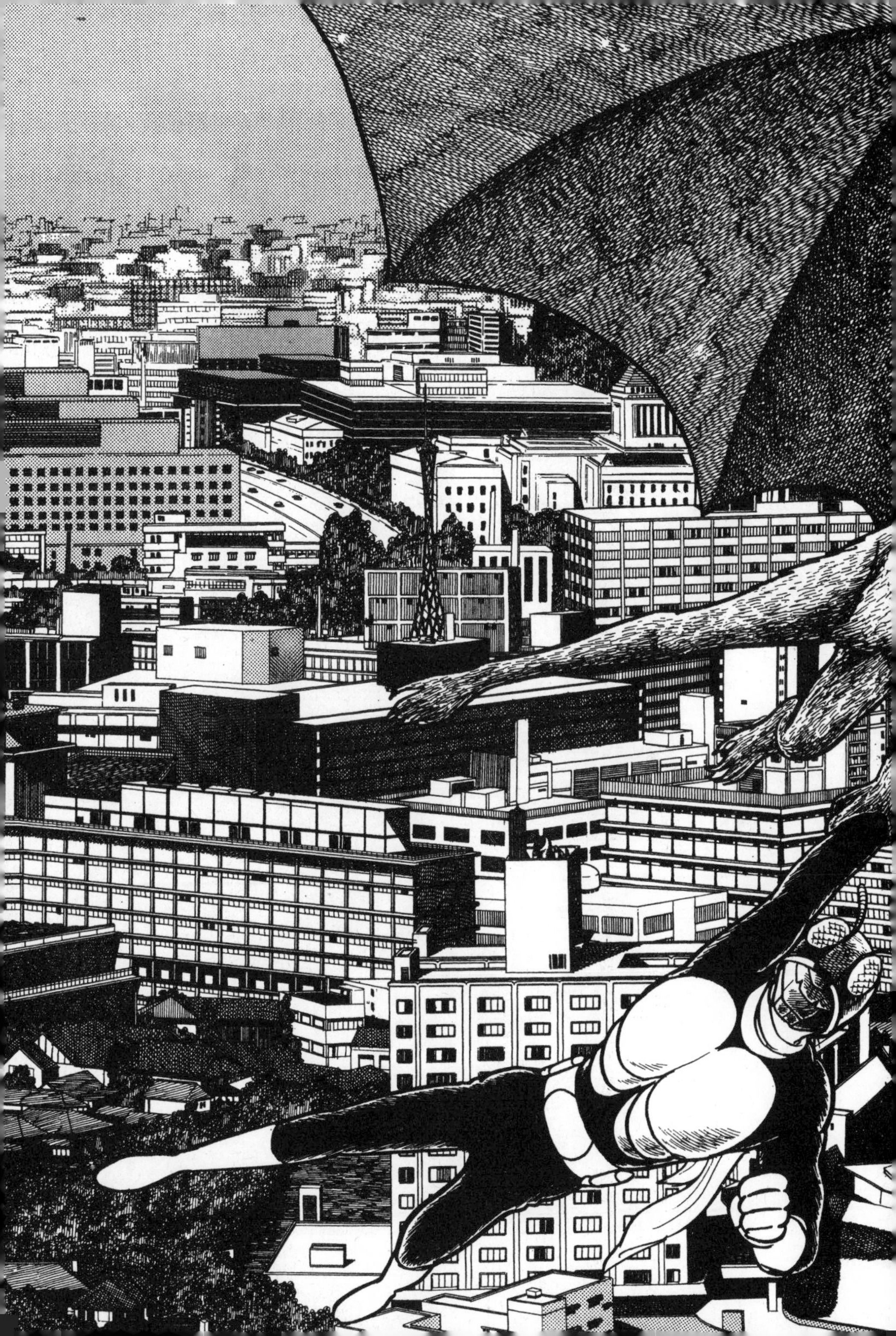

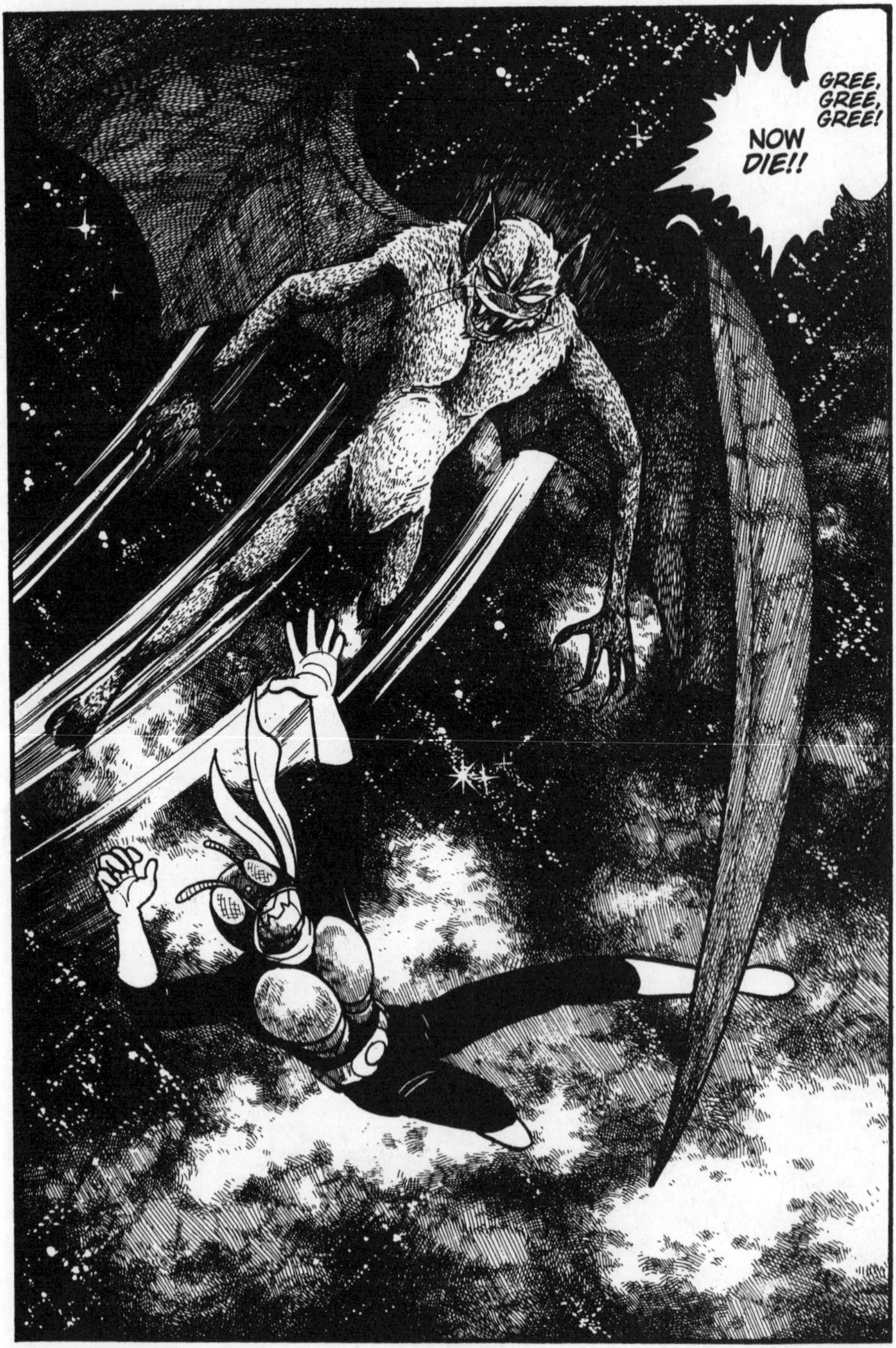
GREE, GREE, GREE!
NOW DIE!!

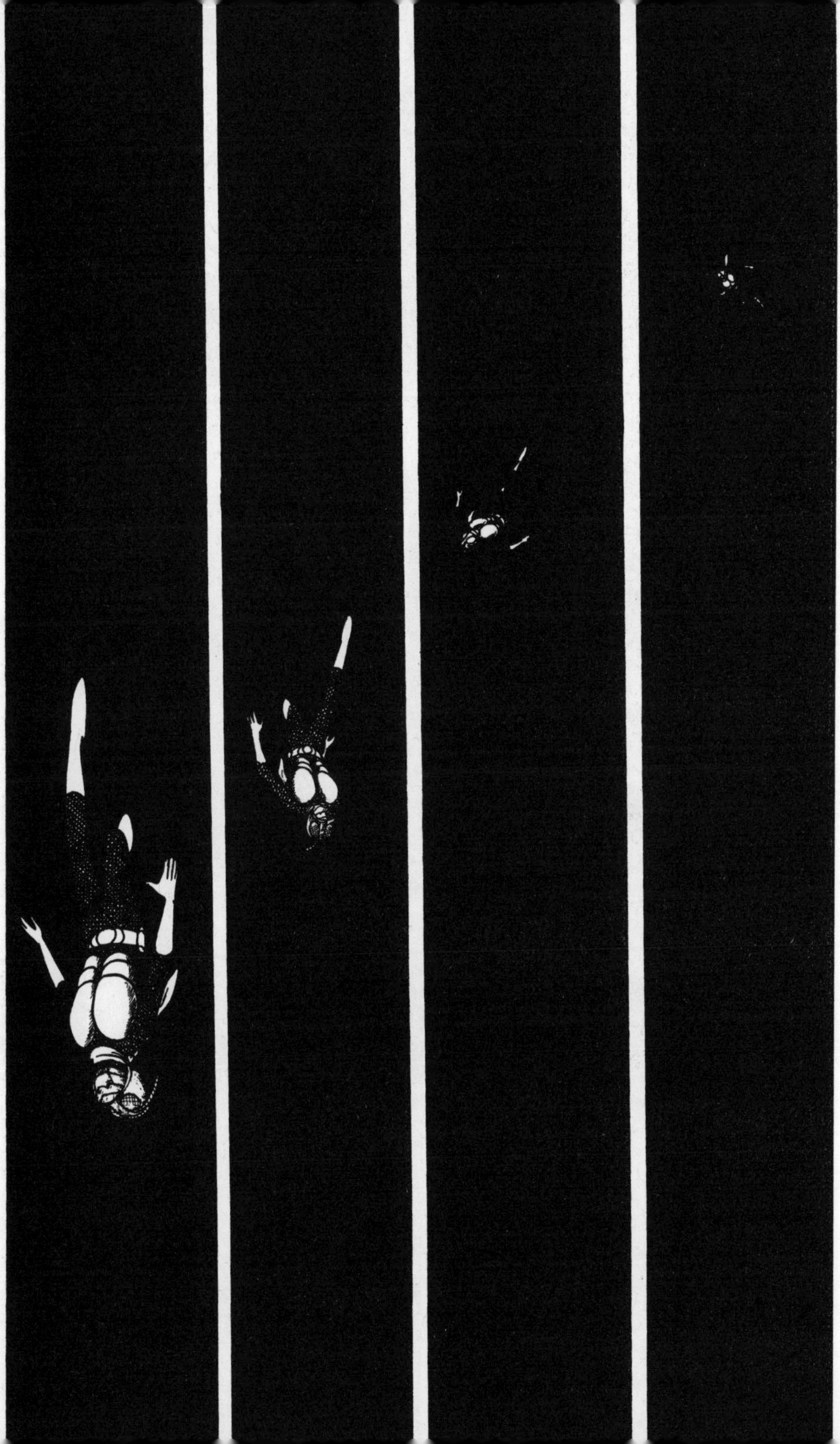

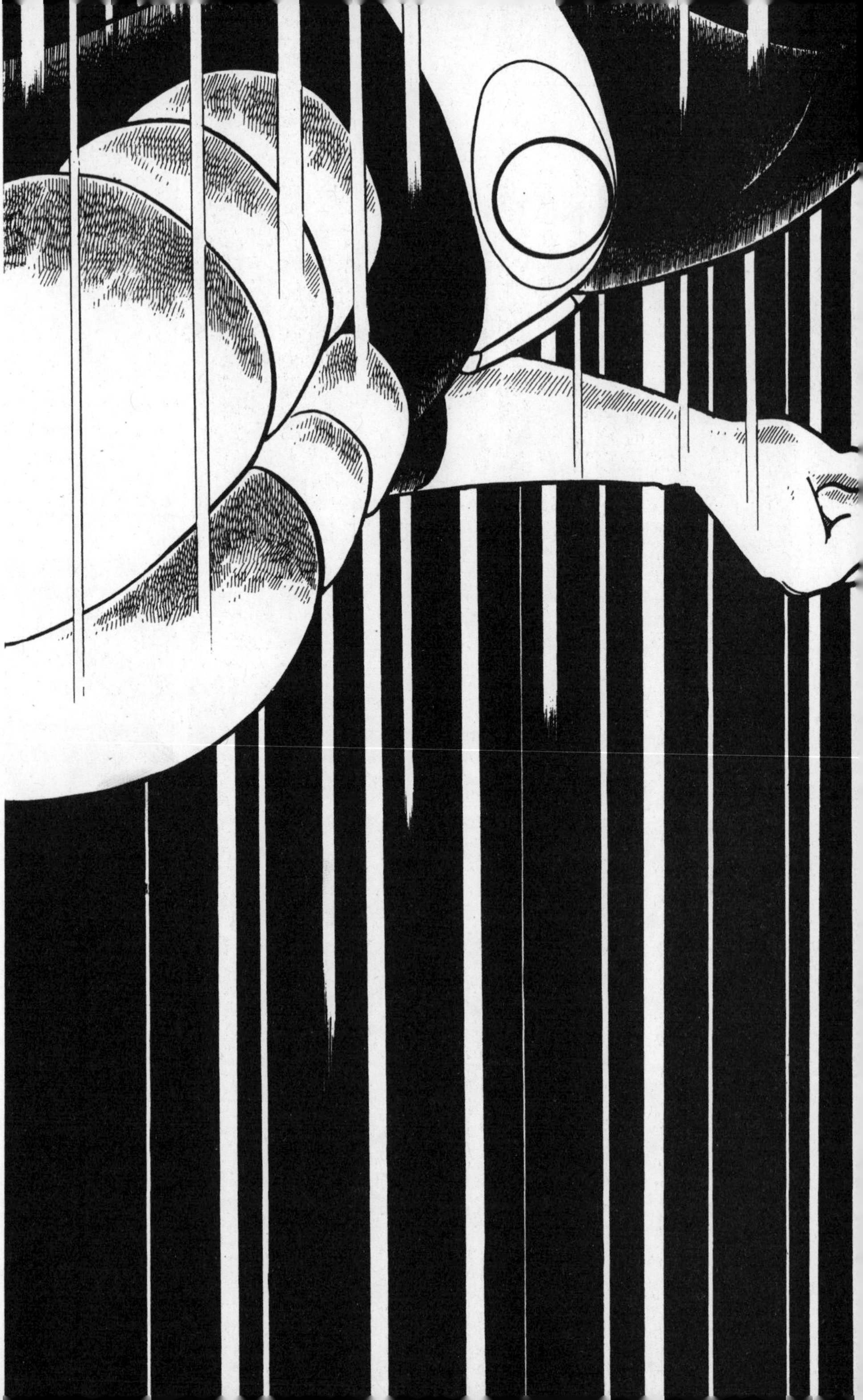

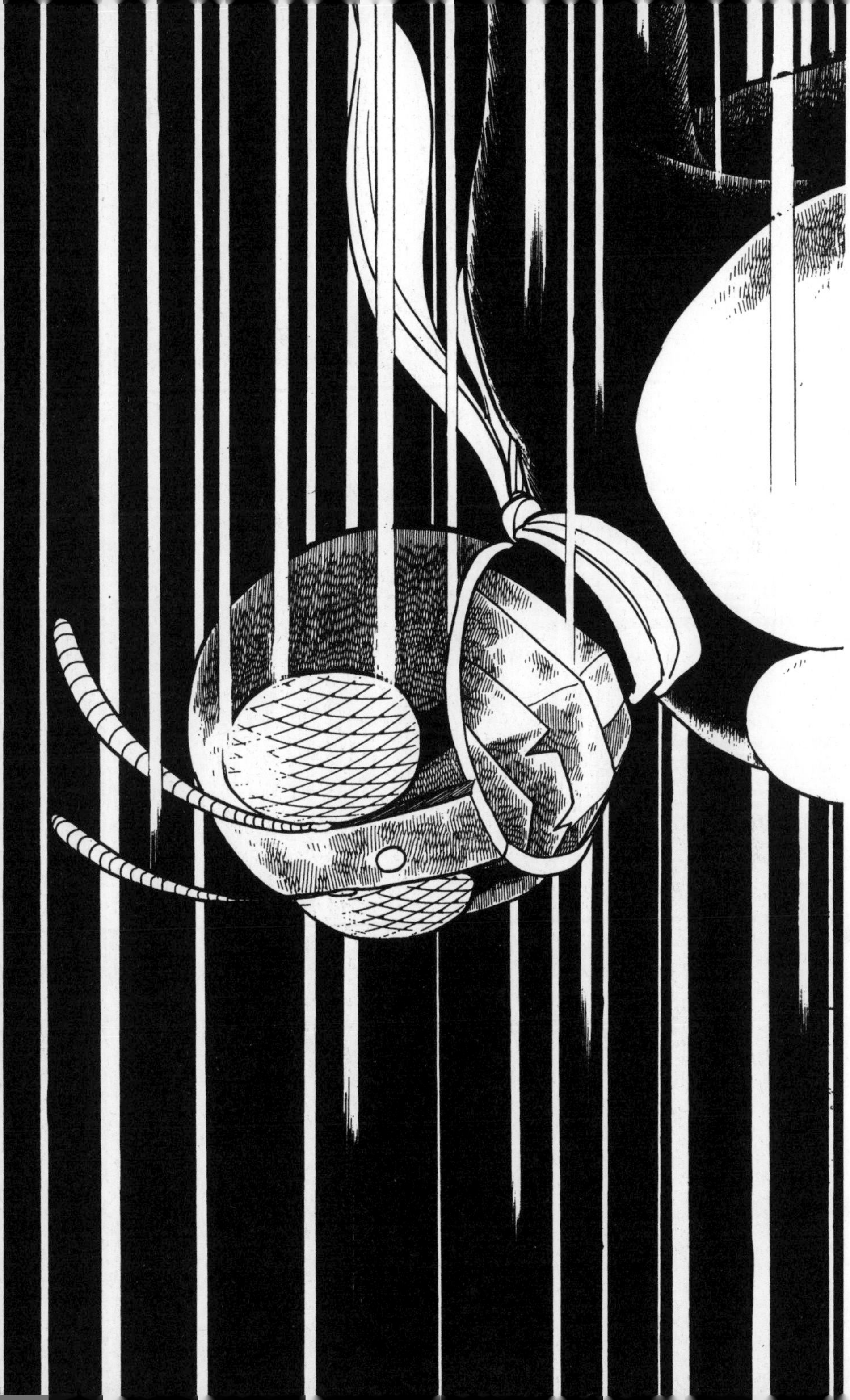

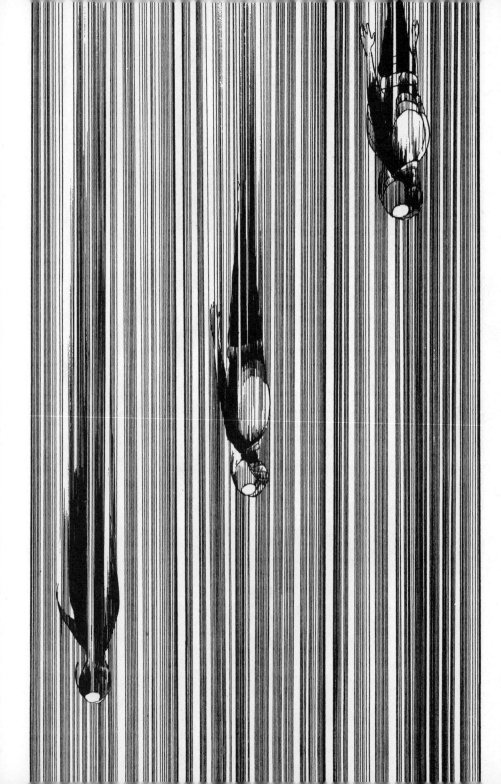

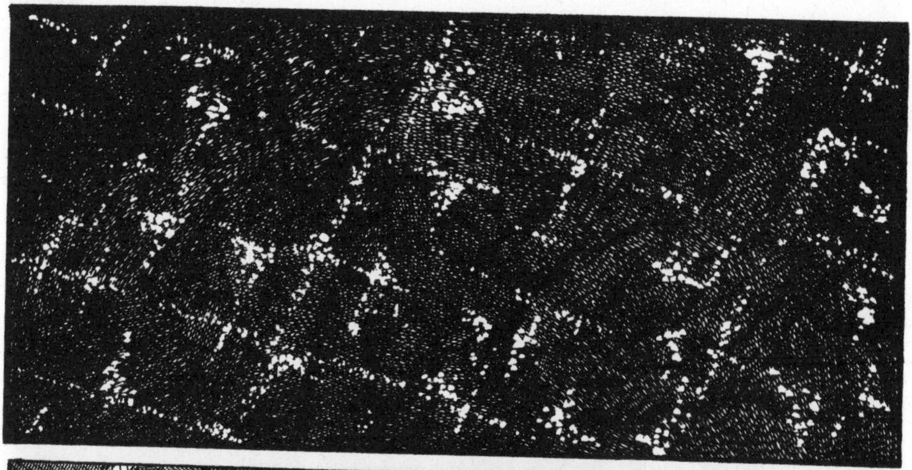
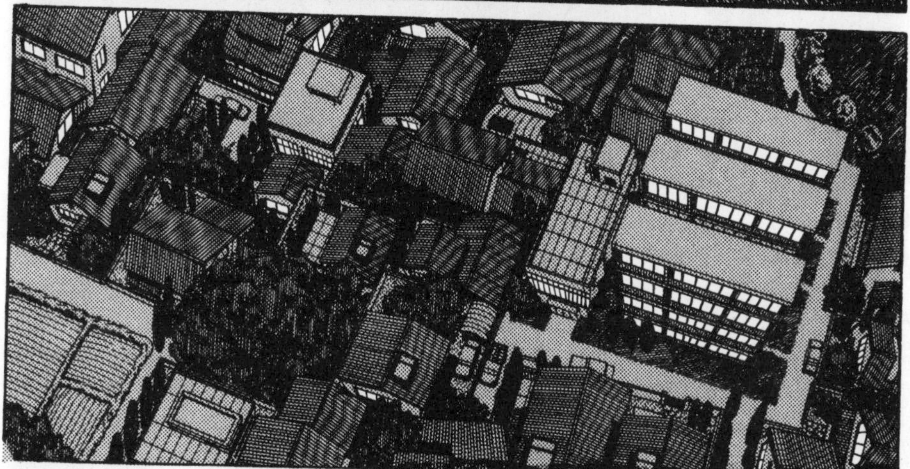
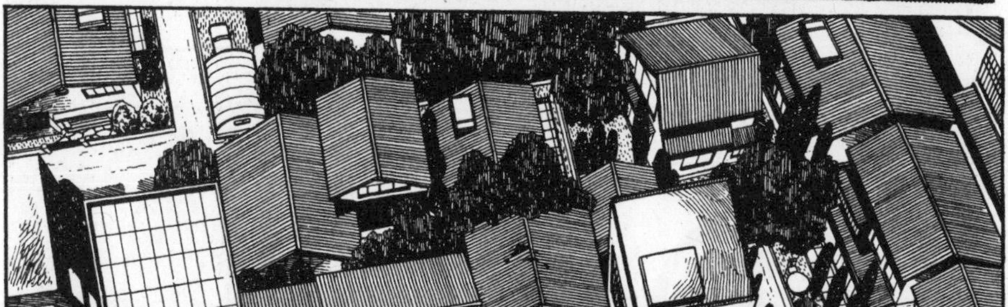

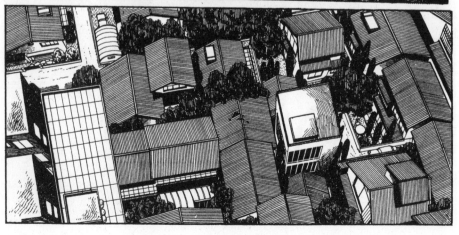

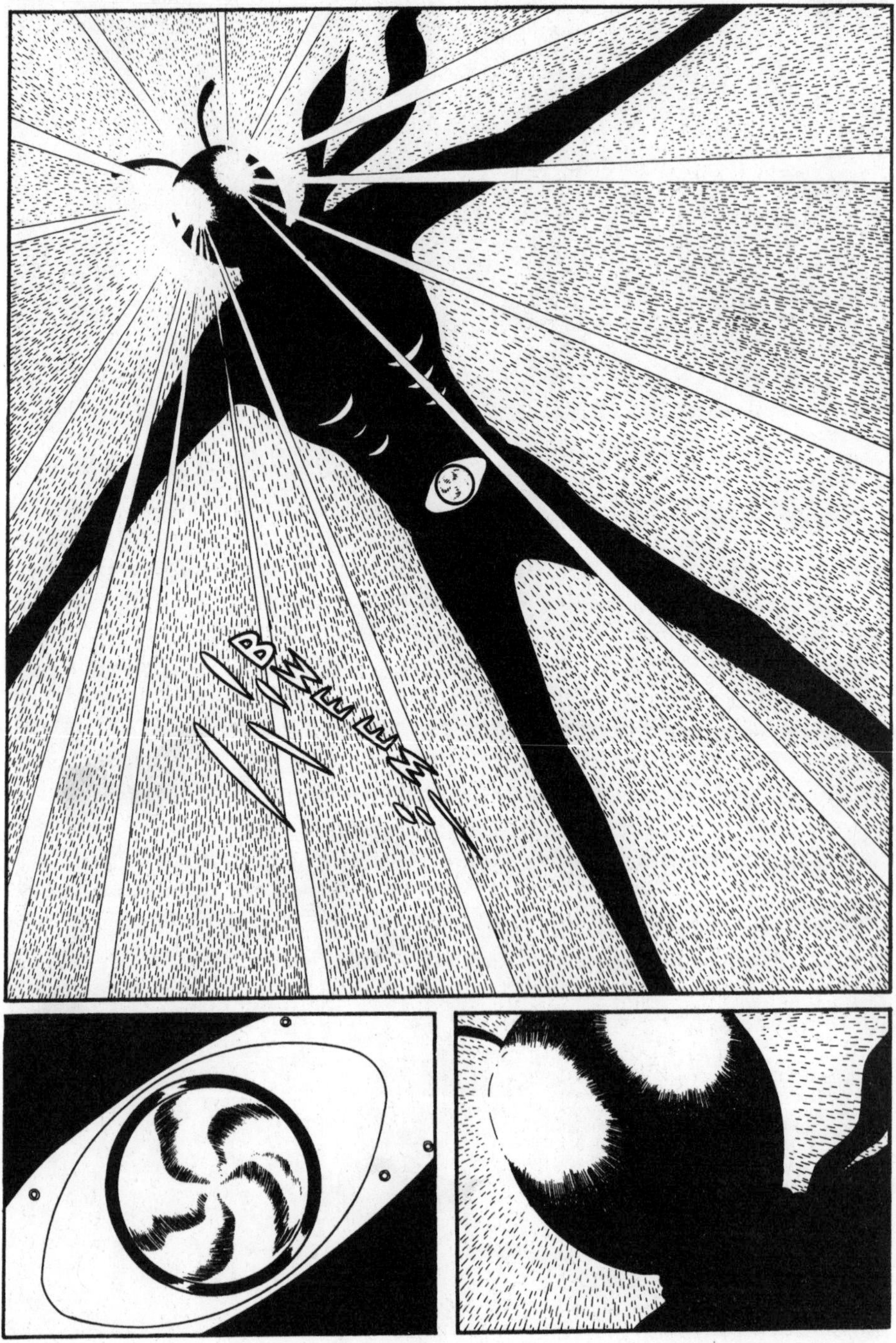

BWUUM!!

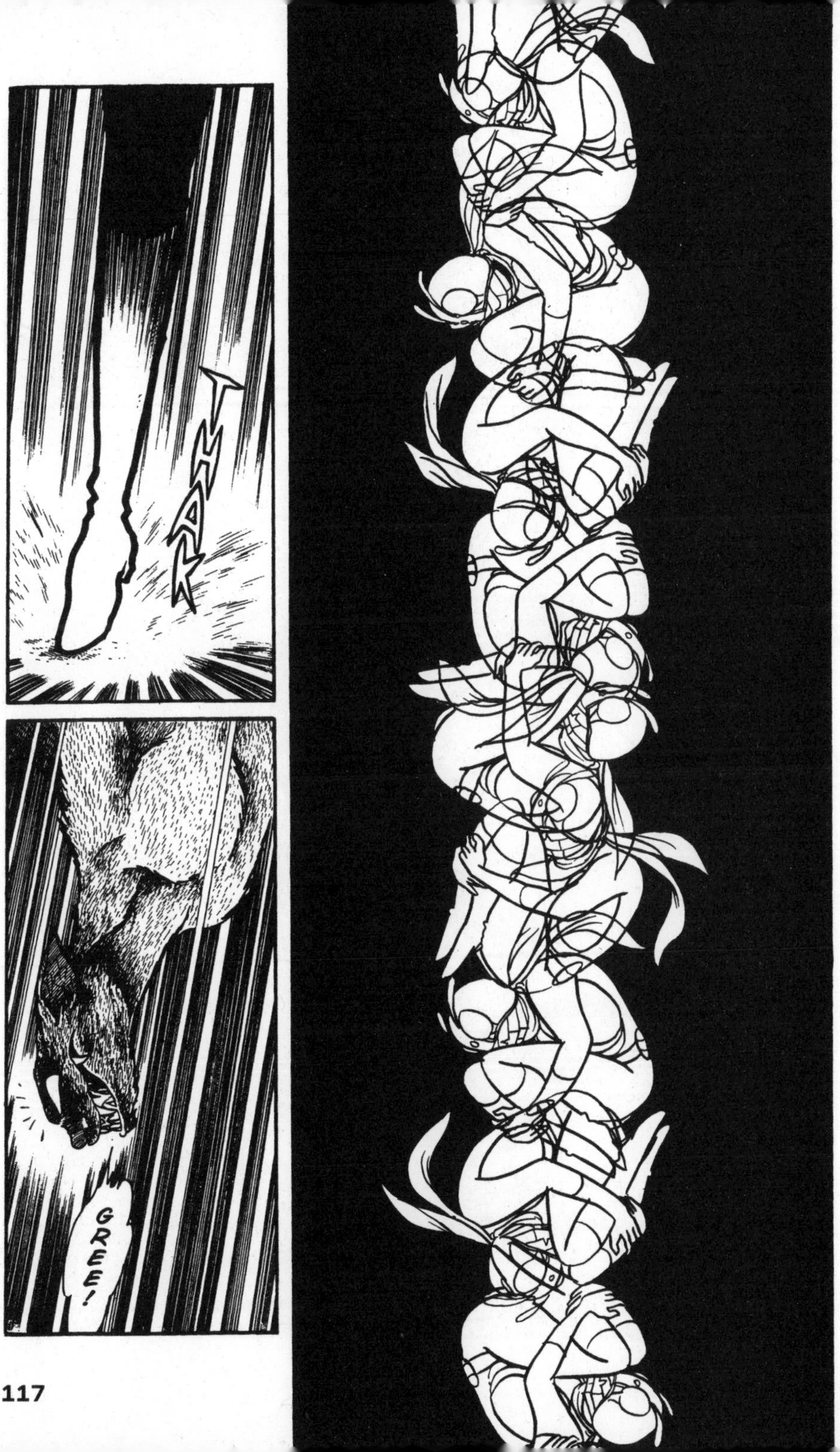
THWAK
GREE!

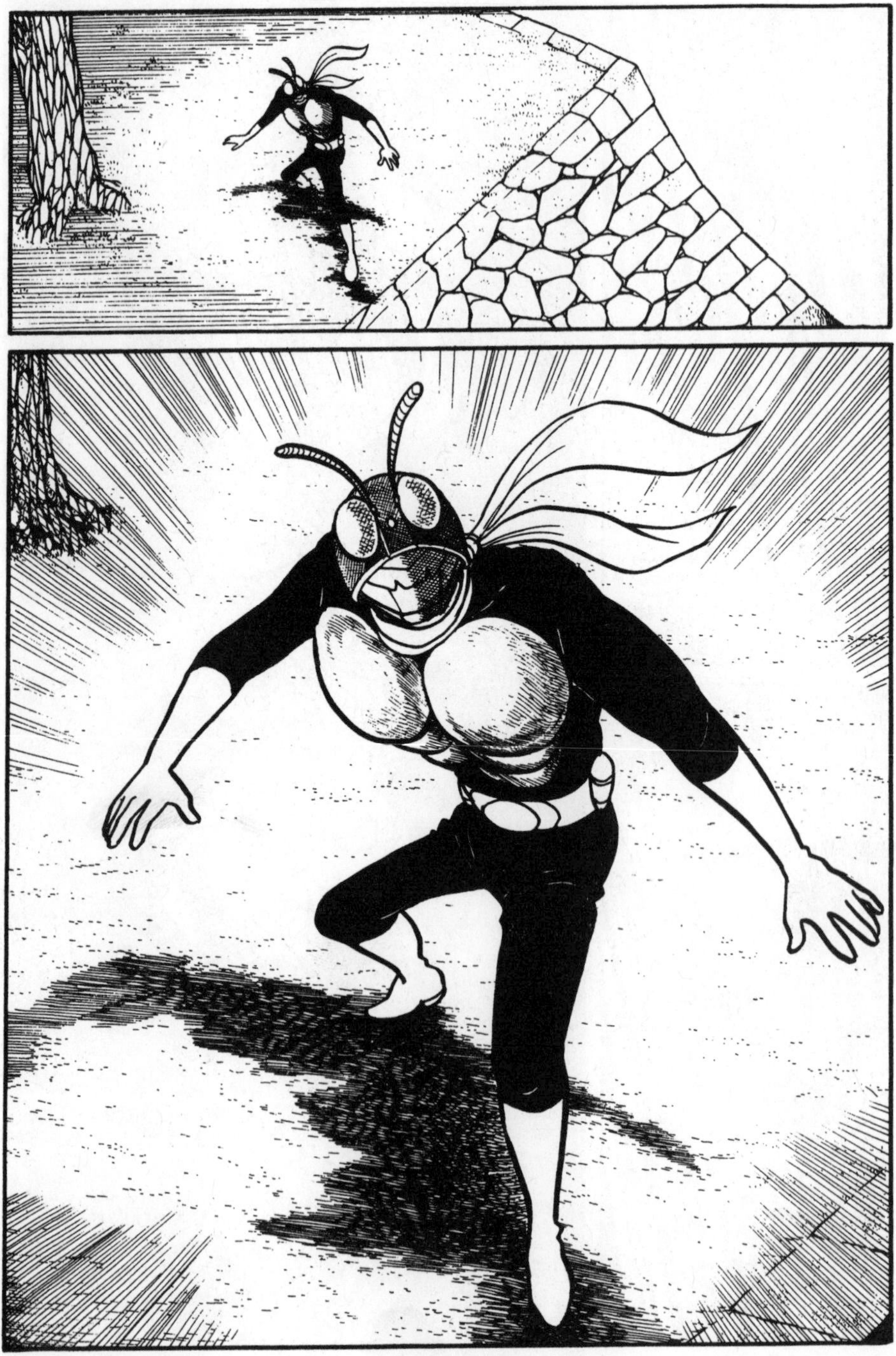

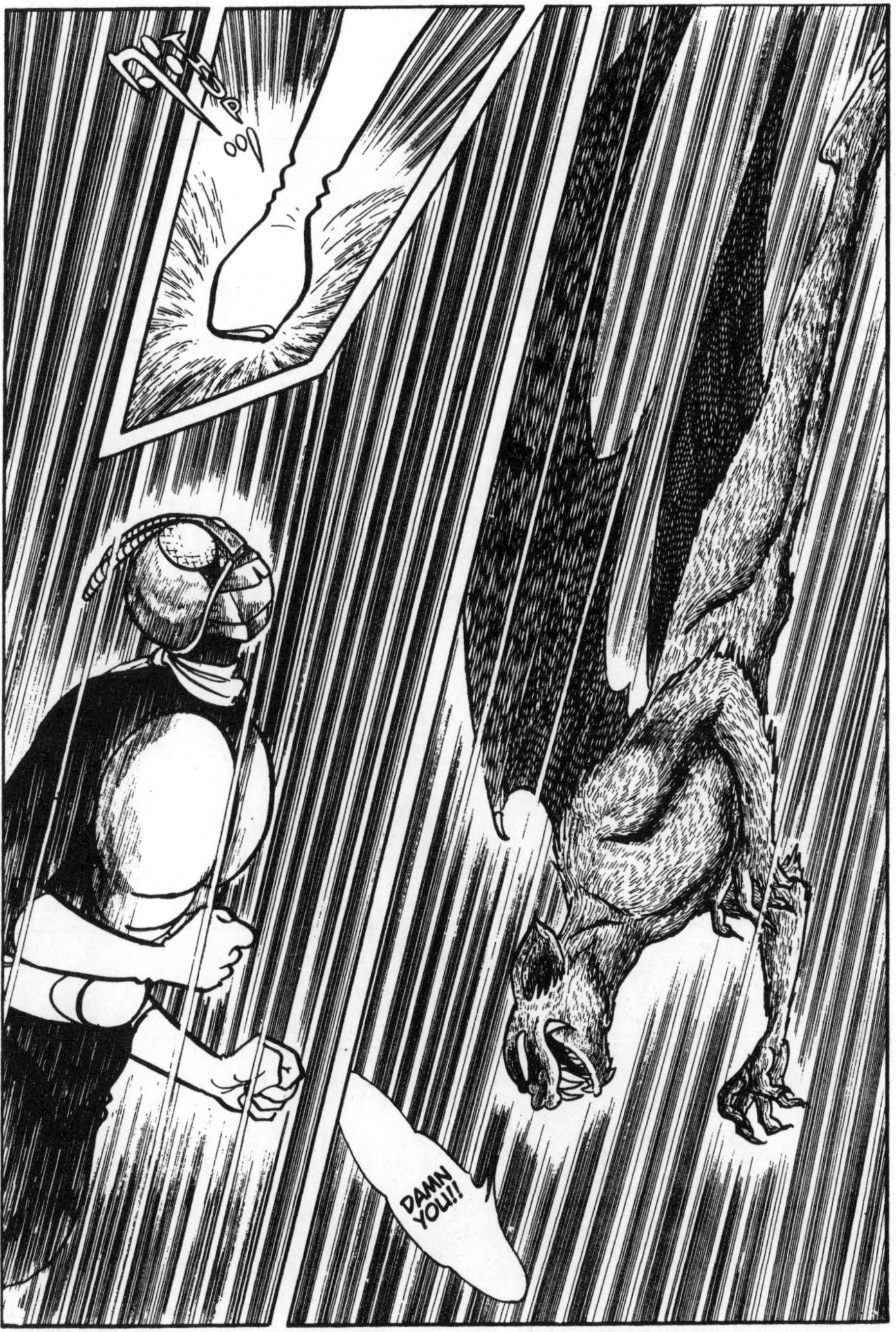
THUD
DAMN YOU!!

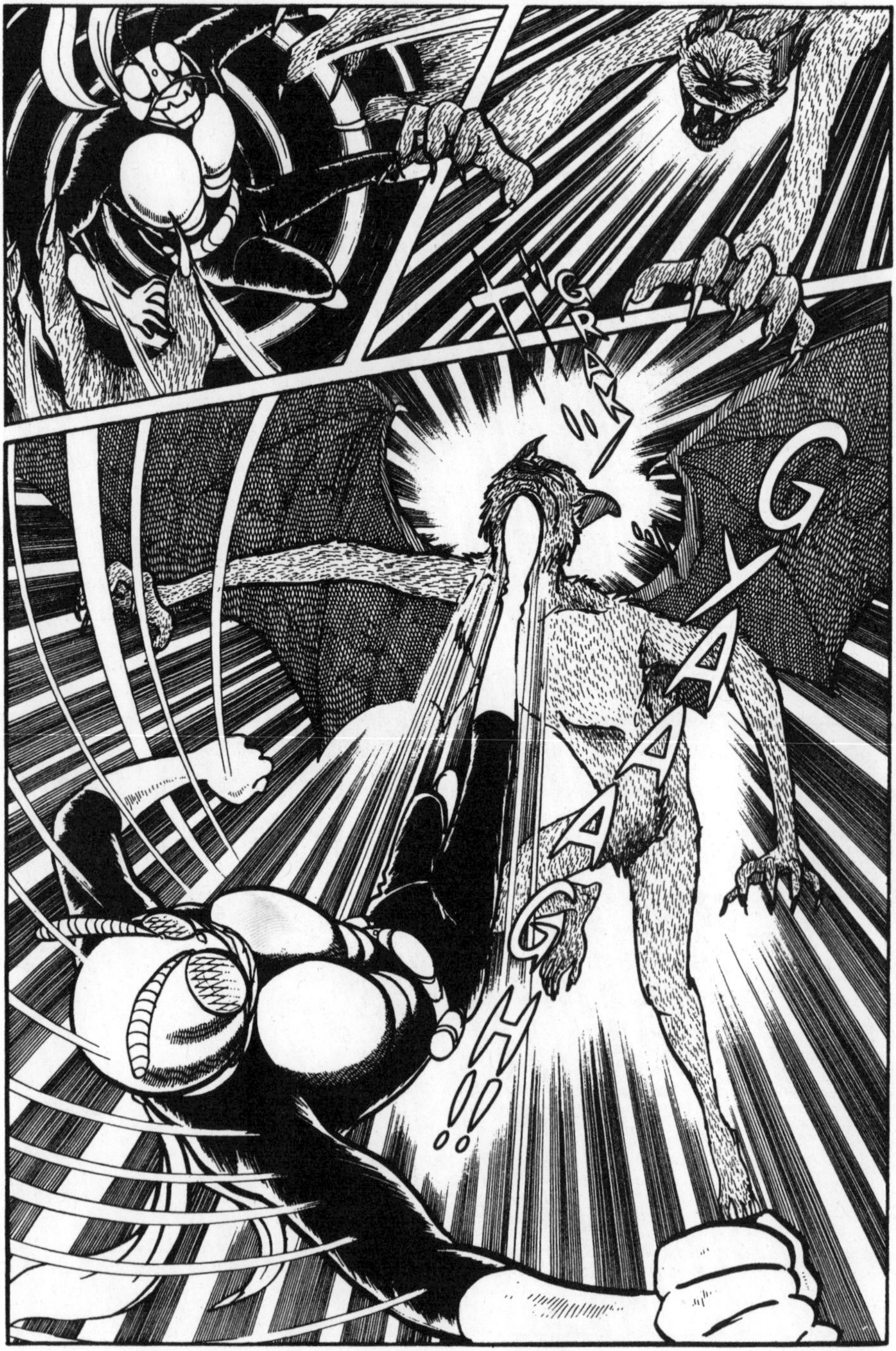
THGRAK!!
GYAAAGH!!

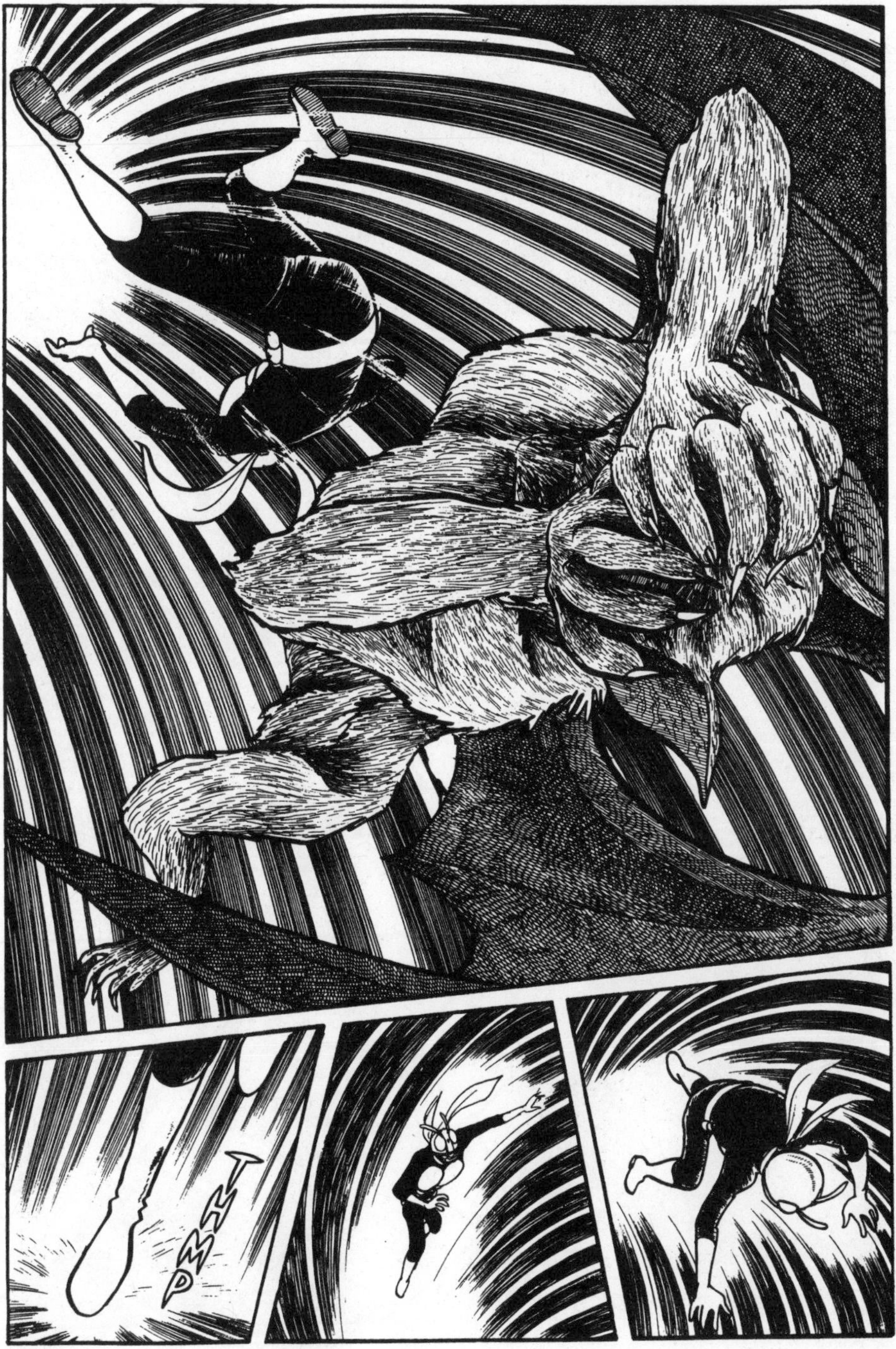
THUMP

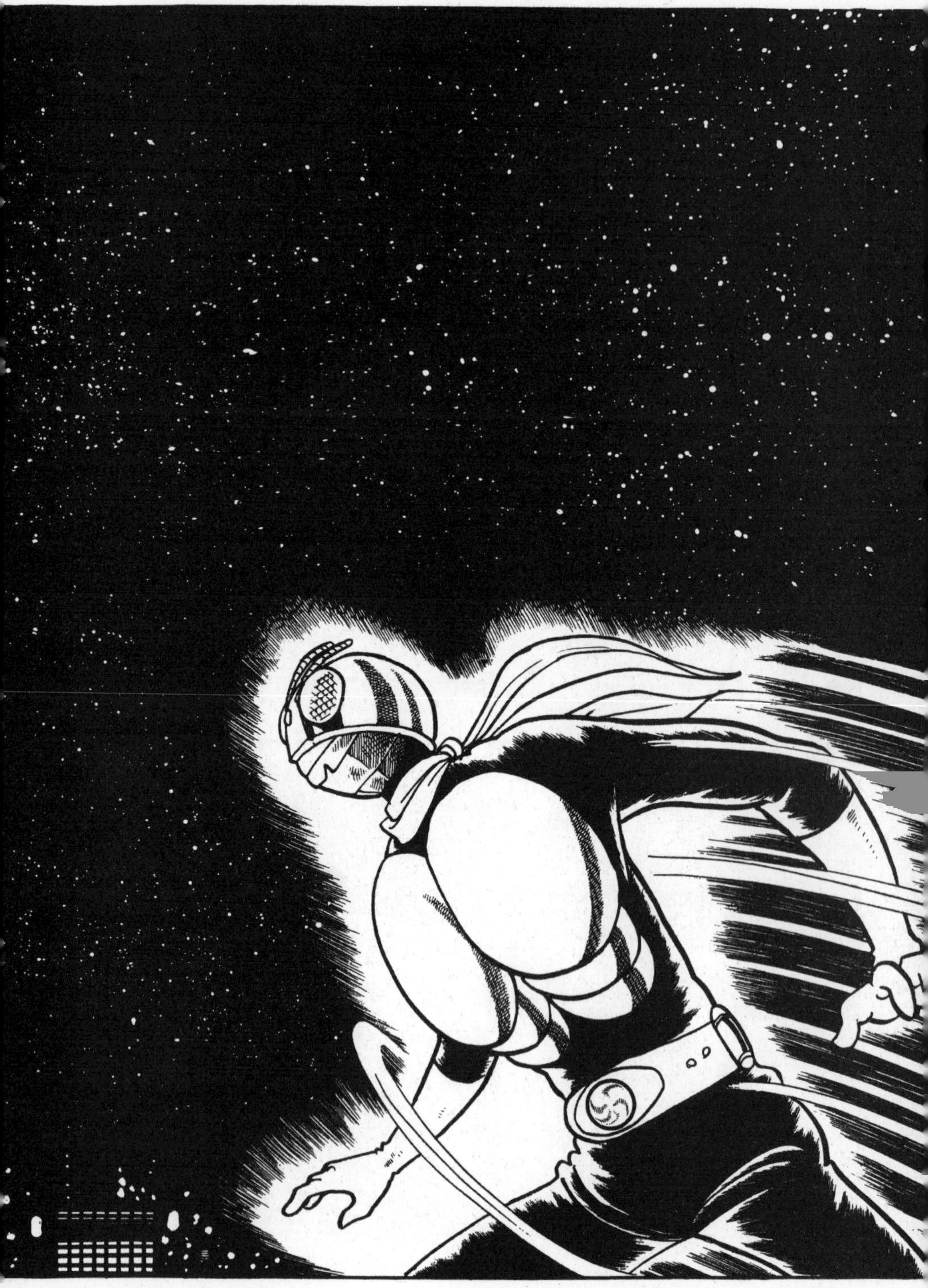

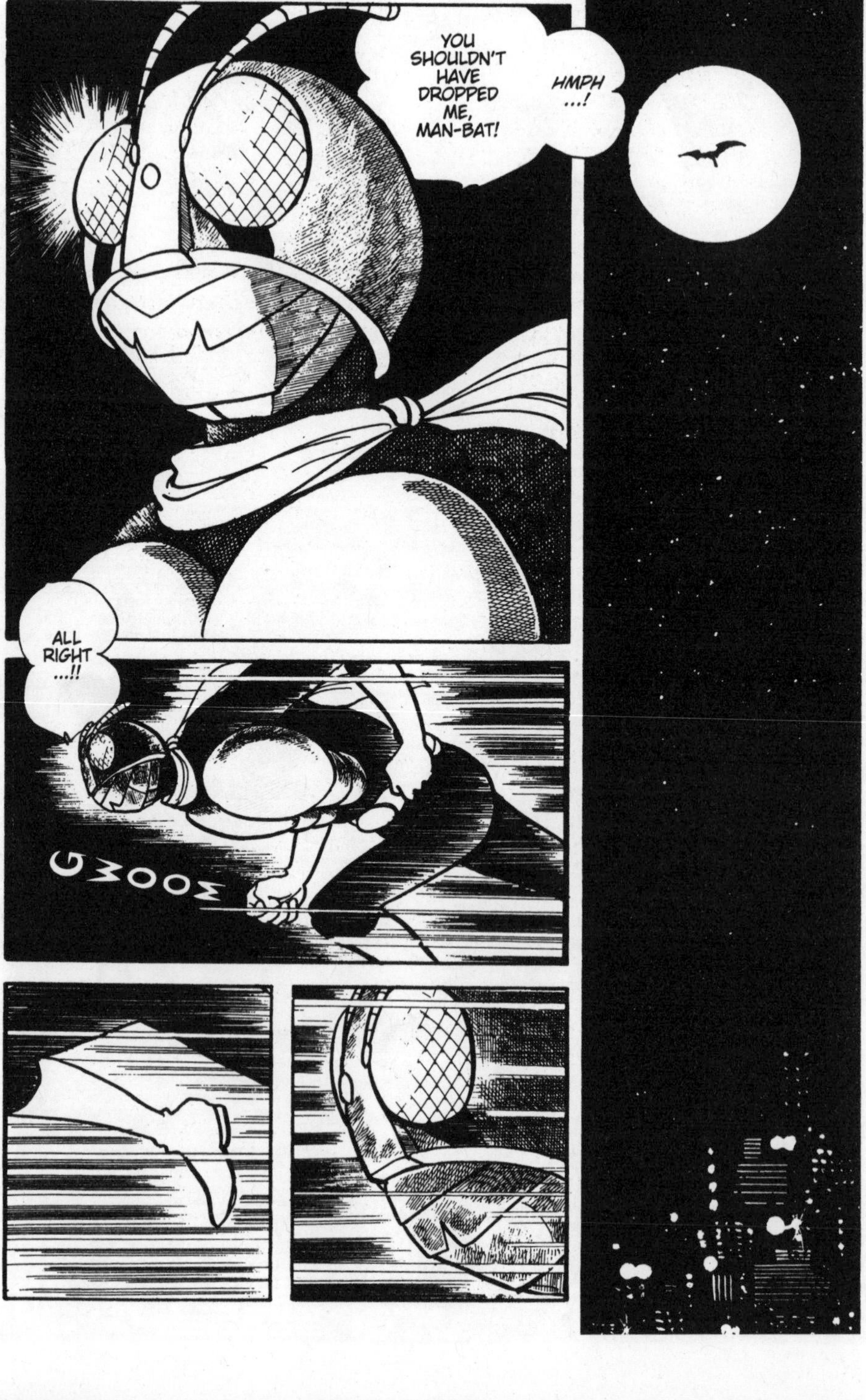
HMPH ...!
YOU SHOULDN'T HAVE DROPPED ME, MAN-BAT!
ALL RIGHT ...!!
GWOOM

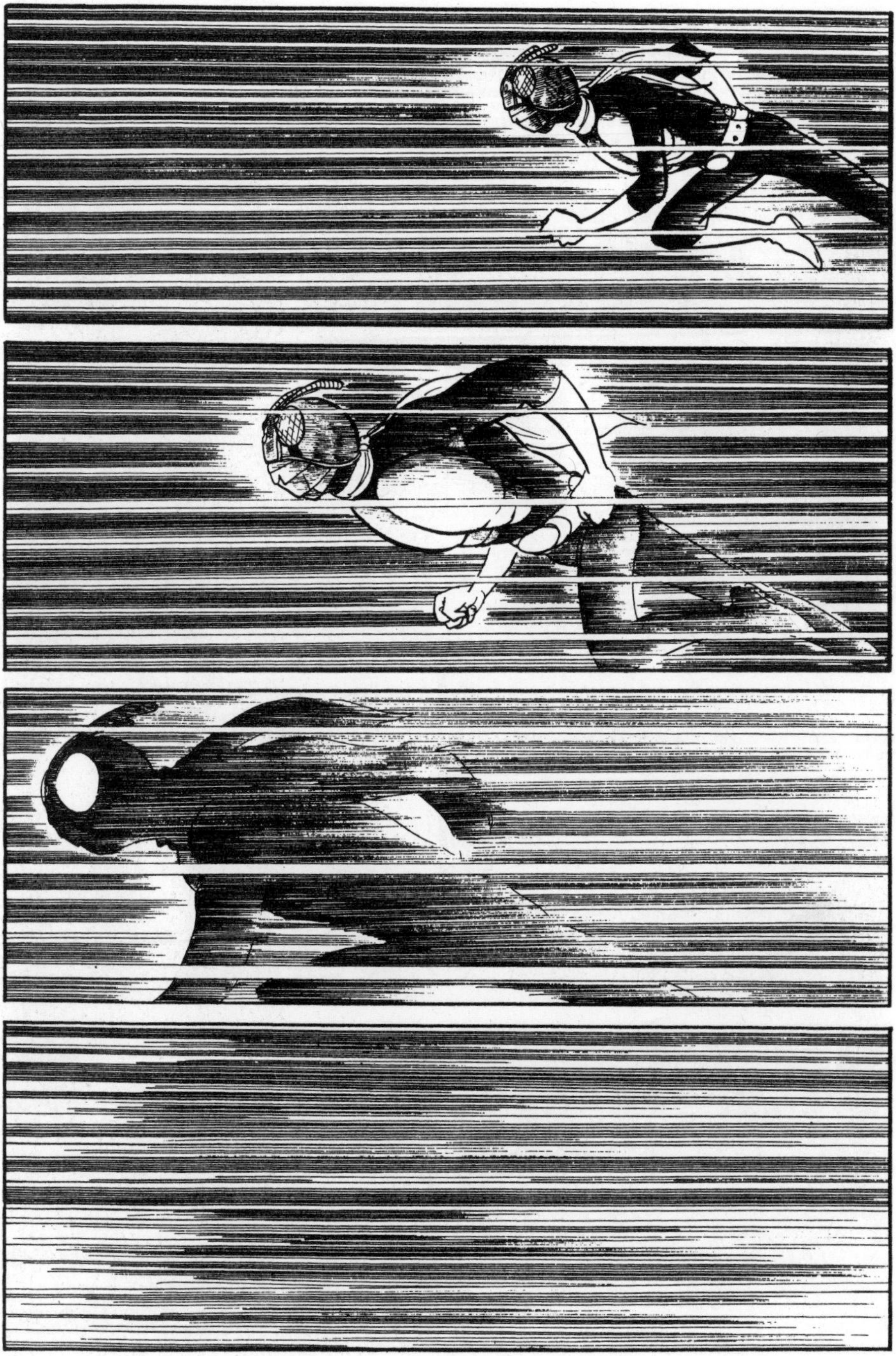

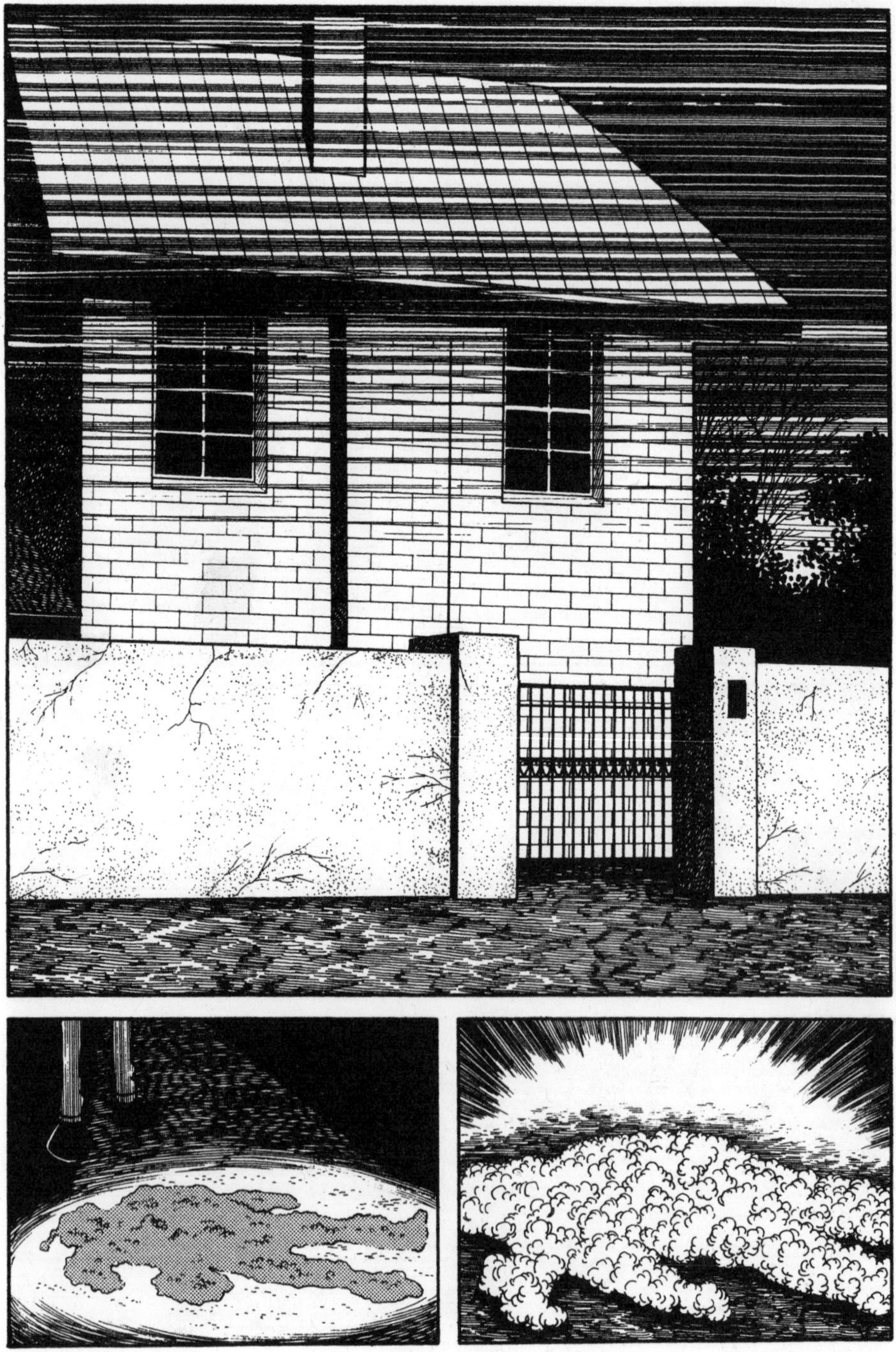

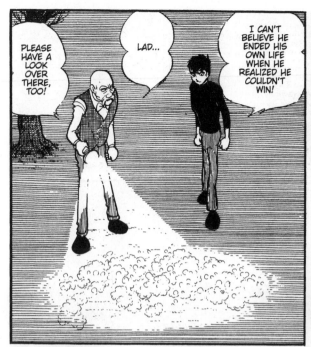

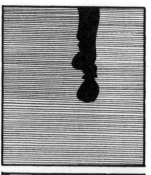

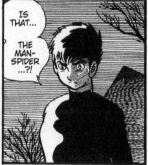

IS THAT... THE MAN-SPIDER ...?!
I CAN'T BELIEVE HE ENDED HIS OWN LIFE WHEN HE REALIZED HE COULDN'T WIN!
LAD...
PLEASE HAVE A LOOK OVER THERE, TOO!
THAT GIRL...
WAS RURIKO-SAMA'S FRIEND!!
HOW COULD THEY BE SO FOUL?!
RRRGH... SHOCKER. DAMN THEM ALL!!
LAD, WHAT ARE YOU DOING?
BEFORE SHE CRUMBLES TO DUST AND BLOWS AWAY...

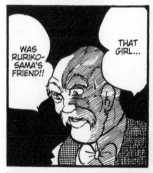

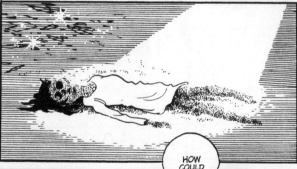

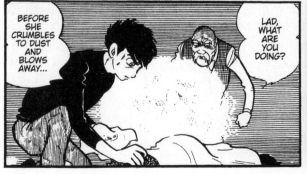

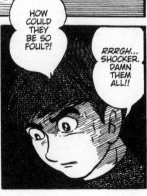

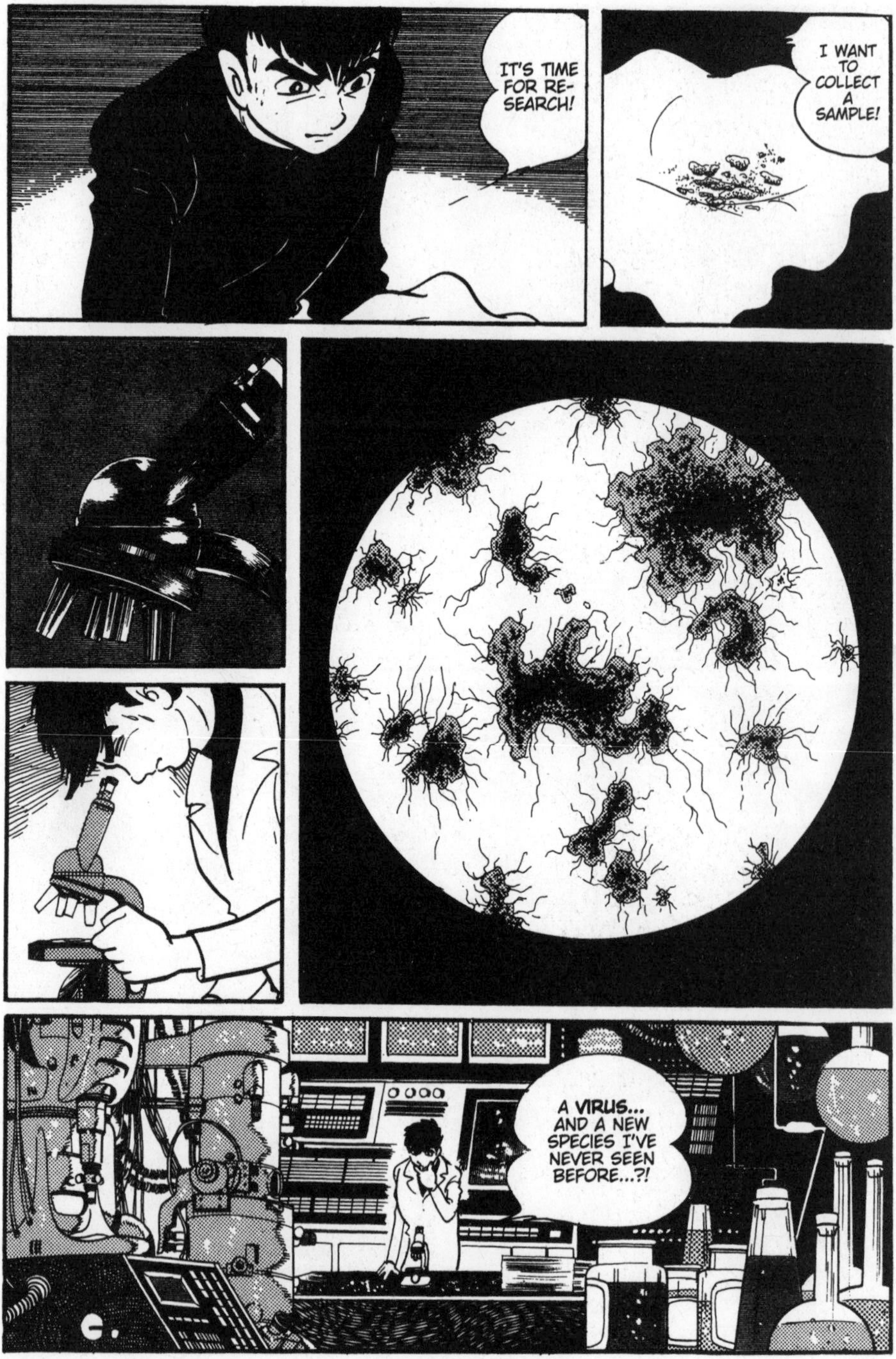
I WANT TO COLLECT A SAMPLE!
IT'S TIME FOR RE-SEARCH!
A VIRUS... AND A NEW SPECIES I'VE NEVER SEEN BEFORE...?!

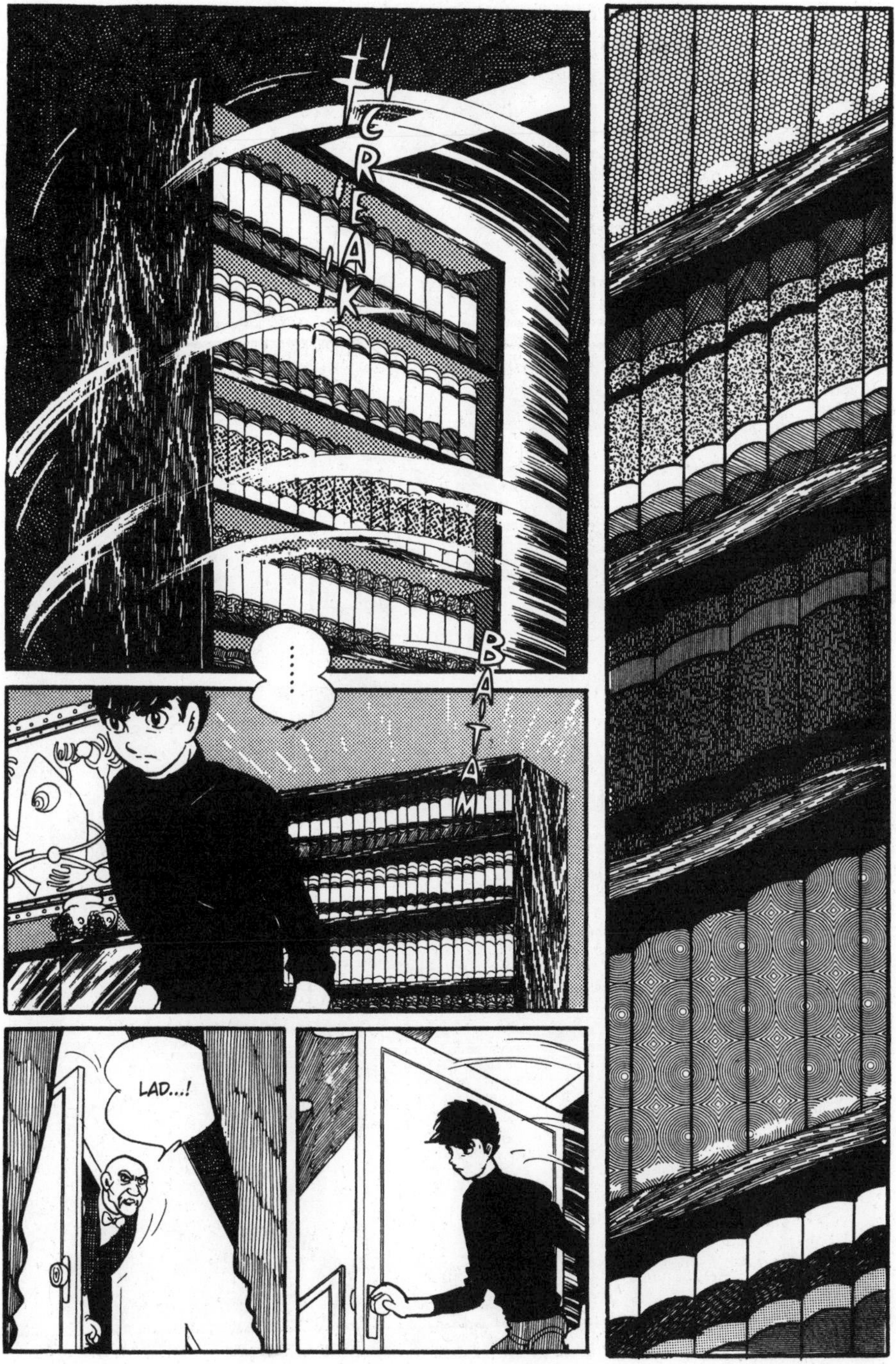
CREAK
BATAM
......
LAD...!

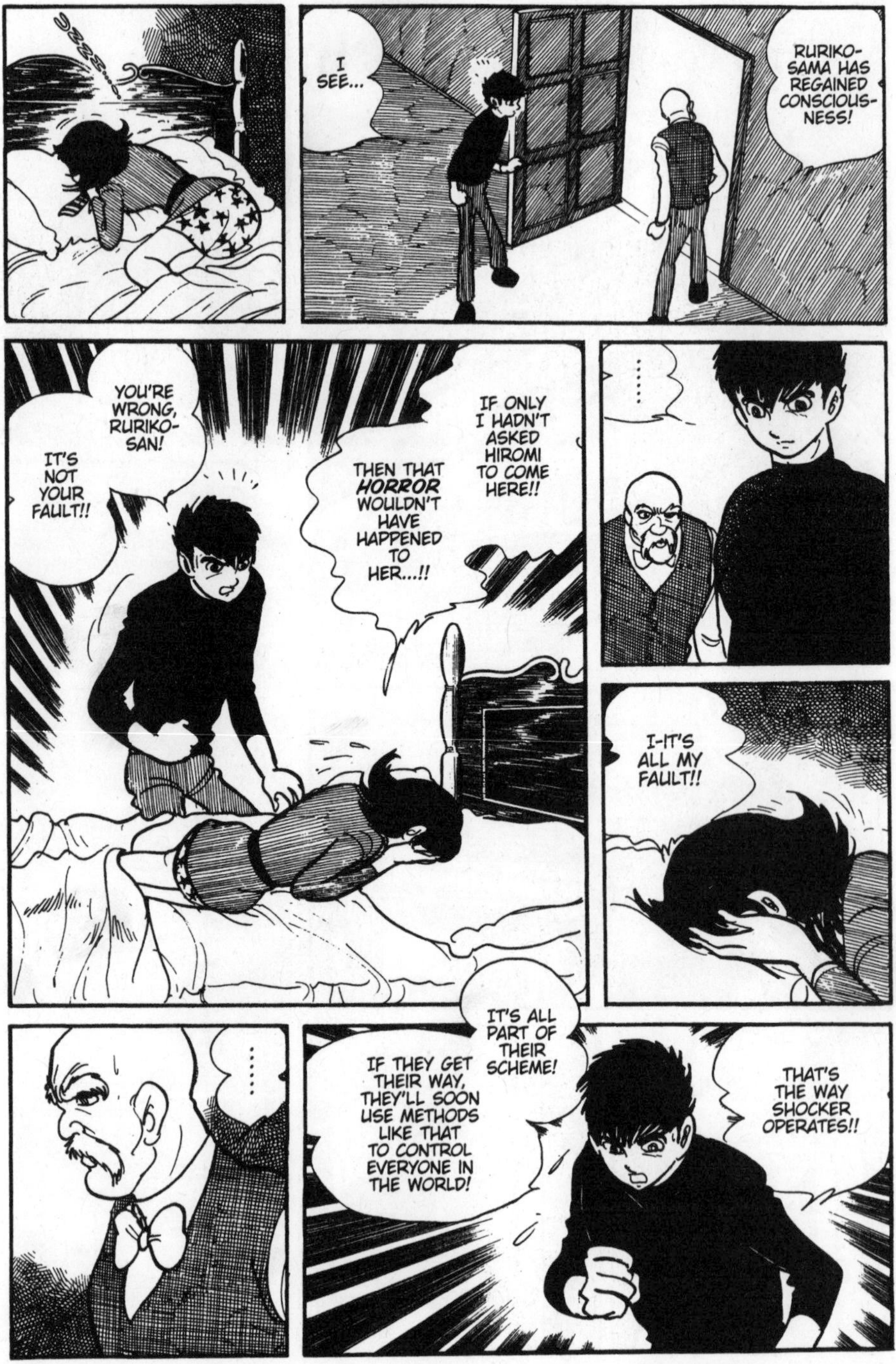
RURIKO-SAMA HAS REGAINED CONSCIOUS-NESS!
I SEE...
......
I-IT'S ALL MY FAULT!!
IF ONLY I HADN'T ASKED HIROMI TO COME HERE!!
THEN THAT **HORROR** WOULDN'T HAVE HAPPENED TO HER...!!
YOU'RE WRONG, RURIKO-SAN!
IT'S NOT YOUR FAULT!!
THAT'S THE WAY SHOCKER OPERATES!!
IT'S ALL PART OF THEIR SCHEME!
IF THEY GET THEIR WAY, THEY'LL SOON USE METHODS LIKE THAT TO CONTROL EVERYONE IN THE WORLD!
......

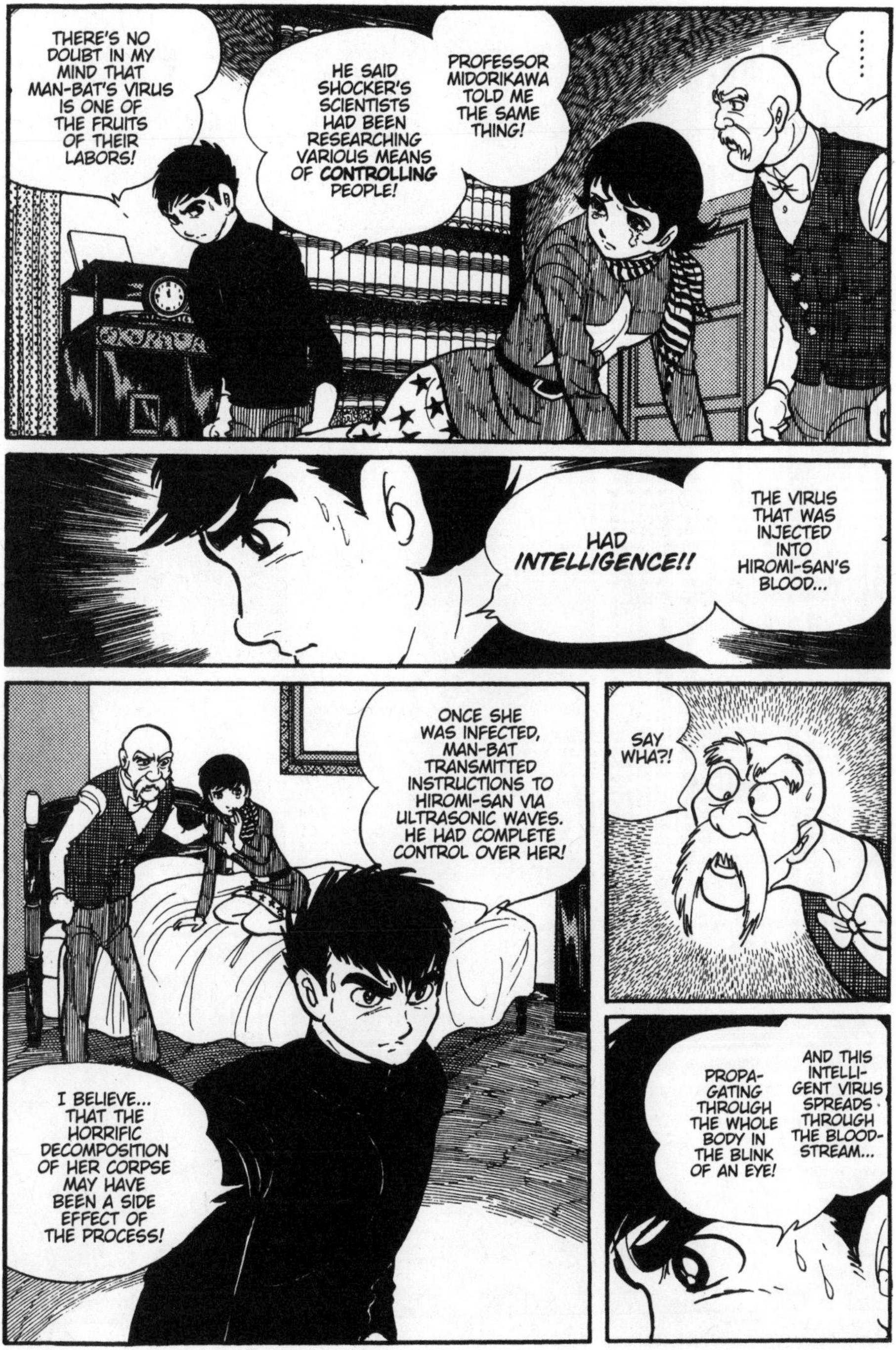
......
PROFESSOR MIDORIKAWA TOLD ME THE SAME THING!
HE SAID SHOCKER'S SCIENTISTS HAD BEEN RESEARCHING VARIOUS MEANS OF **CONTROLLING** PEOPLE!
THERE'S NO DOUBT IN MY MIND THAT MAN-BAT'S VIRUS IS ONE OF THE FRUITS OF THEIR LABORS!
THE VIRUS THAT WAS INJECTED INTO HIROMI-SAN'S BLOOD...
HAD ***INTELLIGENCE!!***
SAY WHA?!
AND THIS INTELLIGENT VIRUS SPREADS THROUGH THE BLOODSTREAM...
PROPAGATING THROUGH THE WHOLE BODY IN THE BLINK OF AN EYE!
ONCE SHE WAS INFECTED, MAN-BAT TRANSMITTED INSTRUCTIONS TO HIROMI-SAN VIA ULTRASONIC WAVES. HE HAD COMPLETE CONTROL OVER HER!
I BELIEVE... THAT THE HORRIFIC DECOMPOSITION OF HER CORPSE MAY HAVE BEEN A SIDE EFFECT OF THE PROCESS!

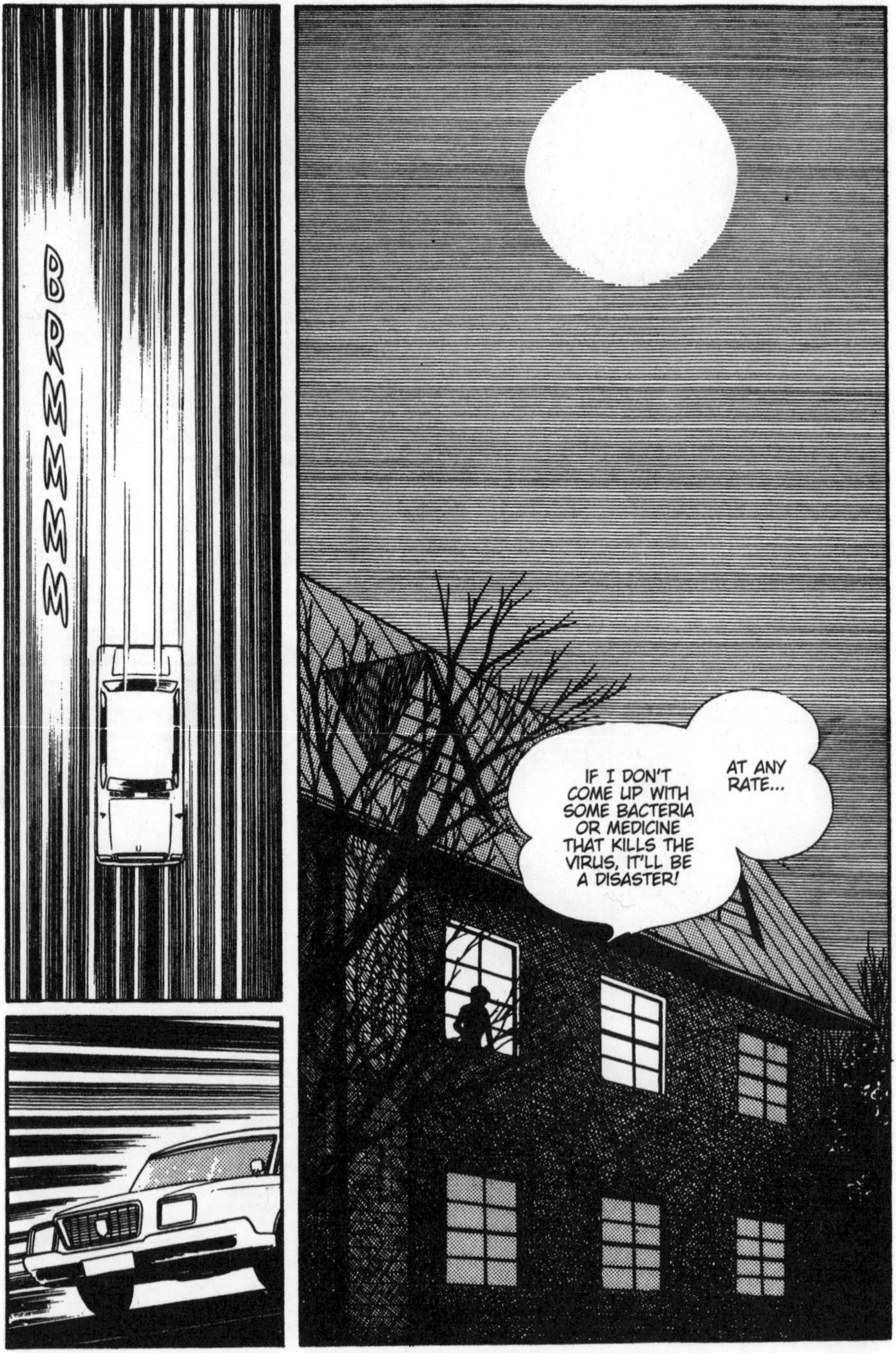
AT ANY RATE...
IF I DON'T COME UP WITH SOME BACTERIA OR MEDICINE THAT KILLS THE VIRUS, IT'LL BE A DISASTER!
BRMMMM

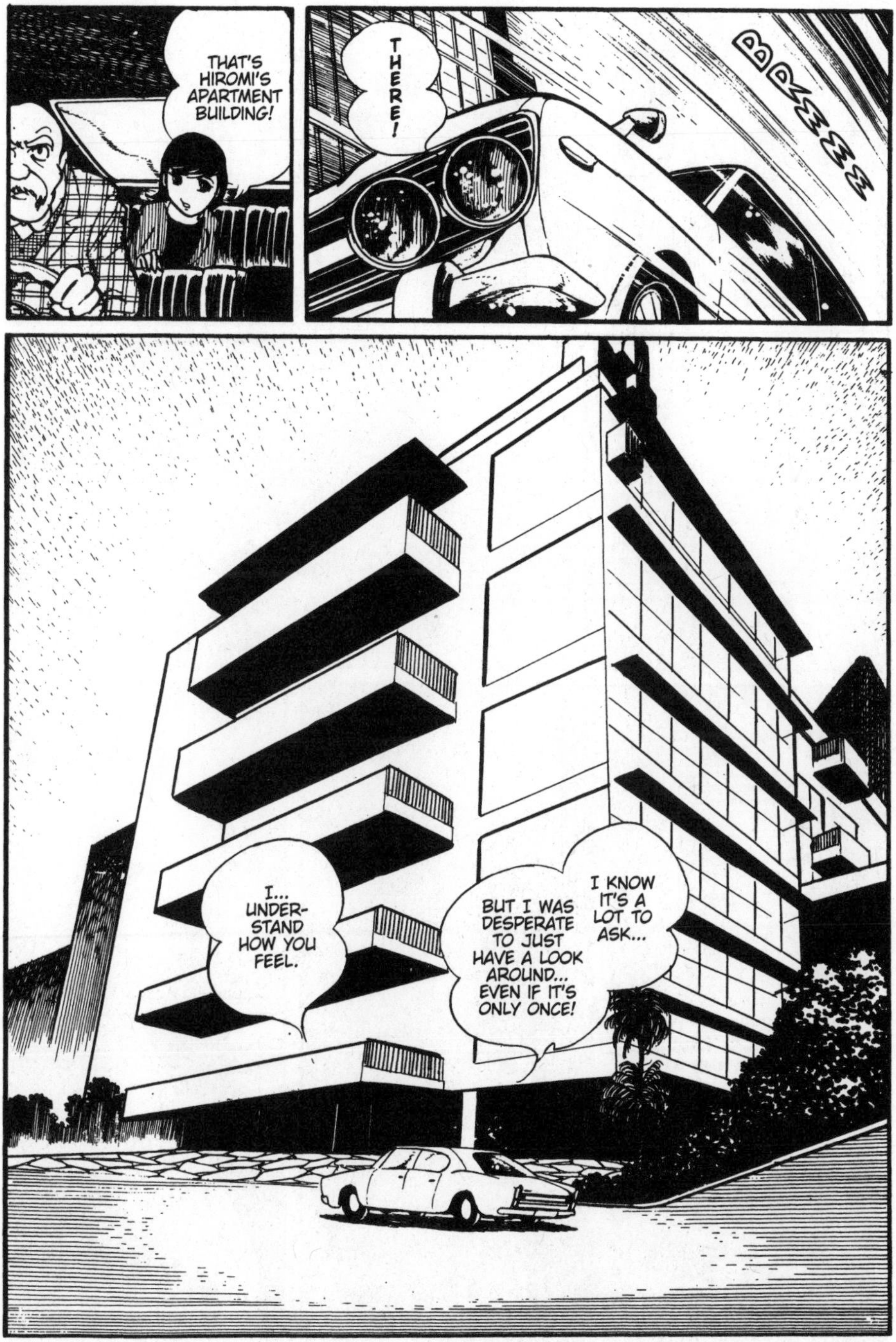
BRMMM
THERE!
THAT'S HIROMI'S APARTMENT BUILDING!
I KNOW IT'S A LOT TO ASK...
BUT I WAS DESPERATE TO JUST HAVE A LOOK AROUND... EVEN IF IT'S ONLY ONCE!
I... UNDERSTAND HOW YOU FEEL.

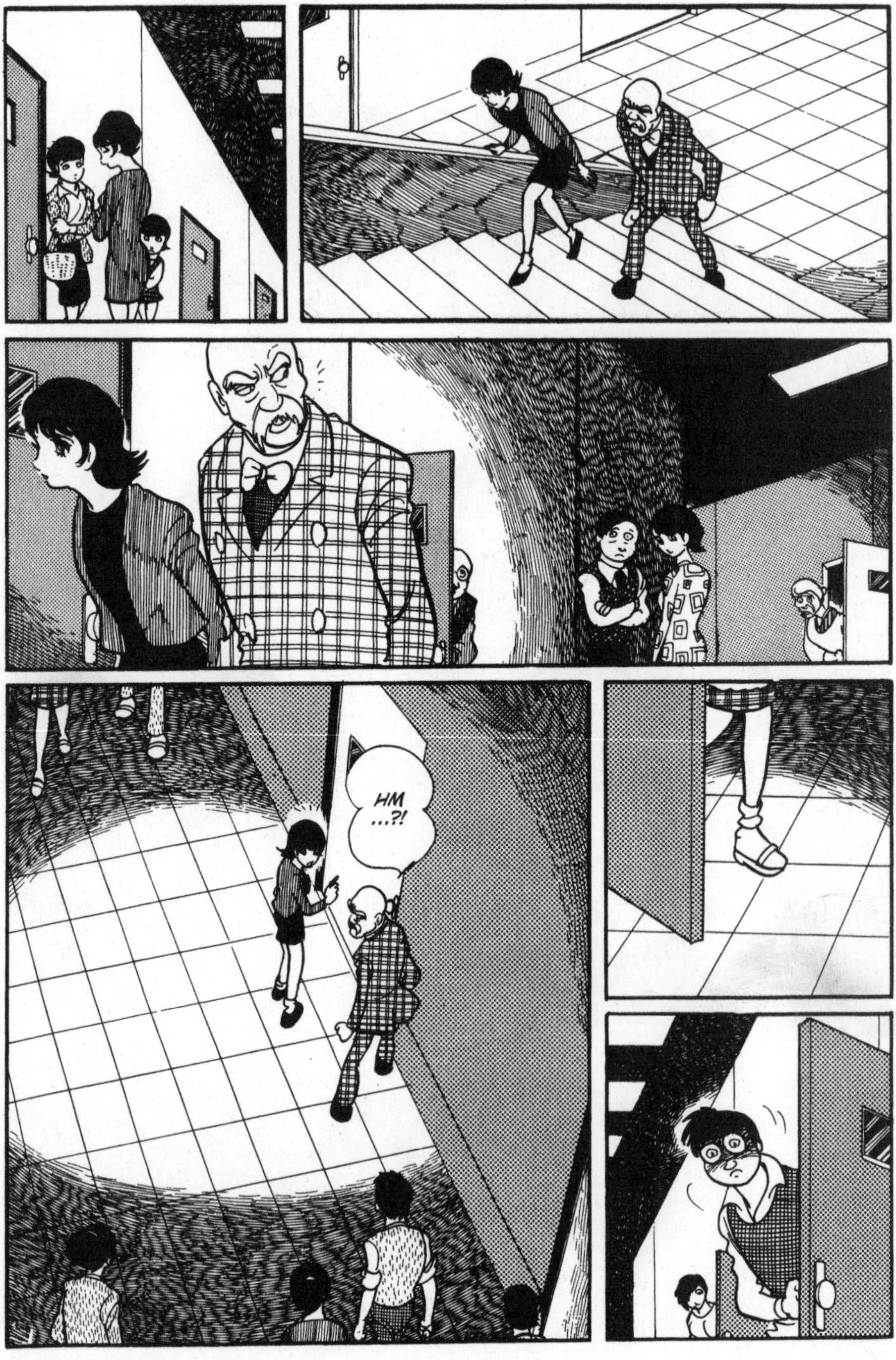
HM ...?!

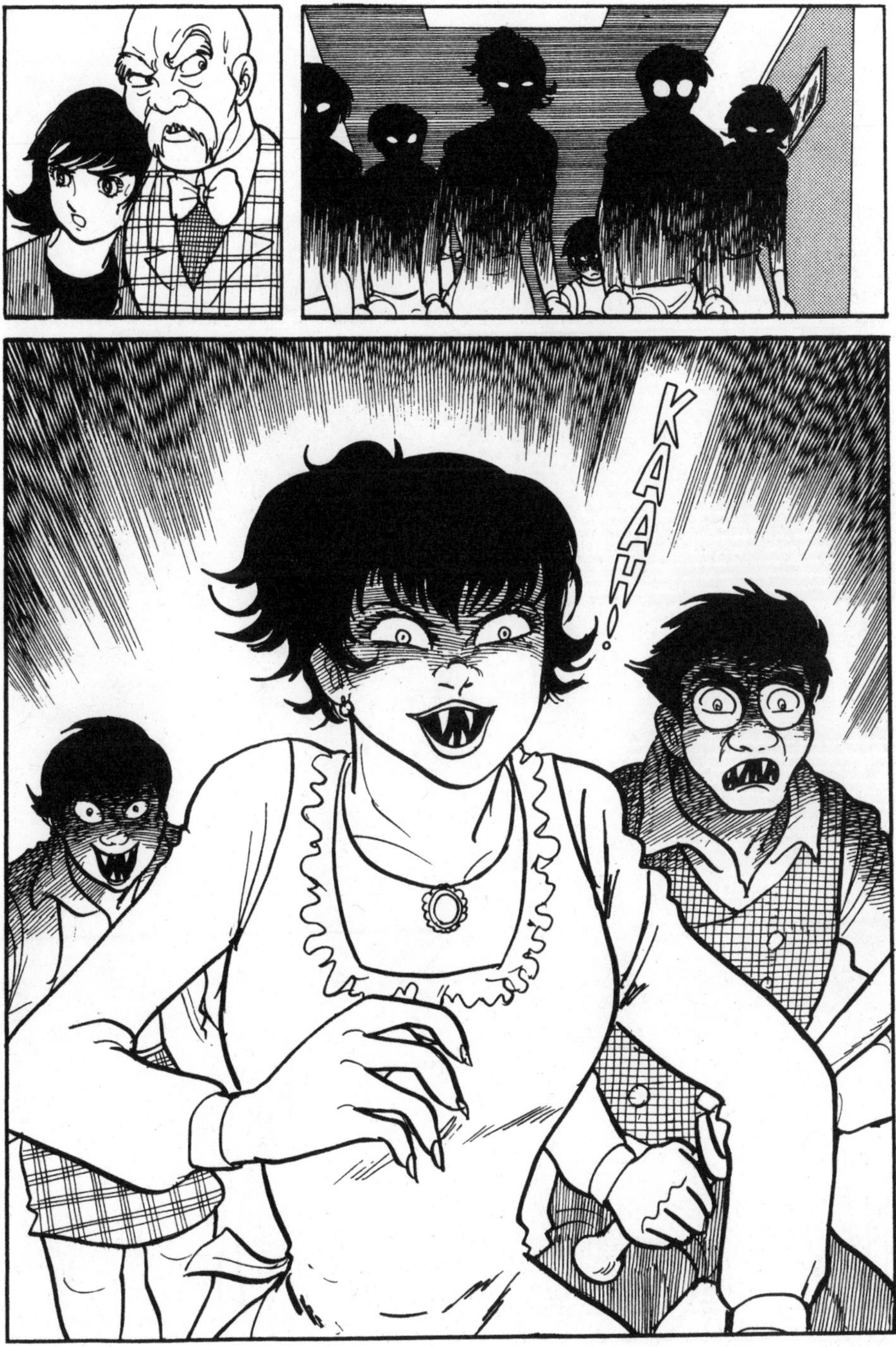
KAAH!

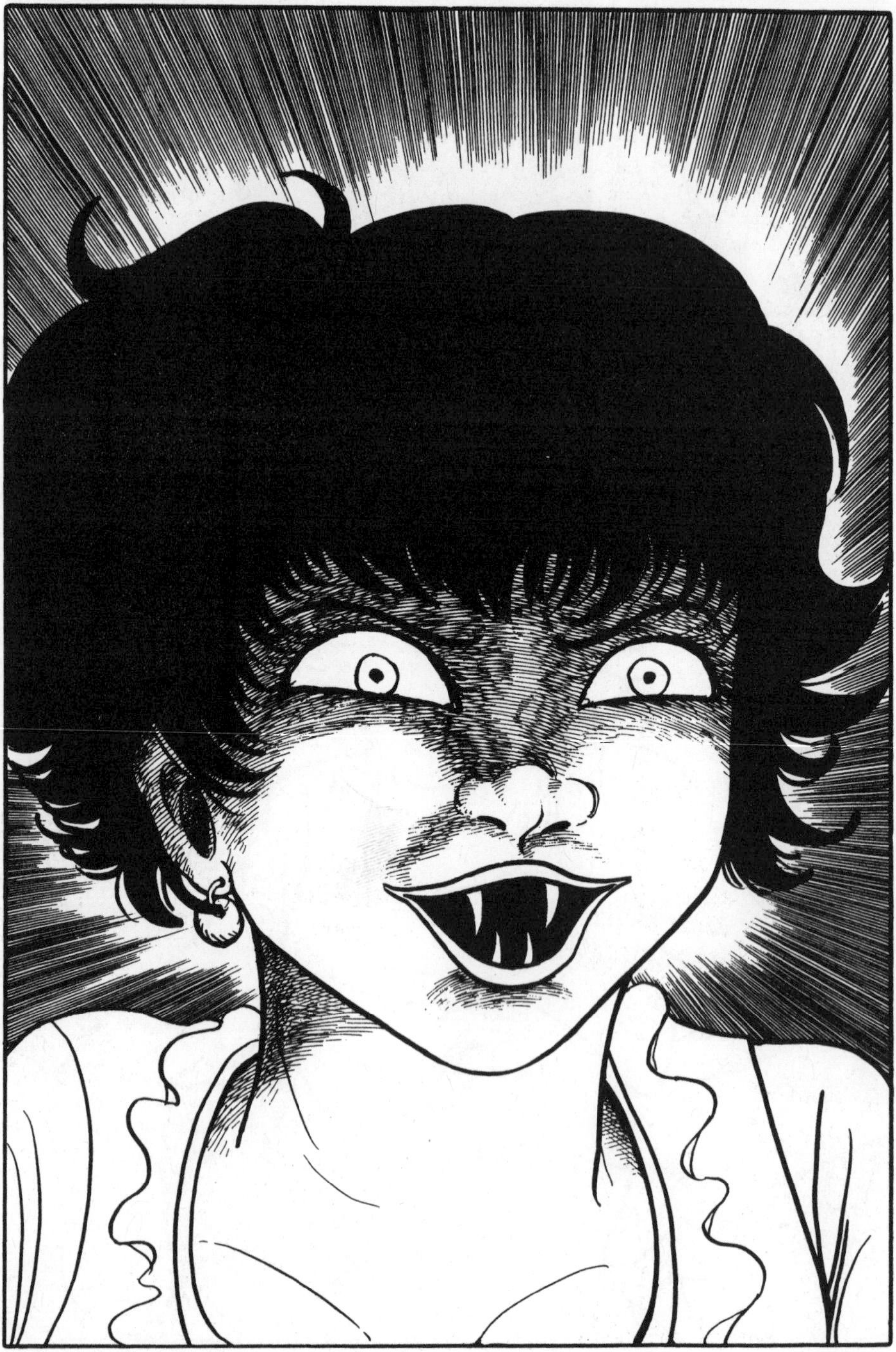

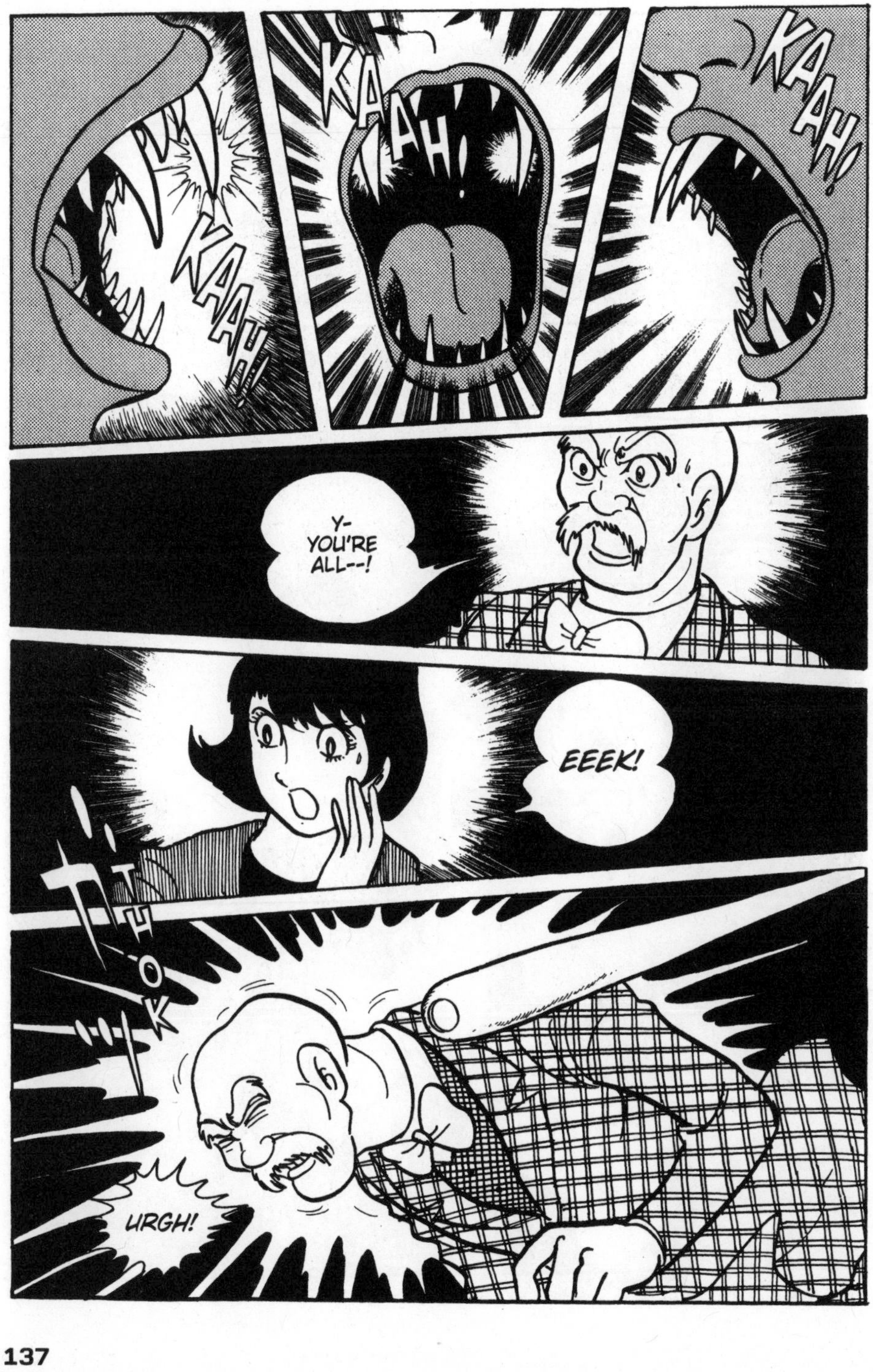
KAAAH!
KAAH!
KAAH!
Y-YOU'RE ALL--!
EEEK!
THOK
URGH!

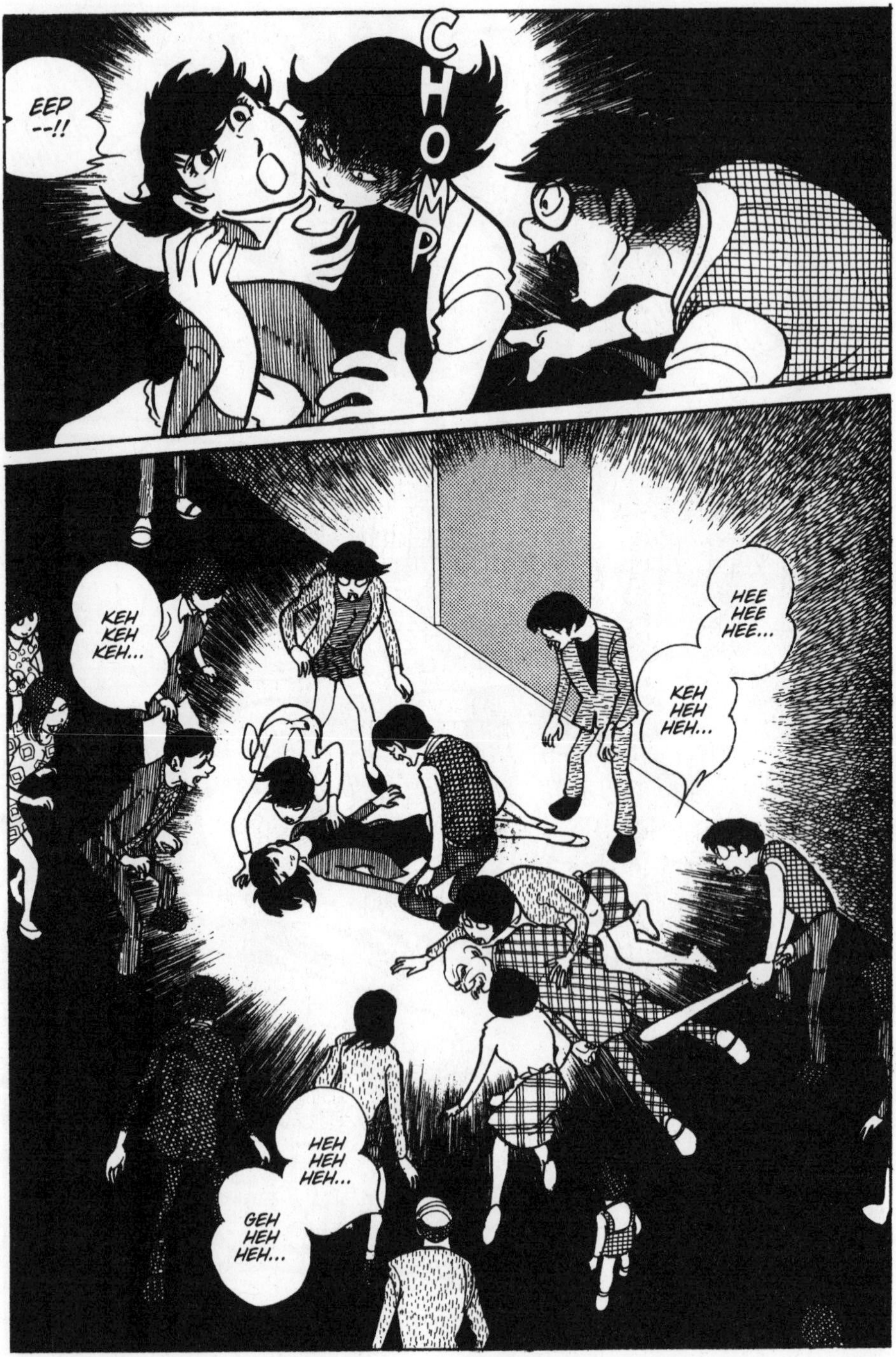
CHOMP
EEP --!!
HEE HEE HEE...
KEH HEH HEH...
KEH KEH KEH...
HEH HEH HEH...
GEH HEH HEH...

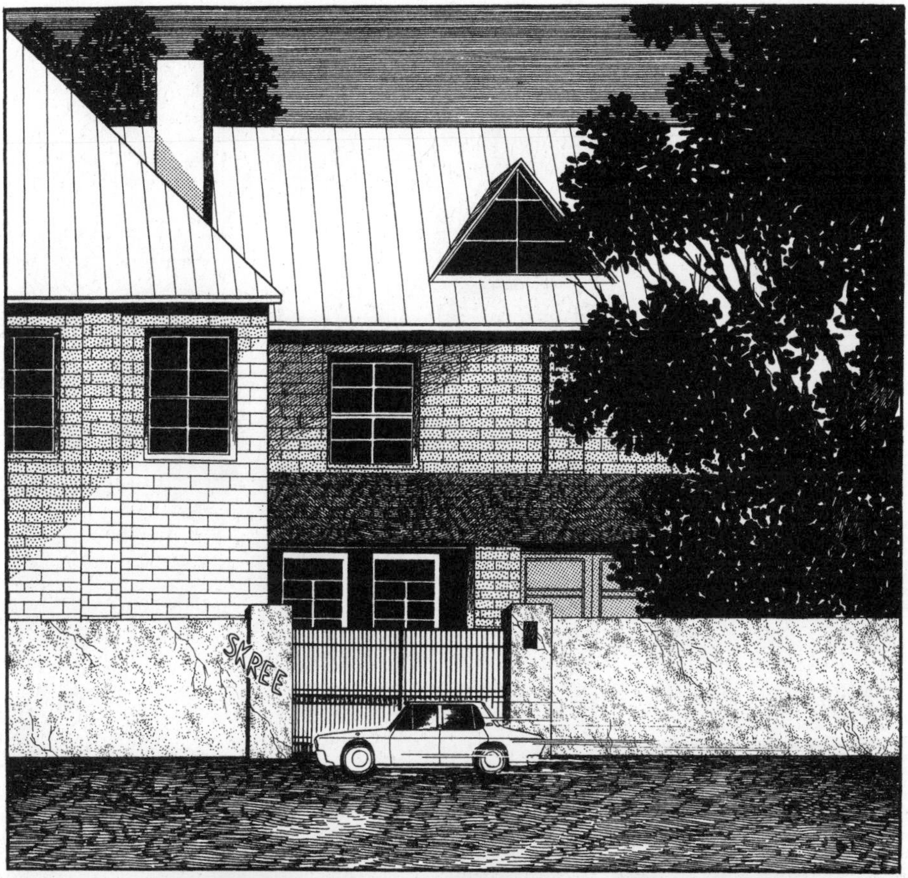
SKREE
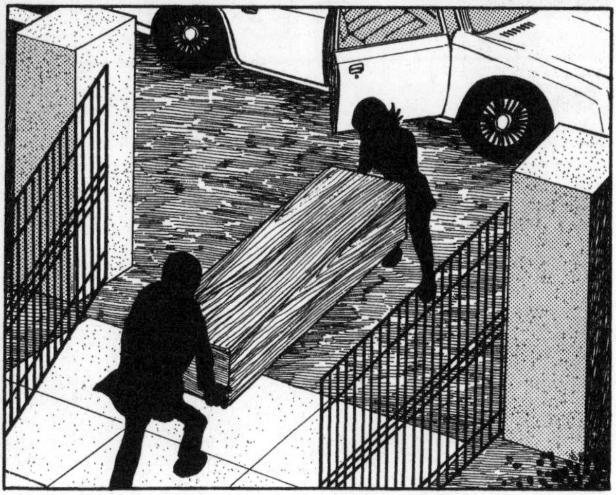
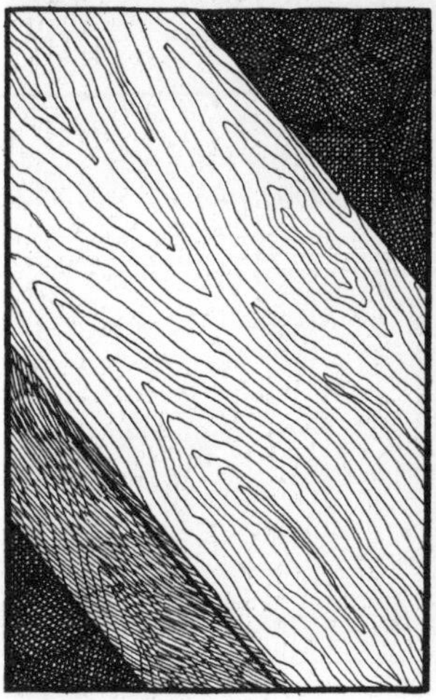

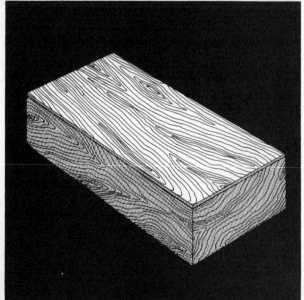

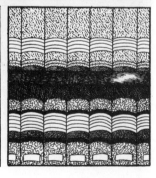

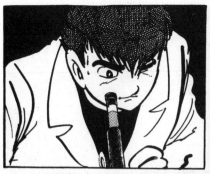

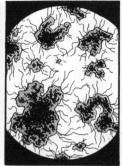

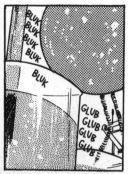

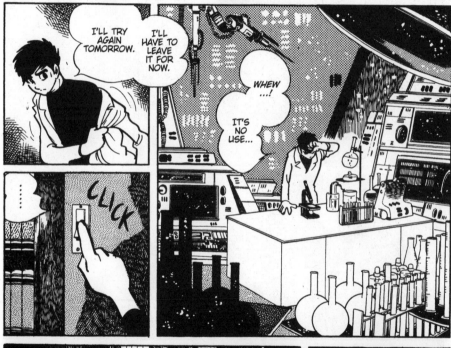

BLUK BLUK BLUK BLUK
BLUK
GLUB GLUB GLUB GLUB
WHEW ...!
IT'S NO USE...
I'LL HAVE TO LEAVE IT FOR NOW.
I'LL TRY AGAIN TOMORROW.
......
CLICK
CREAK
HM?

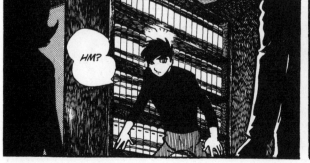

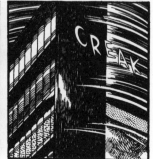

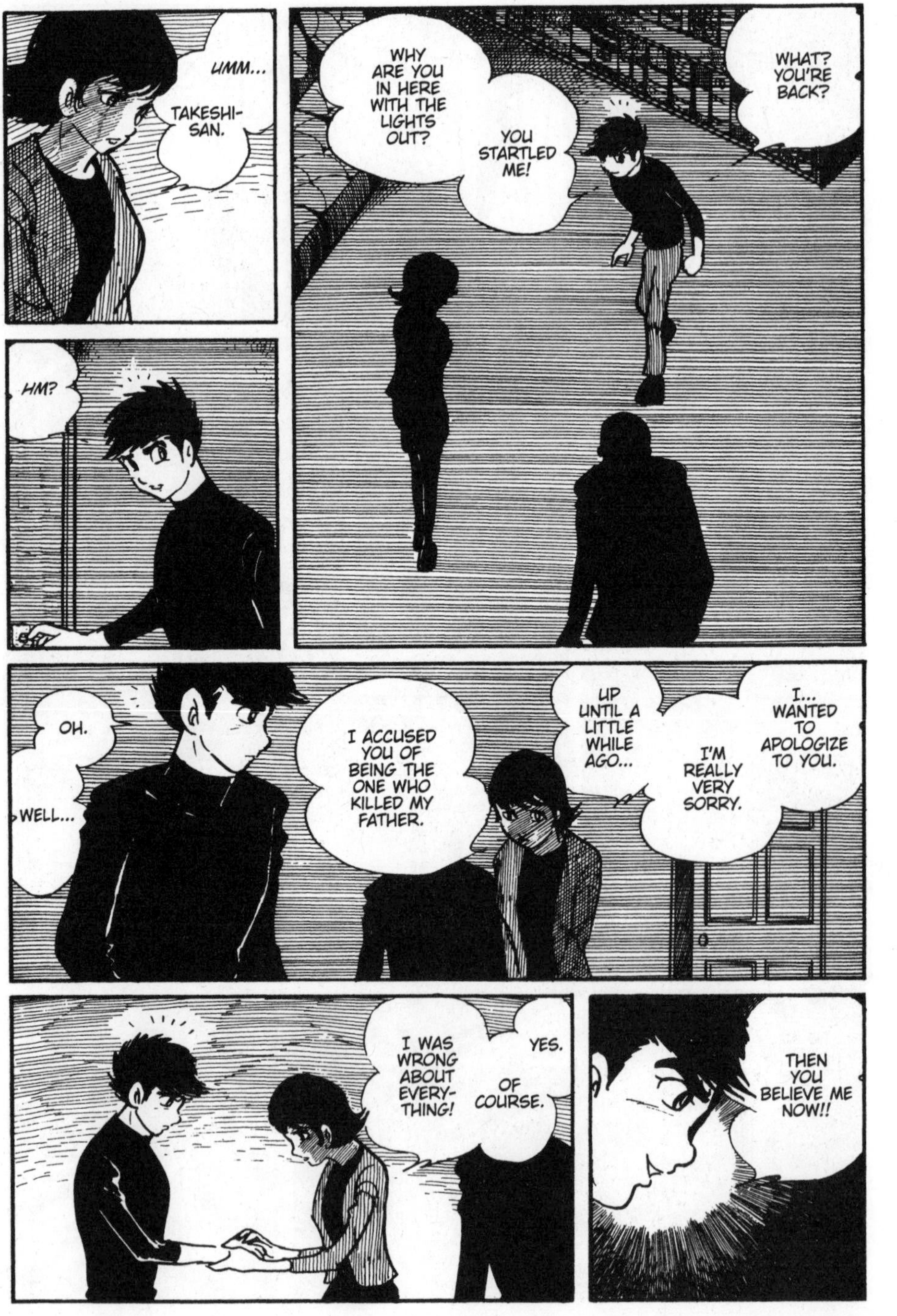
WHAT? YOU'RE BACK?
YOU STARTLED ME!
WHY ARE YOU IN HERE WITH THE LIGHTS OUT?
UMM... TAKESHI-SAN.
HM?
I... WANTED TO APOLOGIZE TO YOU.
I'M REALLY VERY SORRY.
UP UNTIL A LITTLE WHILE AGO...
I ACCUSED YOU OF BEING THE ONE WHO KILLED MY FATHER.
OH.
WELL...
THEN YOU BELIEVE ME NOW!!
YES.
OF COURSE.
I WAS WRONG ABOUT EVERY-THING!

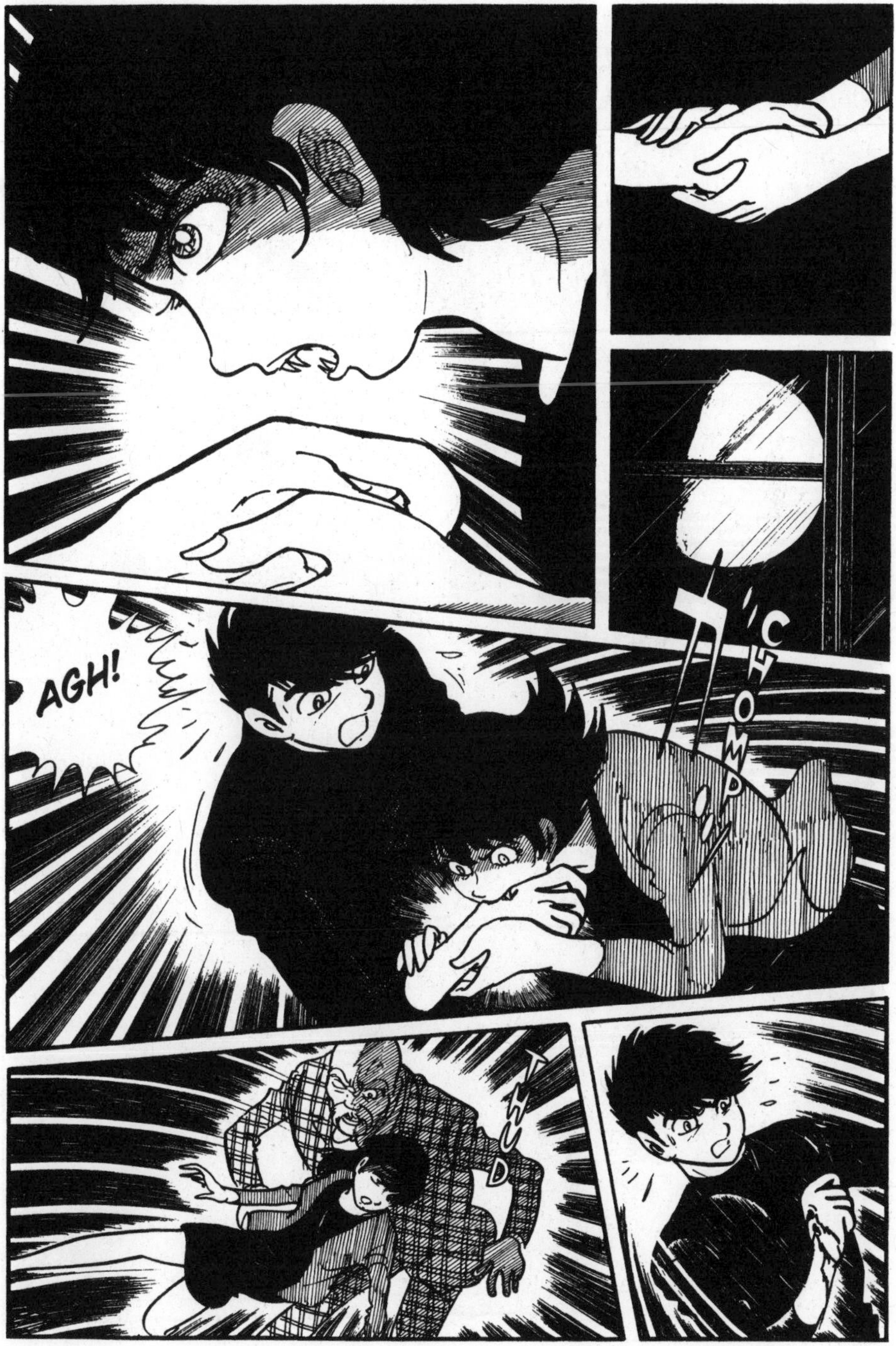
CHOMP
AGH!
THUD

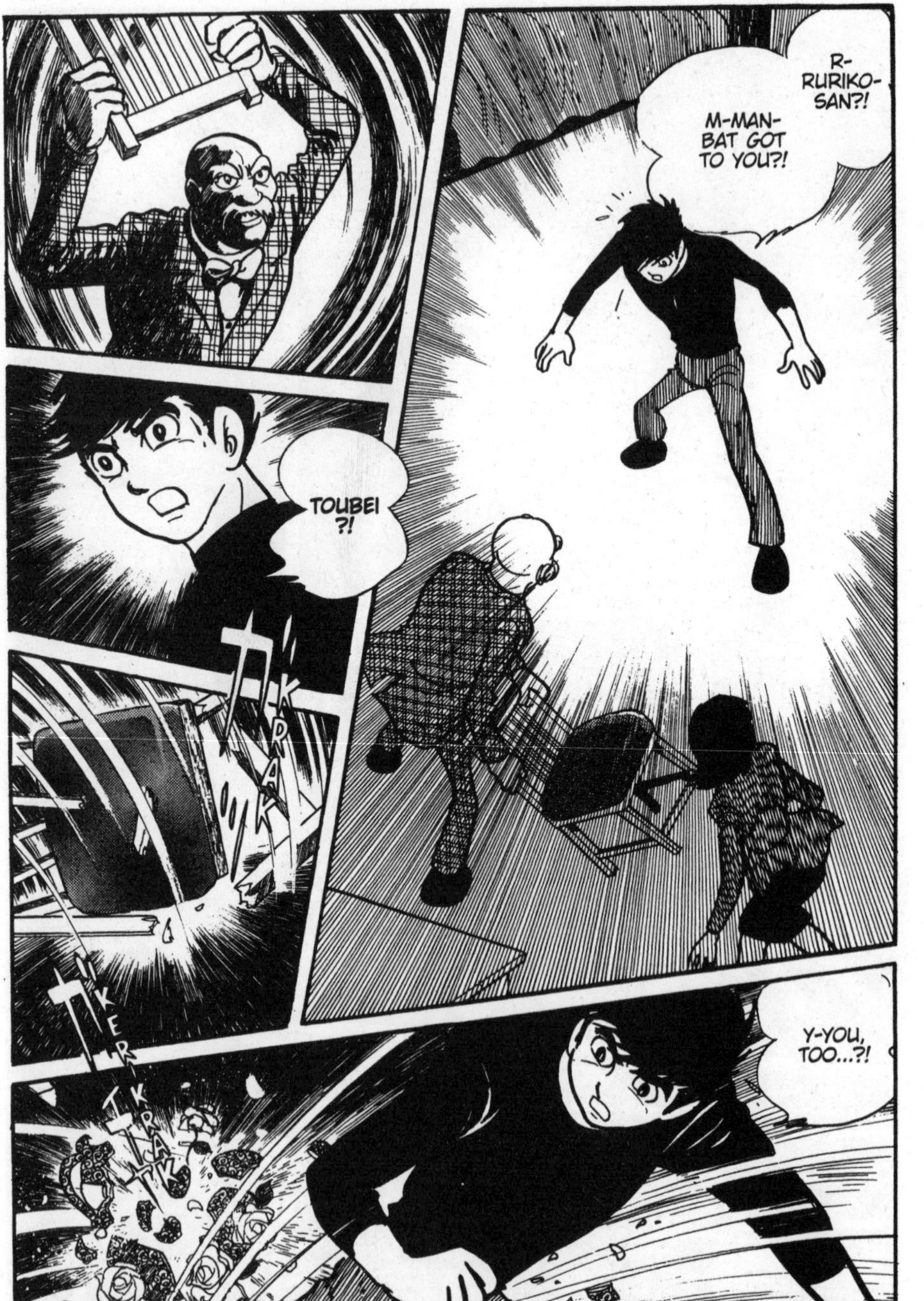
R-RURIKO-SAN?!
M-MAN-BAT GOT TO YOU?!
TOUBEI ?!
KDRAK
Y-YOU, TOO...?!

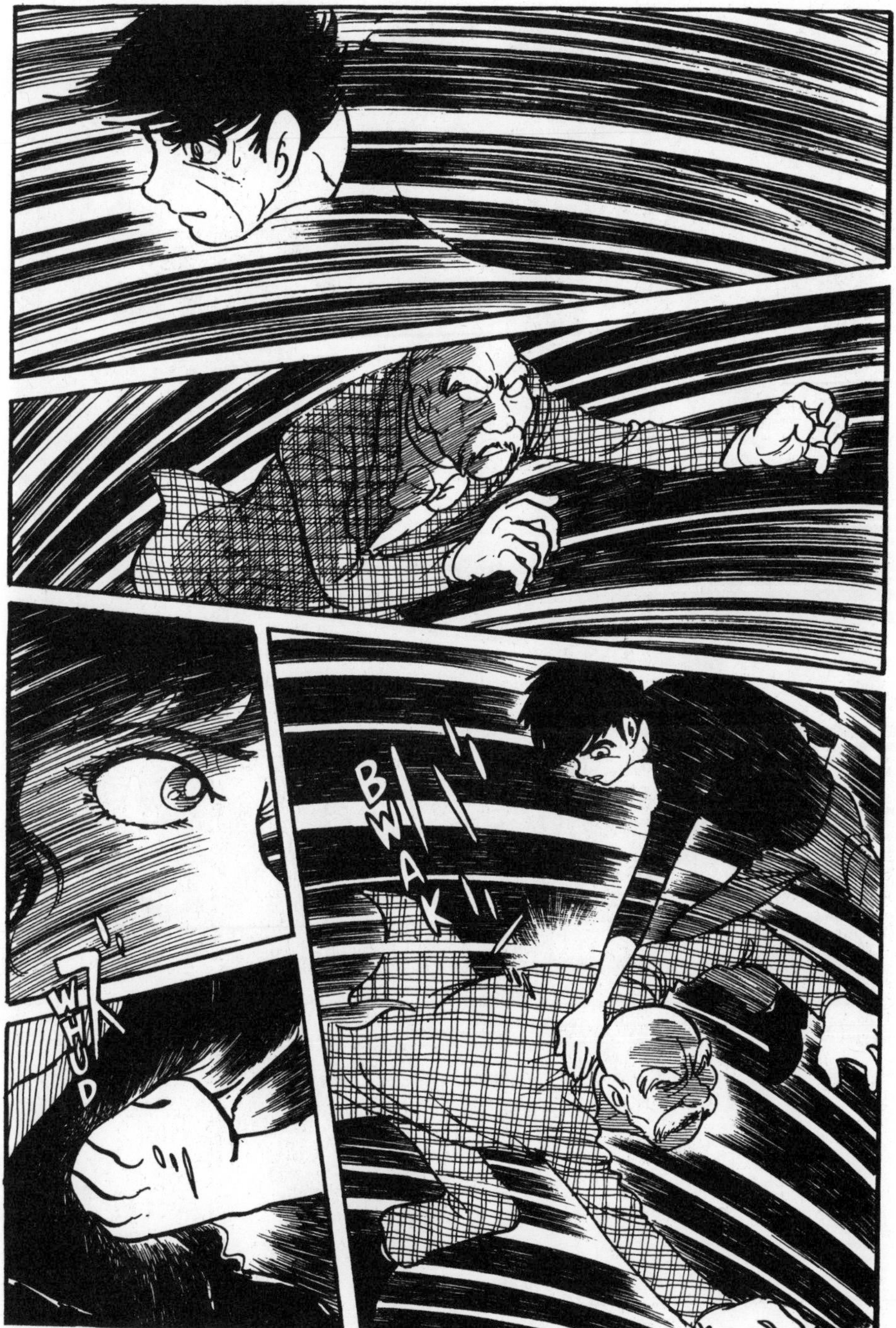
BWAK
WHUD

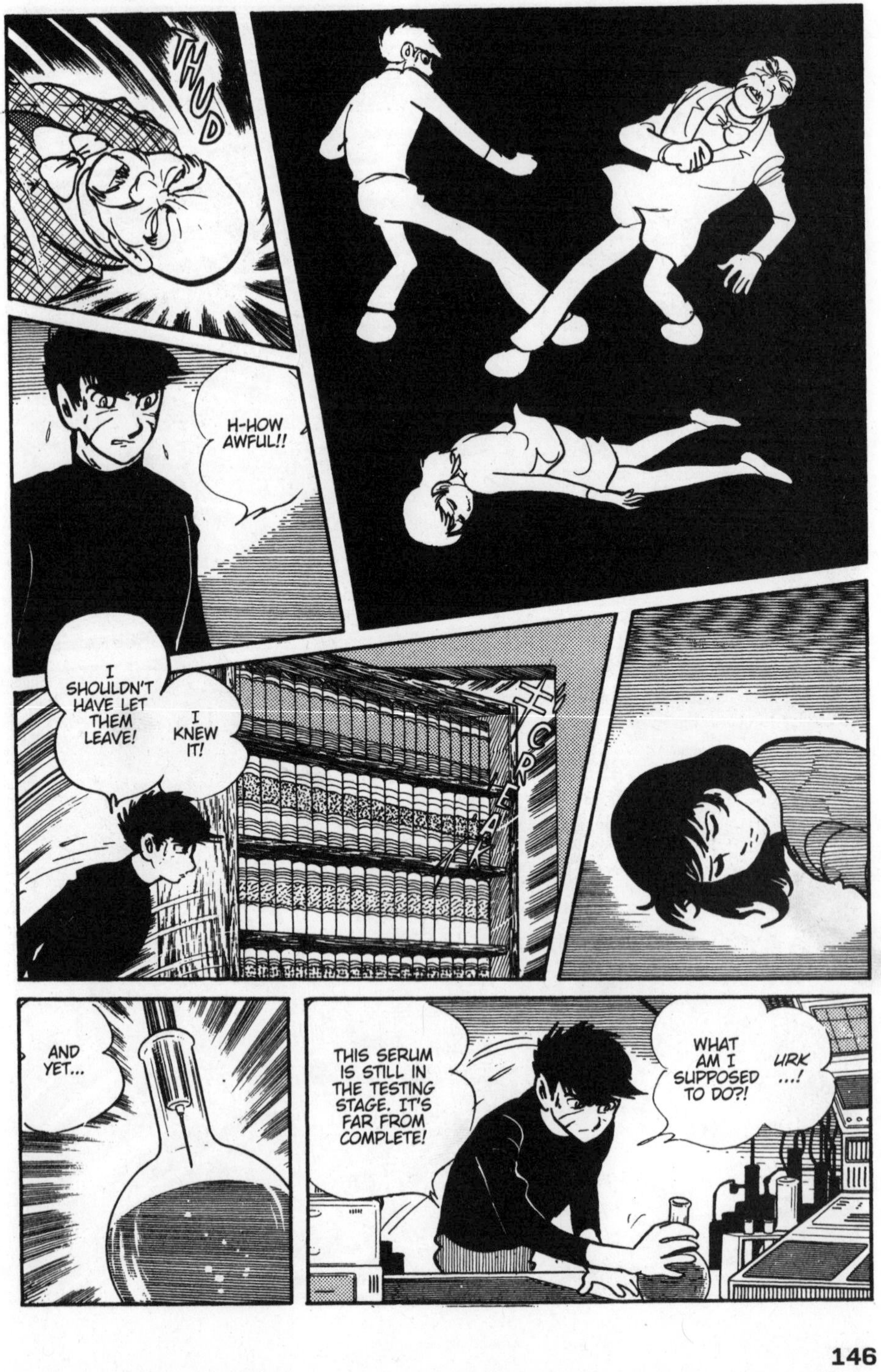
THUD
H-HOW AWFUL!!
I KNEW IT!
I SHOULDN'T HAVE LET THEM LEAVE!
CREAK
URK ...!
WHAT AM I SUPPOSED TO DO?!
THIS SERUM IS STILL IN THE TESTING STAGE. IT'S FAR FROM COMPLETE!
AND YET...

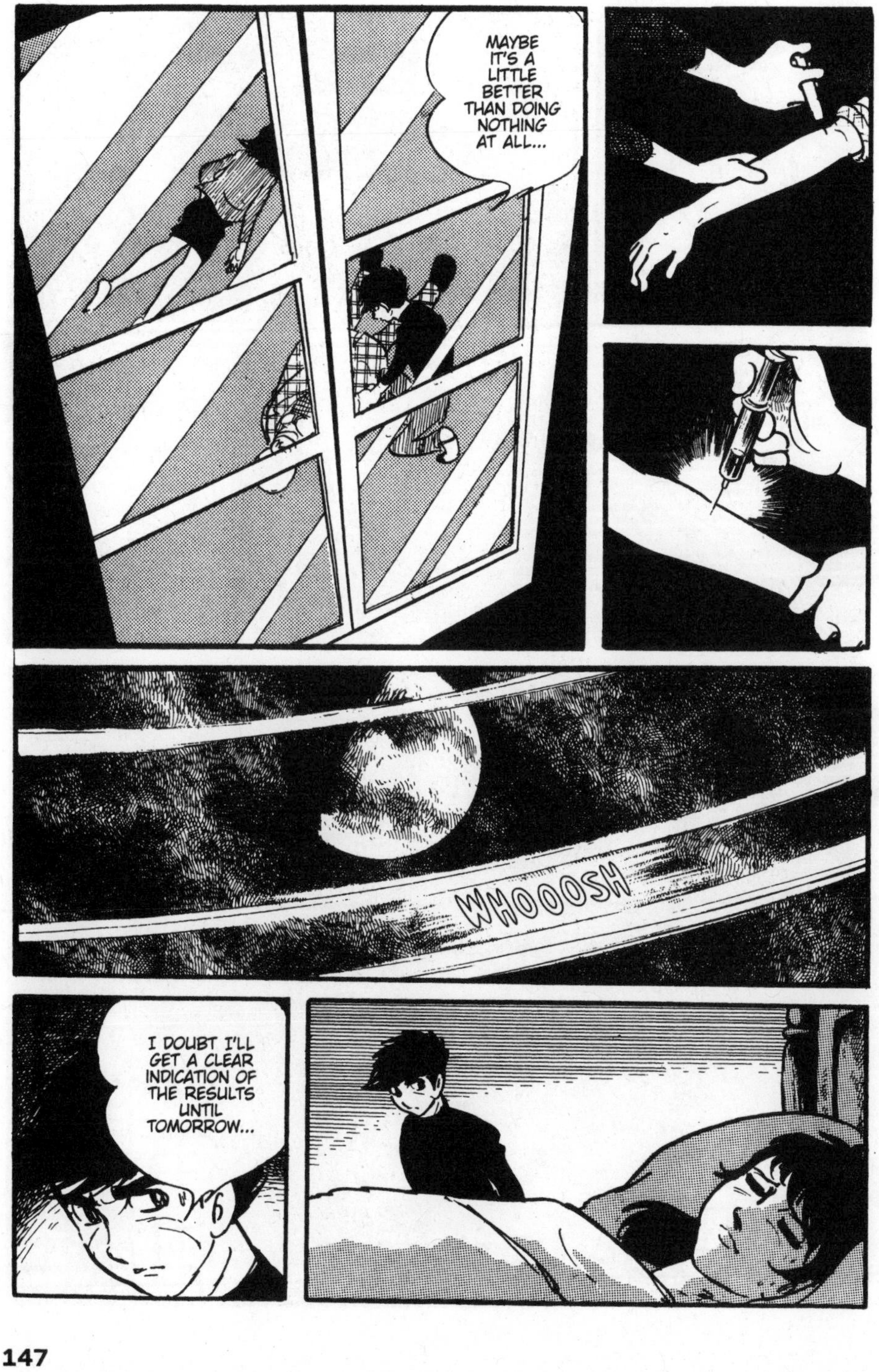

MAYBE IT'S A LITTLE BETTER THAN DOING NOTHING AT ALL...
WHOOOSH
I DOUBT I'LL GET A CLEAR INDICATION OF THE RESULTS UNTIL TOMORROW...

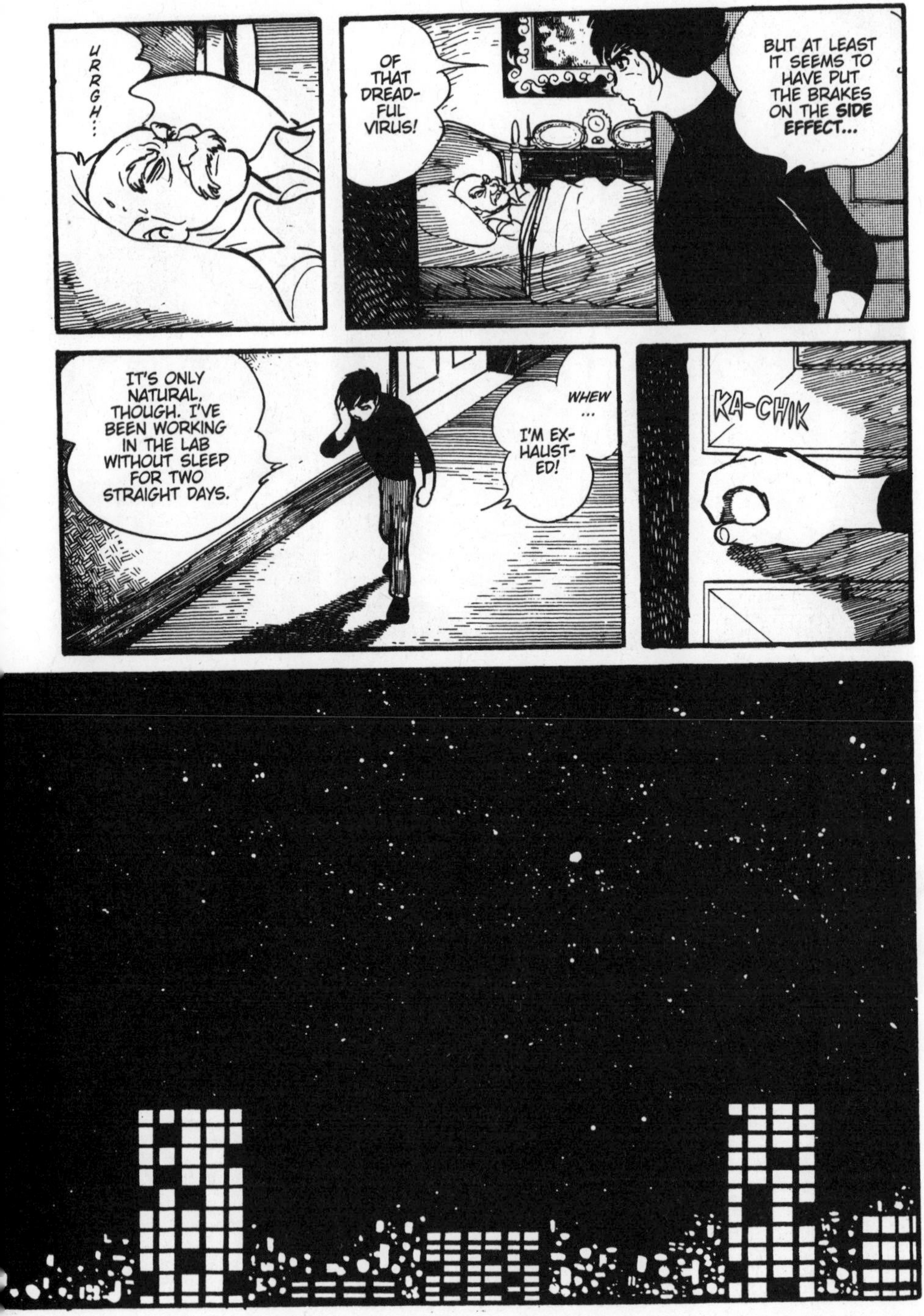
BUT AT LEAST IT SEEMS TO HAVE PUT THE BRAKES ON THE **SIDE EFFECT...**
OF THAT DREAD-FUL VIRUS!
URRGH...
KA-CHIK
WHEW ...
I'M EX-HAUST-ED!
IT'S ONLY NATURAL, THOUGH. I'VE BEEN WORKING IN THE LAB WITHOUT SLEEP FOR TWO STRAIGHT DAYS.

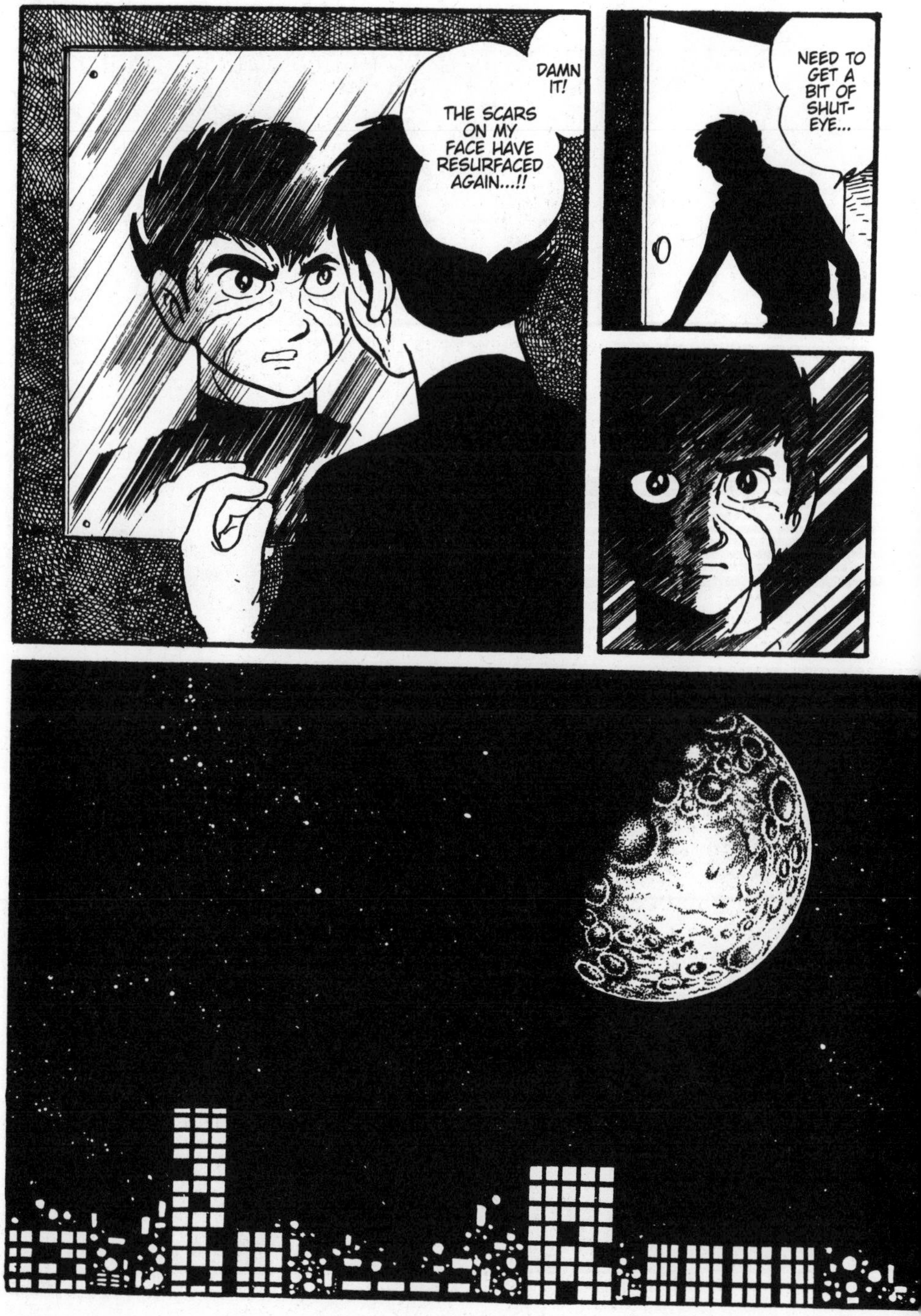
NEED TO GET A BIT OF SHUT-EYE...
DAMN IT!
THE SCARS ON MY FACE HAVE RESURFACED AGAIN...!!

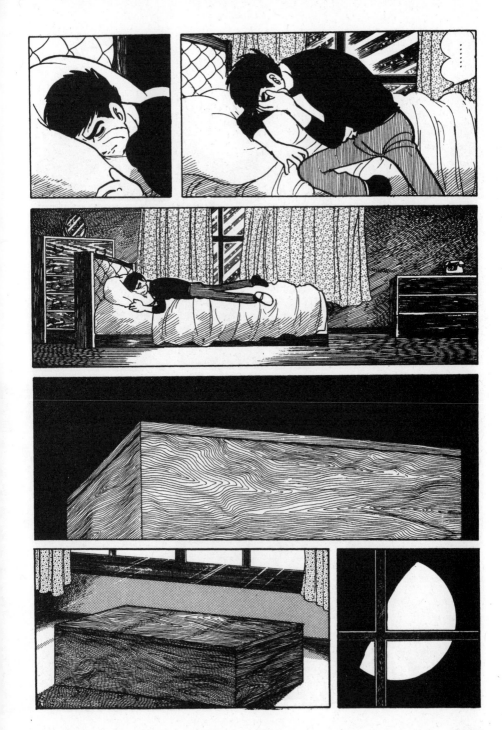

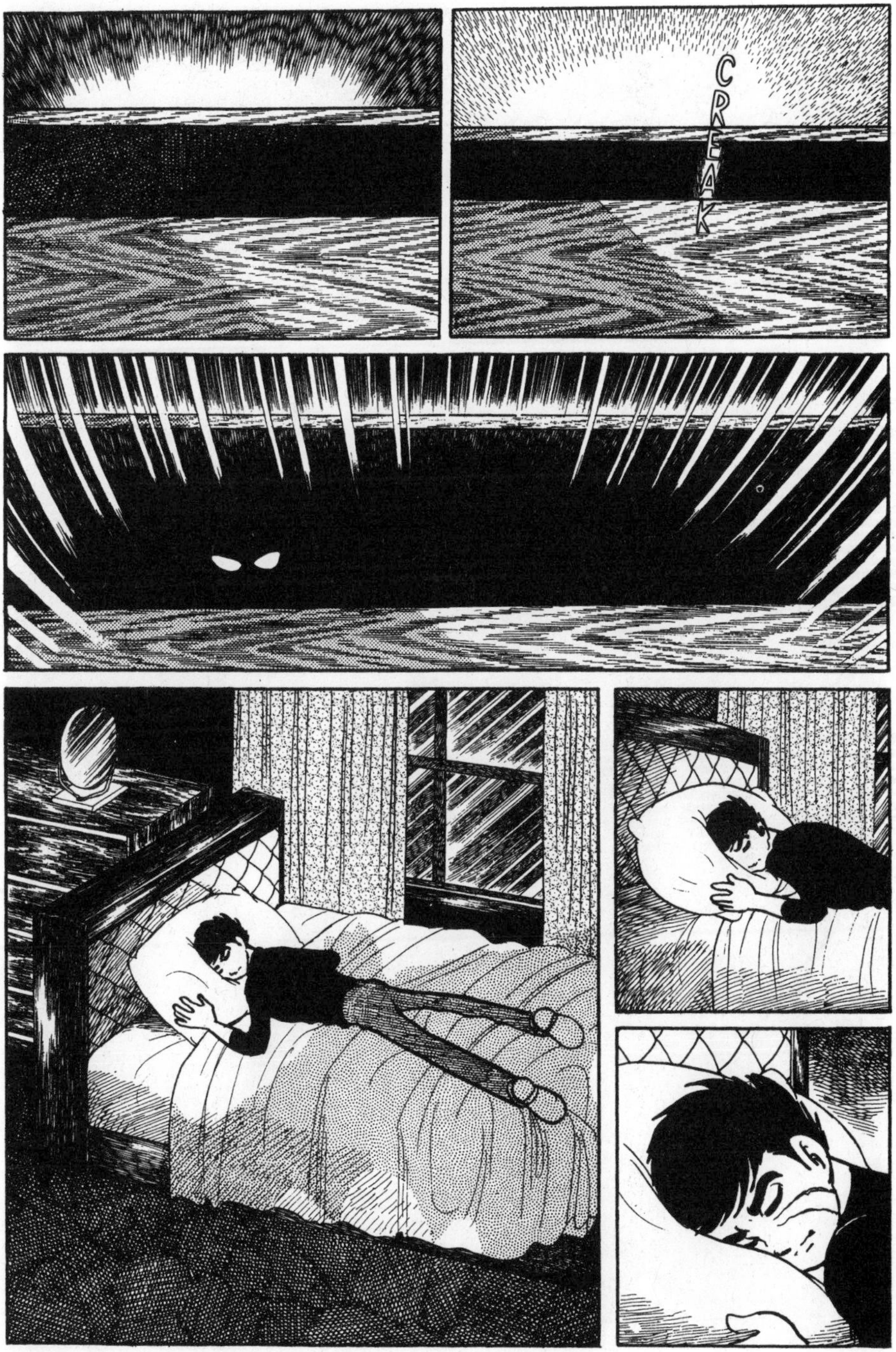
CREAK

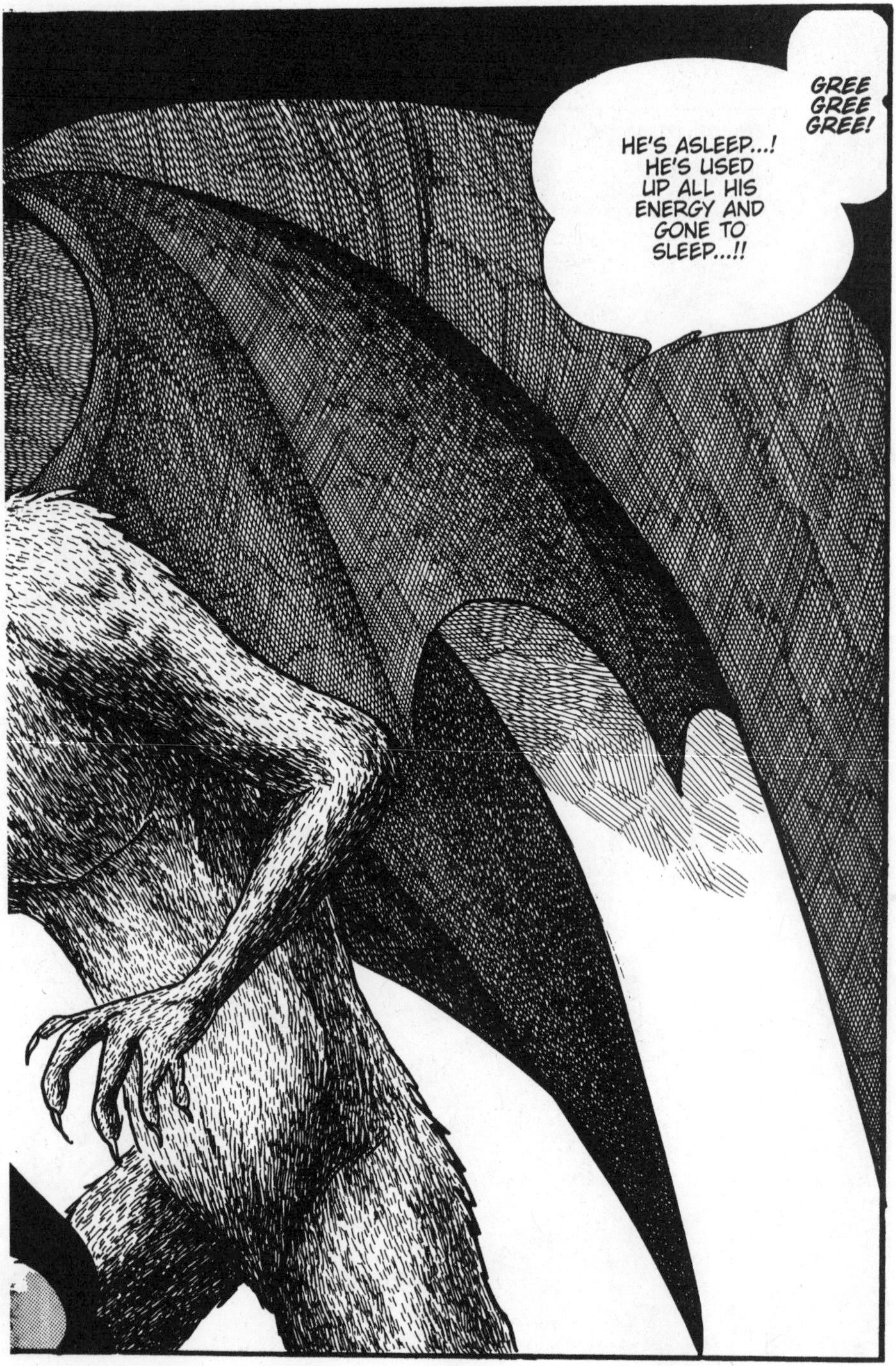
GREE GREE GREE!
HE'S ASLEEP...! HE'S USED UP ALL HIS ENERGY AND GONE TO SLEEP...!!

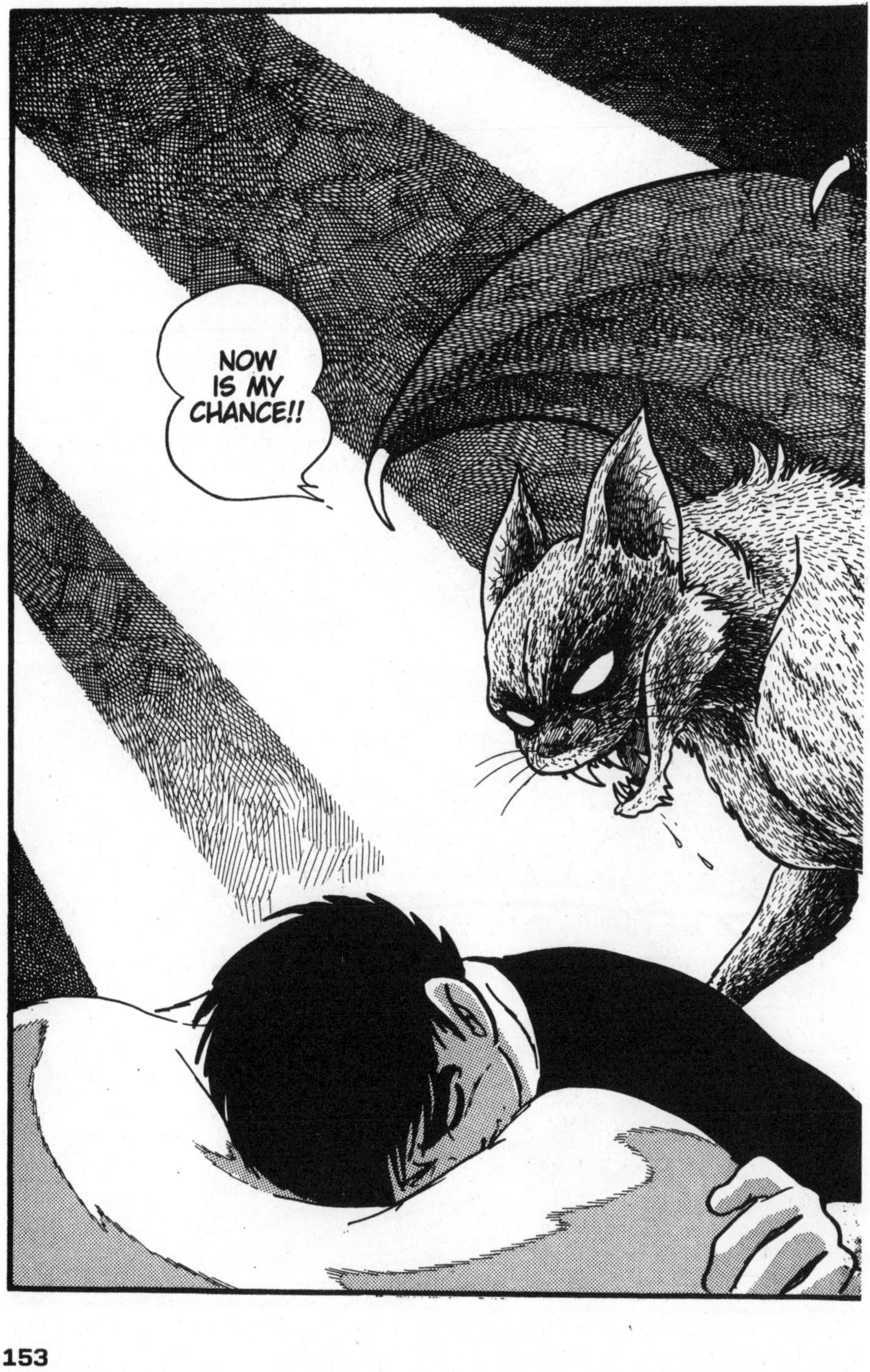
NOW IS MY CHANCE!!

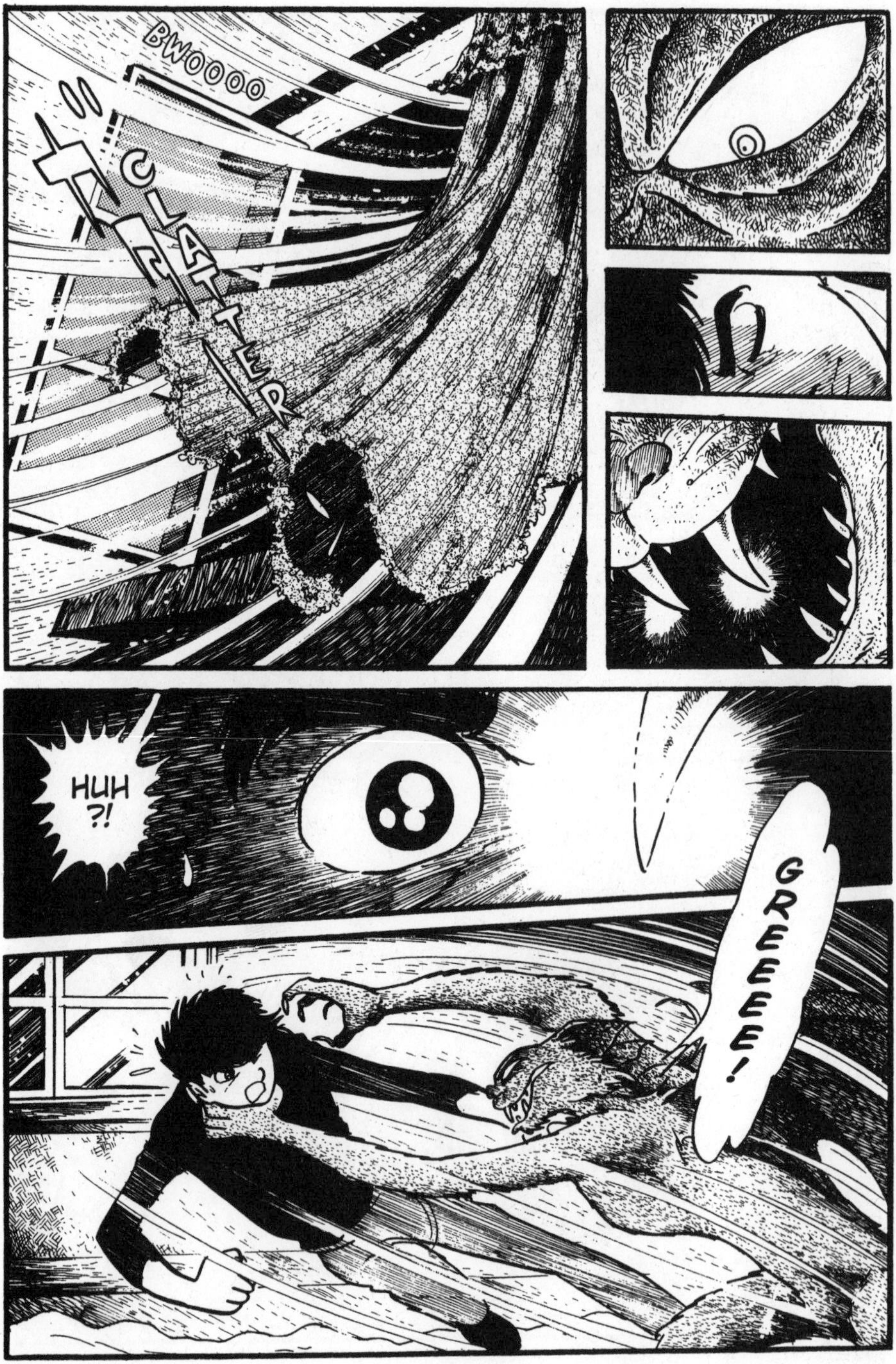
BWOOOO
SCLATTER
HUH?!
GREEEE!

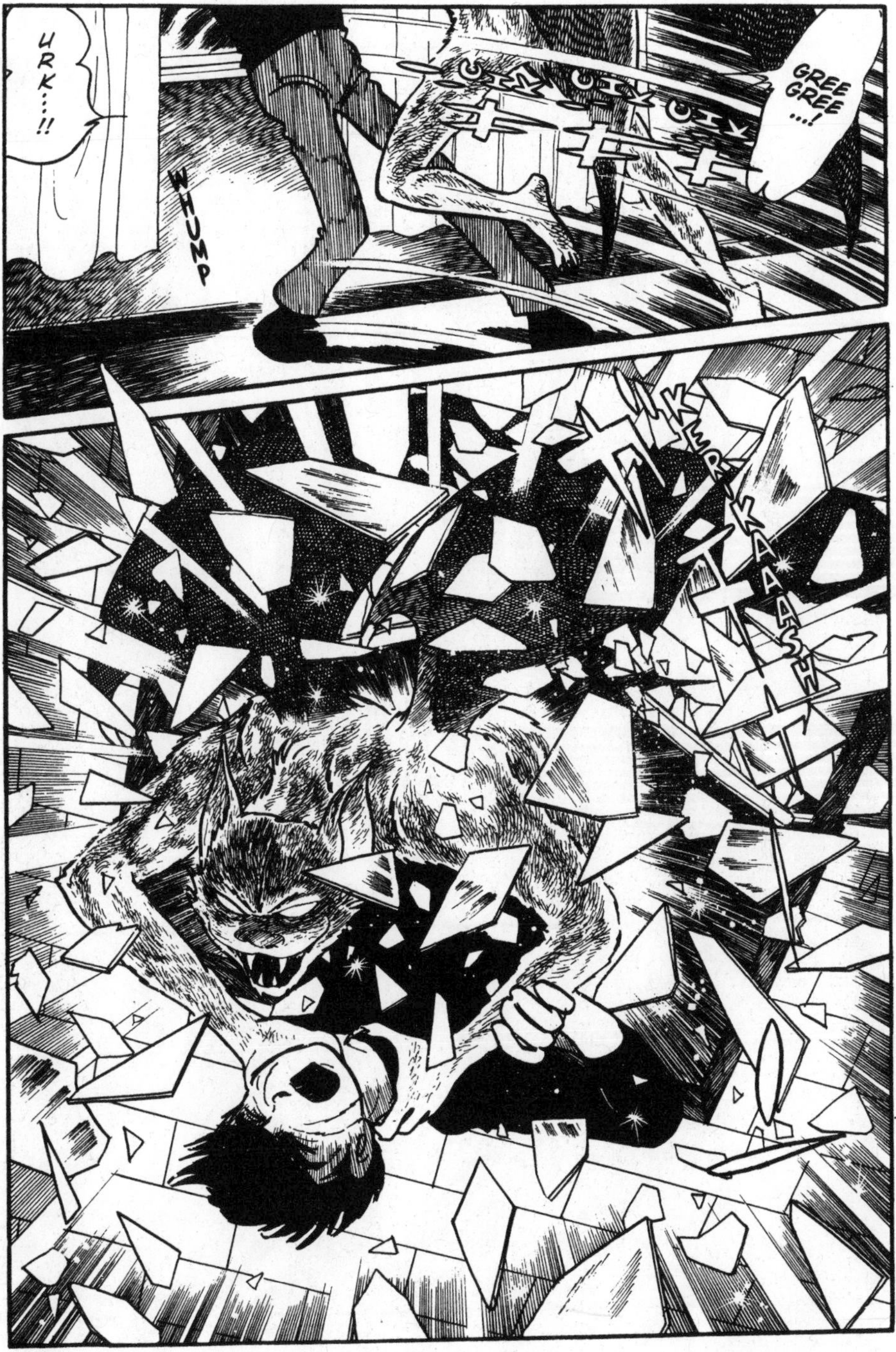
GREE GREE ...!
WHUMP
URK...!!
KERKAAASH

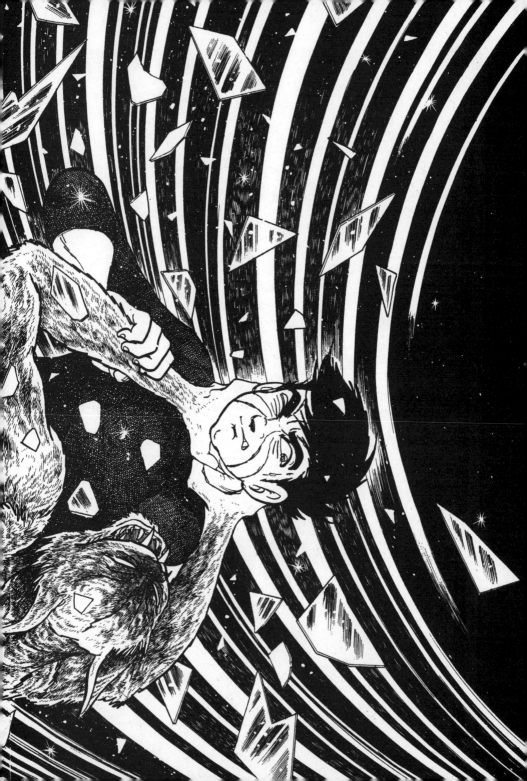

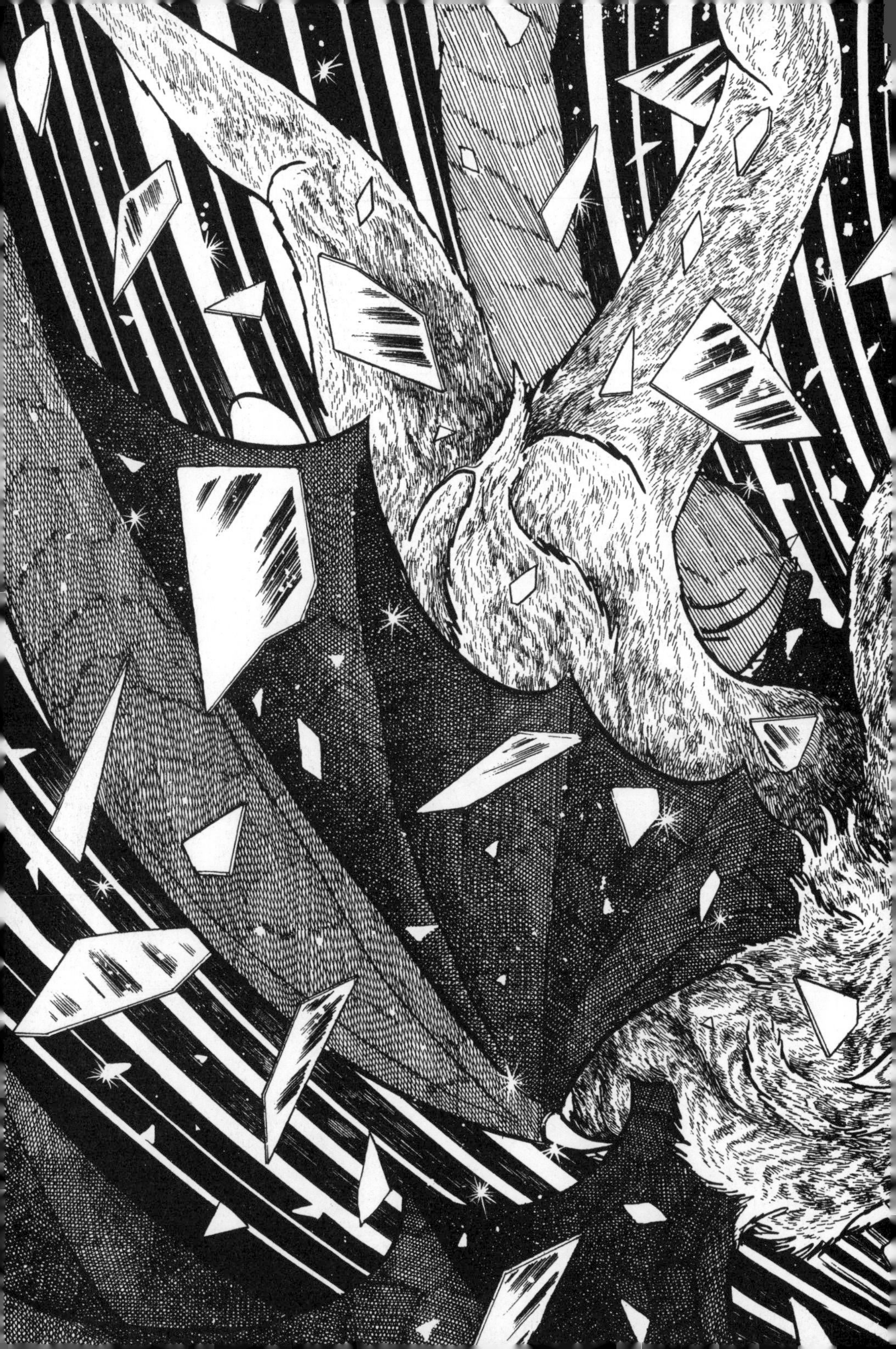

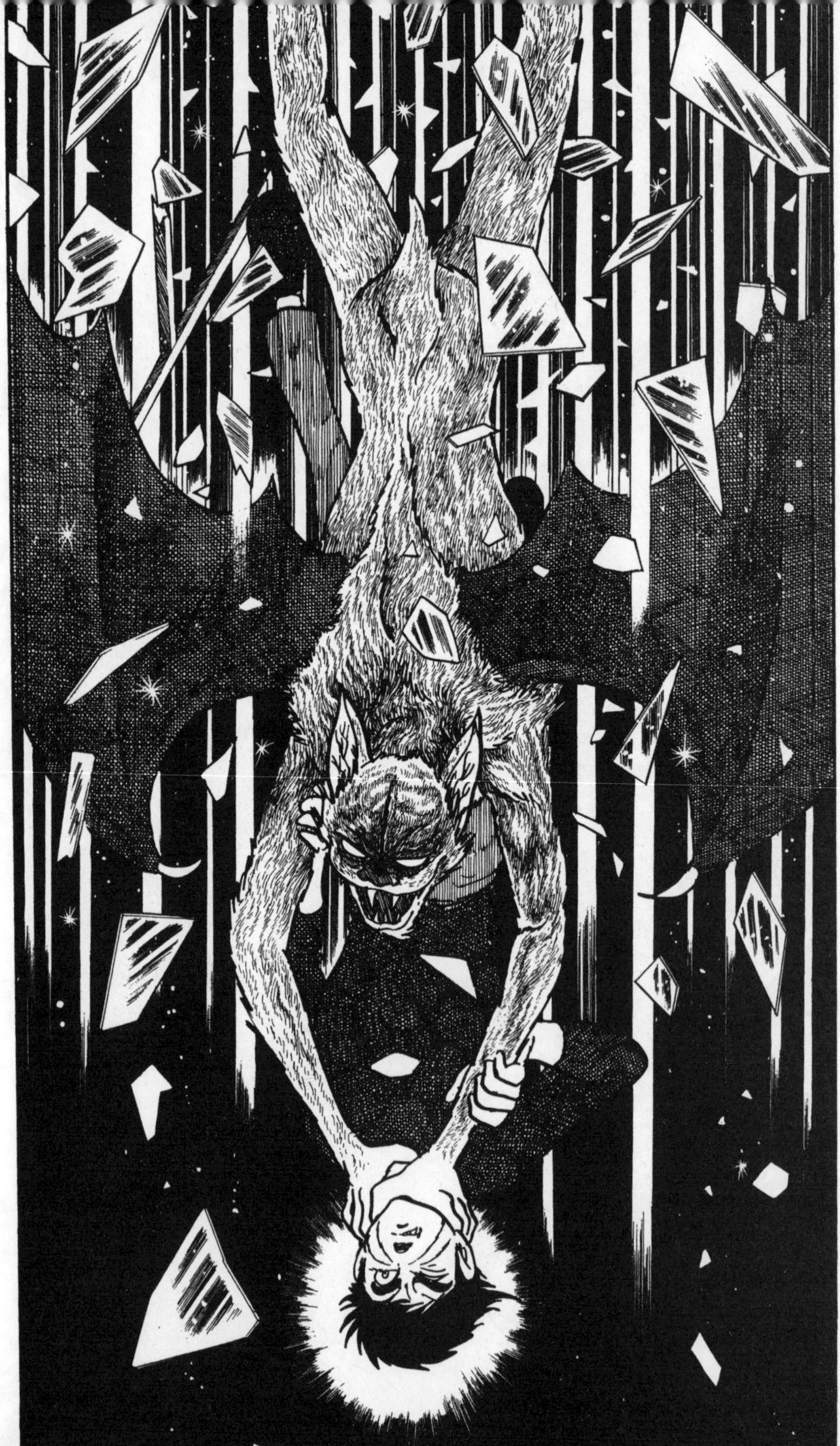

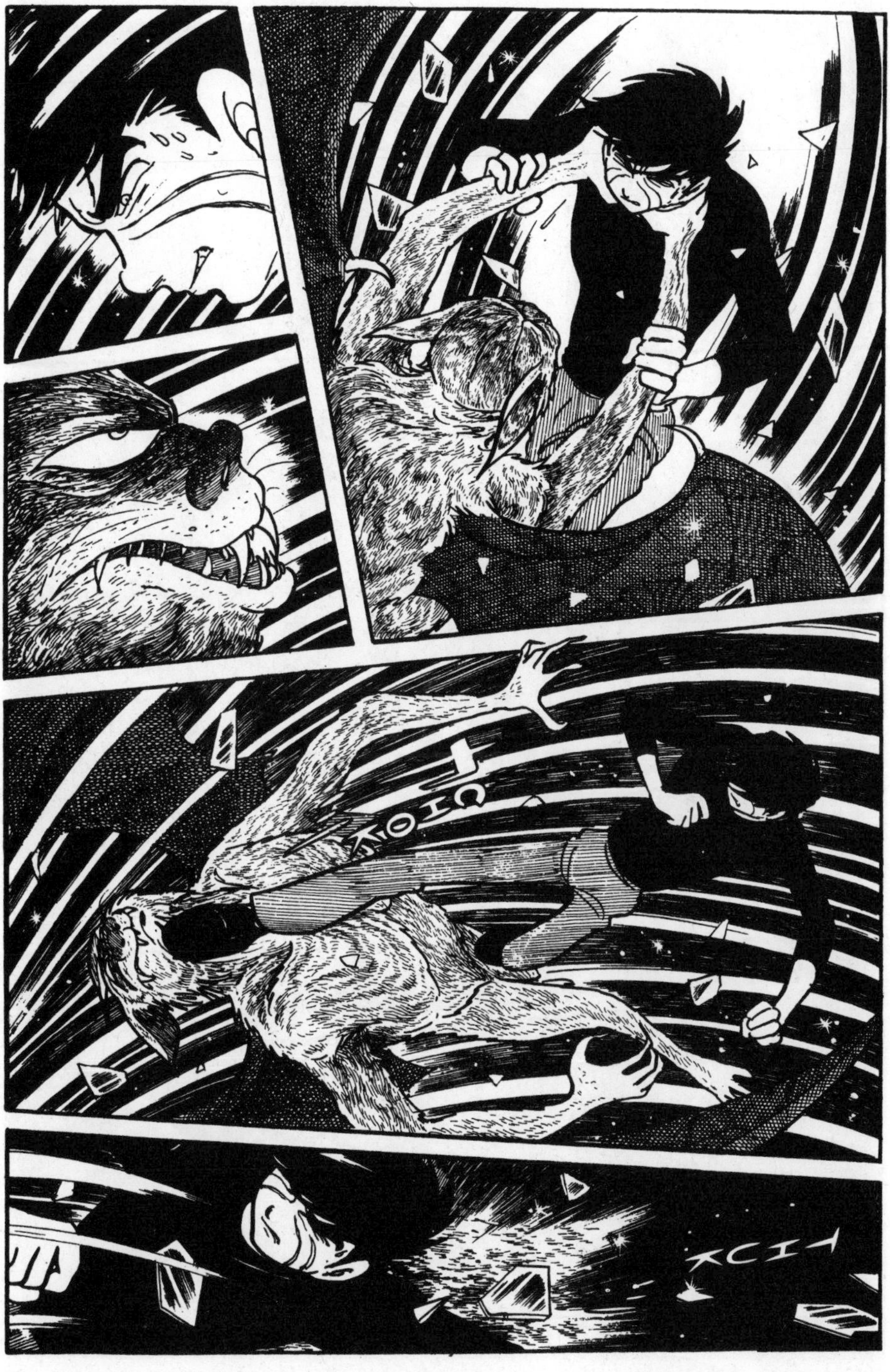

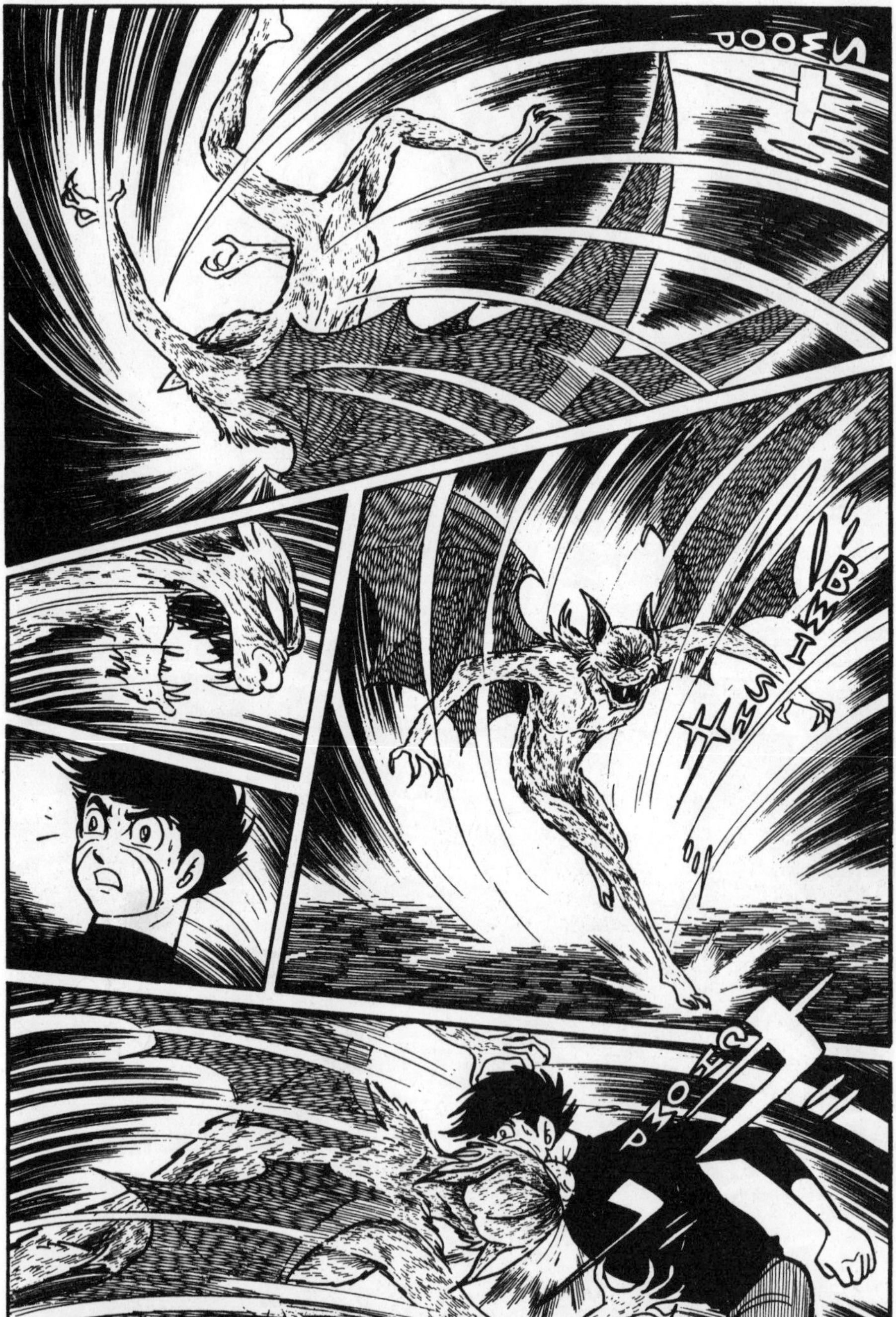
SWOOP
BWISHH
CHOMP

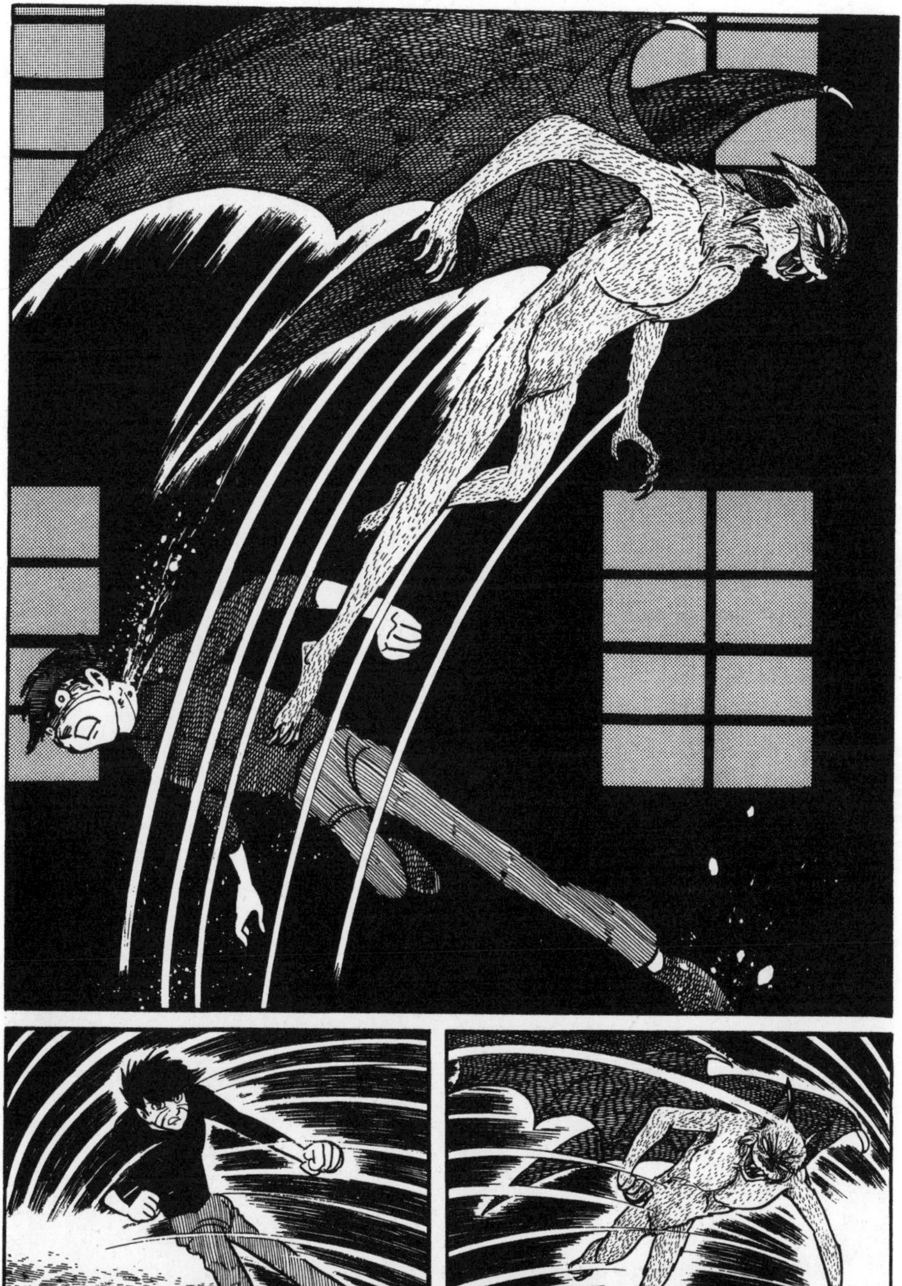

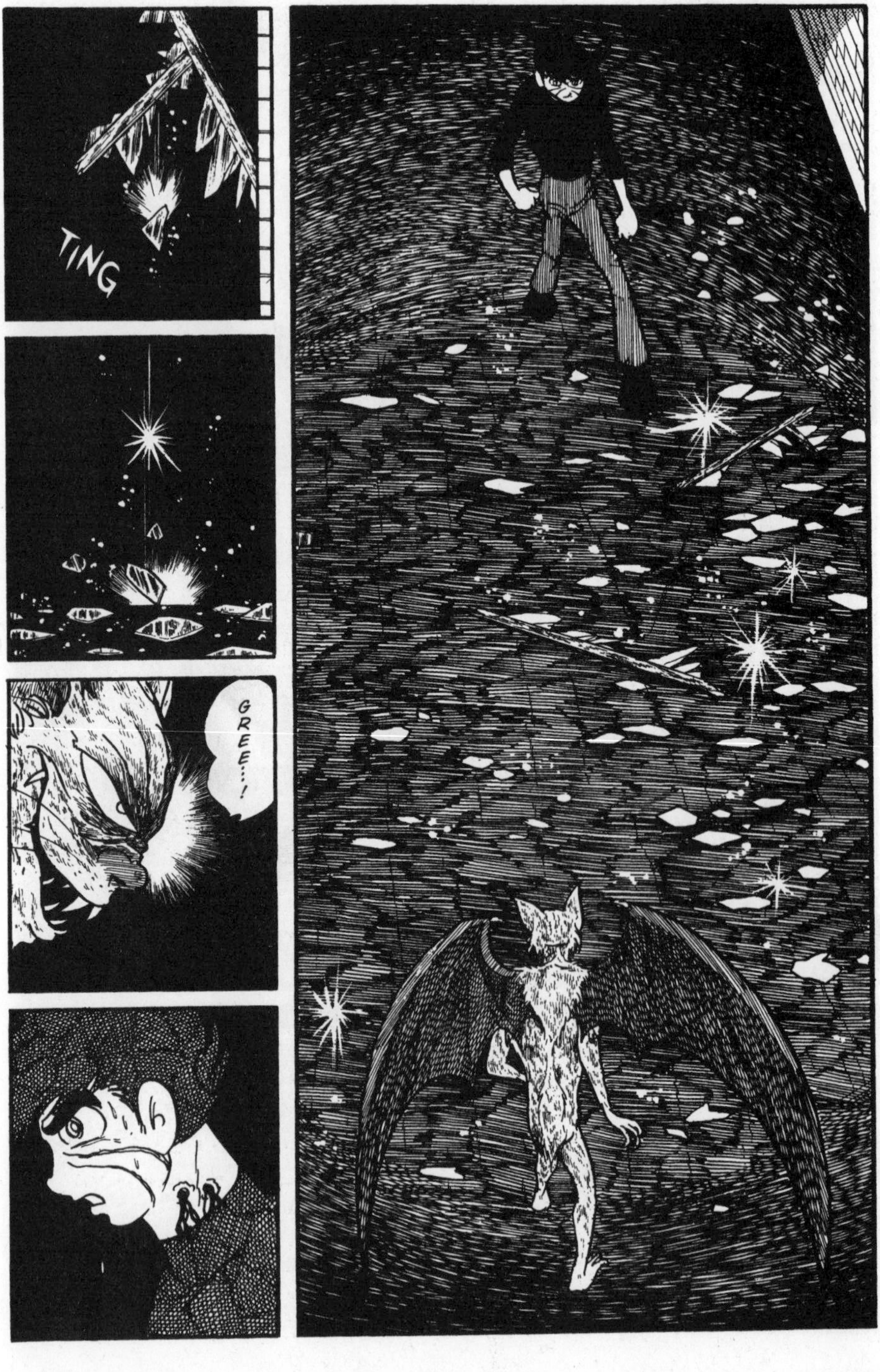
TING
GREE...!

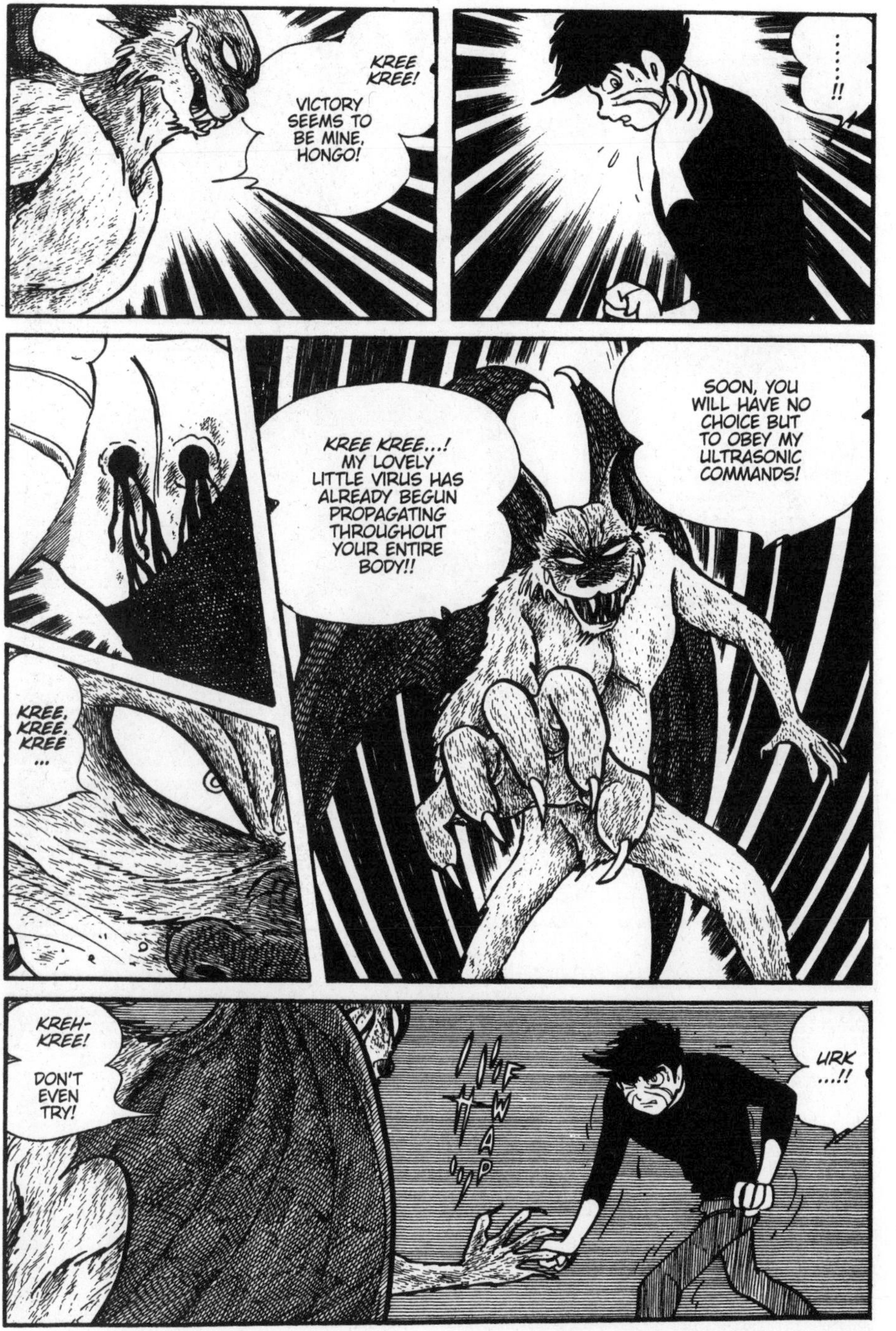

……!!
KREE KREE!
VICTORY SEEMS TO BE MINE, HONGO!
SOON, YOU WILL HAVE NO CHOICE BUT TO OBEY MY ULTRASONIC COMMANDS!
KREE KREE…! MY LOVELY LITTLE VIRUS HAS ALREADY BEGUN PROPAGATING THROUGHOUT YOUR ENTIRE BODY!!
KREE, KREE, KREE …
URK …!!
FWAP
KREH-KREE!
DON'T EVEN TRY!

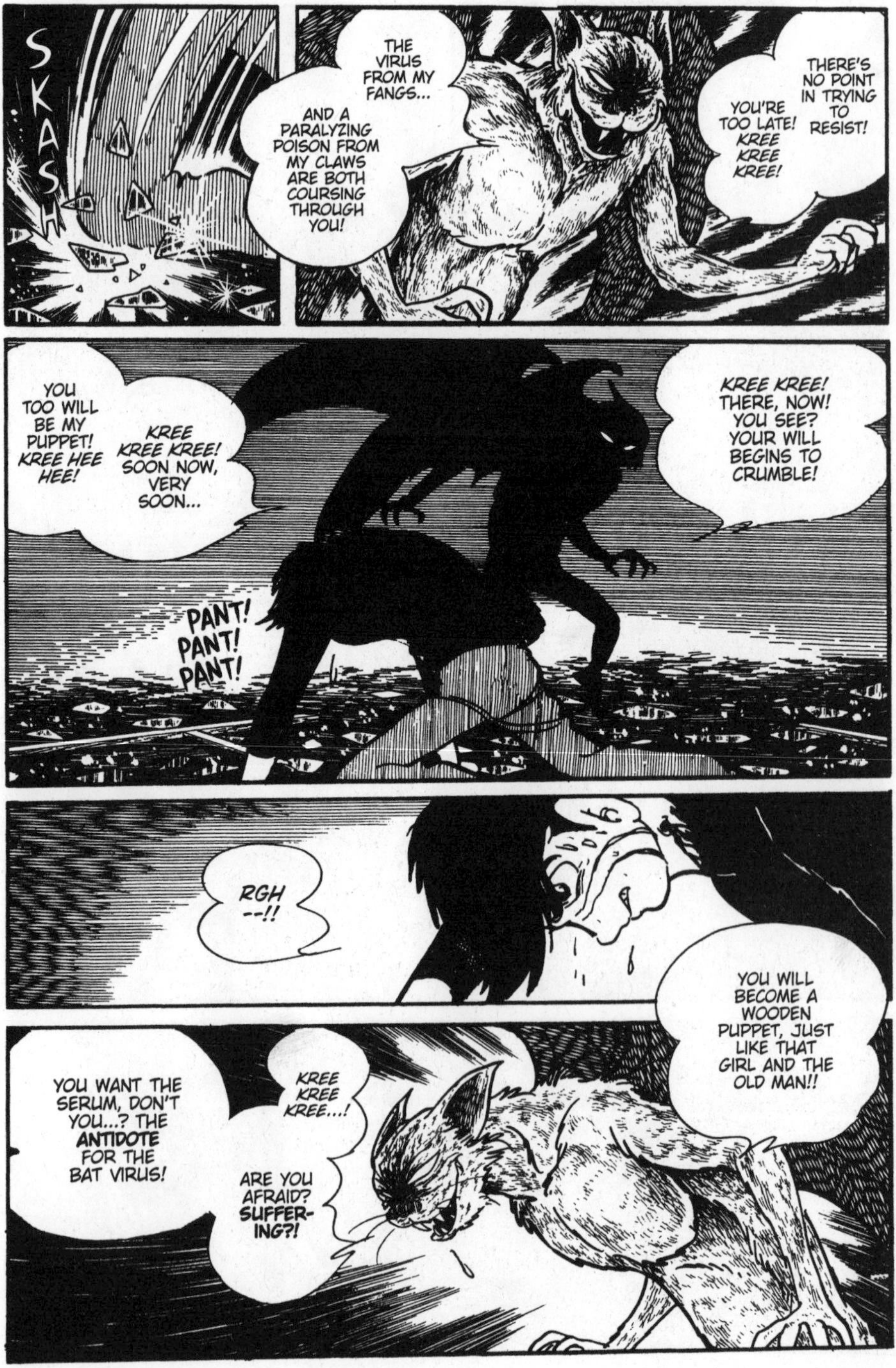
THERE'S NO POINT IN TRYING TO RESIST!
YOU'RE TOO LATE! KREE KREE KREE!
THE VIRUS FROM MY FANGS...
AND A PARALYZING POISON FROM MY CLAWS ARE BOTH COURSING THROUGH YOU!
SKASH
KREE KREE! THERE, NOW! YOU SEE? YOUR WILL BEGINS TO CRUMBLE!
KREE KREE KREE! SOON NOW, VERY SOON...
YOU TOO WILL BE MY PUPPET! KREE HEE HEE!
PANT! PANT! PANT!
RGH--!!
YOU WILL BECOME A WOODEN PUPPET, JUST LIKE THAT GIRL AND THE OLD MAN!!
KREE KREE KREE...!
YOU WANT THE SERUM, DON'T YOU...? THE **ANTIDOTE** FOR THE BAT VIRUS!
ARE YOU AFRAID? **SUFFERING?!**

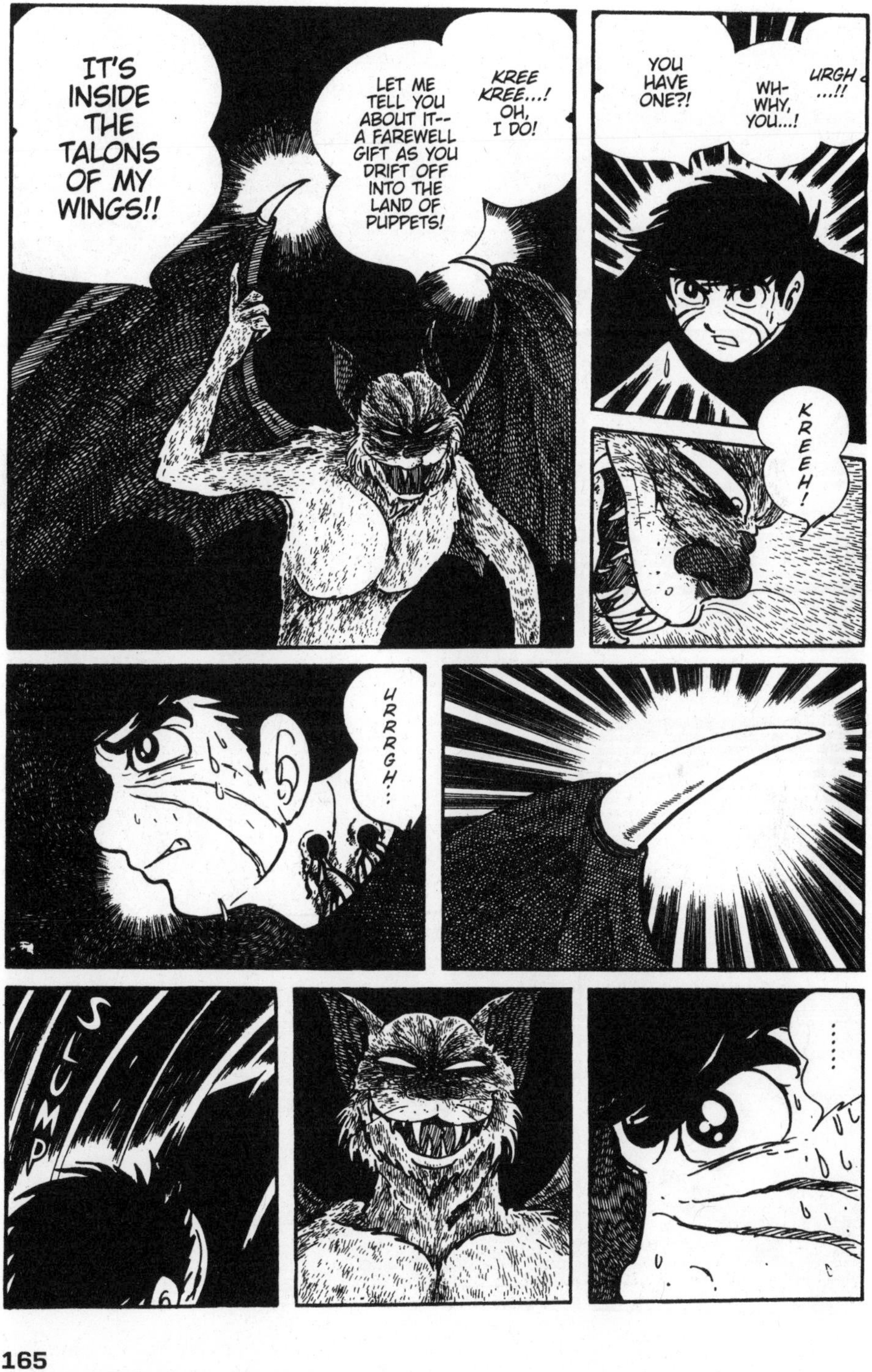
URGH ...!!
WH- WHY, YOU...!
YOU HAVE ONE?!
KREEH!
KREE KREE...! OH, I DO!
LET ME TELL YOU ABOUT IT-- A FAREWELL GIFT AS YOU DRIFT OFF INTO THE LAND OF PUPPETS!
IT'S INSIDE THE TALONS OF MY WINGS!!
URRRGH...
......
SLUMP

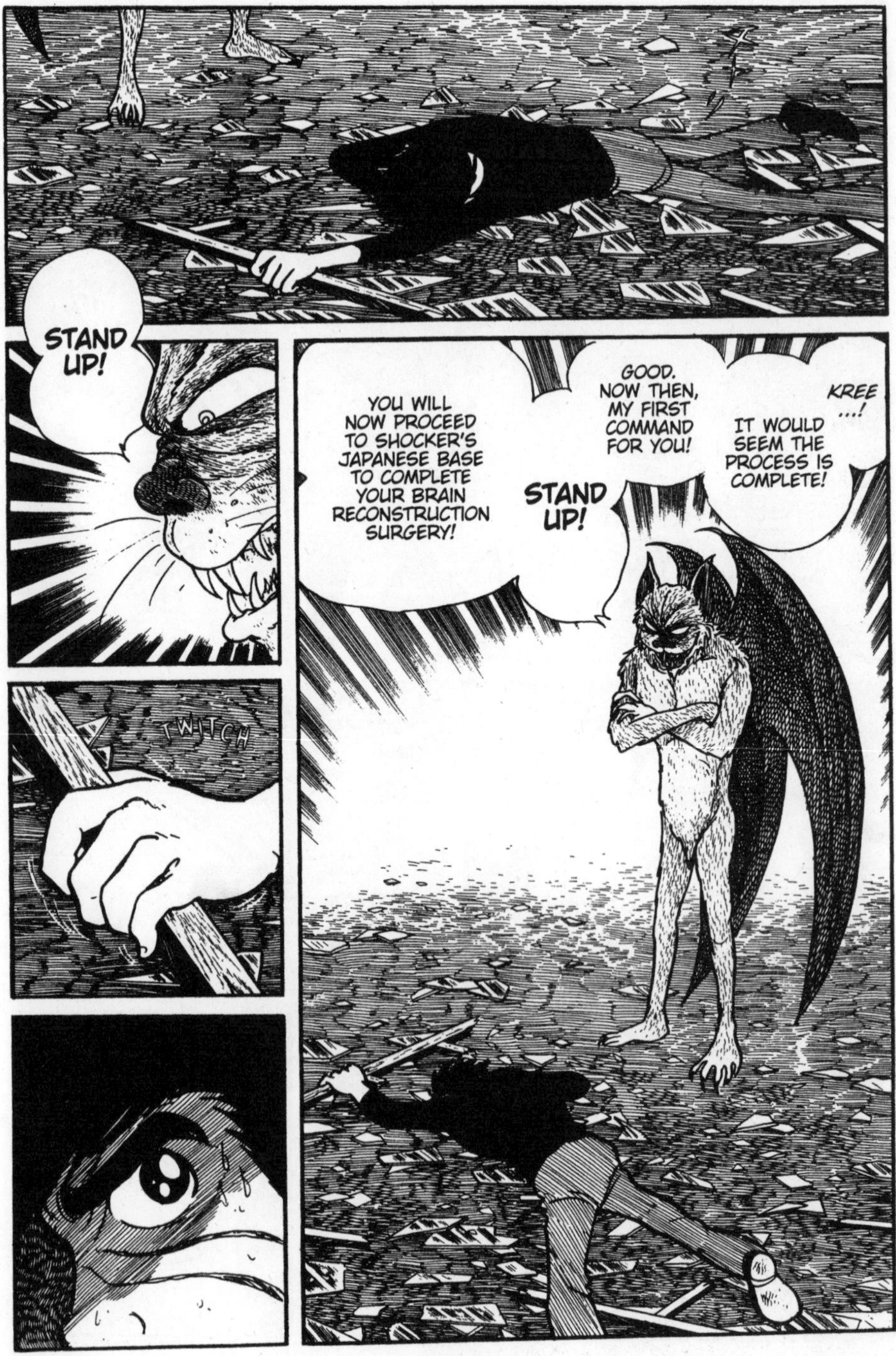
KREE ...!
IT WOULD SEEM THE PROCESS IS COMPLETE!
GOOD. NOW THEN, MY FIRST COMMAND FOR YOU!
STAND UP!
YOU WILL NOW PROCEED TO SHOCKER'S JAPANESE BASE TO COMPLETE YOUR BRAIN RECONSTRUCTION SURGERY!
STAND UP!
TWITCH

KAMEN
RIDER

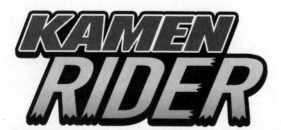

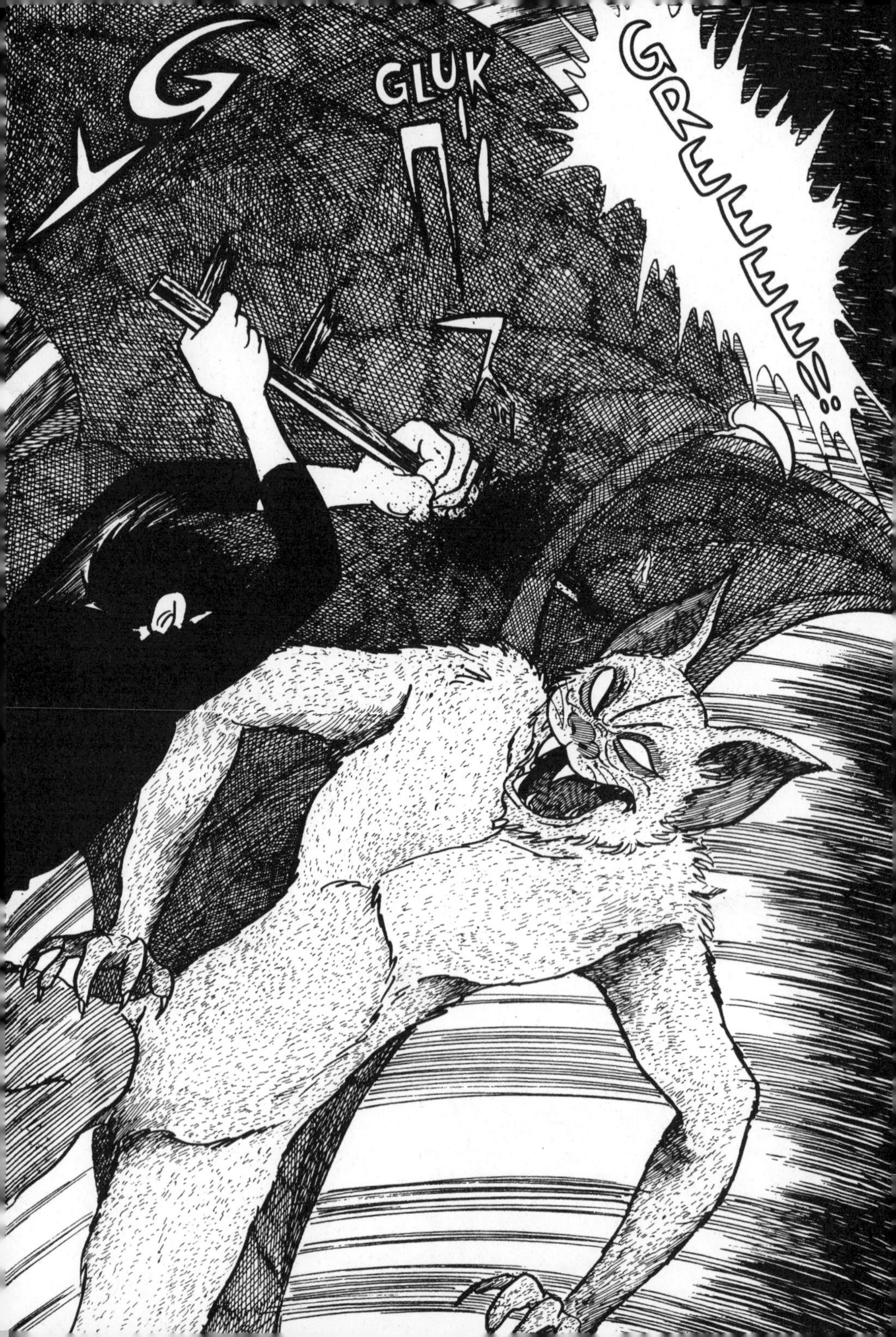
GLUK
GREEEEE!!

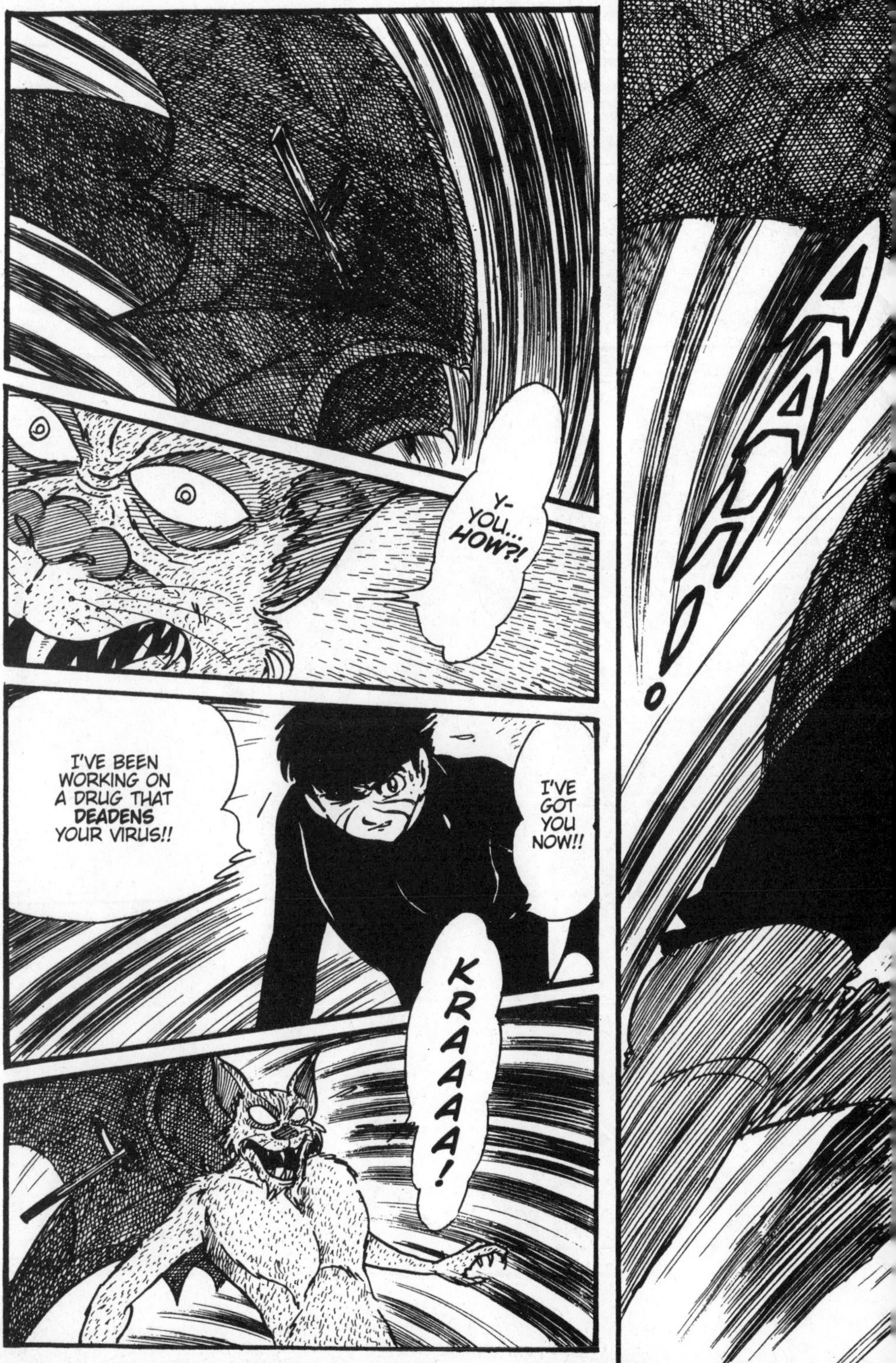

AAAH!!
Y-YOU... HOW?!
I'VE GOT YOU NOW!!
I'VE BEEN WORKING ON A DRUG THAT **DEADENS** YOUR VIRUS!!
KRAAAAA!

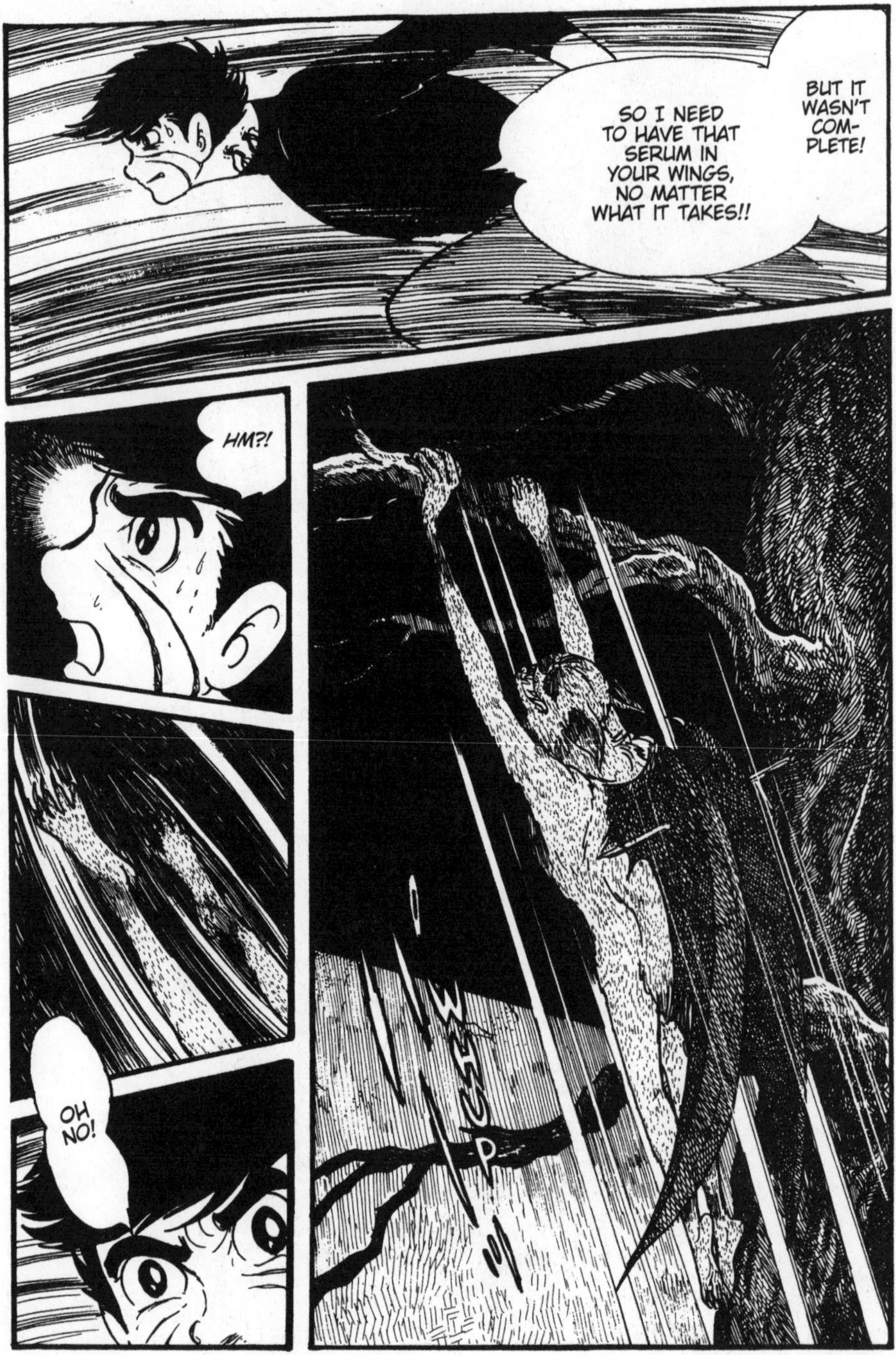
BUT IT WASN'T COM-PLETE!
SO I NEED TO HAVE THAT SERUM IN YOUR WINGS, NO MATTER WHAT IT TAKES!!
WHUP
HM?!
OH NO!

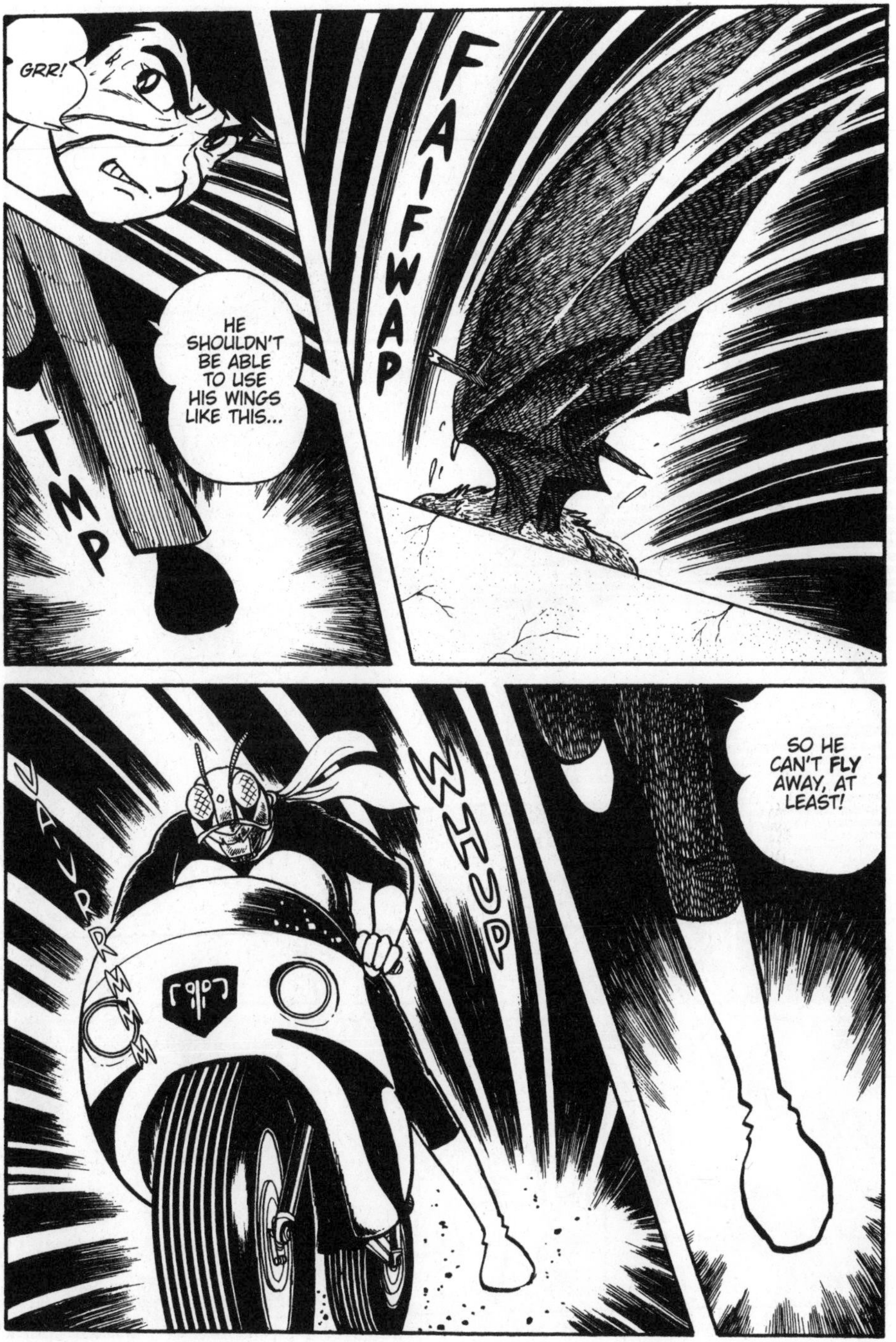
FAIFWAP
GRR!
HE SHOULDN'T BE ABLE TO USE HIS WINGS LIKE THIS...
TMP
SO HE CAN'T **FLY** AWAY, AT LEAST!
WHUP
JA-JRRMMMM

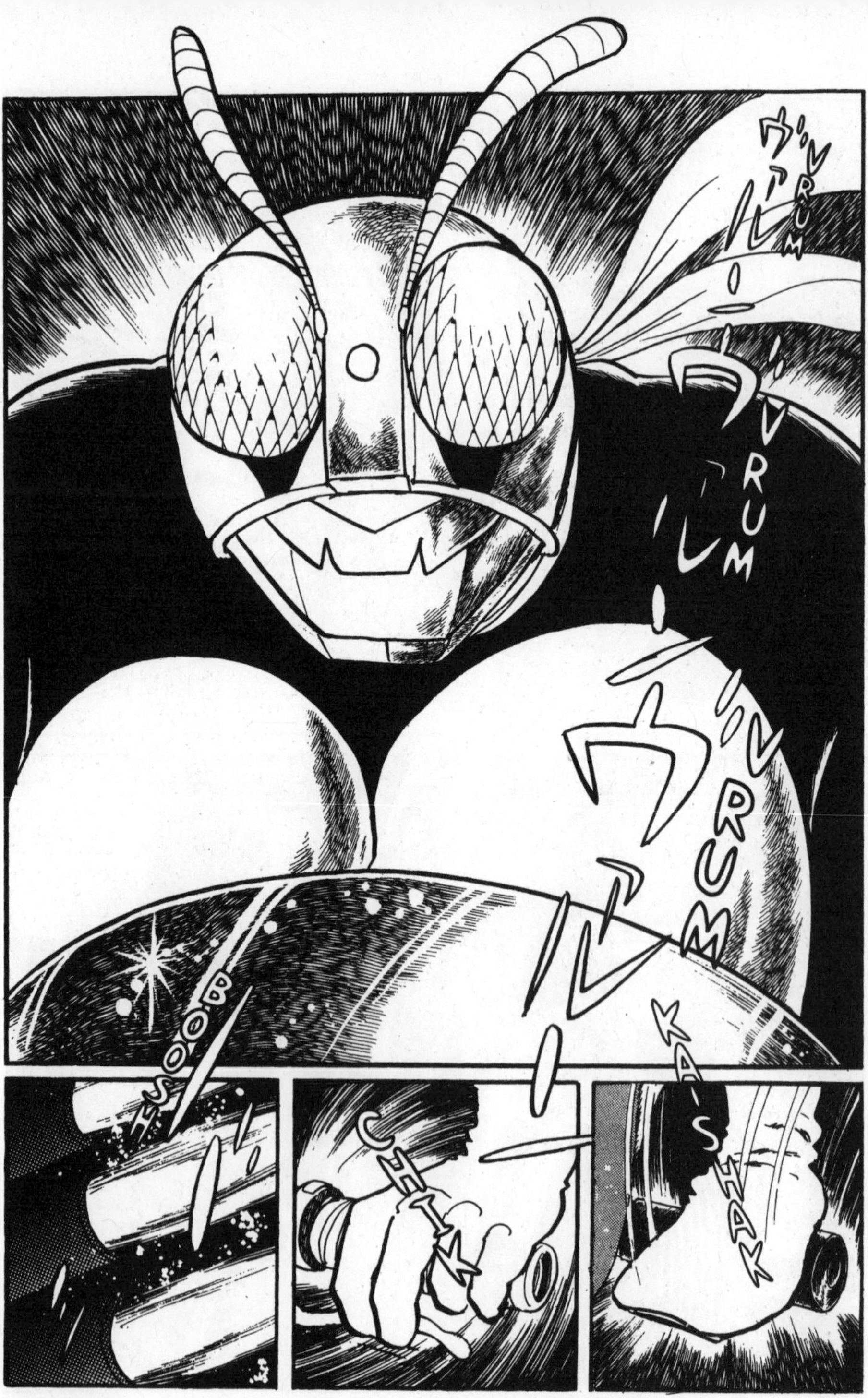
VRUM
VRUM
VRUMM
KA-SHAK
CHIK
BOOSH

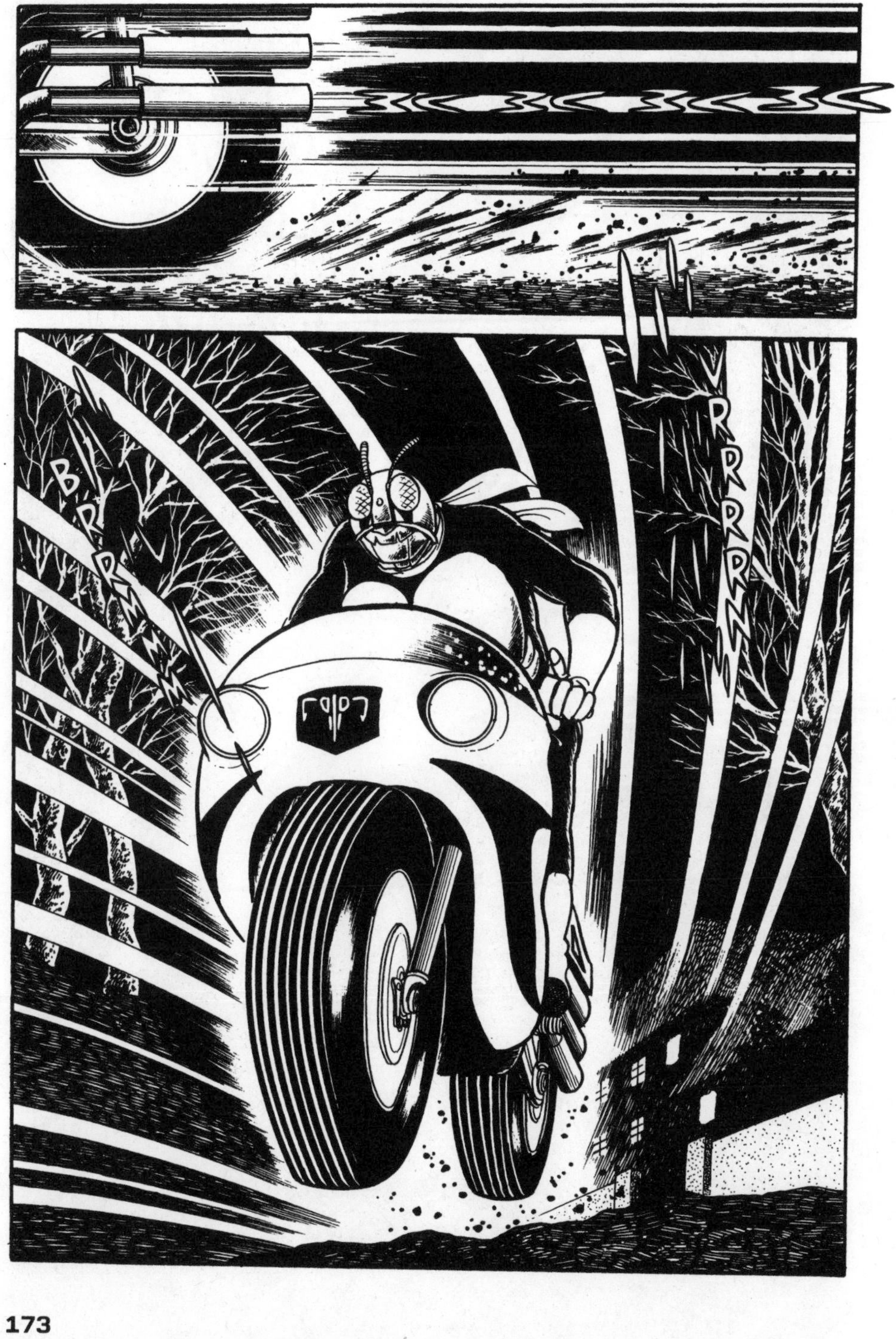
VRRRRN
BRRMMM

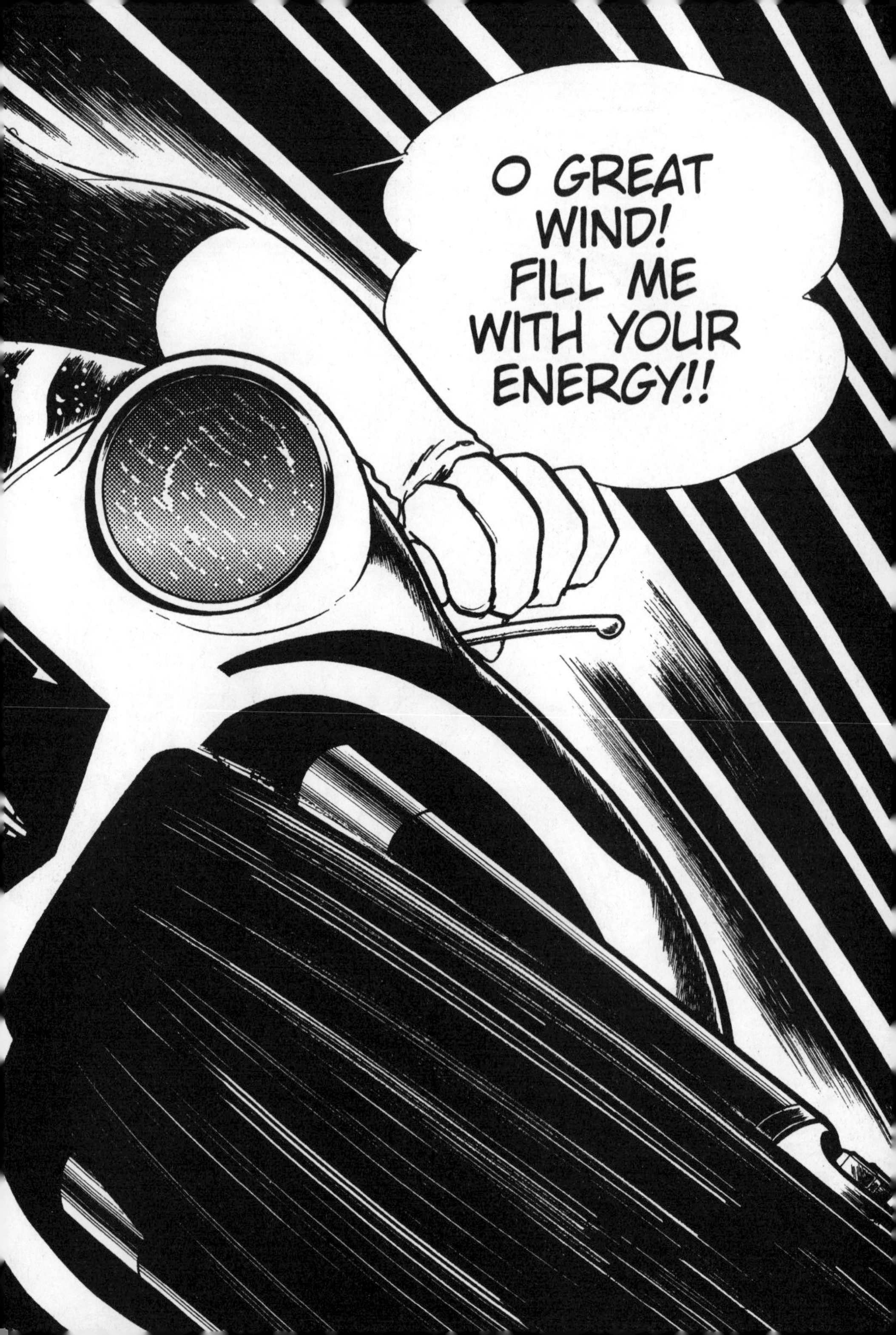
O GREAT WIND! FILL ME WITH YOUR ENERGY!!

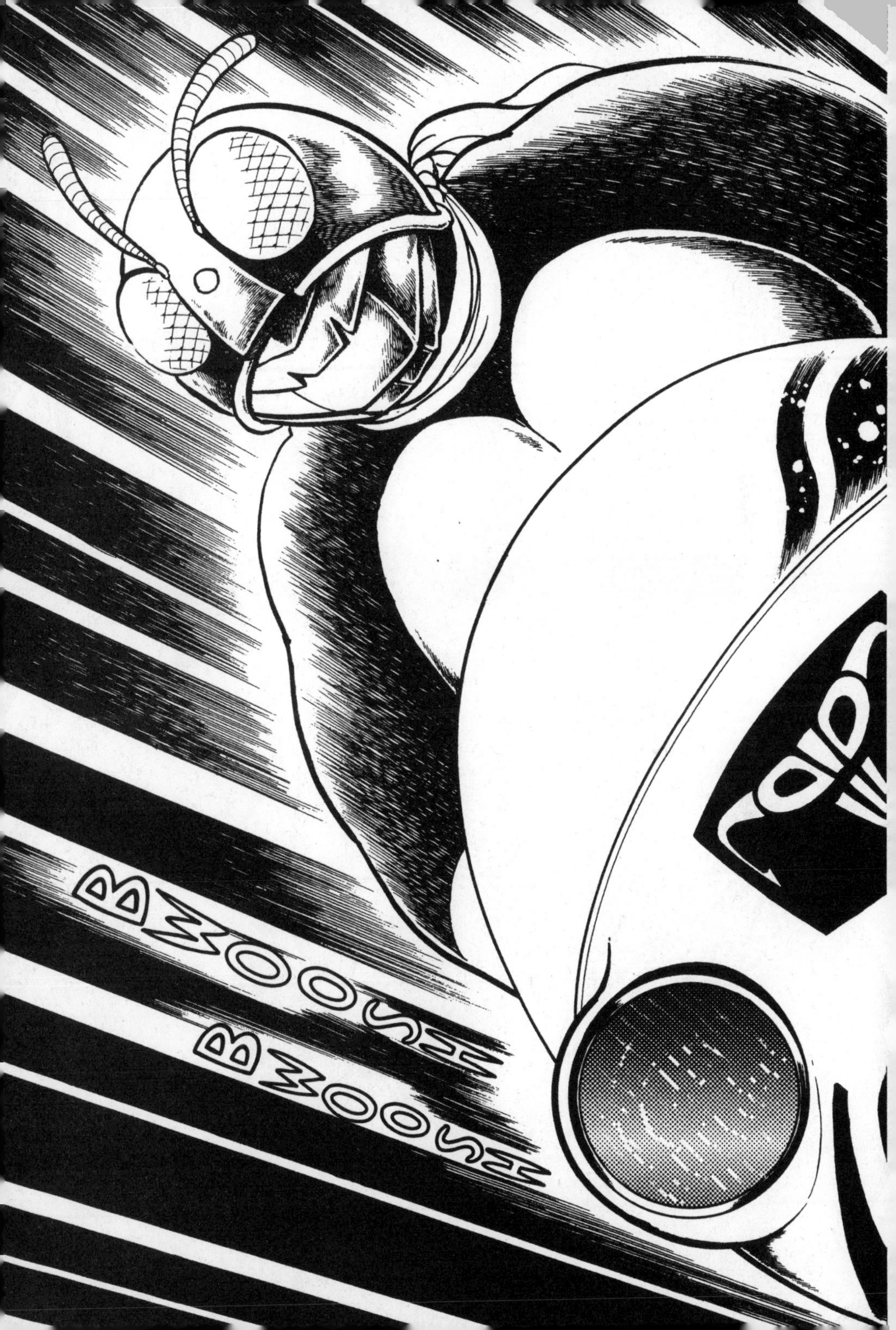
BWOOSH
BWOOSH

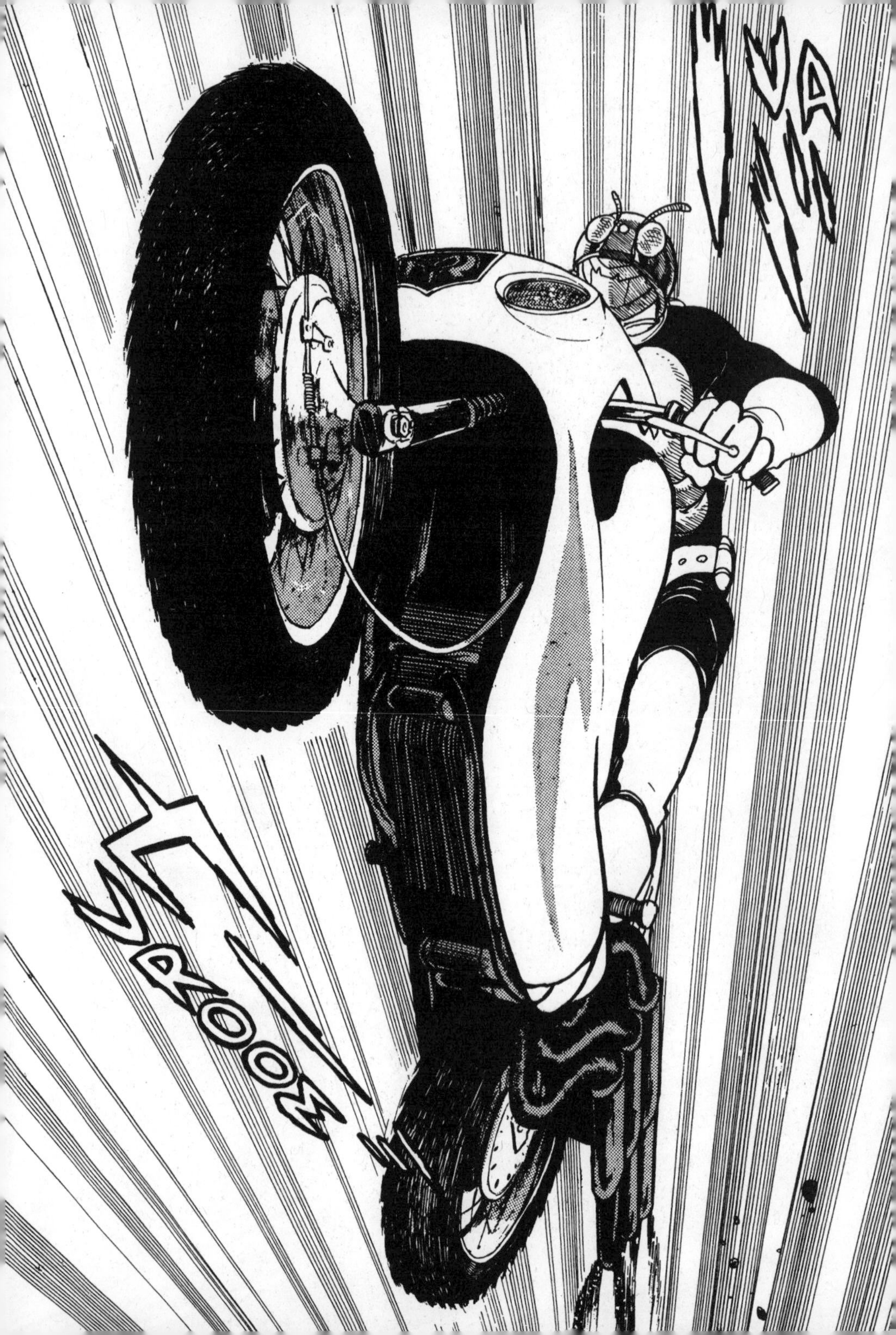
VROOOM

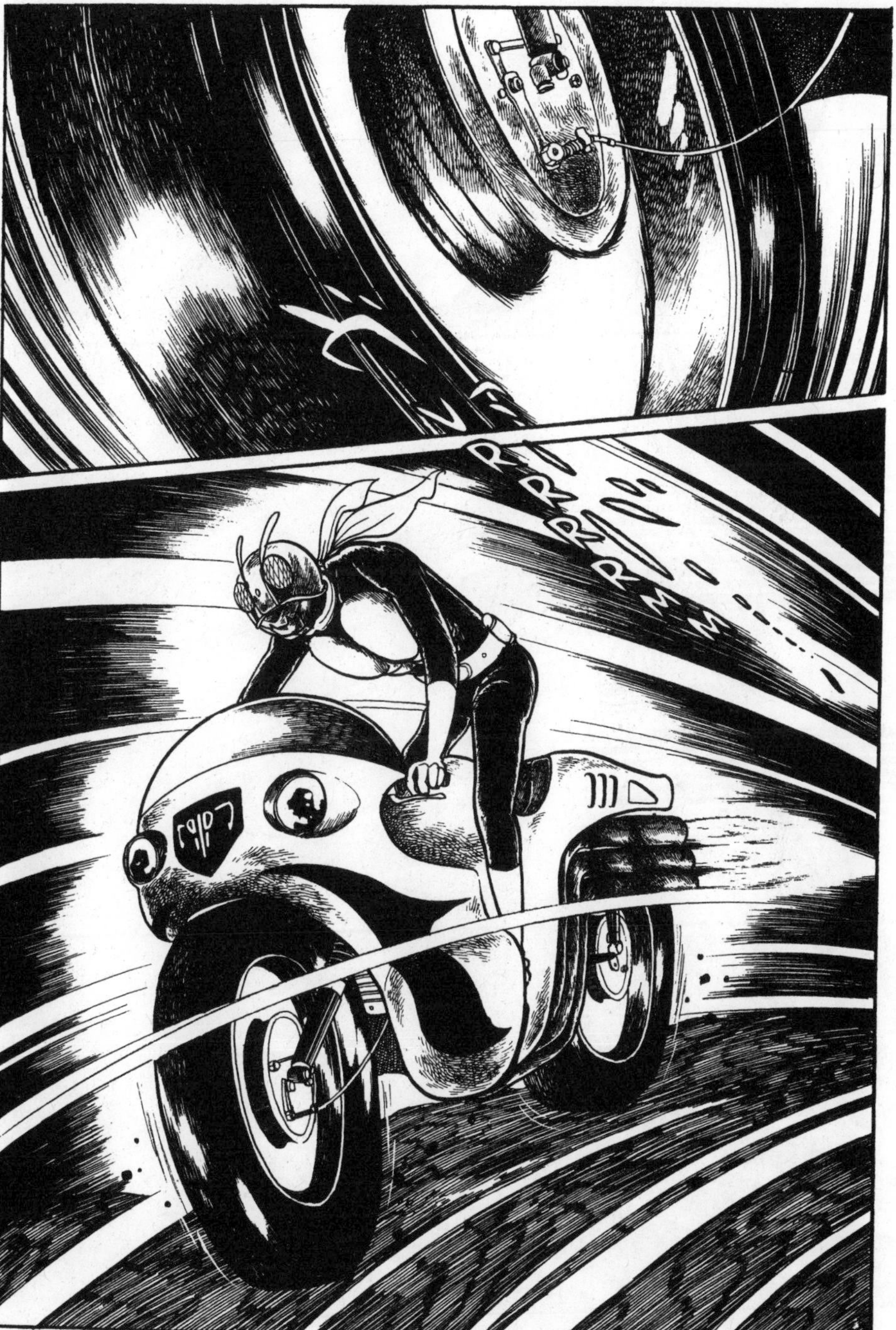
RRRRMM

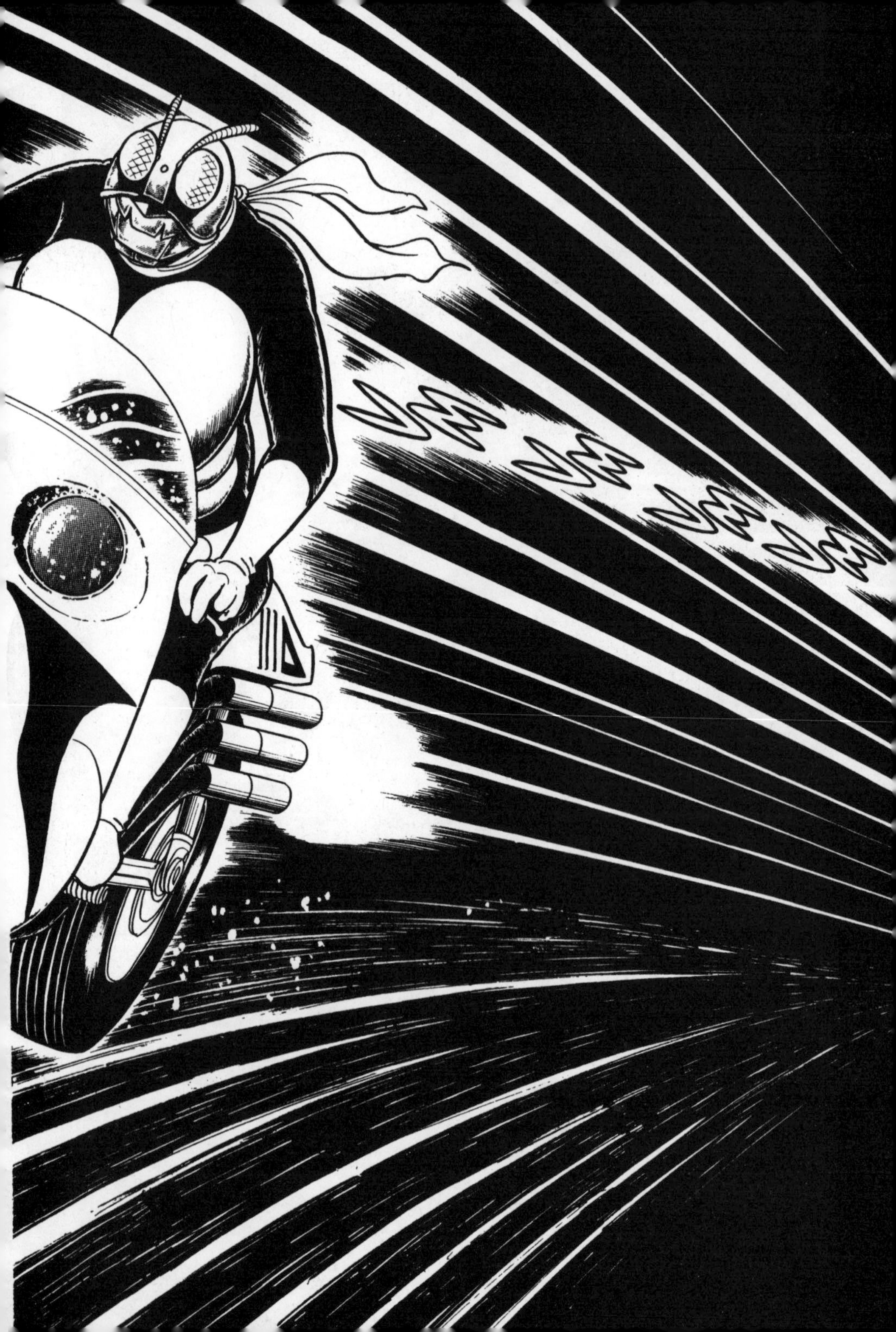

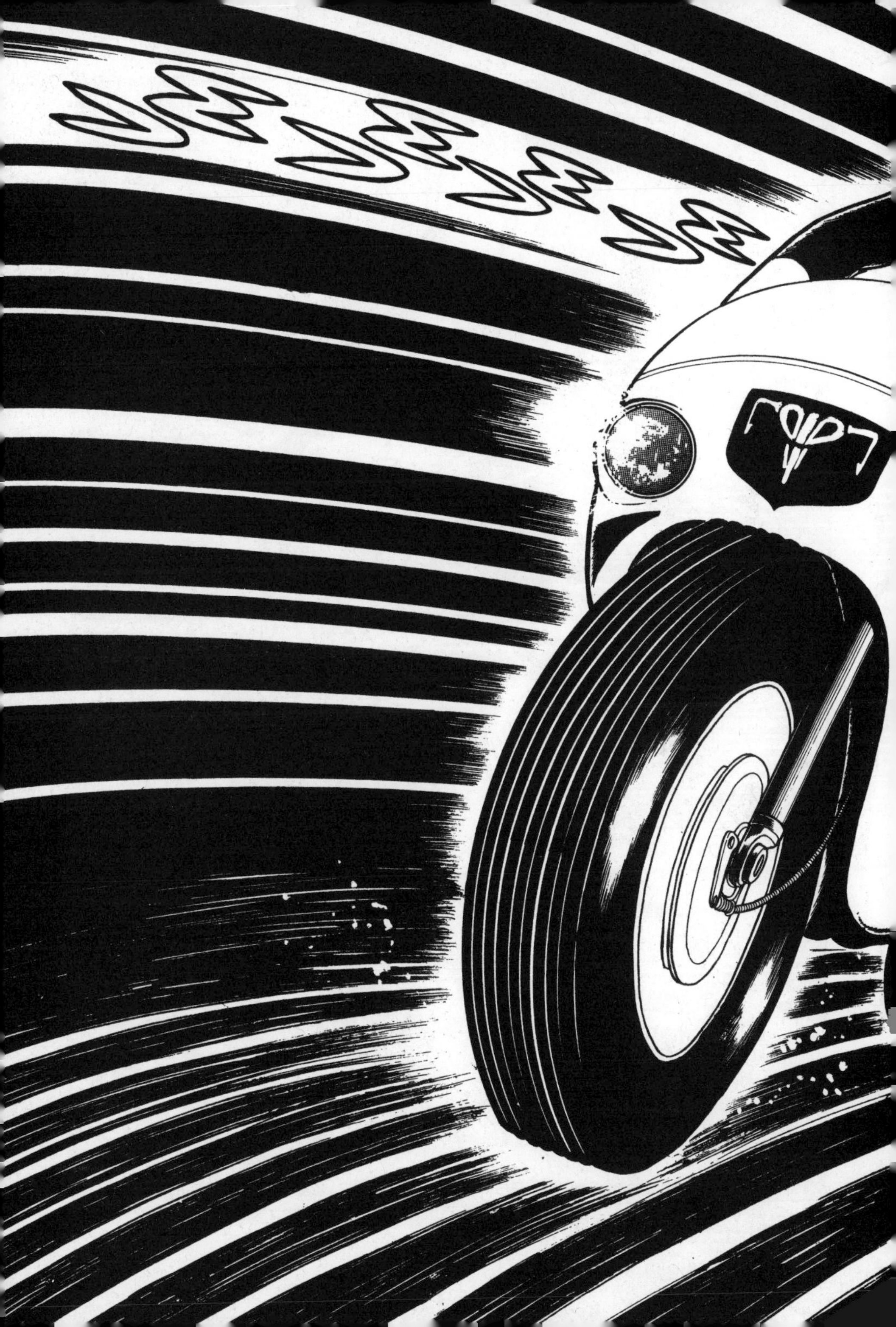

HMPH ...!
I'VE CAUGHT UP WITH YOU, MAN-BAT!
HE'S IN THERE!!

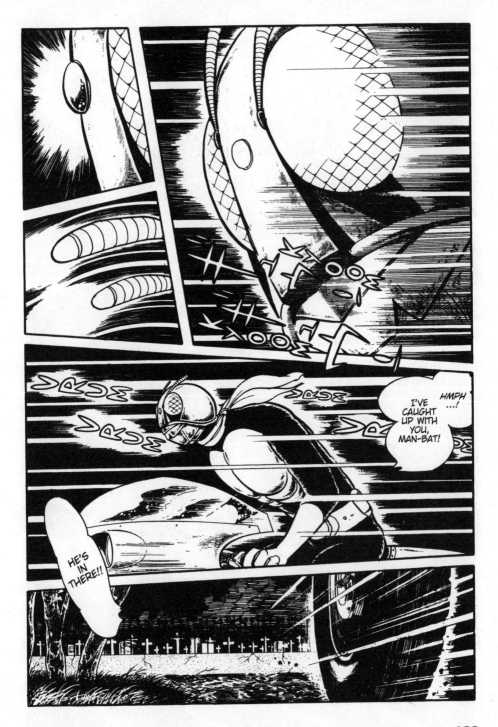

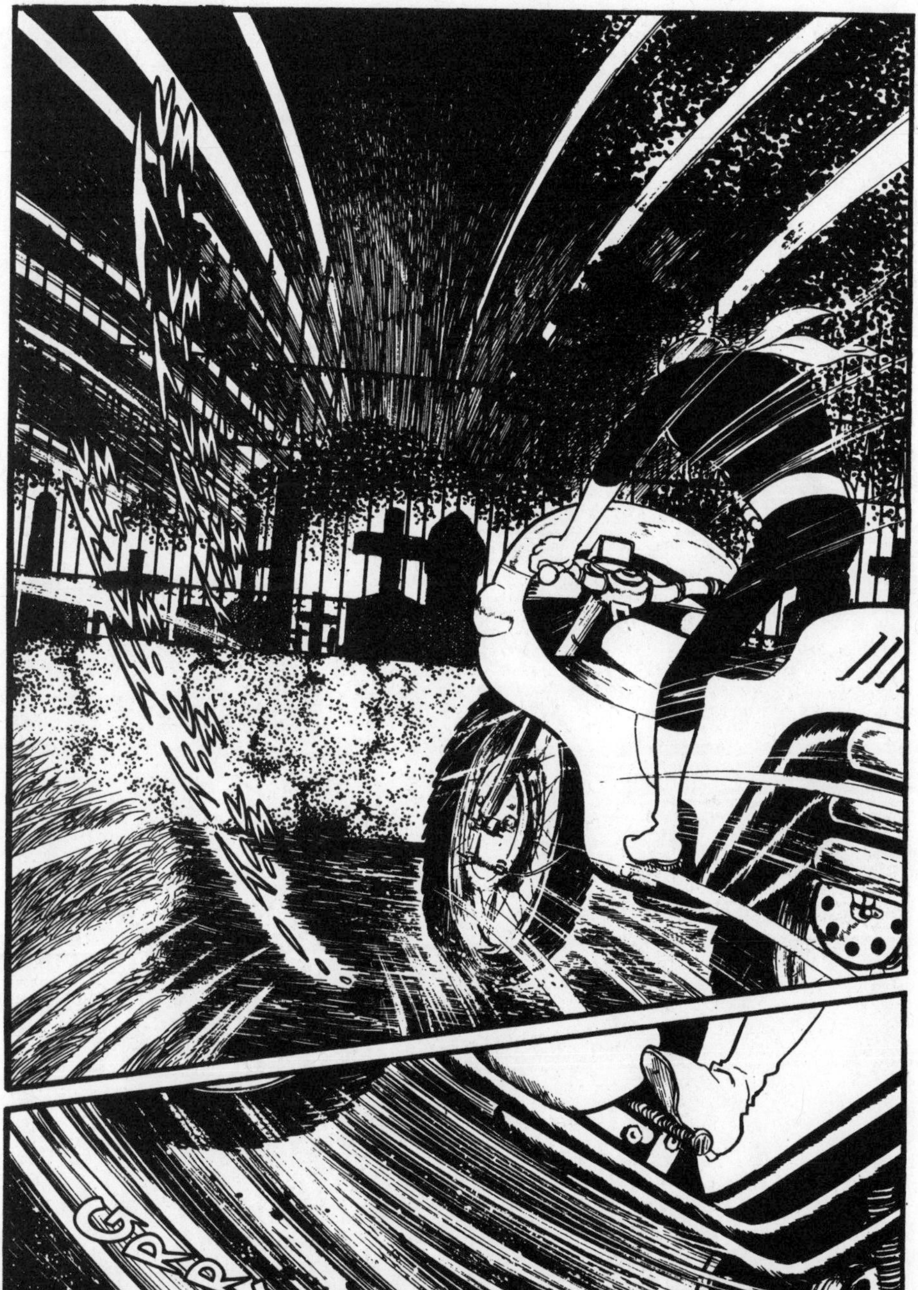

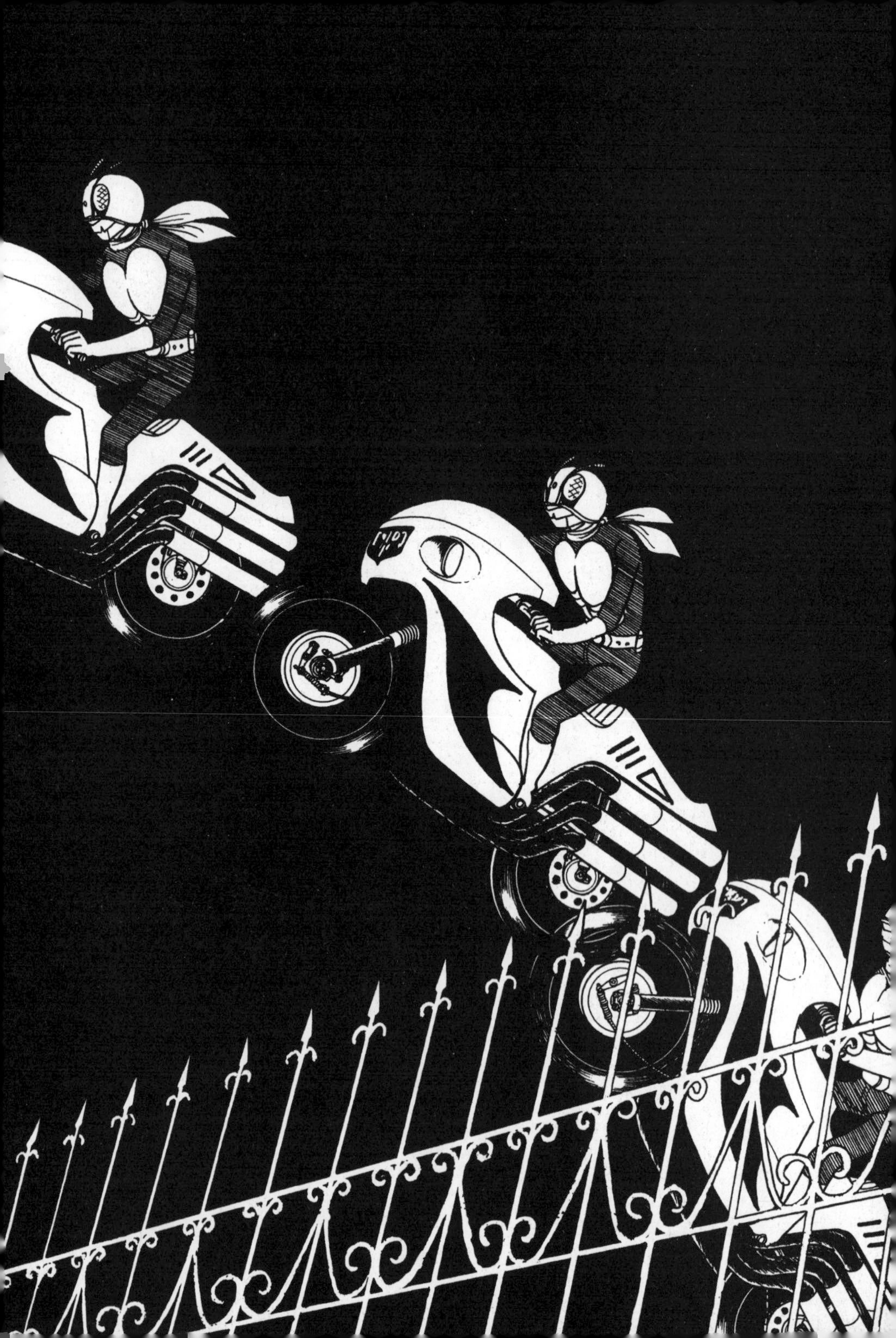

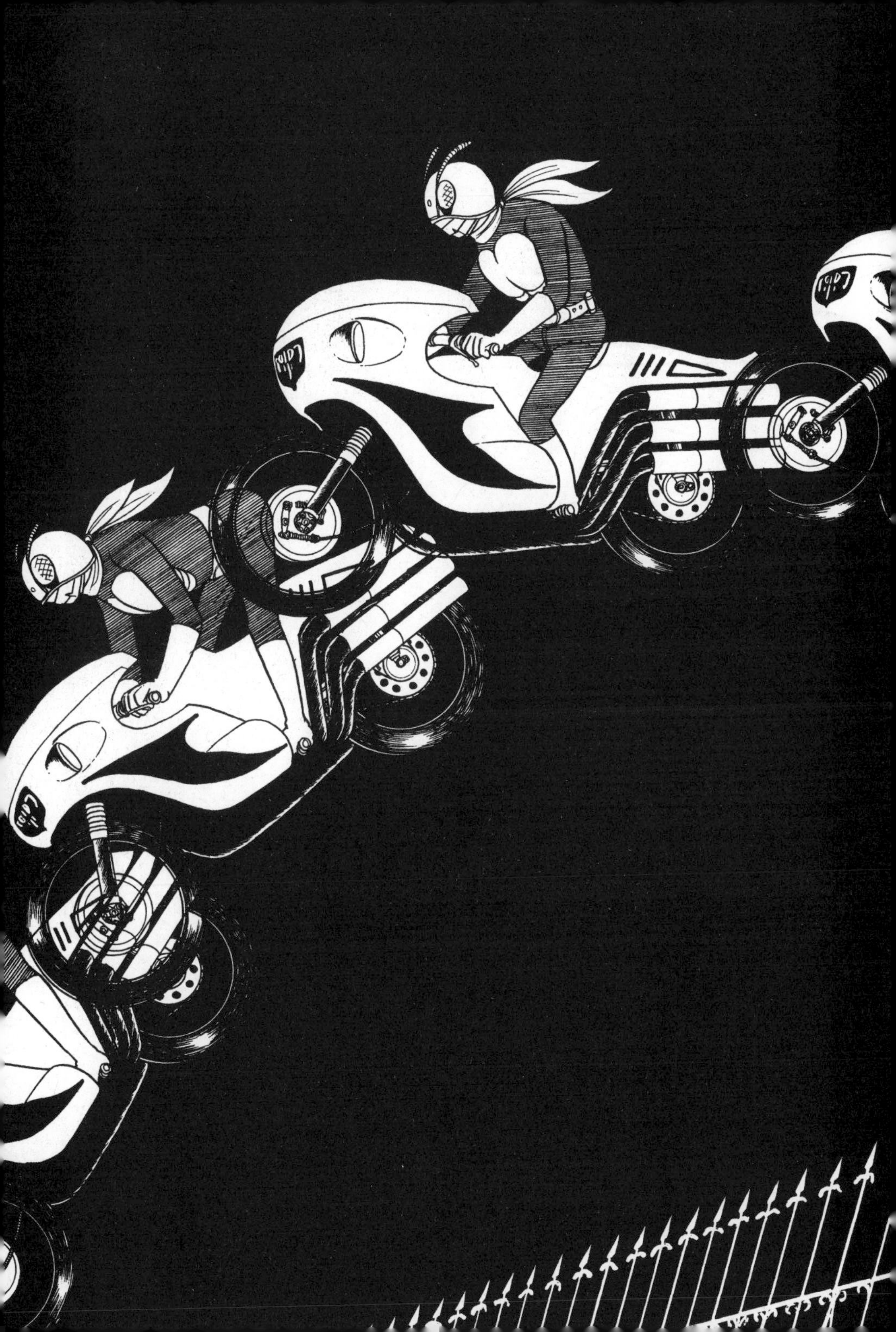

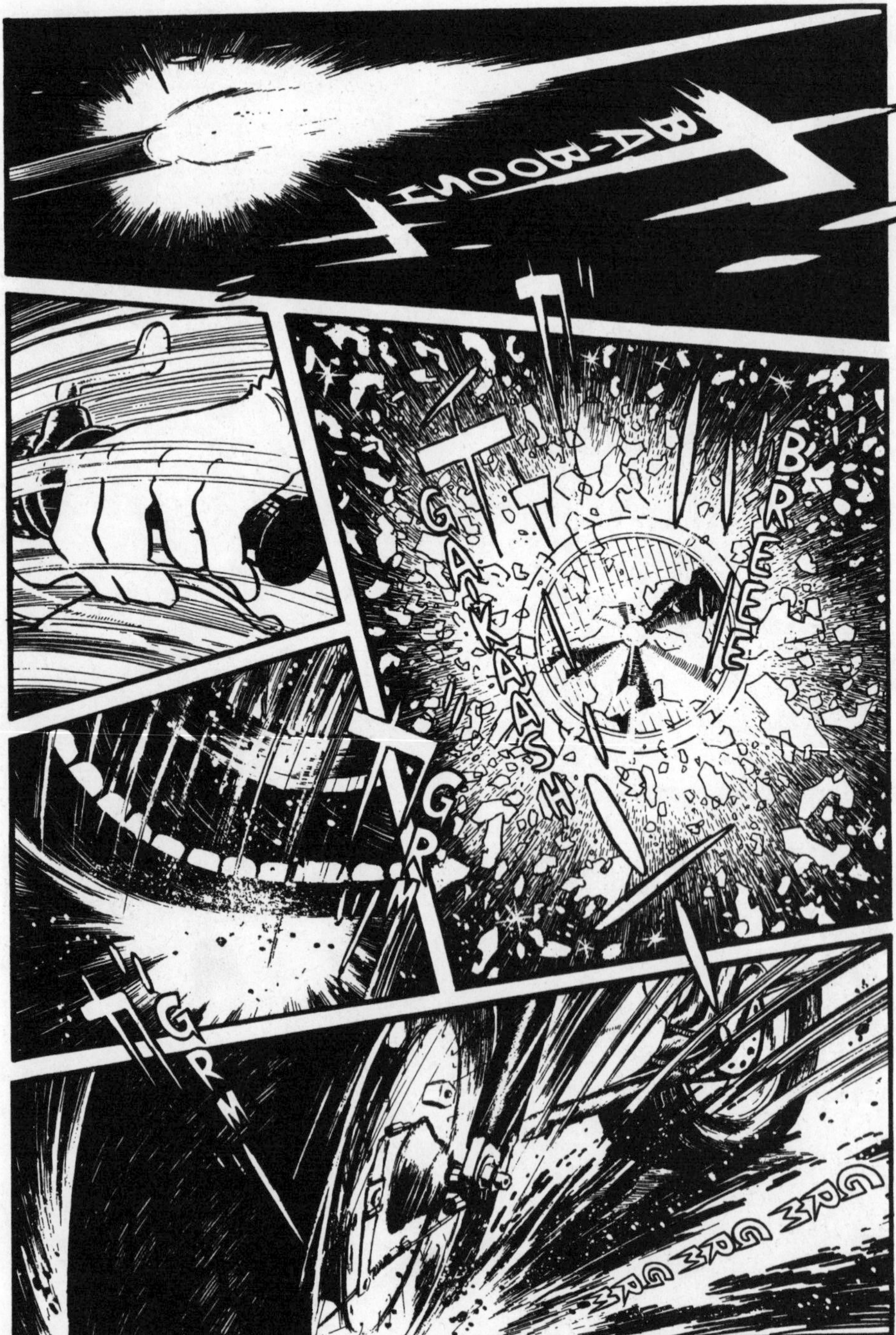
BA-BOOM!
BREEEE
GACKASH
GRM
GRM
GRM GRM GRM

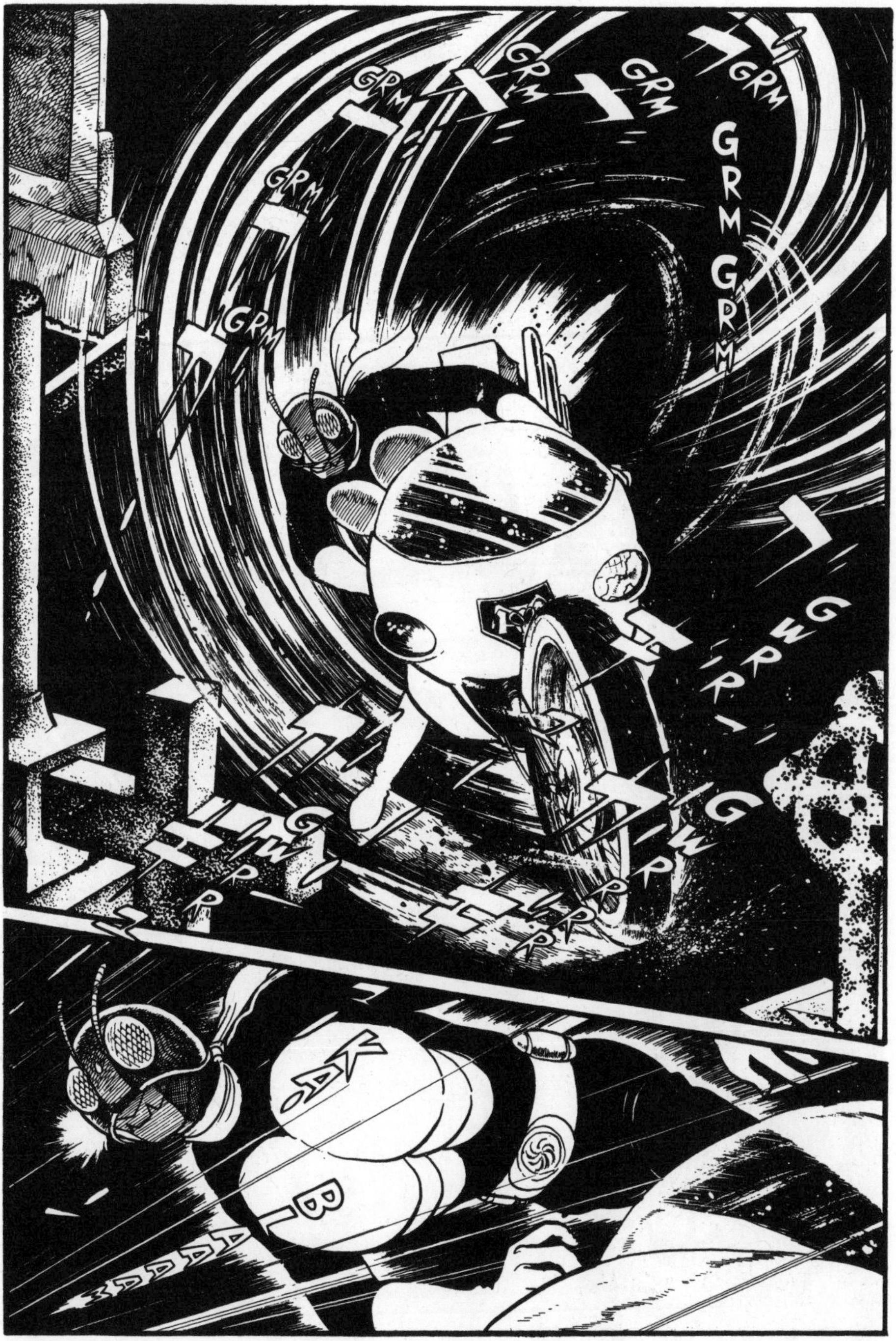
GRM
GRM
GRM
GRM
GRM
GRM
GRM
GRM
GRM
GWRR
GWRRR
GWRRR
KA-
BLAAAAM

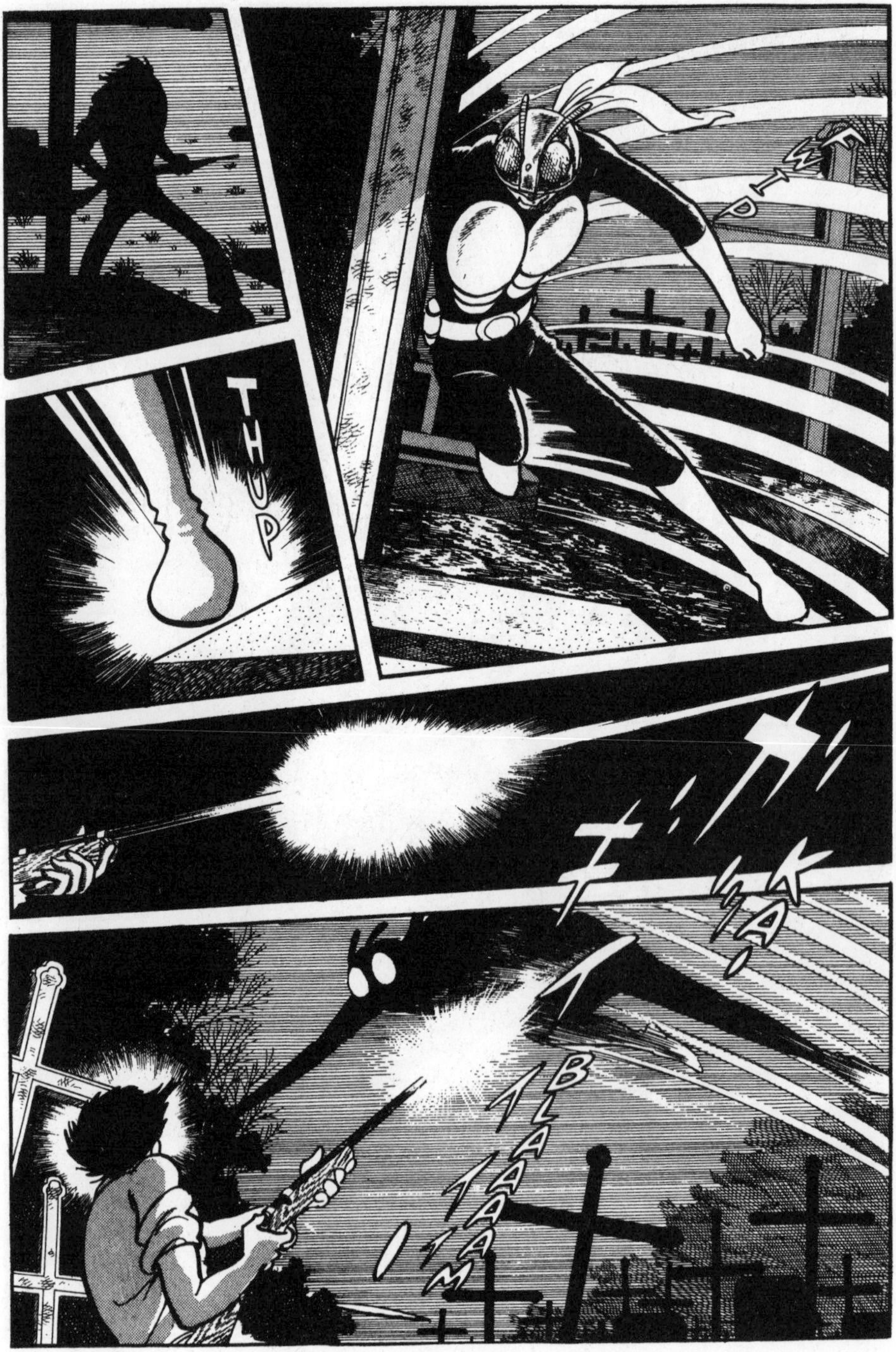
WHIP
THUP
KA!!
BLAAAAAM!!

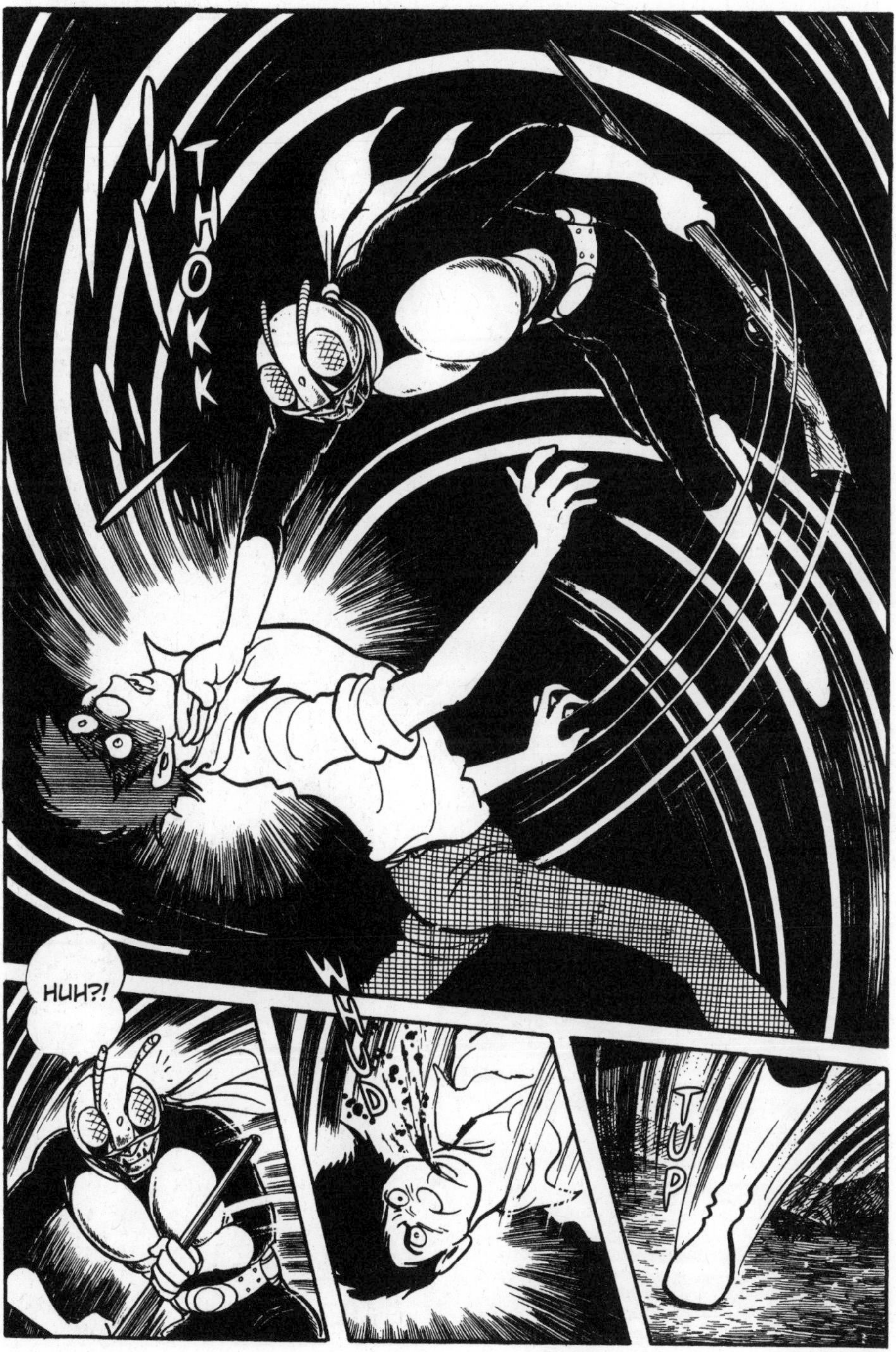
THOKK
TUP
WHUD
HUH?!

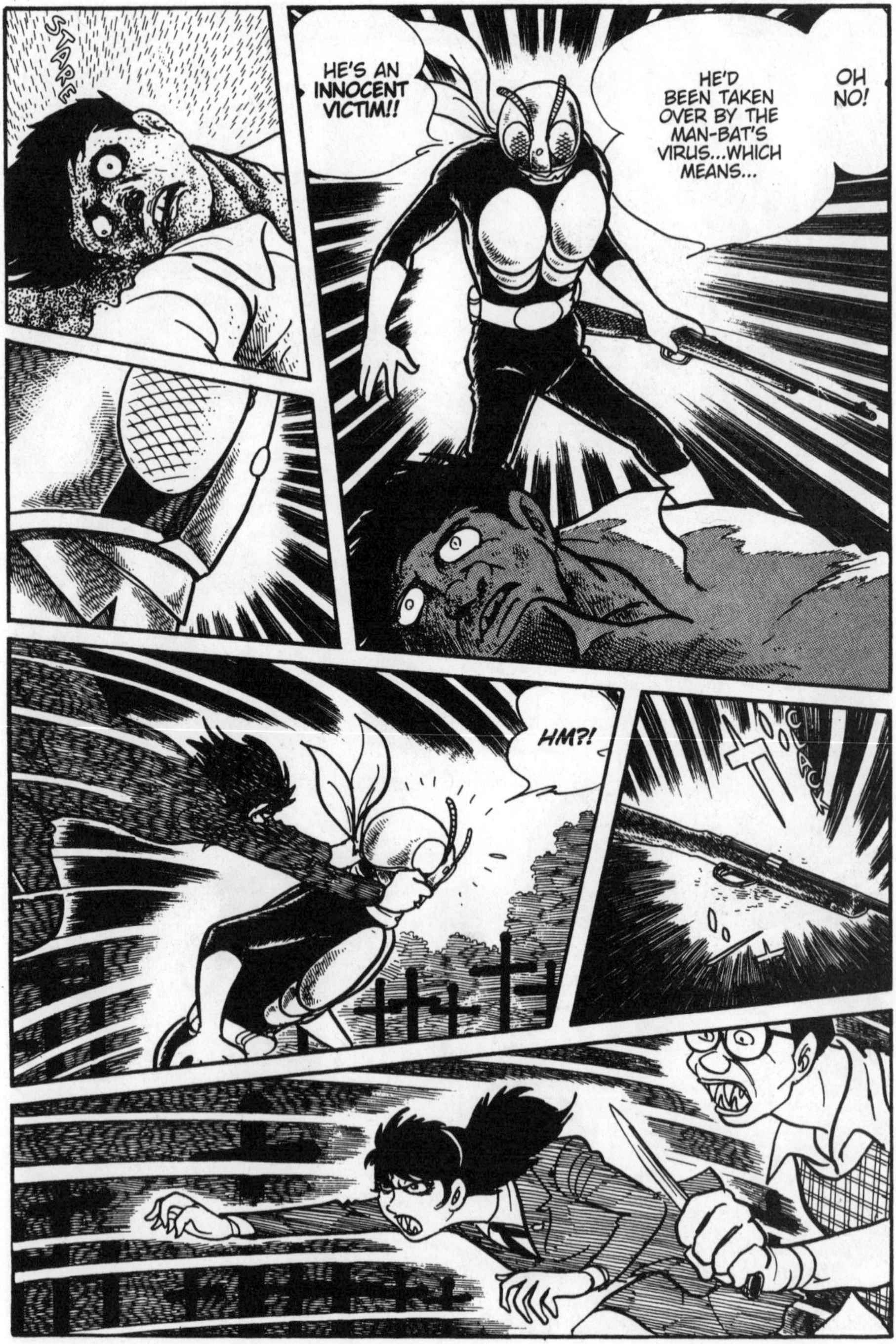
OH NO!
HE'D BEEN TAKEN OVER BY THE MAN-BAT'S VIRUS...WHICH MEANS...
HE'S AN INNOCENT VICTIM!!
STARE
CLACK
HM?!

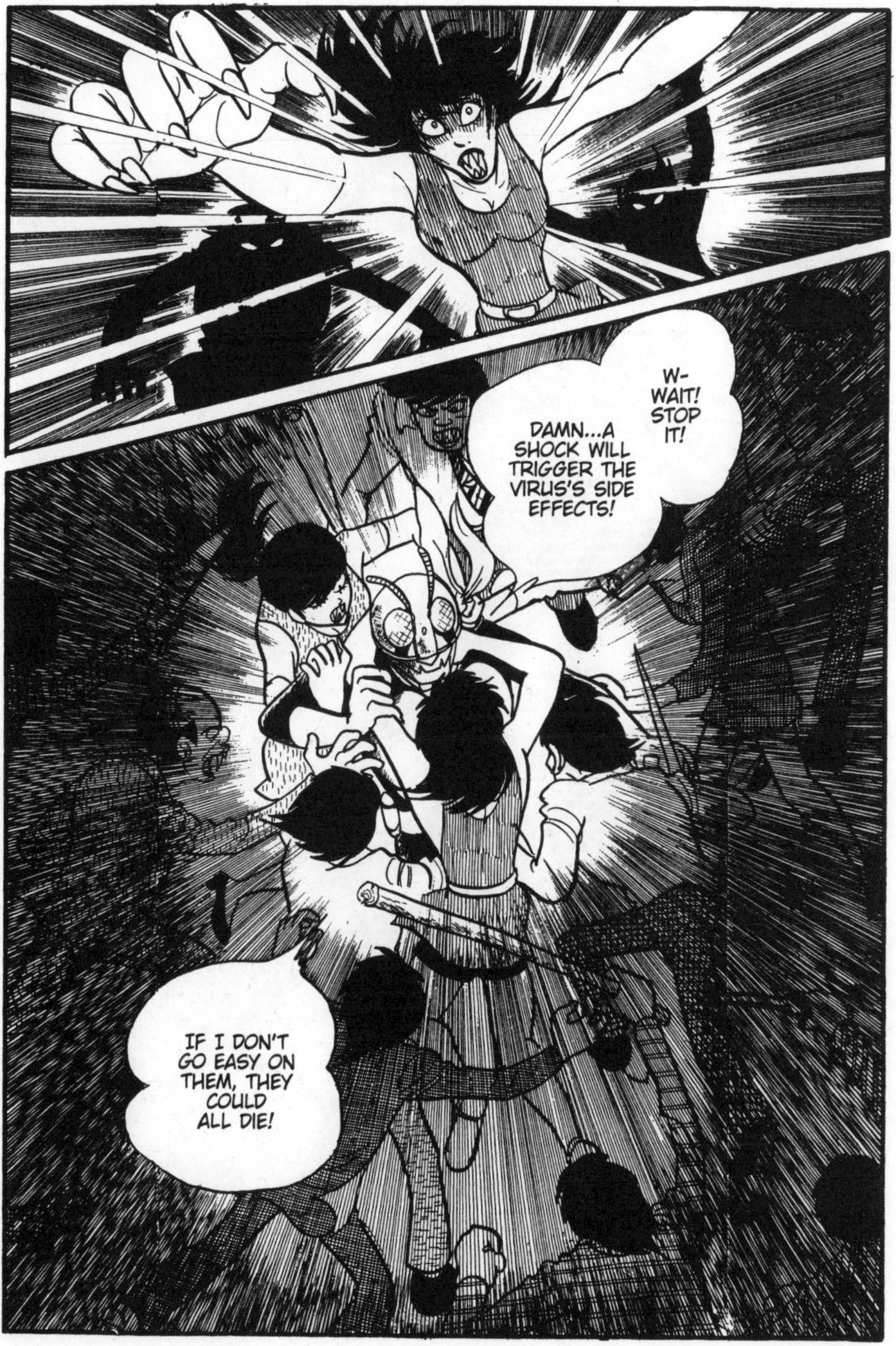
W-WAIT! STOP IT!
DAMN...A SHOCK WILL TRIGGER THE VIRUS'S SIDE EFFECTS!
IF I DON'T GO EASY ON THEM, THEY COULD ALL DIE!

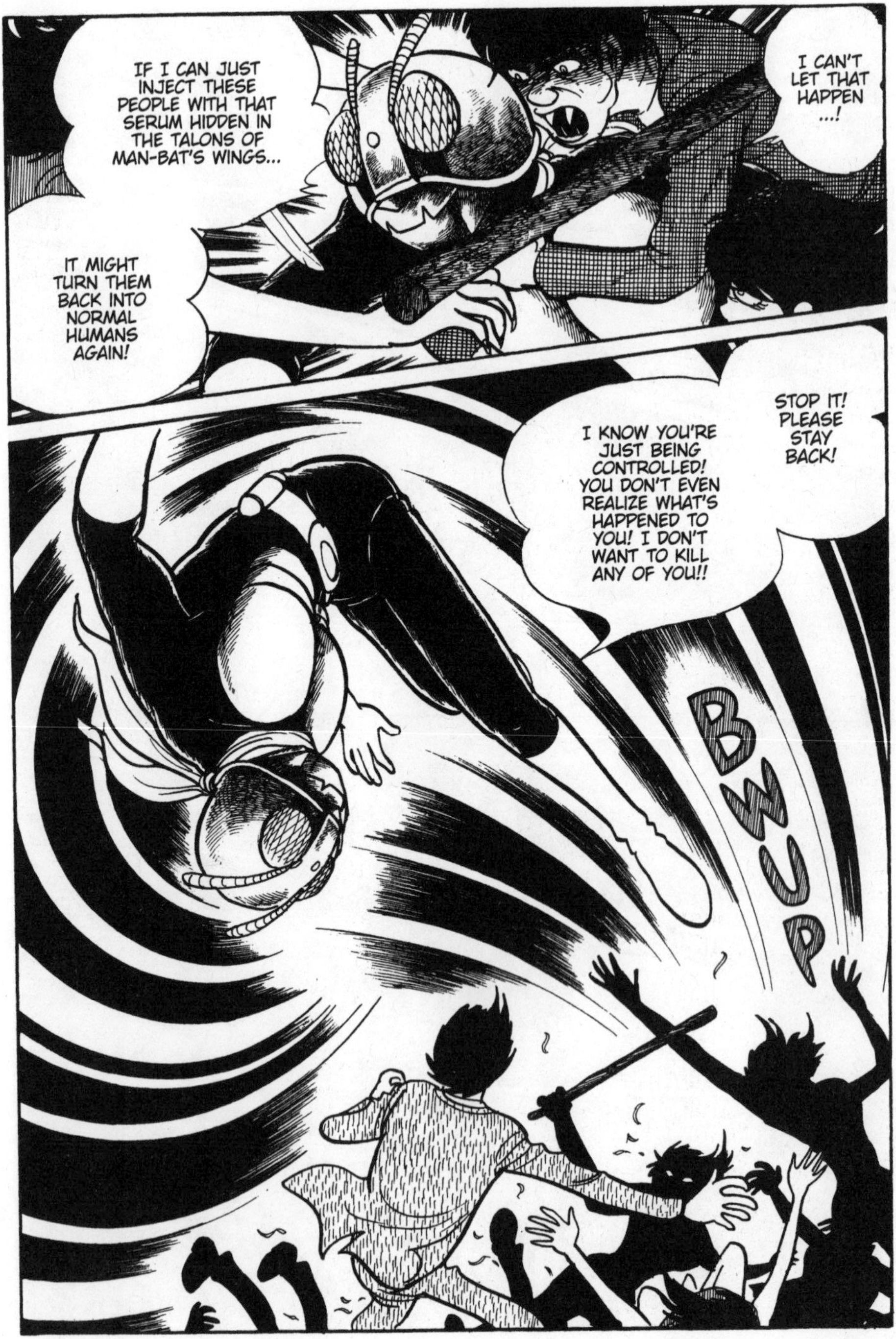

I CAN'T LET THAT HAPPEN ...!
IF I CAN JUST INJECT THESE PEOPLE WITH THAT SERUM HIDDEN IN THE TALONS OF MAN-BAT'S WINGS...
IT MIGHT TURN THEM BACK INTO NORMAL HUMANS AGAIN!
STOP IT! PLEASE STAY BACK!
I KNOW YOU'RE JUST BEING CONTROLLED! YOU DON'T EVEN REALIZE WHAT'S HAPPENED TO YOU! I DON'T WANT TO KILL ANY OF YOU!!
BWUP

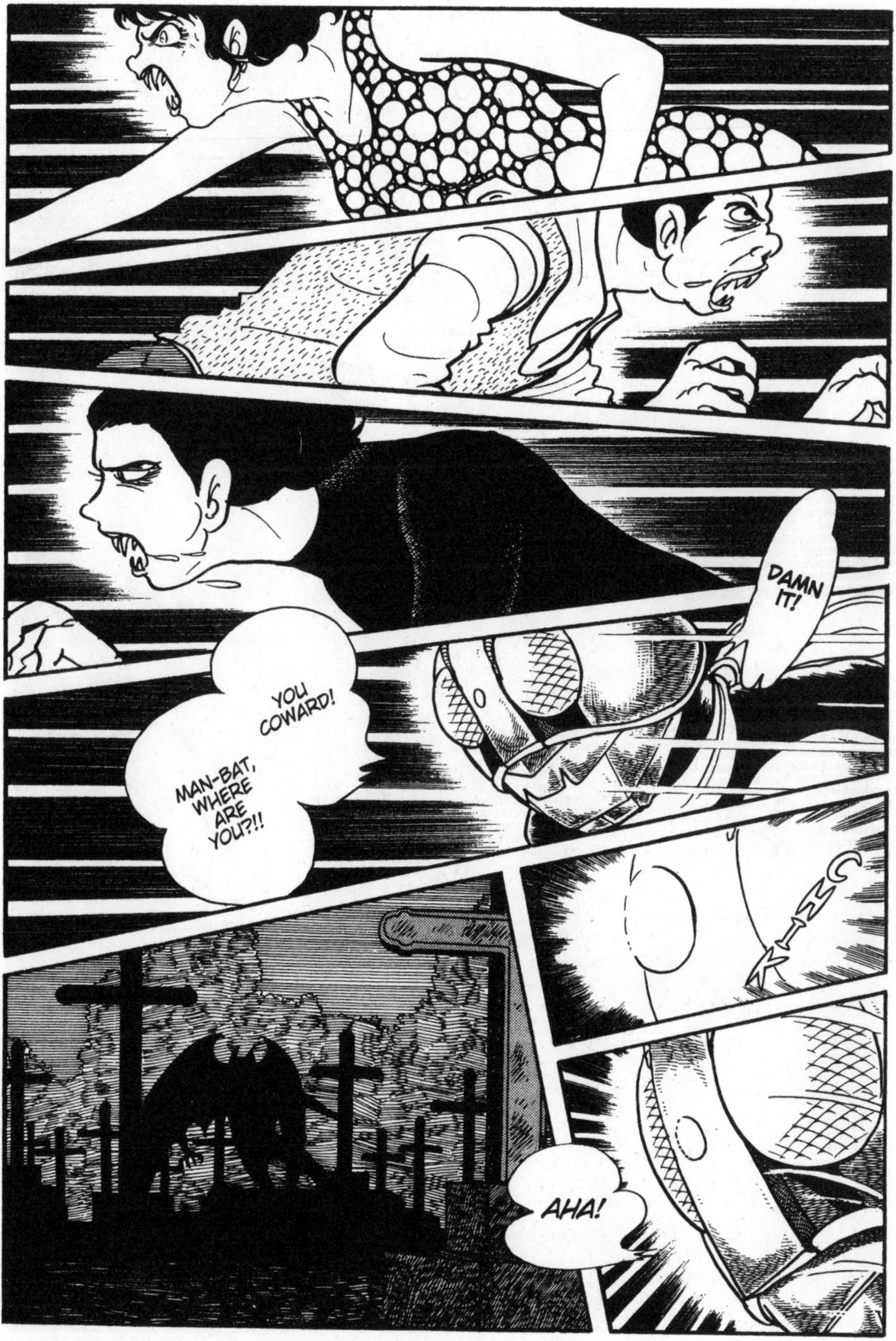
DAMN IT!
YOU COWARD!
MAN-BAT, WHERE ARE YOU?!!
CHIK
AHA!

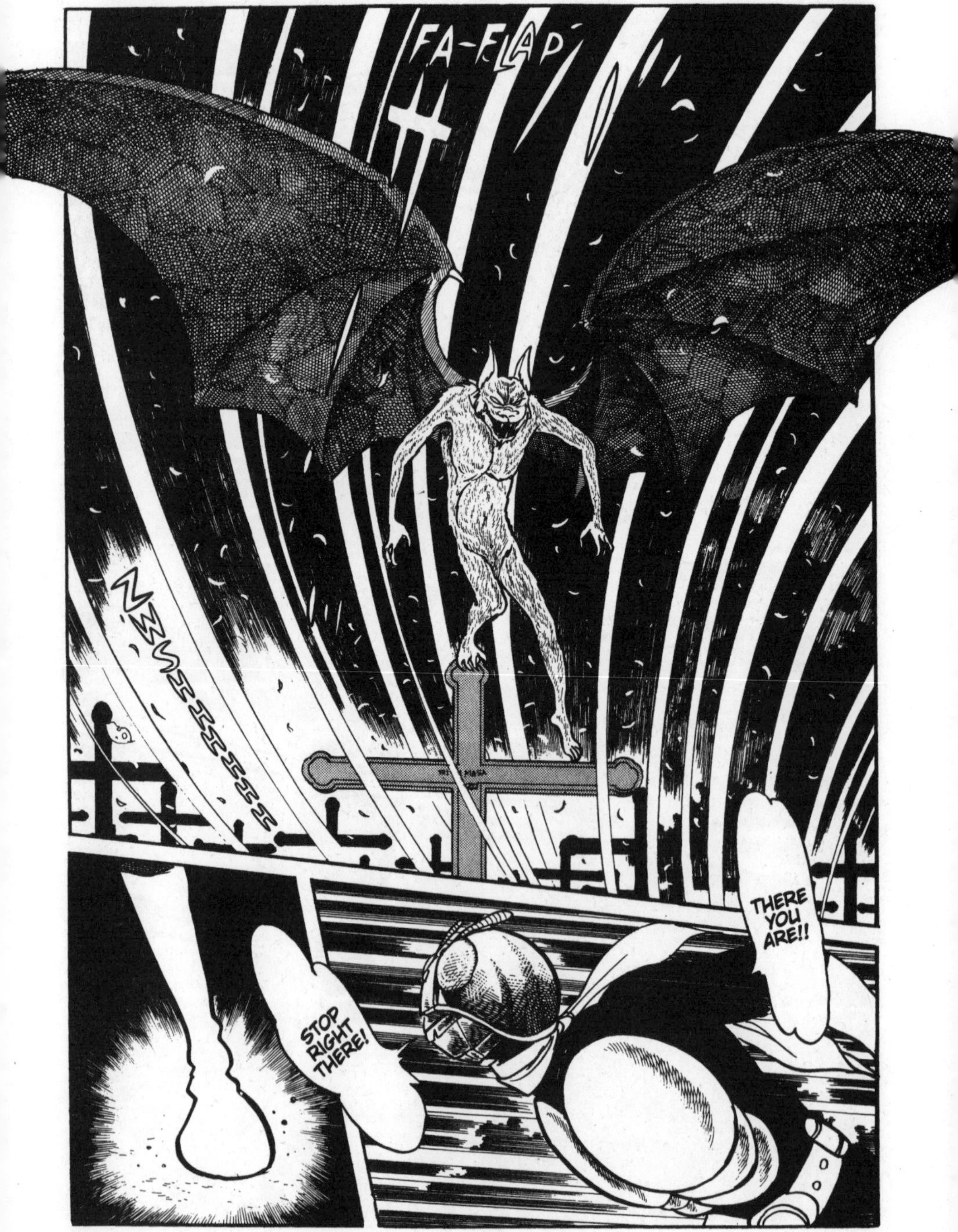
FA-FLAP
NWSHHHHHH
THERE YOU ARE!!
STOP RIGHT THERE!

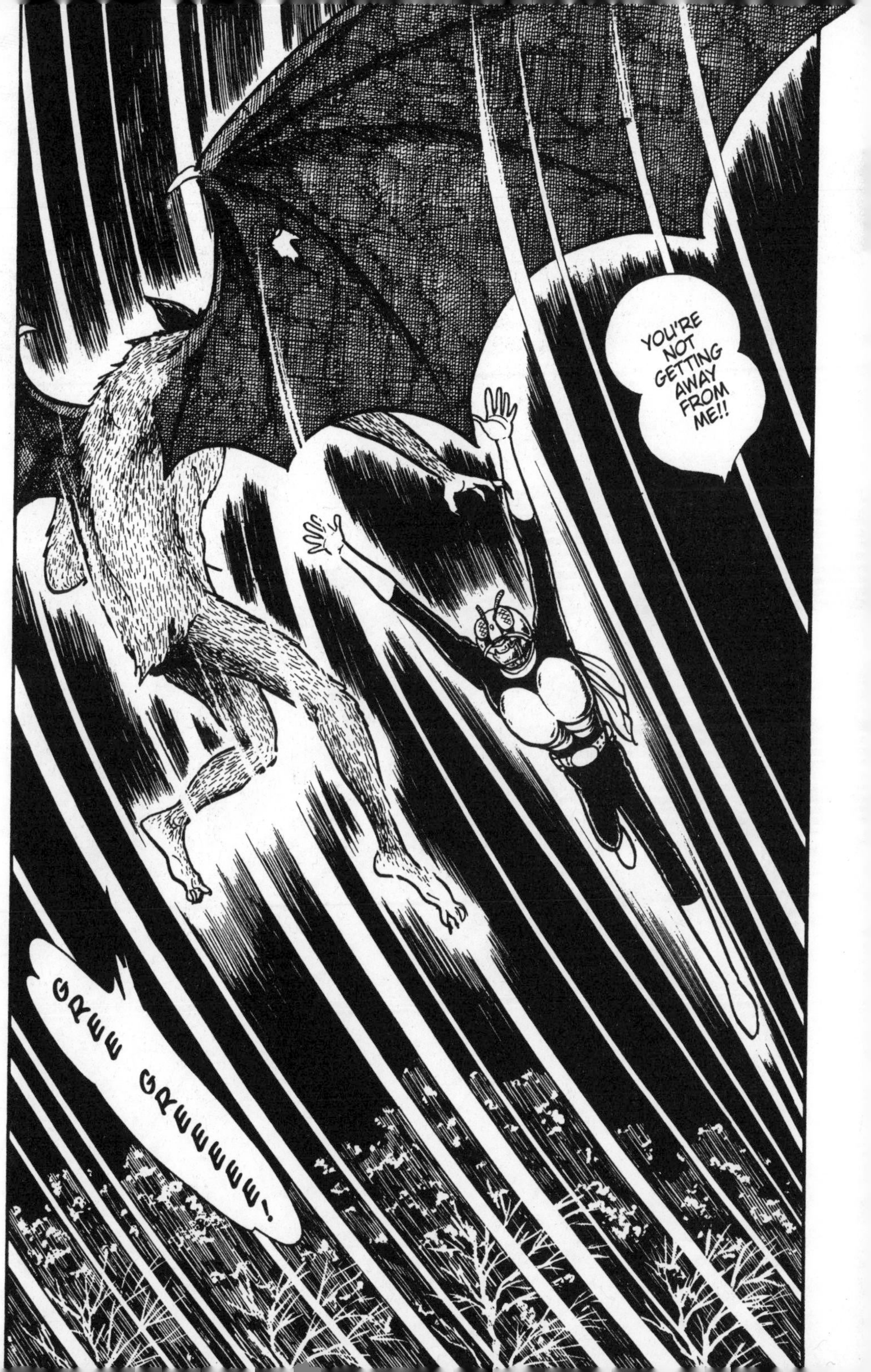
YOU'RE NOT GETTING AWAY FROM ME!!
GREE GREEEEEE!

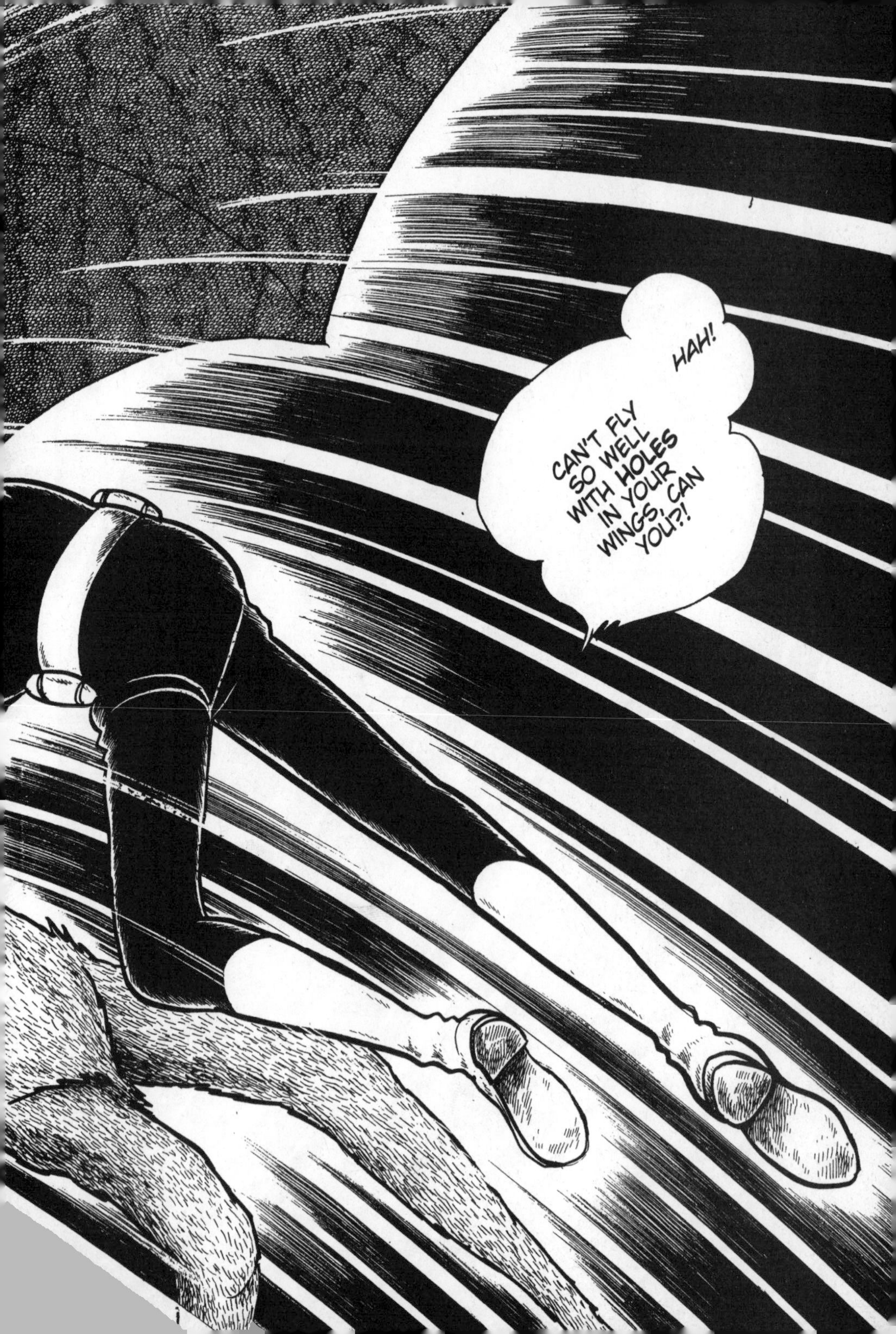
HAH!
CAN'T FLY SO WELL WITH HOLES IN YOUR WINGS, CAN YOU?!

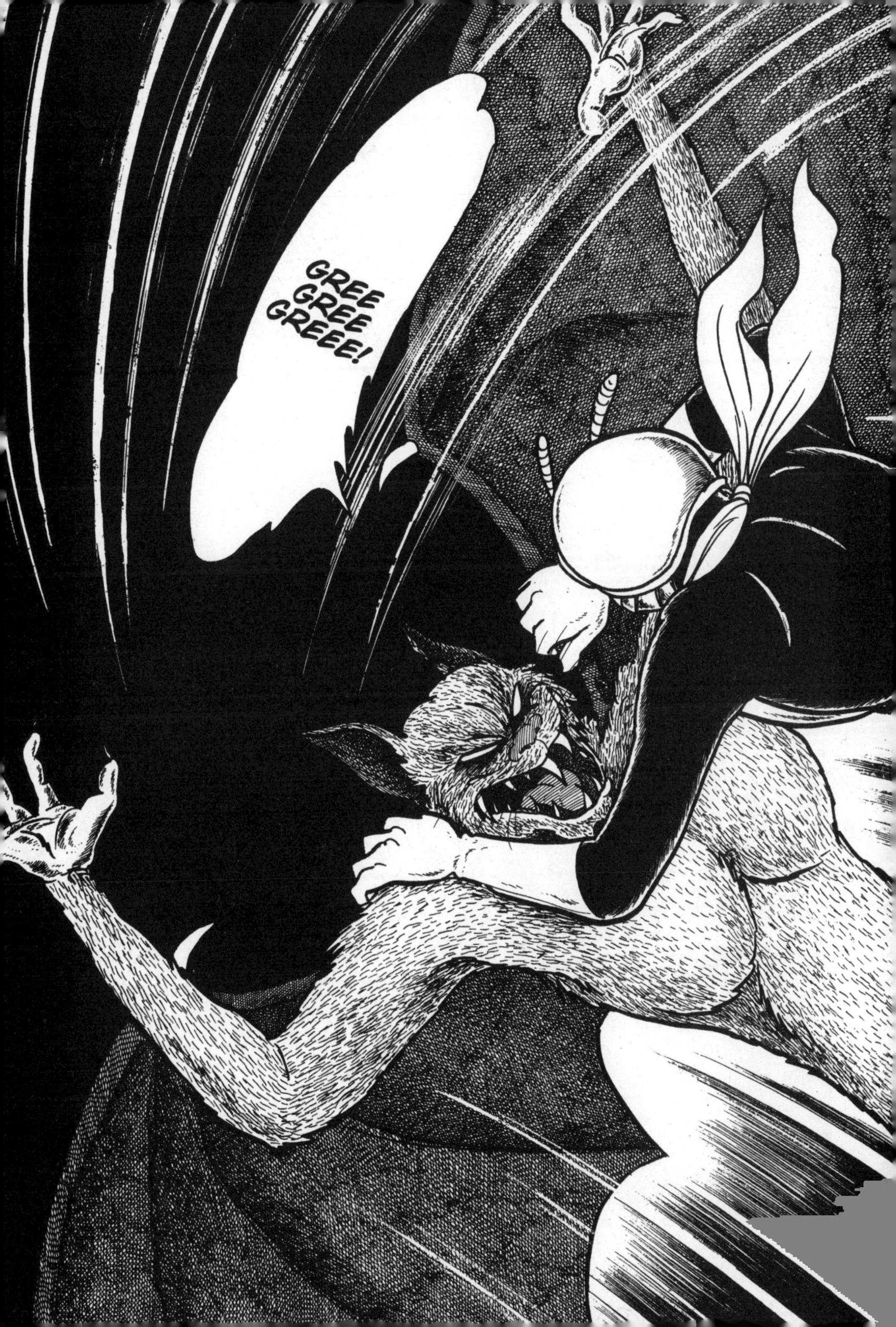
GREE GREE GREEE!

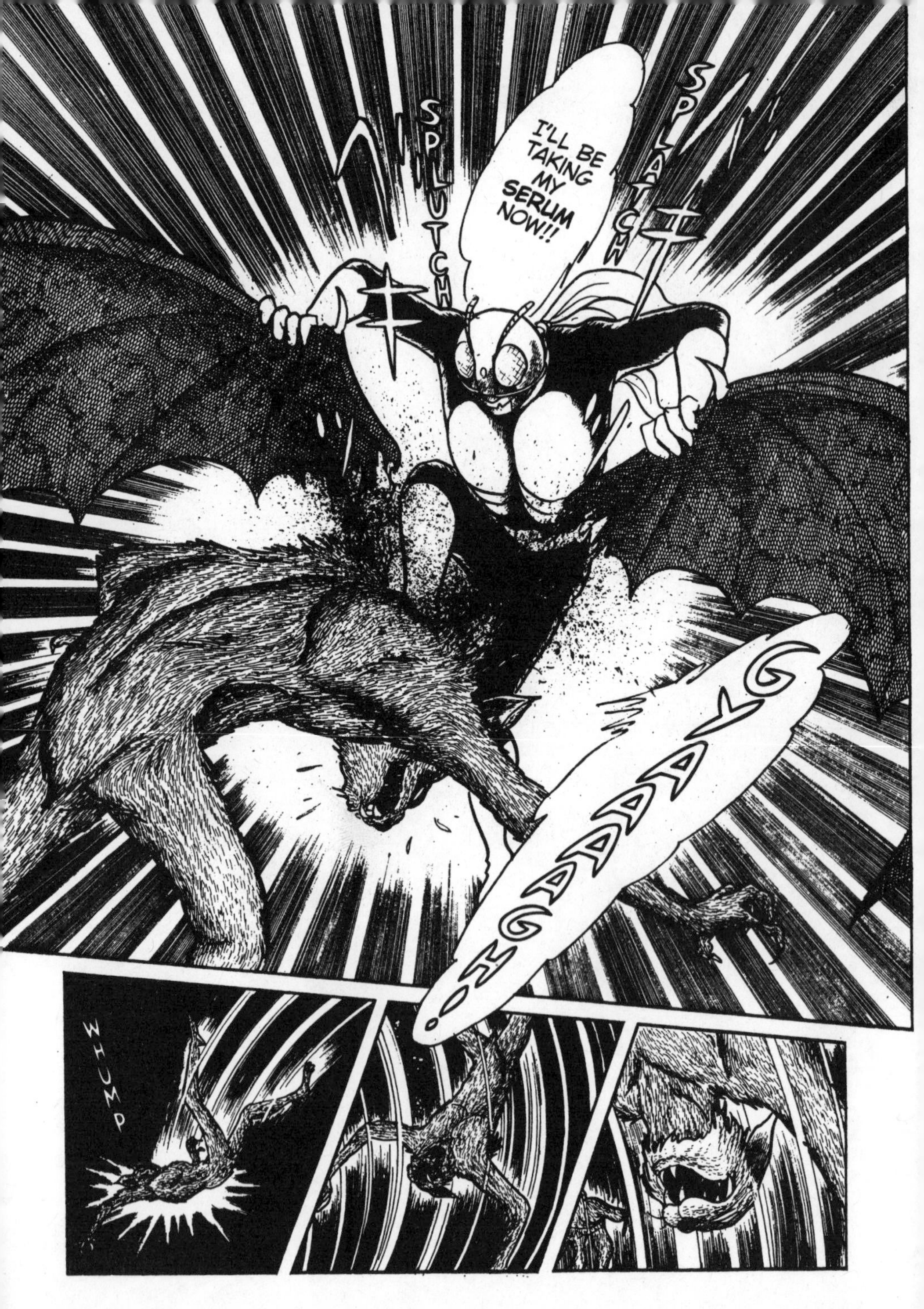
I'LL BE TAKING MY SERUM NOW!!
SPLATCH
SPLUTCH
GYAAAAGH!
WHUMP

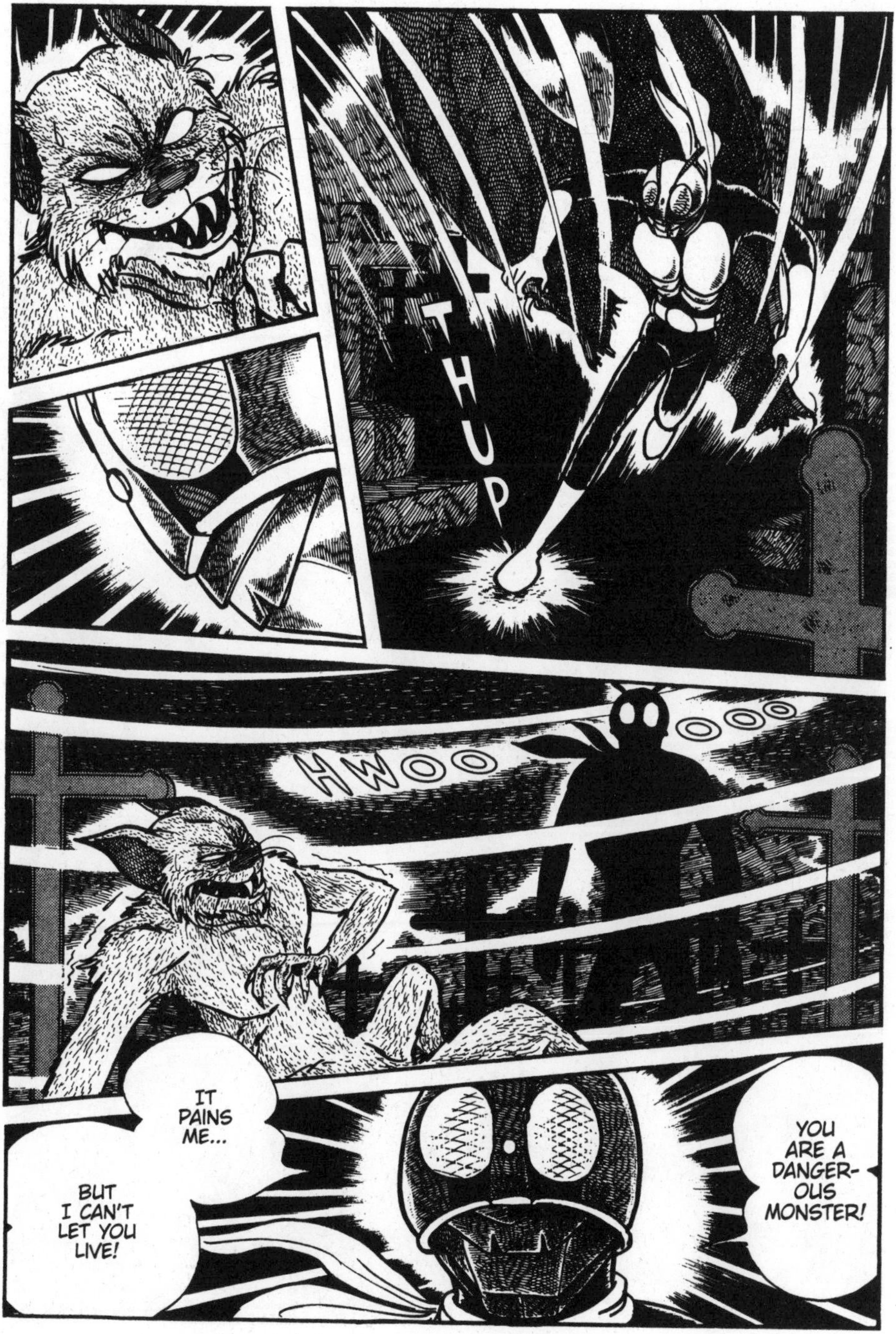
THUP
HWOOOOOO
YOU ARE A DANGER-OUS MONSTER!
IT PAINS ME...
BUT I CAN'T LET YOU LIVE!

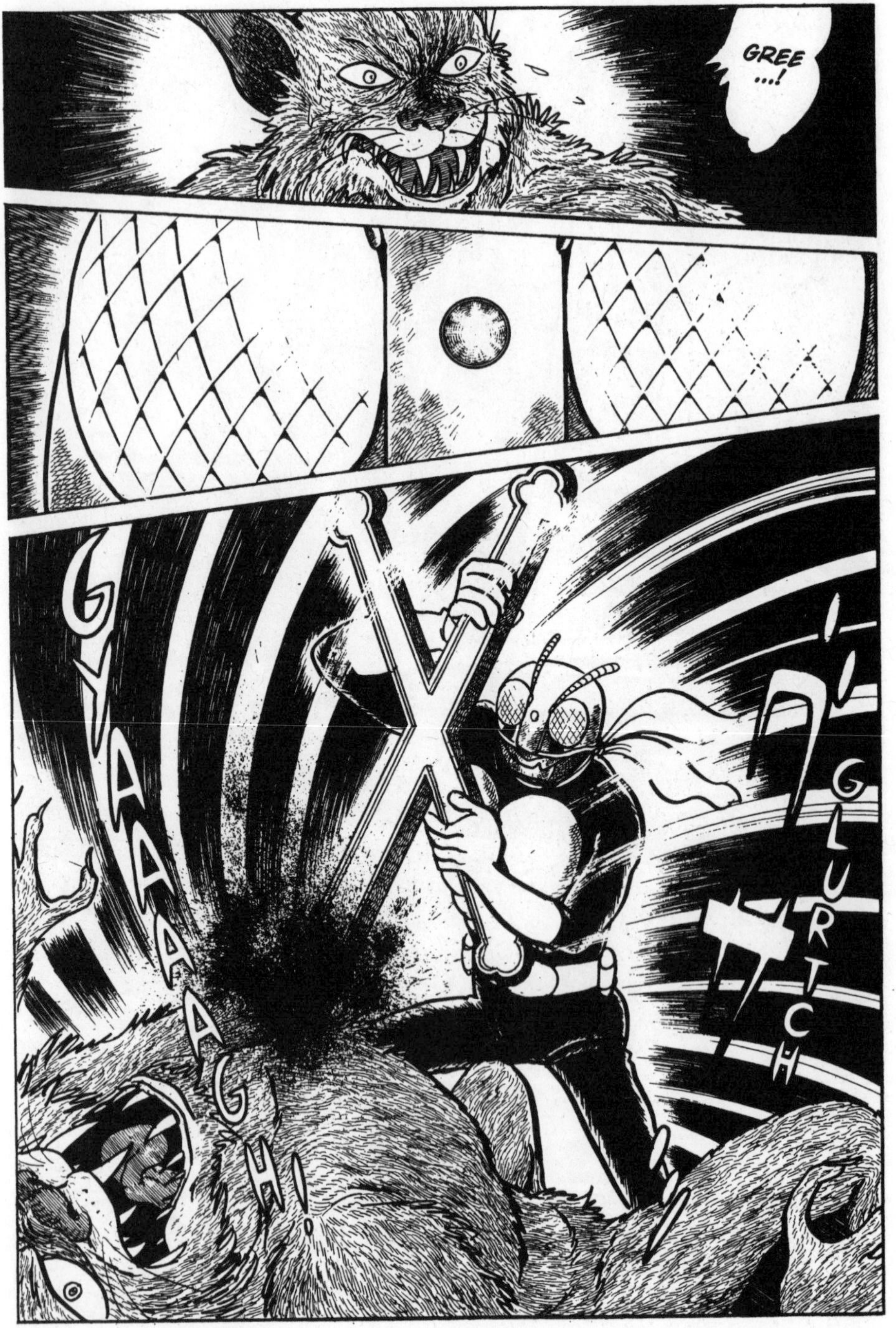
GREE ...!
GLURTCH
GYAAAAAGH!

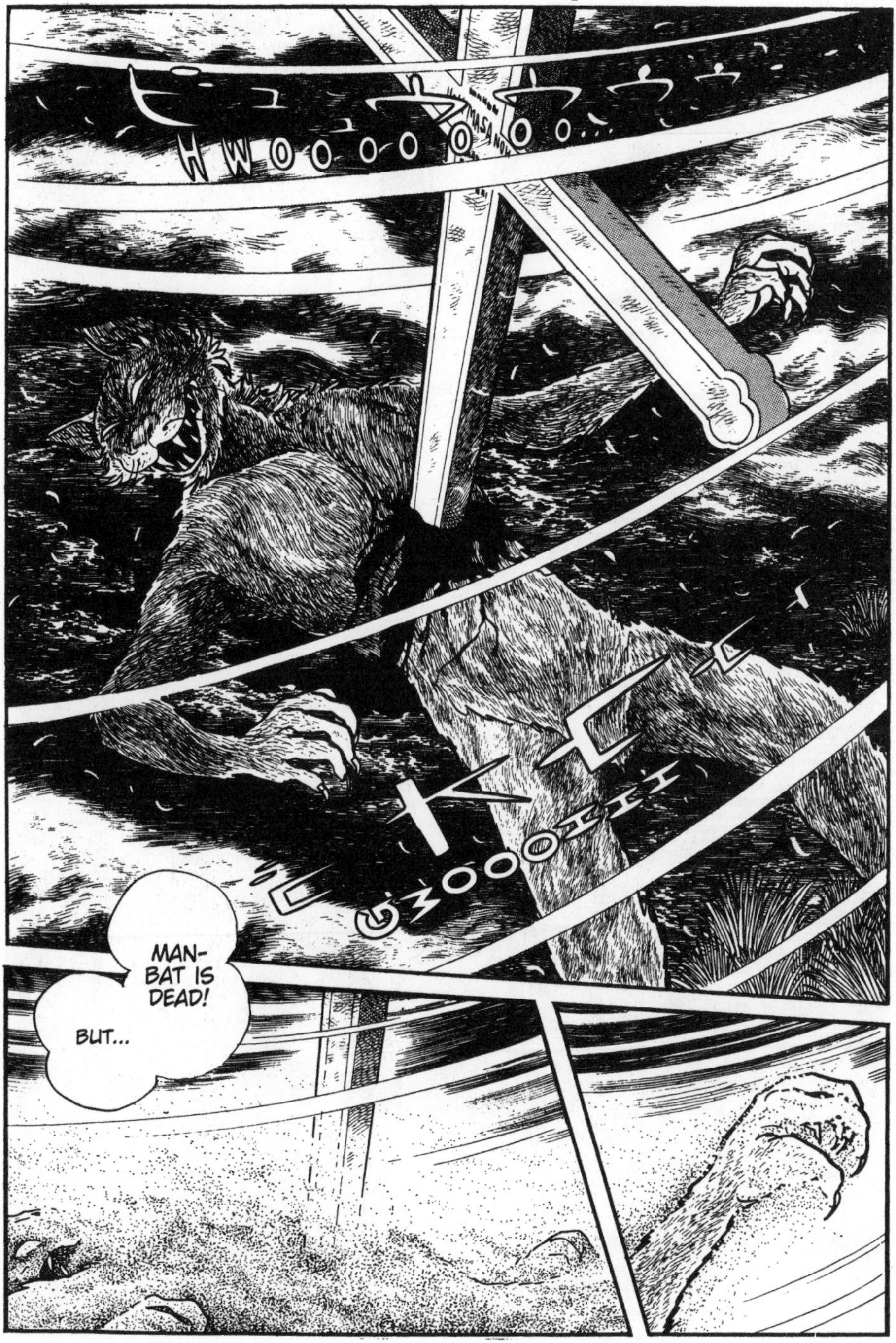
HWOOOOOOO...
GWOOOHHH
MAN-BAT IS DEAD!
BUT...

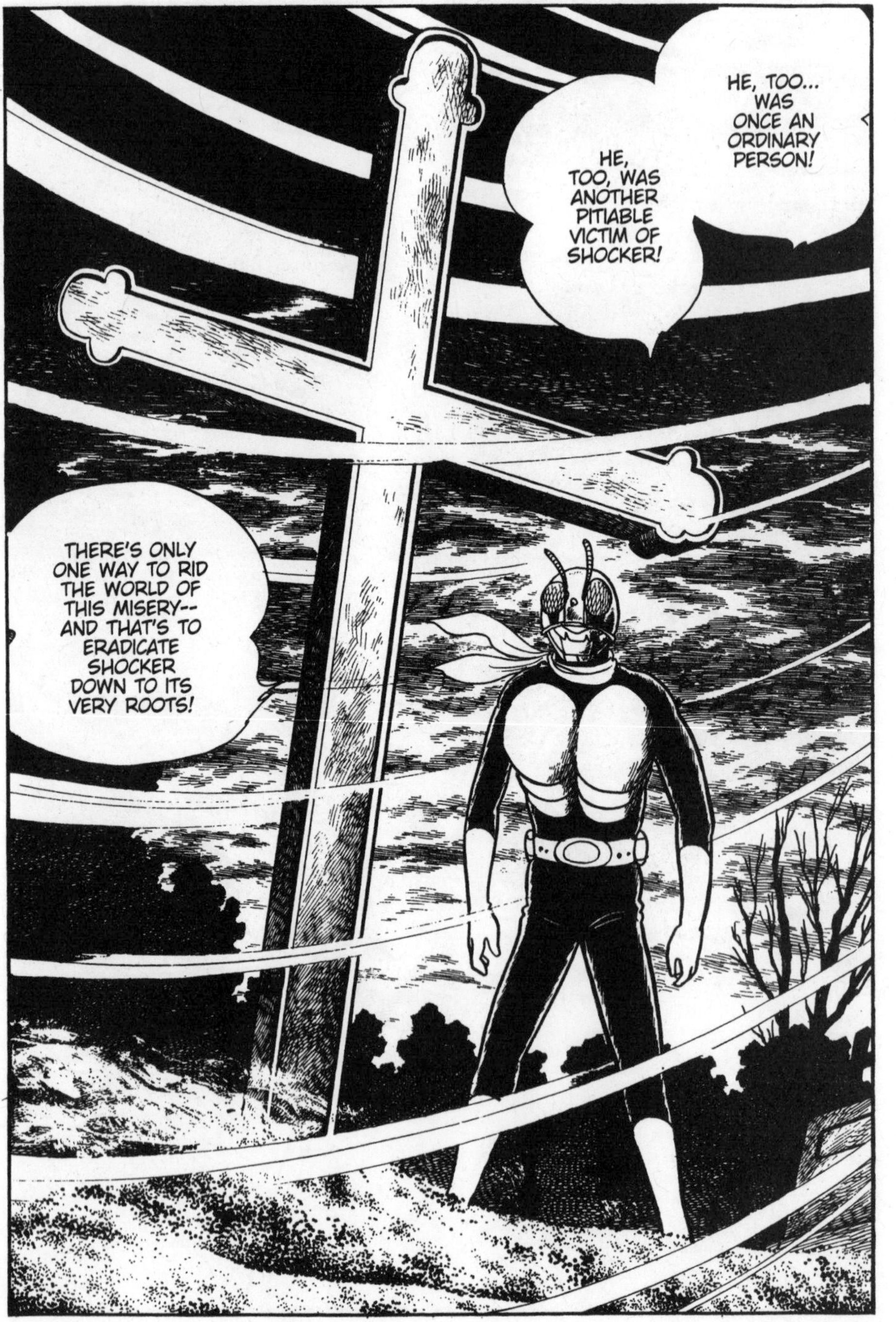
HE, TOO... WAS ONCE AN ORDINARY PERSON!
HE, TOO, WAS ANOTHER PITIABLE VICTIM OF SHOCKER!
THERE'S ONLY ONE WAY TO RID THE WORLD OF THIS MISERY-- AND THAT'S TO ERADICATE SHOCKER DOWN TO ITS VERY ROOTS!

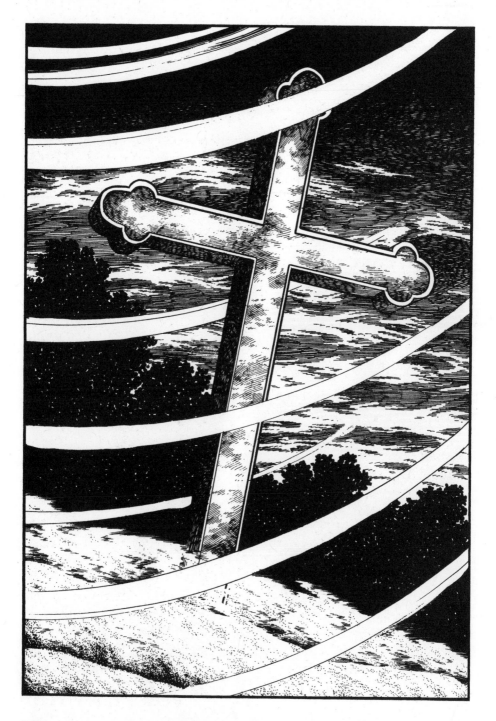

KAMEN RIDER

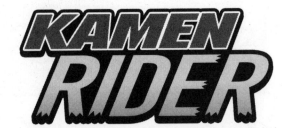

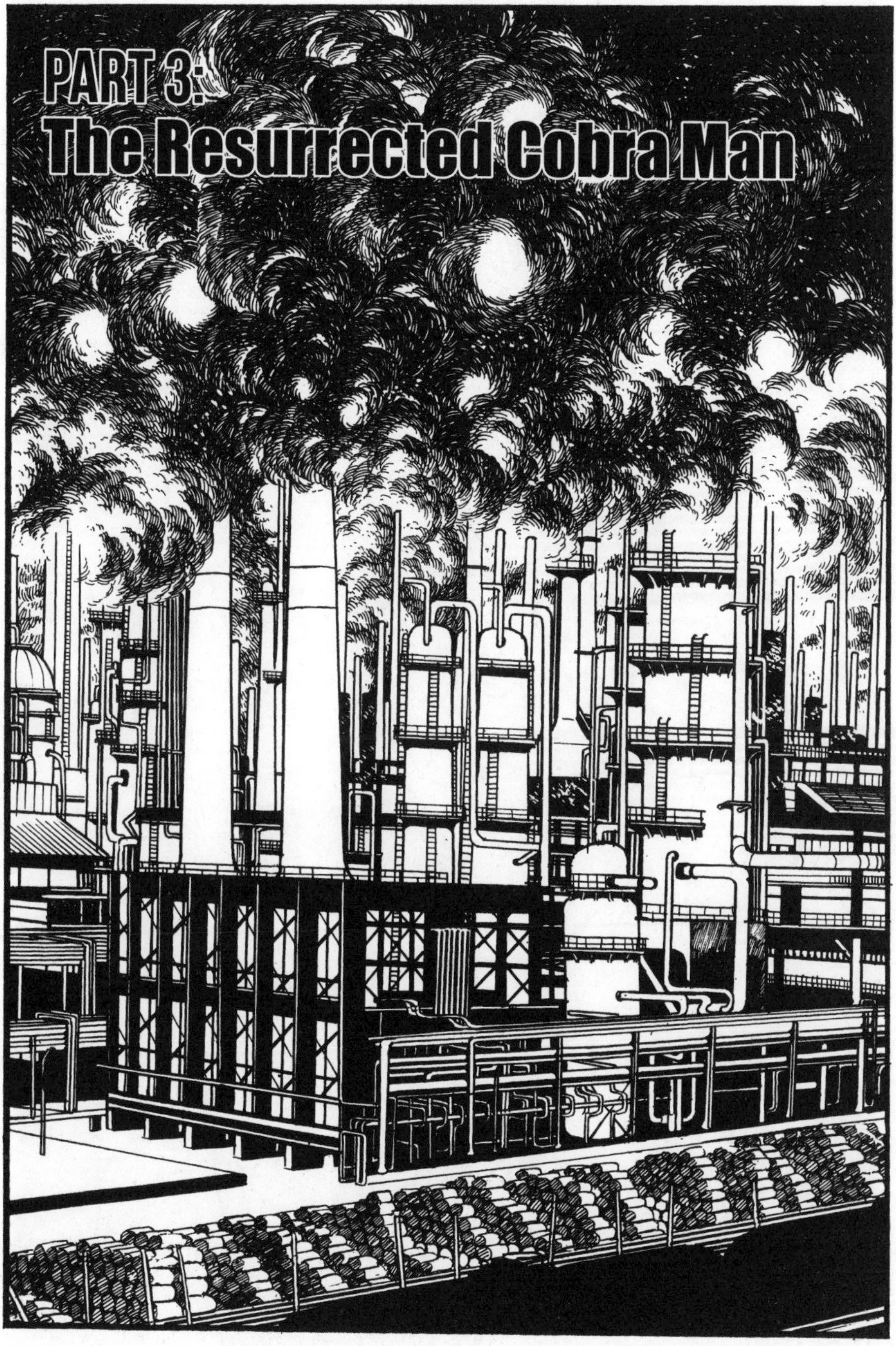
PART 3:
The Resurrected Cobra Man

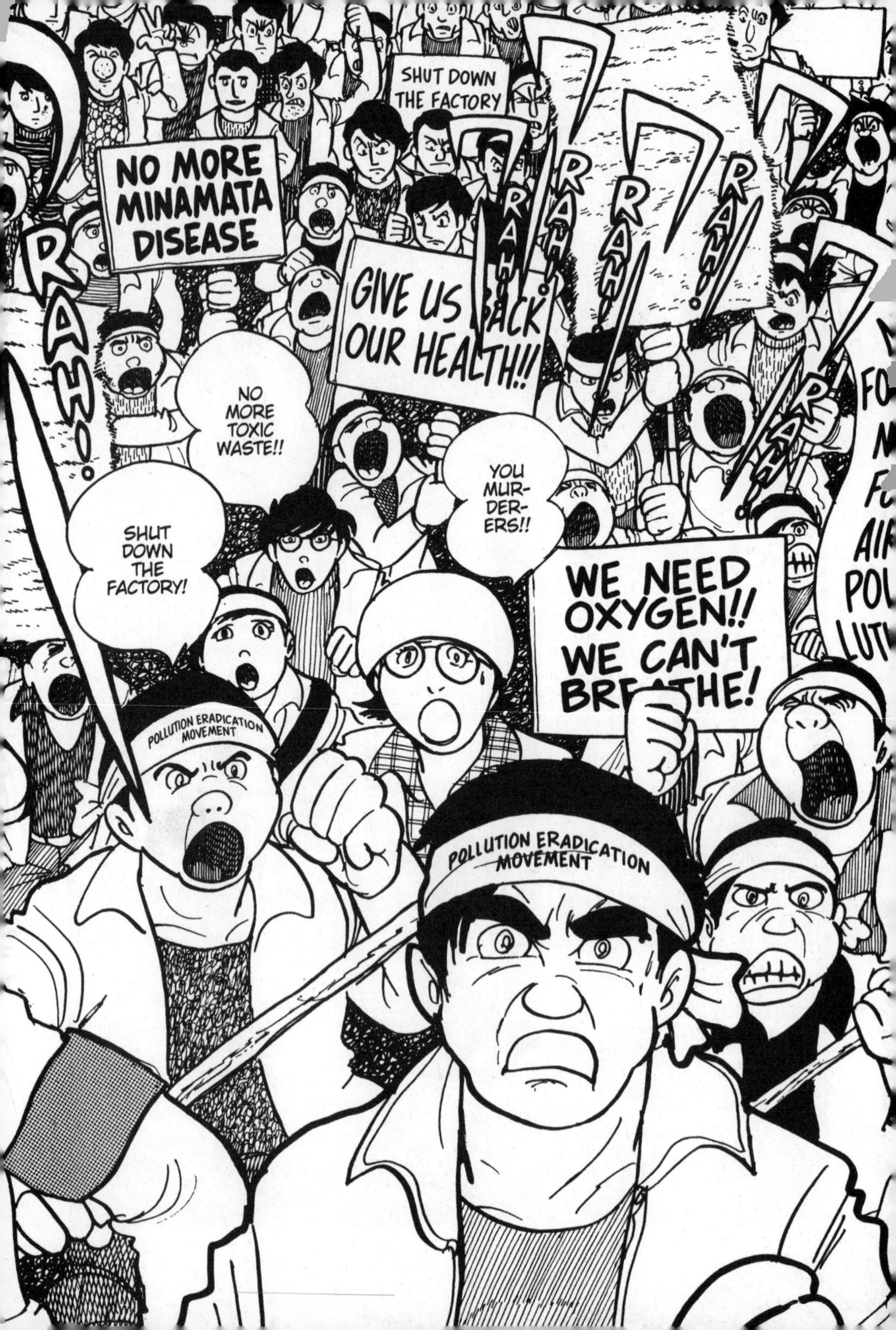
RAH!!
RAH!!
RAH!!
RAH!
SHUT DOWN THE FACTORY
GIVE US BACK OUR HEALTH!!
NO MORE MINAMATA DISEASE
RAH!
WE NEED OXYGEN!! WE CAN'T BREATHE!
YOU MUR-DER-ERS!!
NO MORE TOXIC WASTE!!
SHUT DOWN THE FACTORY!
POLLUTION ERADICATION MOVEMENT
POLLUTION ERADICATION MOVEMENT

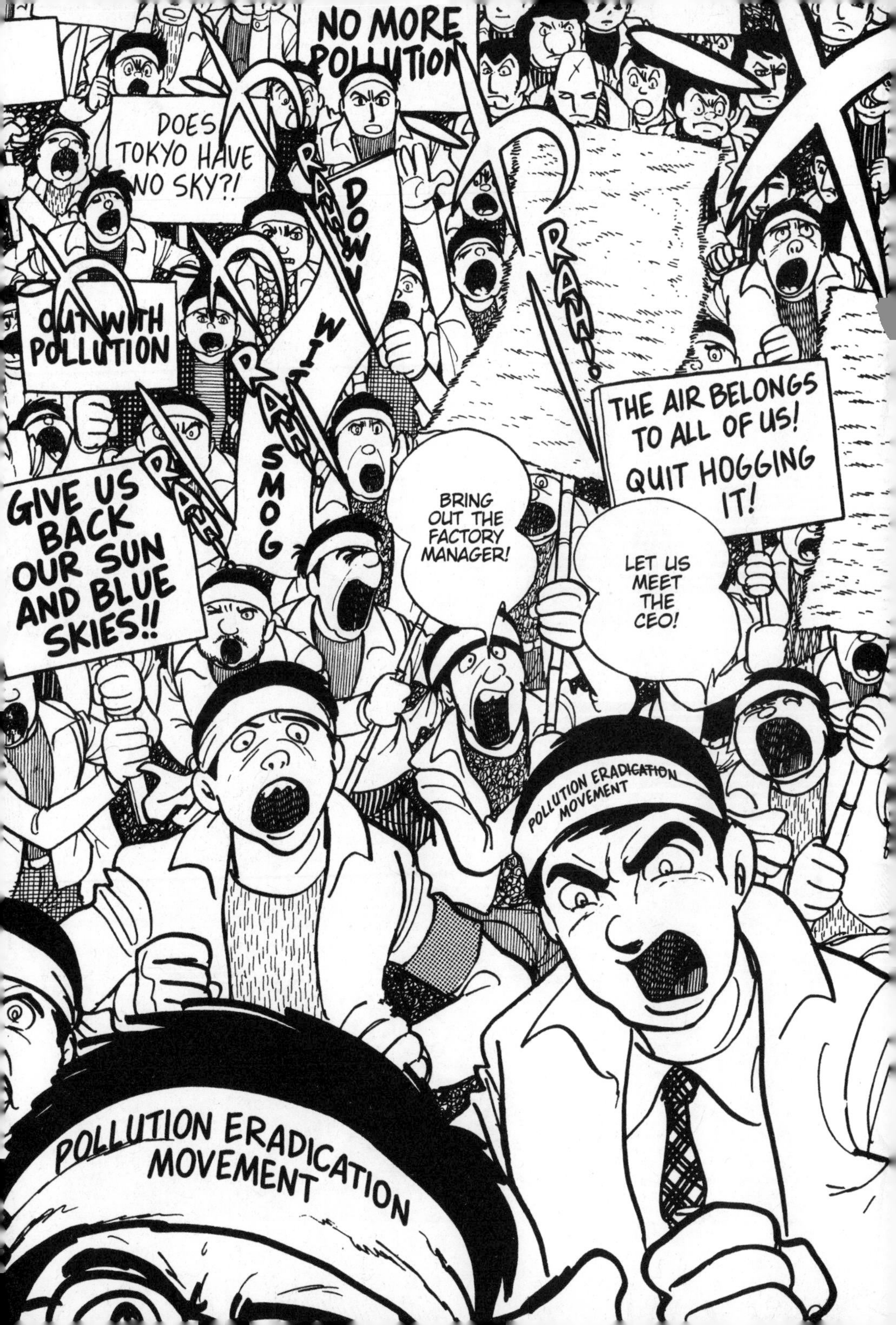
NO MORE POLLUTION
DOES TOKYO HAVE NO SKY?!
THE AIR BELONGS TO ALL OF US! QUIT HOGGING IT!
DOWN WITH SMOG
OUT WITH POLLUTION
LET US MEET THE CEO!
BRING OUT THE FACTORY MANAGER!
GIVE US BACK OUR SUN AND BLUE SKIES!!
POLLUTION ERADICATION MOVEMENT
POLLUTION ERADICATION MOVEMENT

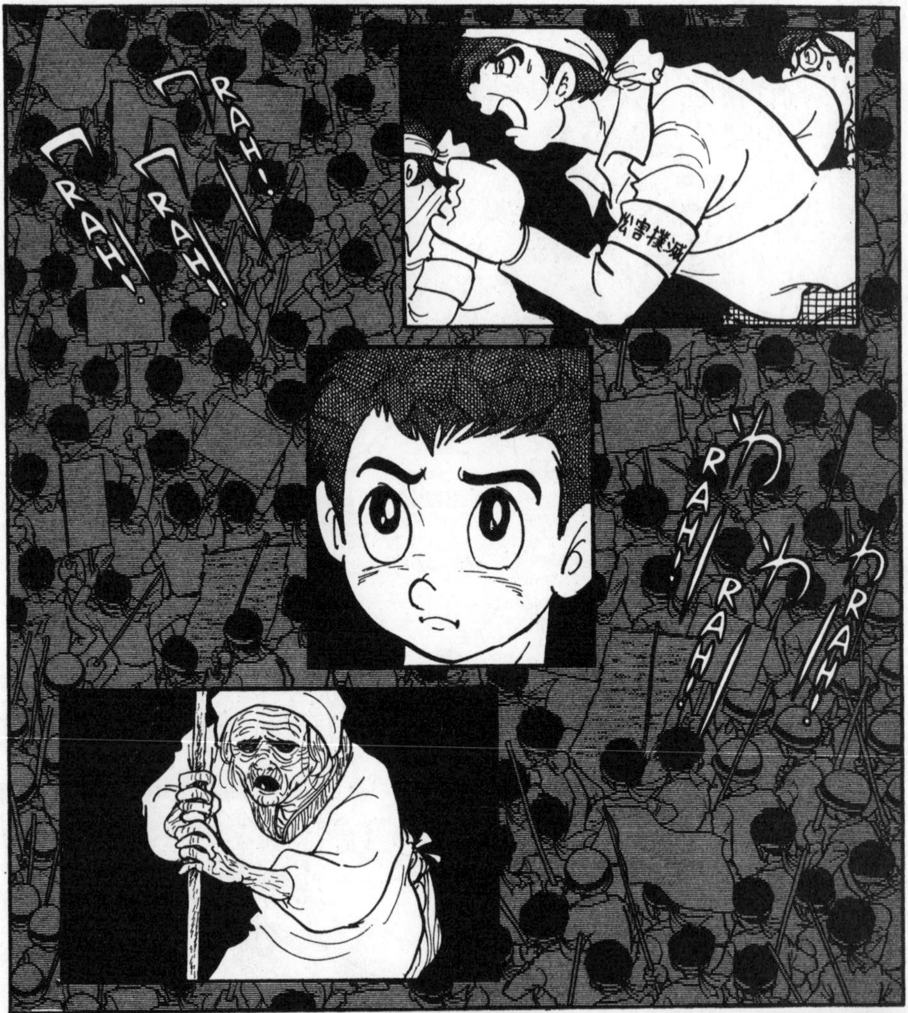

公害撲滅
RAH!
RAH!
RAH!
わ
わ
わ
RAH!
RAH!
RAH!

Armband: Pollution Eradication.

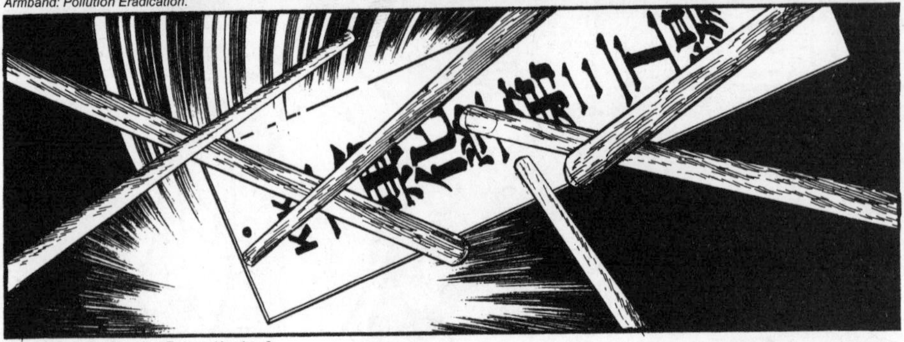
Sign: KK Daikoku Chemical Factory Number 3.

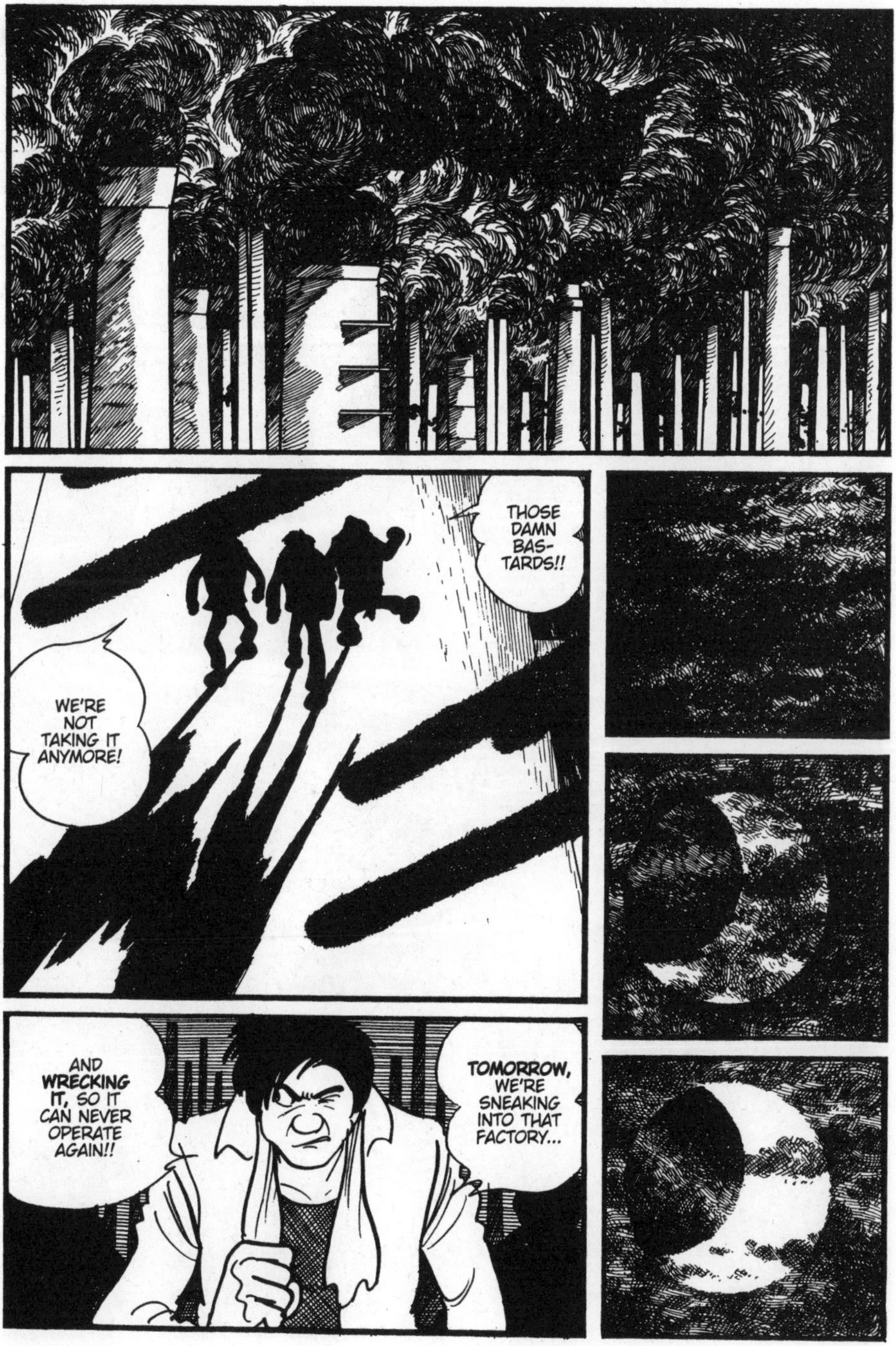
THOSE DAMN BASTARDS!!
WE'RE NOT TAKING IT ANYMORE!
TOMORROW, WE'RE SNEAKING INTO THAT FACTORY...
AND WRECKING IT, SO IT CAN NEVER OPERATE AGAIN!!

LET'S DO IT, LET'S DO IT!
YEAH, YEAH!
LET'S SMASH IT UP!!
HM?
HWSHHHH...
SHH!
SWSH
WHSHHH
SWSH
WH...
WHAT IS THAT?!
SWSH
SWSH
SWSH
THWIP
HUH--?!
URGH!!
WHUH?!

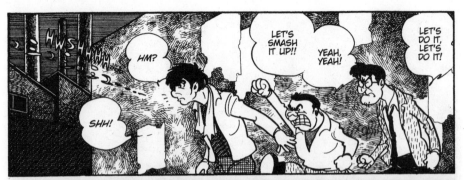

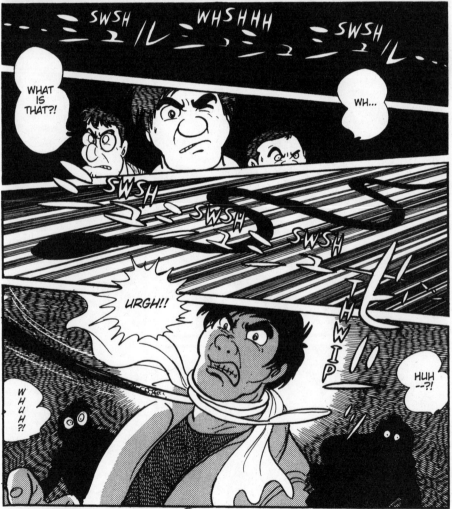

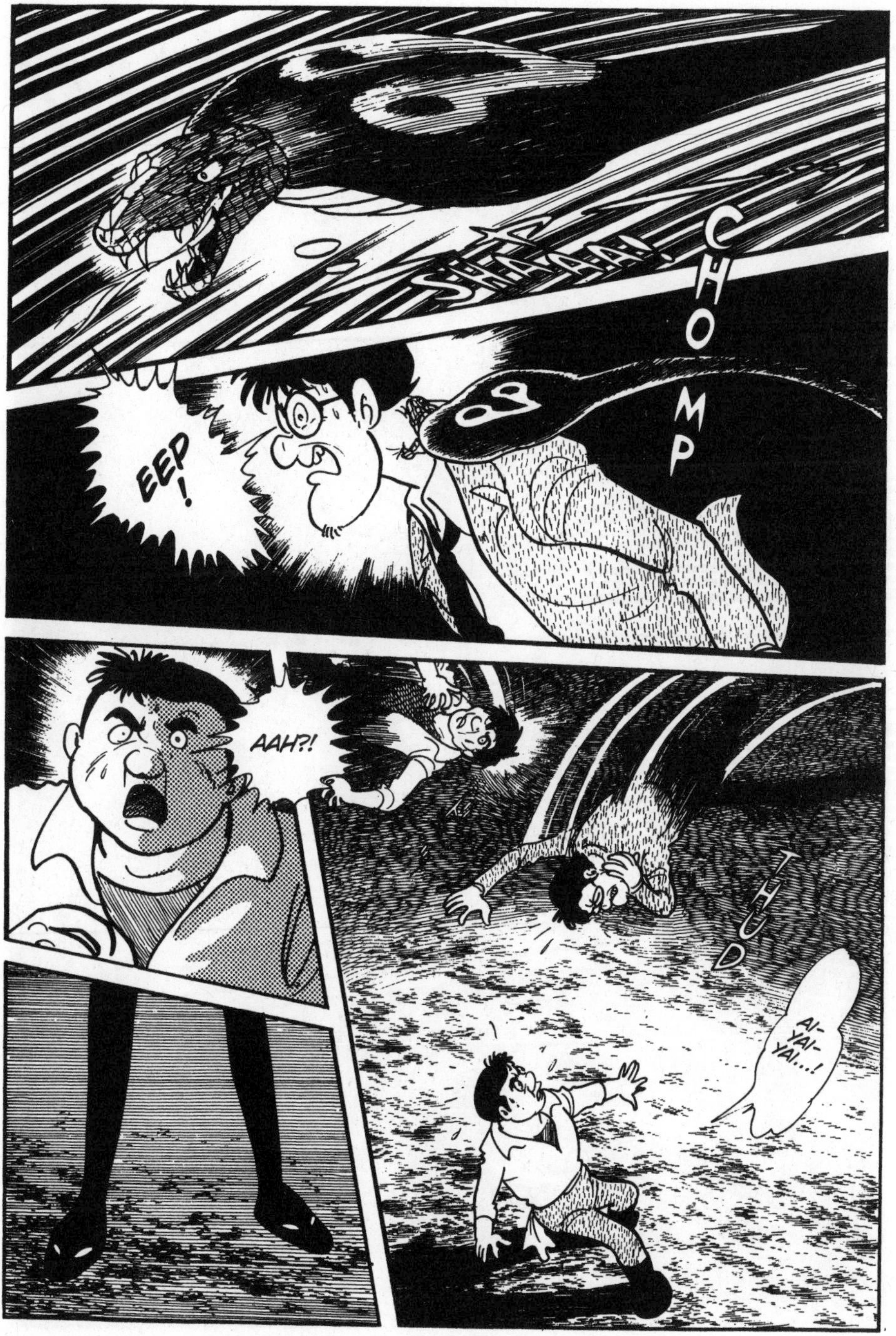
SHAAA!
CHOMP
EEP!
THUD
AI-YAI-YAI...!
AAH?!

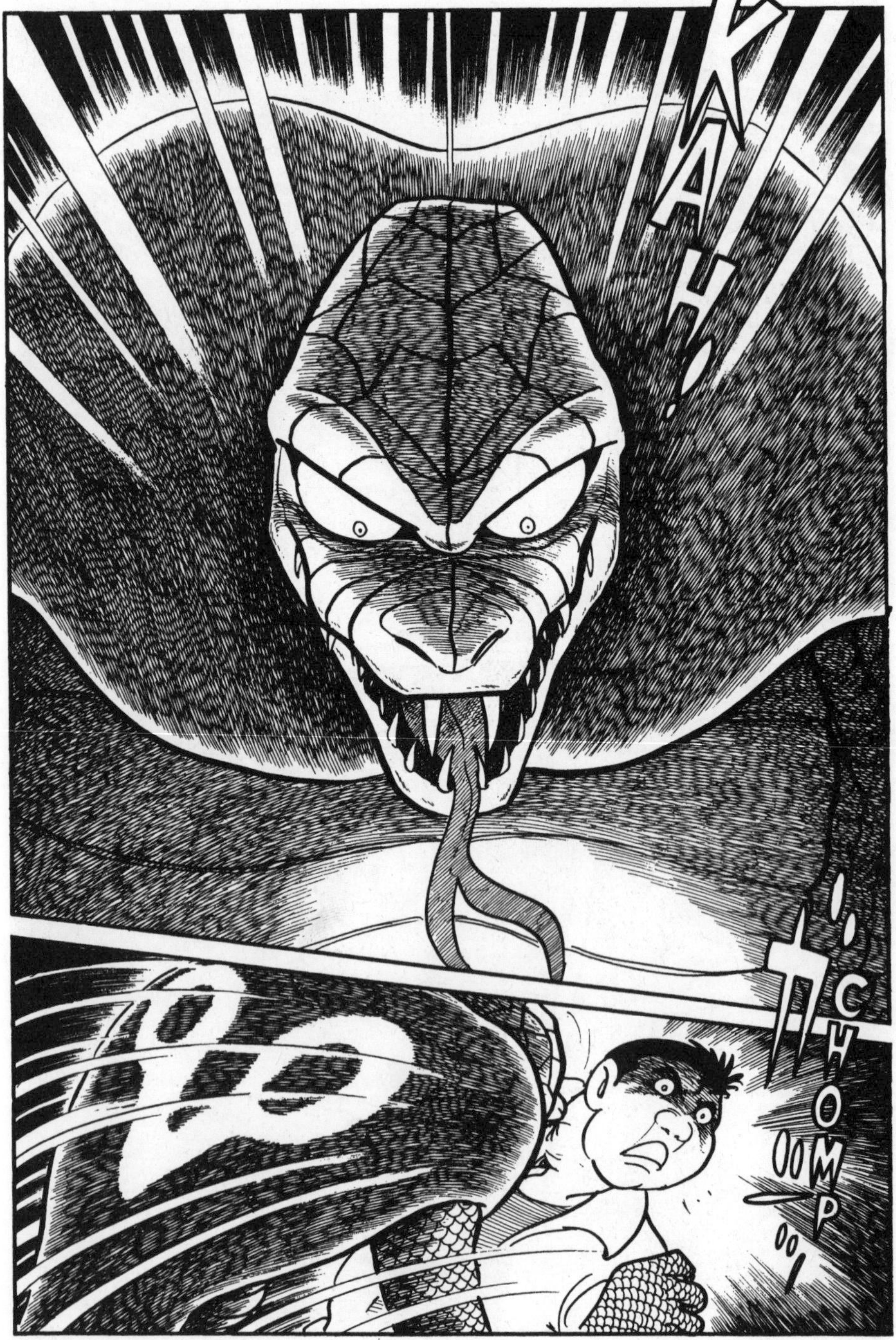
KAAH!!
CHOMP

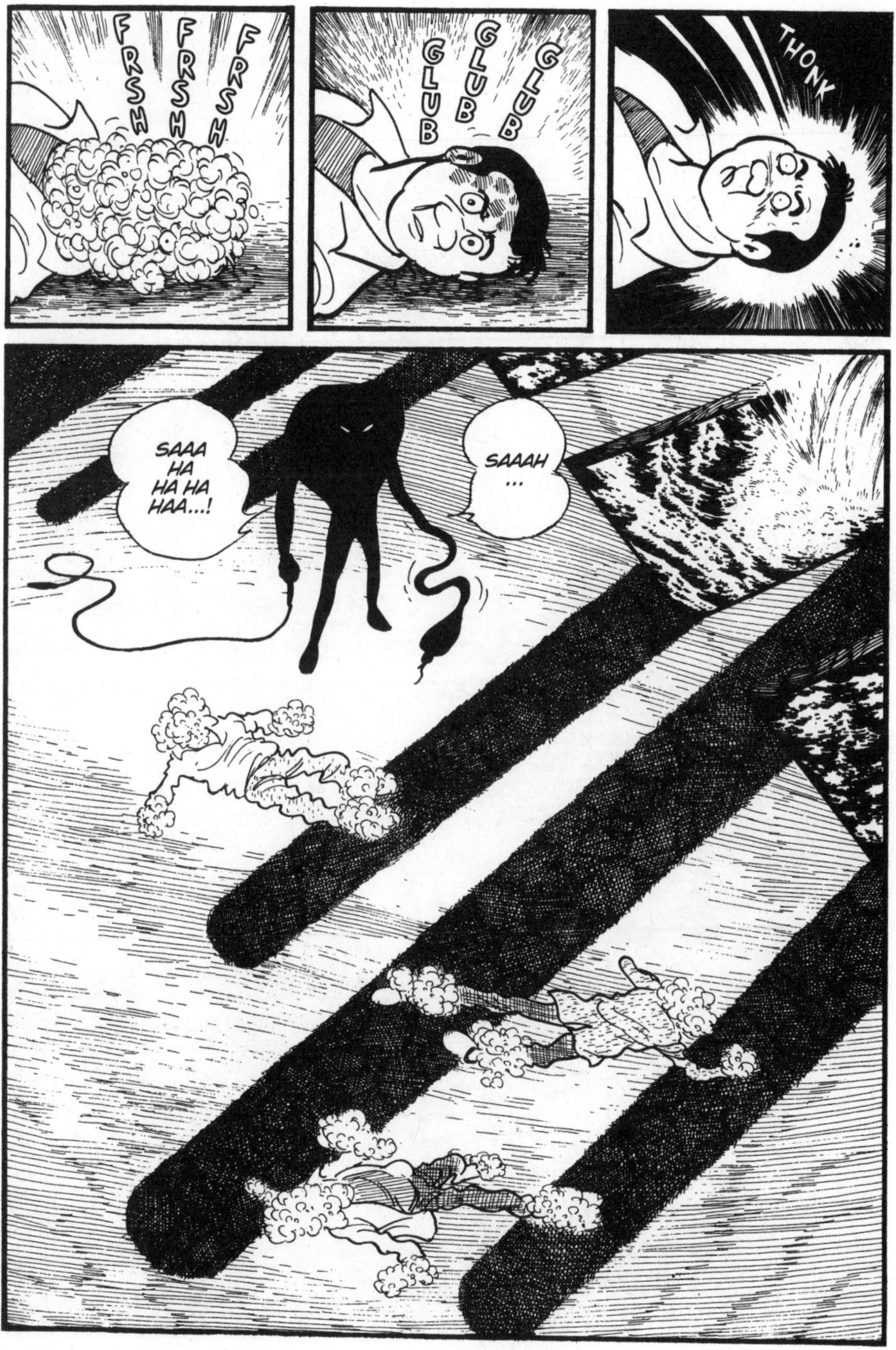
THONK
GLUB GLUB GLUB
FRSH FRSH FRSH
SAAAH ...
SAAA HA HA HA HAA...!

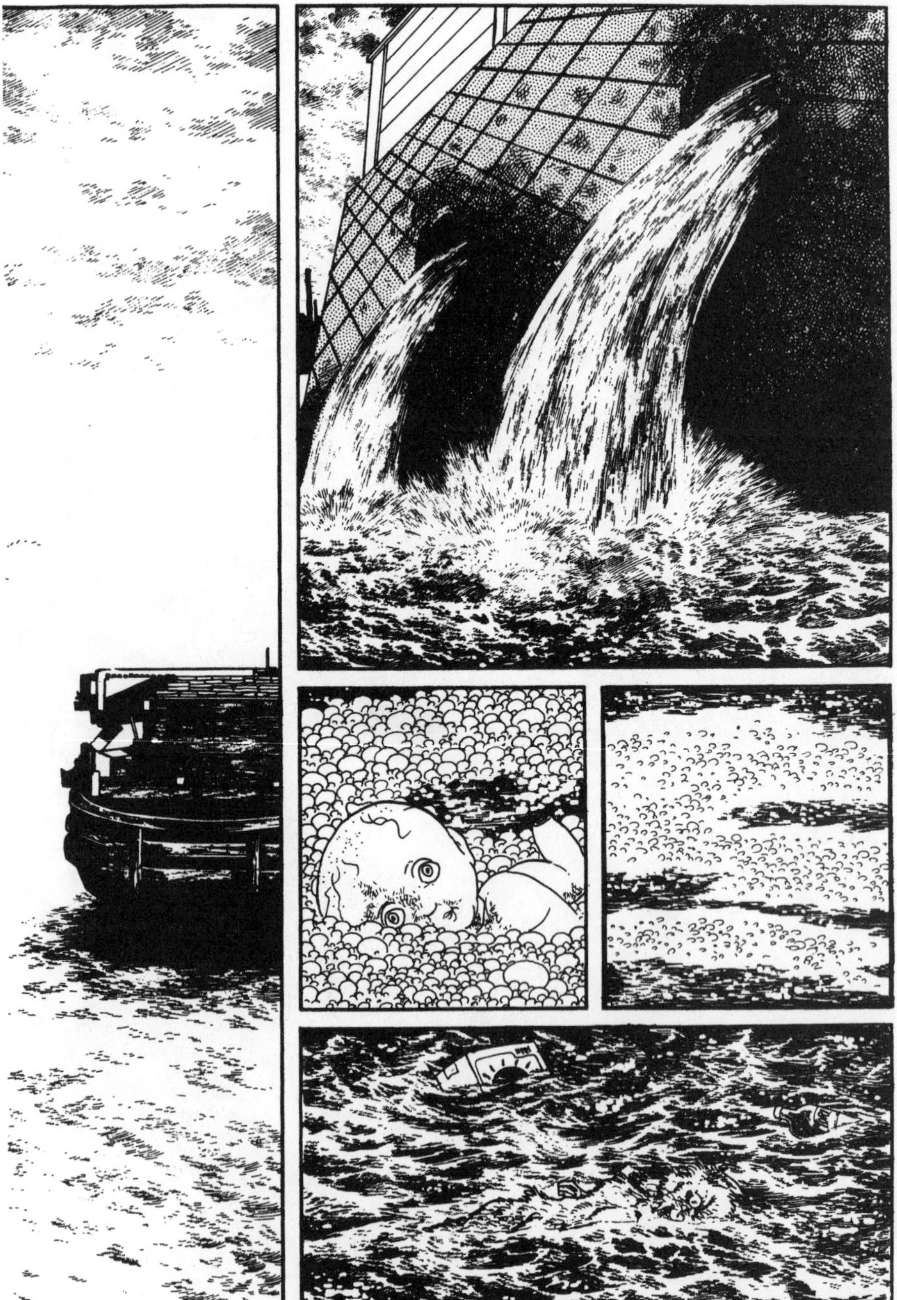

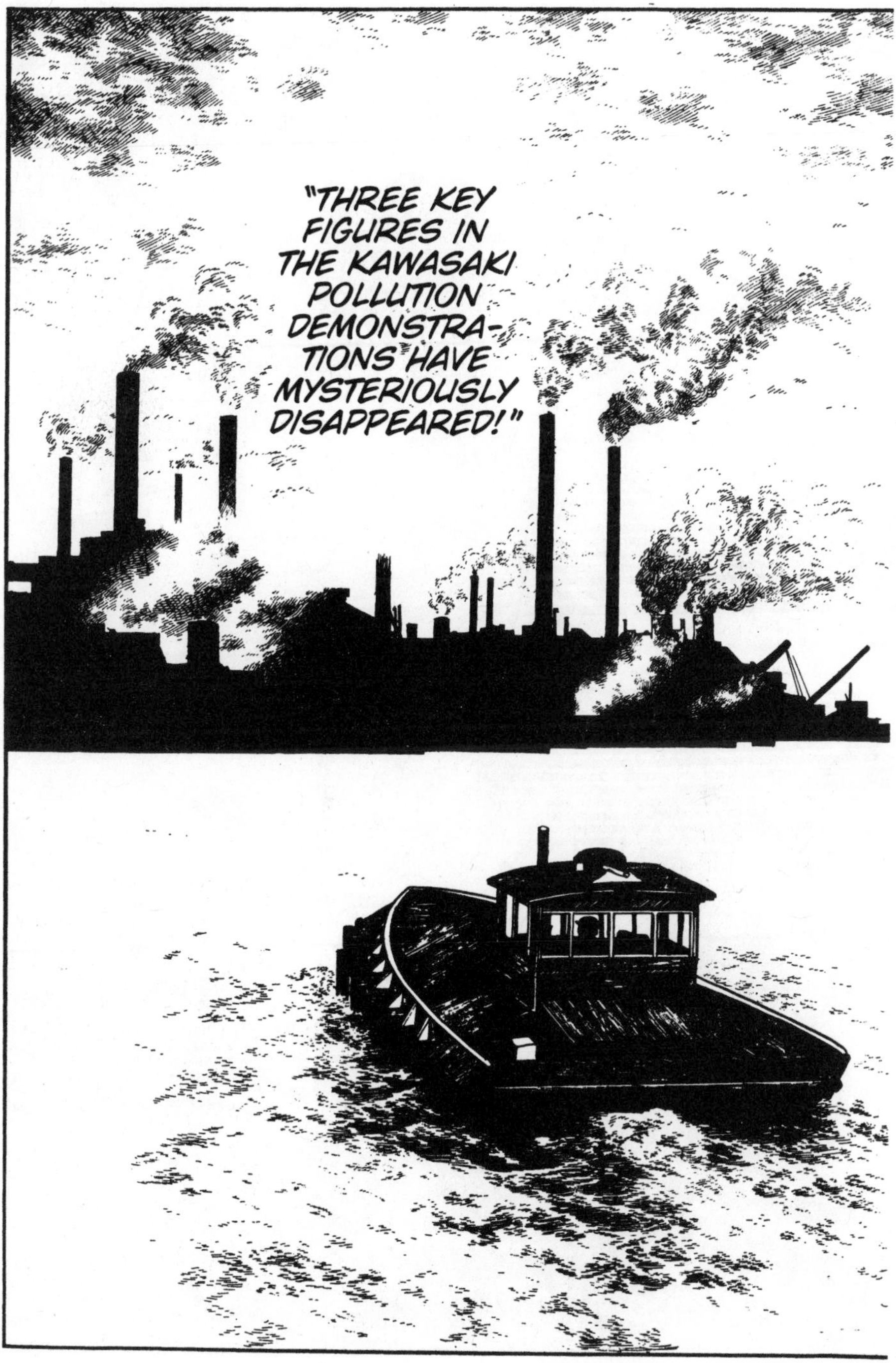
"THREE KEY FIGURES IN THE KAWASAKI POLLUTION DEMONSTRATIONS HAVE MYSTERIOUSLY DISAPPEARED!"

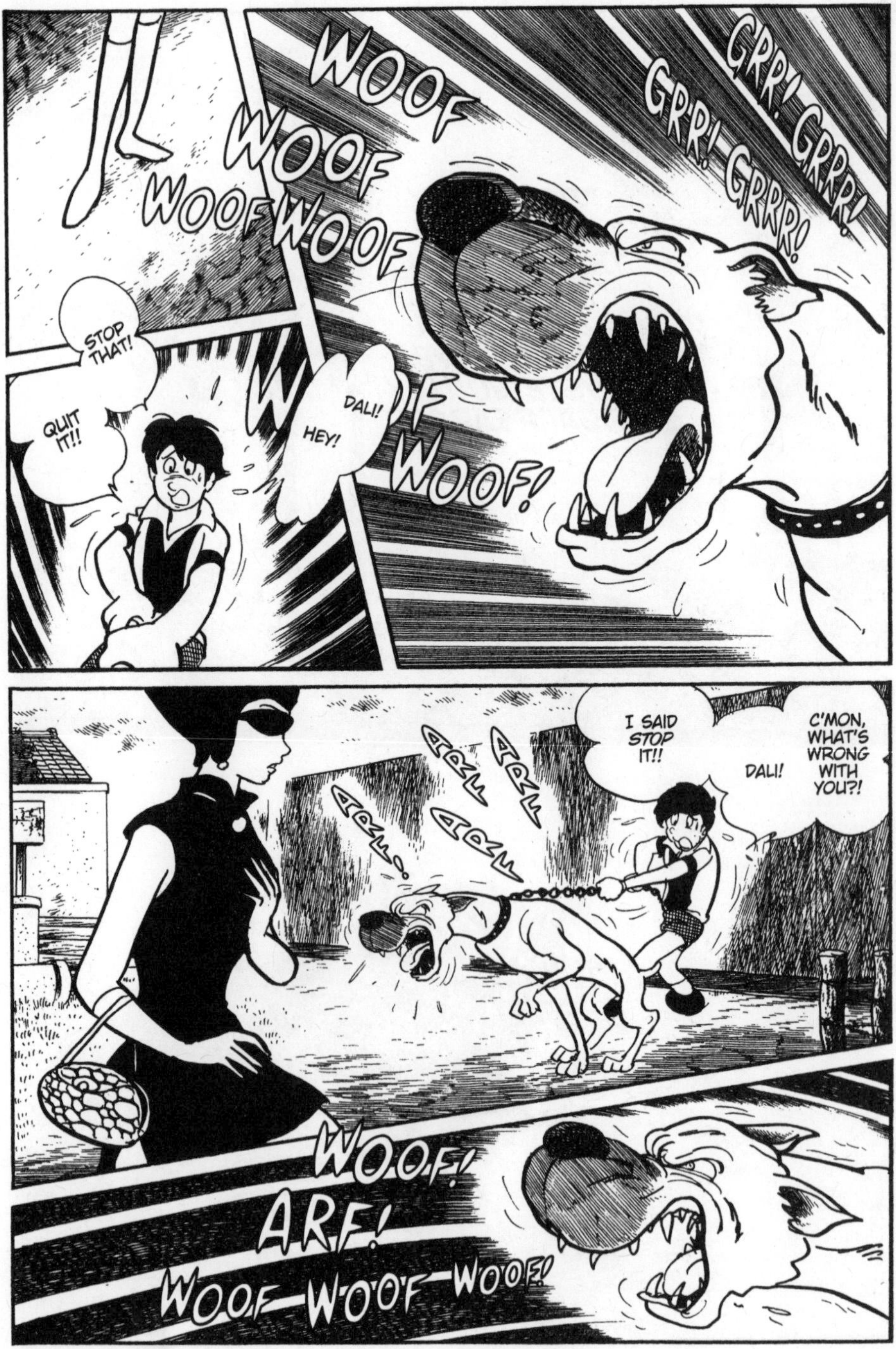
GRR! GRRR!
GRR! GRRR!
WOOF
WOOF
WOOF WOOF
WOOF!
DALI!
HEY!
STOP THAT!
QUIT IT!!
C'MON, WHAT'S WRONG WITH YOU?!
DALI!
I SAID STOP IT!!
ARF ARF
ARF ARF!
WOOF!
ARF!
WOOF WOOF WOOF!

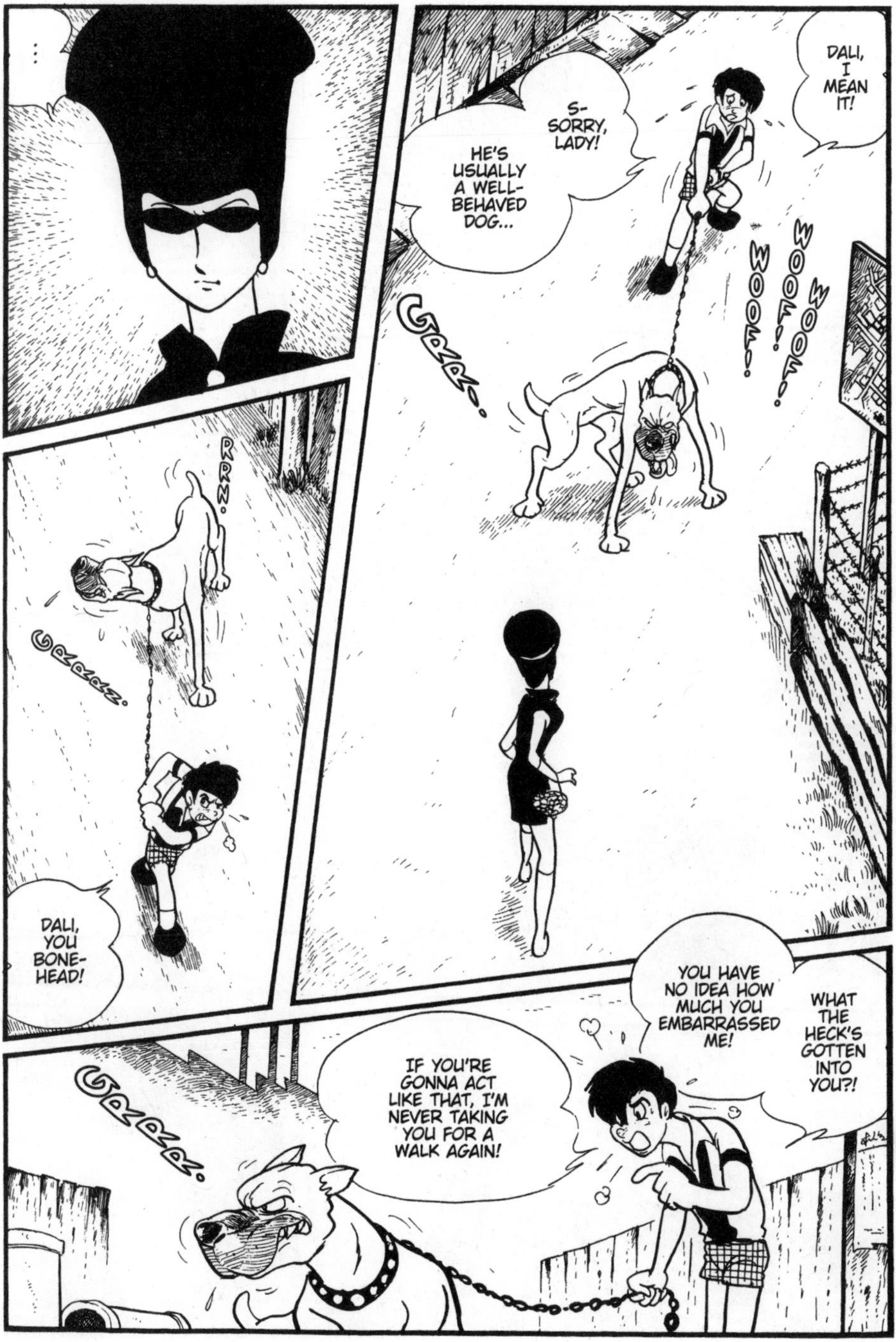
DALI, I MEAN IT!
S-SORRY, LADY!
HE'S USUALLY A WELL-BEHAVED DOG...
WOOF! WOOF! WOOF!
...
RRRN.
DALI, YOU BONEHEAD!
WHAT THE HECK'S GOTTEN INTO YOU?!
YOU HAVE NO IDEA HOW MUCH YOU EMBARRASSED ME!
IF YOU'RE GONNA ACT LIKE THAT, I'M NEVER TAKING YOU FOR A WALK AGAIN!

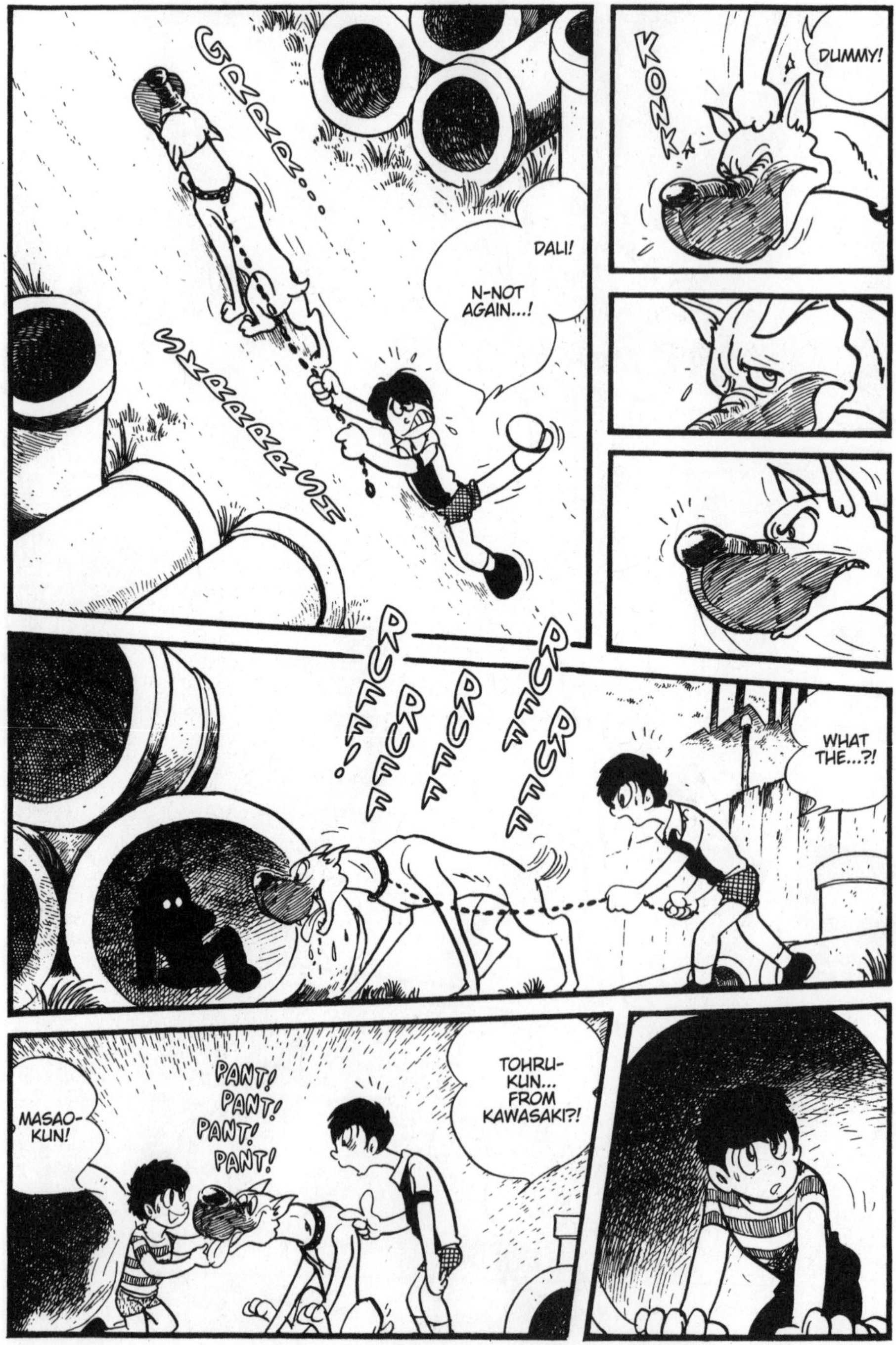
KONK
DUMMY!
DALI!
N-NOT AGAIN...!
GRRRR....
SKRRRRRSH
WHAT THE...?!
RUFF RUFF
RUFF RUFF
RUFF RUFF!
TOHRU-KUN... FROM KAWASAKI?!
PANT! PANT! PANT! PANT!
MASAO-KUN!

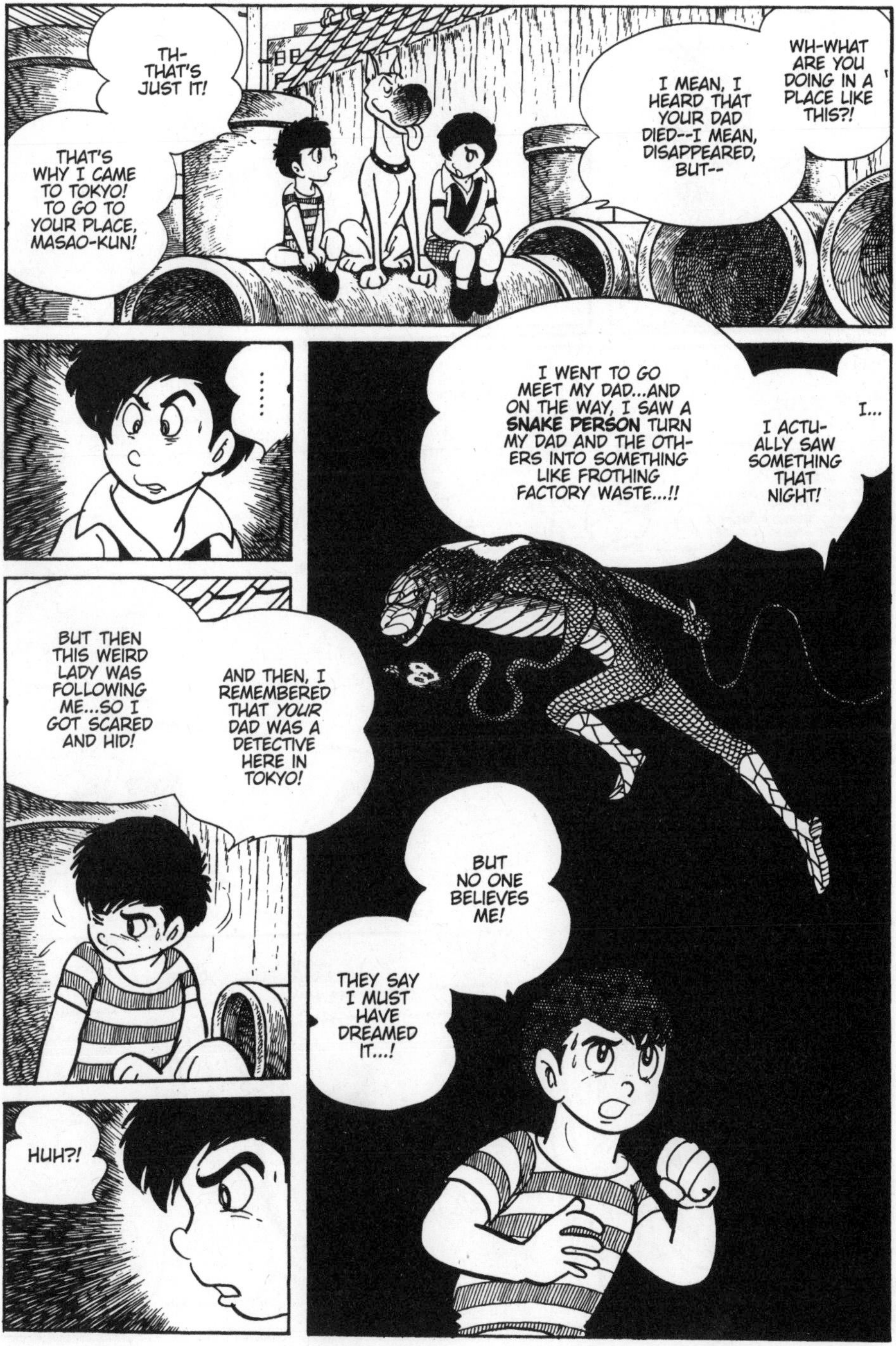
WH-WHAT ARE YOU DOING IN A PLACE LIKE THIS?!
I MEAN, I HEARD THAT YOUR DAD DIED--I MEAN, DISAPPEARED, BUT--
TH- THAT'S JUST IT!
THAT'S WHY I CAME TO TOKYO! TO GO TO YOUR PLACE, MASAO-KUN!
I...
I ACTU-ALLY SAW SOMETHING THAT NIGHT!
I WENT TO GO MEET MY DAD...AND ON THE WAY, I SAW A **SNAKE PERSON** TURN MY DAD AND THE OTH-ERS INTO SOMETHING LIKE FROTHING FACTORY WASTE...!!
BUT NO ONE BELIEVES ME!
THEY SAY I MUST HAVE DREAMED IT...!
......
AND THEN, I REMEMBERED THAT *YOUR* DAD WAS A DETECTIVE HERE IN TOKYO!
BUT THEN THIS WEIRD LADY WAS FOLLOWING ME...SO I GOT SCARED AND HID!
HUH?!

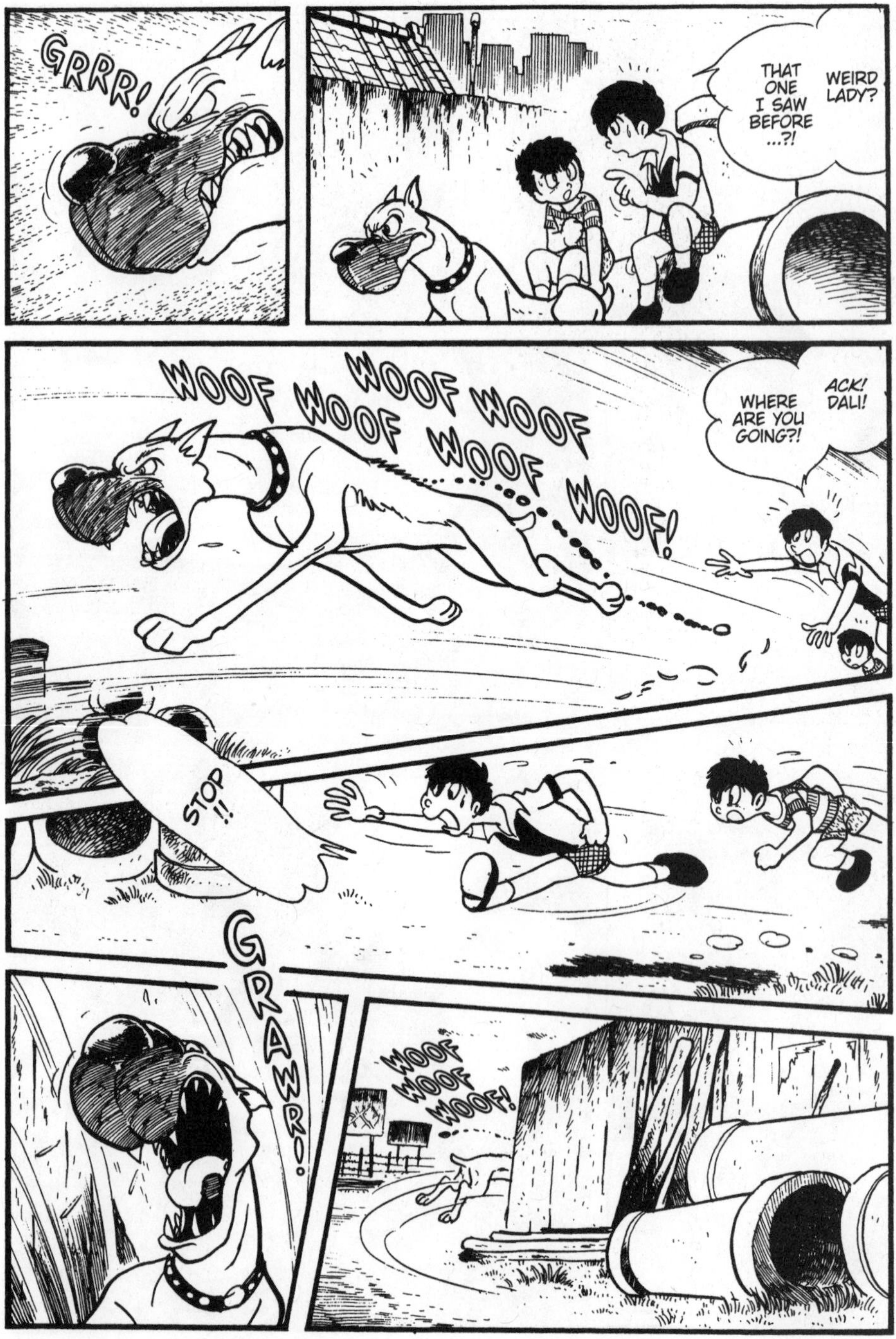
WEIRD LADY?
THAT ONE I SAW BEFORE ...?!
GRRR!
ACK! DALI!
WHERE ARE YOU GOING?!
WOOF WOOF WOOF WOOF WOOF WOOF!
STOP !!
WOOF WOOF WOOF!
GRAWR!

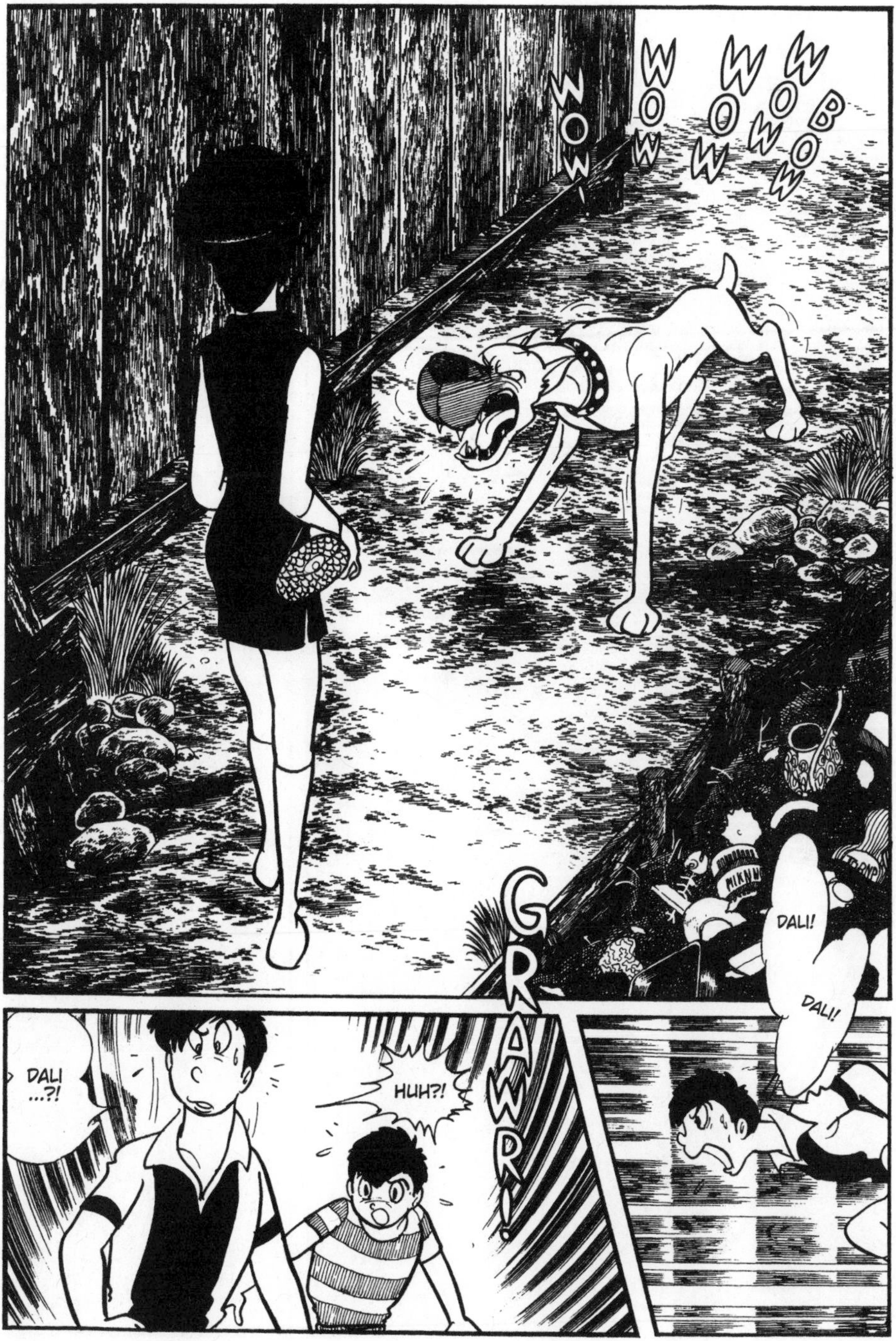

BOW
WOW
WOW
WOW!
GRAWR!
DALI!
DALI!
DALI ...?!
HUH?!

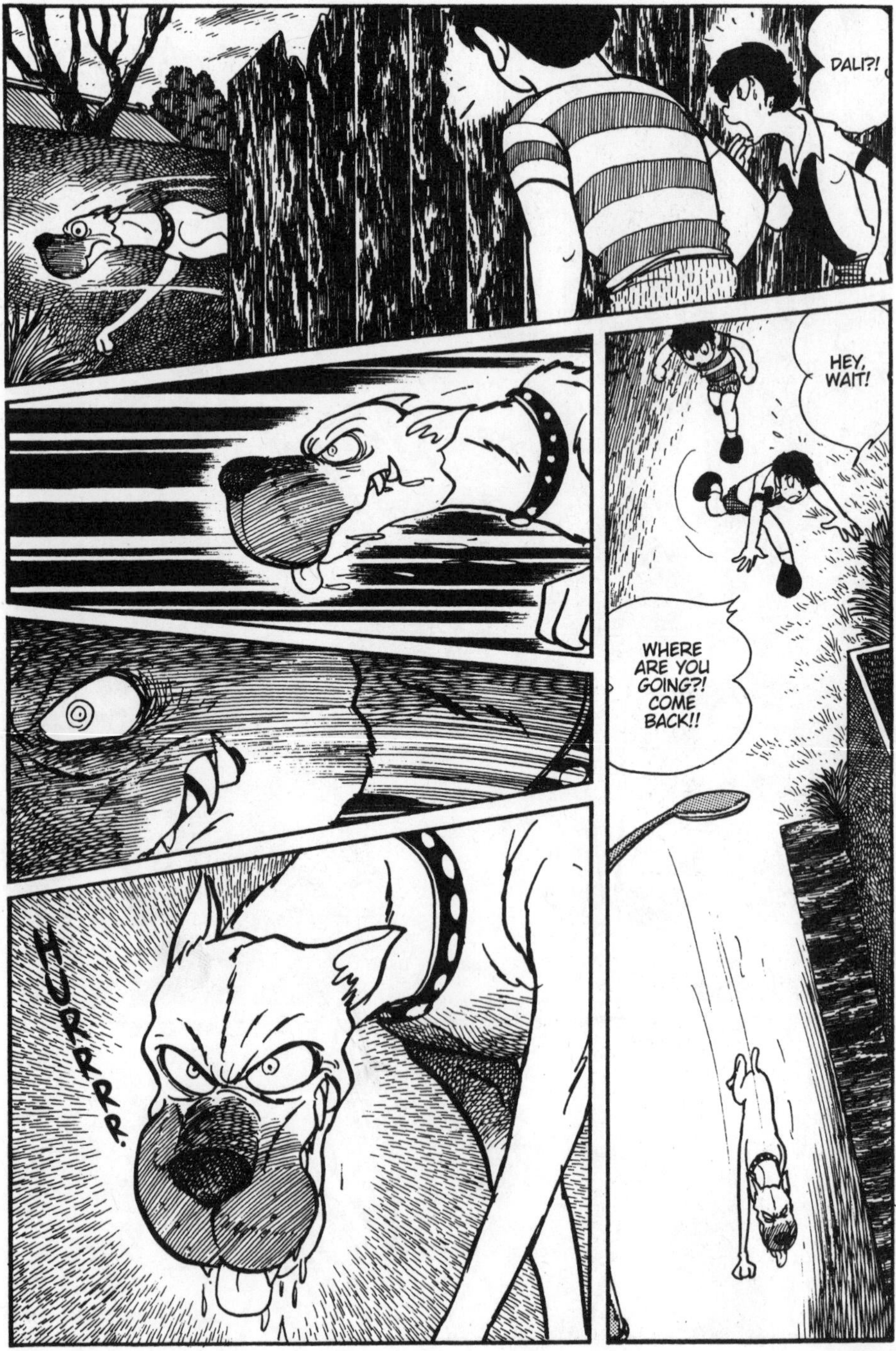
DALI?!
HEY, WAIT!
WHERE ARE YOU GOING?! COME BACK!!
HURRRR.

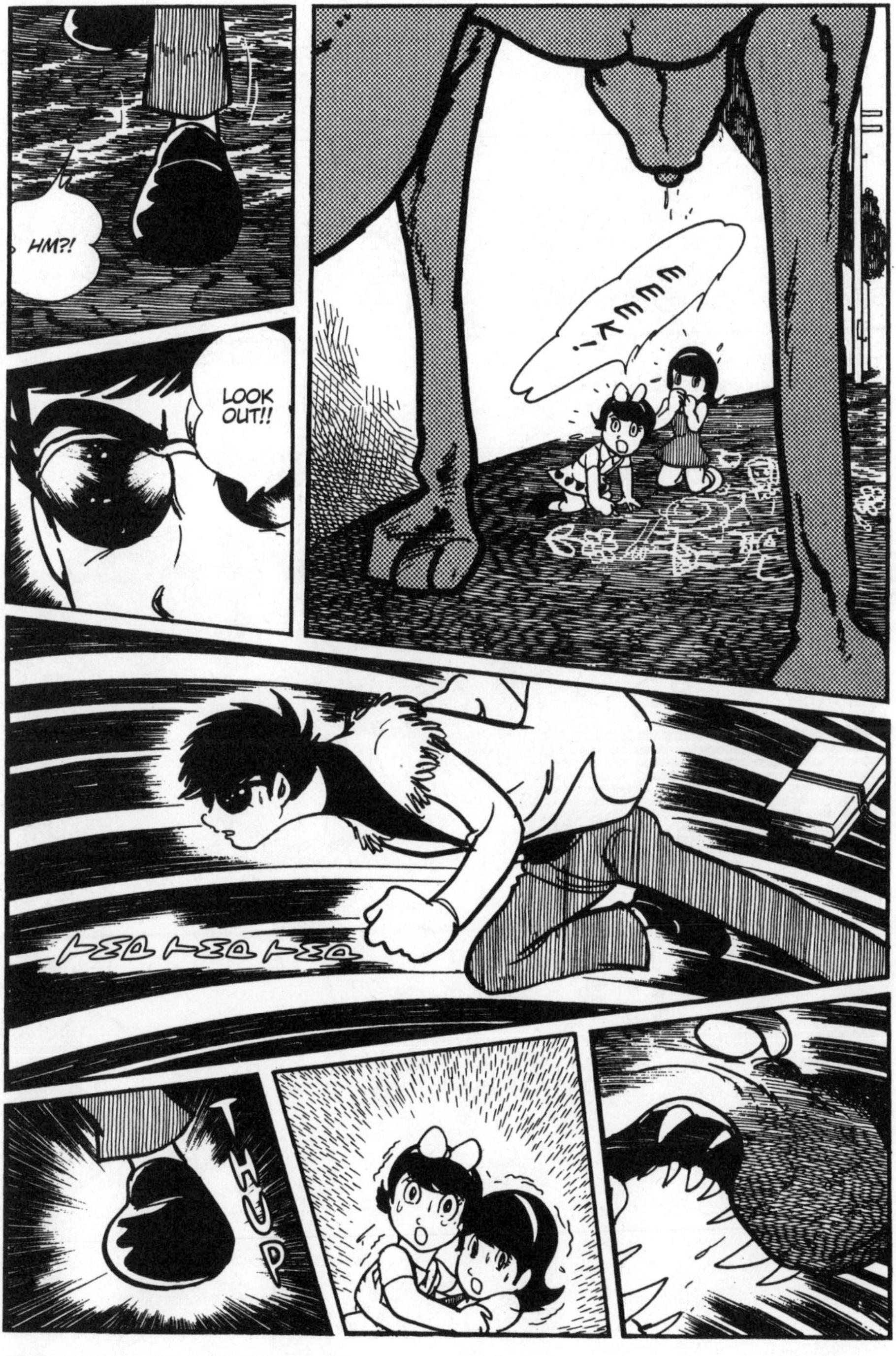
EEEEK!
HM?!
LOOK OUT!!
THUP

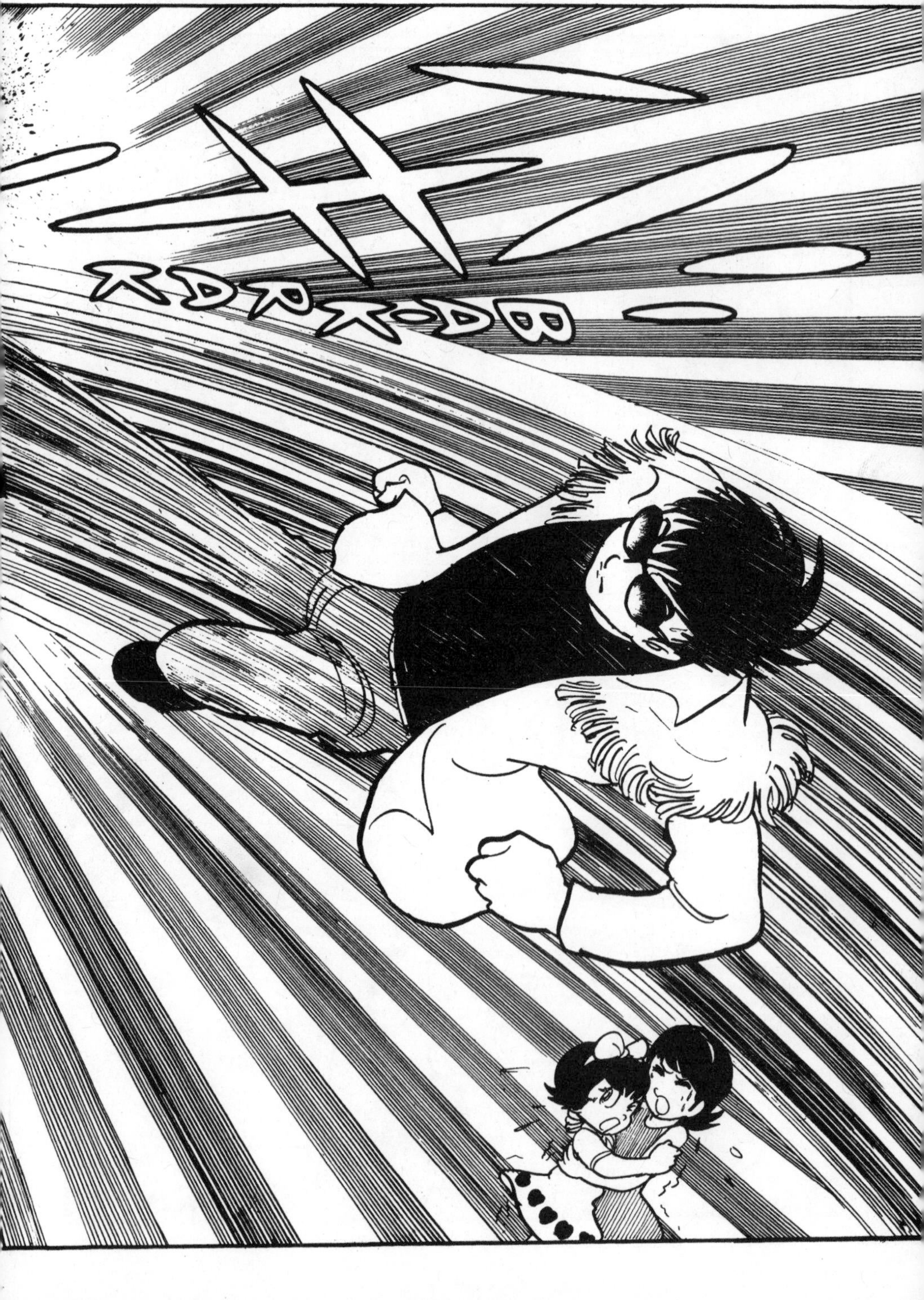

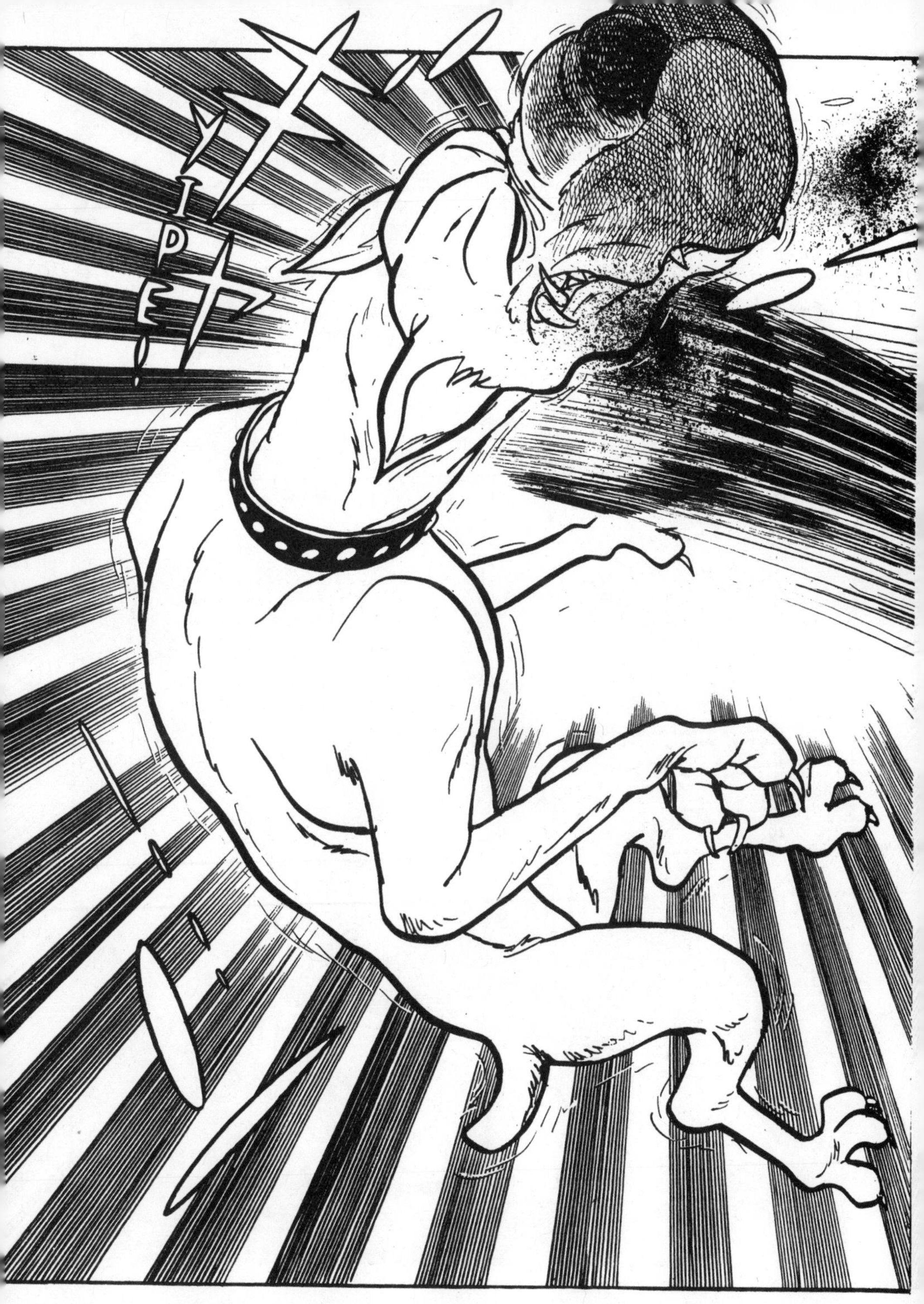
YIPE!

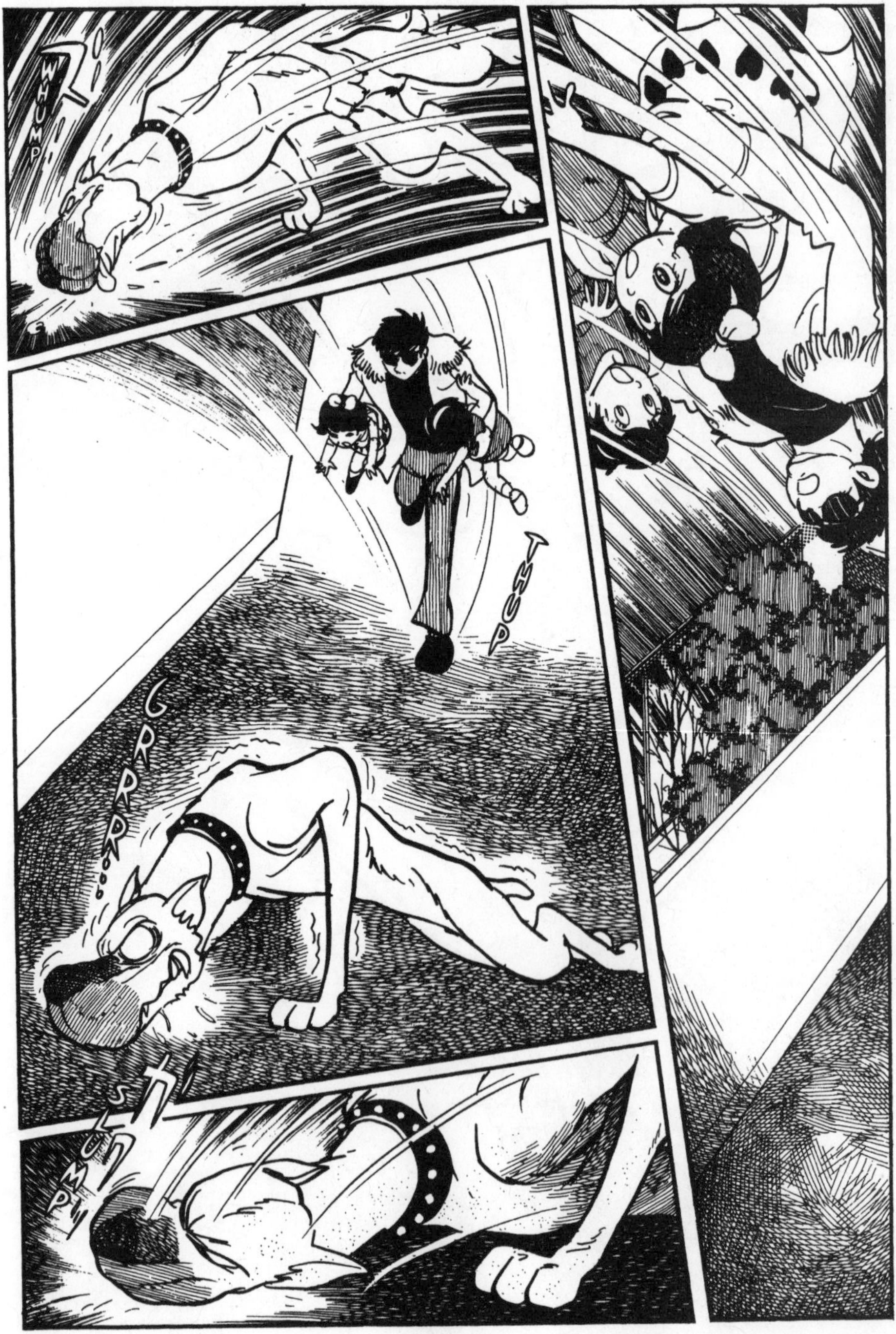
WHUMP
THUP
GRRRR...
SLUMP

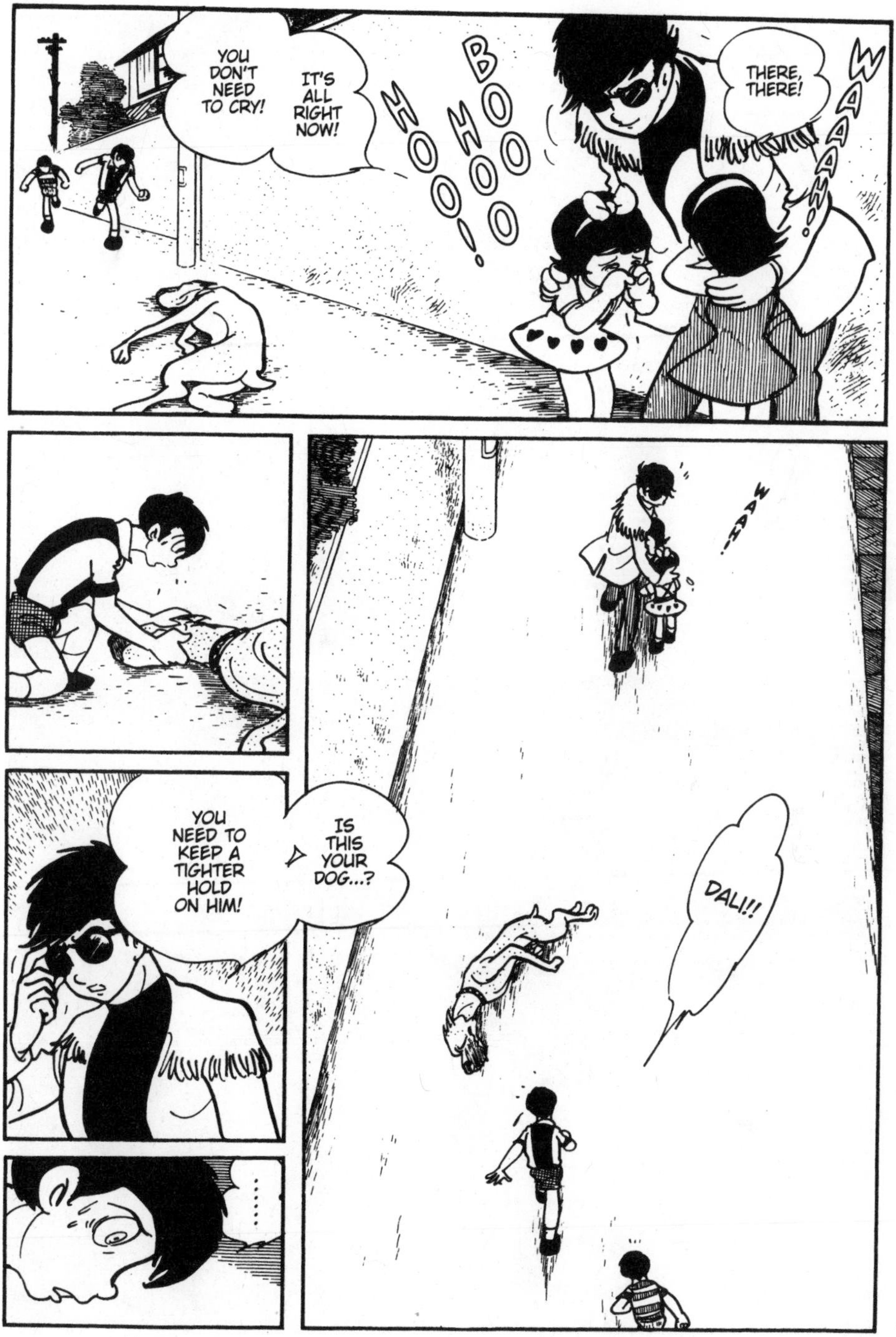
WAAAAAH!!
THERE, THERE!
BOOHOO
HOOO!!
IT'S ALL RIGHT NOW!
YOU DON'T NEED TO CRY!
WAAH...
DALI!!
IS THIS YOUR DOG...?
YOU NEED TO KEEP A TIGHTER HOLD ON HIM!
......

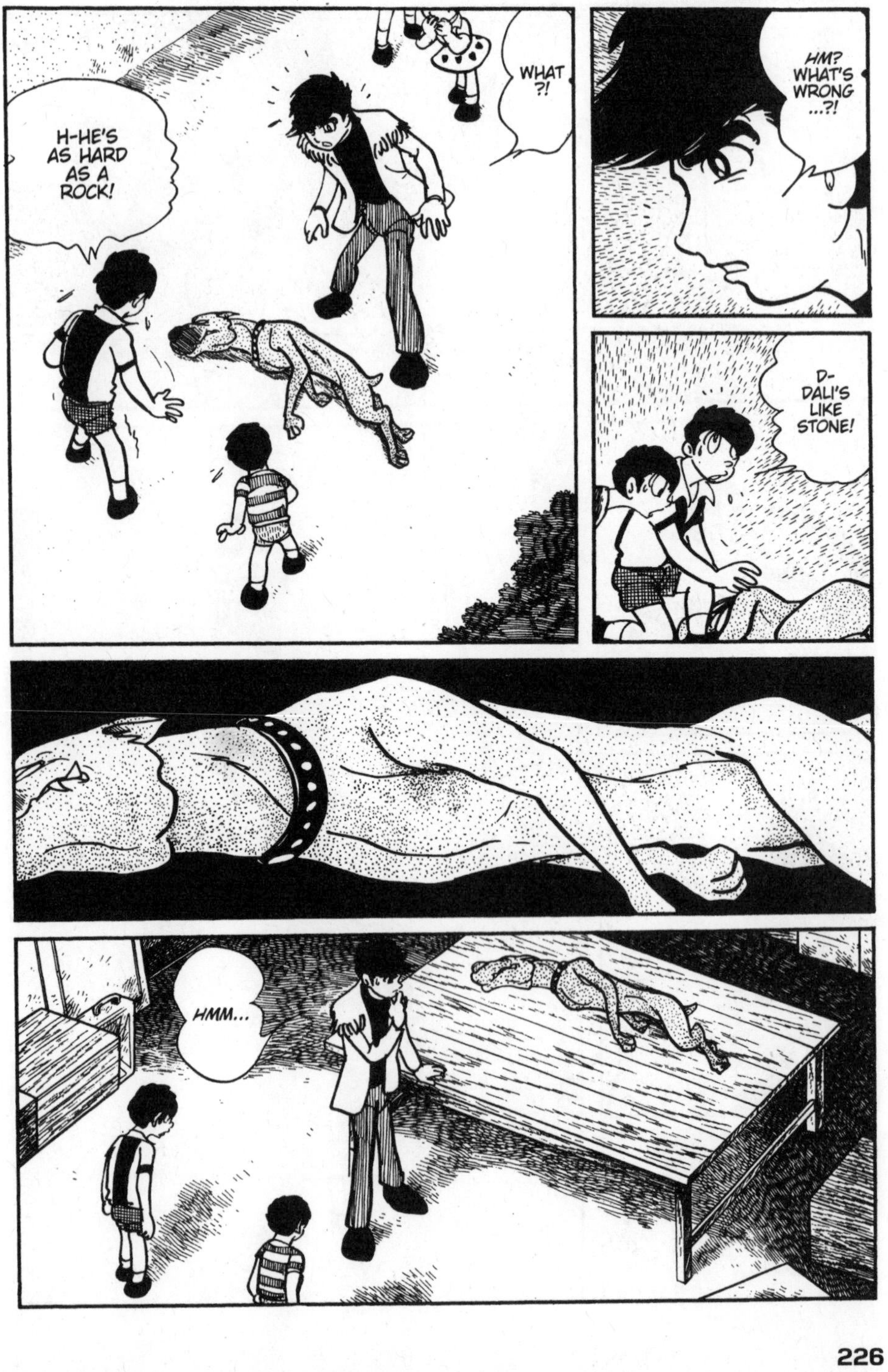
HM? WHAT'S WRONG ...?!
D-DALI'S LIKE STONE!
WHAT ?!
H-HE'S AS HARD AS A ROCK!
HMM...

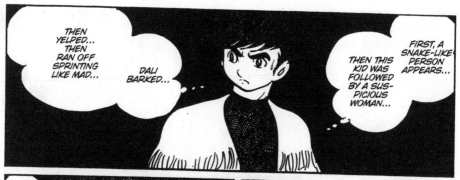

FIRST, A SNAKE-LIKE PERSON APPEARS...
THEN THIS KID WAS FOLLOWED BY A SUS-PICIOUS WOMAN...
DALI BARKED...
THEN YELPED... THEN RAN OFF SPRINTING LIKE MAD...
......
......
IT'S SHOCKER!!
ONE OF SHOCKER'S AGENTS. A CYBORG!
IT'S THE ONLY EXPLANA-TION!
THEY KNOW THIS BOY WITNESSED THE MURDER, AND THEY SENT THE WOMAN TO SILENCE HIM!
IS THAT WOMAN THE SNAKE PERSON...?

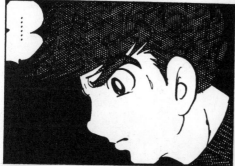

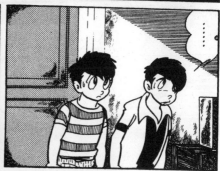

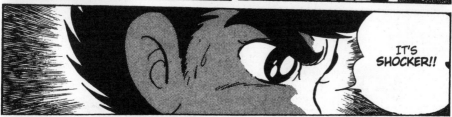

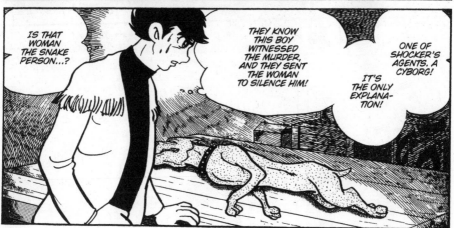

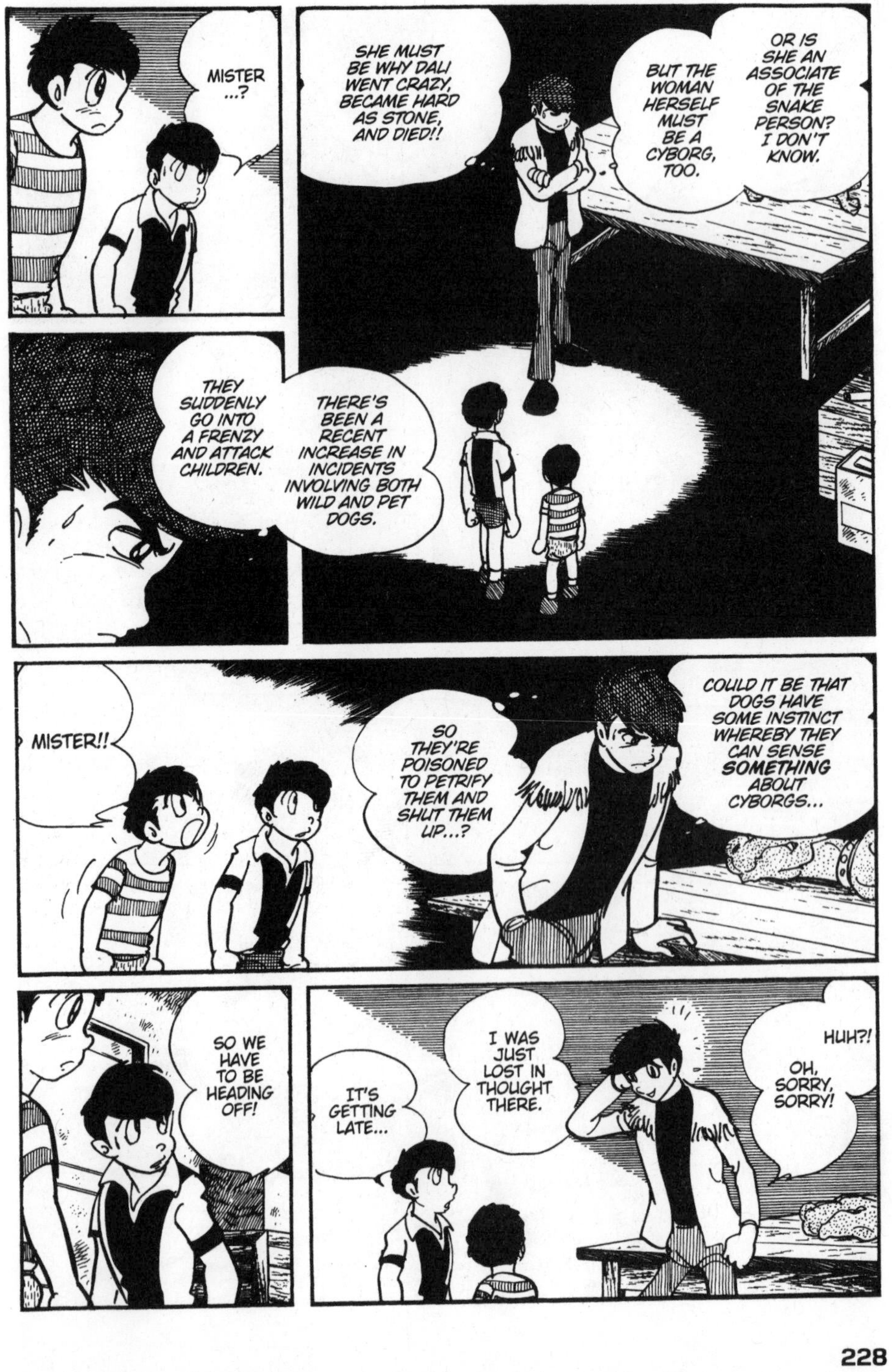
BUT THE WOMAN HERSELF MUST BE A CYBORG, TOO. OR IS SHE AN ASSOCIATE OF THE SNAKE PERSON? I DON'T KNOW.
SHE MUST BE WHY DALI WENT CRAZY, BECAME HARD AS STONE, AND DIED!!
MISTER ...?
THERE'S BEEN A RECENT INCREASE IN INCIDENTS INVOLVING BOTH WILD AND PET DOGS.
THEY SUDDENLY GO INTO A FRENZY AND ATTACK CHILDREN.
COULD IT BE THAT DOGS HAVE SOME INSTINCT WHEREBY THEY CAN SENSE **SOMETHING** ABOUT CYBORGS...
SO THEY'RE POISONED TO PETRIFY THEM AND SHUT THEM UP...?
MISTER!!
HUH?! OH, SORRY, SORRY!
I WAS JUST LOST IN THOUGHT THERE.
IT'S GETTING LATE...
SO WE HAVE TO BE HEADING OFF!

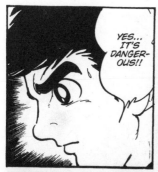

OH, I SEE. OF COURSE!
I'LL DRIVE YOU HOME!
IT'S DANGEROUS OUT THERE!
YES... IT'S DANGER-OUS!!
IF ONE OF SHOCKER'S AGENTS WAS FOLLOWING THIS BOY TOHRU, THEN IT REALLY IS...!!
KREEEEK
SKREEE

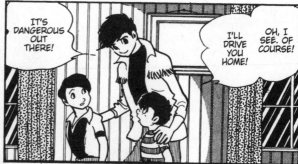

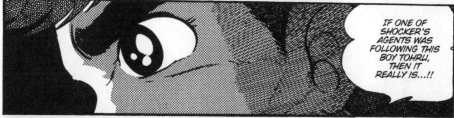

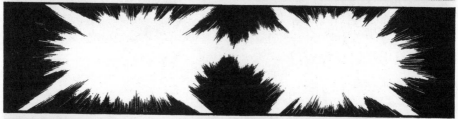

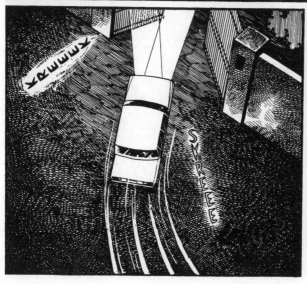

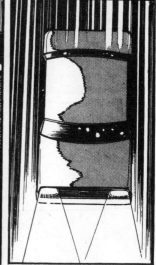

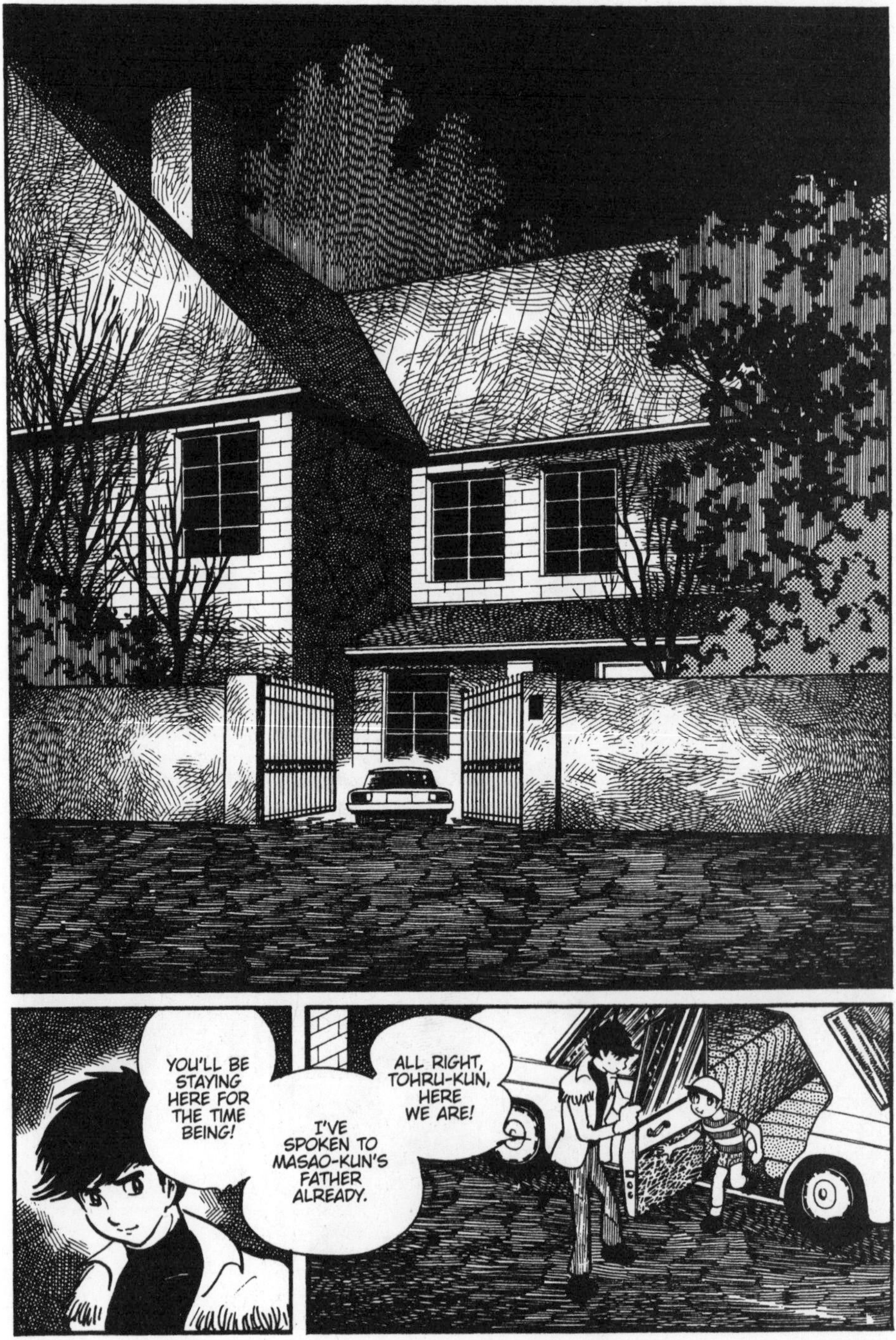
ALL RIGHT, TOHRU-KUN, HERE WE ARE!
YOU'LL BE STAYING HERE FOR THE TIME BEING!
I'VE SPOKEN TO MASAO-KUN'S FATHER ALREADY.

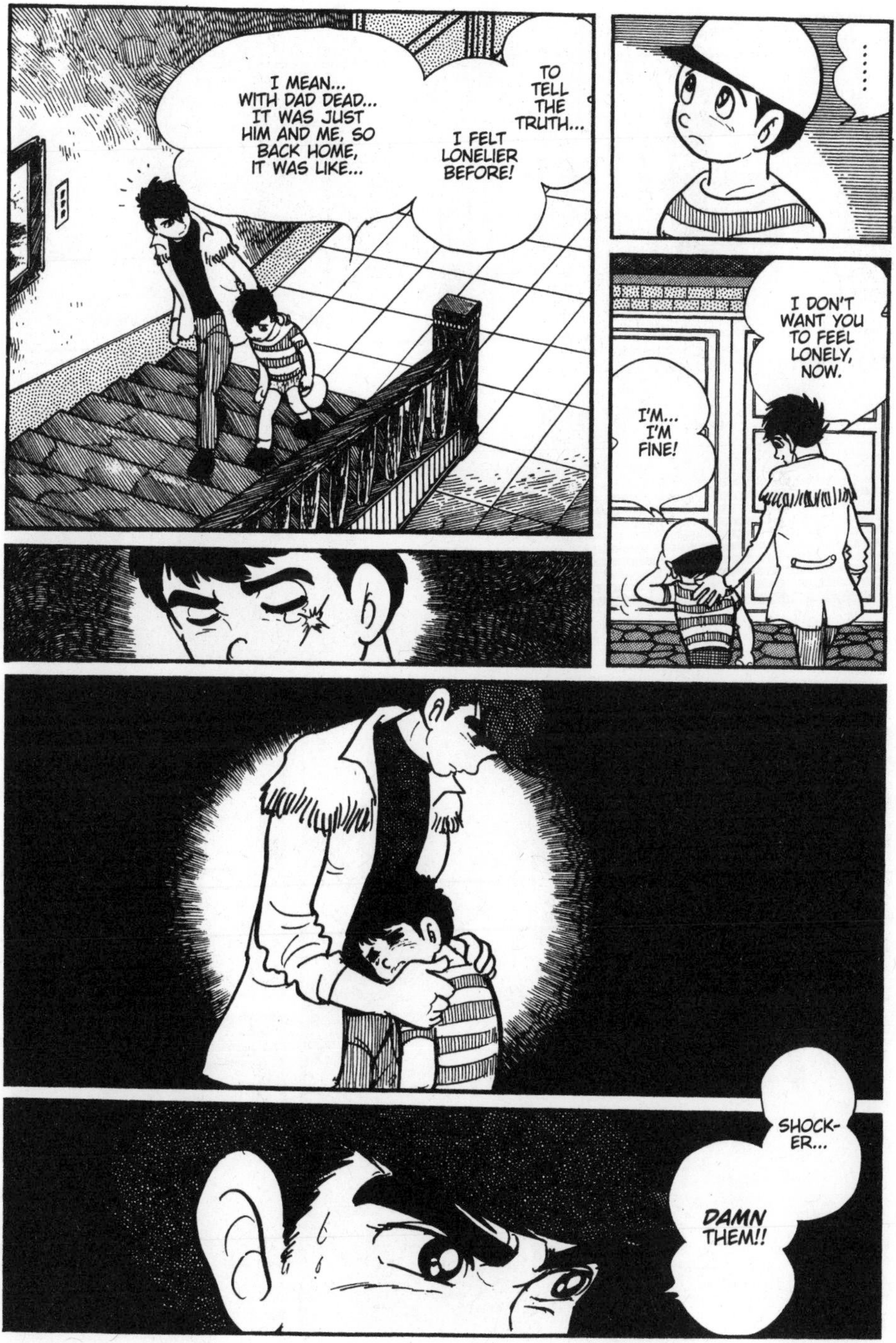
......
I DON'T WANT YOU TO FEEL LONELY, NOW.
I'M... I'M FINE!
TO TELL THE TRUTH...
I FELT LONELIER BEFORE!
I MEAN... WITH DAD DEAD... IT WAS JUST HIM AND ME, SO BACK HOME, IT WAS LIKE...
SHOCKER...
DAMN THEM!!

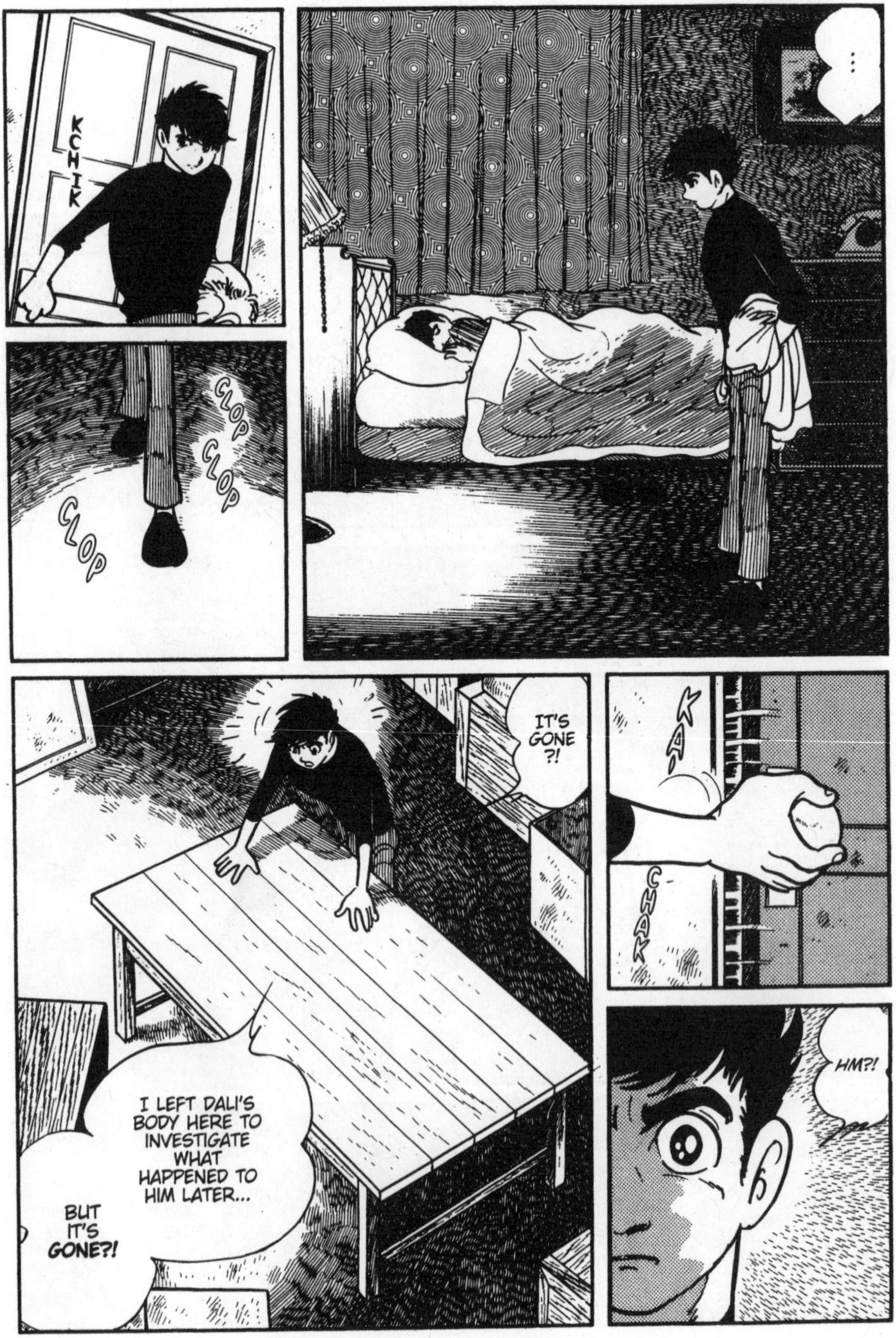
...
KCHIK
CLOP
CLOP
CLOP
KA-CHAK
HM?!
IT'S GONE?!
I LEFT DALI'S BODY HERE TO INVESTIGATE WHAT HAPPENED TO HIM LATER...
BUT IT'S GONE?!

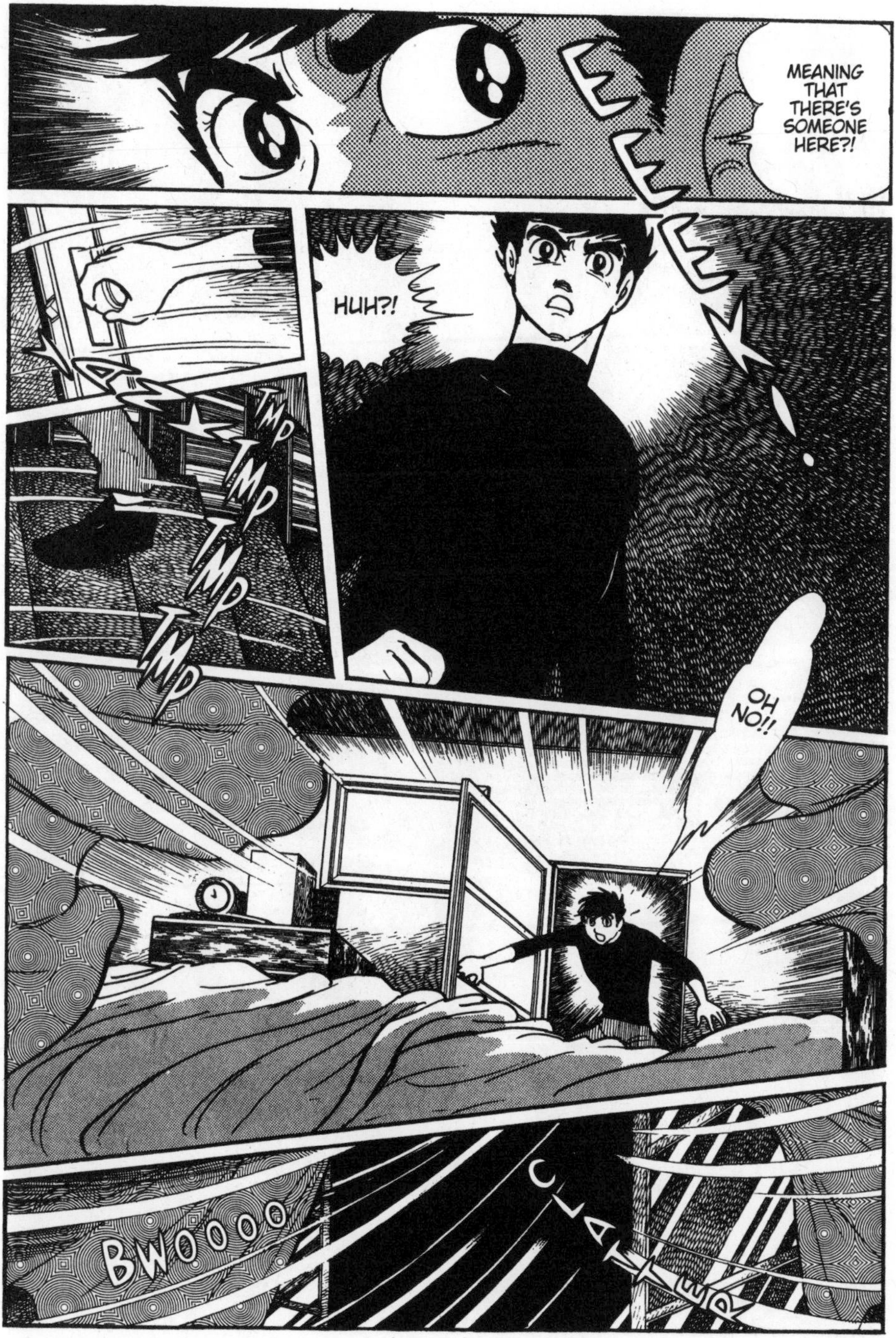
MEANING THAT THERE'S SOMEONE HERE?!
EEEEK...!
HUH?!
TMP TMP TMP TMP TMP
OH NO!!
CLATTER
BWOOOO

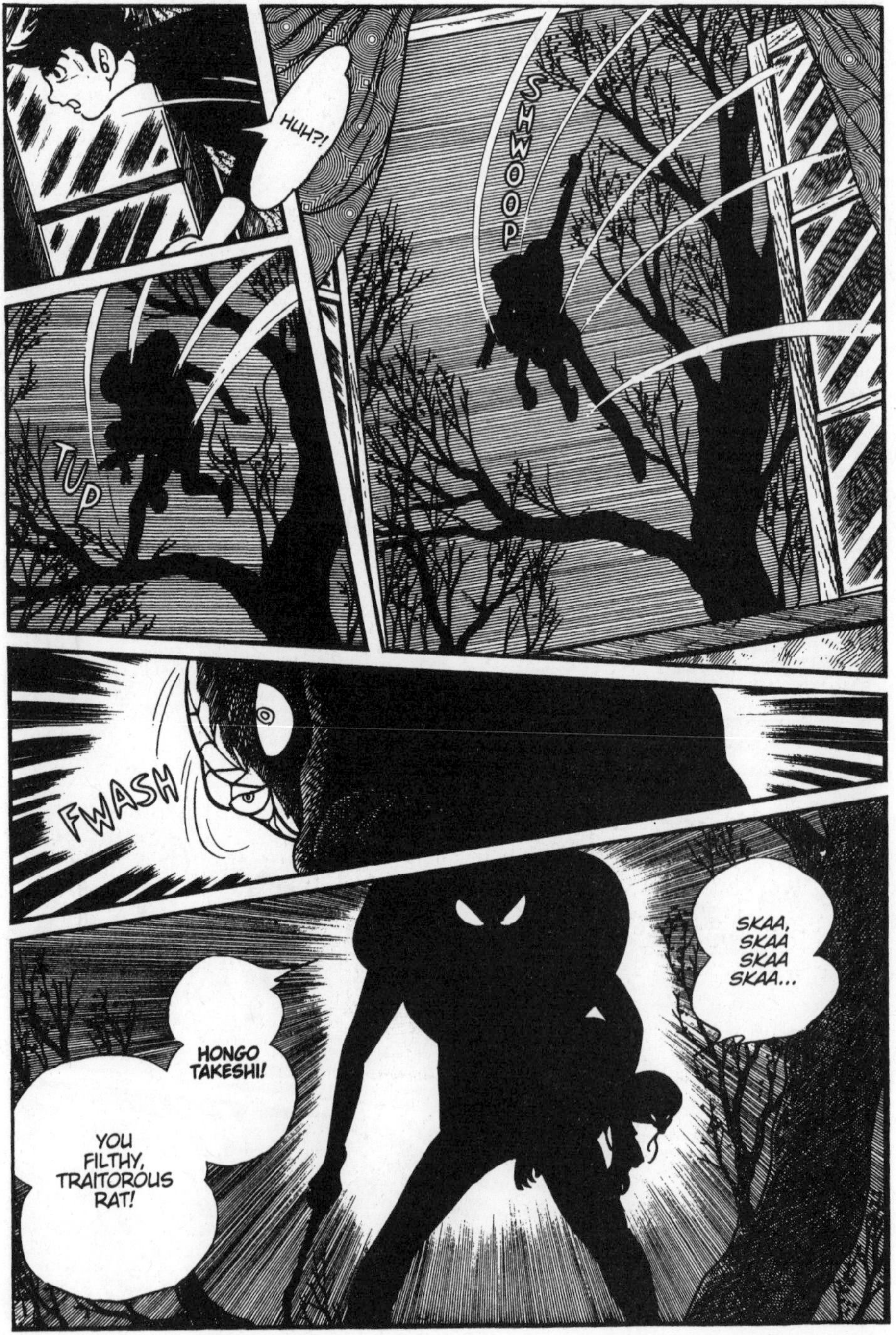
SHWOOP
HUH?!
TUP
FWASH
SKAA, SKAA SKAA SKAA...
HONGO TAKESHI!
YOU FILTHY, TRAITOROUS RAT!

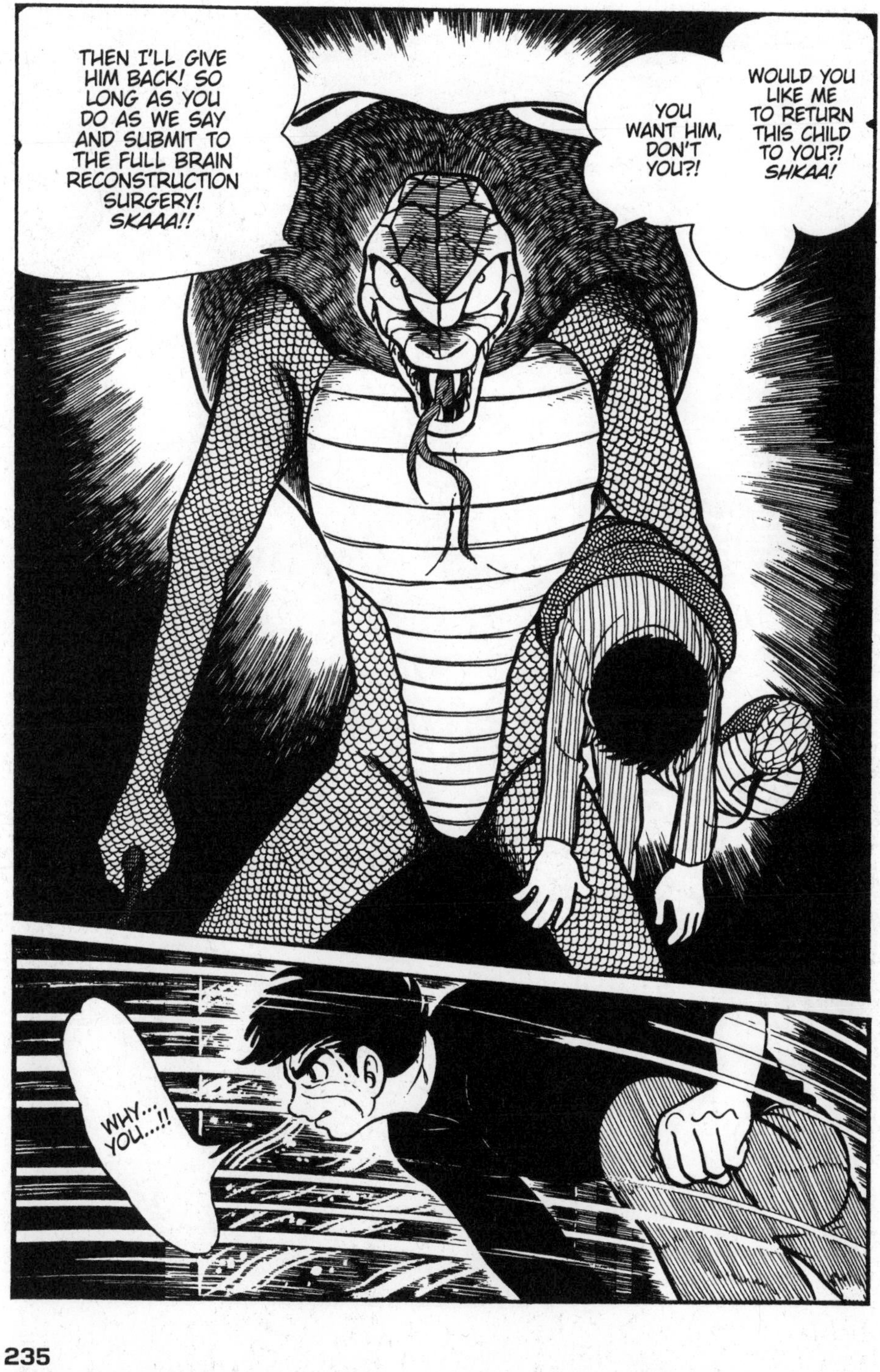
WOULD YOU LIKE ME TO RETURN THIS CHILD TO YOU?! SHKAA!
YOU WANT HIM, DON'T YOU?!
THEN I'LL GIVE HIM BACK! SO LONG AS YOU DO AS WE SAY AND SUBMIT TO THE FULL BRAIN RECONSTRUCTION SURGERY! SKAAA!!
WHY... YOU...!!

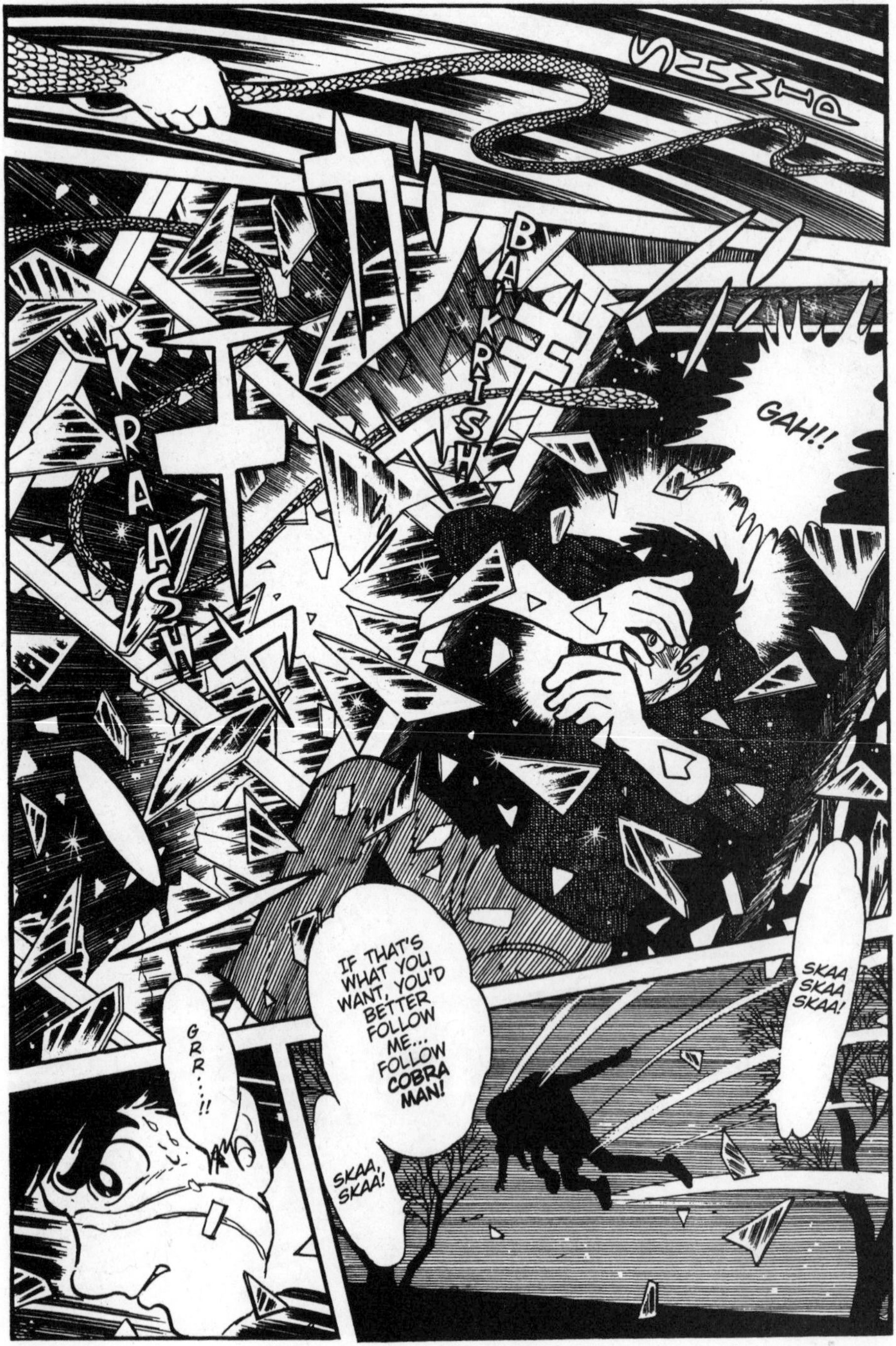
SHWIP
BA-KRISH
KRAASH
GAH!!
SKAA SKAA SKAA!
IF THAT'S WHAT YOU WANT, YOU'D BETTER FOLLOW ME... FOLLOW COBRA MAN!
SKAA, SKAA!
GRR...!!

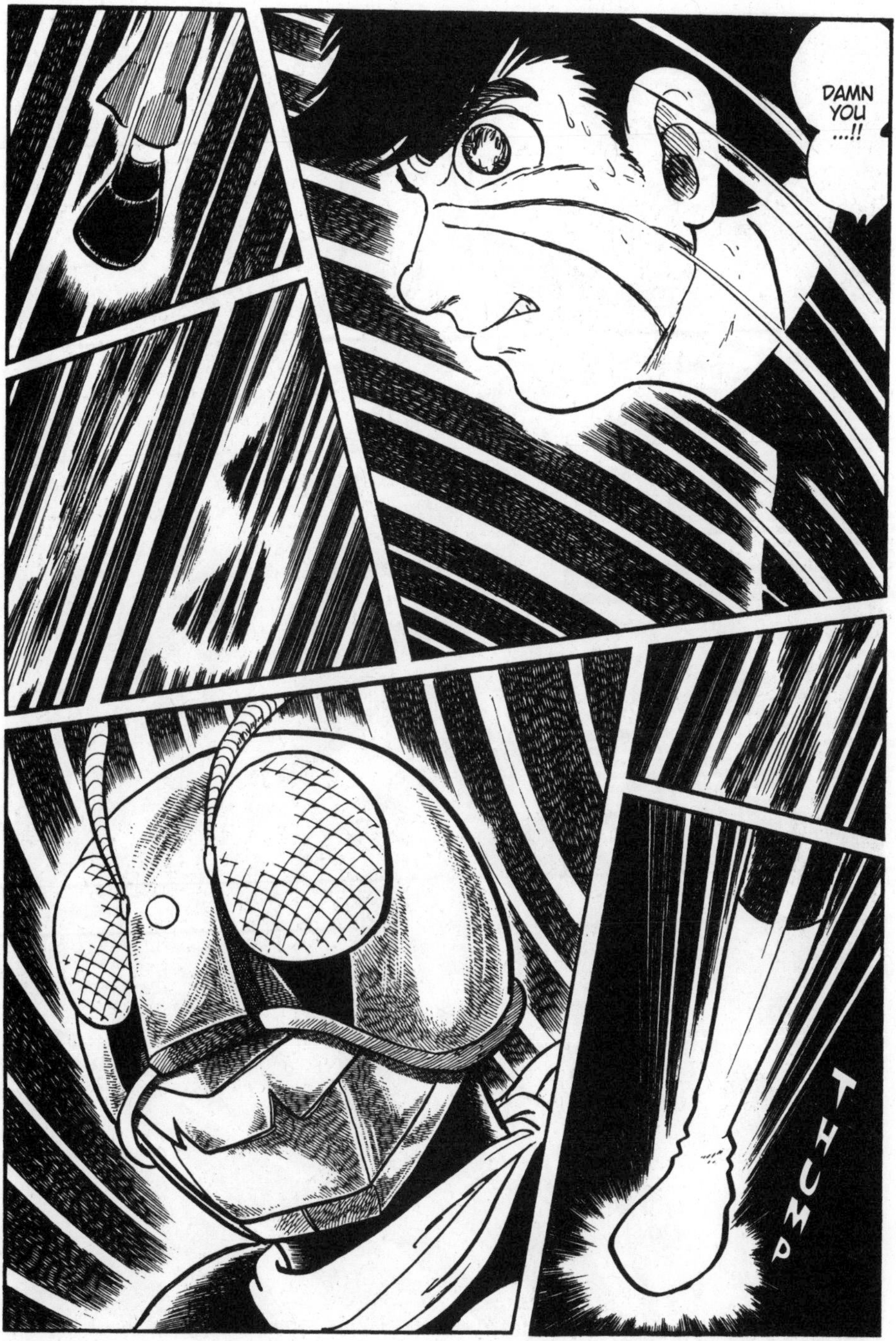
DAMN YOU ...!!
THUMP

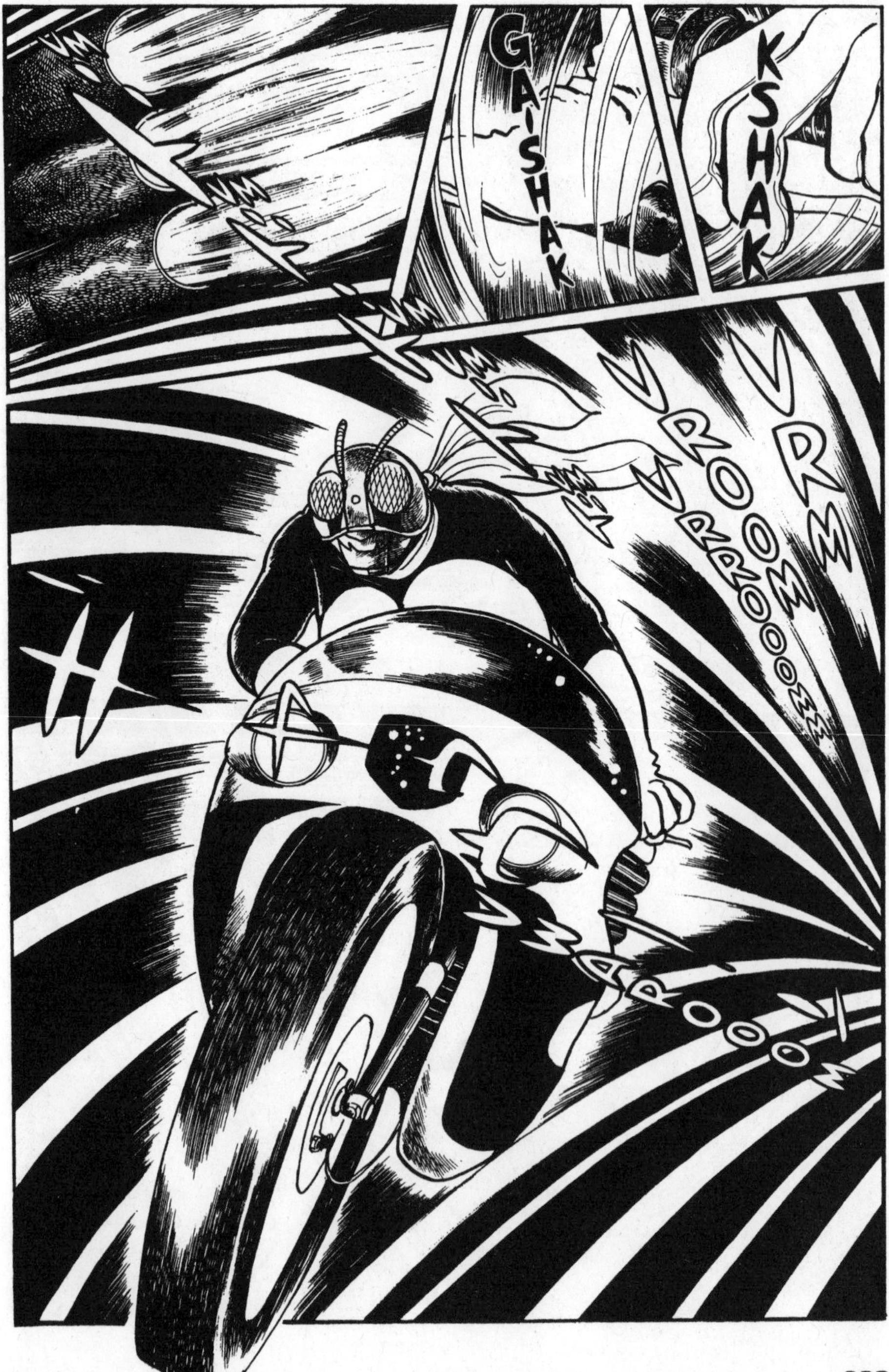
KSHAK
GAISHAK
VRM
VROOM
VWAROOOM

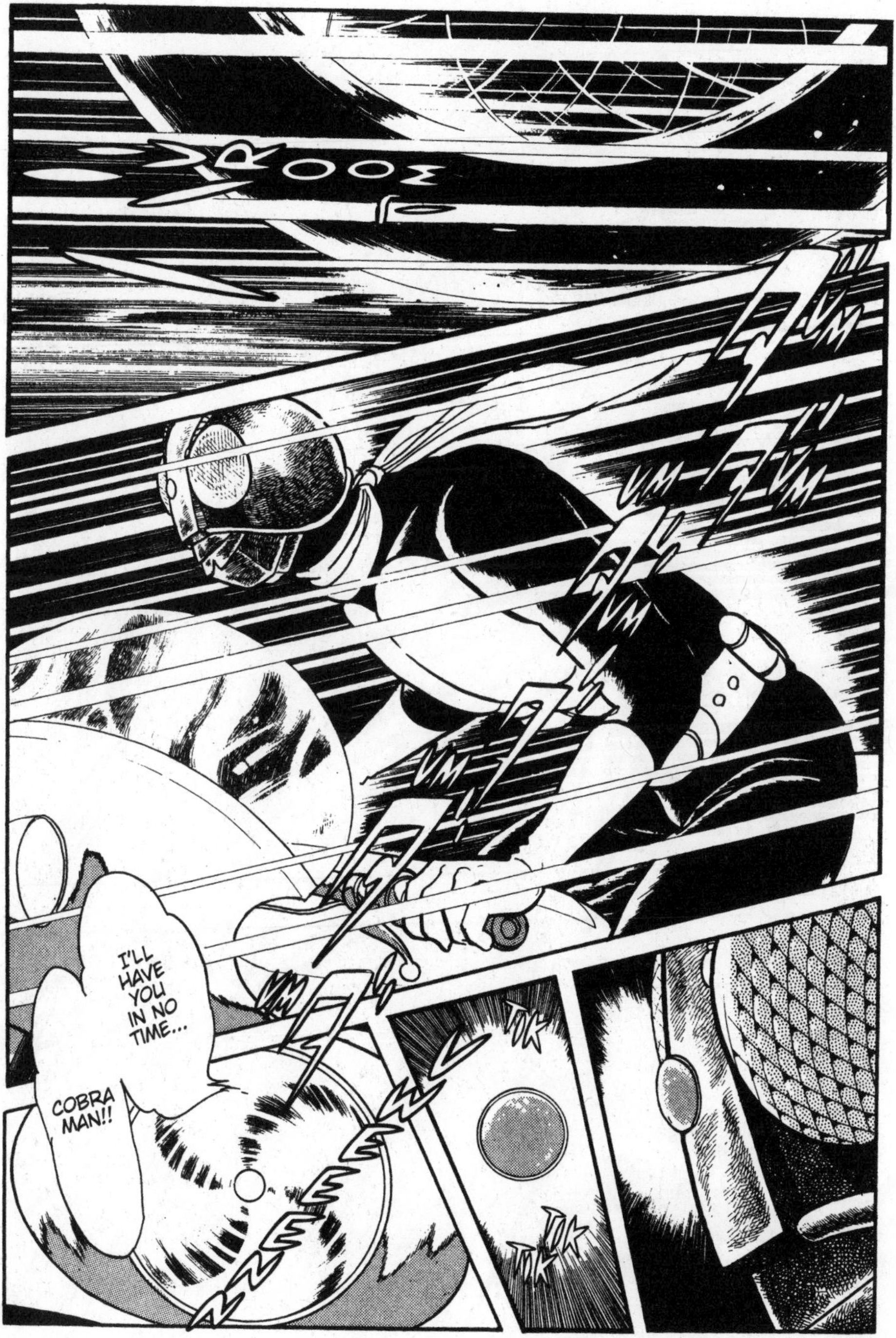
VROOM
I'LL HAVE YOU IN NO TIME...
COBRA MAN!!
TIK
TIK
TIK

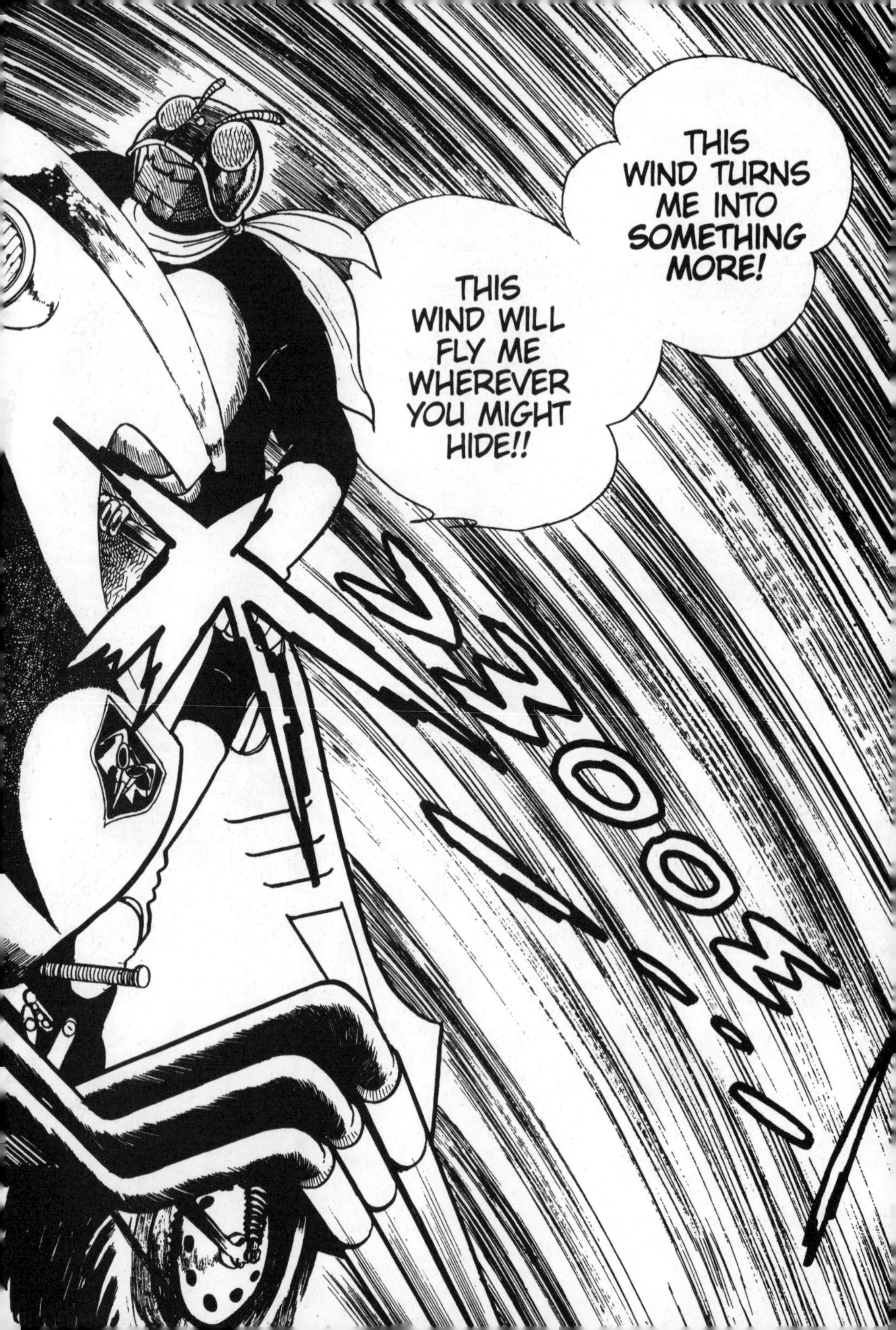
THIS WIND TURNS ME INTO SOMETHING MORE!
THIS WIND WILL FLY ME WHEREVER YOU MIGHT HIDE!!
VWOOOM!!

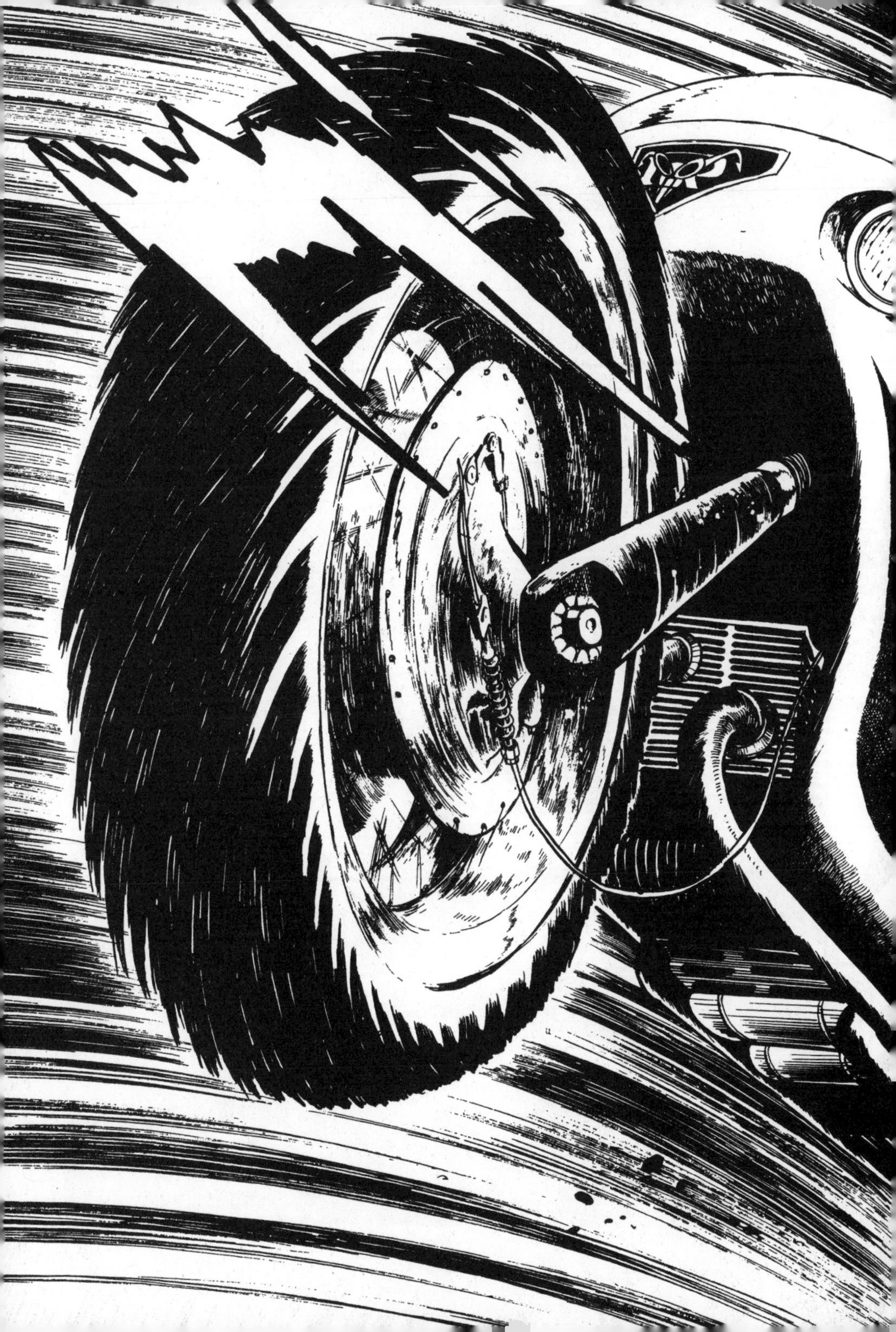

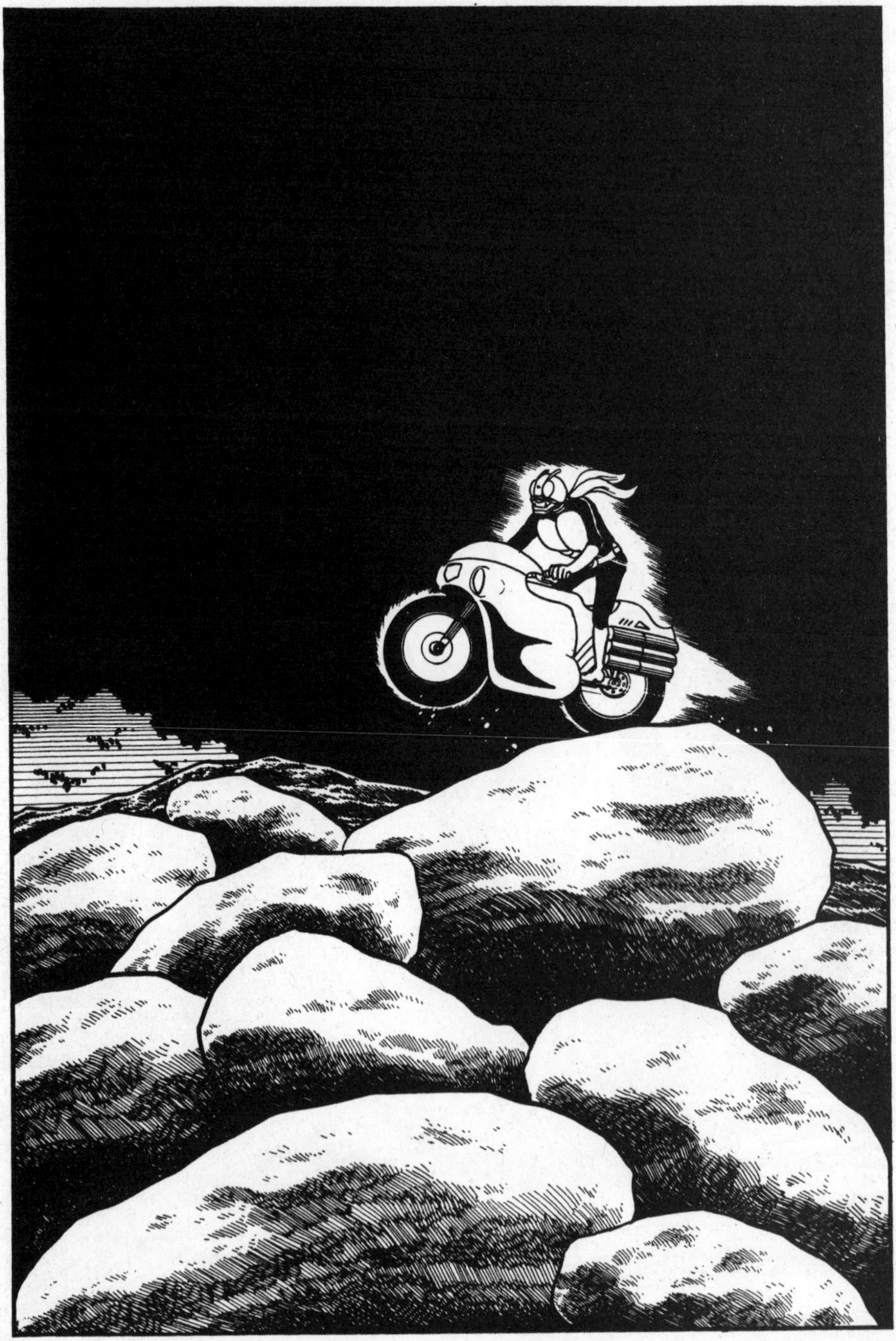

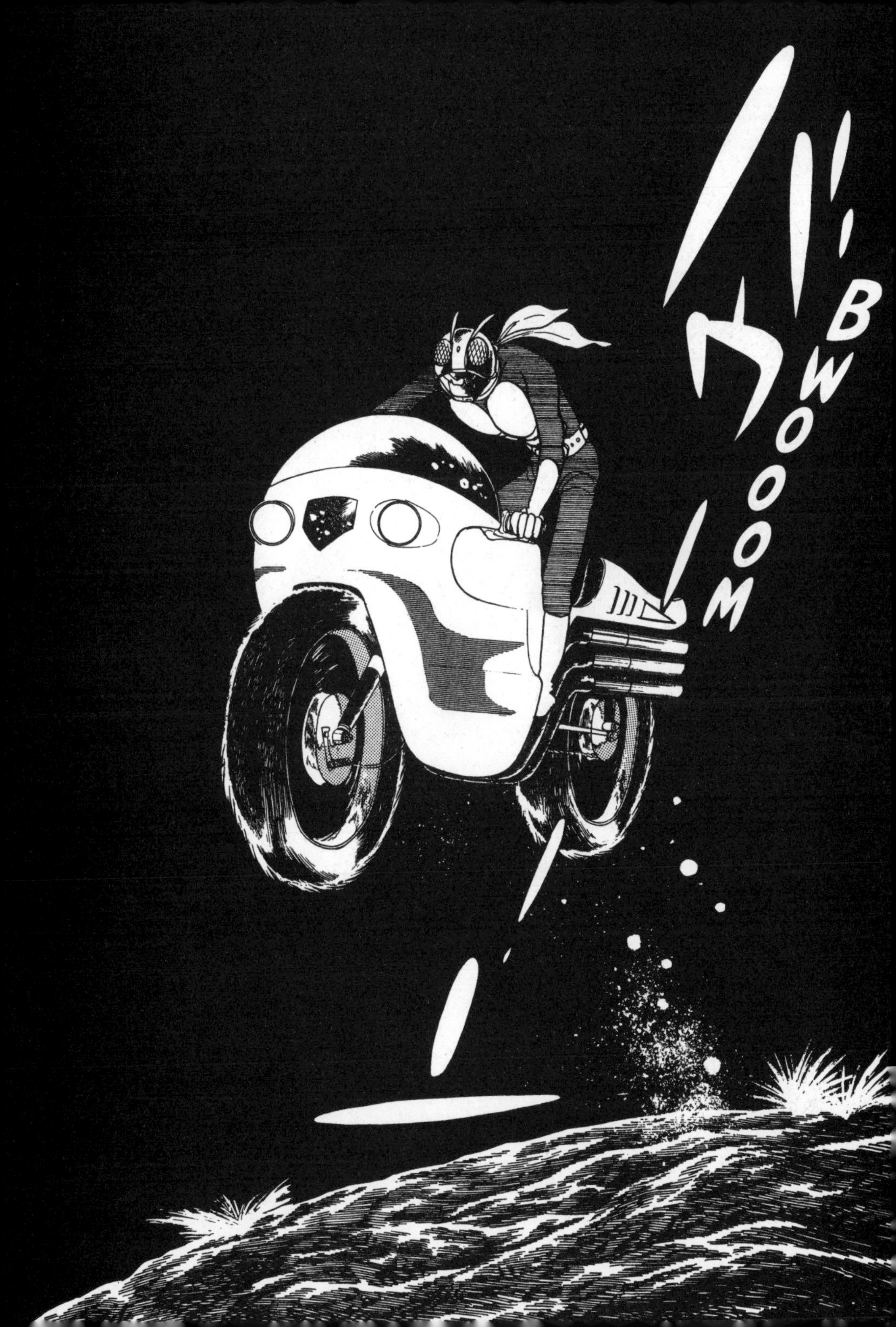
BWOOOOM

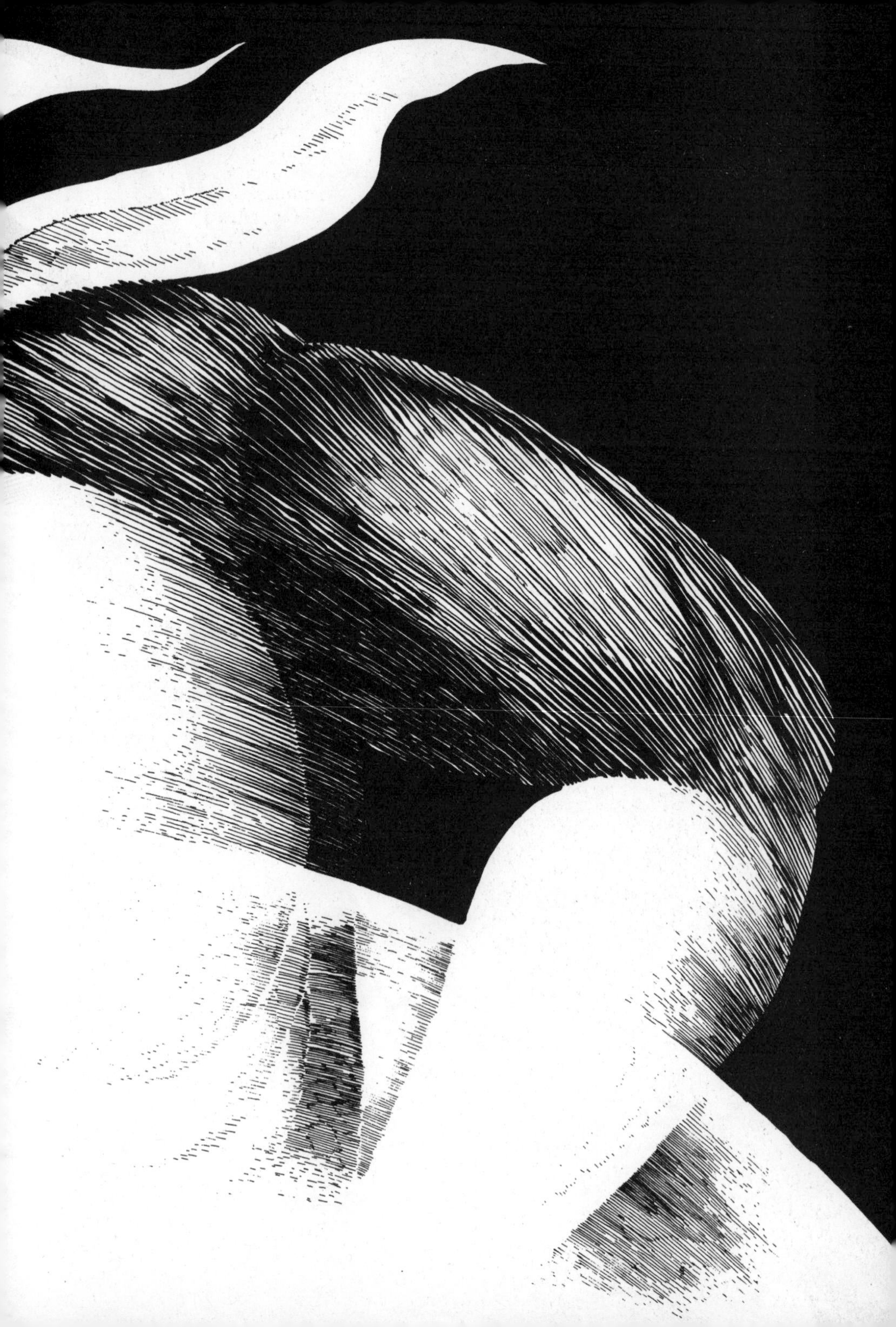

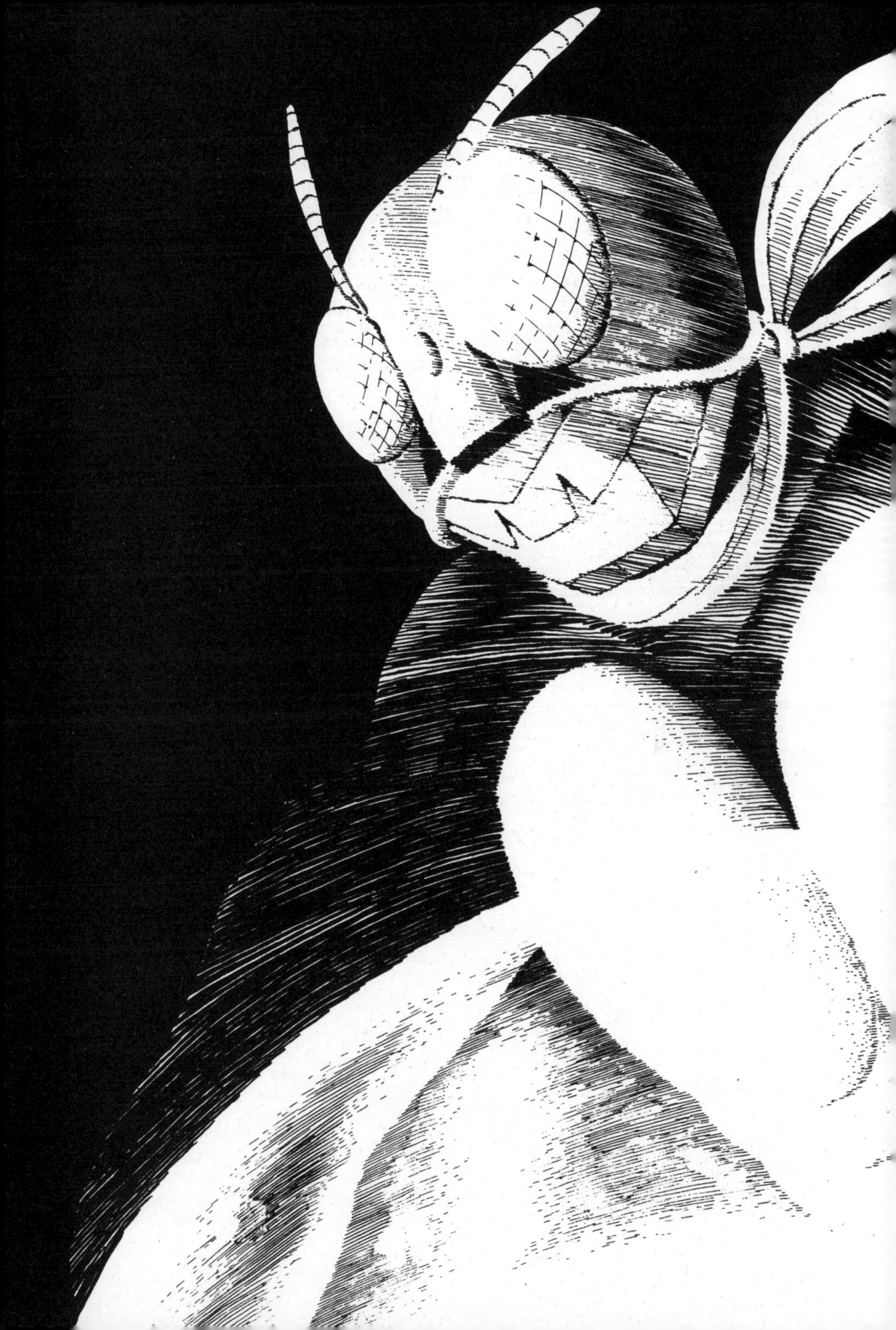

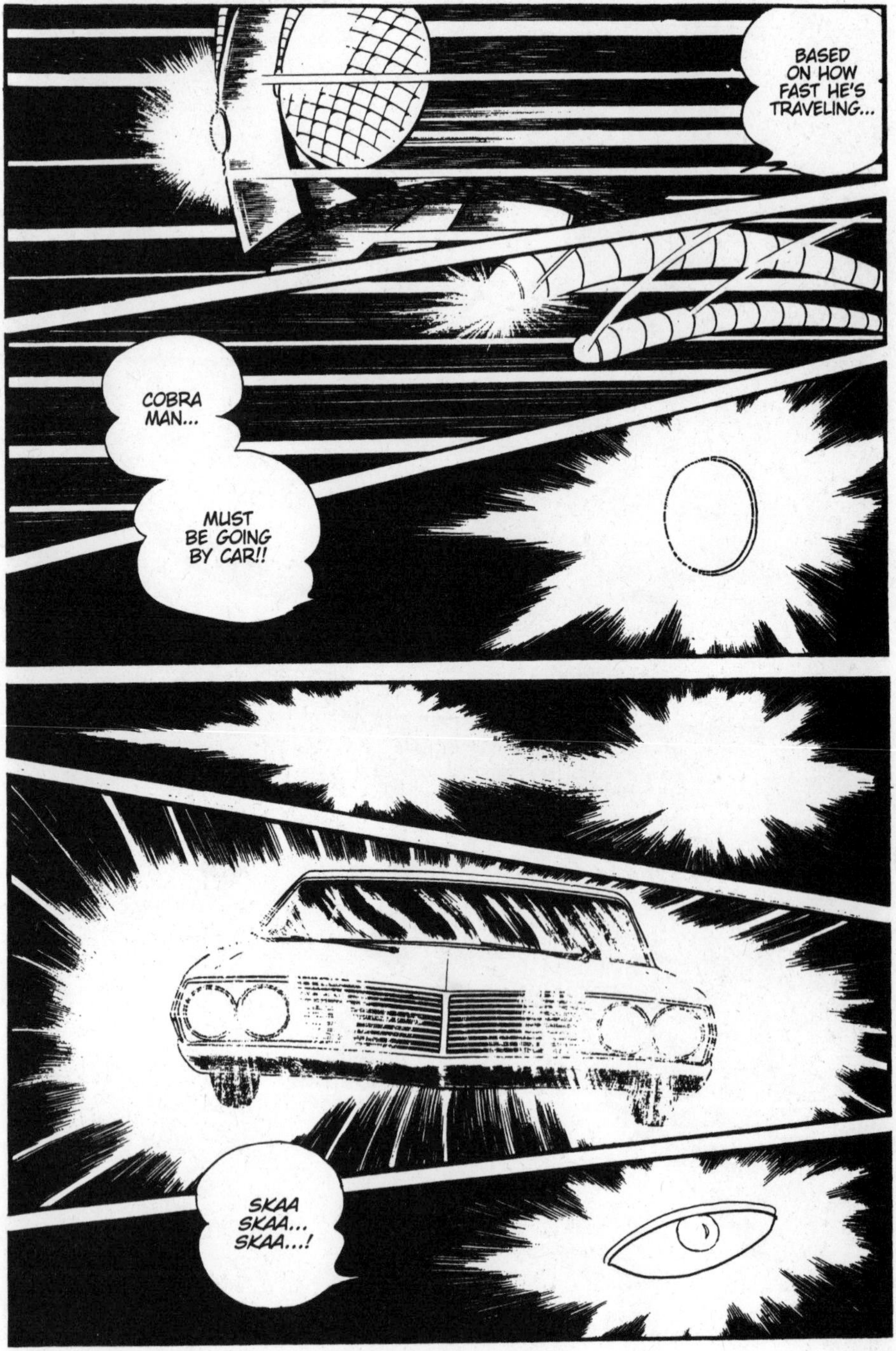
BASED ON HOW FAST HE'S TRAVELING...
COBRA MAN...
MUST BE GOING BY CAR!!
SKAA SKAA... SKAA...!

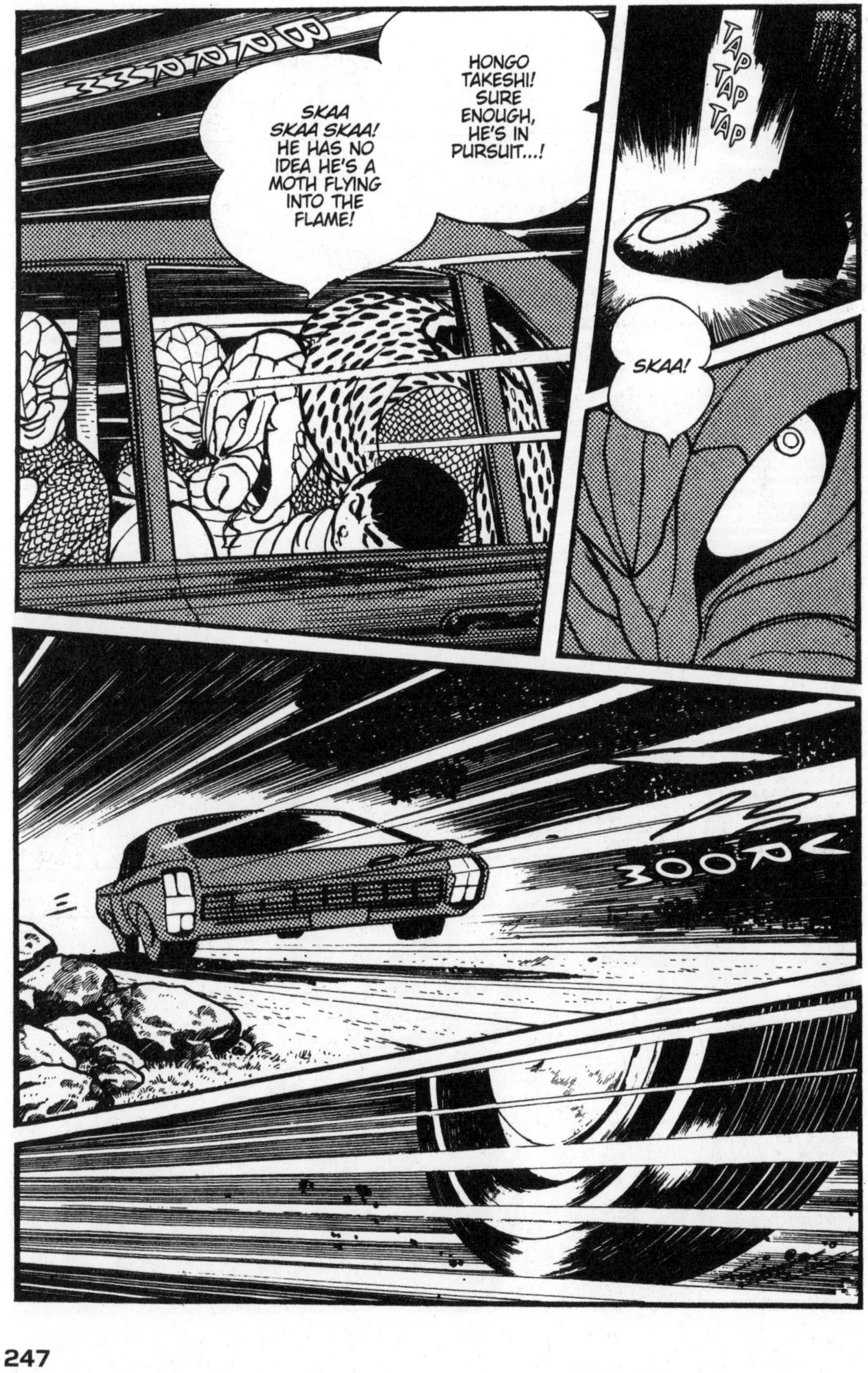
TAP TAP TAP
SKAA!
HONGO TAKESHI! SURE ENOUGH, HE'S IN PURSUIT...!
SKAA SKAA SKAA! HE HAS NO IDEA HE'S A MOTH FLYING INTO THE FLAME!

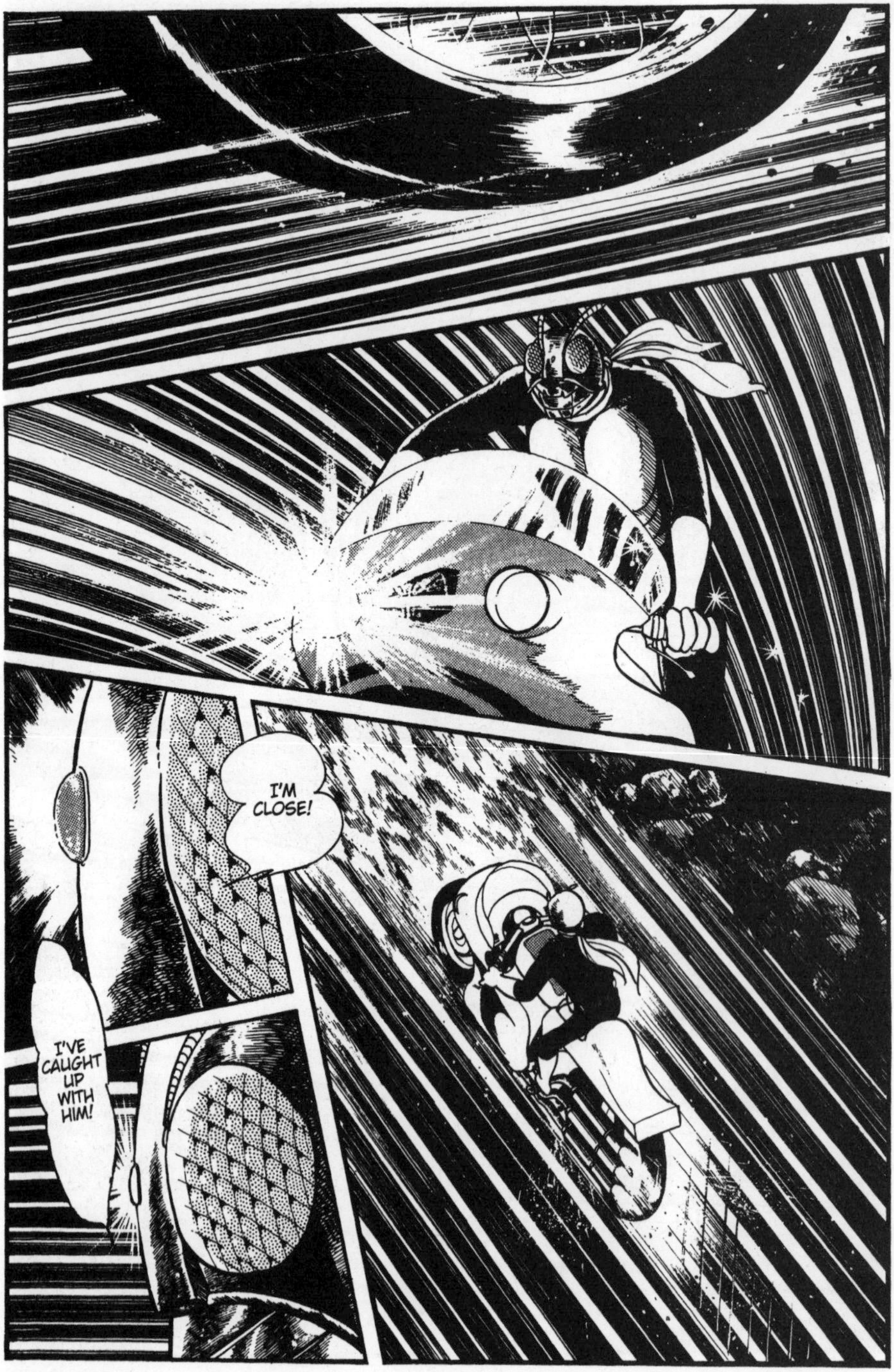
I'M CLOSE!
I'VE CAUGHT UP WITH HIM!

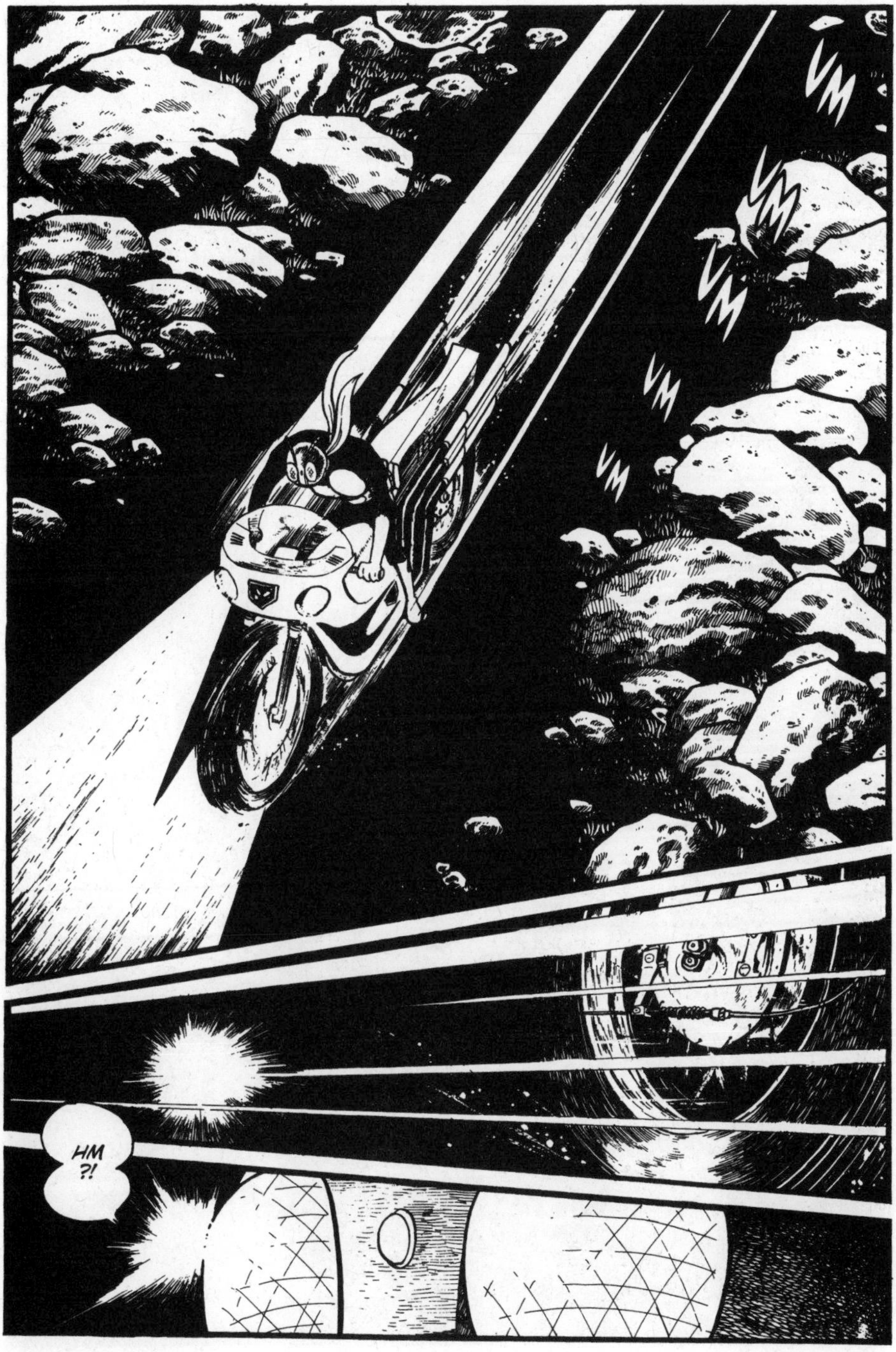
VM
VM
VM
VM
VM
HM ?!

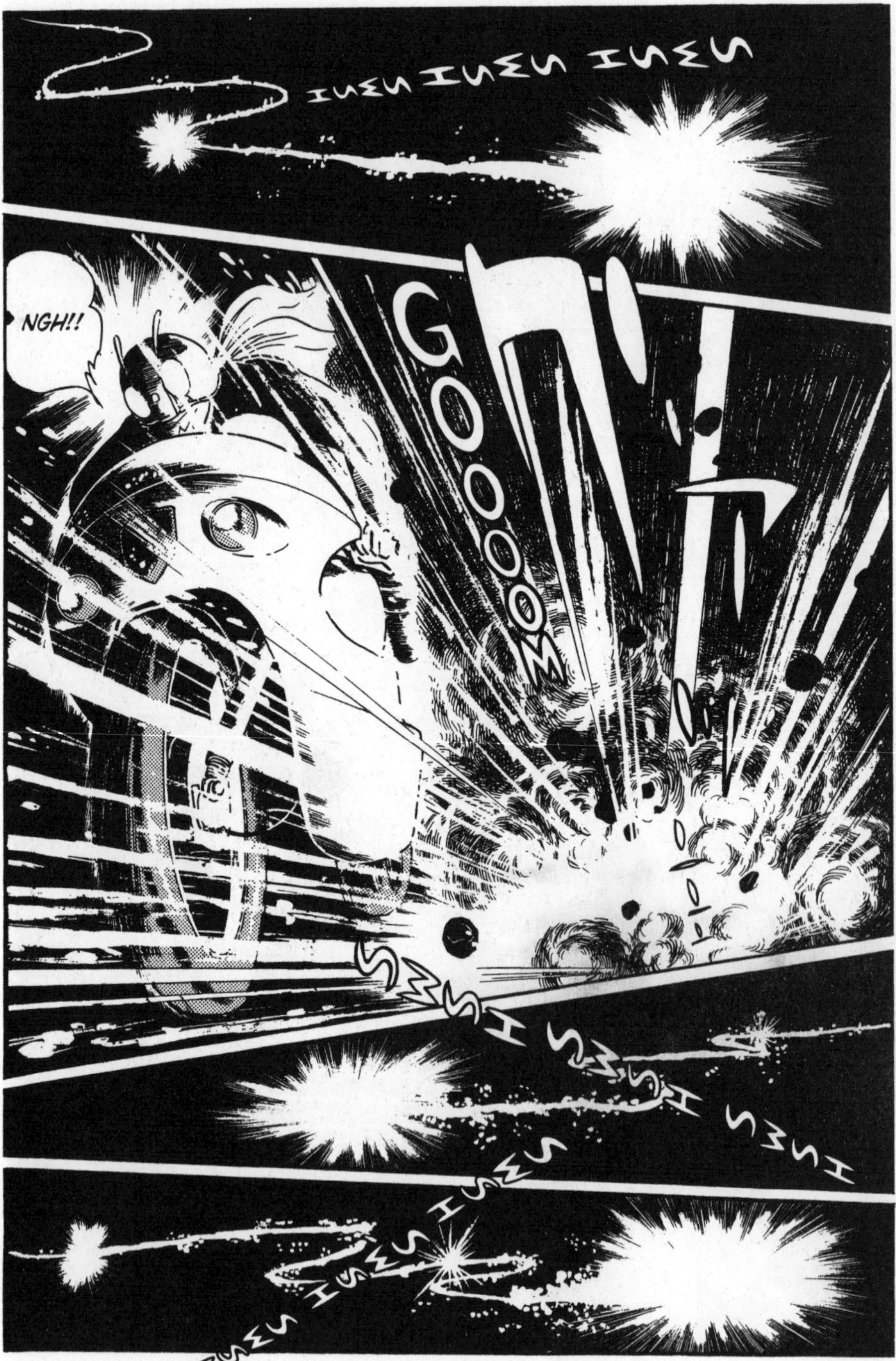
NGH!!
GOOOOOM

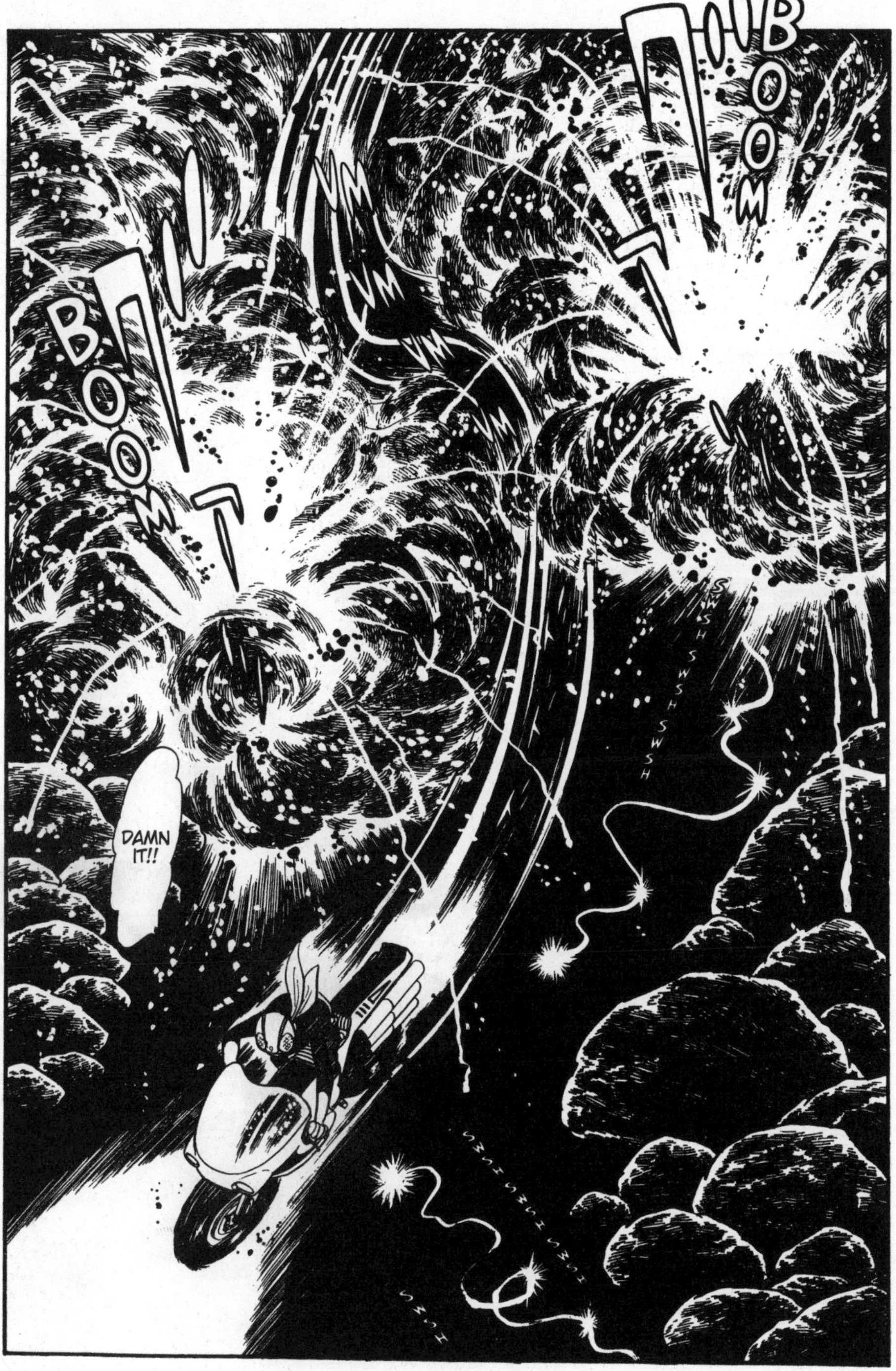

BOOOM
BOOOM
DAMN IT!!
SWSH SWSH SWSH

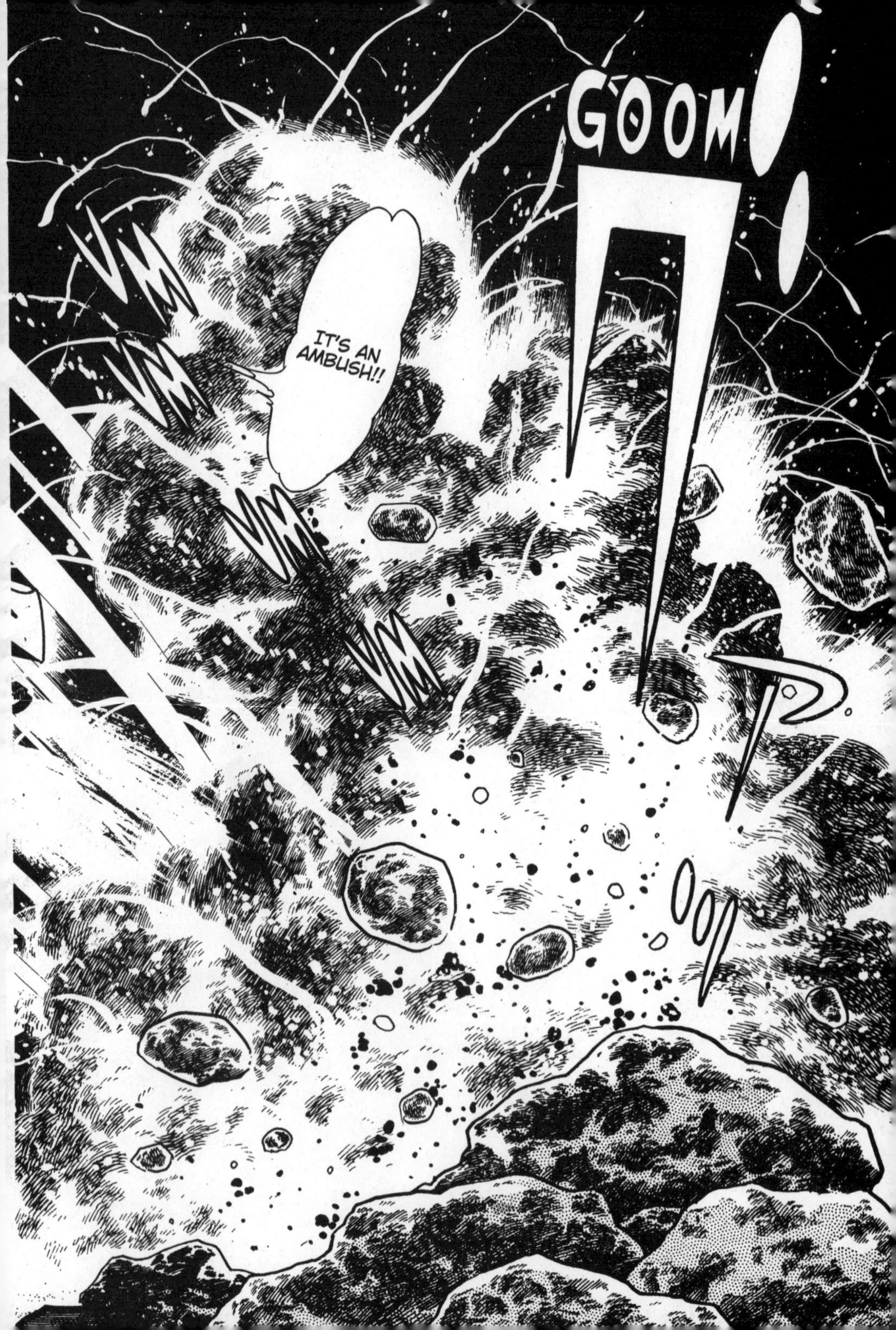
GOOM
IT'S AN AMBUSH!!

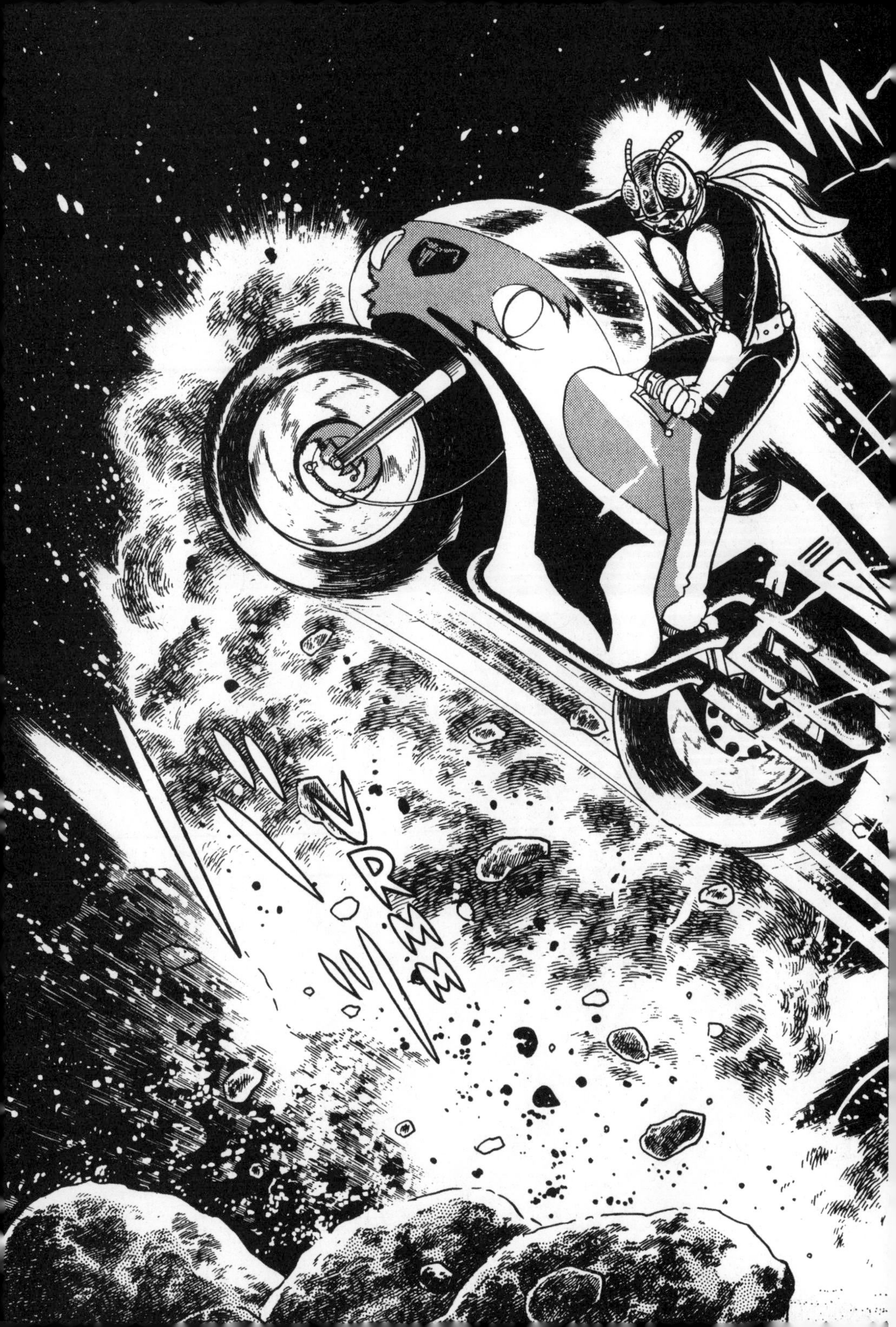
VM
VRMMM

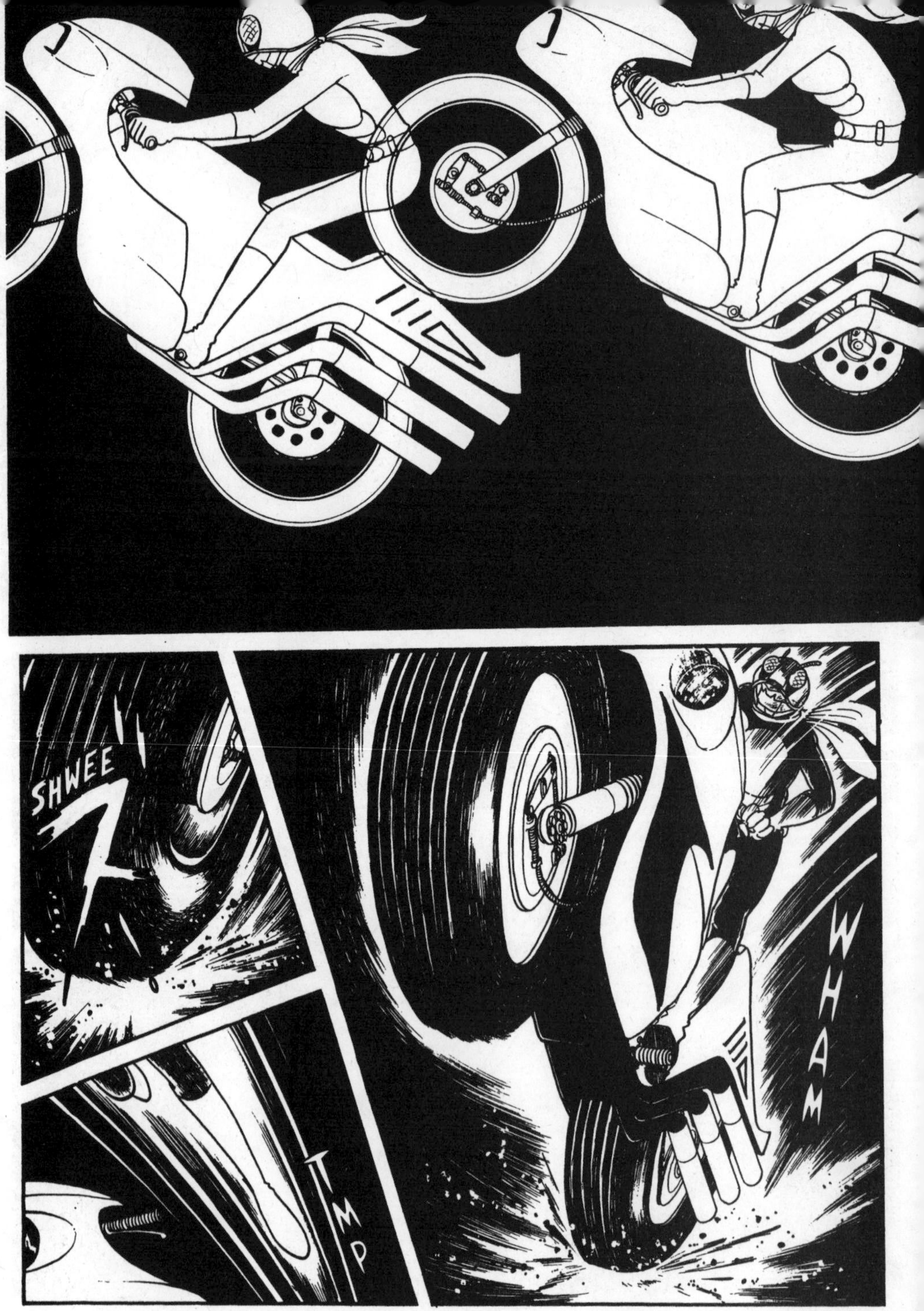
WHAM
SHWEE
TMP

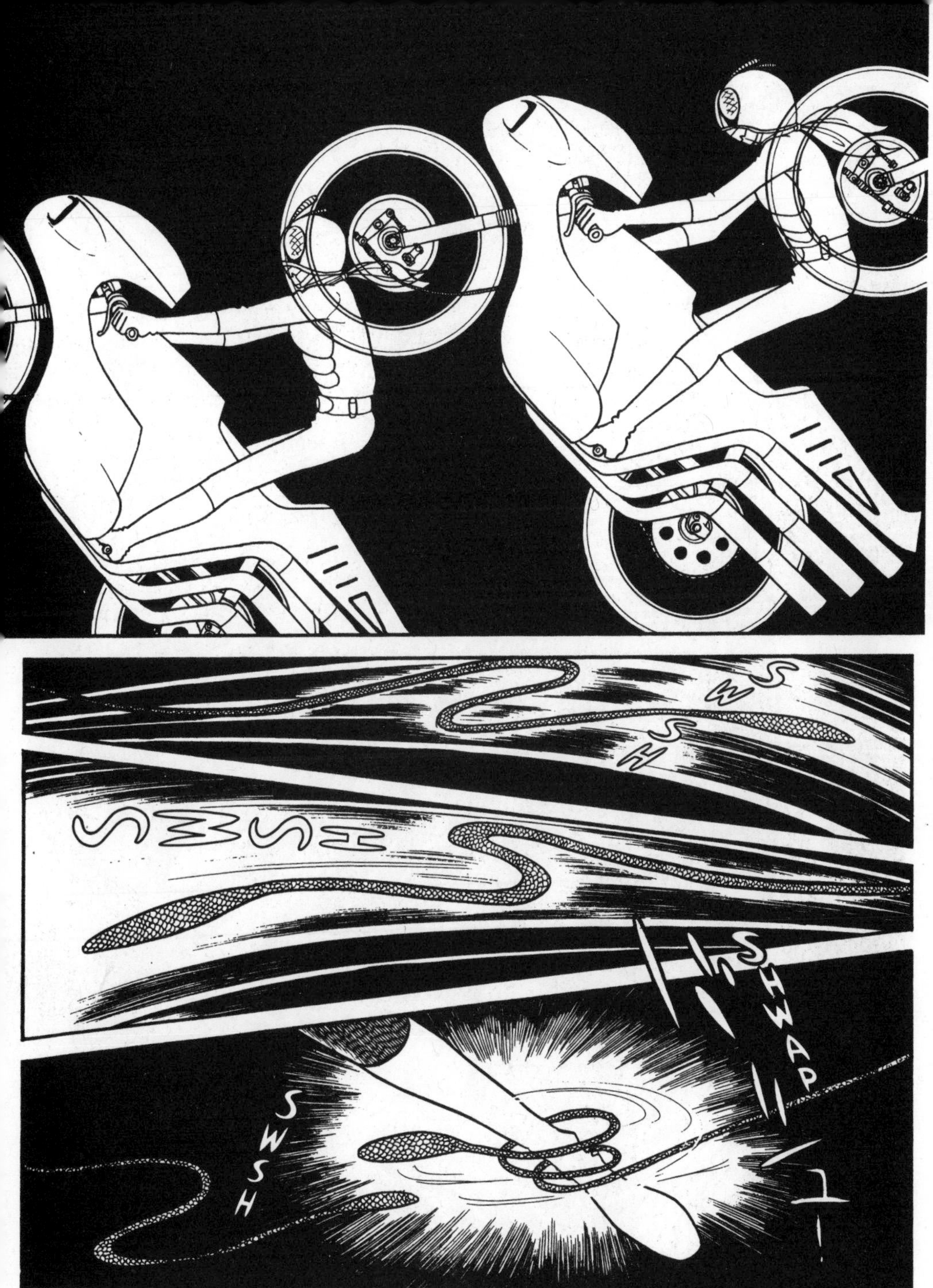
SWSH
SWSH
SHWAP
SWSH

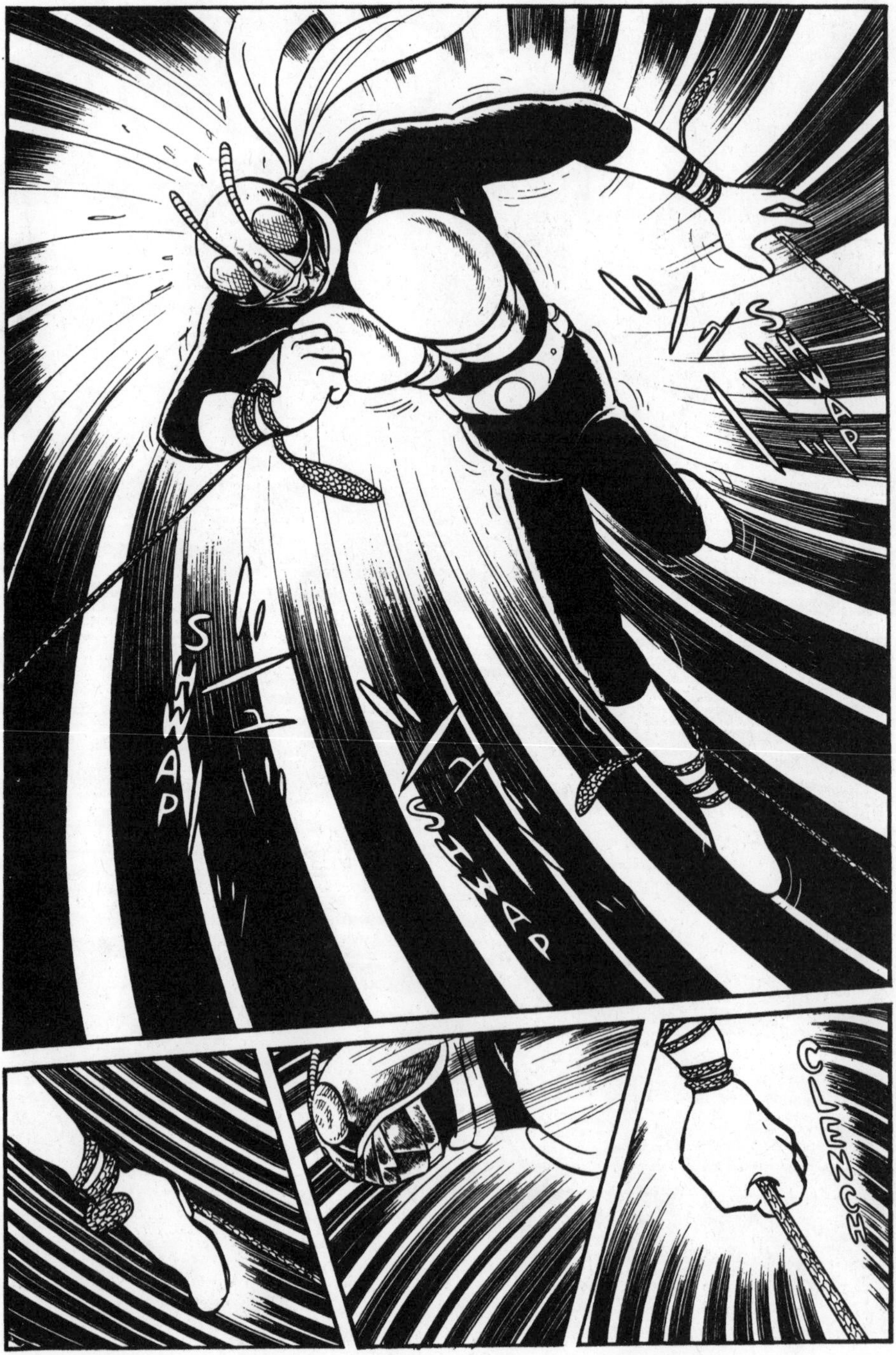
SHWAP
SHWAP
SHWAP
CLENCH

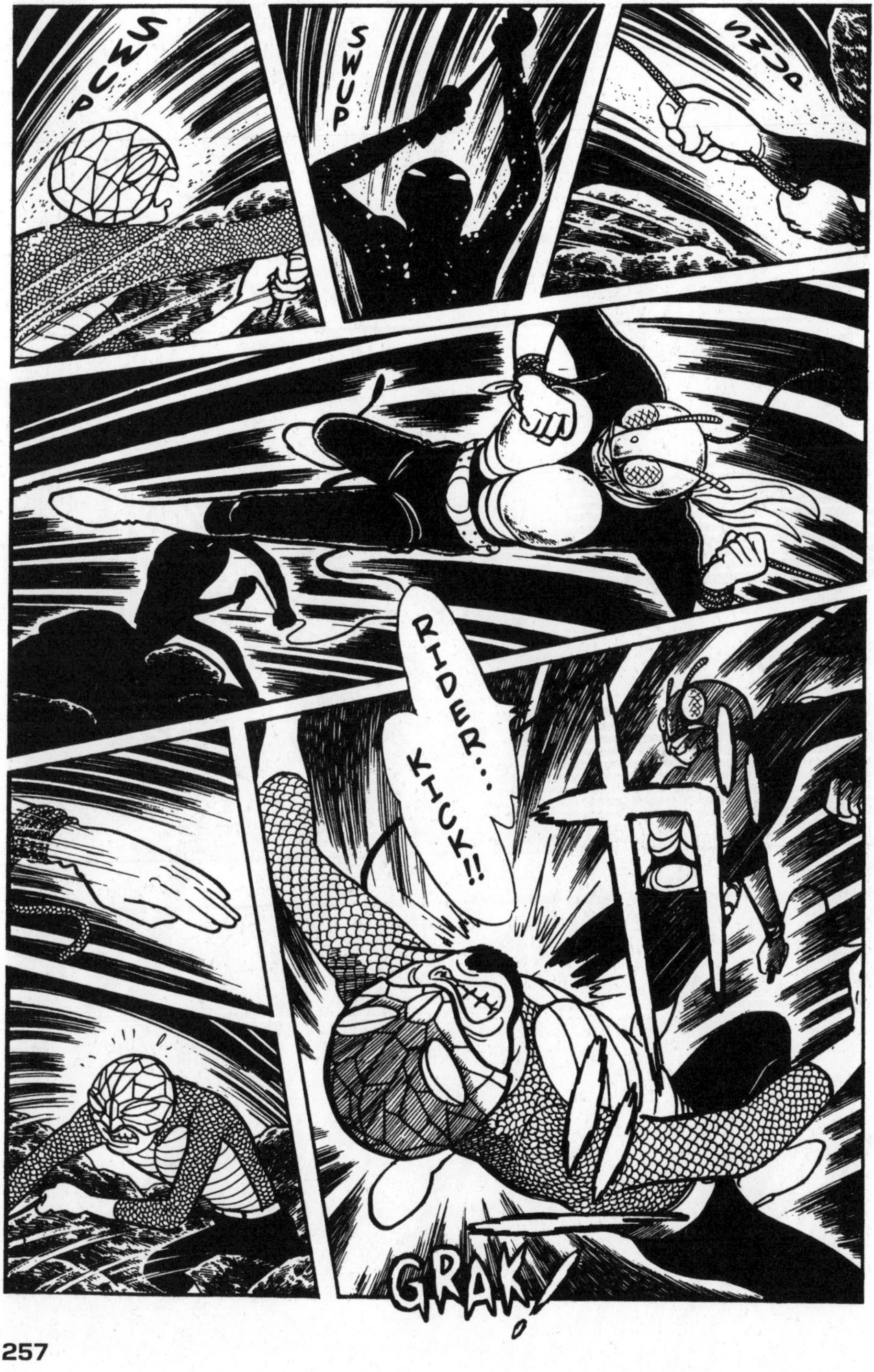
SWUP
SWUP
SWUP
RIDER... KICK!!
GRAK!

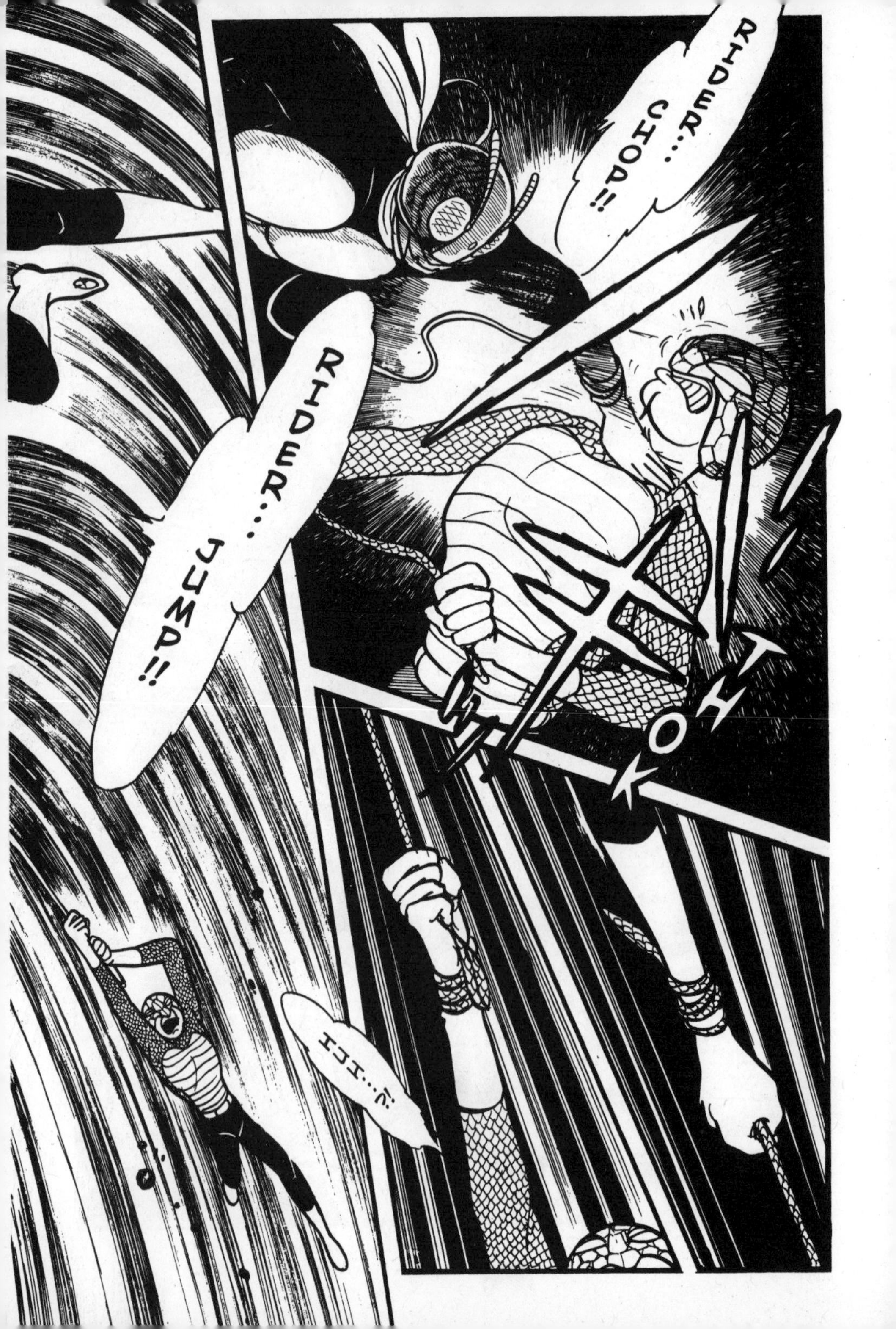
RIDER... CHOP!!
RIDER... JUMP!!
THOK
HUH...?!

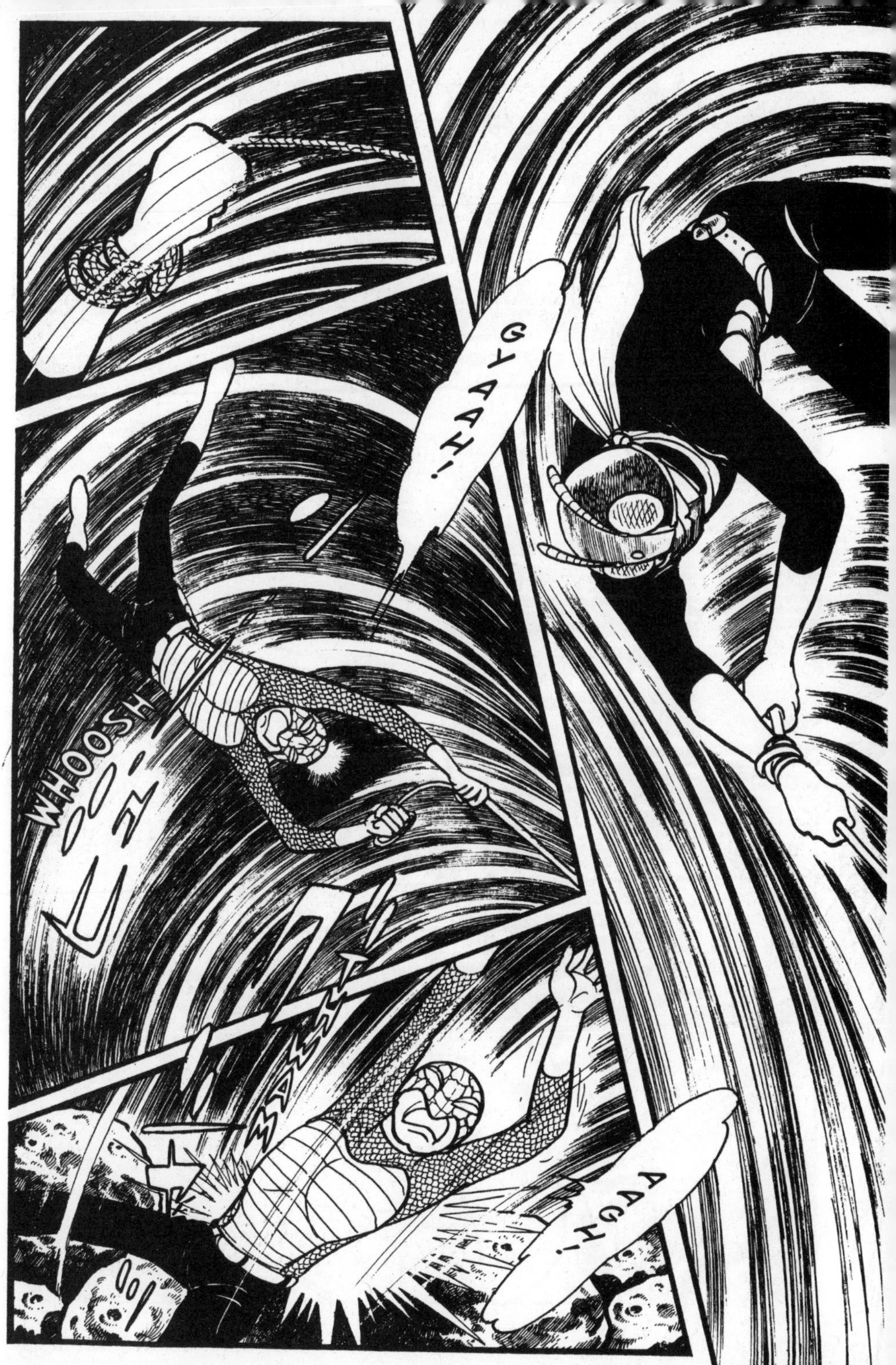
GYAAAH!
WHOOSH
SMASH
AAGH!

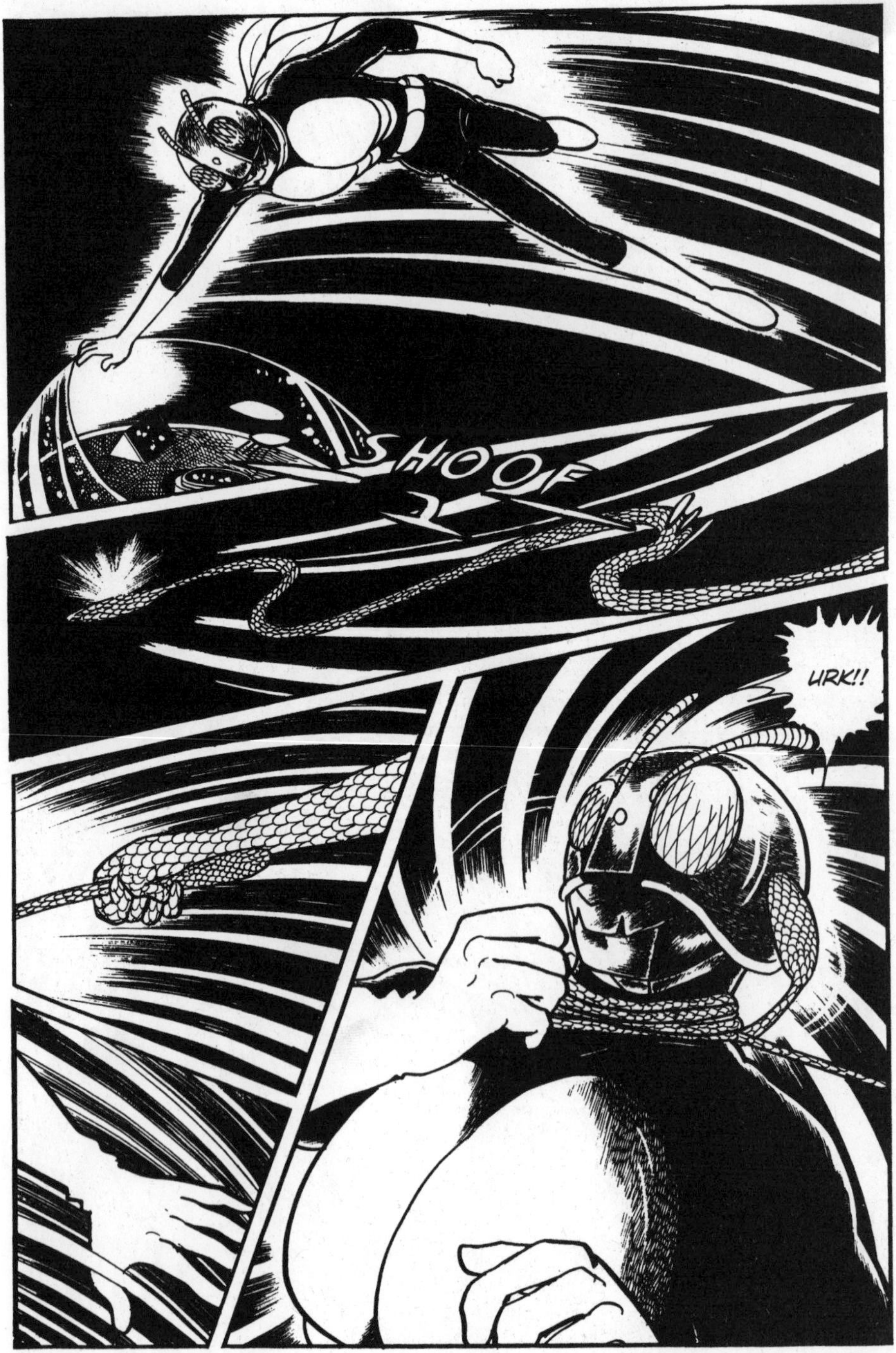
SHOOF
URK!!

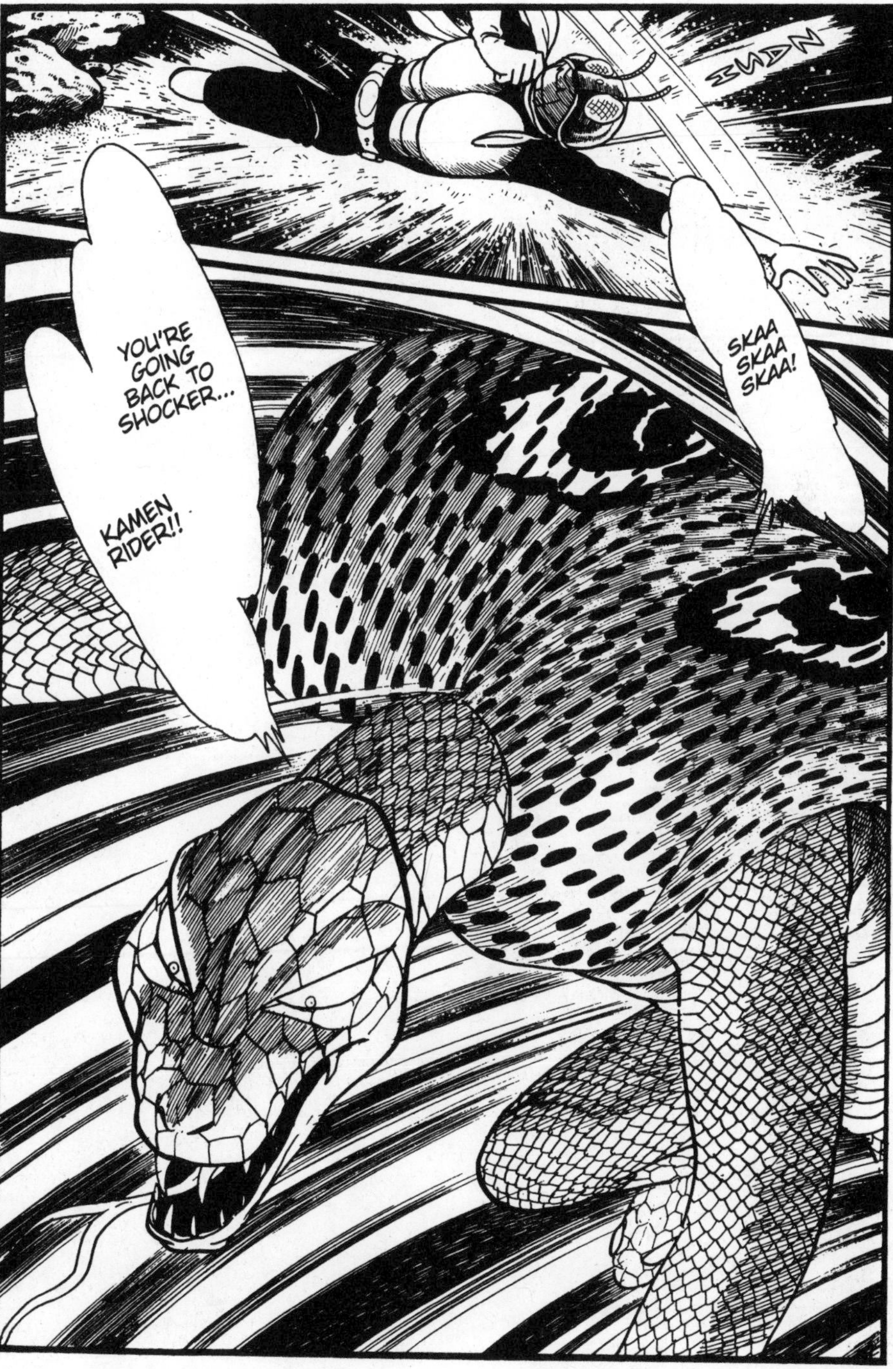
SKAA SKAA SKAA!
YOU'RE GOING BACK TO SHOCKER...
KAMEN RIDER!!

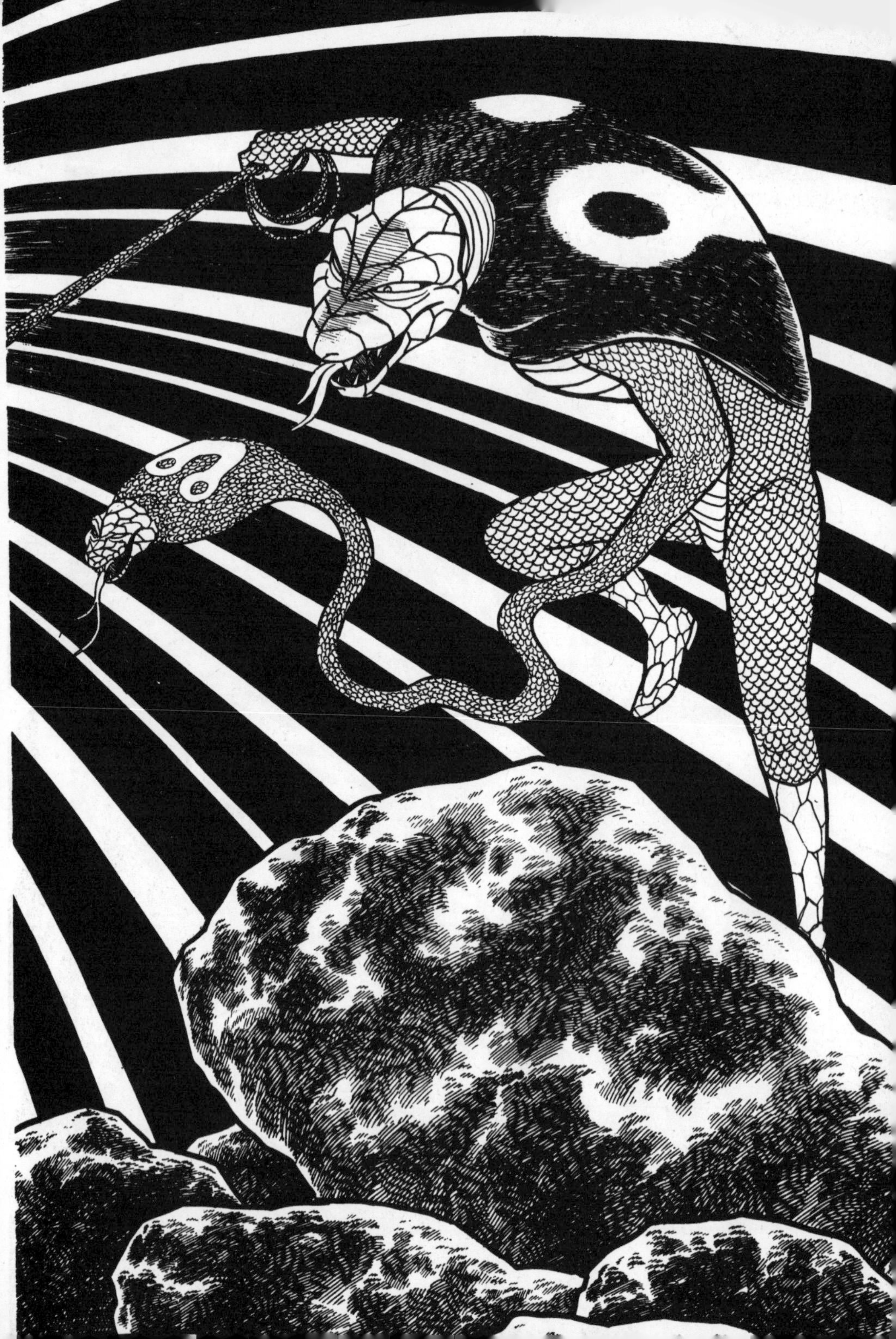

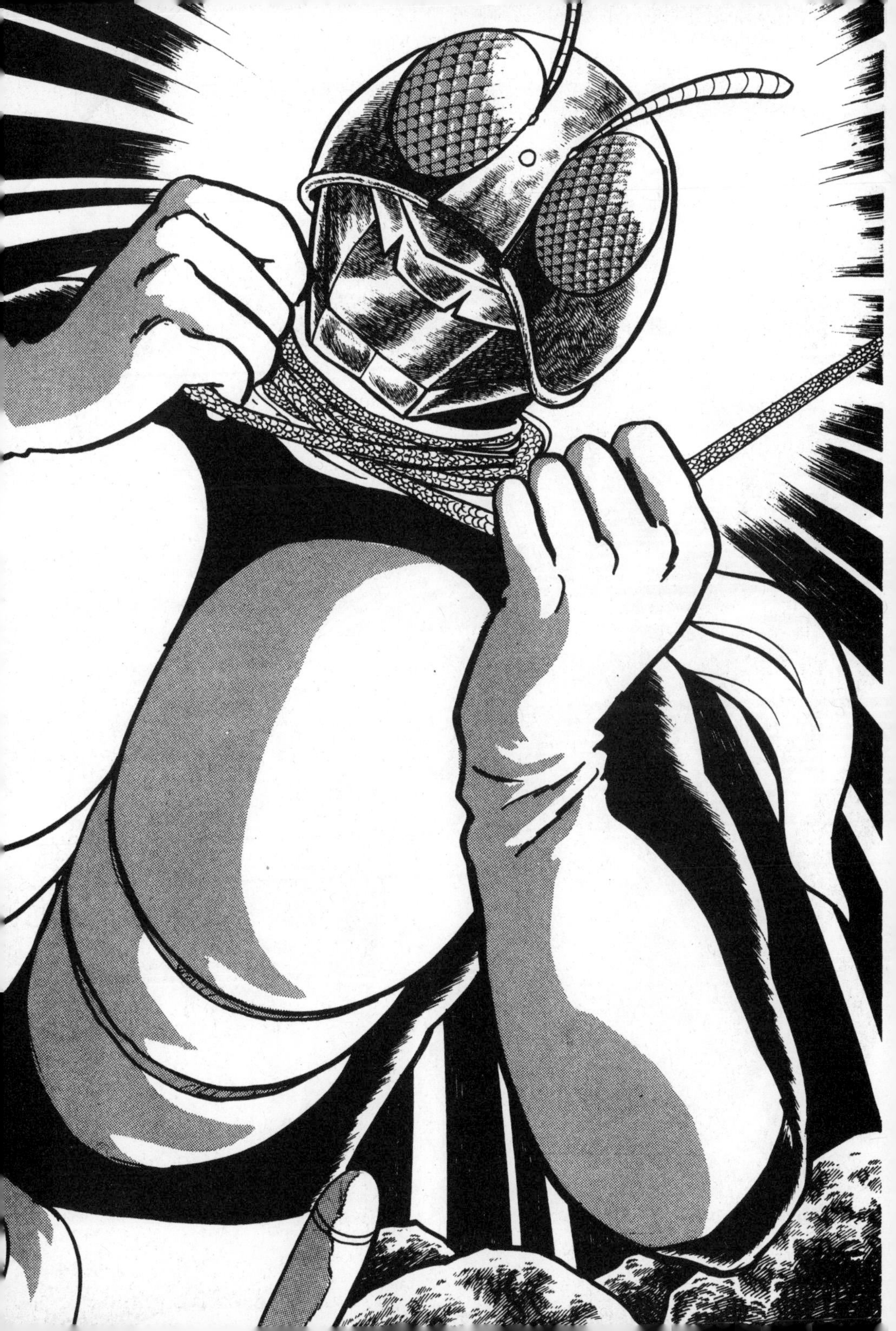

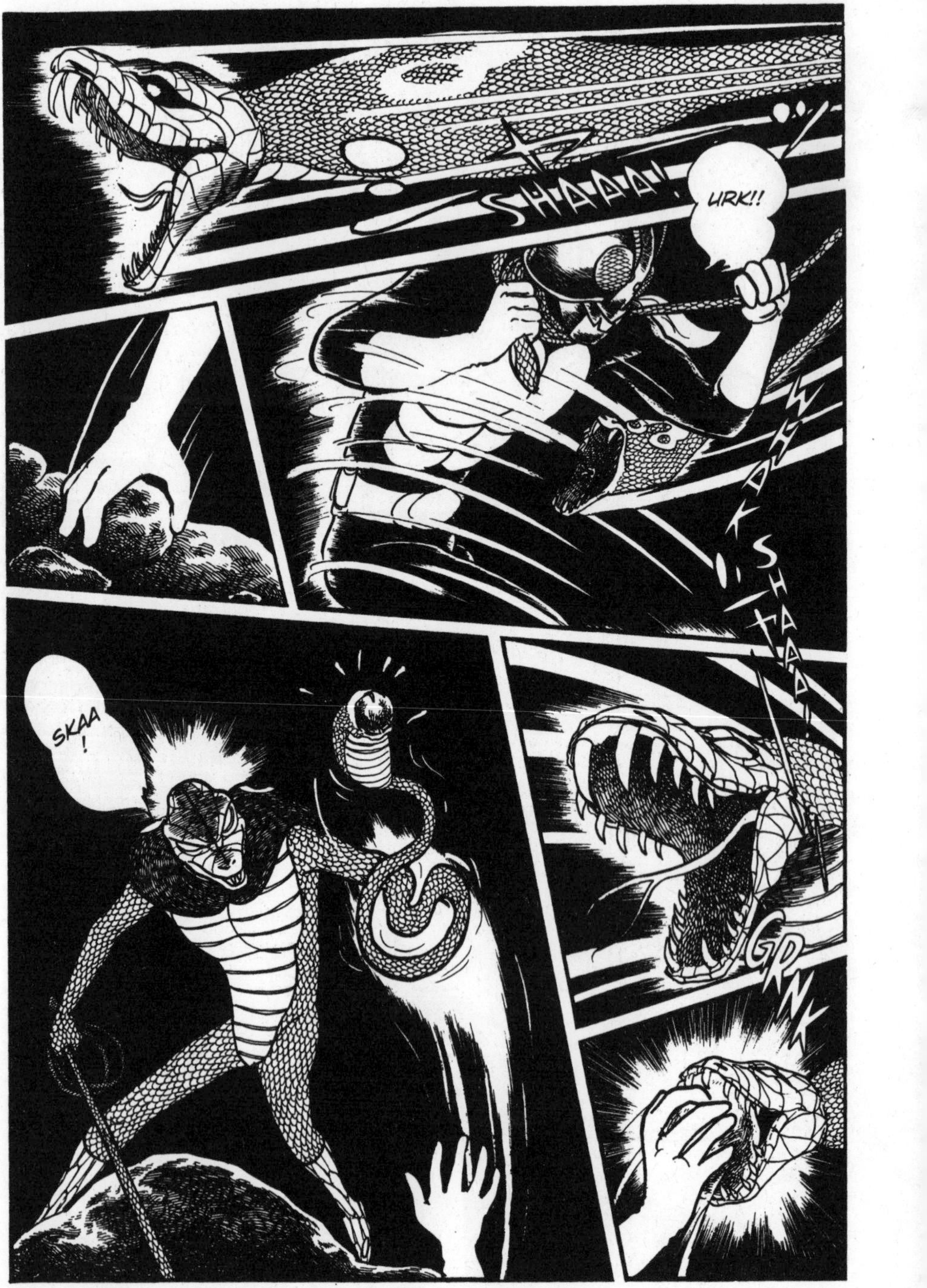
SHAAA!
URK!!
WHAK
SHAAA!
GRNK
SKAA!

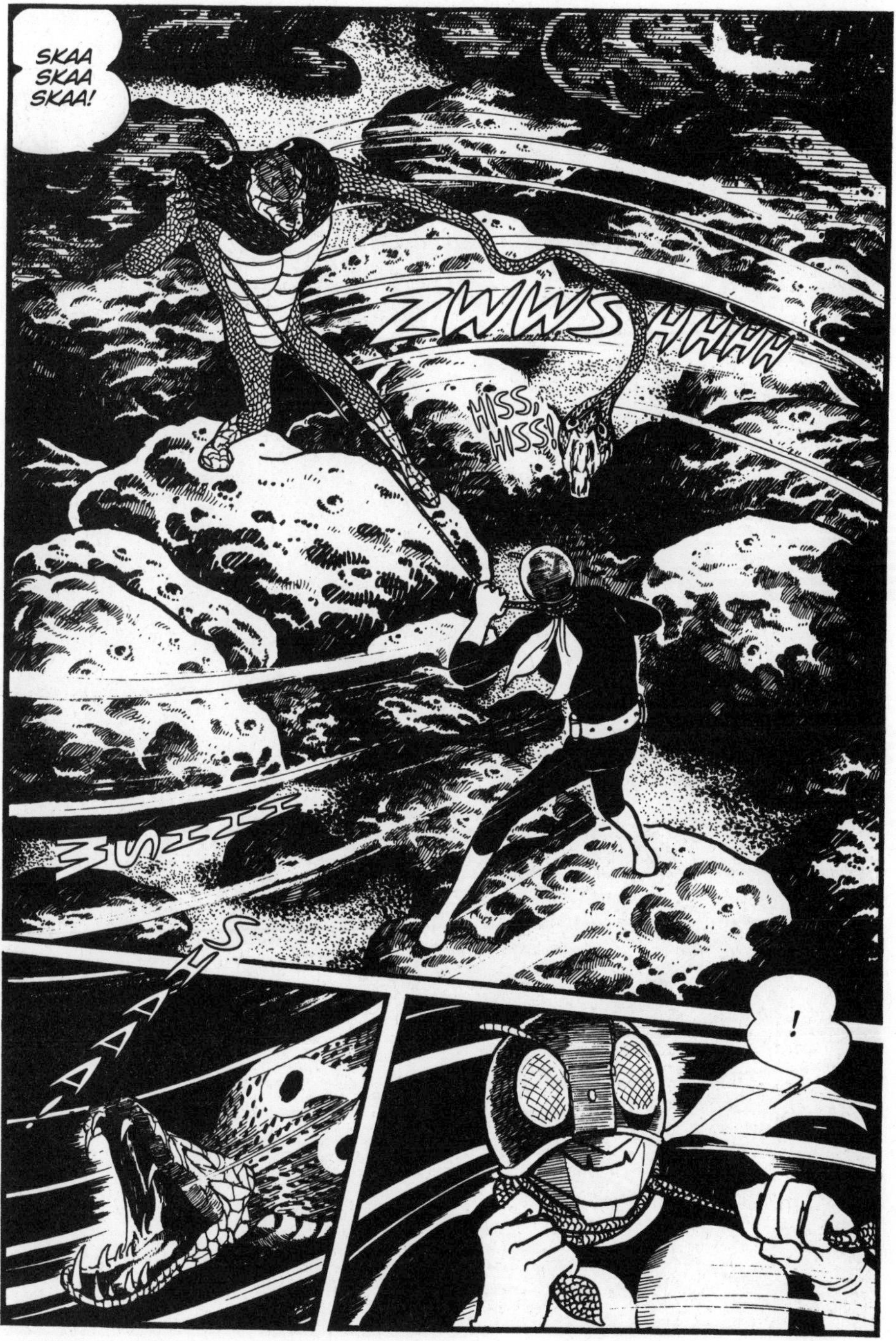
SKAA SKAA SKAA!
ZWWSHHHH
HISS, HISS!
WSHHH
!
SHAAAA!

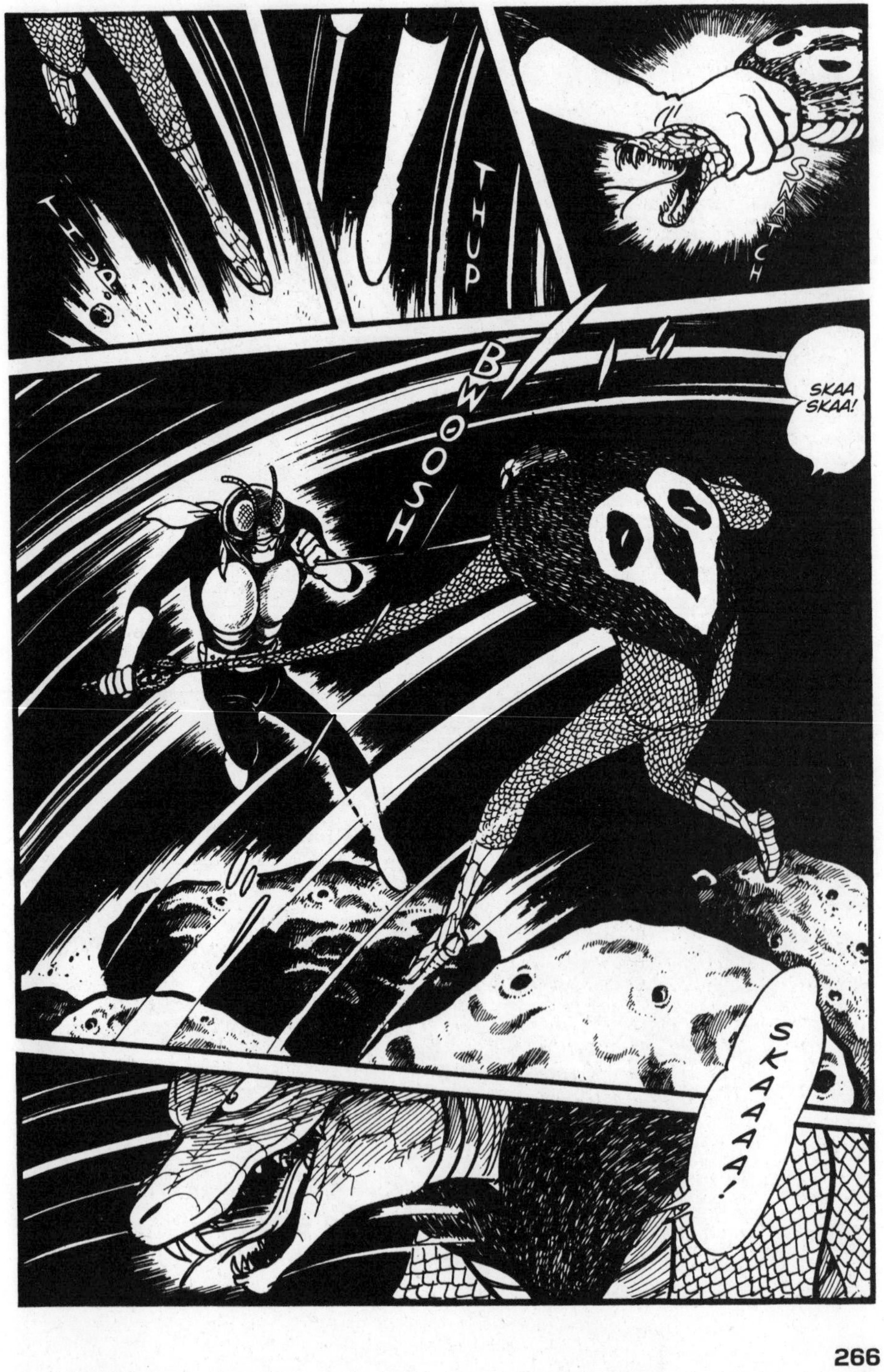
SNATCH
THUP
THUP
SKAA SKAA!
BWOOSH
SKAAAAA!

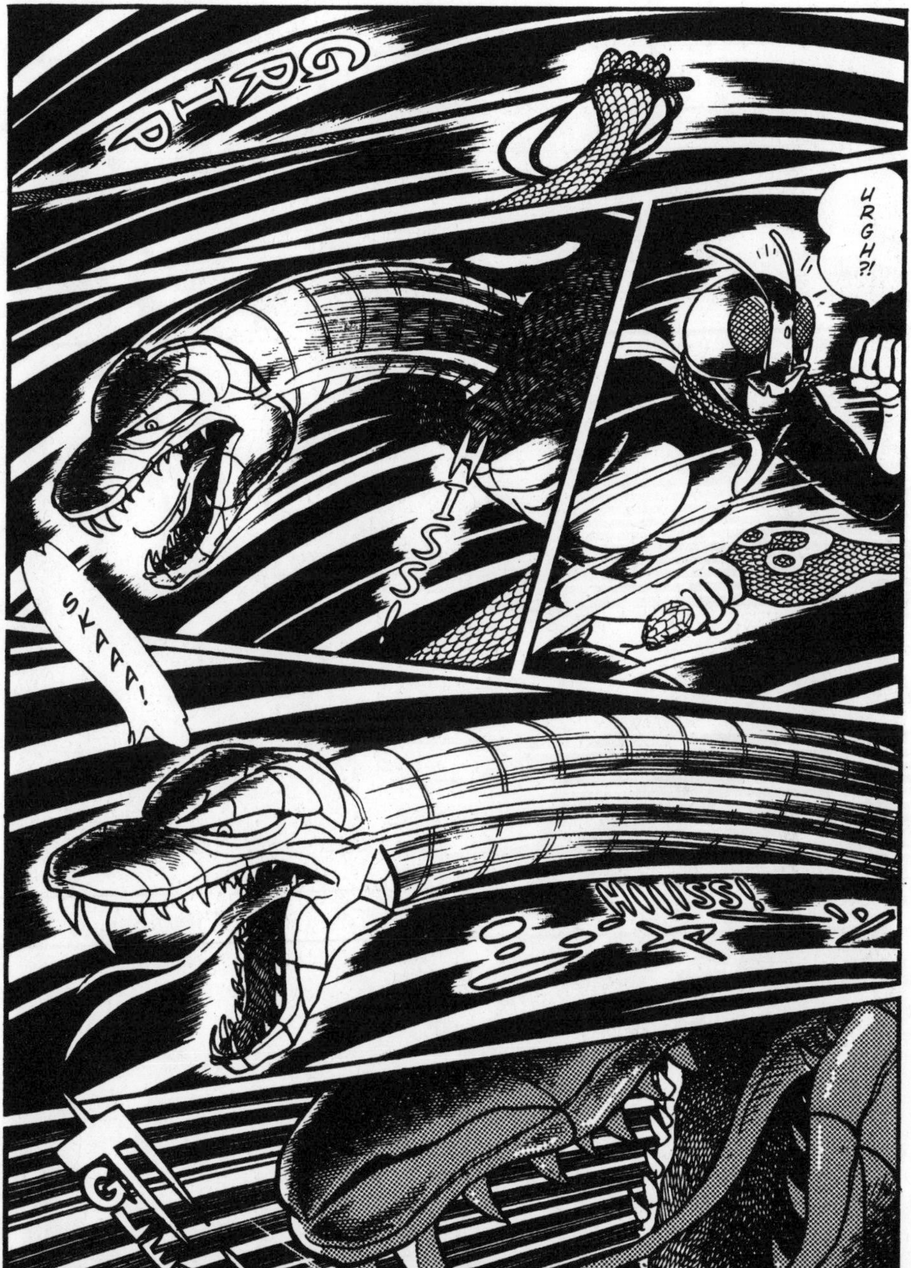
GRIP
URGH?!
HISSS!
SKAAA!
HIIISS!
GLEAM

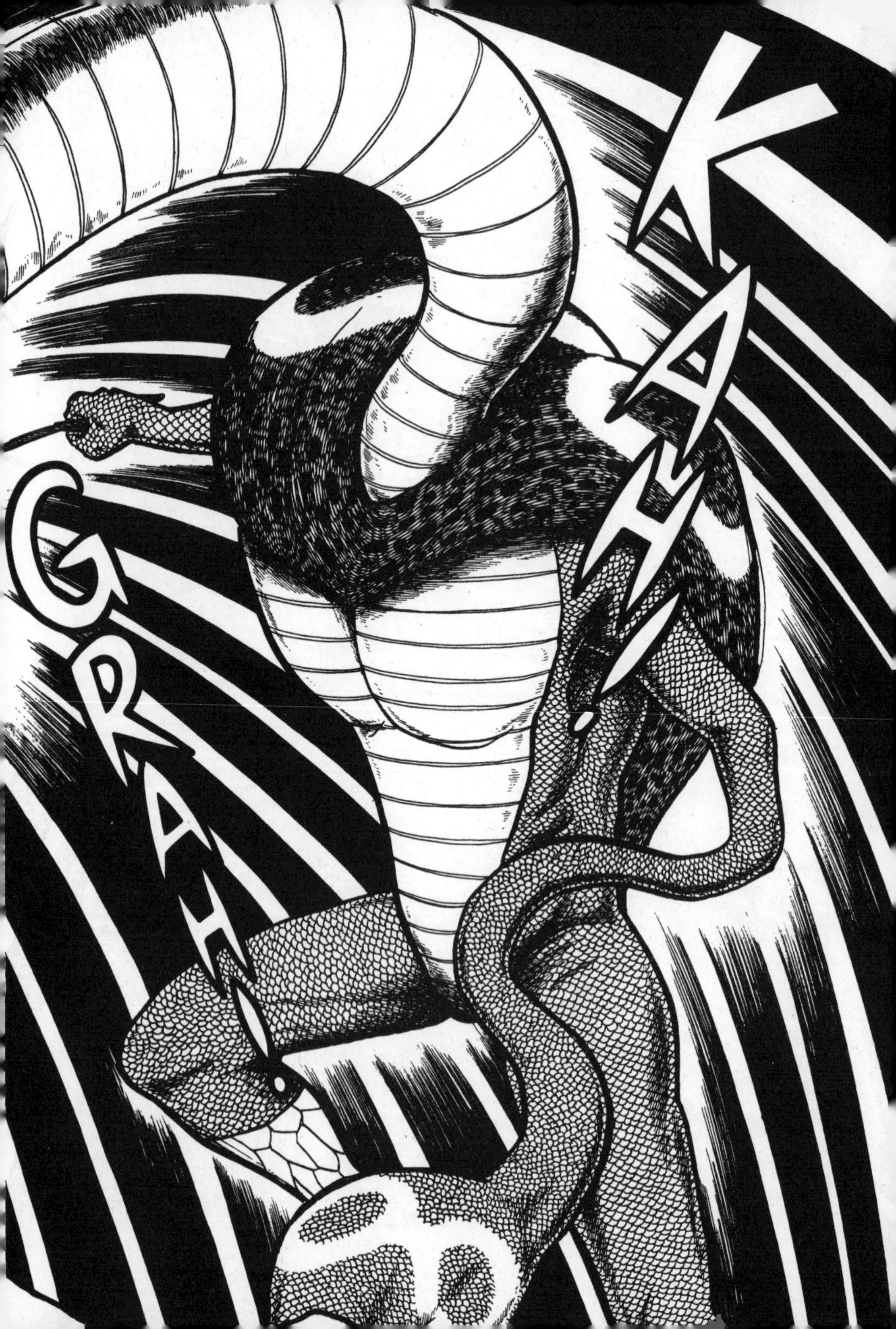
KAAH!
GRAH!

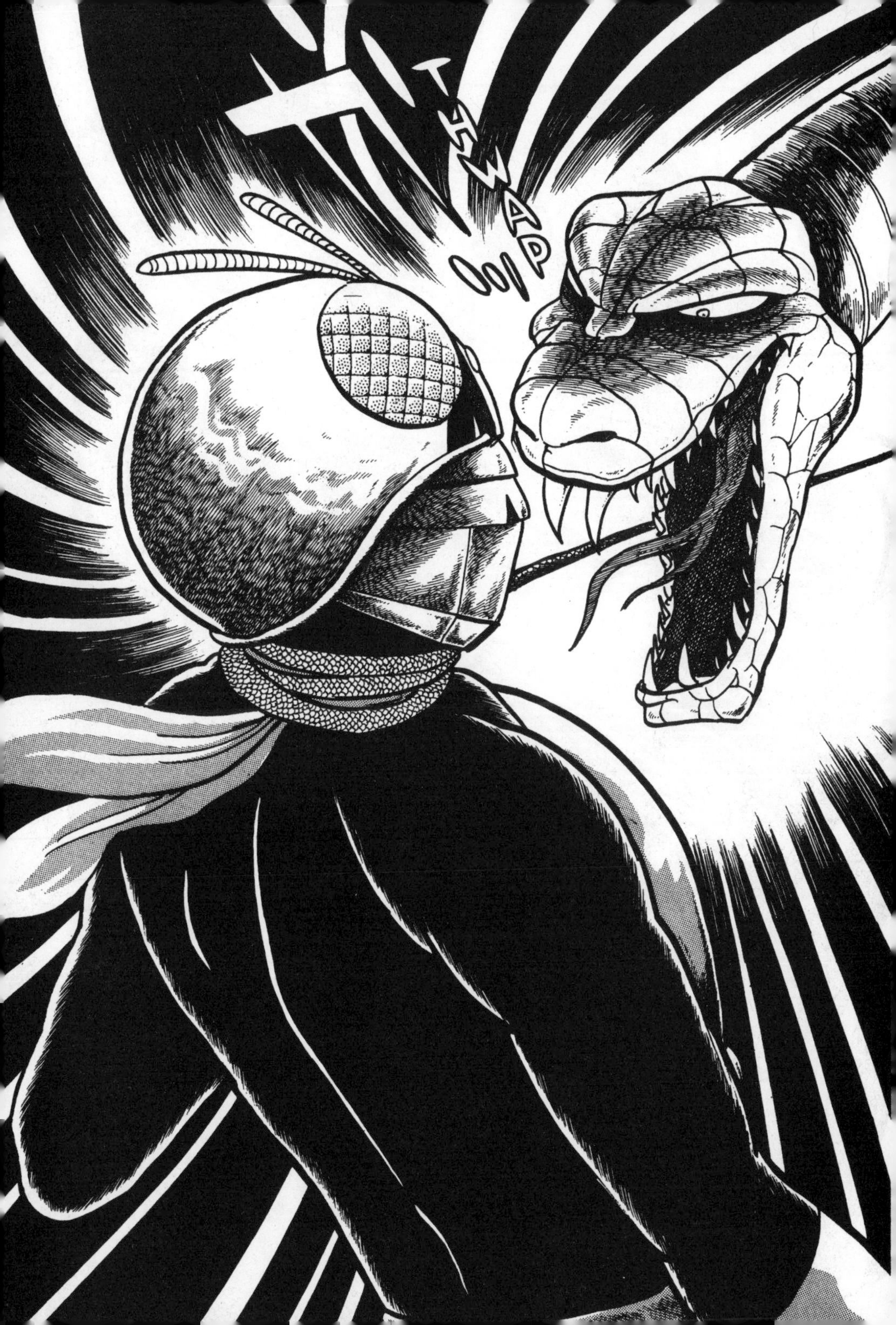
THWAP

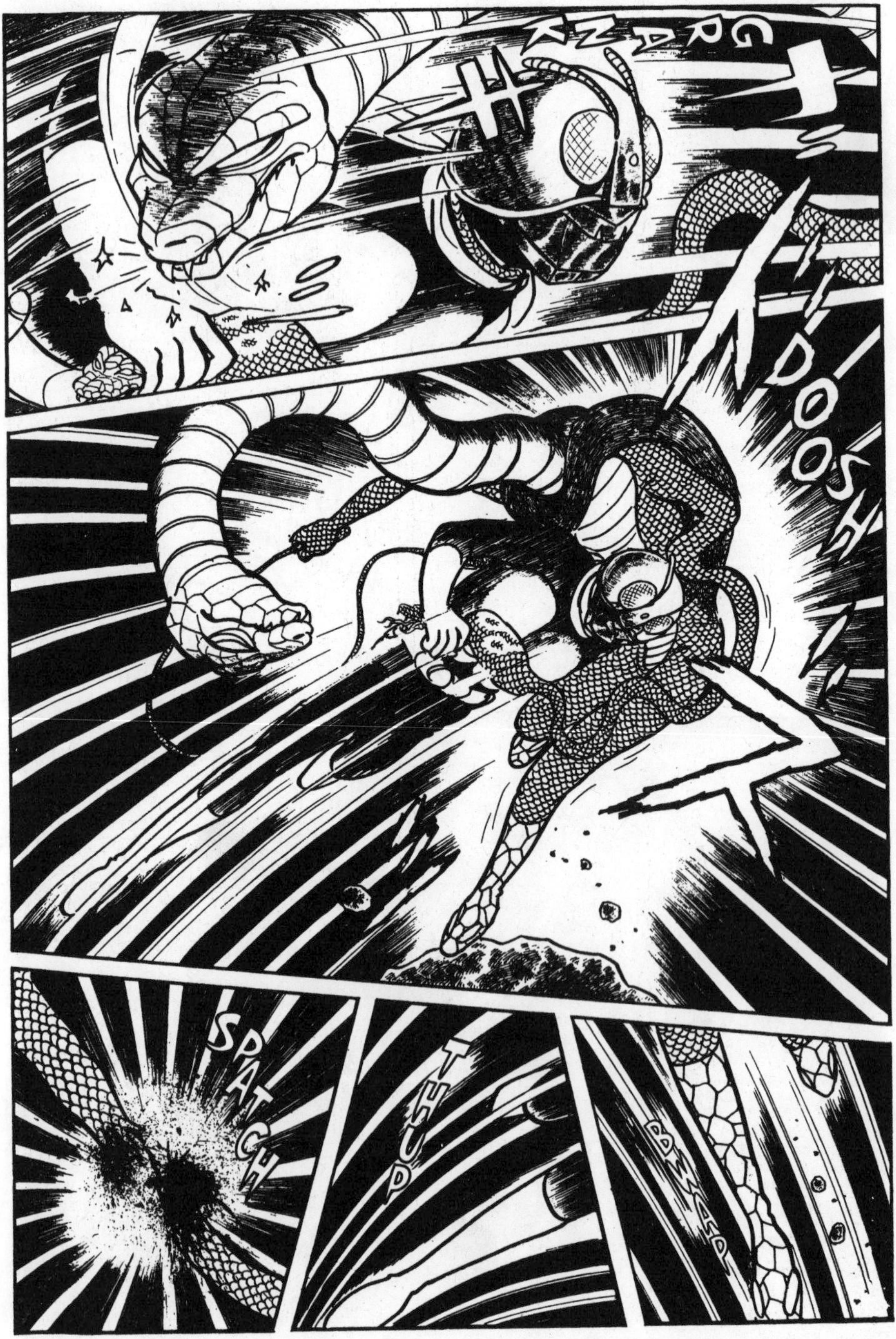
GRANK
DOOSH
THUD
SPATCH

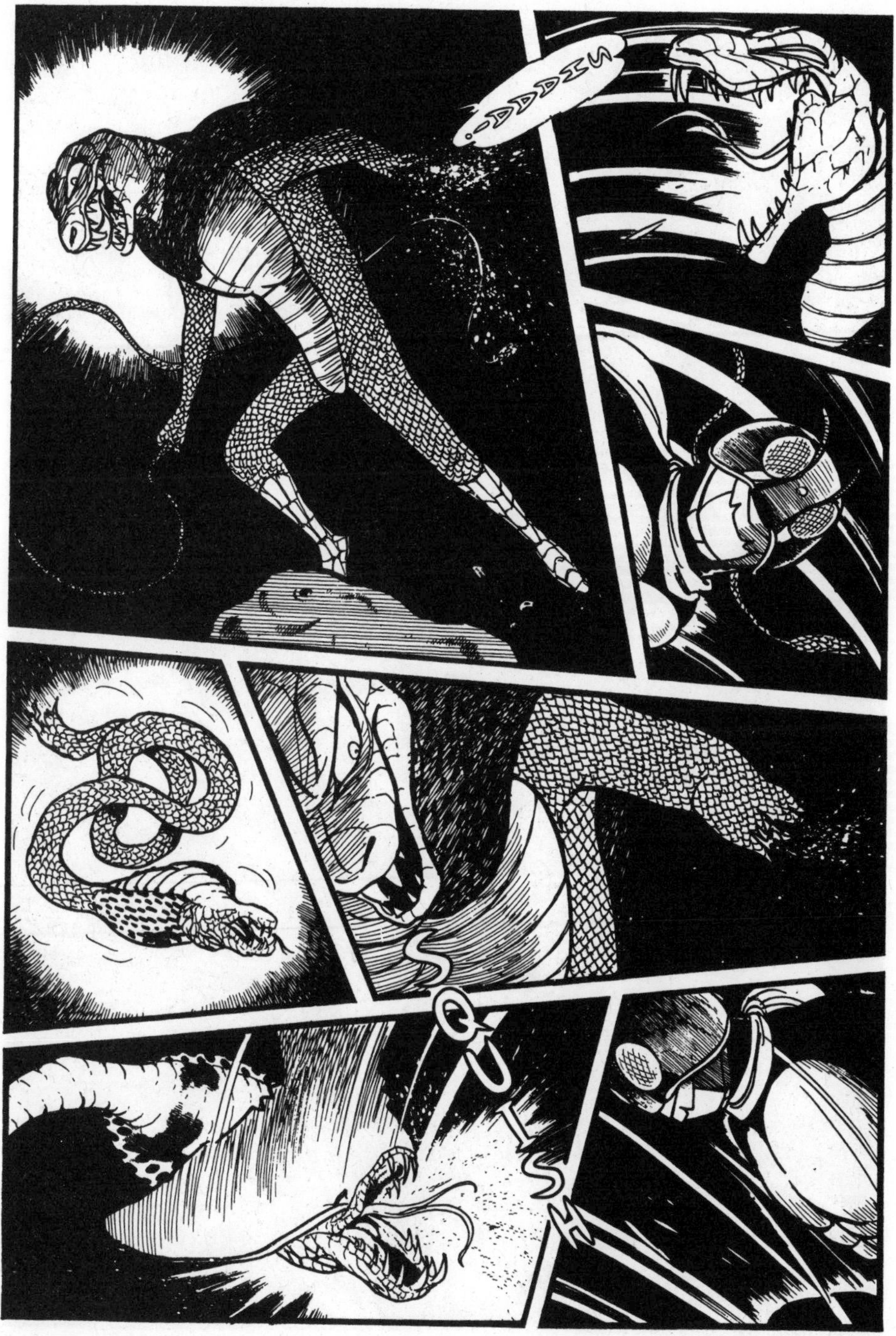
SHAAA-!
SQUISH

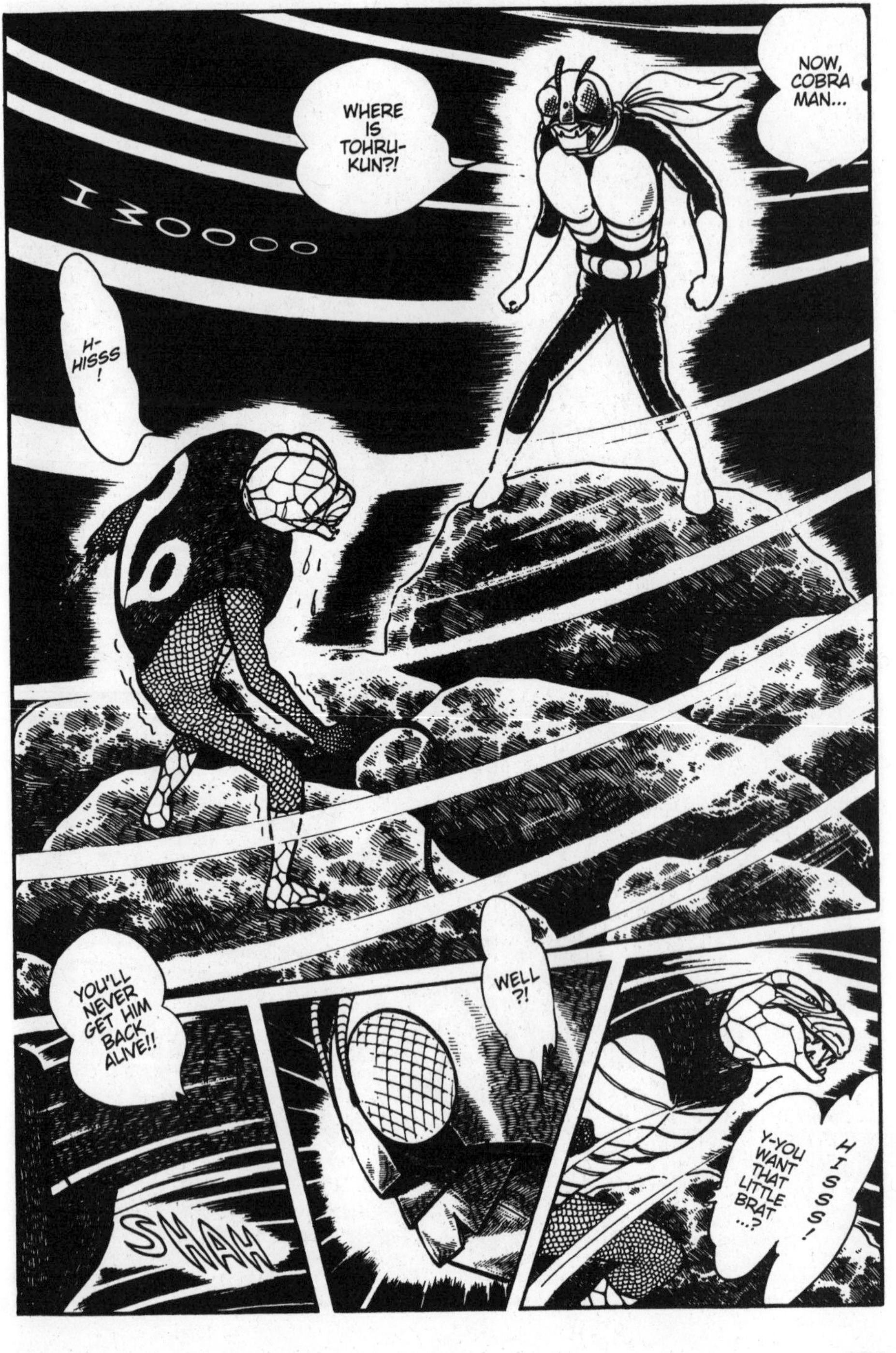
NOW, COBRA MAN...
WHERE IS TOHRU-KUN?!
HWOOOO
H-HISSS!
HISSS!
Y-YOU WANT THAT LITTLE BRAT...?
WELL?!
YOU'LL NEVER GET HIM BACK ALIVE!!
SHAAH

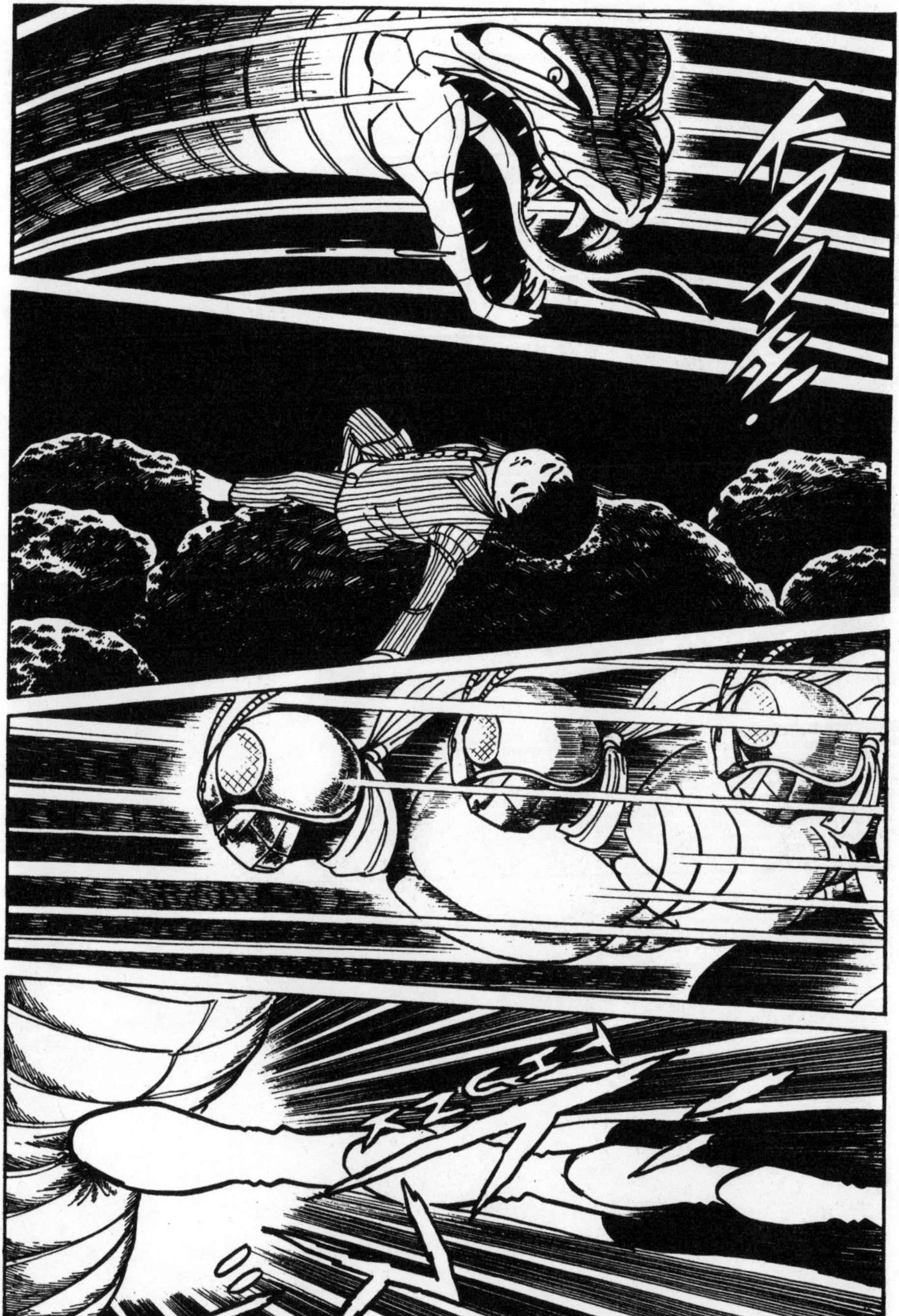
KAAAH!
KZGHT

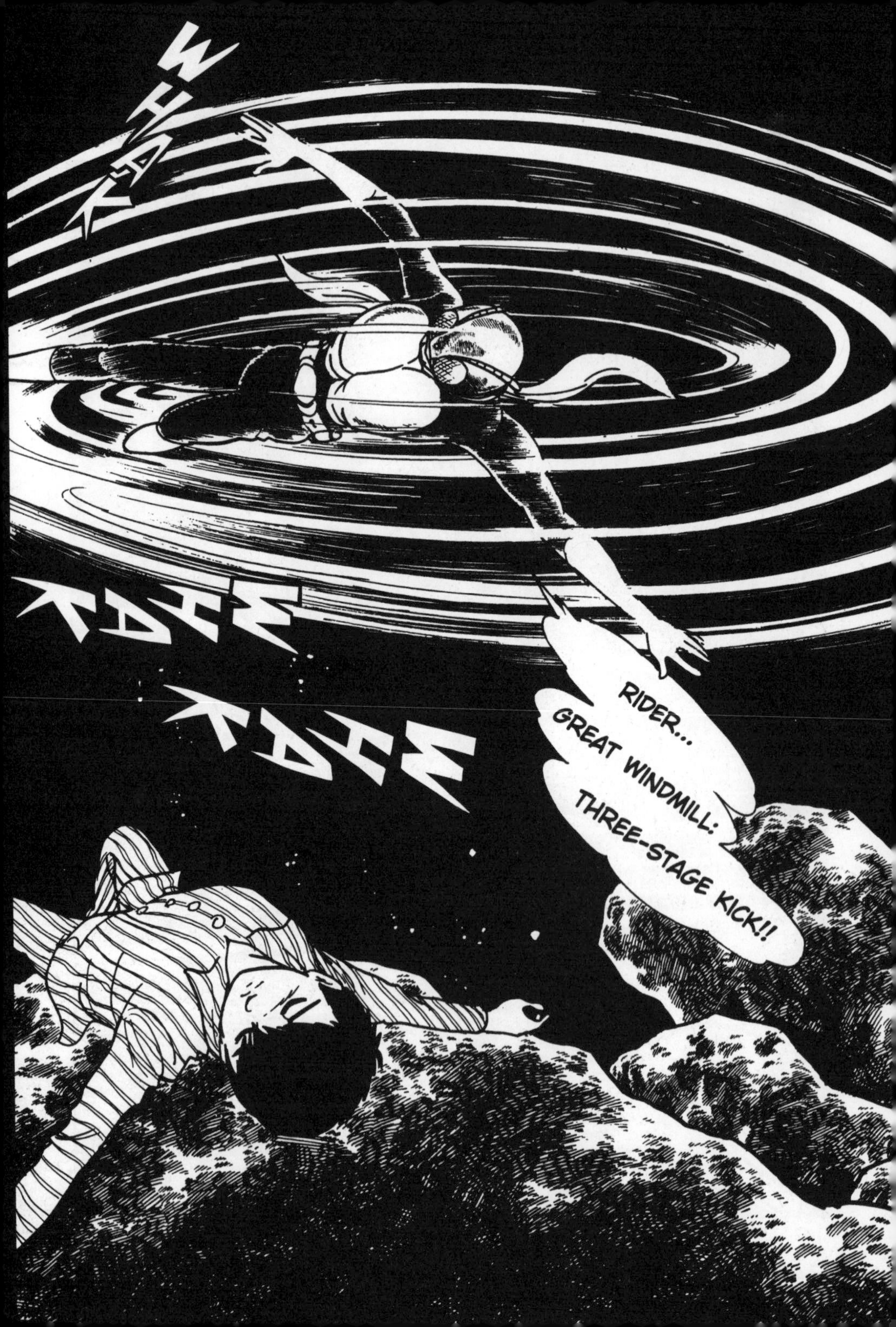
WHAK
WHAK
WHAK
RIDER... GREAT WINDMILL: THREE-STAGE KICK!!

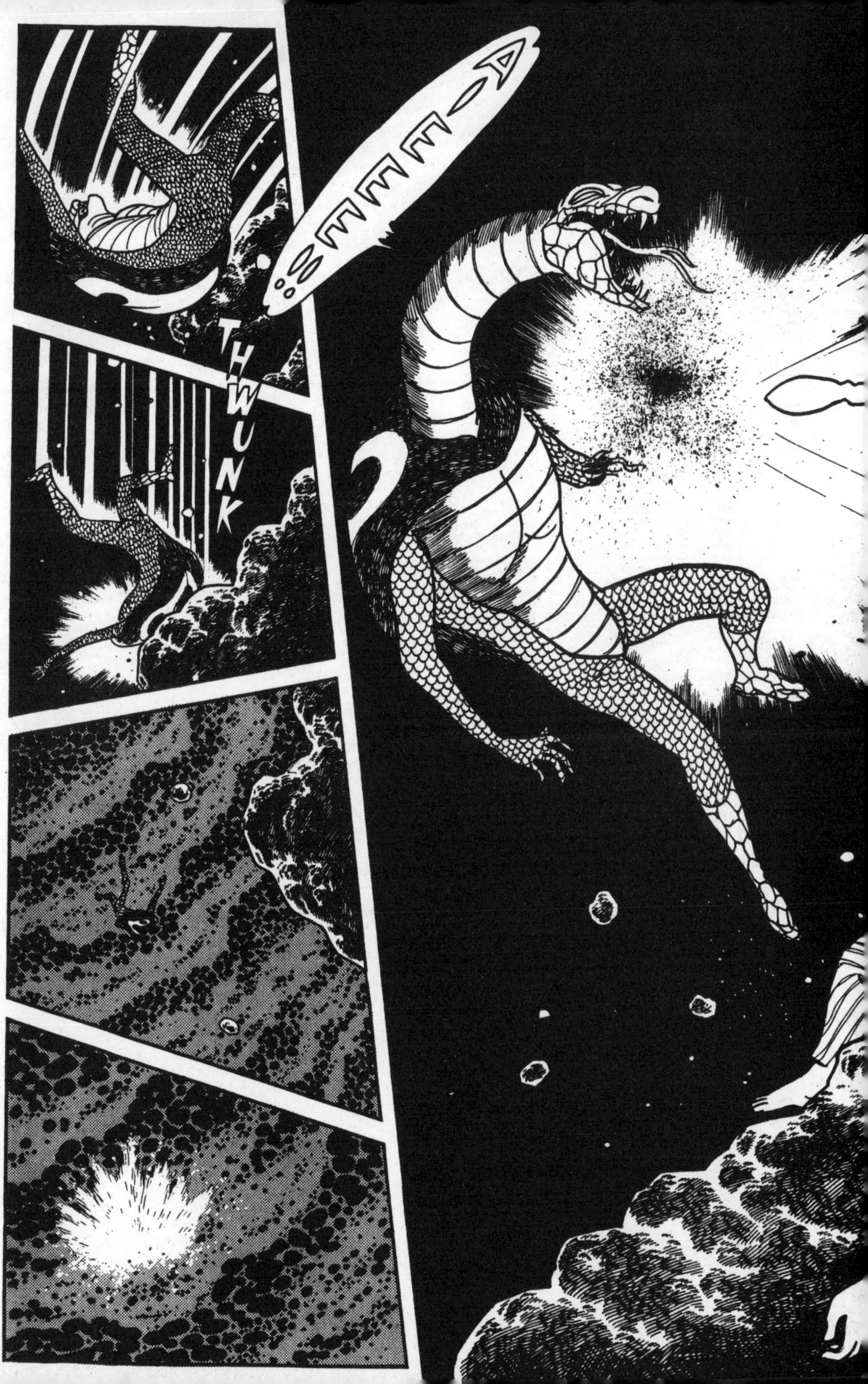
A-EEEE!!
THWUNK

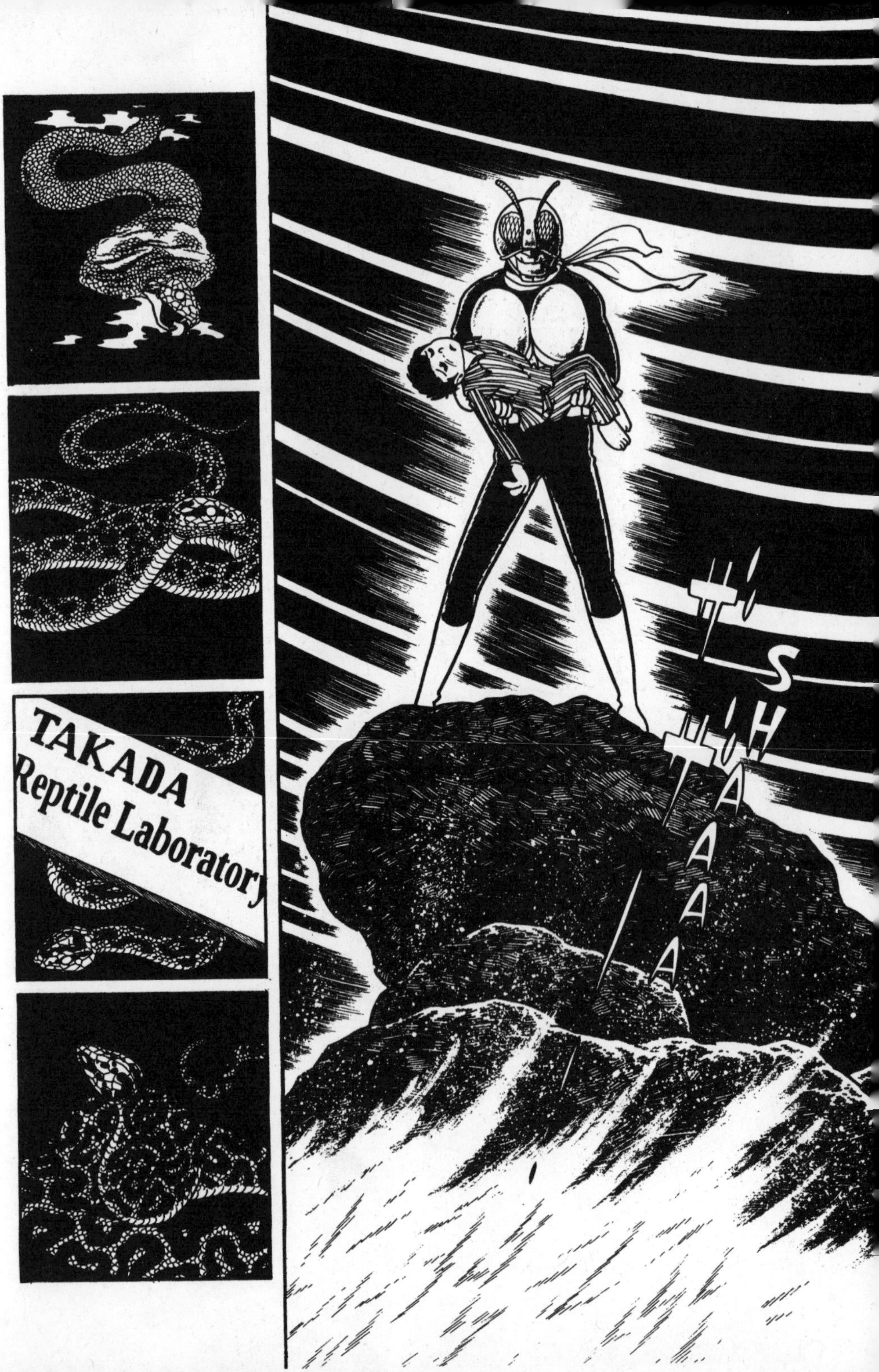
SHAAAA
TAKADA Reptile Laboratory

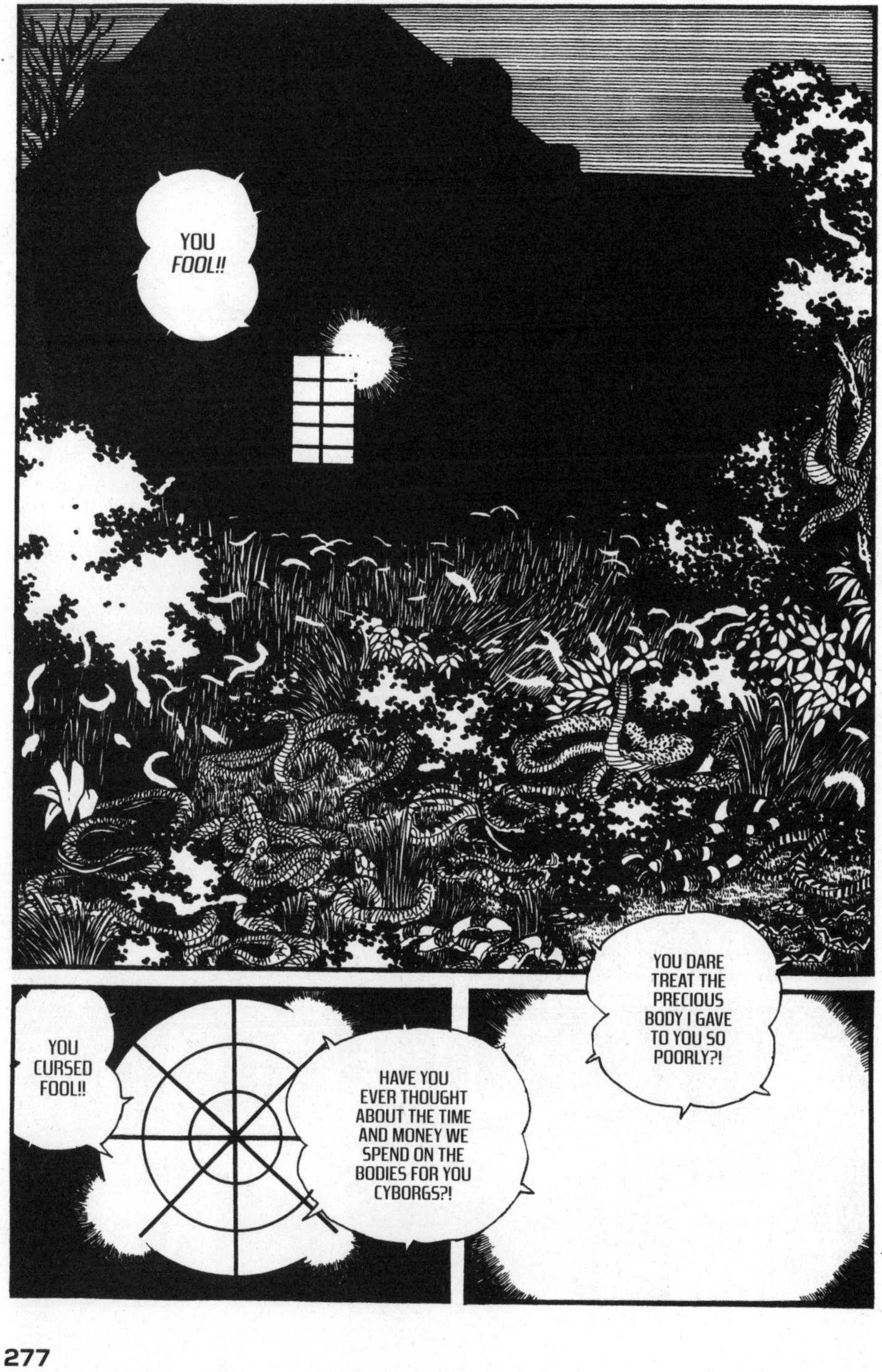
YOU *FOOL!!*
YOU DARE TREAT THE PRECIOUS BODY I GAVE TO YOU SO POORLY?!
HAVE YOU EVER THOUGHT ABOUT THE TIME AND MONEY WE SPEND ON THE BODIES FOR YOU CYBORGS?!
YOU CURSED FOOL!!

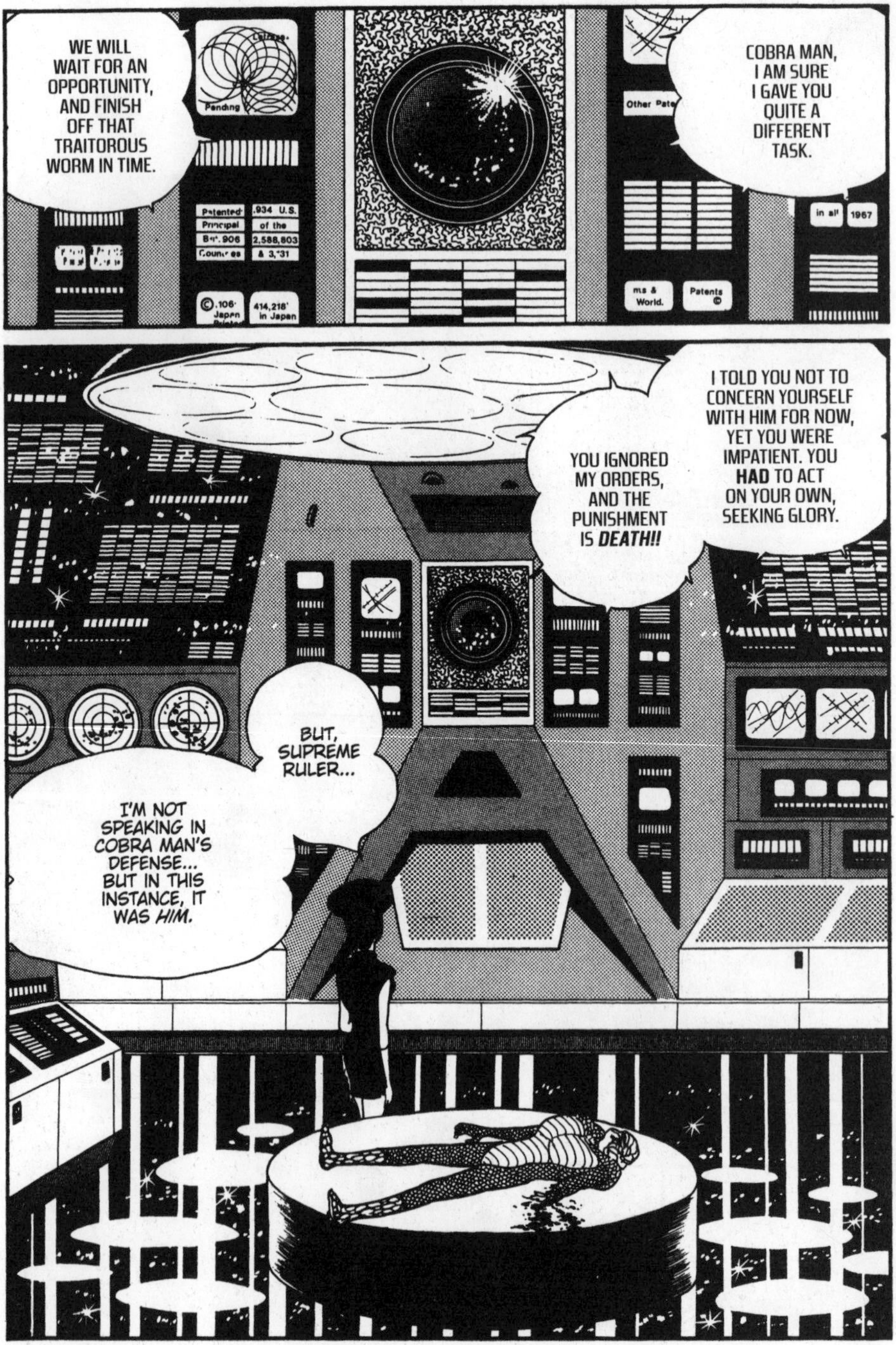
COBRA MAN, I AM SURE I GAVE YOU QUITE A DIFFERENT TASK.
WE WILL WAIT FOR AN OPPORTUNITY, AND FINISH OFF THAT TRAITOROUS WORM IN TIME.
I TOLD YOU NOT TO CONCERN YOURSELF WITH HIM FOR NOW, YET YOU WERE IMPATIENT. YOU **HAD** TO ACT ON YOUR OWN, SEEKING GLORY.
YOU IGNORED MY ORDERS, AND THE PUNISHMENT IS ***DEATH!!***
BUT, SUPREME RULER...
I'M NOT SPEAKING IN COBRA MAN'S DEFENSE... BUT IN THIS INSTANCE, IT WAS *HIM.*

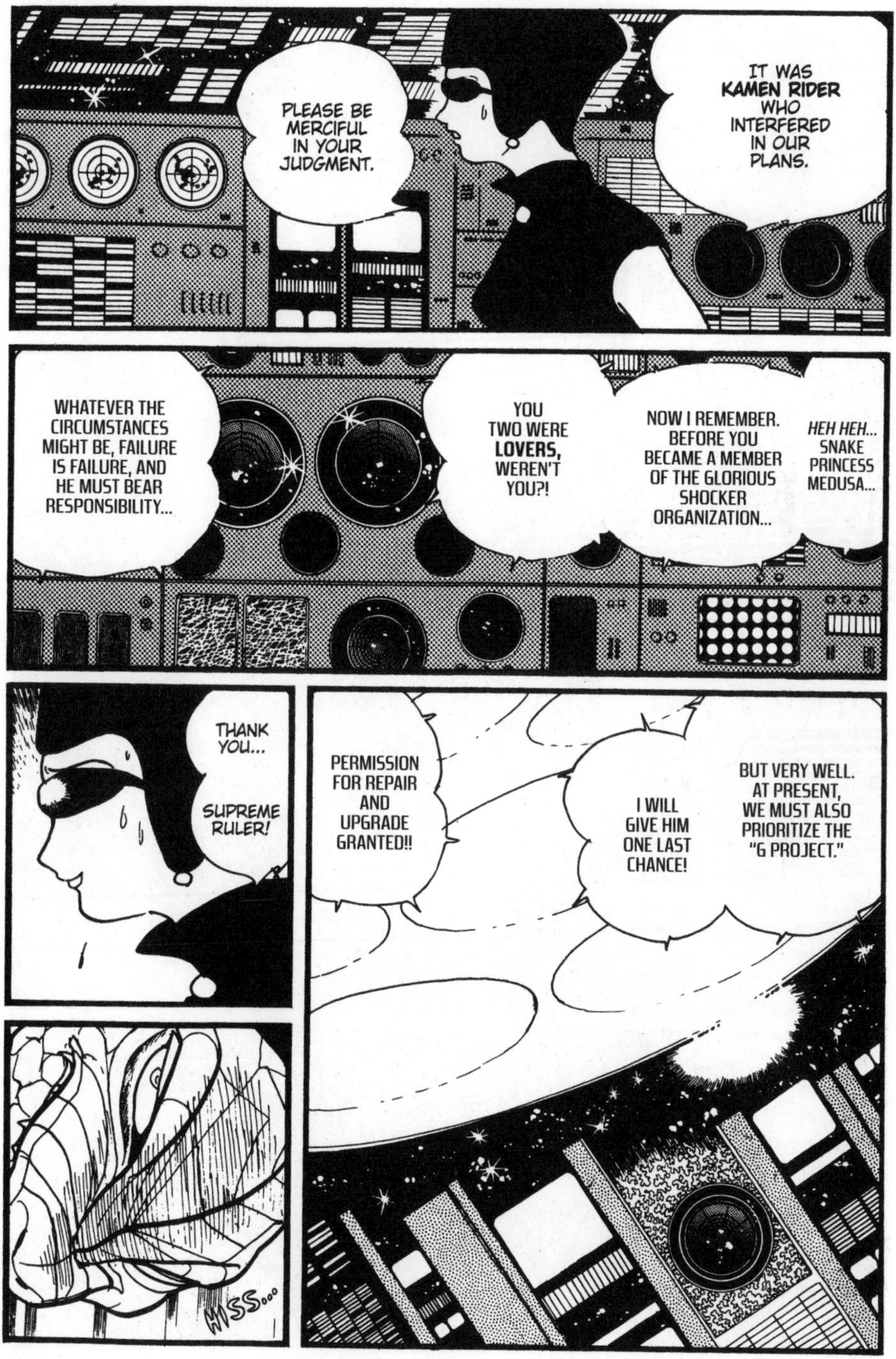

IT WAS KAMEN RIDER WHO INTERFERED IN OUR PLANS.
PLEASE BE MERCIFUL IN YOUR JUDGMENT.
HEH HEH... SNAKE PRINCESS MEDUSA...
NOW I REMEMBER. BEFORE YOU BECAME A MEMBER OF THE GLORIOUS SHOCKER ORGANIZATION...
YOU TWO WERE **LOVERS,** WEREN'T YOU?!
WHATEVER THE CIRCUMSTANCES MIGHT BE, FAILURE IS FAILURE, AND HE MUST BEAR RESPONSIBILITY...
BUT VERY WELL. AT PRESENT, WE MUST ALSO PRIORITIZE THE "G PROJECT."
I WILL GIVE HIM ONE LAST CHANCE!
PERMISSION FOR REPAIR AND UPGRADE GRANTED!!
THANK YOU...
SUPREME RULER!
HISS...

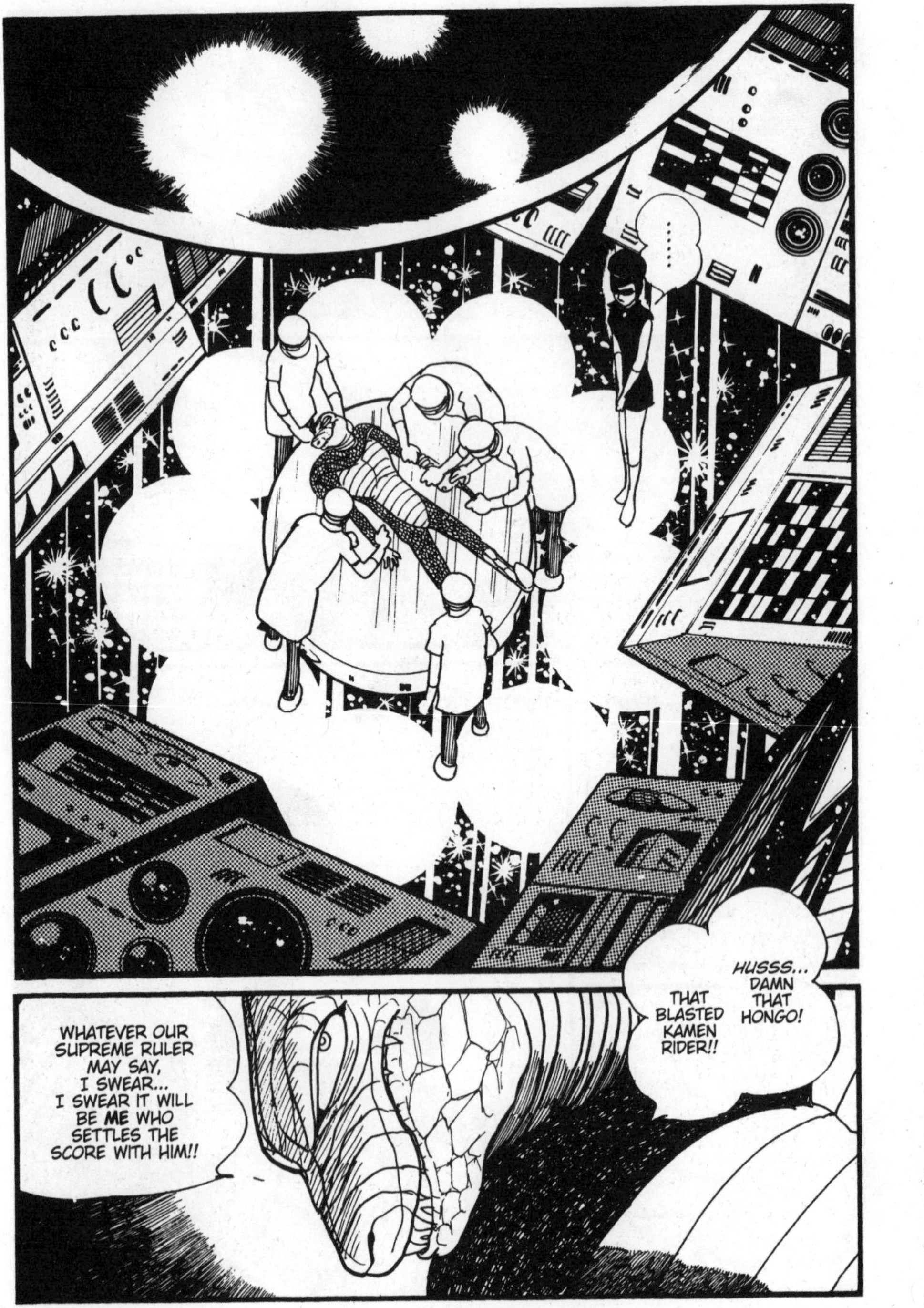
......
HUSSS... DAMN THAT HONGO!
THAT BLASTED KAMEN RIDER!!
WHATEVER OUR SUPREME RULER MAY SAY, I SWEAR... I SWEAR IT WILL BE **ME** WHO SETTLES THE SCORE WITH HIM!!

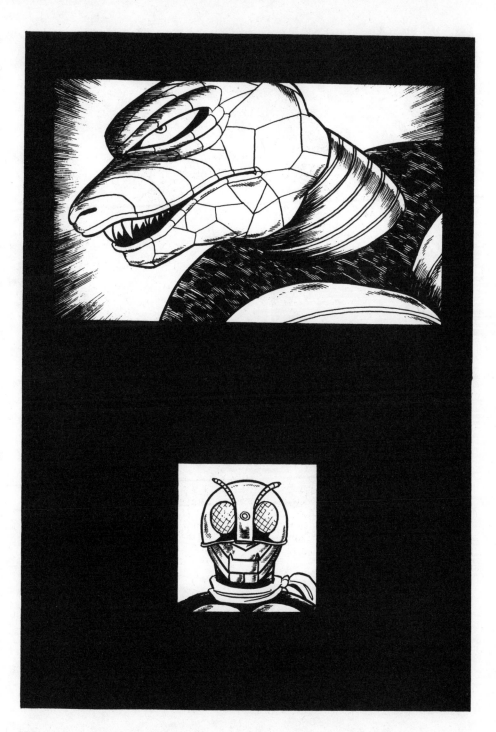

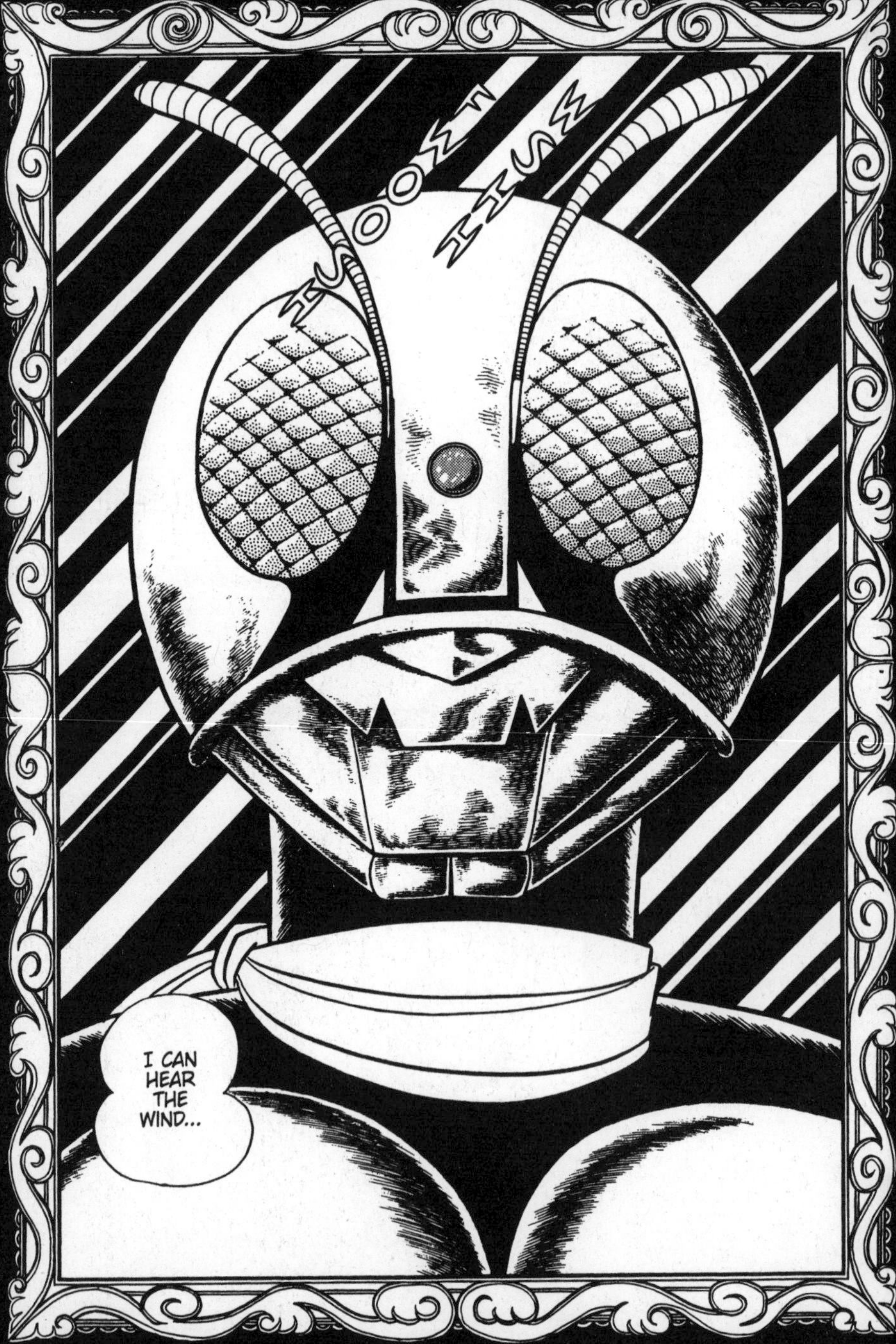
I CAN HEAR THE WIND...

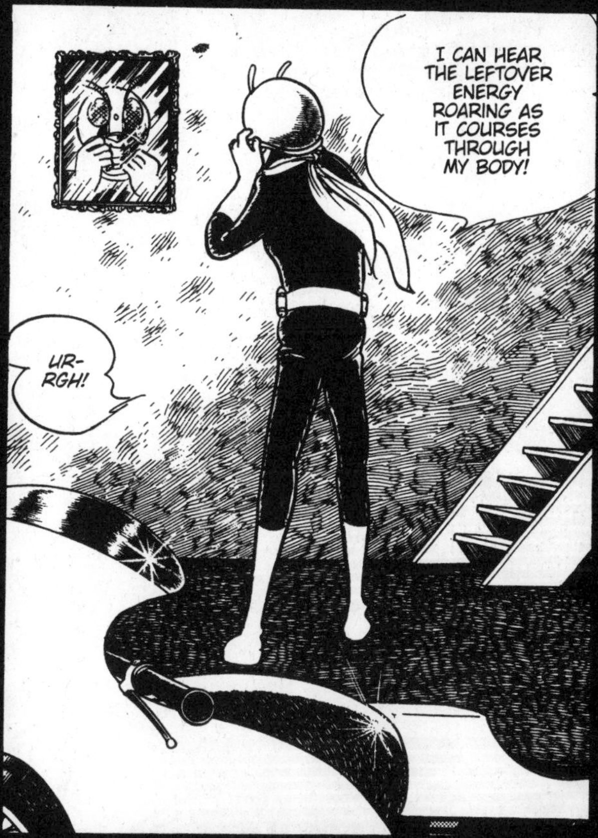
I CAN HEAR THE LEFTOVER ENERGY ROARING AS IT COURSES THROUGH MY BODY!
UR-RGH!
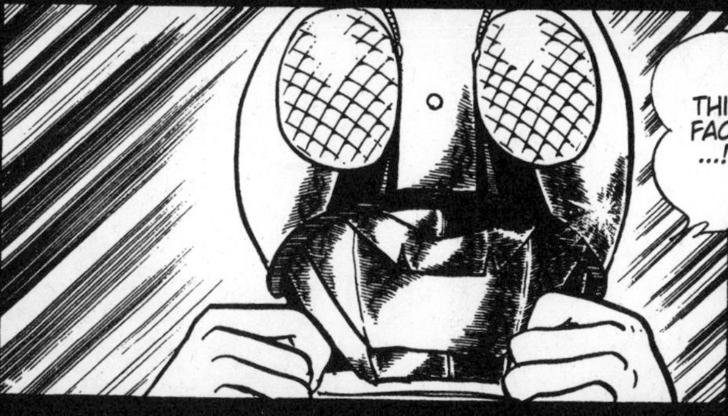
THIS FACE ...!!

THIS FACE IS NOW MY *TRUE* FACE!
AND THIS FACE...
THIS FACE IN WHICH THE SCARS OF MY CYBORG SURGERY RESURFACE WHENEVER I FEEL ANGER OR SADNESS...
IT IS A FALSE ONE!
RIGHT NOW...
I AM BOTH HUMAN AND NOT HUMAN!
VARIOUS ARTIFI-CIAL MECHANISMS WERE IMPLANTED IN THIS BODY AT THE HANDS OF SHOCKER!
I WAS ARMED WITH ARTIFICIAL MUSCLES AND BONES, AND A HEART THAT GIVES ME ABILITIES MANY TIMES BEYOND ORDINARY MEN'S!

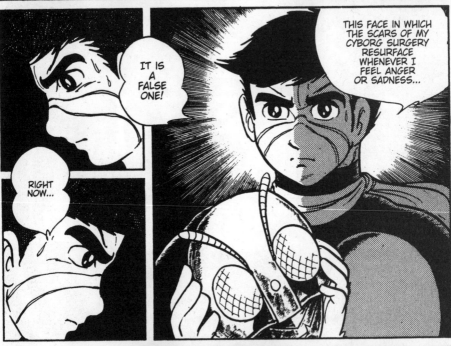

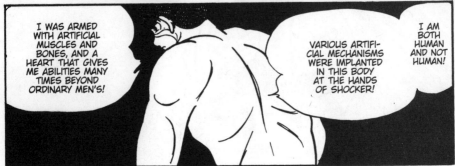

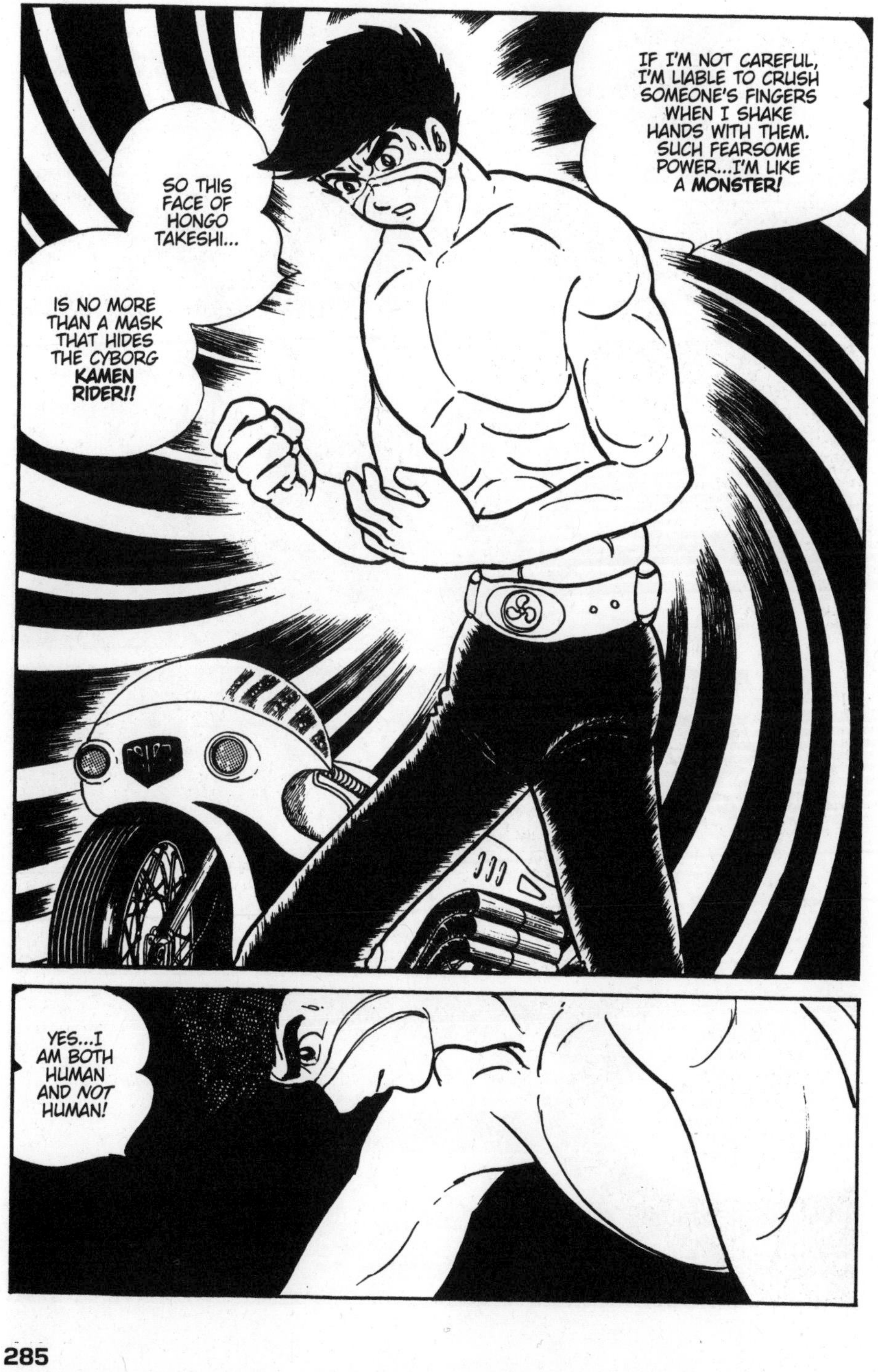
IF I'M NOT CAREFUL, I'M LIABLE TO CRUSH SOMEONE'S FINGERS WHEN I SHAKE HANDS WITH THEM. SUCH FEARSOME POWER...I'M LIKE A **MONSTER!**
SO THIS FACE OF HONGO TAKESHI...
IS NO MORE THAN A MASK THAT HIDES THE CYBORG **KAMEN RIDER!!**
YES...I AM BOTH HUMAN AND *NOT* HUMAN!

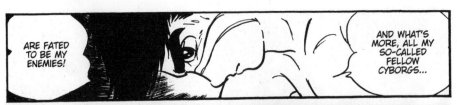

AND WHAT'S MORE, ALL MY SO-CALLED FELLOW CYBORGS...
ARE FATED TO BE MY ENEMIES!
I AM ALL ALONE IN THIS GREAT, WIDE WORLD.
NNH.
URRGH...
BUT...
EVEN IF I'M ALONE...
NO, *BECAUSE* I'M ALONE... I MUST FIGHT!
I HAVE TO FIGHT ON!
SHOCKER IS TRYING TO TAKE OVER THE WORLD, AND I'M THE ONLY ONE WHO CAN STAND AGAINST THEM!!

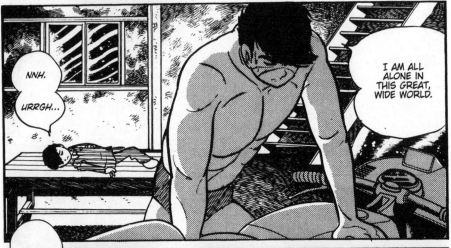

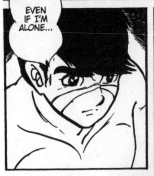

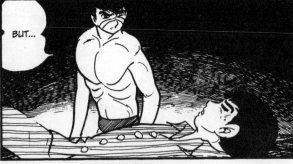

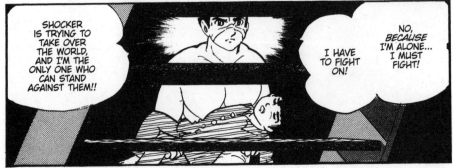

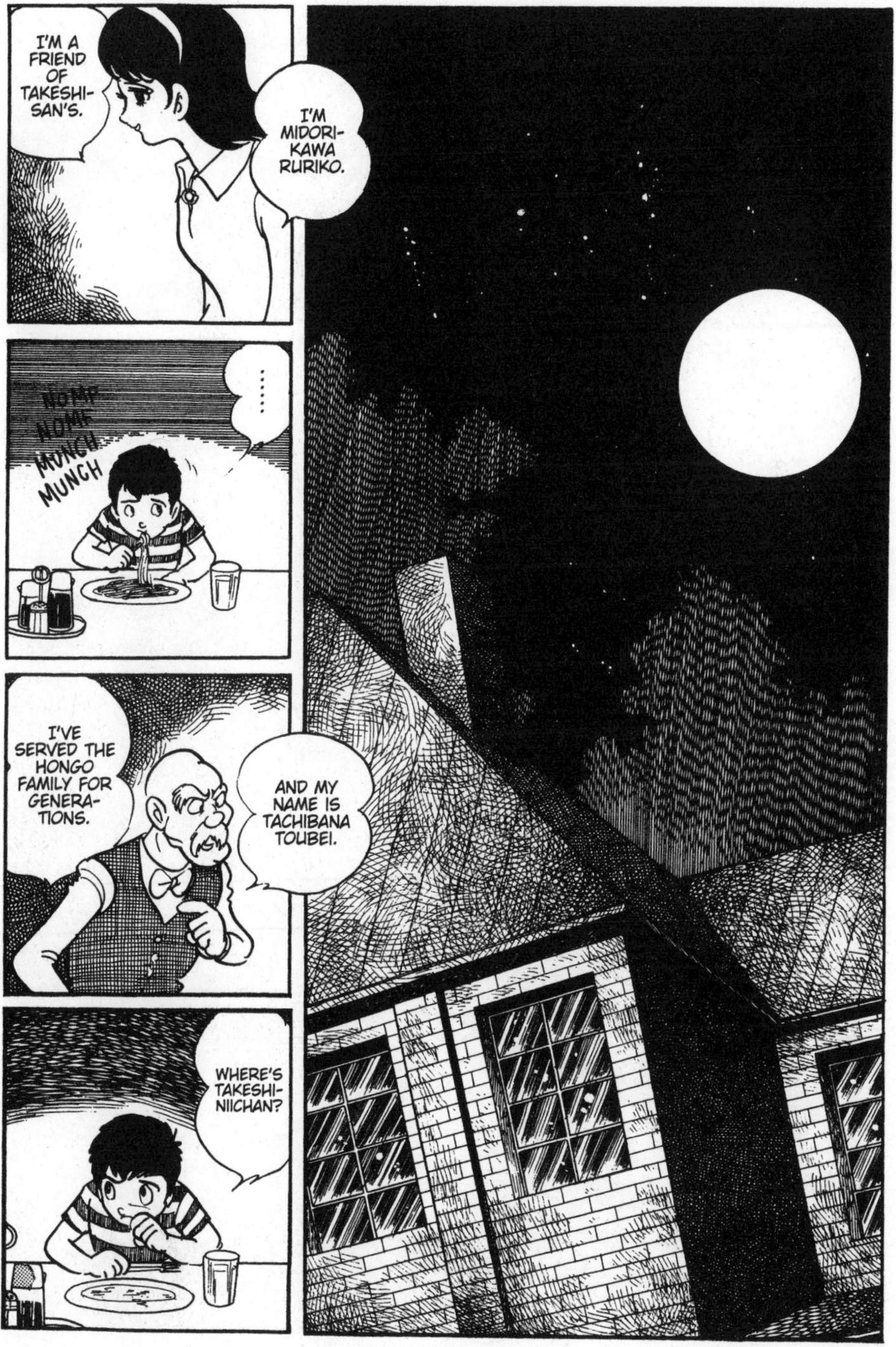
I'M MIDORIKAWA RURIKO.
I'M A FRIEND OF TAKESHI-SAN'S.
......
NOMP NOMP MUNCH MUNCH
AND MY NAME IS TACHIBANA TOUBEI.
I'VE SERVED THE HONGO FAMILY FOR GENERATIONS.
WHERE'S TAKESHI-NIICHAN?

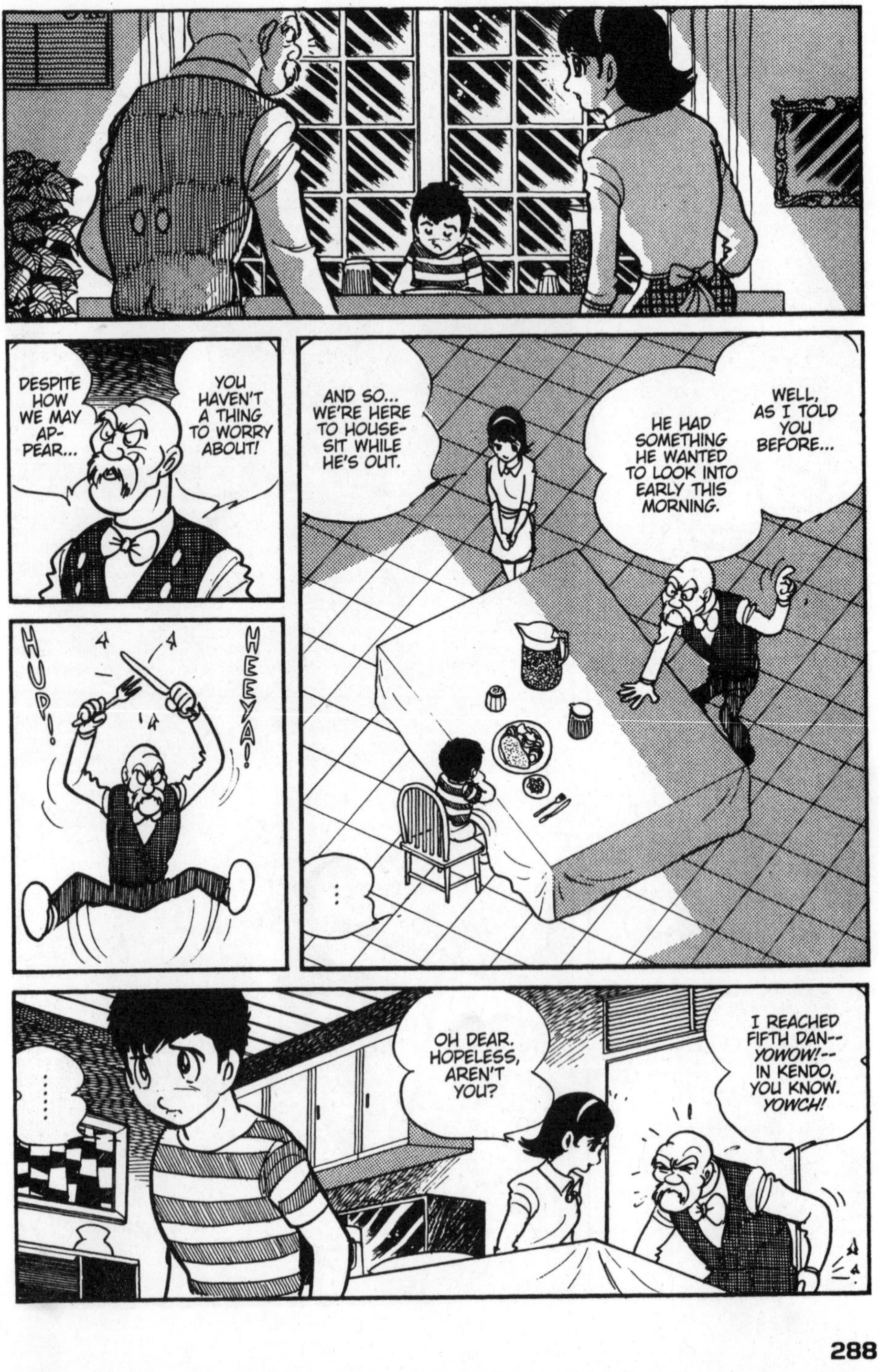
WELL, AS I TOLD YOU BEFORE...
HE HAD SOMETHING HE WANTED TO LOOK INTO EARLY THIS MORNING.
AND SO... WE'RE HERE TO HOUSE-SIT WHILE HE'S OUT.
...
YOU HAVEN'T A THING TO WORRY ABOUT!
DESPITE HOW WE MAY AP-PEAR...
HEEYA!
HUP!
I REACHED FIFTH DAN-- *YOWOW!*-- IN KENDO, YOU KNOW. *YOWCH!*
OH DEAR. HOPELESS, AREN'T YOU?
......

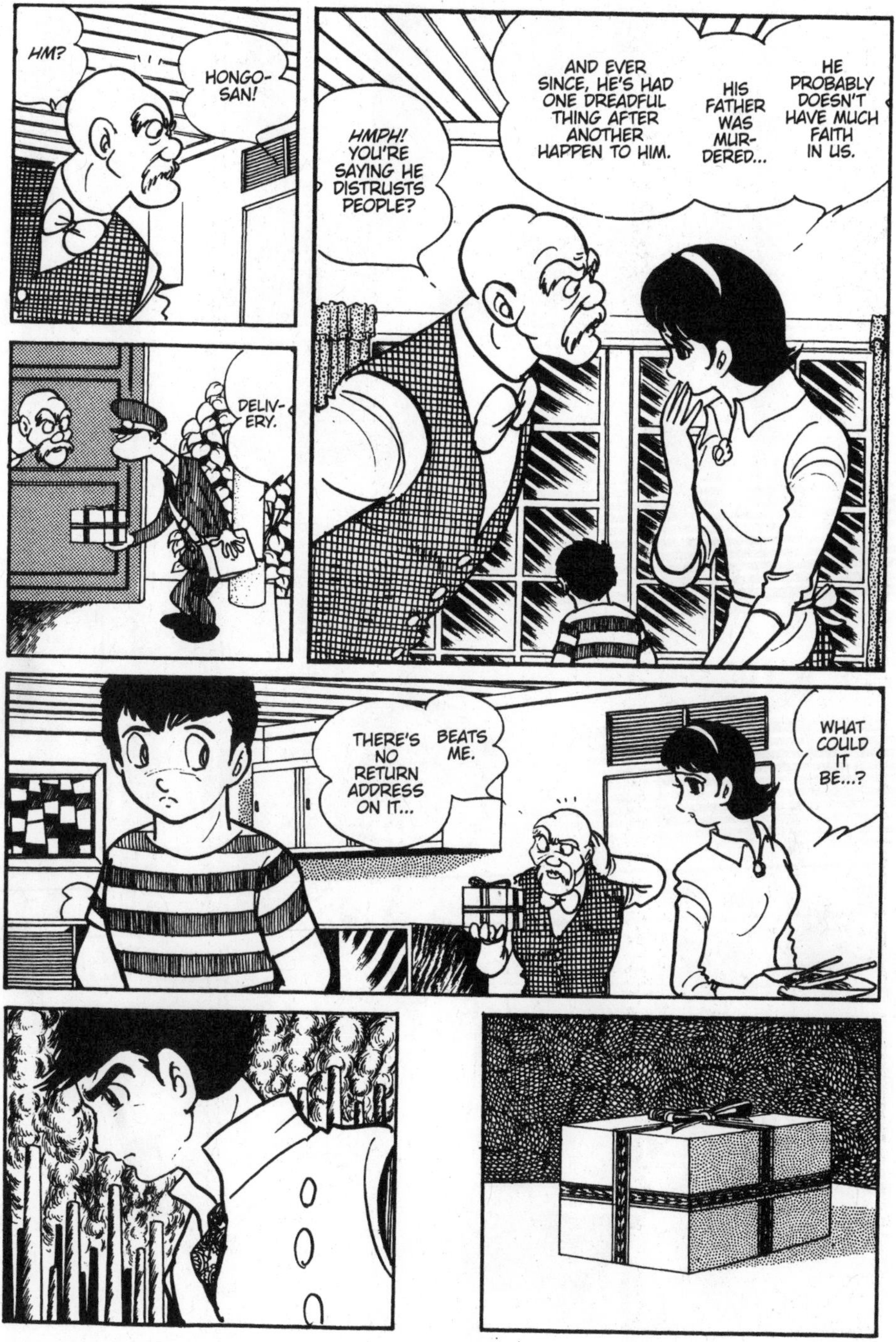
HE PROBABLY DOESN'T HAVE MUCH FAITH IN US.
HIS FATHER WAS MUR-DERED...
AND EVER SINCE, HE'S HAD ONE DREADFUL THING AFTER ANOTHER HAPPEN TO HIM.
HMPH! YOU'RE SAYING HE DISTRUSTS PEOPLE?
HONGO-SAN!
HM?
DELIV-ERY.
WHAT COULD IT BE...?
BEATS ME.
THERE'S NO RETURN ADDRESS ON IT...

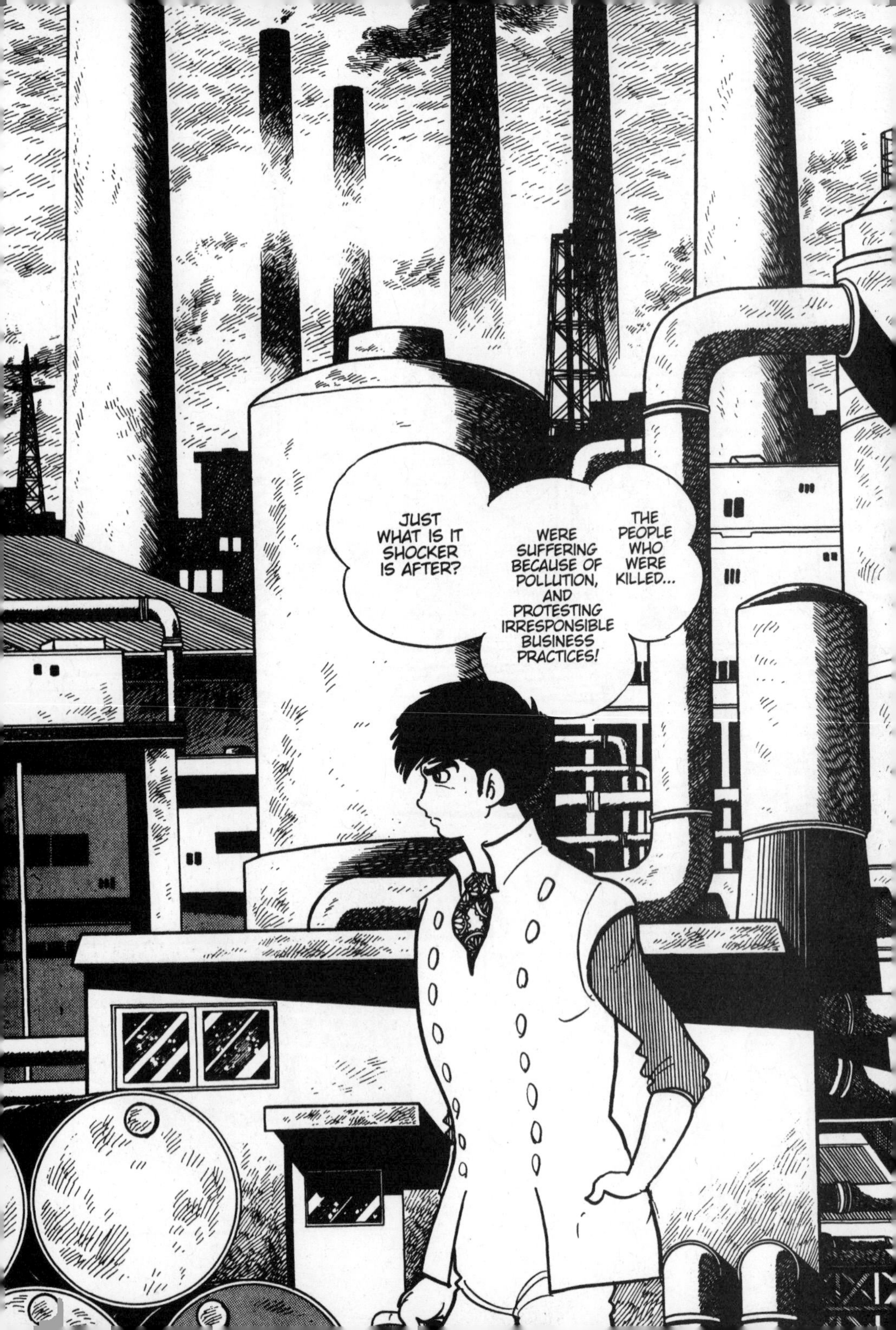
THE PEOPLE WHO WERE KILLED...
WERE SUFFERING BECAUSE OF POLLUTION, AND PROTESTING IRRESPONSIBLE BUSINESS PRACTICES!
JUST WHAT IS IT SHOCKER IS AFTER?

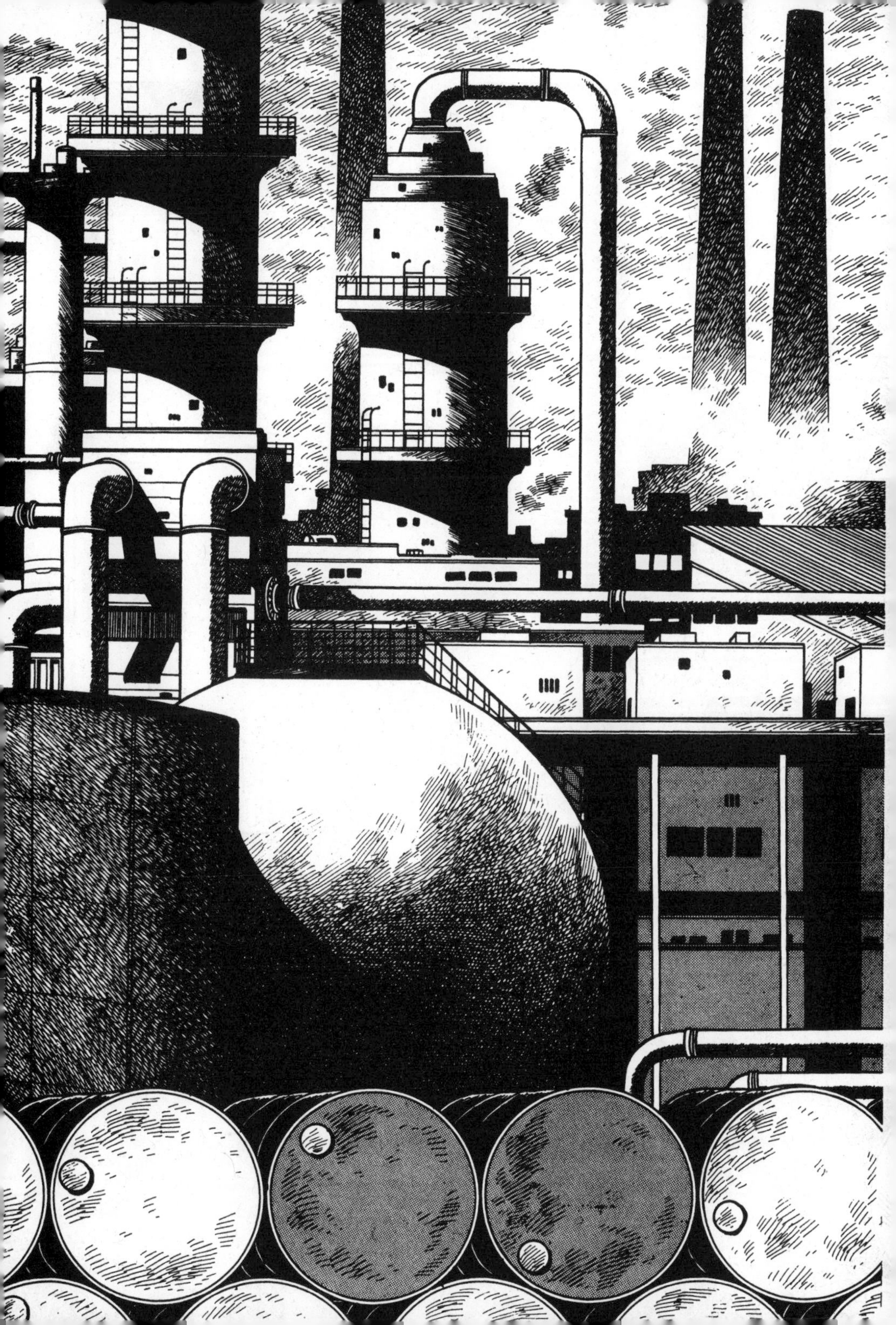

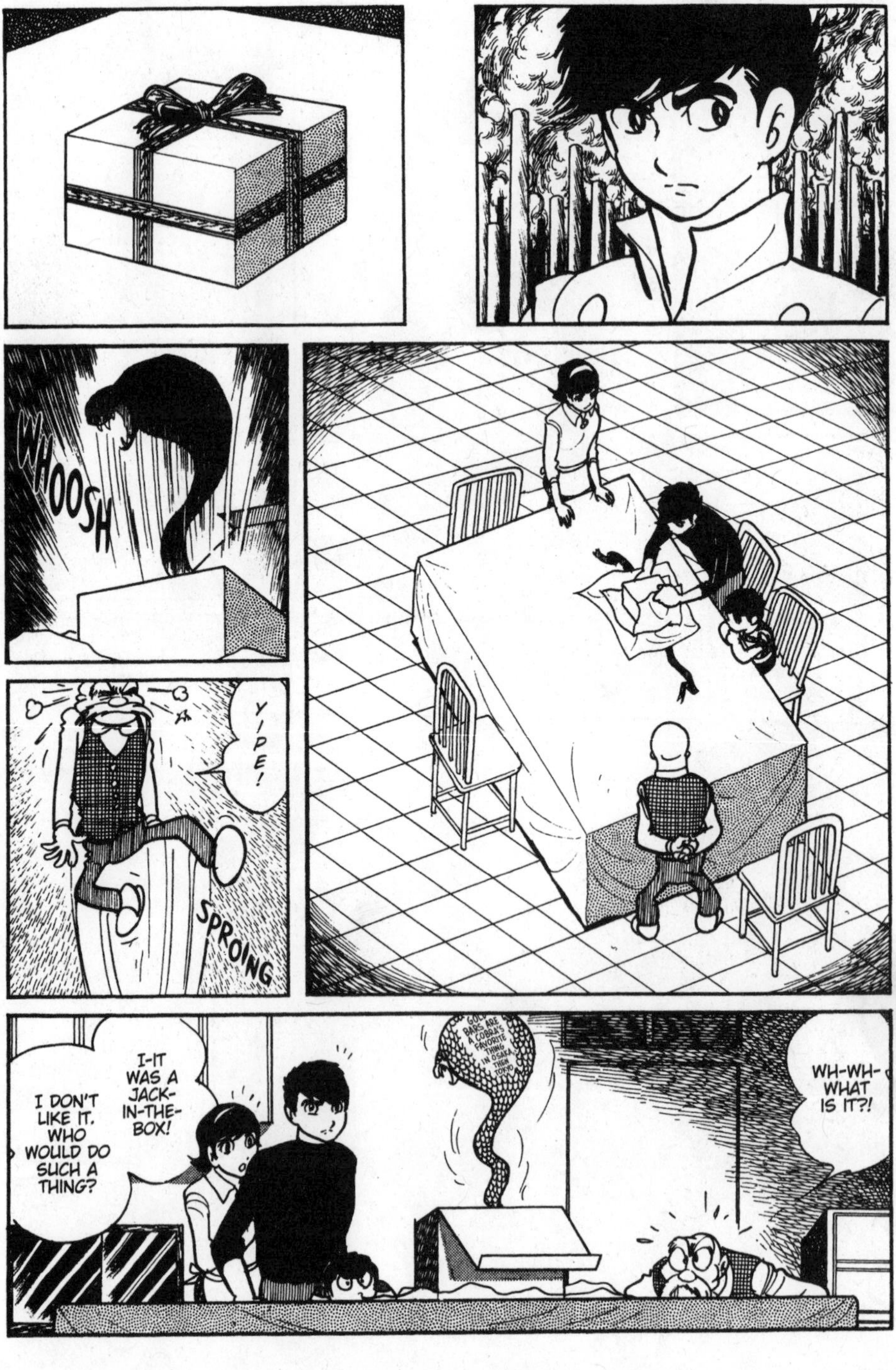
WHOOSH
YIPE!
SPROING
WH-WH-WHAT IS IT?!
GOLD BARS ARE A COBRA'S FAVORITE THING IN OSAKA, THEN TOKYO
I-IT WAS A JACK-IN-THE-BOX!
I DON'T LIKE IT. WHO WOULD DO SUCH A THING?

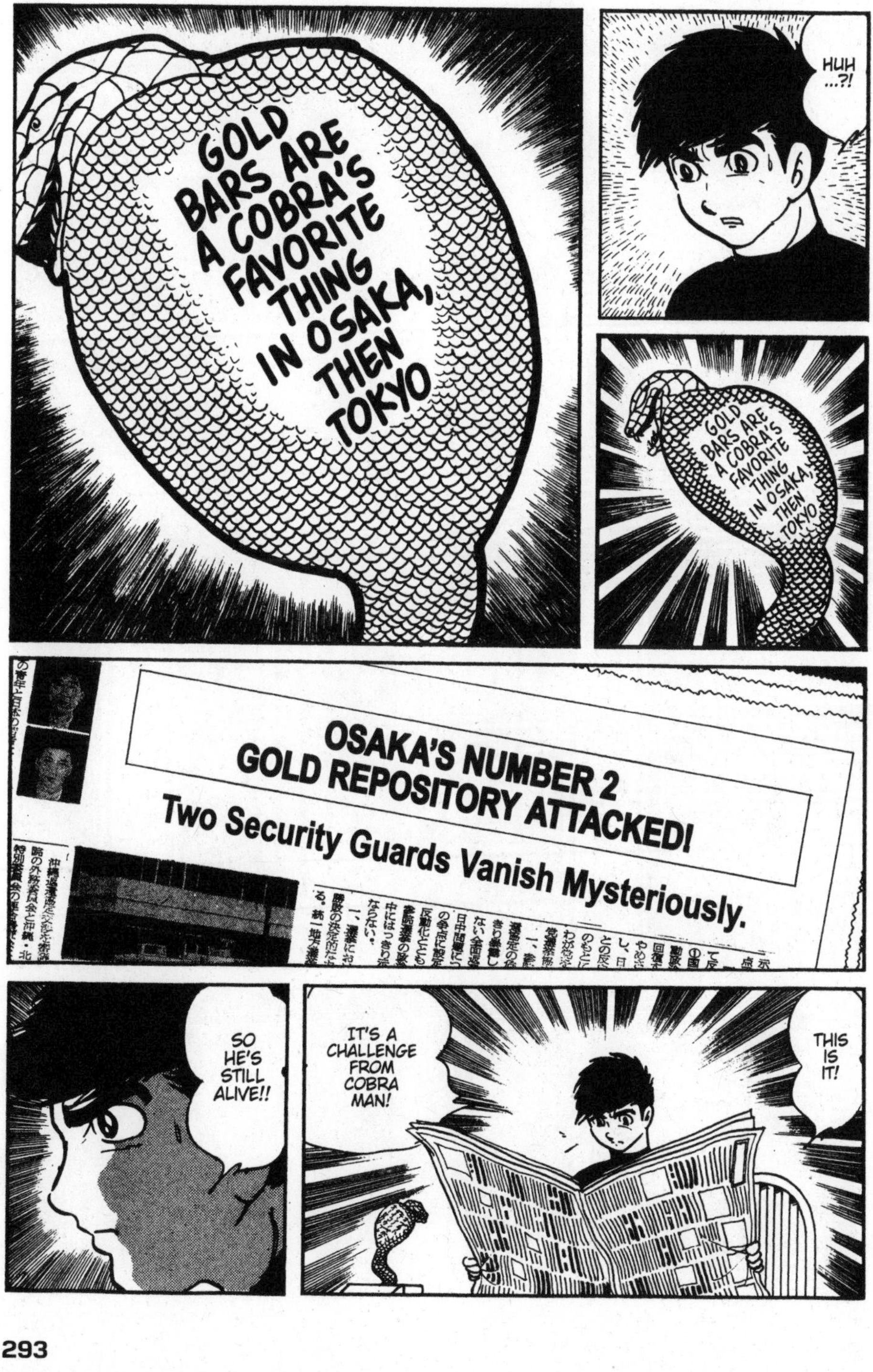
HUH ...?!
GOLD BARS ARE A COBRA'S FAVORITE THING IN OSAKA, THEN TOKYO
GOLD BARS ARE A COBRA'S FAVORITE THING IN OSAKA, THEN TOKYO
OSAKA'S NUMBER 2 GOLD REPOSITORY ATTACKED!
Two Security Guards Vanish Mysteriously.
THIS IS IT!
IT'S A CHALLENGE FROM COBRA MAN!
SO HE'S STILL ALIVE!!

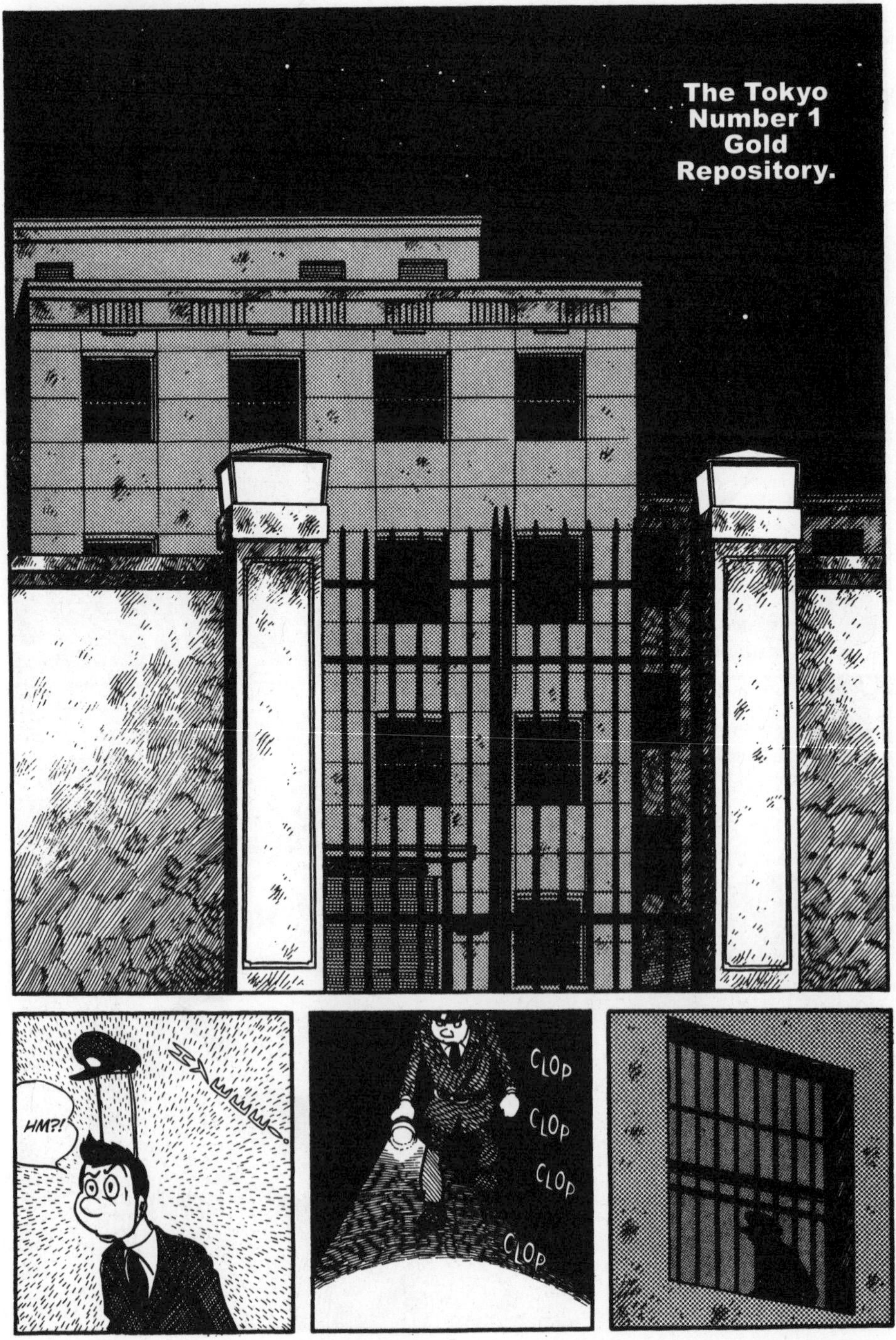
The Tokyo Number 1 Gold Repository.
CLOP
CLOP
CLOP
CLOP
HM?!

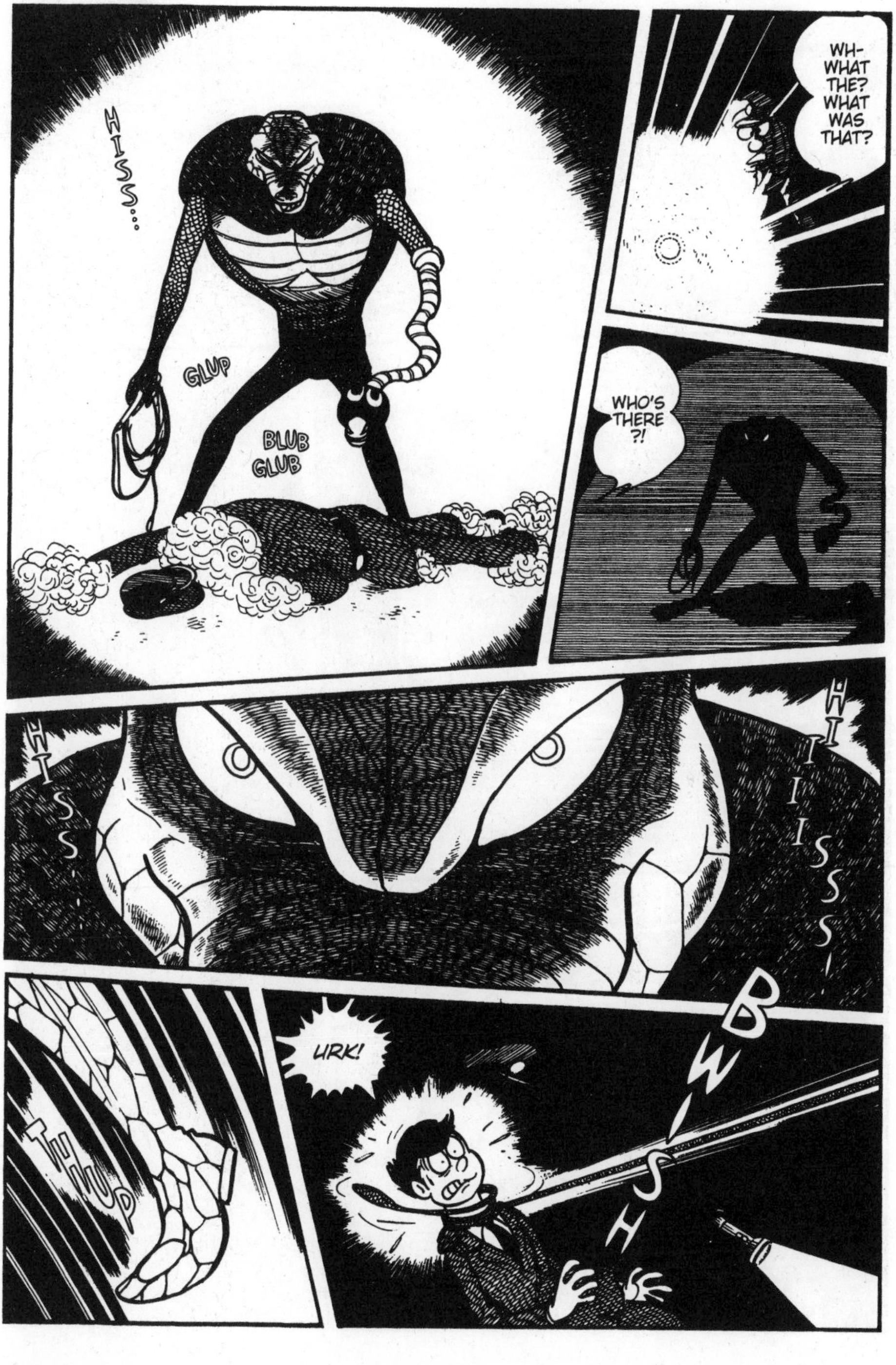
WH-WHAT THE? WHAT WAS THAT?
WHO'S THERE?!
HISS...
GLUP
BLUB GLUB
HISSS...
HISS...
BWISH
URK!
THUP

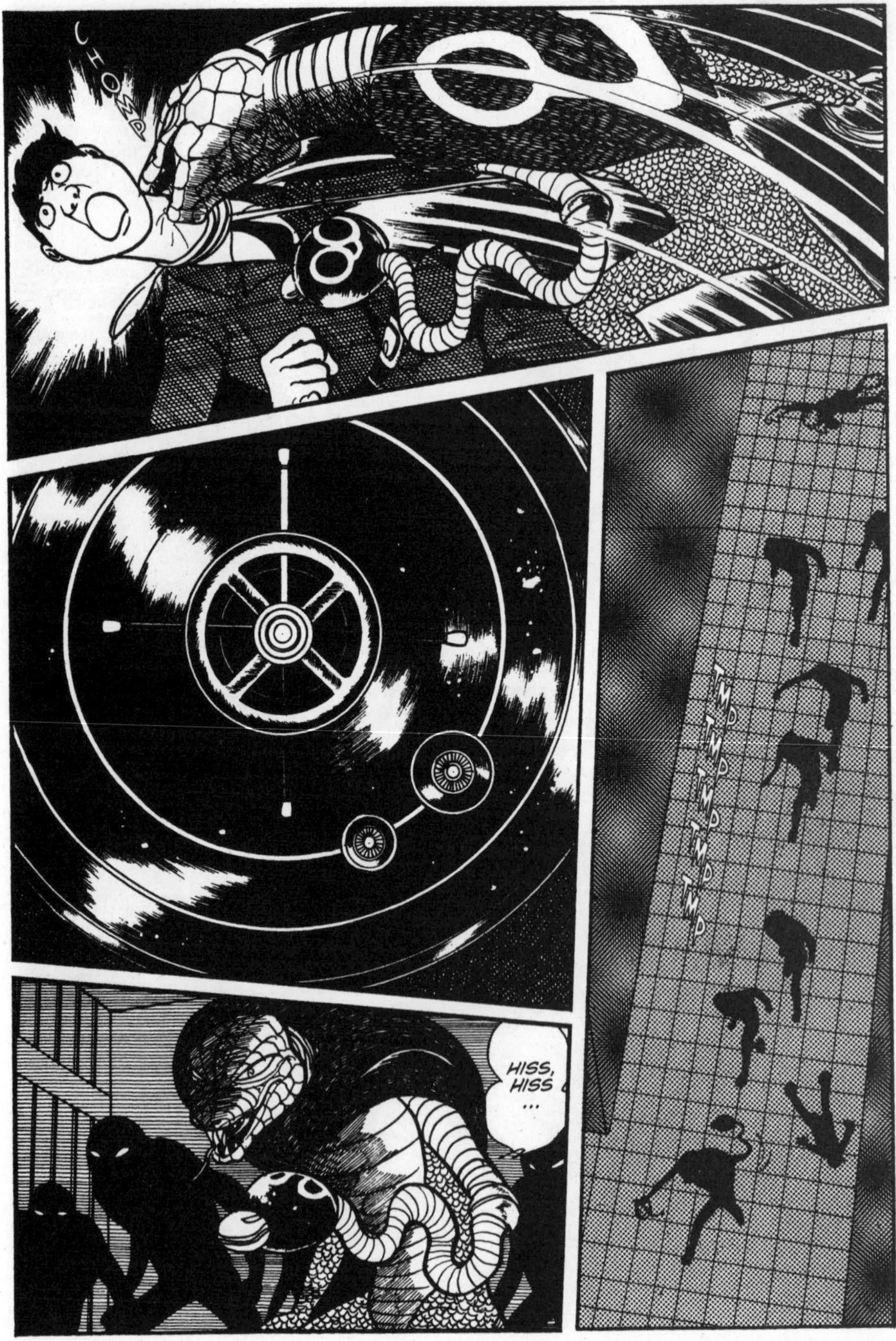
CHOMP
TMP TMP TMP TMP TMP
HISS, HISS ...

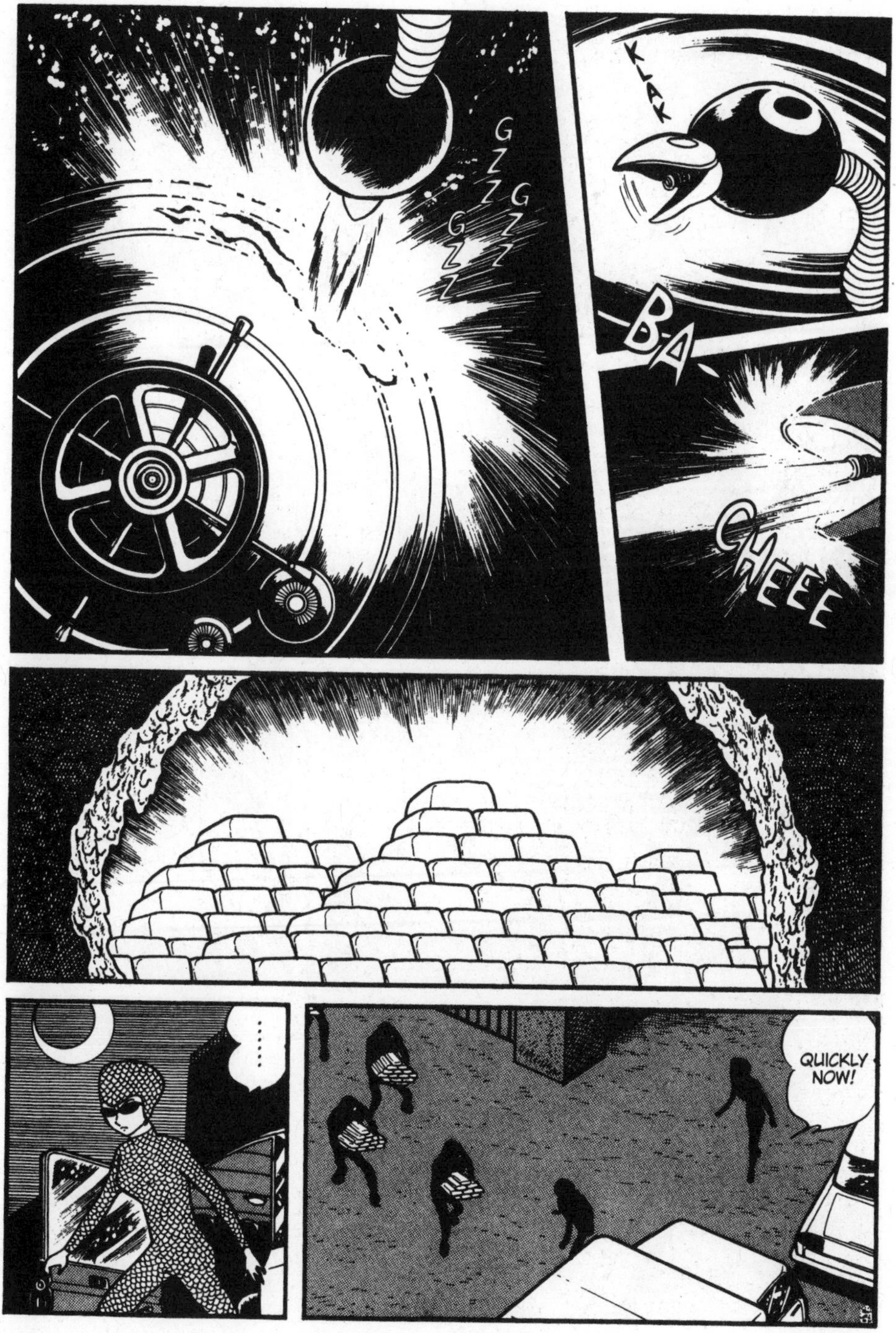
KLAK
BA-CHEEE
GZZZ GZZZ
QUICKLY NOW!

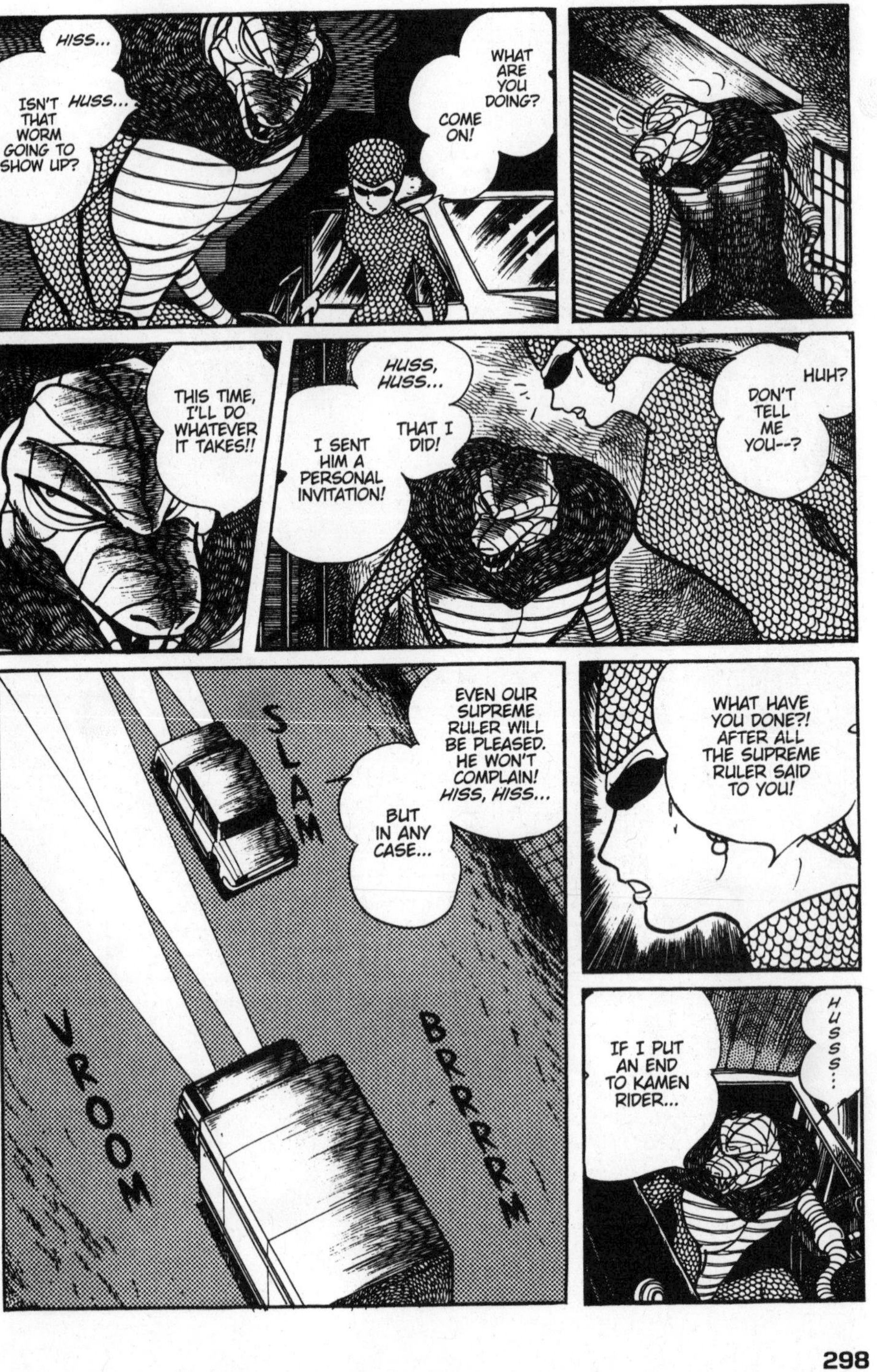
WHAT ARE YOU DOING?
COME ON!
HISS...
ISN'T *HUSS...* THAT WORM GOING TO SHOW UP?
HUH?
DON'T TELL ME YOU--?
HUSS, HUSS...
THAT I DID!
I SENT HIM A PERSONAL INVITATION!
THIS TIME, I'LL DO WHATEVER IT TAKES!!
WHAT HAVE YOU DONE?! AFTER ALL THE SUPREME RULER SAID TO YOU!
HUSSS...
IF I PUT AN END TO KAMEN RIDER...
EVEN OUR SUPREME RULER WILL BE PLEASED. HE WON'T COMPLAIN! *HISS, HISS...*
BUT IN ANY CASE...
SLAM
BRRRRRM
VROOM

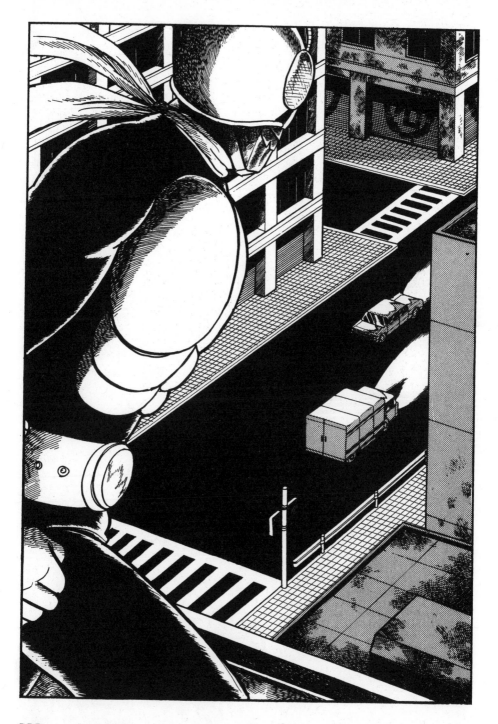

KAMEN RIDER

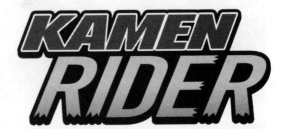

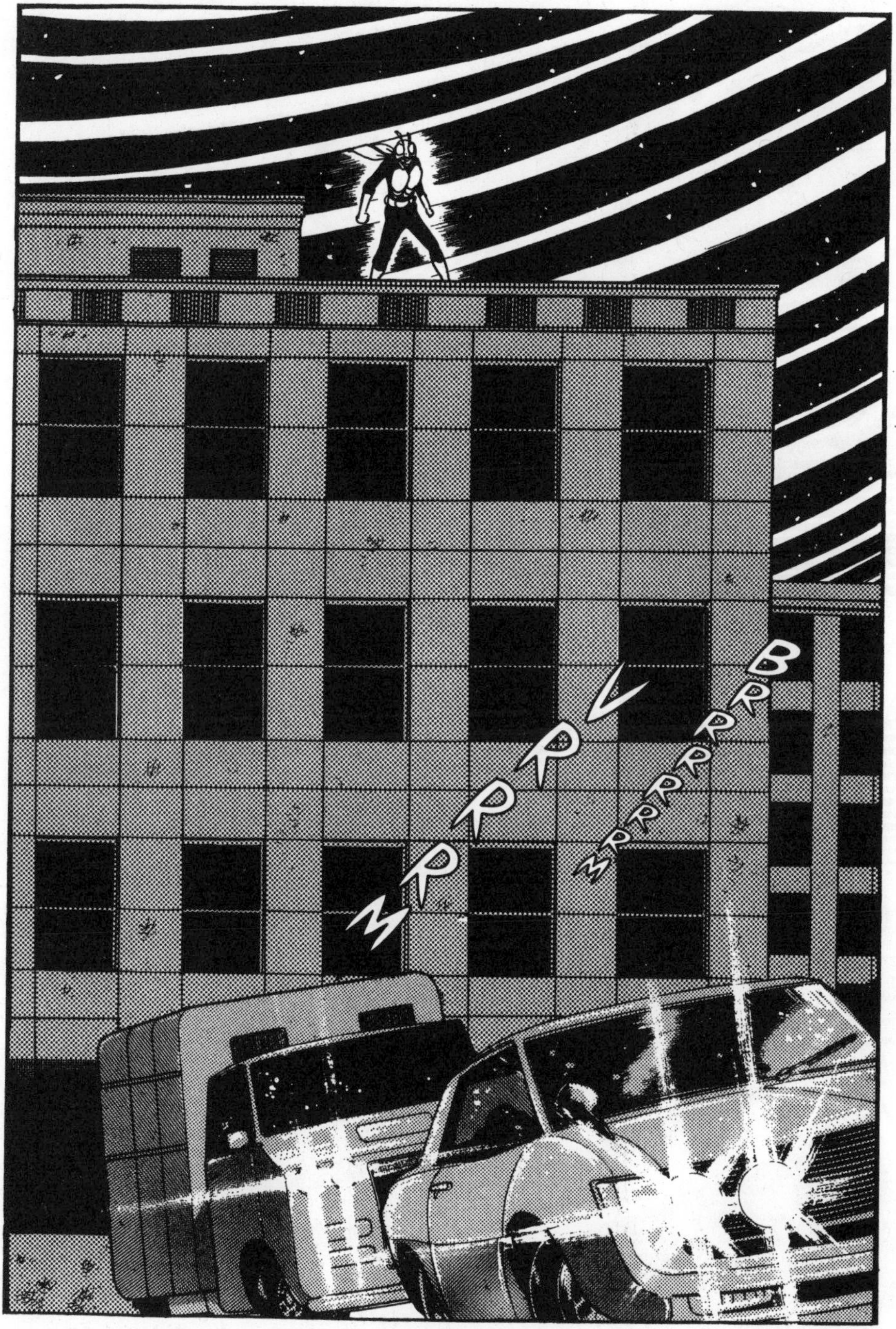
BRRRRRRM
VRRRM

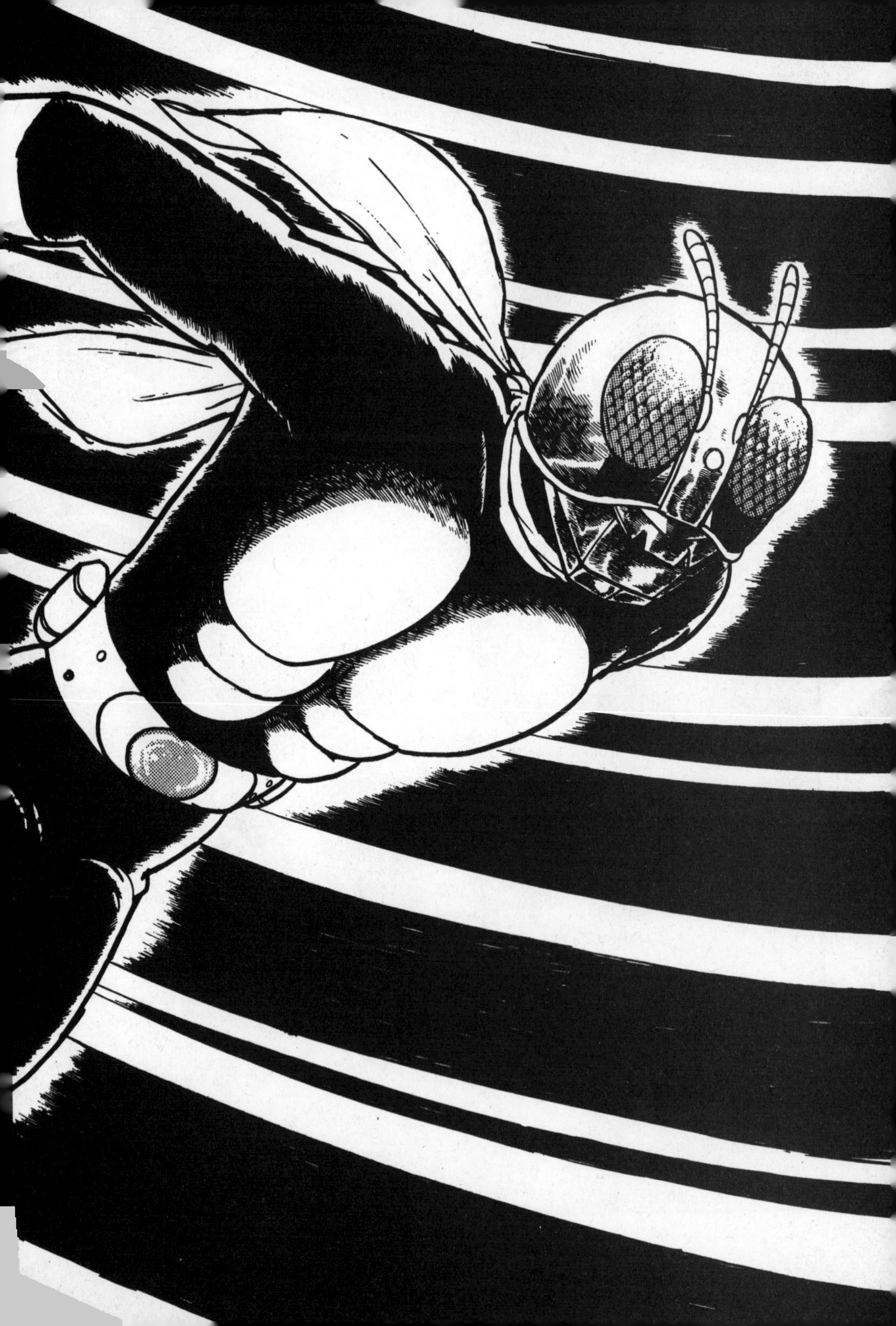

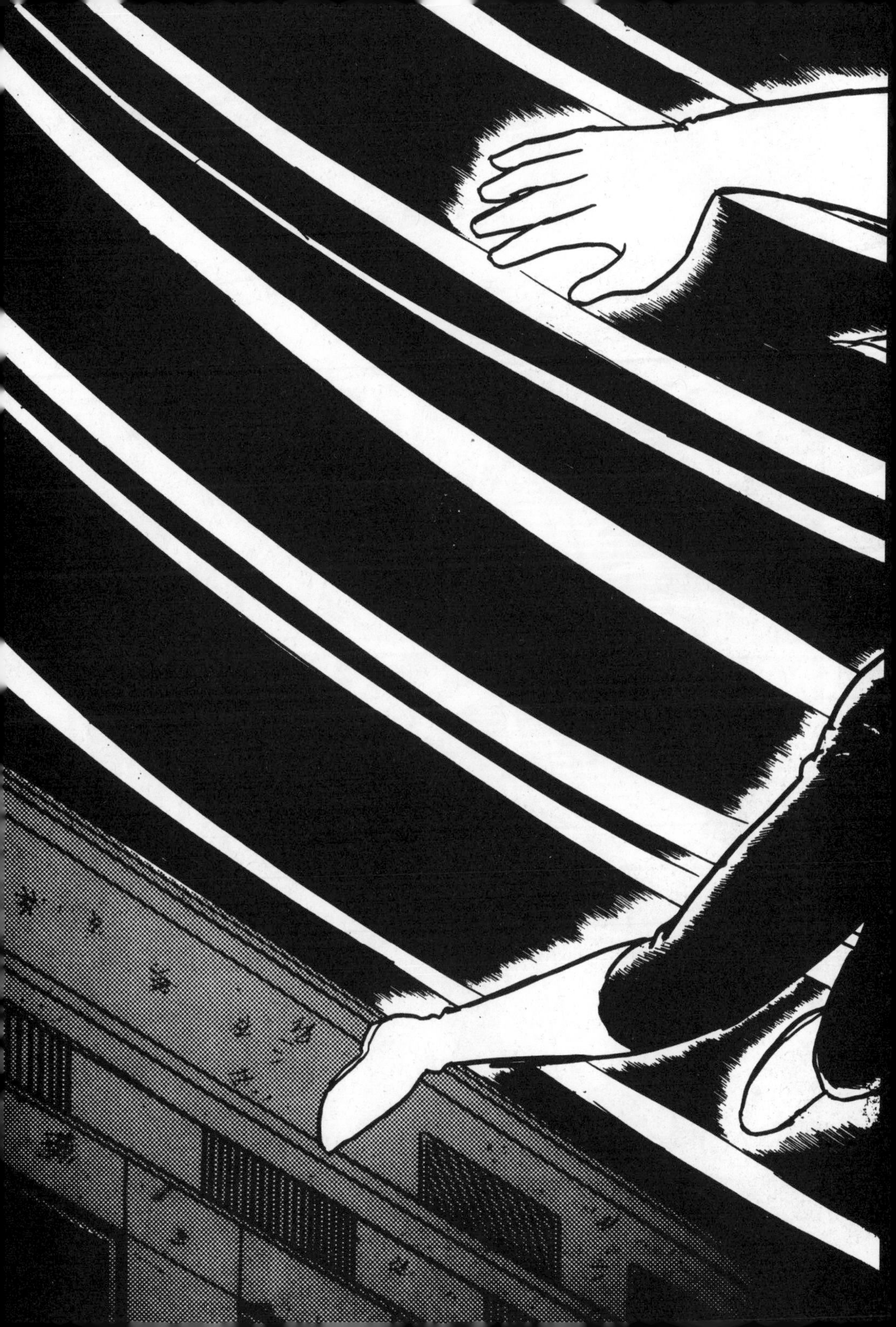

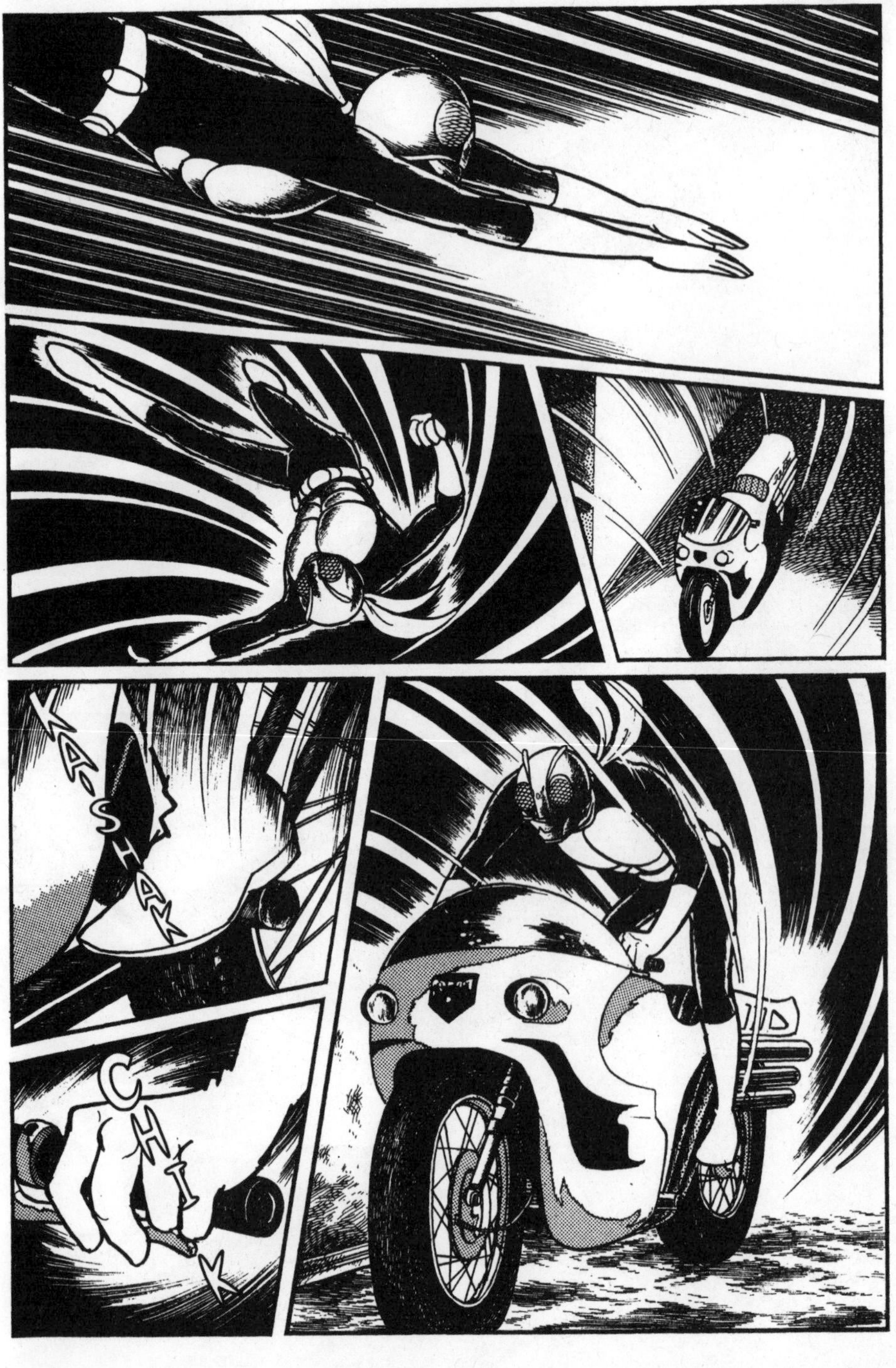
KA-SHAK
CHIK

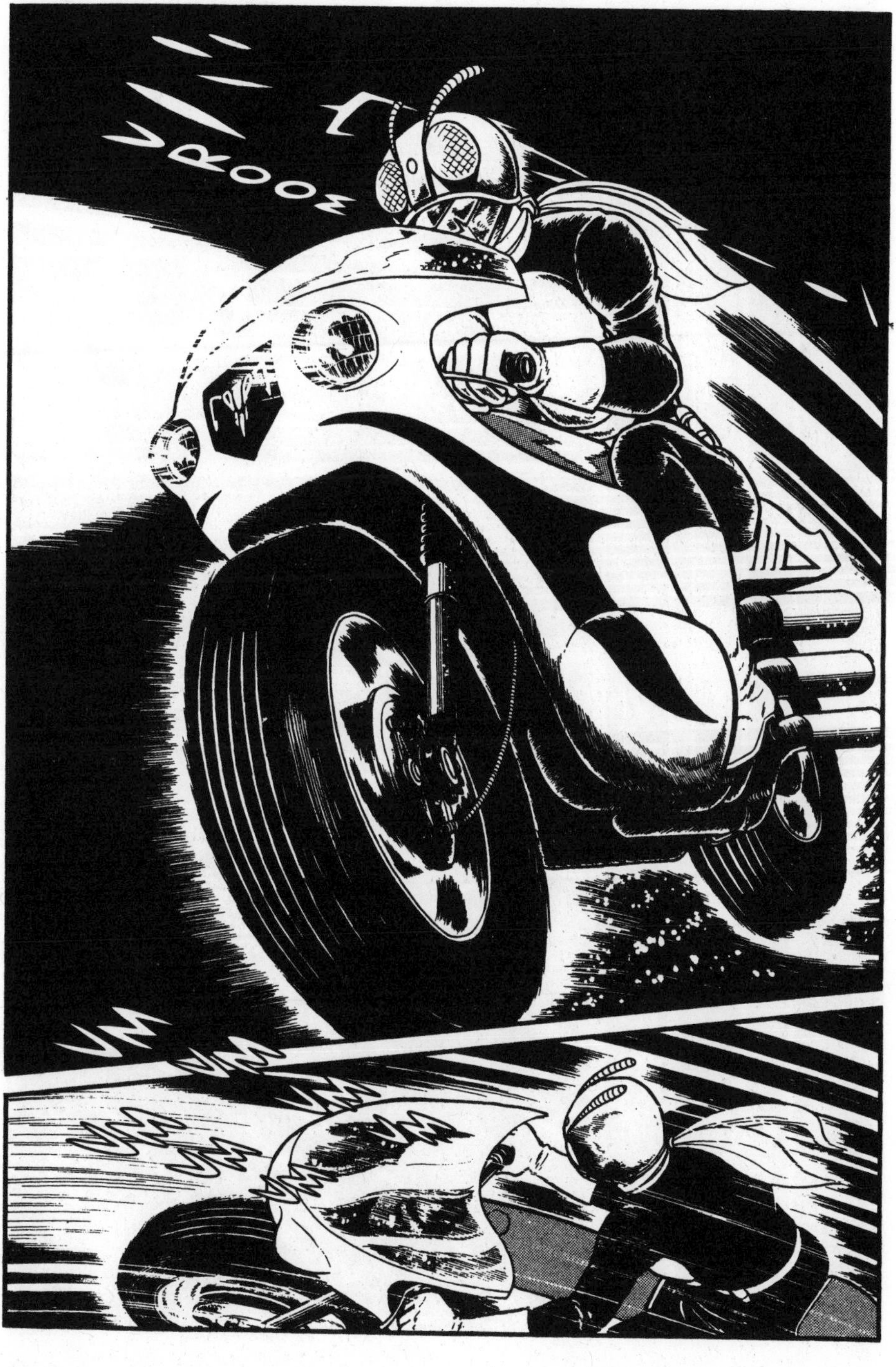
VROOM

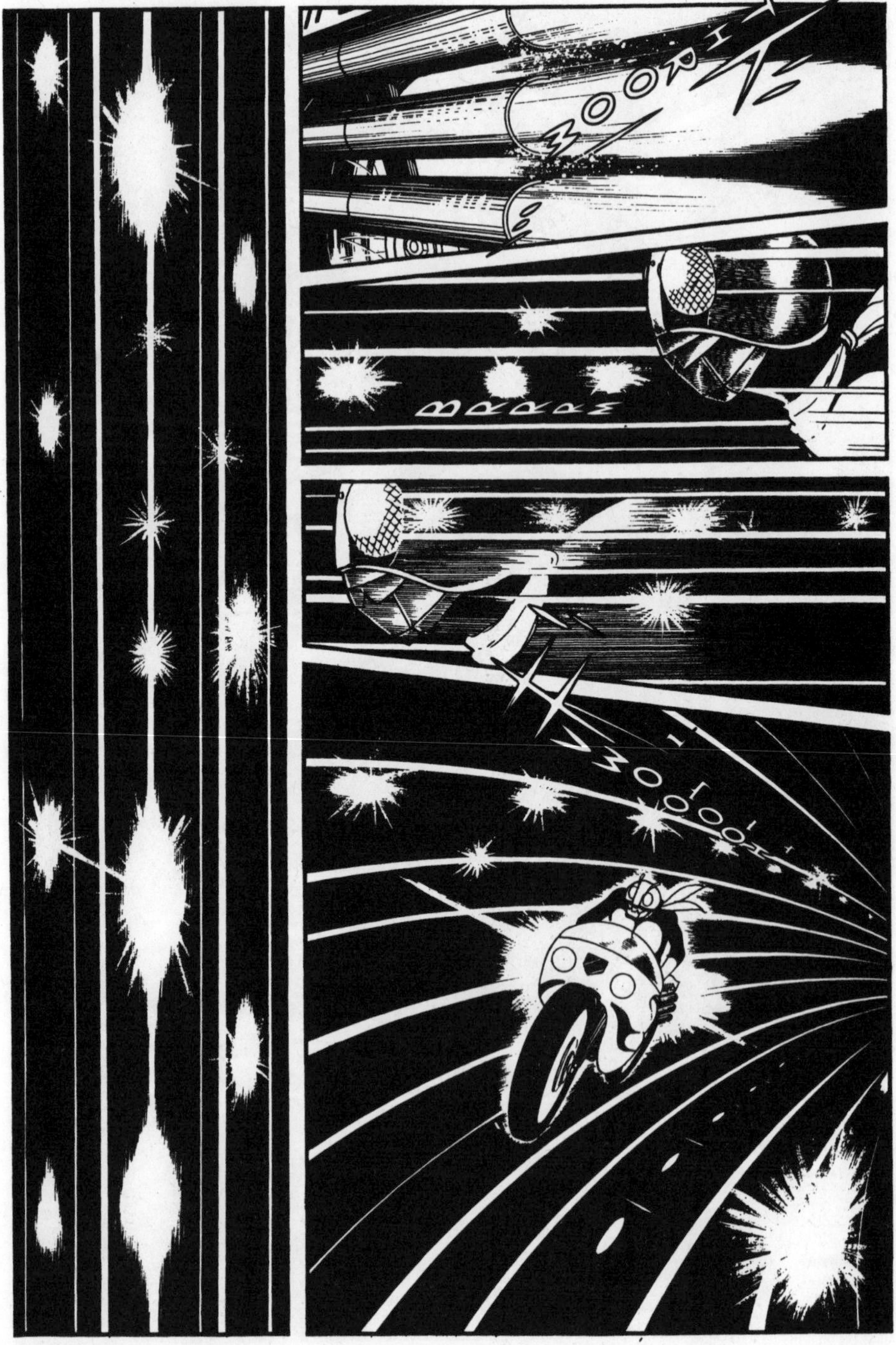
BRRRM

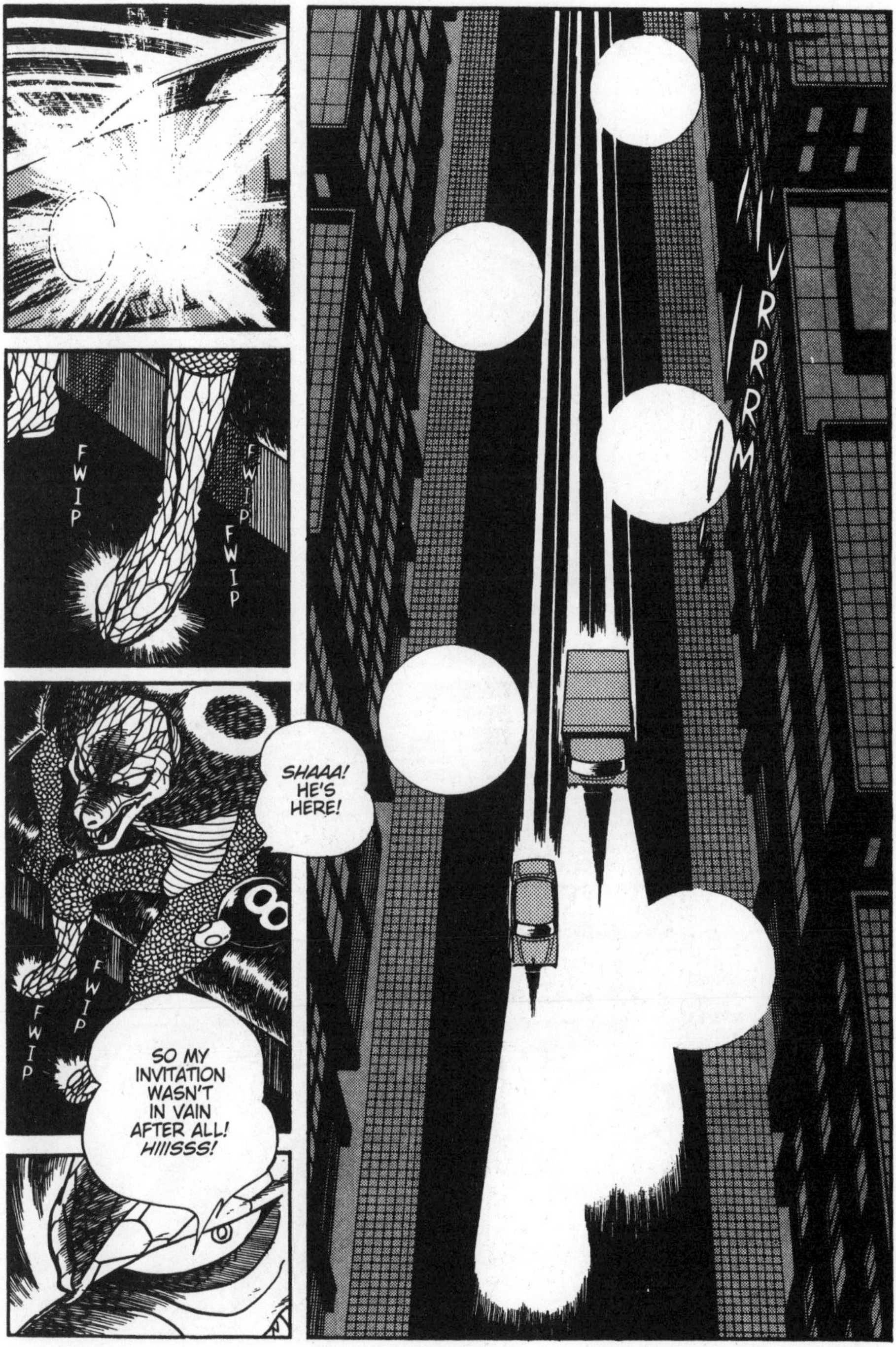
VRRRM
FWIP
FWIP
FWIP
SHAAA! HE'S HERE!
FWIP
FWIP
SO MY INVITATION WASN'T IN VAIN AFTER ALL! HIIISSS!

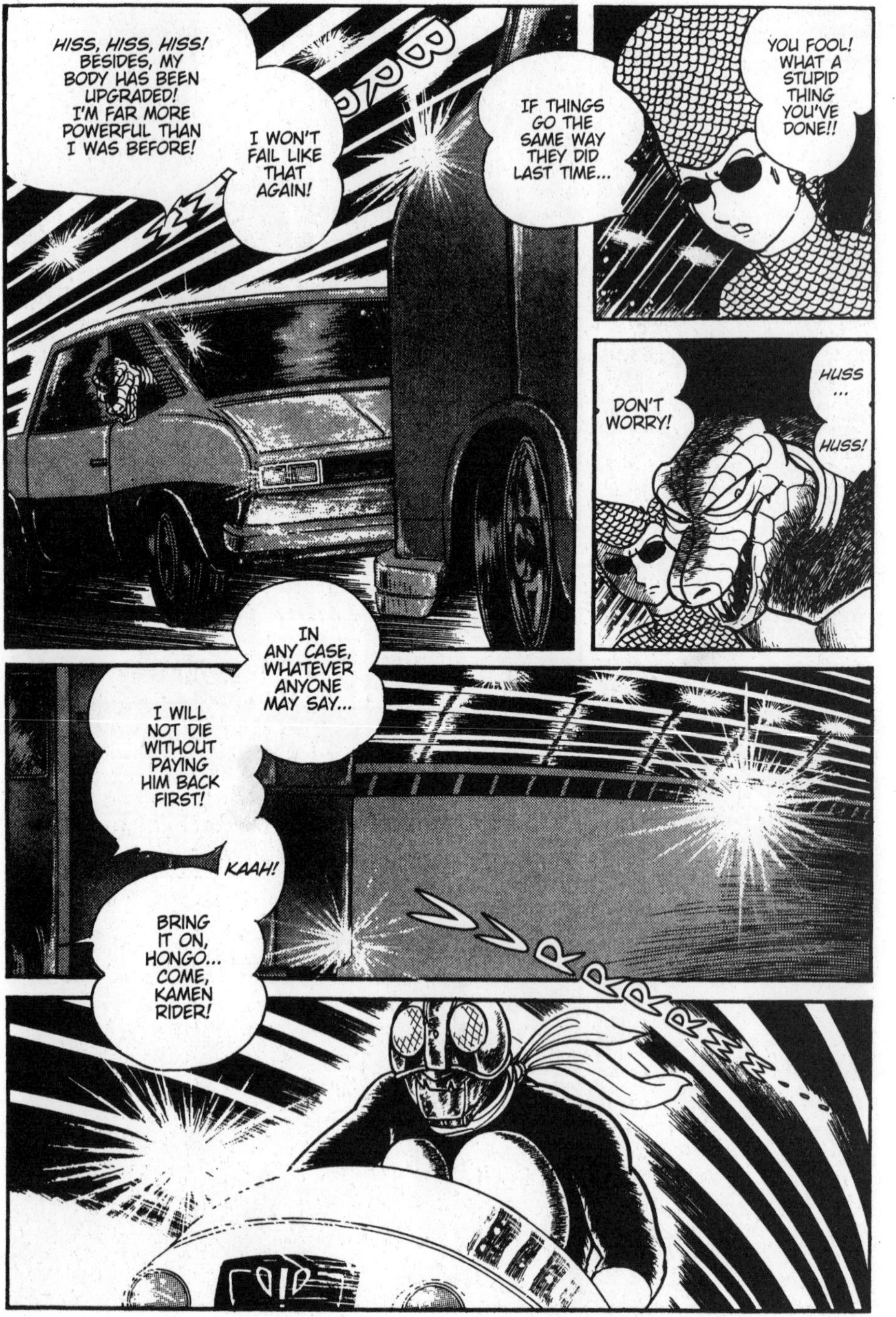
YOU FOOL! WHAT A STUPID THING YOU'VE DONE!!
HUSS ... HUSS!
DON'T WORRY!
IF THINGS GO THE SAME WAY THEY DID LAST TIME...
BRR
I WON'T FAIL LIKE THAT AGAIN!
HISS, HISS, HISS! BESIDES, MY BODY HAS BEEN UPGRADED! I'M FAR MORE POWERFUL THAN I WAS BEFORE!
IN ANY CASE, WHATEVER ANYONE MAY SAY...
I WILL NOT DIE WITHOUT PAYING HIM BACK FIRST!
KAAH!
BRING IT ON, HONGO... COME, KAMEN RIDER!
VVRRRRMMM...

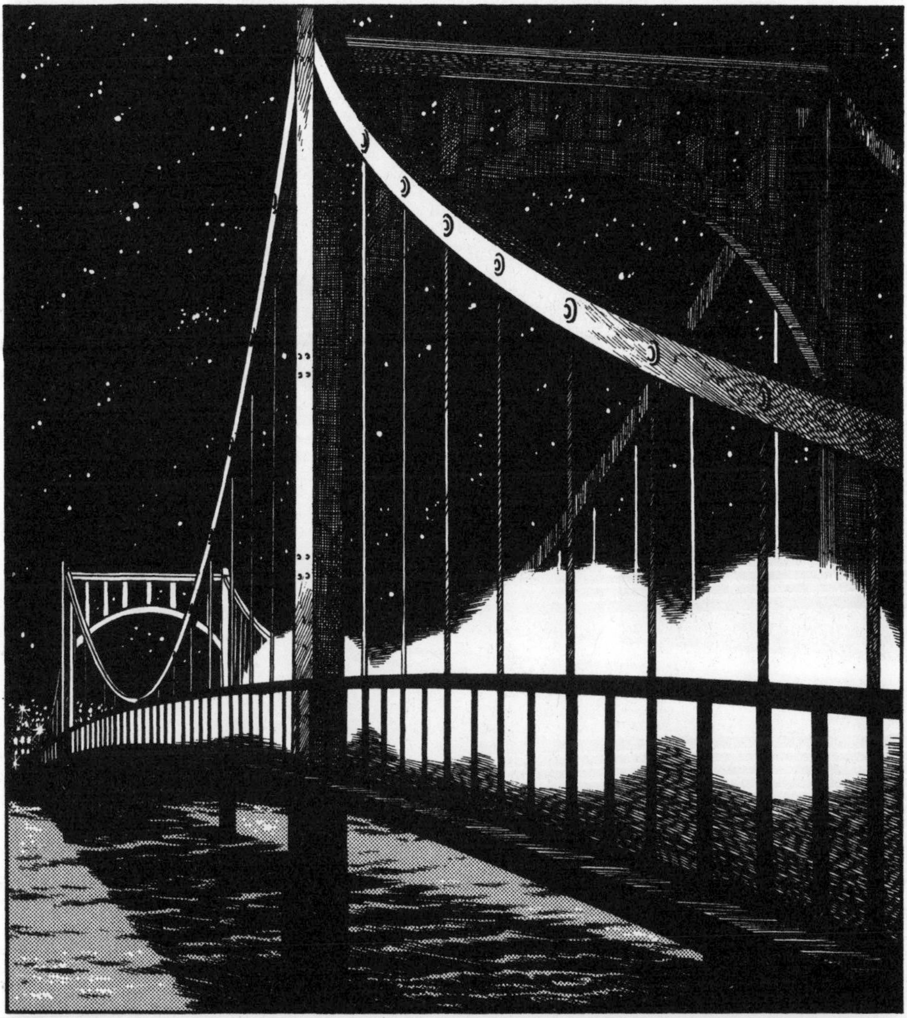
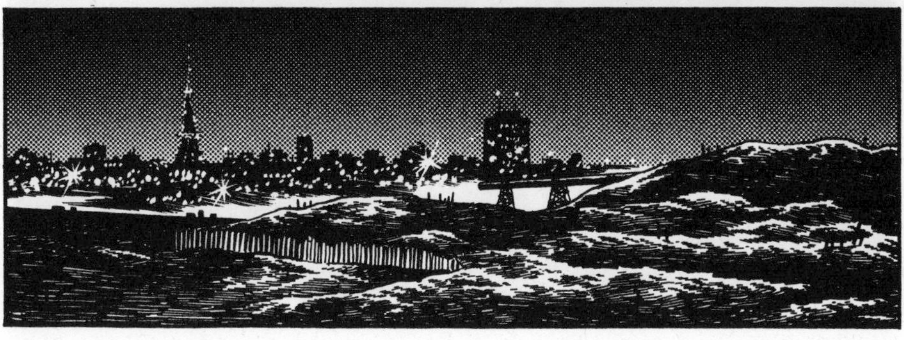

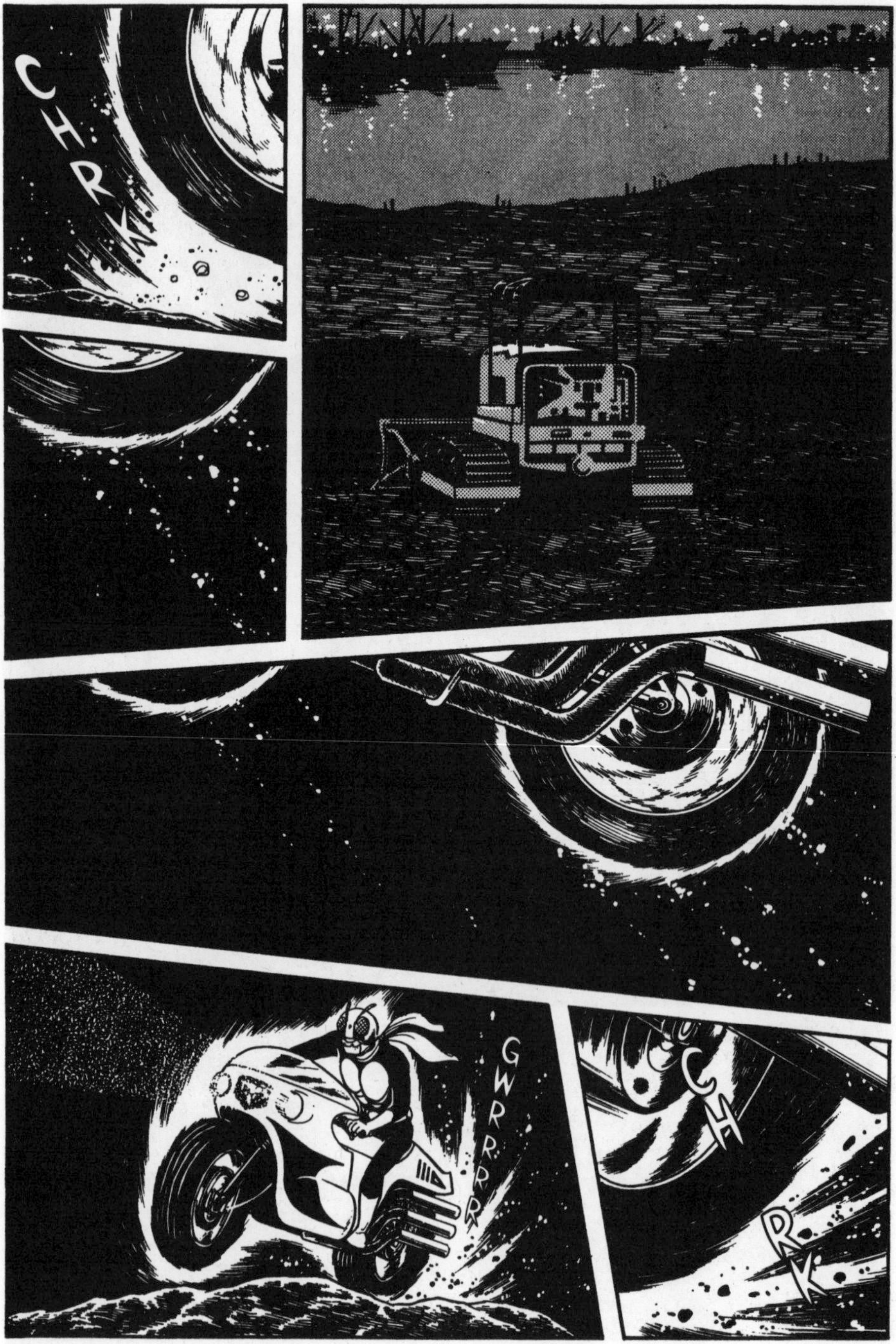
CHRK
CHRK
GWRRRRR

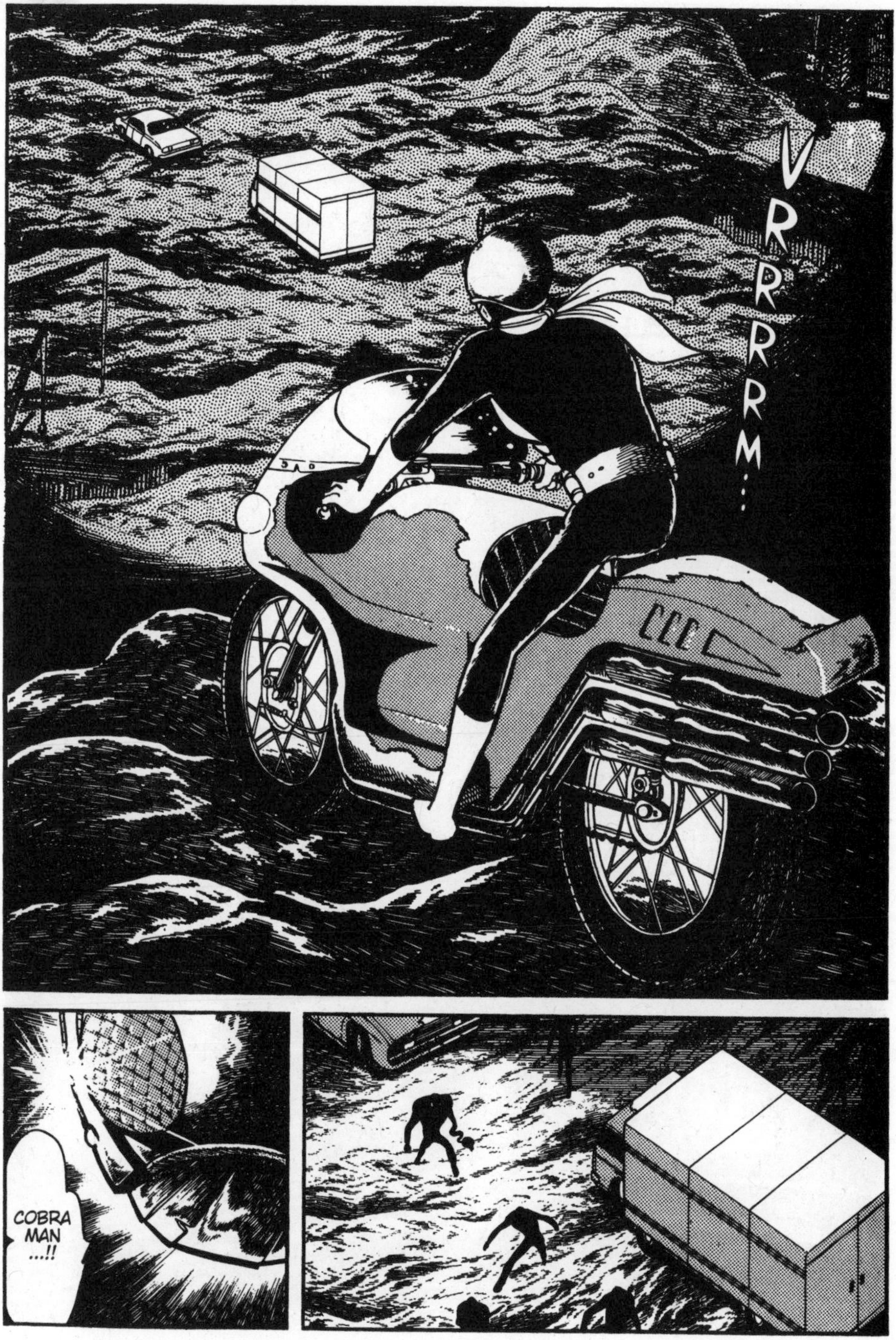
VRRRRM...
COBRA MAN ...!!

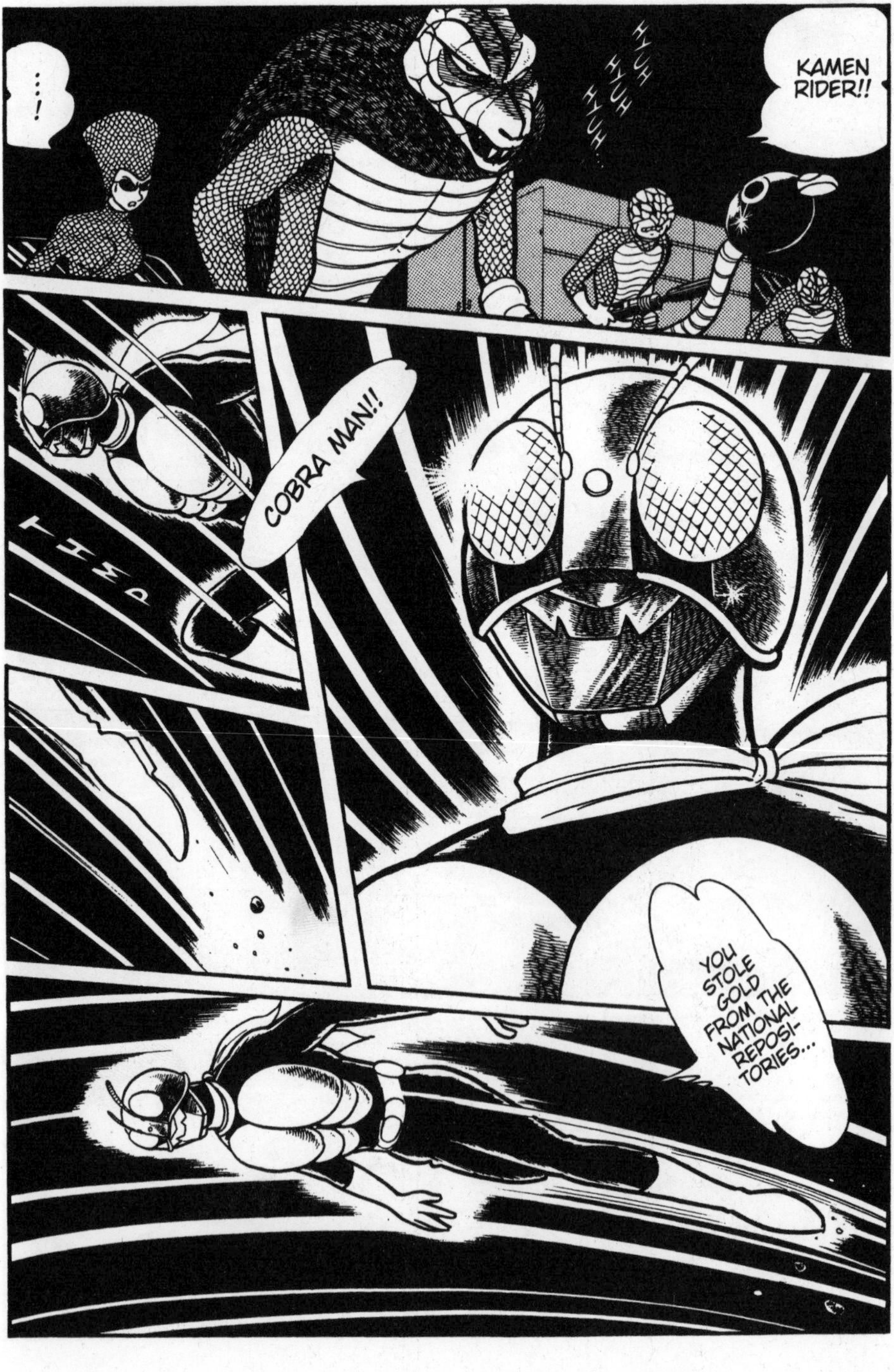
KAMEN RIDER!!
HYUH HYUH HYUH...
...!
COBRA MAN!!
YOU STOLE GOLD FROM THE NATIONAL REPOSITORIES...

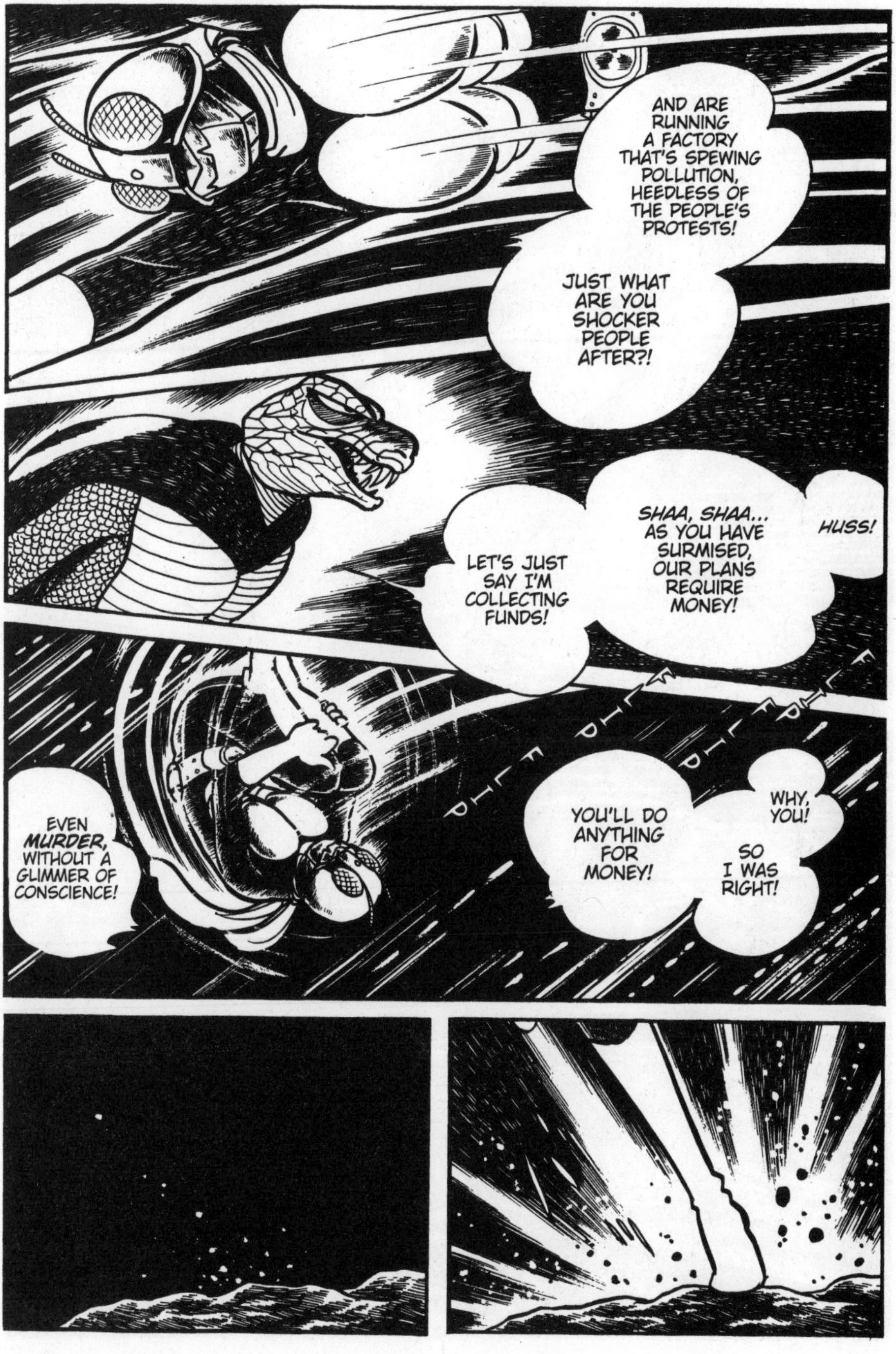
AND ARE RUNNING A FACTORY THAT'S SPEWING POLLUTION, HEEDLESS OF THE PEOPLE'S PROTESTS!
JUST WHAT ARE YOU SHOCKER PEOPLE AFTER?!
HUSS!
SHAA, SHAA... AS YOU HAVE SURMISED, OUR PLANS REQUIRE MONEY!
LET'S JUST SAY I'M COLLECTING FUNDS!
WHY, YOU!
SO I WAS RIGHT!
YOU'LL DO ANYTHING FOR MONEY!
FLIP FLIP FLIP
EVEN MURDER, WITHOUT A GLIMMER OF CONSCIENCE!

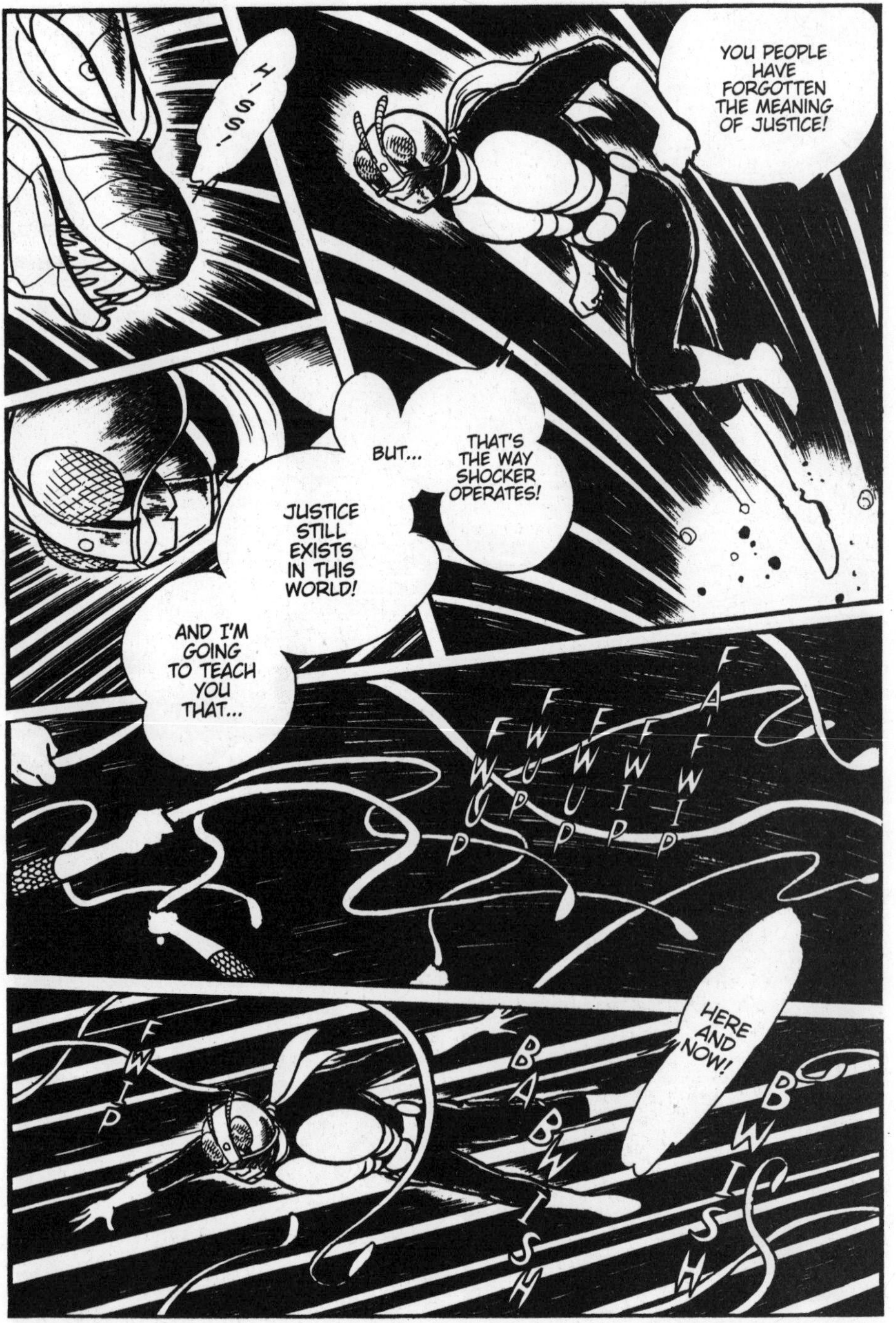
YOU PEOPLE HAVE FORGOTTEN THE MEANING OF JUSTICE!
HISS!
THAT'S THE WAY SHOCKER OPERATES!
BUT...
JUSTICE STILL EXISTS IN THIS WORLD!
AND I'M GOING TO TEACH YOU THAT...
FAFWIPP
FWIPP
FWUPP
FWUPP
FWUP
HERE AND NOW!
BWISH
BABWISH
FWIP

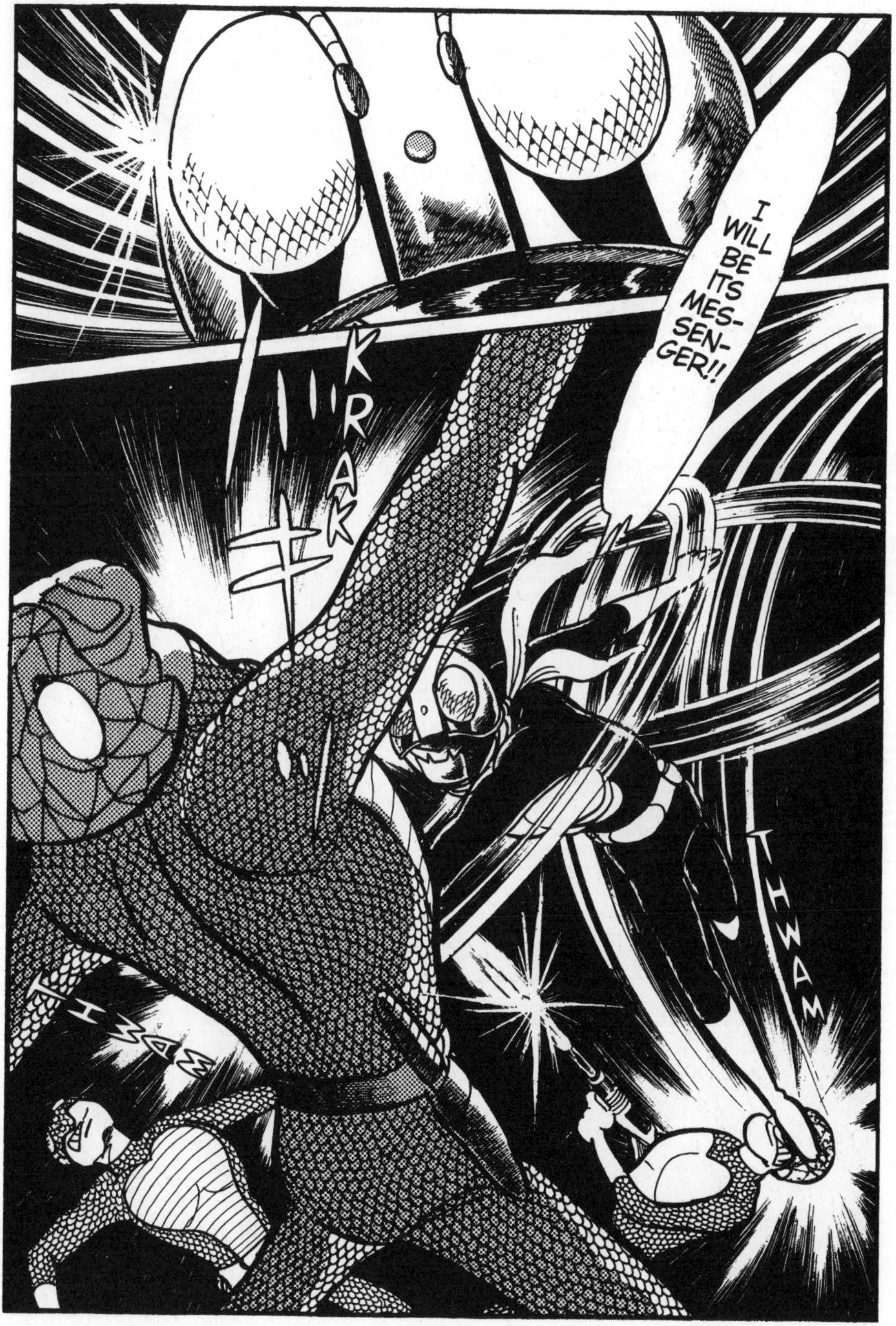
I WILL BE ITS MES-SENGER!!
KRAK
THWAM
THWAM

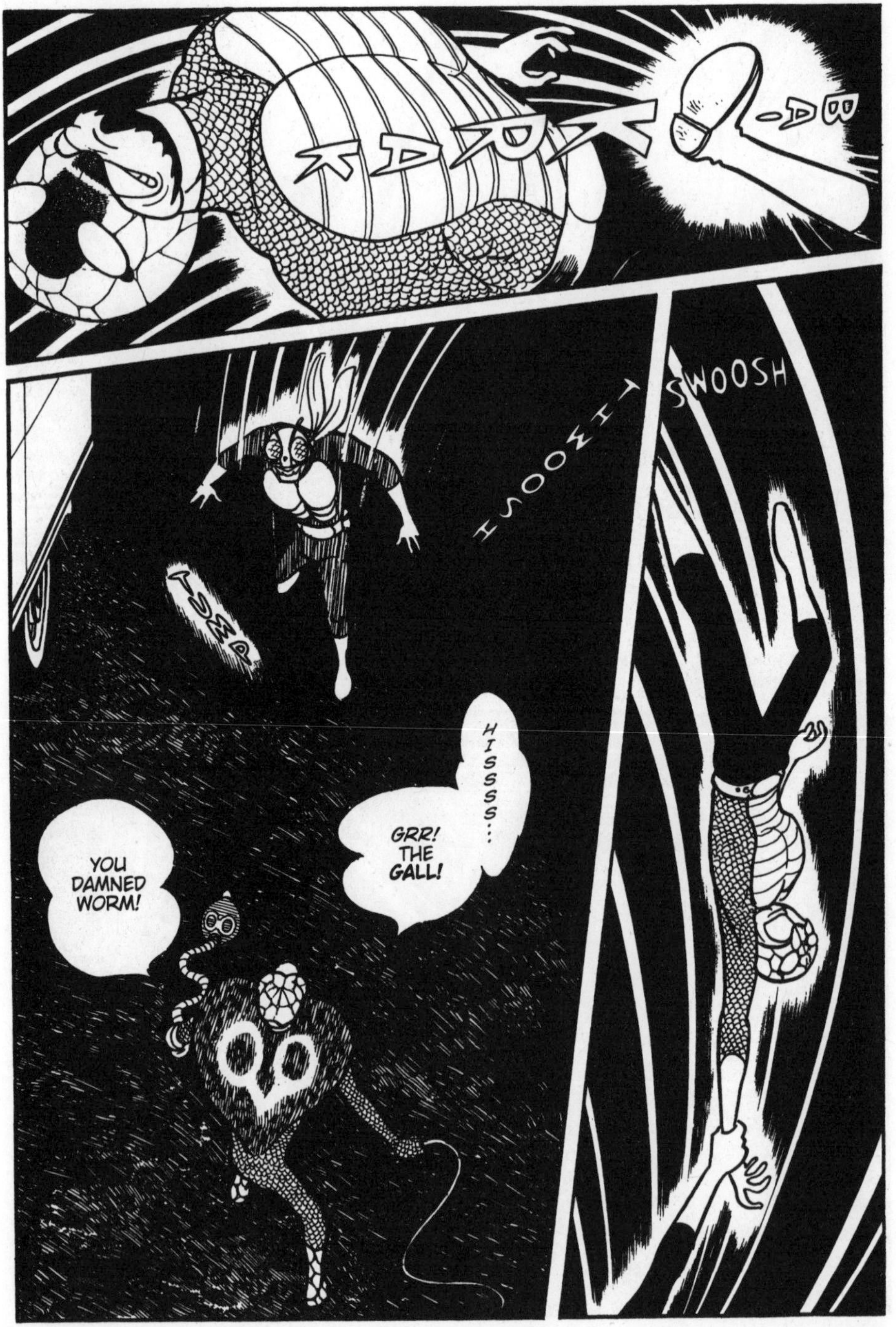
BA-KRAK
SWOOSH
WHOOSH
TUMP
HISSSS...
GRR! THE GALL!
YOU DAMNED WORM!

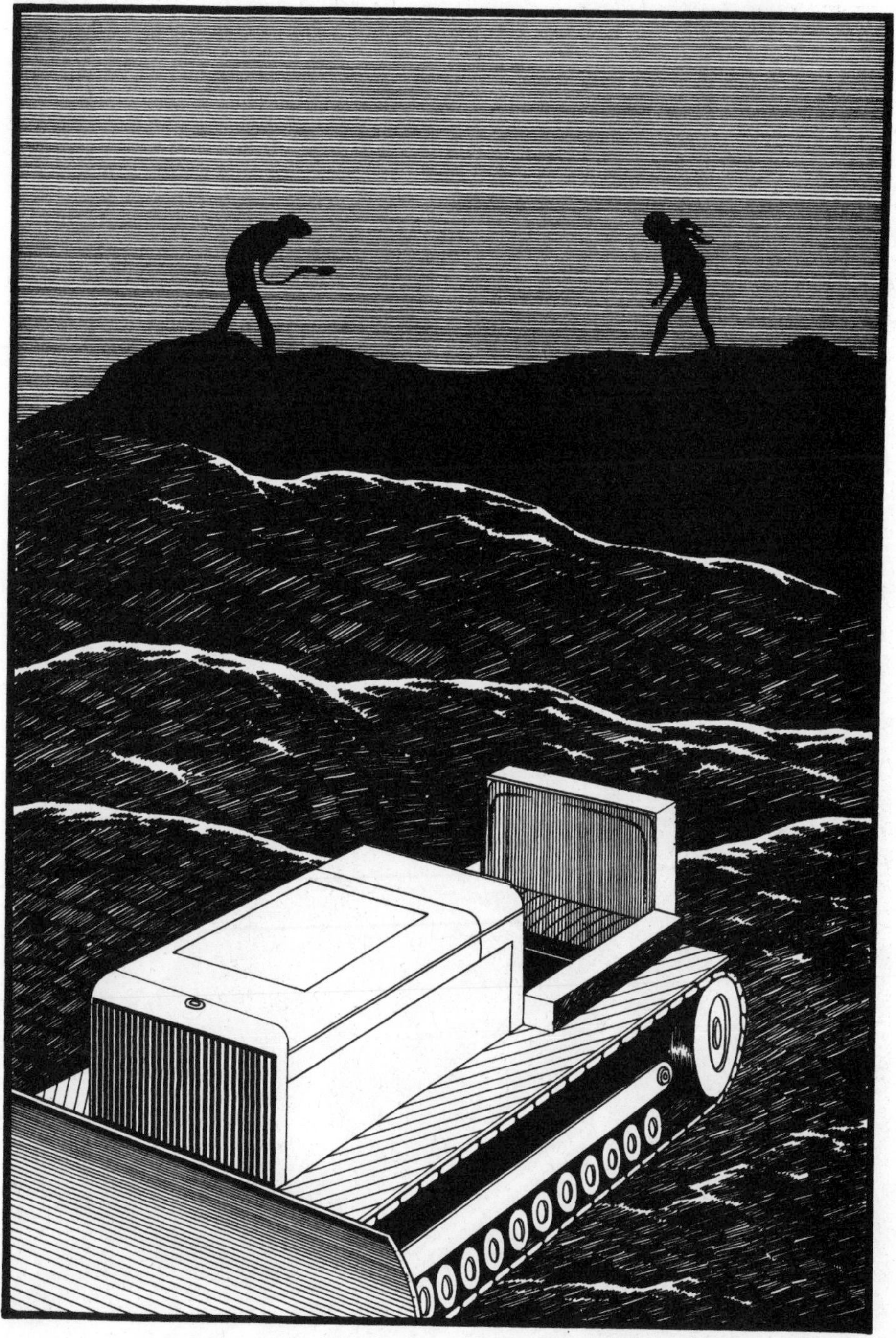

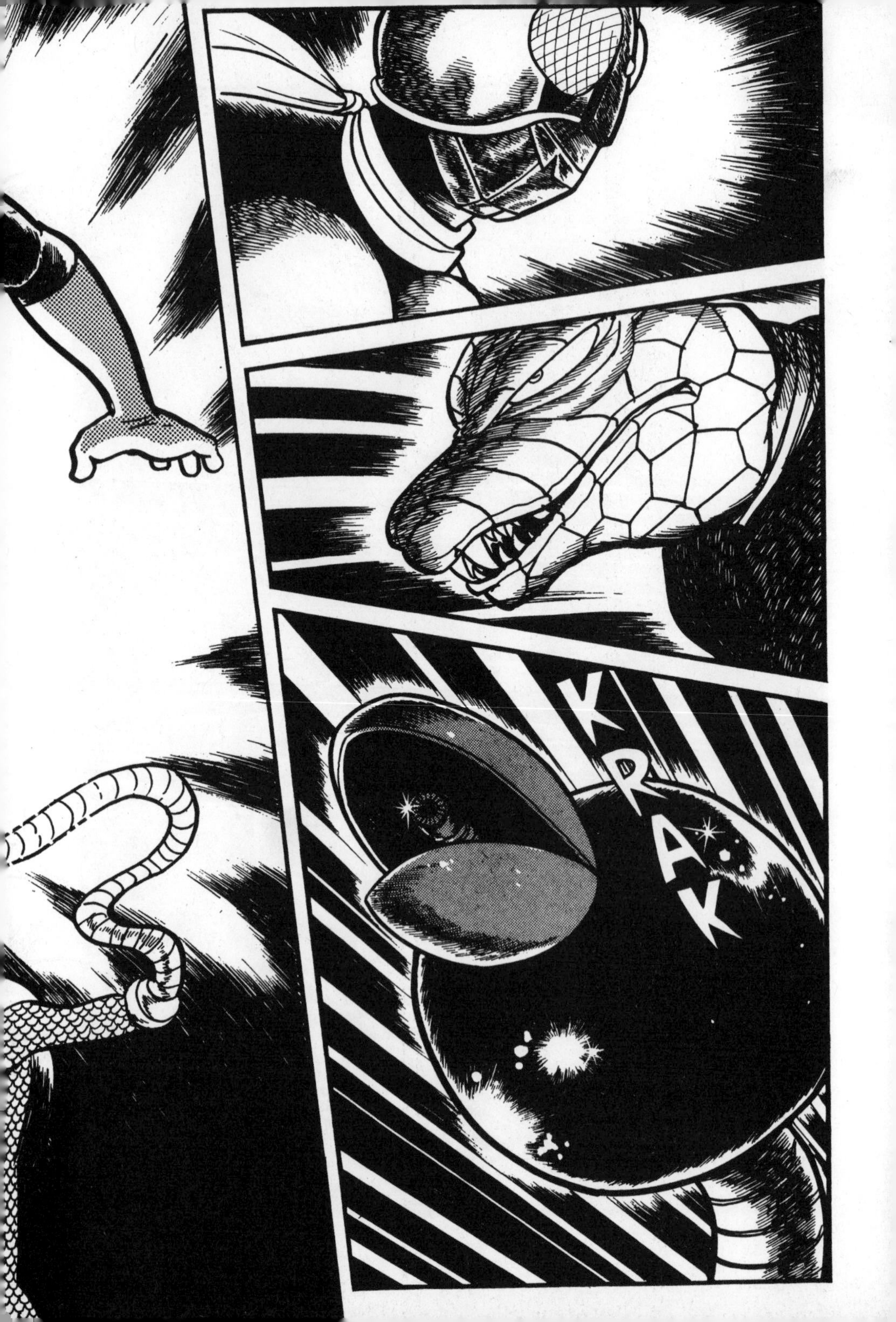
KRAK

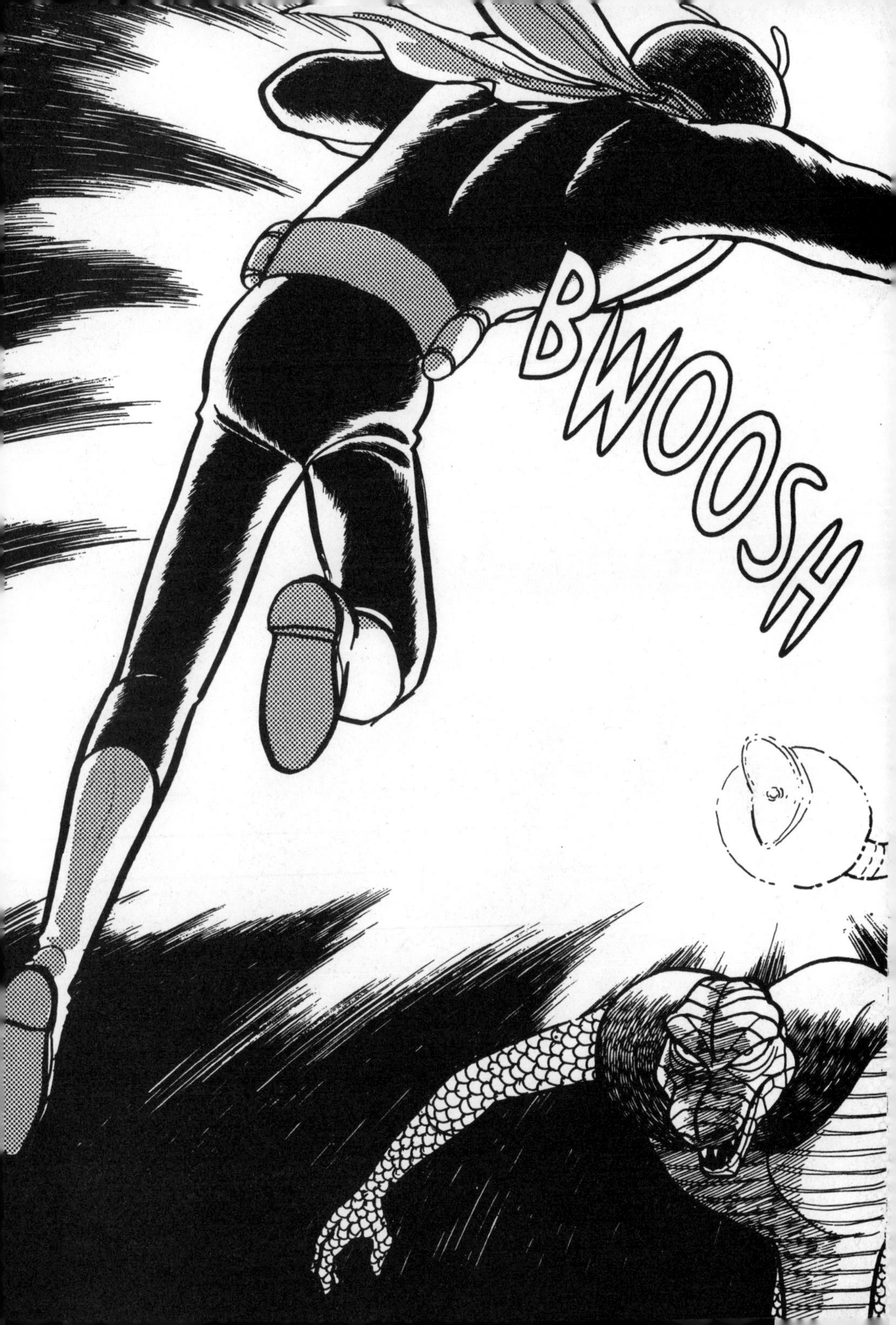
BWOOSH

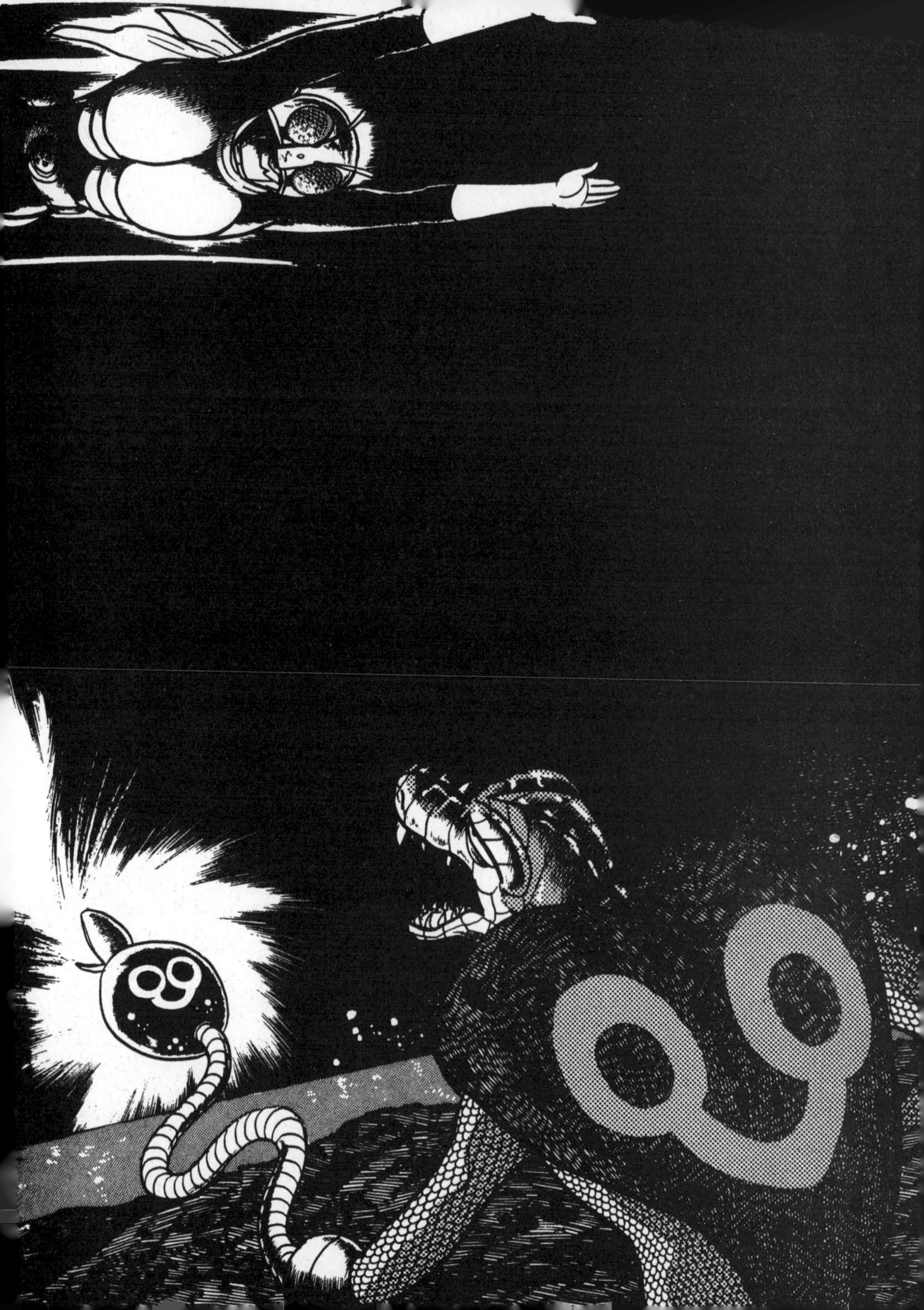

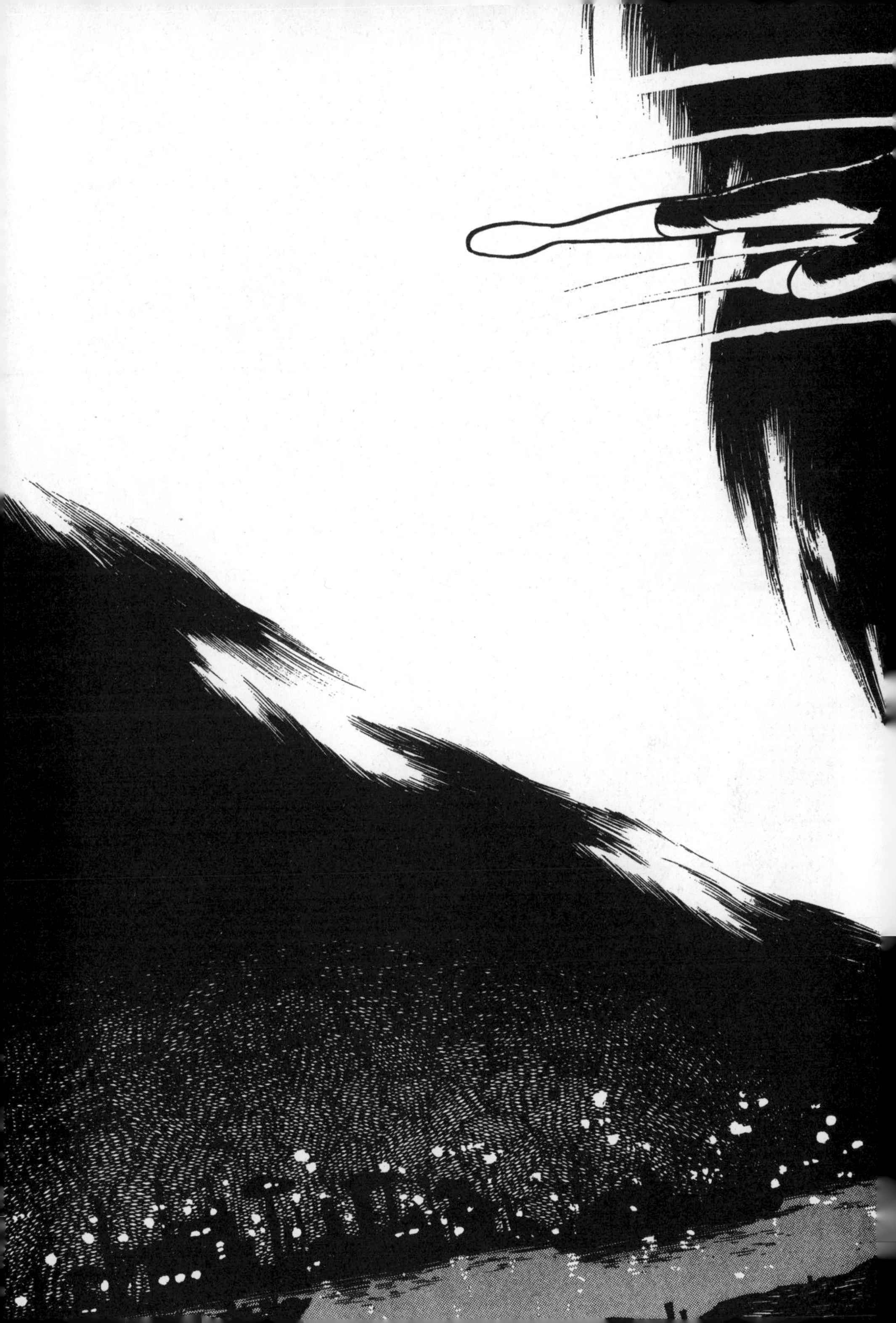

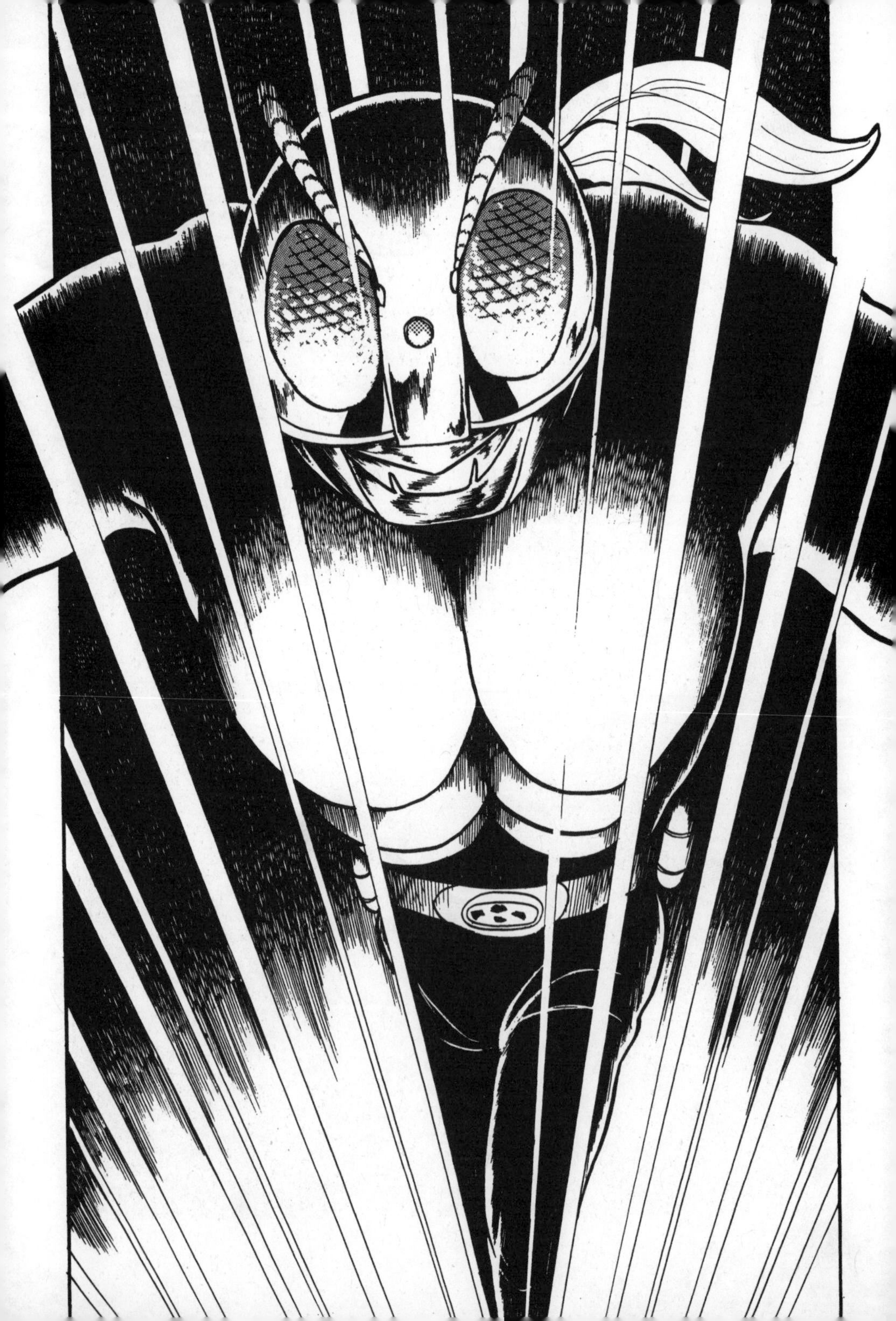

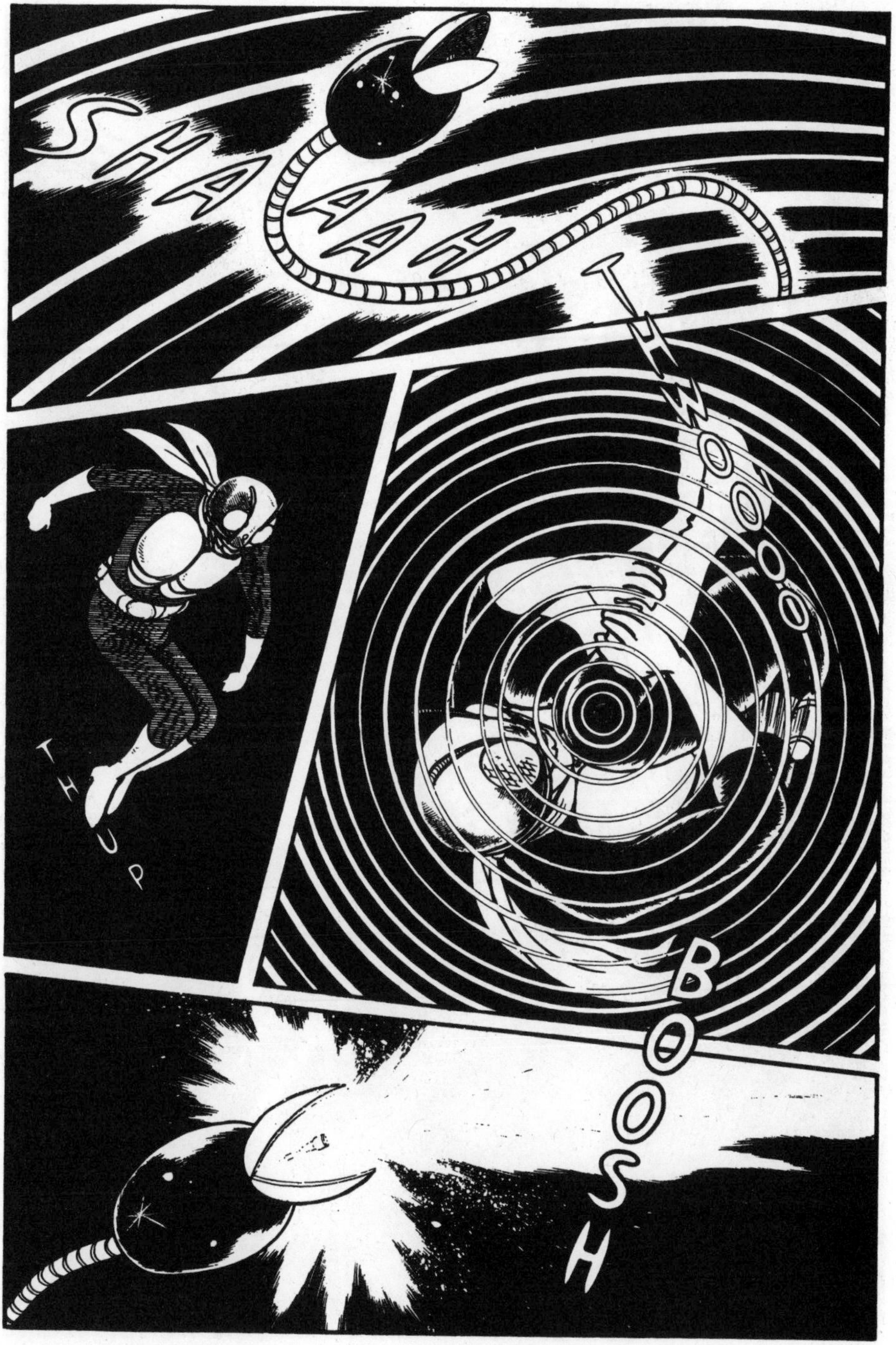
SHAAAH
THWOOOOO
BOOSH
THUP

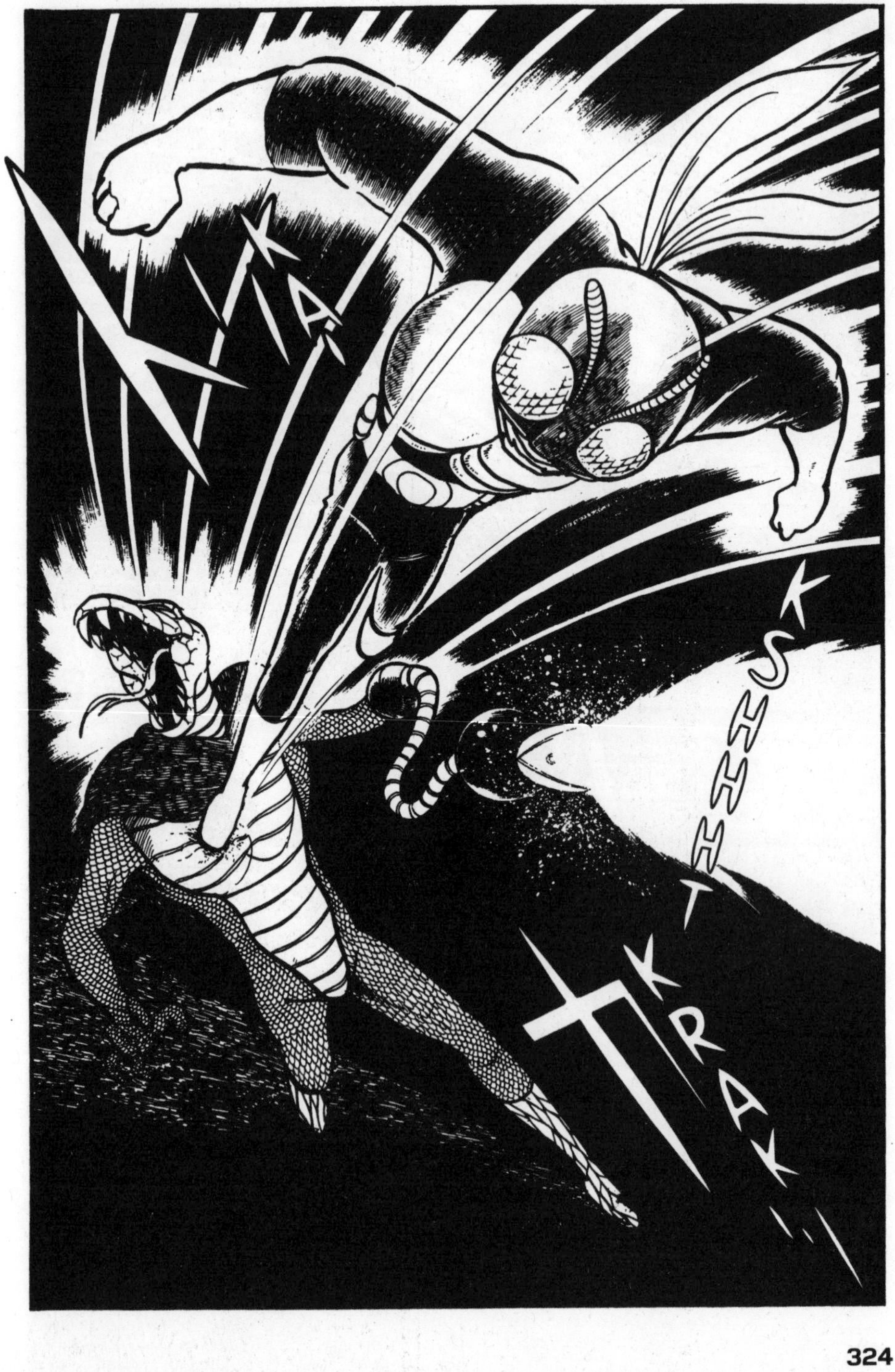
KA!
KSHHHHT
TKRAK

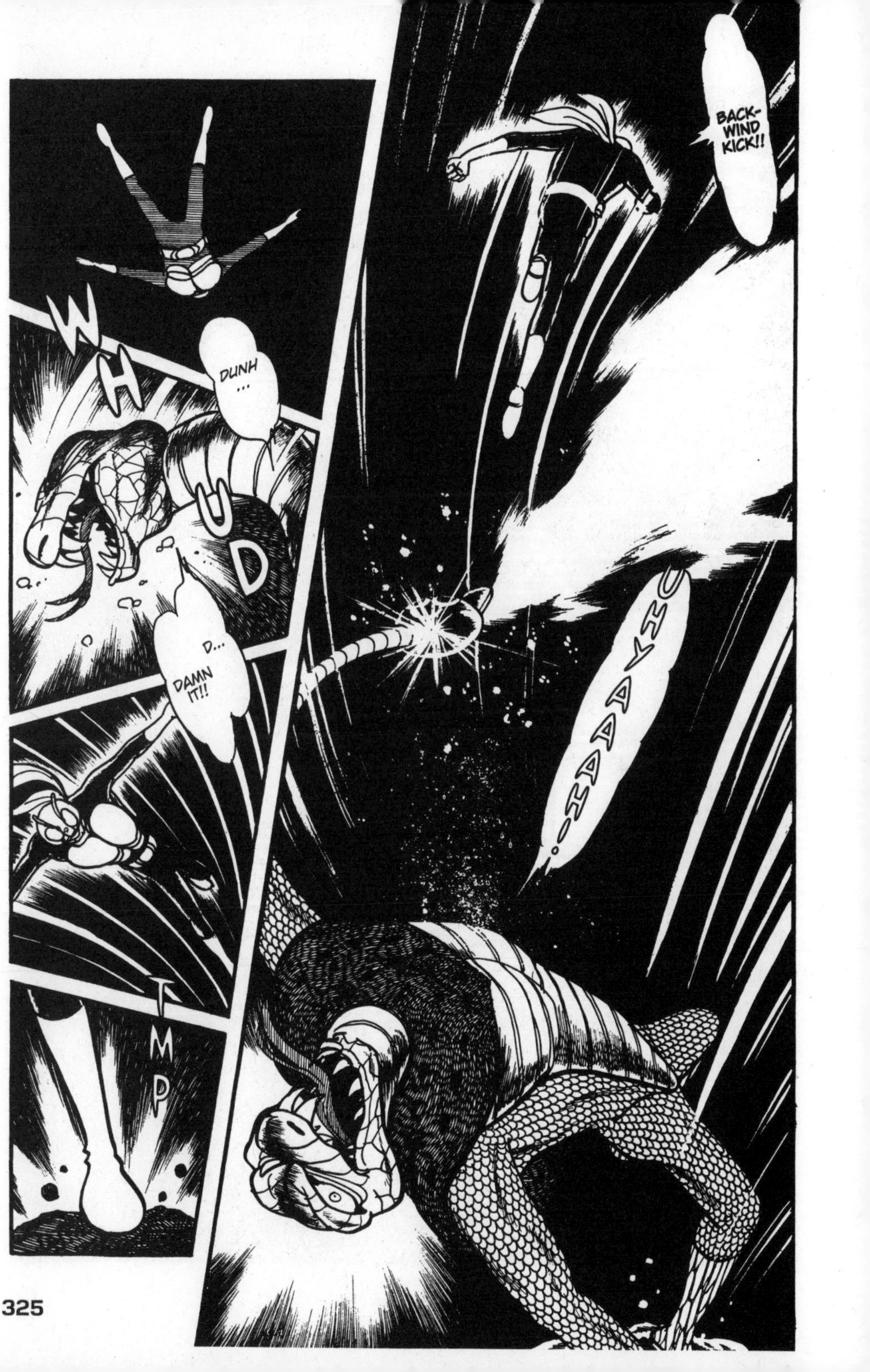
BACK-WIND KICK!!
UHYAAAAAH--!
DUNH ...
WHUD
D... DAMN IT!!
TMP

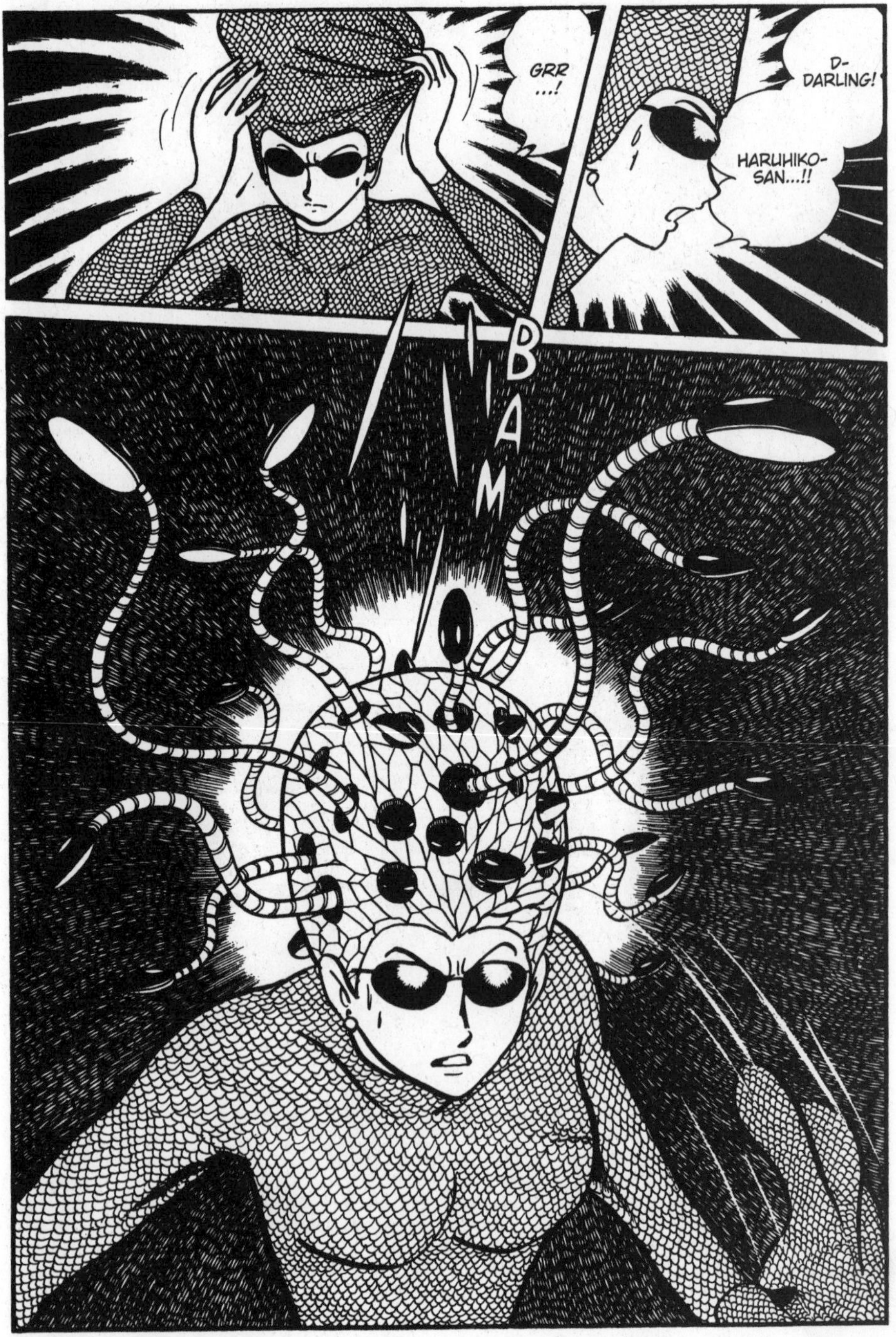
D-DARLING!
HARUHIKO-SAN...!!
GRR ...!
BAM

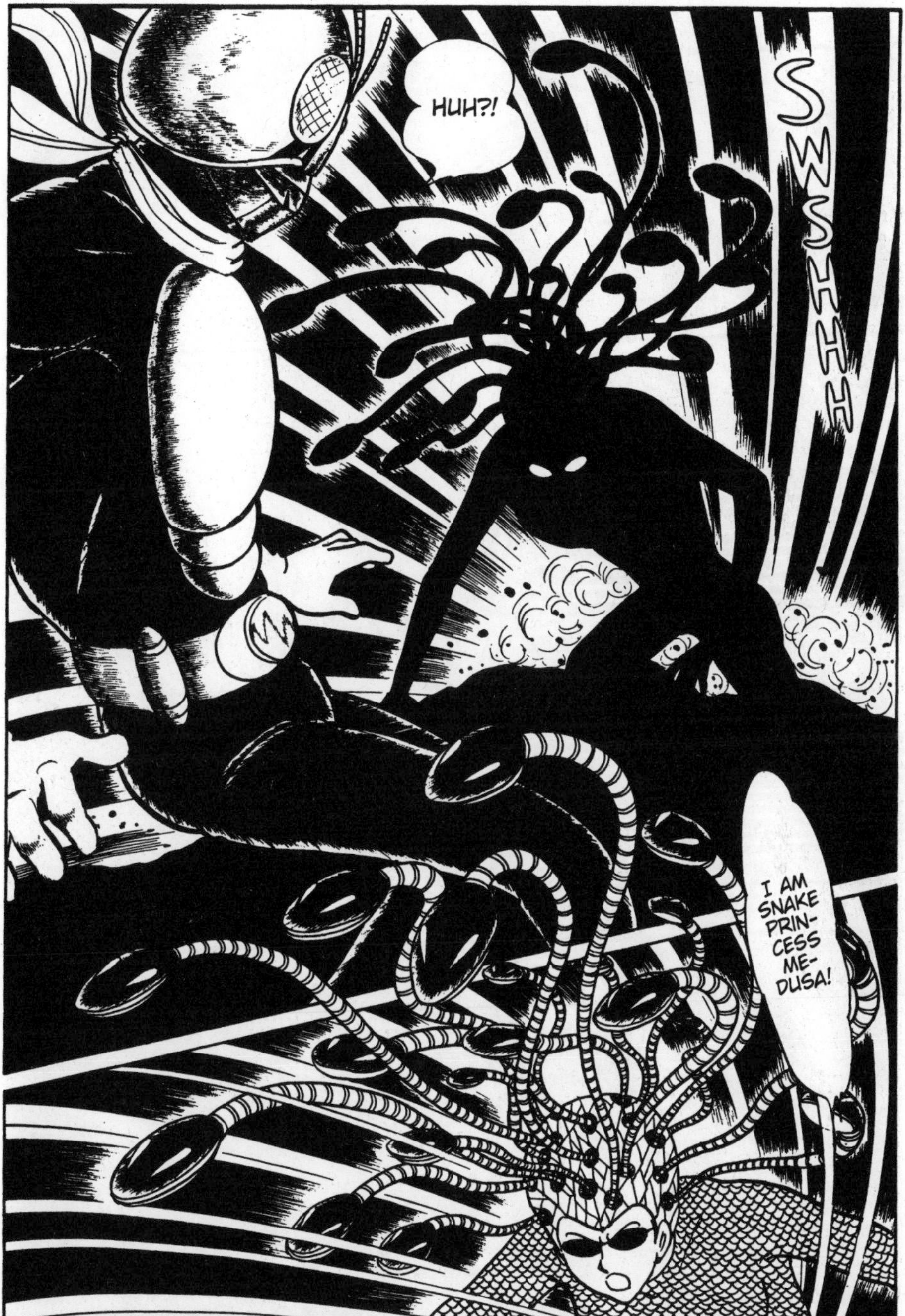
HUH?!
SWSHHH
I AM SNAKE PRIN-CESS ME-DUSA!

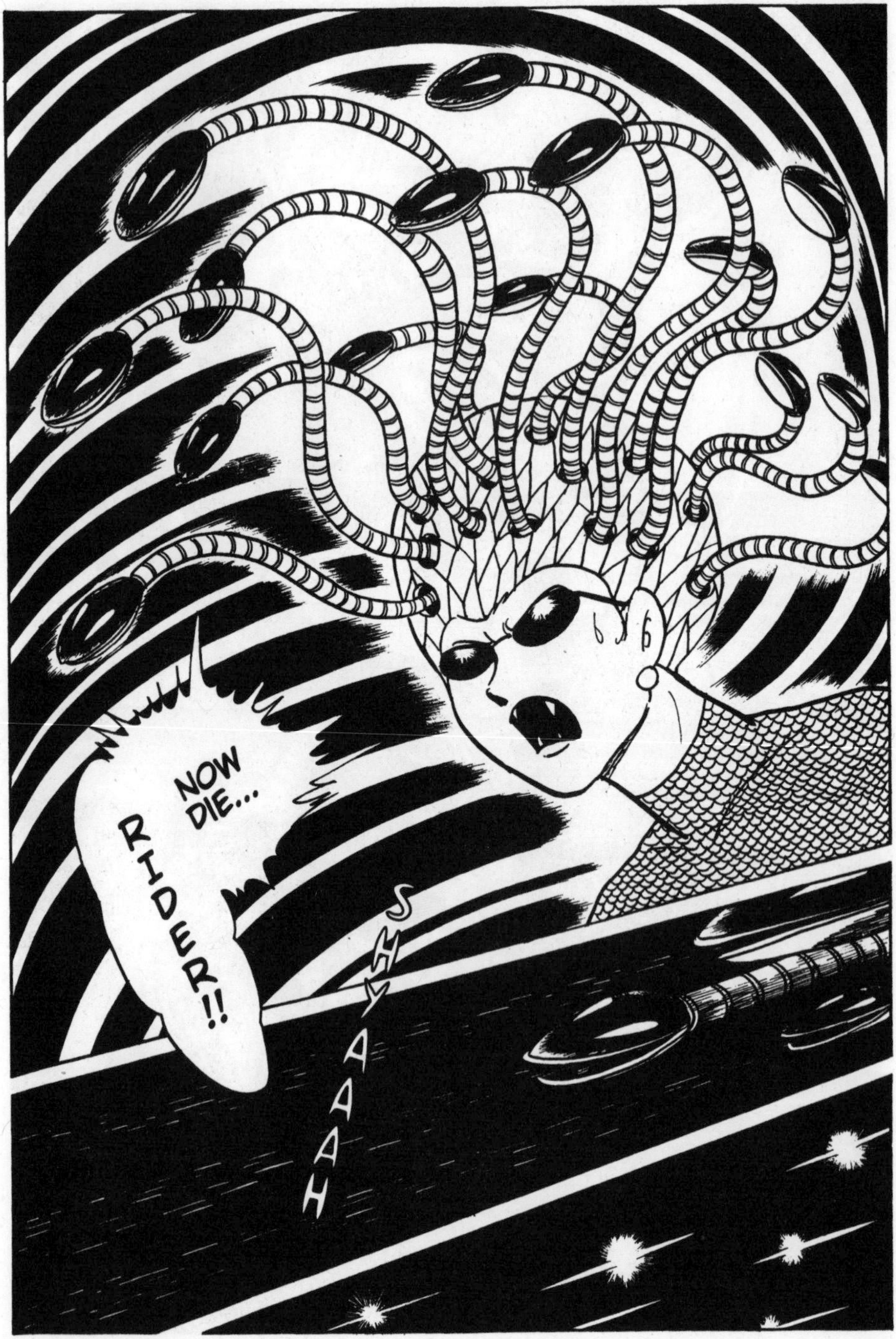
NOW DIE... RIDER!!
SHYAAAAH

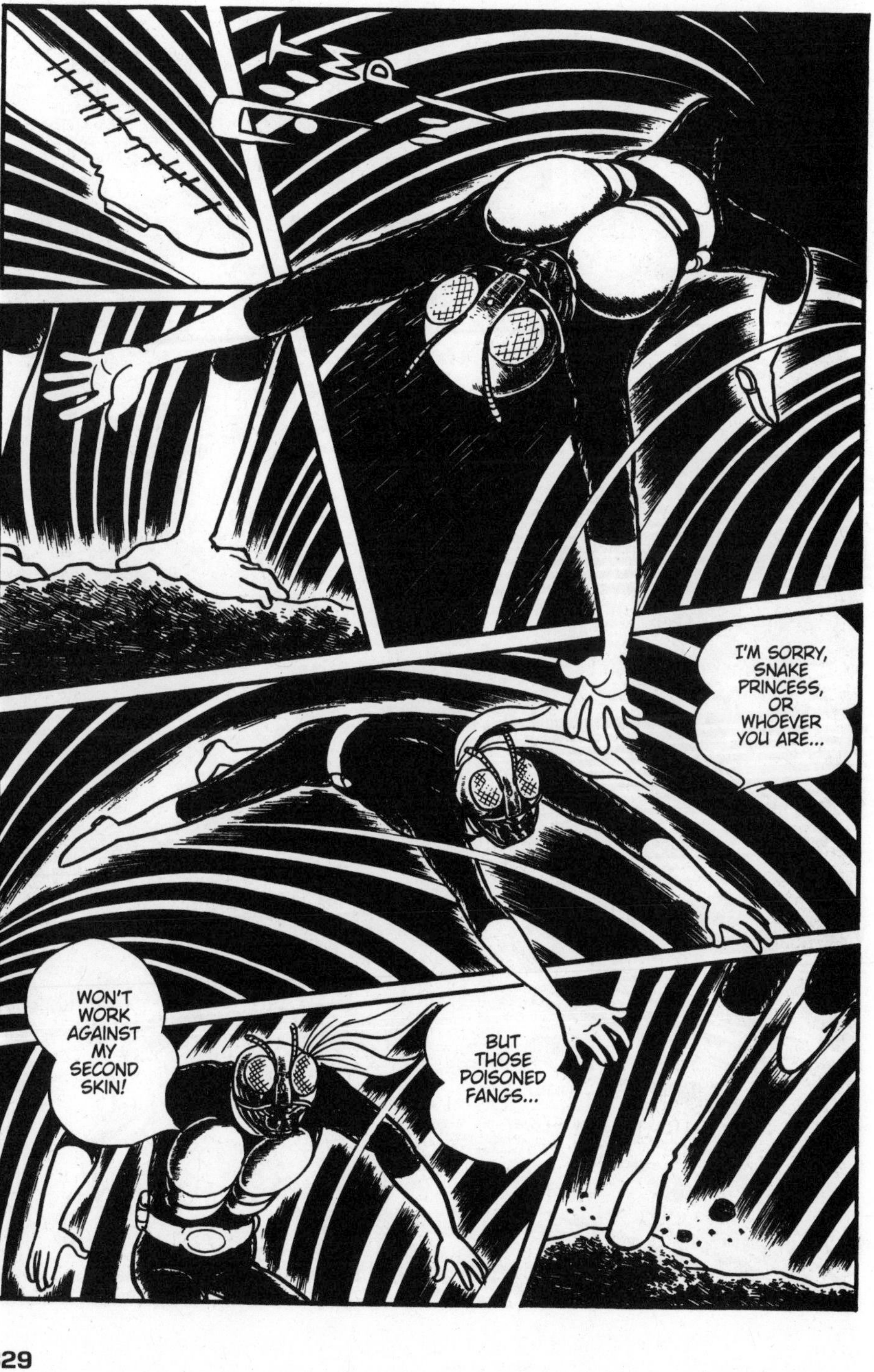
I'M SORRY, SNAKE PRINCESS, OR WHOEVER YOU ARE...
BUT THOSE POISONED FANGS...
WON'T WORK AGAINST MY SECOND SKIN!

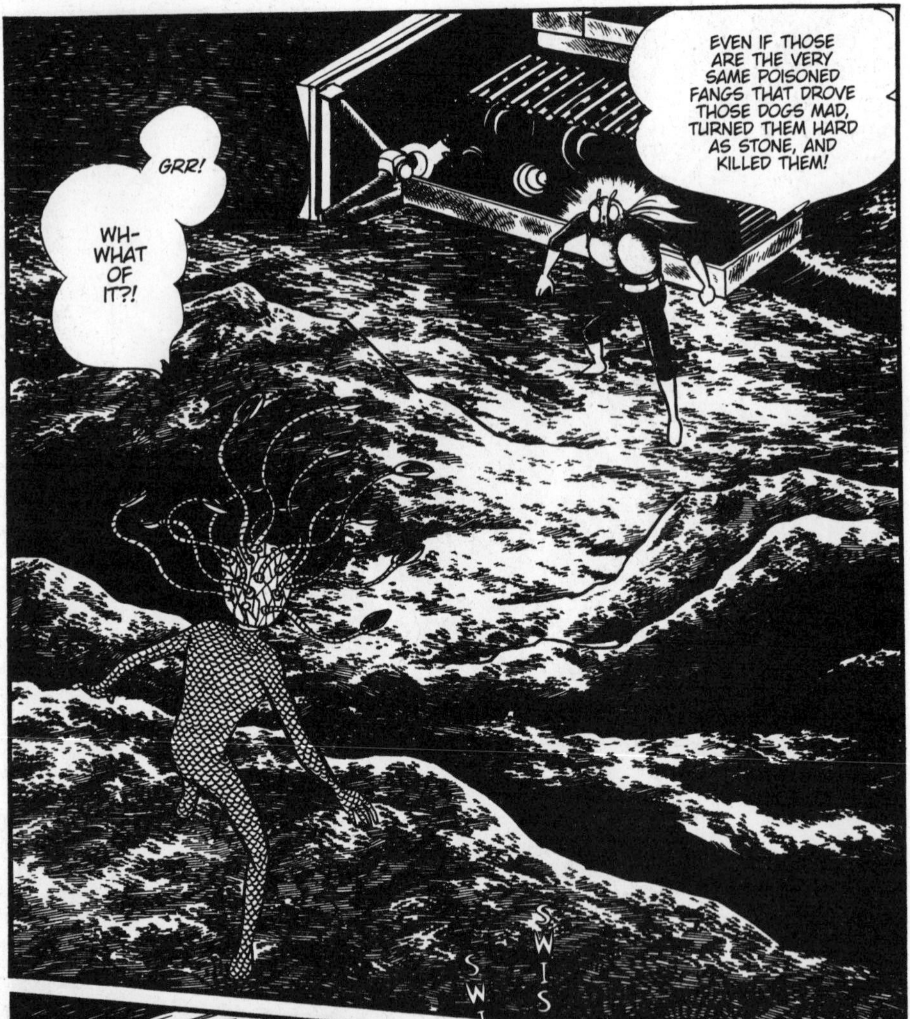
EVEN IF THOSE ARE THE VERY SAME POISONED FANGS THAT DROVE THOSE DOGS MAD, TURNED THEM HARD AS STONE, AND KILLED THEM!
GRR!
WH-WHAT OF IT?!

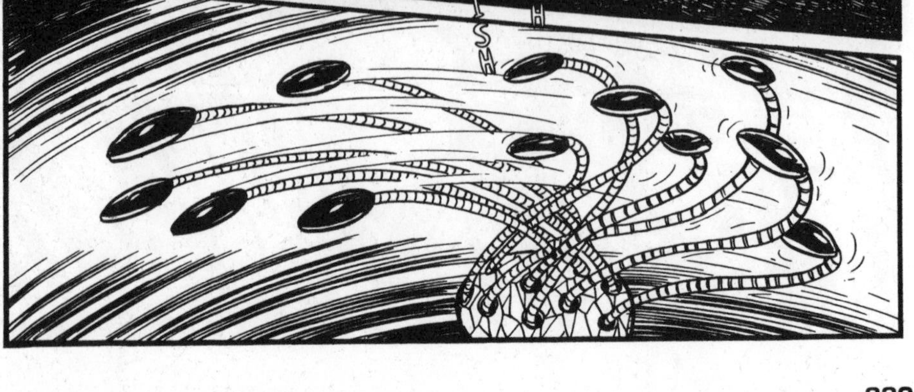
SWISH
SWISH

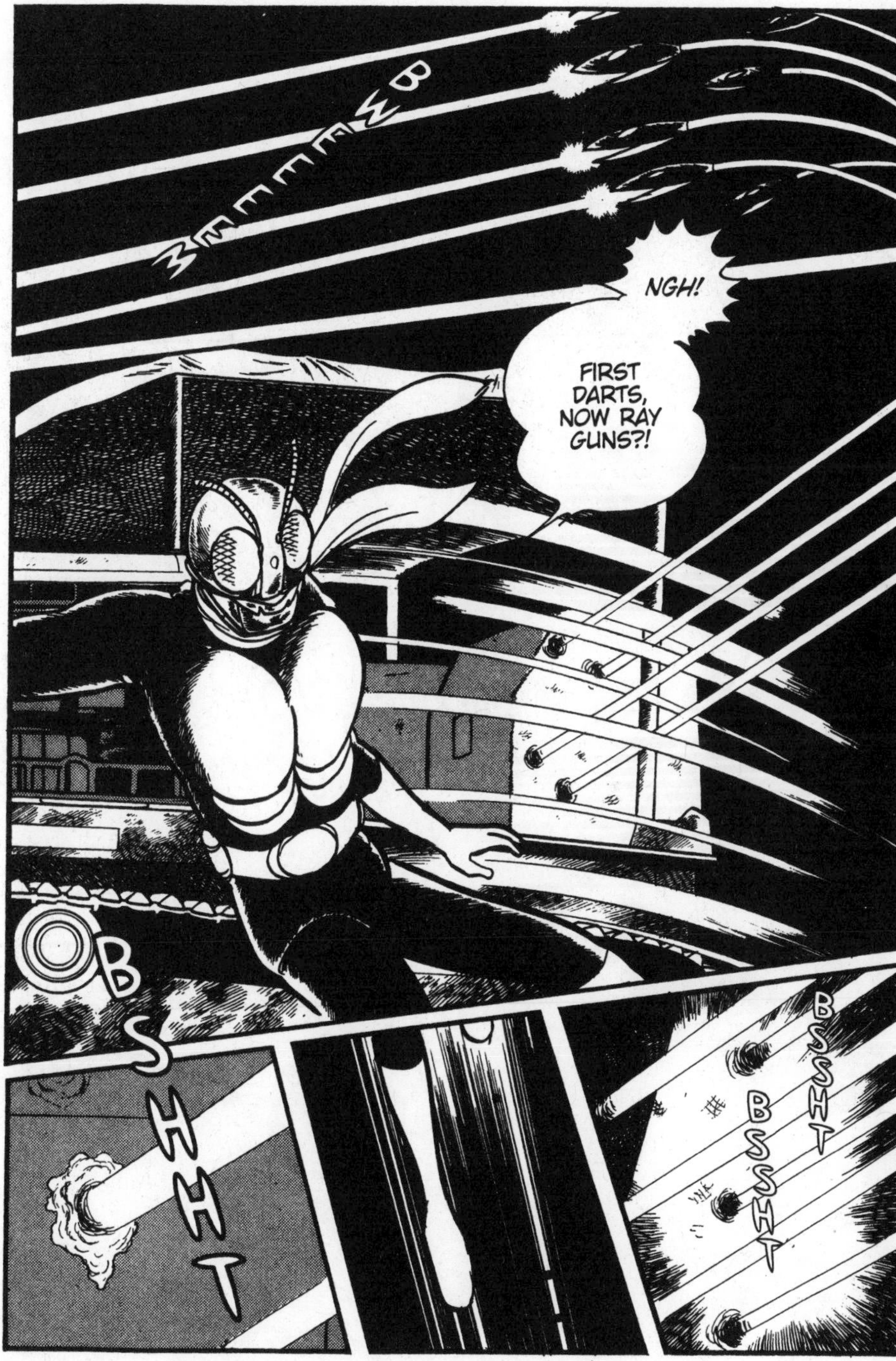
BWEEEEEM
NGH!
FIRST DARTS, NOW RAY GUNS?!
BSSHT
BSSHT
BSHHT

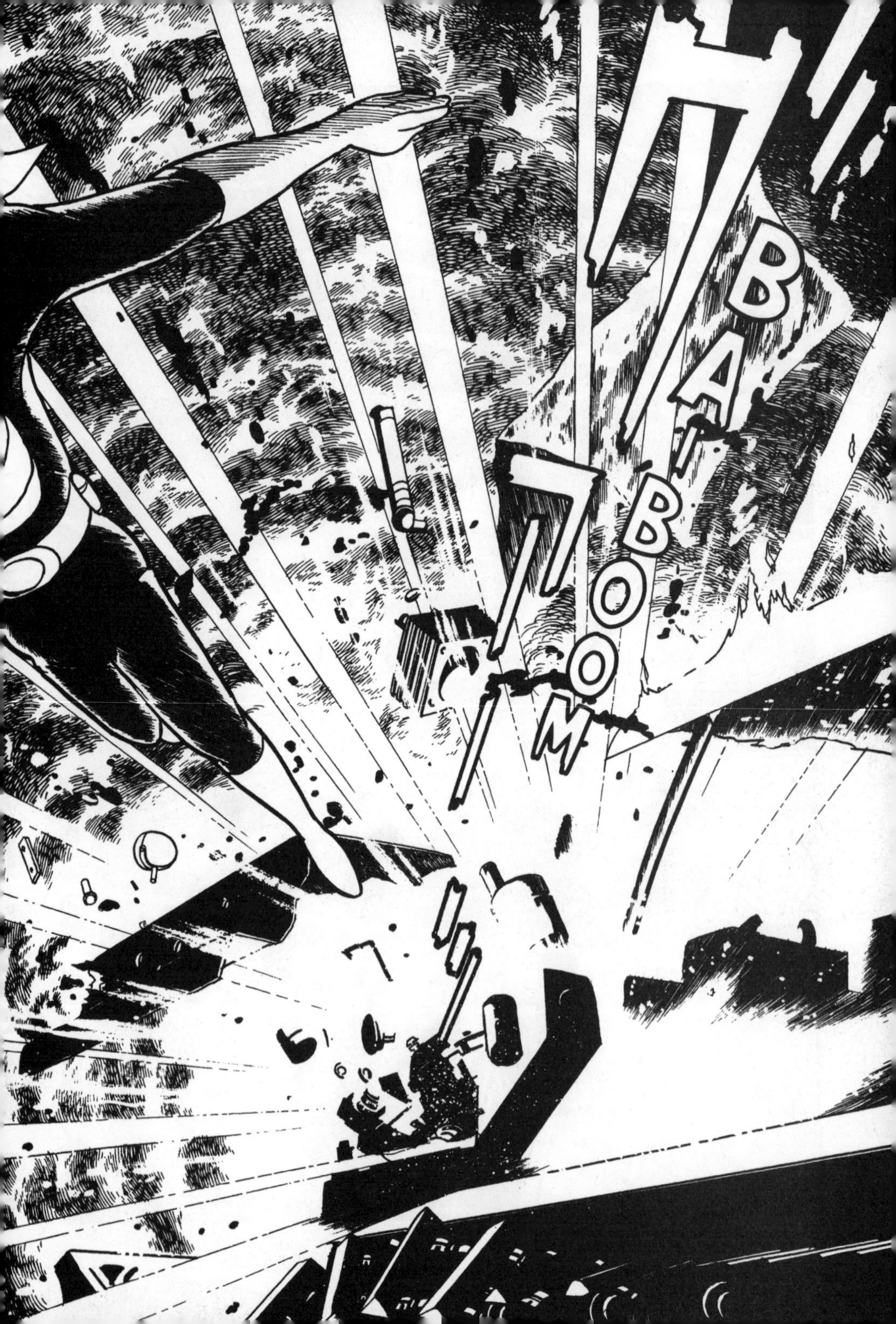
BA-BOOM

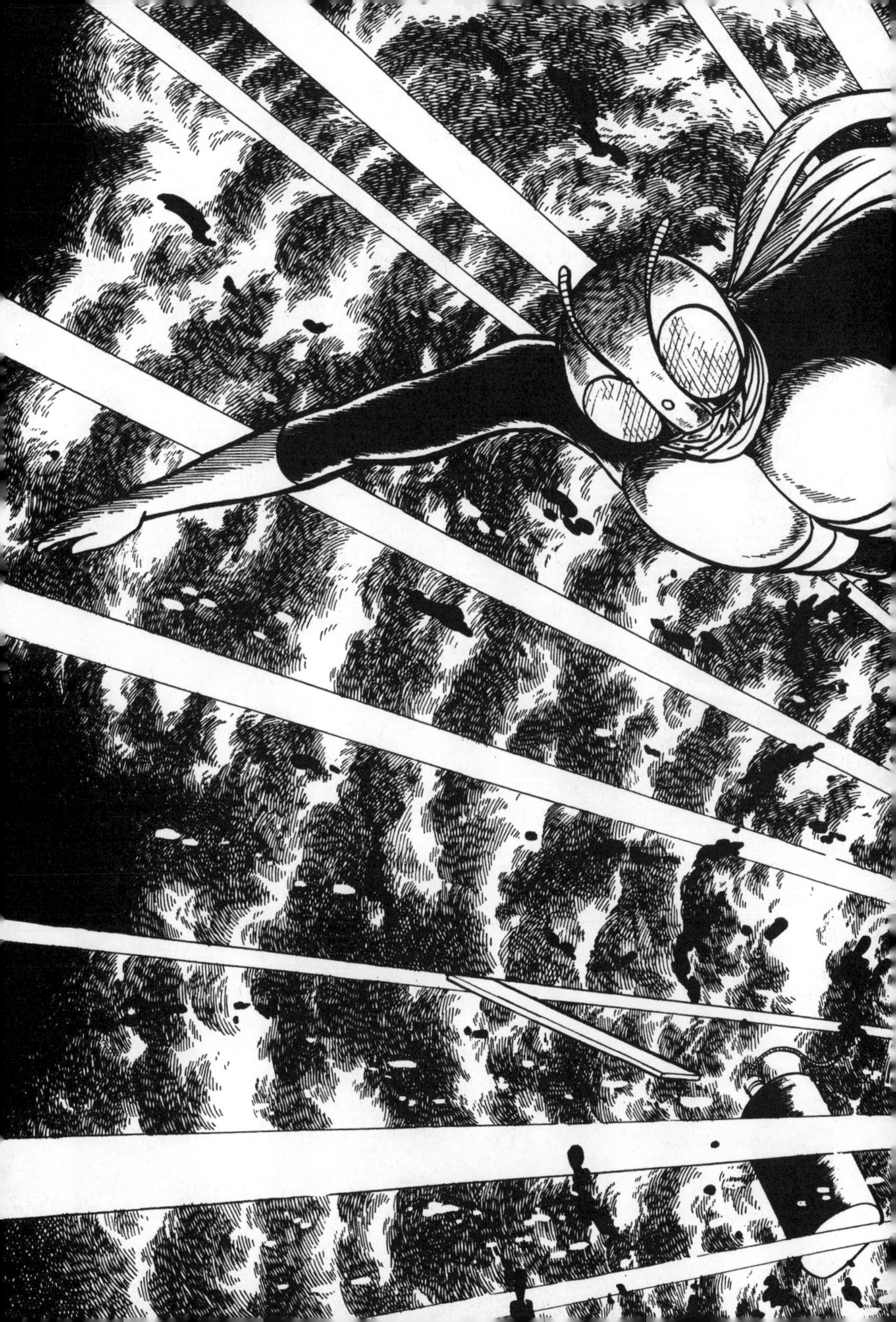

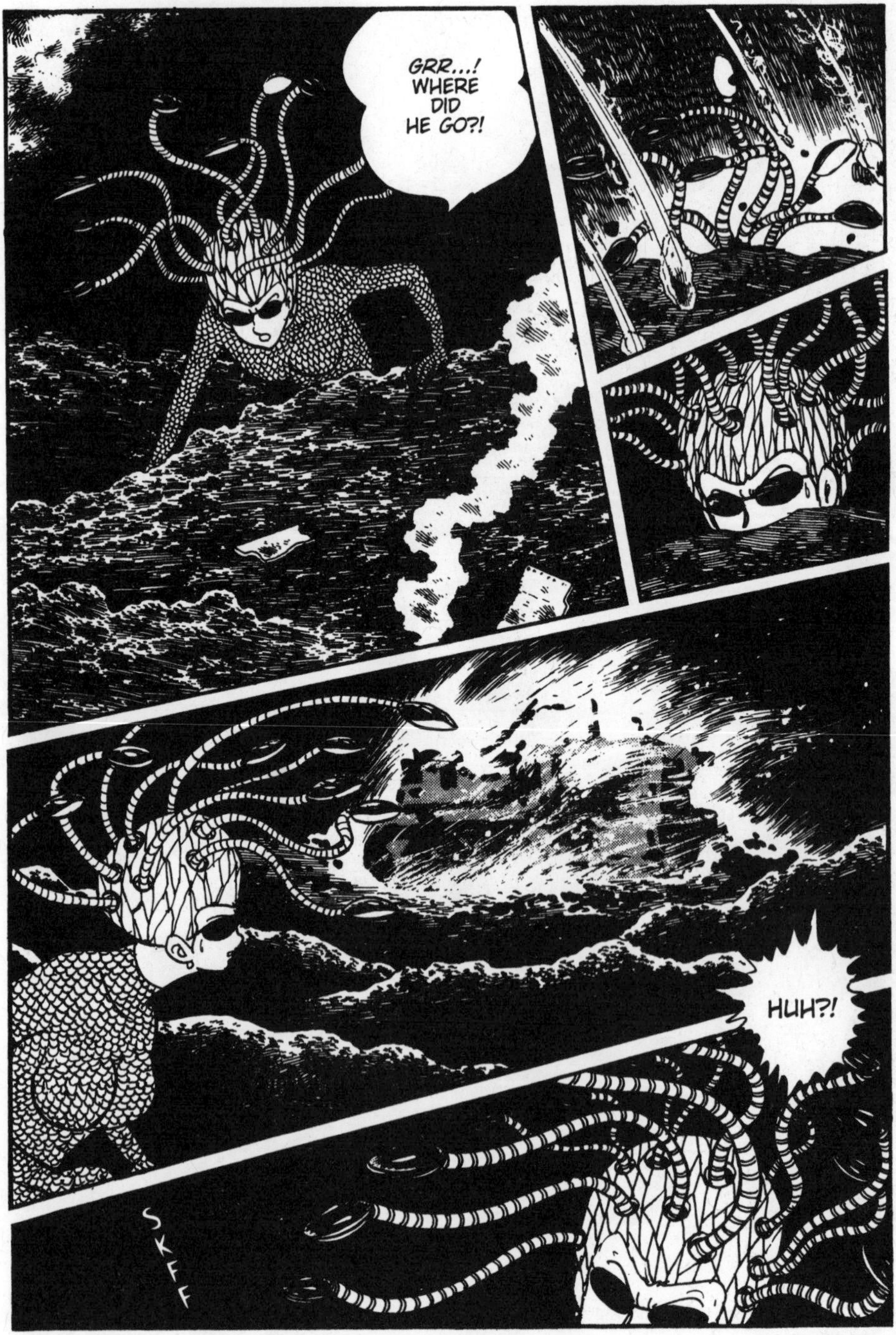
GRR...! WHERE DID HE GO?!
HUH?!
SKFF

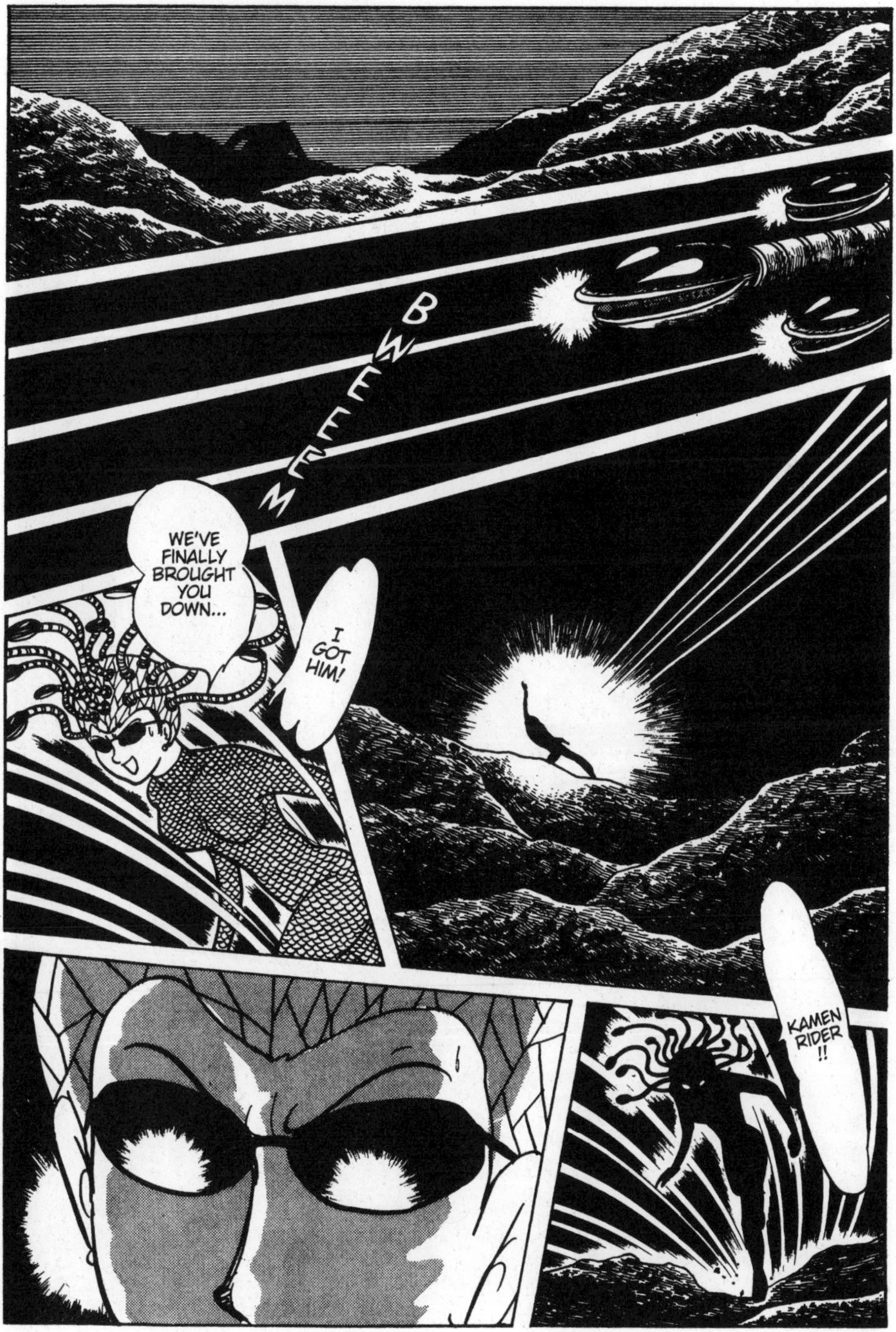
BWEEEM
WE'VE FINALLY BROUGHT YOU DOWN...
I GOT HIM!
KAMEN RIDER!!

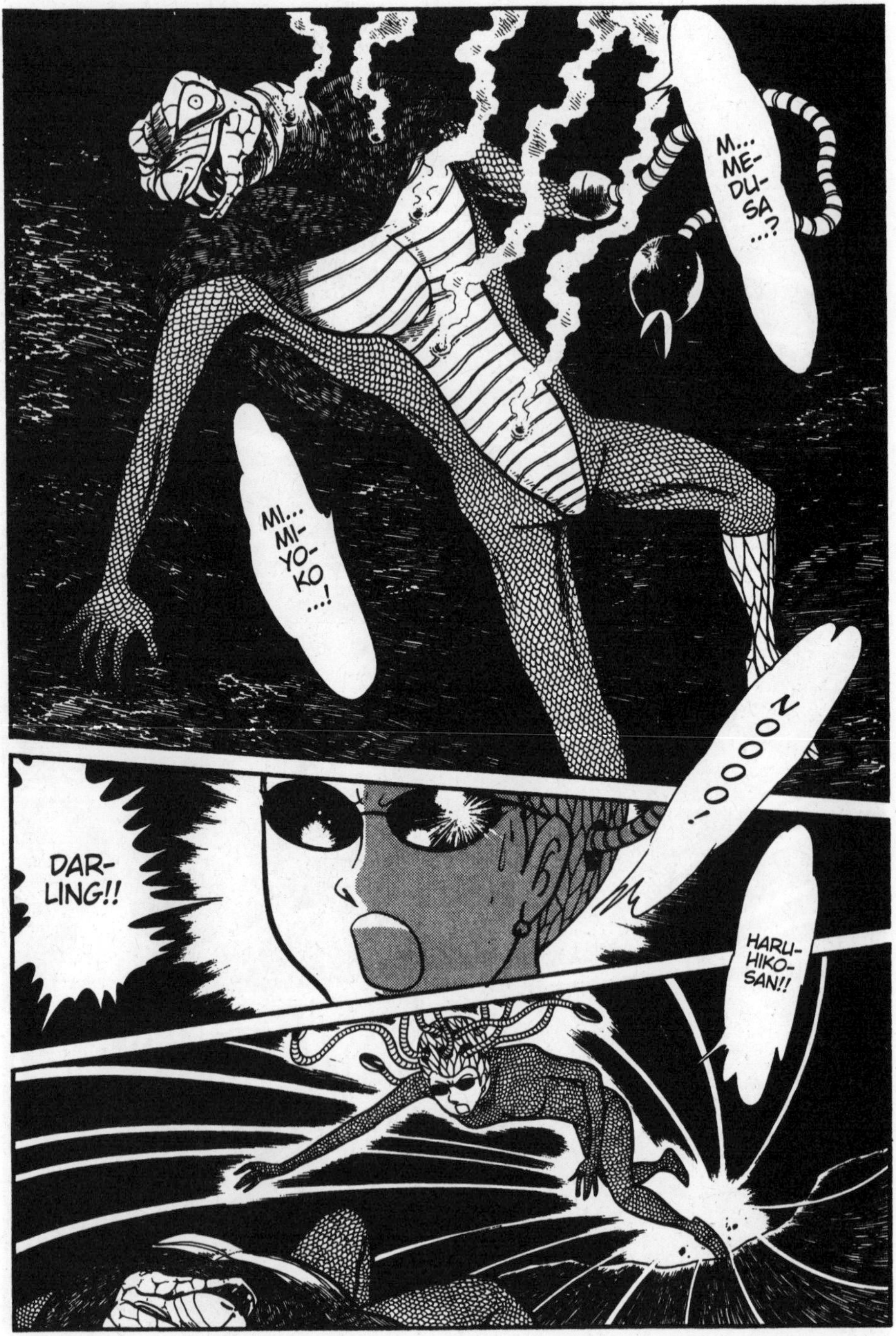

M... ME-DU-SA ...?
MI... MI-YO-KO ...!
NOOOO...!
DAR-LING!!
HARU-HIKO-SAN!!

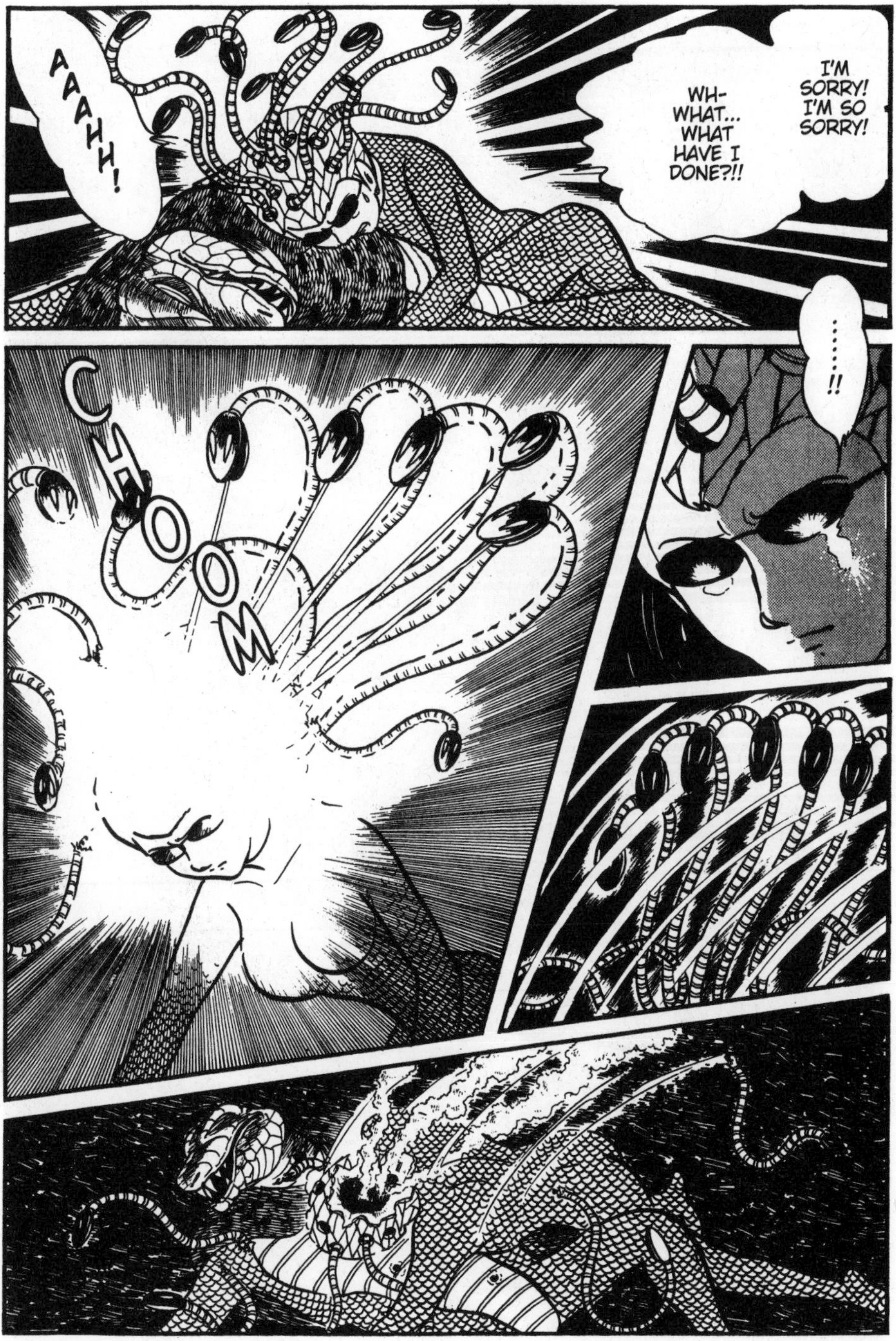
I'M SORRY! I'M SO SORRY!
WH- WHAT... WHAT HAVE I DONE?!!
AAAHH!
......!!
CHOOOM

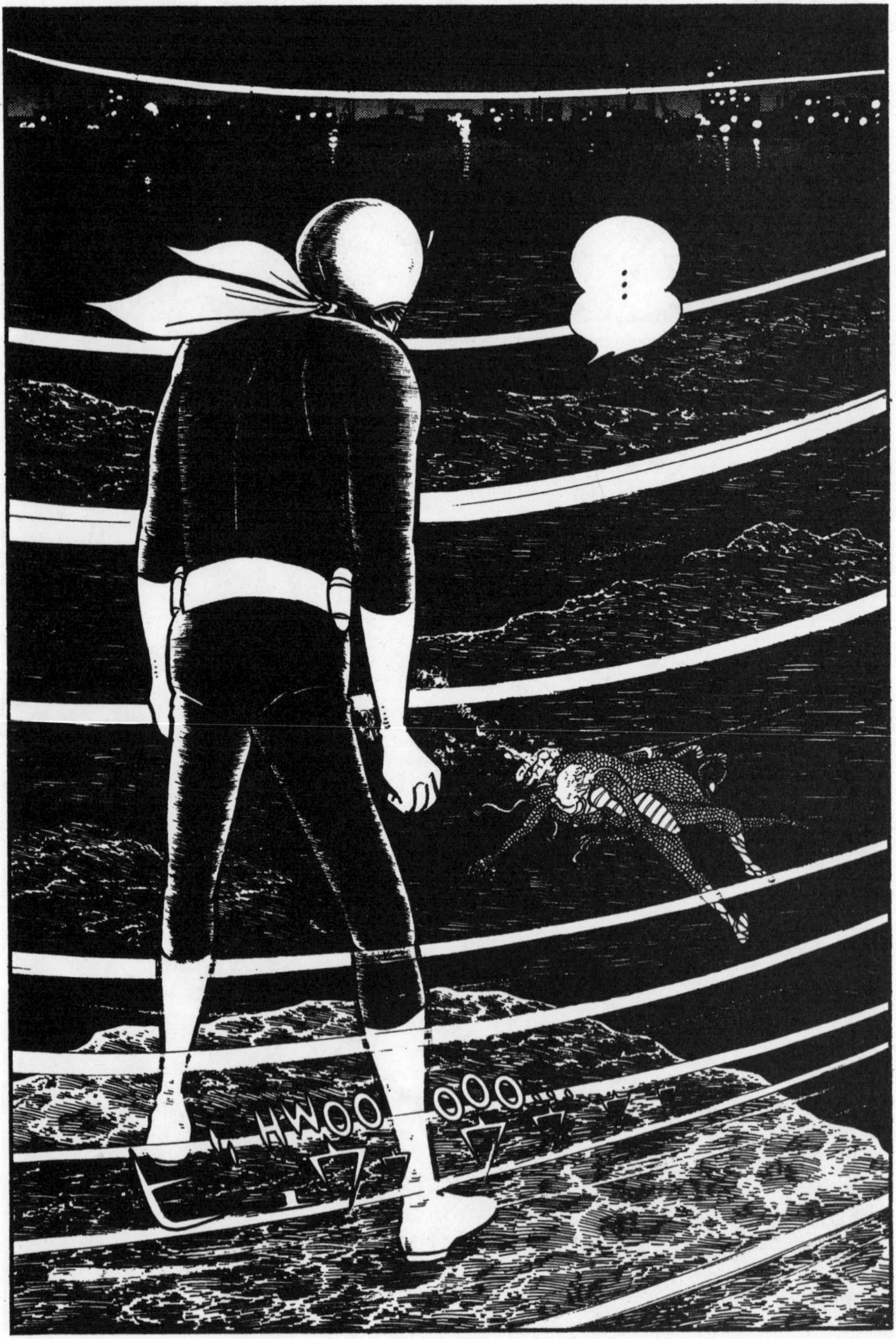
...
HWOO OOO...

KAMEN RIDER

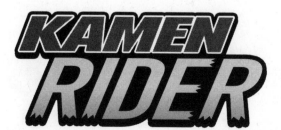

KAMEN RIDER

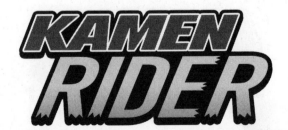

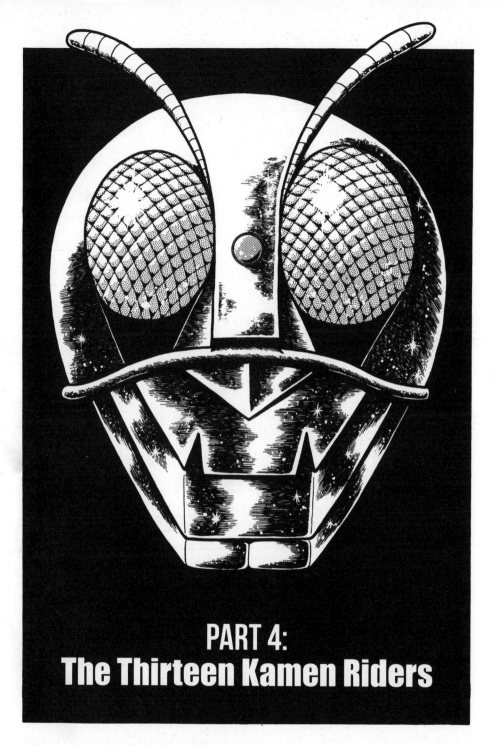

PART 4:
The Thirteen Kamen Riders

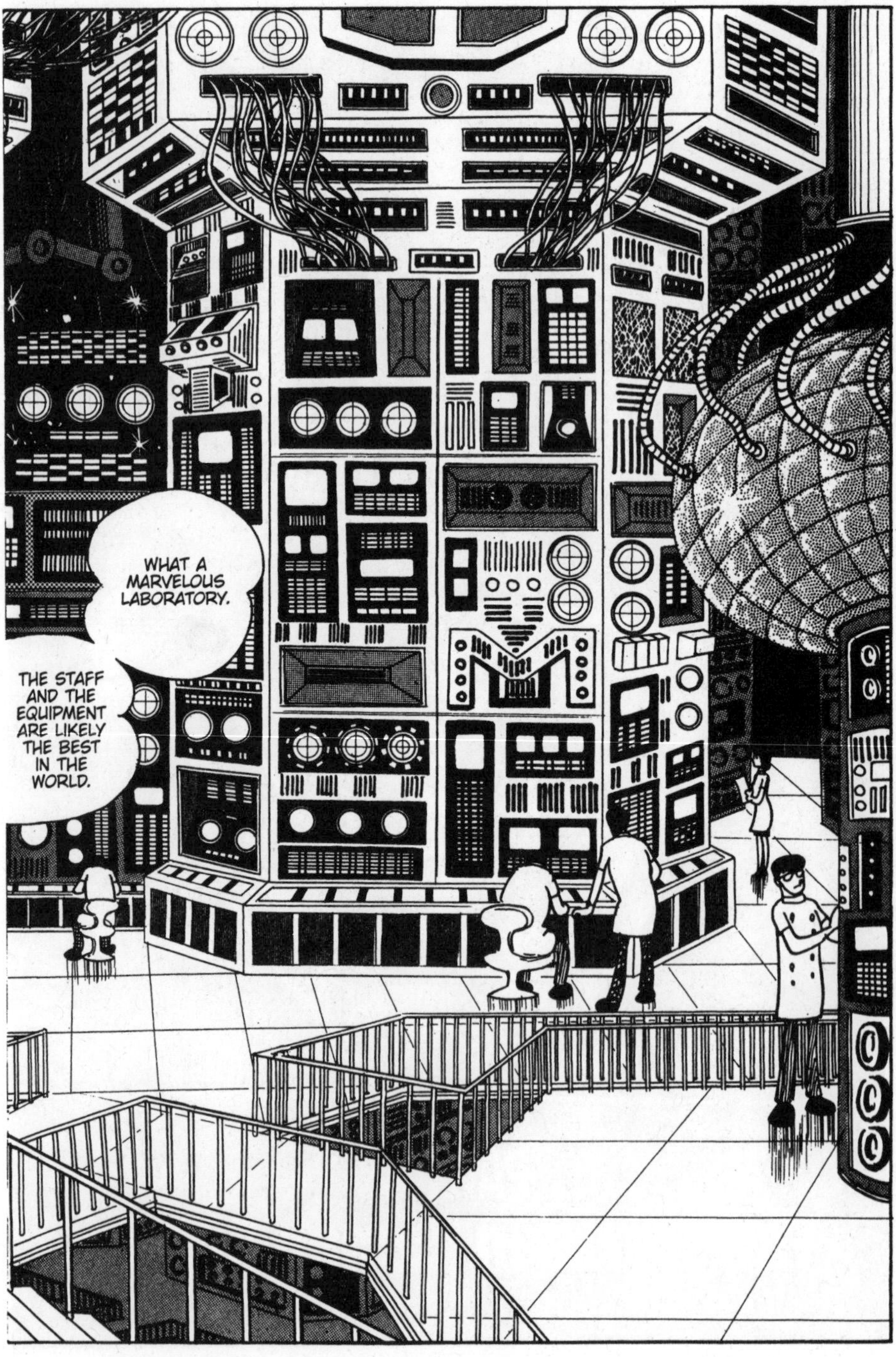
WHAT A MARVELOUS LABORATORY.
THE STAFF AND THE EQUIPMENT ARE LIKELY THE BEST IN THE WORLD.

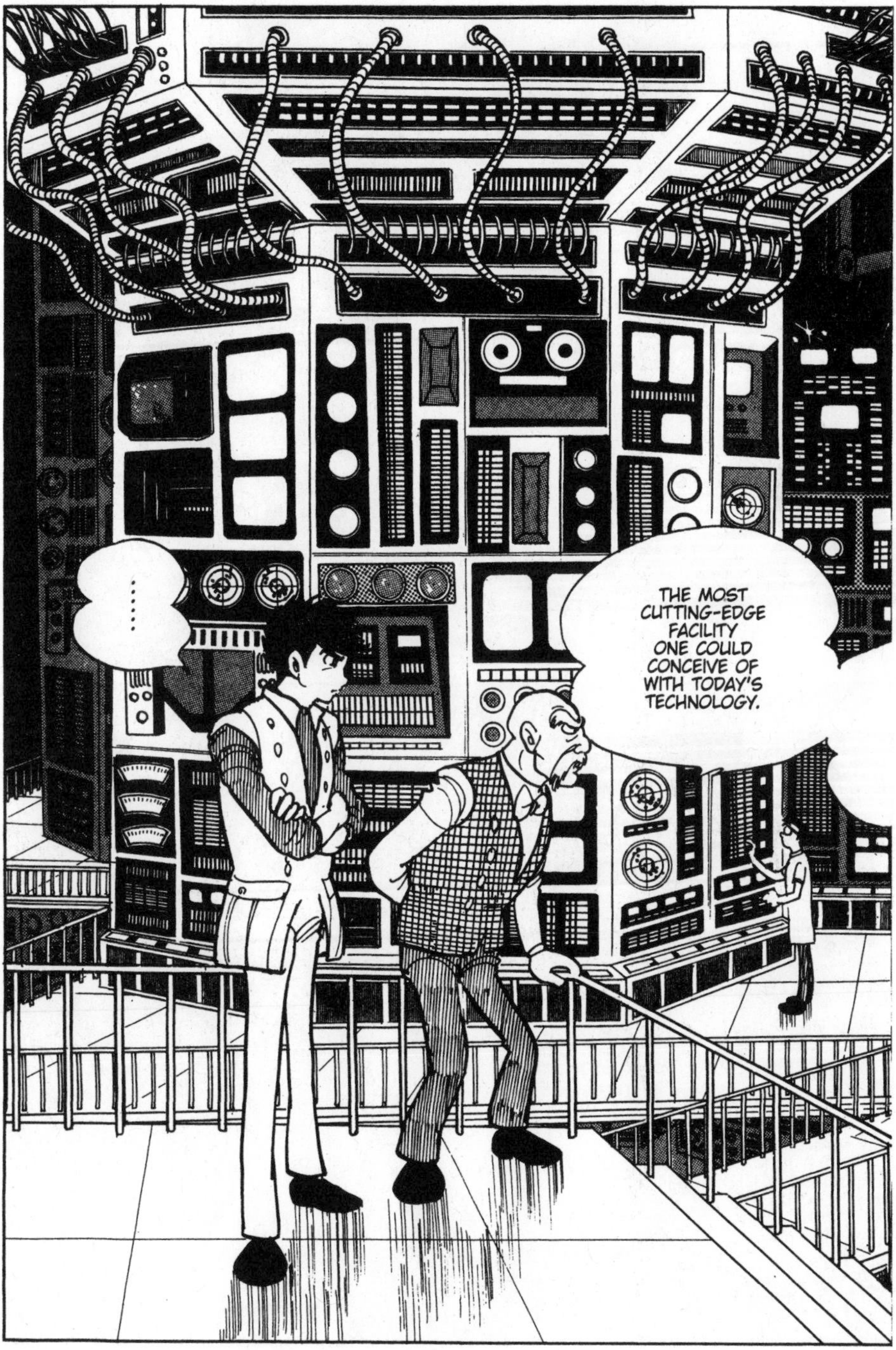
THE MOST CUTTING-EDGE FACILITY ONE COULD CONCEIVE OF WITH TODAY'S TECHNOLOGY.
......

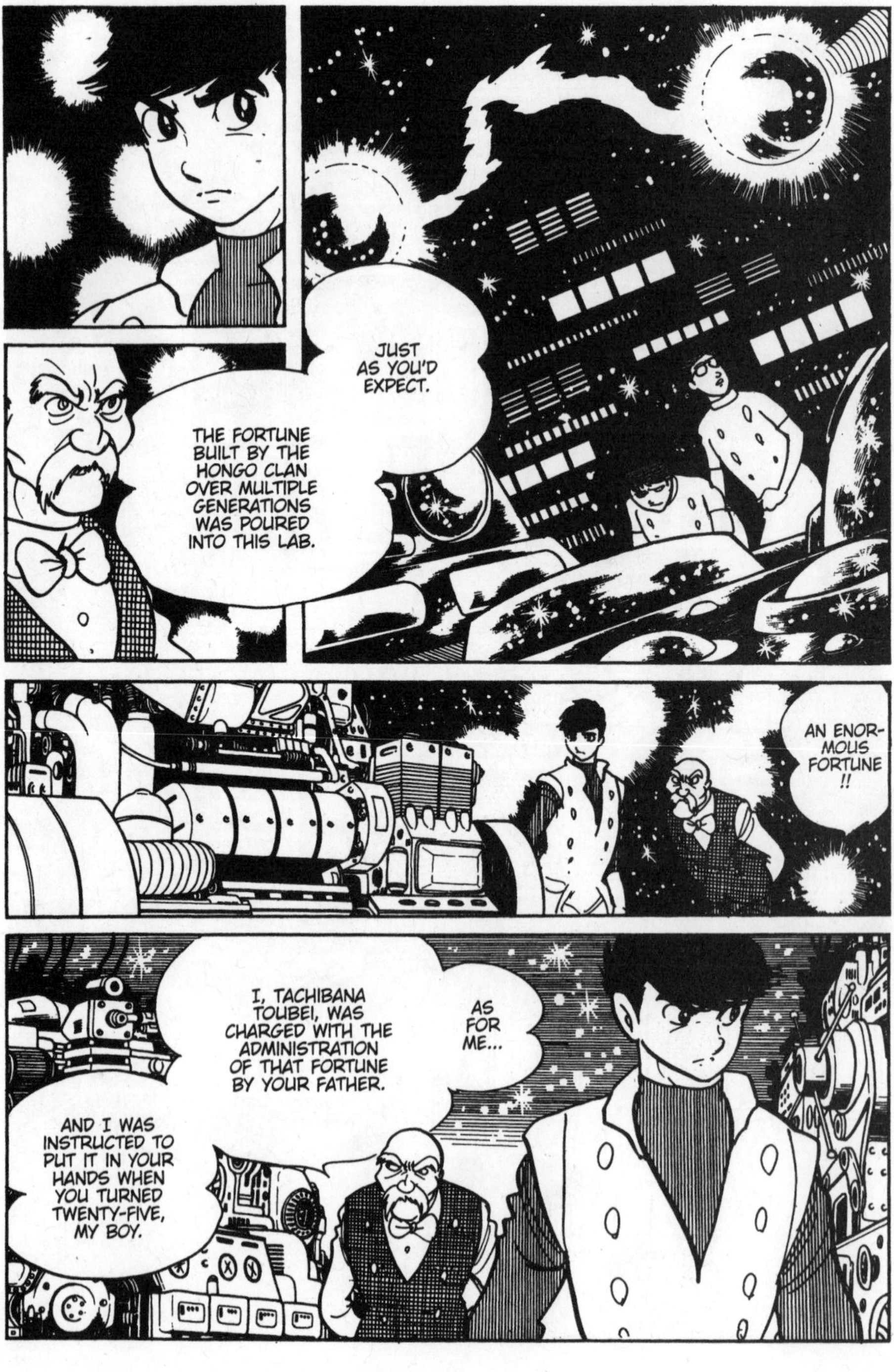
JUST AS YOU'D EXPECT.
THE FORTUNE BUILT BY THE HONGO CLAN OVER MULTIPLE GENERATIONS WAS POURED INTO THIS LAB.
AN ENOR-MOUS FORTUNE !!
AS FOR ME...
I, TACHIBANA TOUBEI, WAS CHARGED WITH THE ADMINISTRATION OF THAT FORTUNE BY YOUR FATHER.
AND I WAS INSTRUCTED TO PUT IT IN YOUR HANDS WHEN YOU TURNED TWENTY-FIVE, MY BOY.

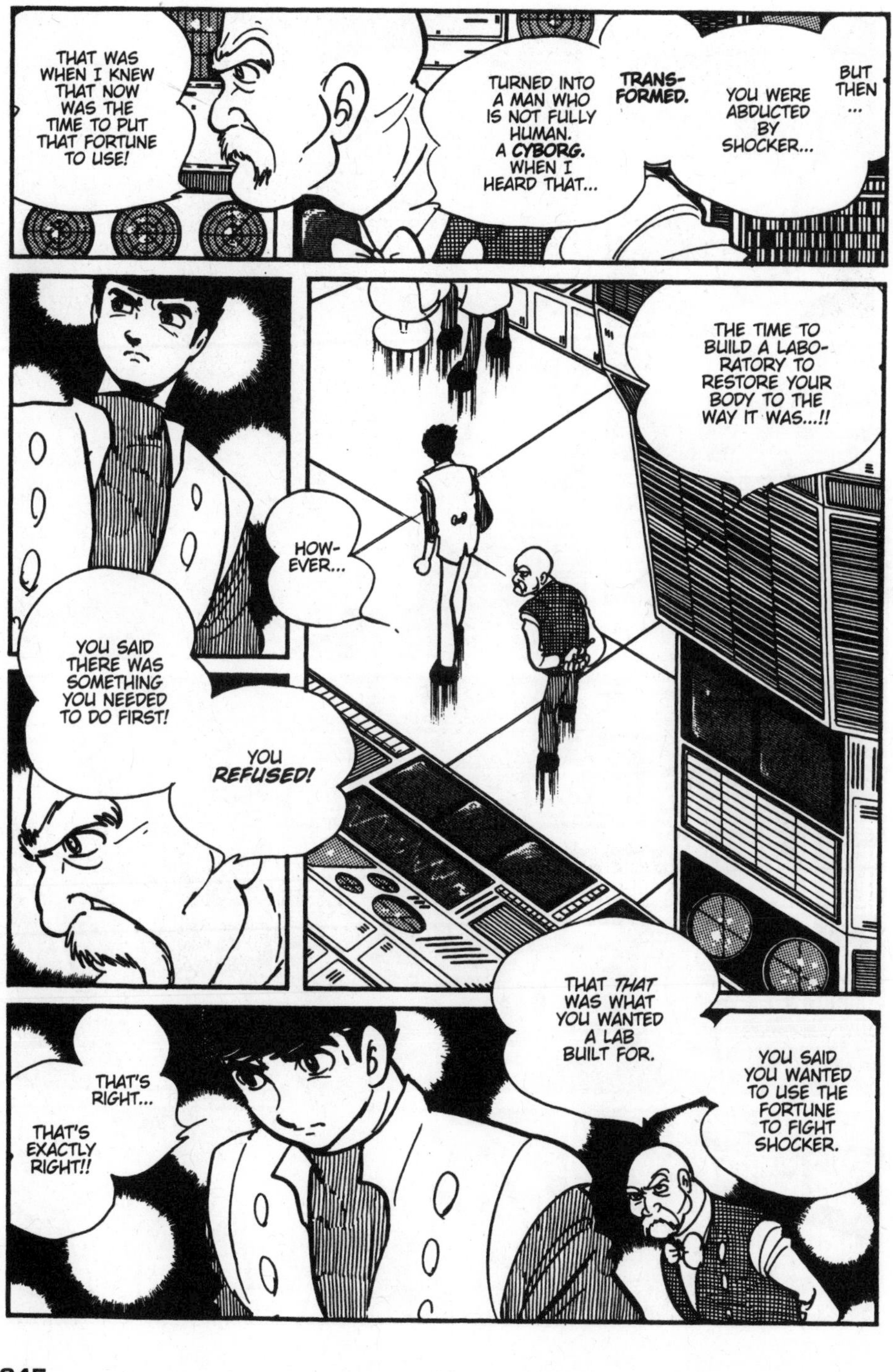
BUT THEN ...
YOU WERE ABDUCTED BY SHOCKER...
TRANS-FORMED.
TURNED INTO A MAN WHO IS NOT FULLY HUMAN. A CYBORG. WHEN I HEARD THAT...
THAT WAS WHEN I KNEW THAT NOW WAS THE TIME TO PUT THAT FORTUNE TO USE!
THE TIME TO BUILD A LABO-RATORY TO RESTORE YOUR BODY TO THE WAY IT WAS...!!
HOW-EVER...
YOU SAID THERE WAS SOMETHING YOU NEEDED TO DO FIRST!
YOU REFUSED!
YOU SAID YOU WANTED TO USE THE FORTUNE TO FIGHT SHOCKER.
THAT THAT WAS WHAT YOU WANTED A LAB BUILT FOR.
THAT'S RIGHT...
THAT'S EXACTLY RIGHT!!

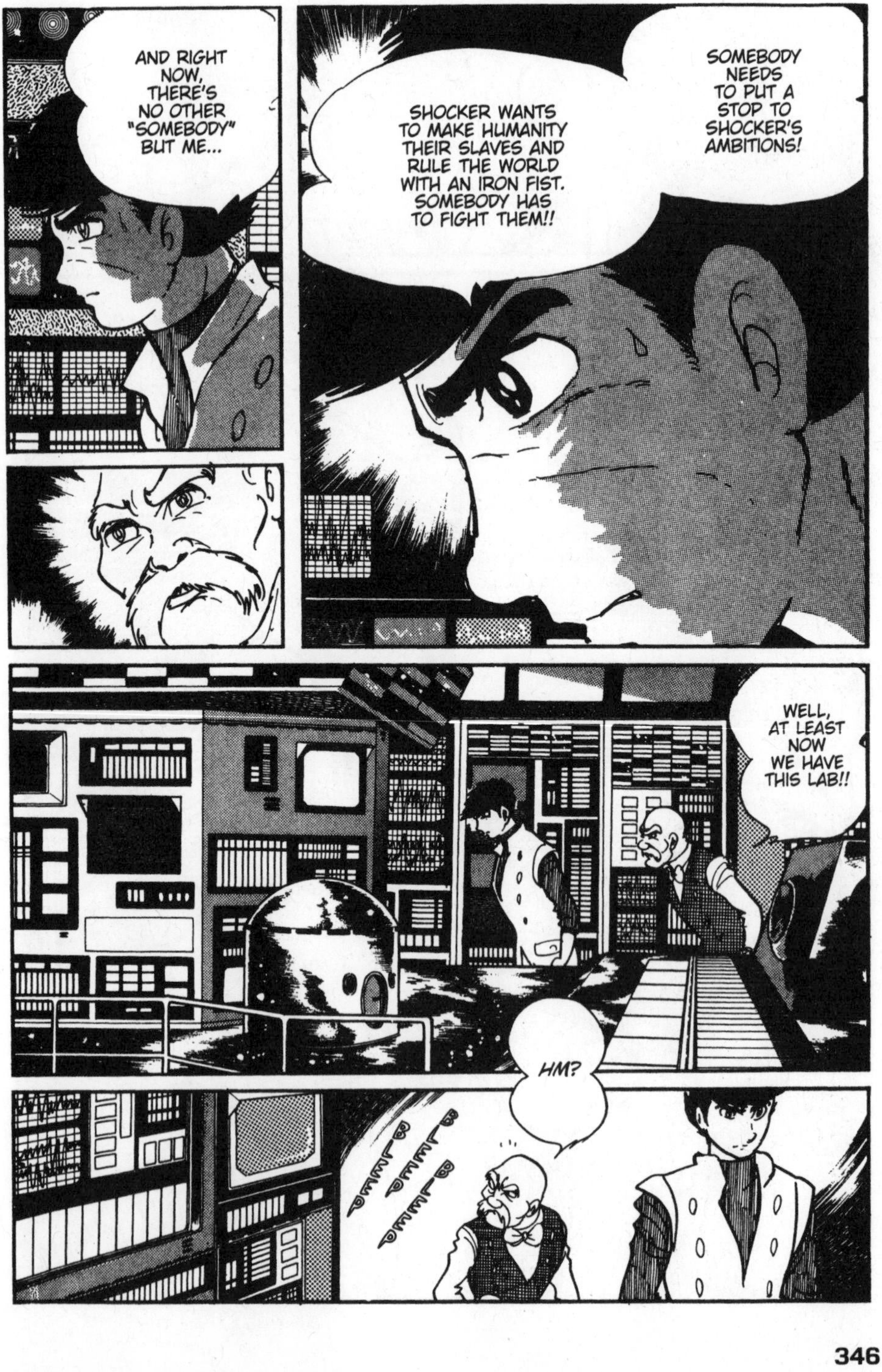
SOMEBODY NEEDS TO PUT A STOP TO SHOCKER'S AMBITIONS!
SHOCKER WANTS TO MAKE HUMANITY THEIR SLAVES AND RULE THE WORLD WITH AN IRON FIST. SOMEBODY HAS TO FIGHT THEM!!
AND RIGHT NOW, THERE'S NO OTHER "SOMEBODY" BUT ME...
WELL, AT LEAST NOW WE HAVE THIS LAB!!
HM?

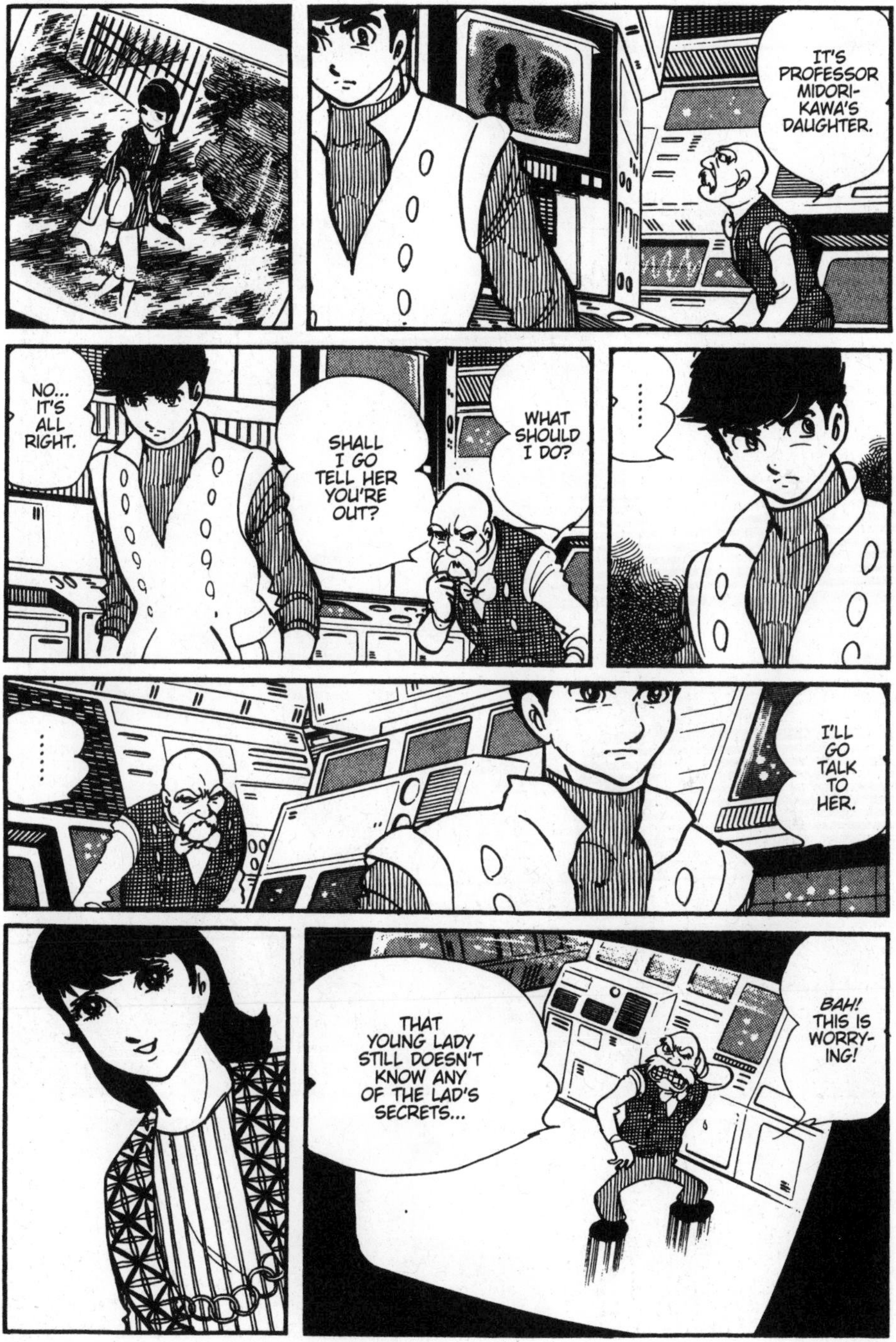
IT'S PROFESSOR MIDORI-KAWA'S DAUGHTER.
......
WHAT SHOULD I DO?
SHALL I GO TELL HER YOU'RE OUT?
NO... IT'S ALL RIGHT.
I'LL GO TALK TO HER.
......
BAH! THIS IS WORRY-ING!
THAT YOUNG LADY STILL DOESN'T KNOW ANY OF THE LAD'S SECRETS...

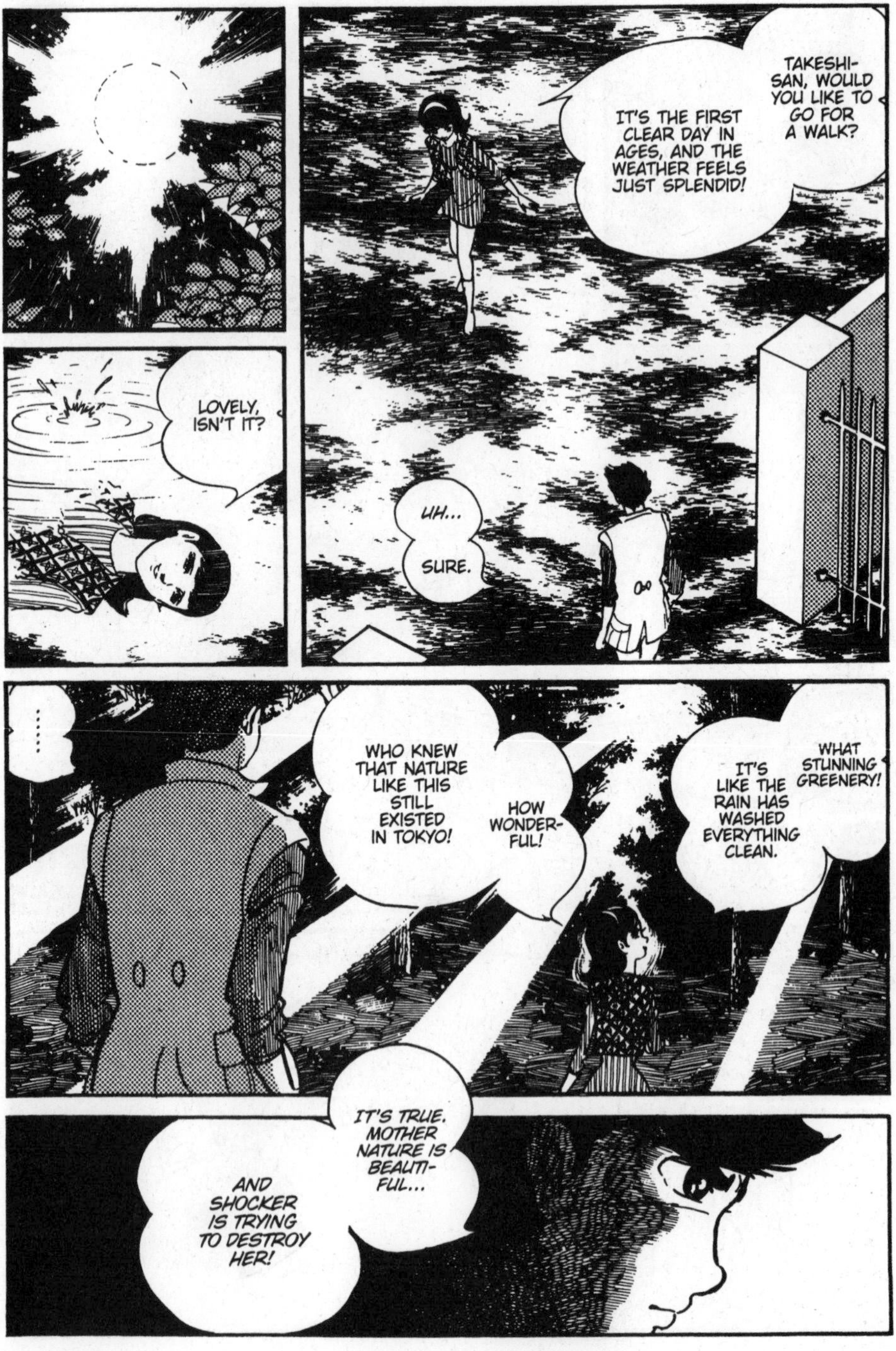
TAKESHI-SAN, WOULD YOU LIKE TO GO FOR A WALK?
IT'S THE FIRST CLEAR DAY IN AGES, AND THE WEATHER FEELS JUST SPLENDID!
UH...
SURE.
LOVELY, ISN'T IT?
WHAT STUNNING GREENERY!
IT'S LIKE THE RAIN HAS WASHED EVERYTHING CLEAN.
HOW WONDER-FUL!
WHO KNEW THAT NATURE LIKE THIS STILL EXISTED IN TOKYO!
......
IT'S TRUE. MOTHER NATURE IS BEAUTI-FUL...
AND SHOCKER IS TRYING TO DESTROY HER!

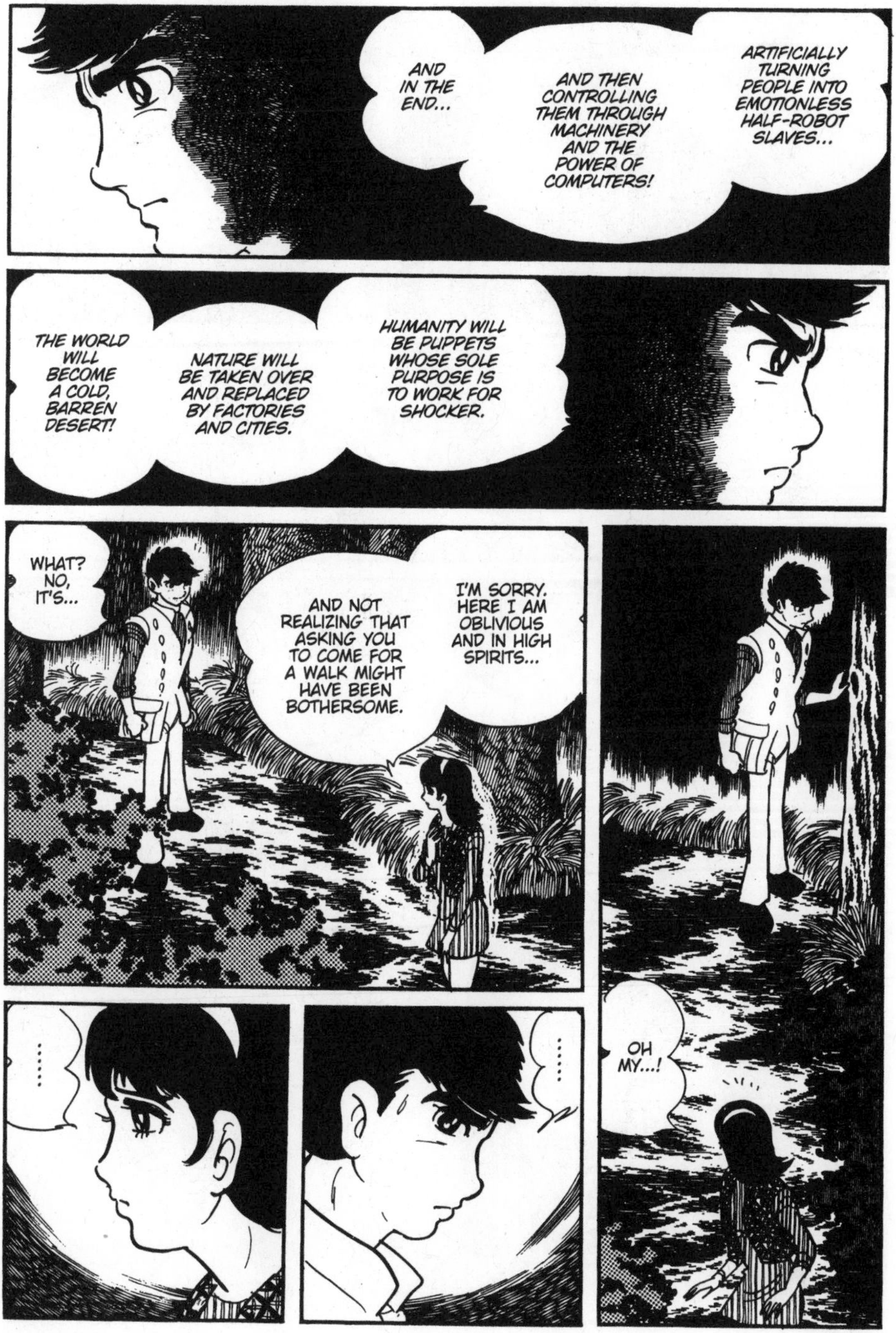
ARTIFICIALLY TURNING PEOPLE INTO EMOTIONLESS HALF-ROBOT SLAVES...
AND THEN CONTROLLING THEM THROUGH MACHINERY AND THE POWER OF COMPUTERS!
AND IN THE END...
HUMANITY WILL BE PUPPETS WHOSE SOLE PURPOSE IS TO WORK FOR SHOCKER.
NATURE WILL BE TAKEN OVER AND REPLACED BY FACTORIES AND CITIES.
THE WORLD WILL BECOME A COLD, BARREN DESERT!
OH MY...!
I'M SORRY. HERE I AM OBLIVIOUS AND IN HIGH SPIRITS...
AND NOT REALIZING THAT ASKING YOU TO COME FOR A WALK MIGHT HAVE BEEN BOTHERSOME.
WHAT? NO, IT'S...
......
......

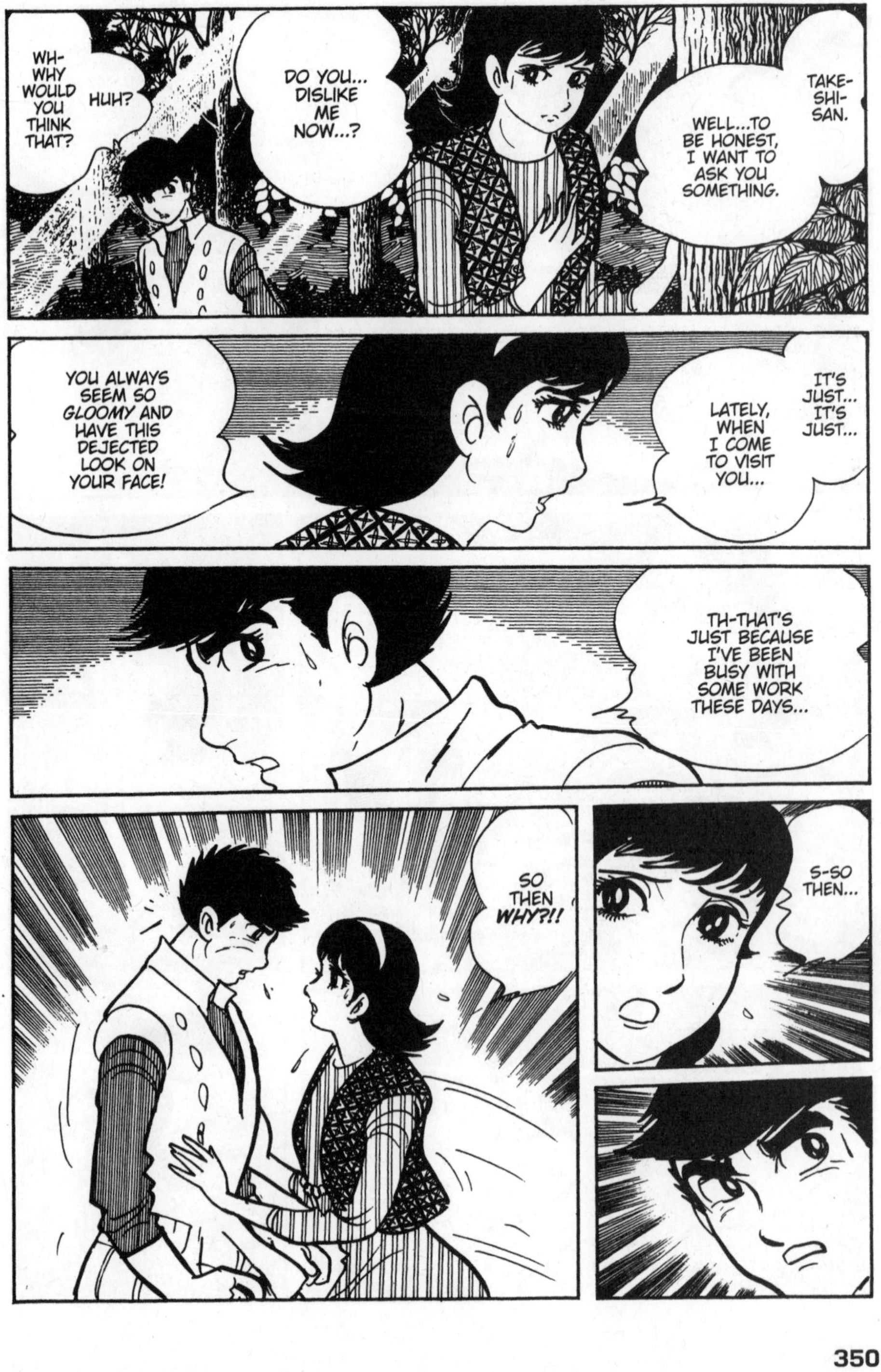

TAKE-SHI-SAN.
WELL...TO BE HONEST, I WANT TO ASK YOU SOMETHING.
DO YOU... DISLIKE ME NOW...?
HUH?
WH-WHY WOULD YOU THINK THAT?
IT'S JUST... IT'S JUST...
LATELY, WHEN I COME TO VISIT YOU...
YOU ALWAYS SEEM SO *GLOOMY* AND HAVE THIS DEJECTED LOOK ON YOUR FACE!
TH-THAT'S JUST BECAUSE I'VE BEEN BUSY WITH SOME WORK THESE DAYS...
S-SO THEN...
SO THEN ***WHY?!!***

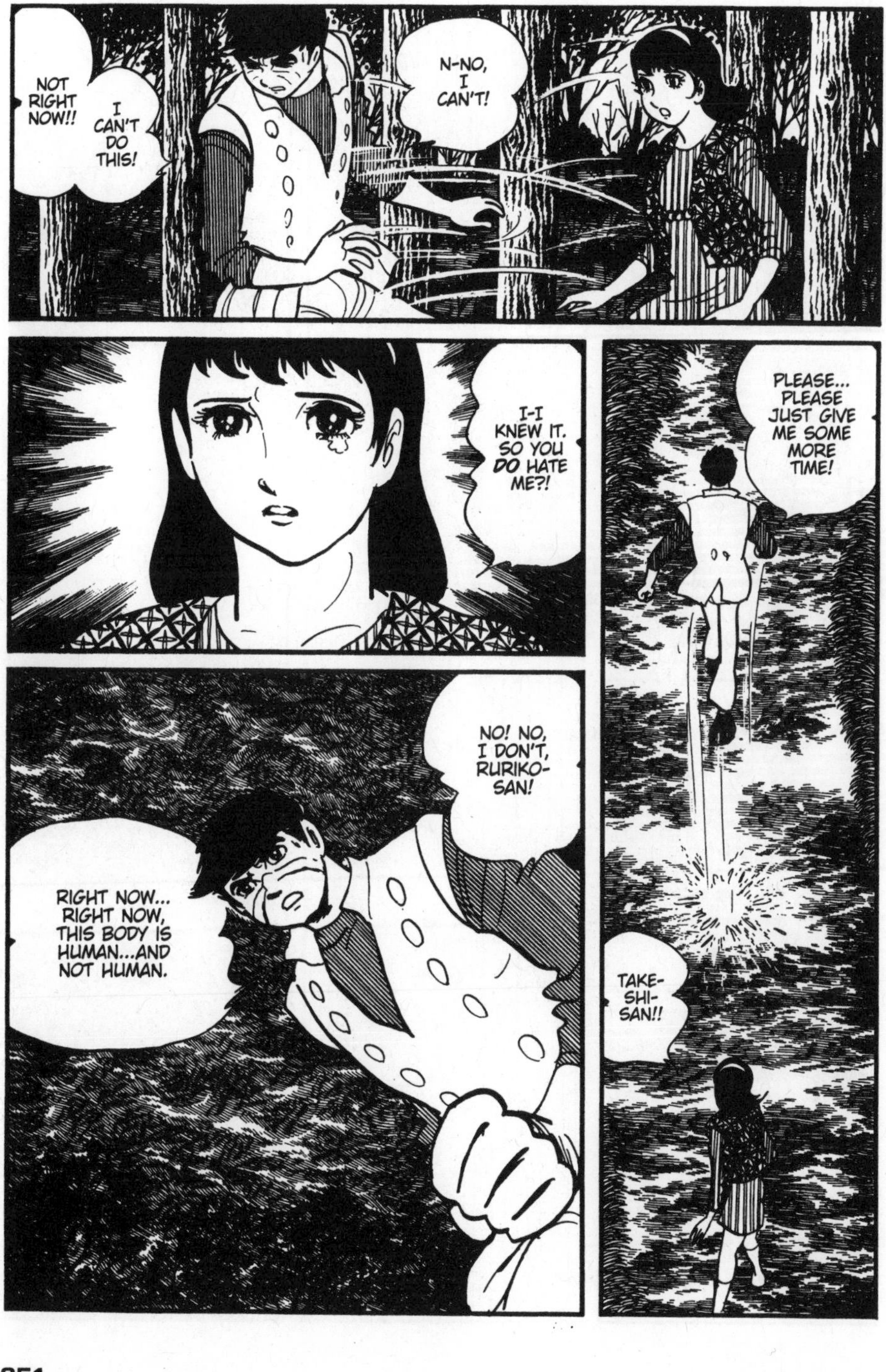
N-NO, I CAN'T!
I CAN'T DO THIS!
NOT RIGHT NOW!!
PLEASE... PLEASE JUST GIVE ME SOME MORE TIME!
TAKESHI-SAN!!
I-I KNEW IT. SO YOU **DO** HATE ME?!
NO! NO, I DON'T, RURIKO-SAN!
RIGHT NOW... RIGHT NOW, THIS BODY IS HUMAN...AND NOT HUMAN.

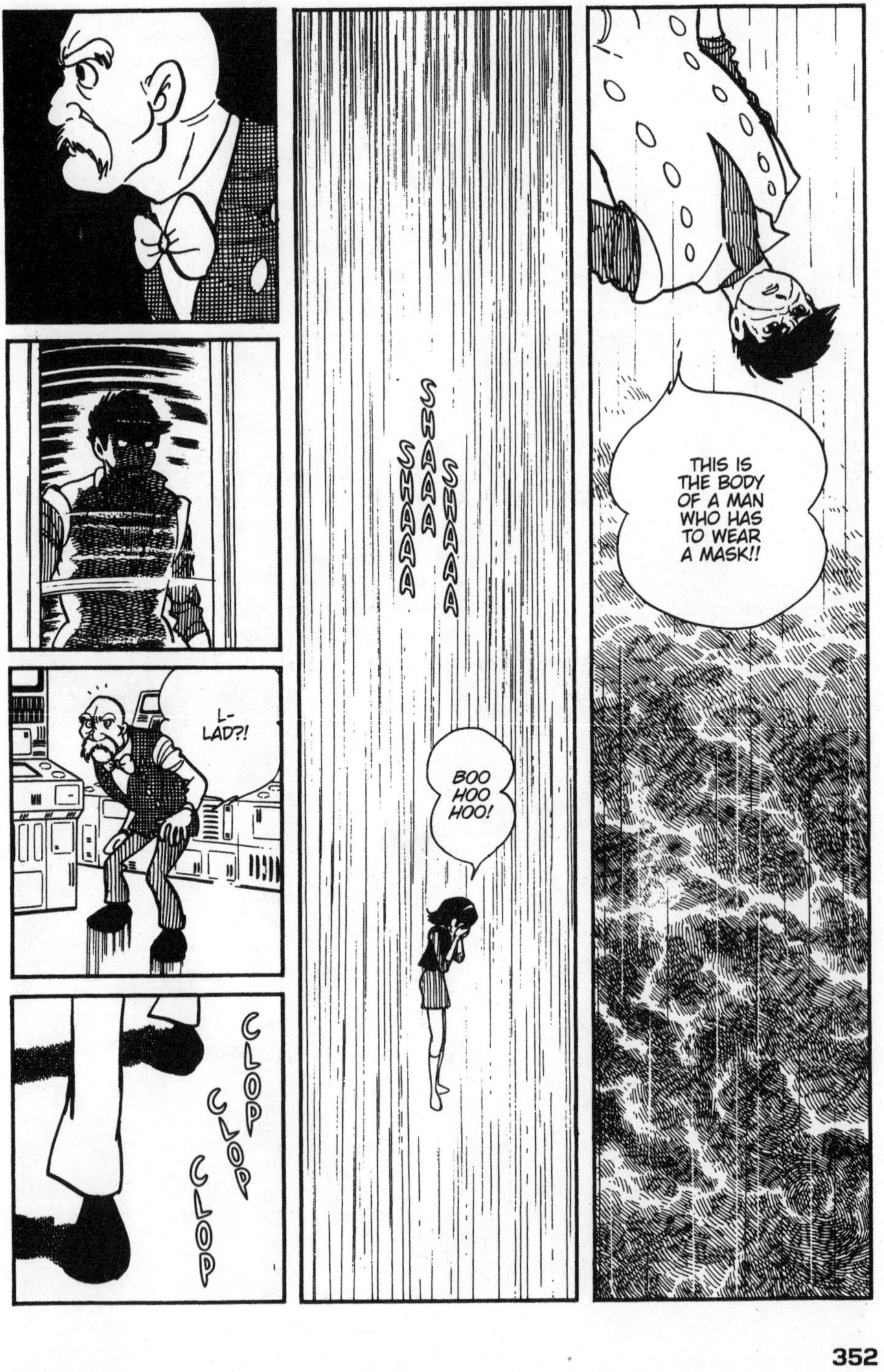
THIS IS THE BODY OF A MAN WHO HAS TO WEAR A MASK!!
SHAAAA SHAAAA SHAAAA
BOO HOO HOO!
L-LAD?!
CLOP CLOP CLOP

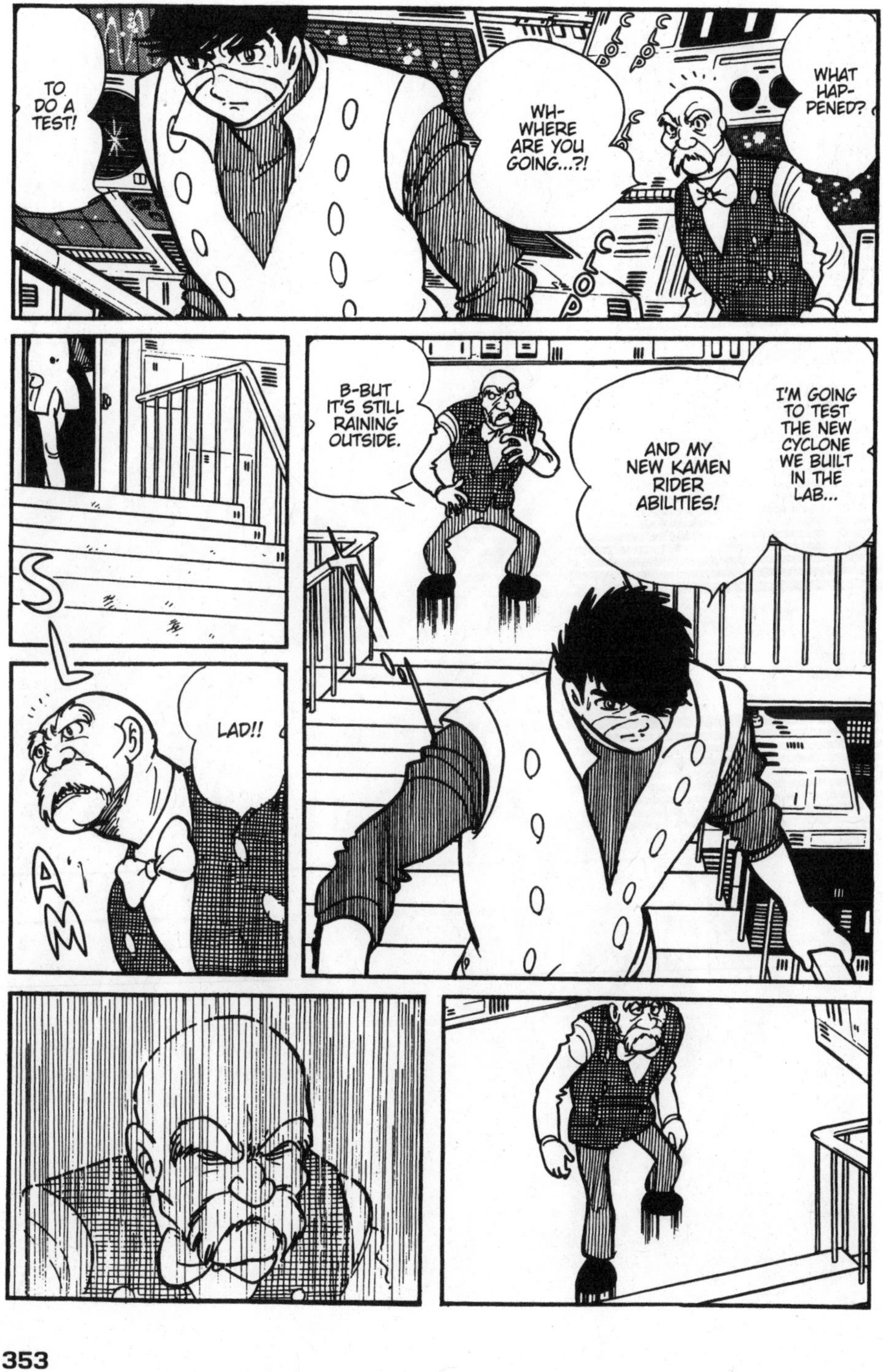
WHAT HAP-PENED?
CLOP
CLOP
CLOP
WH-WHERE ARE YOU GOING...?!
TO DO A TEST!
I'M GOING TO TEST THE NEW CYCLONE WE BUILT IN THE LAB...
AND MY NEW KAMEN RIDER ABILITIES!
B-BUT IT'S STILL RAINING OUTSIDE.
SLAM
LAD!!

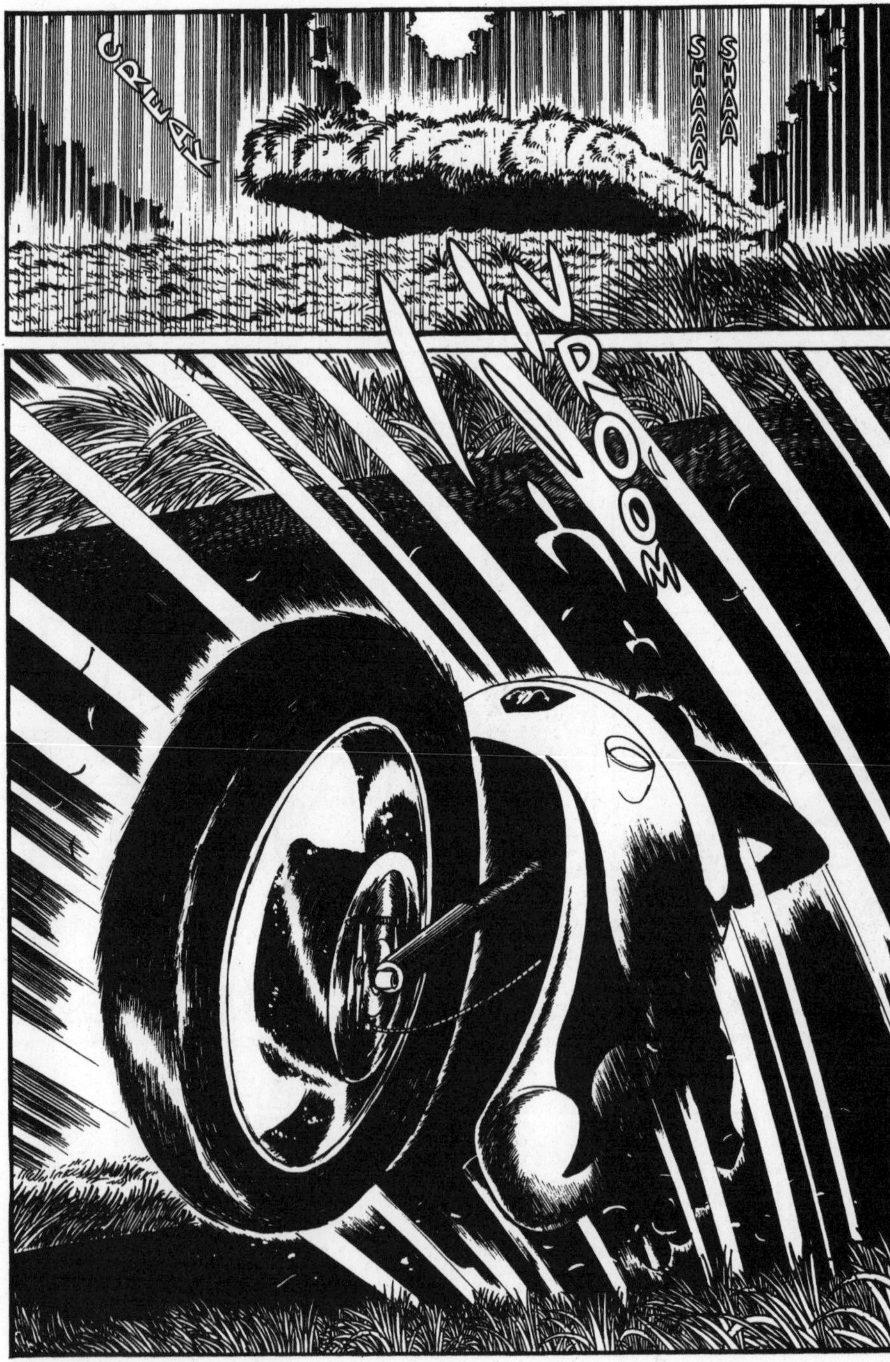
SHAAA
SHAAA
CREAK
VROOM

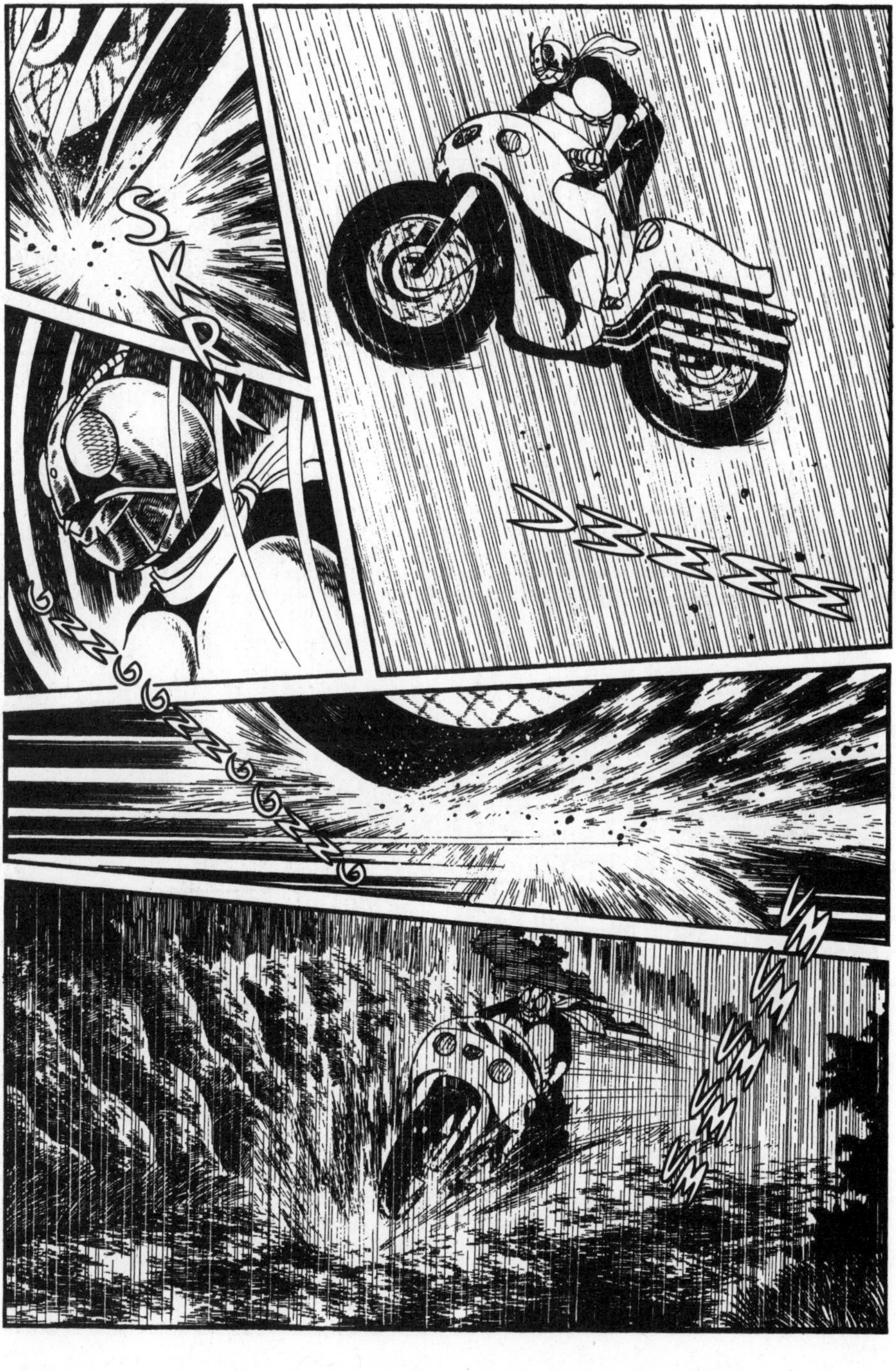
DZZZZ
SKRK
VMVMVMVMVM

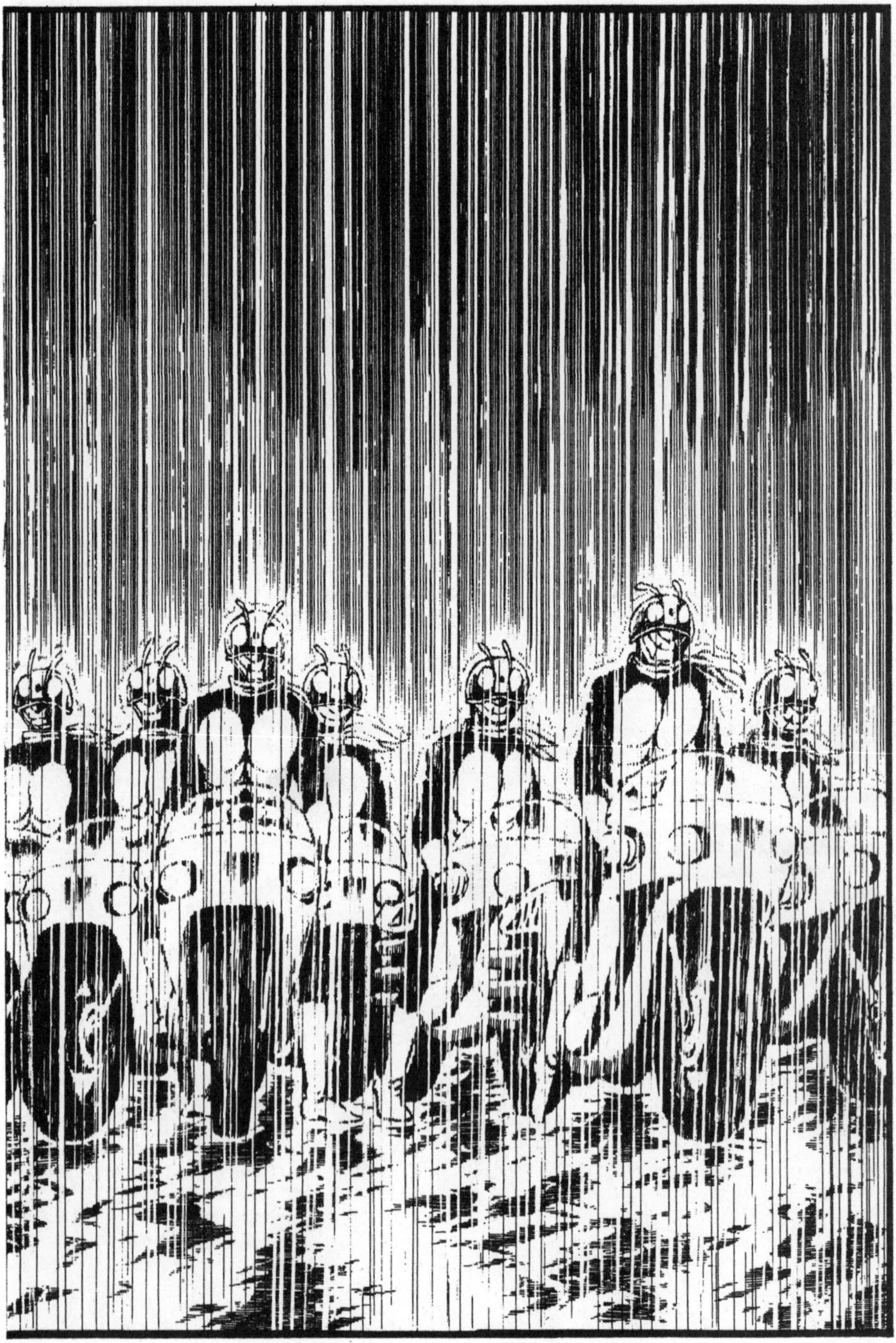

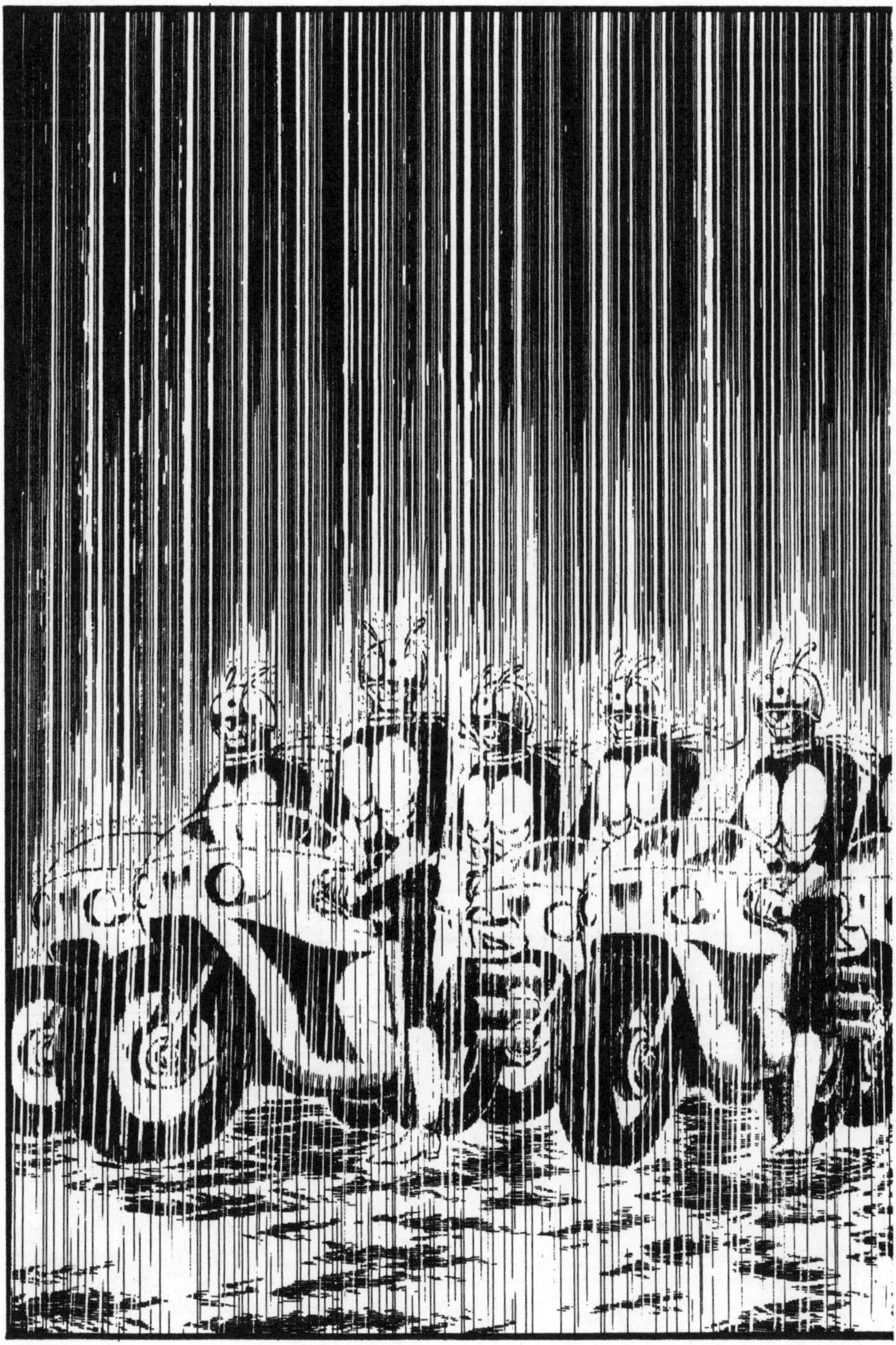

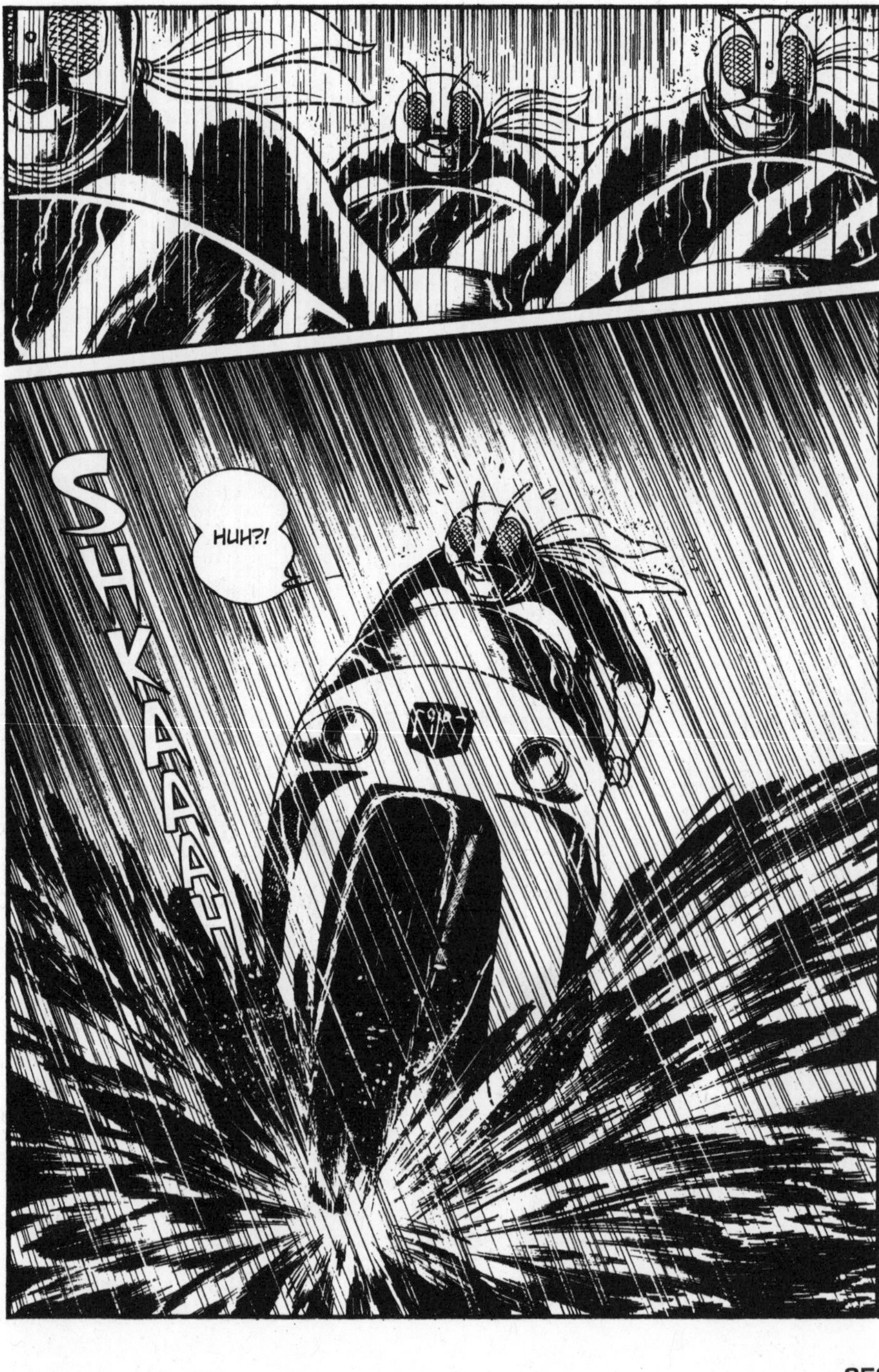
HUH?!
SHKAAAAH

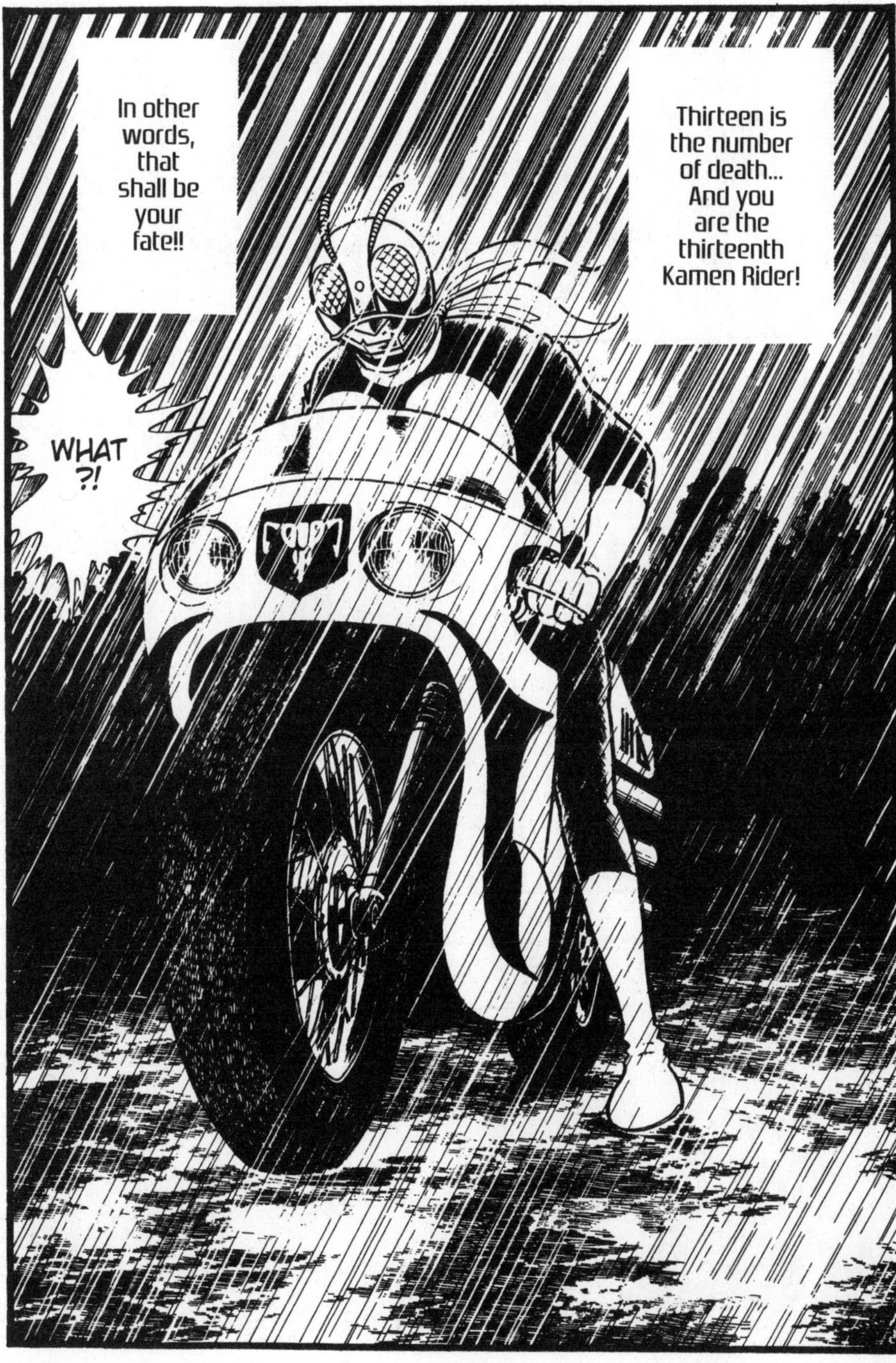
Thirteen is the number of death... And you are the thirteenth Kamen Rider!
In other words, that shall be your fate!!
WHAT ?!

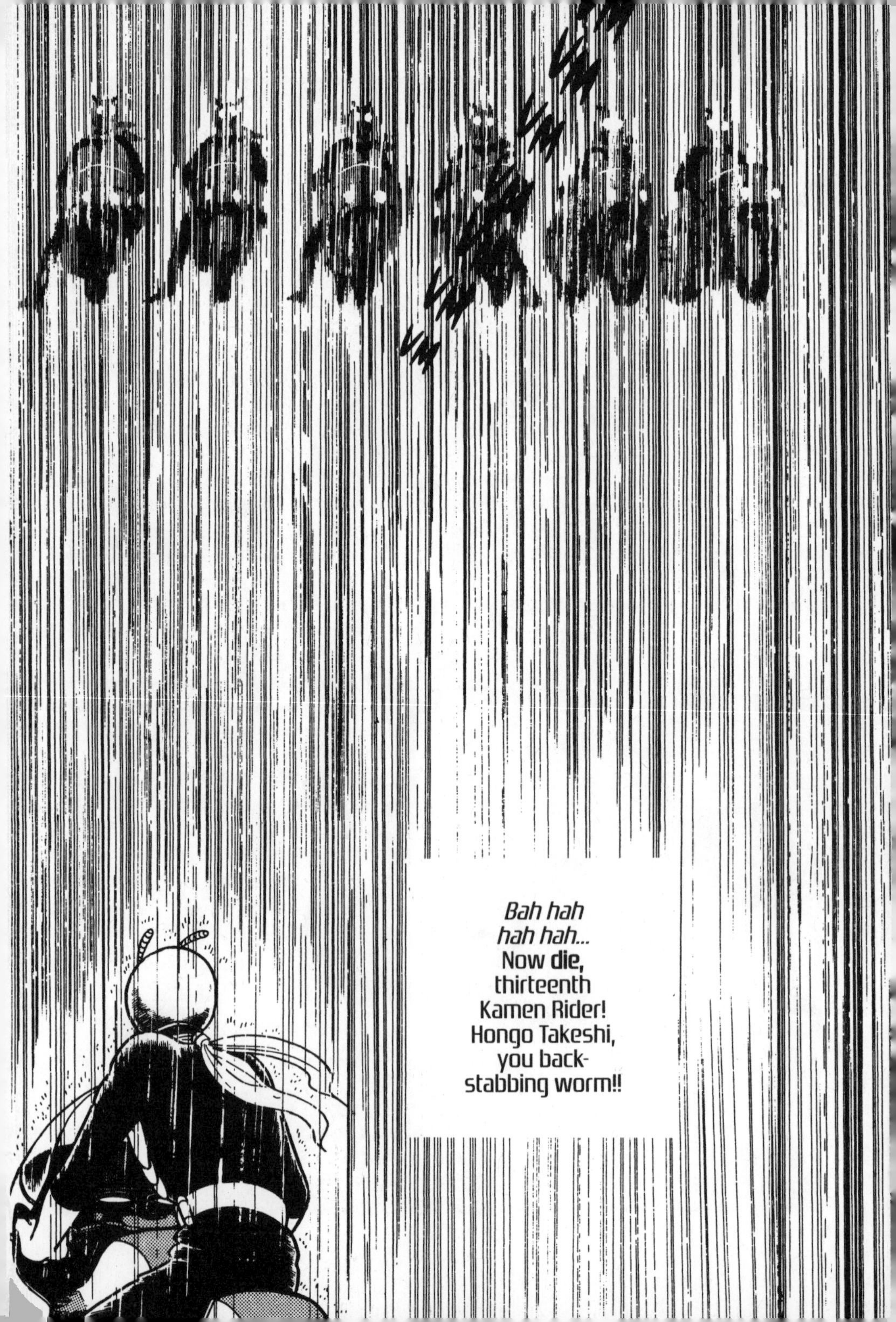
Bah hah hah hah... Now **die**, thirteenth Kamen Rider! Hongo Takeshi, you back-stabbing worm!!

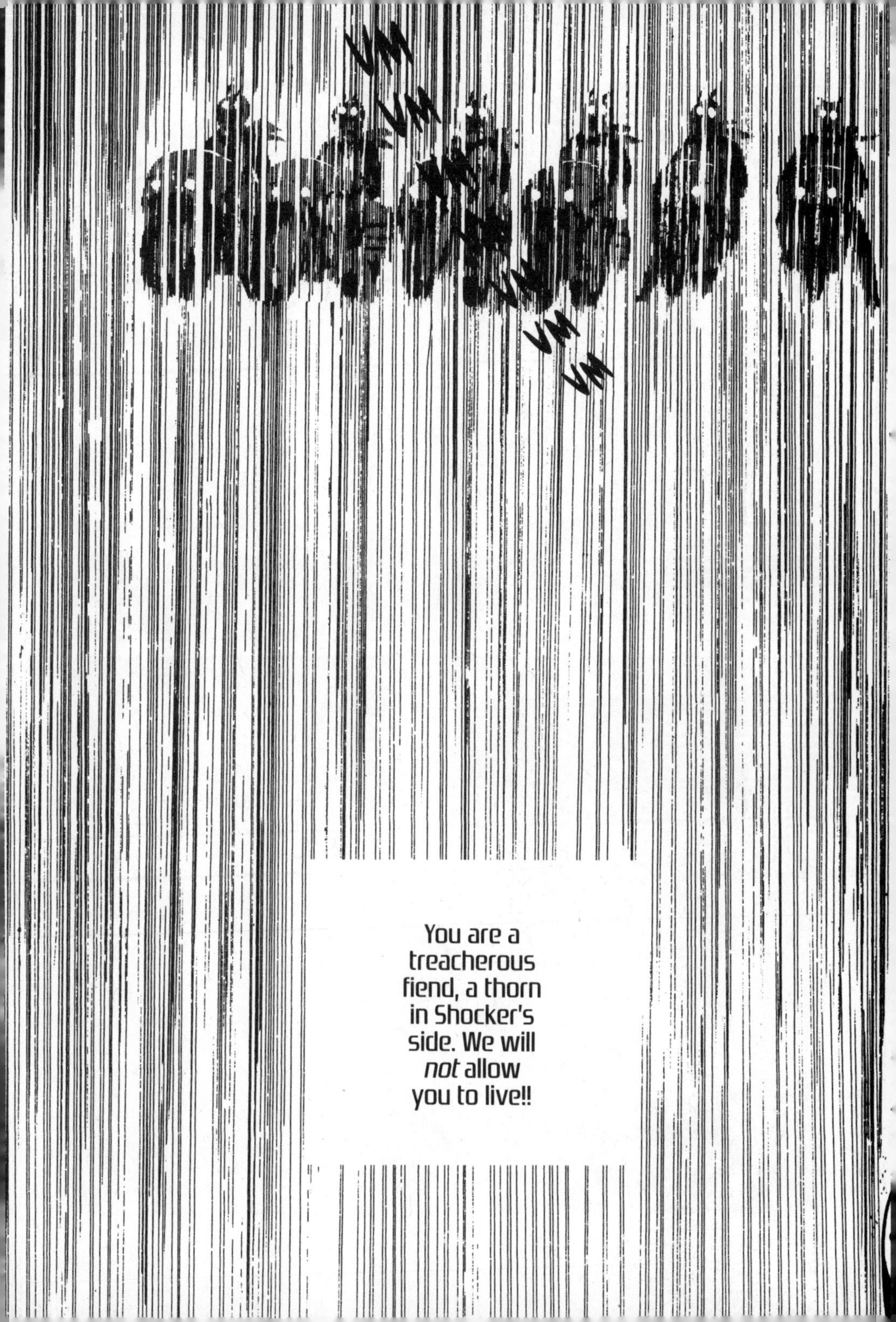
VM VM VM VM VM VM VM
You are a treacherous fiend, a thorn in Shocker's side. We will *not* allow you to live!!

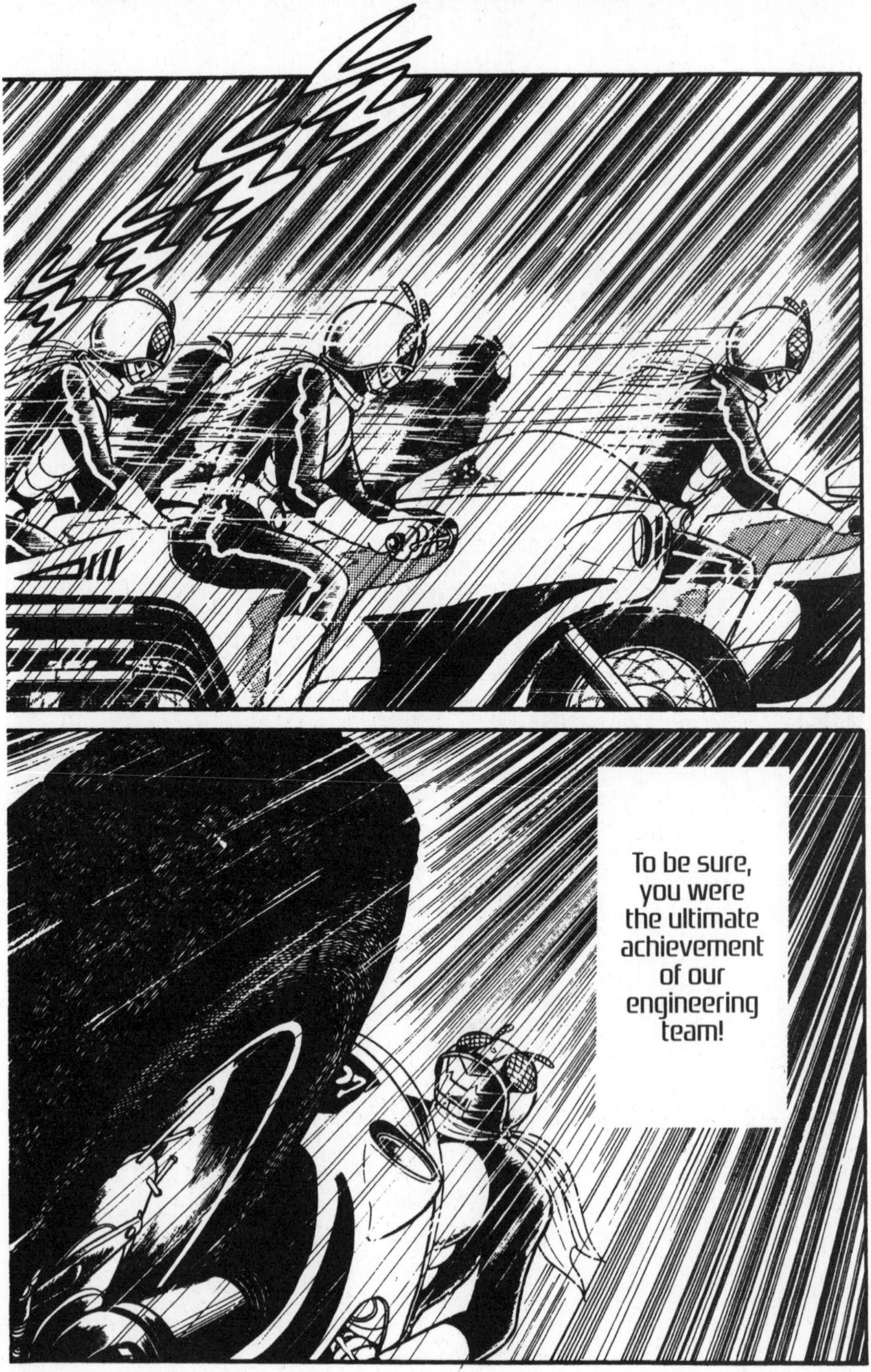
To be sure, you were the ultimate achievement of our engineering team!

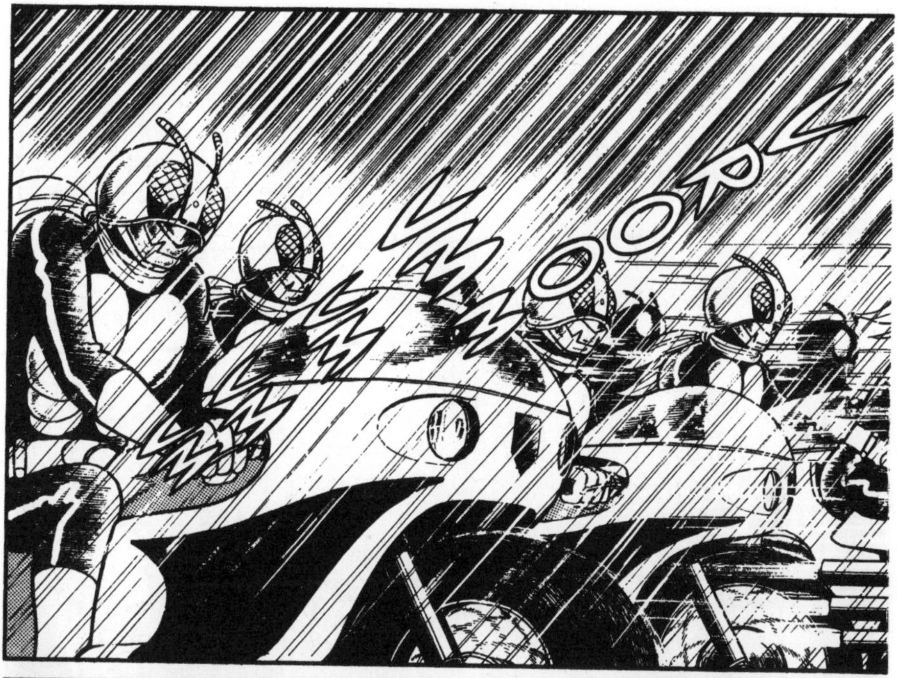
VROOOMMM

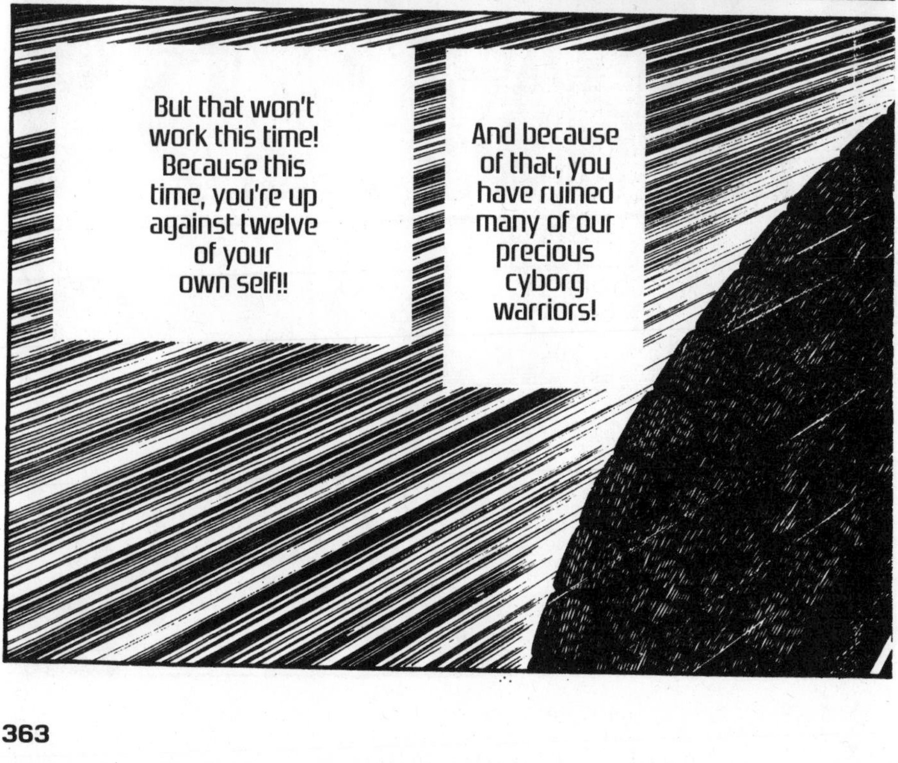
And because of that, you have ruined many of our precious cyborg warriors!
But that won't work this time! Because this time, you're up against twelve of your own self!!

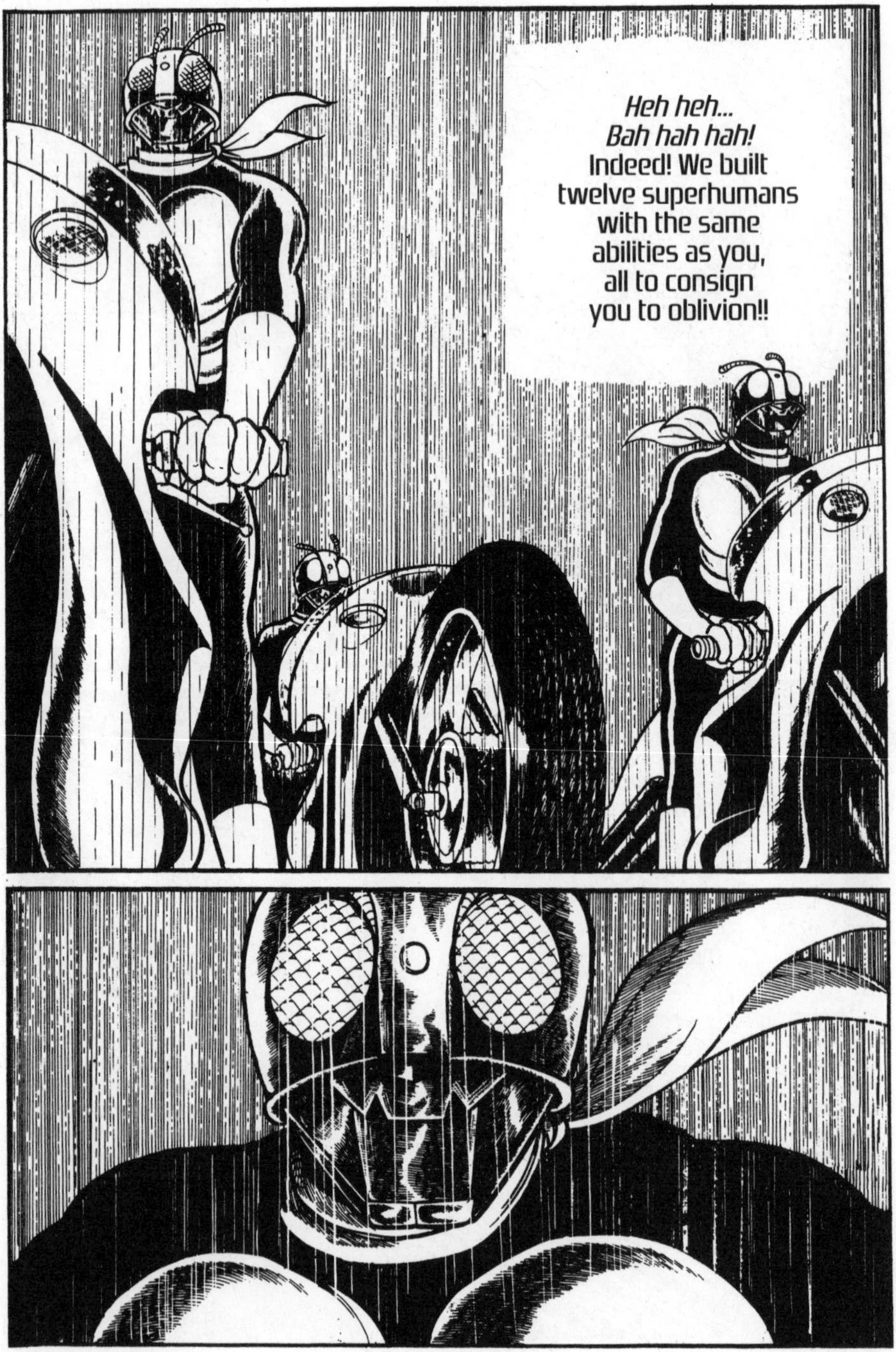
Heh heh... Bah hah hah! Indeed! We built twelve superhumans with the same abilities as you, all to consign you to oblivion!!

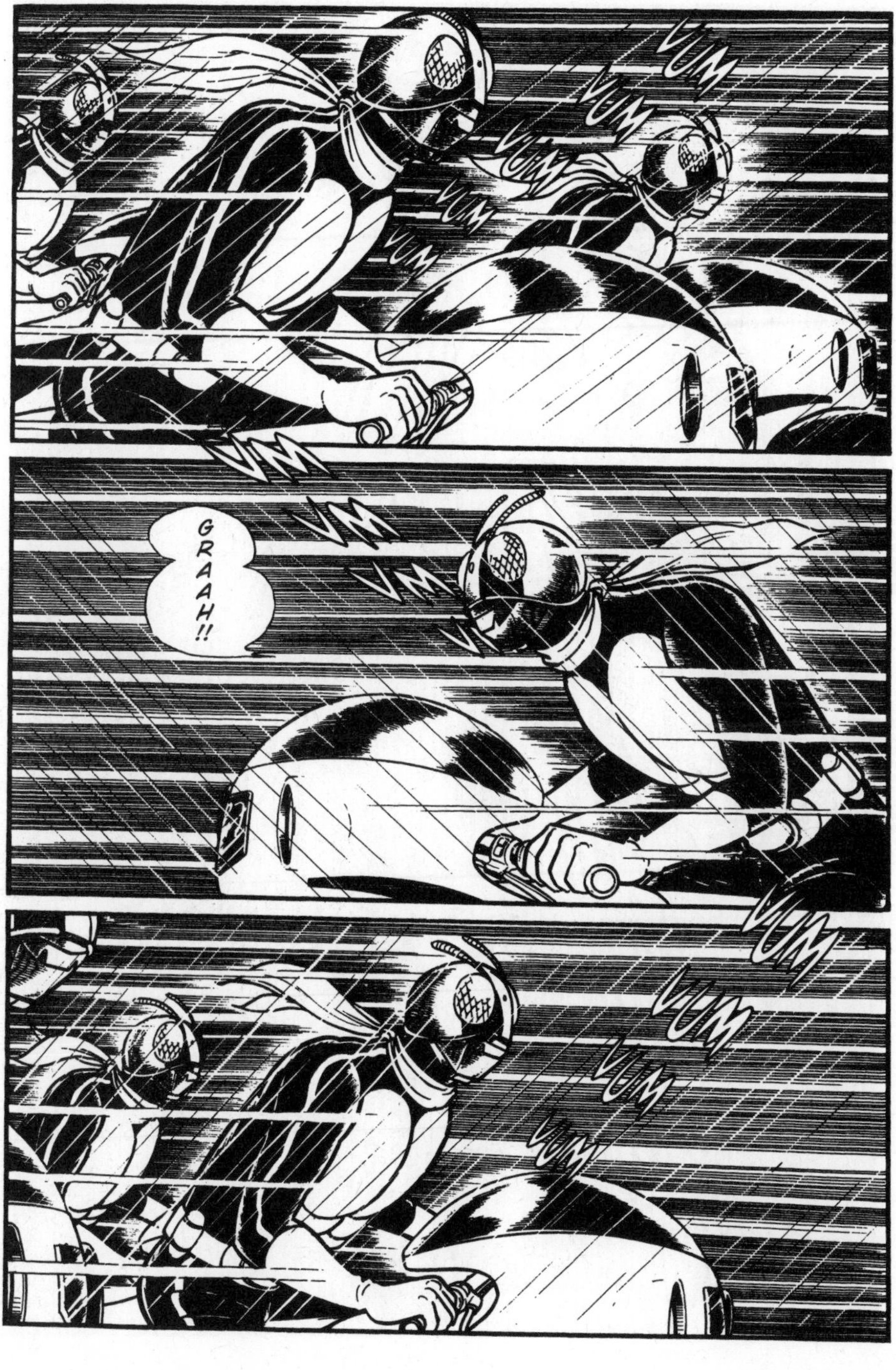
VUM
VUM
VUM
VUM
VUM
VUM
GRAAAH!!
VUM
VUM
VUM
VUM
VUM

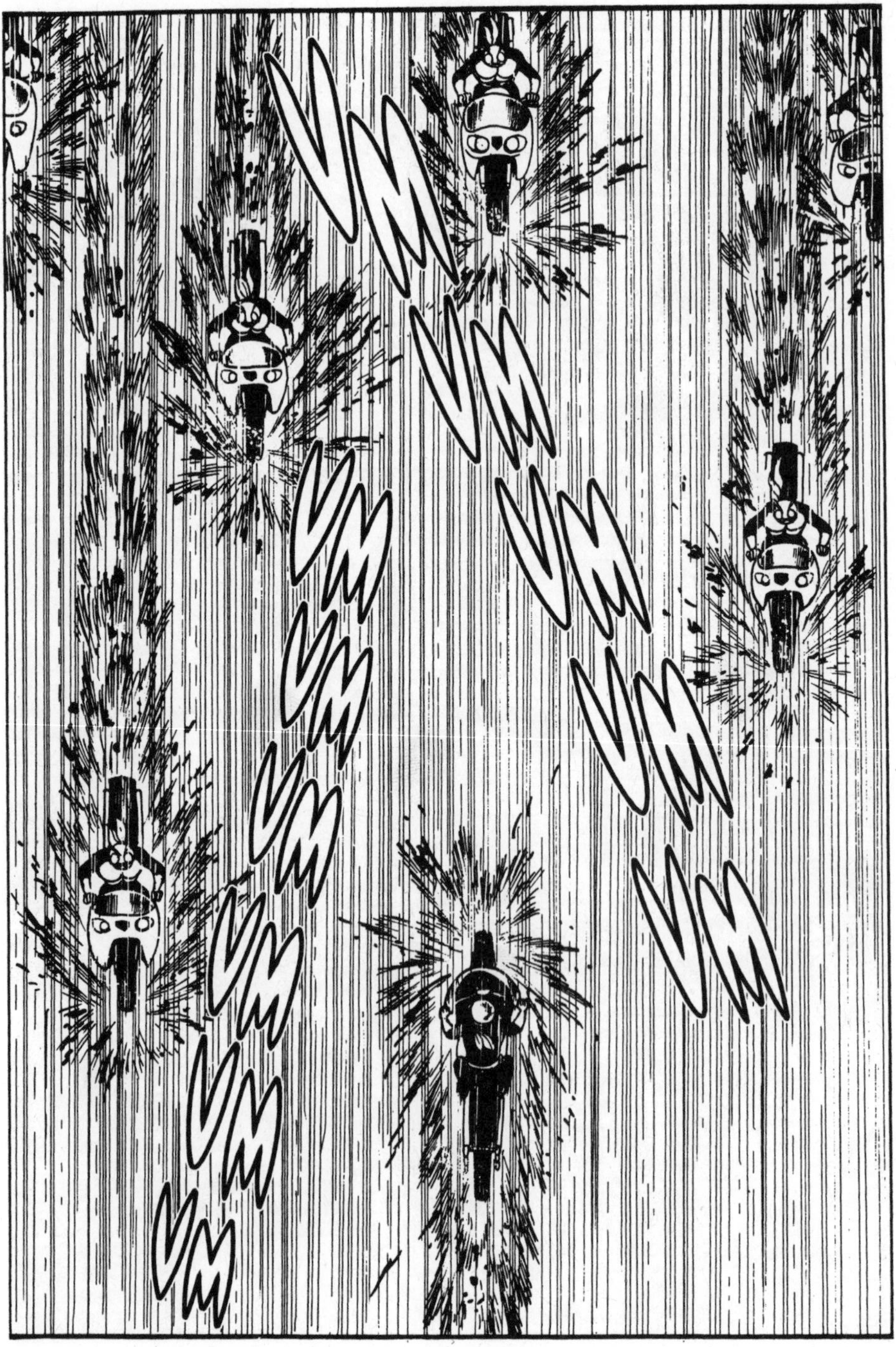

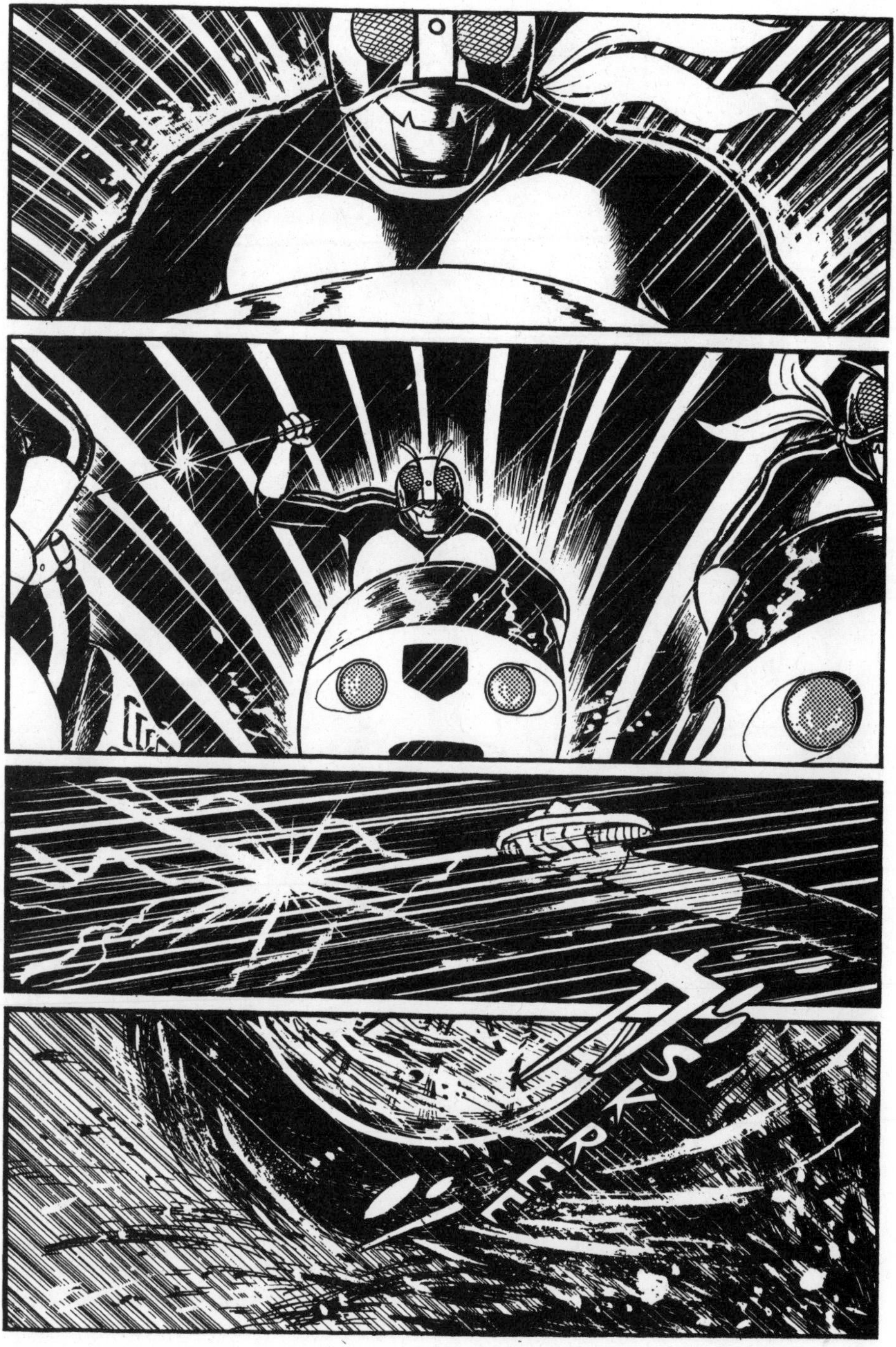
SKREE

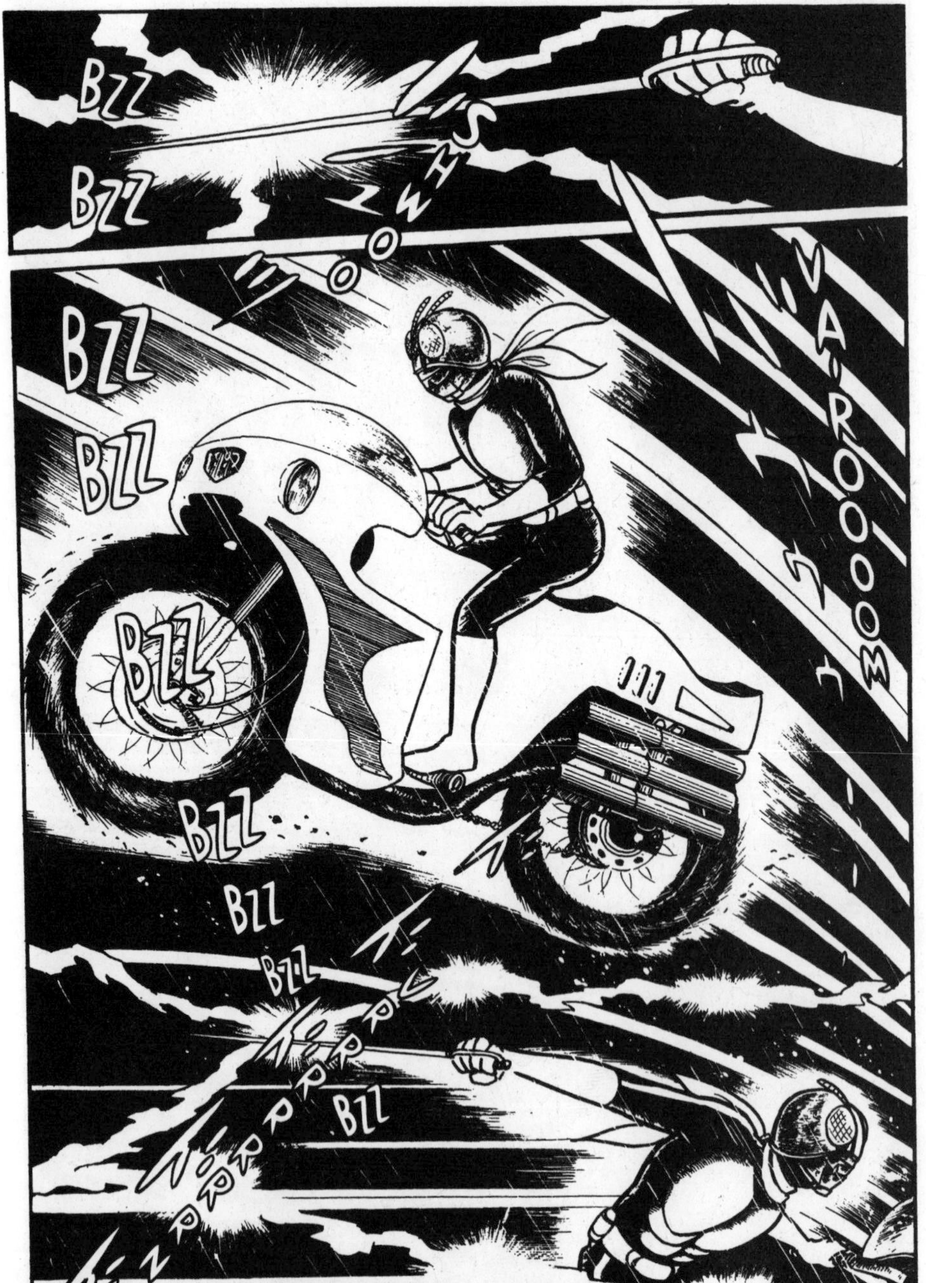
BZZ
BZZ
SHWOO
VAROOOOOM
BZZ
BZZ
BZZ
BZZ
BZZ
BZZ
BZZ

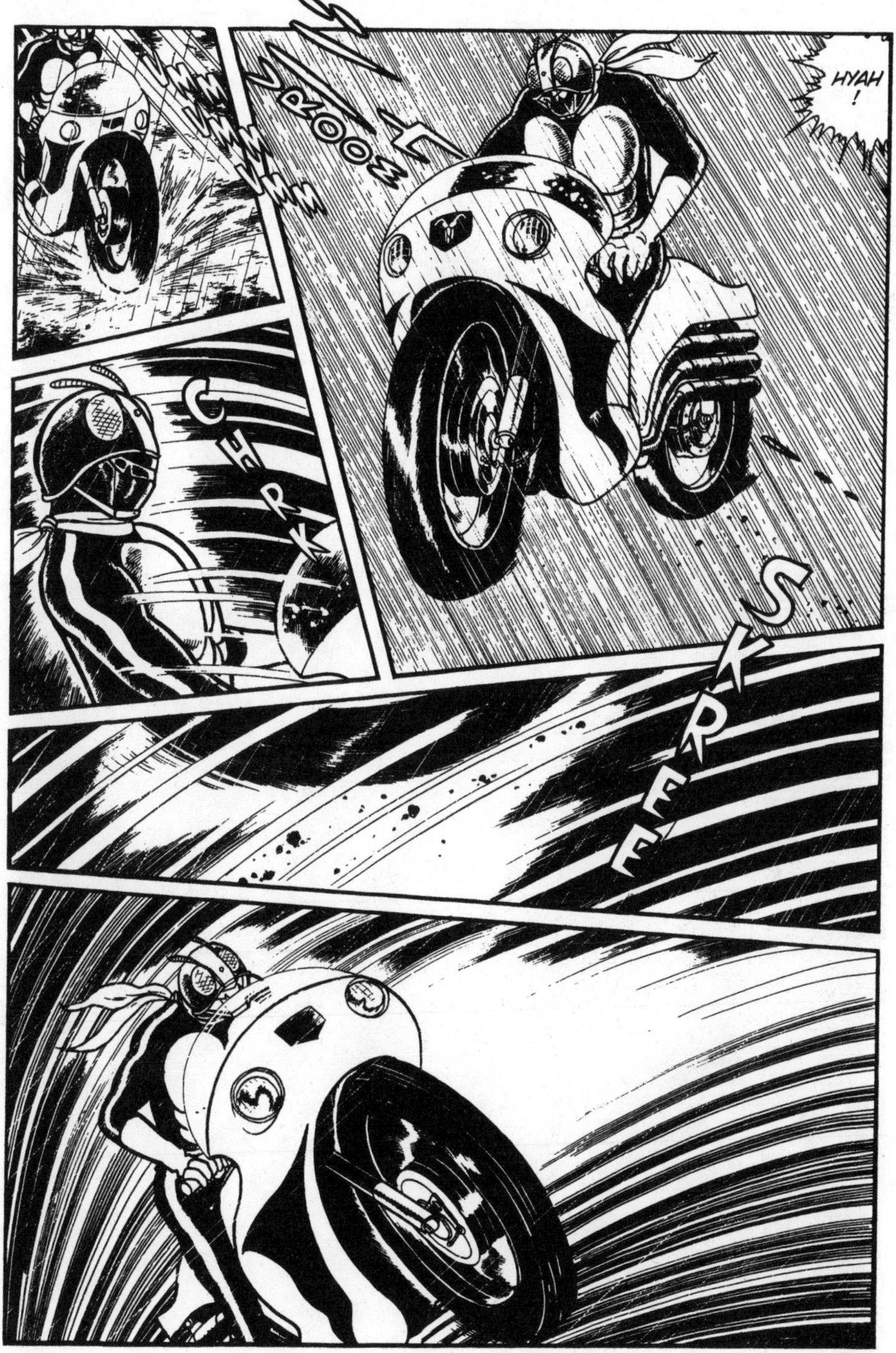
HYAH!
VROOM
VMMMM
CHRK
SKREE

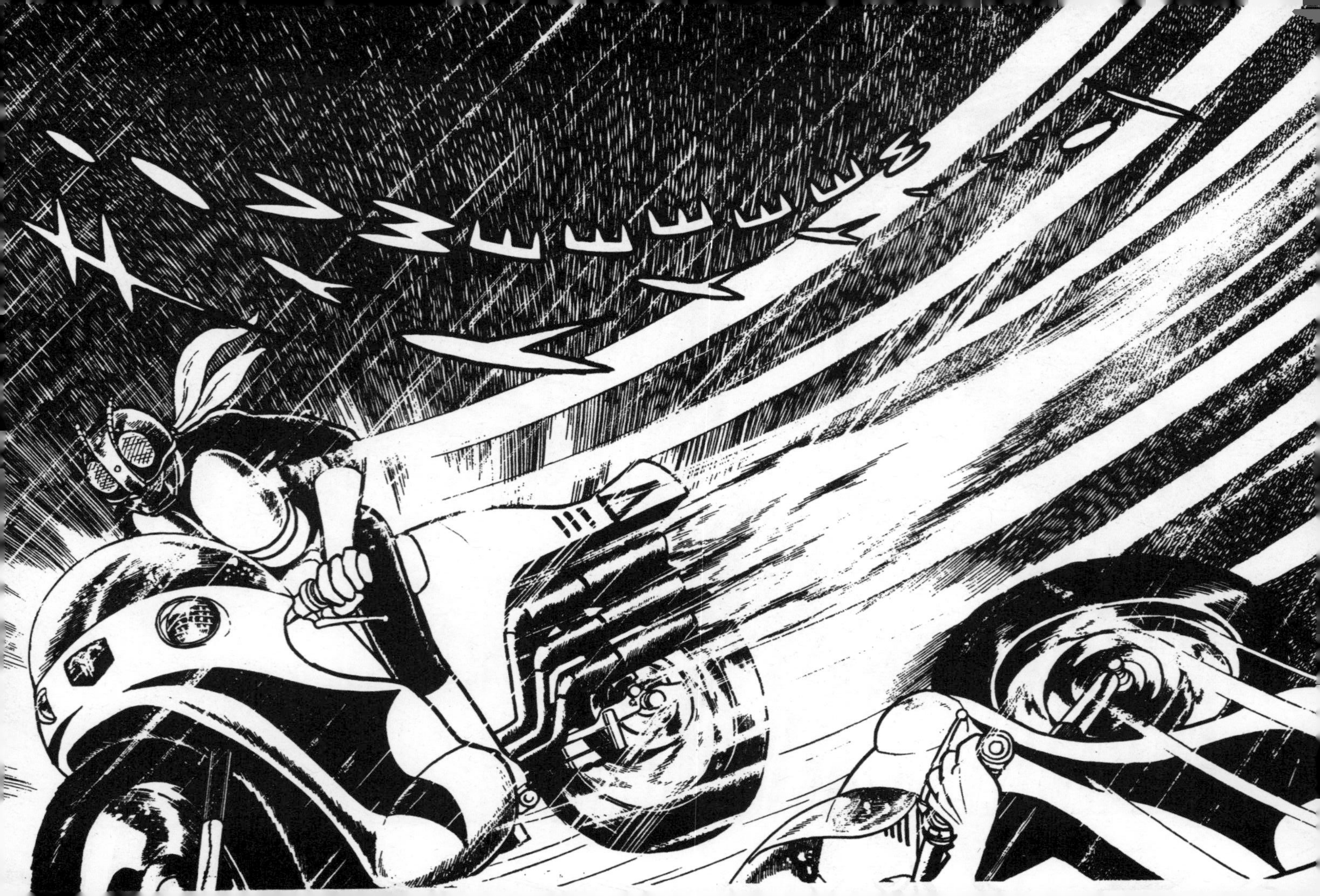
VWEEEEEEM

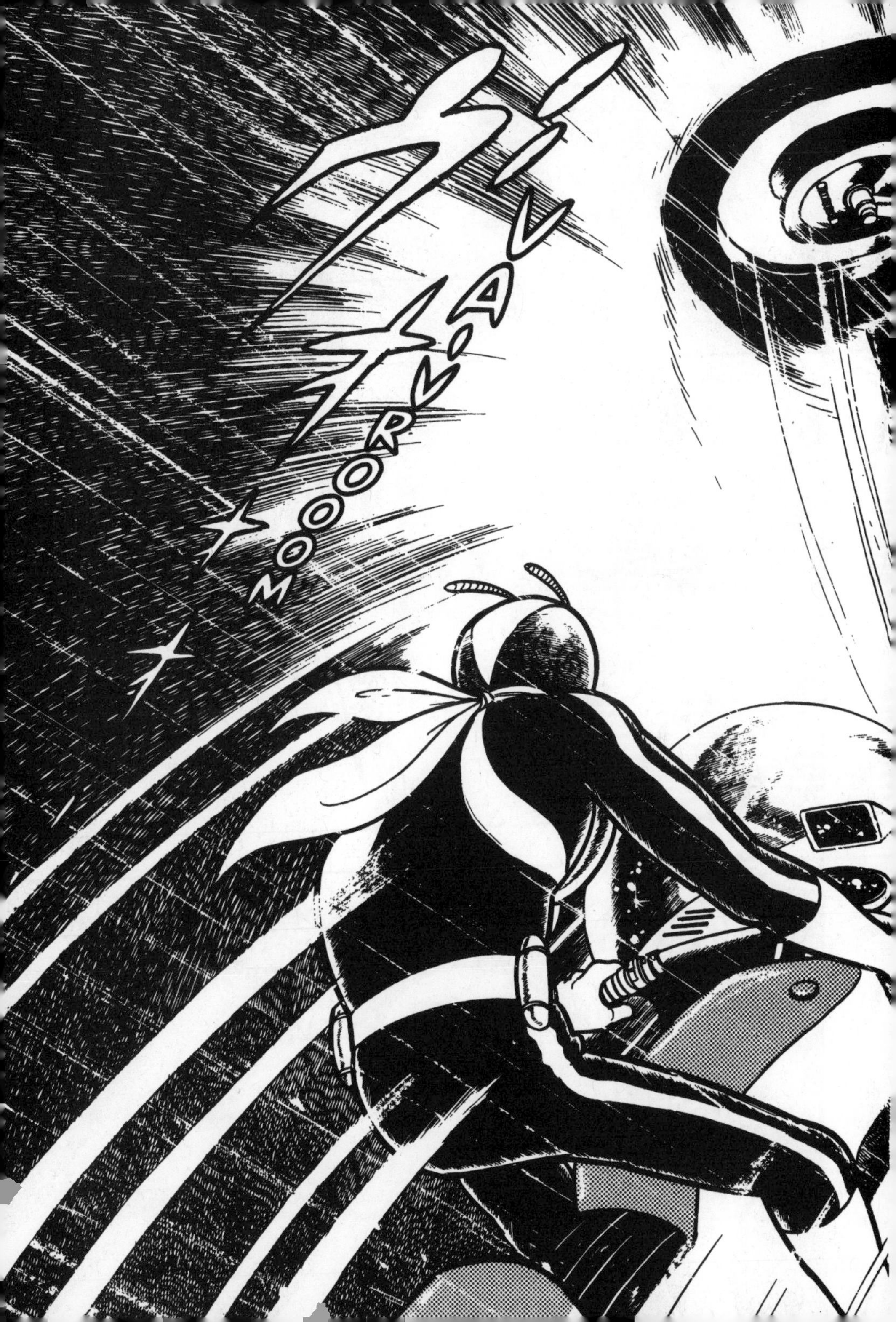
VVVRROOOOM

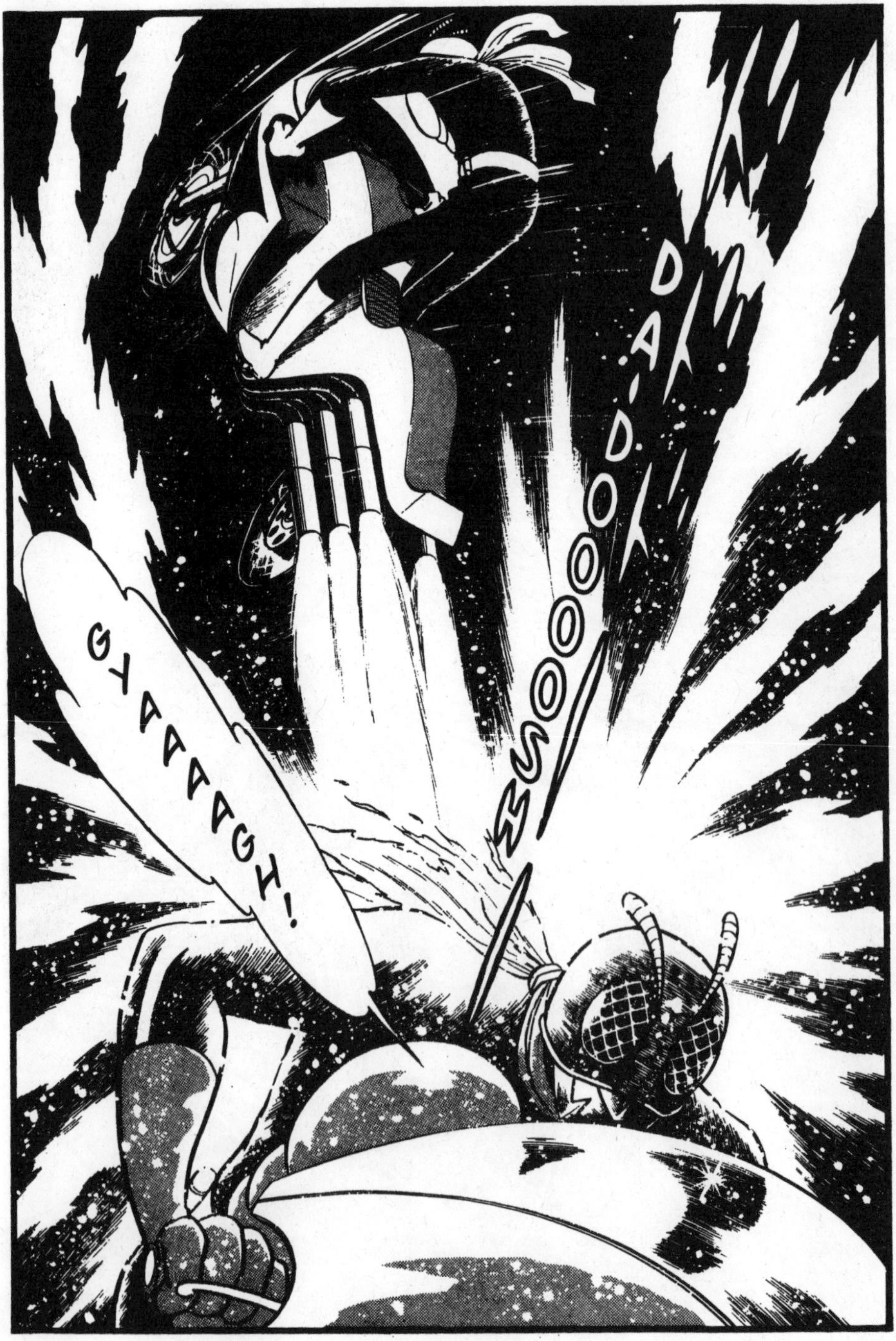
DADOOOOOSH
GYAAAAAGH!

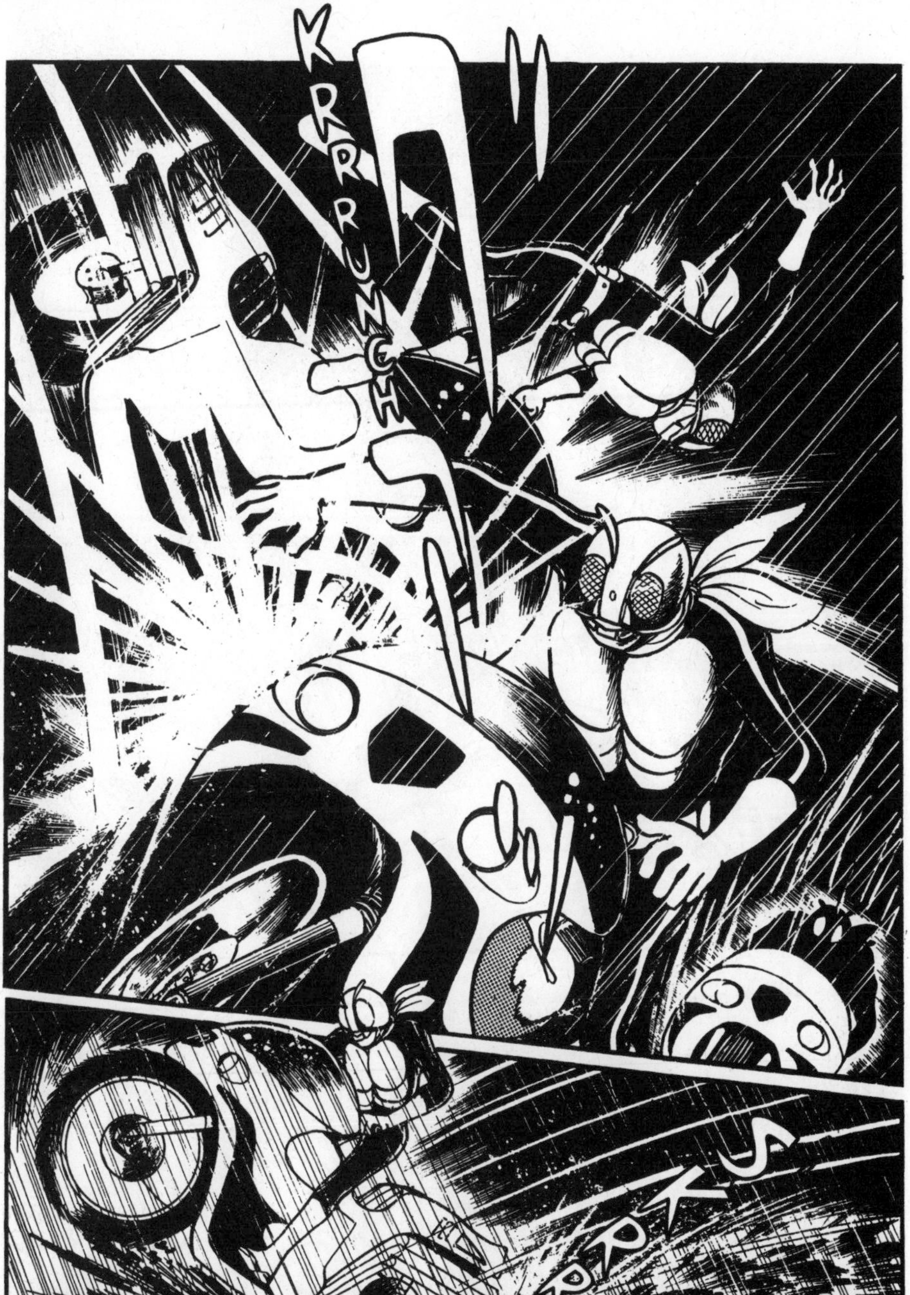
KRRRUNCH
SKRRR

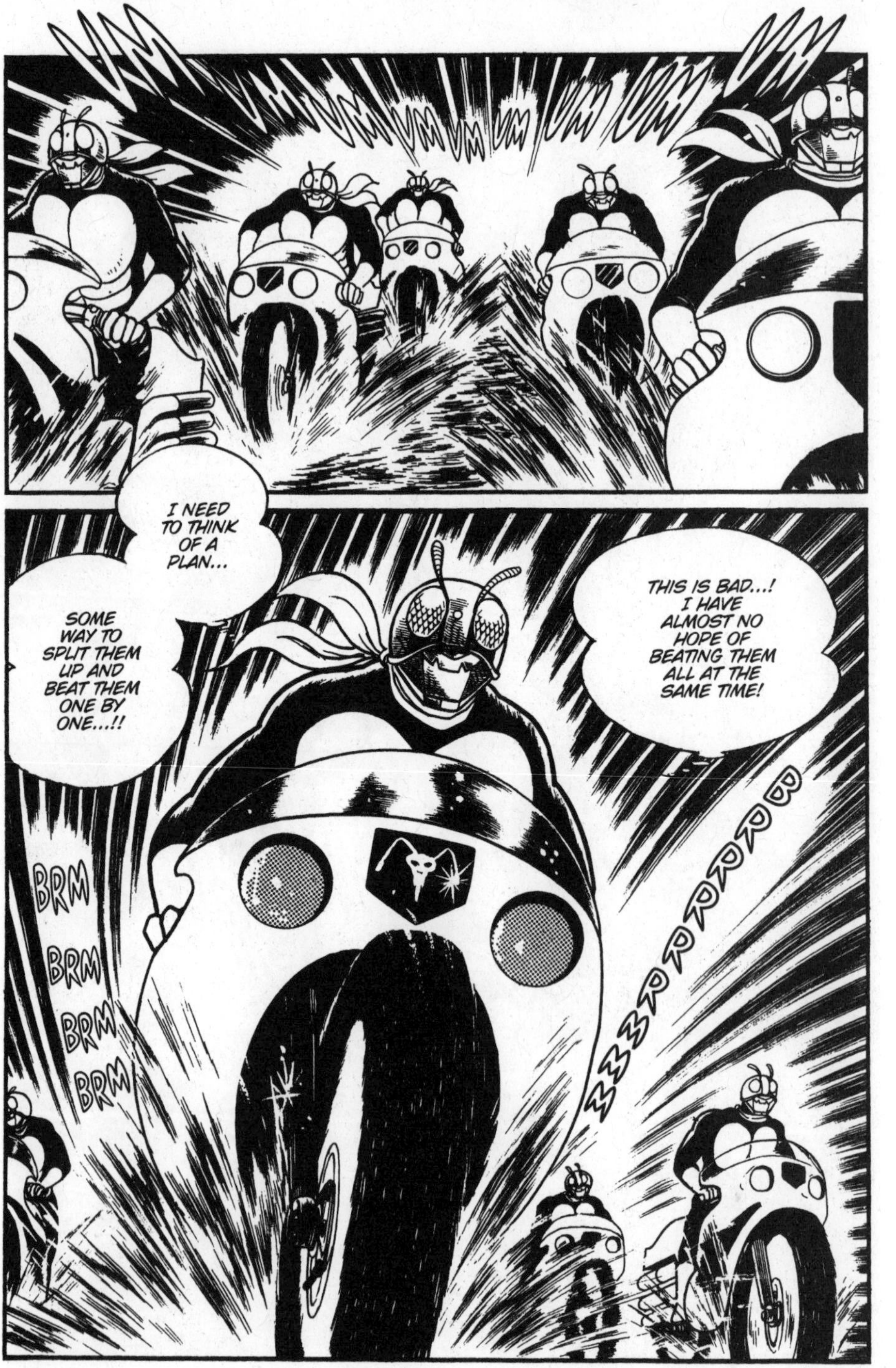
VM VM VM VM VM VM
THIS IS BAD...! I HAVE ALMOST NO HOPE OF BEATING THEM ALL AT THE SAME TIME!
I NEED TO THINK OF A PLAN...
SOME WAY TO SPLIT THEM UP AND BEAT THEM ONE BY ONE...!!
BRRRRRRRRMMMM
BRM
BRM
BRM
BRM

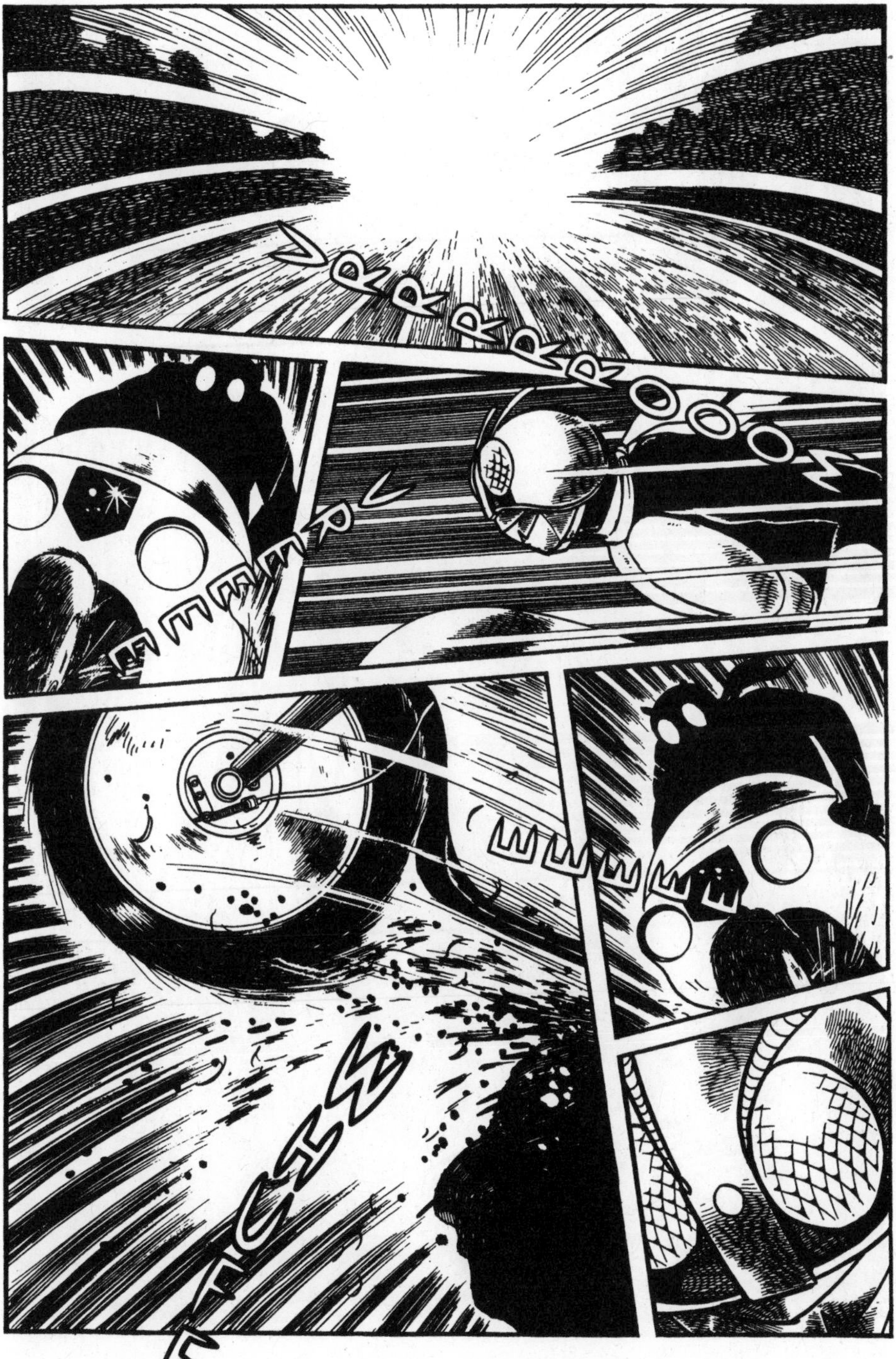
VRRRRROOOOM
VREEEE

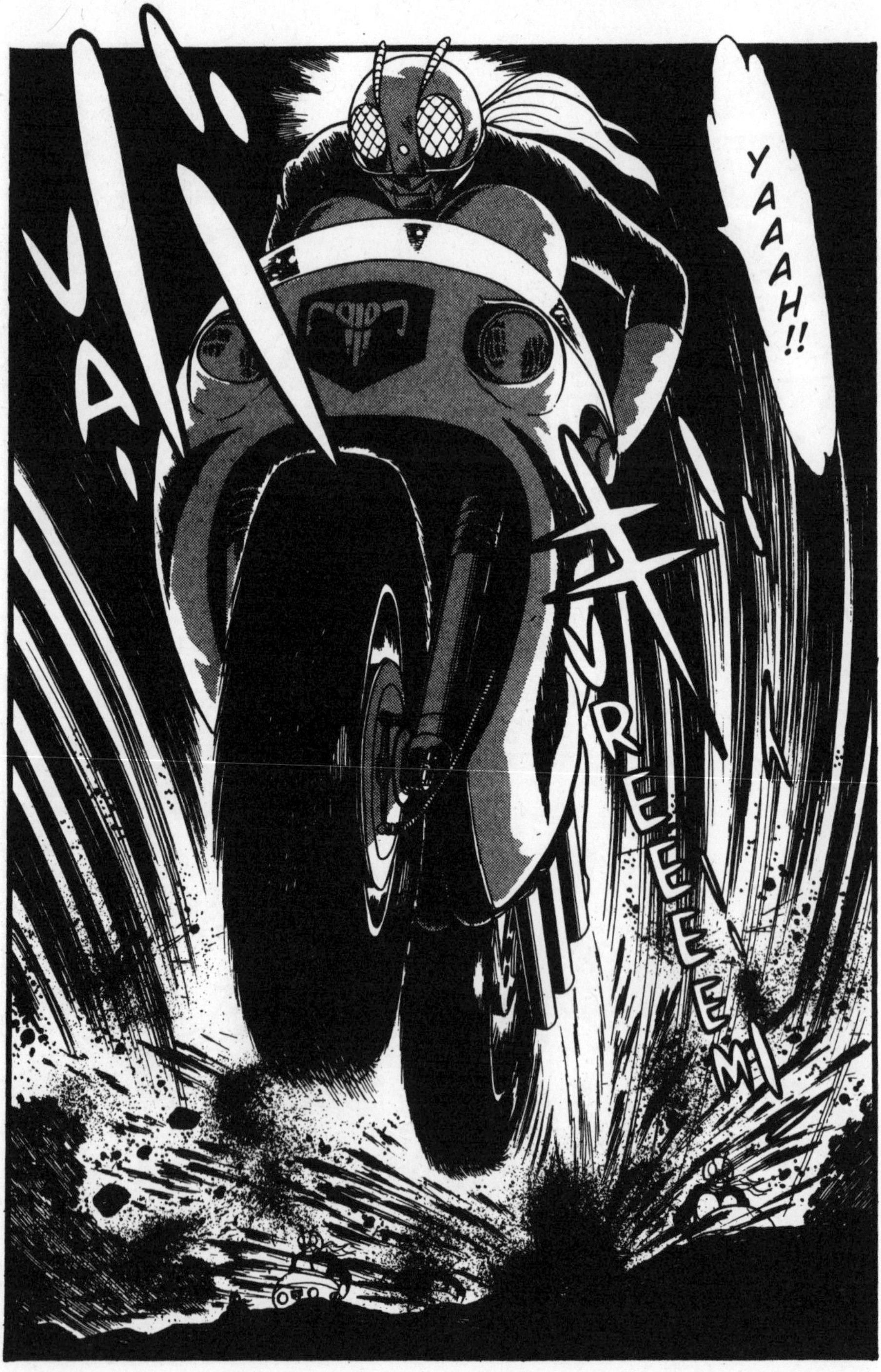
YAAAAH!!
VA!!
VURREEEEEM!

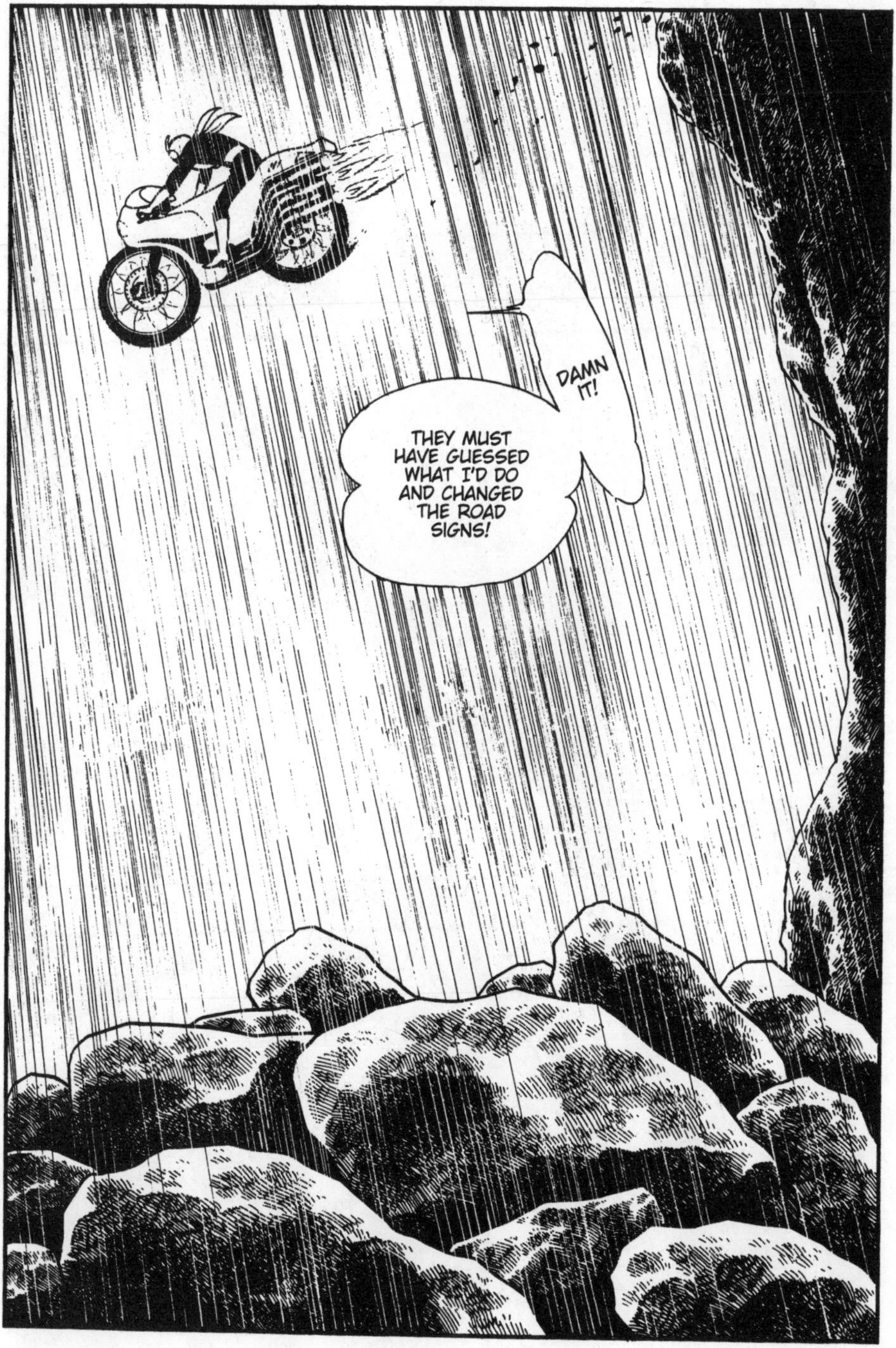
DAMN IT!
THEY MUST HAVE GUESSED WHAT I'D DO AND CHANGED THE ROAD SIGNS!

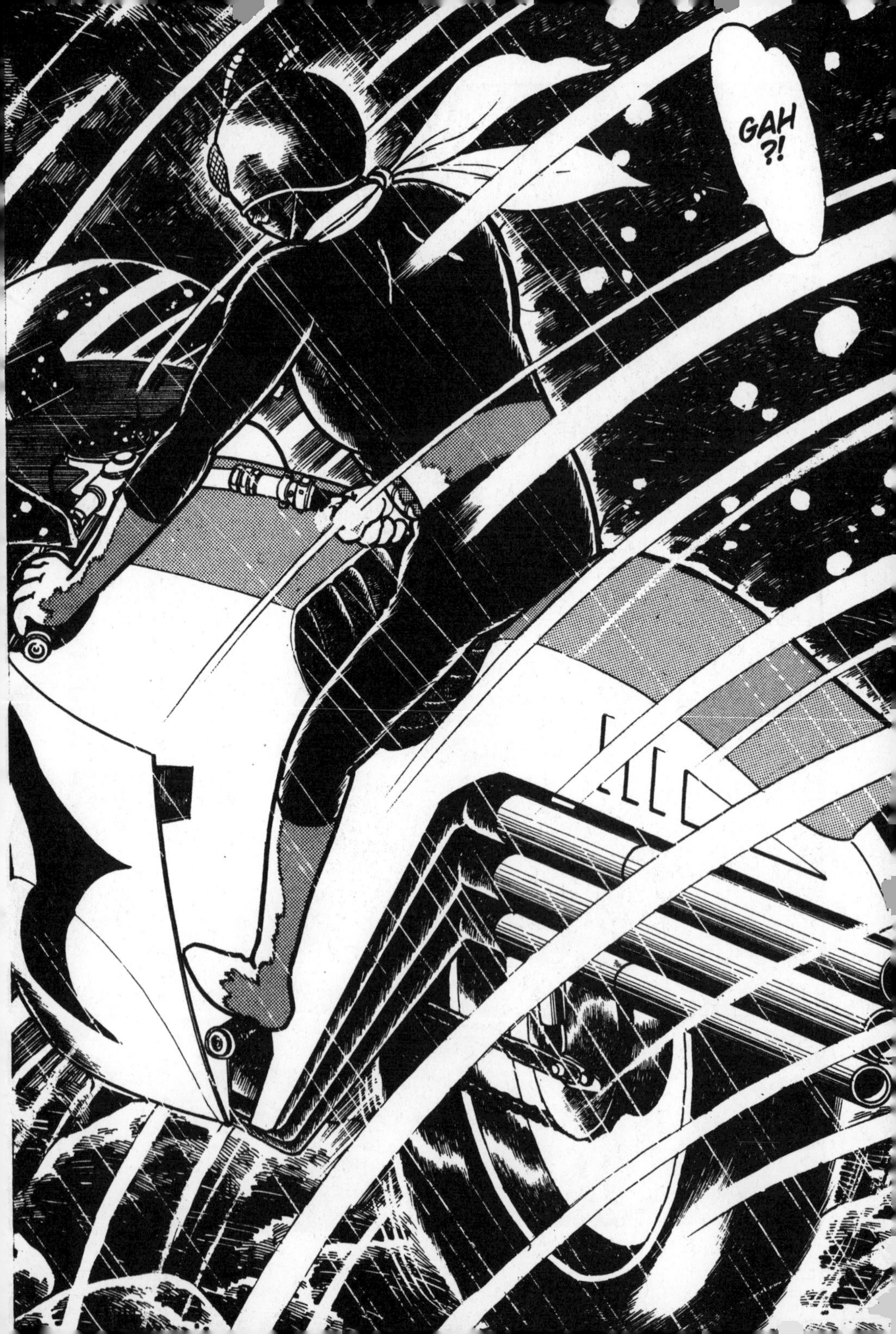
GAH ?!

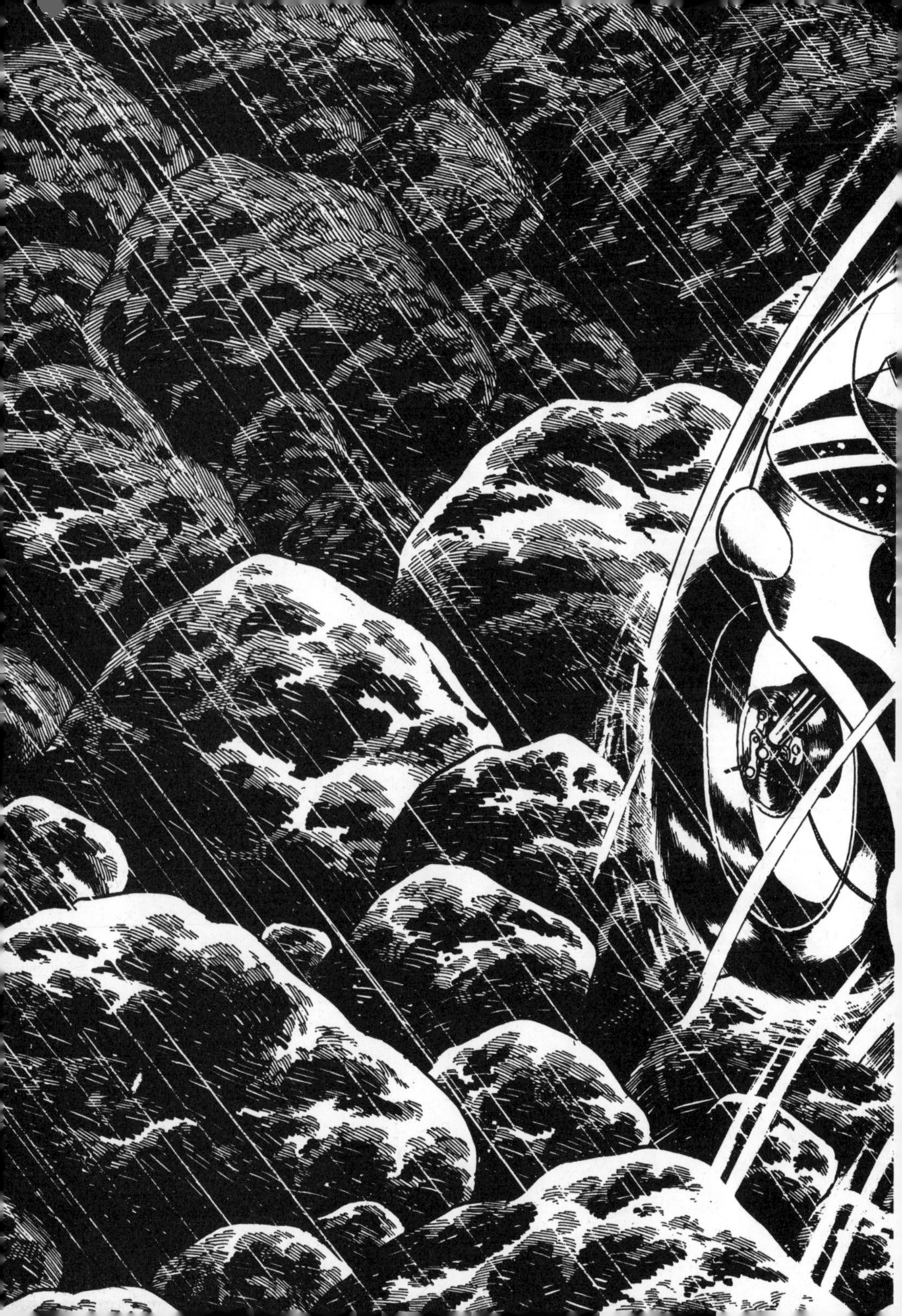

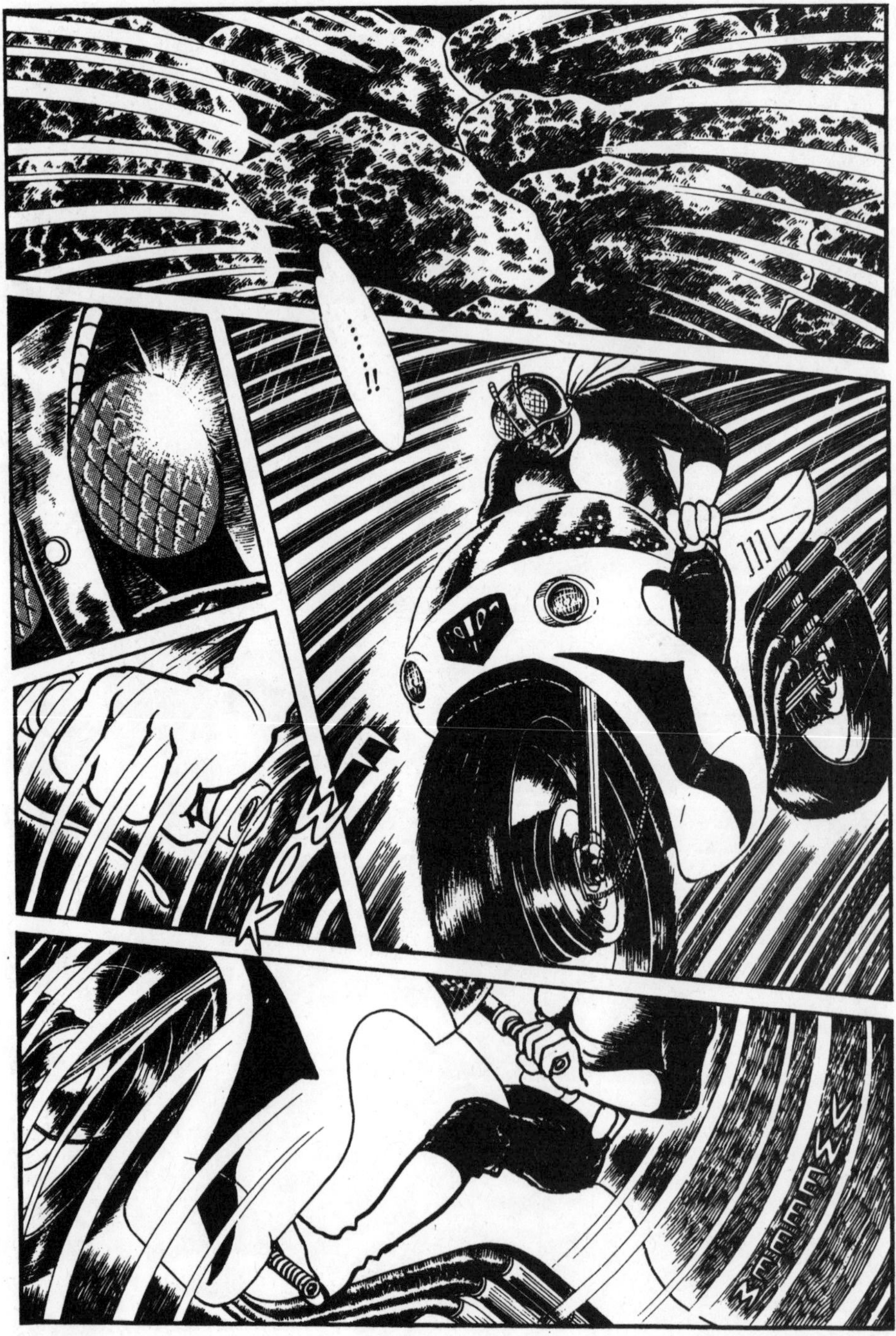
......!!
KOWF

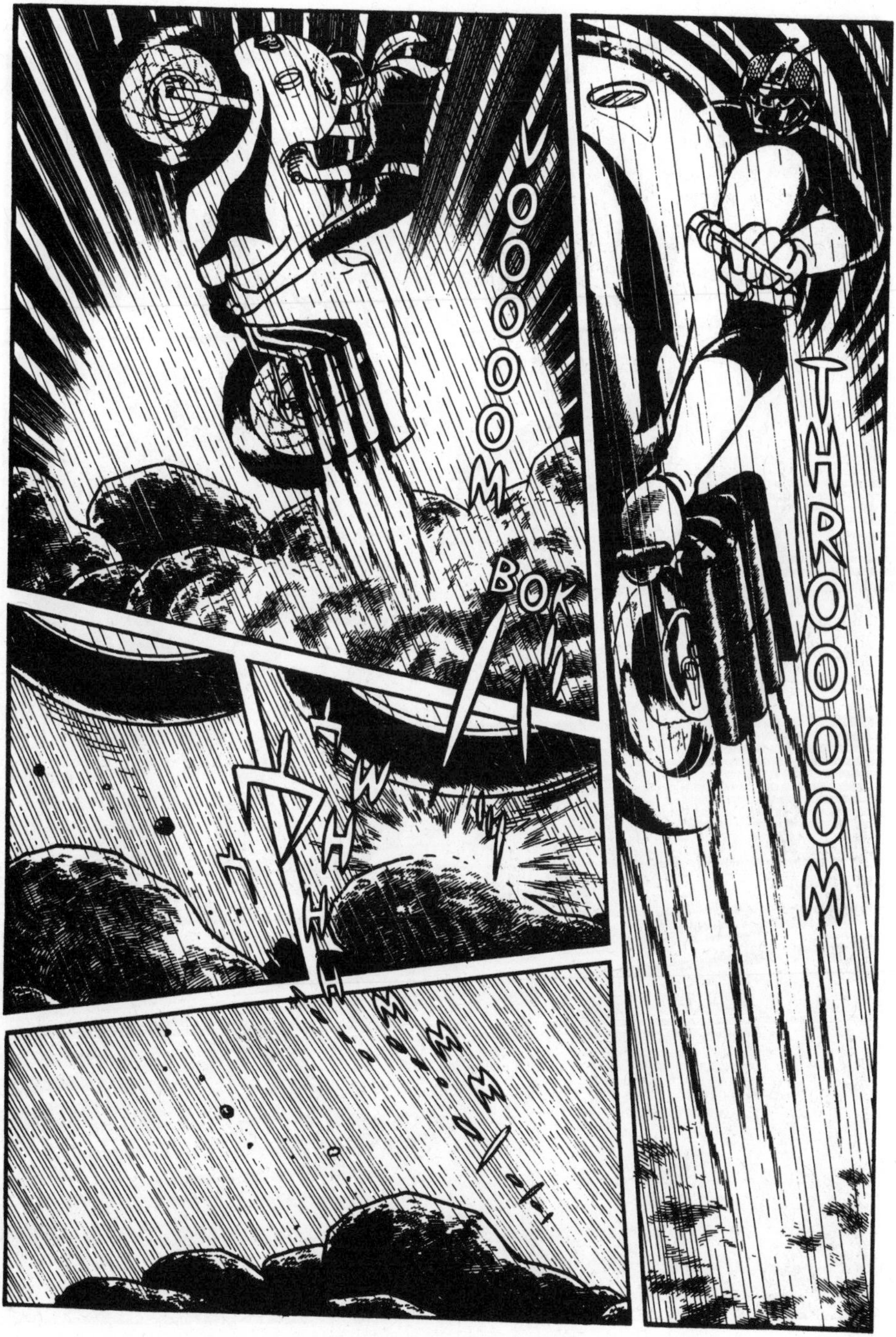
THROOOOM
VOOOOOM
BOK
DWHHHMMM

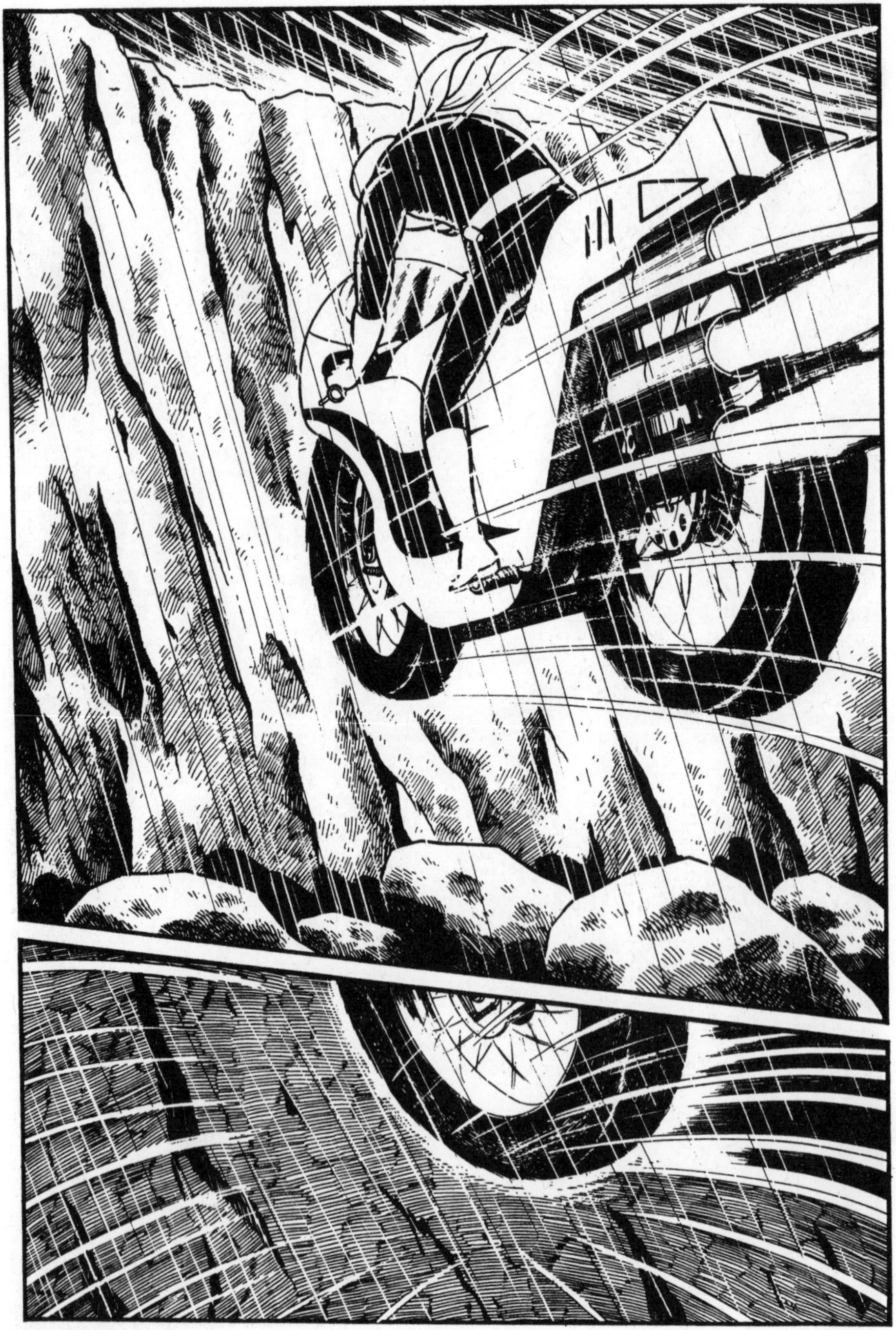

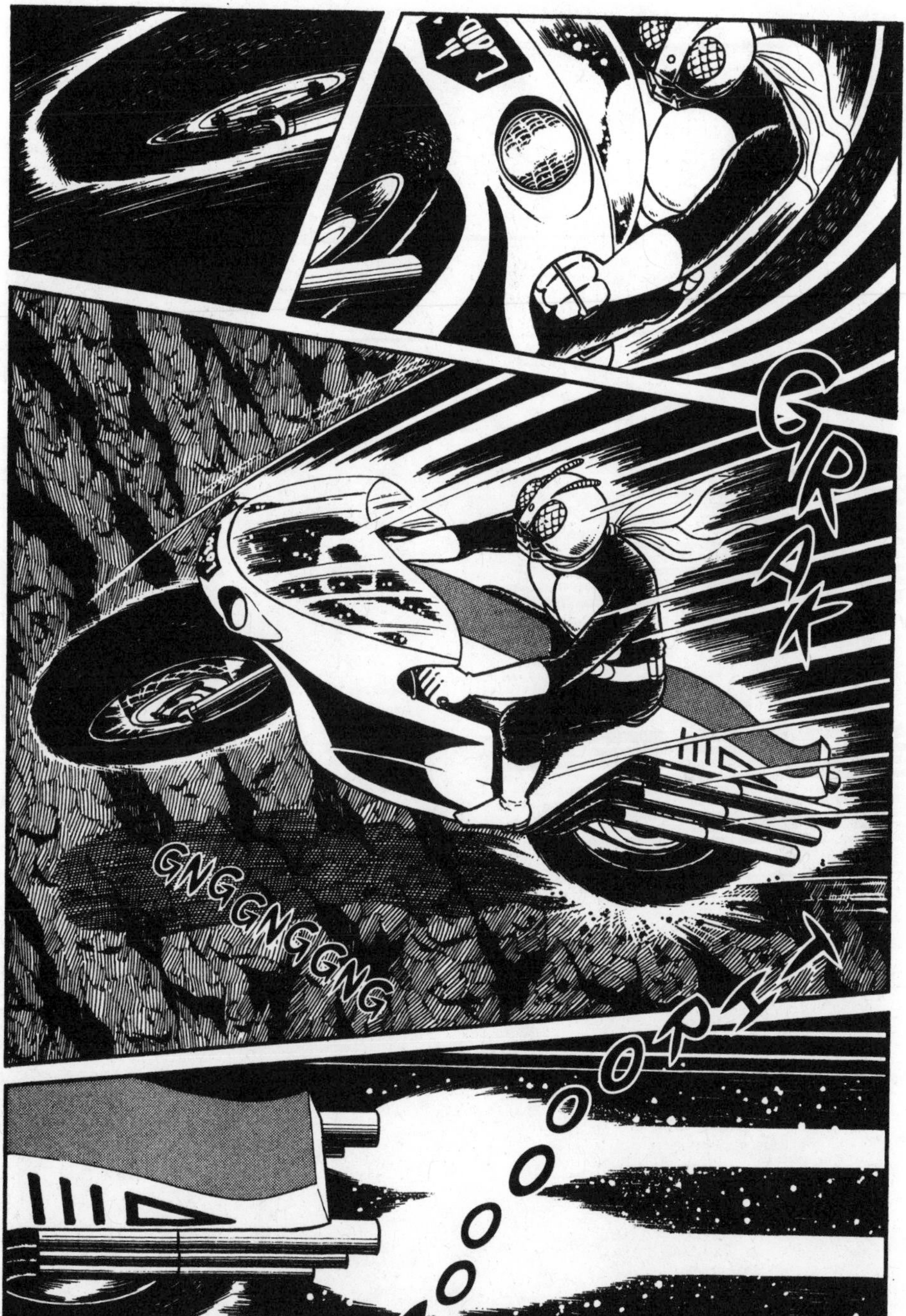

GRAK
GNGGNGGNG
WOOOOORHT

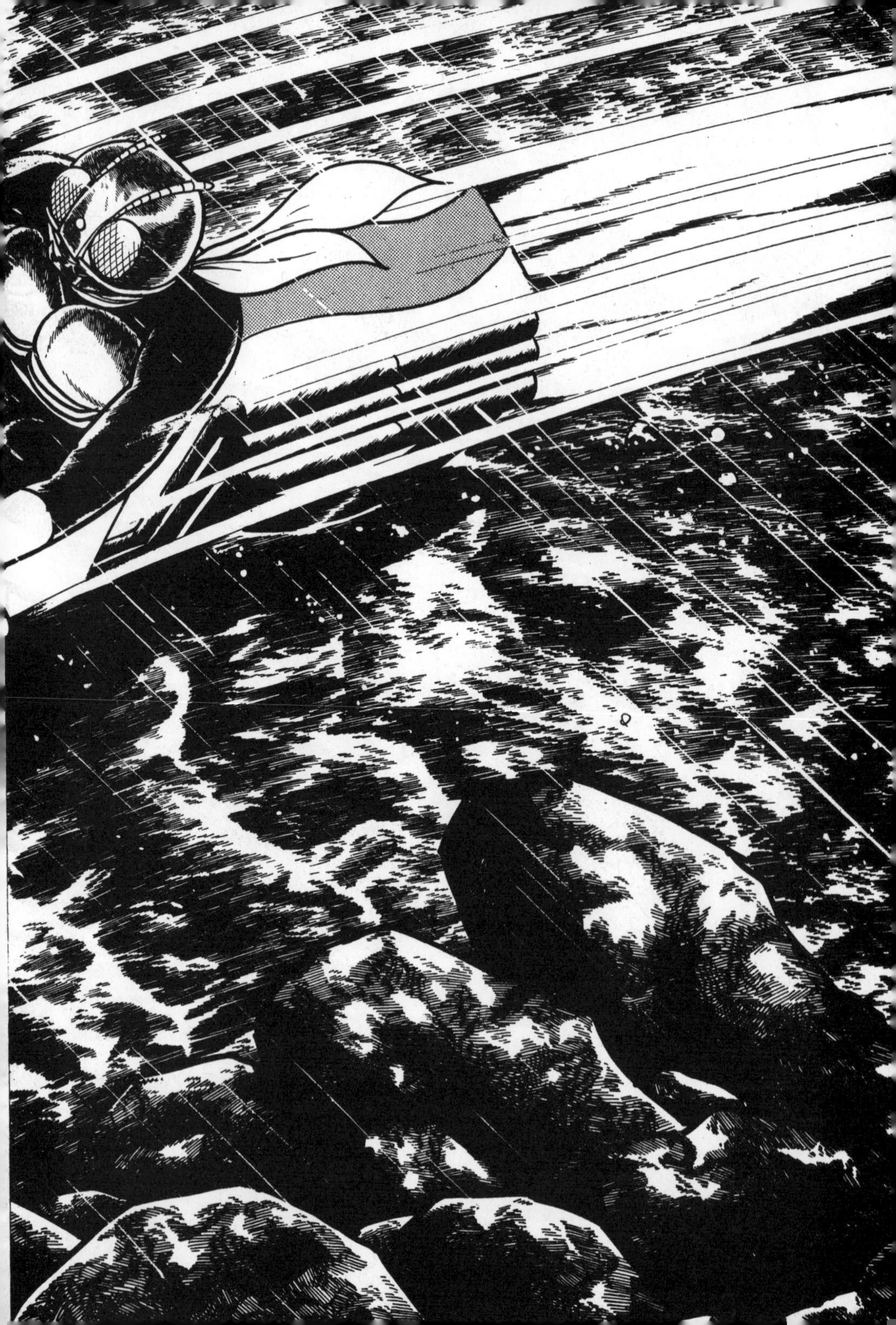

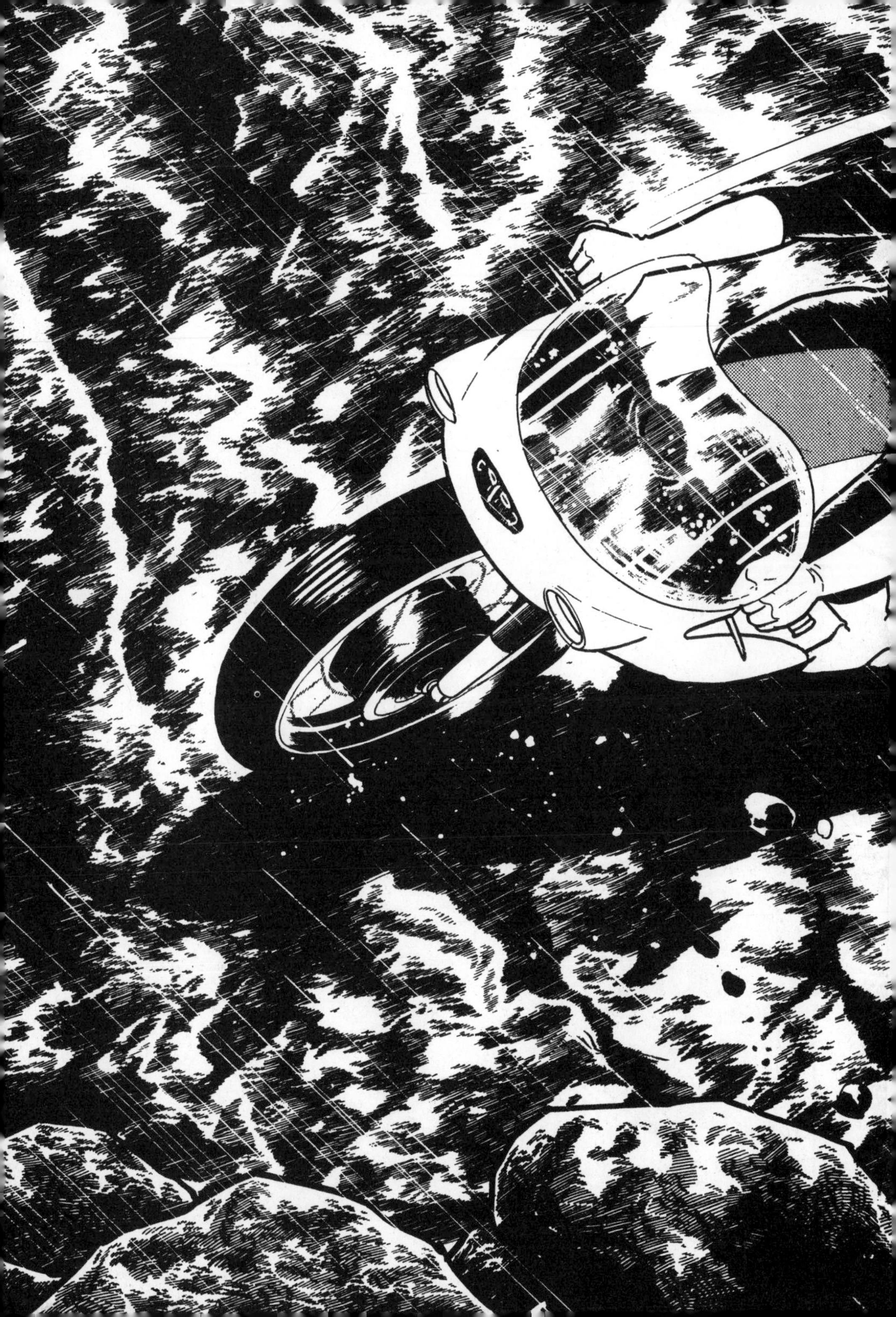

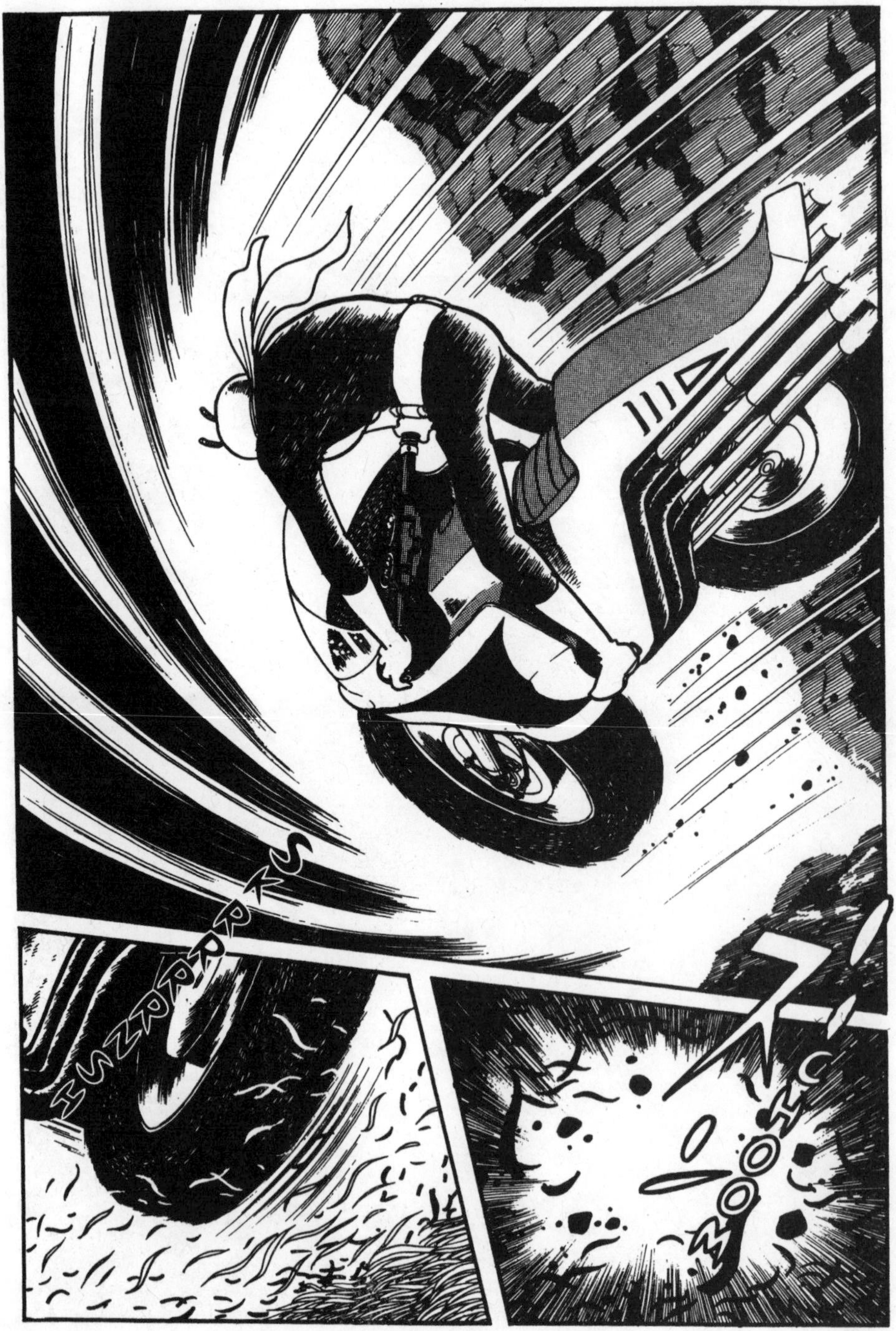
SKRRR
CHOOOM
HSZZRRR

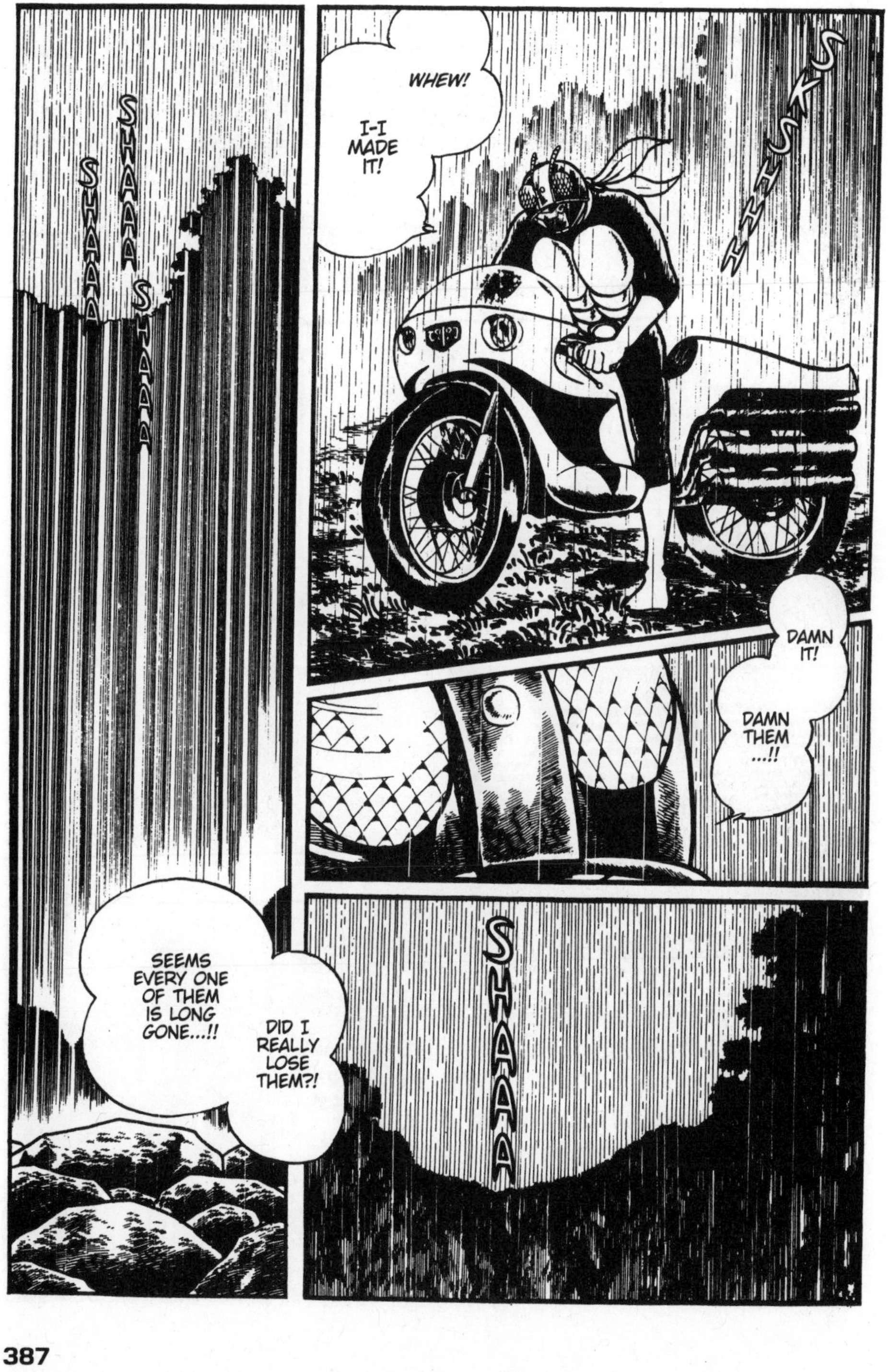
SHHSKS
WHEW!
I-I MADE IT!
DAMN IT!
DAMN THEM ...!!
SHAAAA
DID I REALLY LOSE THEM?!
SEEMS EVERY ONE OF THEM IS LONG GONE...!!
SHAAAA
SHAAAA
SHAAAAA

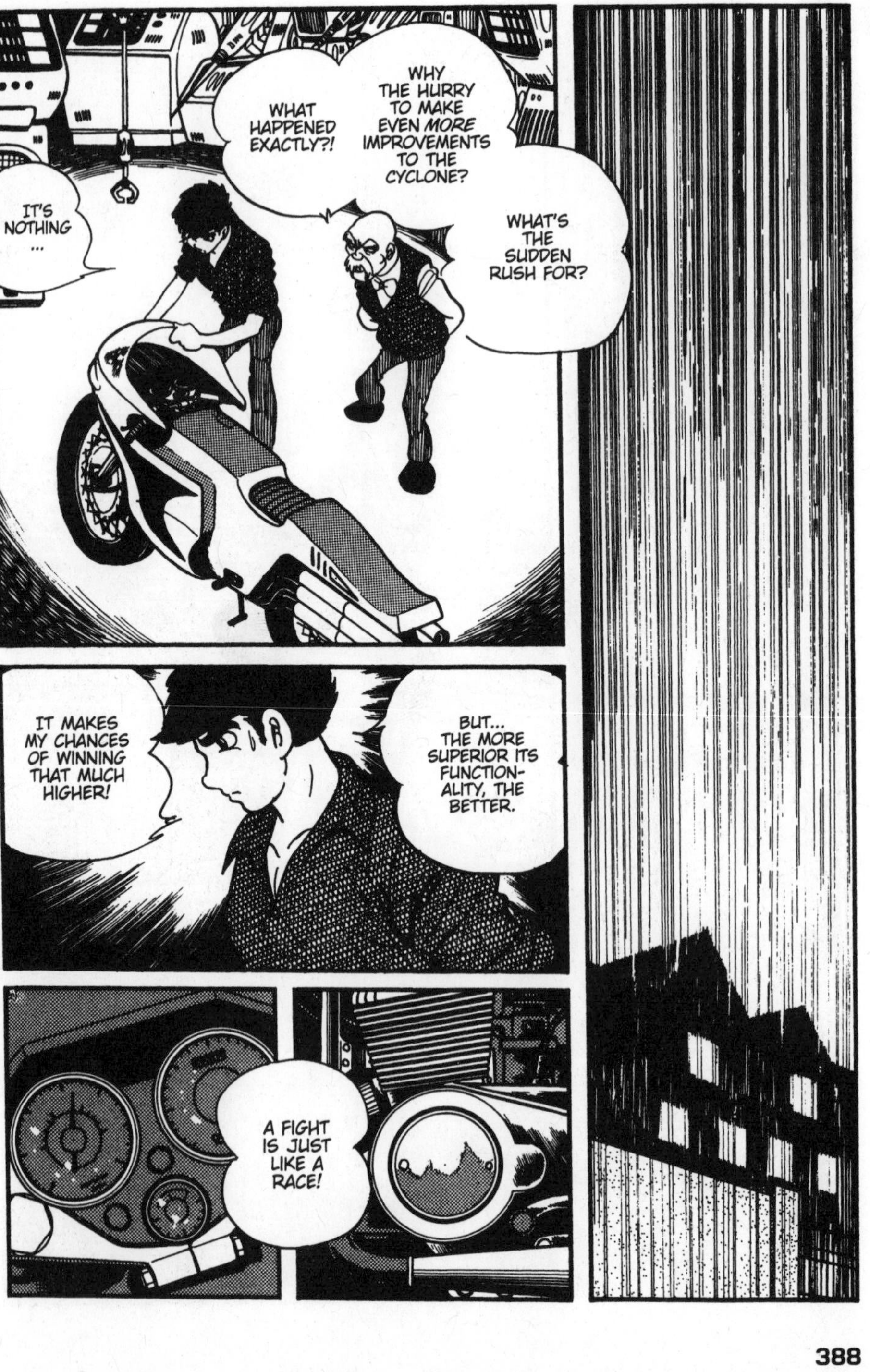
WHY THE HURRY TO MAKE EVEN *MORE* IMPROVEMENTS TO THE CYCLONE?
WHAT'S THE SUDDEN RUSH FOR?
WHAT HAPPENED EXACTLY?!
IT'S NOTHING ...
BUT... THE MORE SUPERIOR ITS FUNCTION-ALITY, THE BETTER.
IT MAKES MY CHANCES OF WINNING THAT MUCH HIGHER!
A FIGHT IS JUST LIKE A RACE!

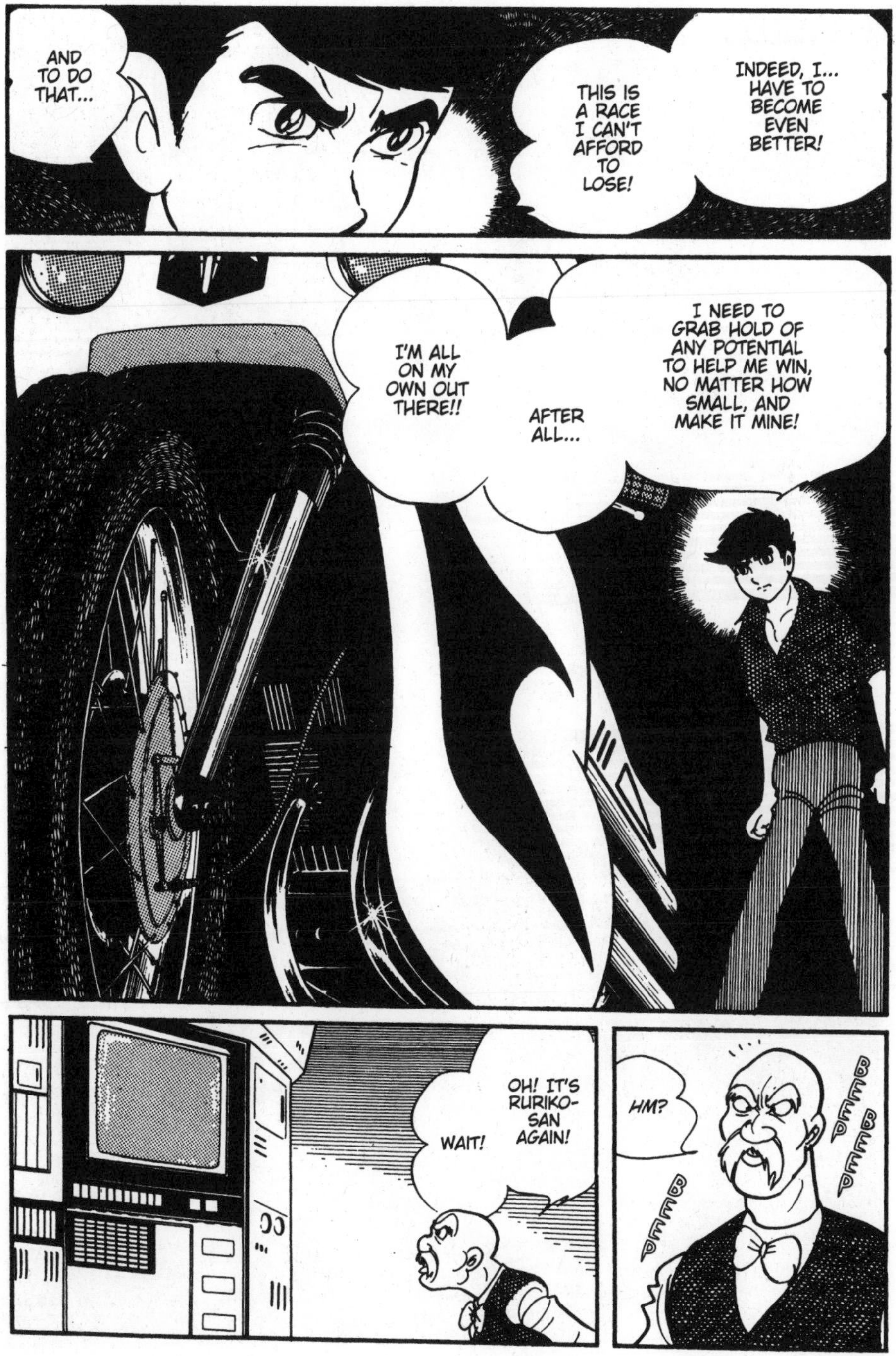

INDEED, I... HAVE TO BECOME EVEN BETTER!
THIS IS A RACE I CAN'T AFFORD TO LOSE!
AND TO DO THAT...
I NEED TO GRAB HOLD OF ANY POTENTIAL TO HELP ME WIN, NO MATTER HOW SMALL, AND MAKE IT MINE!
AFTER ALL...
I'M ALL ON MY OWN OUT THERE!!
BEEP BEEP
HM?
BEEP
OH! IT'S RURIKO-SAN AGAIN!
WAIT!

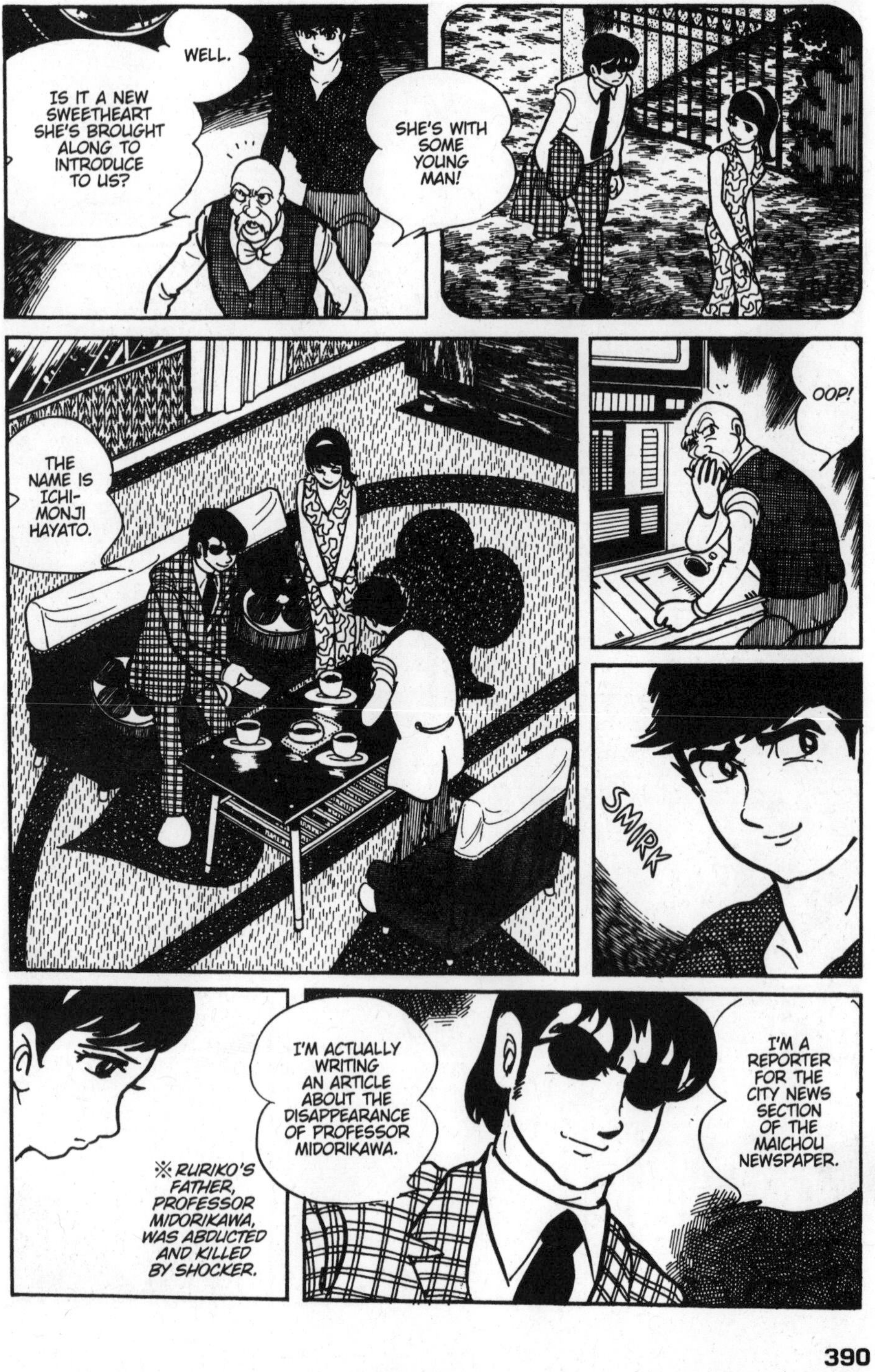
SHE'S WITH SOME YOUNG MAN!
WELL.
IS IT A NEW SWEETHEART SHE'S BROUGHT ALONG TO INTRODUCE TO US?
OOP!
SMIRK
THE NAME IS ICHIMONJI HAYATO.
I'M A REPORTER FOR THE CITY NEWS SECTION OF THE MAICHOU NEWSPAPER.
I'M ACTUALLY WRITING AN ARTICLE ABOUT THE DISAPPEARANCE OF PROFESSOR MIDORIKAWA.
※RURIKO'S FATHER, PROFESSOR MIDORIKAWA, WAS ABDUCTED AND KILLED BY SHOCKER.

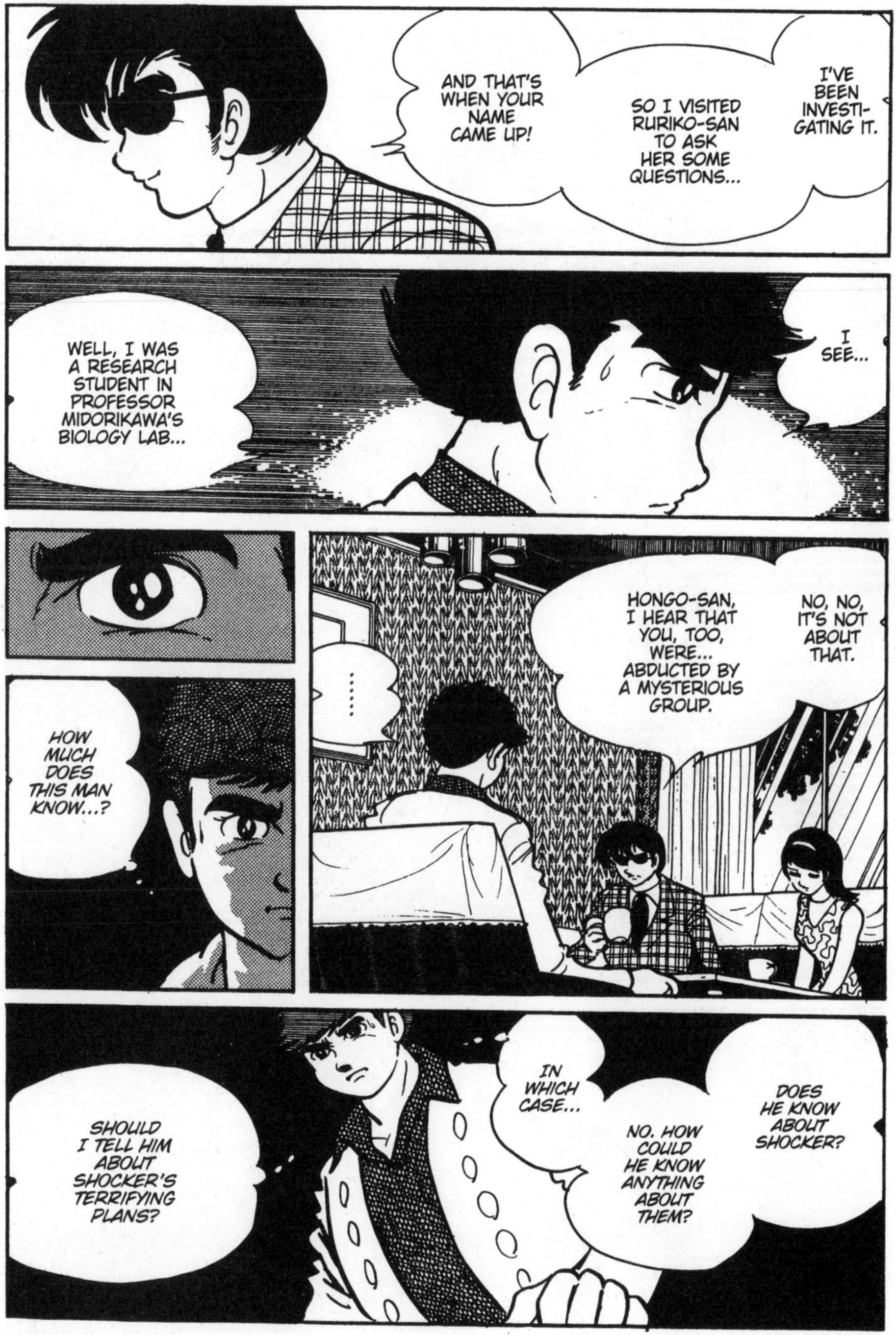
I'VE BEEN INVESTI-GATING IT.
SO I VISITED RURIKO-SAN TO ASK HER SOME QUESTIONS...
AND THAT'S WHEN YOUR NAME CAME UP!
I SEE...
WELL, I WAS A RESEARCH STUDENT IN PROFESSOR MIDORIKAWA'S BIOLOGY LAB...
NO, NO, IT'S NOT ABOUT THAT.
HONGO-SAN, I HEAR THAT YOU, TOO, WERE... ABDUCTED BY A MYSTERIOUS GROUP.
......
HOW MUCH DOES THIS MAN KNOW...?
DOES HE KNOW ABOUT SHOCKER?
NO. HOW COULD HE KNOW ANYTHING ABOUT THEM?
IN WHICH CASE...
SHOULD I TELL HIM ABOUT SHOCKER'S TERRIFYING PLANS?

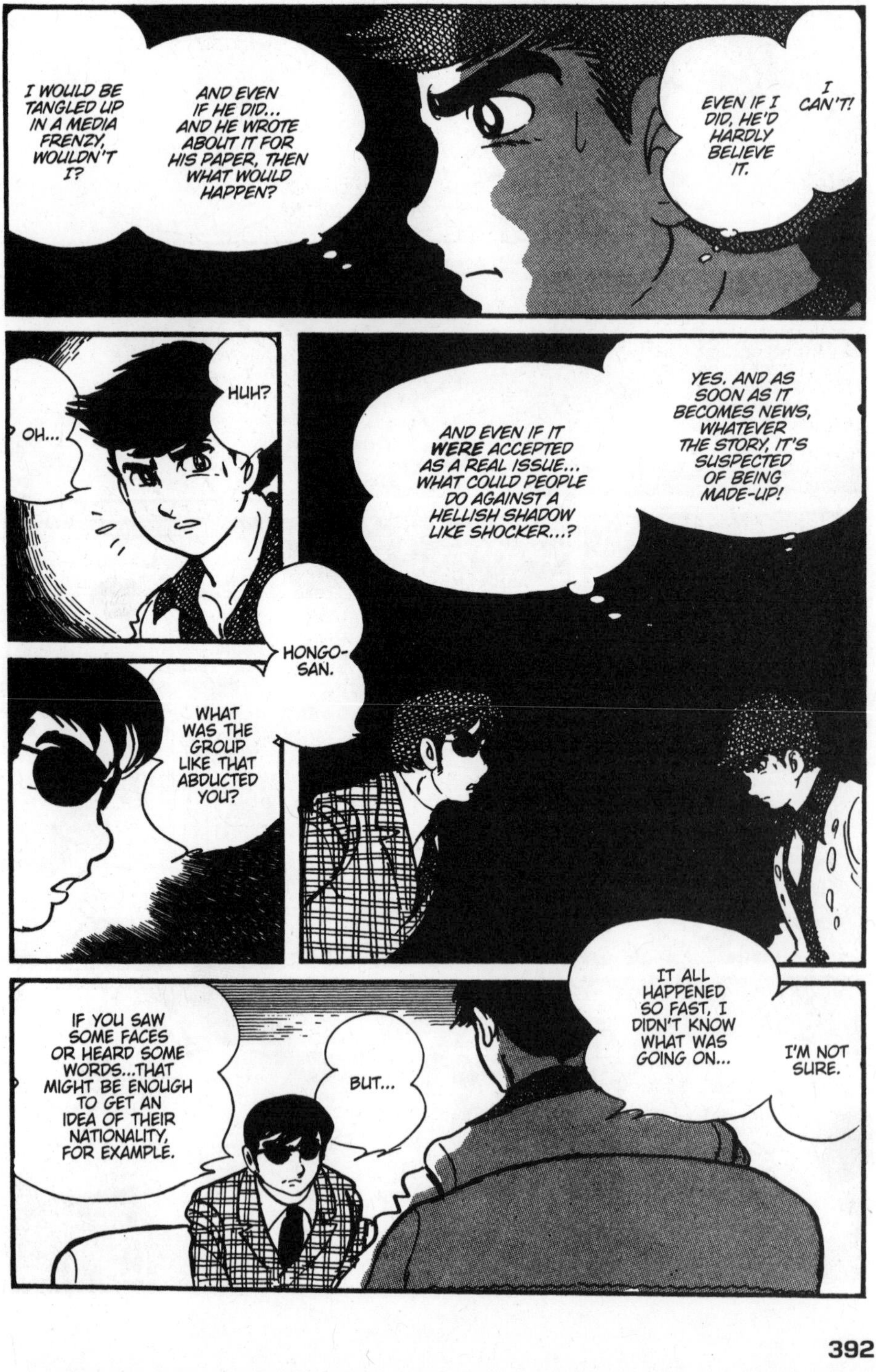
I CAN'T!
EVEN IF I DID, HE'D HARDLY BELIEVE IT.
AND EVEN IF HE DID... AND HE WROTE ABOUT IT FOR HIS PAPER, THEN WHAT WOULD HAPPEN?
I WOULD BE TANGLED UP IN A MEDIA FRENZY, WOULDN'T I?
YES. AND AS SOON AS IT BECOMES NEWS, WHATEVER THE STORY, IT'S SUSPECTED OF BEING MADE-UP!
AND EVEN IF IT WERE ACCEPTED AS A REAL ISSUE... WHAT COULD PEOPLE DO AGAINST A HELLISH SHADOW LIKE SHOCKER...?
HONGO-SAN.
HUH?
OH...
WHAT WAS THE GROUP LIKE THAT ABDUCTED YOU?
I'M NOT SURE.
IT ALL HAPPENED SO FAST, I DIDN'T KNOW WHAT WAS GOING ON...
BUT...
IF YOU SAW SOME FACES OR HEARD SOME WORDS...THAT MIGHT BE ENOUGH TO GET AN IDEA OF THEIR NATIONALITY, FOR EXAMPLE.

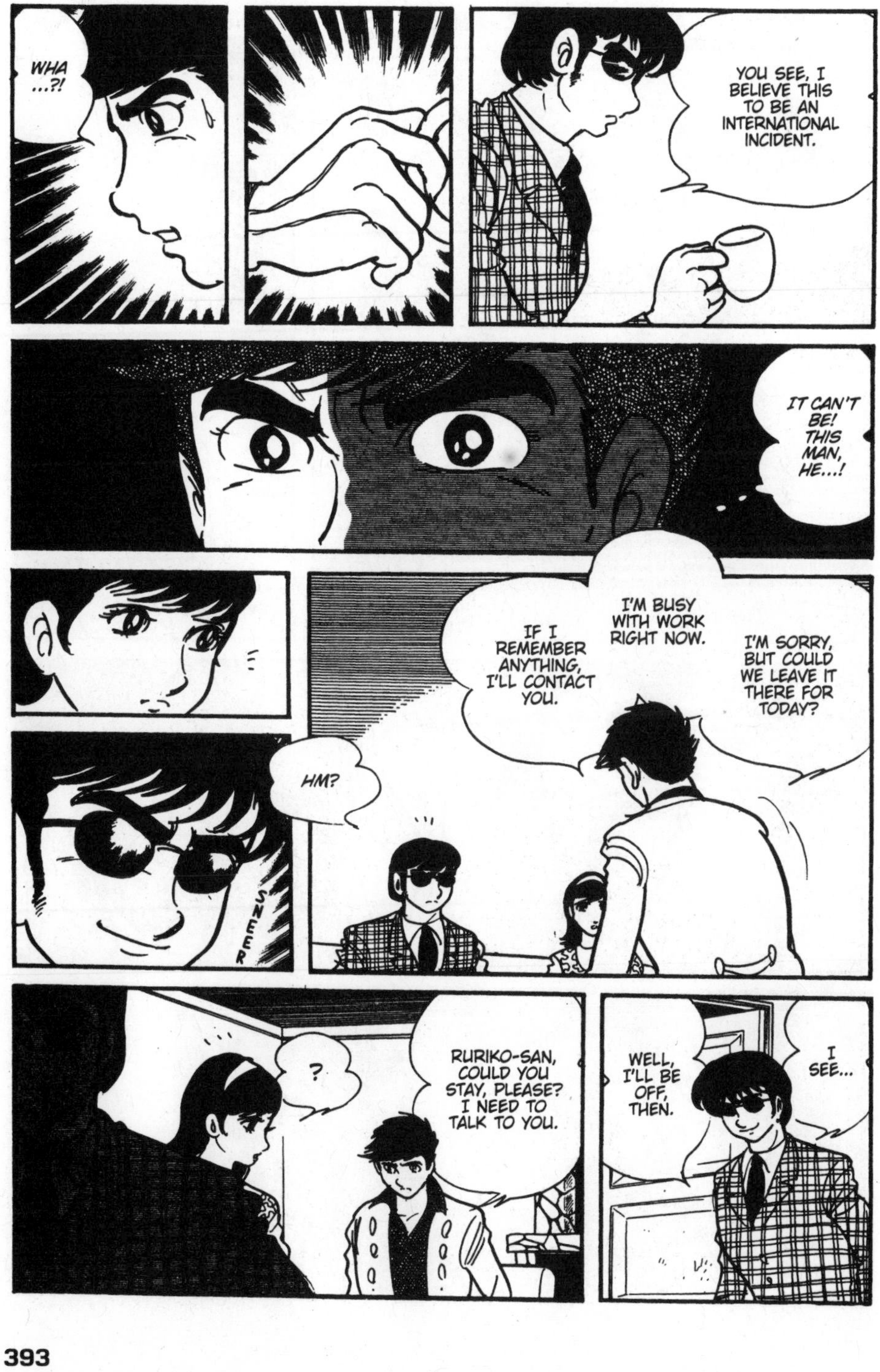
YOU SEE, I BELIEVE THIS TO BE AN INTERNATIONAL INCIDENT.
WHA ...?!
IT CAN'T BE! THIS MAN, HE...!
I'M SORRY, BUT COULD WE LEAVE IT THERE FOR TODAY?
I'M BUSY WITH WORK RIGHT NOW.
IF I REMEMBER ANYTHING, I'LL CONTACT YOU.
HM?
SNEER
I SEE...
WELL, I'LL BE OFF, THEN.
RURIKO-SAN, COULD YOU STAY, PLEASE? I NEED TO TALK TO YOU.
?

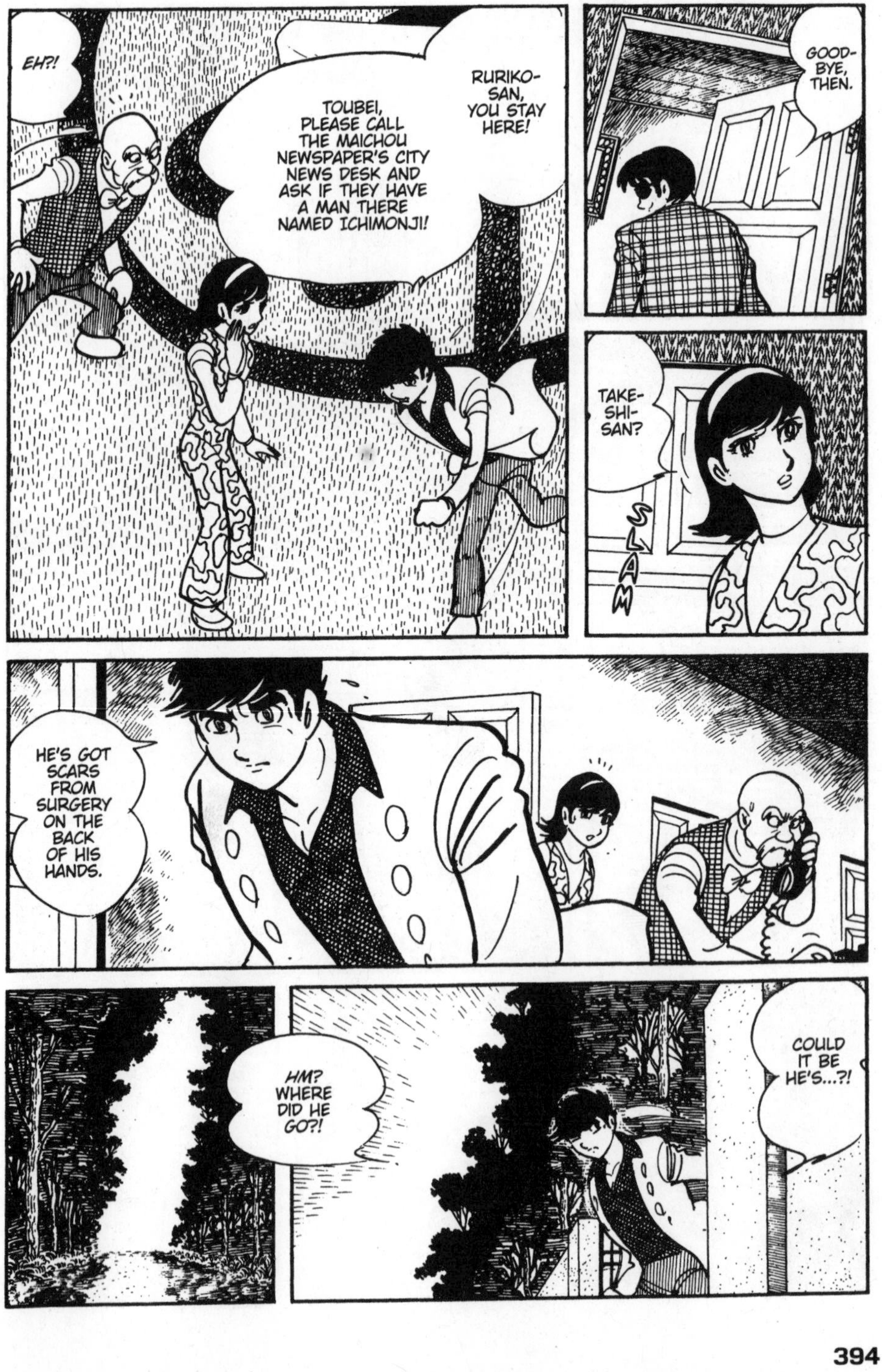
GOOD-BYE, THEN.
TAKE-SHI-SAN?
SLAM
RURIKO-SAN, YOU STAY HERE!
TOUBEI, PLEASE CALL THE MAICHOU NEWSPAPER'S CITY NEWS DESK AND ASK IF THEY HAVE A MAN THERE NAMED ICHIMONJI!
EH?!
HE'S GOT SCARS FROM SURGERY ON THE BACK OF HIS HANDS.
COULD IT BE HE'S...?!
HM? WHERE DID HE GO?!

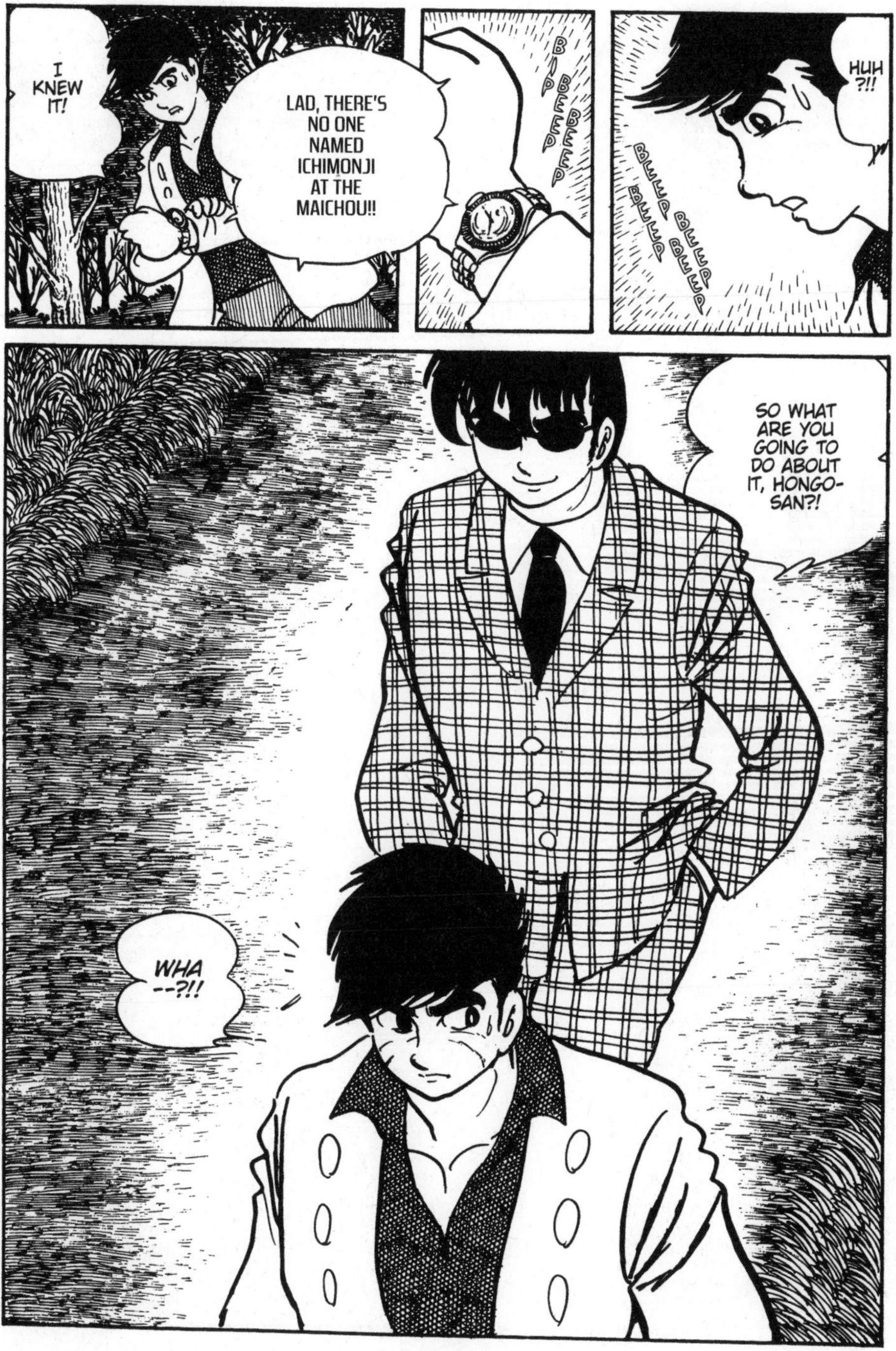
HUH ?!!
BLEEP BLEEP BLEEP BLEEP
BIP BEEEP BEEEP
LAD, THERE'S NO ONE NAMED ICHIMONJI AT THE MAICHOU!!
I KNEW IT!
SO WHAT ARE YOU GOING TO DO ABOUT IT, HONGO-SAN?!
WHA --?!!

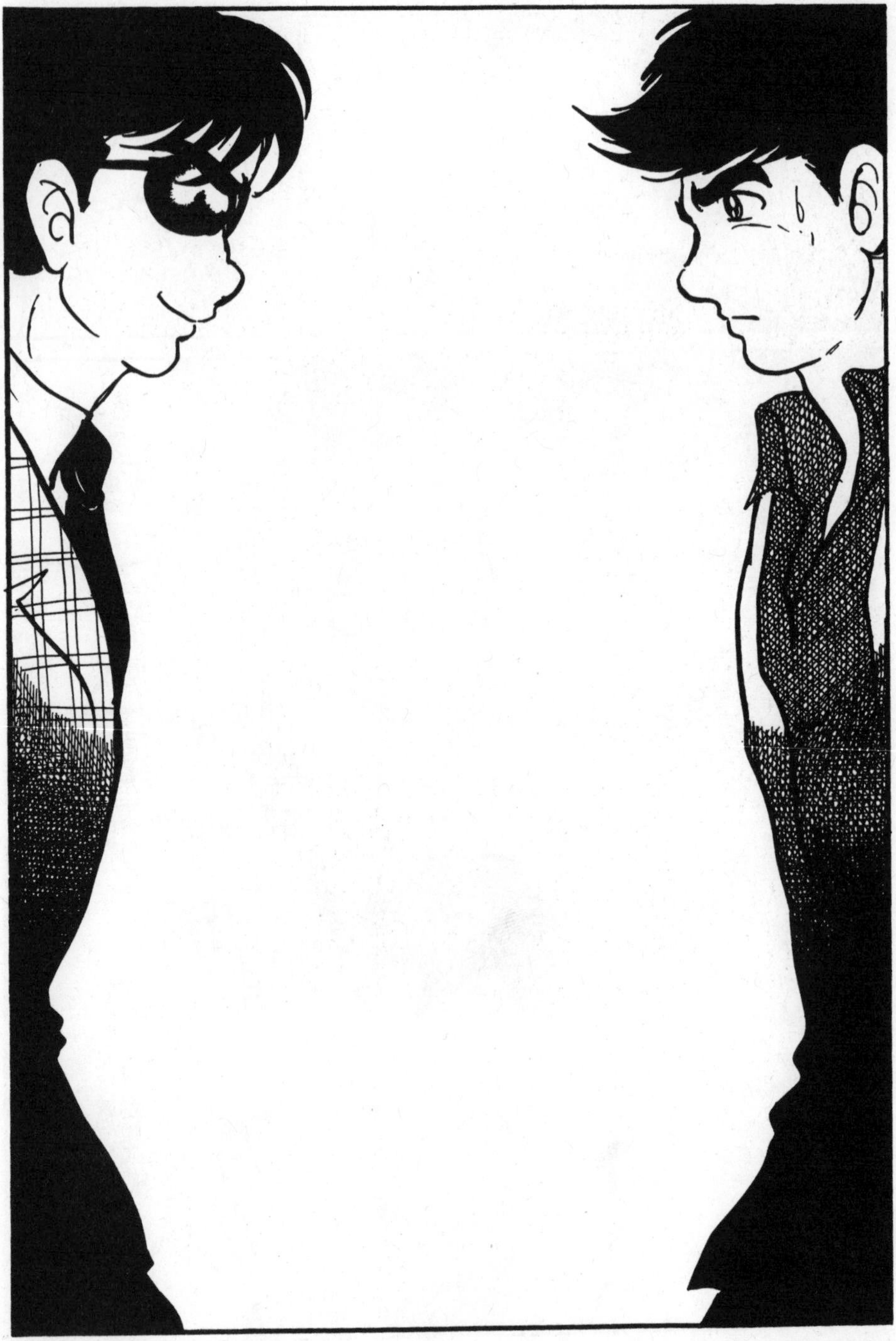

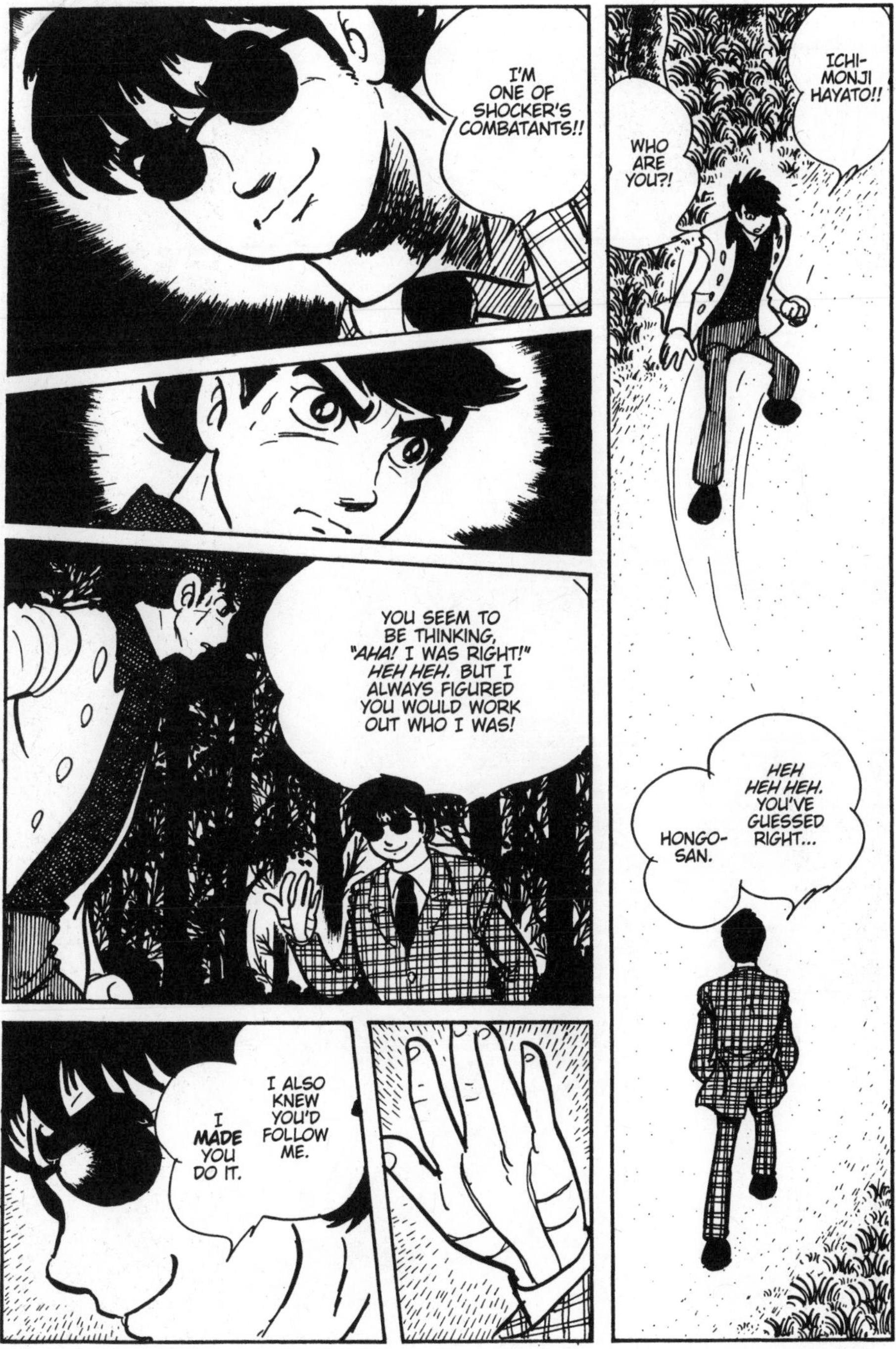
ICHI-MONJI HAYATO!!
WHO ARE YOU?!
HEH HEH HEH. YOU'VE GUESSED RIGHT...
HONGO-SAN.
I'M ONE OF SHOCKER'S COMBATANTS!!
YOU SEEM TO BE THINKING, "AHA! I WAS RIGHT!" HEH HEH. BUT I ALWAYS FIGURED YOU WOULD WORK OUT WHO I WAS!
I ALSO KNEW YOU'D FOLLOW ME.
I MADE YOU DO IT.

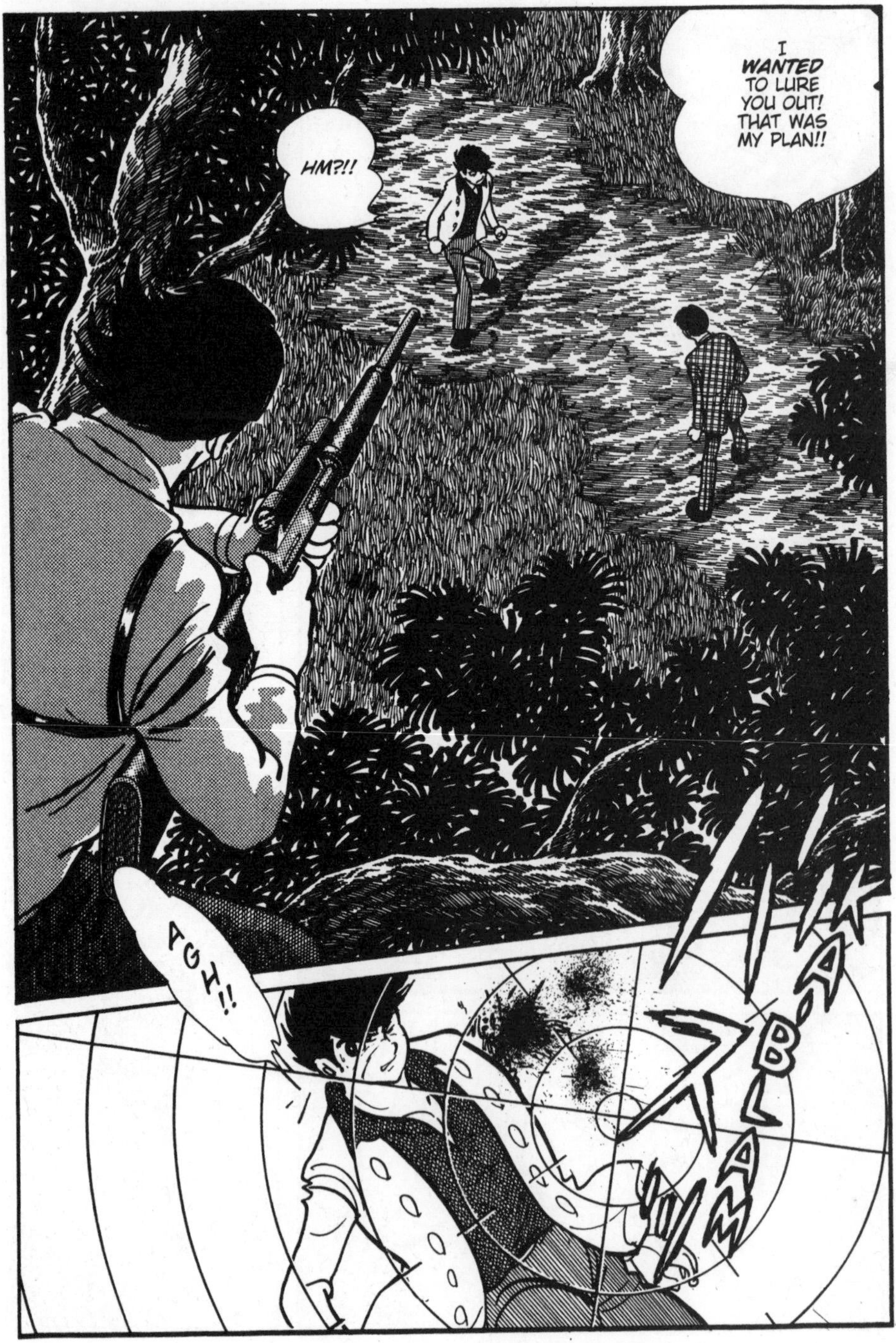
I WANTED TO LURE YOU OUT! THAT WAS MY PLAN!!
HM?!!
KA-BLAM
AGH!!

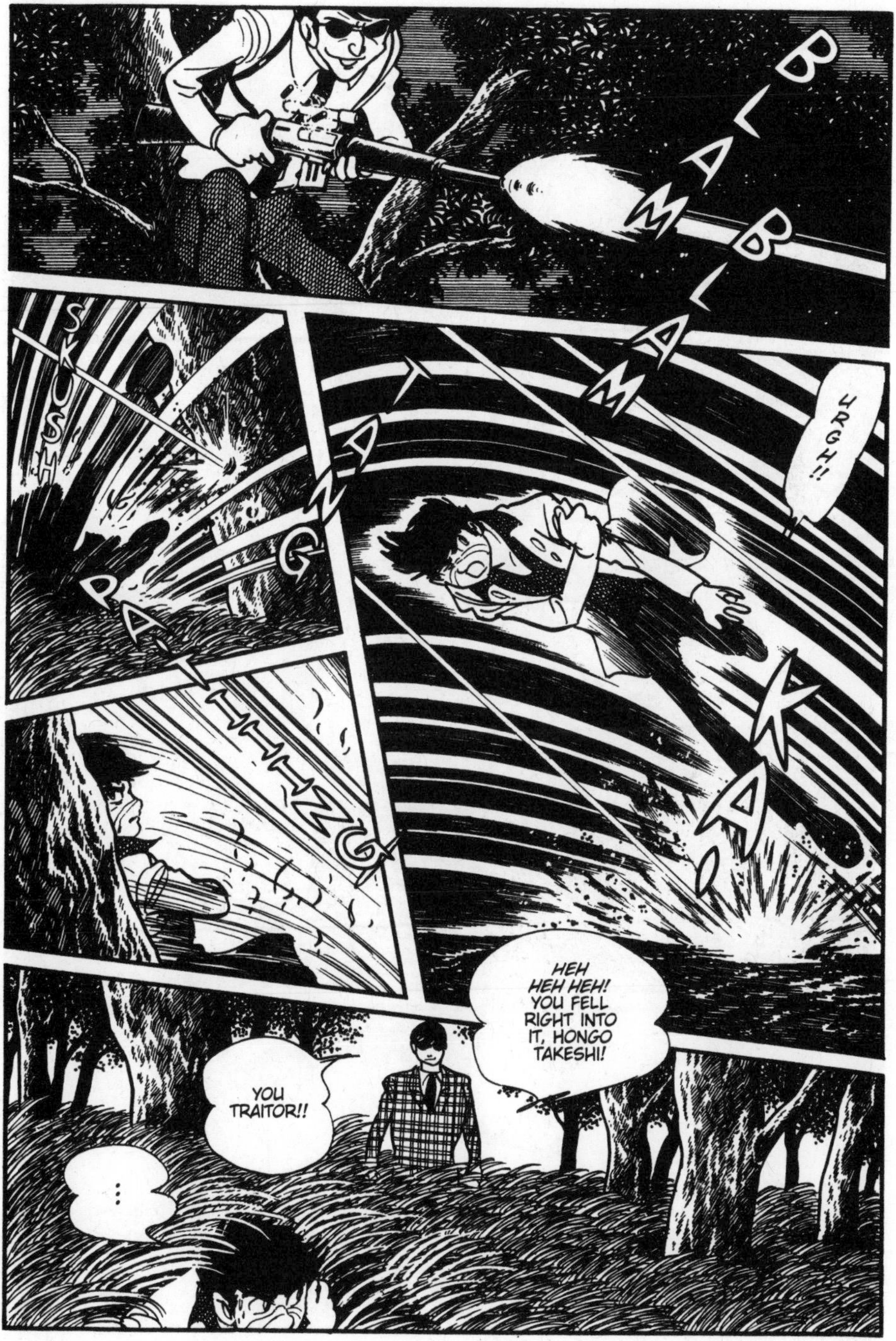
BLAMBLAM
TANG
URGH!!
KA!
SKUSH!
PATIIIING
HEH HEH HEH! YOU FELL RIGHT INTO IT, HONGO TAKESHI!
YOU TRAITOR!!
...

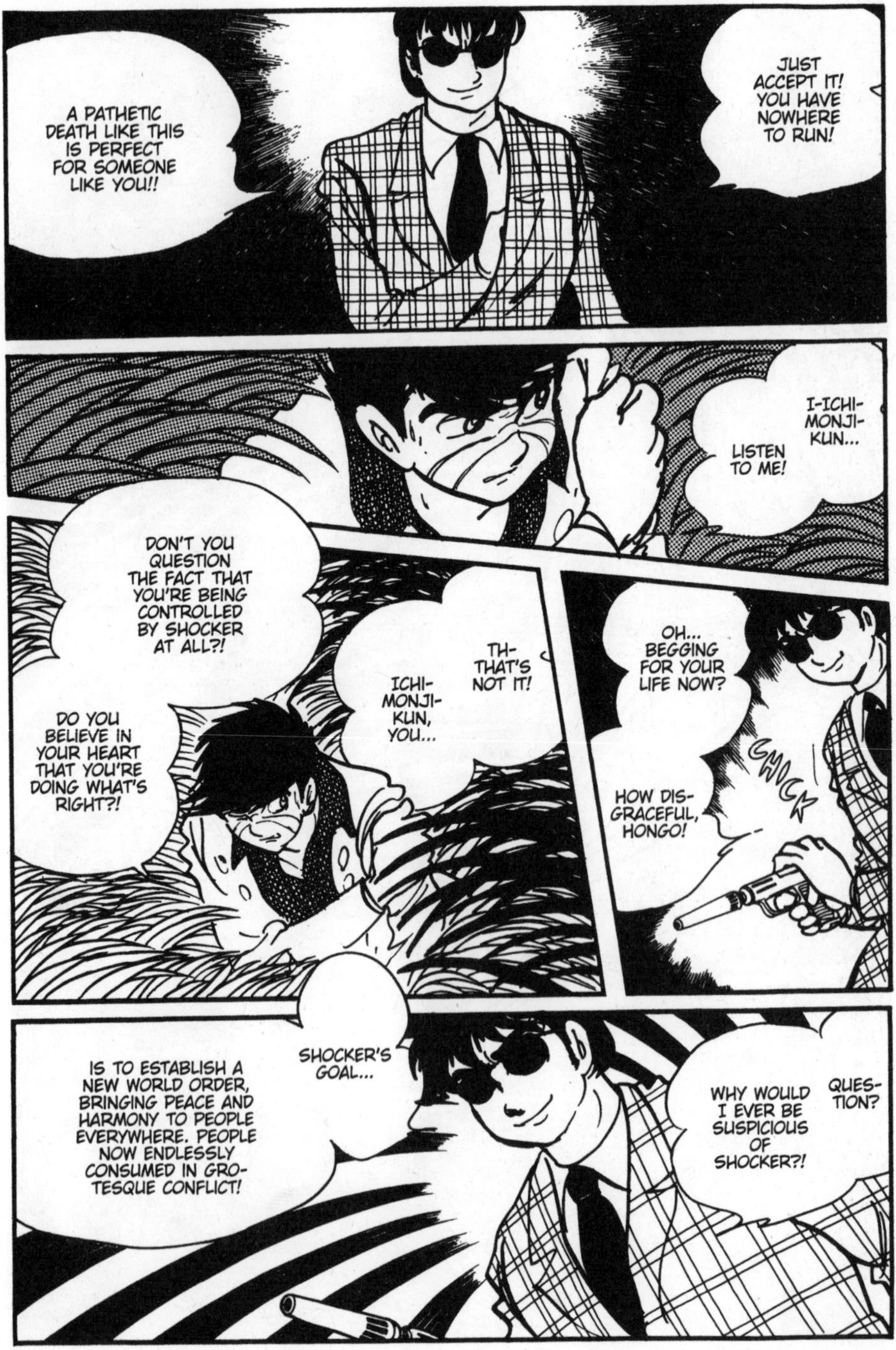
JUST ACCEPT IT! YOU HAVE NOWHERE TO RUN!
A PATHETIC DEATH LIKE THIS IS PERFECT FOR SOMEONE LIKE YOU!!
I-ICHI-MONJI-KUN...
LISTEN TO ME!
OH... BEGGING FOR YOUR LIFE NOW?
CHICK
HOW DIS-GRACEFUL, HONGO!
TH-THAT'S NOT IT!
ICHI-MONJI-KUN, YOU...
DON'T YOU QUESTION THE FACT THAT YOU'RE BEING CONTROLLED BY SHOCKER AT ALL?!
DO YOU BELIEVE IN YOUR HEART THAT YOU'RE DOING WHAT'S RIGHT?!
QUES-TION?
WHY WOULD I EVER BE SUSPICIOUS OF SHOCKER?!
SHOCKER'S GOAL...
IS TO ESTABLISH A NEW WORLD ORDER, BRINGING PEACE AND HARMONY TO PEOPLE EVERYWHERE. PEOPLE NOW ENDLESSLY CONSUMED IN GRO-TESQUE CONFLICT!

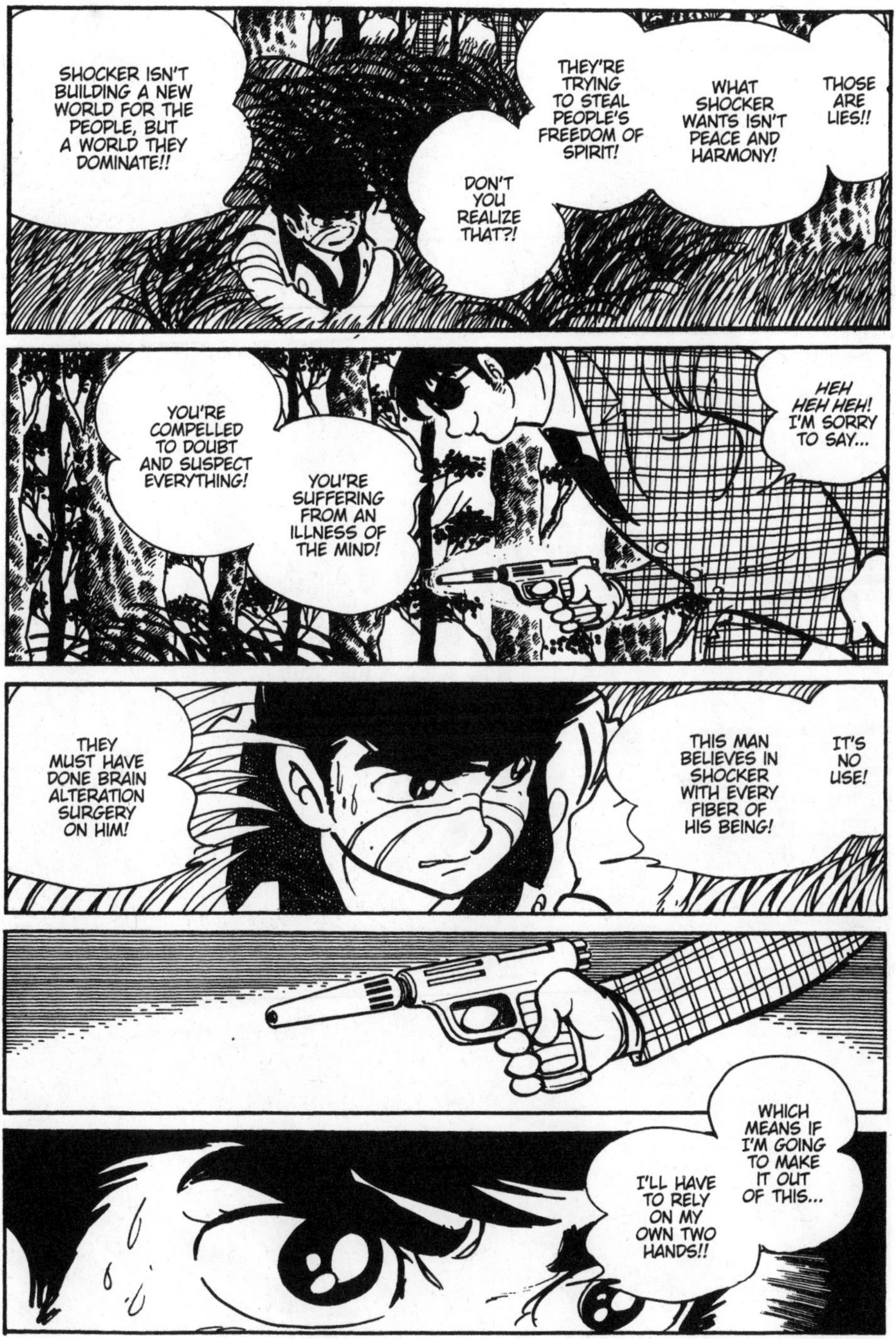
THOSE ARE LIES!!
WHAT SHOCKER WANTS ISN'T PEACE AND HARMONY!
THEY'RE TRYING TO STEAL PEOPLE'S FREEDOM OF SPIRIT!
DON'T YOU REALIZE THAT?!
SHOCKER ISN'T BUILDING A NEW WORLD FOR THE PEOPLE, BUT A WORLD THEY DOMINATE!!
HEH HEH HEH! I'M SORRY TO SAY...
YOU'RE SUFFERING FROM AN ILLNESS OF THE MIND!
YOU'RE COMPELLED TO DOUBT AND SUSPECT EVERYTHING!
IT'S NO USE!
THIS MAN BELIEVES IN SHOCKER WITH EVERY FIBER OF HIS BEING!
THEY MUST HAVE DONE BRAIN ALTERATION SURGERY ON HIM!
WHICH MEANS IF I'M GOING TO MAKE IT OUT OF THIS...
I'LL HAVE TO RELY ON MY OWN TWO HANDS!!

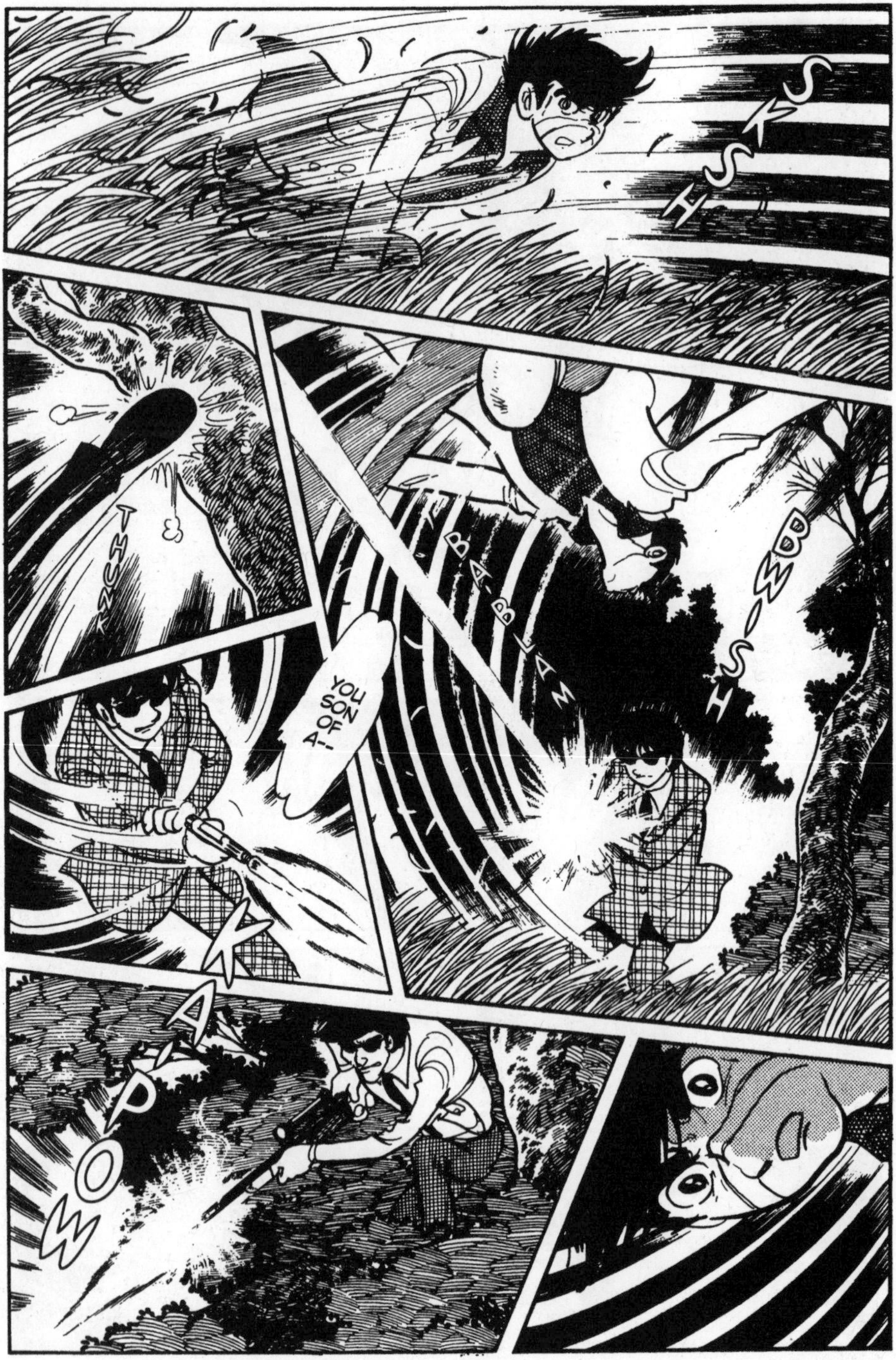
SKSH
BWISH
BA-BLAM
THUNK
YOU SON OF A--
KAPOW

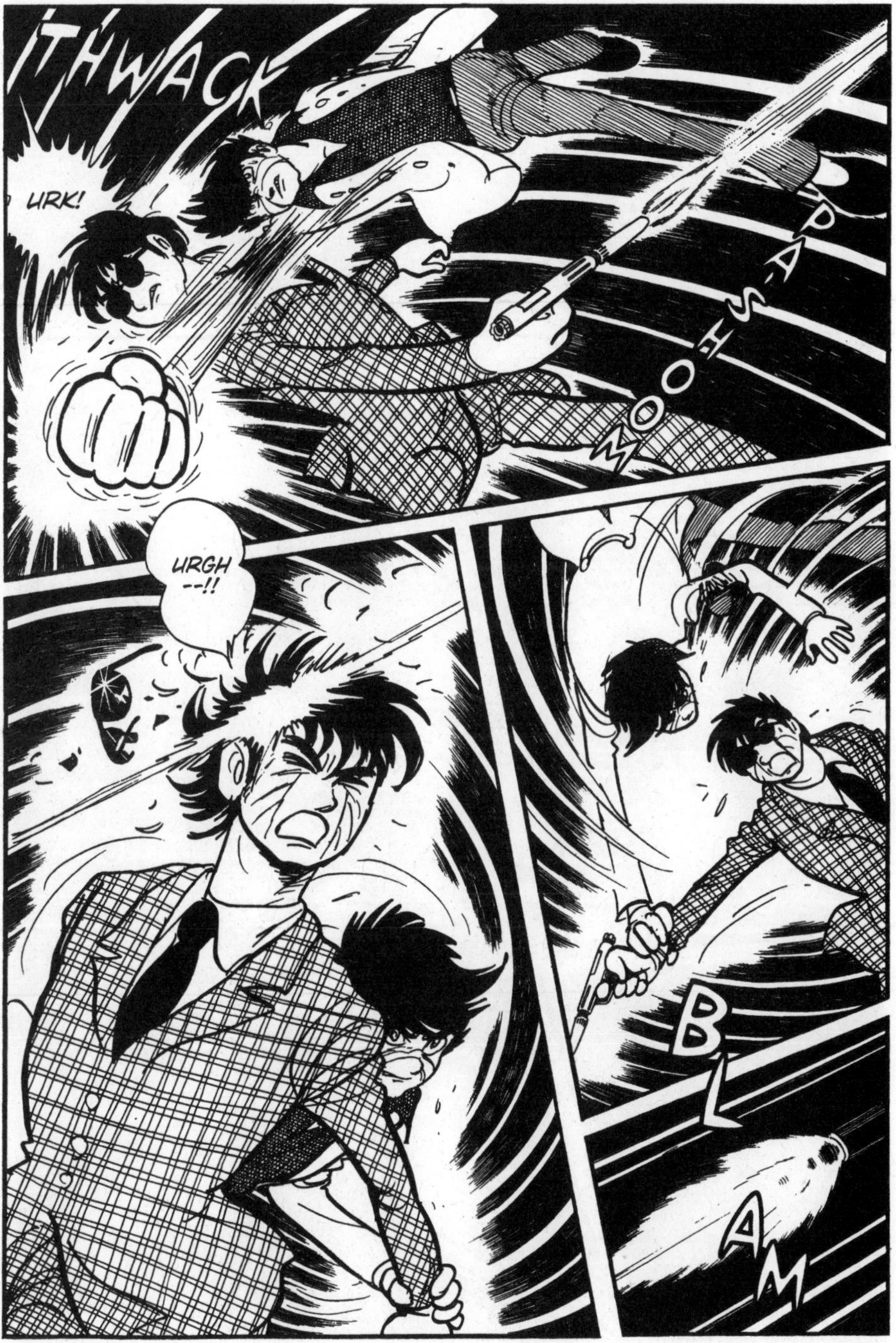
THWACK
URK!
PA-SHOOM
BLAM
URGH
--!!

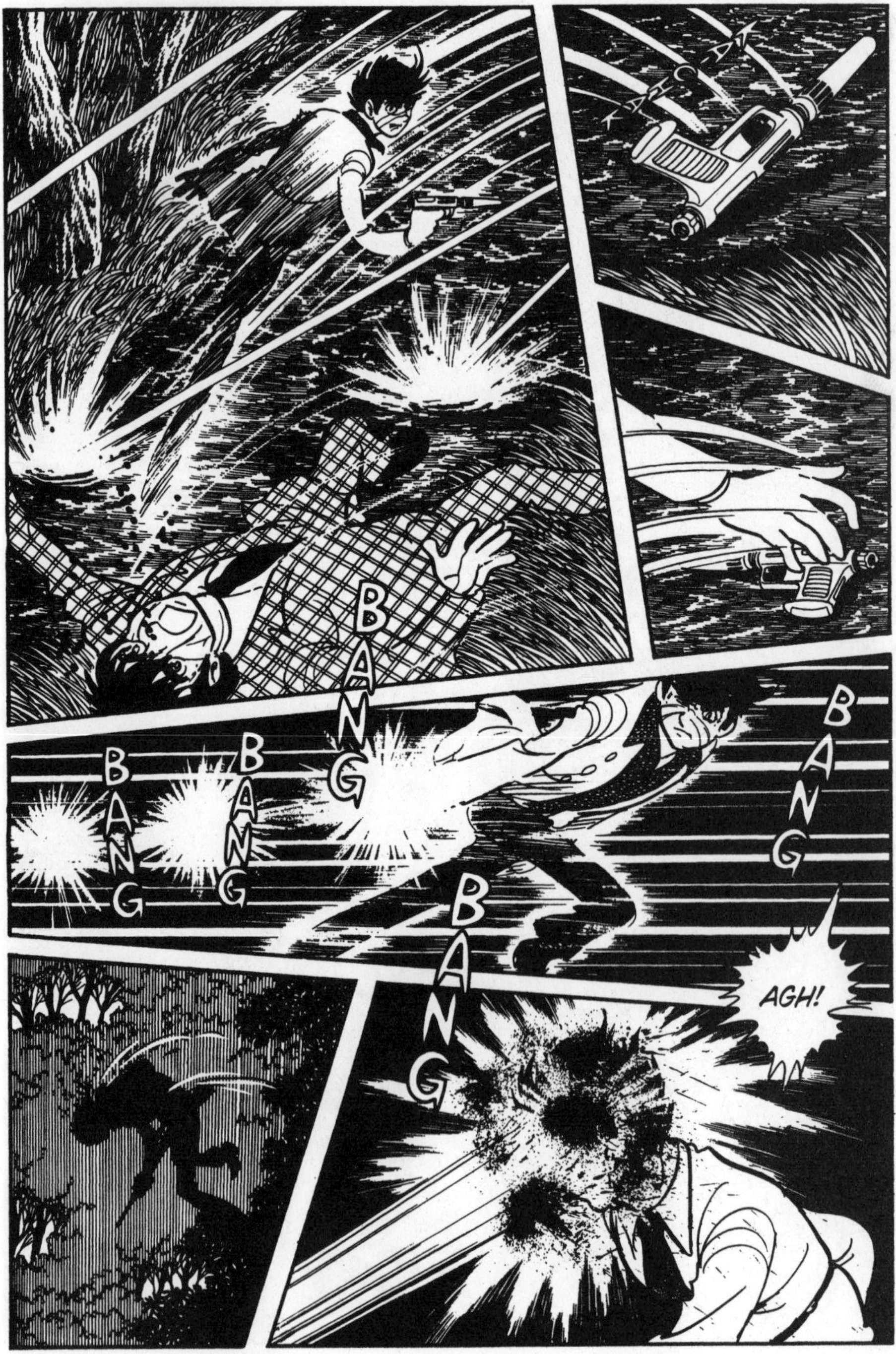
KACHAK
BANG
BANG
BANG
BANG
BANG
AGH!

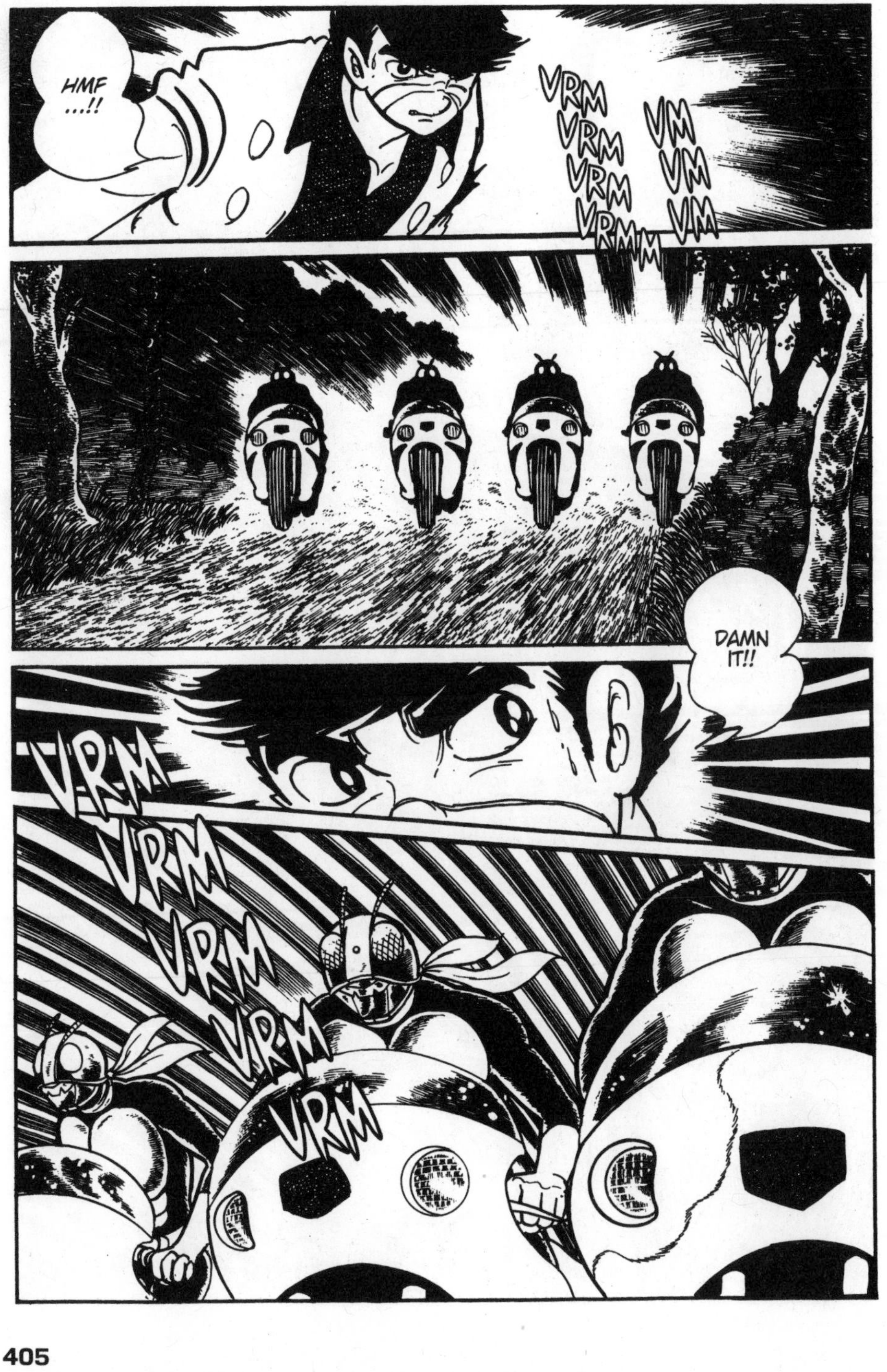
VRM VRM VRM VRMM
VM VM VM VM
HMF ...!!
DAMN IT!!
VRM VRM VRM VRM VRM

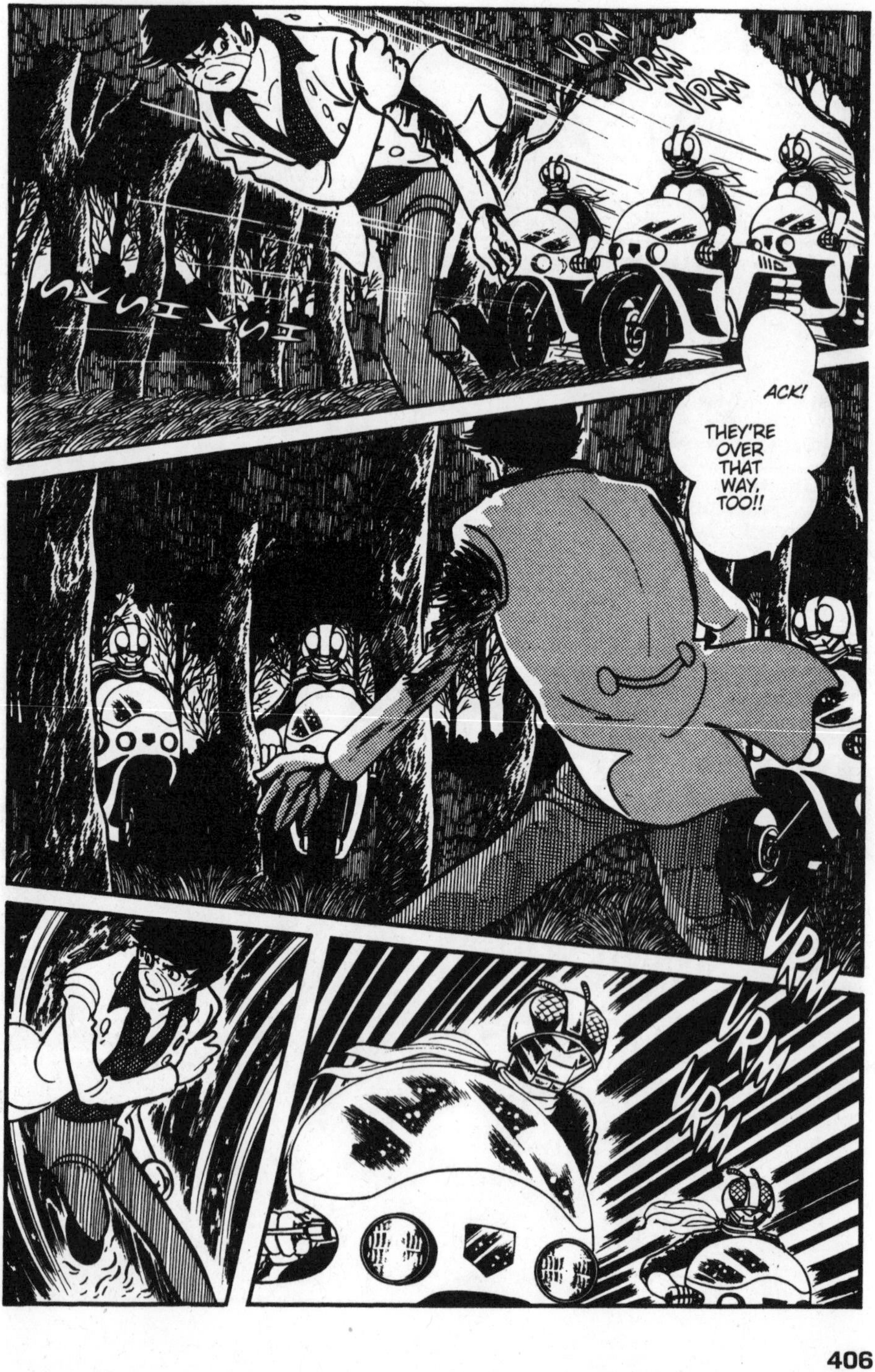
VRM
VRM
VRM
ACK!
THEY'RE OVER THAT WAY, TOO!!
VRM
VRM
VRM
VRM

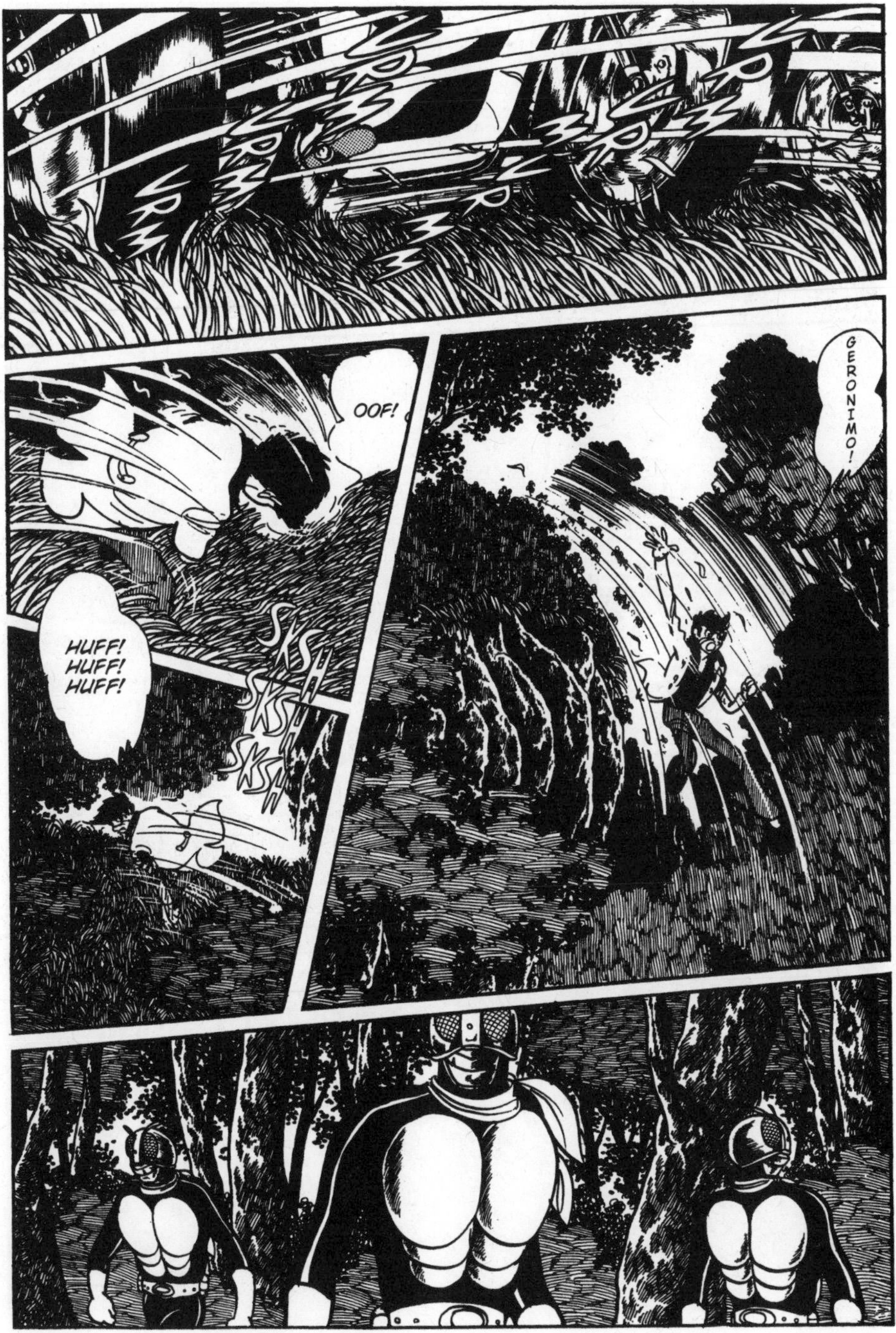
VRM
VRMMM
VRMM
VRMM
VRM
GERONIMO!
OOF!
HUFF! HUFF! HUFF!
SKSH SKSH SKSH

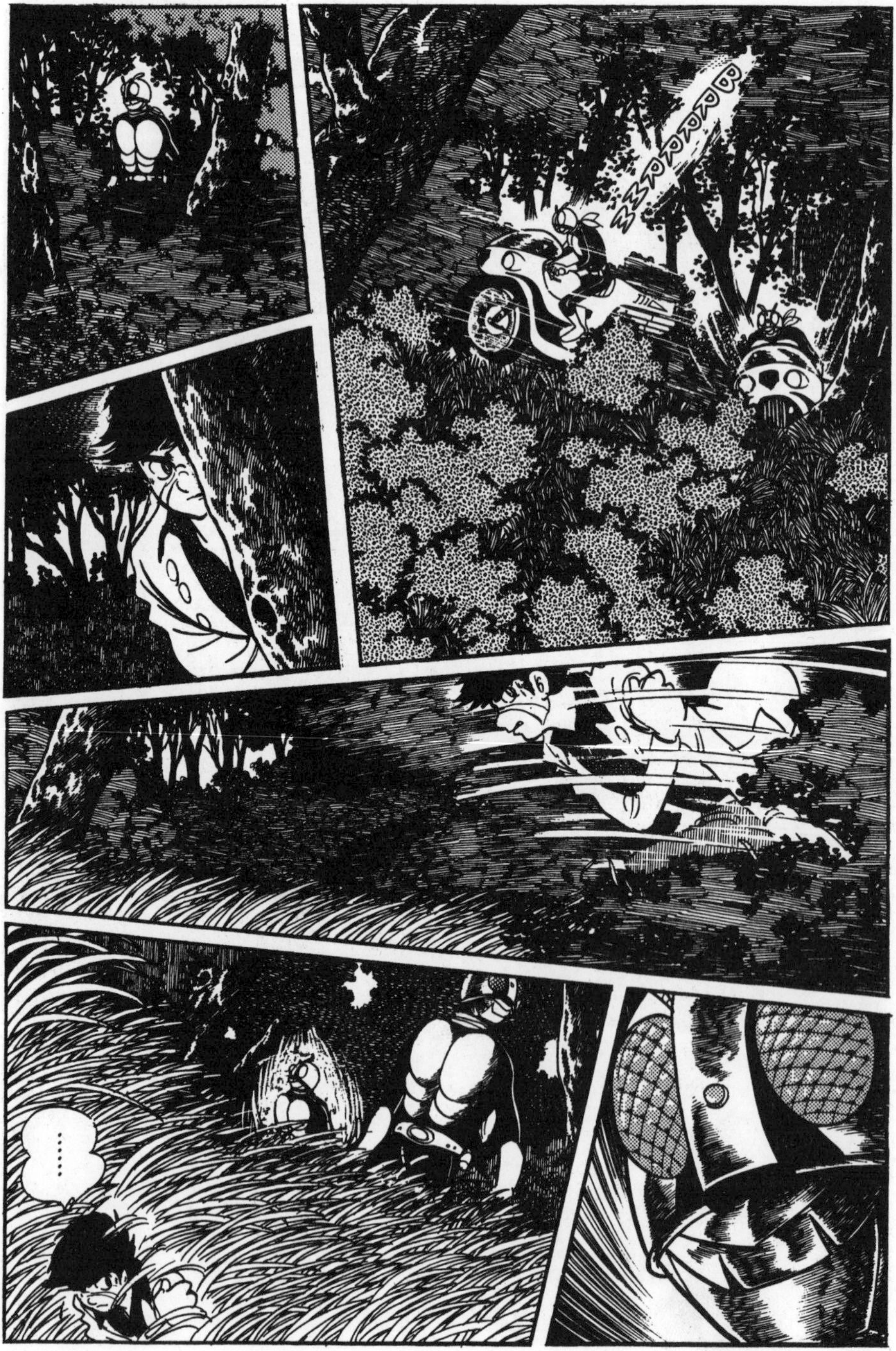
BRRRRMM
……

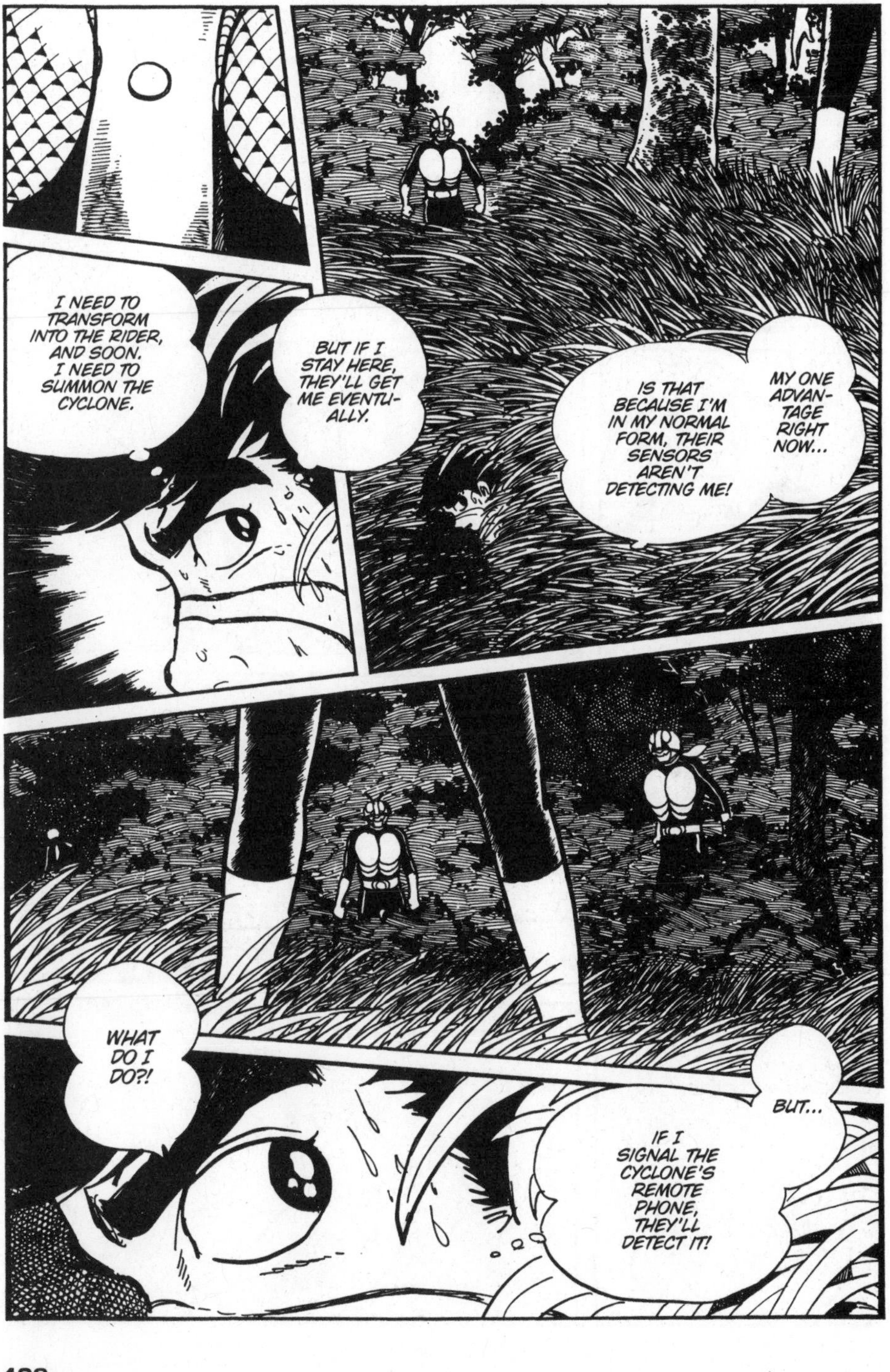
MY ONE ADVANTAGE RIGHT NOW...
IS THAT BECAUSE I'M IN MY NORMAL FORM, THEIR SENSORS AREN'T DETECTING ME!
BUT IF I STAY HERE, THEY'LL GET ME EVENTUALLY.
I NEED TO TRANSFORM INTO THE RIDER, AND SOON. I NEED TO SUMMON THE CYCLONE.
BUT...
IF I SIGNAL THE CYCLONE'S REMOTE PHONE, THEY'LL DETECT IT!
WHAT DO I DO?!

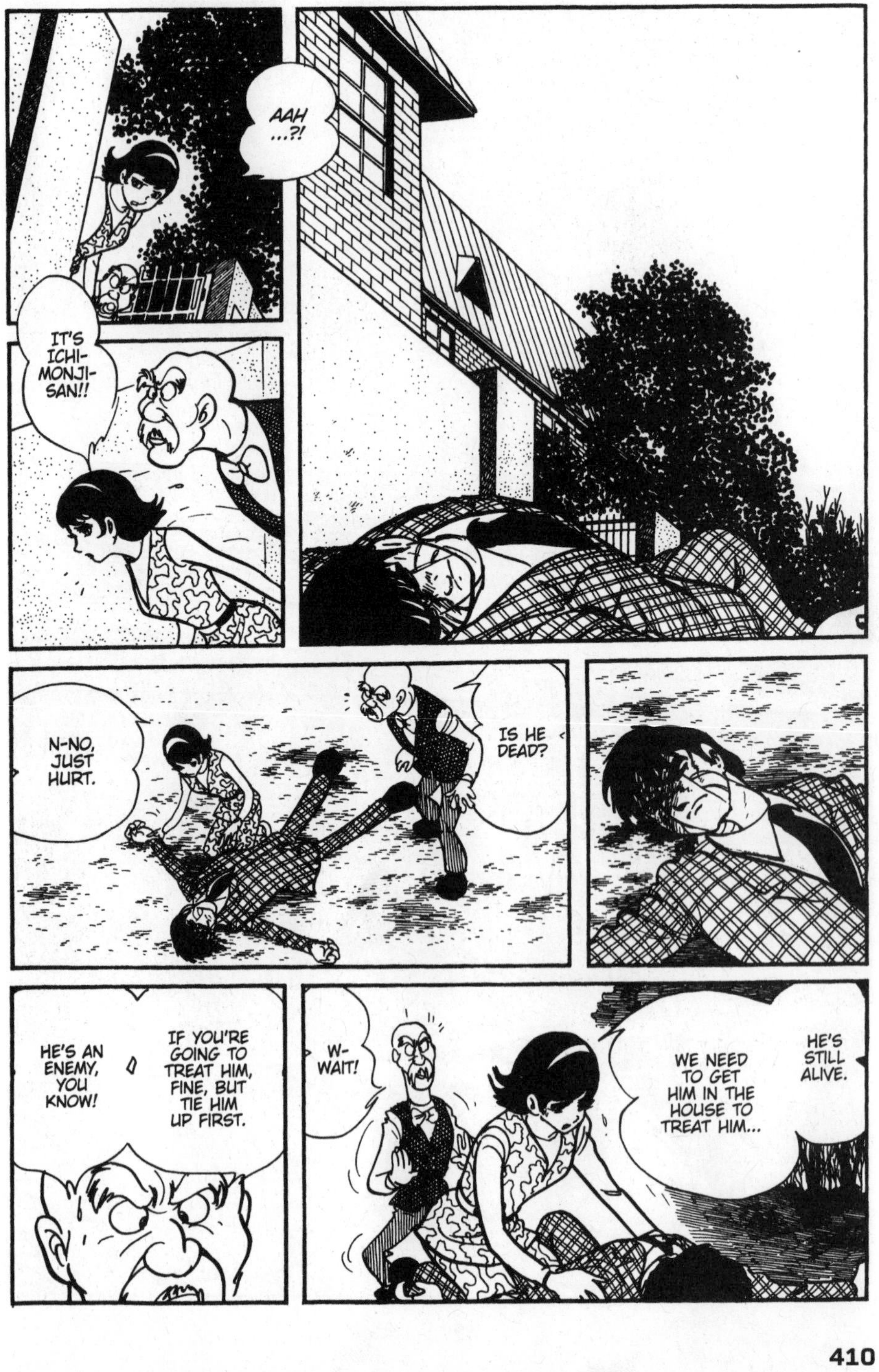
AAH ...?!
IT'S ICHIMONJI-SAN!!
IS HE DEAD?
N-NO, JUST HURT.
HE'S STILL ALIVE.
WE NEED TO GET HIM IN THE HOUSE TO TREAT HIM...
W-WAIT!
IF YOU'RE GOING TO TREAT HIM, FINE, BUT TIE HIM UP FIRST.
HE'S AN ENEMY, YOU KNOW!

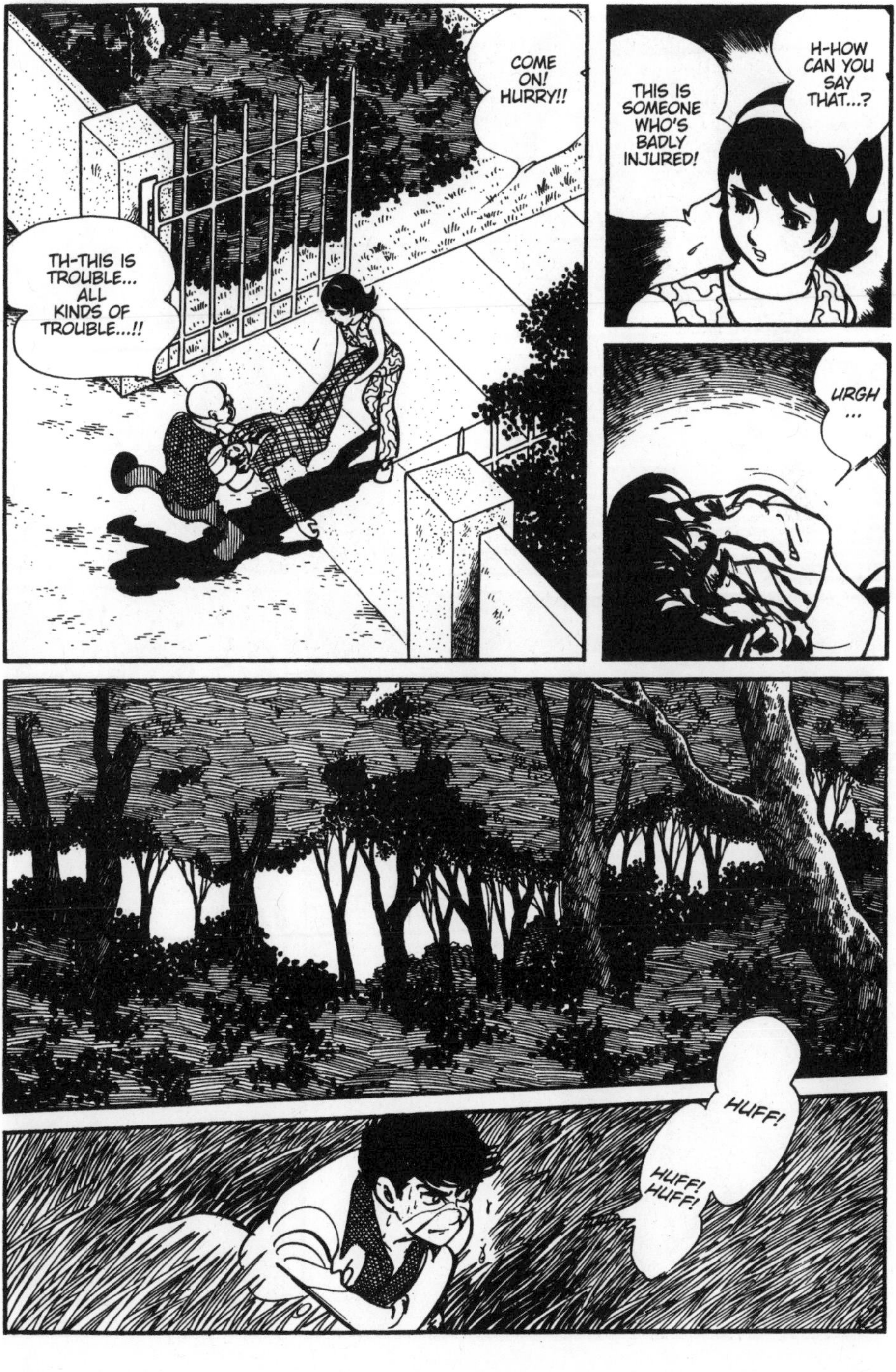
H-HOW CAN YOU SAY THAT...?
THIS IS SOMEONE WHO'S BADLY INJURED!
URGH ...
COME ON! HURRY!!
TH-THIS IS TROUBLE... ALL KINDS OF TROUBLE...!!
HUFF!
HUFF! HUFF!

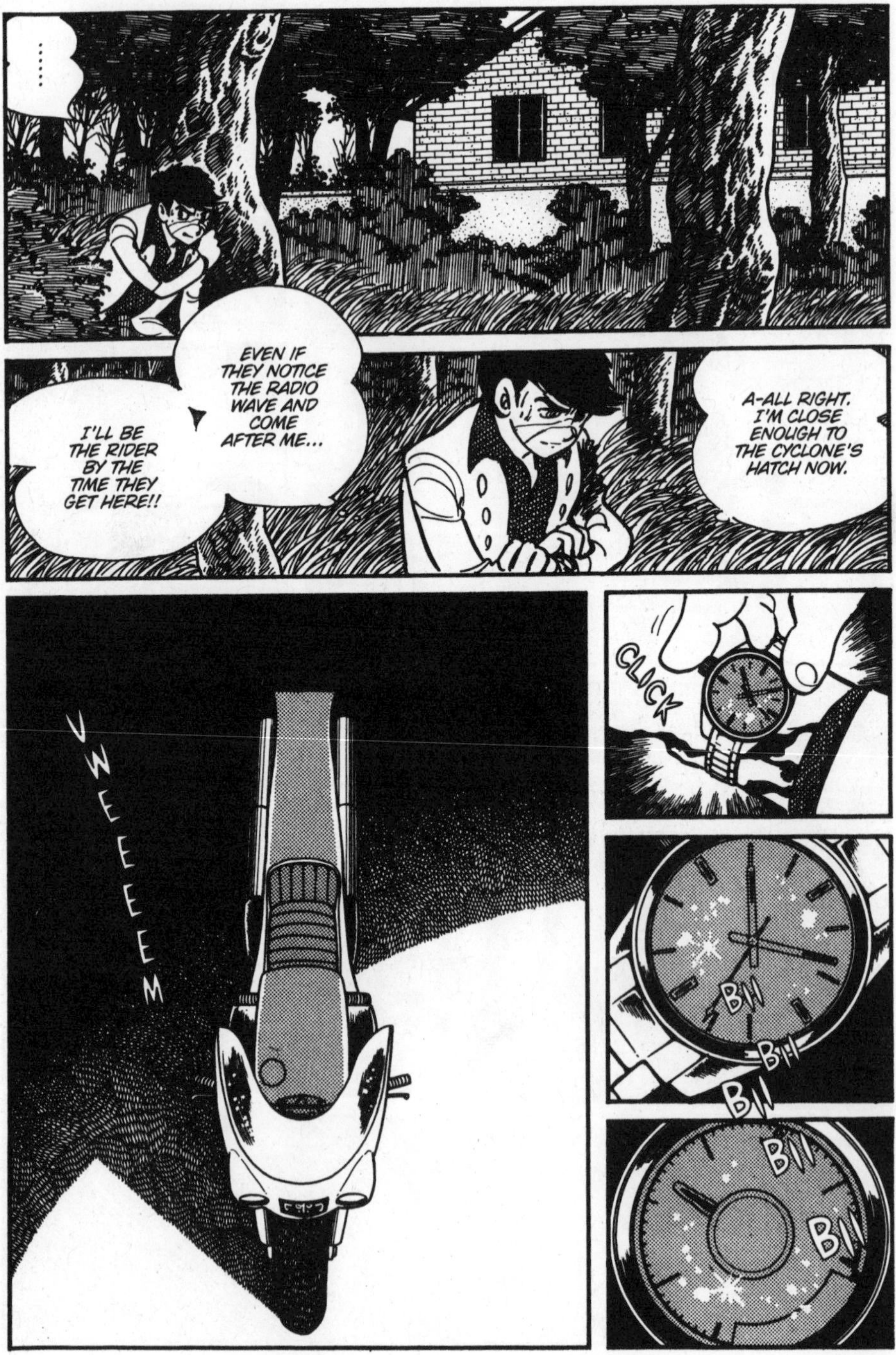
……
A-ALL RIGHT. I'M CLOSE ENOUGH TO THE CYCLONE'S HATCH NOW.
EVEN IF THEY NOTICE THE RADIO WAVE AND COME AFTER ME...
I'LL BE THE RIDER BY THE TIME THEY GET HERE!!
CLICK
BI
BI
BI
BI
BI
VWEEEEM

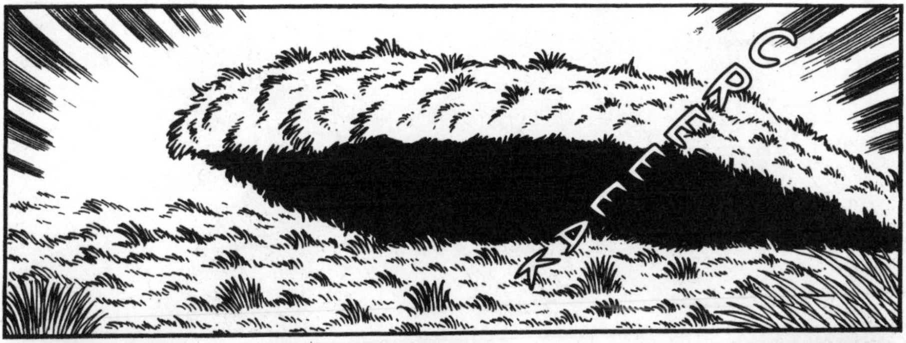
CREEEAK
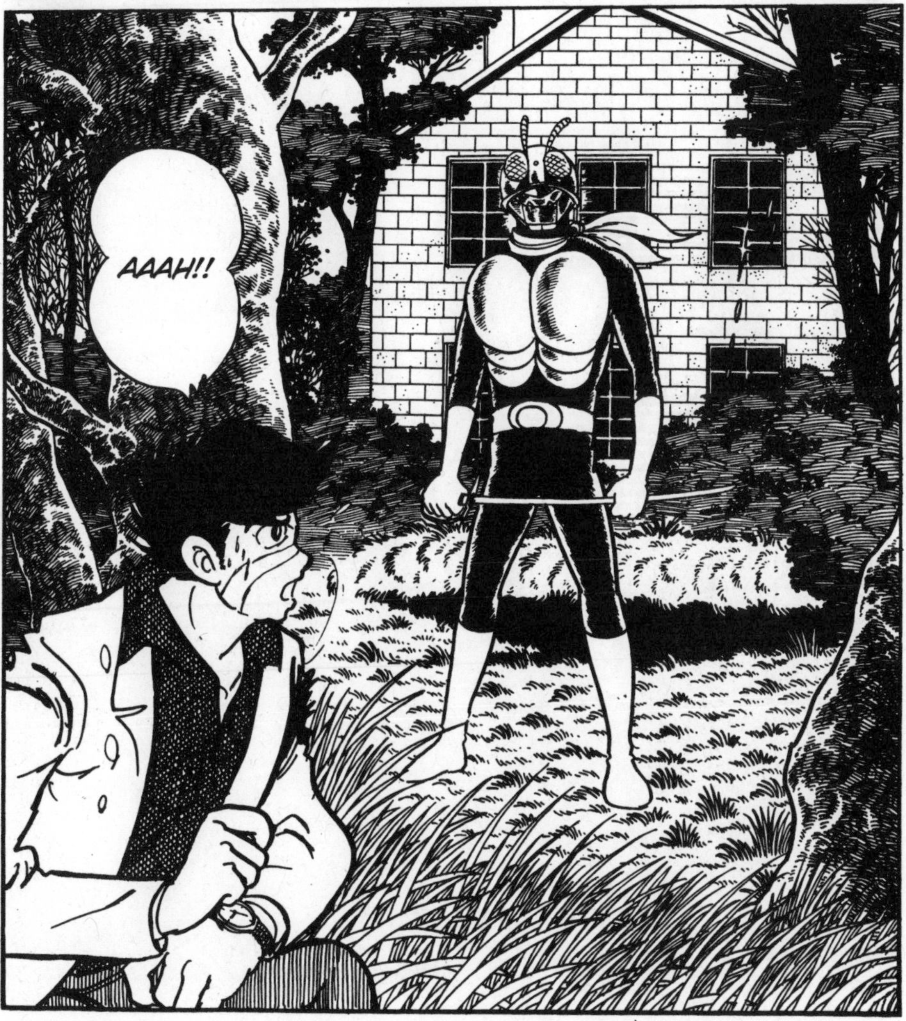
AAAH!!

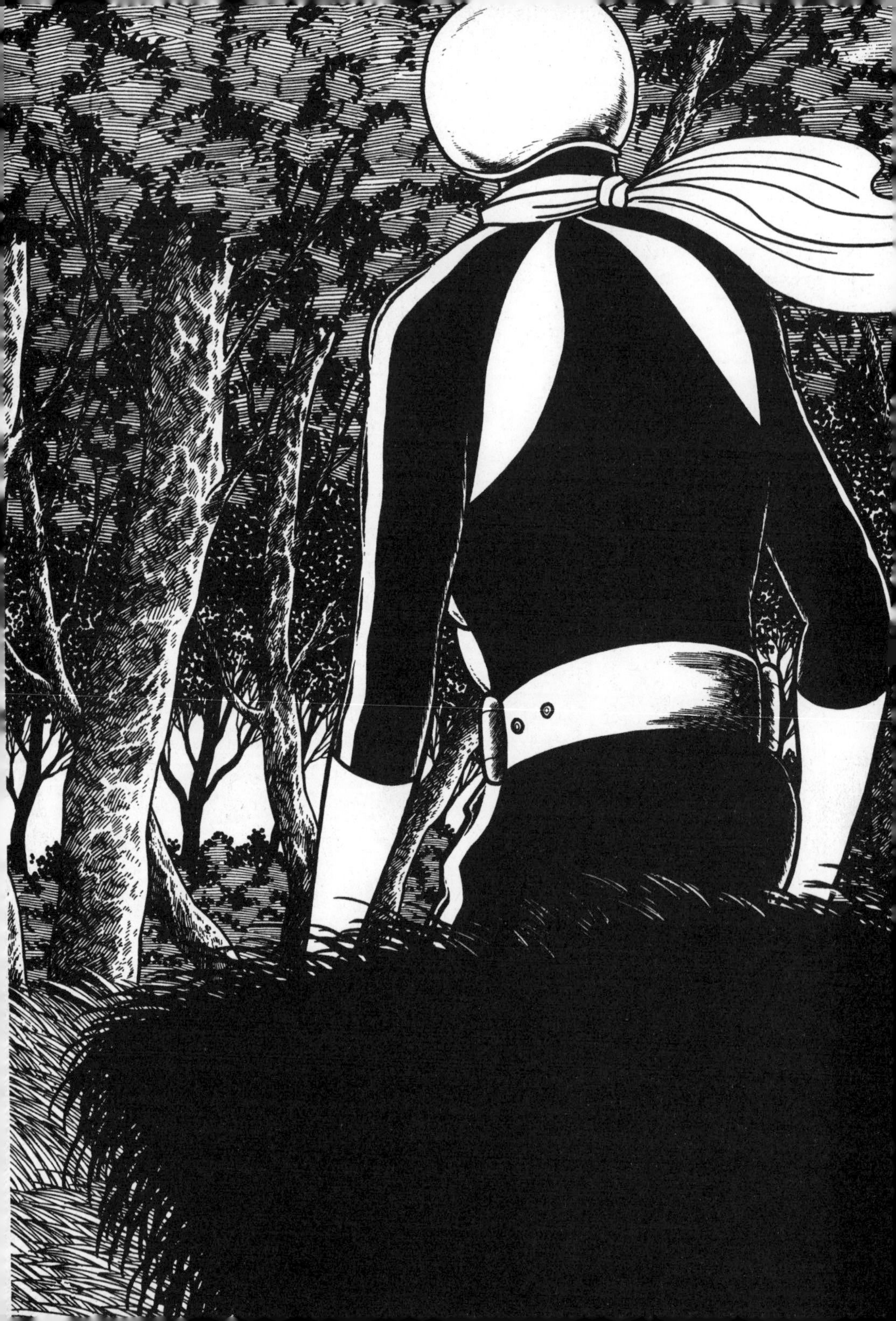

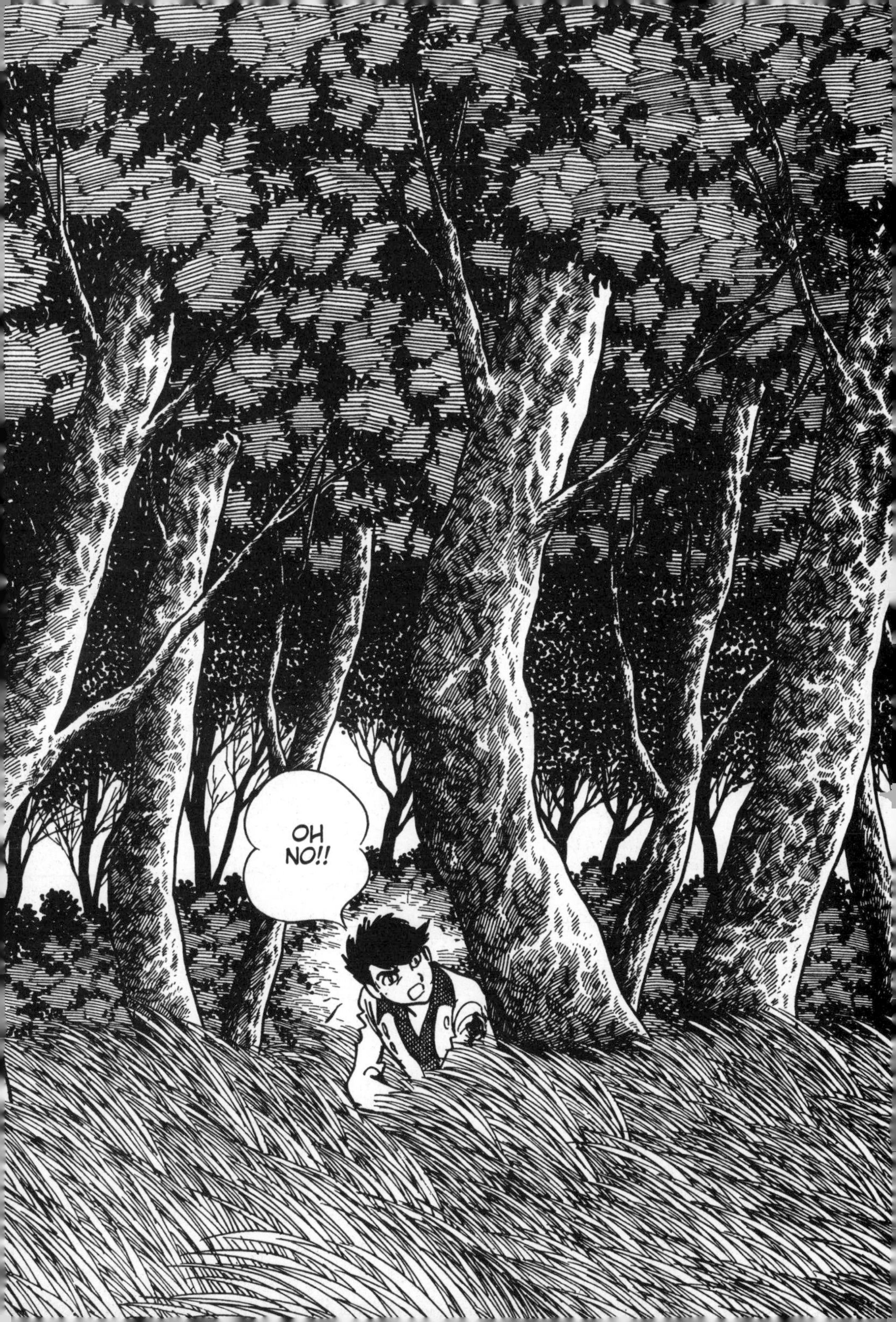
OH NO!!

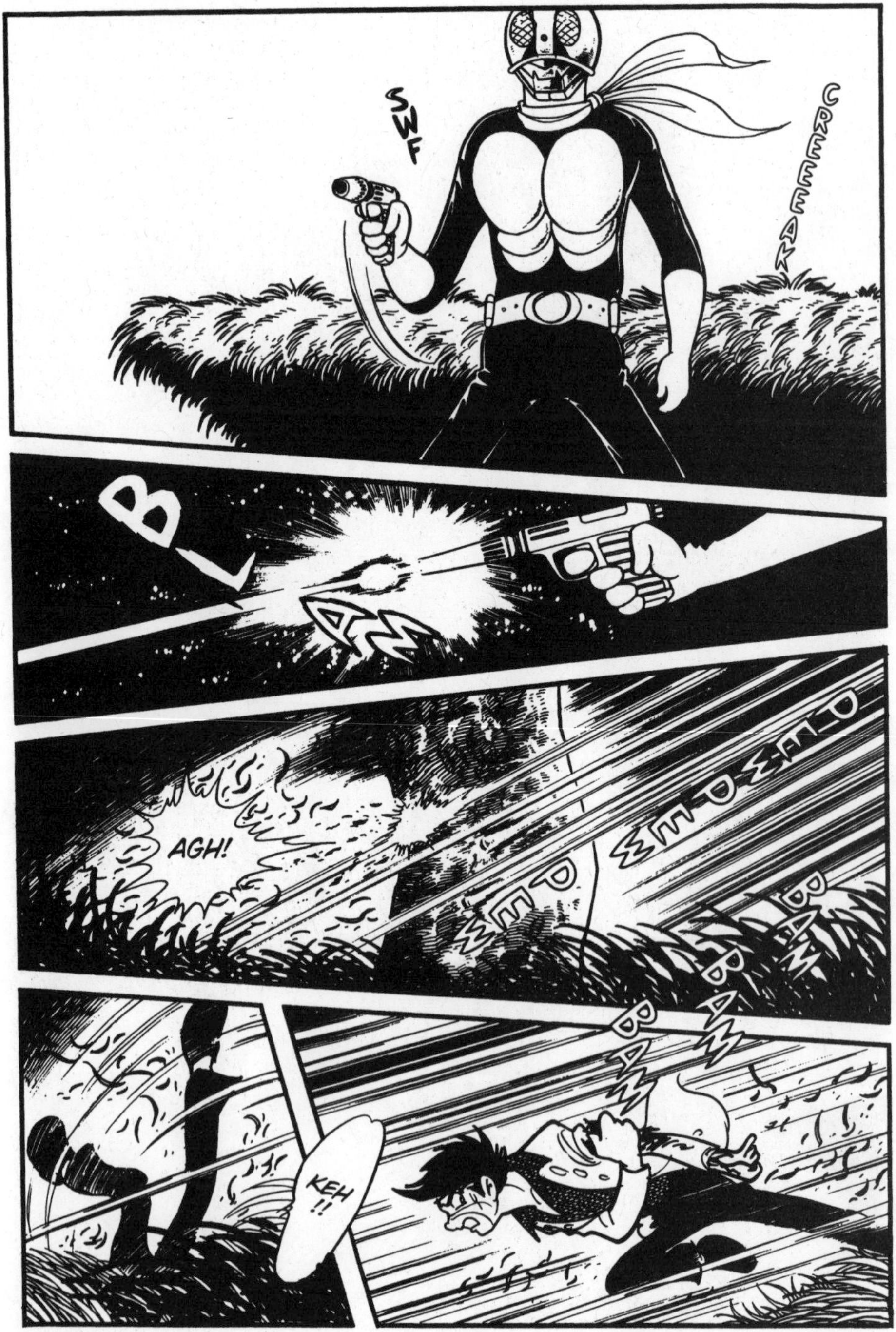
CREEEAK
SWF
BLAM
PEW PEW
PEW
AGH!
BAM BAM BAM
KEH!!

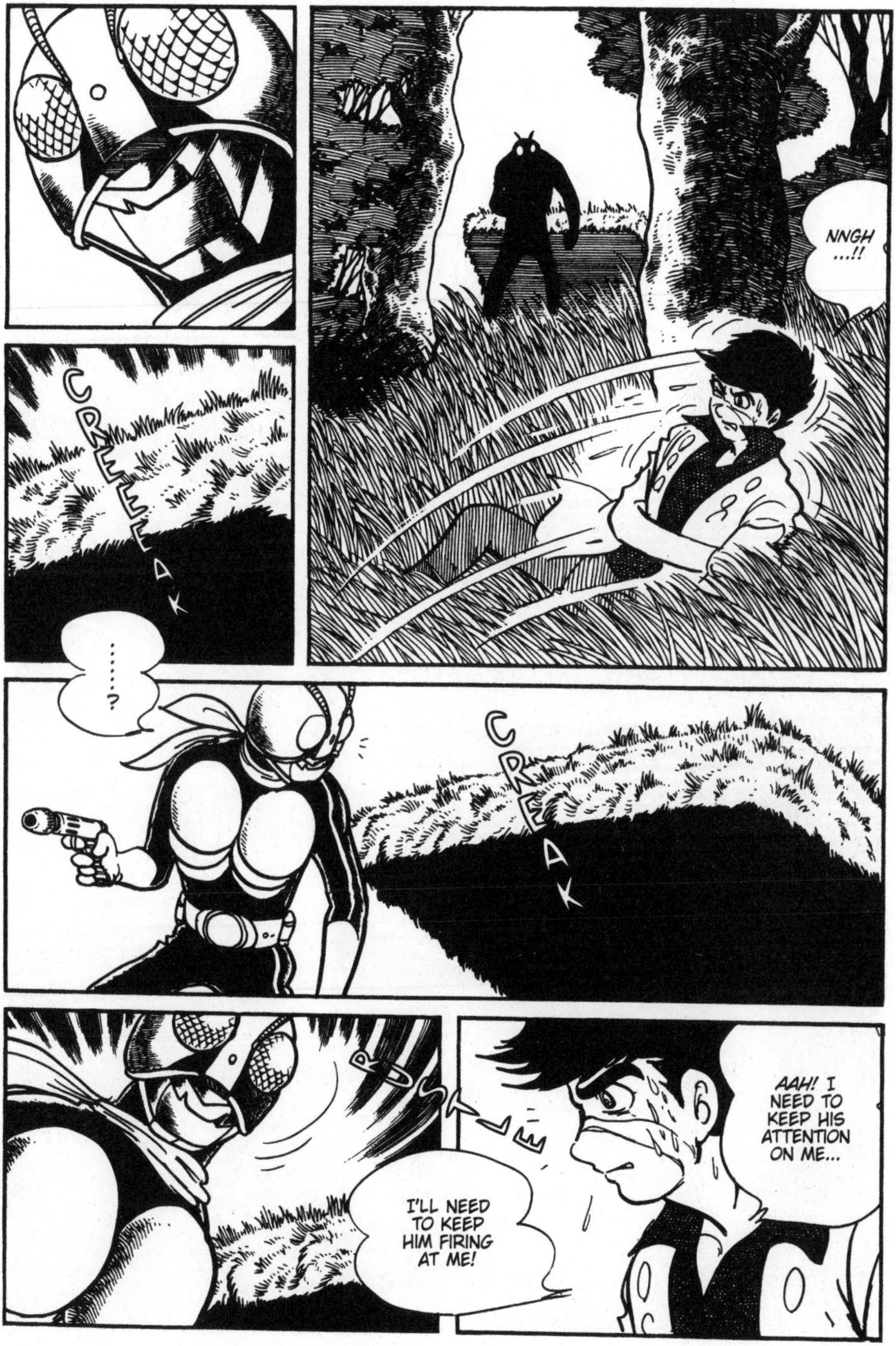
NNGH ...!!
CREEEAK
......?
CREAK
AAH! I NEED TO KEEP HIS ATTENTION ON ME...
I'LL NEED TO KEEP HIM FIRING AT ME!
RUSTLE

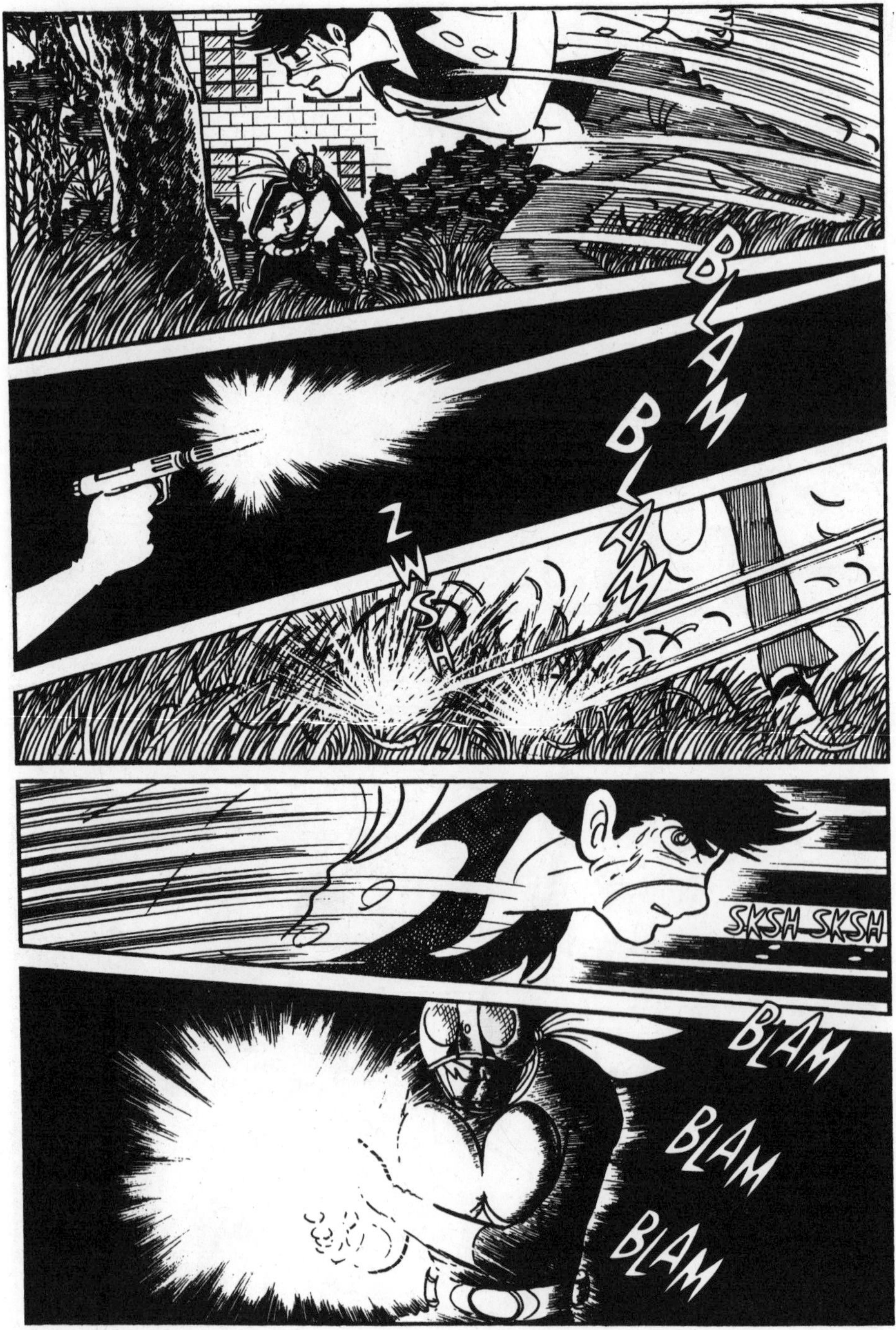
BLAM
BLAM
ZWSH
SKSH SKSH
BLAM
BLAM
BLAM

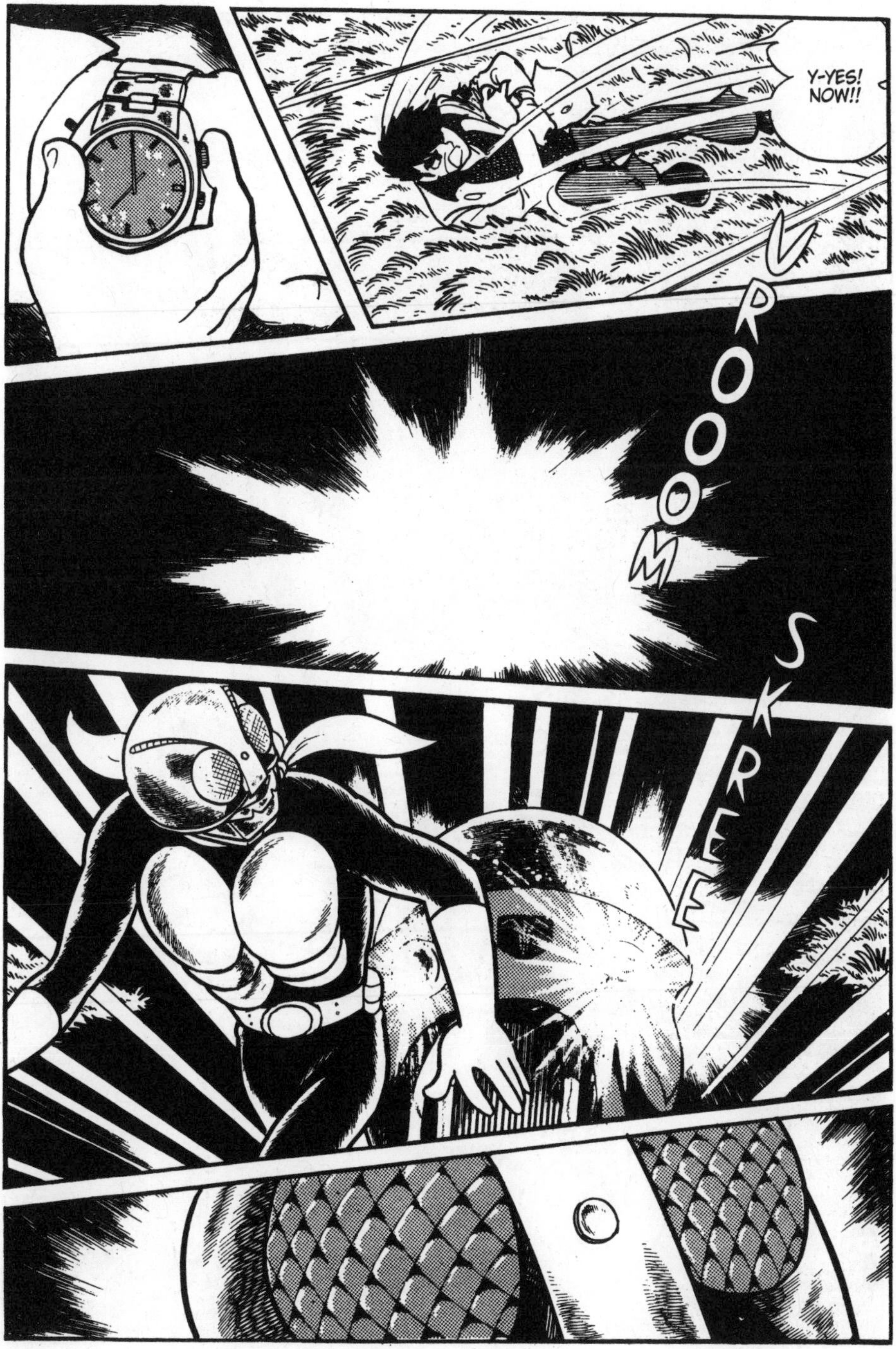
Y-YES! NOW!!
VROOOOM
SKREE

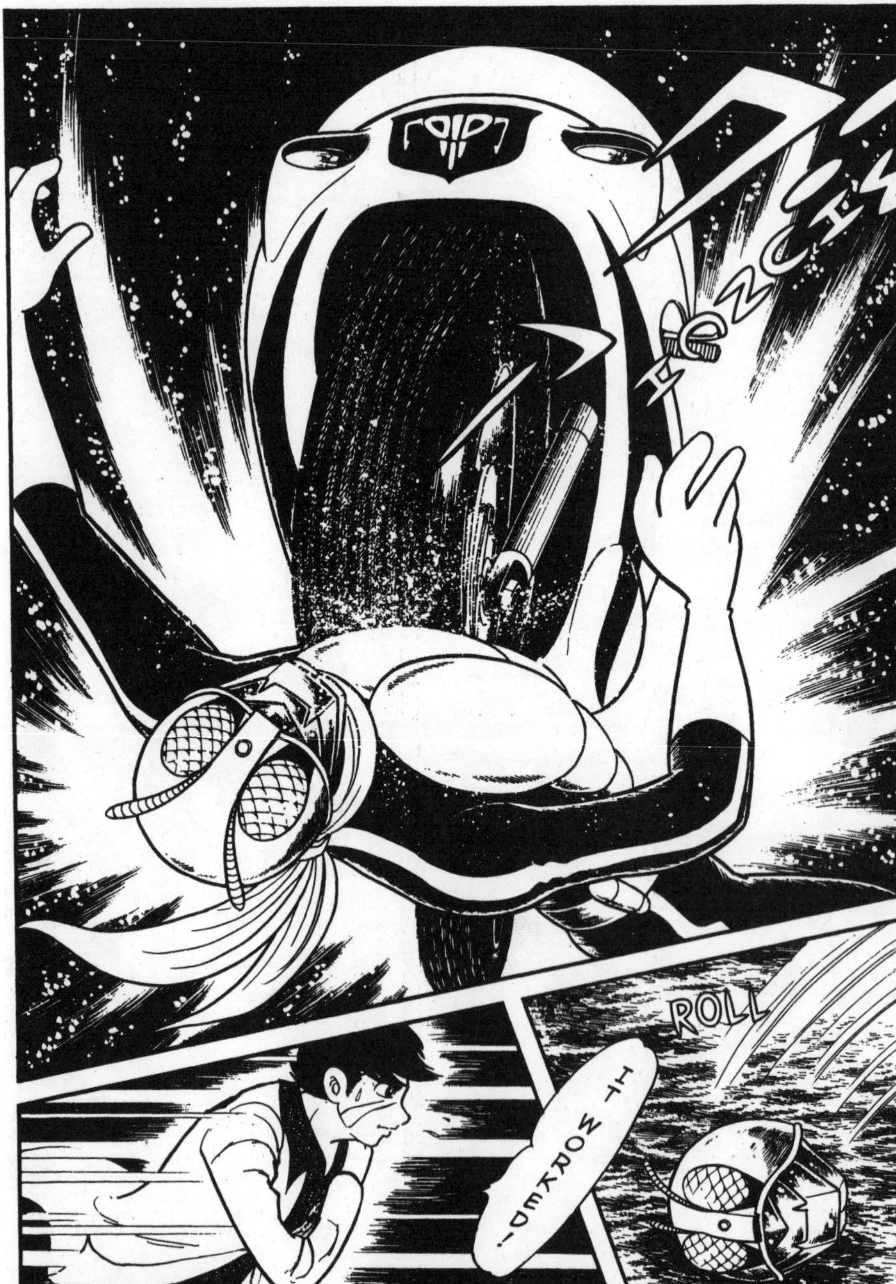
ROLL
IT WORKED!

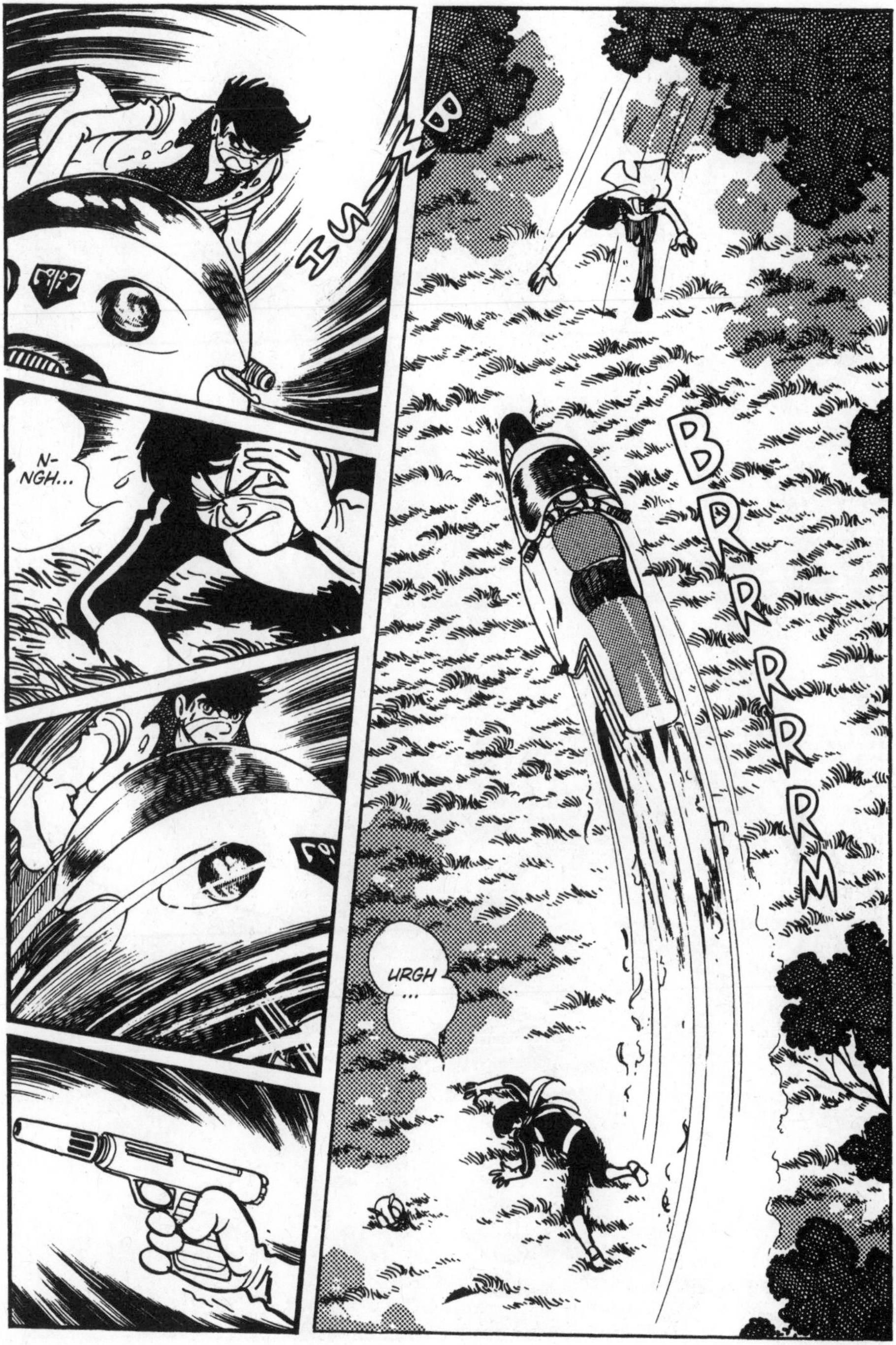
BRRRRRRM
URGH ...
BWSSH
N-NGH...

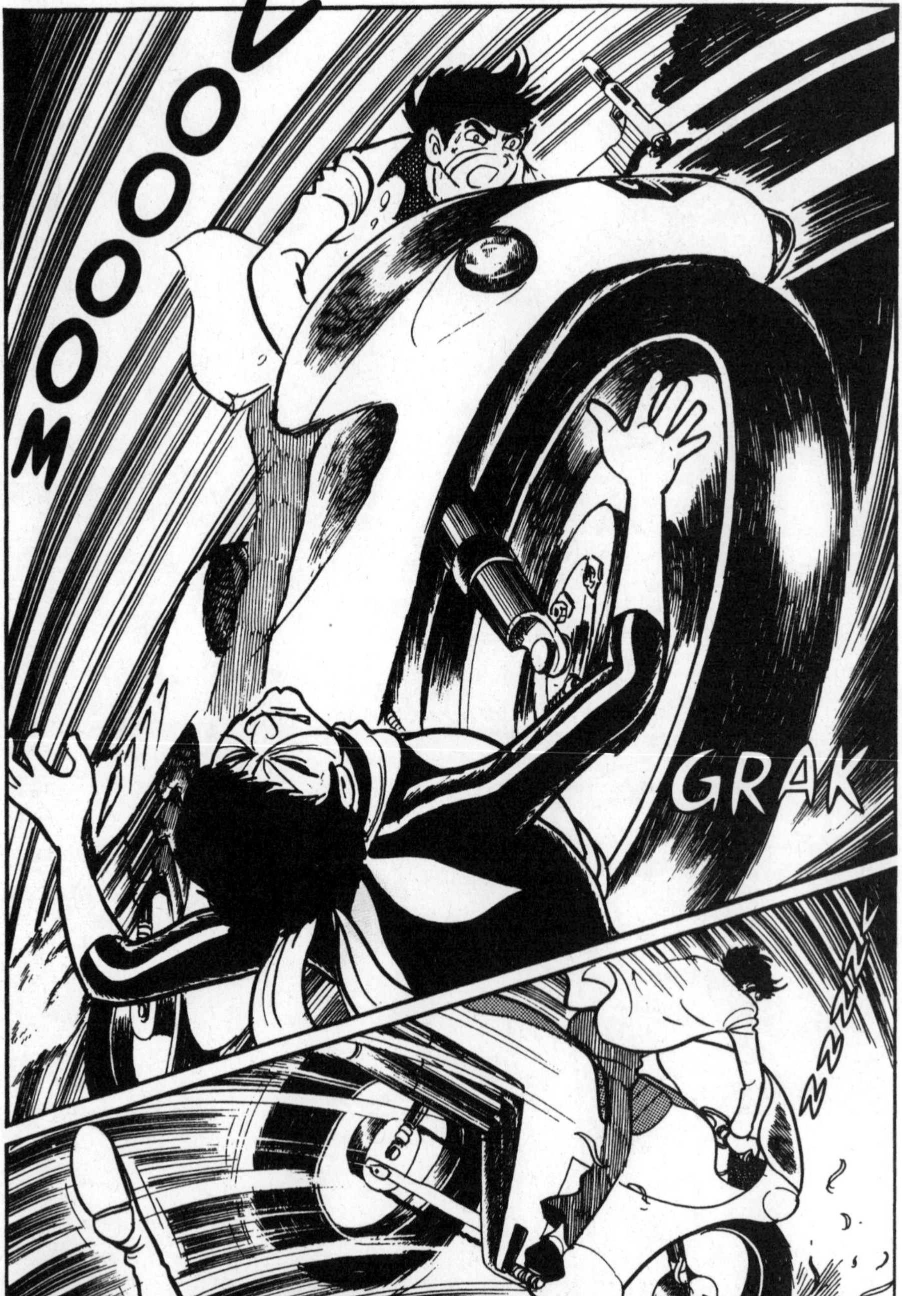
VOOOOM
GRAK

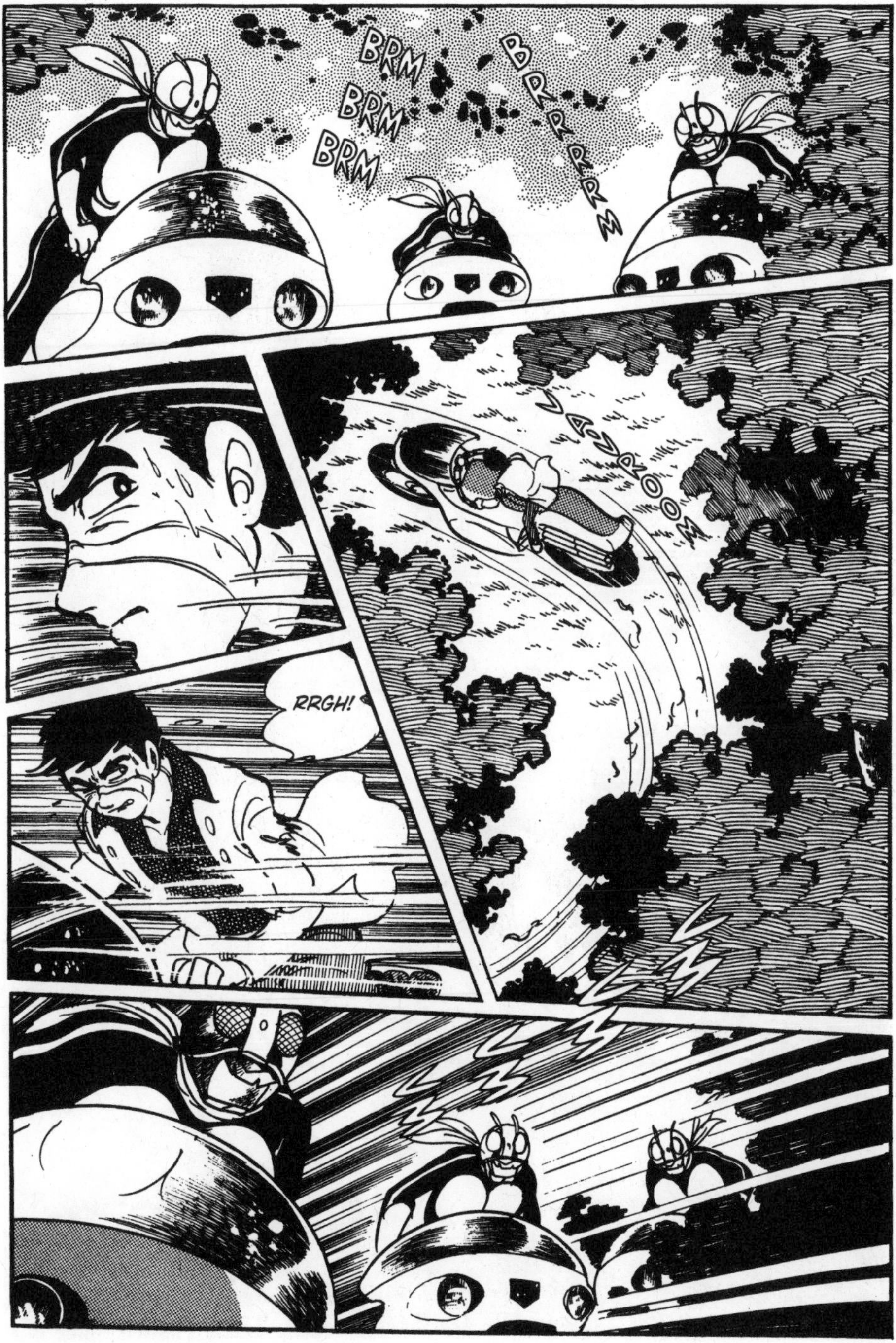
BRM BRM BRM
BRRRRRRM
VA-VROOM
RRGH!

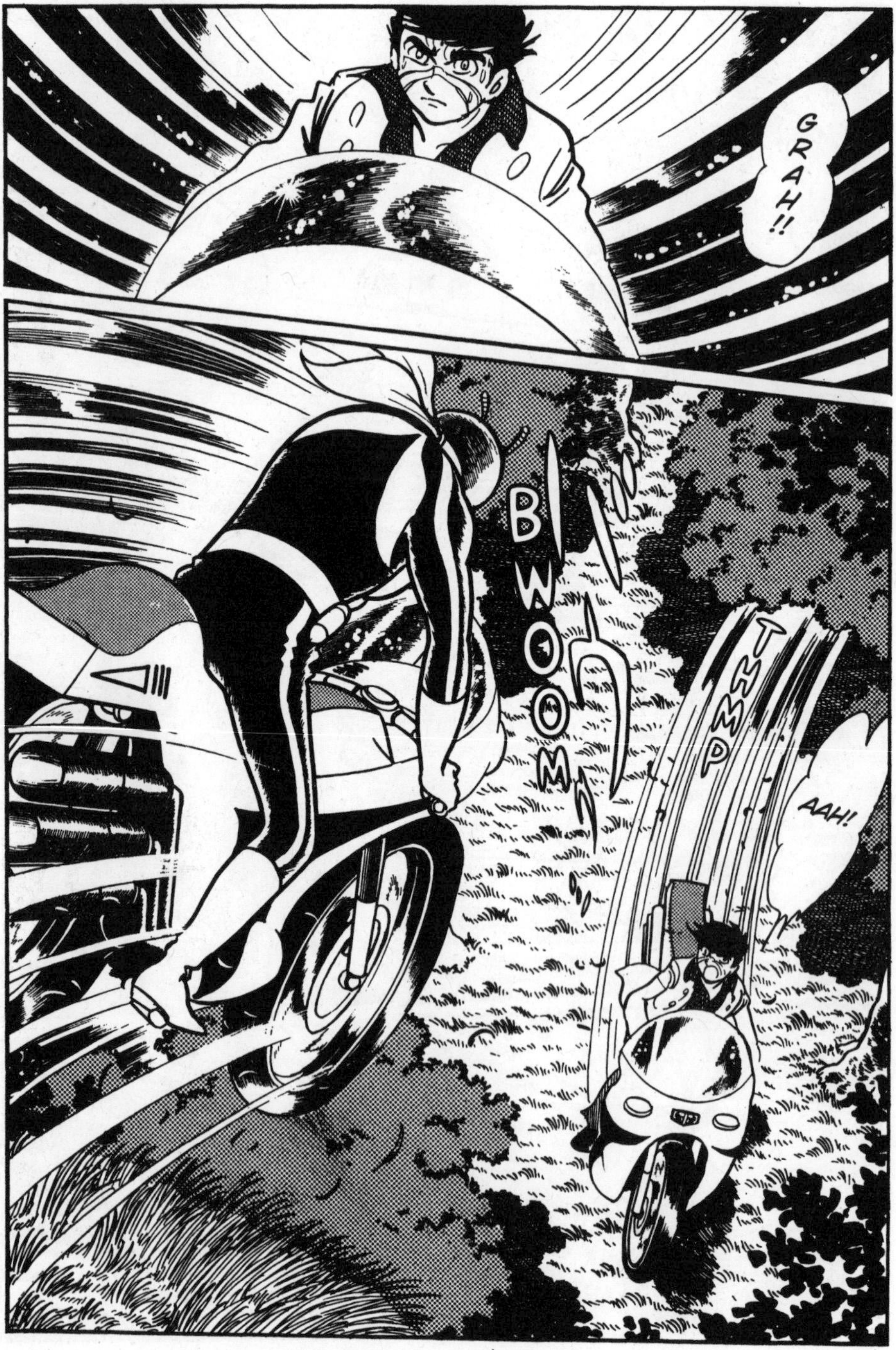
GRAH!!
BWOOM
THMP
AAH!

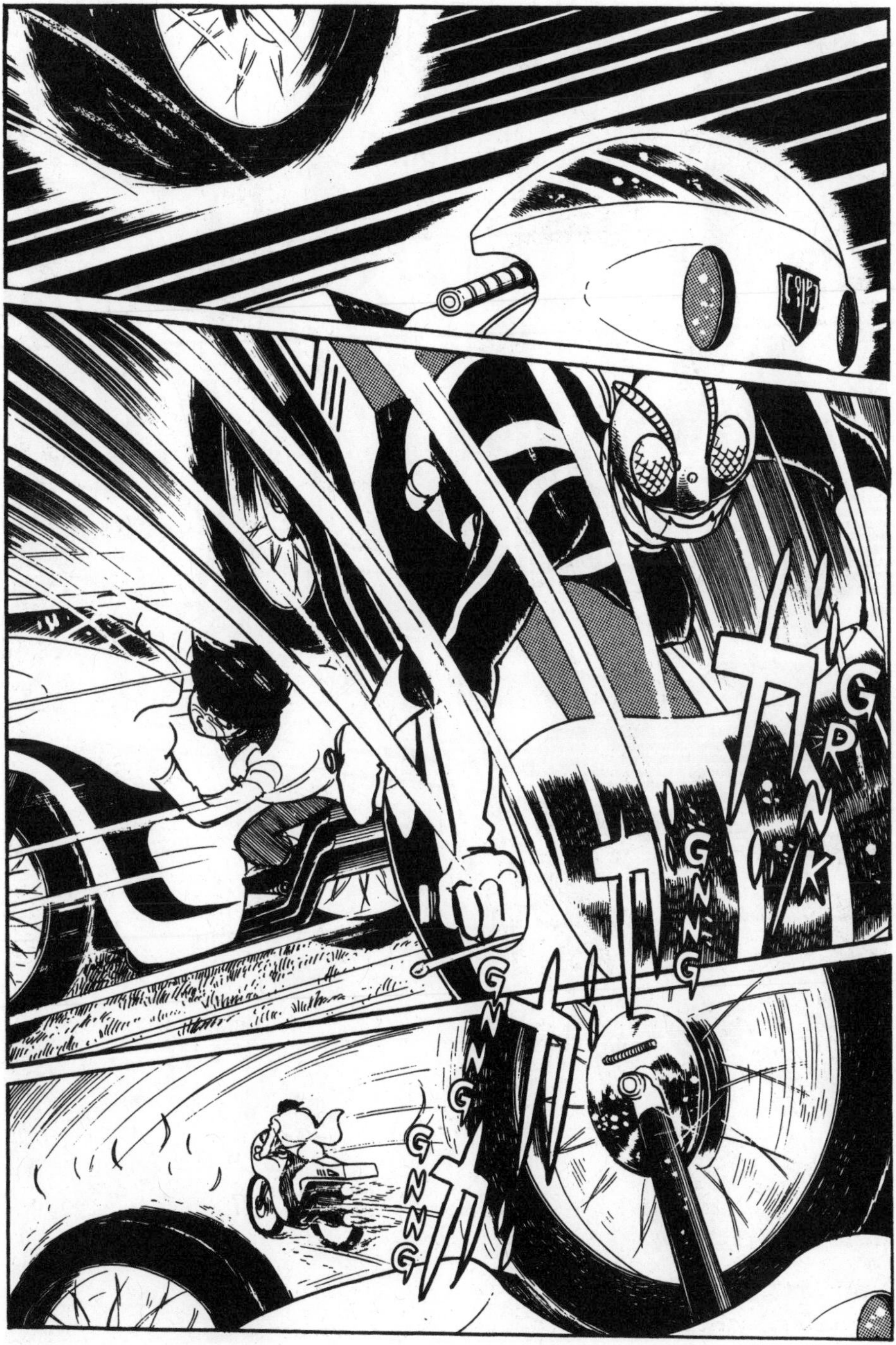
GRNK
GNNG
GNNNG
GNNG

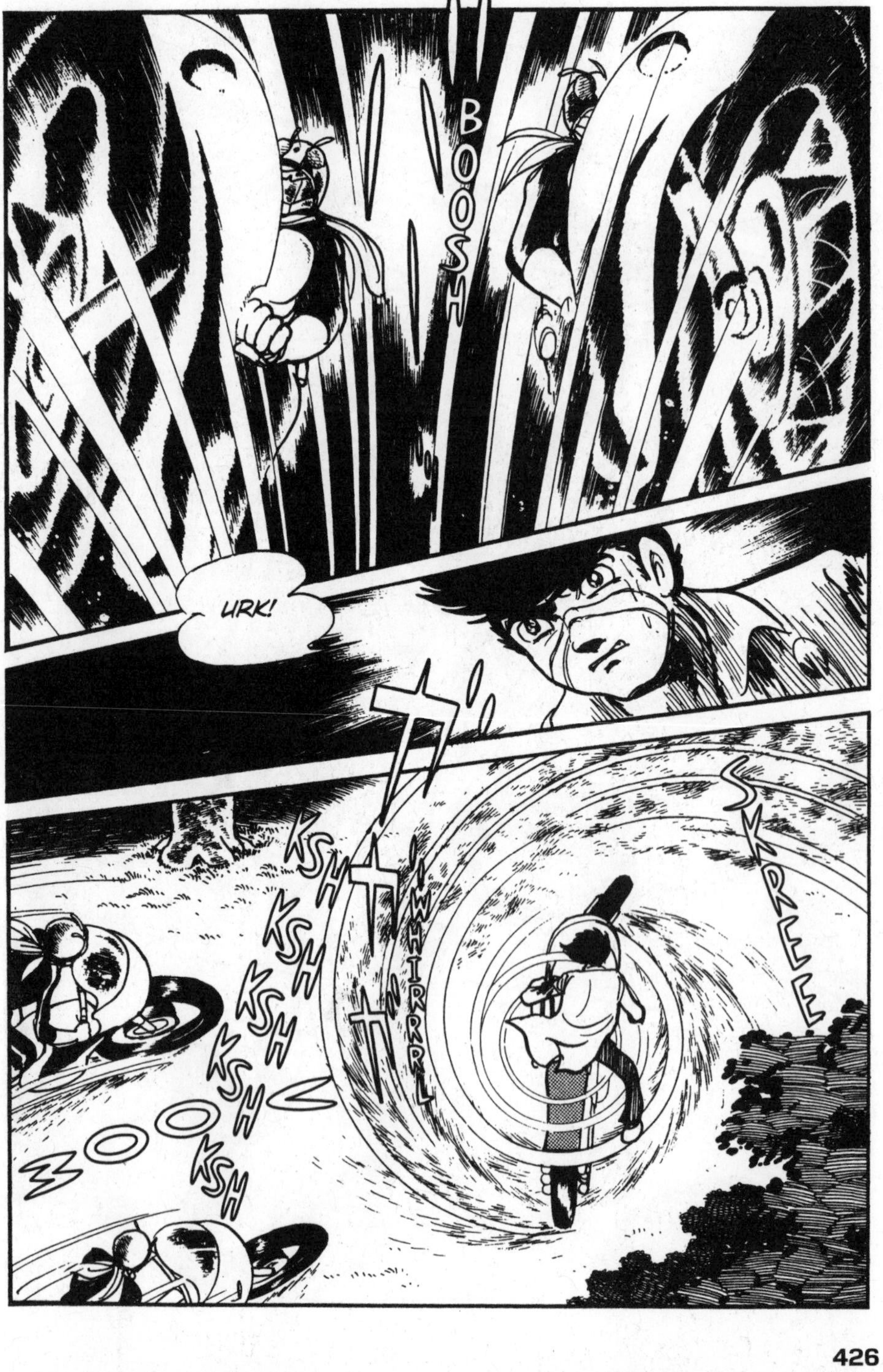
BOOSH
URK!
SKREE
WHIRRRL
KSH
KSH
KSH
KSH
KSH
KSH
VOOOM

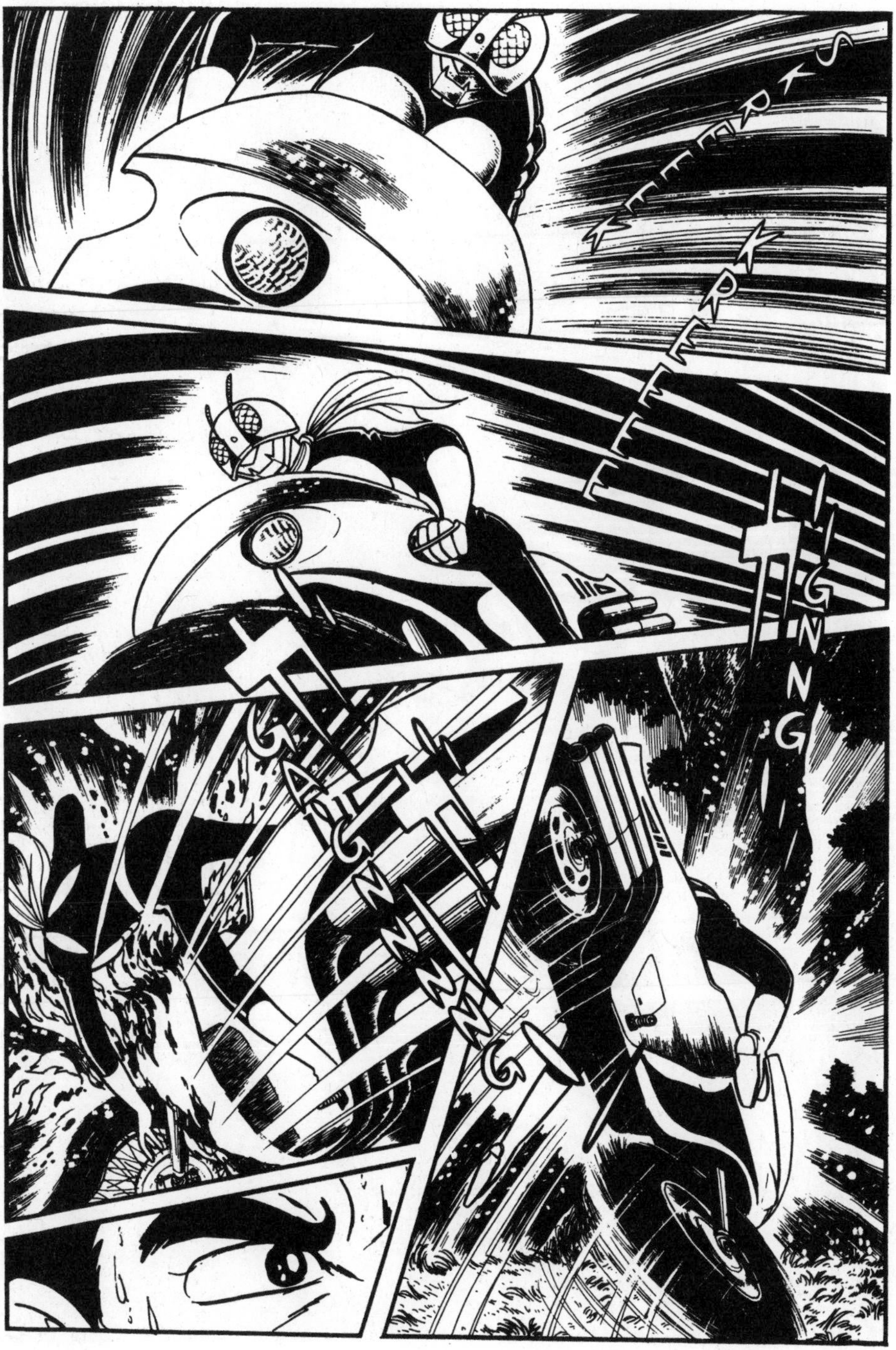
SKREEEEE
KREEEEEE
GNNG
GAGNNNNG

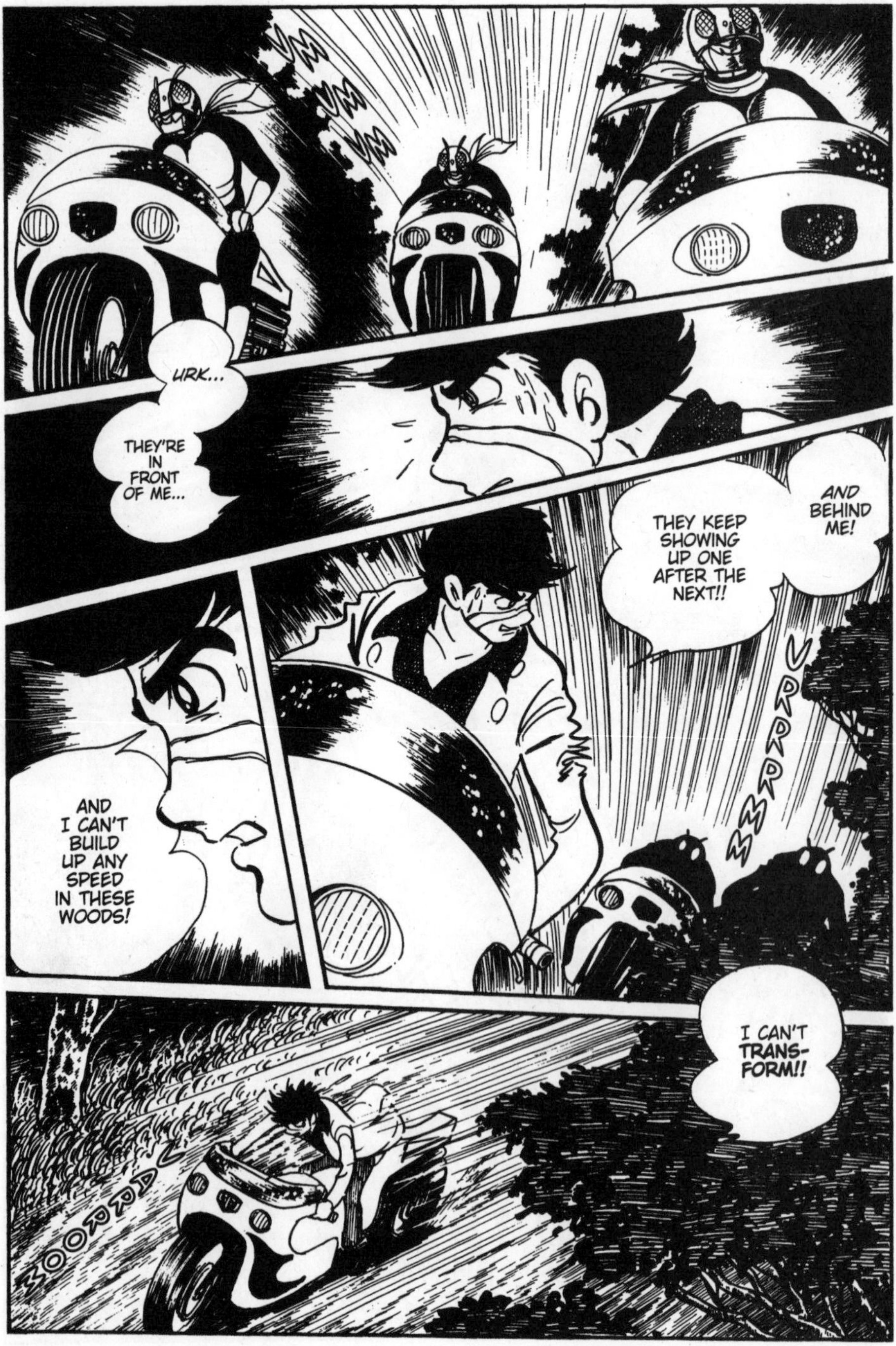
VMM VMM VM
URK...
THEY'RE IN FRONT OF ME...
AND BEHIND ME!
THEY KEEP SHOWING UP ONE AFTER THE NEXT!!
VRRRRMMM
AND I CAN'T BUILD UP ANY SPEED IN THESE WOODS!
I CAN'T TRANS-FORM!!
VARROOM

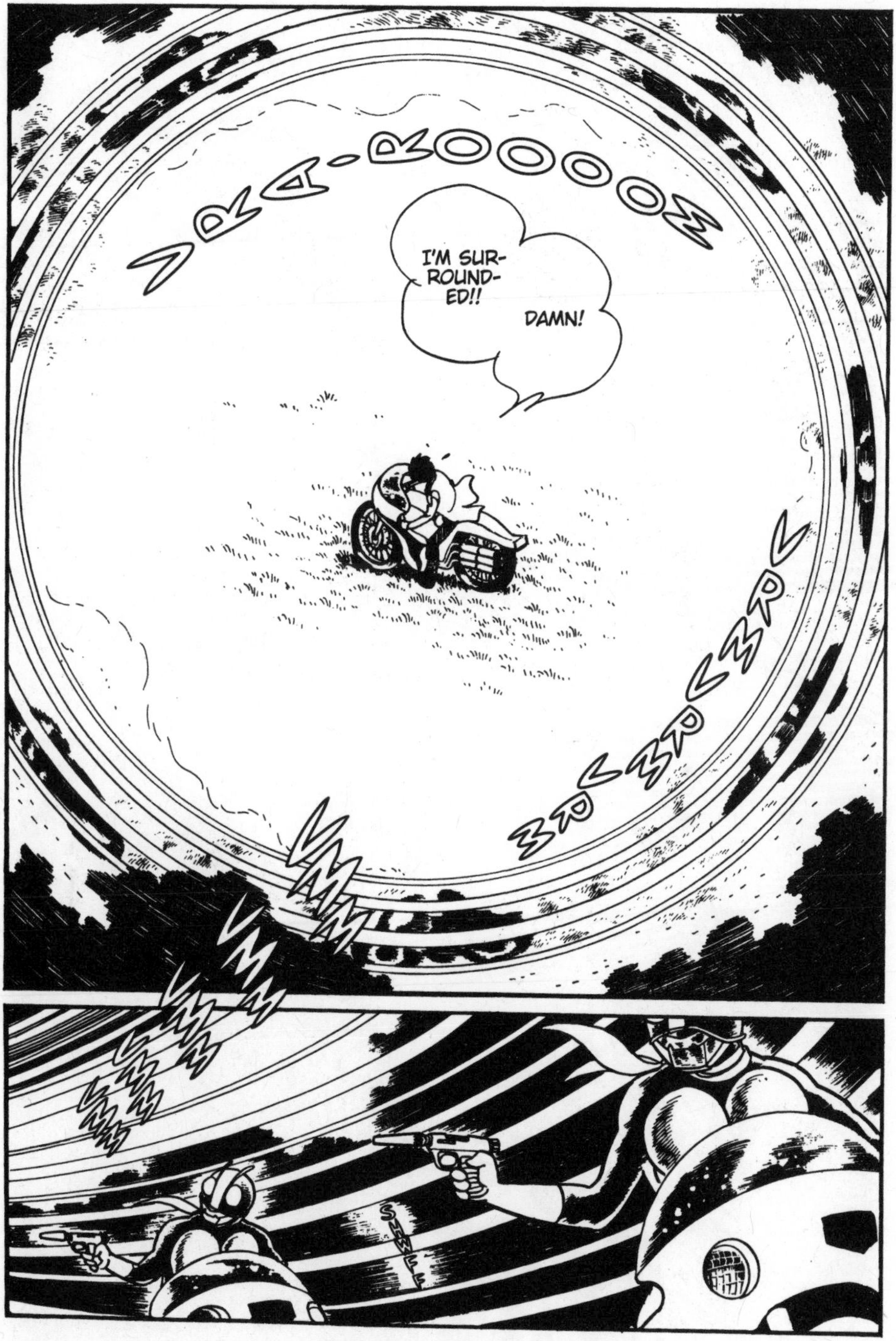
VRA-ROOOOM
I'M SURROUNDED!! DAMN!
SHWFF

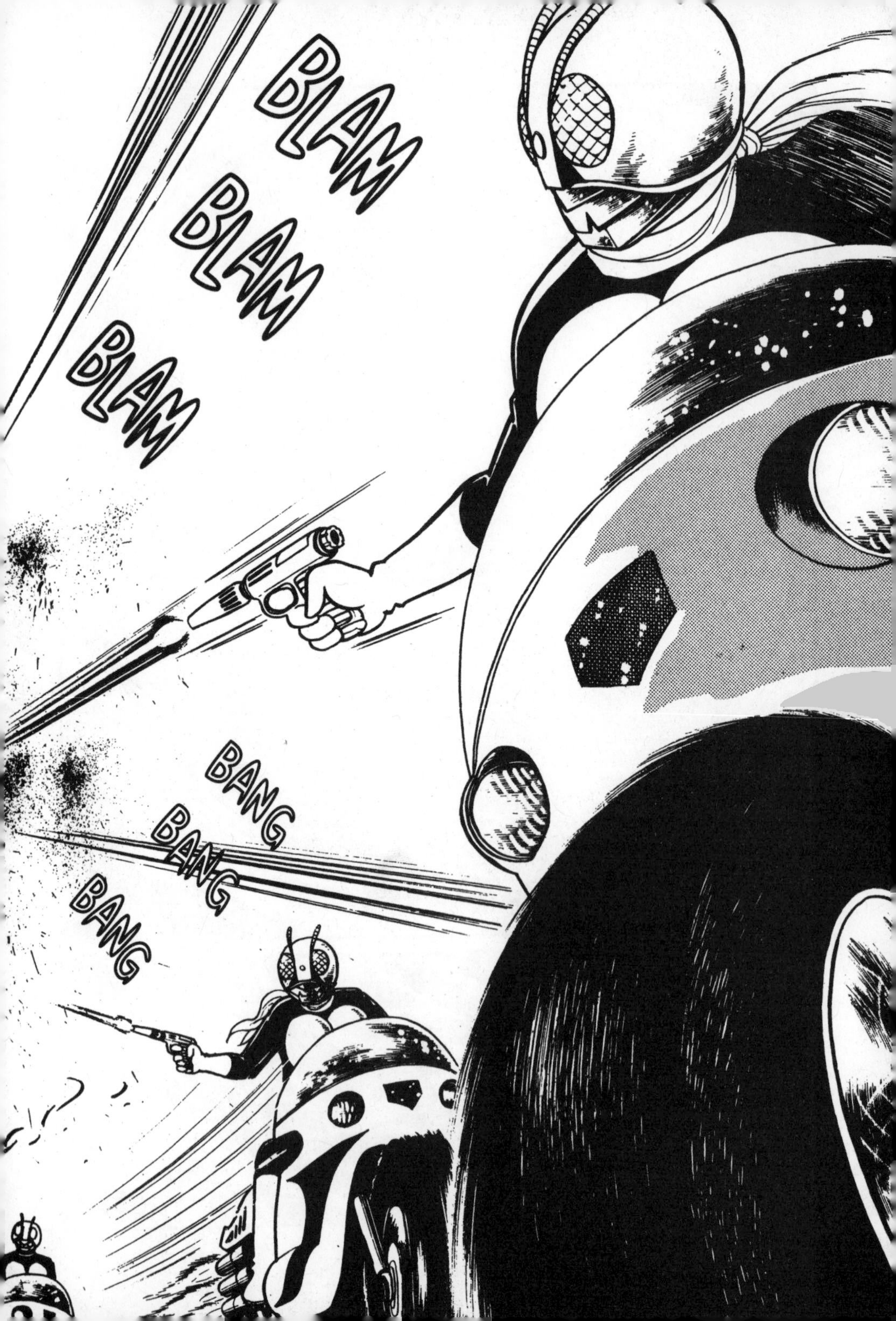
BLAM
BLAM
BLAM
BANG
BANG
BANG

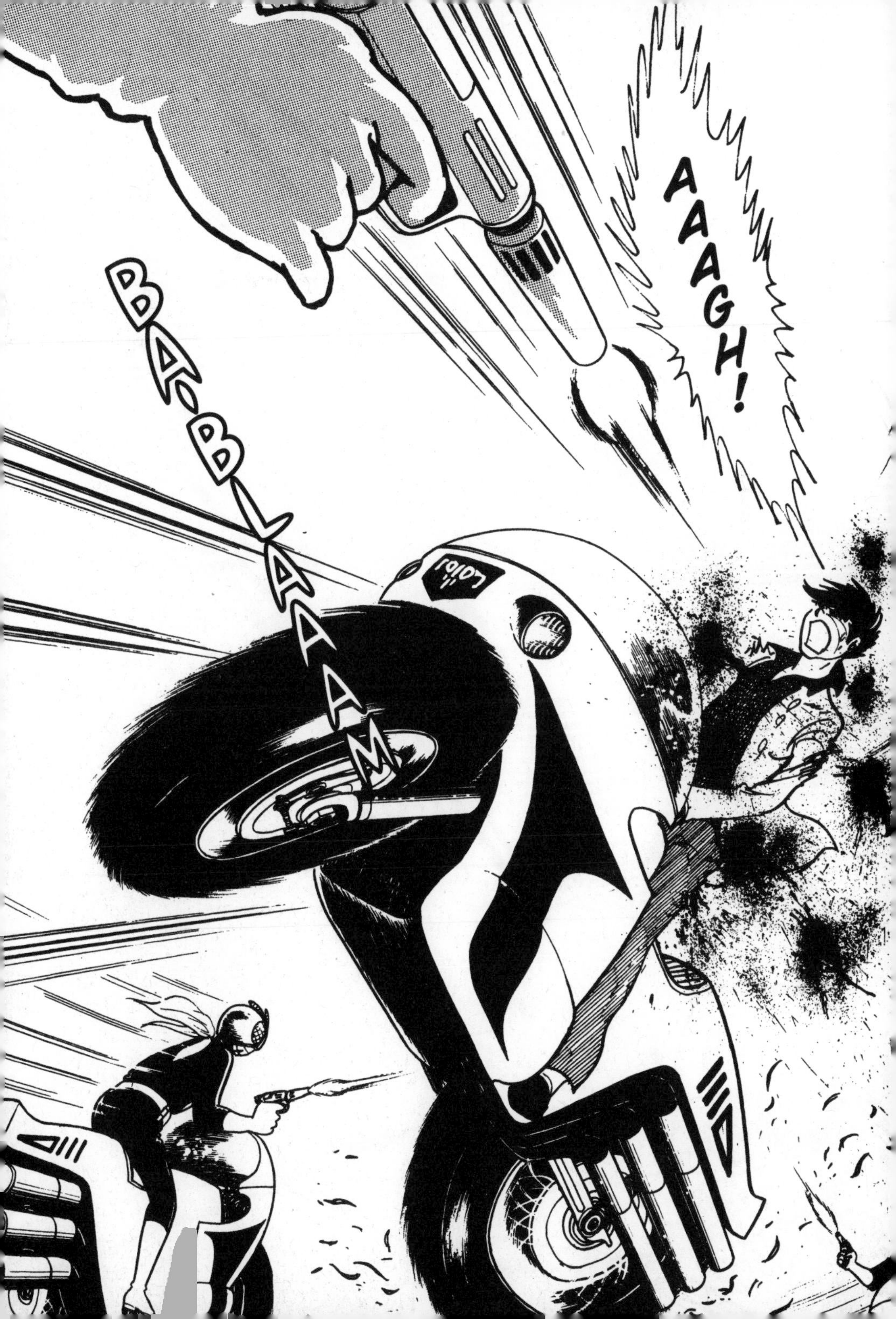
AAAGH!
BA-BLAAAM

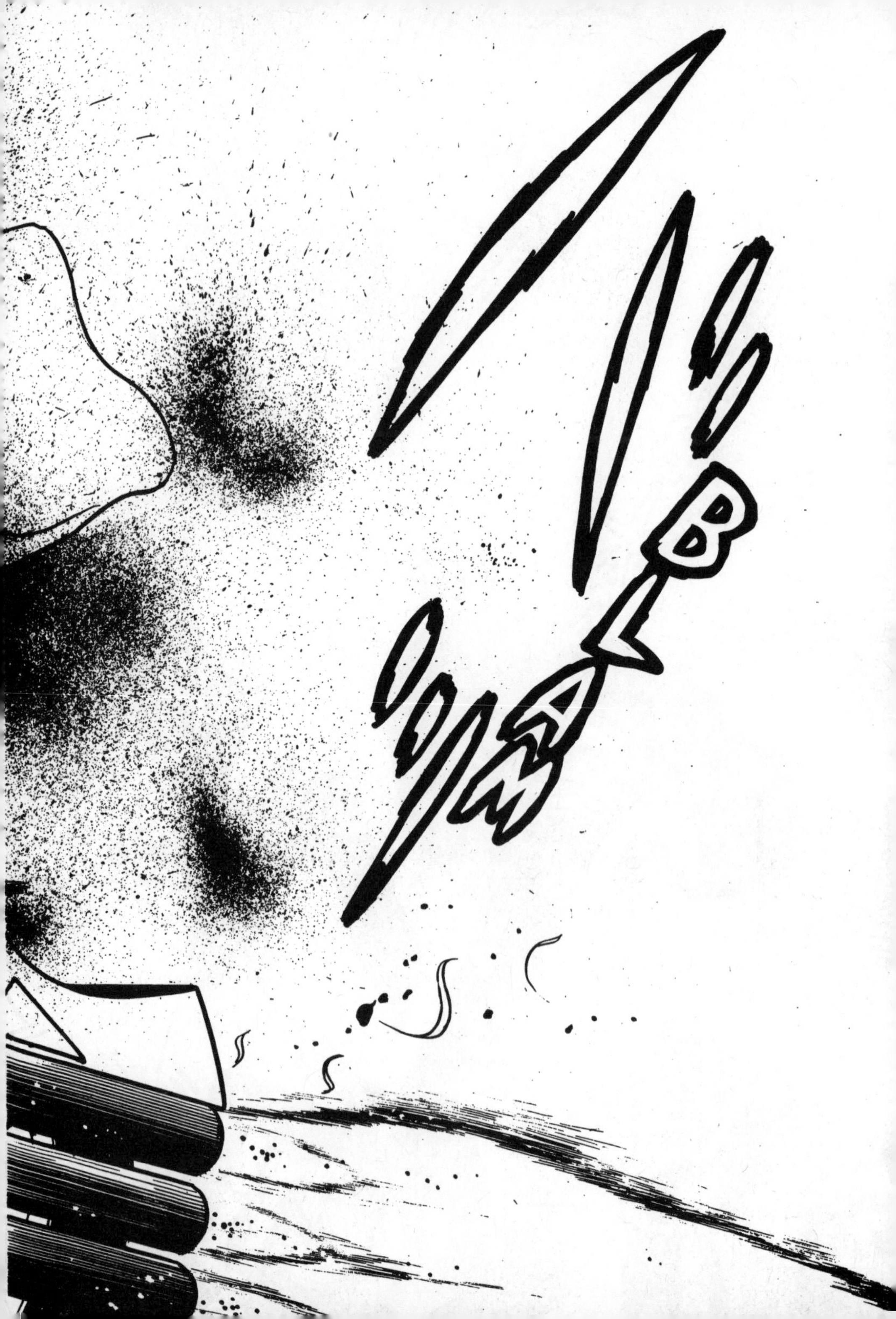
BLAM

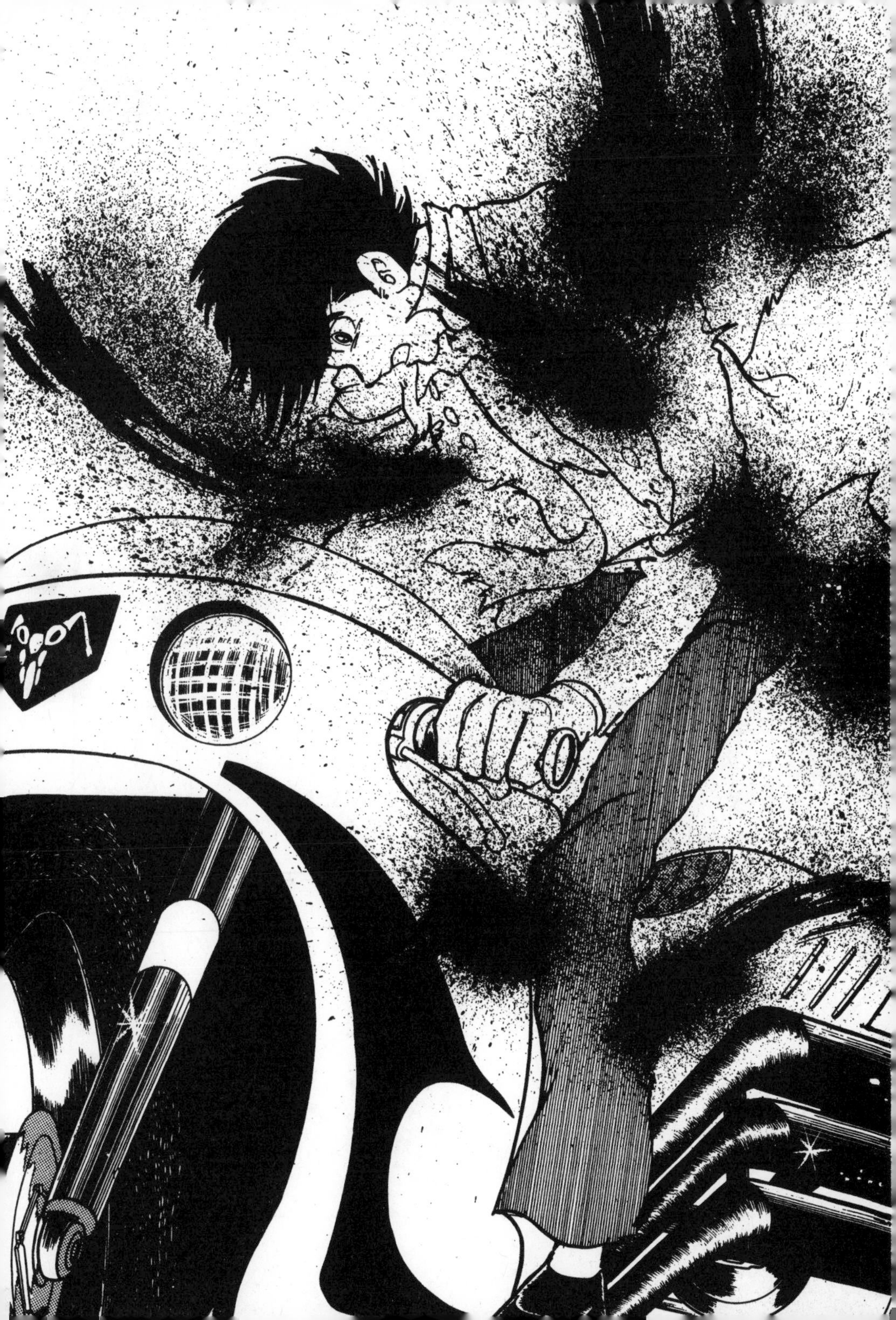

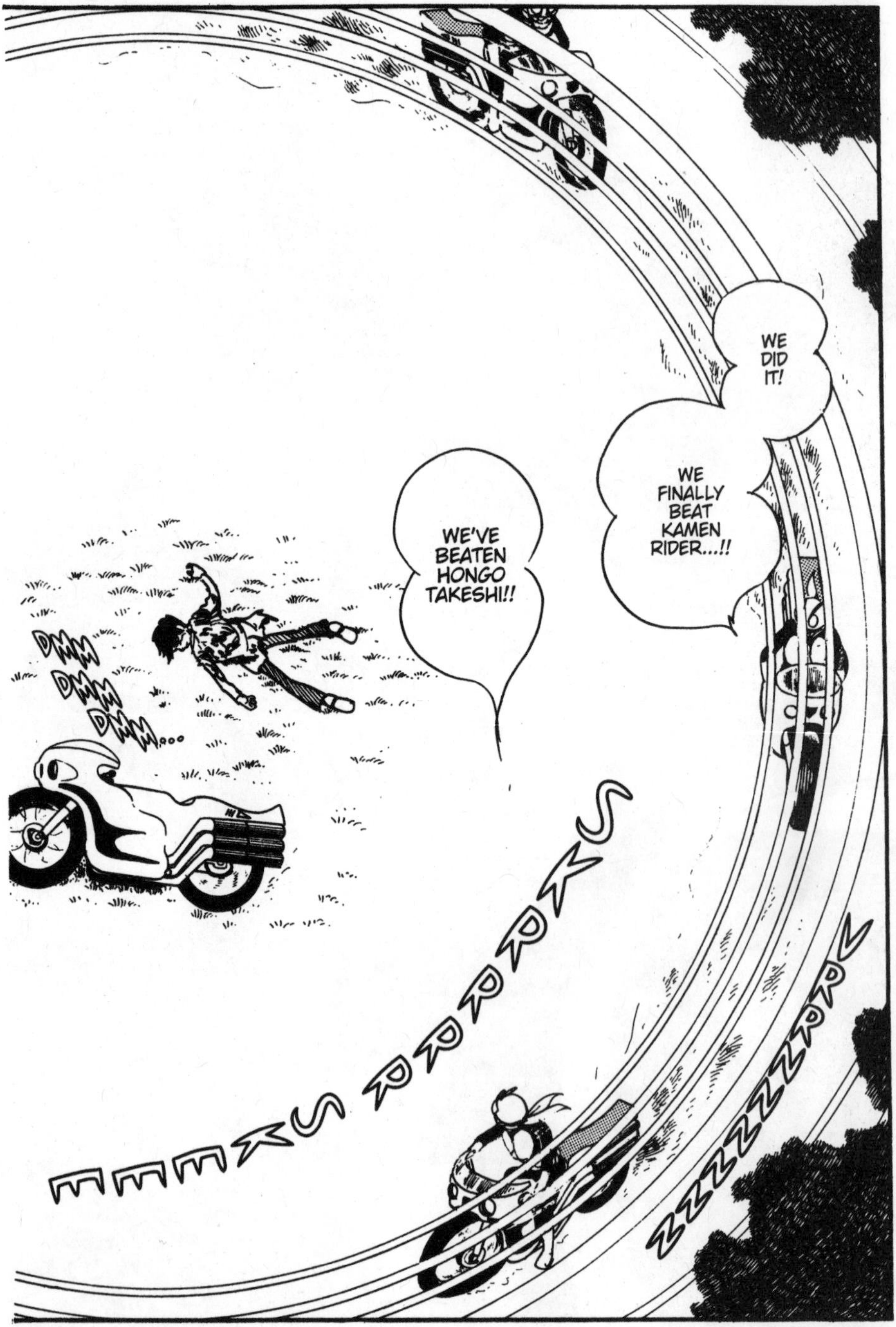
WE DID IT!
WE FINALLY BEAT KAMEN RIDER...!!
WE'VE BEATEN HONGO TAKESHI!!
ZZZZZZZRRRV
EEEEEKS RRRRRKS
DMMM DMMM DMMM...

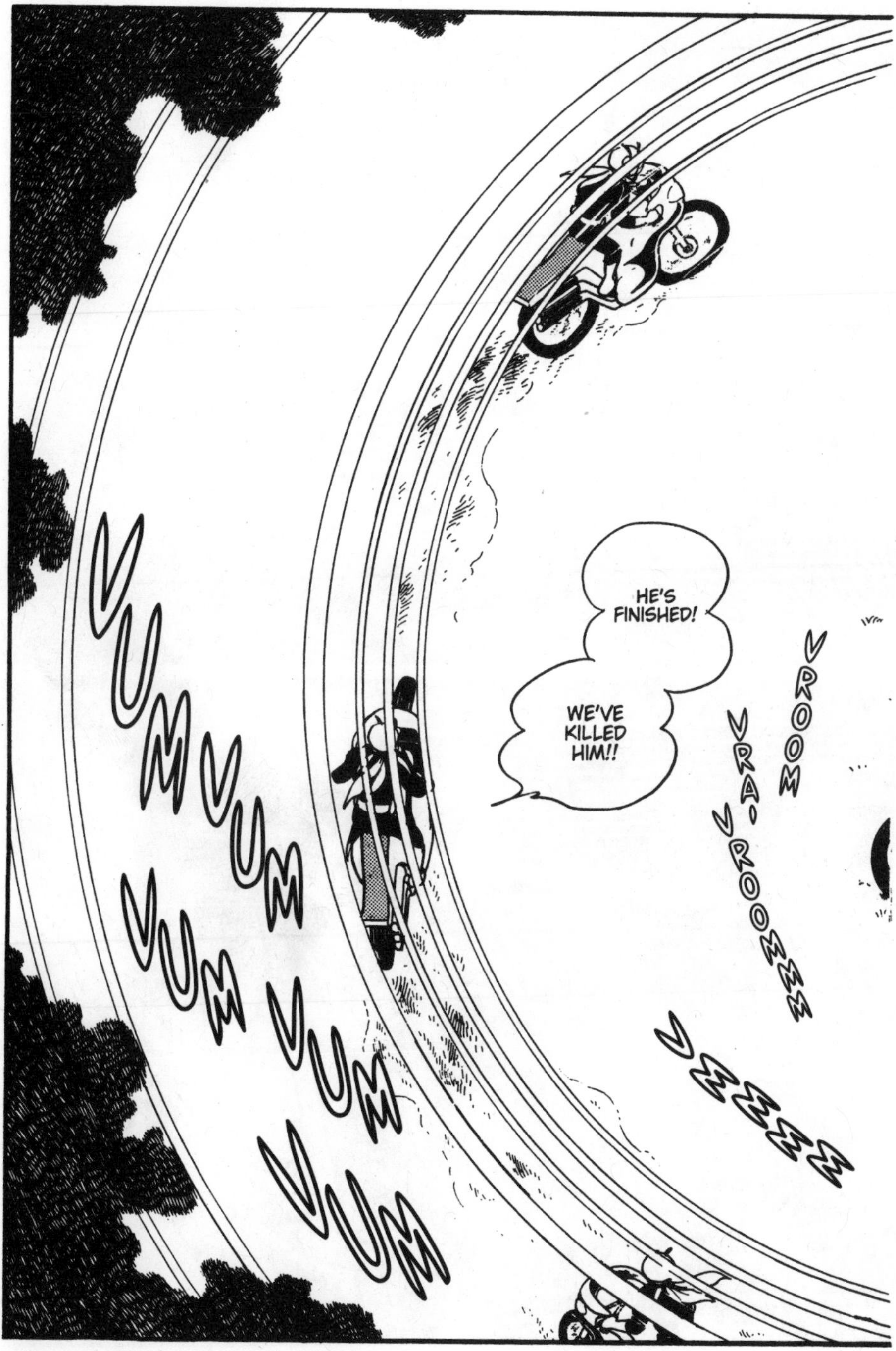
VROOM
HE'S FINISHED!
WE'VE KILLED HIM!!
VRA! VROOMMMM
VMMMM
VUM VUM
VUM VUM VUM

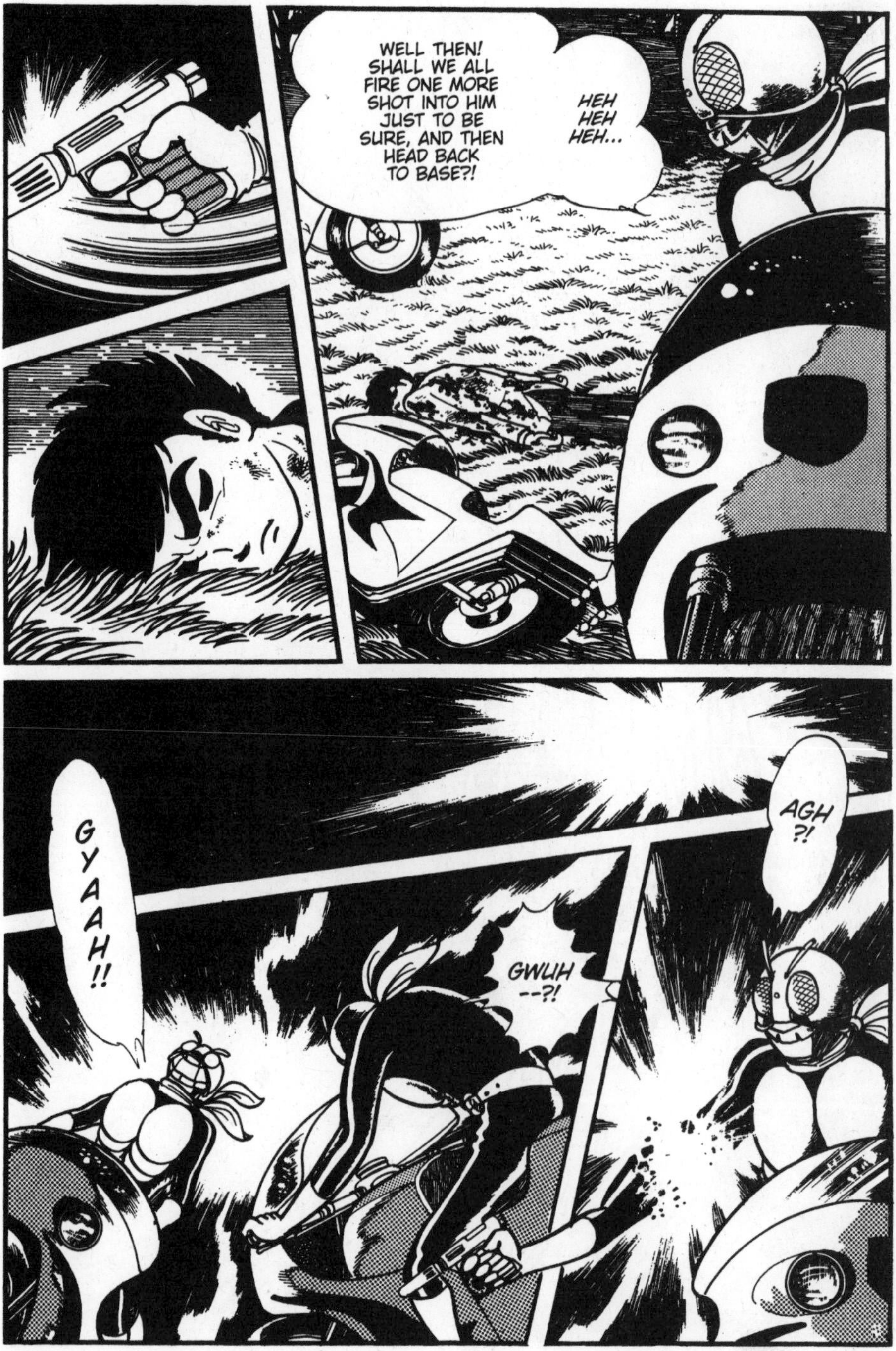
WELL THEN! SHALL WE ALL FIRE ONE MORE SHOT INTO HIM JUST TO BE SURE, AND THEN HEAD BACK TO BASE?!
HEH HEH HEH...
AGH ?!
GWUH --?!
GYAAAH!!

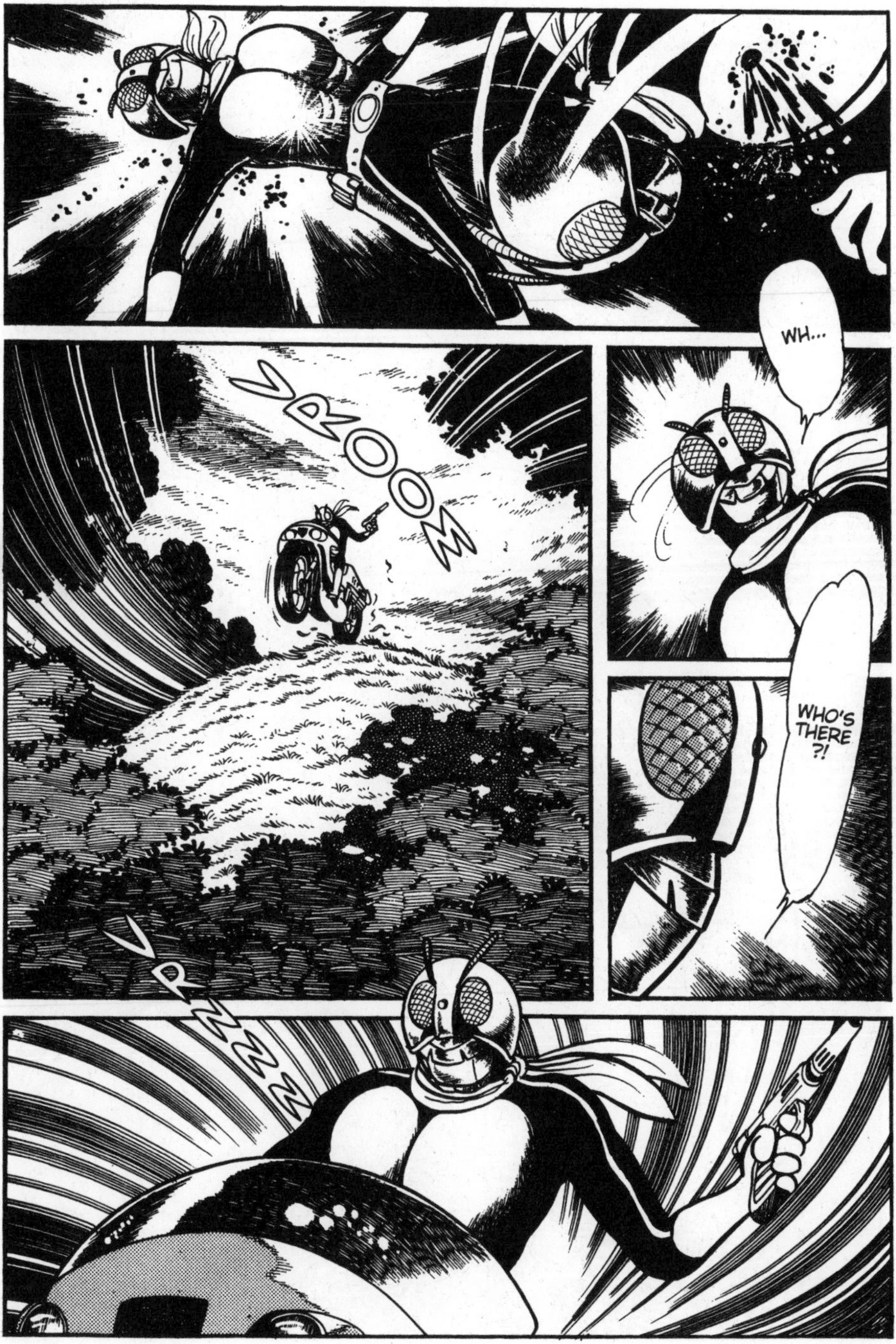
WH...
WHO'S THERE ?!
VROOOM
VRZZZ

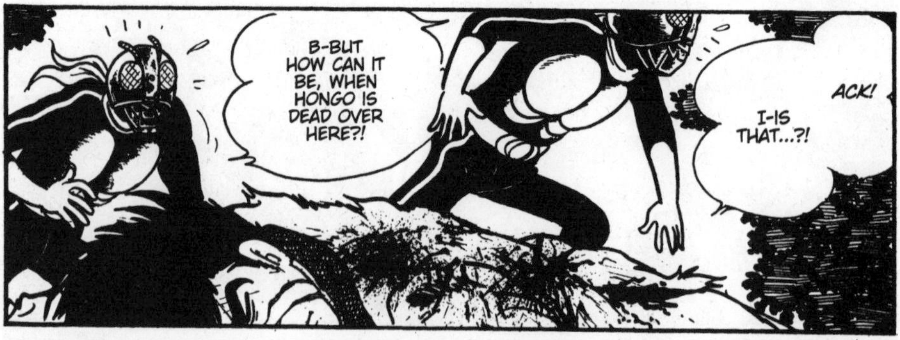
ACK!
I-IS THAT...?!
B-BUT HOW CAN IT BE, WHEN HONGO IS DEAD OVER HERE?!

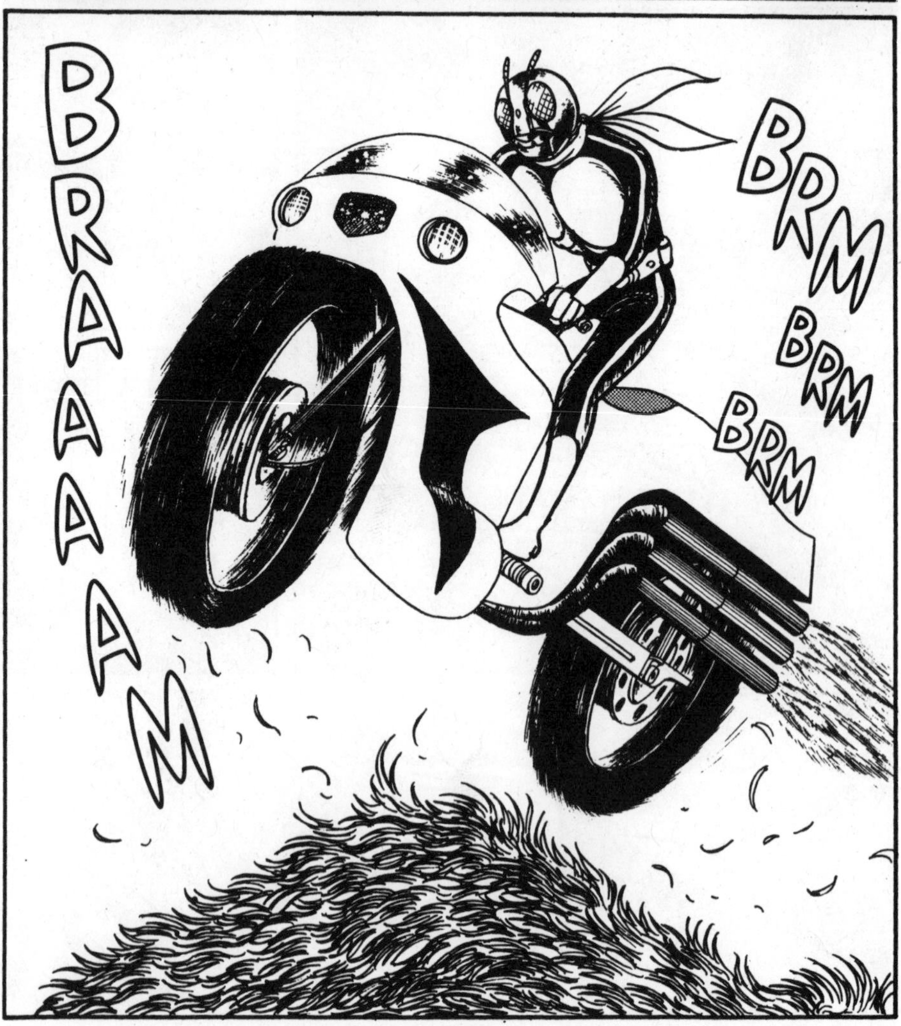
BRM BRM BRM BRM
BRAAAAAM

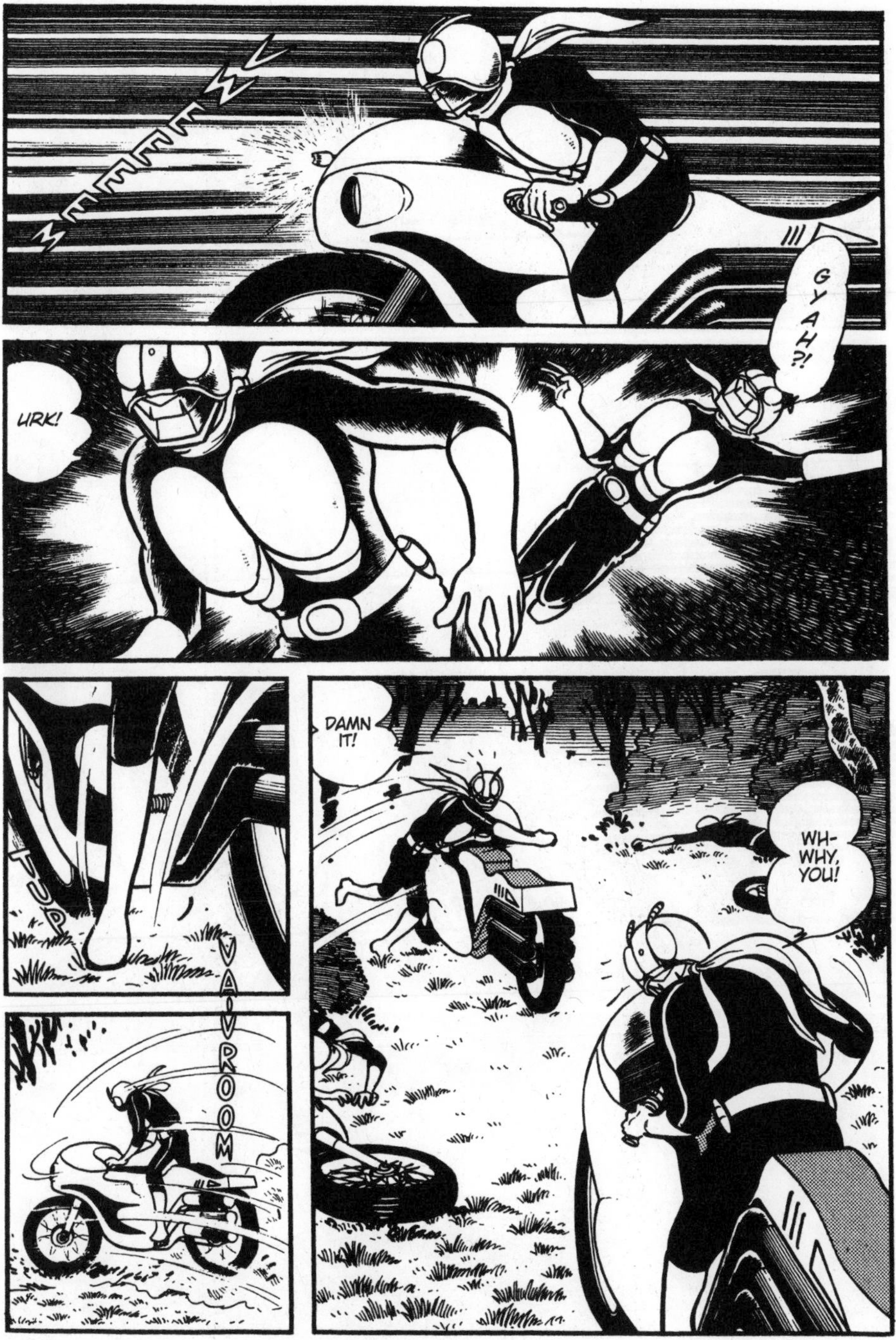
WEEEEEEEW
GYAH?!
URK!
WH-WHY, YOU!
DAMN IT!
TUD
VAVROOM

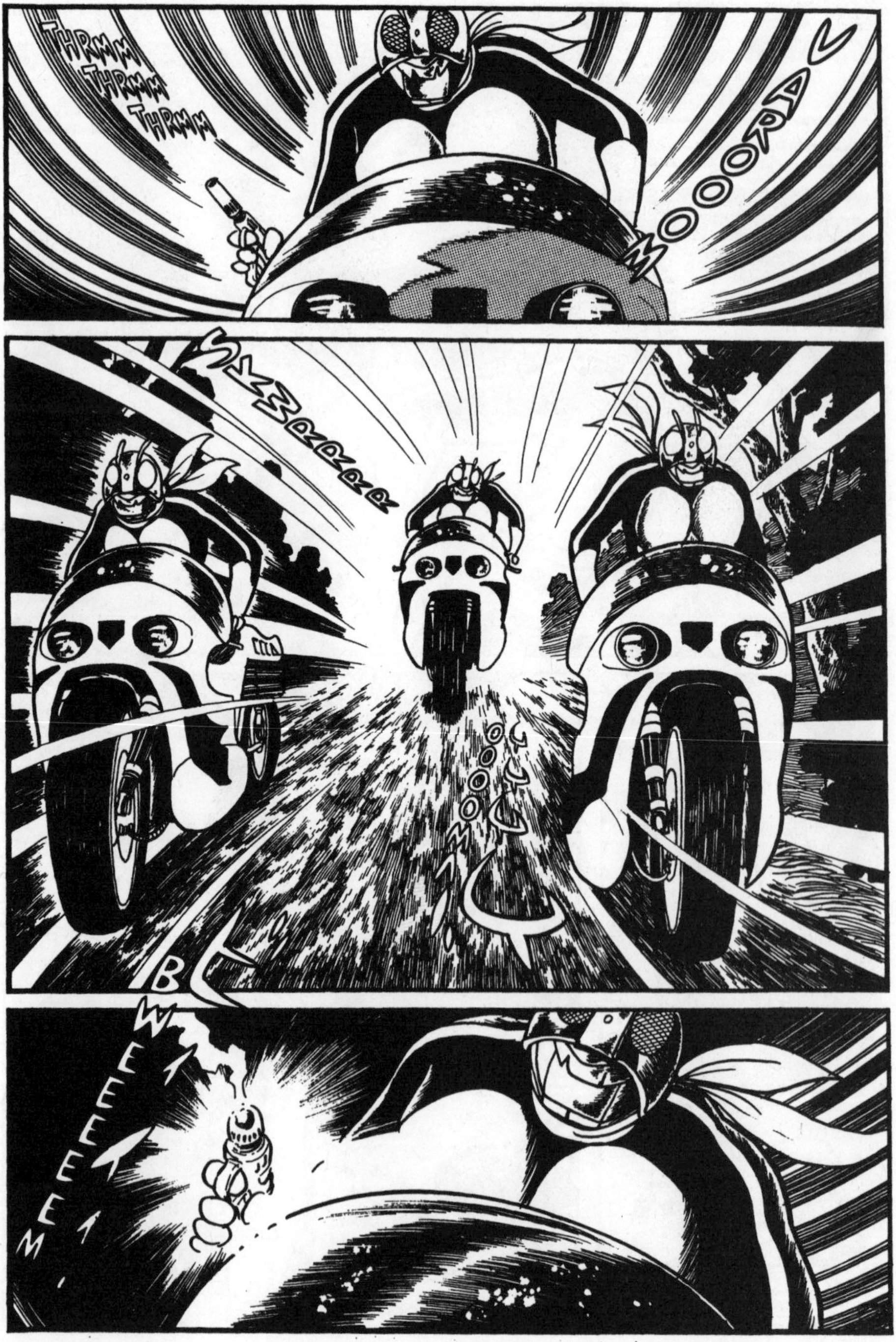
VAROOOM
THRMM
THRMM
THRMM
SKWRRRRR
BWEEEEEEM

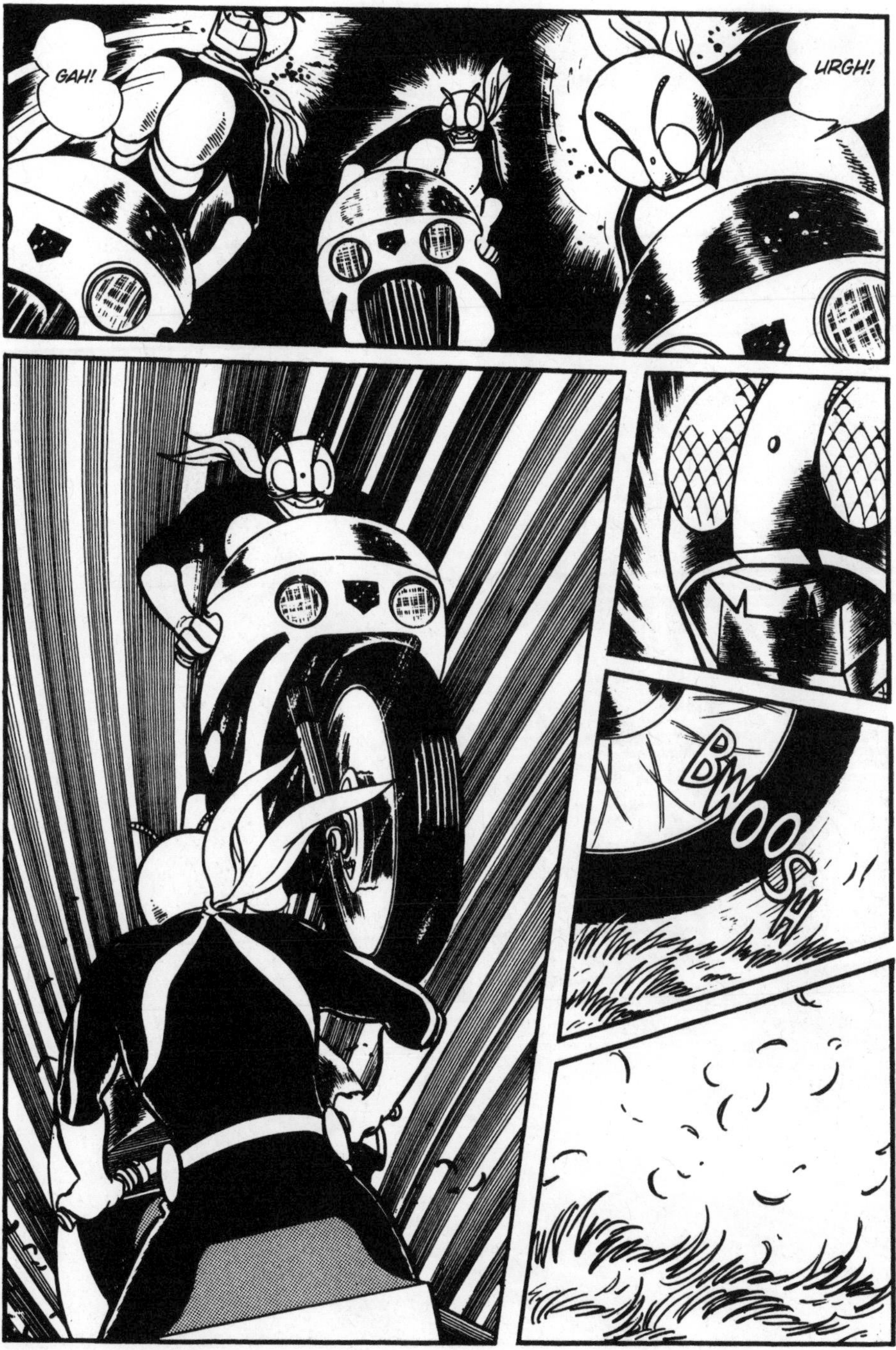
URGH!
GAH!
BWOOSH

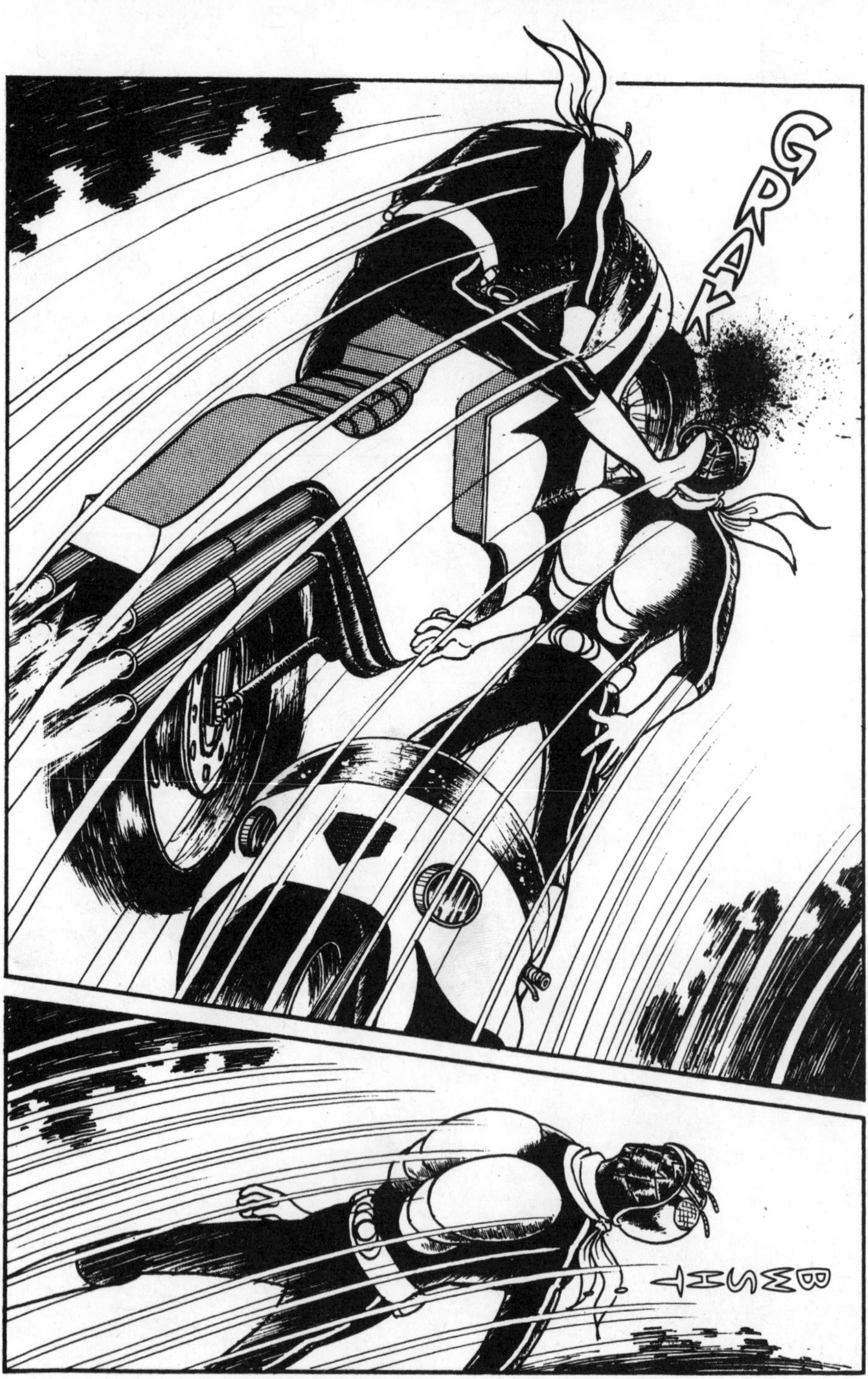
GRAK
BWSHT

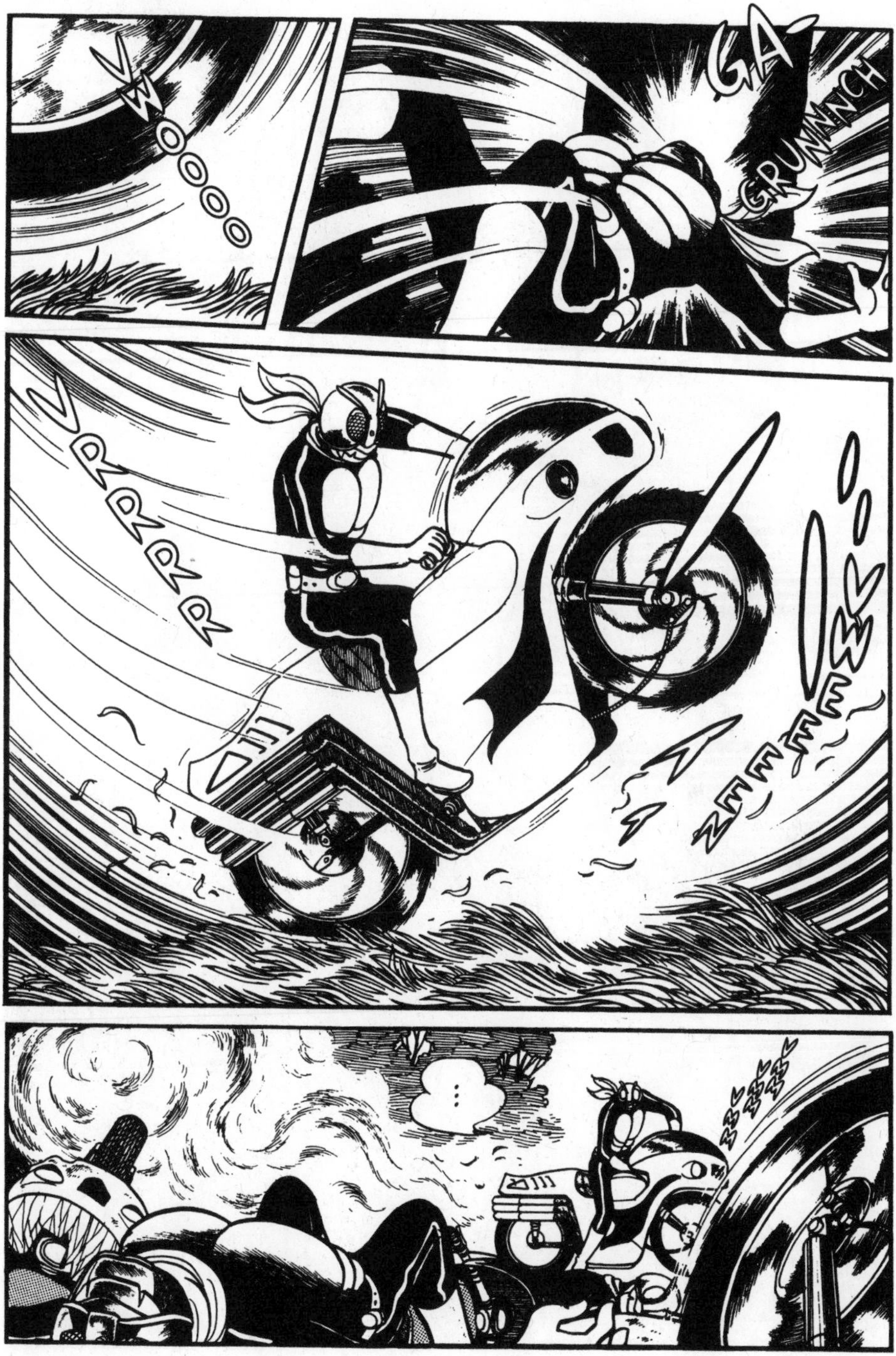
GA
GRUNNNCH
VWOOOO
ZEEEEEW
VRRRRR
…

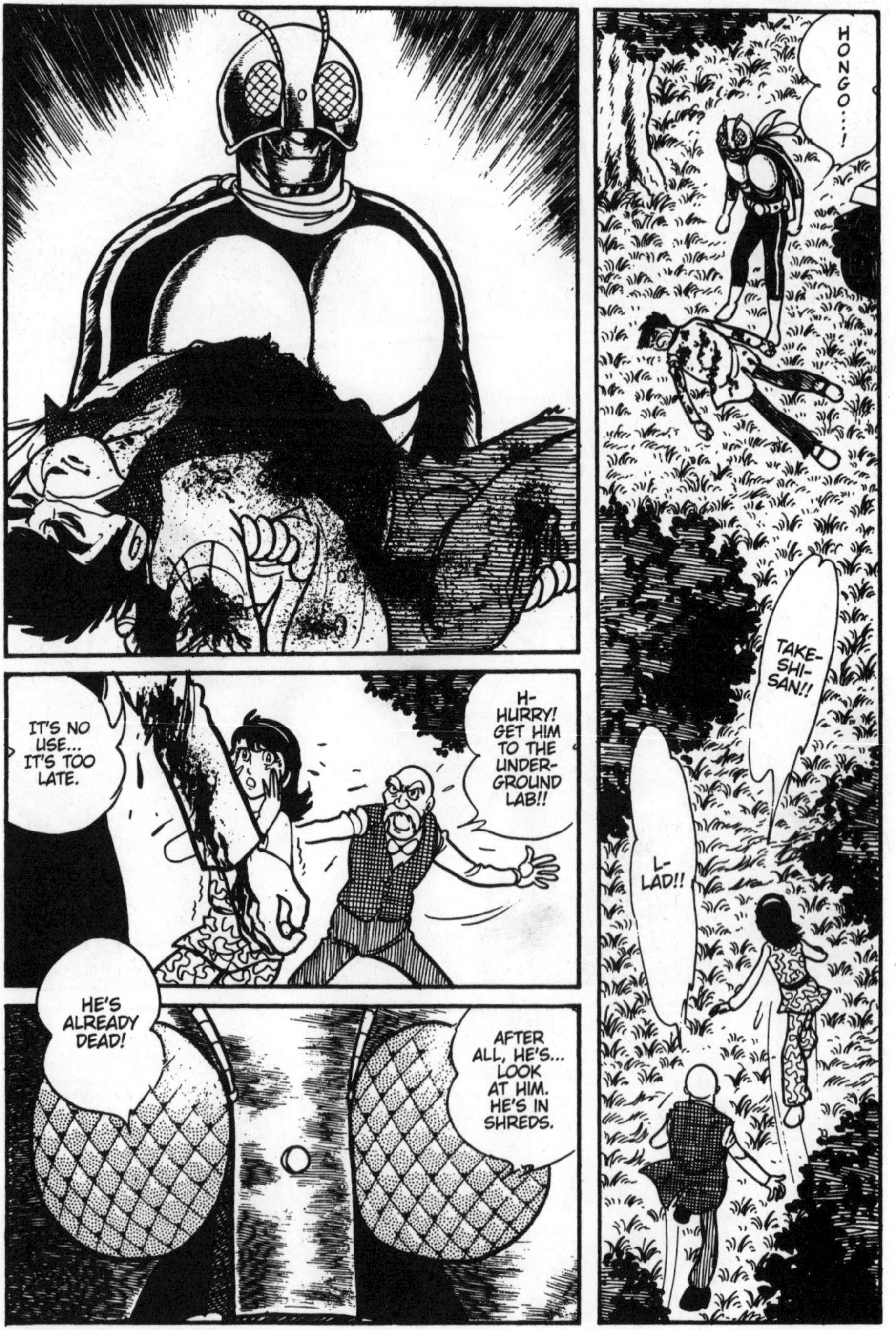
HONGO...!
TAKESHI-SAN!!
L-LAD!!
H-HURRY! GET HIM TO THE UNDERGROUND LAB!!
IT'S NO USE... IT'S TOO LATE.
HE'S ALREADY DEAD!
AFTER ALL, HE'S... LOOK AT HIM. HE'S IN SHREDS.

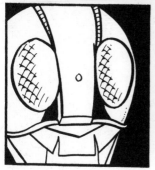

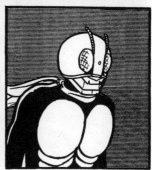

445

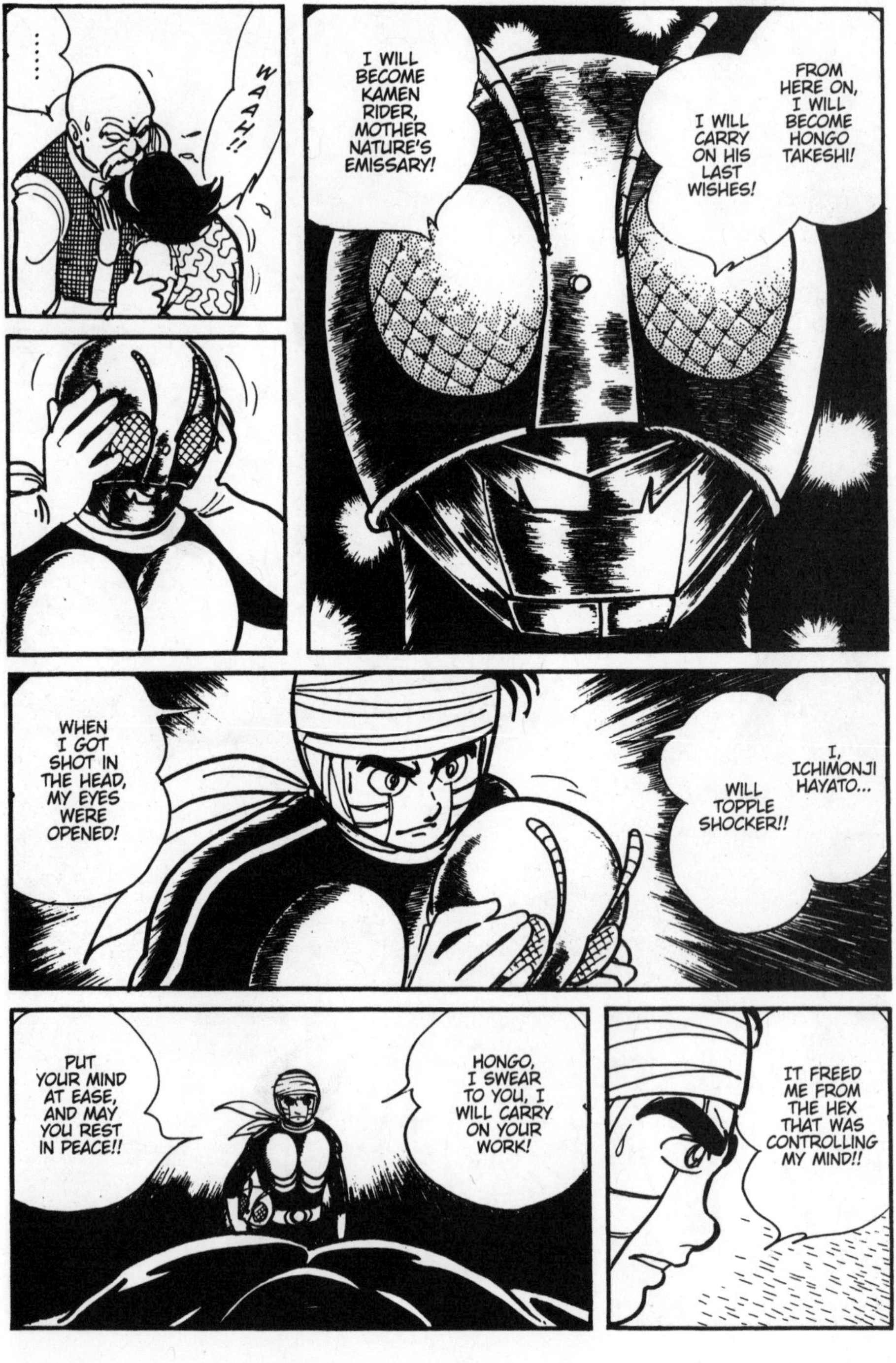
FROM HERE ON, I WILL BECOME HONGO TAKESHI!
I WILL CARRY ON HIS LAST WISHES!
I WILL BECOME KAMEN RIDER, MOTHER NATURE'S EMISSARY!
WAAH!!
......
I, ICHIMONJI HAYATO...
WILL TOPPLE SHOCKER!!
WHEN I GOT SHOT IN THE HEAD, MY EYES WERE OPENED!
IT FREED ME FROM THE HEX THAT WAS CONTROLLING MY MIND!!
HONGO, I SWEAR TO YOU, I WILL CARRY ON YOUR WORK!
PUT YOUR MIND AT EASE, AND MAY YOU REST IN PEACE!!

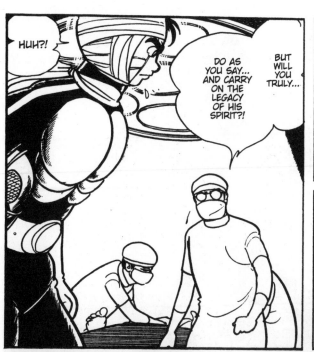

...
HM?
BUT WILL YOU TRULY...
DO AS YOU SAY... AND CARRY ON THE LEGACY OF HIS SPIRIT?!
HUH?!
THE SPIRIT OF HONGO TAKESHI...!!

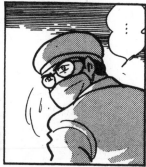

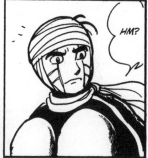

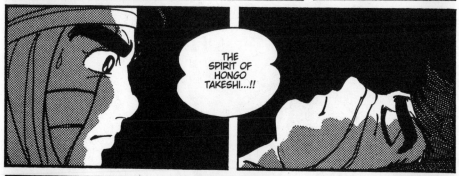

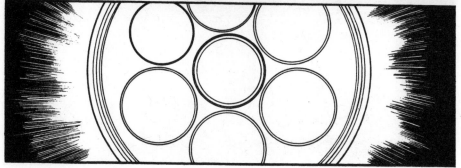

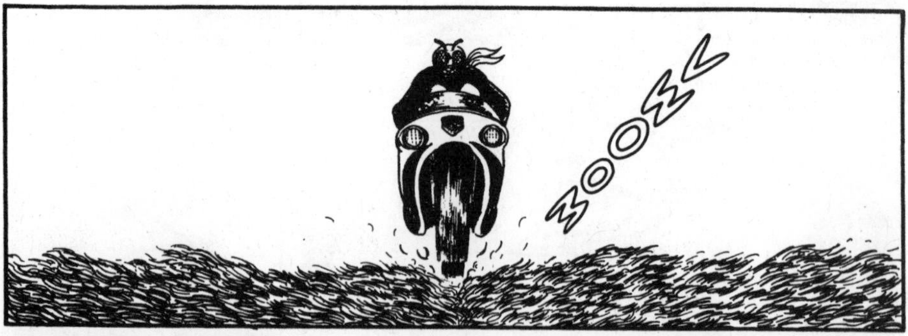
VROOM
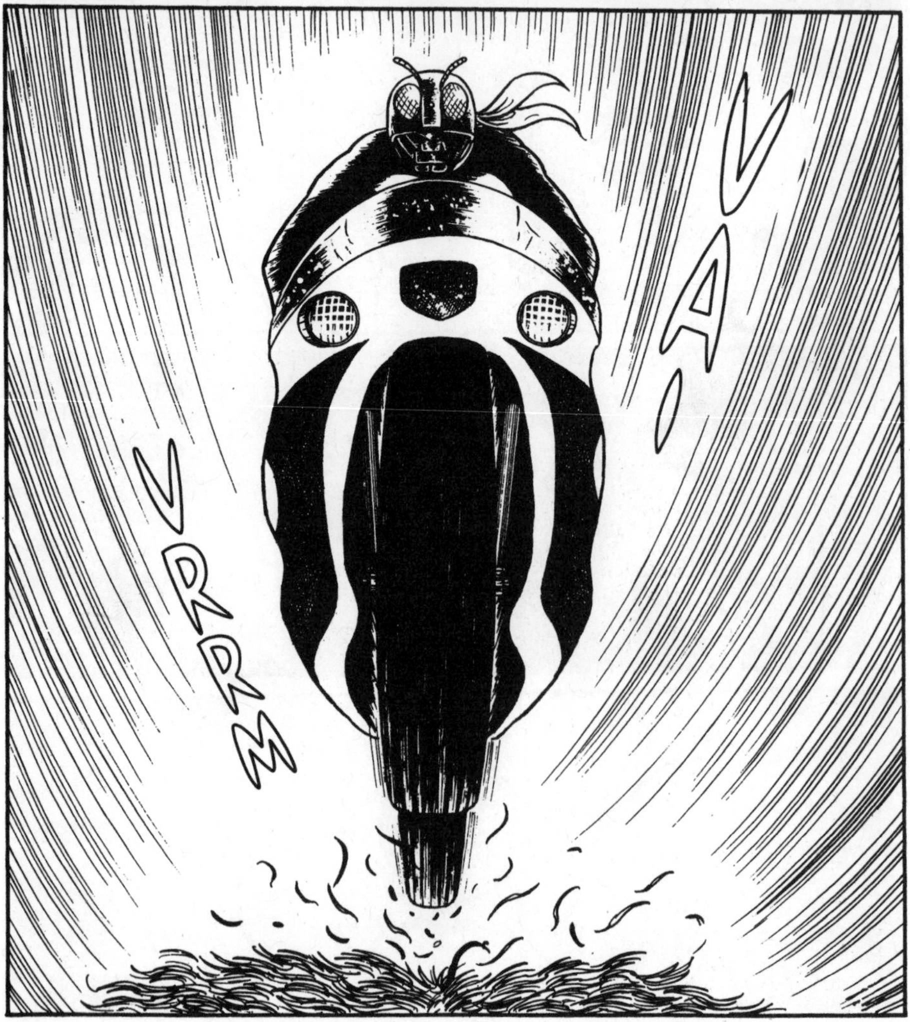
VA
VRRRM

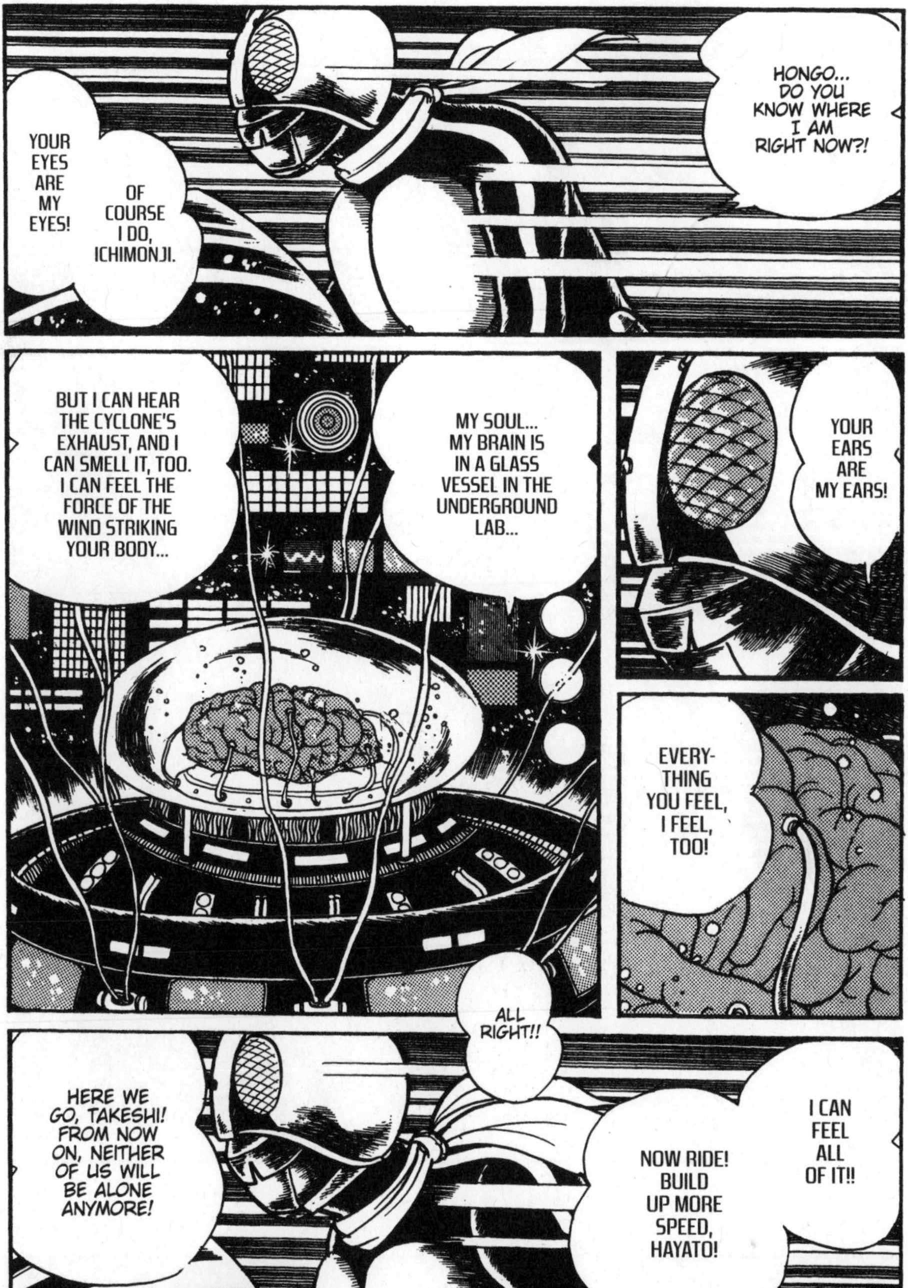
HONGO... DO YOU KNOW WHERE I AM RIGHT NOW?!
OF COURSE I DO, ICHIMONJI.
YOUR EYES ARE MY EYES!
YOUR EARS ARE MY EARS!
EVERY-THING YOU FEEL, I FEEL, TOO!
MY SOUL... MY BRAIN IS IN A GLASS VESSEL IN THE UNDERGROUND LAB...
BUT I CAN HEAR THE CYCLONE'S EXHAUST, AND I CAN SMELL IT, TOO. I CAN FEEL THE FORCE OF THE WIND STRIKING YOUR BODY...
I CAN FEEL ALL OF IT!!
ALL RIGHT!!
NOW RIDE! BUILD UP MORE SPEED, HAYATO!
HERE WE GO, TAKESHI! FROM NOW ON, NEITHER OF US WILL BE ALONE ANYMORE!

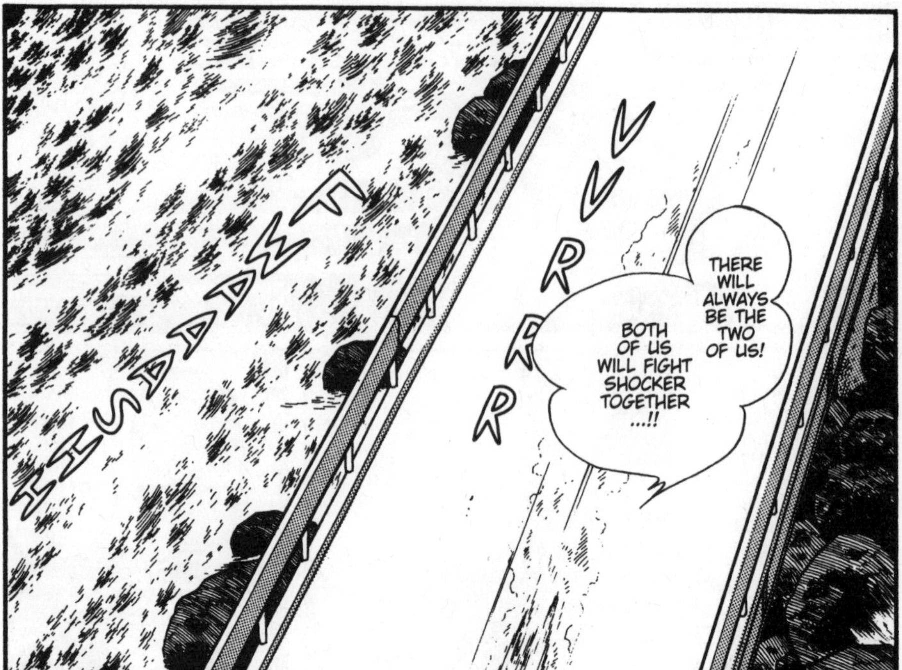
FWAAASH
VVRRRR
THERE WILL ALWAYS BE THE TWO OF US!
BOTH OF US WILL FIGHT SHOCKER TOGETHER ...!!
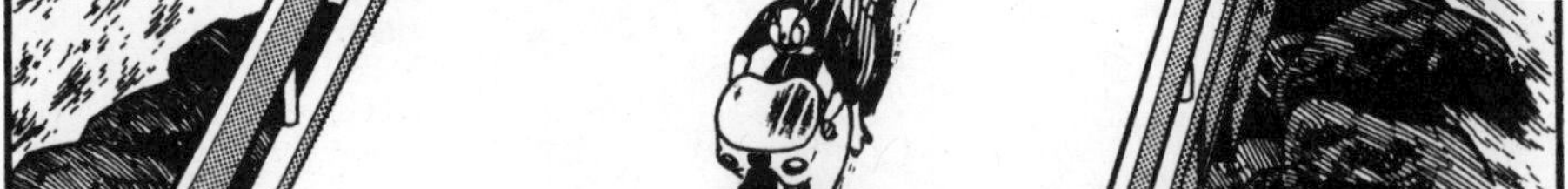

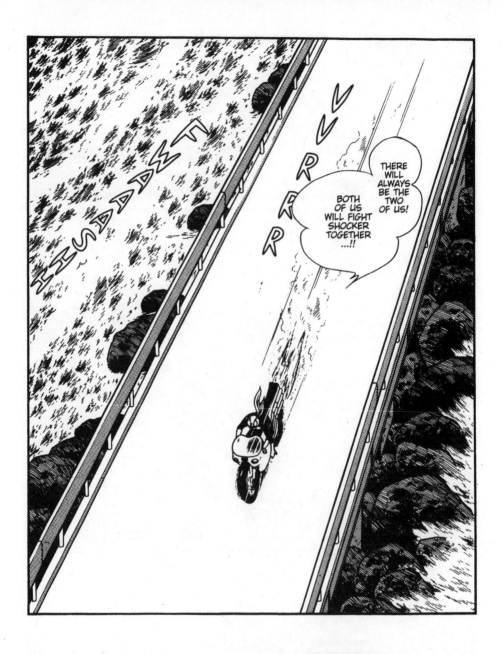

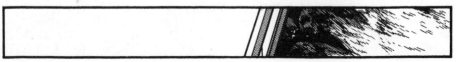

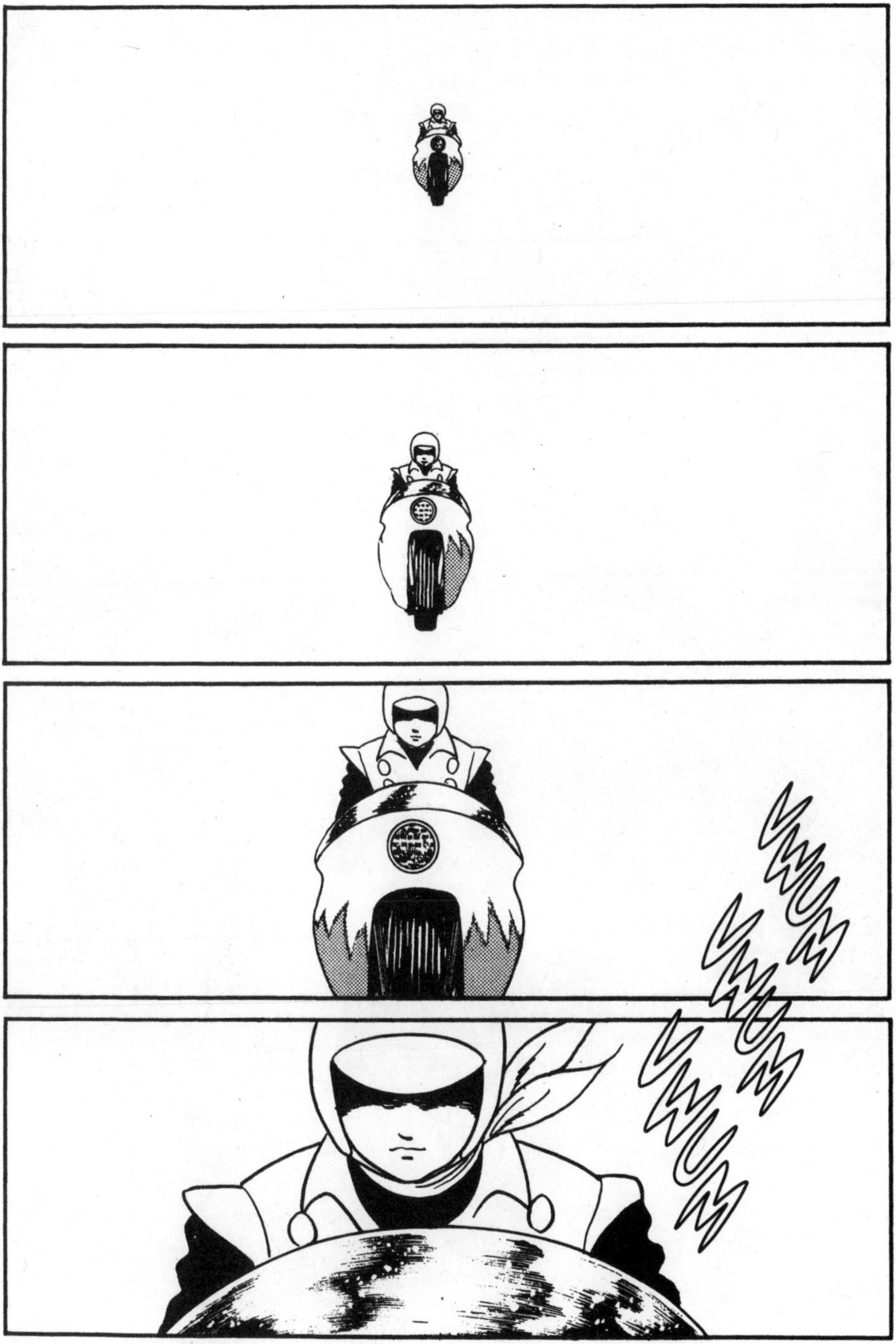
VMUM
VMUM
VMUM

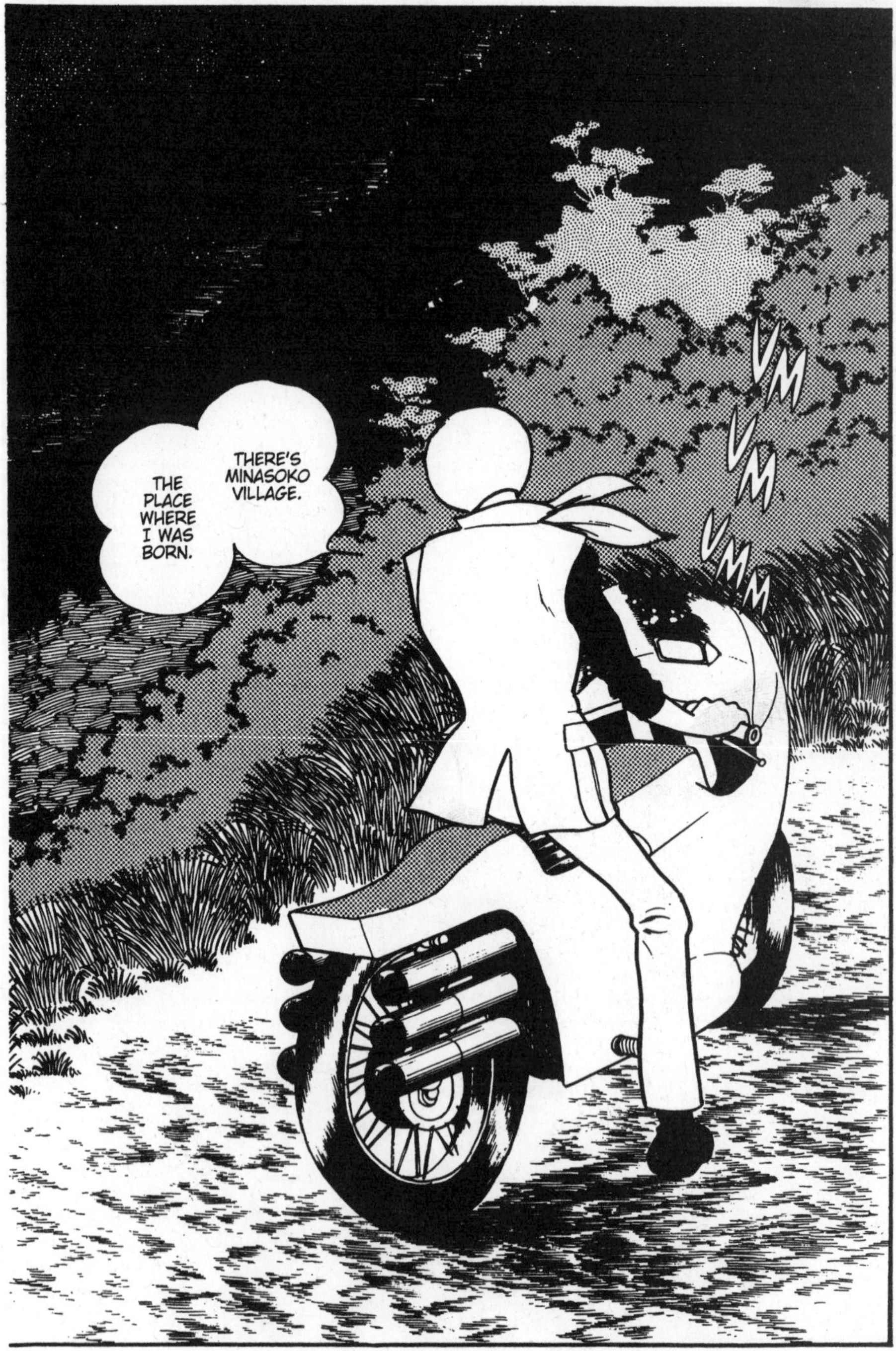
THERE'S MINASOKO VILLAGE.
THE PLACE WHERE I WAS BORN.
VM VM VMM

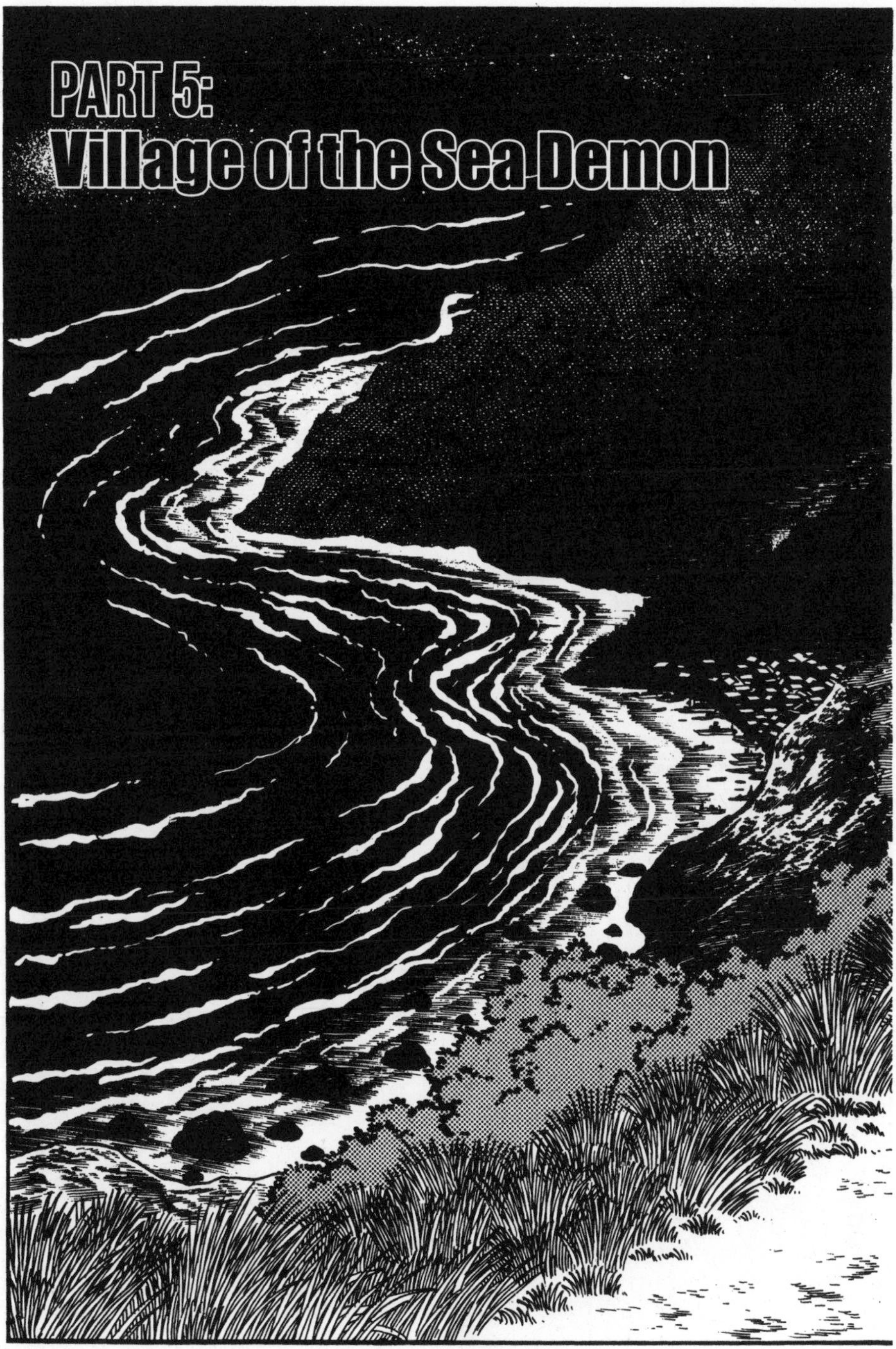
PART 5:
Village of the Sea Demon

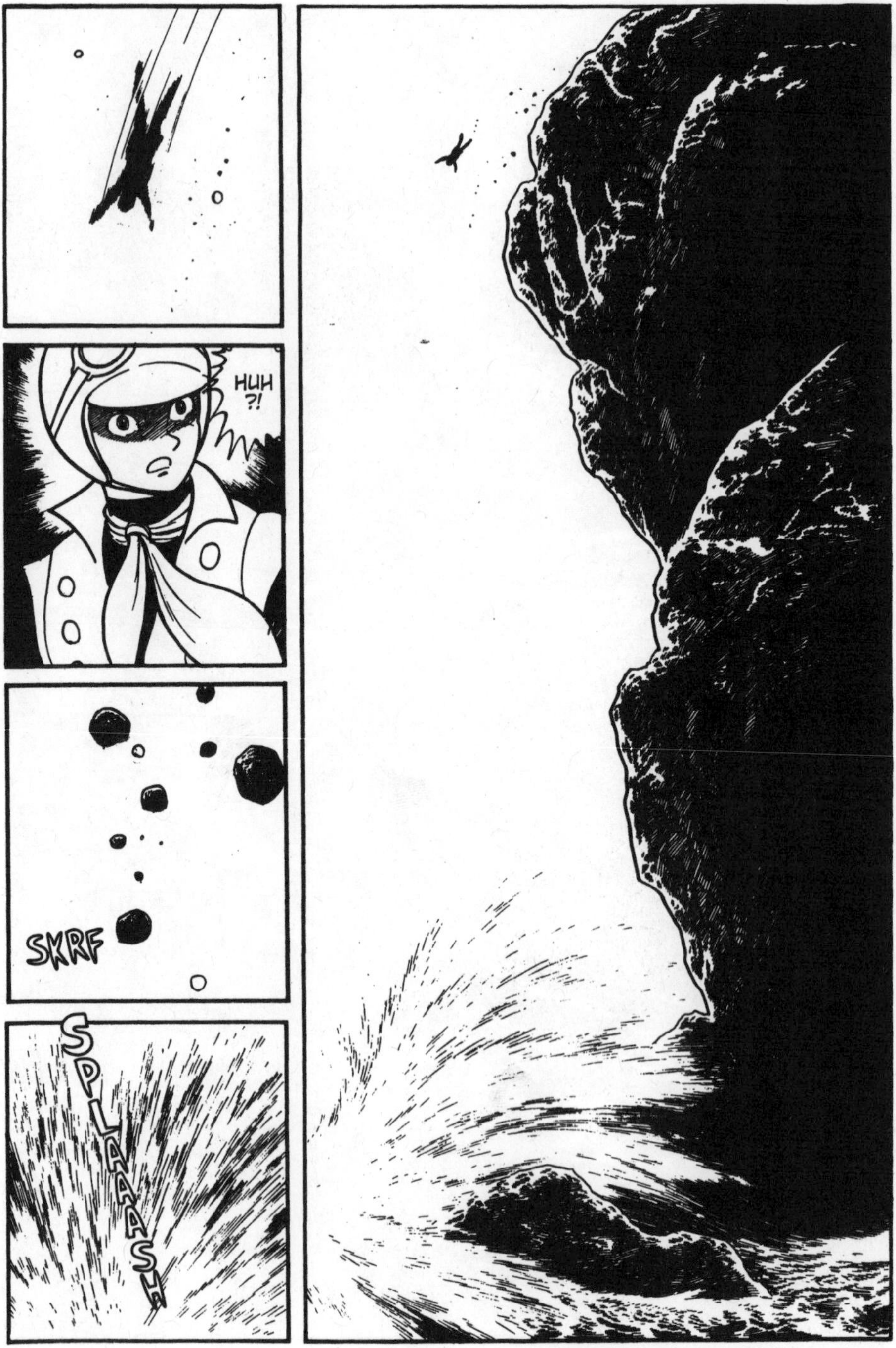
HUH ?!
SKRF
SPLAAAASH

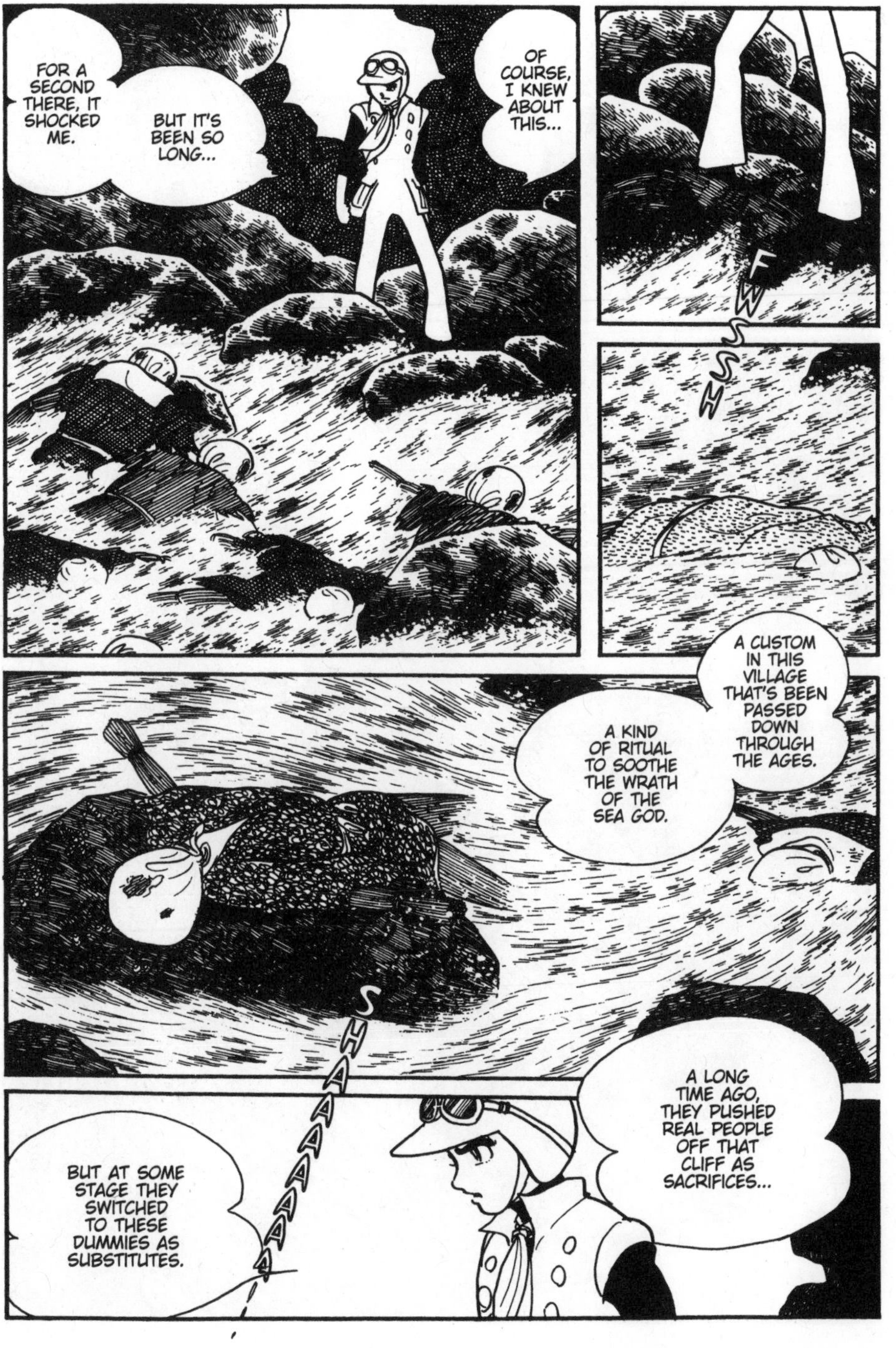
FWSSH
OF COURSE, I KNEW ABOUT THIS...
BUT IT'S BEEN SO LONG...
FOR A SECOND THERE, IT SHOCKED ME.
A CUSTOM IN THIS VILLAGE THAT'S BEEN PASSED DOWN THROUGH THE AGES.
A KIND OF RITUAL TO SOOTHE THE WRATH OF THE SEA GOD.
SHAAAAAAA
A LONG TIME AGO, THEY PUSHED REAL PEOPLE OFF THAT CLIFF AS SACRIFICES...
BUT AT SOME STAGE THEY SWITCHED TO THESE DUMMIES AS SUBSTITUTES.

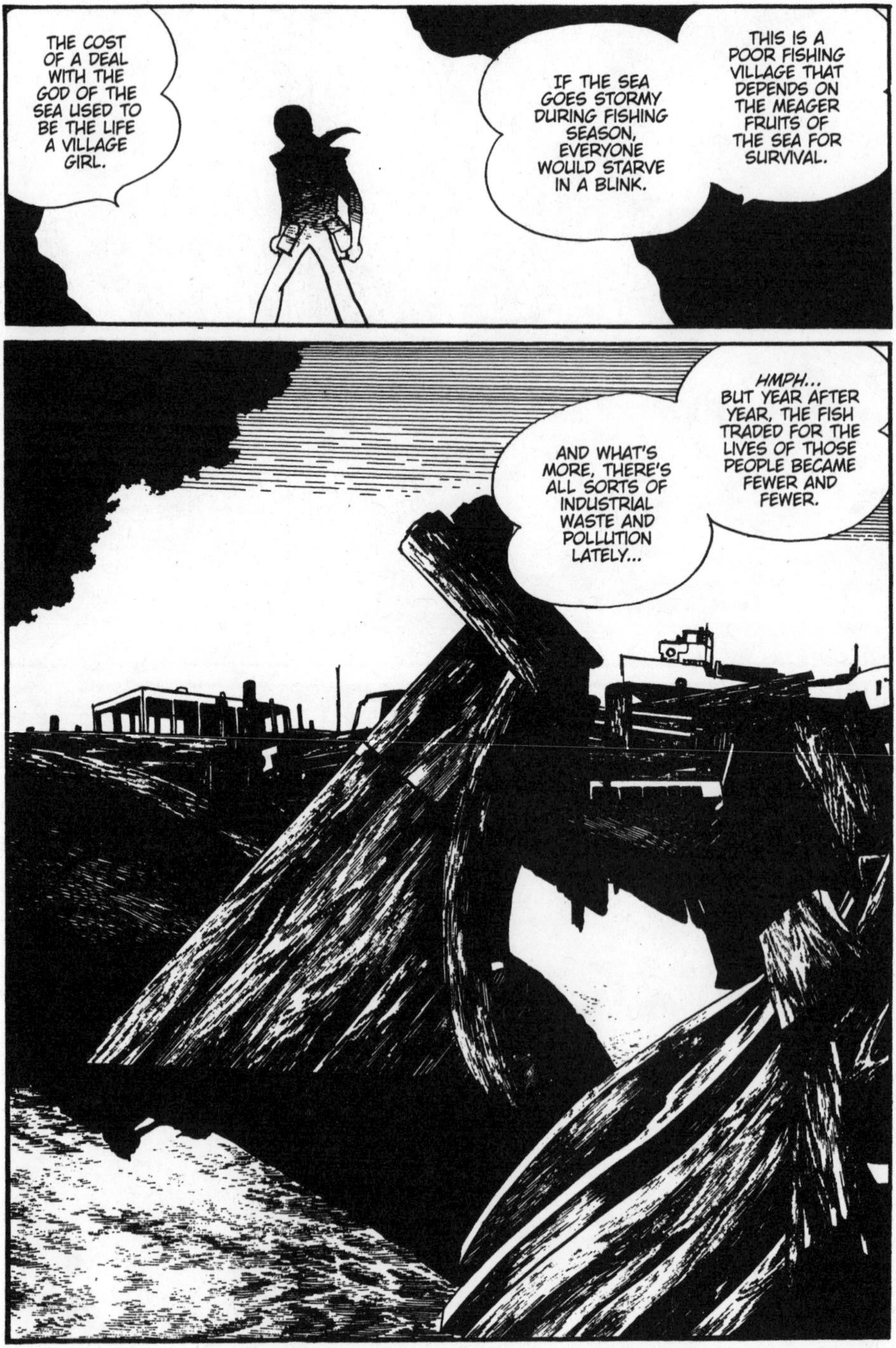
THIS IS A POOR FISHING VILLAGE THAT DEPENDS ON THE MEAGER FRUITS OF THE SEA FOR SURVIVAL.
IF THE SEA GOES STORMY DURING FISHING SEASON, EVERYONE WOULD STARVE IN A BLINK.
THE COST OF A DEAL WITH THE GOD OF THE SEA USED TO BE THE LIFE A VILLAGE GIRL.
HMPH... BUT YEAR AFTER YEAR, THE FISH TRADED FOR THE LIVES OF THOSE PEOPLE BECAME FEWER AND FEWER.
AND WHAT'S MORE, THERE'S ALL SORTS OF INDUSTRIAL WASTE AND POLLUTION LATELY...

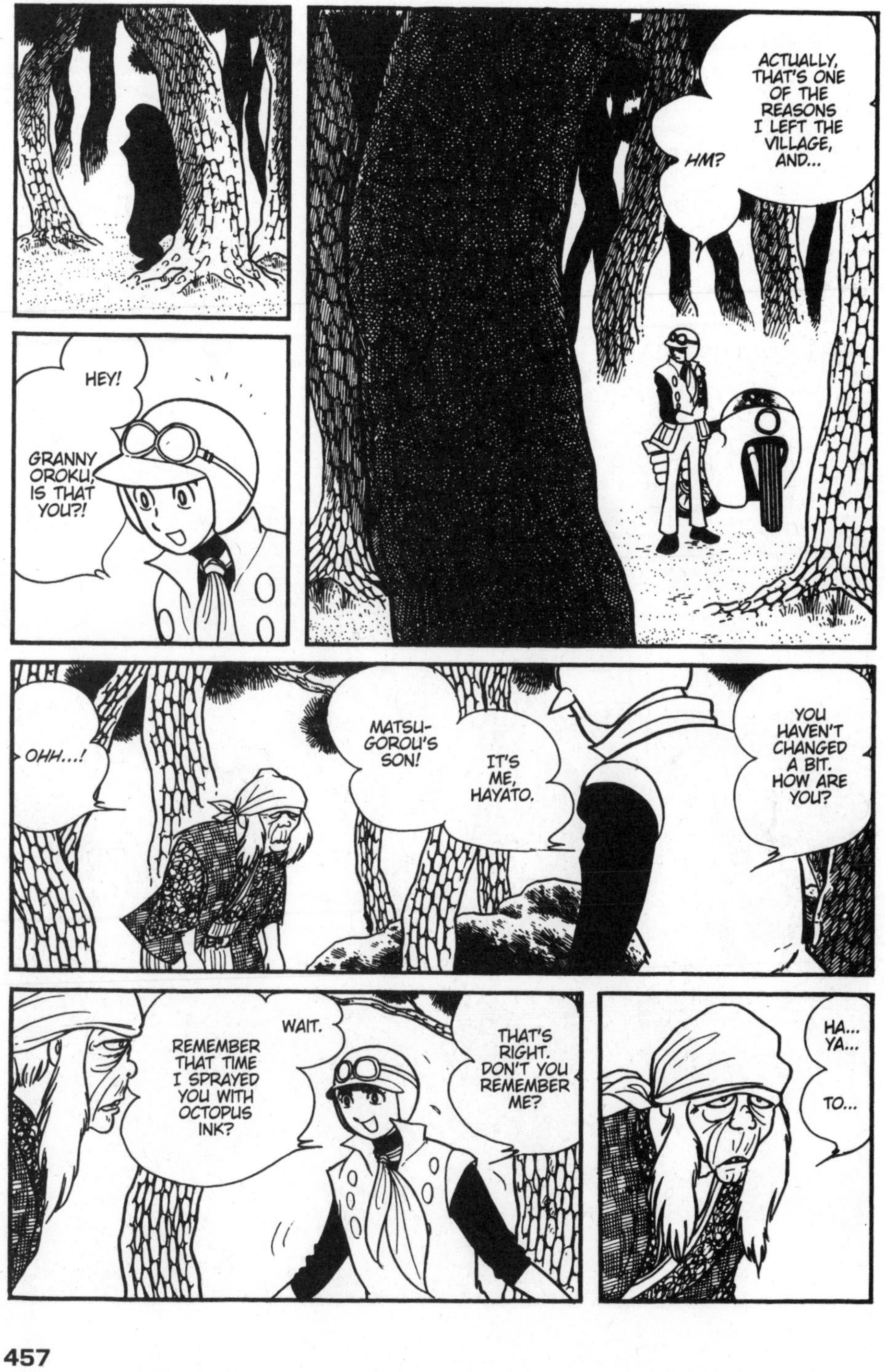
ACTUALLY, THAT'S ONE OF THE REASONS I LEFT THE VILLAGE, AND...
HM?
HEY!
GRANNY OROKU, IS THAT YOU?!
YOU HAVEN'T CHANGED A BIT. HOW ARE YOU?
IT'S ME, HAYATO.
MATSU-GOROU'S SON!
OHH...!
HA... YA...
TO...
THAT'S RIGHT. DON'T YOU REMEMBER ME?
WAIT.
REMEMBER THAT TIME I SPRAYED YOU WITH OCTOPUS INK?

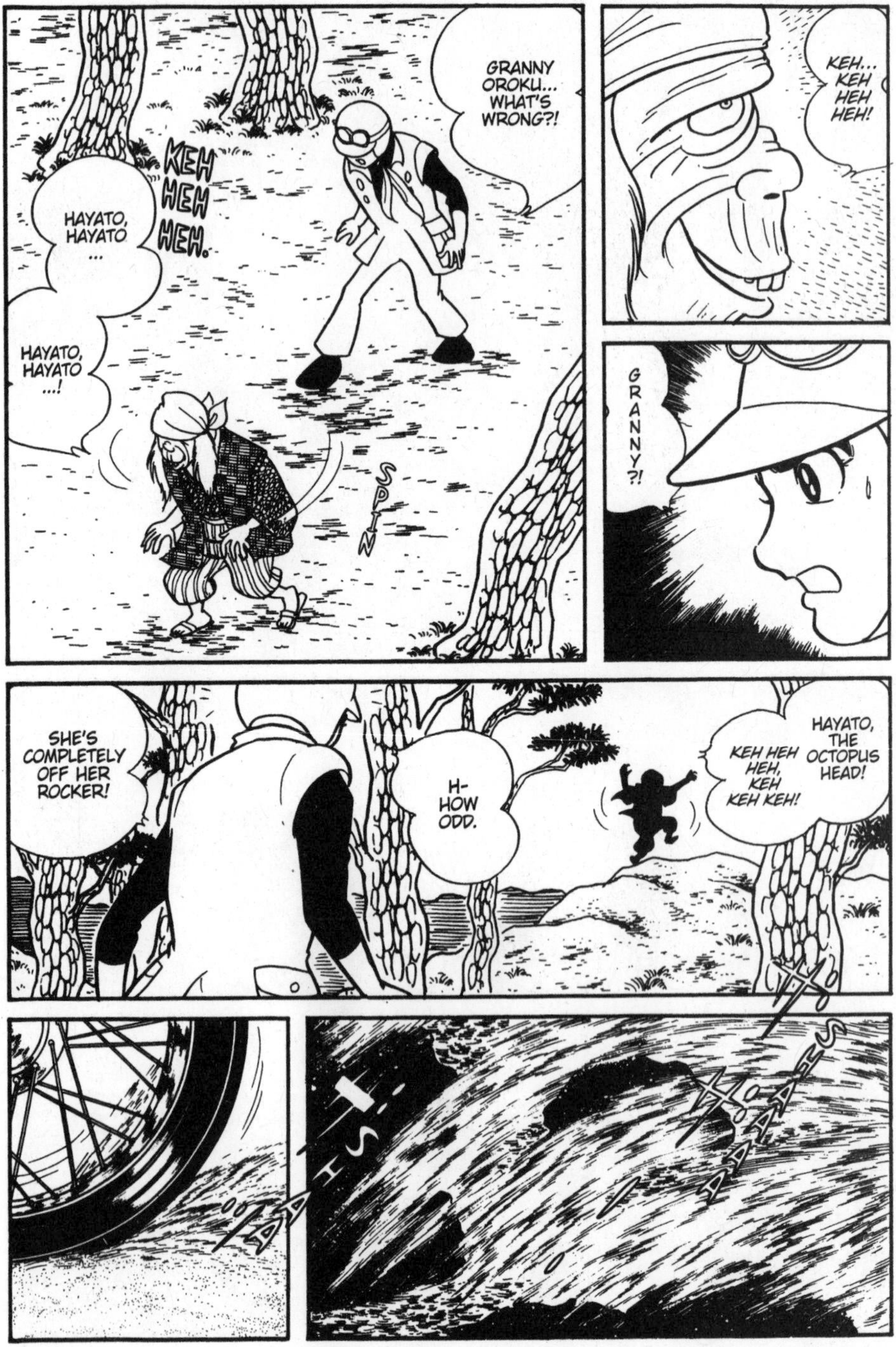
KEH... KEH HEH HEH!
GRANNY?!
GRANNY OROKU... WHAT'S WRONG?!
KEH HEH HEH.
HAYATO, HAYATO ...
HAYATO, HAYATO ...!
SPIN
HAYATO, THE OCTOPUS HEAD!
KEH HEH HEH, KEH KEH KEH!
H- HOW ODD.
SHE'S COMPLETELY OFF HER ROCKER!

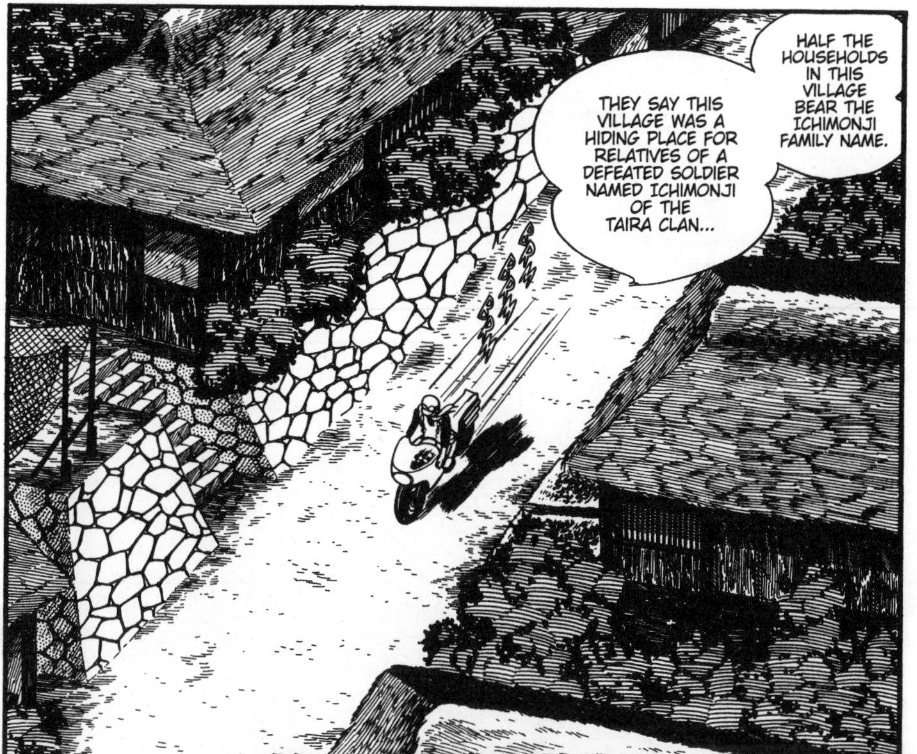
HALF THE HOUSEHOLDS IN THIS VILLAGE BEAR THE ICHIMONJI FAMILY NAME.
THEY SAY THIS VILLAGE WAS A HIDING PLACE FOR RELATIVES OF A DEFEATED SOLDIER NAMED ICHIMONJI OF THE TAIRA CLAN...
BRM BRM BRM
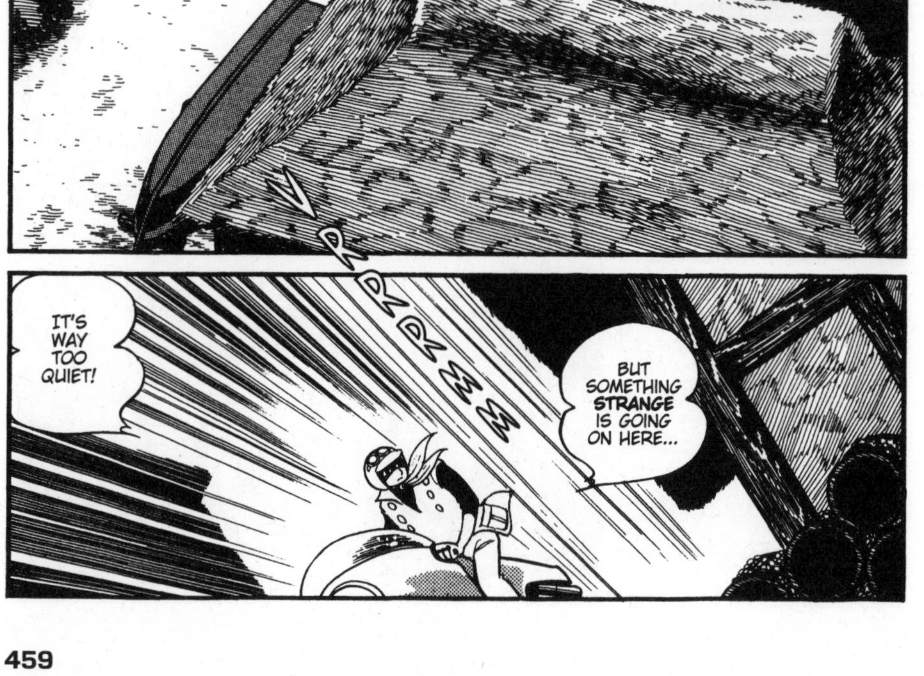
BUT SOMETHING **STRANGE** IS GOING ON HERE...
VRRRRMMM
IT'S WAY TOO QUIET!

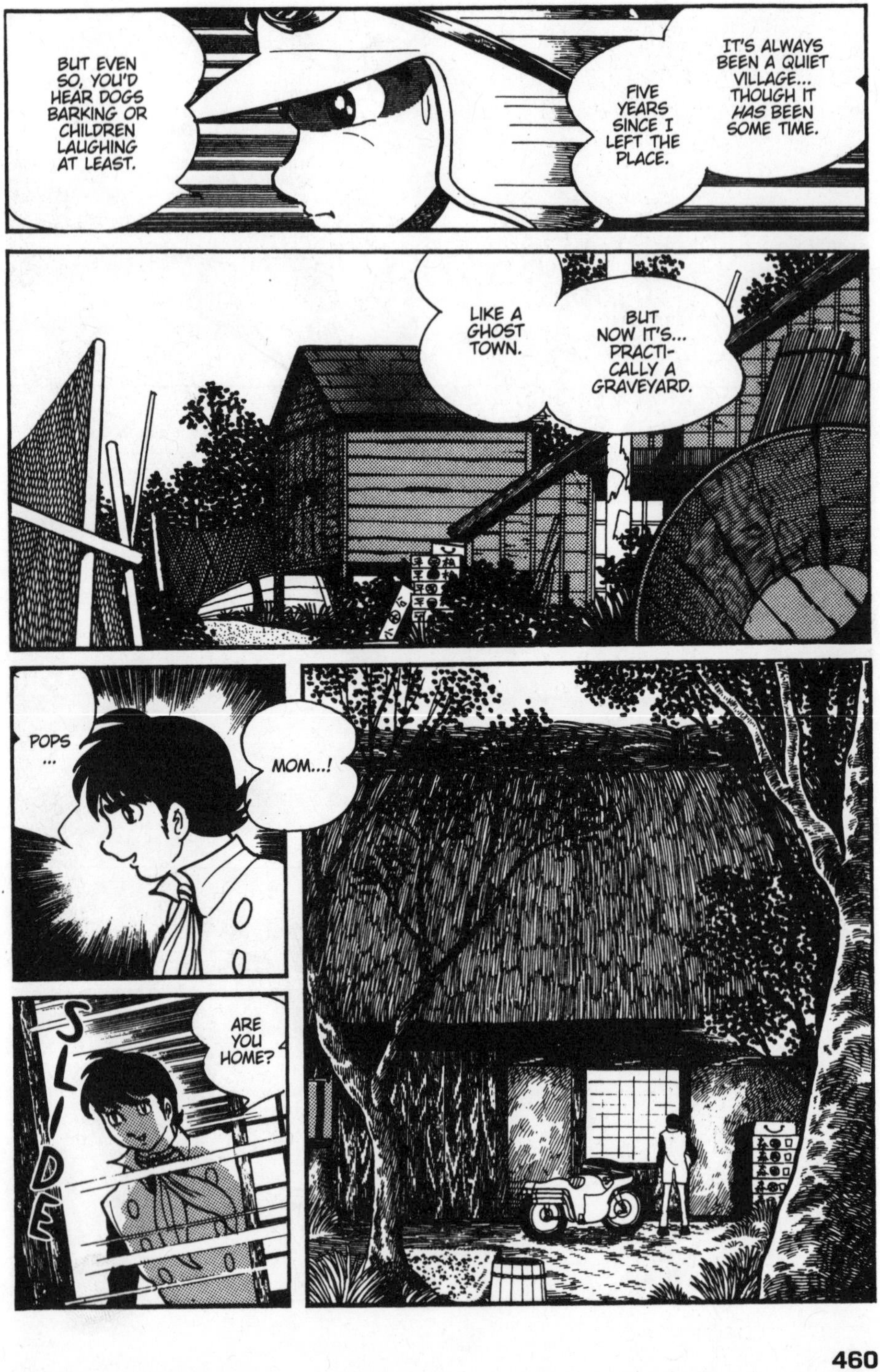
IT'S ALWAYS BEEN A QUIET VILLAGE... THOUGH IT *HAS* BEEN SOME TIME.
FIVE YEARS SINCE I LEFT THE PLACE.
BUT EVEN SO, YOU'D HEAR DOGS BARKING OR CHILDREN LAUGHING AT LEAST.
BUT NOW IT'S... PRACTI-CALLY A GRAVEYARD.
LIKE A GHOST TOWN.
MOM...!
POPS ...
ARE YOU HOME?
SLIDE

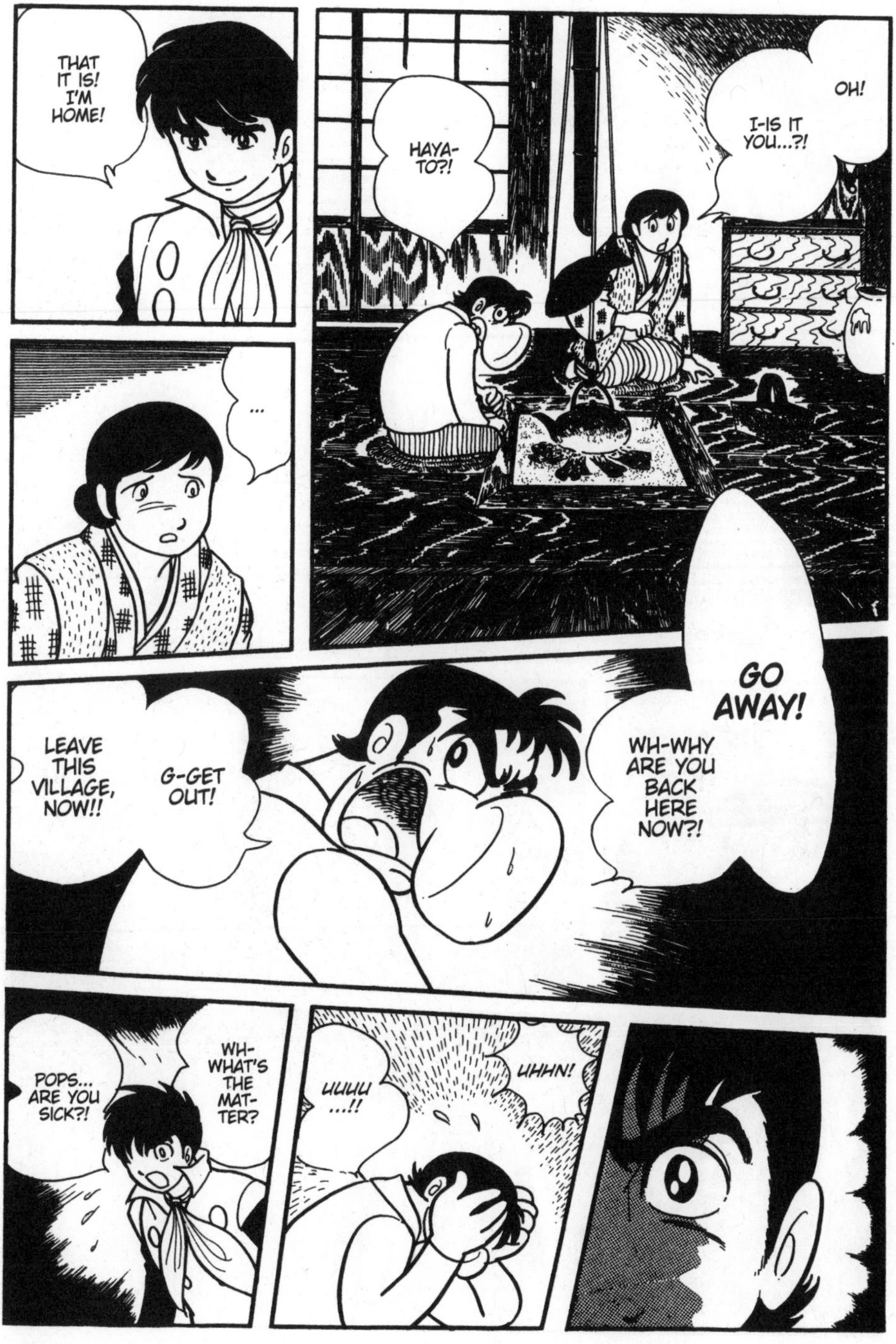

OH!
I-IS IT YOU...?!
HAYA-TO?!
THAT IT IS! I'M HOME!
...
GO AWAY!
WH-WHY ARE YOU BACK HERE NOW?!
G-GET OUT!
LEAVE THIS VILLAGE, NOW!!
UHHN!
uuuu ...!!
WH-WHAT'S THE MAT-TER?
POPS... ARE YOU SICK?!

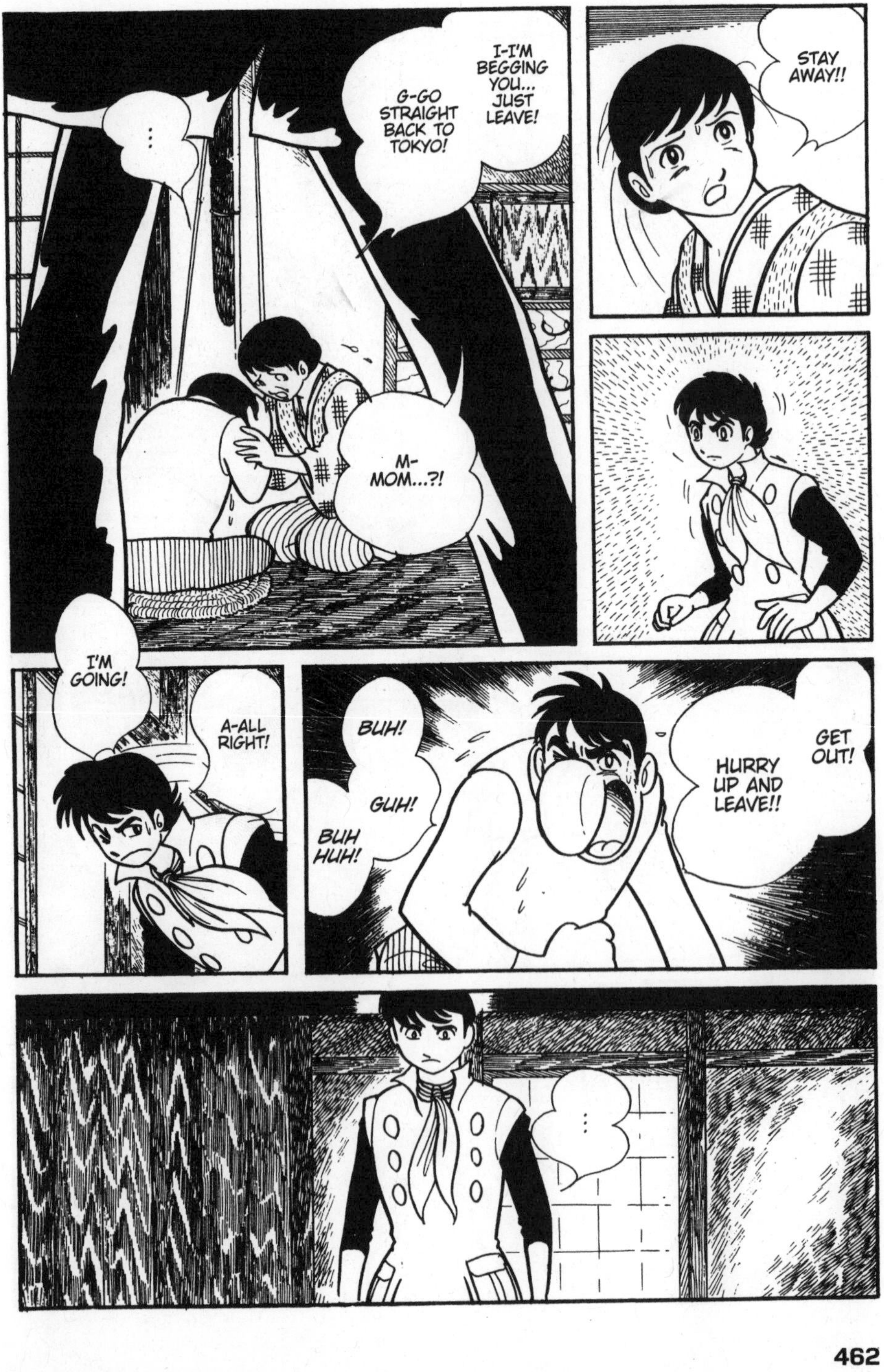
STAY AWAY!!
I-I'M BEGGING YOU... JUST LEAVE!
G-GO STRAIGHT BACK TO TOKYO!
...
M-MOM...?!
GET OUT!
HURRY UP AND LEAVE!!
BUH!
GUH!
BUH HUH!
A-ALL RIGHT!
I'M GOING!
...

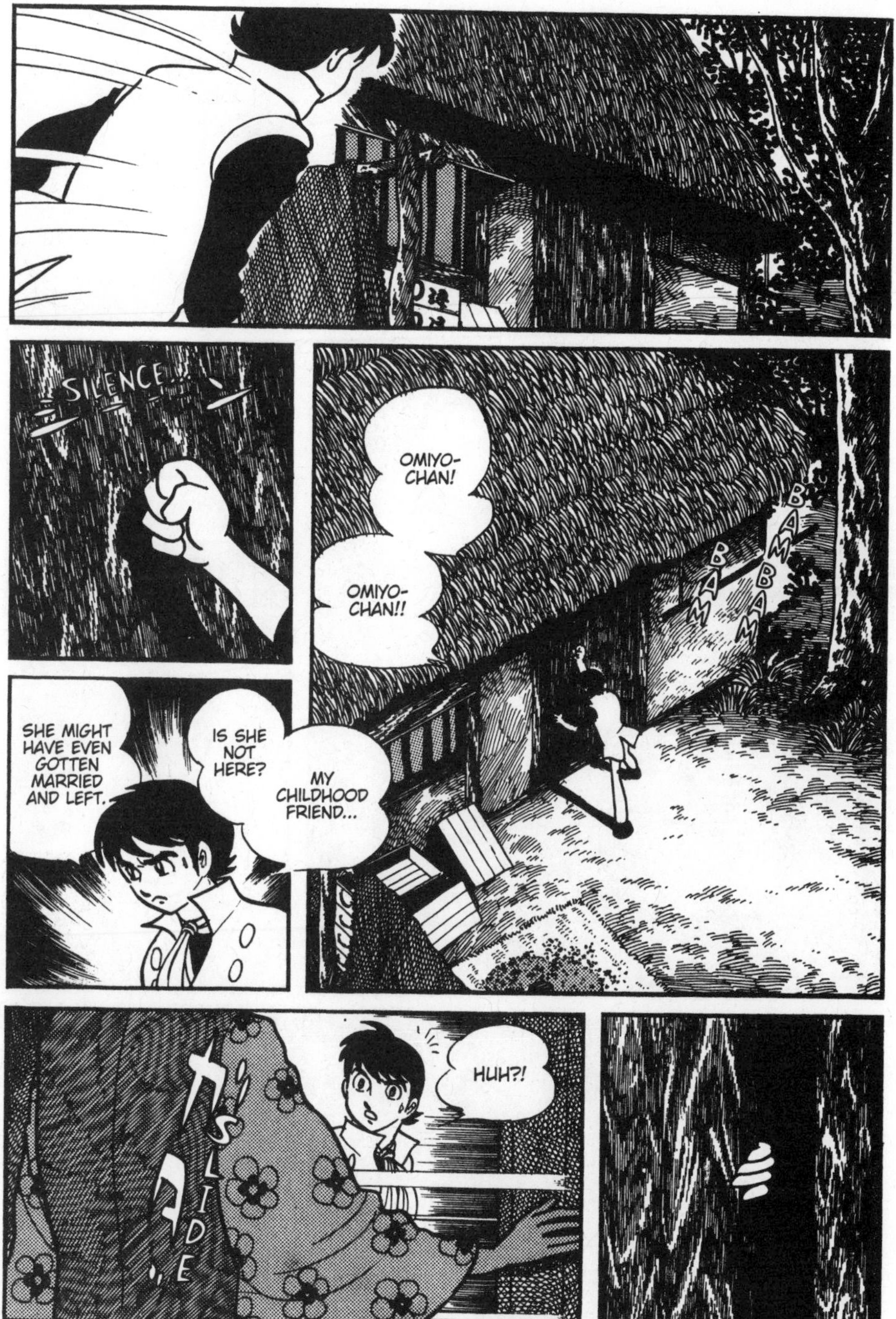
OMIYO-CHAN!
OMIYO-CHAN!!
BAM BAM BAM
BAM BAM
SILENCE...
MY CHILDHOOD FRIEND...
IS SHE NOT HERE?
SHE MIGHT HAVE EVEN GOTTEN MARRIED AND LEFT.
HUH?!
SLIDE

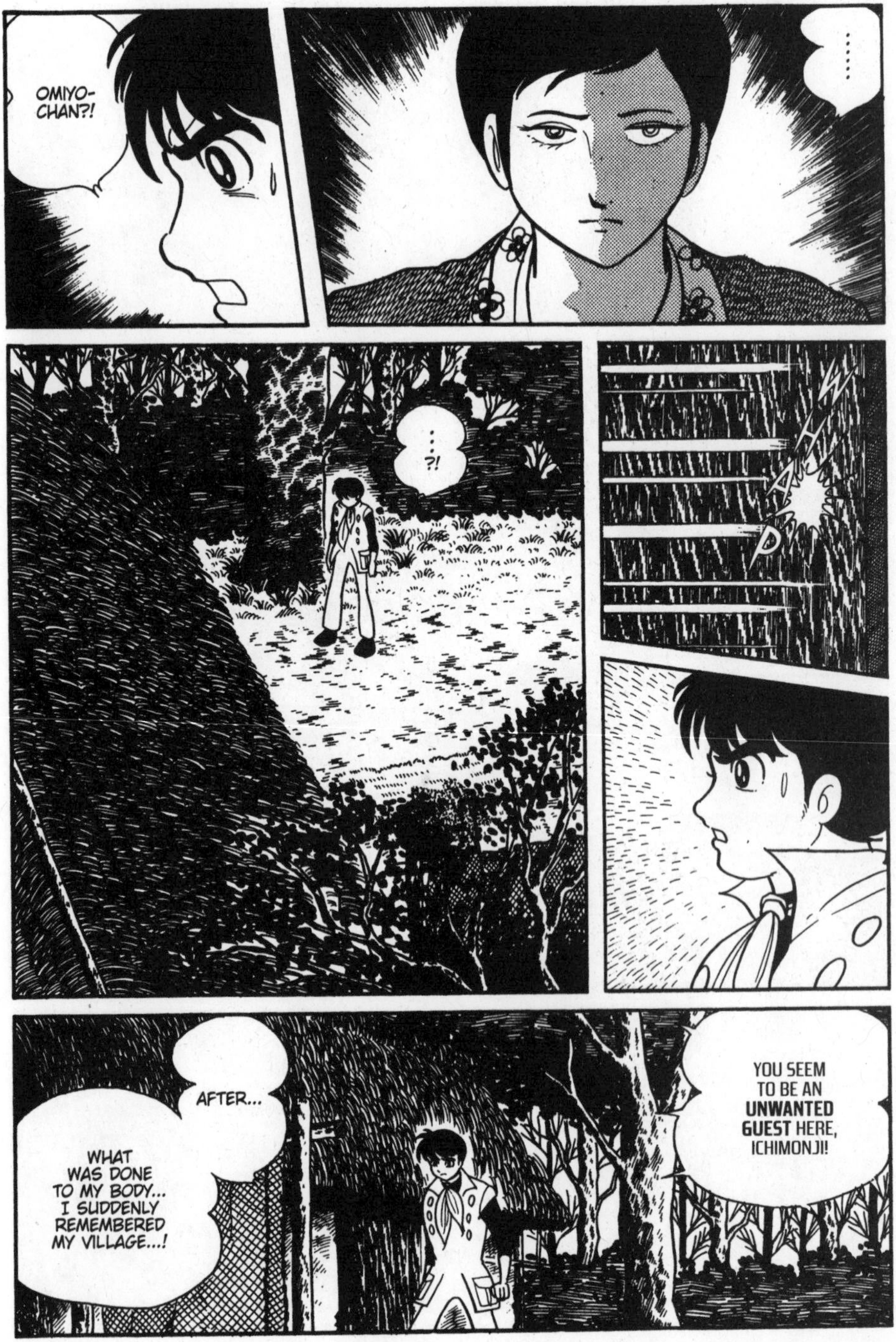
……
OMIYO-CHAN?!
WHAP
……?!
YOU SEEM TO BE AN UNWANTED GUEST HERE, ICHIMONJI!
AFTER…
WHAT WAS DONE TO MY BODY… I SUDDENLY REMEMBERED MY VILLAGE…!

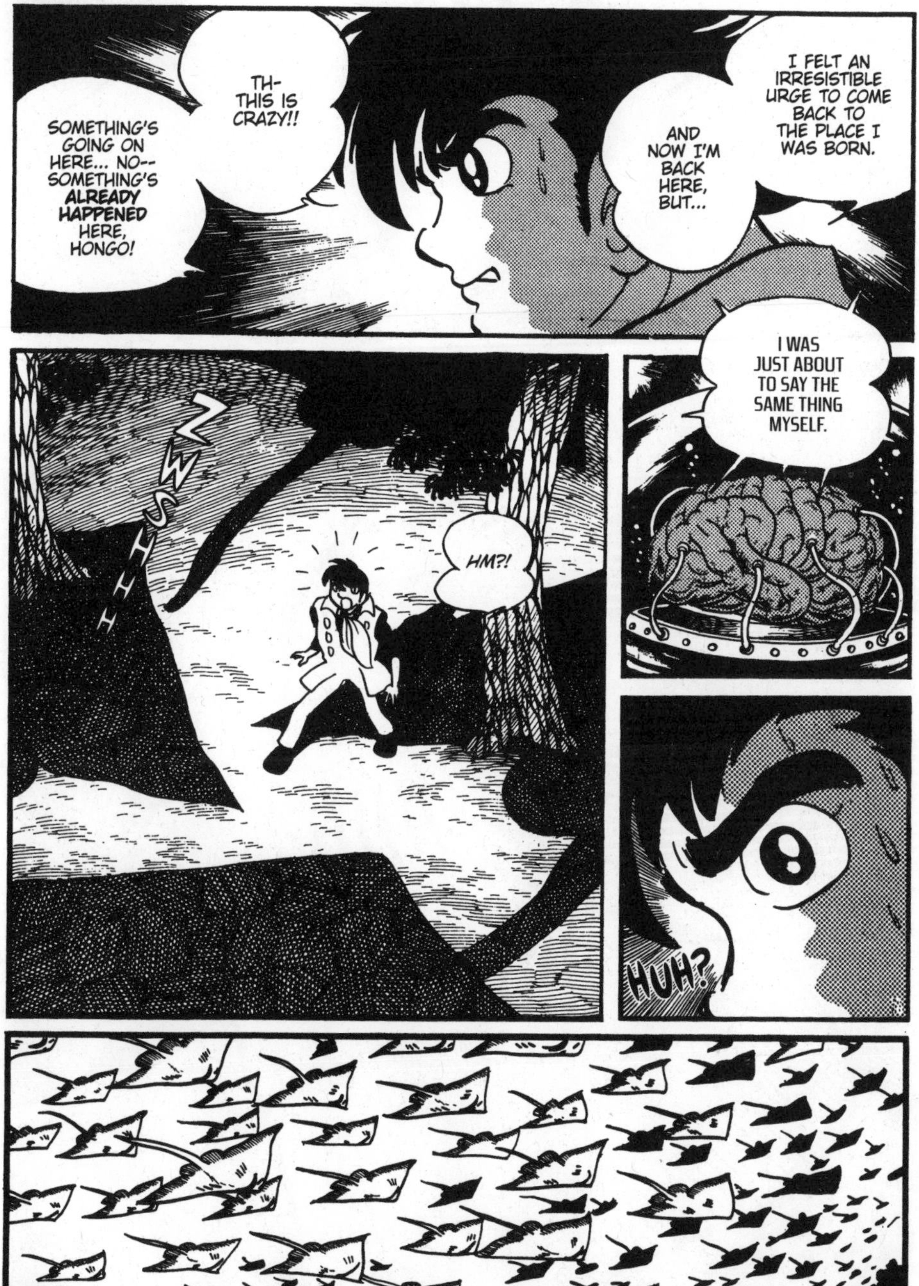
I FELT AN IRRESISTIBLE URGE TO COME BACK TO THE PLACE I WAS BORN.
AND NOW I'M BACK HERE, BUT...
TH- THIS IS CRAZY!!
SOMETHING'S GOING ON HERE... NO-- SOMETHING'S **ALREADY HAPPENED** HERE, HONGO!
I WAS JUST ABOUT TO SAY THE SAME THING MYSELF.
HUH?
ZWSHHH
HM?!

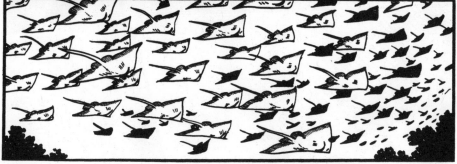

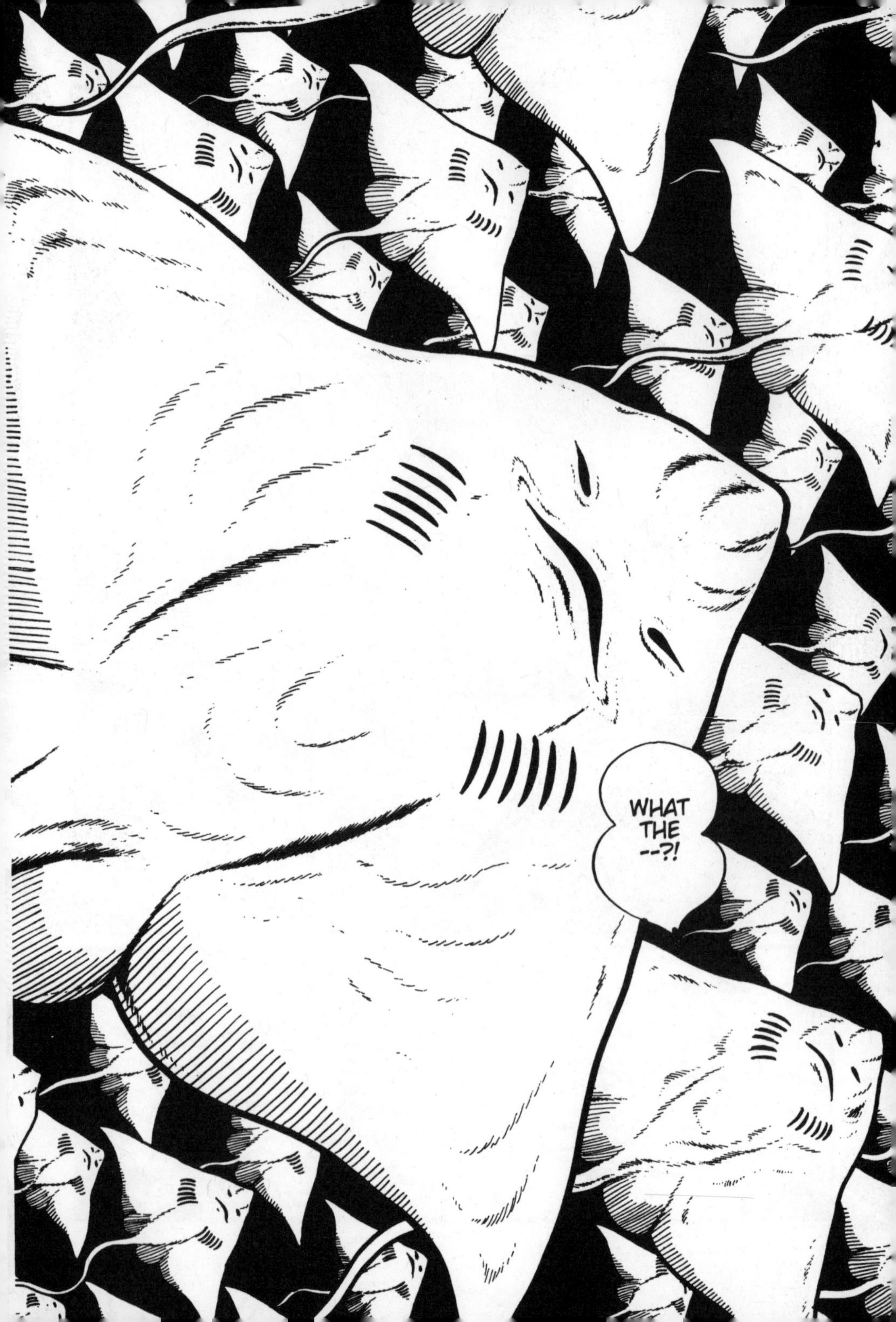
WHAT THE --?!

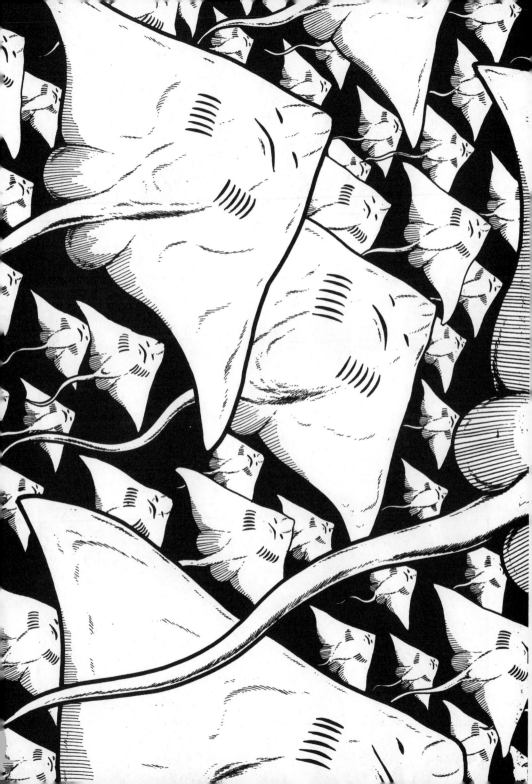

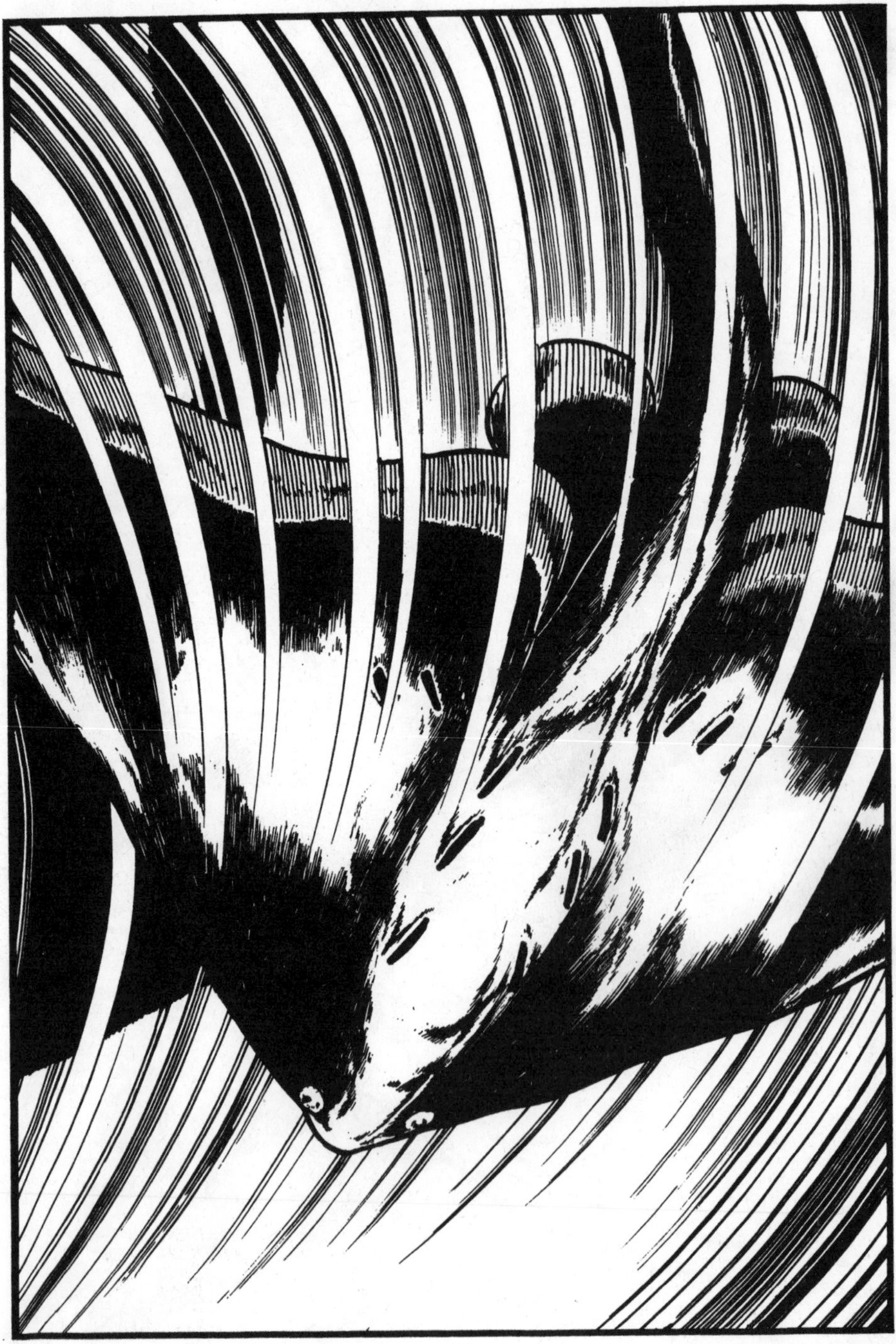

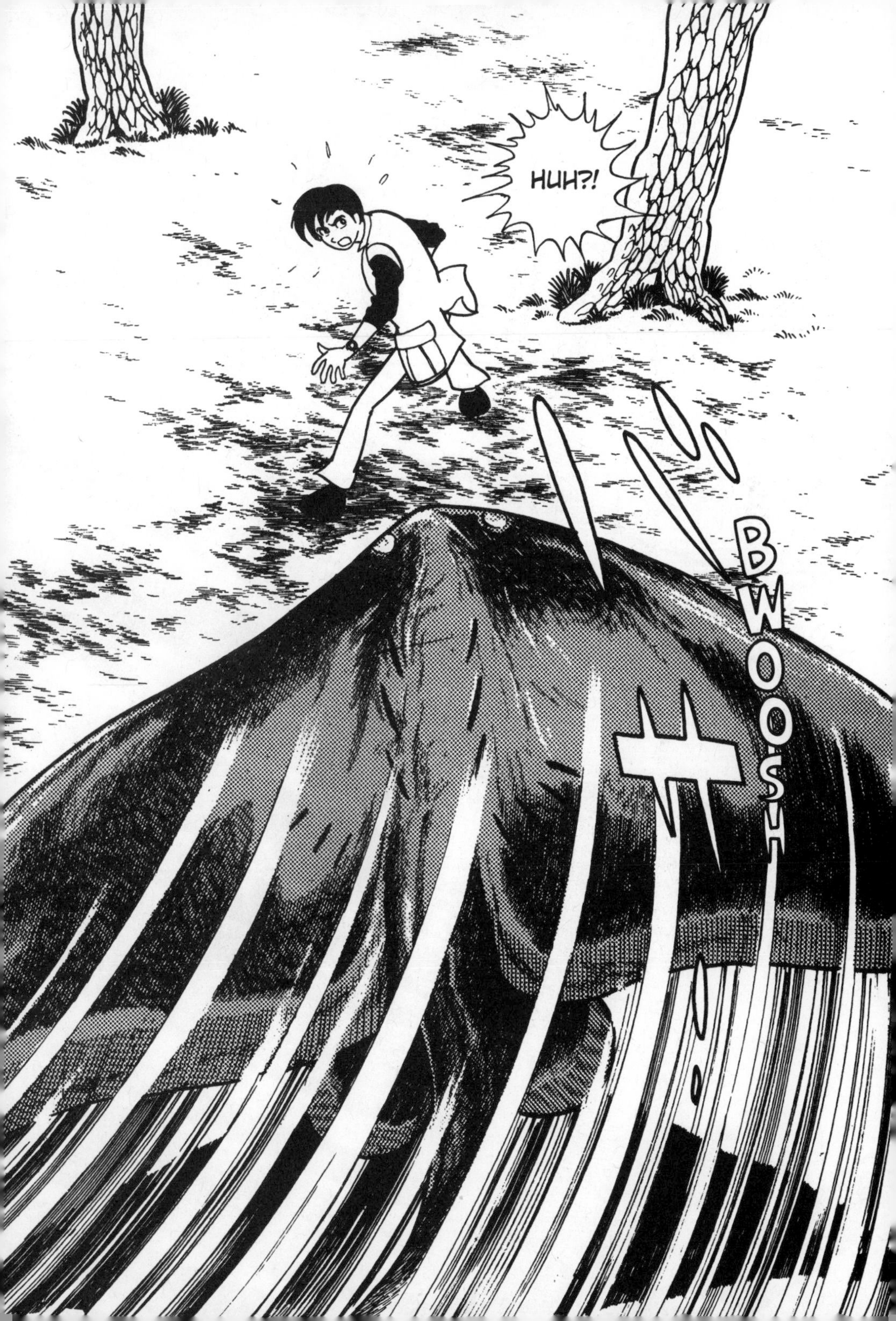
HUH?!
BWOOSH

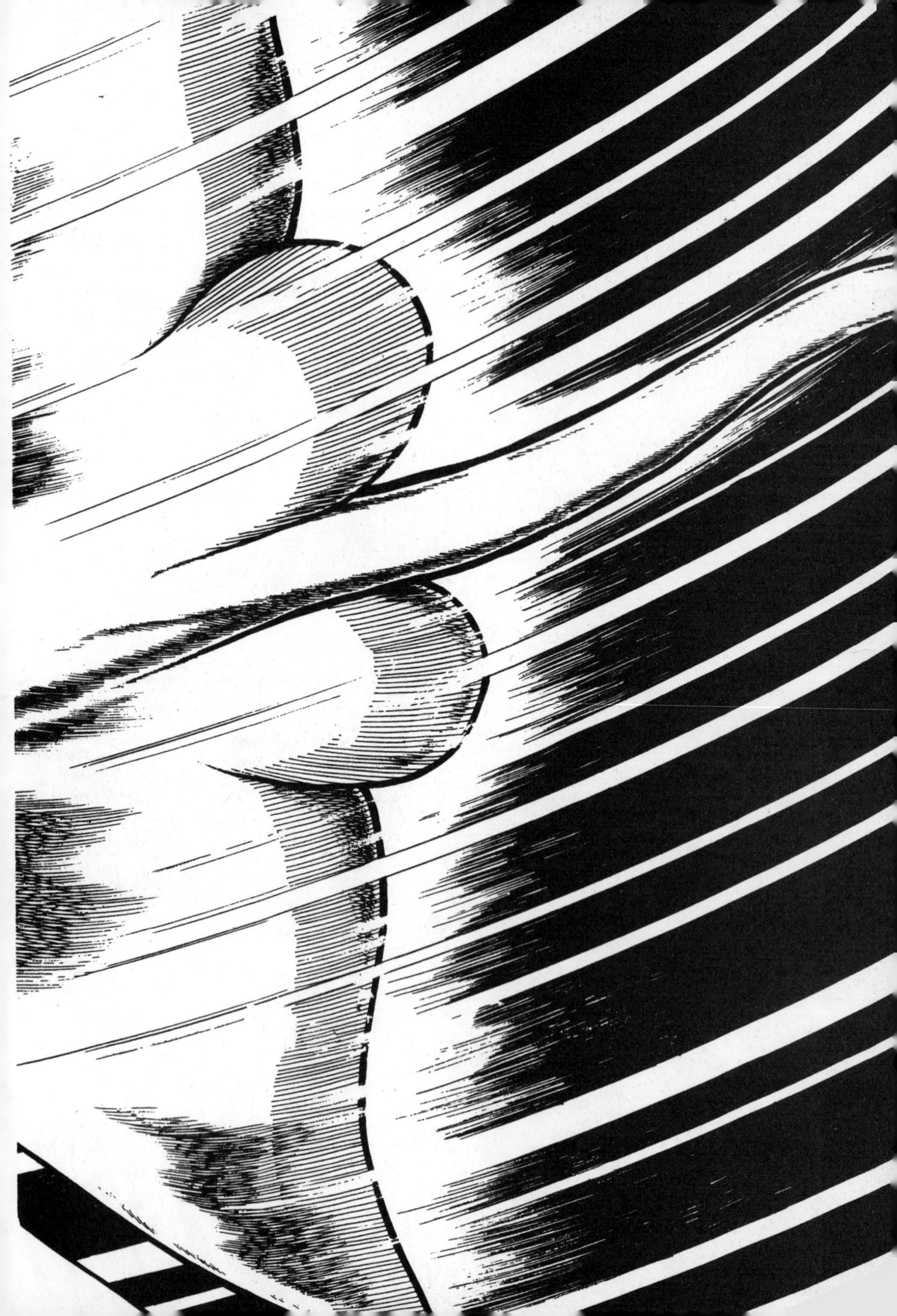

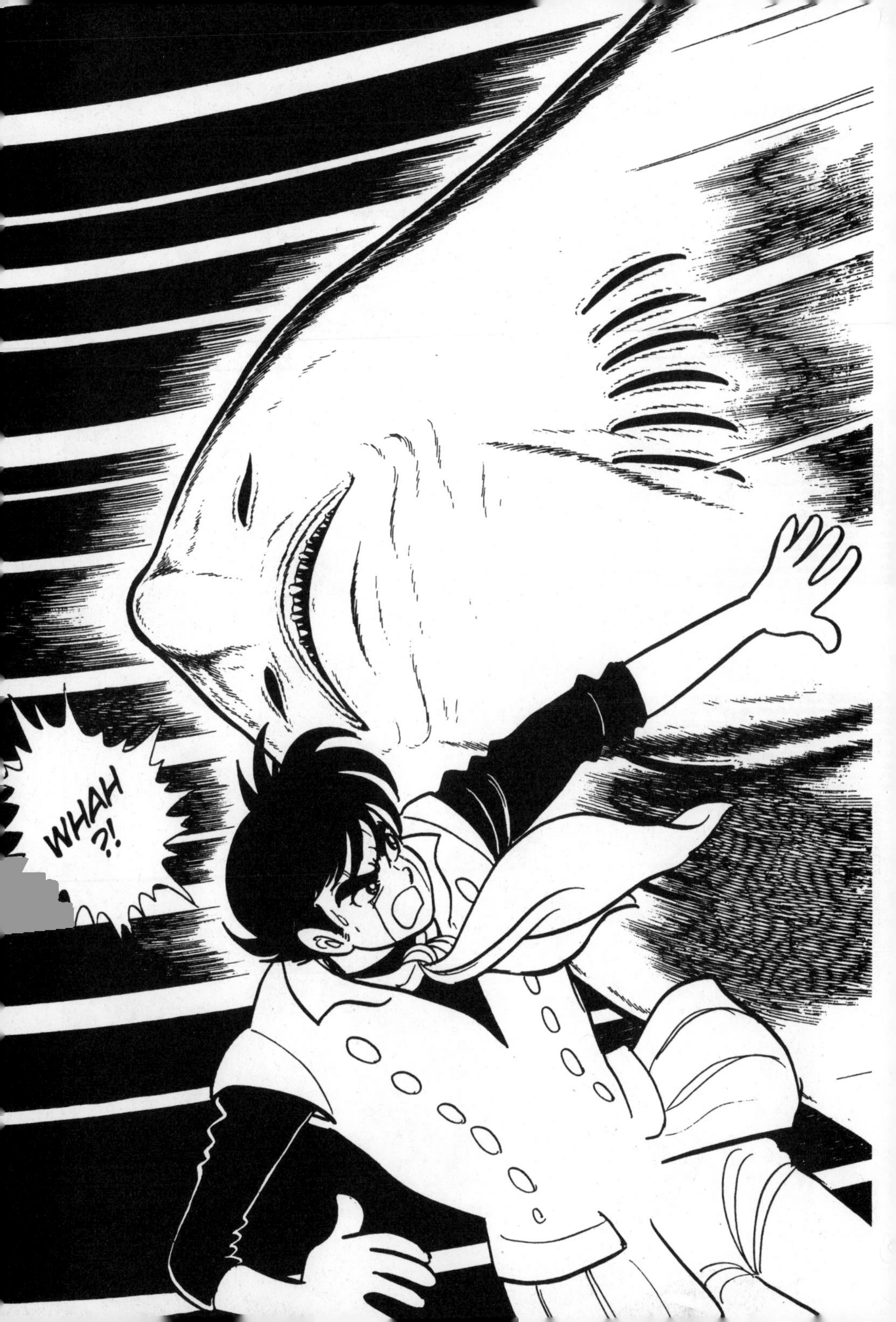
WHAH ?!

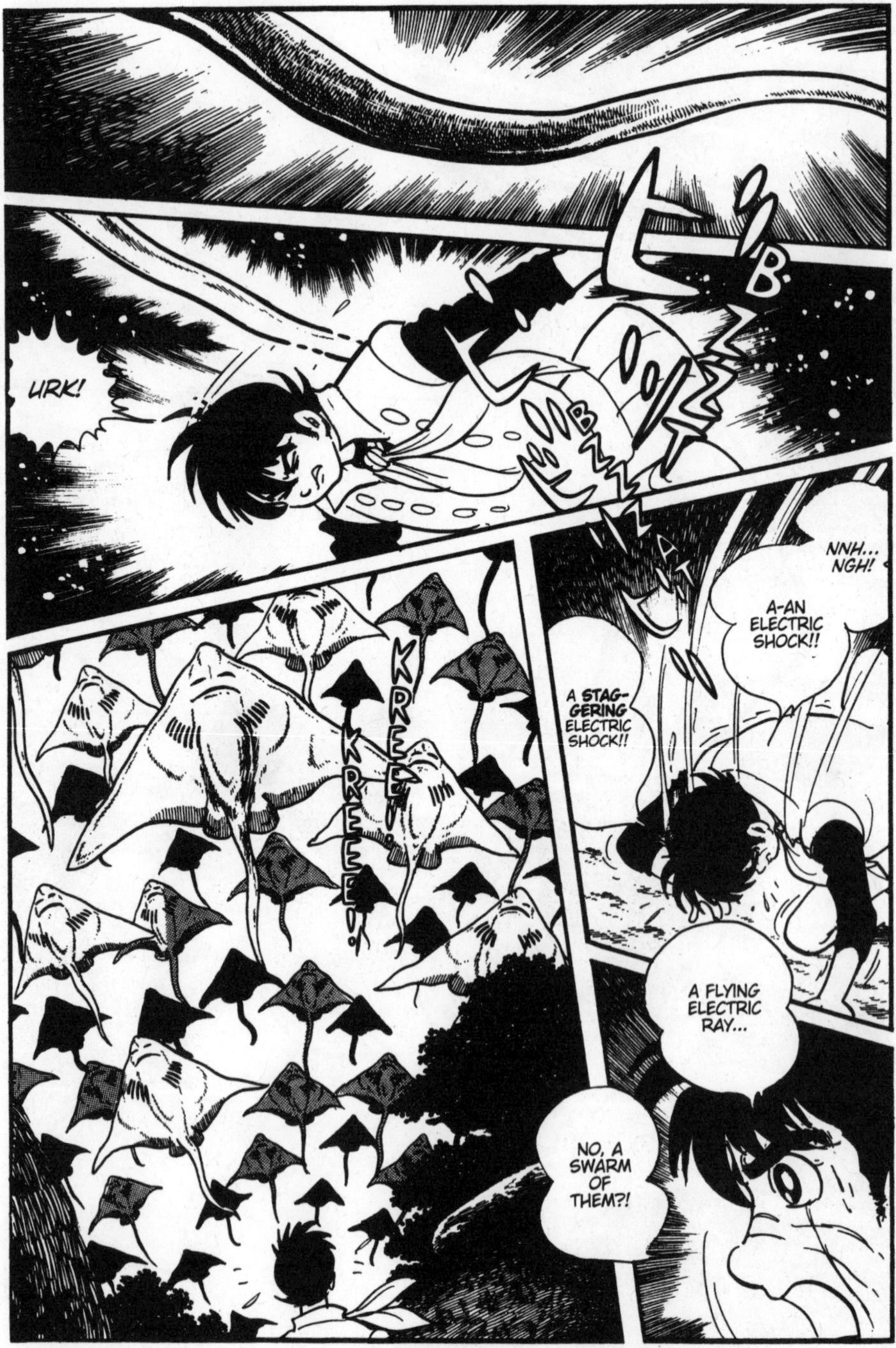
URK!
NNH... NGH!
A-AN ELECTRIC SHOCK!!
A STAG-GERING ELECTRIC SHOCK!!
A FLYING ELECTRIC RAY...
NO, A SWARM OF THEM?!
KREEE!

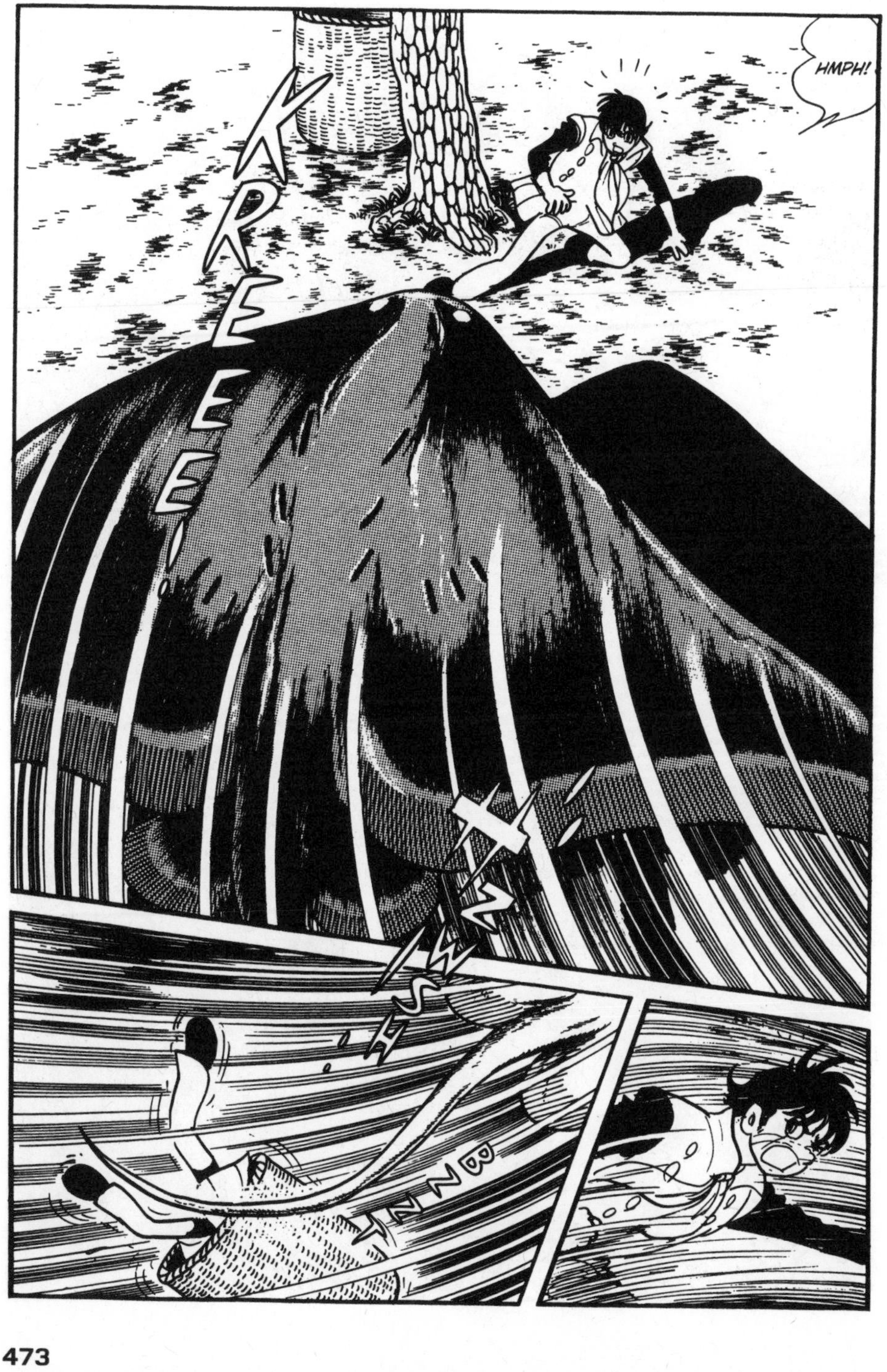
HMPH!
KREEEE!!
BNNT

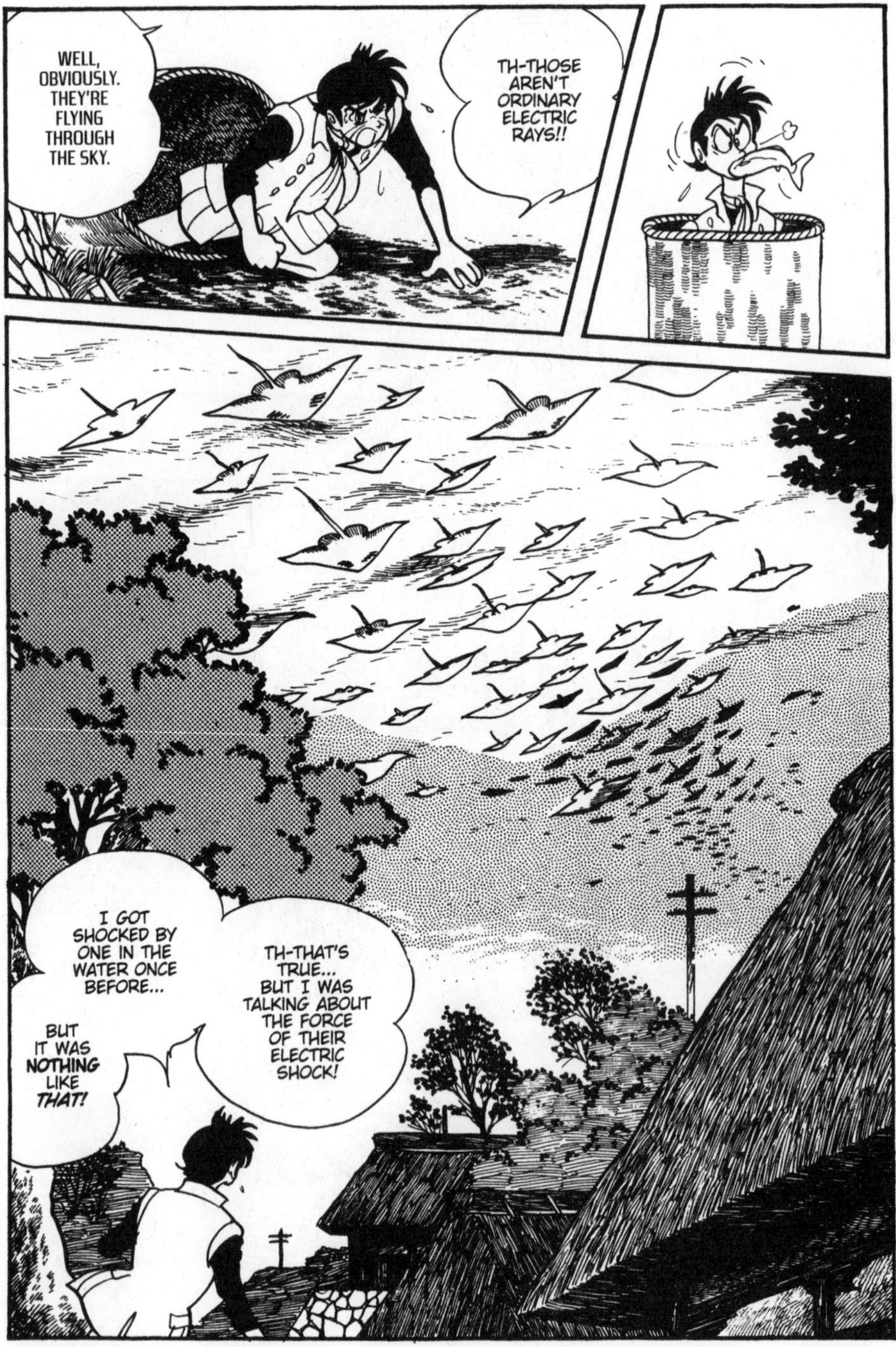
TH-THOSE AREN'T ORDINARY ELECTRIC RAYS!!
WELL, OBVIOUSLY. THEY'RE FLYING THROUGH THE SKY.
TH-THAT'S TRUE... BUT I WAS TALKING ABOUT THE FORCE OF THEIR ELECTRIC SHOCK!
I GOT SHOCKED BY ONE IN THE WATER ONCE BEFORE...
BUT IT WAS **NOTHING** LIKE ***THAT!***

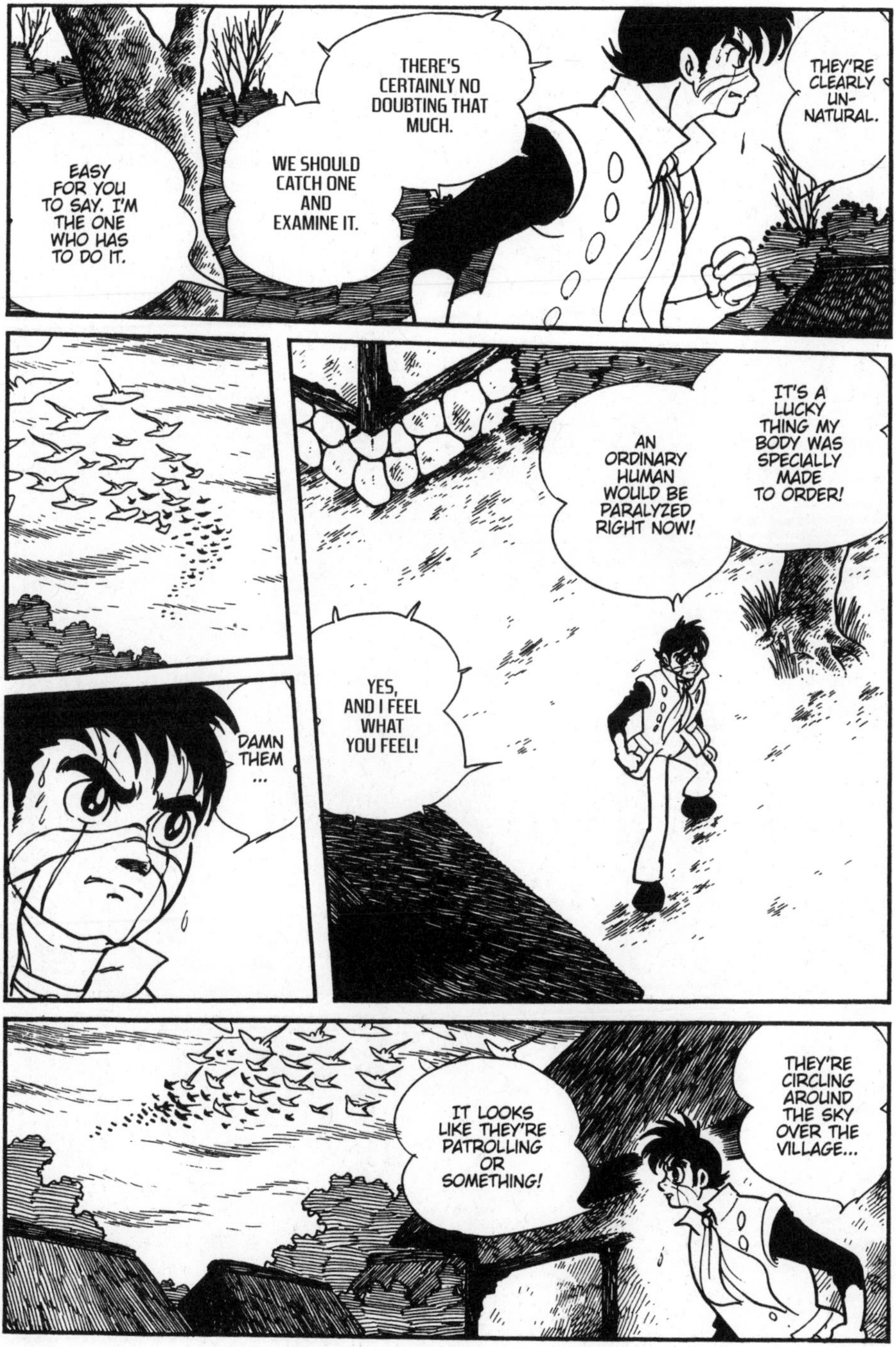
THEY'RE CLEARLY UN-NATURAL.
THERE'S CERTAINLY NO DOUBTING THAT MUCH.
WE SHOULD CATCH ONE AND EXAMINE IT.
EASY FOR YOU TO SAY. I'M THE ONE WHO HAS TO DO IT.
IT'S A LUCKY THING MY BODY WAS SPECIALLY MADE TO ORDER!
AN ORDINARY HUMAN WOULD BE PARALYZED RIGHT NOW!
YES, AND I FEEL WHAT YOU FEEL!
DAMN THEM ...
THEY'RE CIRCLING AROUND THE SKY OVER THE VILLAGE...
IT LOOKS LIKE THEY'RE PATROLLING OR SOMETHING!

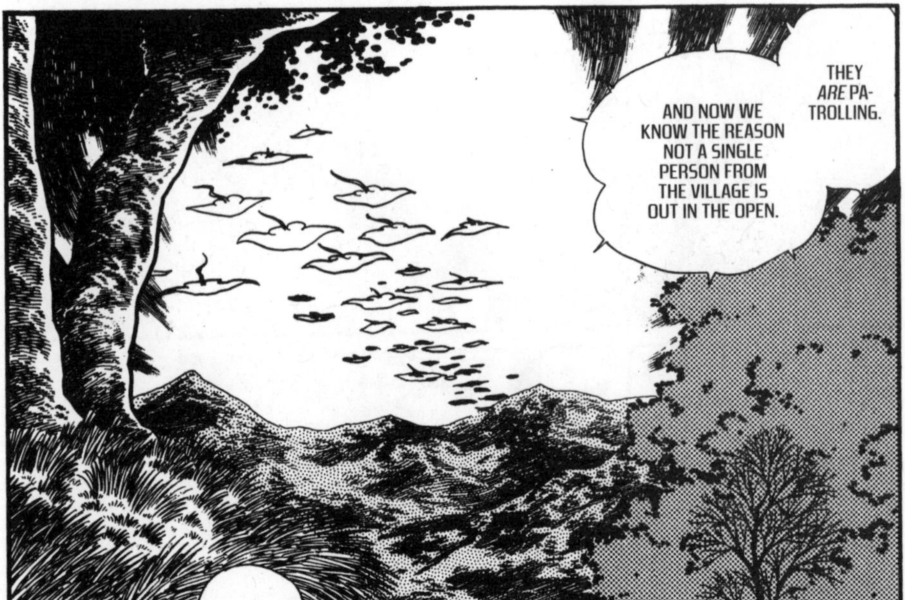
THEY *ARE* PA-TROLLING.
AND NOW WE KNOW THE REASON NOT A SINGLE PERSON FROM THE VILLAGE IS OUT IN THE OPEN.
GRR...
ALL RIGHT, LET'S FOLLOW THEM!
WHERE WILL THEY RETREAT TO...?

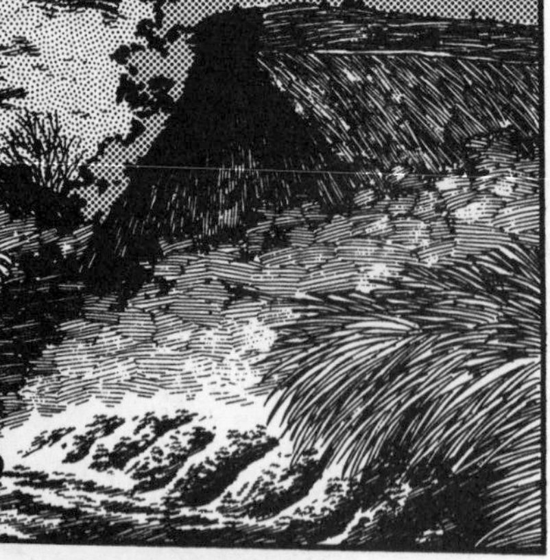
WE KNOW THAT, TOO. THEIR DWELLING PLACE IS THE **SEA!**

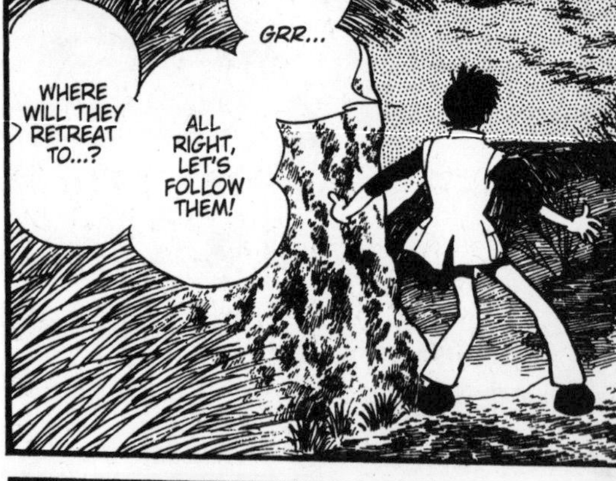

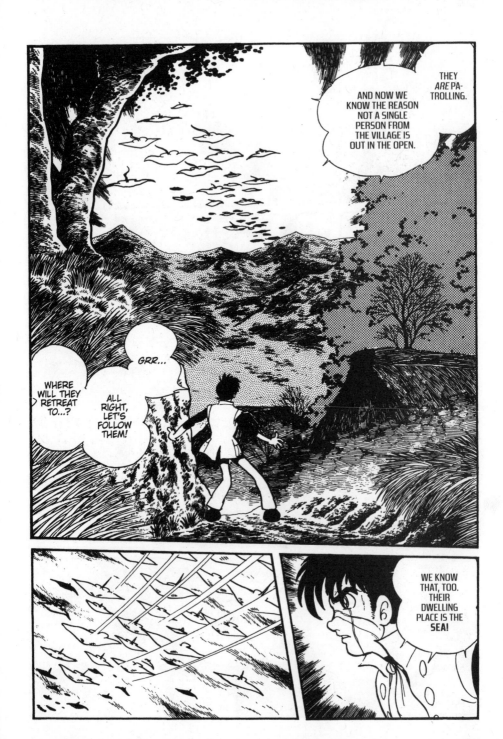

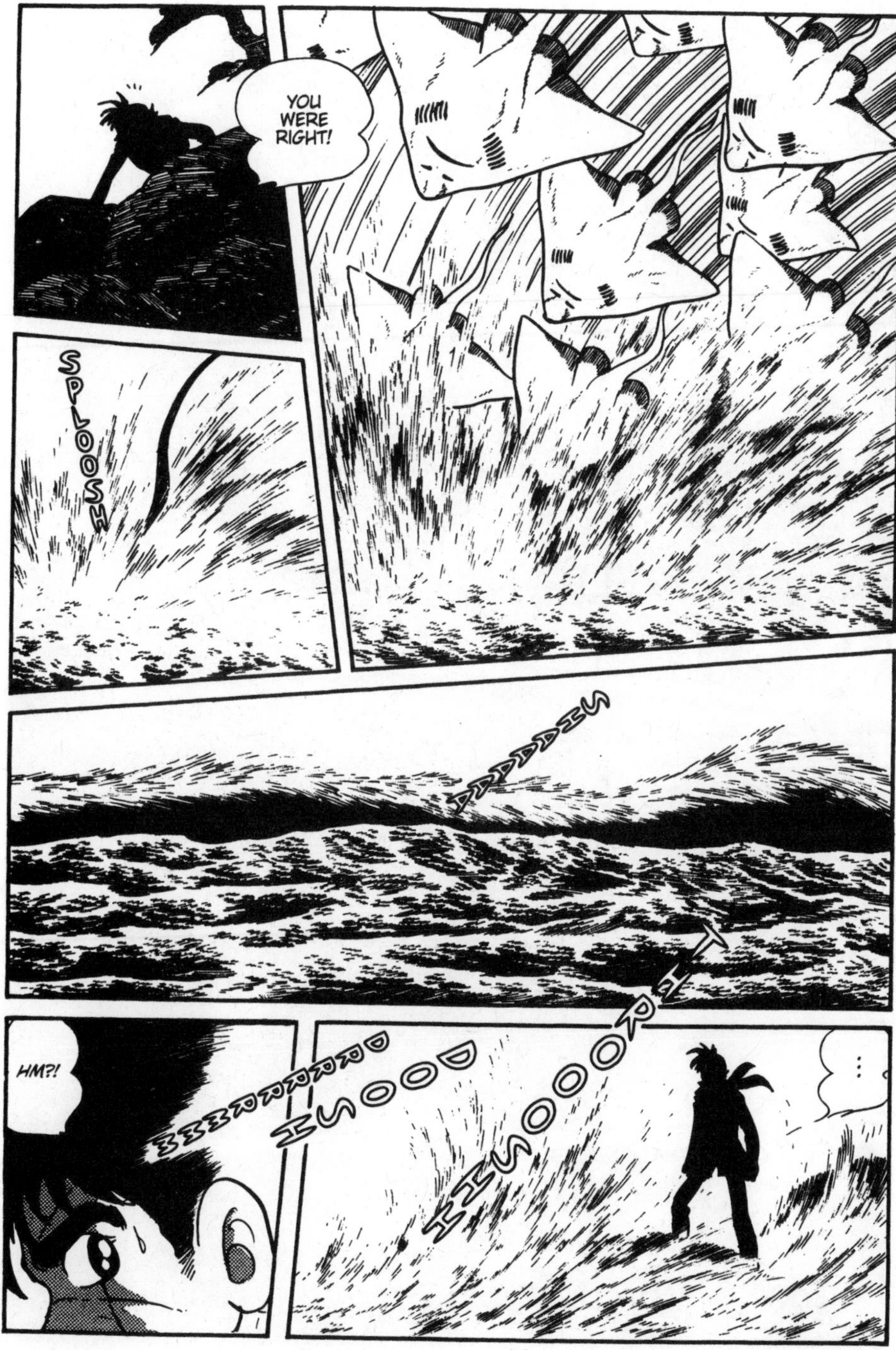
YOU WERE RIGHT!
SPLOOSH
…
HM?!

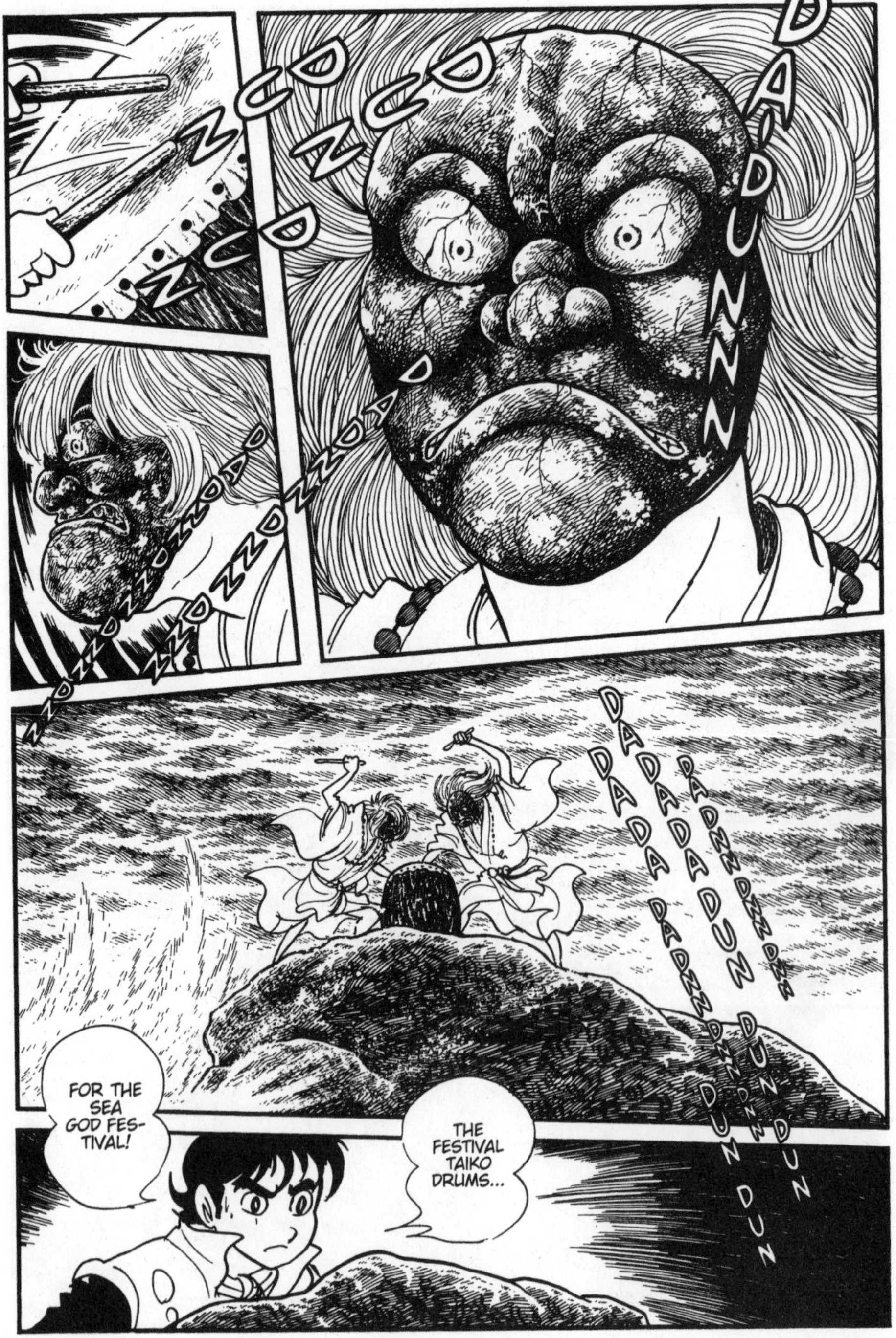
DADUNNNN
DUN DUN DUN
DADUNNN
DADUNNN
DADA DADADUNN DUN DUN
DADADADUN DUN DUN
THE FESTIVAL TAIKO DRUMS...
FOR THE SEA GOD FES-TIVAL!

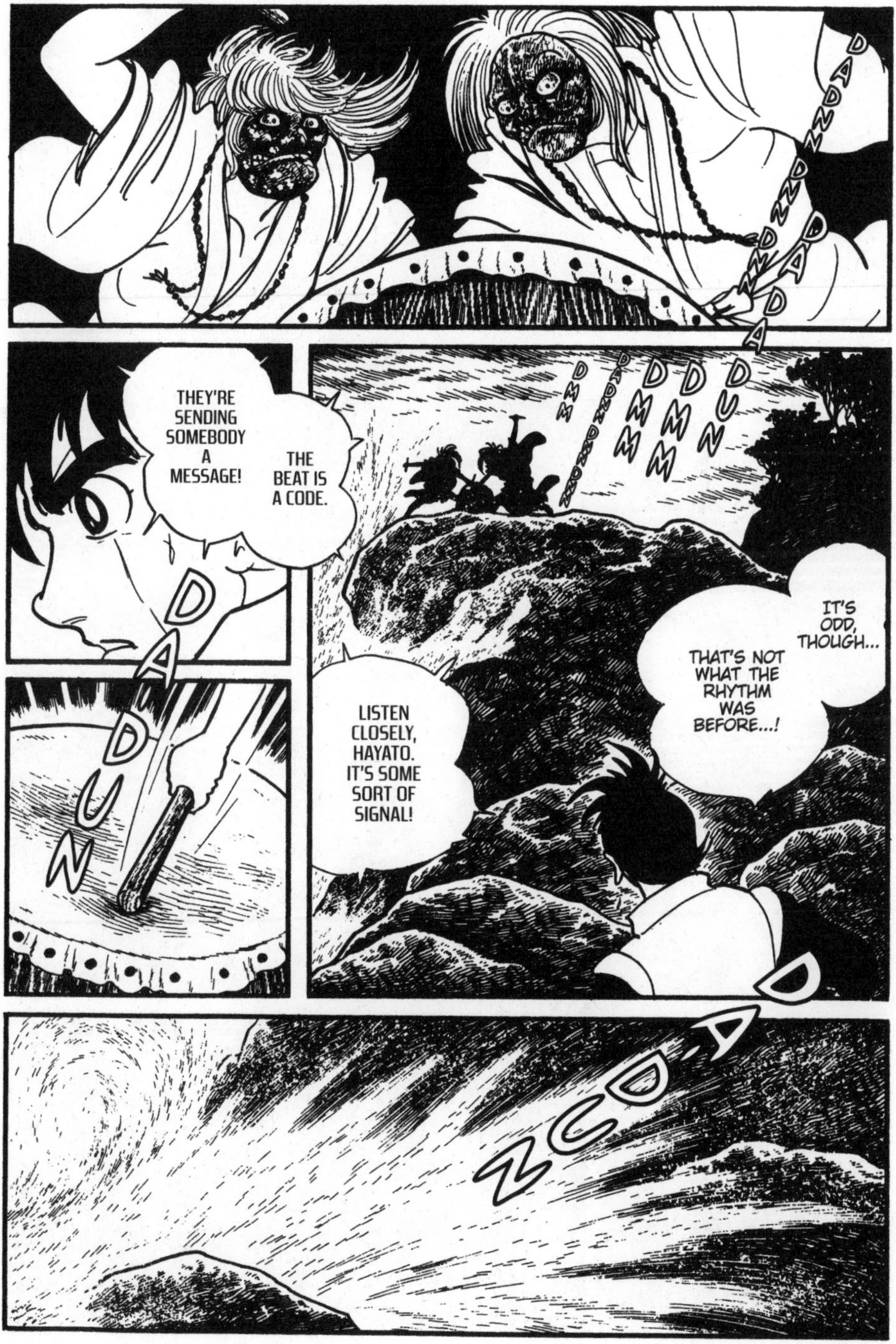
DUN
IT'S ODD, THOUGH...
THAT'S NOT WHAT THE RHYTHM WAS BEFORE...!
LISTEN CLOSELY, HAYATO. IT'S SOME SORT OF SIGNAL!
THE BEAT IS A CODE.
THEY'RE SENDING SOMEBODY A MESSAGE!
DADUN

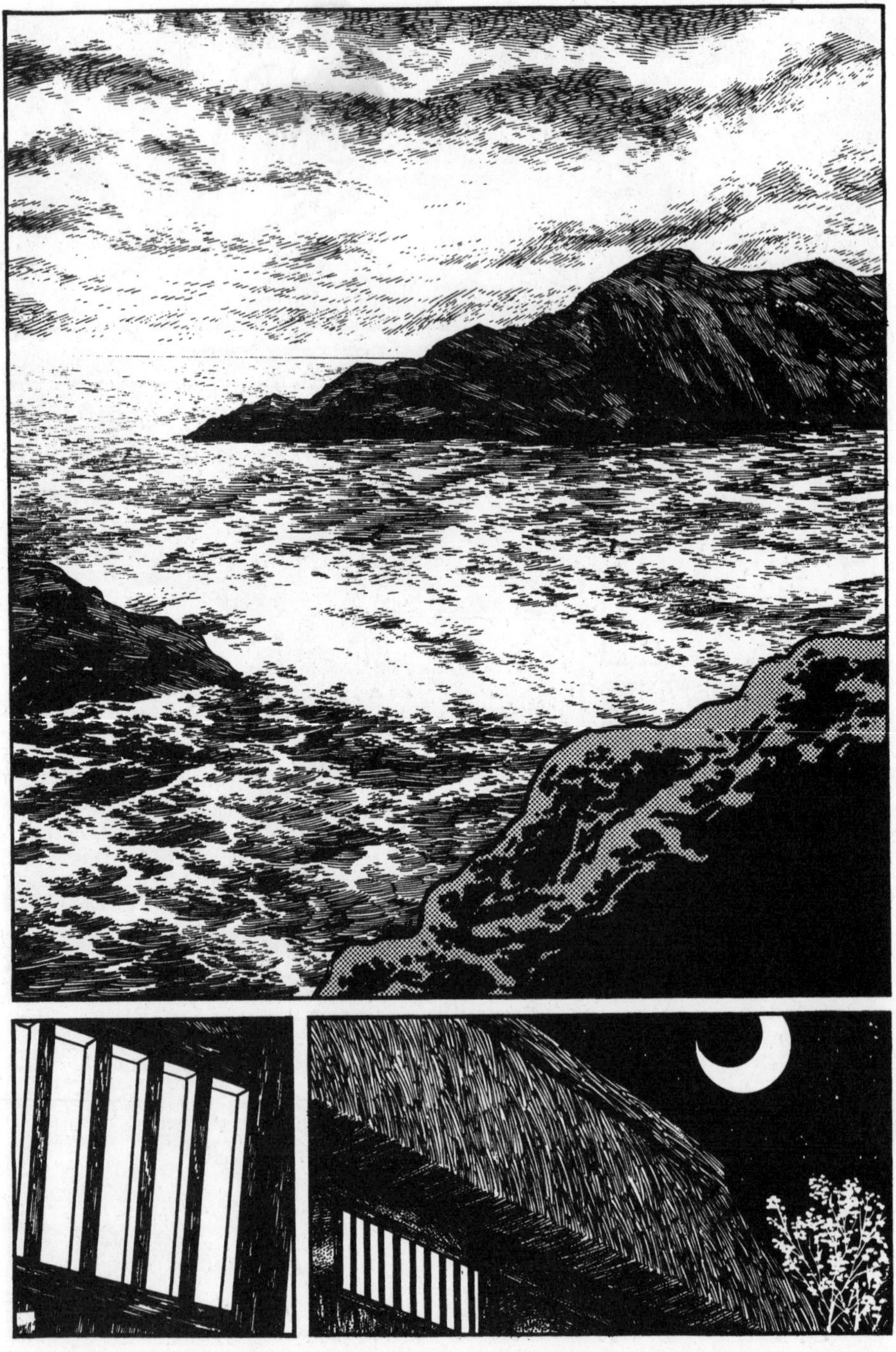

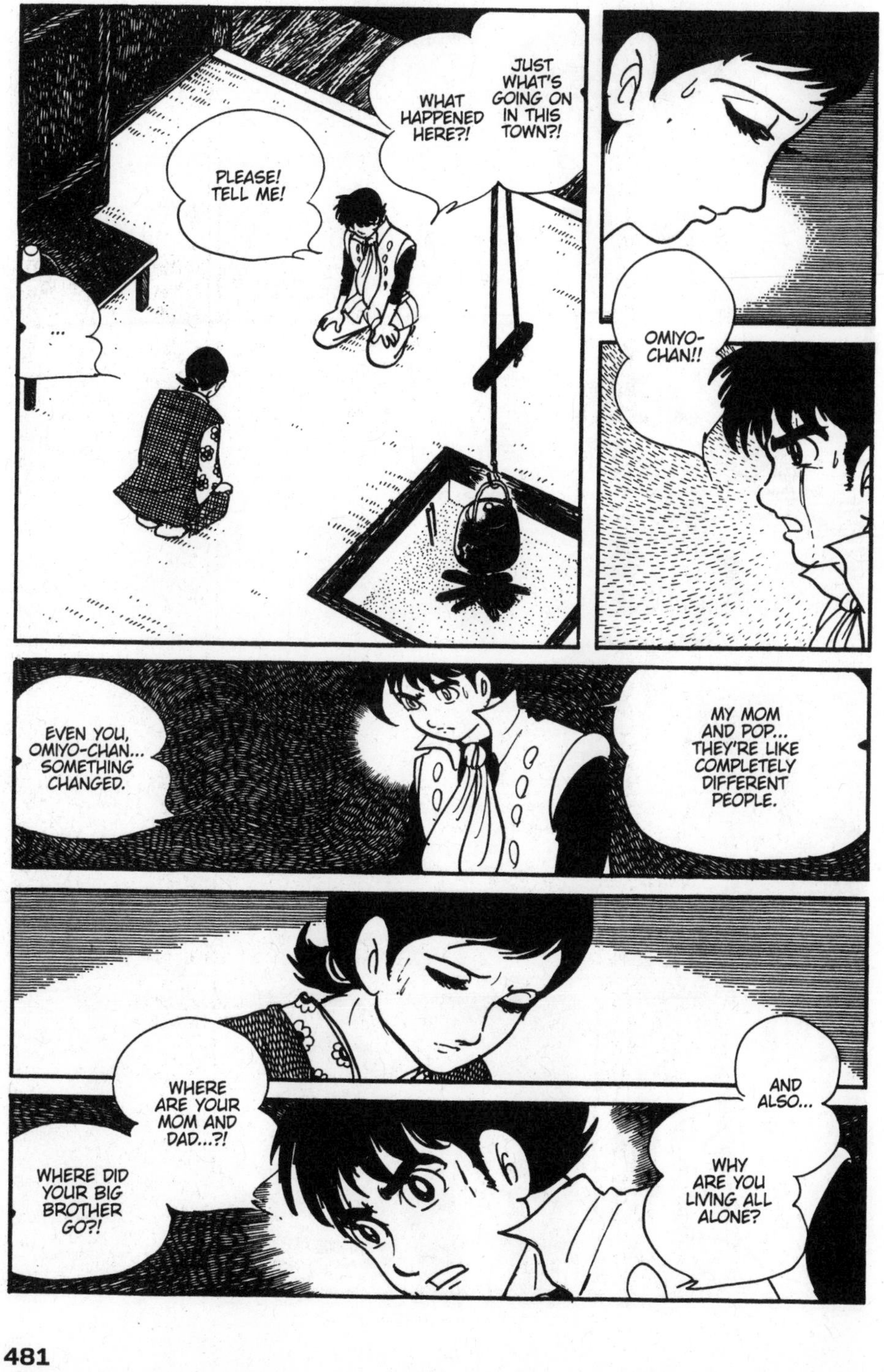
OMIYO-CHAN!!
JUST WHAT'S GOING ON IN THIS TOWN?!
WHAT HAPPENED HERE?!
PLEASE! TELL ME!
...
MY MOM AND POP... THEY'RE LIKE COMPLETELY DIFFERENT PEOPLE.
EVEN YOU, OMIYO-CHAN... SOMETHING CHANGED.
AND ALSO...
WHY ARE YOU LIVING ALL ALONE?
WHERE ARE YOUR MOM AND DAD...?!
WHERE DID YOUR BIG BROTHER GO?!

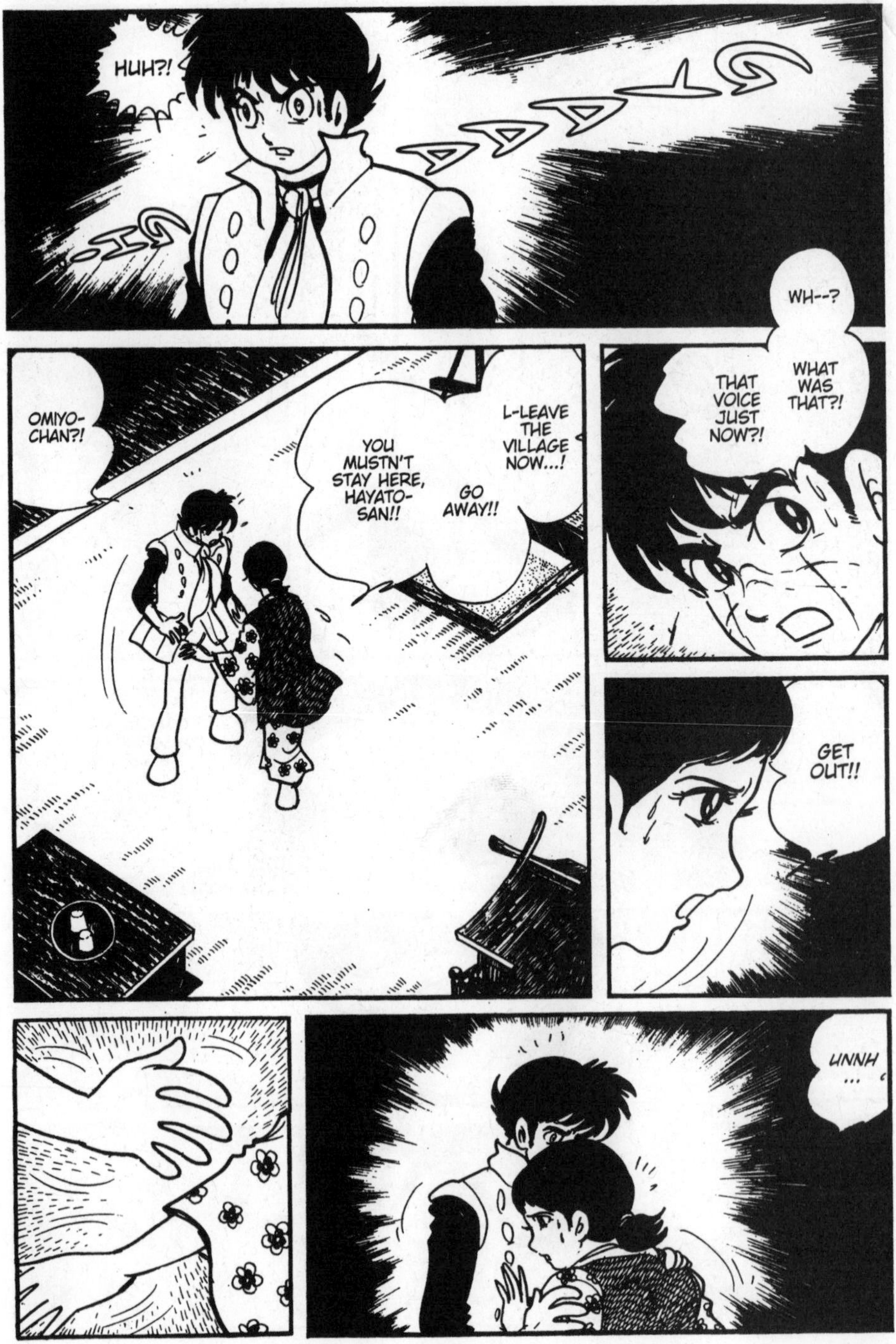
HUH?!
WH--?
WHAT WAS THAT?!
THAT VOICE JUST NOW?!
GET OUT!!
L-LEAVE THE VILLAGE NOW...!
GO AWAY!!
YOU MUSTN'T STAY HERE, HAYATO-SAN!!
OMIYO-CHAN?!
UNNH ...

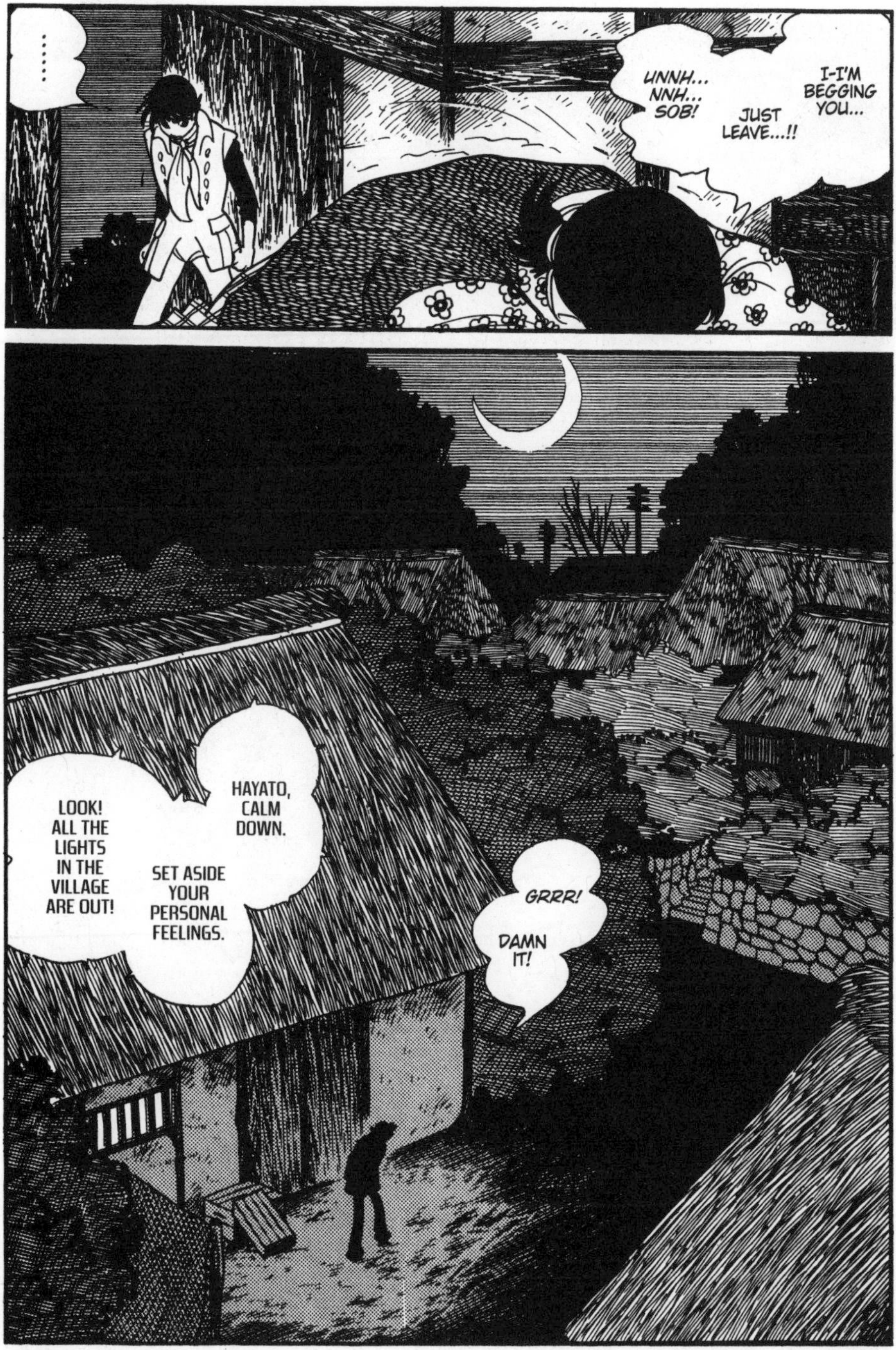

I-I'M BEGGING YOU...
JUST LEAVE...!!
UNNH... NNH... SOB!
......
HAYATO, CALM DOWN.
SET ASIDE YOUR PERSONAL FEELINGS.
LOOK! ALL THE LIGHTS IN THE VILLAGE ARE OUT!
GRRR!
DAMN IT!

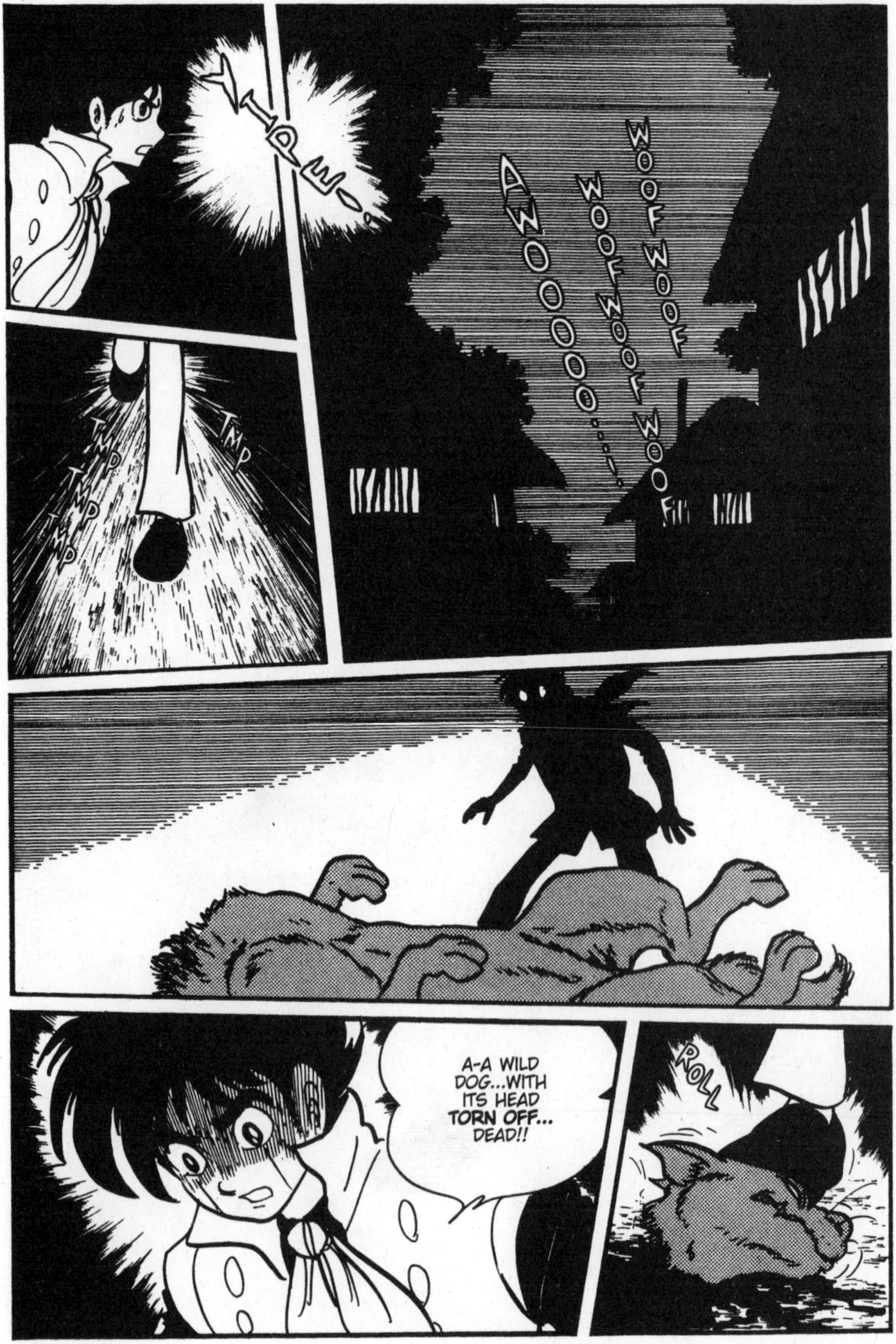
WOOF WOOF WOOF
WOOF WOOF...!
AWOOOOOO...!
YIPE...!
TMP TMP TMP
TMP
ROLL
A-A WILD DOG...WITH ITS HEAD **TORN OFF**... DEAD!!

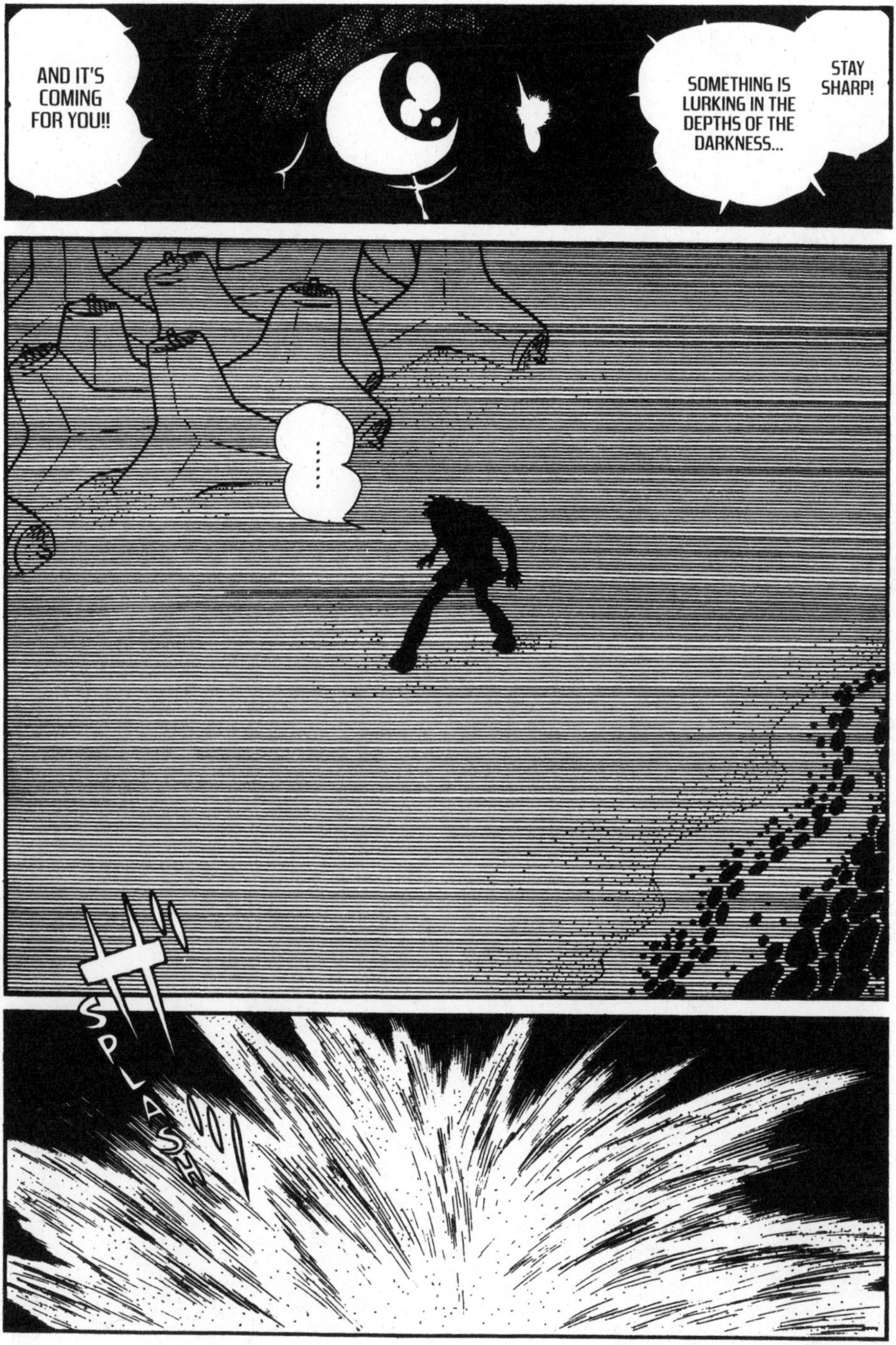
STAY SHARP!
SOMETHING IS LURKING IN THE DEPTHS OF THE DARKNESS...
AND IT'S COMING FOR YOU!!
......
SPLASH

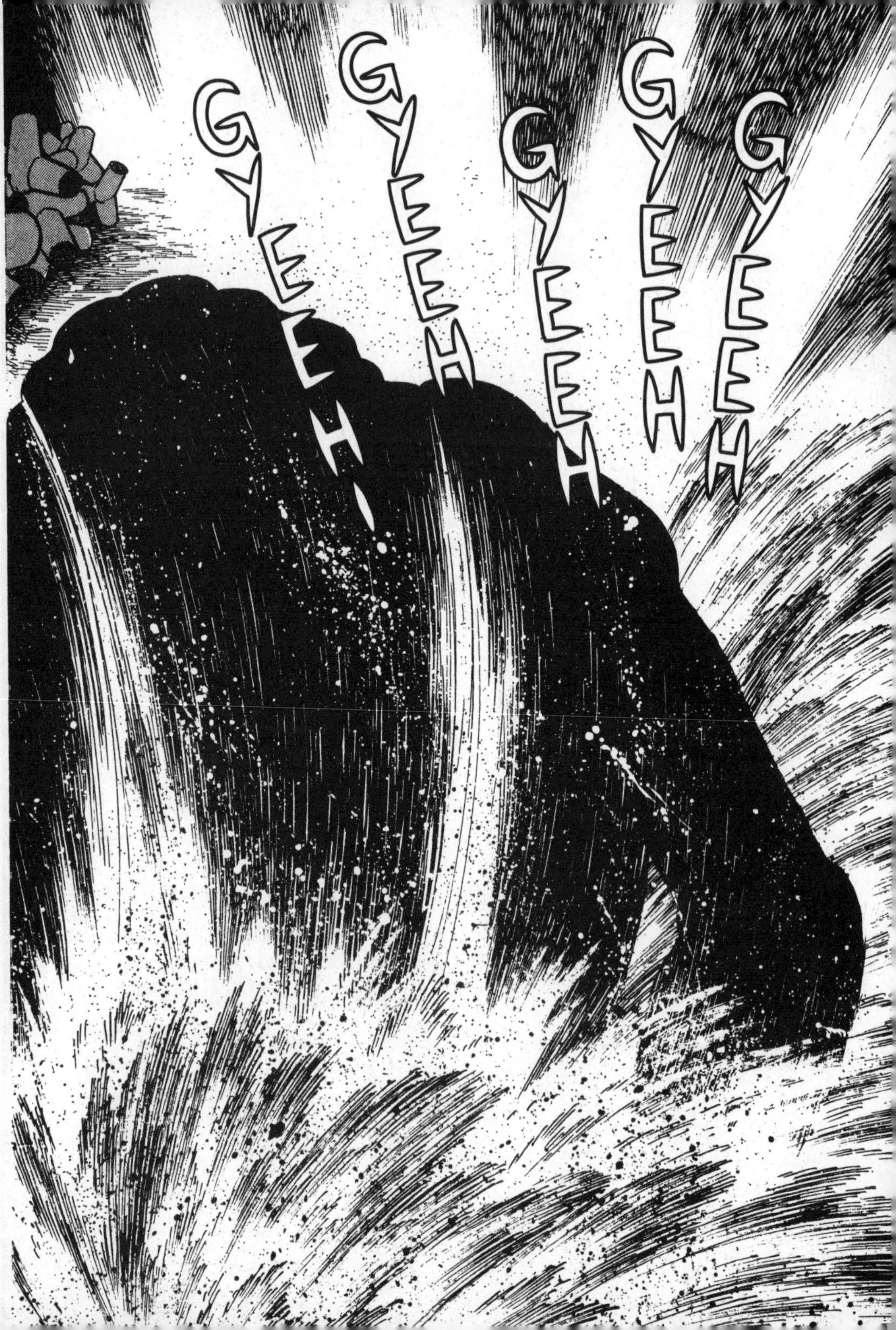
GYEEEH
GYEEEH
GYEEEH
GYEEEH
GYEEEH!

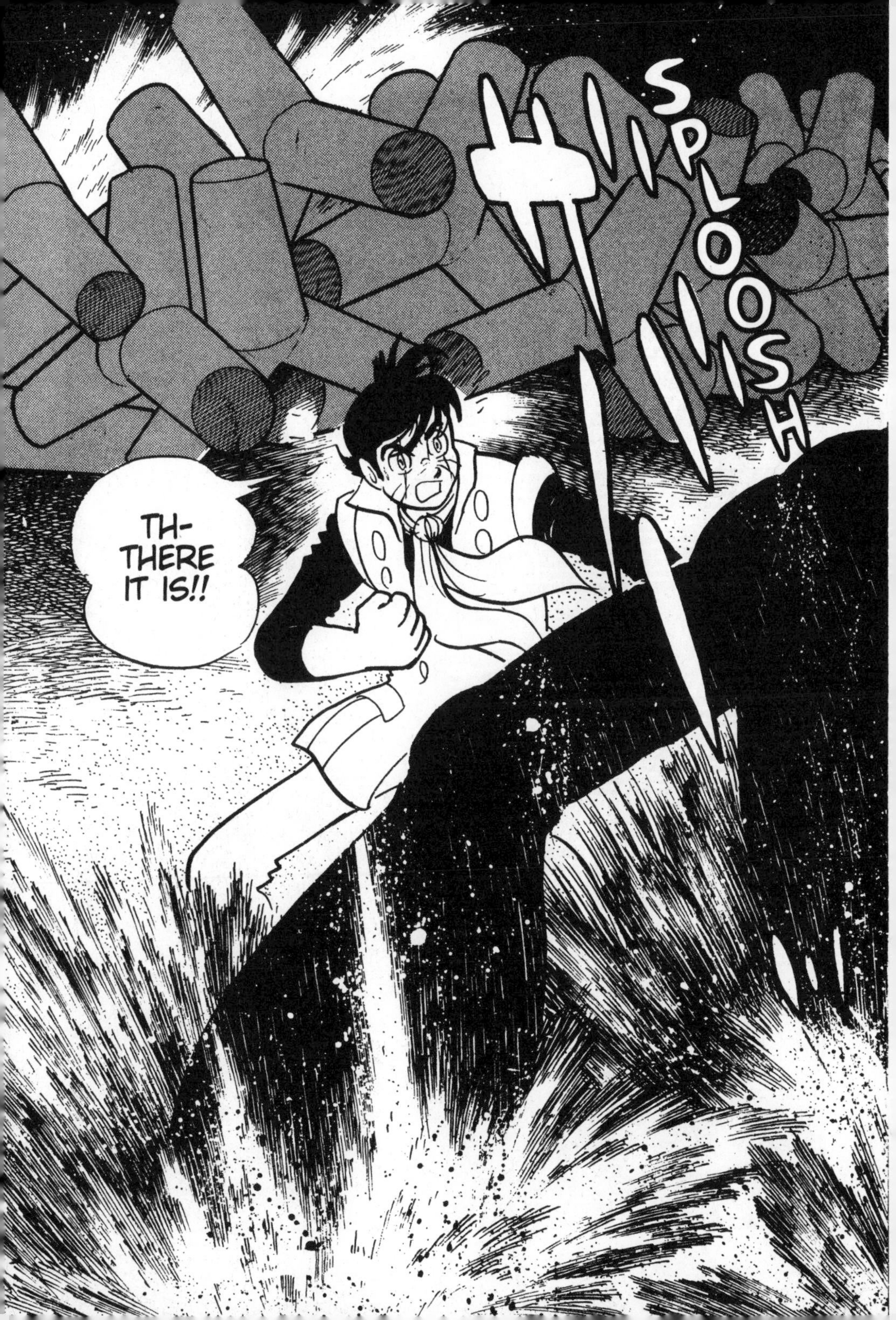
SPLOOSH
TH- THERE IT IS!!

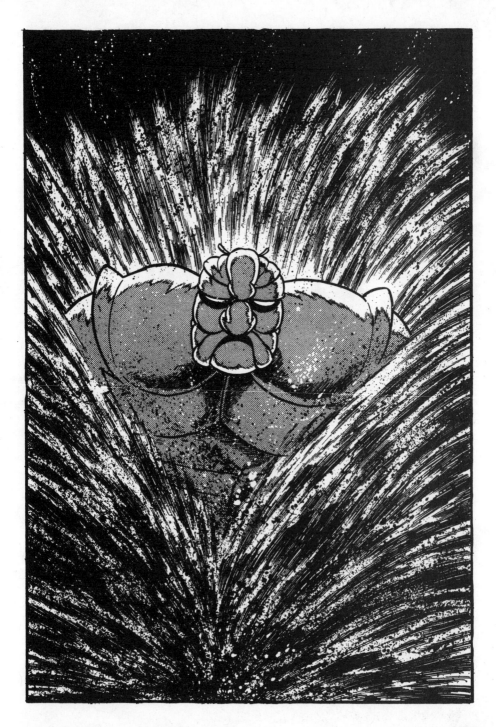

KAMEN RIDER

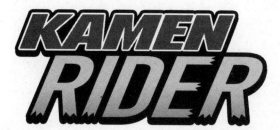

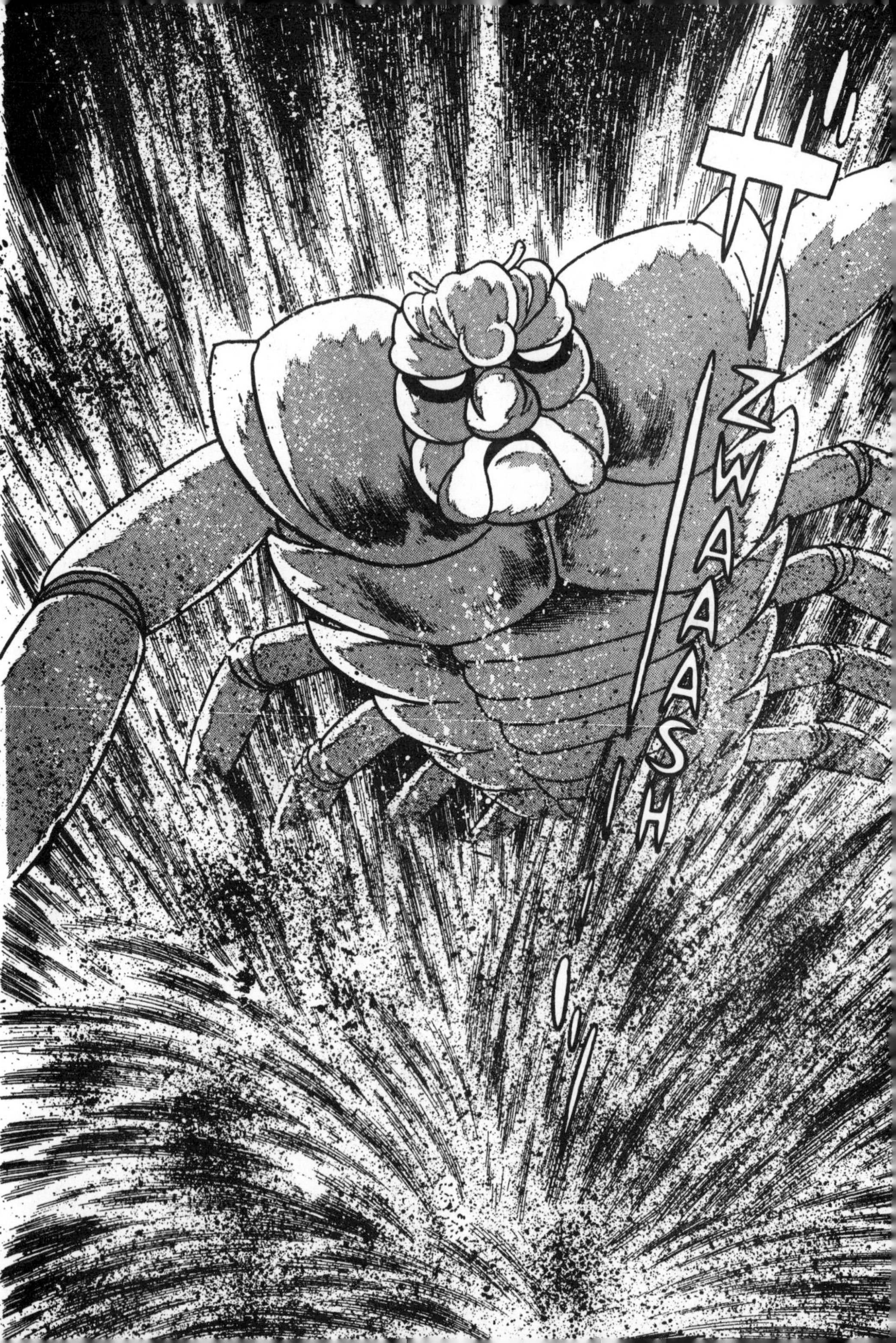
ZWAAAASH

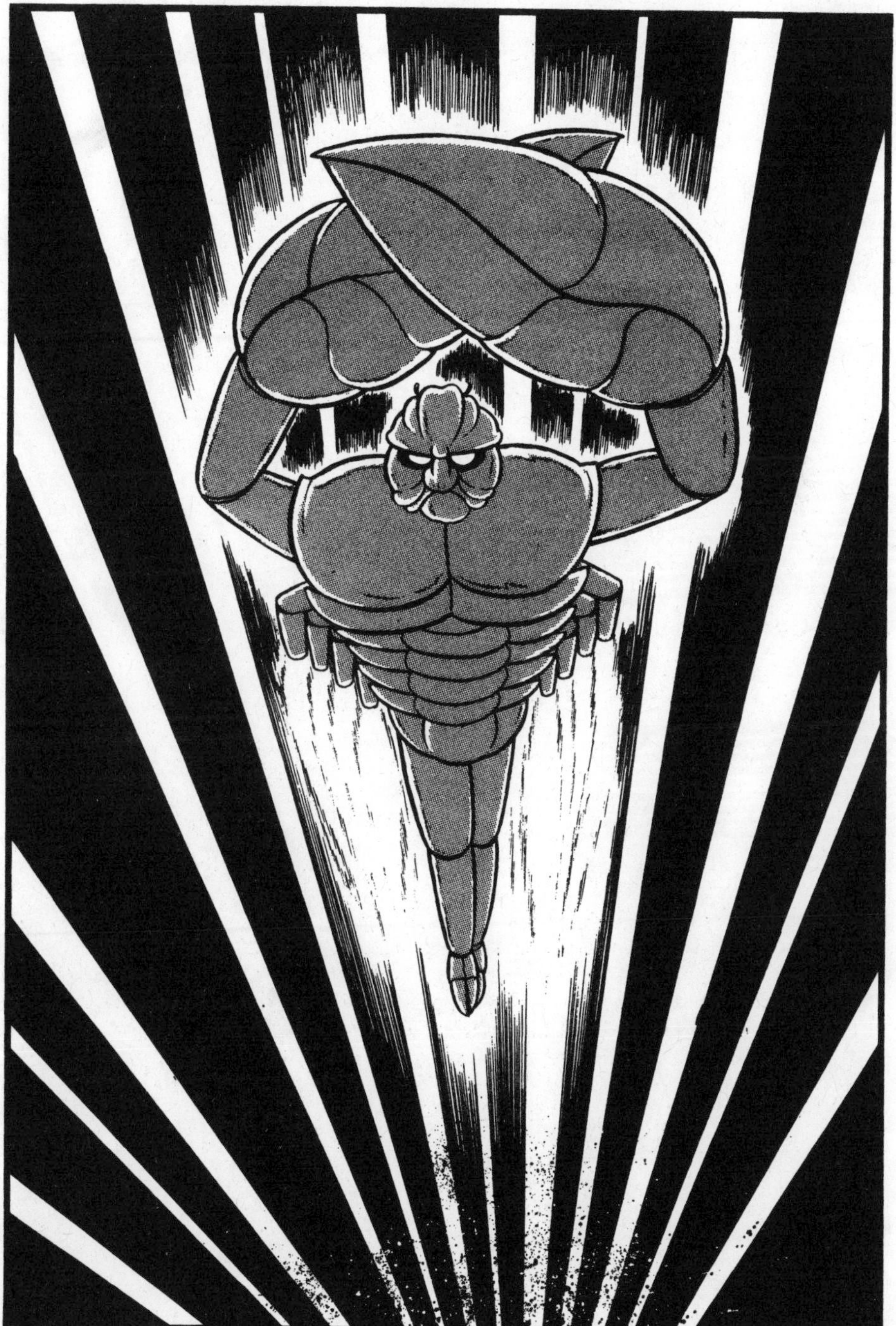

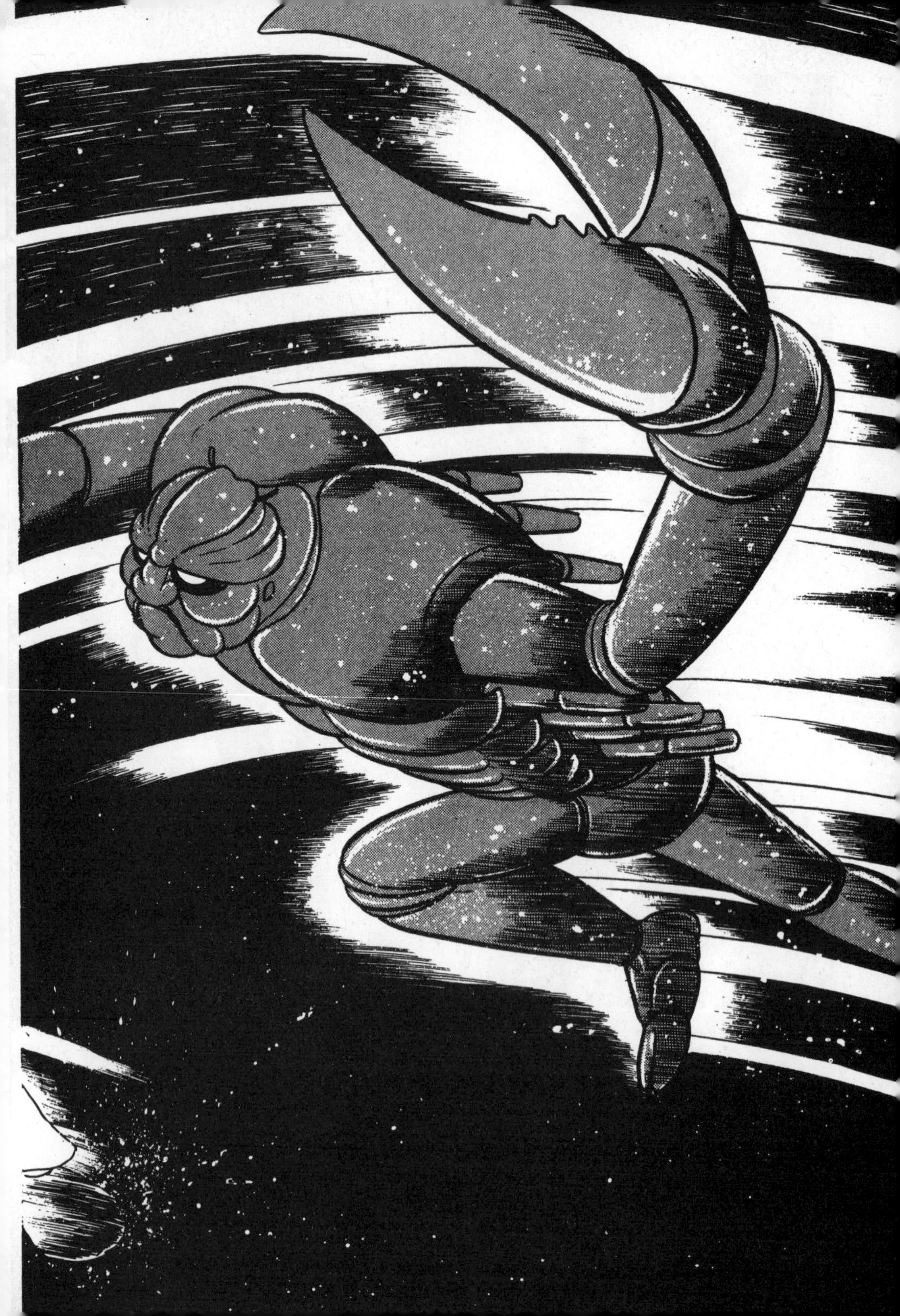

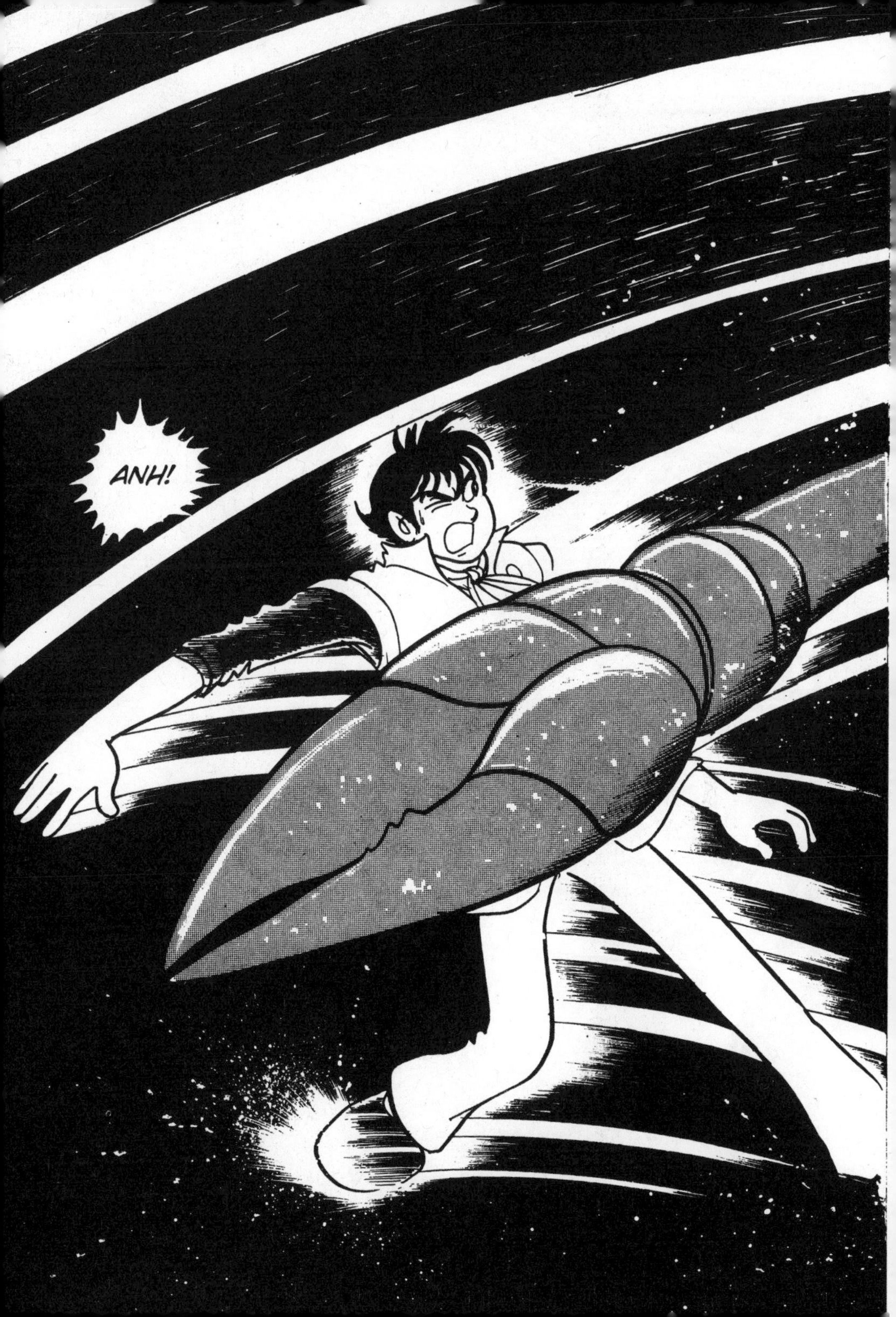
ANH!

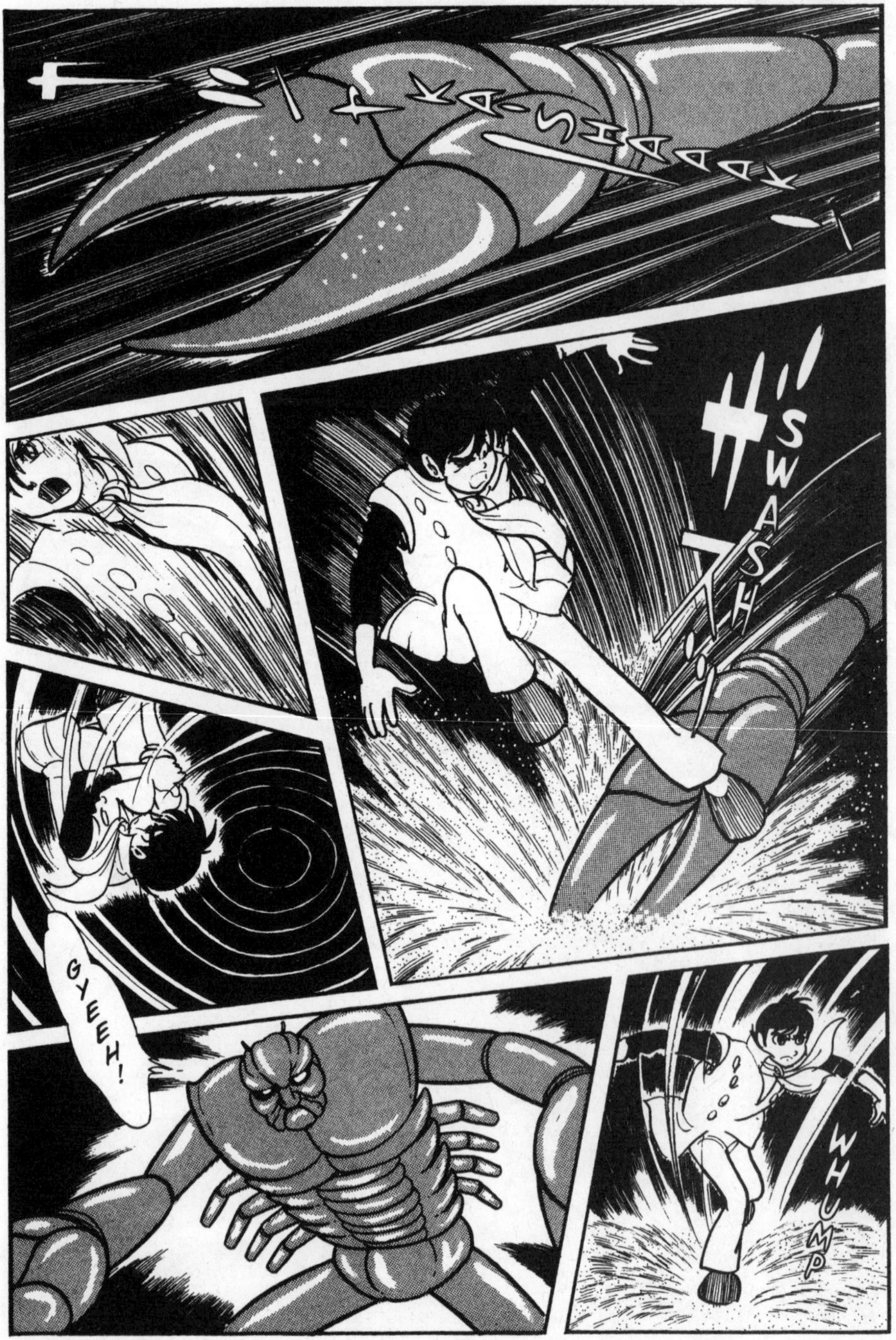
SWASH
GYEEH!
WHUMP

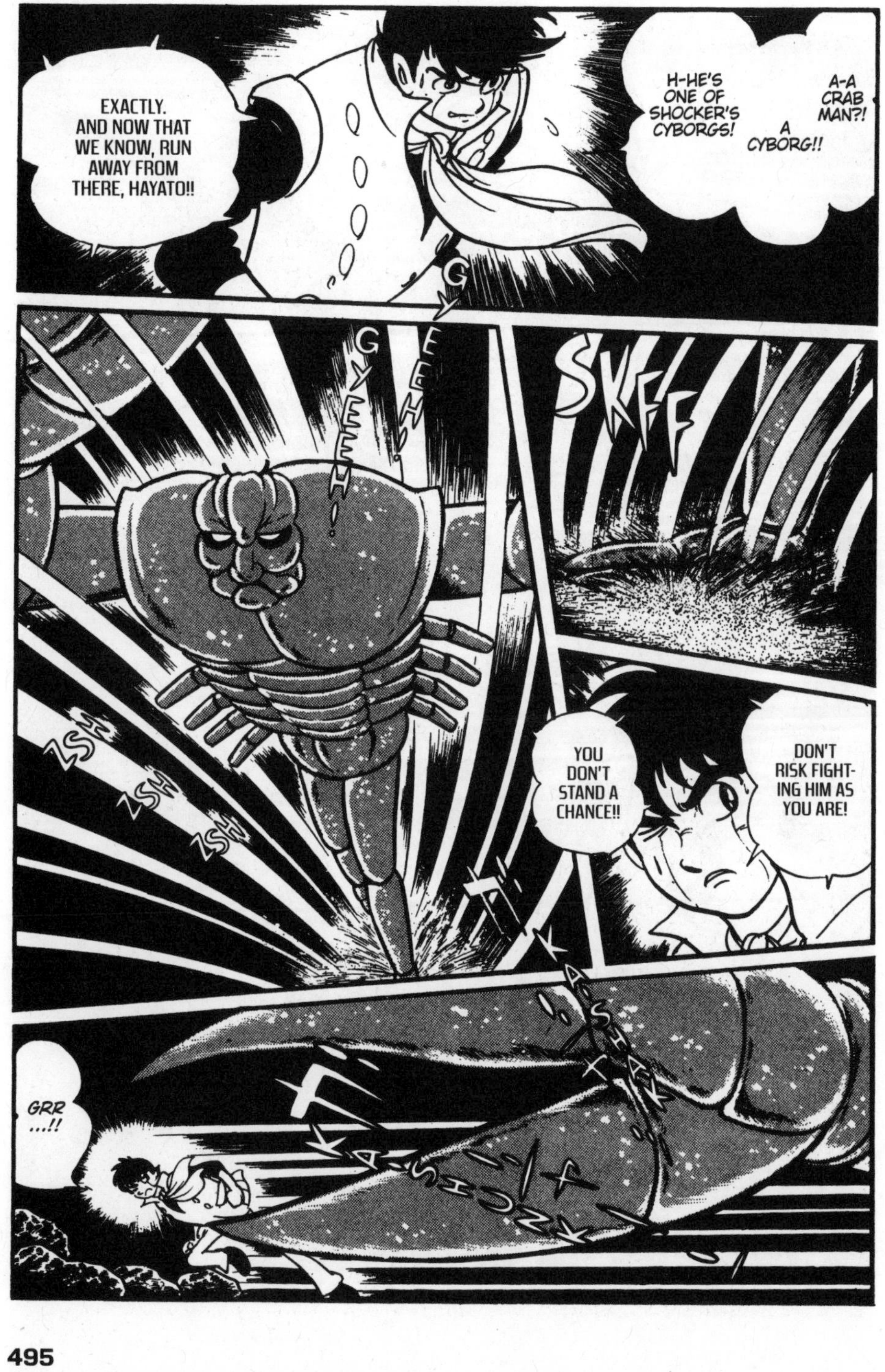

A-A CRAB MAN?!
A CYBORG!!
H-HE'S ONE OF SHOCKER'S CYBORGS!
EXACTLY. AND NOW THAT WE KNOW, RUN AWAY FROM THERE, HAYATO!!
GYEEEH
SKFFF
DON'T RISK FIGHTING HIM AS YOU ARE!
YOU DON'T STAND A CHANCE!!
GYEEEH!
ZSH
ZSH
ZSH
GRR ...!!

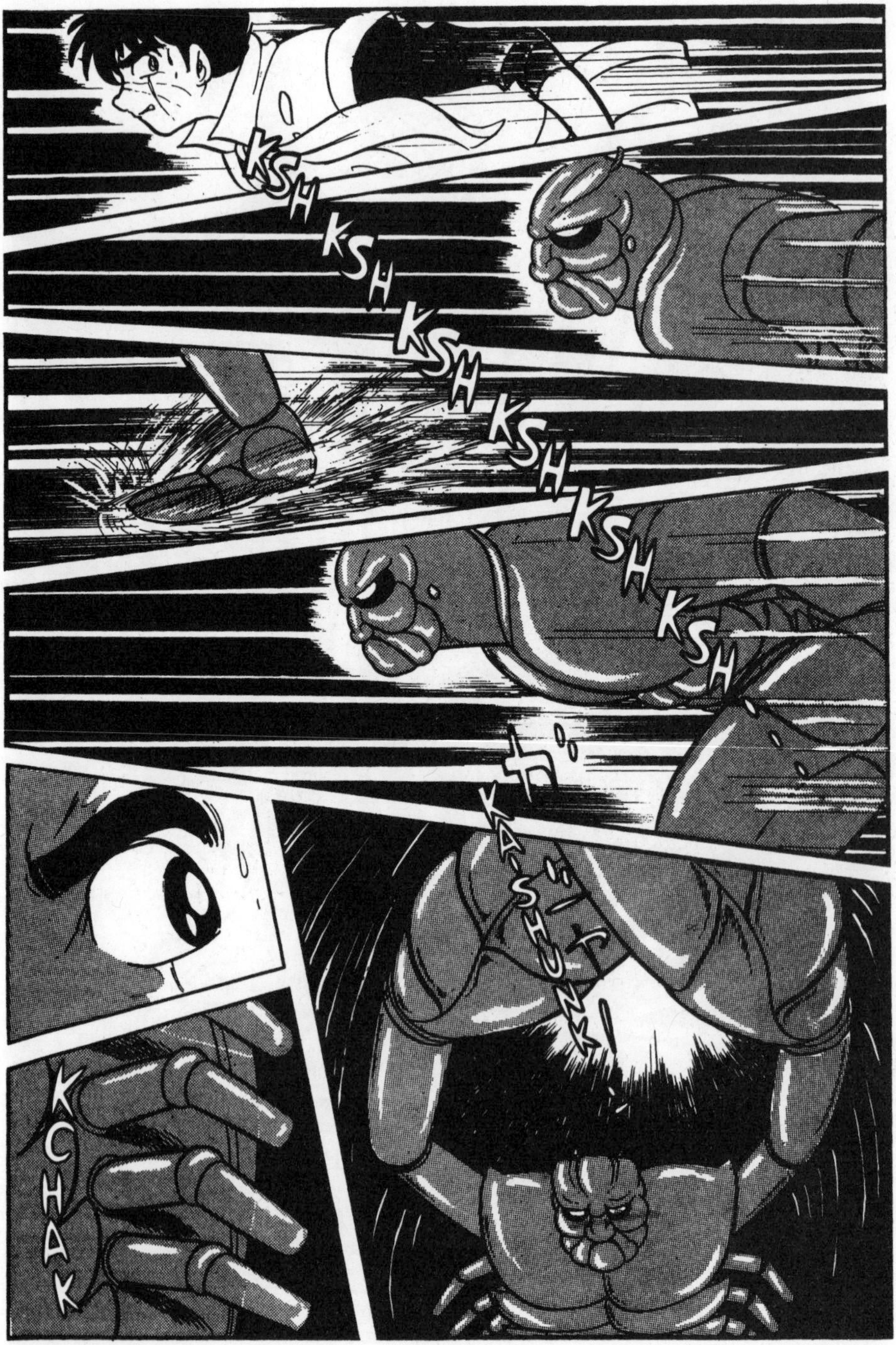
KSHKSHKSHKSHKSHKSH
KA-SHUNK!
KCHAK

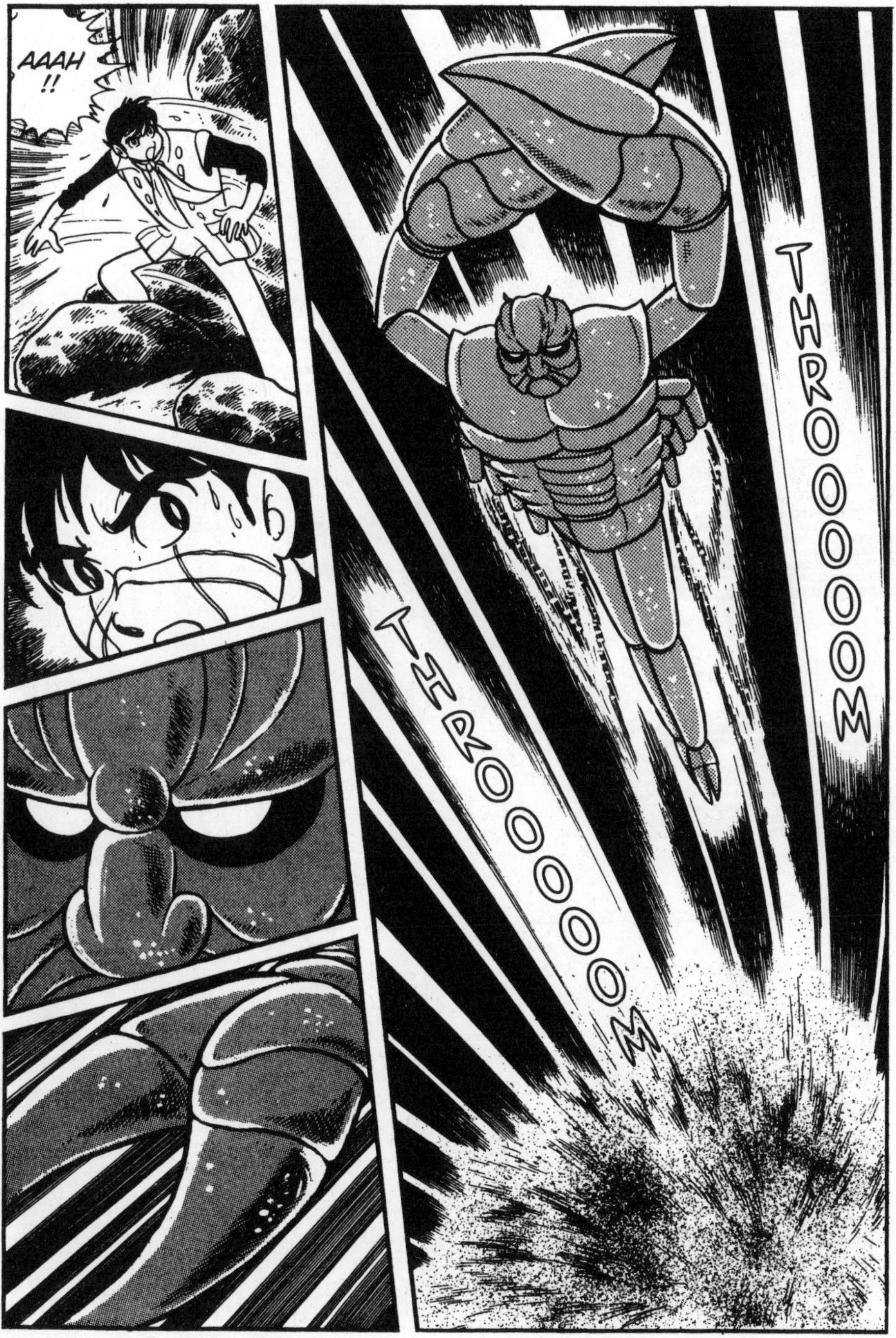
THROOOOOM
THROOOOOM
AAAH!!

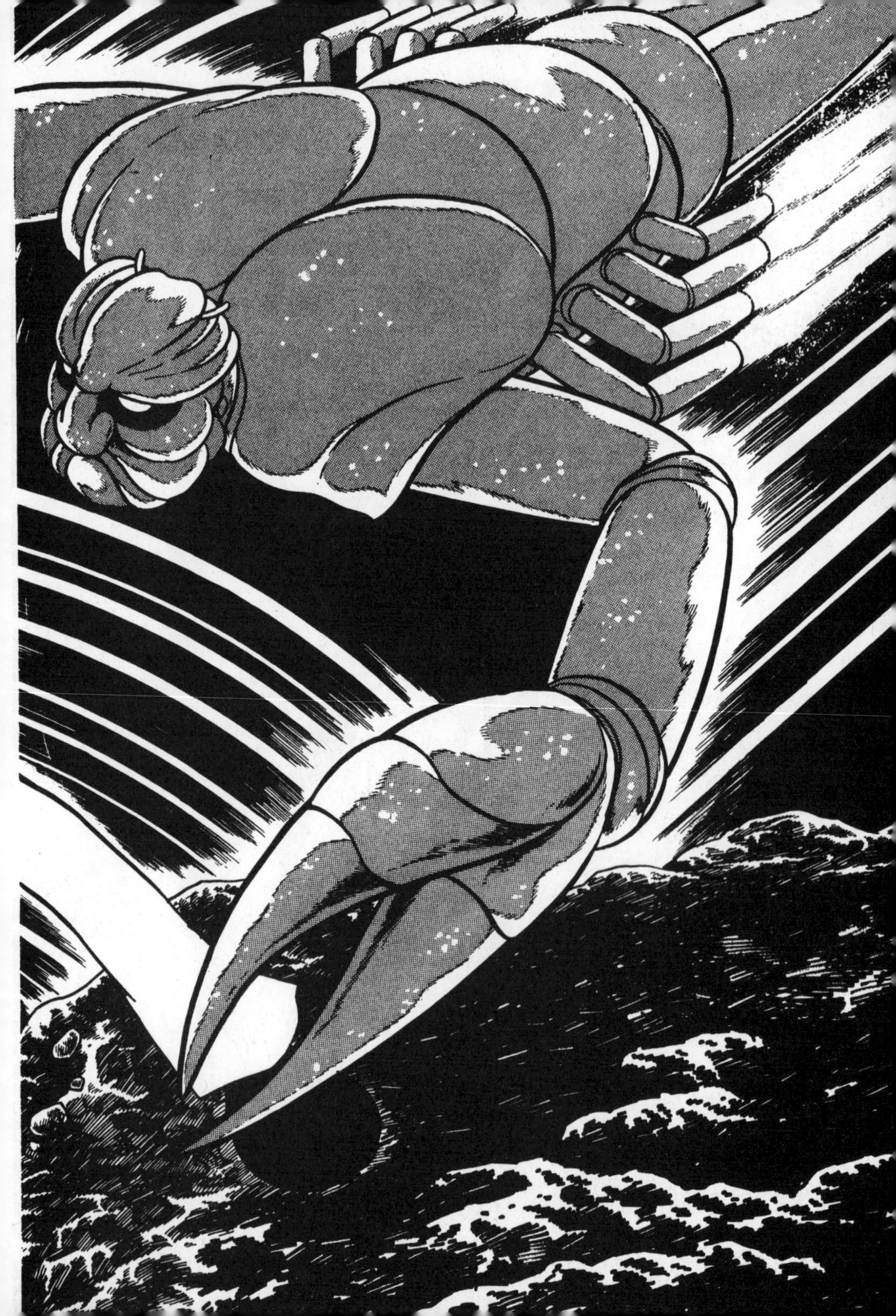

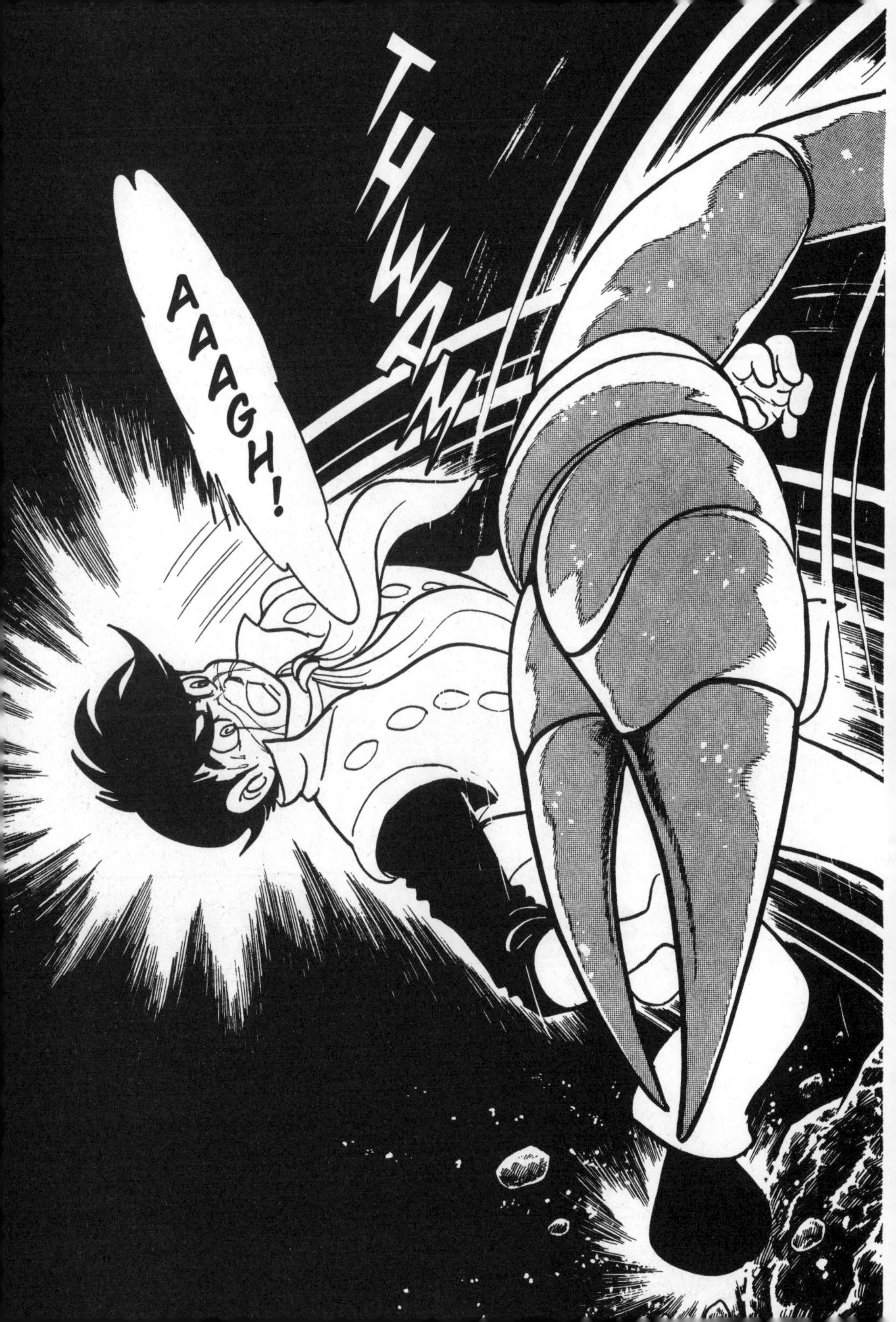
THWAM
AAAGH!

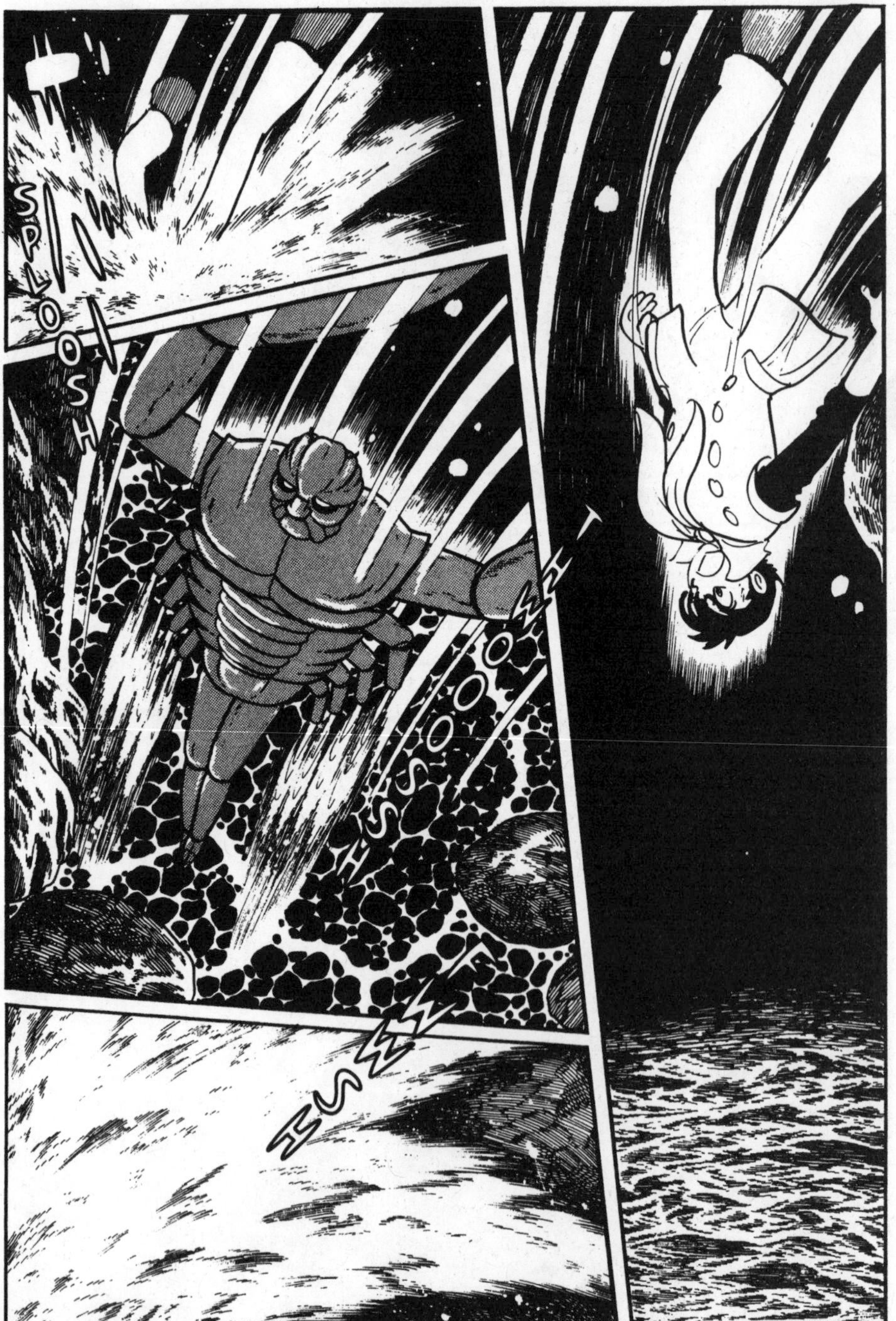
SPLOOSH

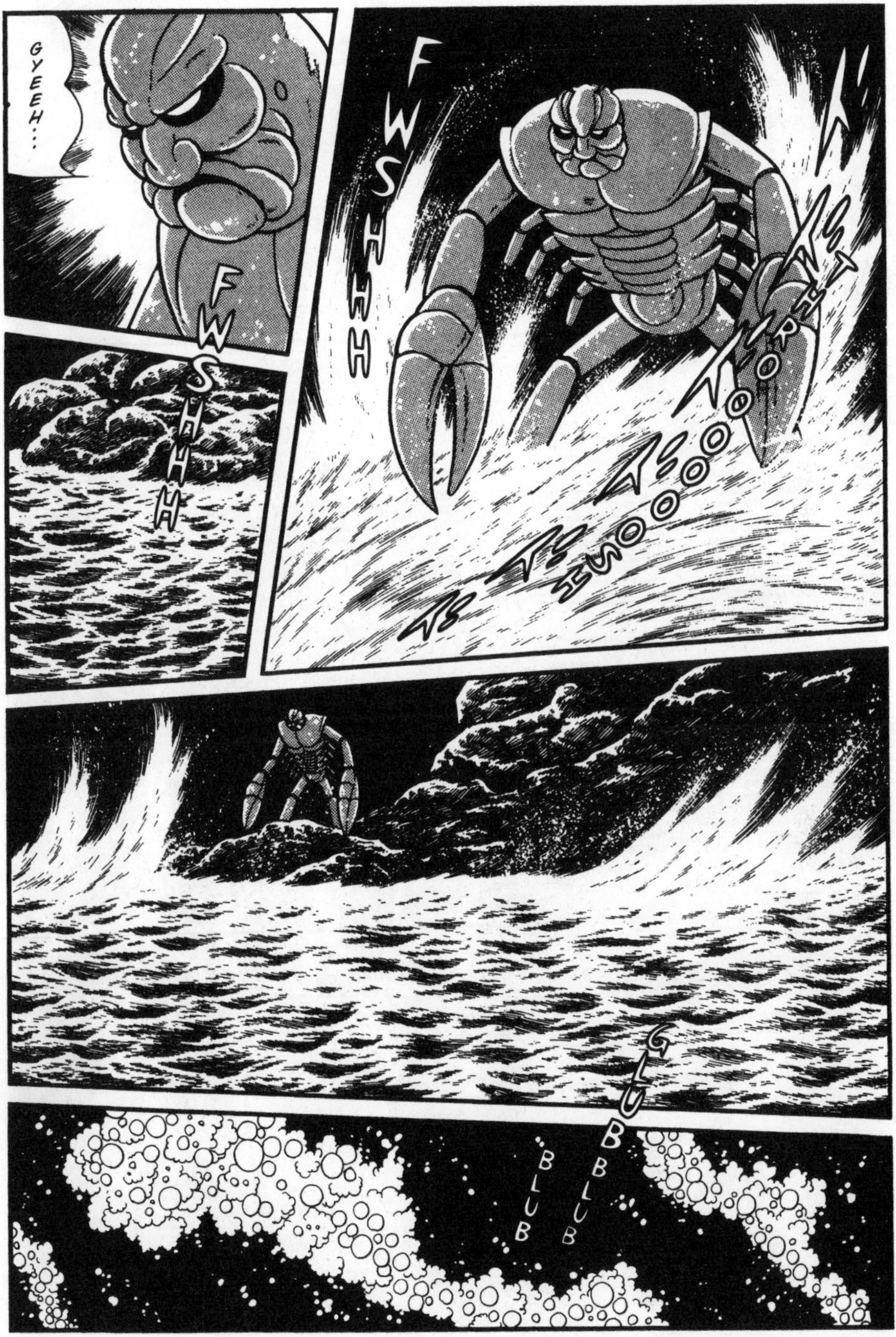
FWSHHHH
THROOOOOOOSH
GYEEH...
FWSHHHH
GLUB
BLUB
BLUB

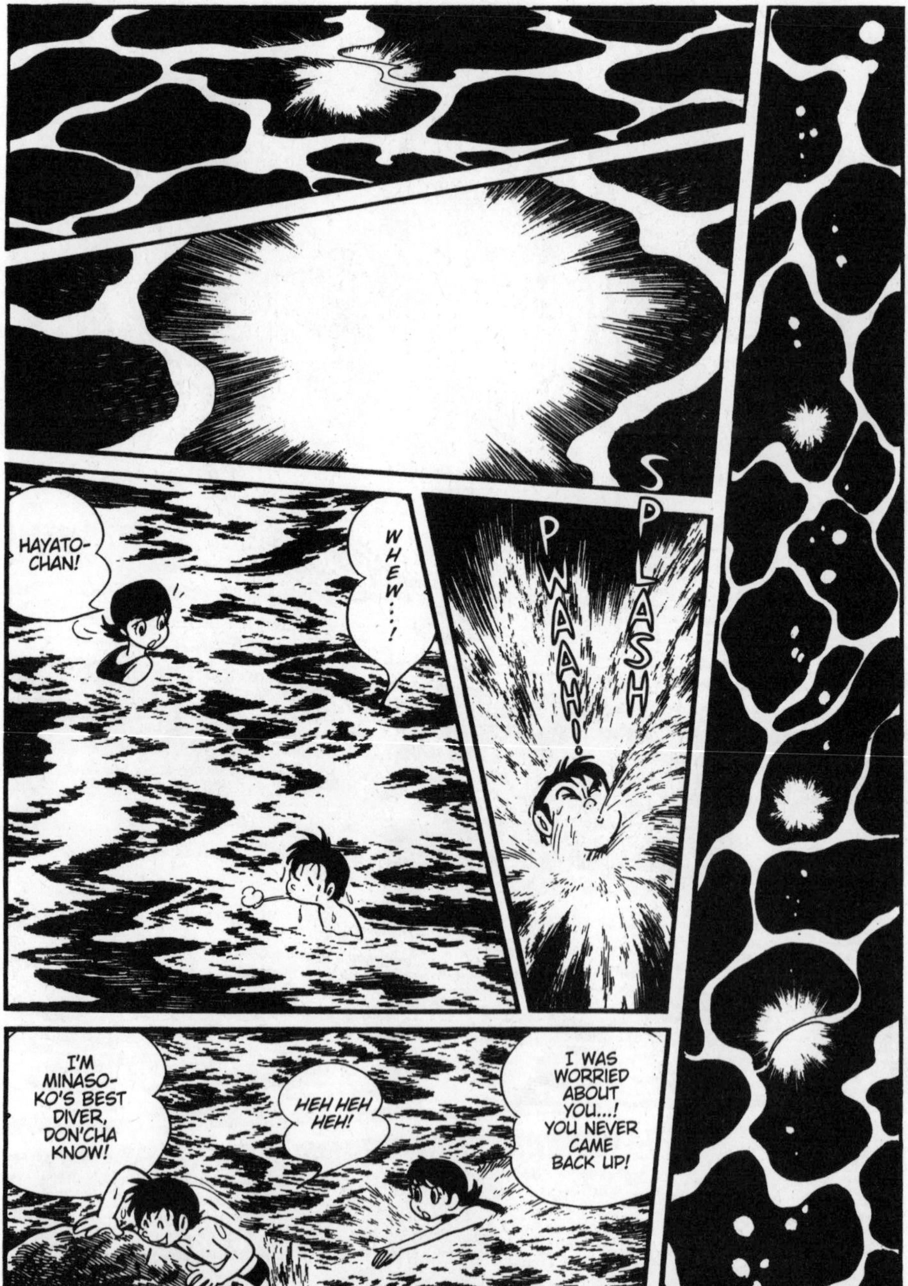
SPLASH
PWAAAH!!
WHEW...!
HAYATO-CHAN!
I WAS WORRIED ABOUT YOU...! YOU NEVER CAME BACK UP!
HEH HEH HEH!
I'M MINASOKO'S BEST DIVER, DON'CHA KNOW!

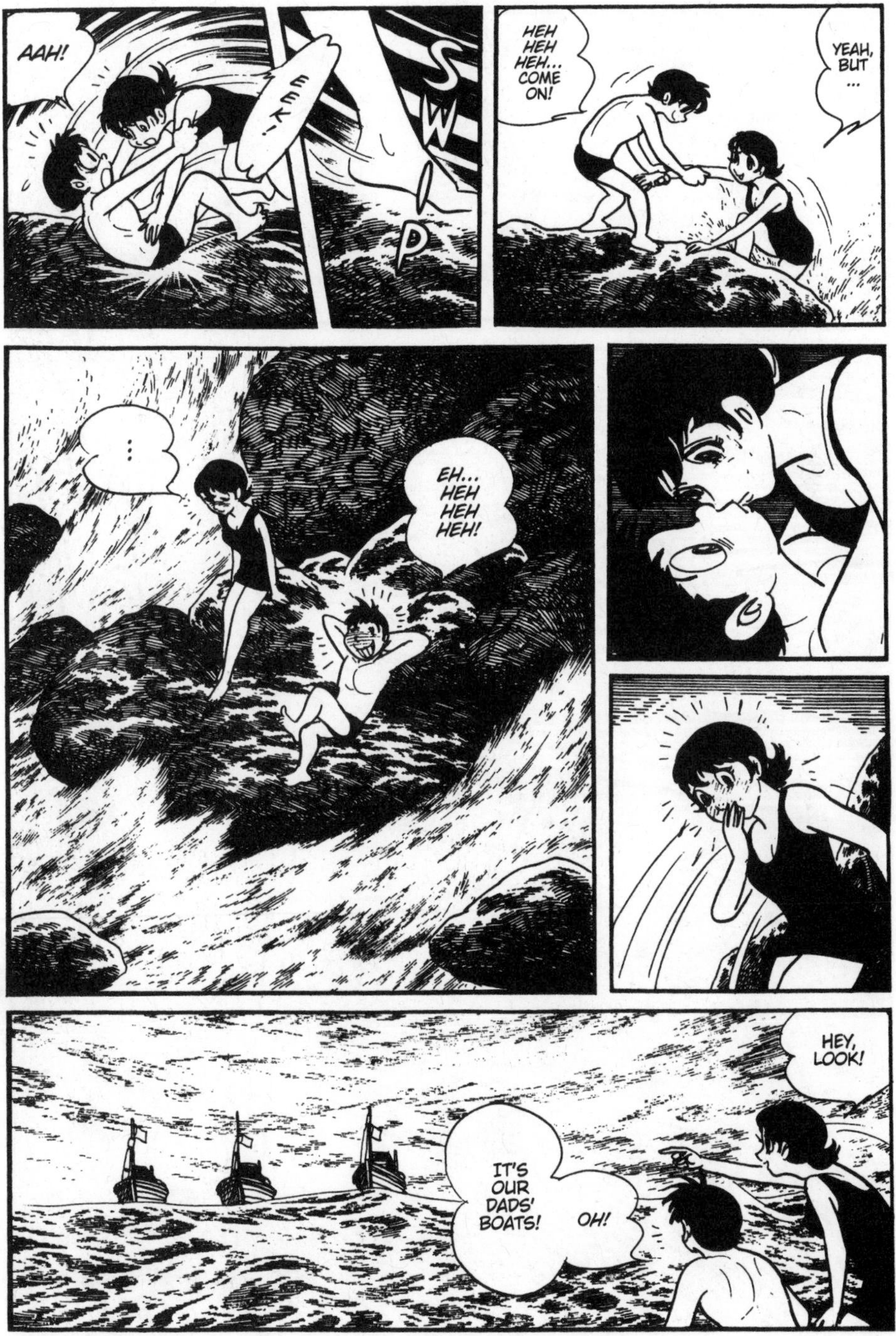
YEAH, BUT ...
HEH HEH HEH... COME ON!
SWIP
EEK!
AAH!
EH... HEH HEH HEH!
...
HEY, LOOK!
OH!
IT'S OUR DADS' BOATS!

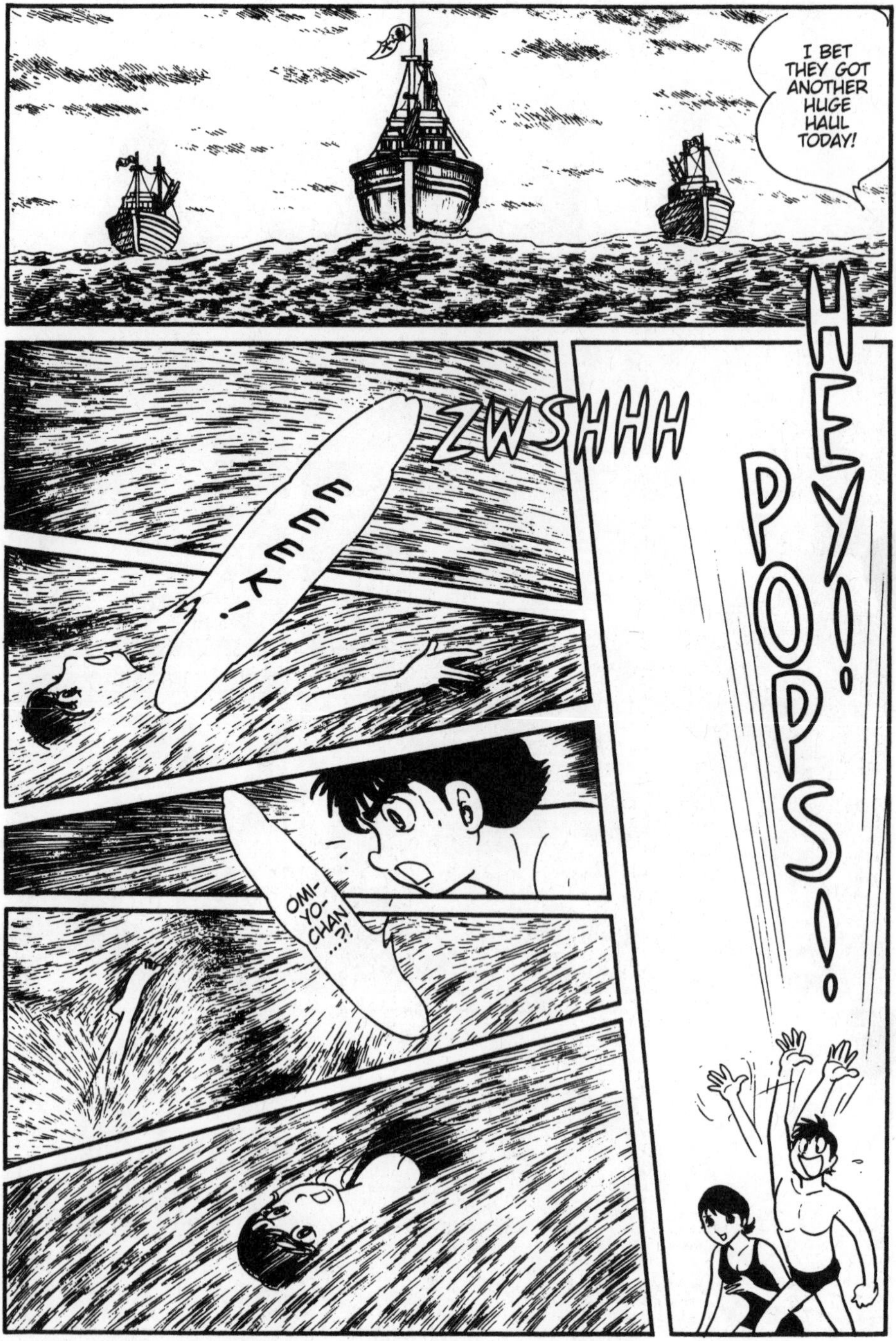
I BET THEY GOT ANOTHER HUGE HAUL TODAY!
HEY!! POPS!!
ZWSHHH
EEEEK!
OMI-YO-CHAN...?!

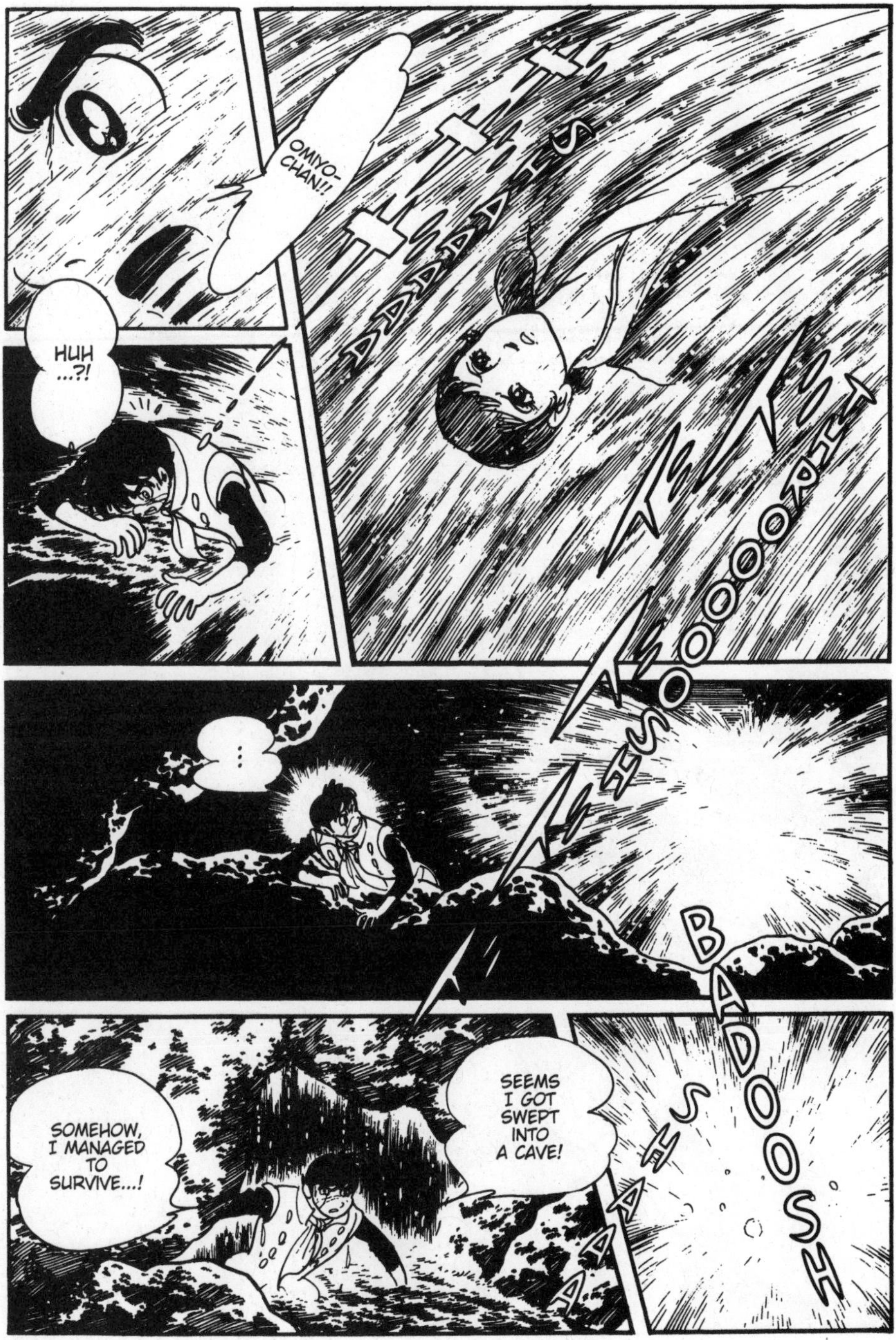
SHAAAAA
OMIYO-CHAN!!
HUH ...?!
ROOOOOOOSH
...
BADOOSH
SHAAAA
SEEMS I GOT SWEPT INTO A CAVE!
SOMEHOW, I MANAGED TO SURVIVE...!

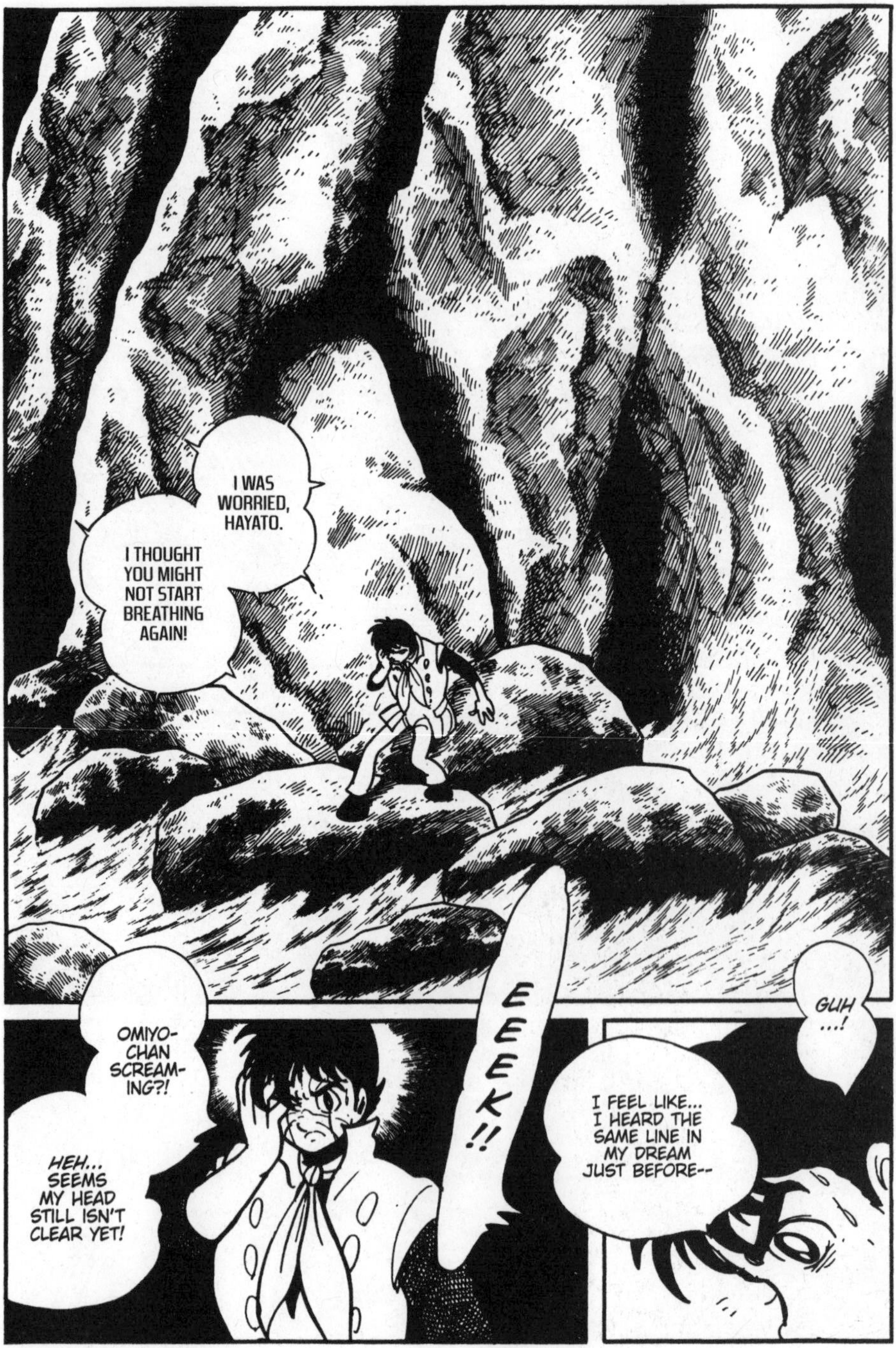
I WAS WORRIED, HAYATO.
I THOUGHT YOU MIGHT NOT START BREATHING AGAIN!
GUH ...!
I FEEL LIKE... I HEARD THE SAME LINE IN MY DREAM JUST BEFORE--
EEEEK!!
OMIYO-CHAN SCREAM-ING?!
HEH... SEEMS MY HEAD STILL ISN'T CLEAR YET!

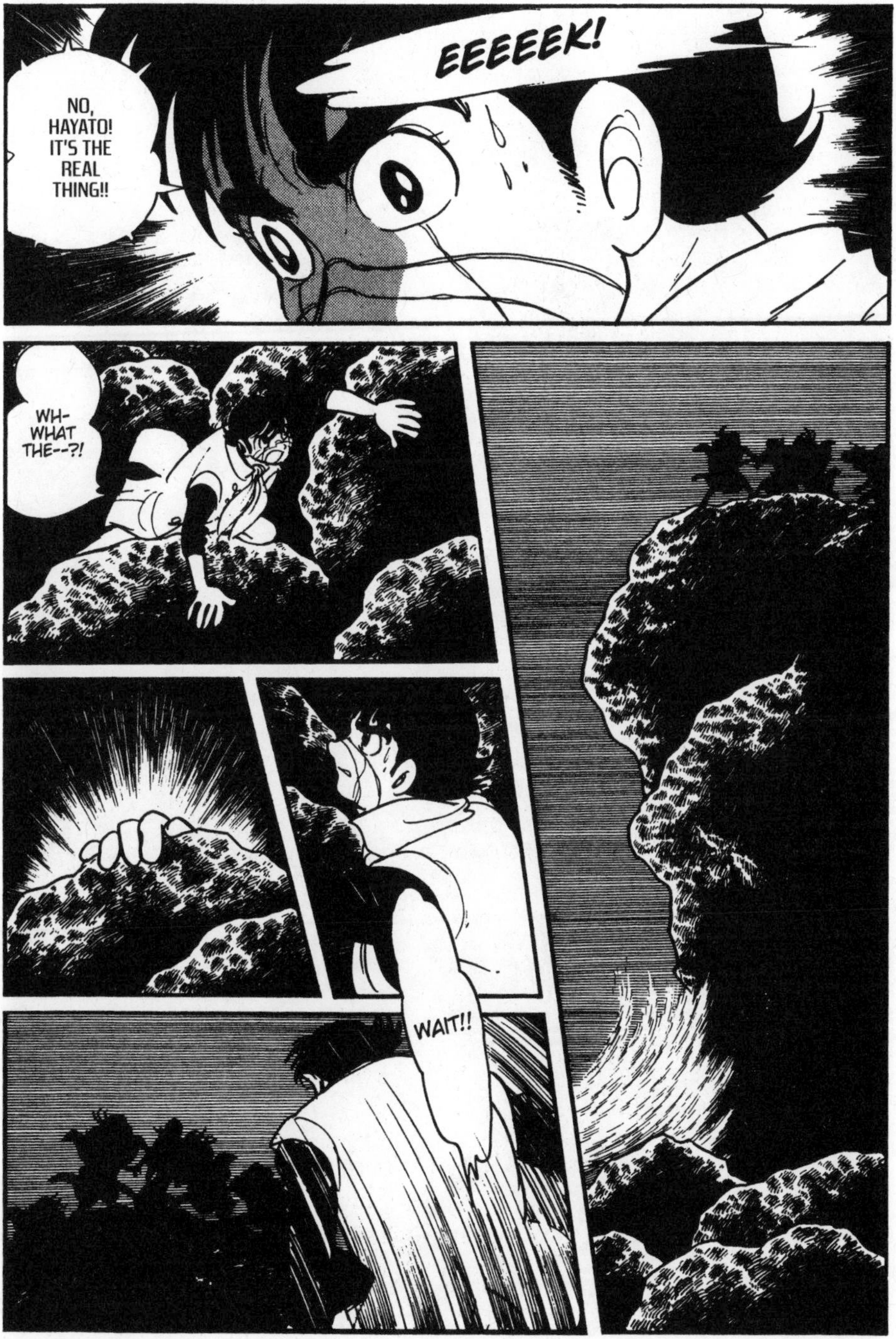
EEEEEK!
NO, HAYATO! IT'S THE REAL THING!!
WH- WHAT THE--?!
WAIT!!

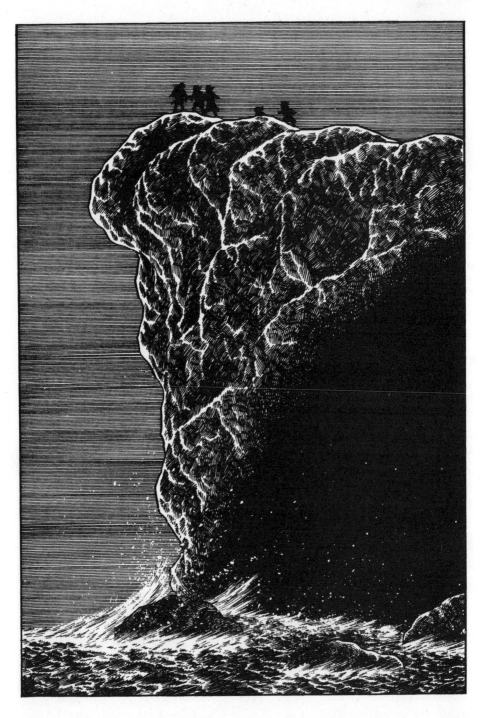

508

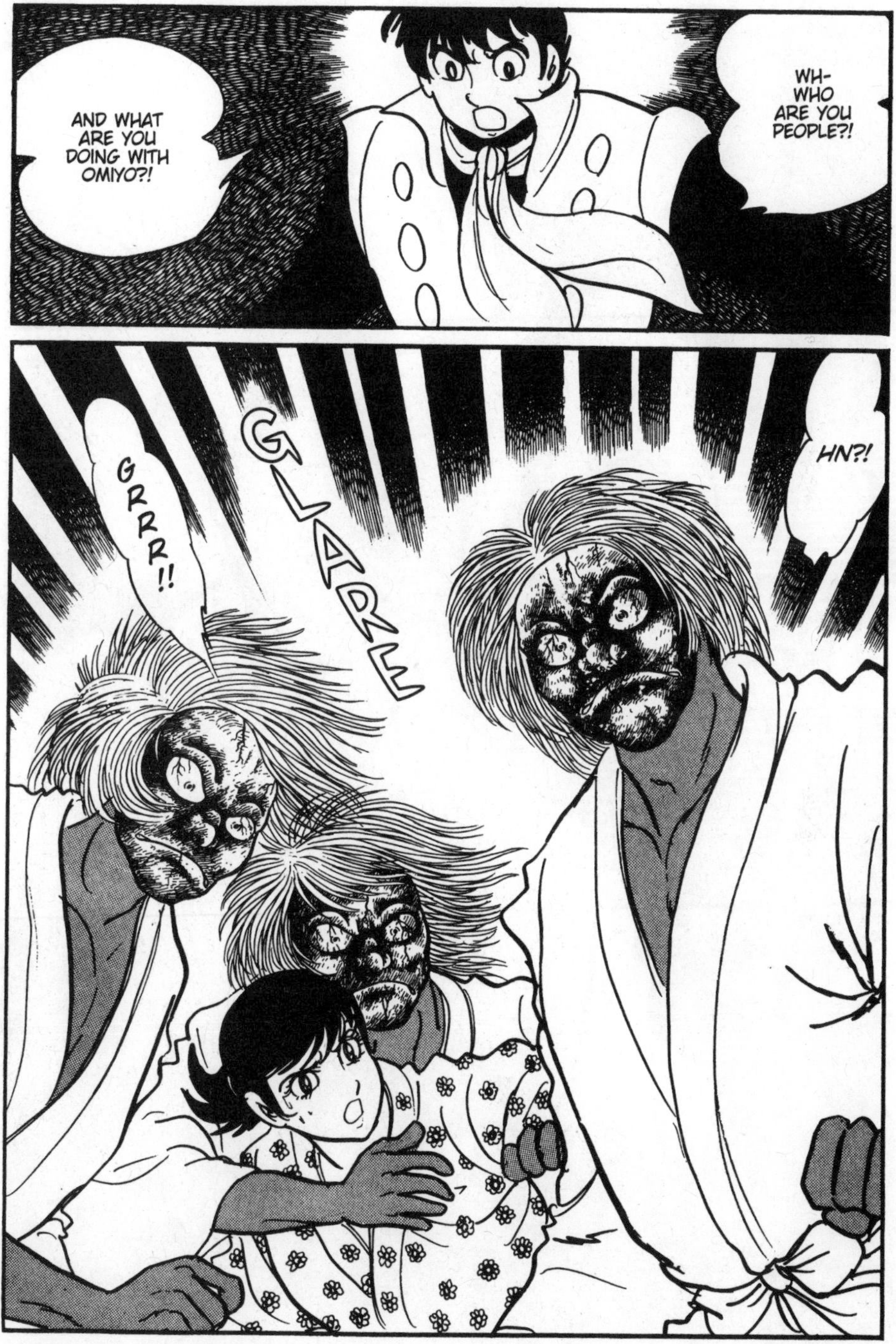
WH- WHO ARE YOU PEOPLE?!
AND WHAT ARE YOU DOING WITH OMIYO?!
HN?!
GLARE
GRRR!!

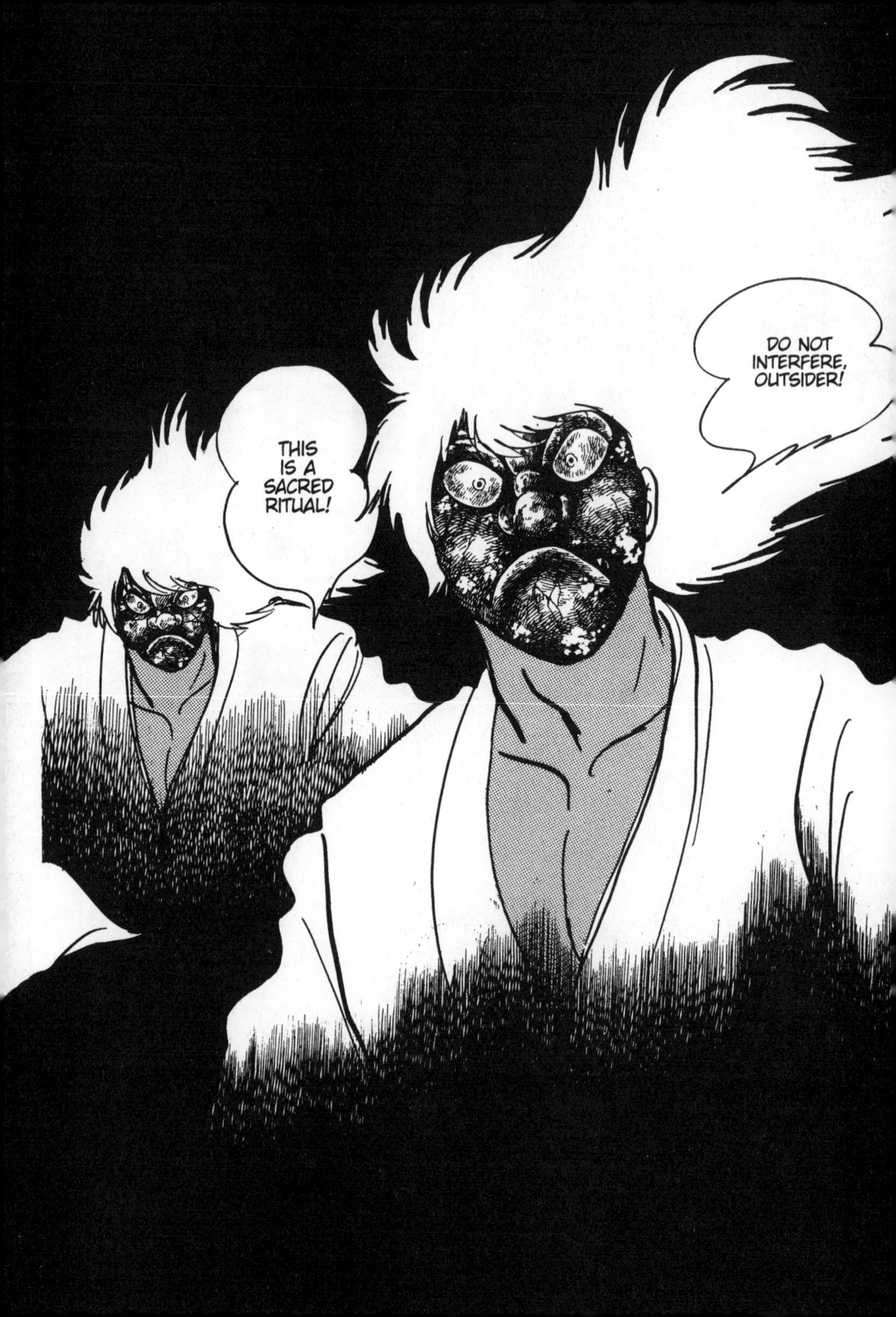
DO NOT INTERFERE, OUTSIDER!
THIS IS A SACRED RITUAL!

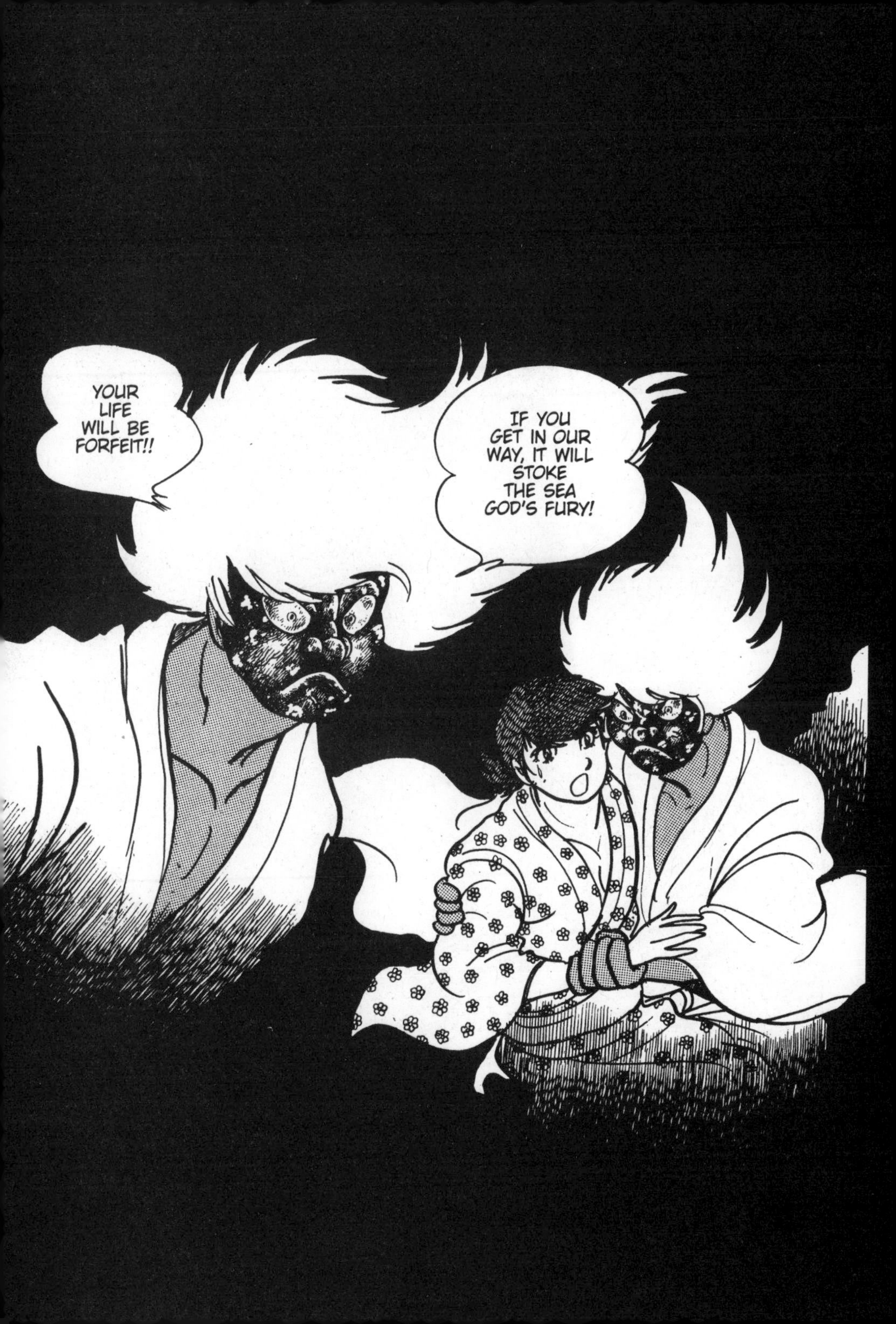
IF YOU GET IN OUR WAY, IT WILL STOKE THE SEA GOD'S FURY!
YOUR LIFE WILL BE FORFEIT!!

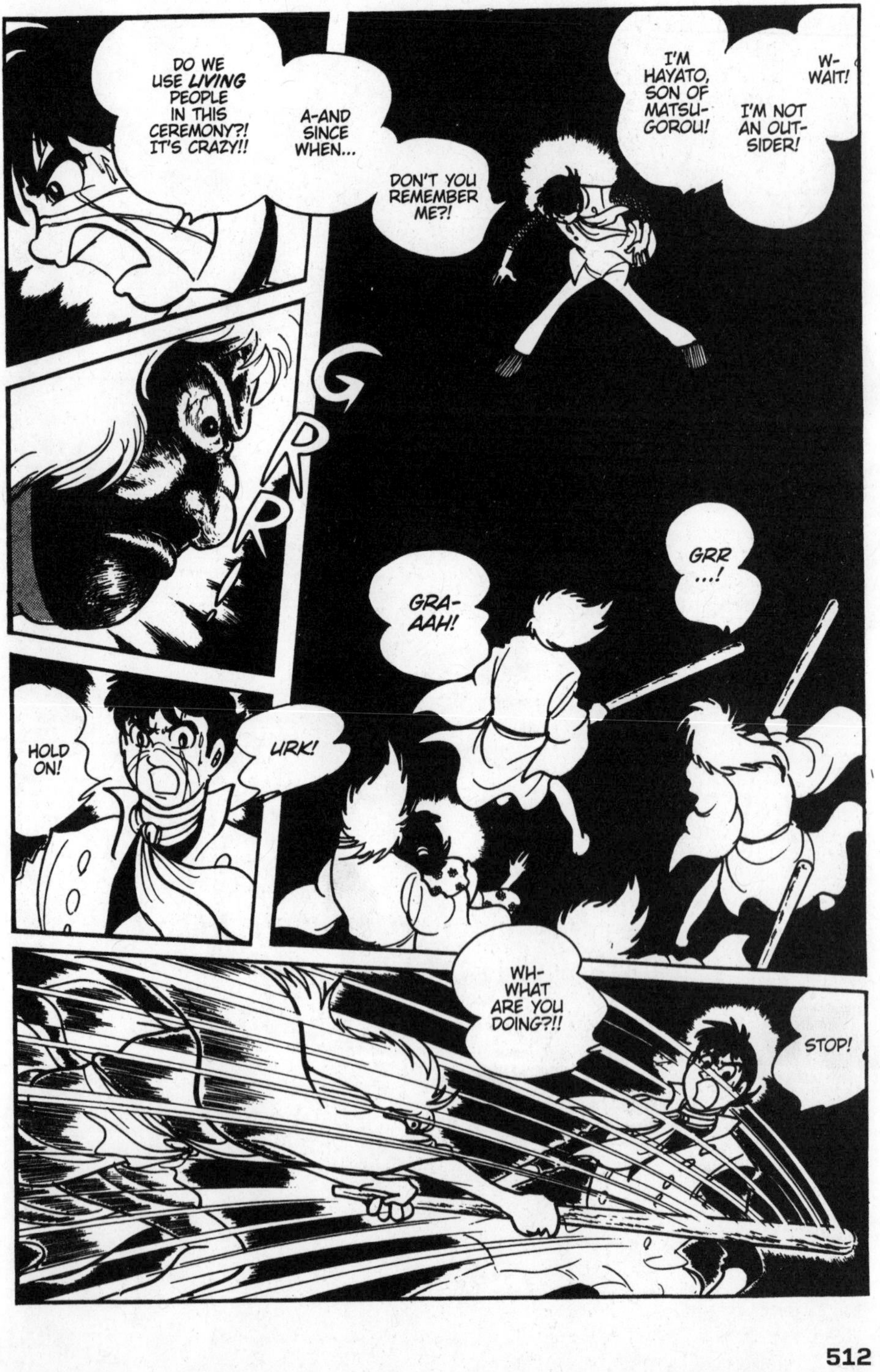
W-WAIT!
I'M NOT AN OUT-SIDER!
I'M HAYATO, SON OF MATSU-GOROU!
DON'T YOU REMEMBER ME?!
GRR ...!
GRA-AAH!
A-AND SINCE WHEN...
DO WE USE *LIVING* PEOPLE IN THIS CEREMONY?! IT'S CRAZY!!
GRRR!
URK!
HOLD ON!
STOP!
WH-WHAT ARE YOU DOING?!!

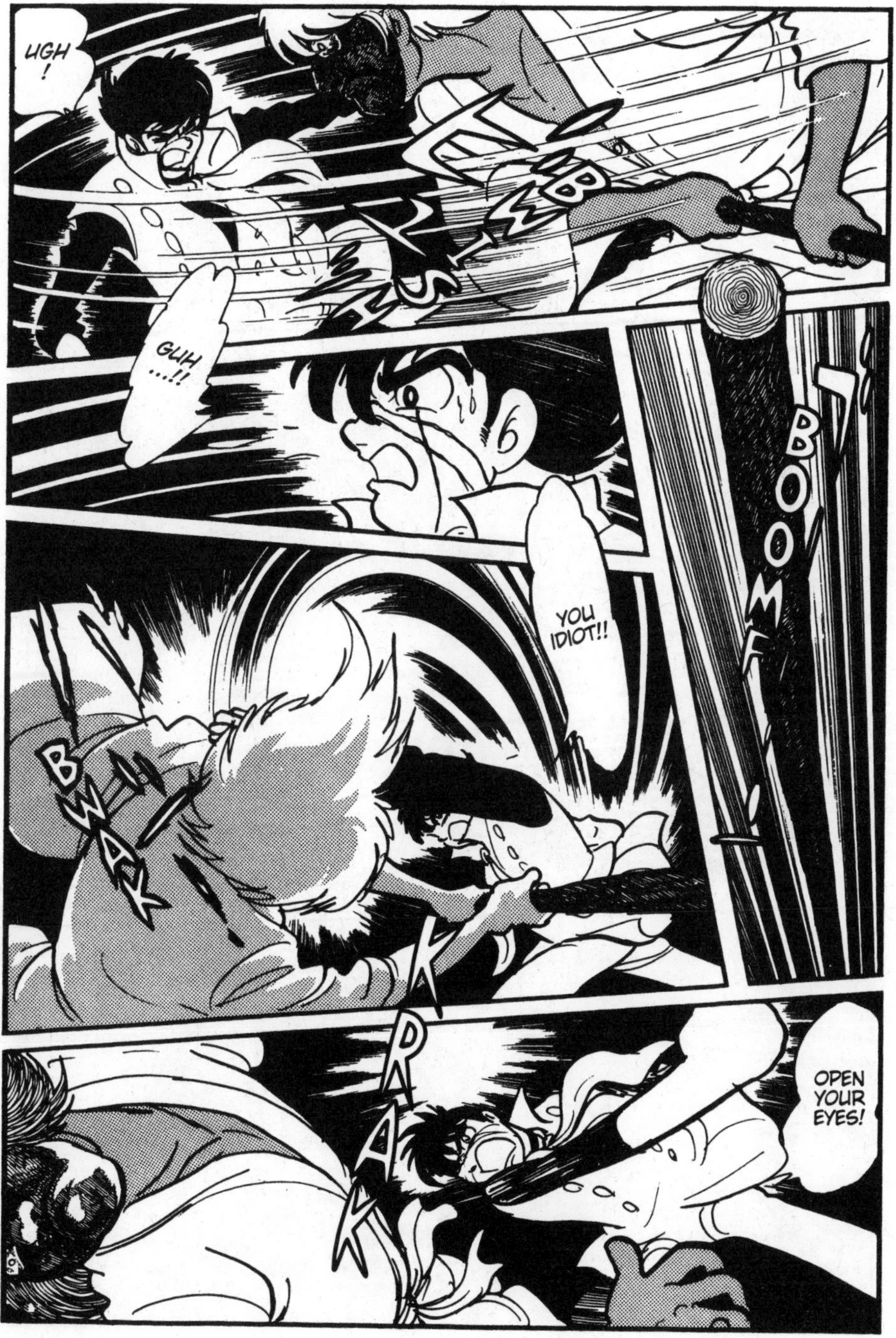
UGH!
BOOMF
GUH ...!!
YOU IDIOT!!
OPEN YOUR EYES!

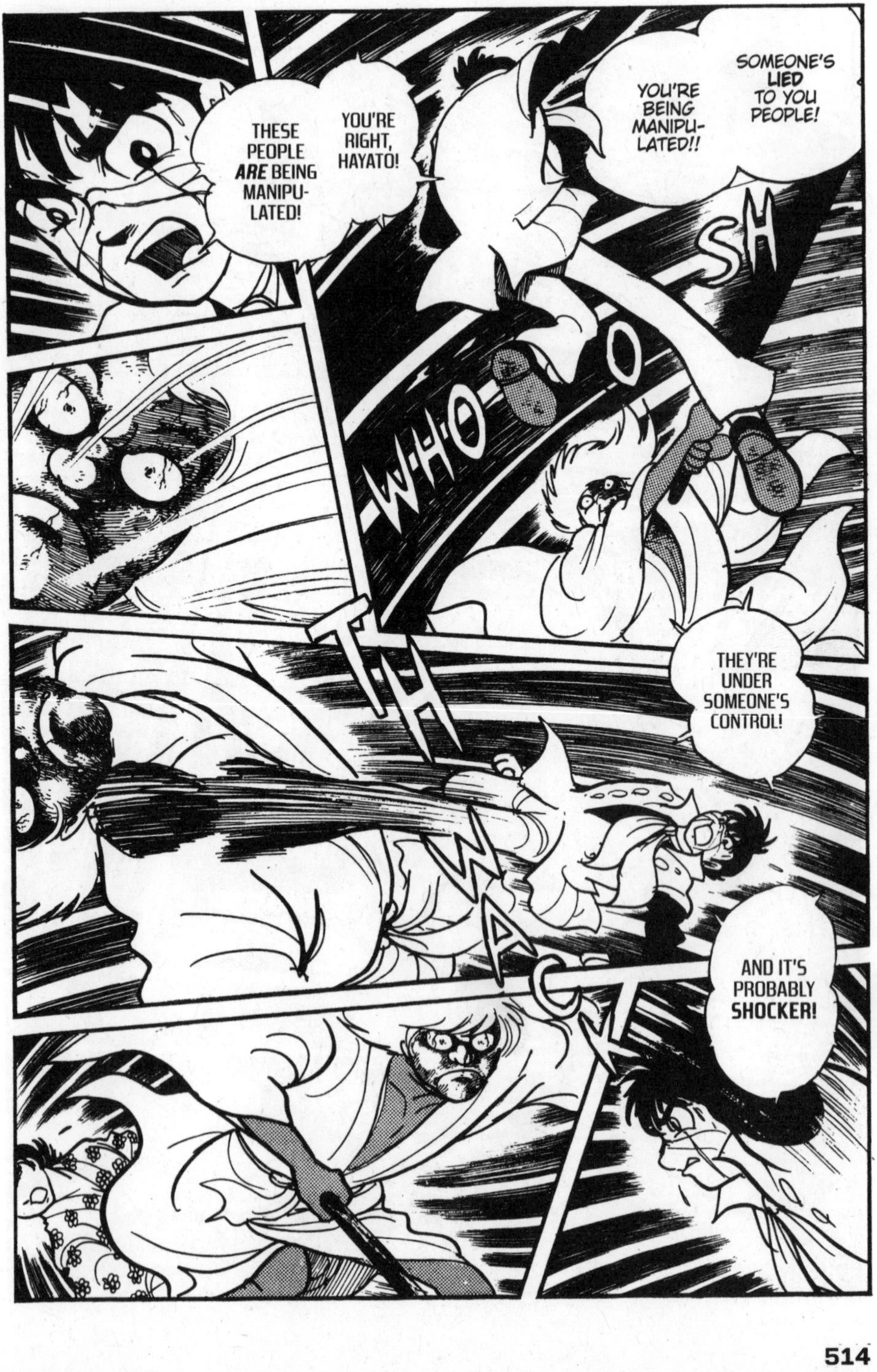
SOMEONE'S LIED TO YOU PEOPLE!
YOU'RE BEING MANIPULATED!!
WHOOOSH
YOU'RE RIGHT, HAYATO!
THESE PEOPLE ARE BEING MANIPULATED!
THEY'RE UNDER SOMEONE'S CONTROL!
THWACK
AND IT'S PROBABLY SHOCKER!

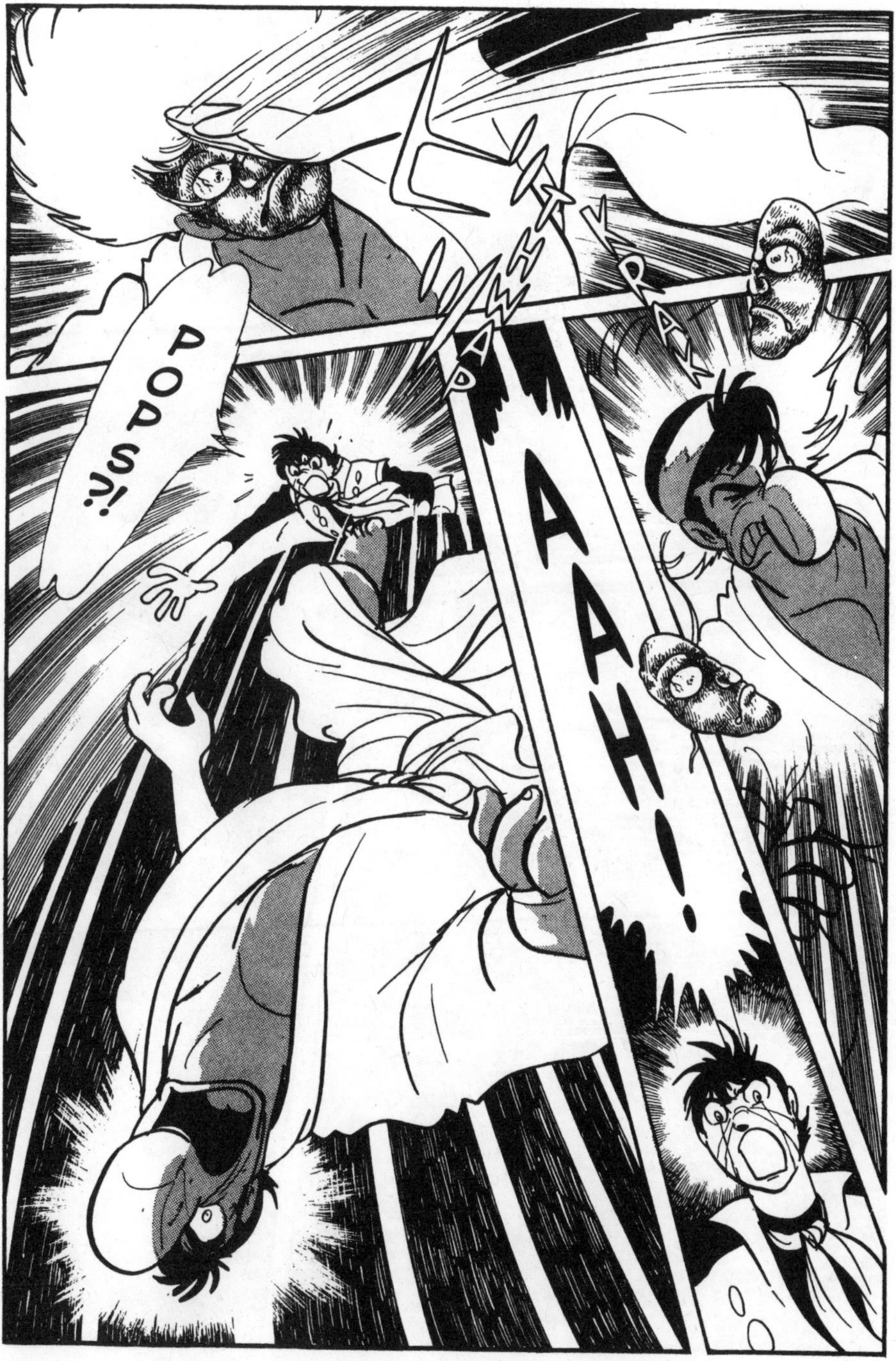
KRAK
WHAP
AAH!!
POPS?!

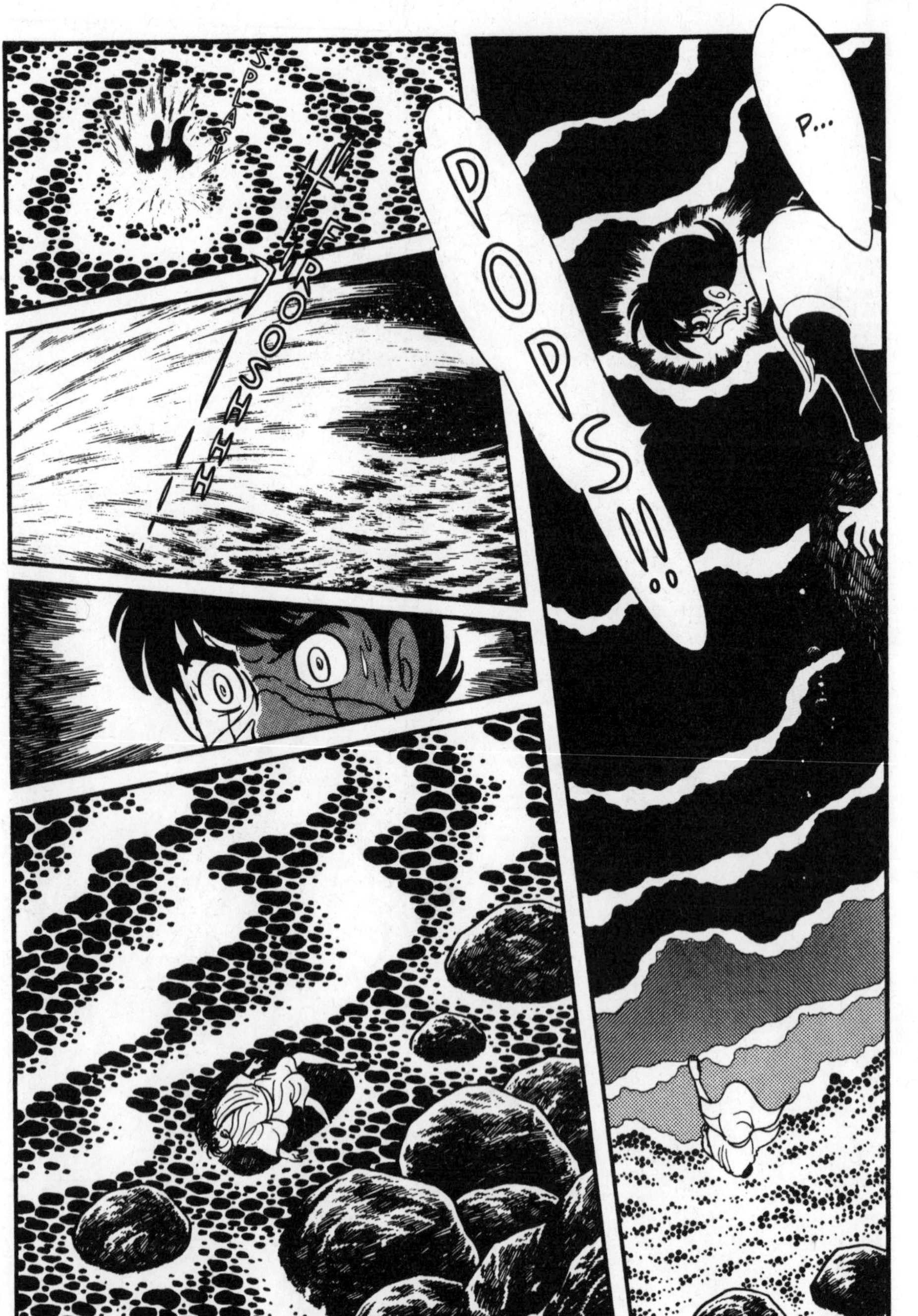
P...
POPS!!
SPLASH

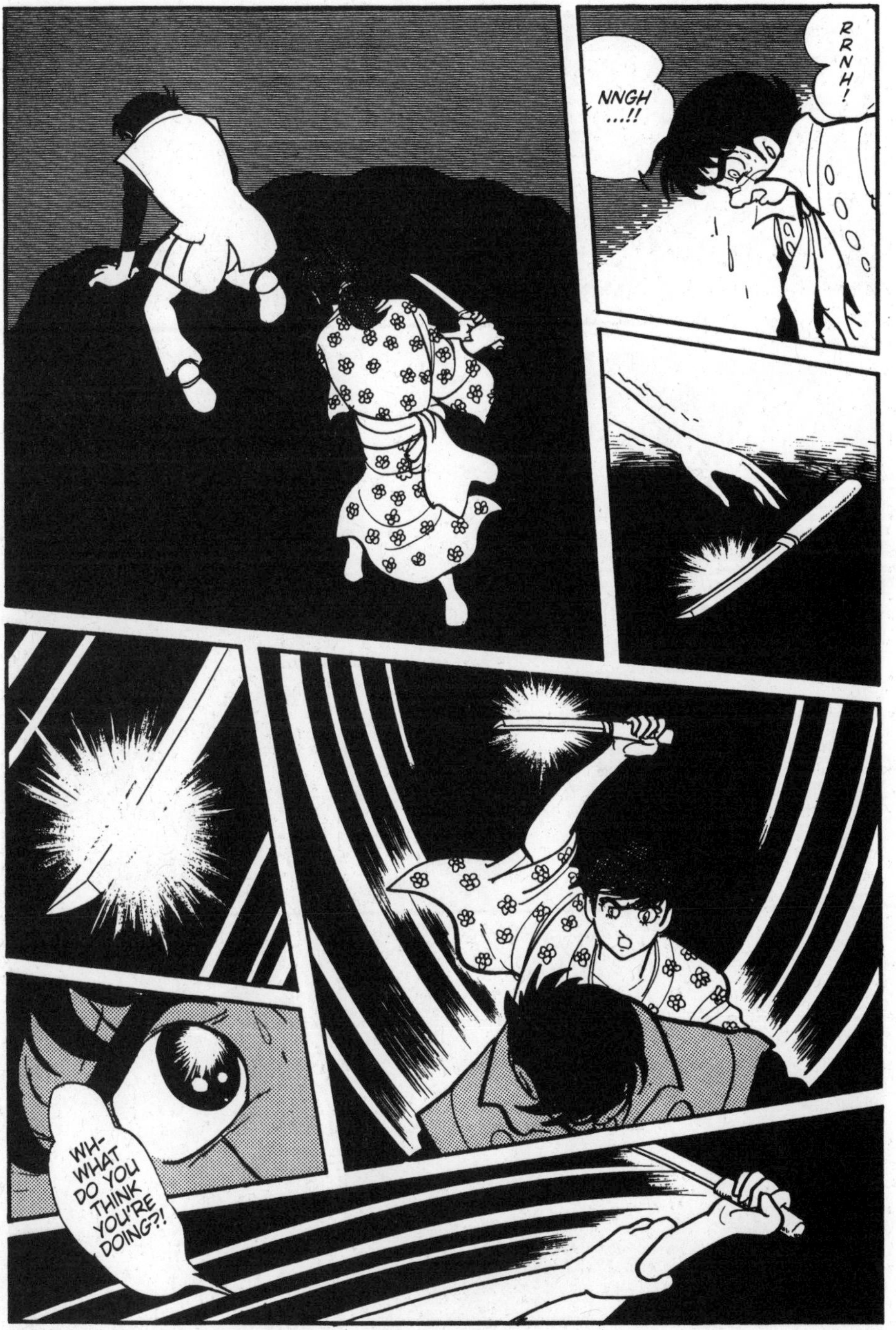
RRNH!
NNGH ...!!
WH-WHAT DO YOU THINK YOU'RE DOING?!

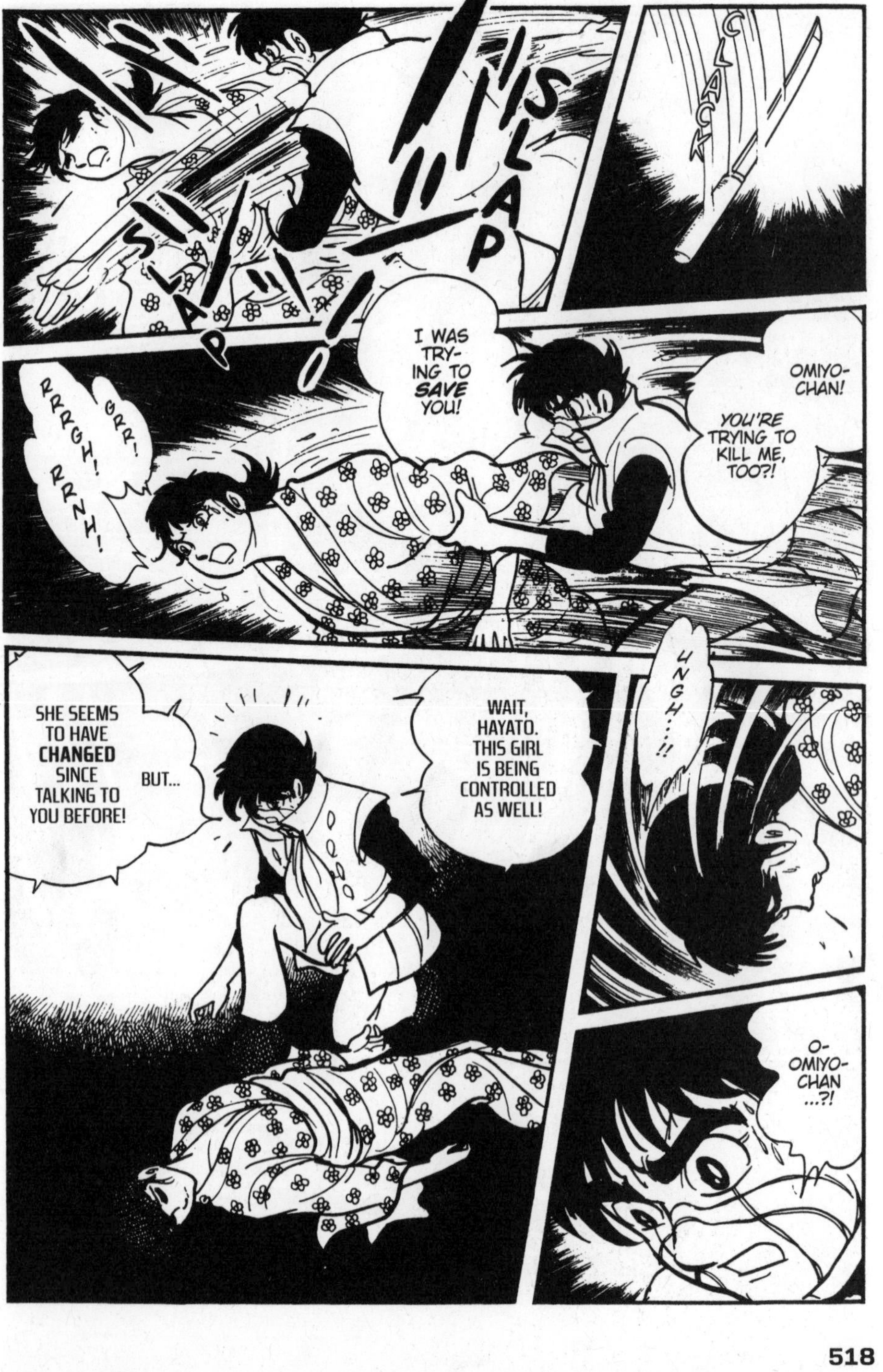
CLACK
SLAP
SLAP
OMIYO-CHAN!
YOU'RE TRYING TO KILL ME, TOO?!
I WAS TRYING TO SAVE YOU!
GRR! RRRGH! RRNH!
UNGH...!!
O-OMIYO-CHAN...?!
WAIT, HAYATO. THIS GIRL IS BEING CONTROLLED AS WELL!
BUT...
SHE SEEMS TO HAVE CHANGED SINCE TALKING TO YOU BEFORE!

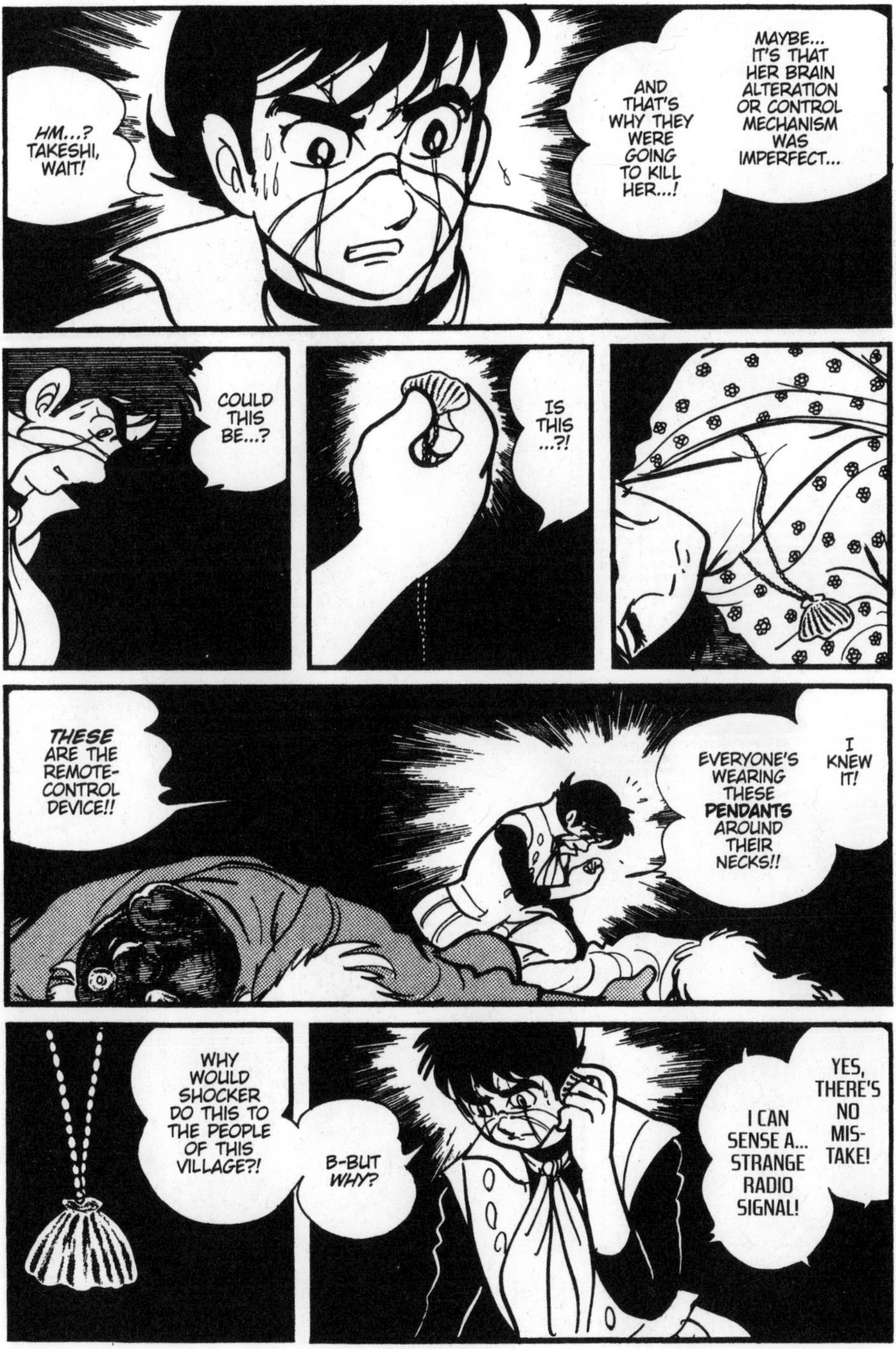
MAYBE... IT'S THAT HER BRAIN ALTERATION OR CONTROL MECHANISM WAS IMPERFECT...
AND THAT'S WHY THEY WERE GOING TO KILL HER...!
HM...? TAKESHI, WAIT!
IS THIS ...?!
COULD THIS BE...?
I KNEW IT!
EVERYONE'S WEARING THESE **PENDANTS** AROUND THEIR NECKS!!
THESE ARE THE REMOTE-CONTROL DEVICE!!
YES, THERE'S NO MIS-TAKE!
I CAN SENSE A... STRANGE RADIO SIGNAL!
B-BUT *WHY?*
WHY WOULD SHOCKER DO THIS TO THE PEOPLE OF THIS VILLAGE?!

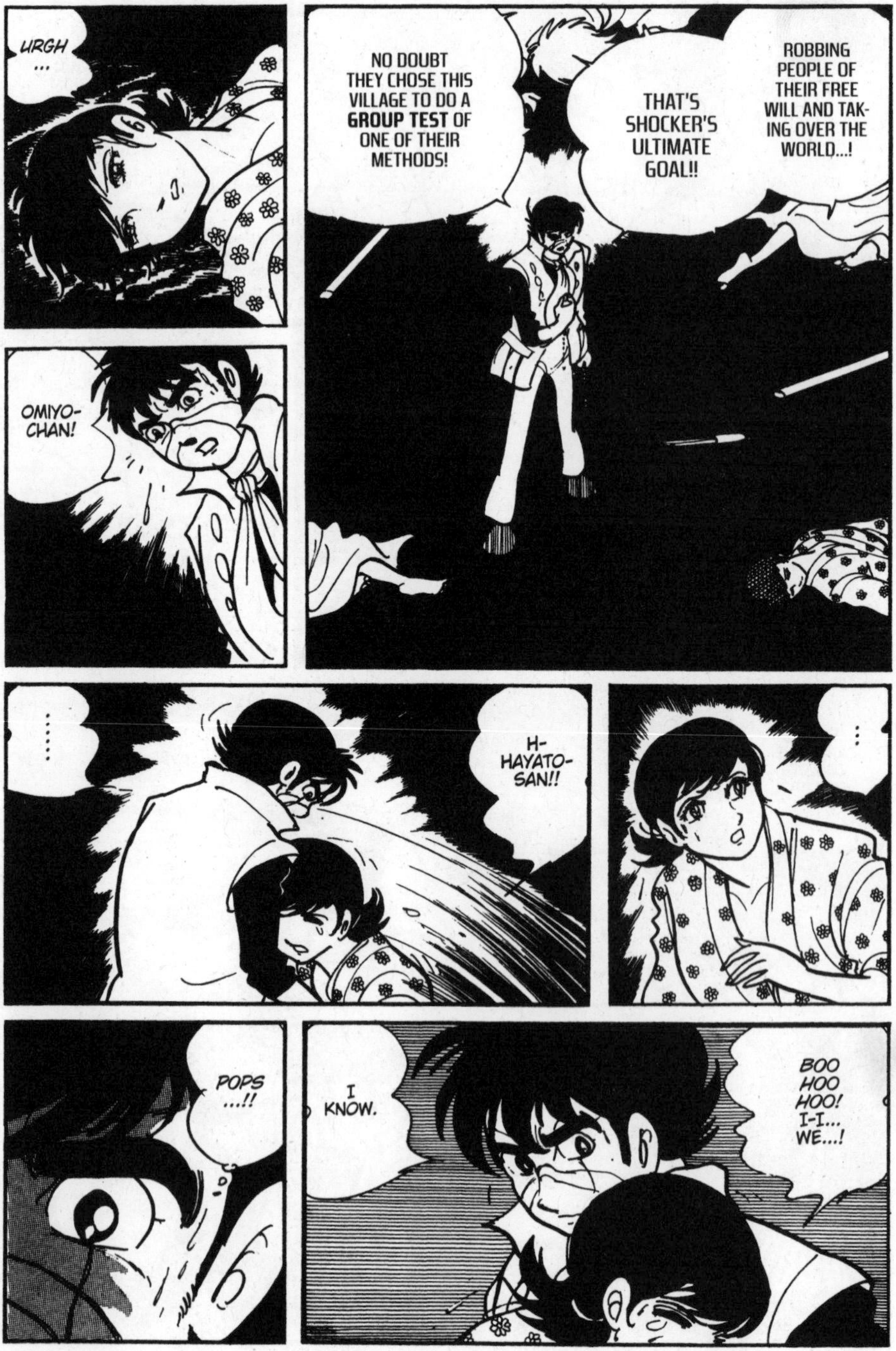
ROBBING PEOPLE OF THEIR FREE WILL AND TAKING OVER THE WORLD...!
THAT'S SHOCKER'S ULTIMATE GOAL!!
NO DOUBT THEY CHOSE THIS VILLAGE TO DO A **GROUP TEST** OF ONE OF THEIR METHODS!
URGH ...
OMIYO-CHAN!
...
H-HAYATO-SAN!!
......
BOO HOO HOO! I-I... WE...!
I KNOW.
POPS ...!!

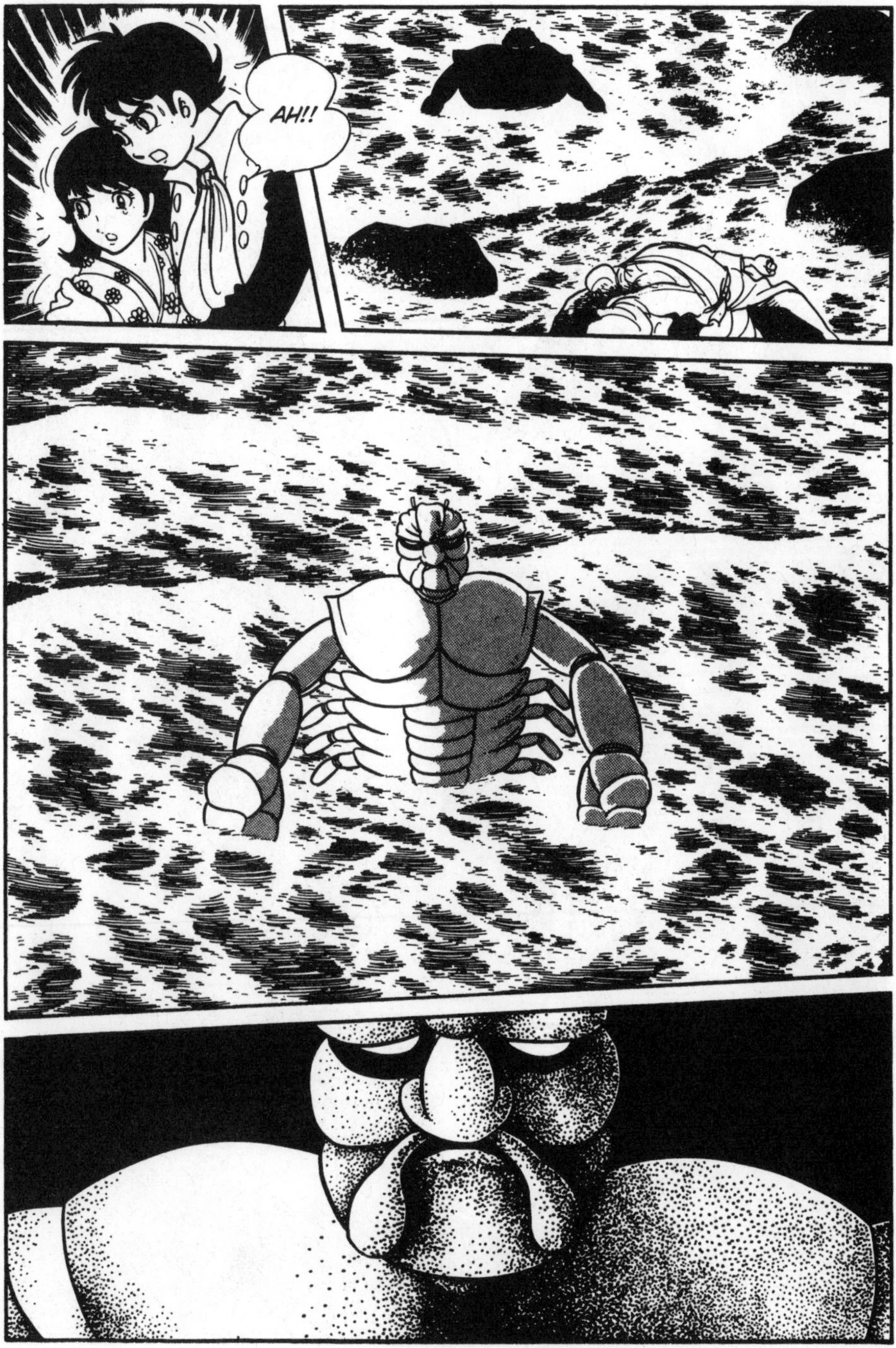
AH!!

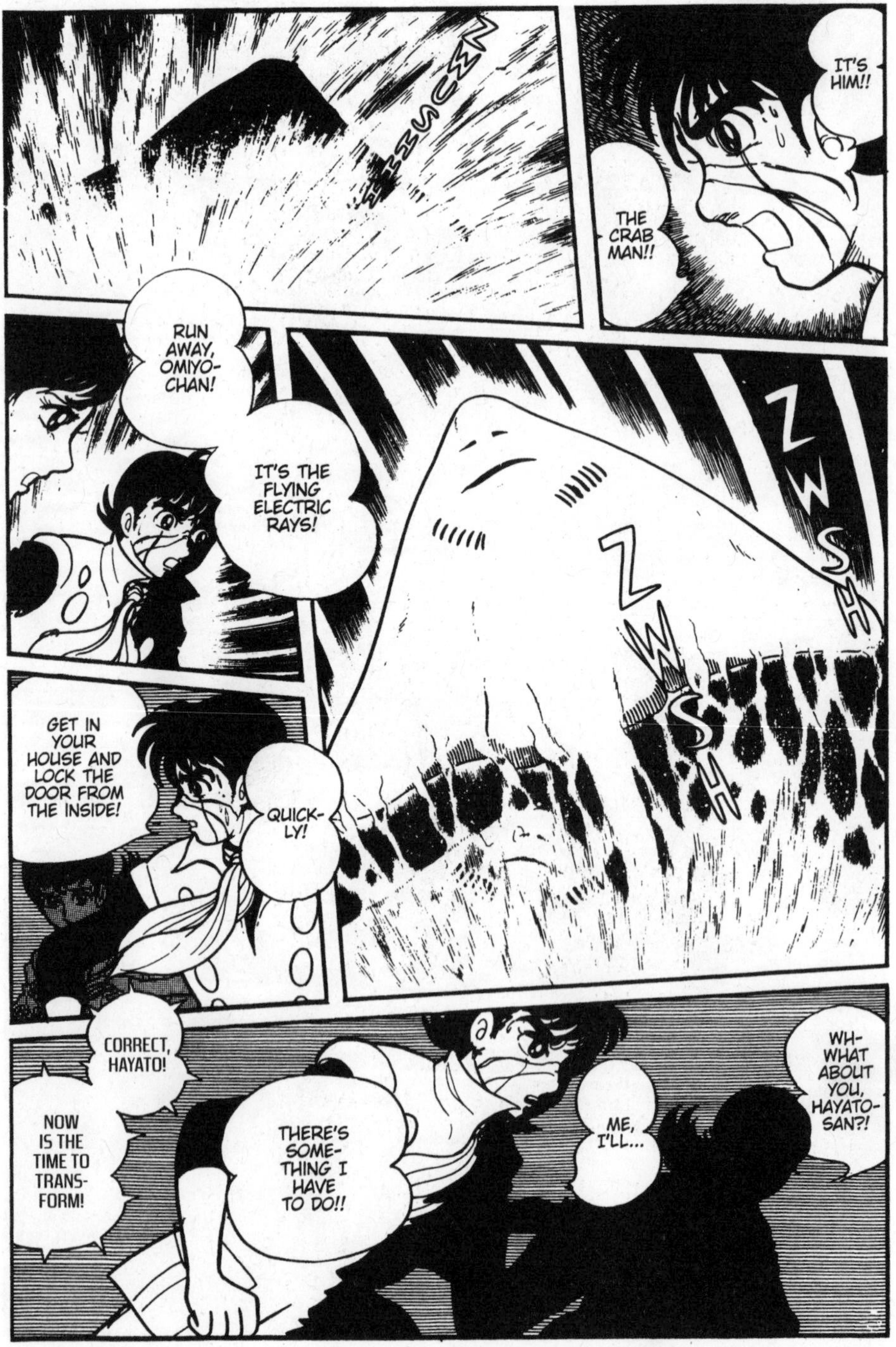
IT'S HIM!!
THE CRAB MAN!!
ZWSH
ZWSH
RUN AWAY, OMIYO-CHAN!
IT'S THE FLYING ELECTRIC RAYS!
GET IN YOUR HOUSE AND LOCK THE DOOR FROM THE INSIDE!
QUICK-LY!
WH-WHAT ABOUT YOU, HAYATO-SAN?!
ME, I'LL...
THERE'S SOME-THING I HAVE TO DO!!
CORRECT, HAYATO!
NOW IS THE TIME TO TRANS-FORM!

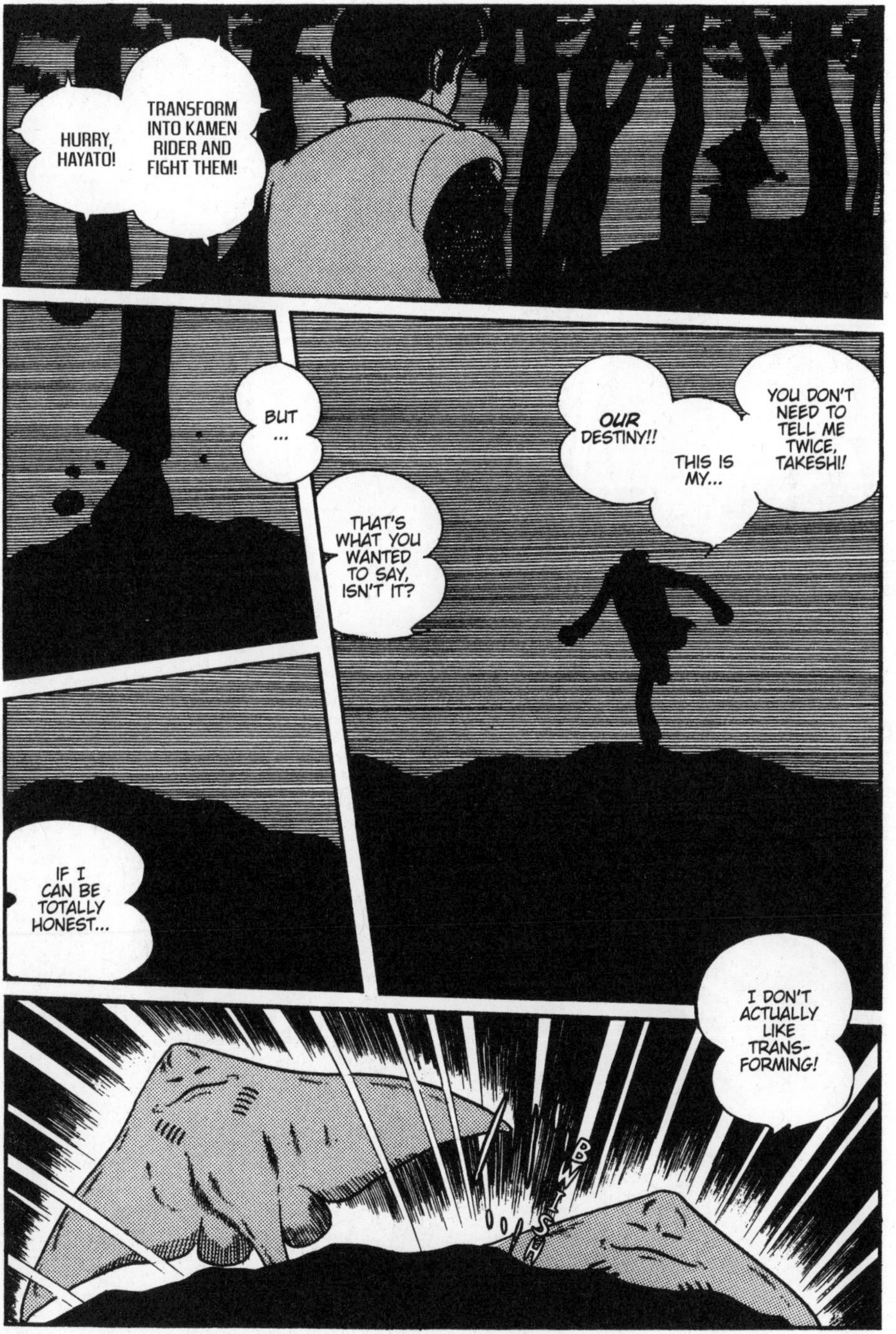
TRANSFORM INTO KAMEN RIDER AND FIGHT THEM!
HURRY, HAYATO!
YOU DON'T NEED TO TELL ME TWICE, TAKESHI!
THIS IS MY...
OUR DESTINY!!
THAT'S WHAT YOU WANTED TO SAY, ISN'T IT?
BUT ...
IF I CAN BE TOTALLY HONEST...
I DON'T ACTUALLY LIKE TRANS-FORMING!
BWISH

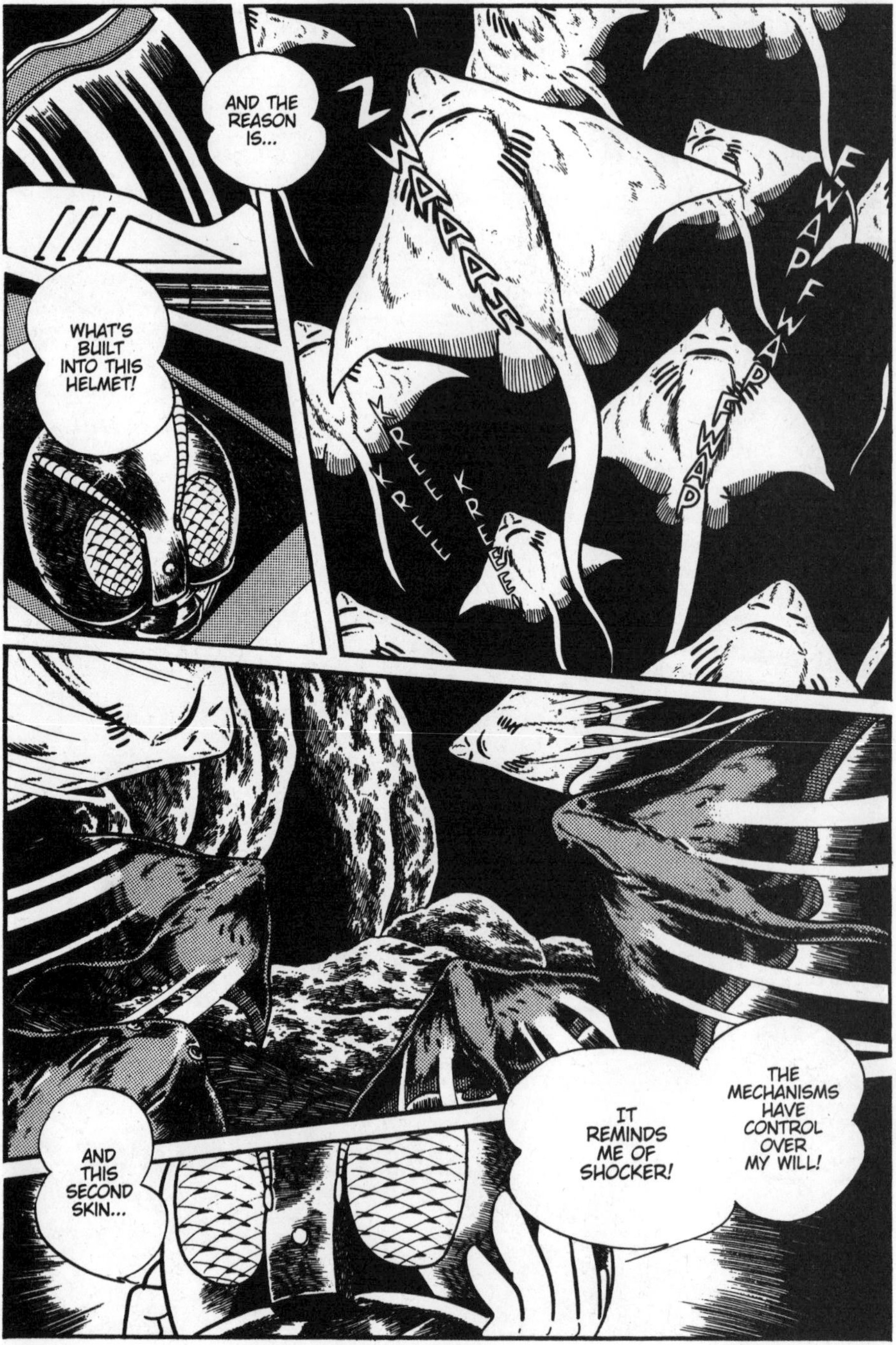
ZWAAAASH
FWAPFWAP
KREEE
KREEE
AND THE REASON IS...
WHAT'S BUILT INTO THIS HELMET!
THE MECHANISMS HAVE CONTROL OVER MY WILL!
IT REMINDS ME OF SHOCKER!
AND THIS SECOND SKIN...

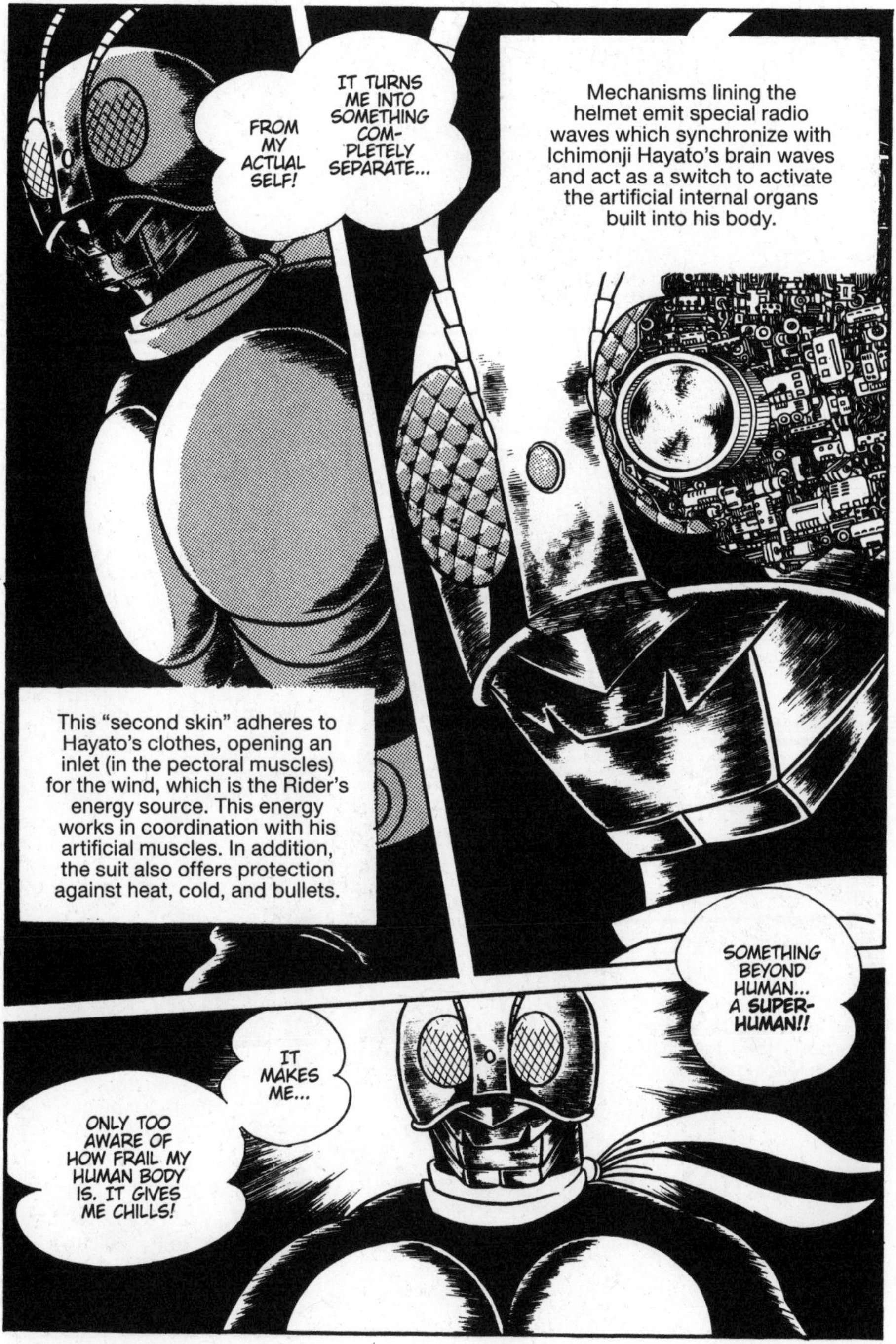

Mechanisms lining the helmet emit special radio waves which synchronize with Ichimonji Hayato's brain waves and act as a switch to activate the artificial internal organs built into his body.
IT TURNS ME INTO SOMETHING COM-PLETELY SEPARATE...
FROM MY ACTUAL SELF!
This "second skin" adheres to Hayato's clothes, opening an inlet (in the pectoral muscles) for the wind, which is the Rider's energy source. This energy works in coordination with his artificial muscles. In addition, the suit also offers protection against heat, cold, and bullets.
SOMETHING BEYOND HUMAN... A SUPER-HUMAN!!
IT MAKES ME...
ONLY TOO AWARE OF HOW FRAIL MY HUMAN BODY IS. IT GIVES ME CHILLS!

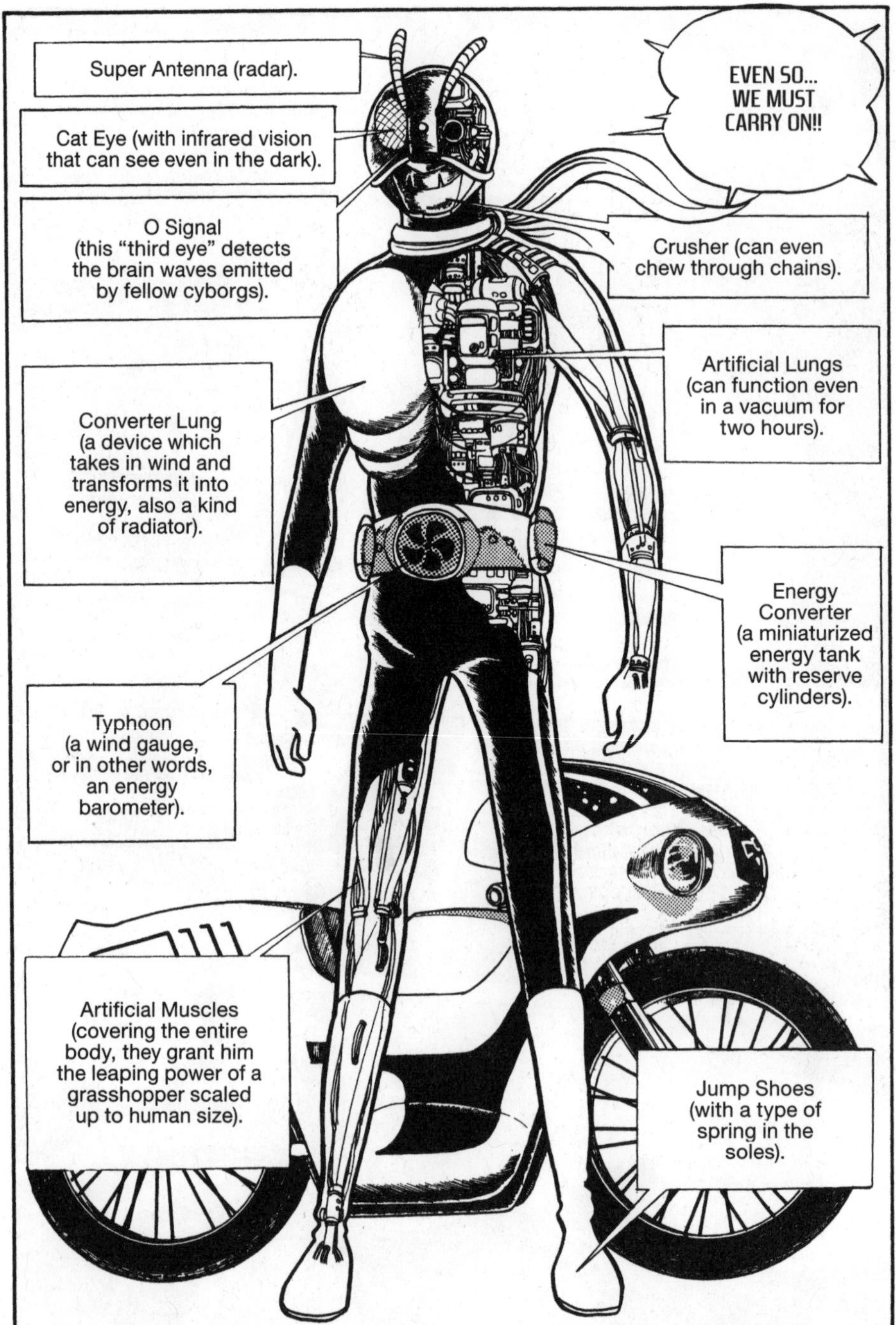
EVEN SO... WE MUST CARRY ON!!
Super Antenna (radar).
Cat Eye (with infrared vision that can see even in the dark).
Crusher (can even chew through chains).
O Signal (this “third eye” detects the brain waves emitted by fellow cyborgs).
Artificial Lungs (can function even in a vacuum for two hours).
Converter Lung (a device which takes in wind and transforms it into energy, also a kind of radiator).
Energy Converter (a miniaturized energy tank with reserve cylinders).
Typhoon (a wind gauge, or in other words, an energy barometer).
Jump Shoes (with a type of spring in the soles).
Artificial Muscles (covering the entire body, they grant him the leaping power of a grasshopper scaled up to human size).

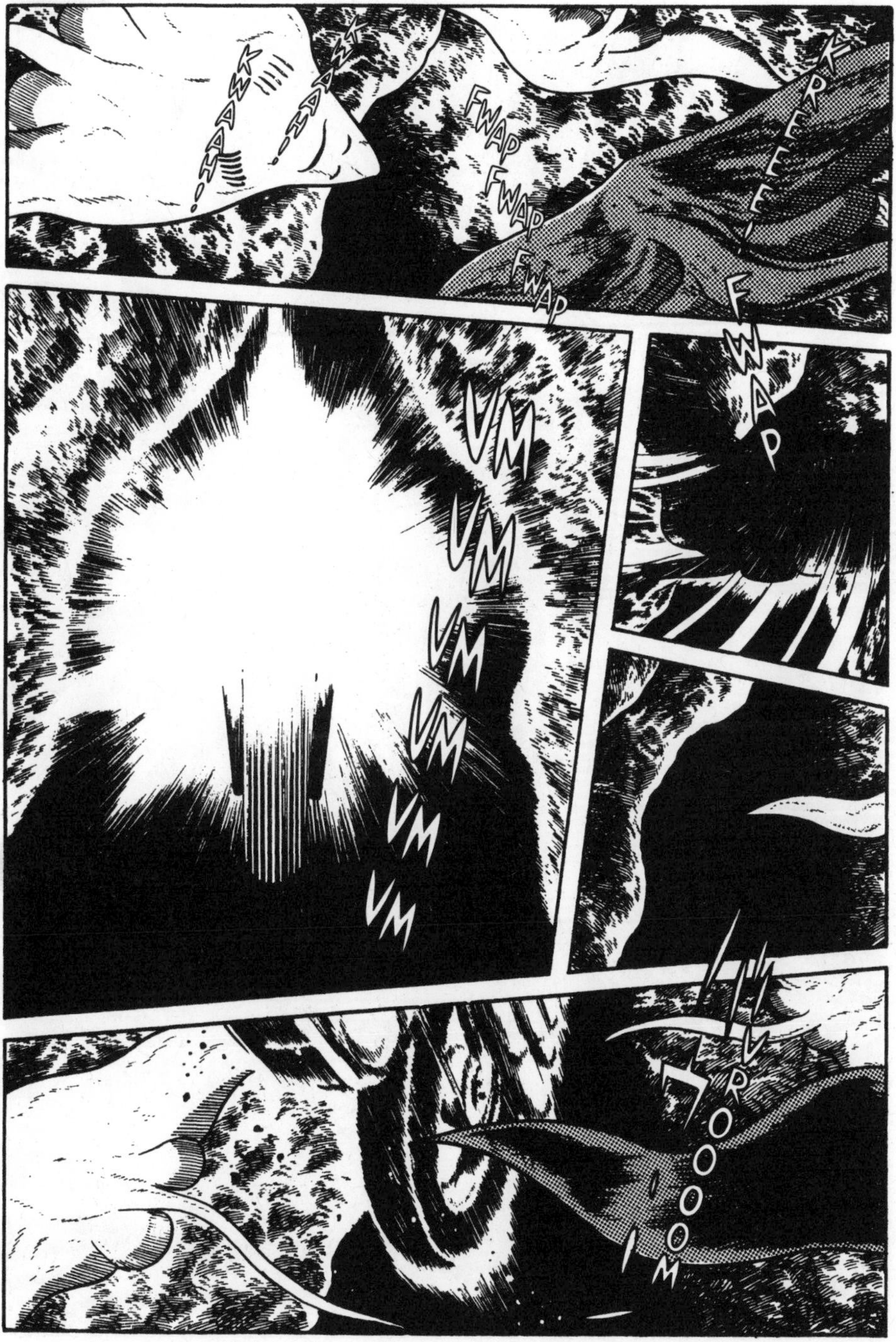
KREEEE!
FWAP FWAP FWAP FWAP
KWAAH!!
KWAAAH!!
FWAP
VM VM VM VM VM VM VM VM
VVROOOOOM

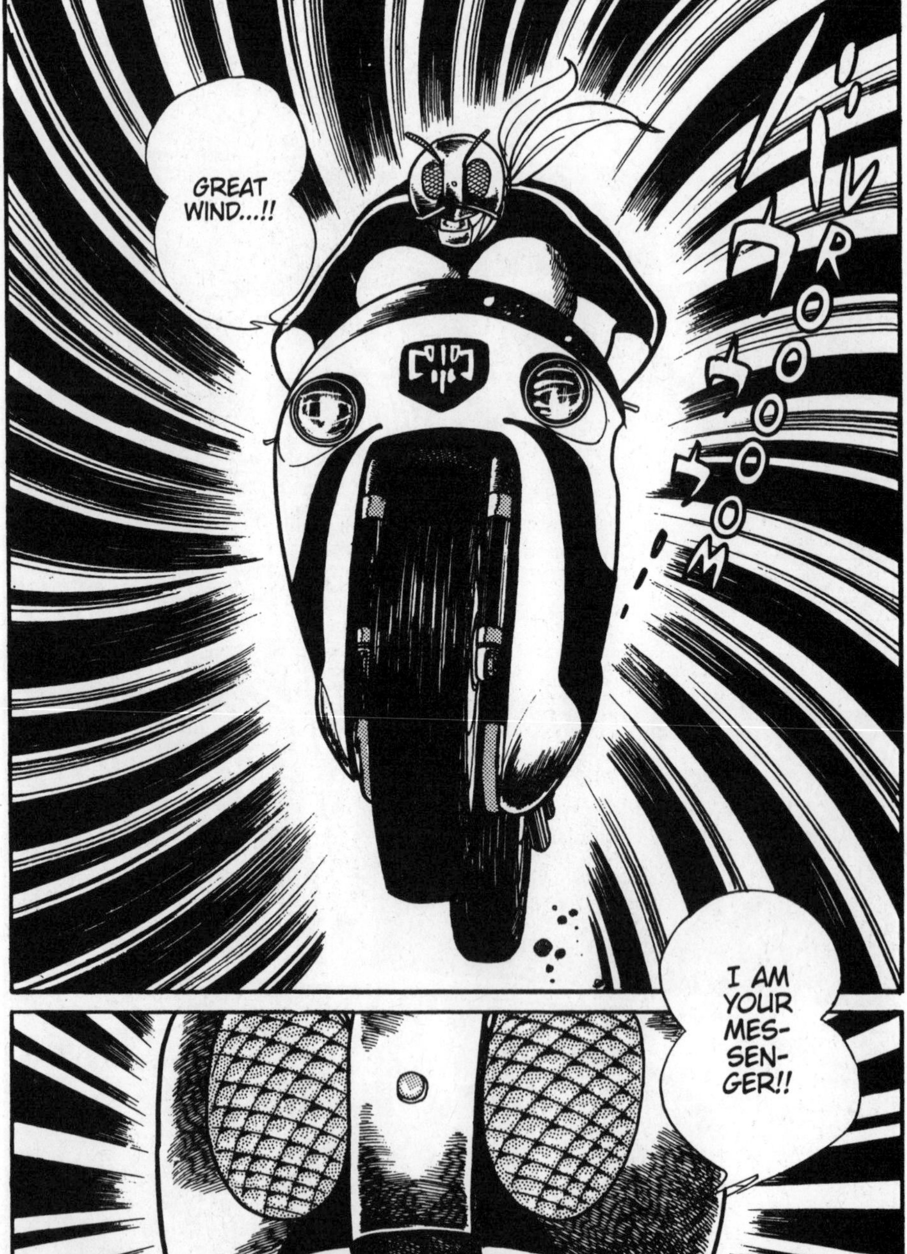
GREAT WIND...!!
ROOOOOOM
I AM YOUR MES-SEN-GER!!

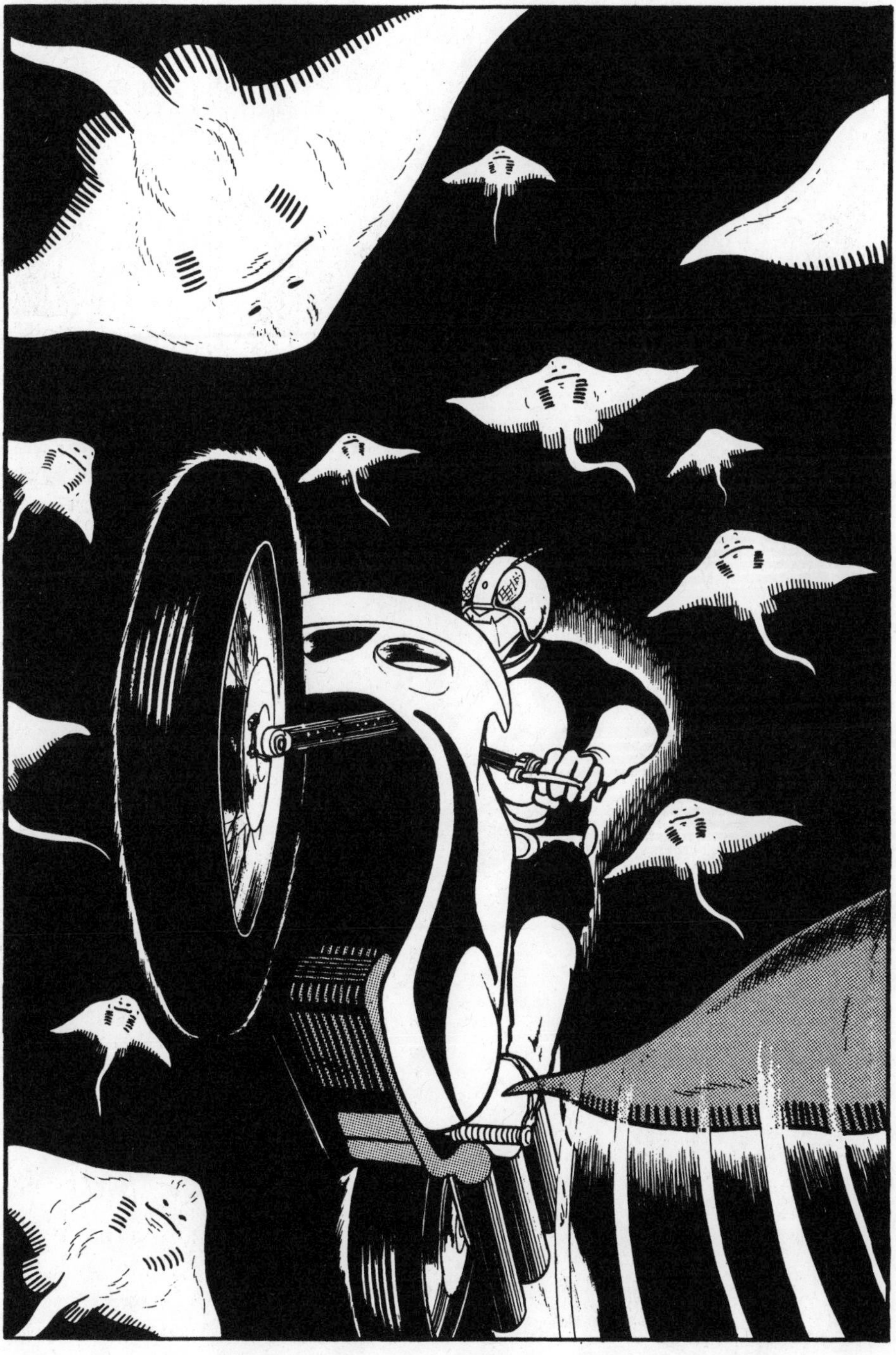

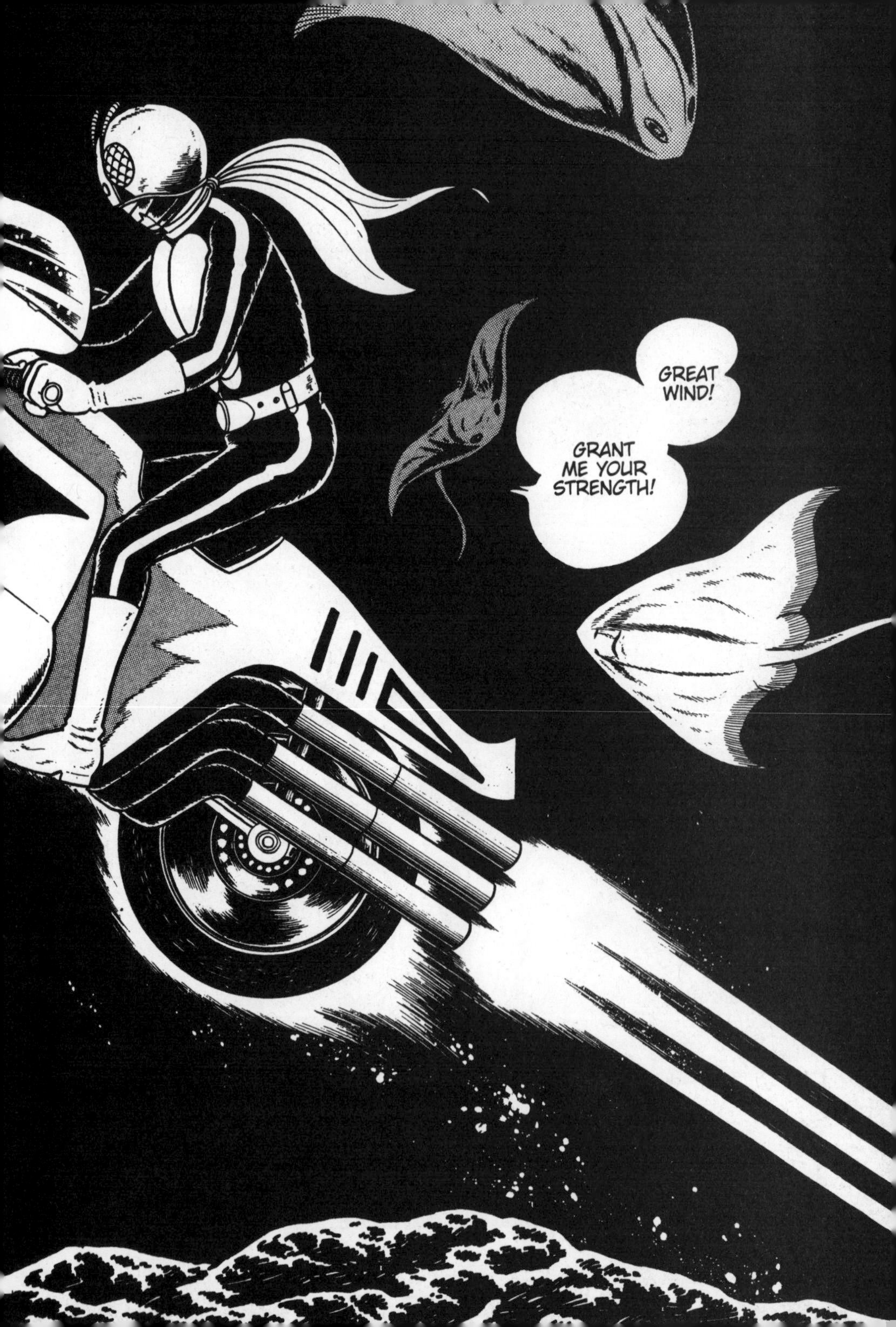
GREAT WIND!
GRANT ME YOUR STRENGTH!

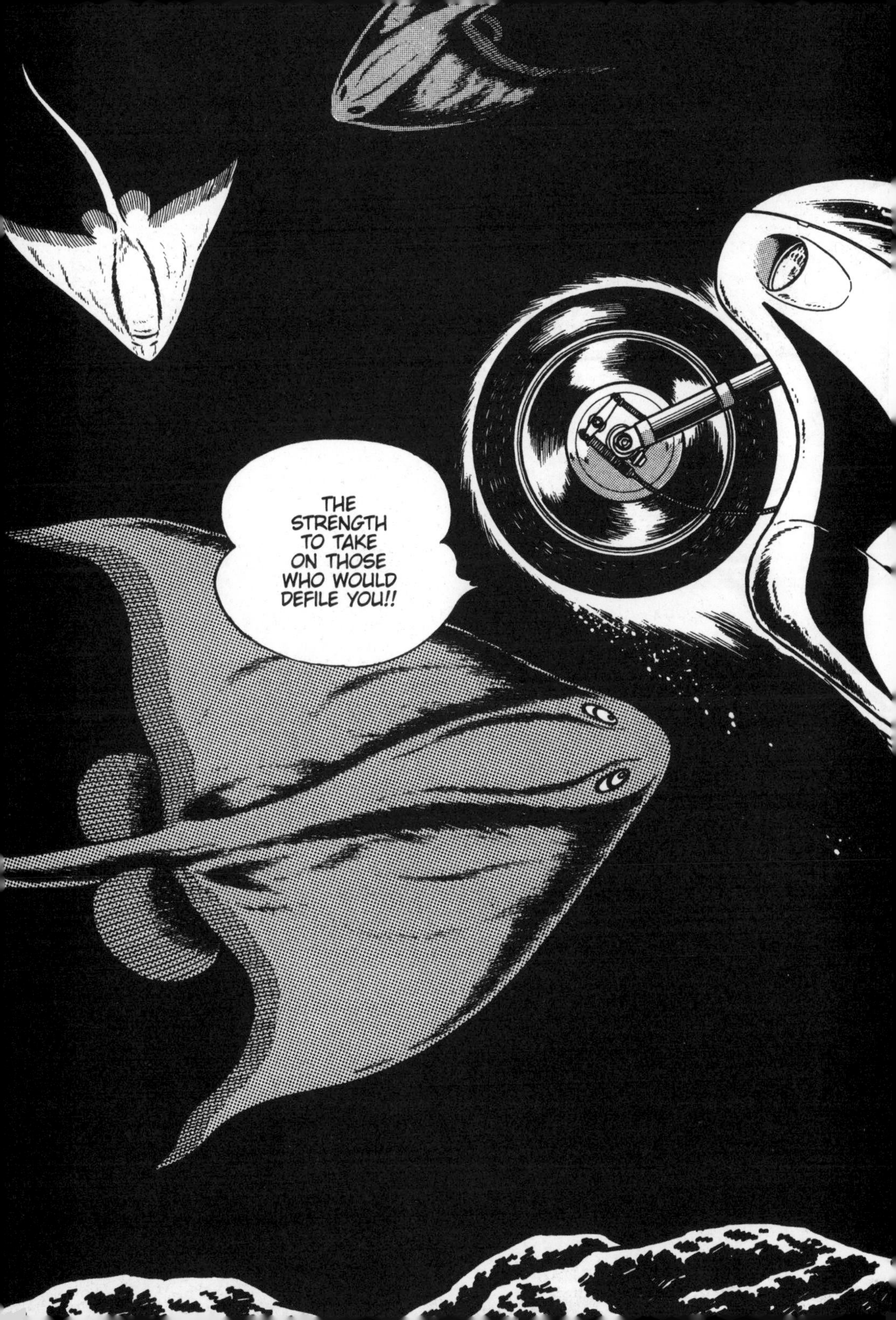
THE STRENGTH TO TAKE ON THOSE WHO WOULD DEFILE YOU!!

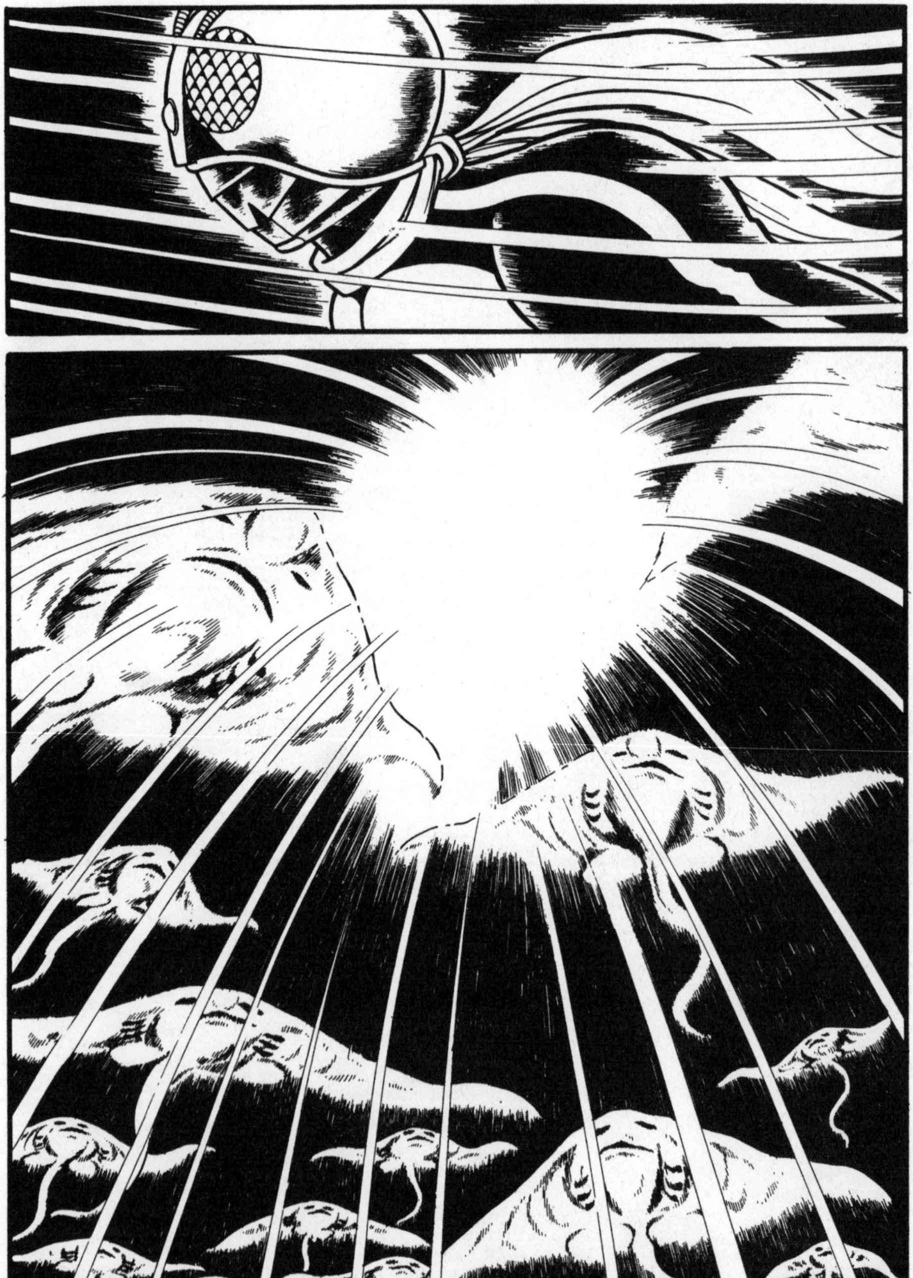

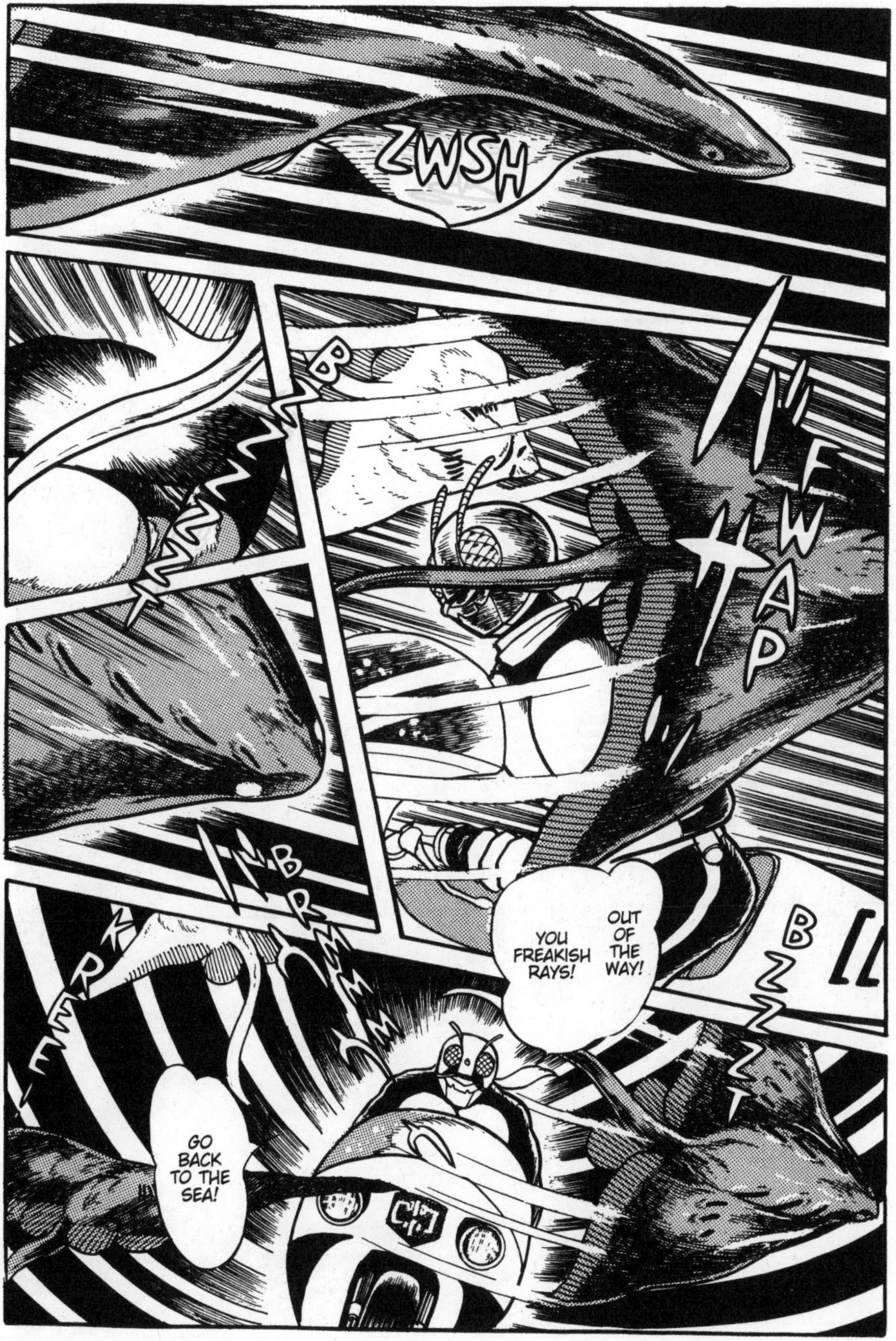
ZWSH
FWAP
OUT OF THE WAY!
YOU FREAKISH RAYS!
BZZZZT
BRRRMMM
KREEEE
GO BACK TO THE SEA!

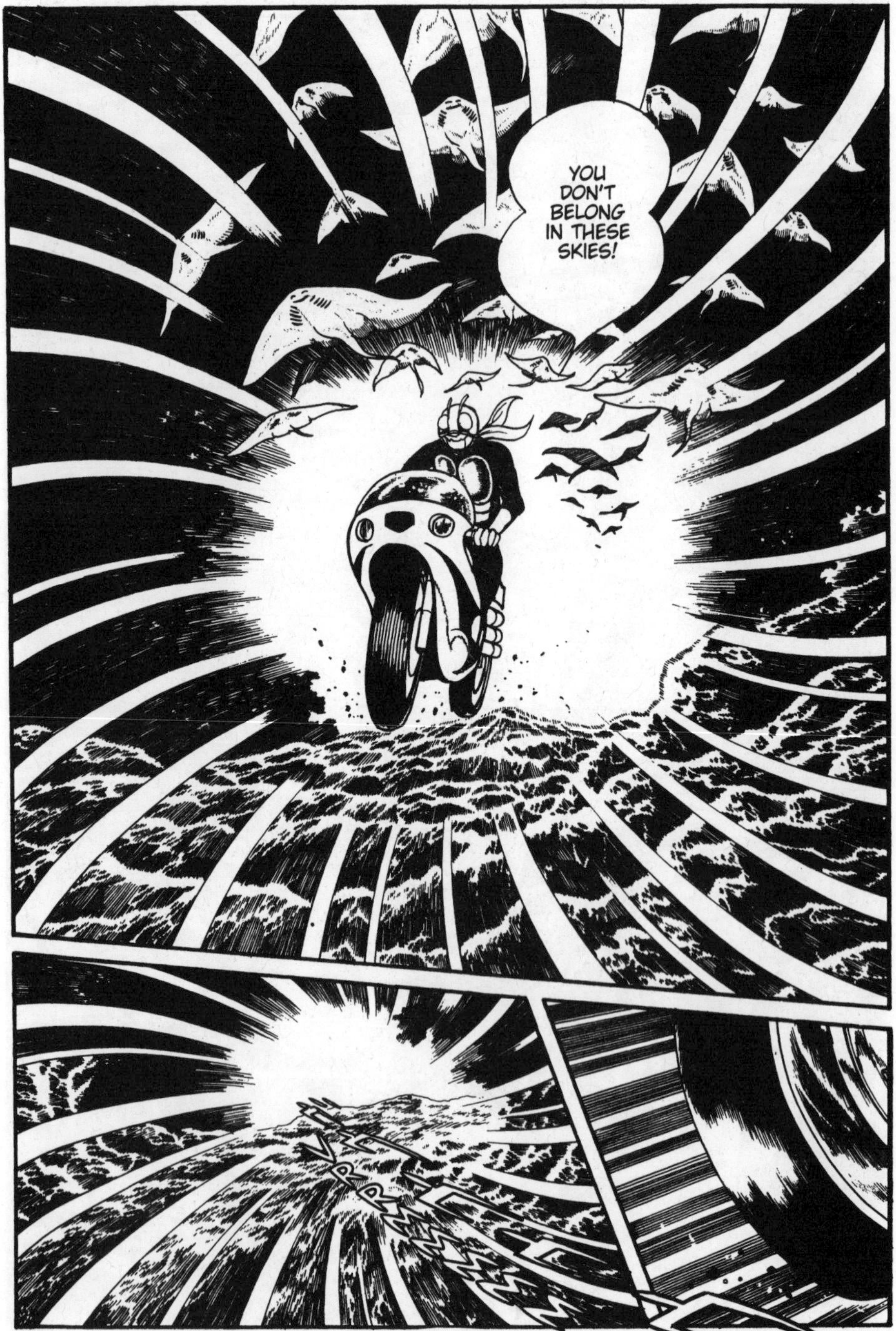
YOU DON'T BELONG IN THESE SKIES!

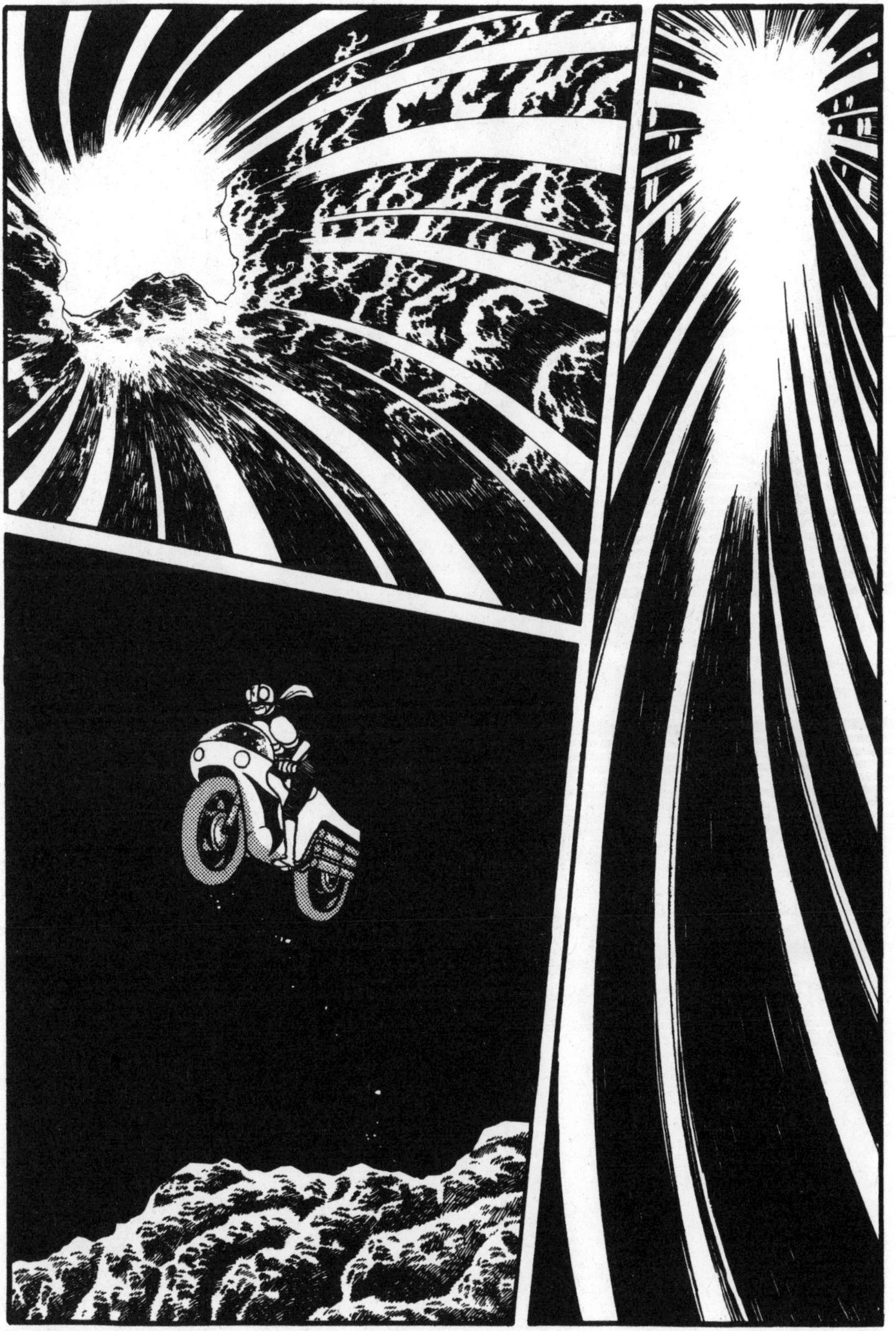

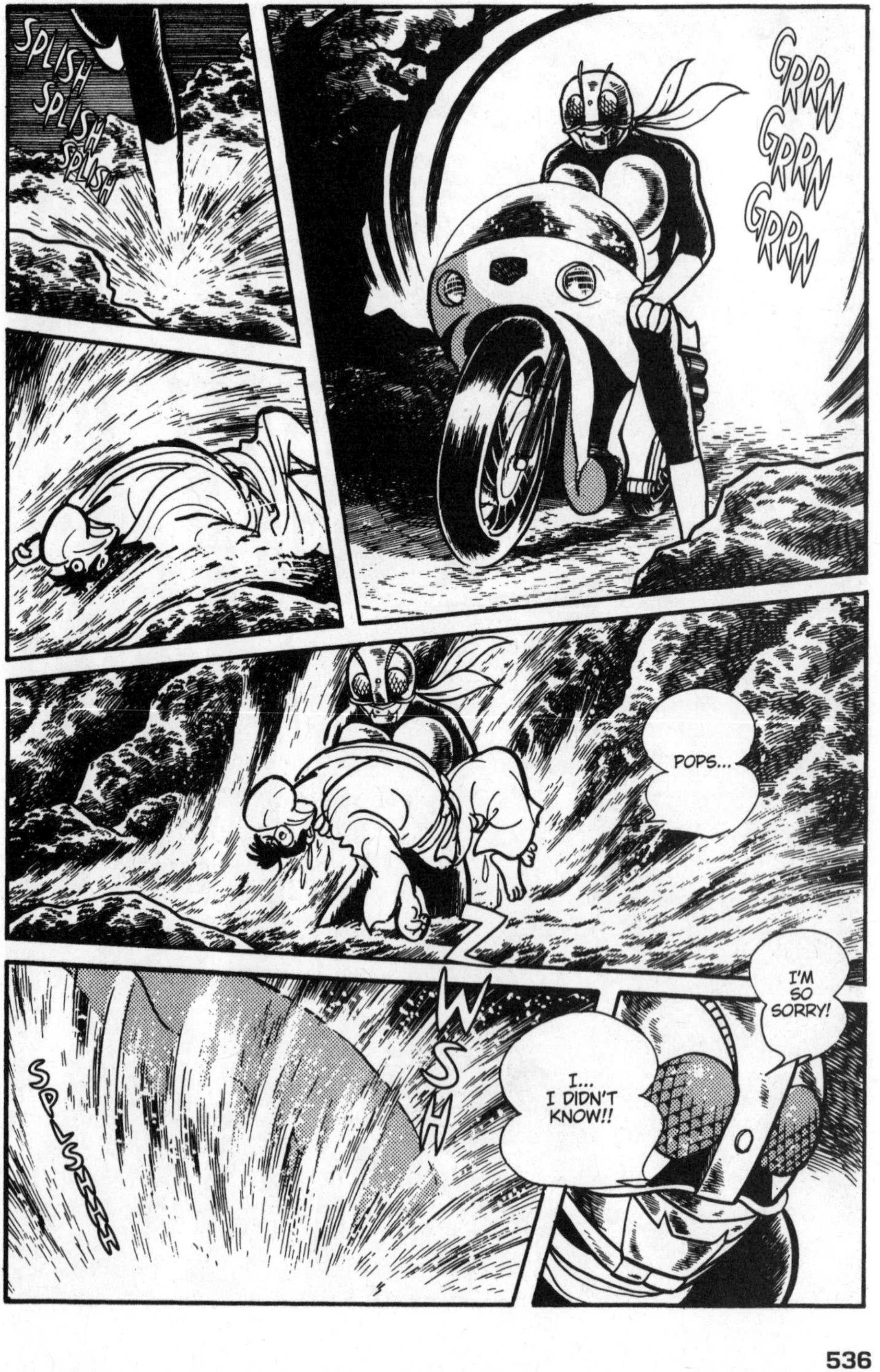
GRRN
GRRN
GRRN
SPLISH
SPLISH
SPLISH
SPLISH
POPS...
WSH
I'M SO SORRY!
I... I DIDN'T KNOW!!
SPLSHHHH

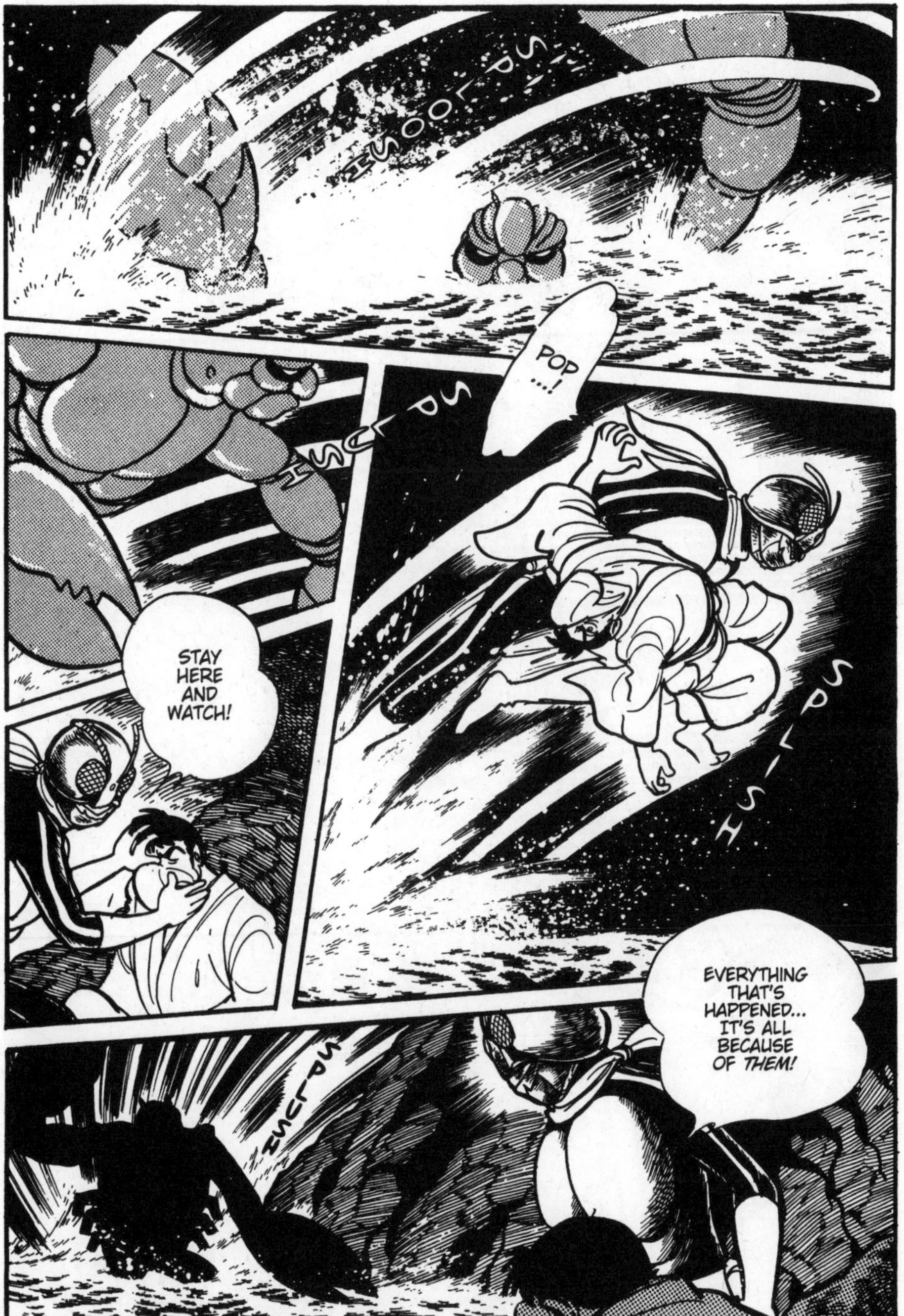
SPLOOSH
POP ...!
SPLISH
SPLASH
STAY HERE AND WATCH!
EVERYTHING THAT'S HAPPENED... IT'S ALL BECAUSE OF *THEM!*
SPLASH

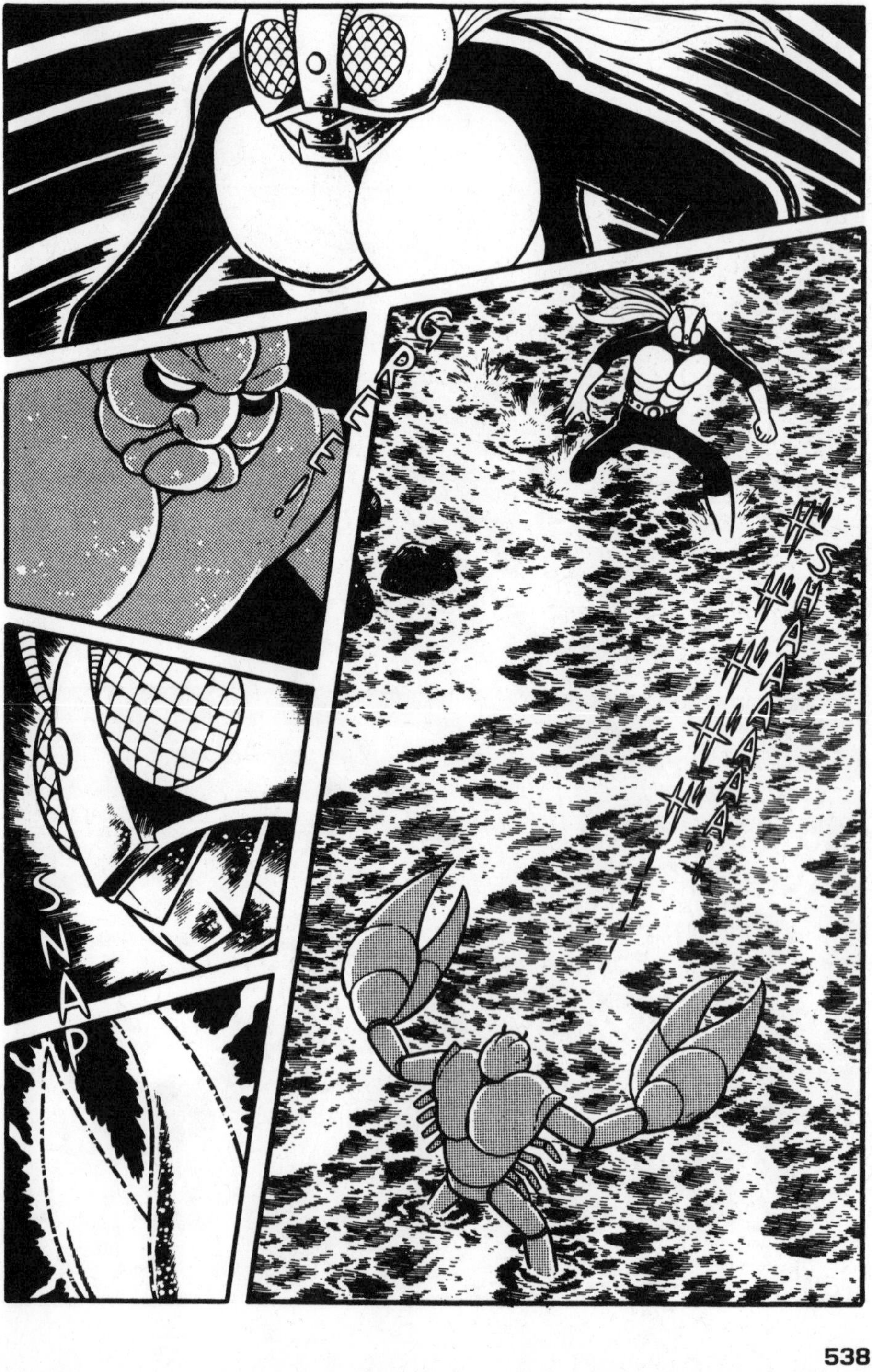
SHAAAAAAA...
GREEE
SNAP

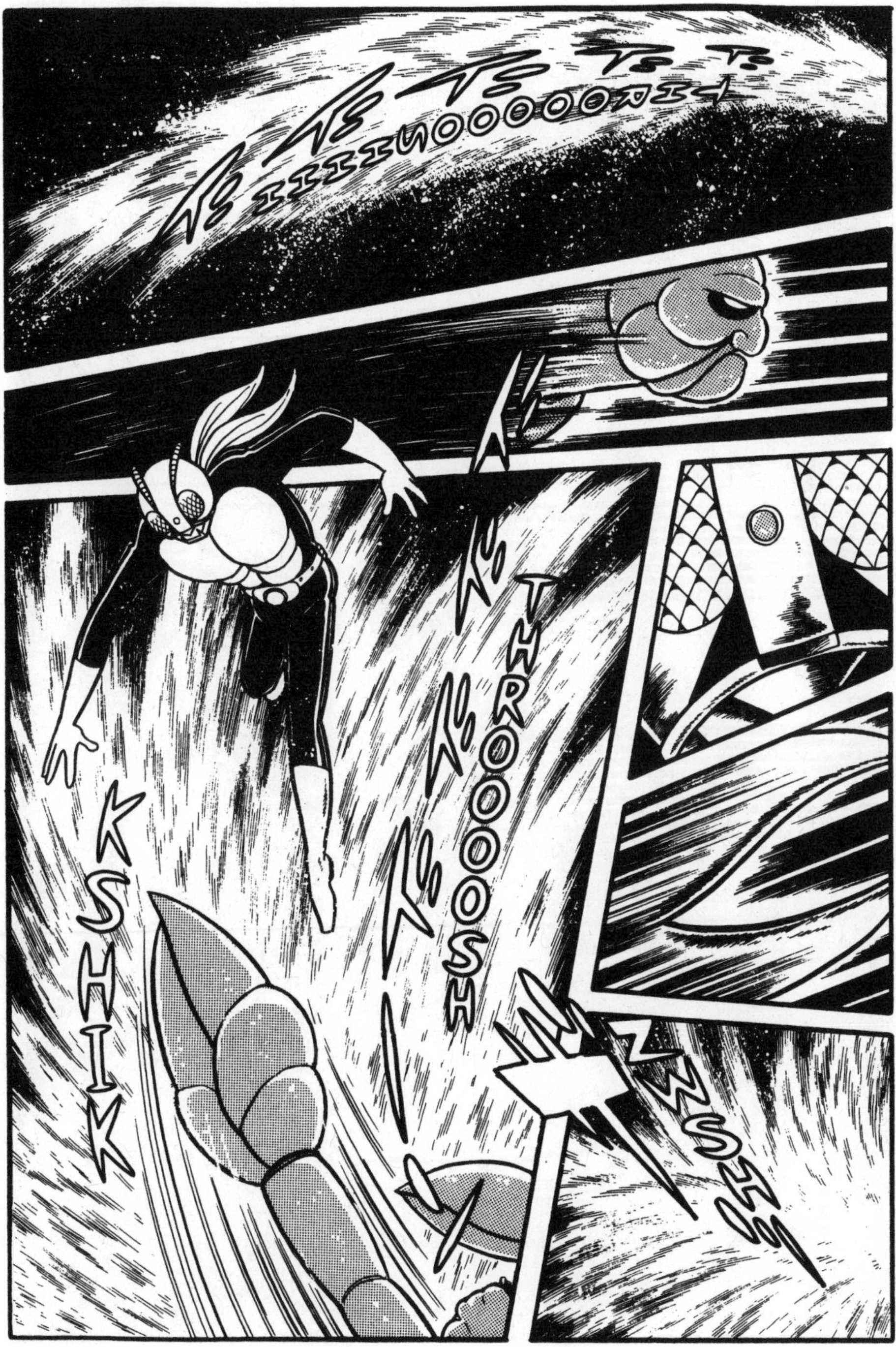
THROOOOOOOSH
KSHIK
ZWSH

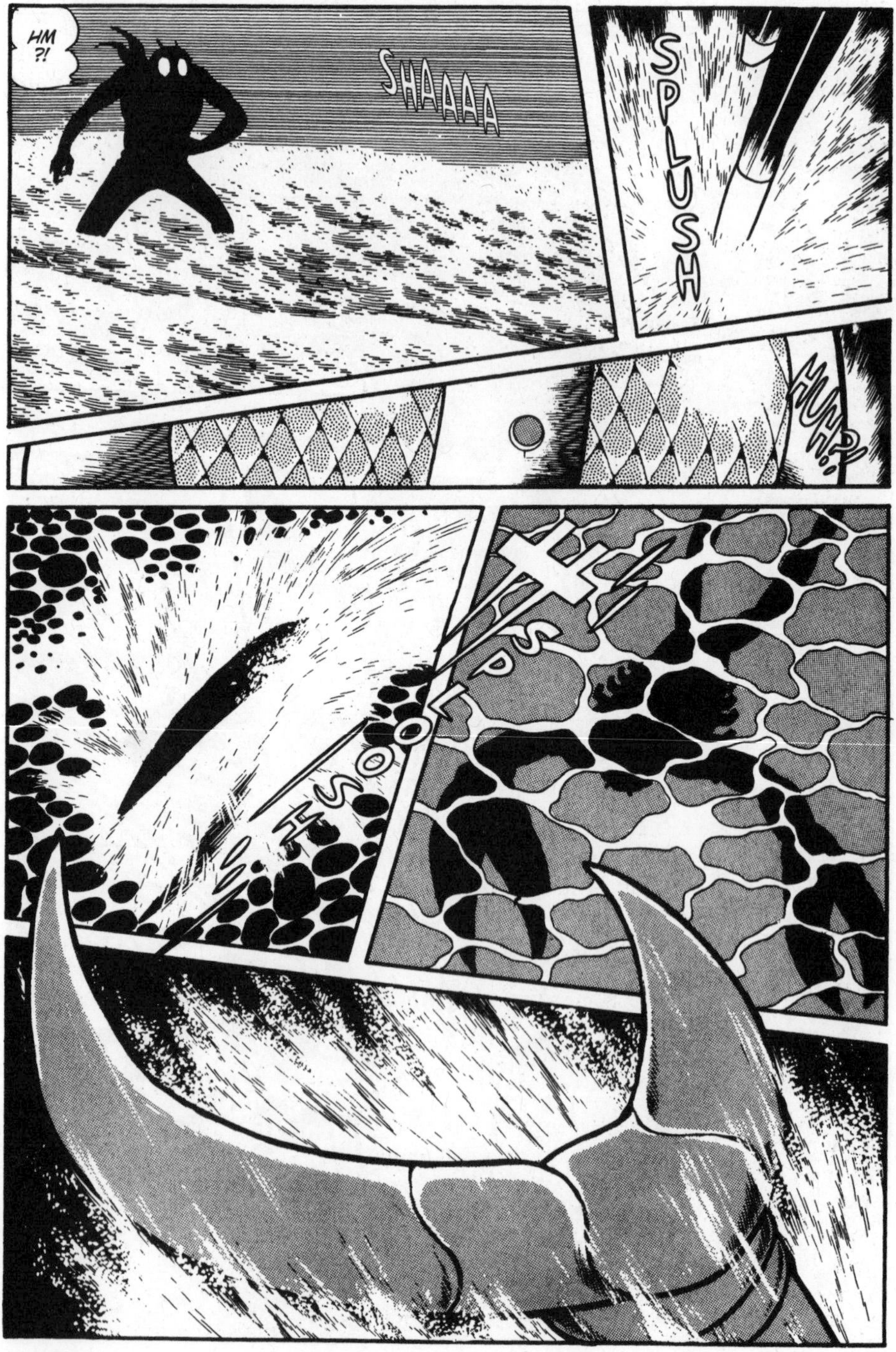
SPLUSH
HM ?!
SHAAAA
HUH?!
SPLOOSH!!

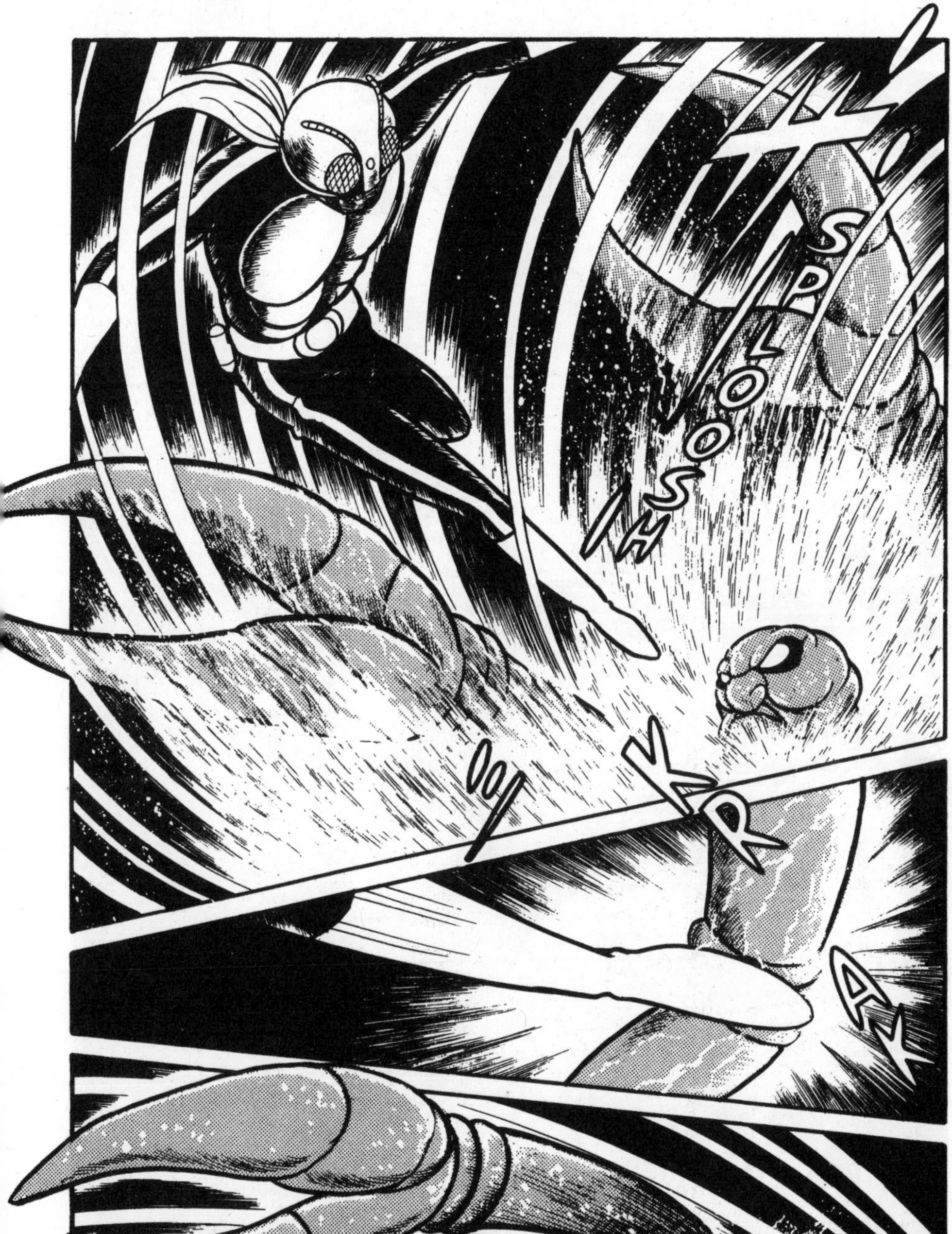
SPLOOSH
KR
AK

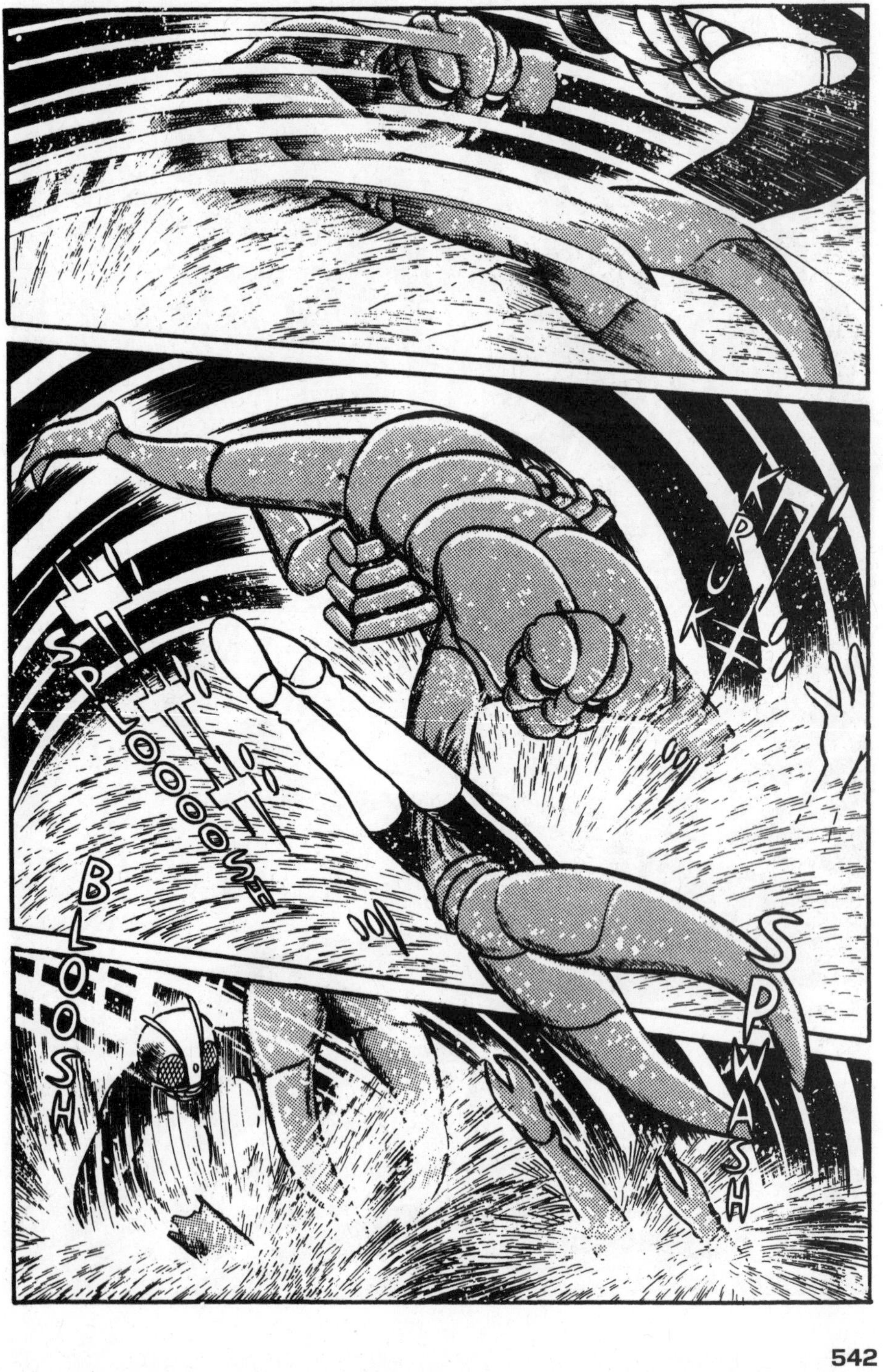
KRUKX
SPLOOOOSH
SPWASH
BLOOSH

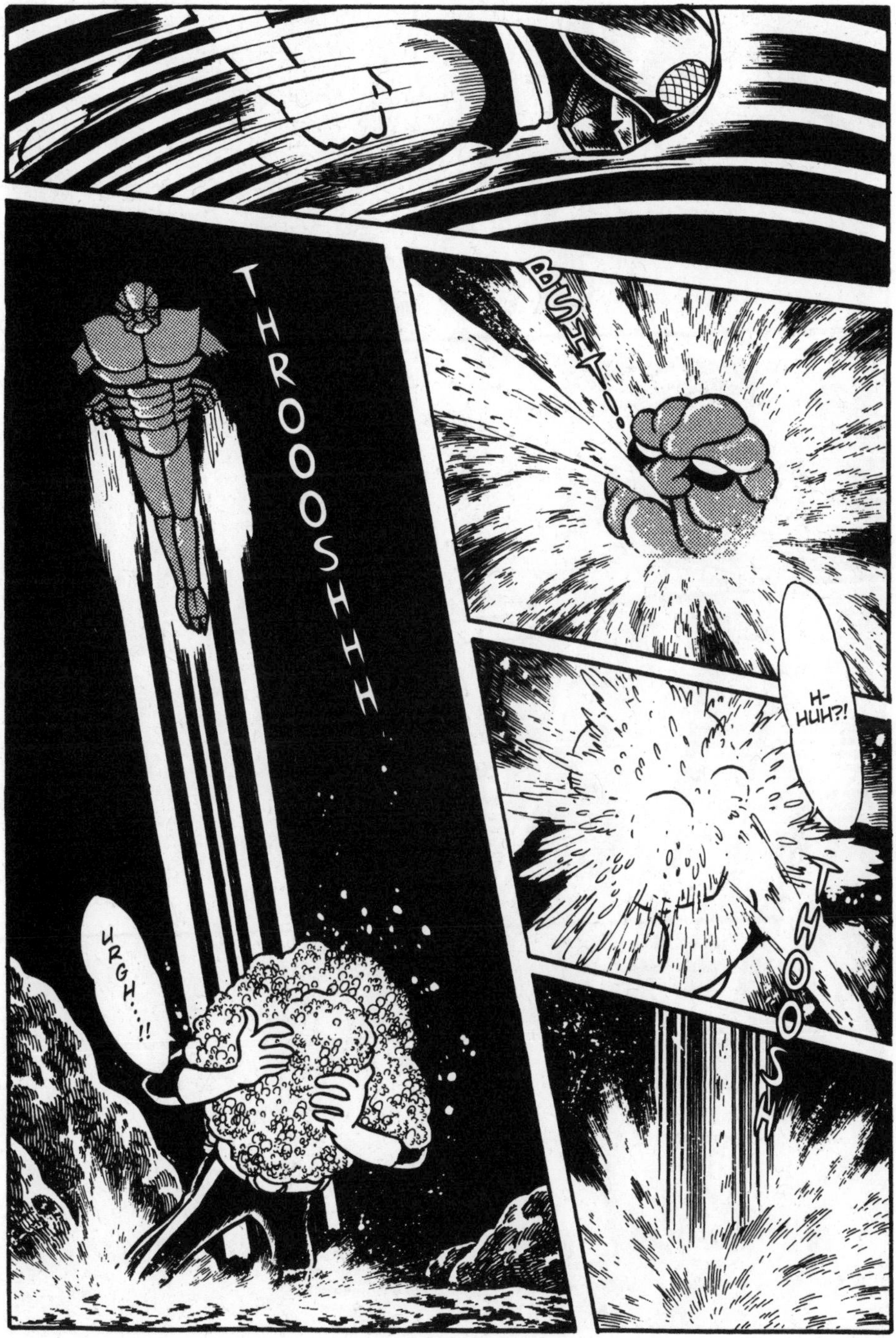
BSHT!!
H-HUH?!
THOOOSH
THROOOSHHH
URGH...!!

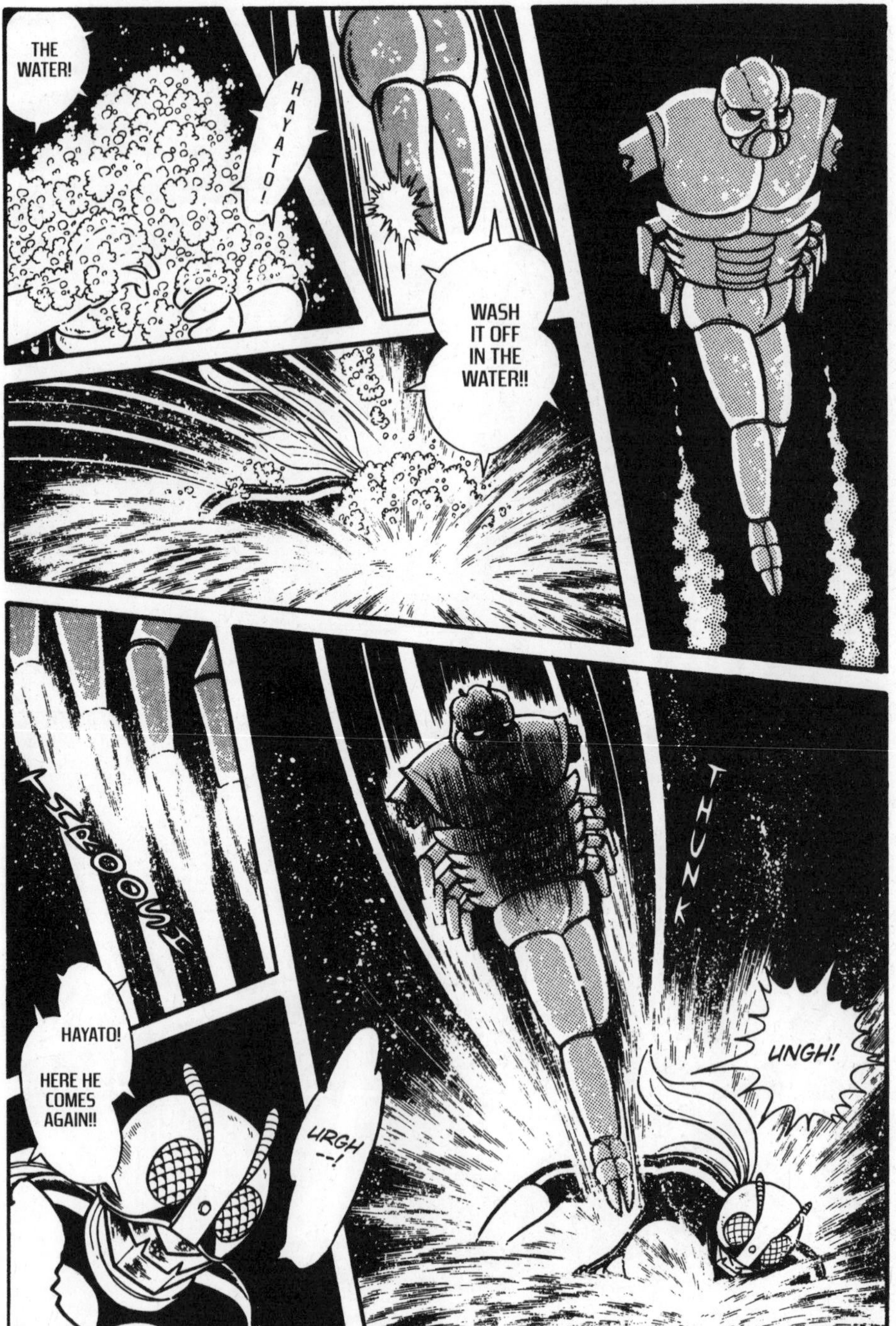
HAYATO!
THE WATER!
WASH IT OFF IN THE WATER!!
THUNK
UNGH!
HAYATO!
HERE HE COMES AGAIN!!
URGH--!

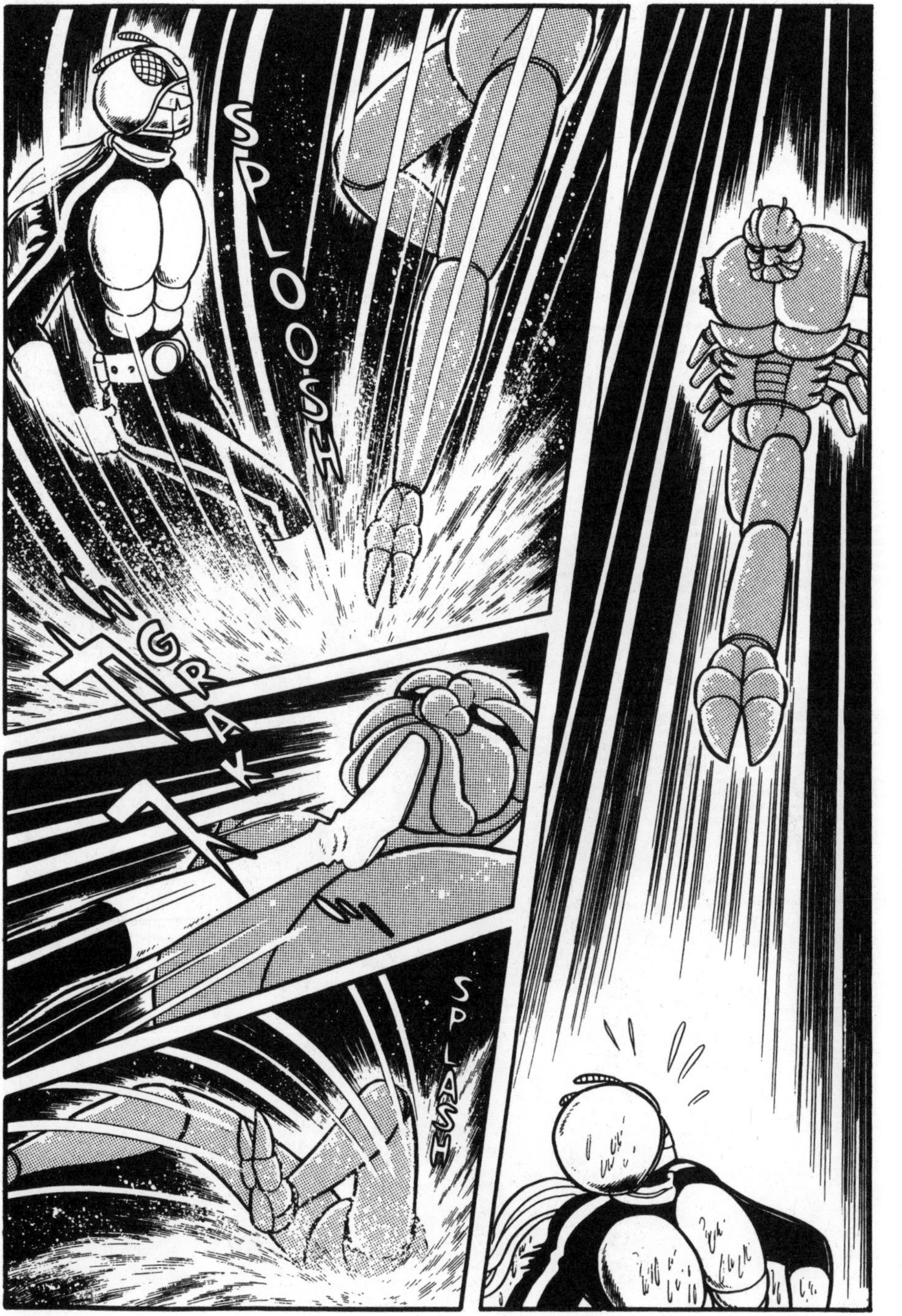
SPLOOSH
GRAK
SPLASH

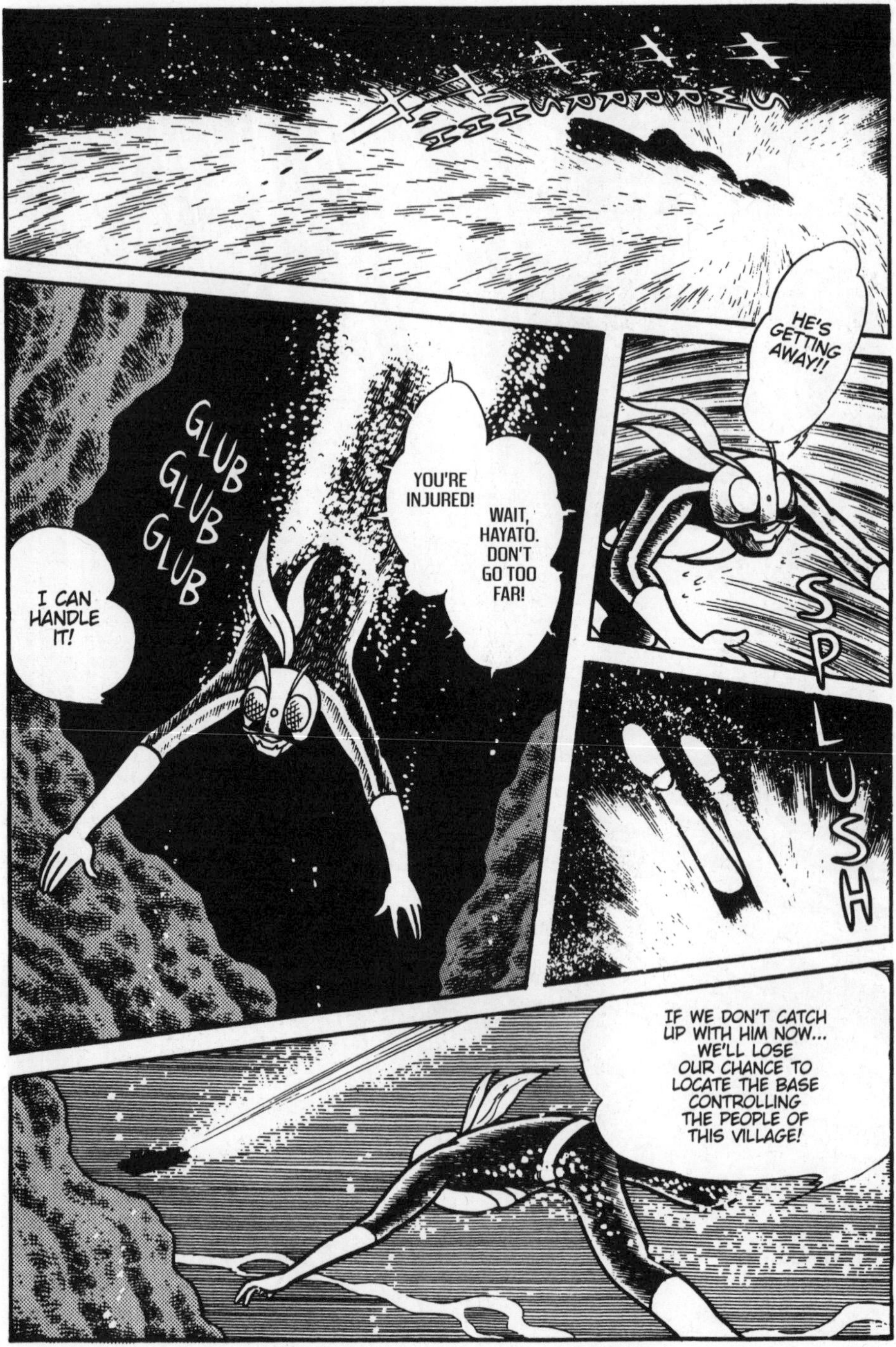
SWRRRUSHHH
HE'S GETTING AWAY!!
SPLUSH
YOU'RE INJURED!
WAIT, HAYATO. DON'T GO TOO FAR!
GLUB GLUB GLUB
I CAN HANDLE IT!
IF WE DON'T CATCH UP WITH HIM NOW... WE'LL LOSE OUR CHANCE TO LOCATE THE BASE CONTROLLING THE PEOPLE OF THIS VILLAGE!

HUH ?!

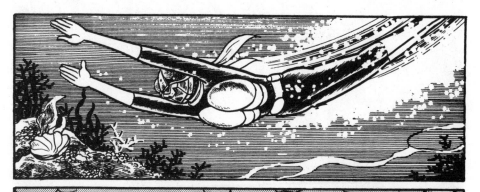

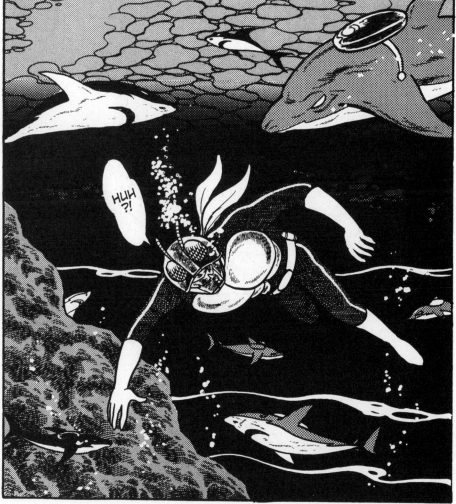

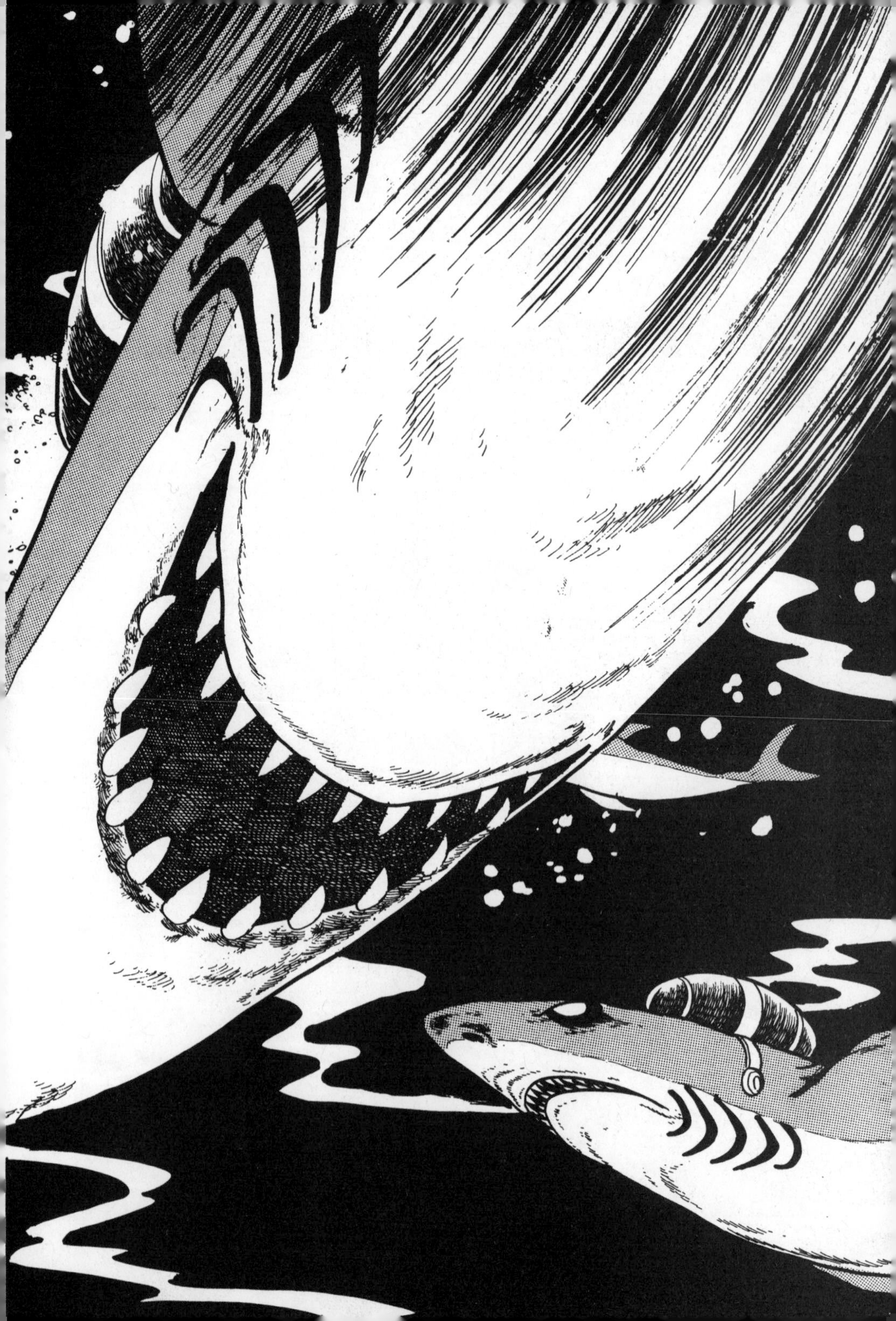

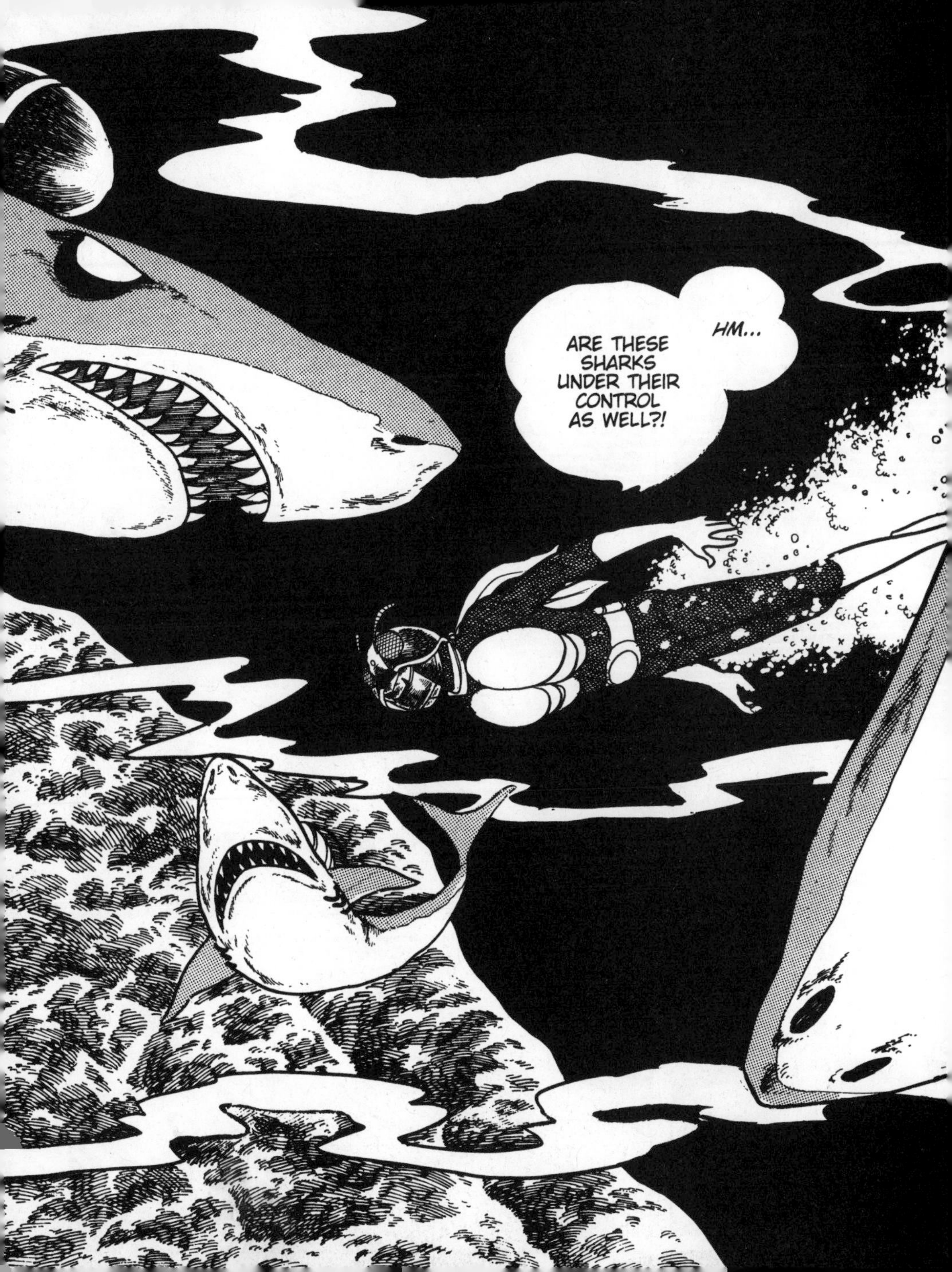
HM...
ARE THESE SHARKS UNDER THEIR CONTROL AS WELL?!

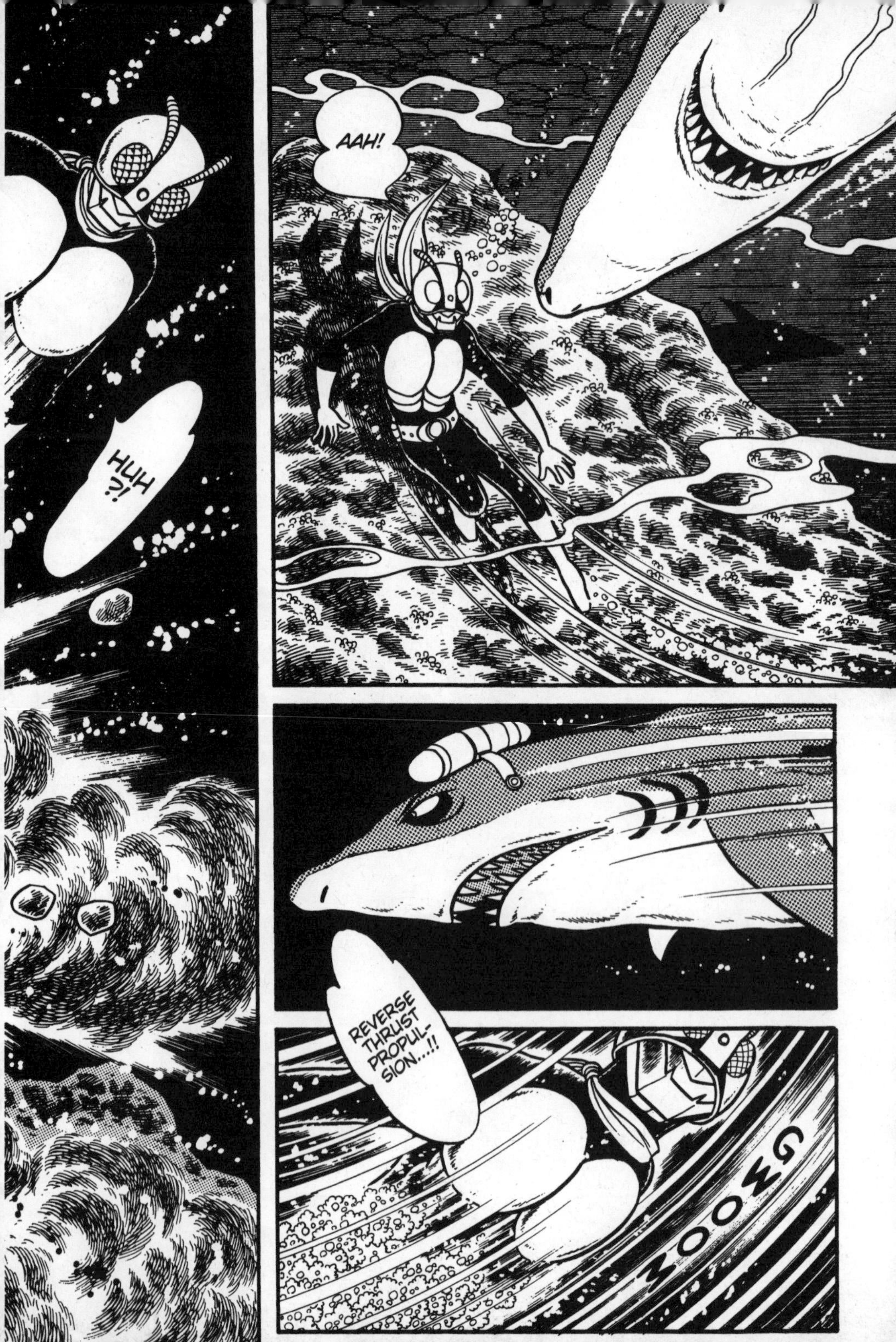
AAH!
HUH?!
REVERSE THRUST PROPUL-SION...!!
ZOOMG

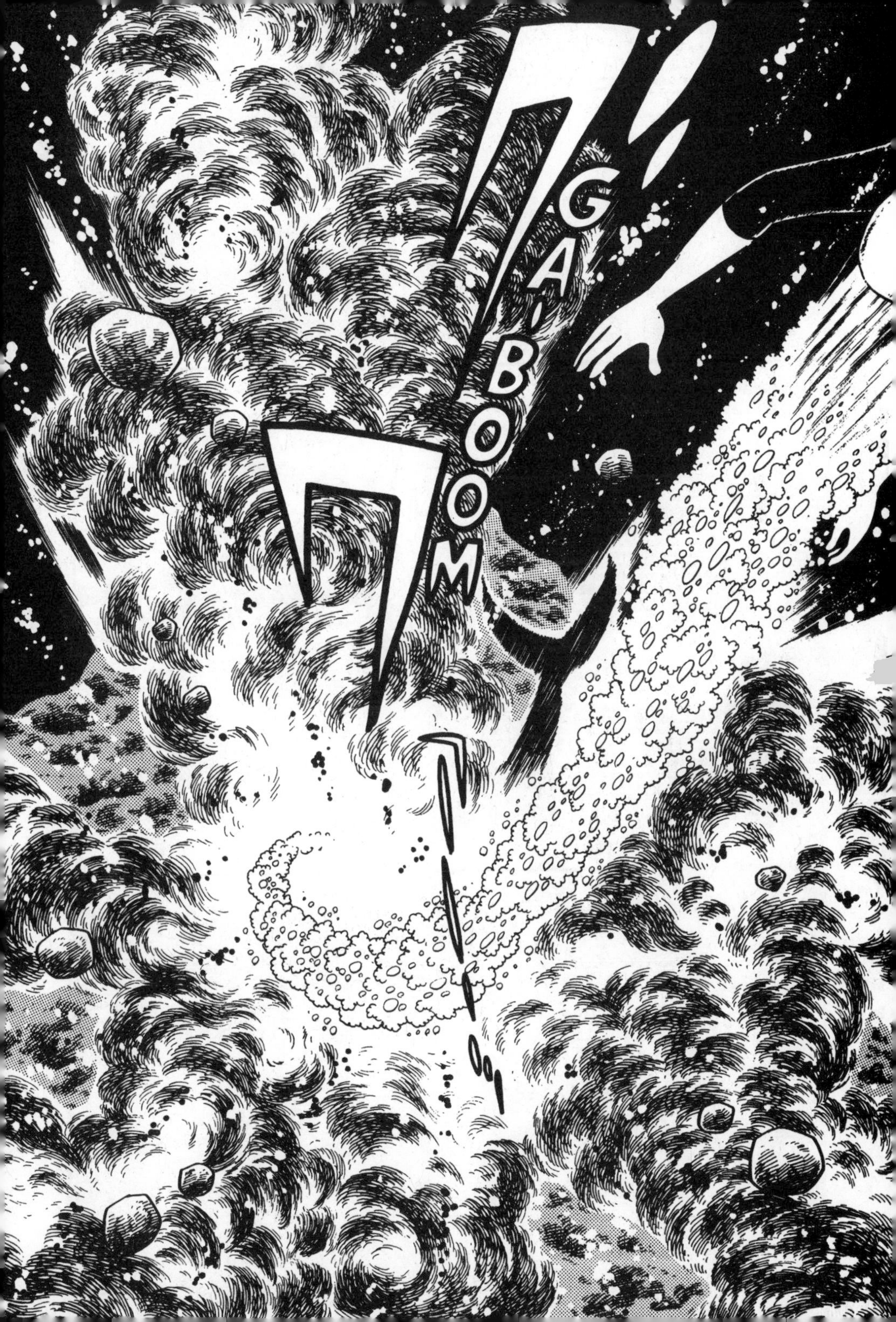
GA-BOOOM

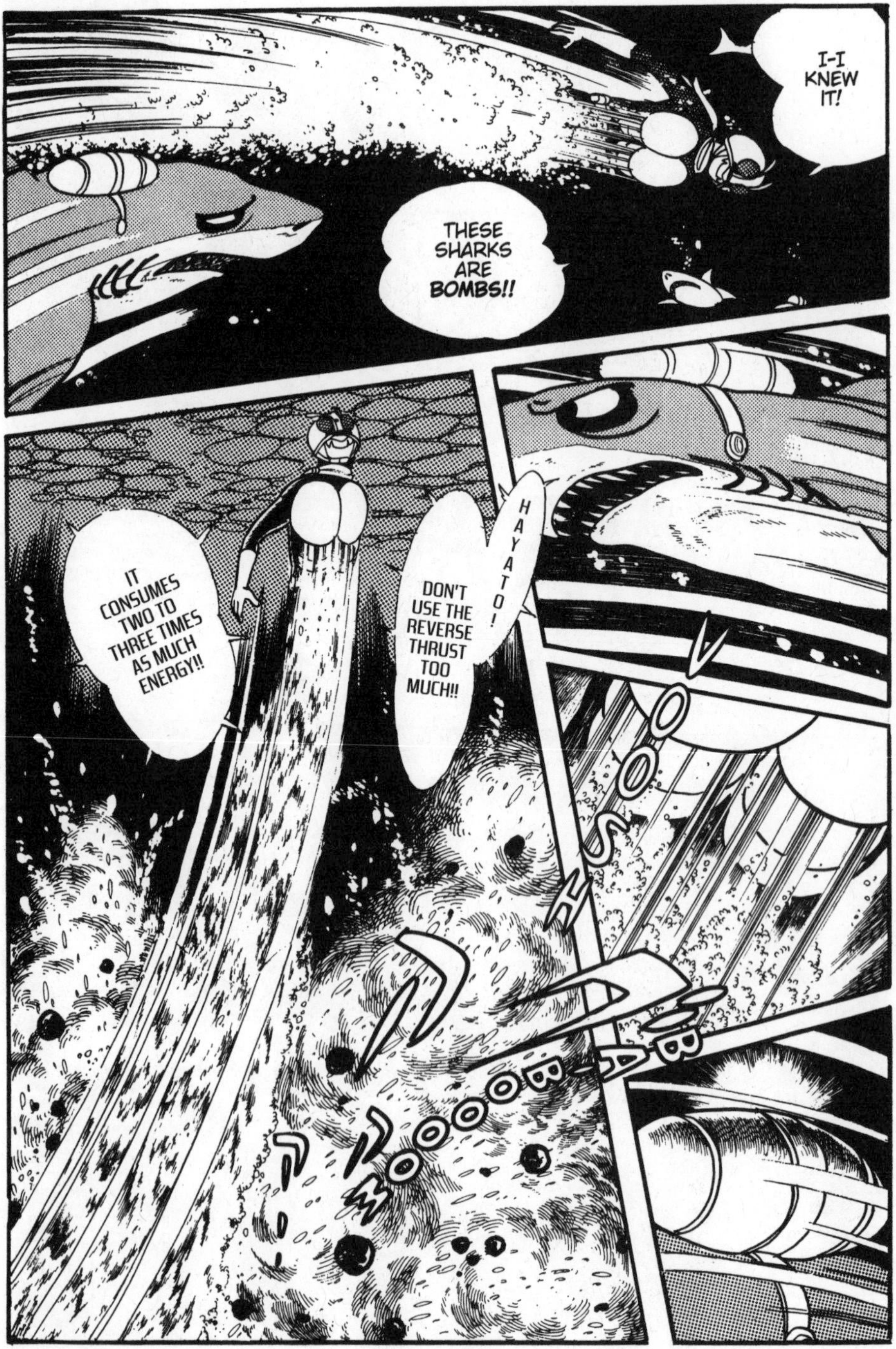
I-I KNEW IT!
THESE SHARKS ARE BOMBS!!
HAYATO!
DON'T USE THE REVERSE THRUST TOO MUCH!!
IT CONSUMES TWO TO THREE TIMES AS MUCH ENERGY!!
VOOOSH
BA-BOOOOOM

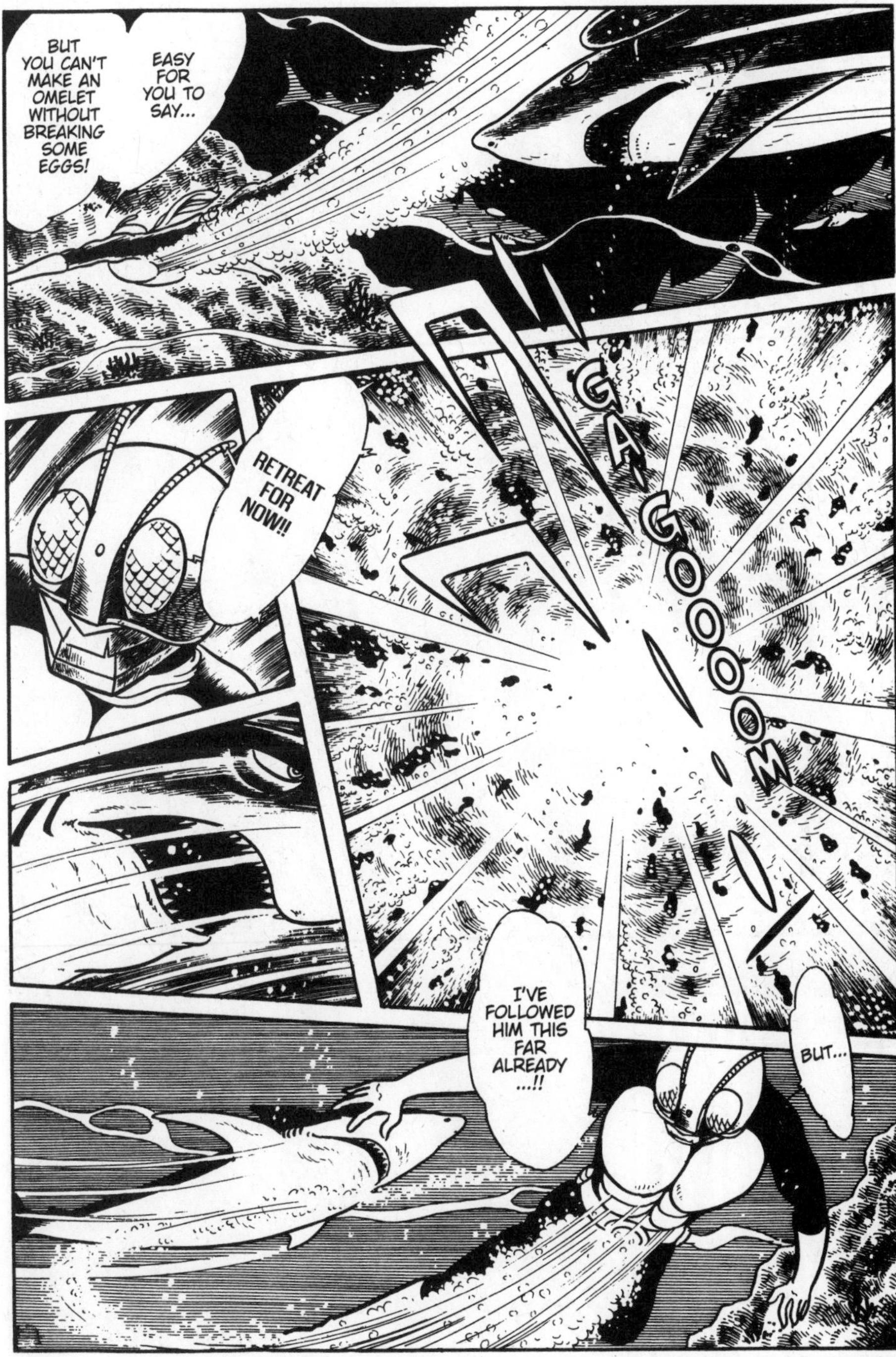
EASY FOR YOU TO SAY...
BUT YOU CAN'T MAKE AN OMELET WITHOUT BREAKING SOME EGGS!
GA GOOOOOM
RETREAT FOR NOW!!
I'VE FOLLOWED HIM THIS FAR ALREADY ...!!
BUT...

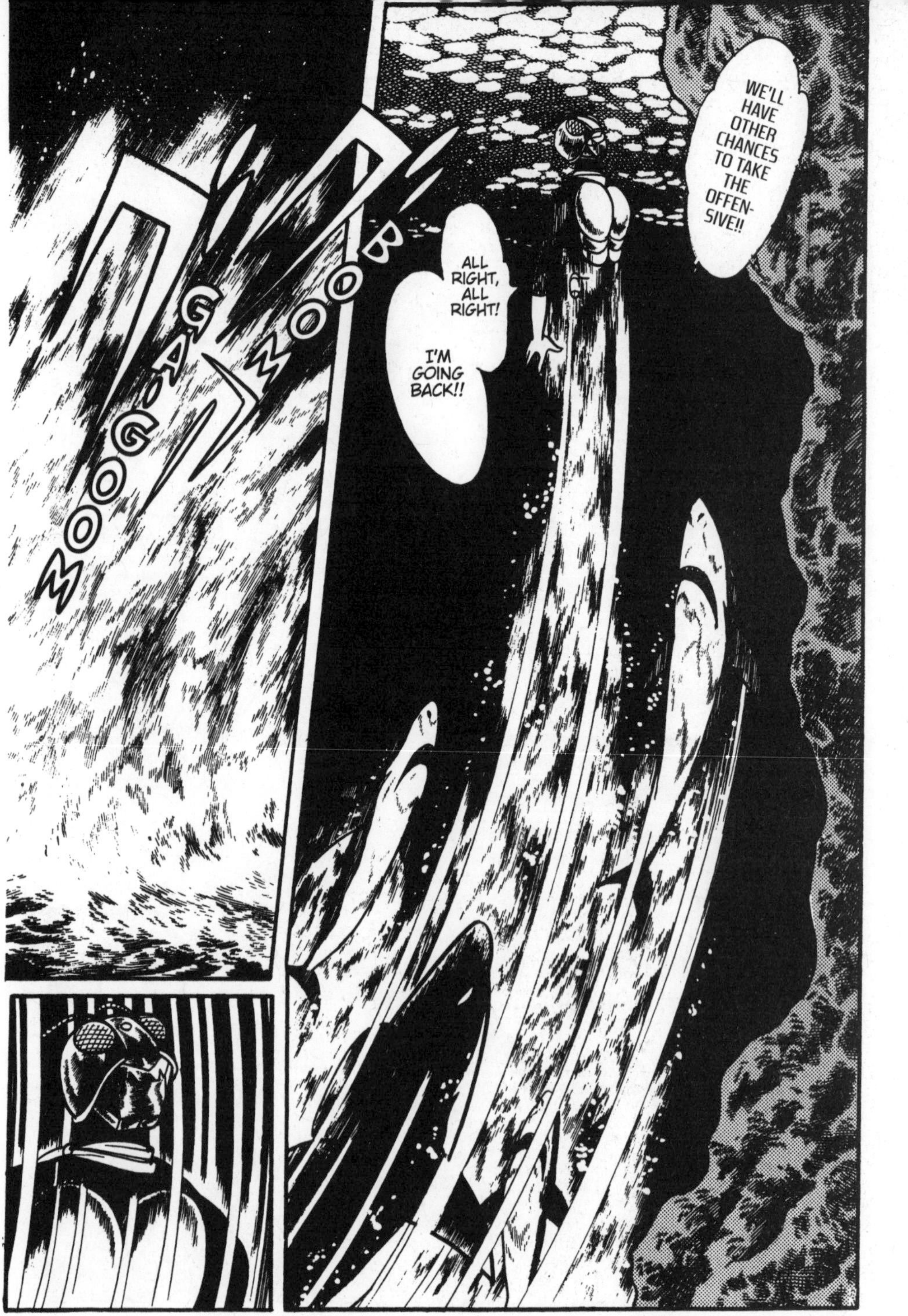
WE'LL HAVE OTHER CHANCES TO TAKE THE OFFEN-SIVE!!
ALL RIGHT, ALL RIGHT!
I'M GOING BACK!!
BOOOM
GAGOOOM

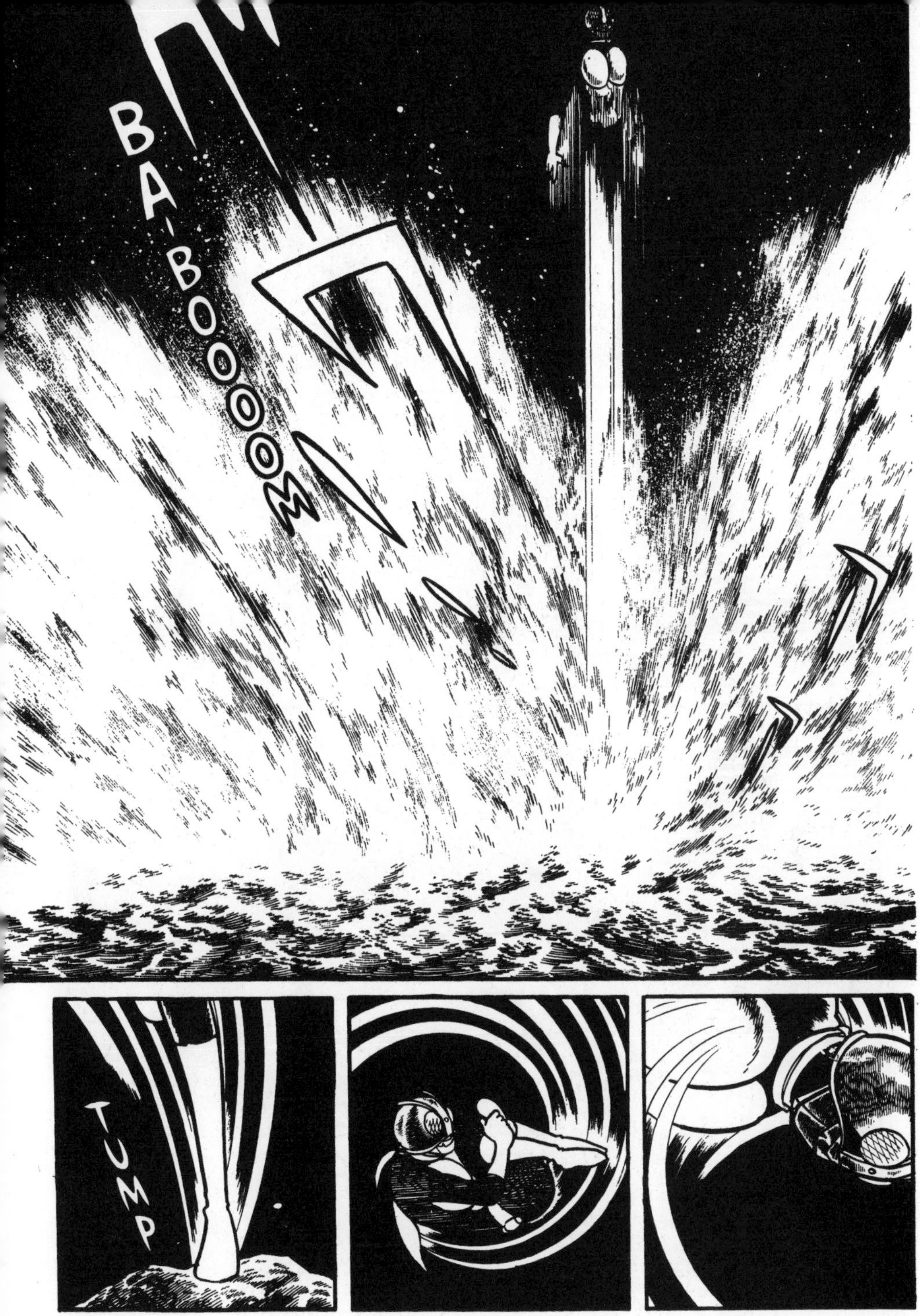
BA-BOOOOOM
TUMP

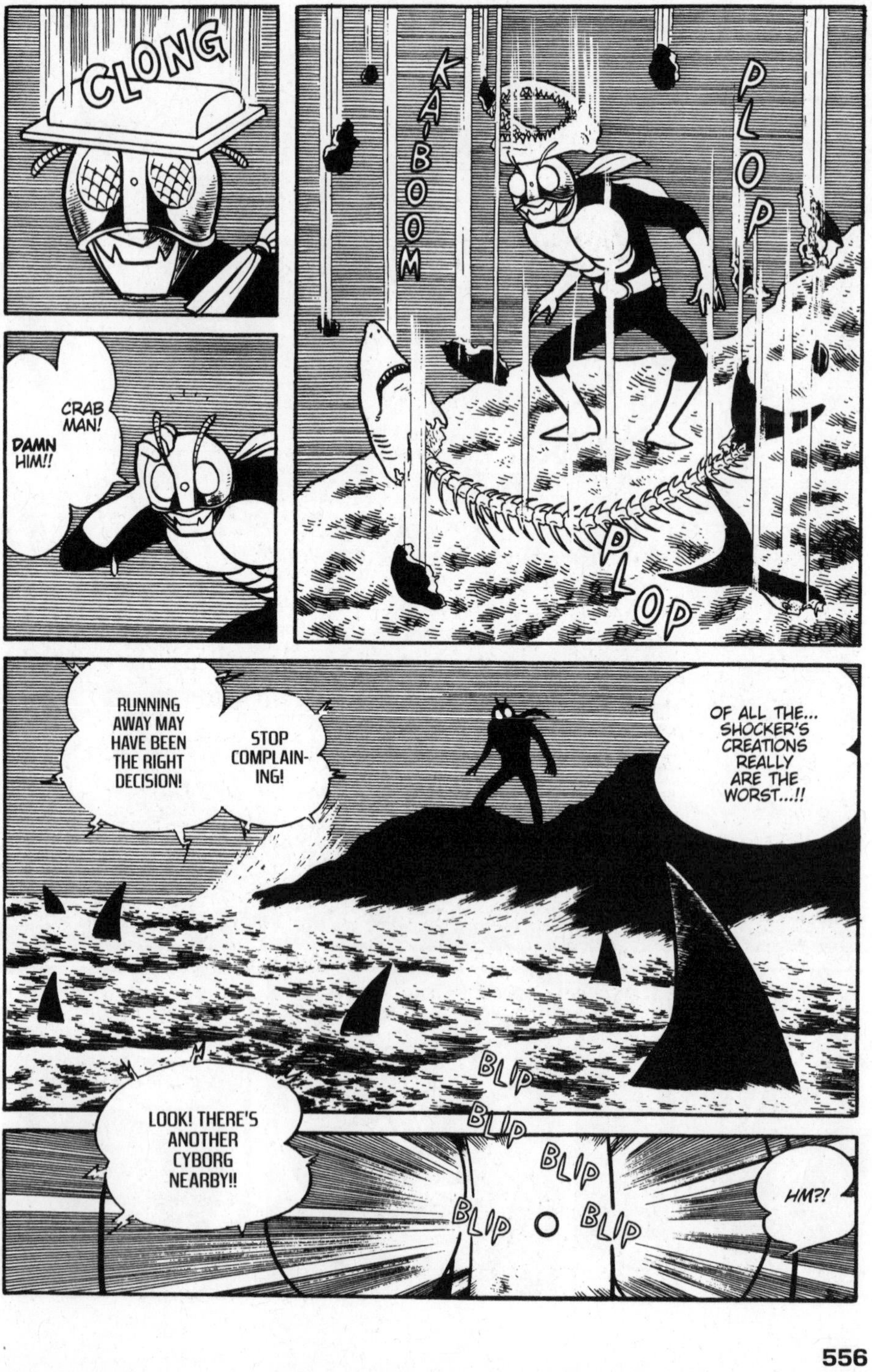
PLOP
KA-BOOM
PLOP
CLONG
CRAB MAN!
DAMN HIM!!
OF ALL THE... SHOCKER'S CREATIONS REALLY ARE THE WORST...!!
STOP COMPLAINING!
RUNNING AWAY MAY HAVE BEEN THE RIGHT DECISION!
BLIP
BLIP
HM?!
BLIP
BLIP
BLIP
LOOK! THERE'S ANOTHER CYBORG NEARBY!!

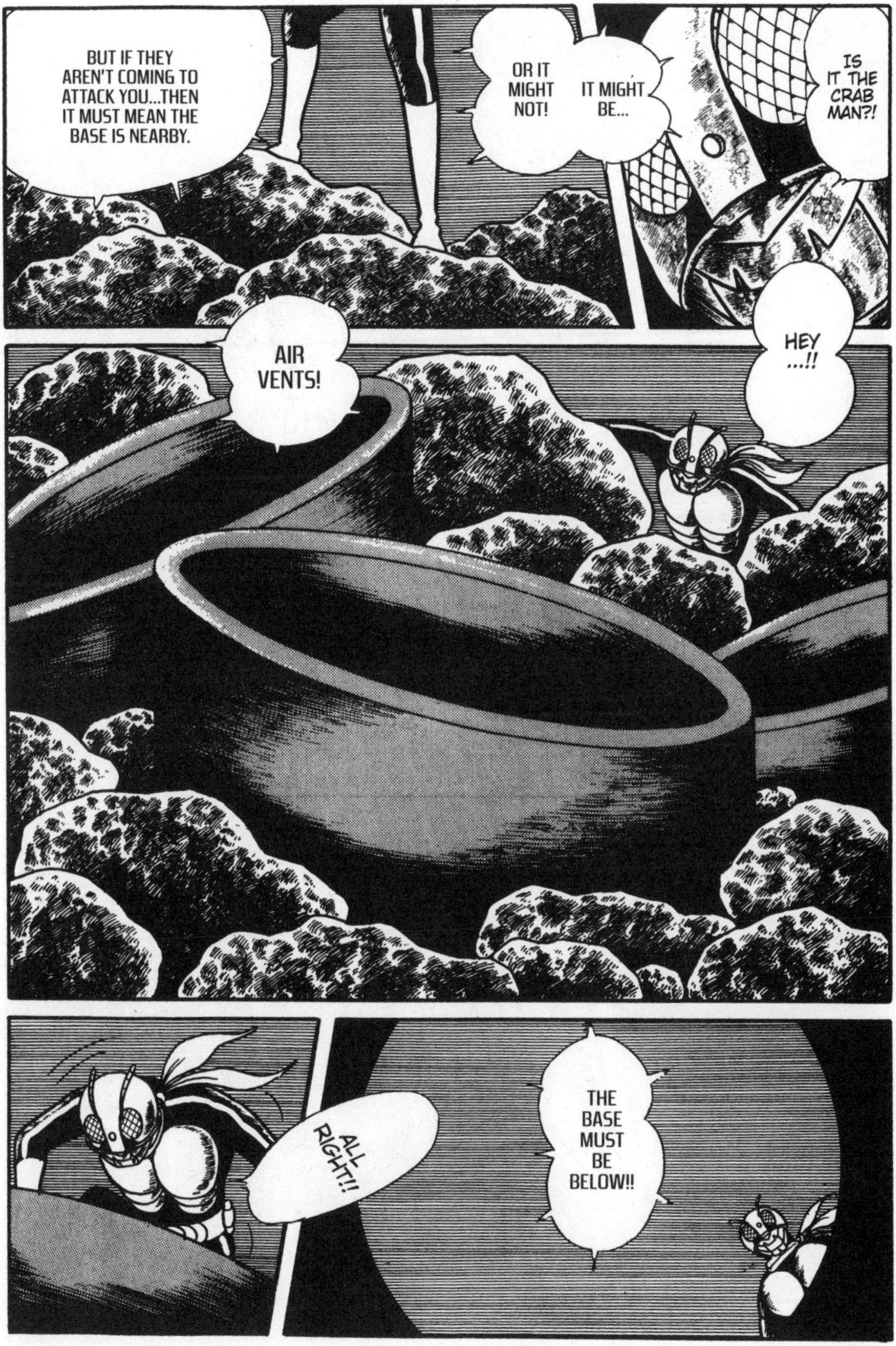
IS IT THE CRAB MAN?!
IT MIGHT BE...
OR IT MIGHT NOT!
BUT IF THEY AREN'T COMING TO ATTACK YOU...THEN IT MUST MEAN THE BASE IS NEARBY.
HEY ...!!
AIR VENTS!
THE BASE MUST BE BELOW!!
ALL RIGHT!!

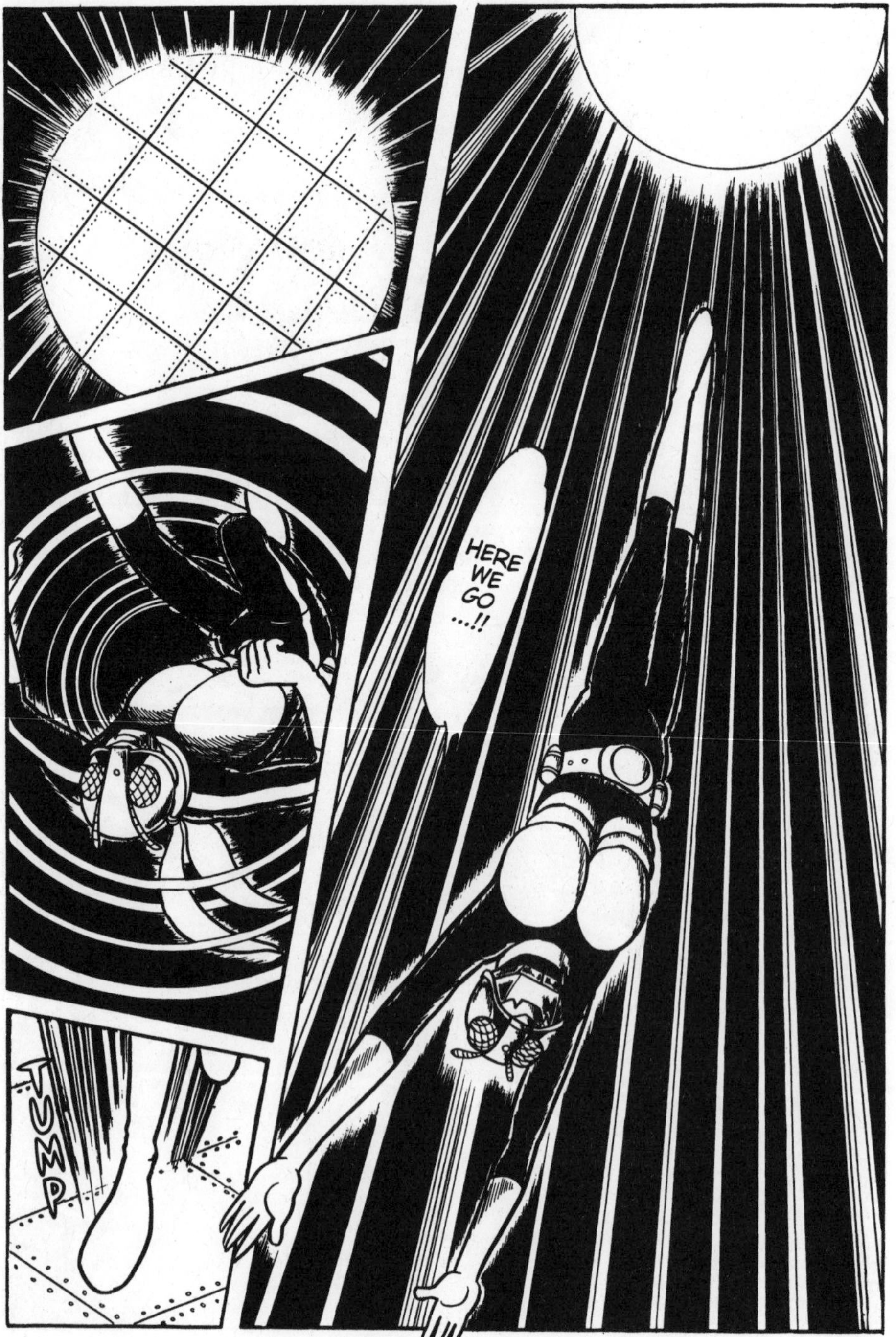
HERE WE GO ...!!
TUMP

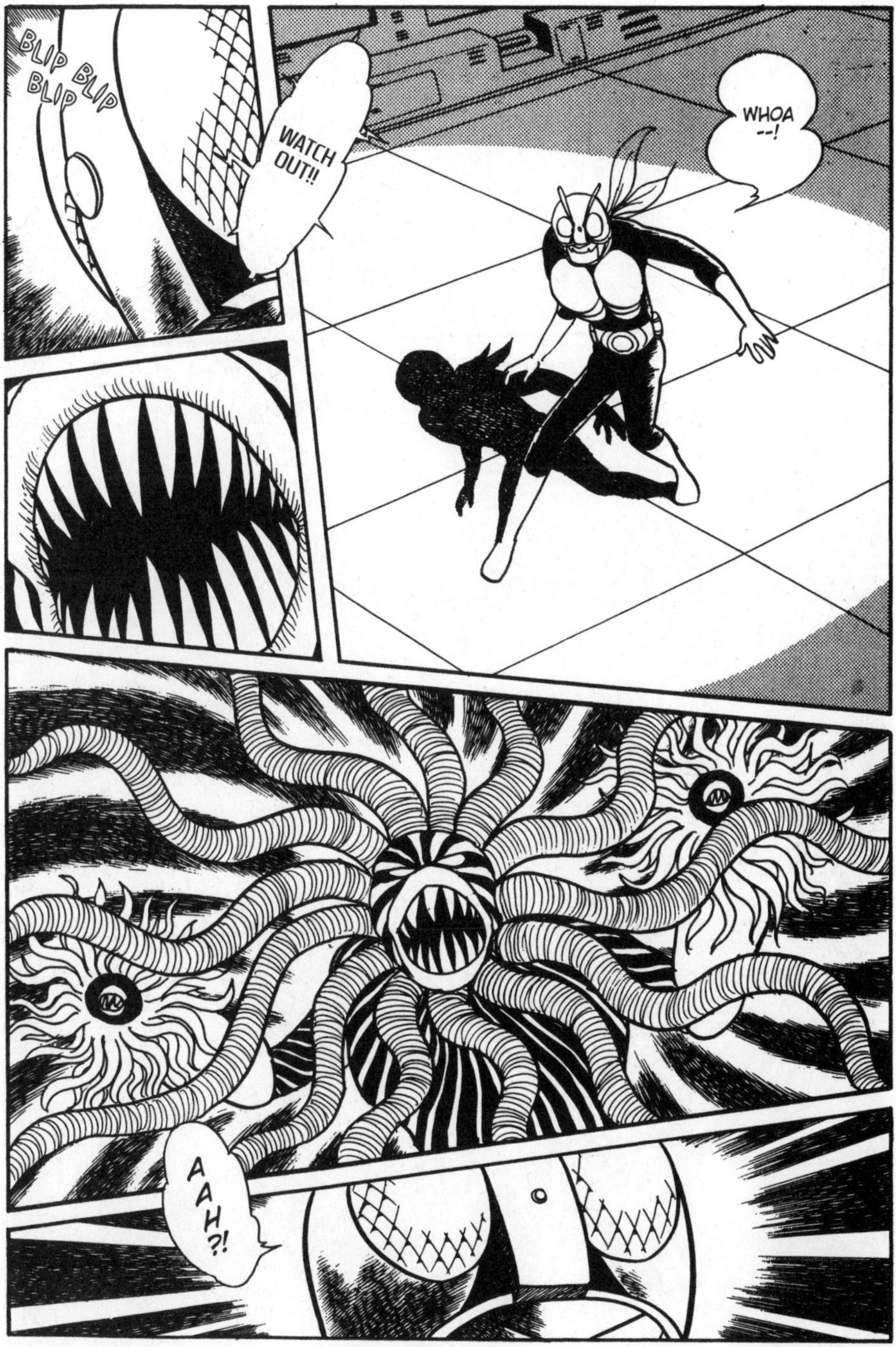
WHOA --!
WATCH OUT!!
BLIP BLIP BLIP
AAH?!

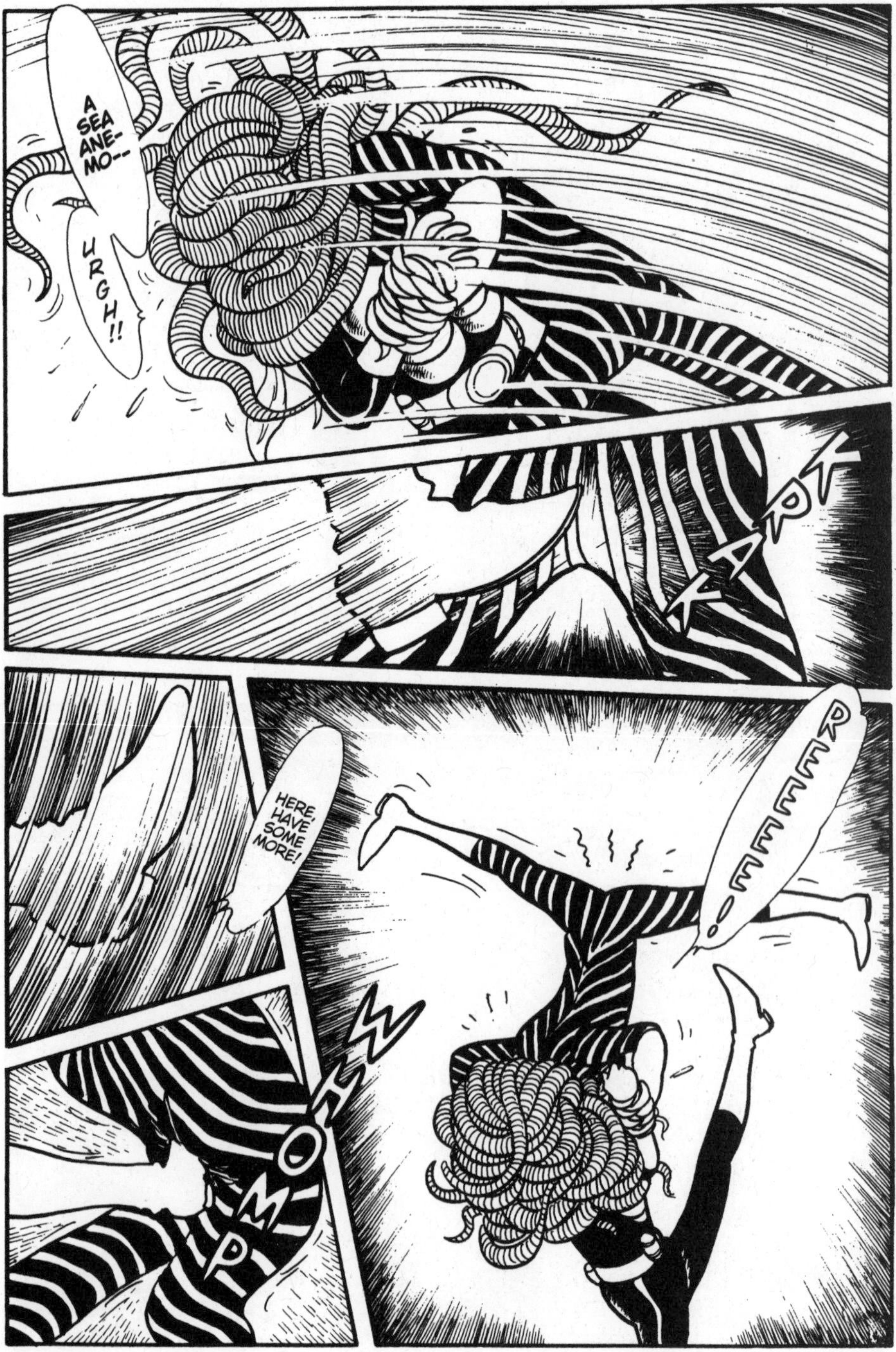
A SEA ANE- MO--
URGH!!
KRAK
REEEEE!
HERE, HAVE SOME MORE!
WHOMP

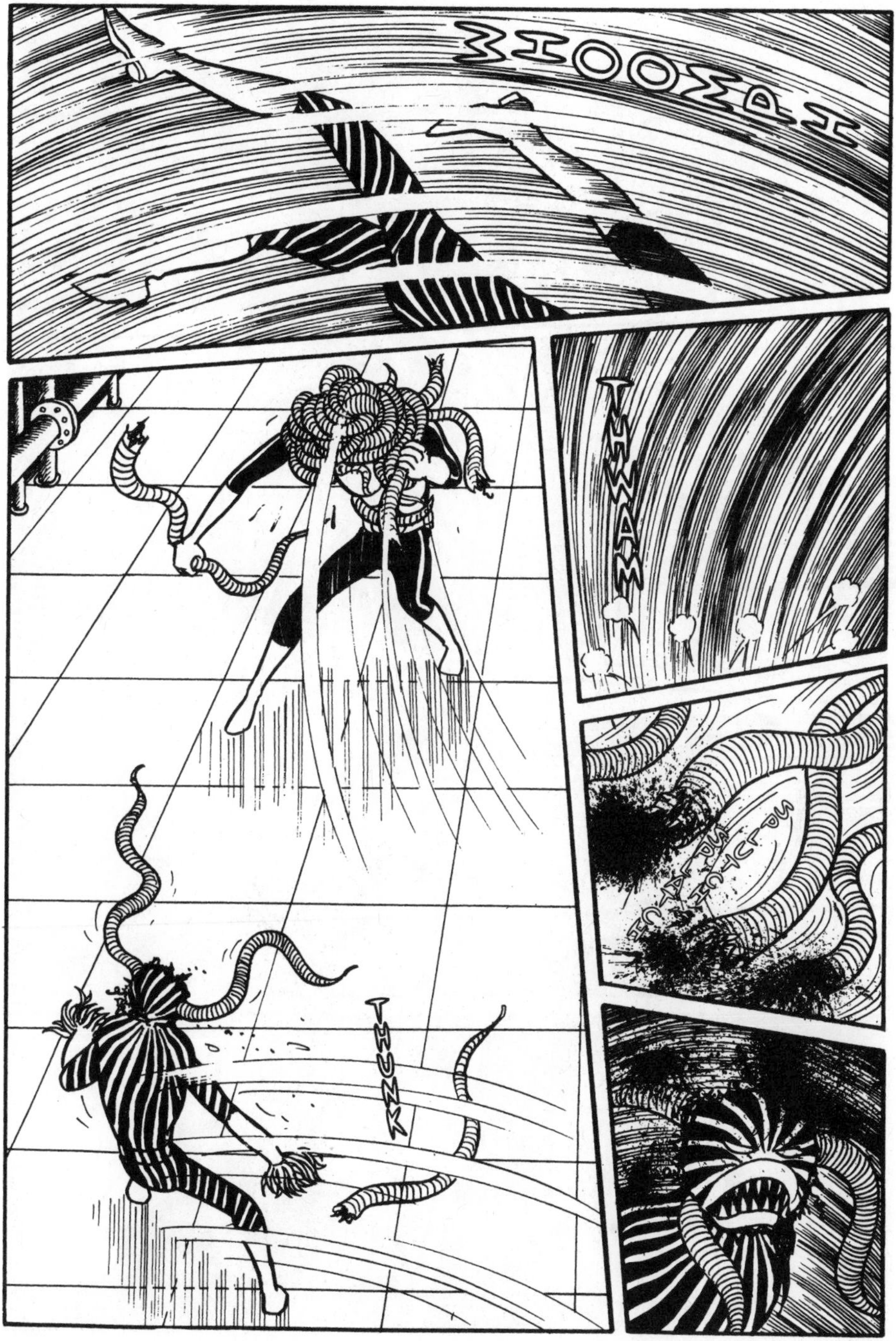
WHOOSH
THWAM
SPLUTCH
SPLATCH
THUNK

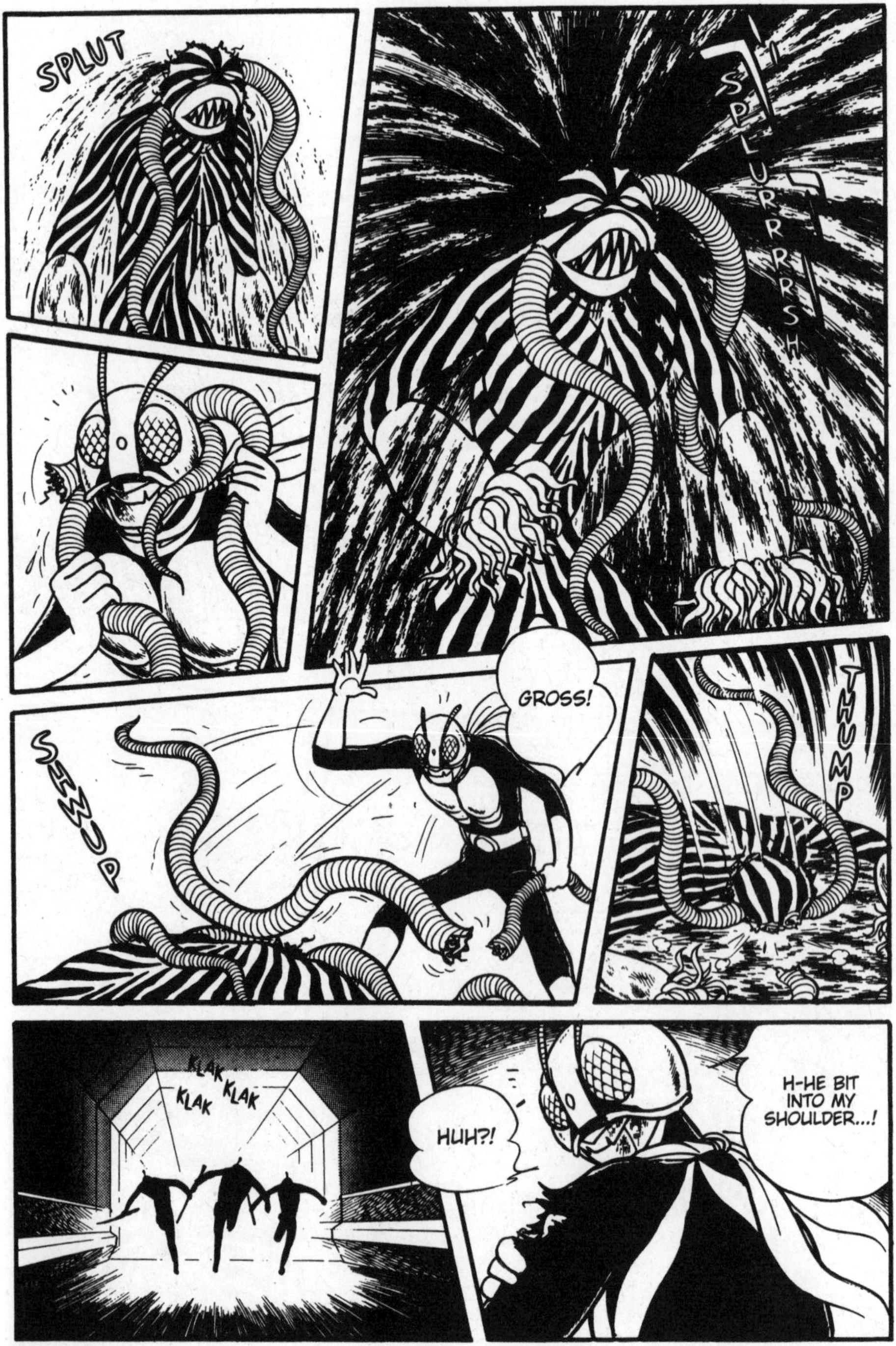
SPLURRRRSH
SPLUT
THUMP
GROSS!
SHWUP
H-HE BIT INTO MY SHOULDER...!
HUH?!
KLAK KLAK KLAK

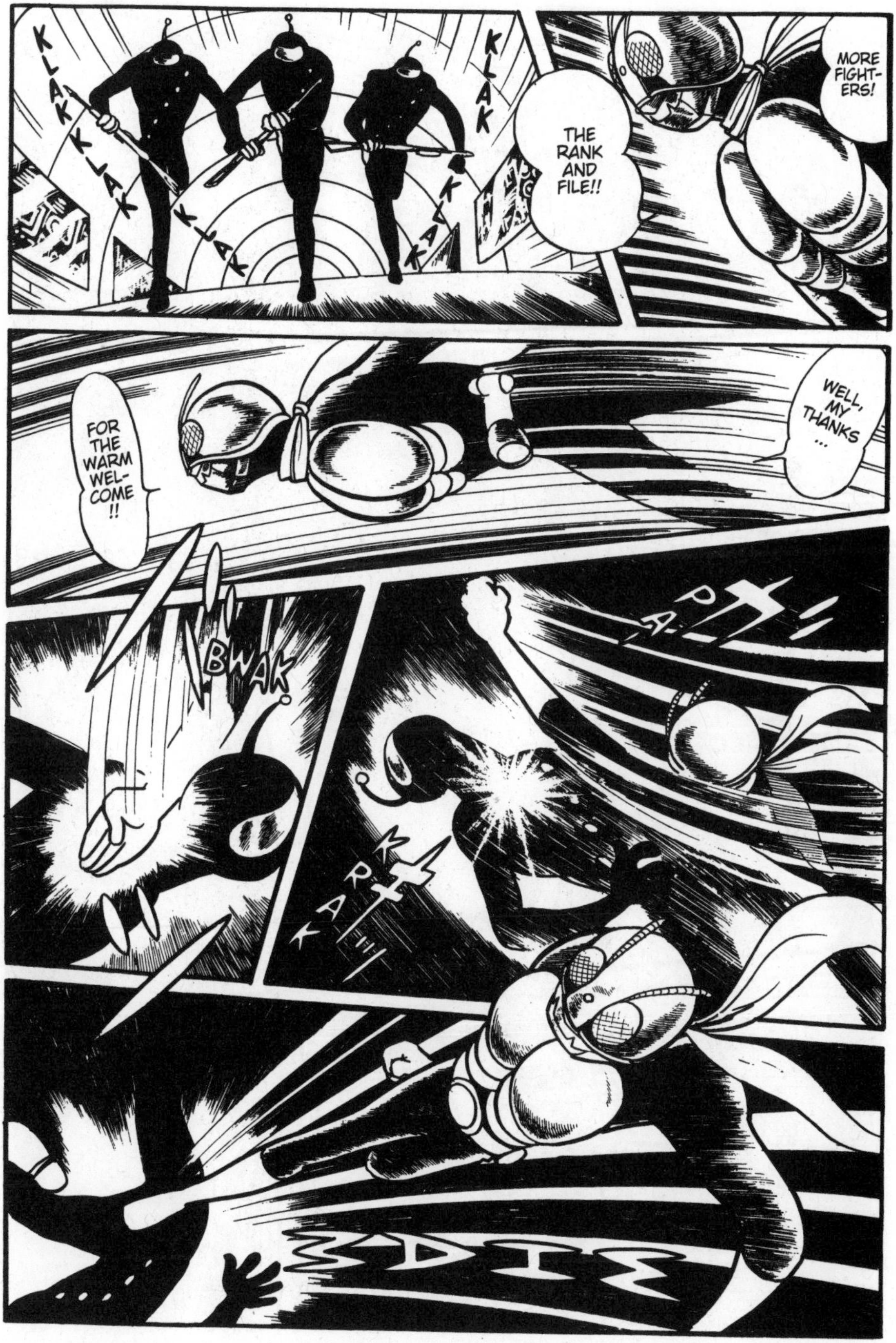
MORE FIGHT-ERS!
THE RANK AND FILE!!
KLAK KLAK
KLAK KLAK
KLAK KLAK
KLAK KLAK
WELL, MY THANKS ...
FOR THE WARM WEL-COME!!
PA-!!
KRRAK
BWAK

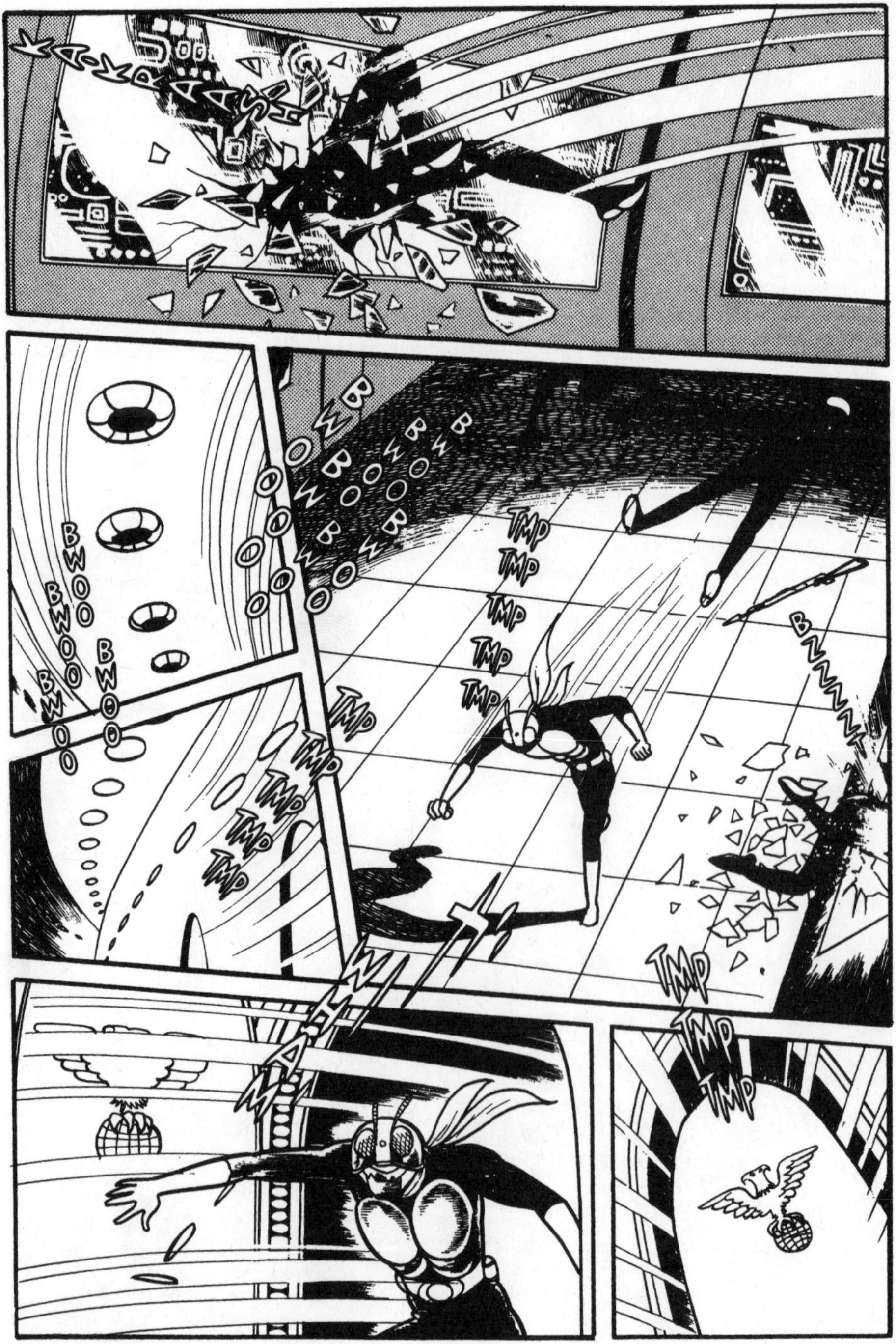
KA-KRAASH
BWOOBWO
BWOOBWOO
BWOOOOO
BWOO
BWOO
BWOOO
BWOO
TMP
TMP
TMP
TMP
TMP
TMP
TMP
TMP
TMP
TMP
BZZZZZT
WHAAM
TMP
TMP
TMP

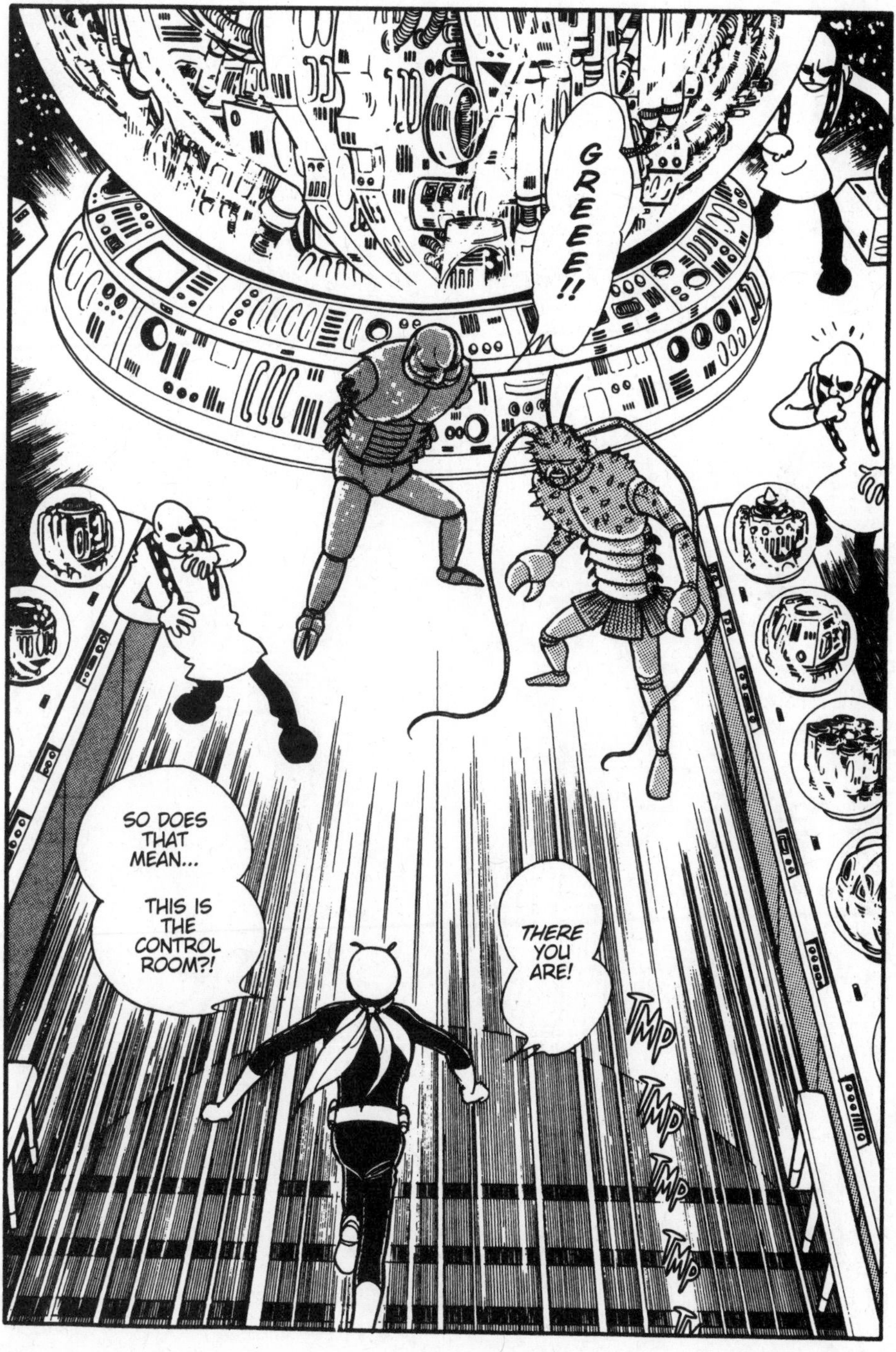
GREEEE!!
THERE YOU ARE!
TMP
TMP
TMP
TMP
SO DOES THAT MEAN...
THIS IS THE CONTROL ROOM?!

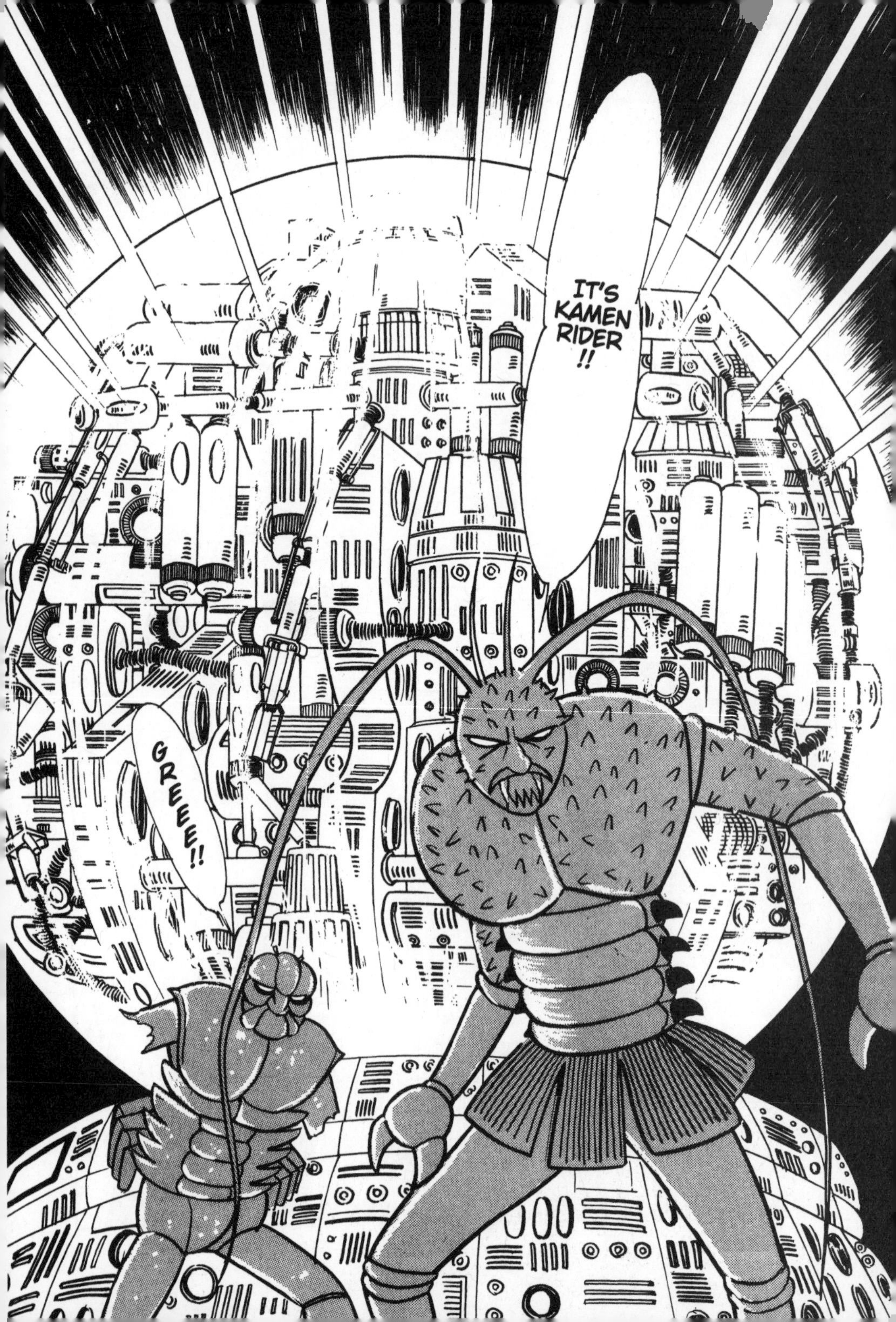
IT'S KAMEN RIDER !!
GREEEE!!

KAMEN
RIDER

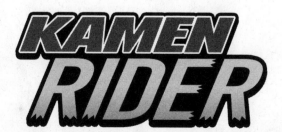

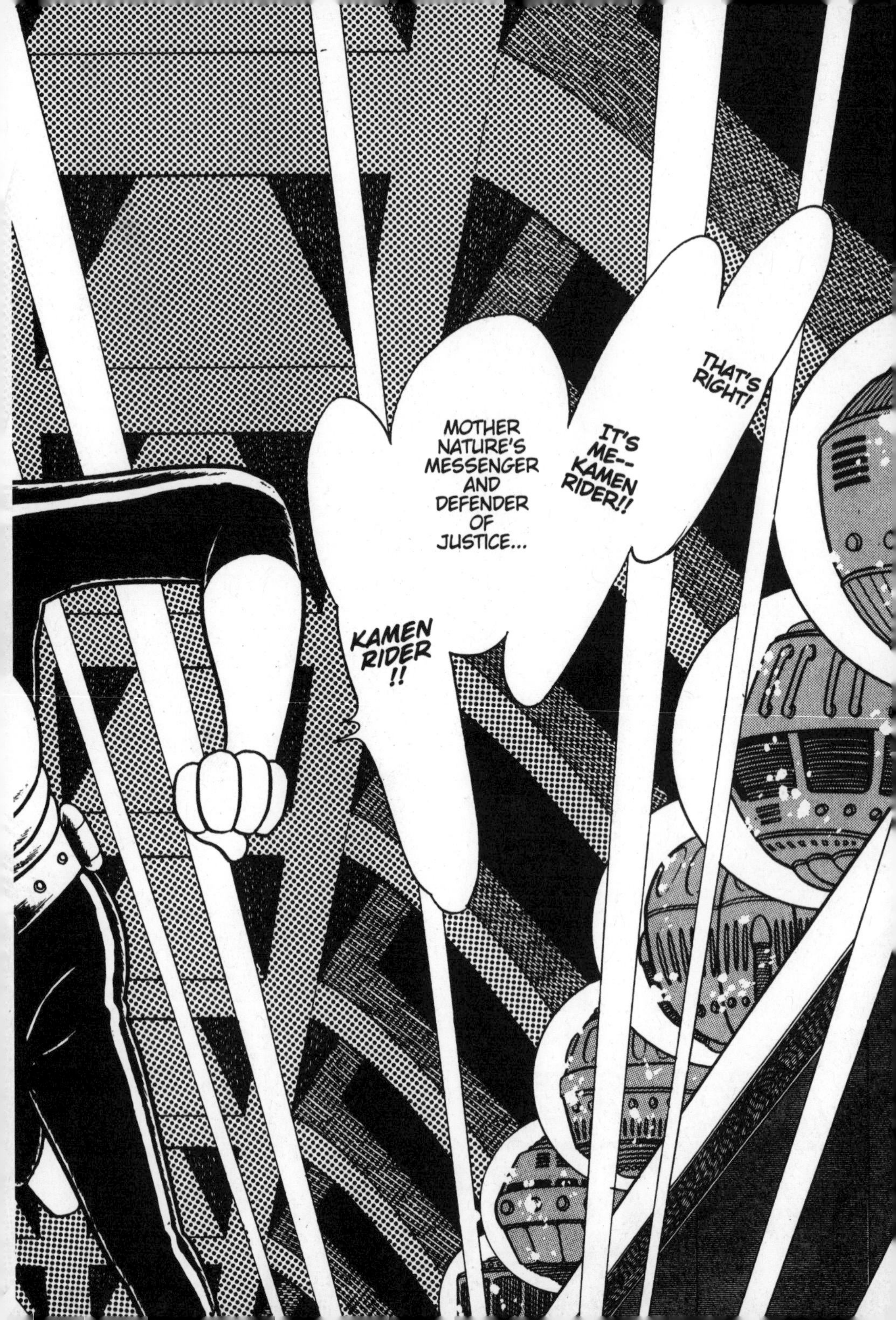
THAT'S RIGHT!
IT'S ME-- KAMEN RIDER!!
MOTHER NATURE'S MESSENGER AND DEFENDER OF JUSTICE...
KAMEN RIDER !!

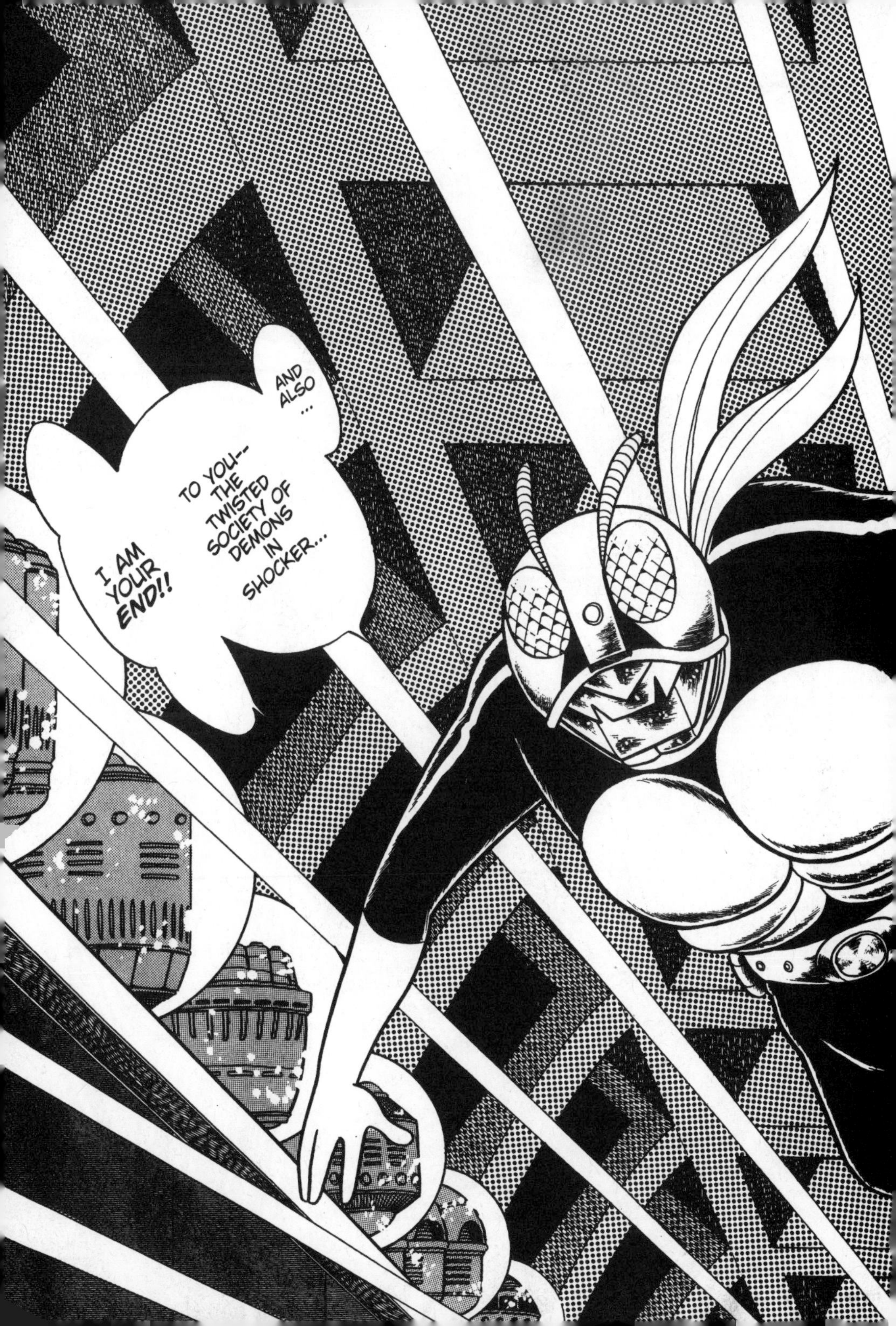
AND ALSO...
TO YOU-- THE TWISTED SOCIETY OF DEMONS IN SHOCKER...
I AM YOUR END!!

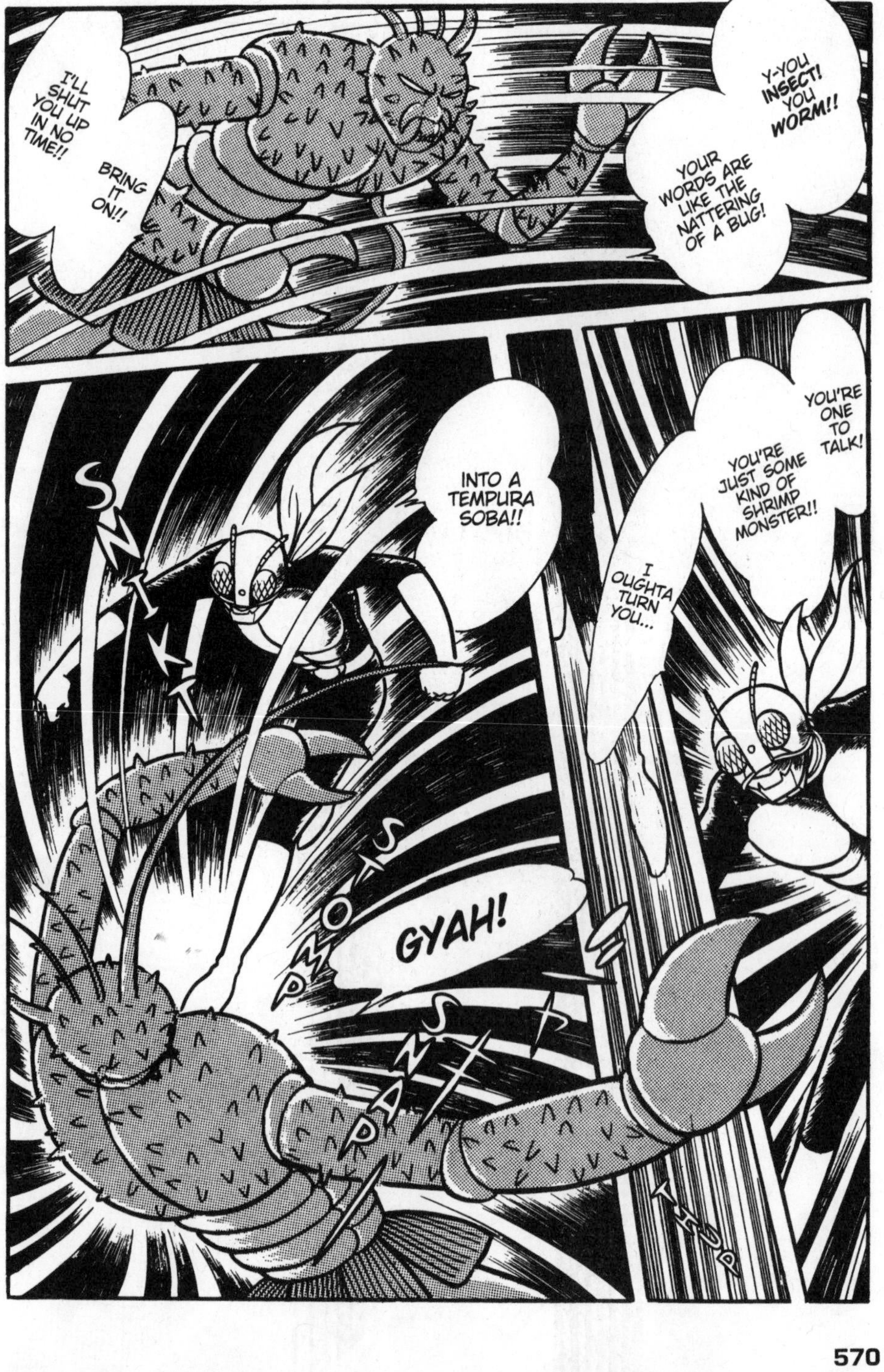
Y-YOU INSECT! YOU WORM!!
YOUR WORDS ARE LIKE THE NATTERING OF A BUG!
I'LL SHUT YOU UP IN NO TIME!!
BRING IT ON!!
YOU'RE ONE TO TALK!
YOU'RE JUST SOME KIND OF SHRIMP MONSTER!!
I OUGHTA TURN YOU...
INTO A TEMPURA SOBA!!
SNIKT
STOMP
GYAH!
SNAP
THUD

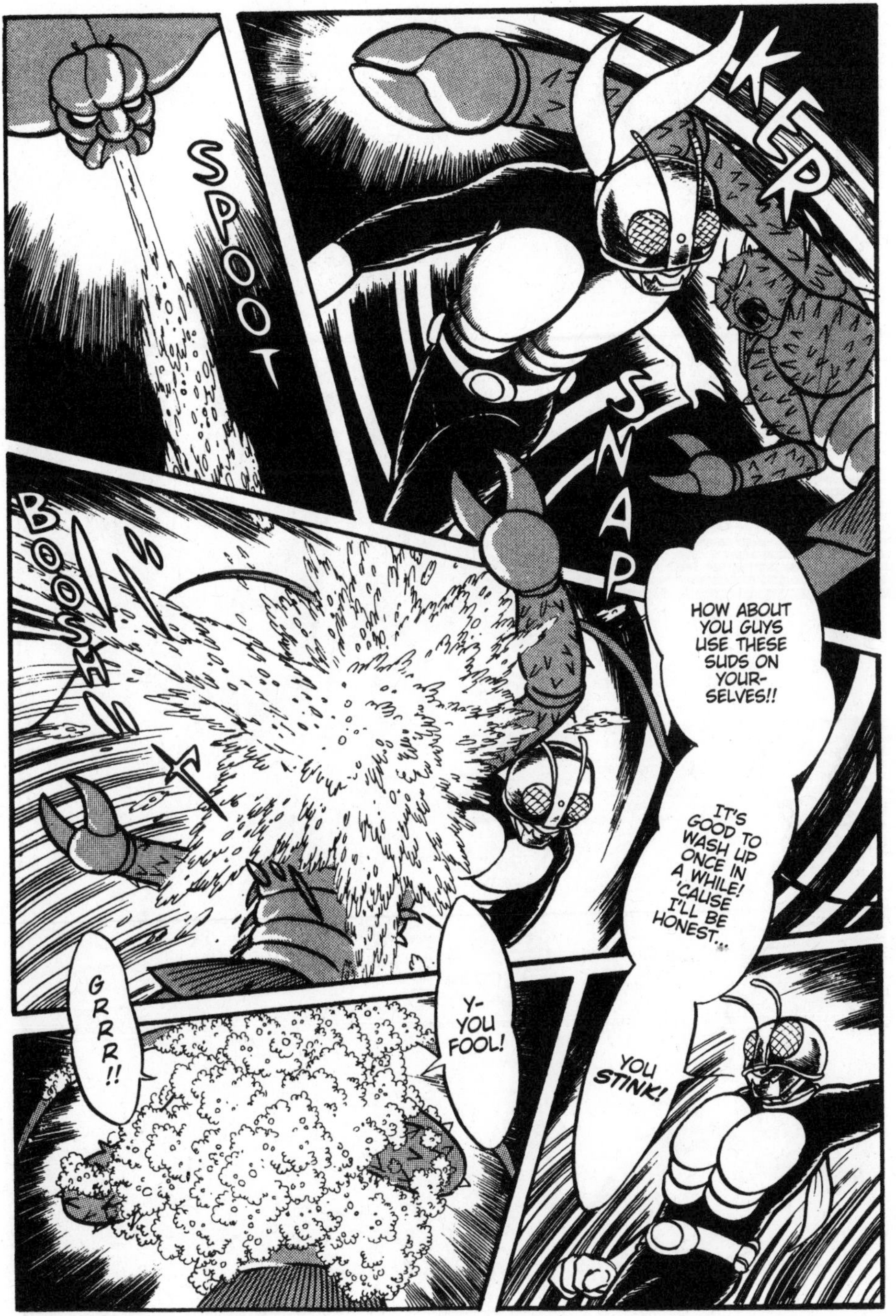
KER
SNAP
SPOOT
HOW ABOUT YOU GUYS USE THESE SUDS ON YOUR-SELVES!!
BOOSH!!
IT'S GOOD TO WASH UP ONCE IN A WHILE! 'CAUSE I'LL BE HONEST...
YOU STINK!
Y-YOU FOOL!
GRRR!!

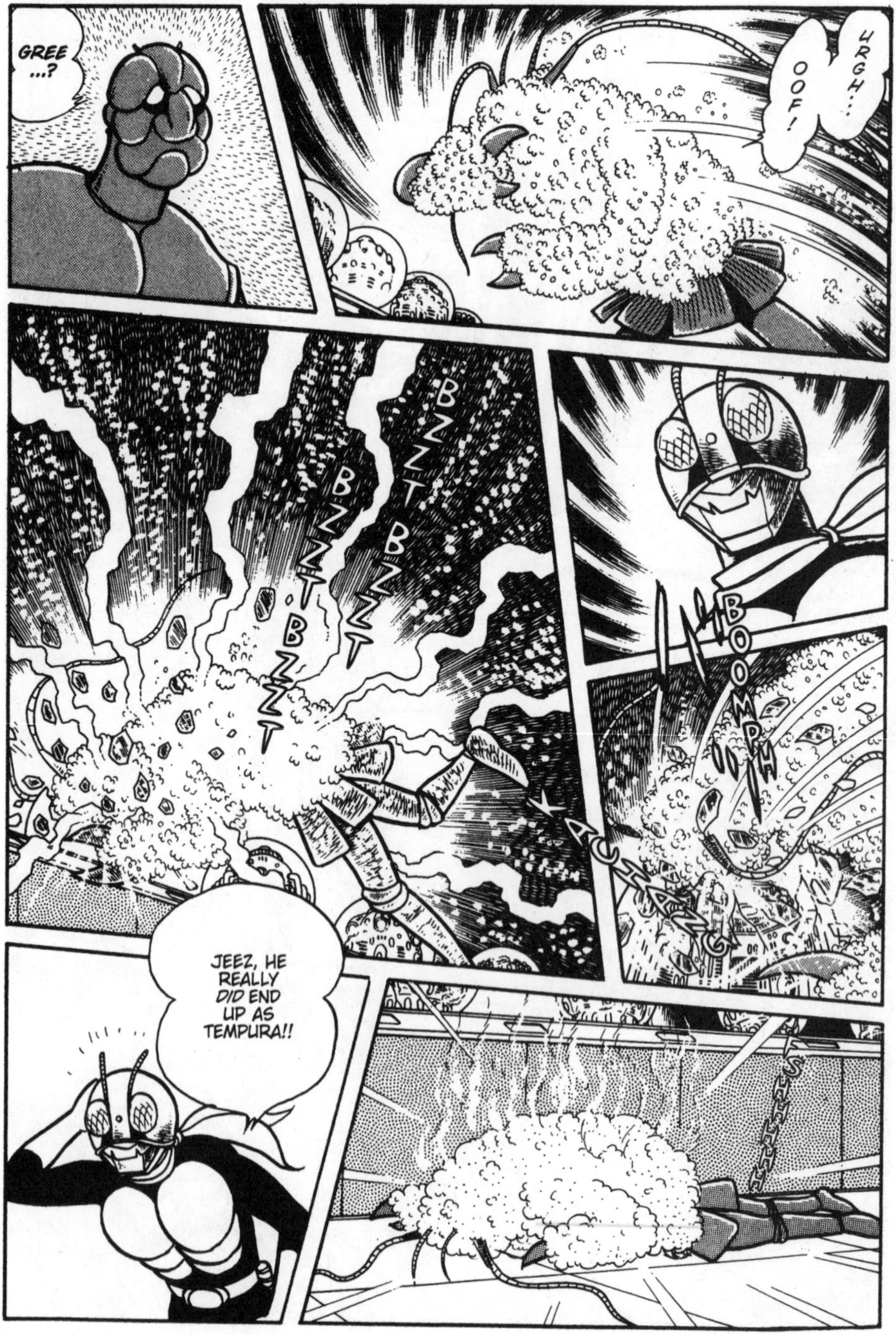
URGH... OOF!
GREE ...?
BOOMPH
KACHANG
BZZZT BZZZT BZZZT
TSHHHHHHH
JEEZ, HE REALLY *DID* END UP AS TEMPURA!!

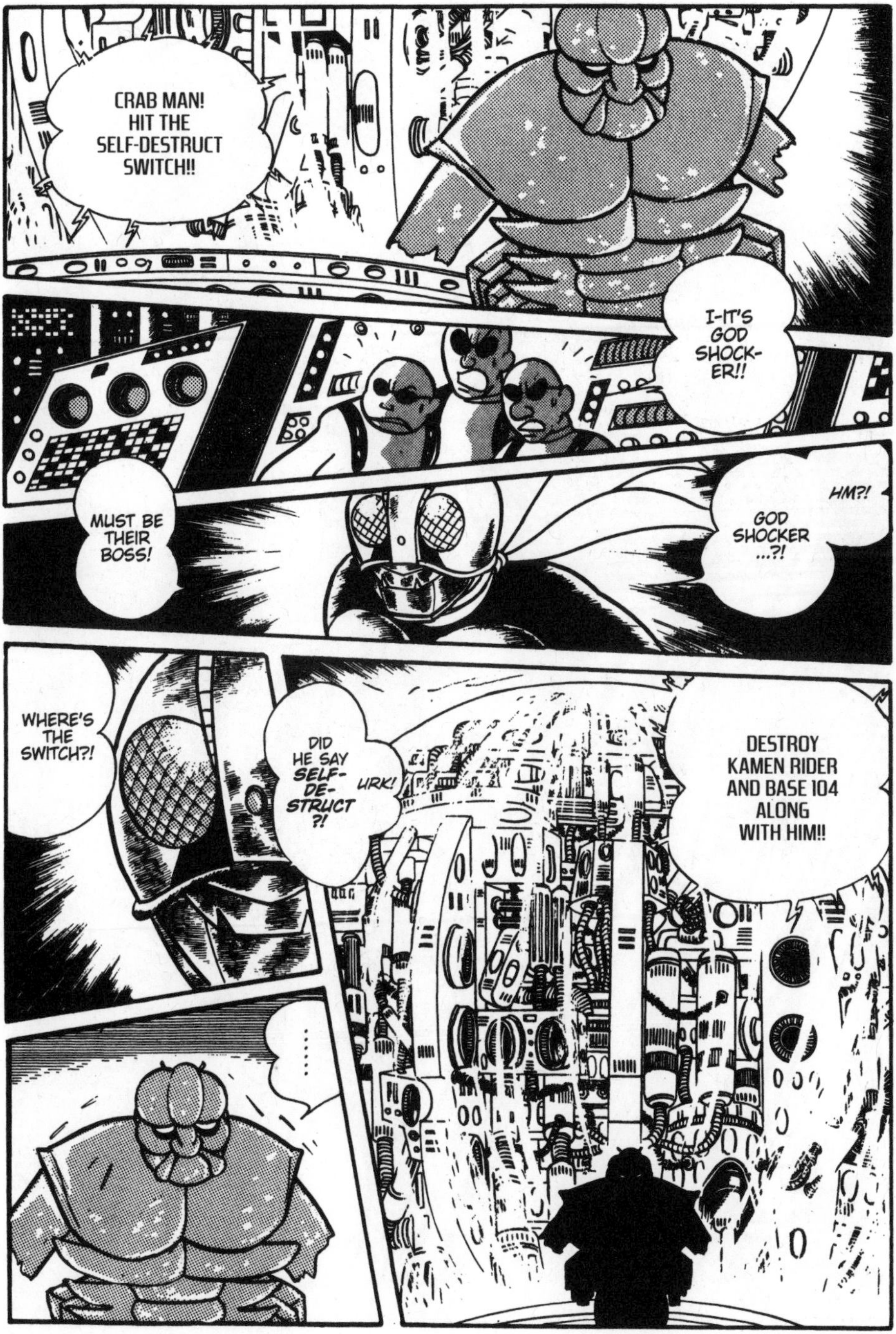
CRAB MAN! HIT THE SELF-DESTRUCT SWITCH!!
I-IT'S GOD SHOCKER!!
HM?!
GOD SHOCKER ...?!
MUST BE THEIR BOSS!
DESTROY KAMEN RIDER AND BASE 104 ALONG WITH HIM!!
URK!
DID HE SAY SELF-DESTRUCT ?!
WHERE'S THE SWITCH?!
......

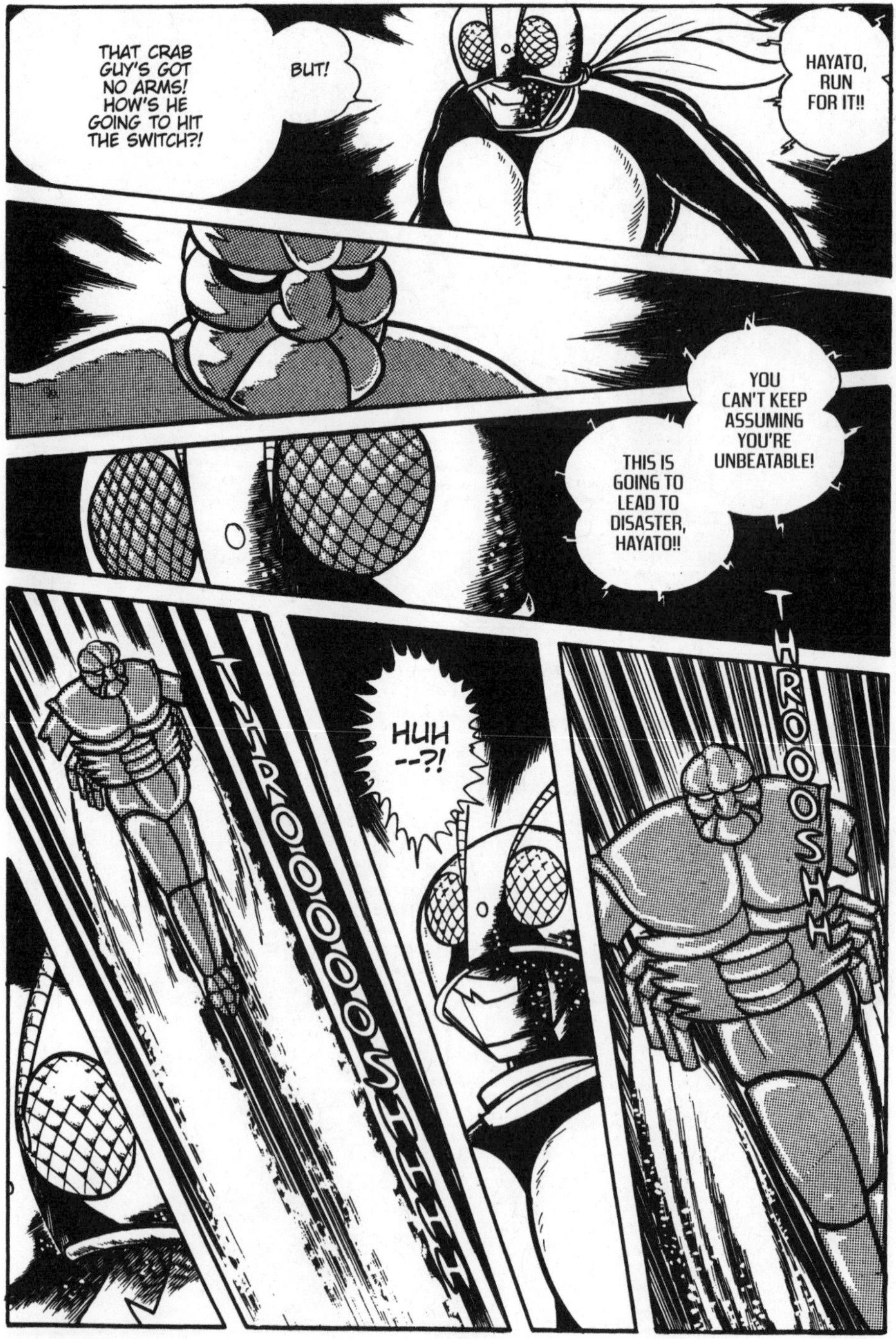
HAYATO, RUN FOR IT!!
BUT!
THAT CRAB GUY'S GOT NO ARMS! HOW'S HE GOING TO HIT THE SWITCH?!
YOU CAN'T KEEP ASSUMING YOU'RE UNBEATABLE!
THIS IS GOING TO LEAD TO DISASTER, HAYATO!!
THROOOOSHH
HUH --?!
THROOOOOOOSHHH

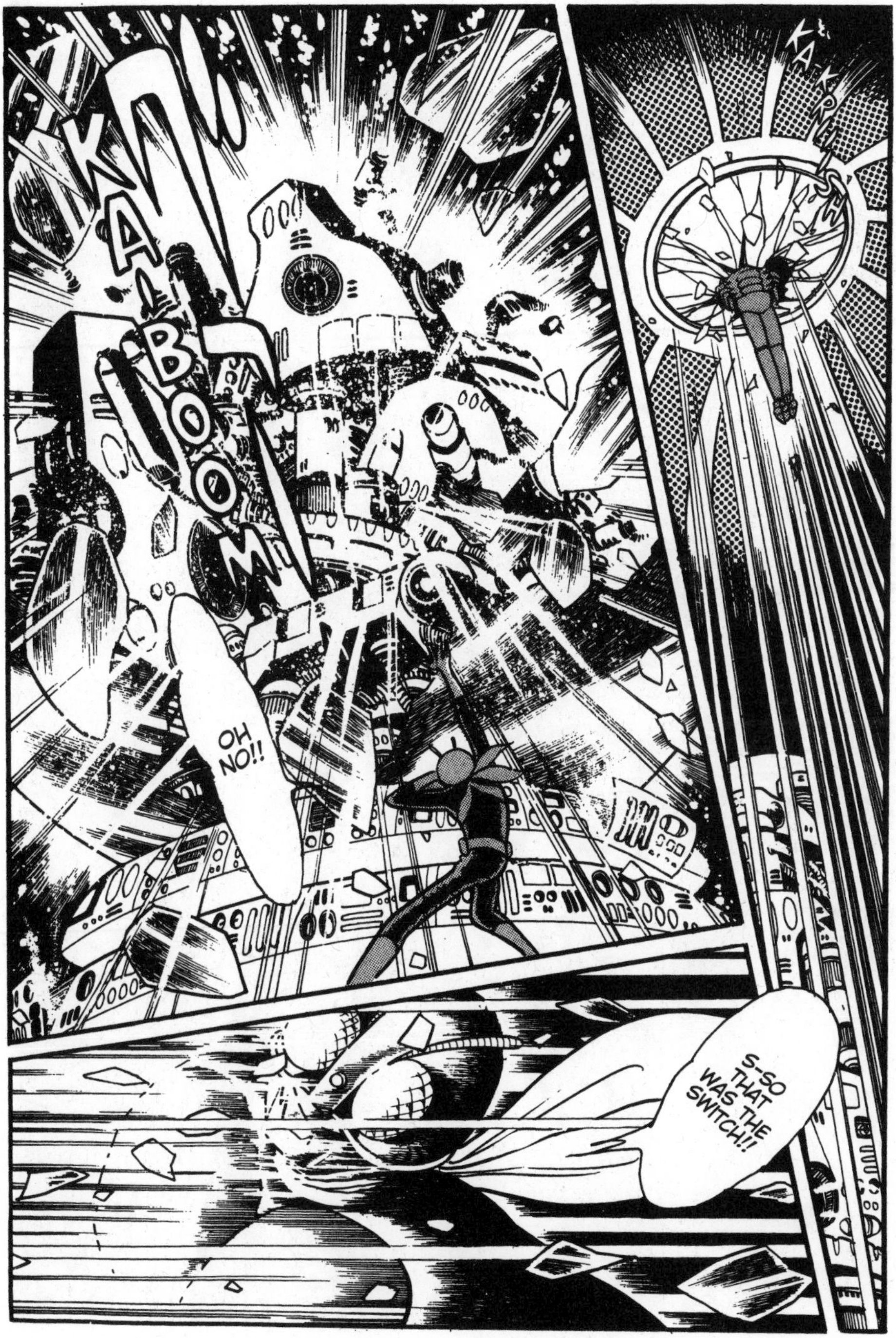
KA-KRISH
KABOOM
OH NO!!
S-SO THAT WAS THE SWITCH!!

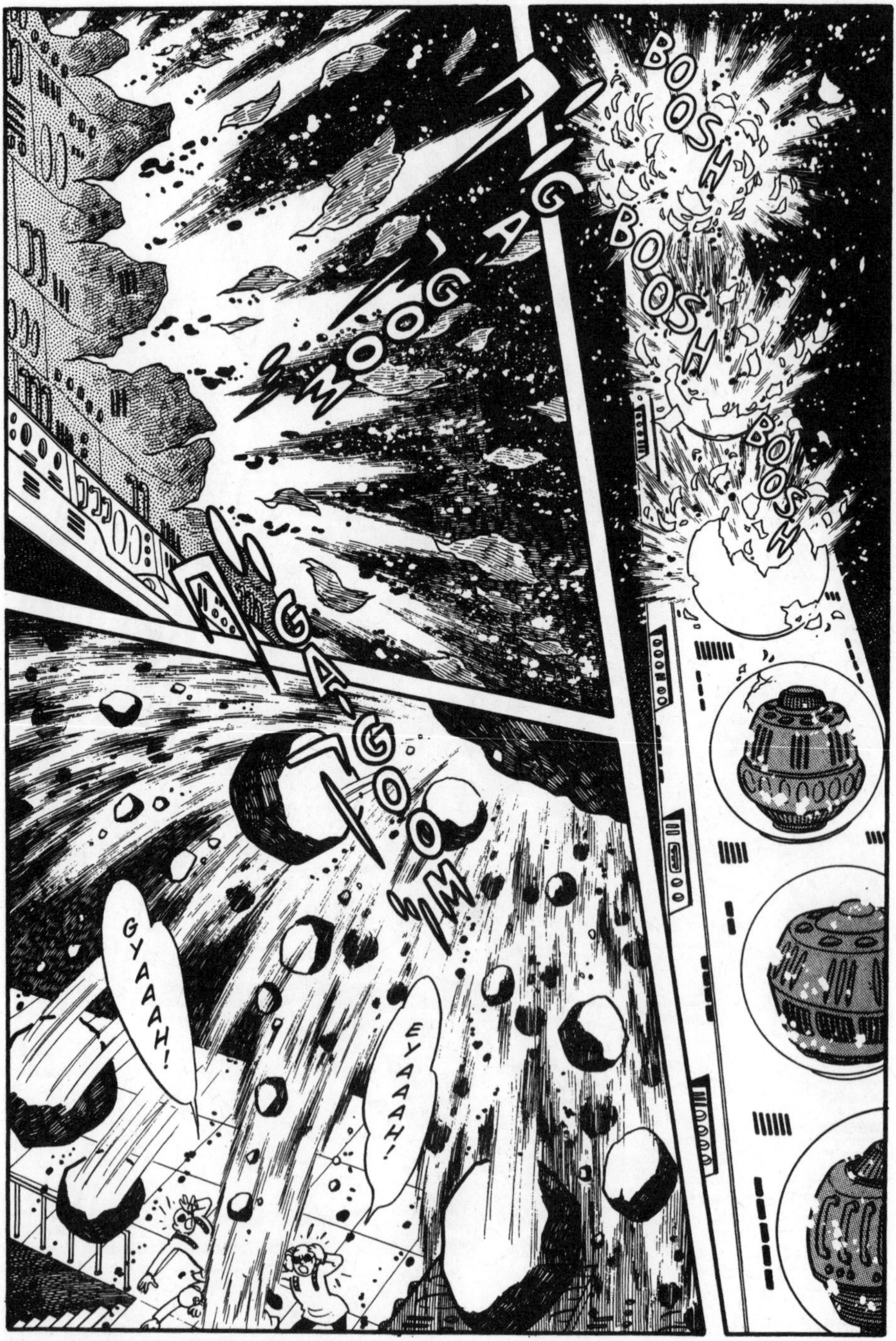
BOOSH
BOOSH
BOOSH
GAGOOM
GAGOOM
EYAAAH!
GYAAAH!

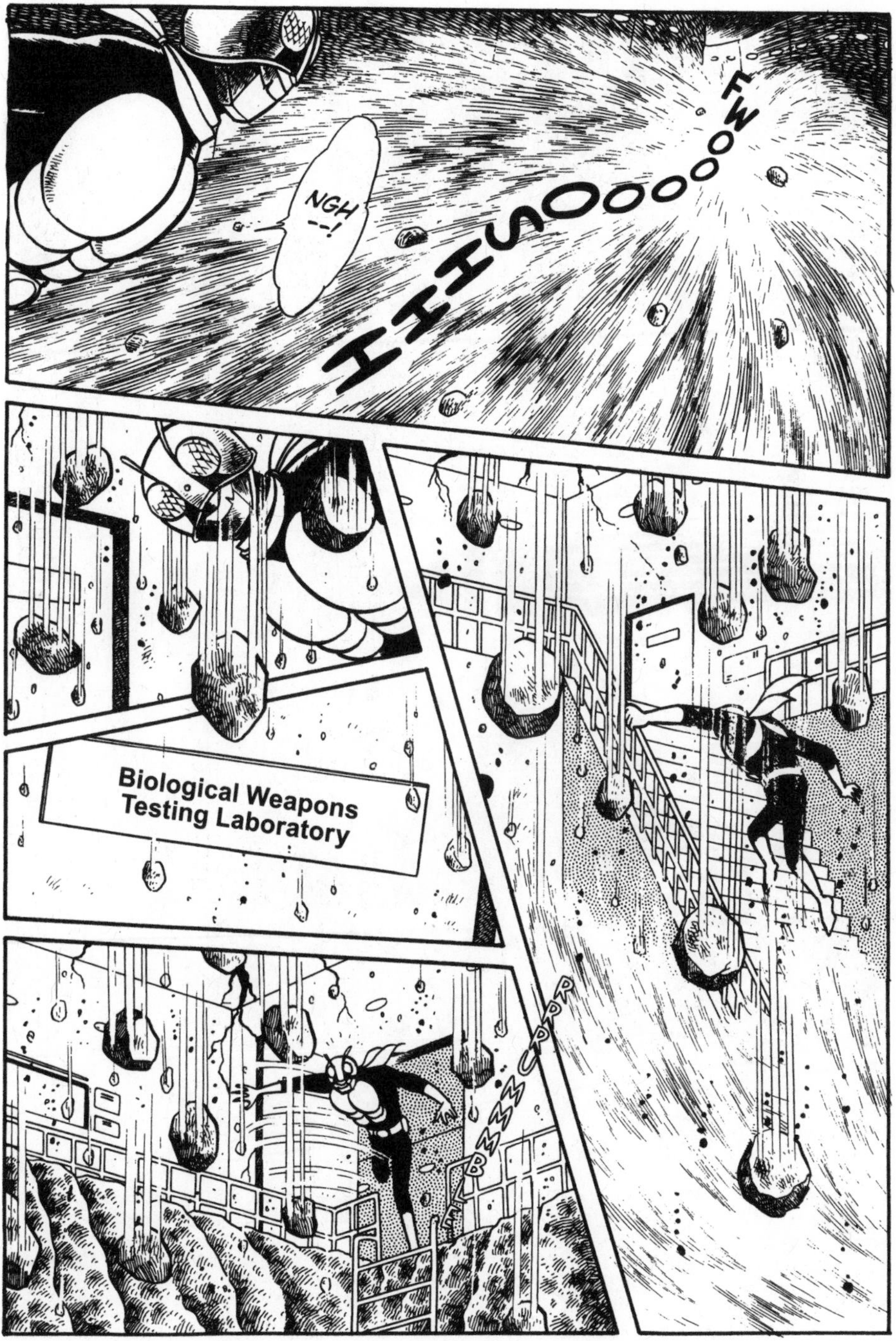
FWOOOOOSHHH
NGH --!
Biological Weapons Testing Laboratory
RRRUMMMB

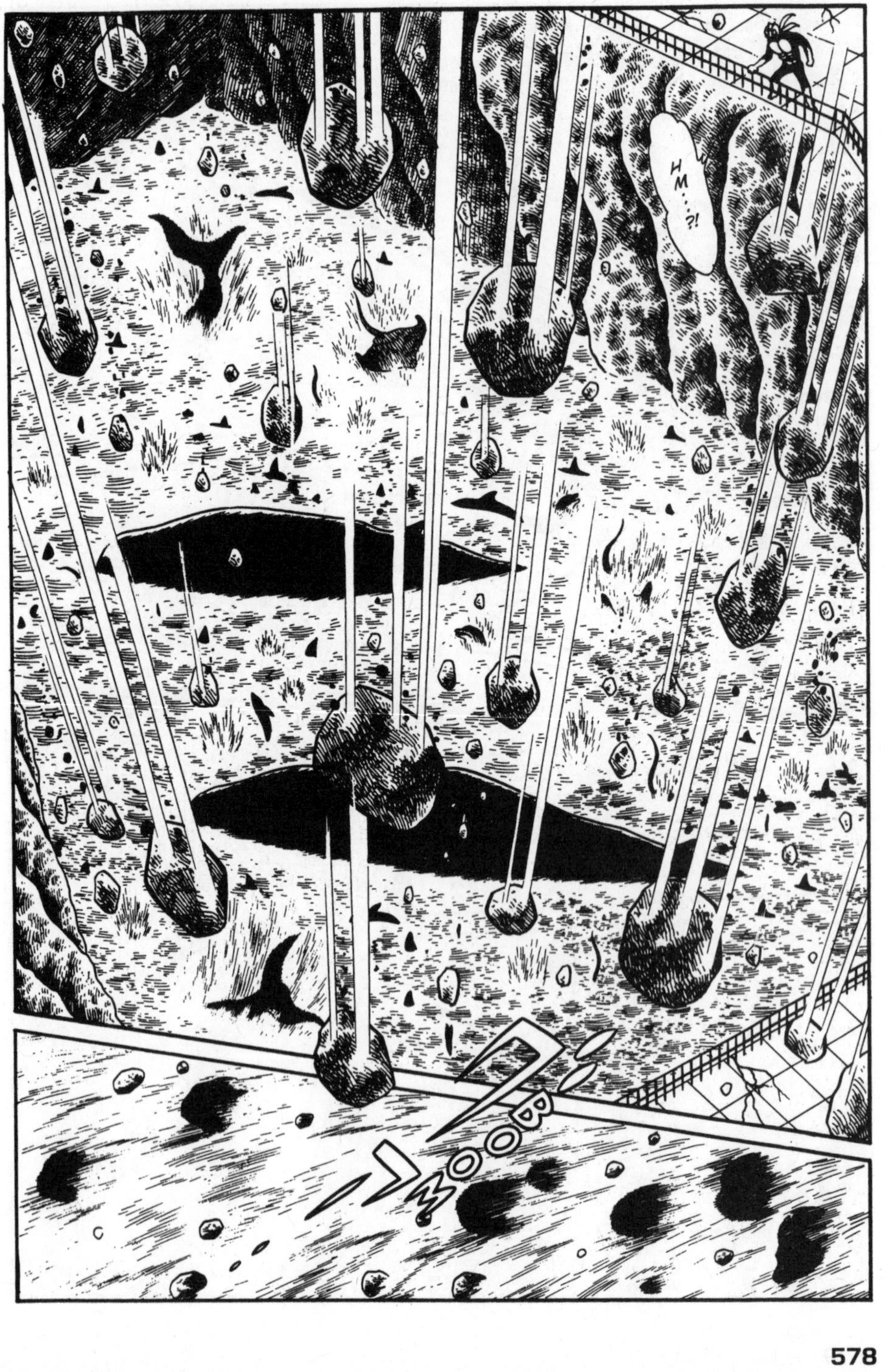
HM...?!
BOOOM!

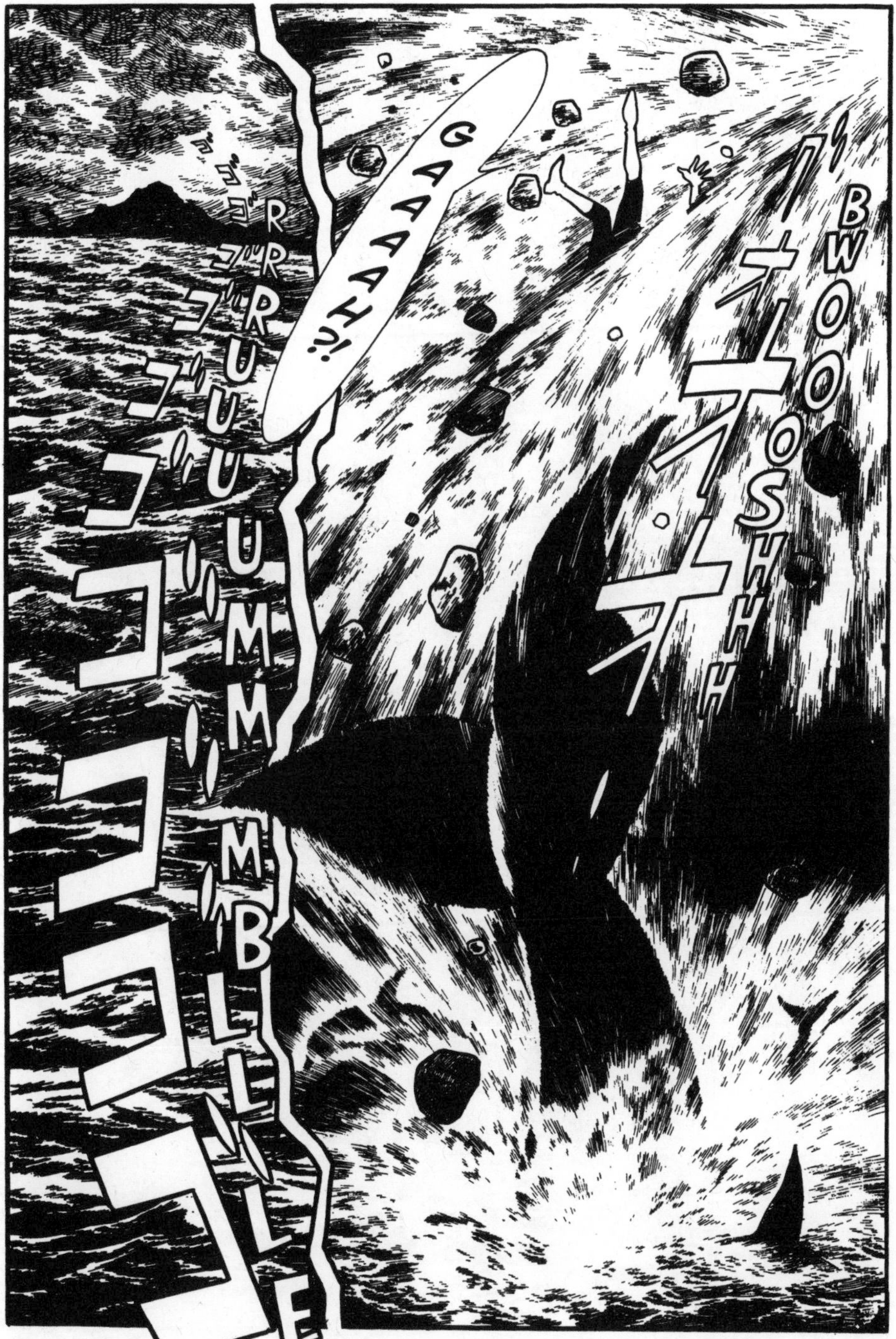
BWOOOSHHH
GAAAAAH?!
RRRUUUUMMMBLLLE

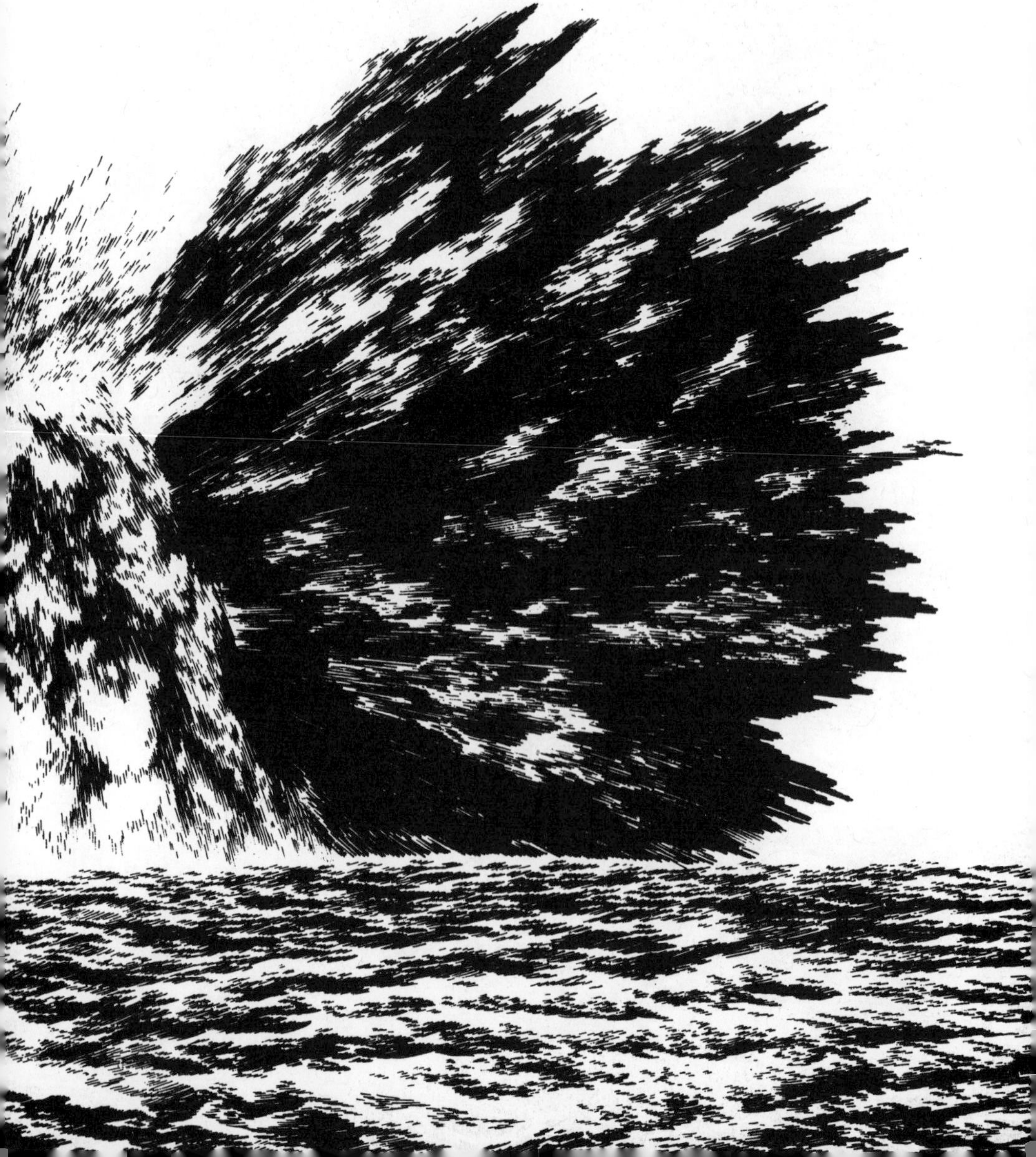

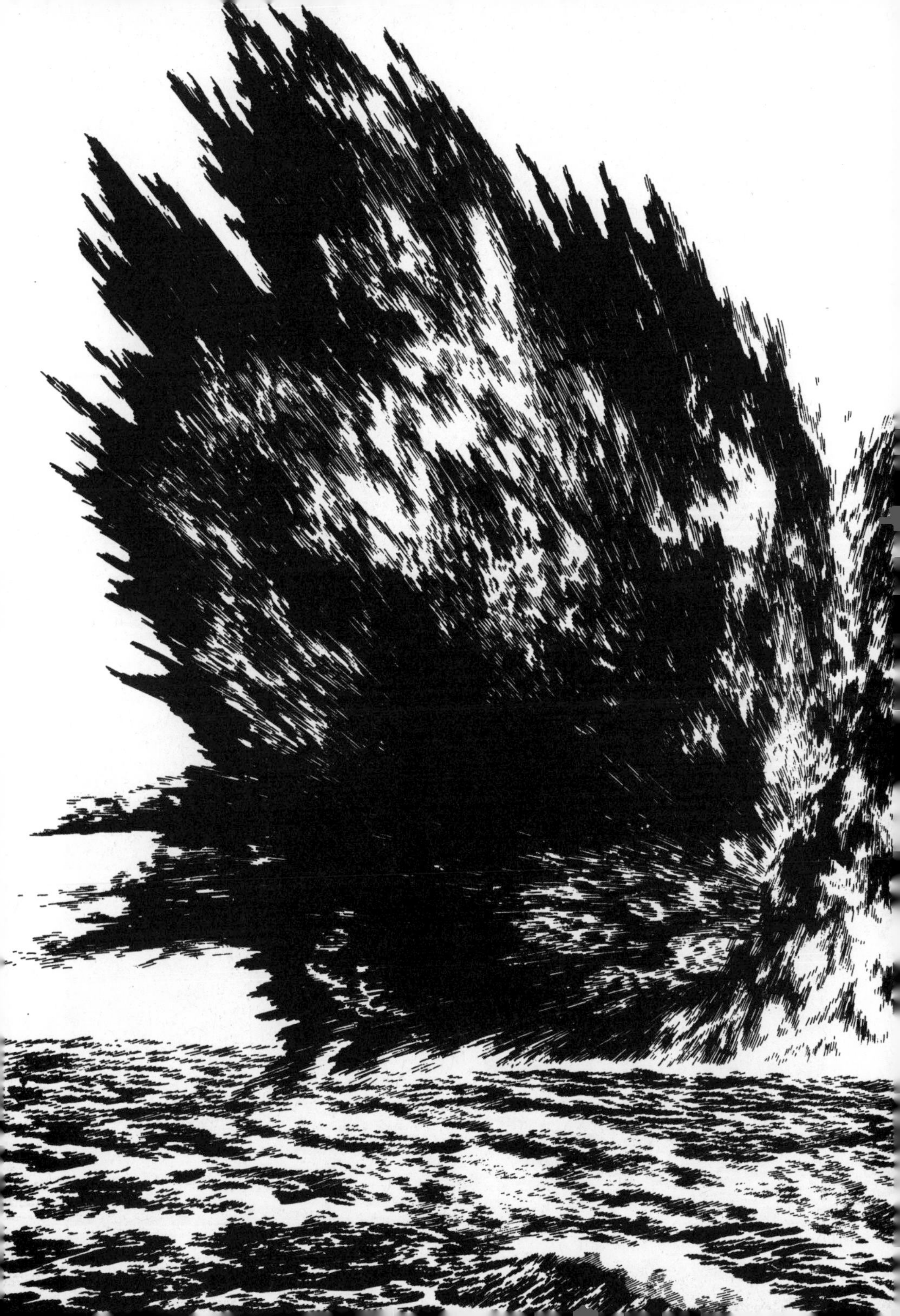

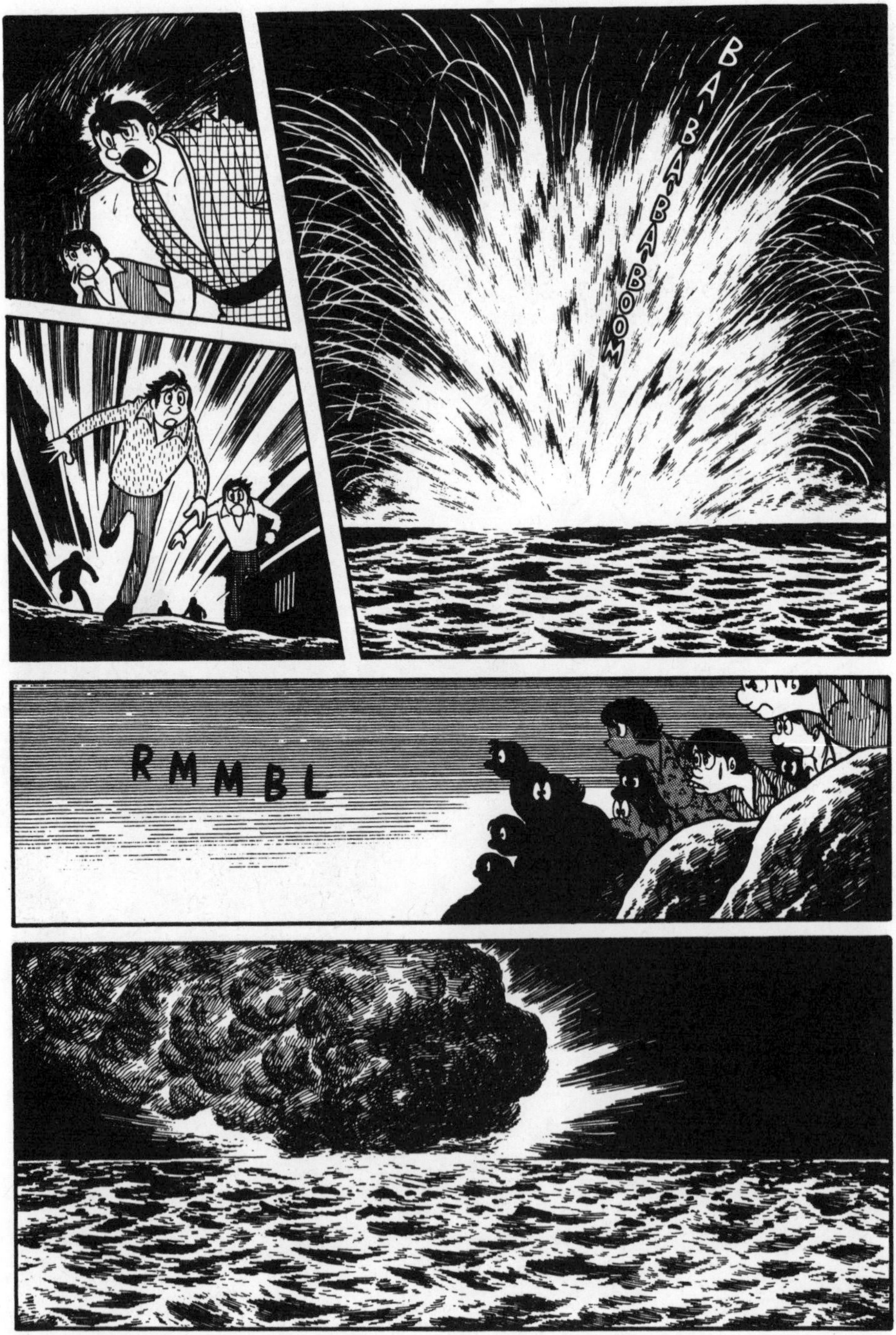
BA-BA-BA-BA-BOOM
RMMBL

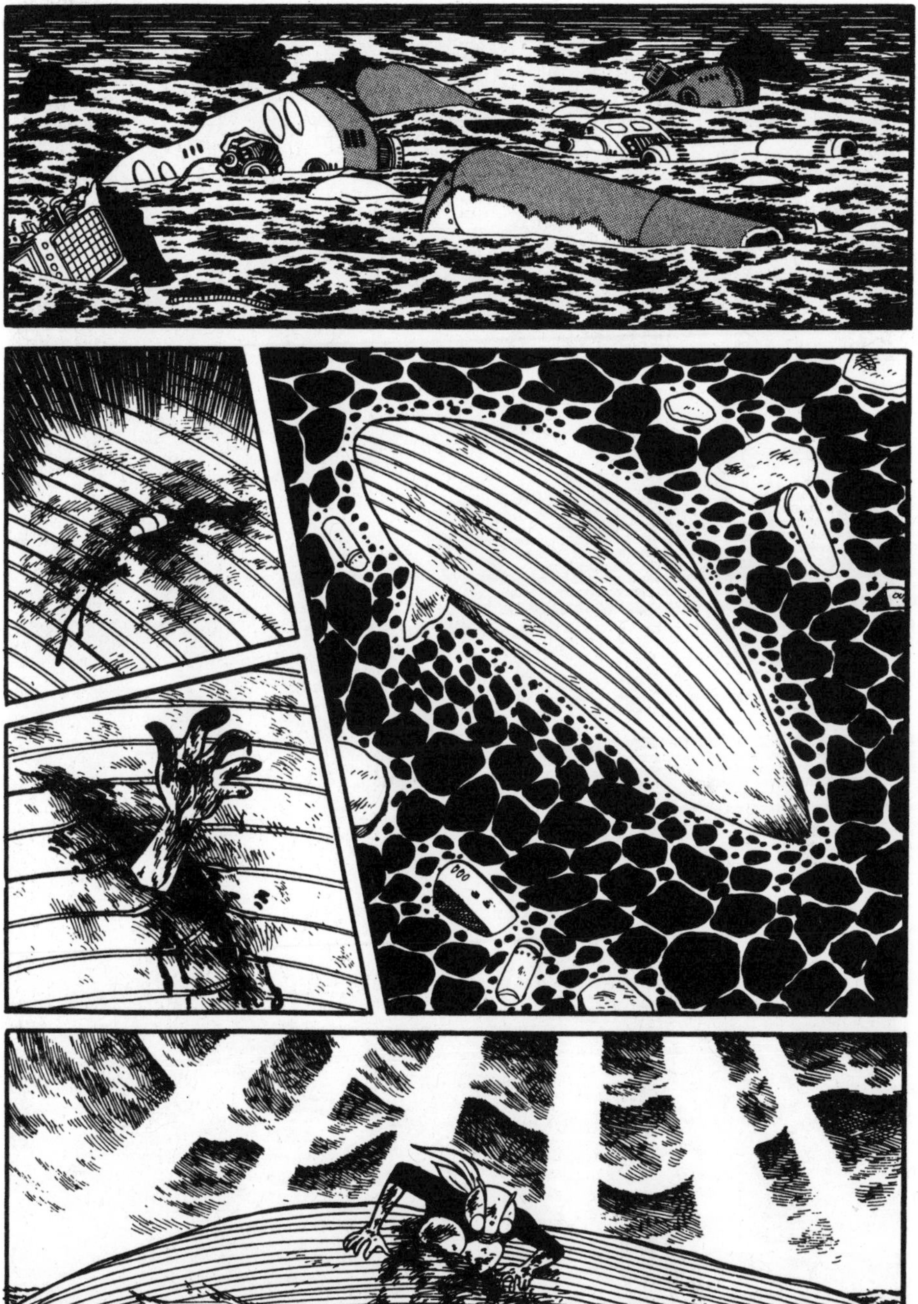

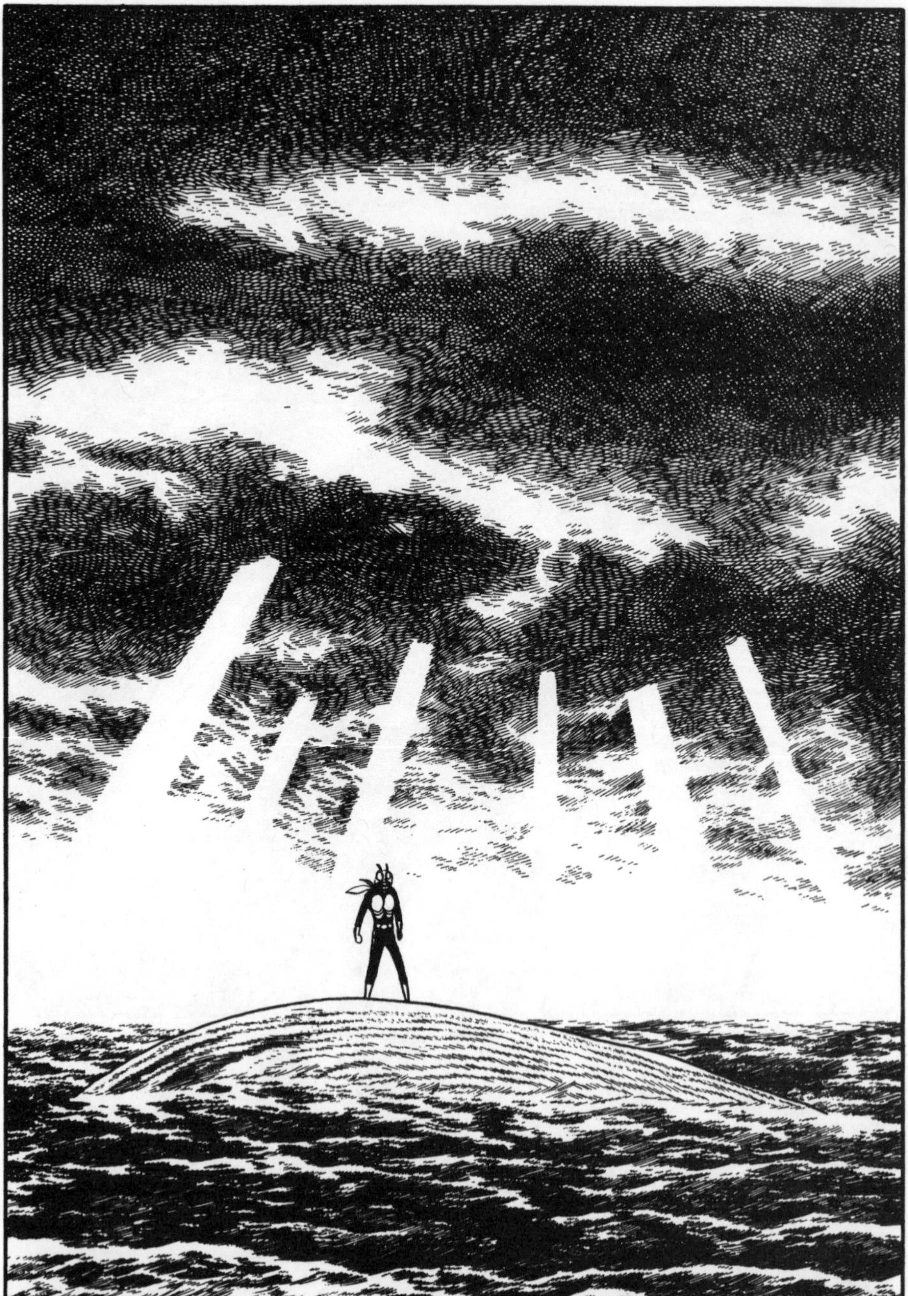

KAMEN
RIDER

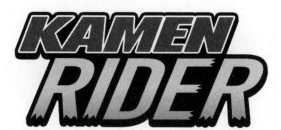

KAMEN RIDER

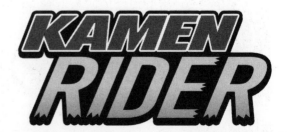

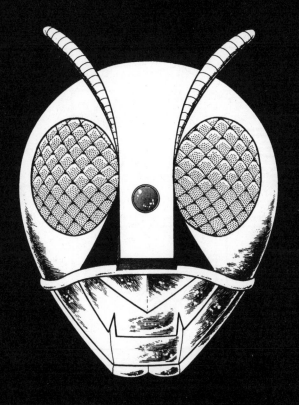

PART 6:
World of Masks

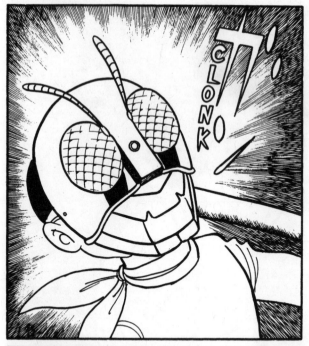

"ALL PEOPLE WEAR MASKS. BENEATH THAT MASK LIES THEIR TRUE FACE."

CLONK
YOW OW OW!!
Y-YOU BLOCK-HEAD!!
WHAT THE HECK'RE YOU DOING?!!
S-SORRY.

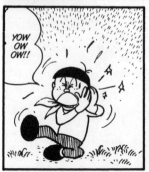

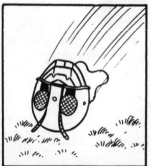

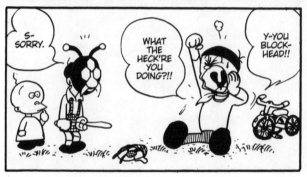

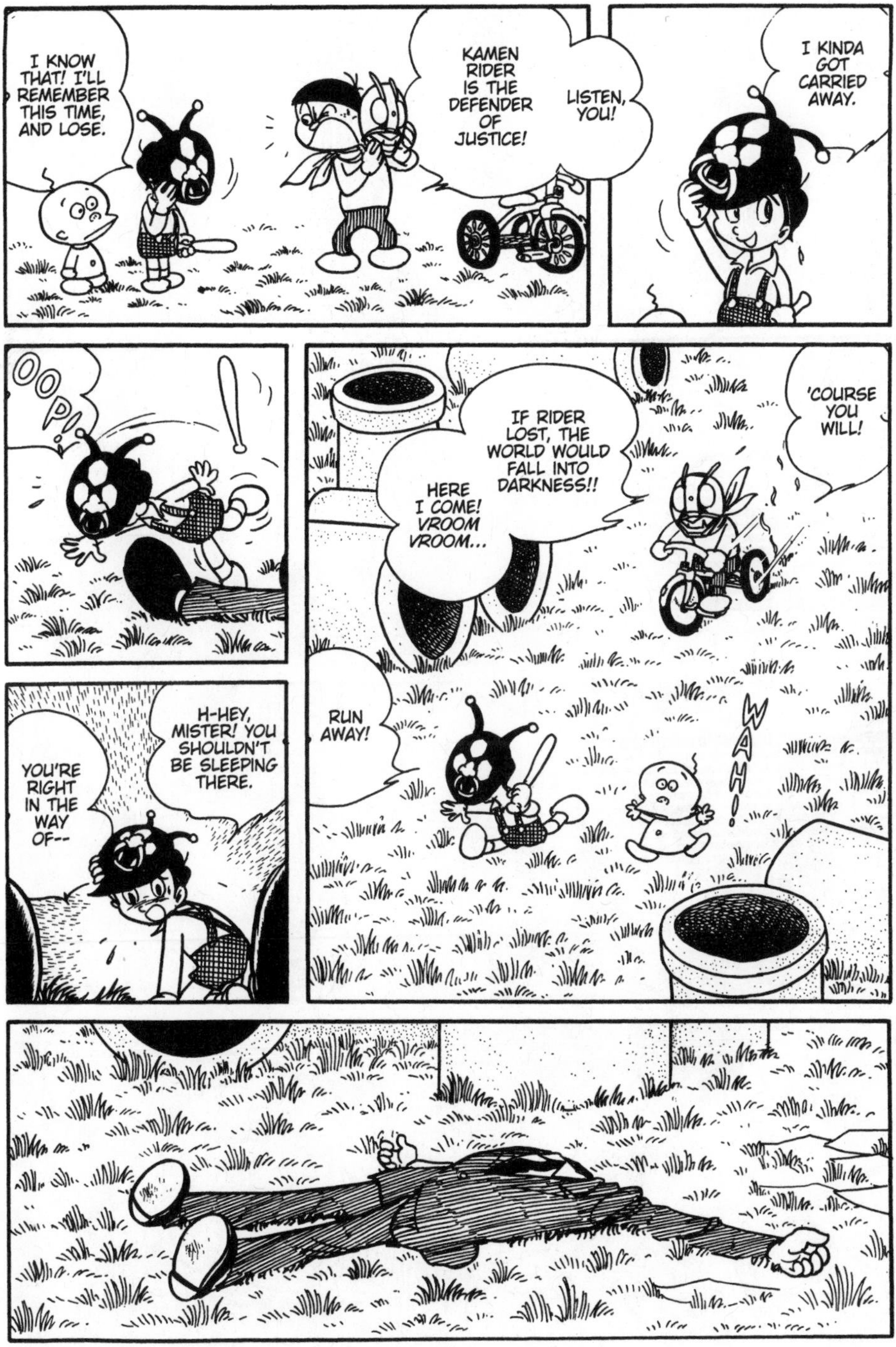
I KINDA GOT CARRIED AWAY.
LISTEN, YOU!
KAMEN RIDER IS THE DEFENDER OF JUSTICE!
I KNOW THAT! I'LL REMEMBER THIS TIME, AND LOSE.
'COURSE YOU WILL!
IF RIDER LOST, THE WORLD WOULD FALL INTO DARKNESS!!
HERE I COME! VROOM VROOM...
WAAH!
RUN AWAY!
OOP!
!
H-HEY, MISTER! YOU SHOULDN'T BE SLEEPING THERE.
YOU'RE RIGHT IN THE WAY OF--

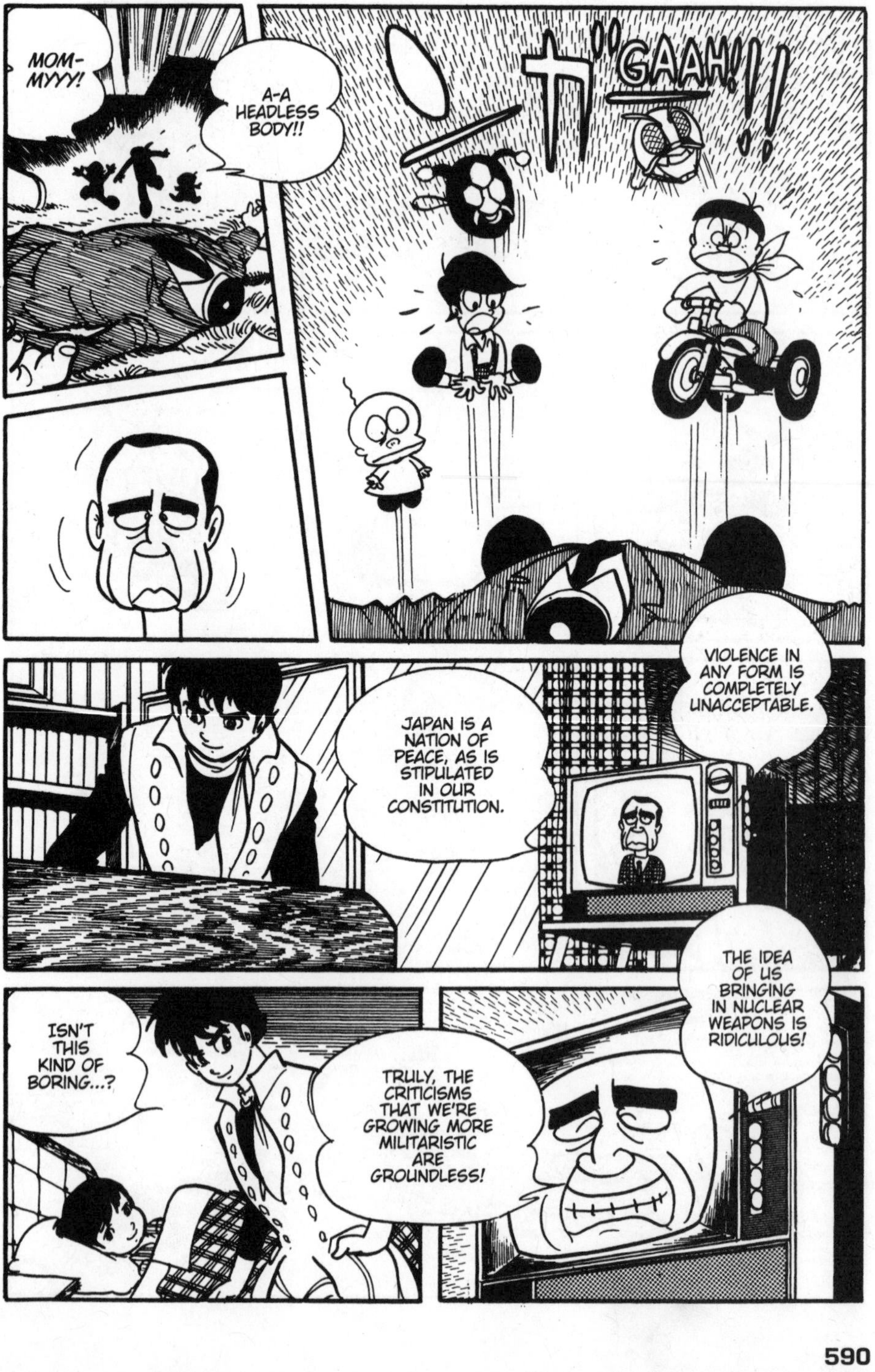
ガ
GAAH!!
MOM-MYYY!
A-A HEADLESS BODY!!
VIOLENCE IN ANY FORM IS COMPLETELY UNACCEPTABLE.
JAPAN IS A NATION OF PEACE, AS IS STIPULATED IN OUR CONSTITUTION.
THE IDEA OF US BRINGING IN NUCLEAR WEAPONS IS RIDICULOUS!
TRULY, THE CRITICISMS THAT WE'RE GROWING MORE MILITARISTIC ARE GROUNDLESS!
ISN'T THIS KIND OF BORING...?

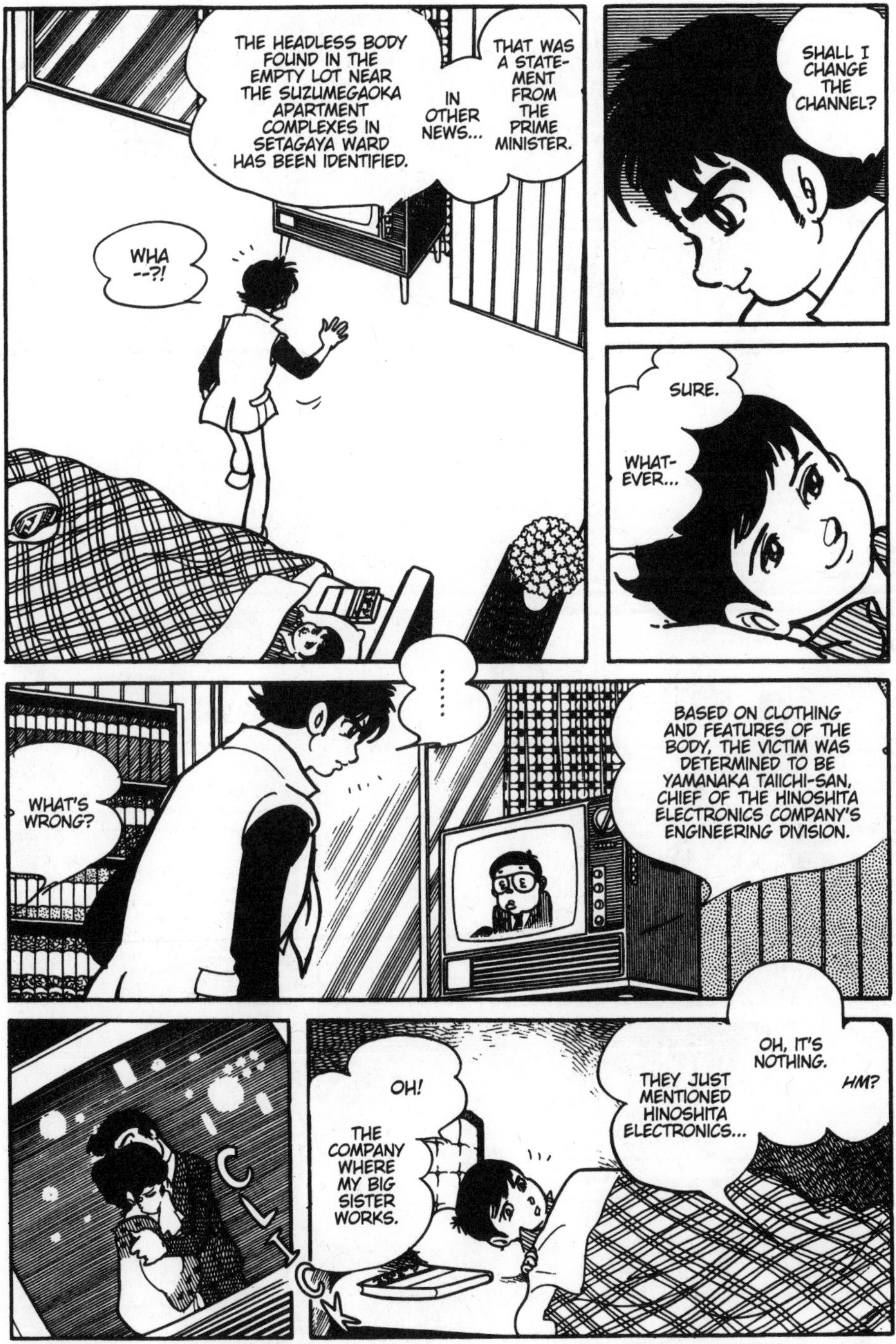

SHALL I CHANGE THE CHANNEL?
SURE.
WHAT-EVER...
THAT WAS A STATE-MENT FROM THE PRIME MINISTER.
IN OTHER NEWS...
THE HEADLESS BODY FOUND IN THE EMPTY LOT NEAR THE SUZUMEGAOKA APARTMENT COMPLEXES IN SETAGAYA WARD HAS BEEN IDENTIFIED.
WHA--?!
BASED ON CLOTHING AND FEATURES OF THE BODY, THE VICTIM WAS DETERMINED TO BE YAMANAKA TAIICHI-SAN, CHIEF OF THE HINOSHITA ELECTRONICS COMPANY'S ENGINEERING DIVISION.
......
WHAT'S WRONG?
HM?
OH, IT'S NOTHING.
THEY JUST MENTIONED HINOSHITA ELECTRONICS...
OH!
THE COMPANY WHERE MY BIG SISTER WORKS.
CLICK

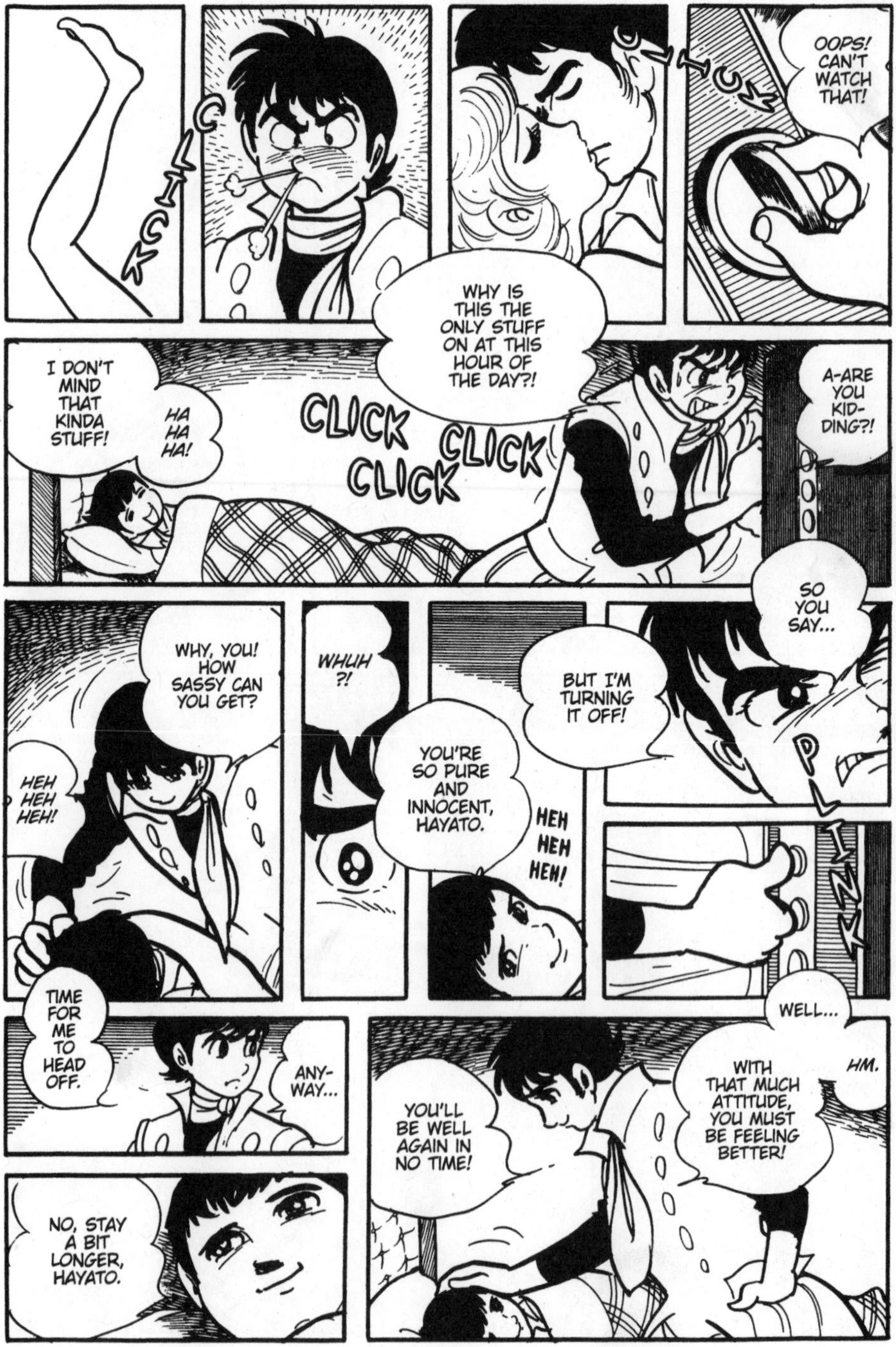
OOPS! CAN'T WATCH THAT!
CLICK
CLICK
CLICK
WHY IS THIS THE ONLY STUFF ON AT THIS HOUR OF THE DAY?!
A-ARE YOU KIDDING?!
CLICK
CLICK
CLICK
I DON'T MIND THAT KINDA STUFF!
HA HA HA!
SO YOU SAY...
BUT I'M TURNING IT OFF!
PLINK
YOU'RE SO PURE AND INNOCENT, HAYATO.
HEH HEH HEH!
WHUH ?!
WHY, YOU! HOW SASSY CAN YOU GET?
HEH HEH HEH!
WELL...
HM.
WITH THAT MUCH ATTITUDE, YOU MUST BE FEELING BETTER!
YOU'LL BE WELL AGAIN IN NO TIME!
ANYWAY...
TIME FOR ME TO HEAD OFF.
NO, STAY A BIT LONGER, HAYATO.

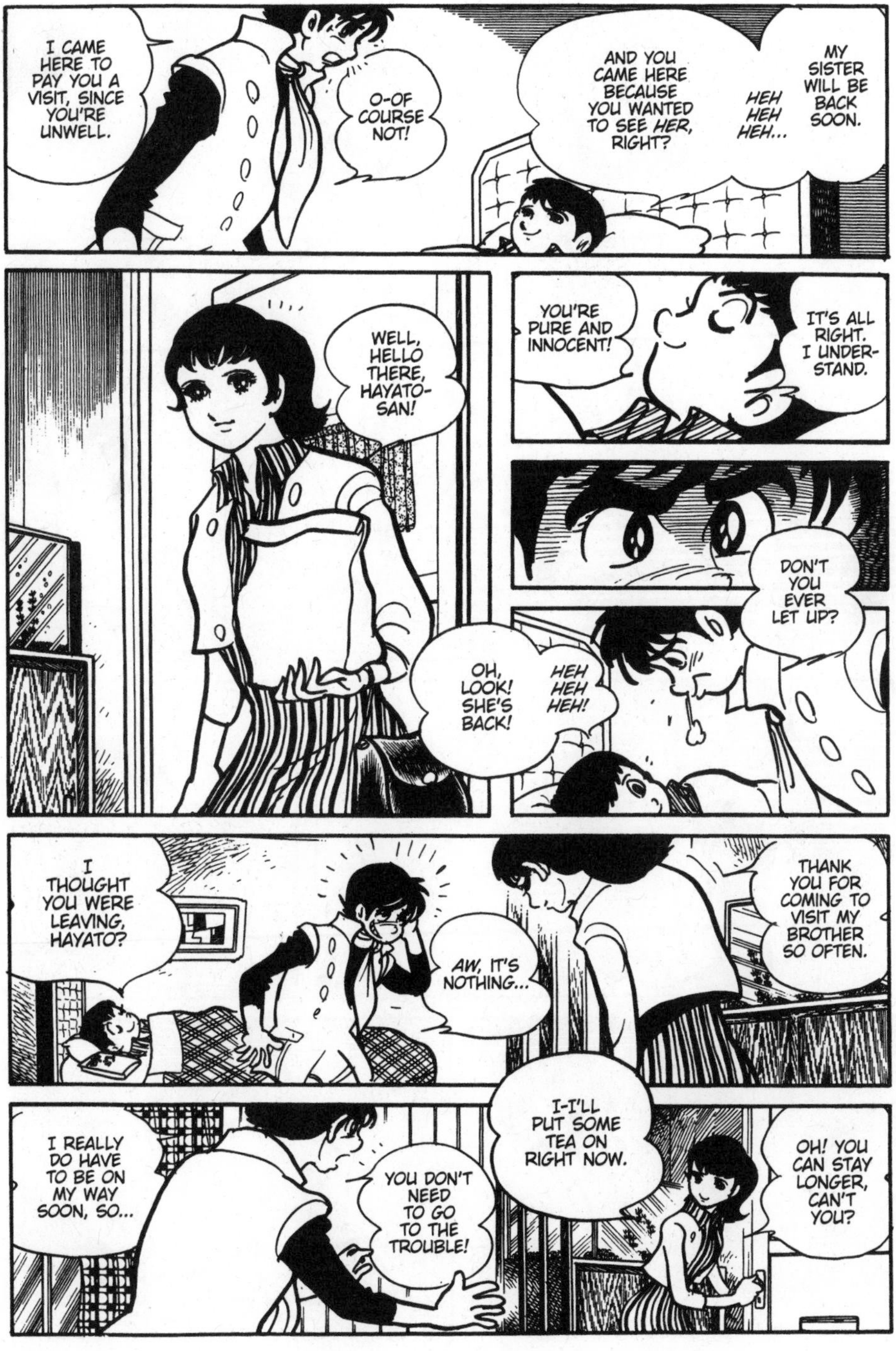
MY SISTER WILL BE BACK SOON.
HEH HEH HEH...
AND YOU CAME HERE BECAUSE YOU WANTED TO SEE *HER*, RIGHT?
O-OF COURSE NOT!
I CAME HERE TO PAY YOU A VISIT, SINCE YOU'RE UNWELL.
IT'S ALL RIGHT. I UNDERSTAND.
YOU'RE PURE AND INNOCENT!
DON'T YOU EVER LET UP?
HEH HEH HEH!
OH, LOOK! SHE'S BACK!
WELL, HELLO THERE, HAYATO-SAN!
THANK YOU FOR COMING TO VISIT MY BROTHER SO OFTEN.
AW, IT'S NOTHING...
I THOUGHT YOU WERE LEAVING, HAYATO?
OH! YOU CAN STAY LONGER, CAN'T YOU?
I-I'LL PUT SOME TEA ON RIGHT NOW.
YOU DON'T NEED TO GO TO THE TROUBLE!
I REALLY DO HAVE TO BE ON MY WAY SOON, SO...

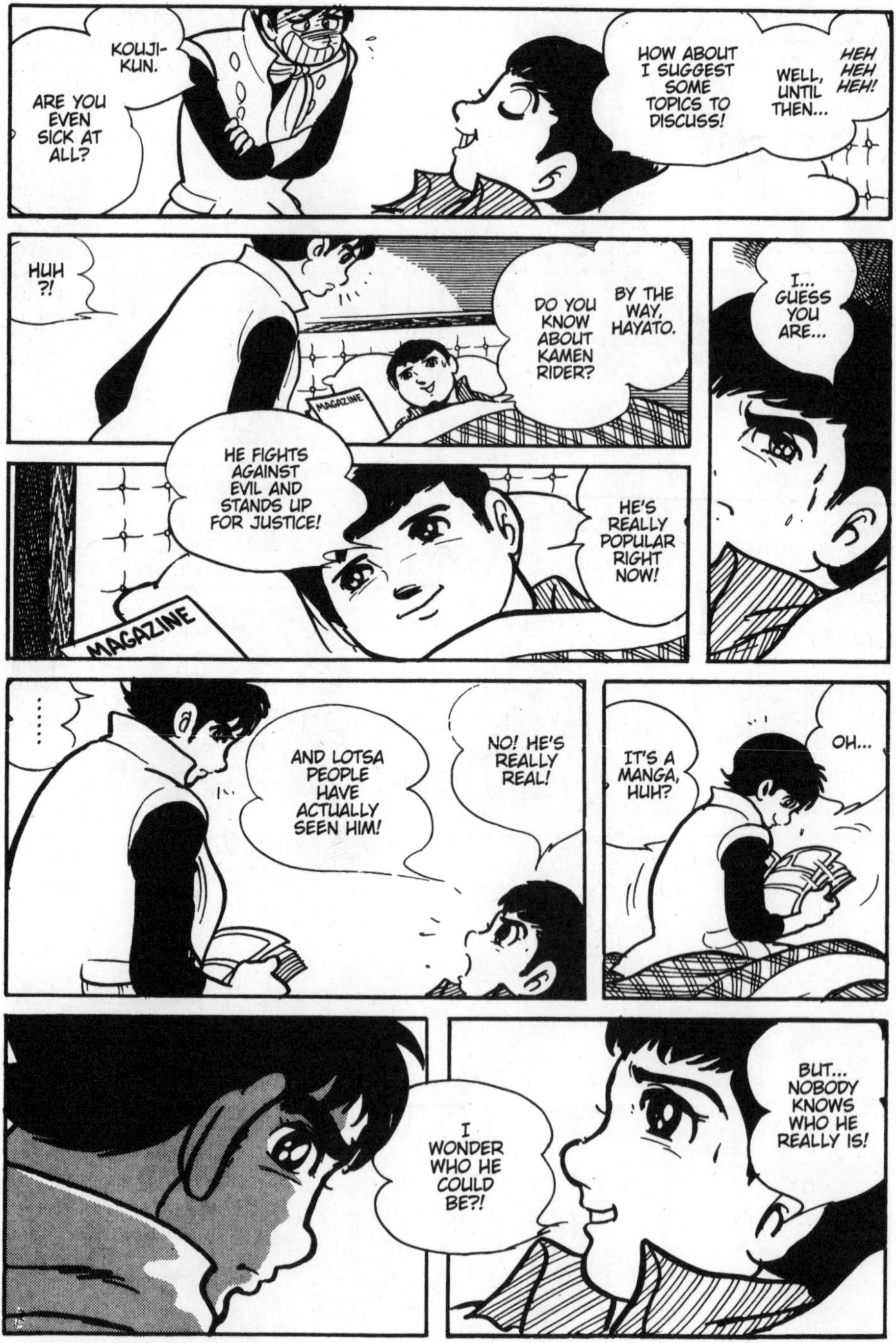
HEH HEH HEH!
WELL, UNTIL THEN...
HOW ABOUT I SUGGEST SOME TOPICS TO DISCUSS!
KOUJI-KUN.
ARE YOU EVEN SICK AT ALL?
I... GUESS YOU ARE...
BY THE WAY, HAYATO.
DO YOU KNOW ABOUT KAMEN RIDER?
HUH?!
MAGAZINE
HE'S REALLY POPULAR RIGHT NOW!
HE FIGHTS AGAINST EVIL AND STANDS UP FOR JUSTICE!
MAGAZINE
OH...
IT'S A MANGA, HUH?
NO! HE'S REALLY REAL!
AND LOTSA PEOPLE HAVE ACTUALLY SEEN HIM!
......
BUT... NOBODY KNOWS WHO HE REALLY IS!
I WONDER WHO HE COULD BE?!

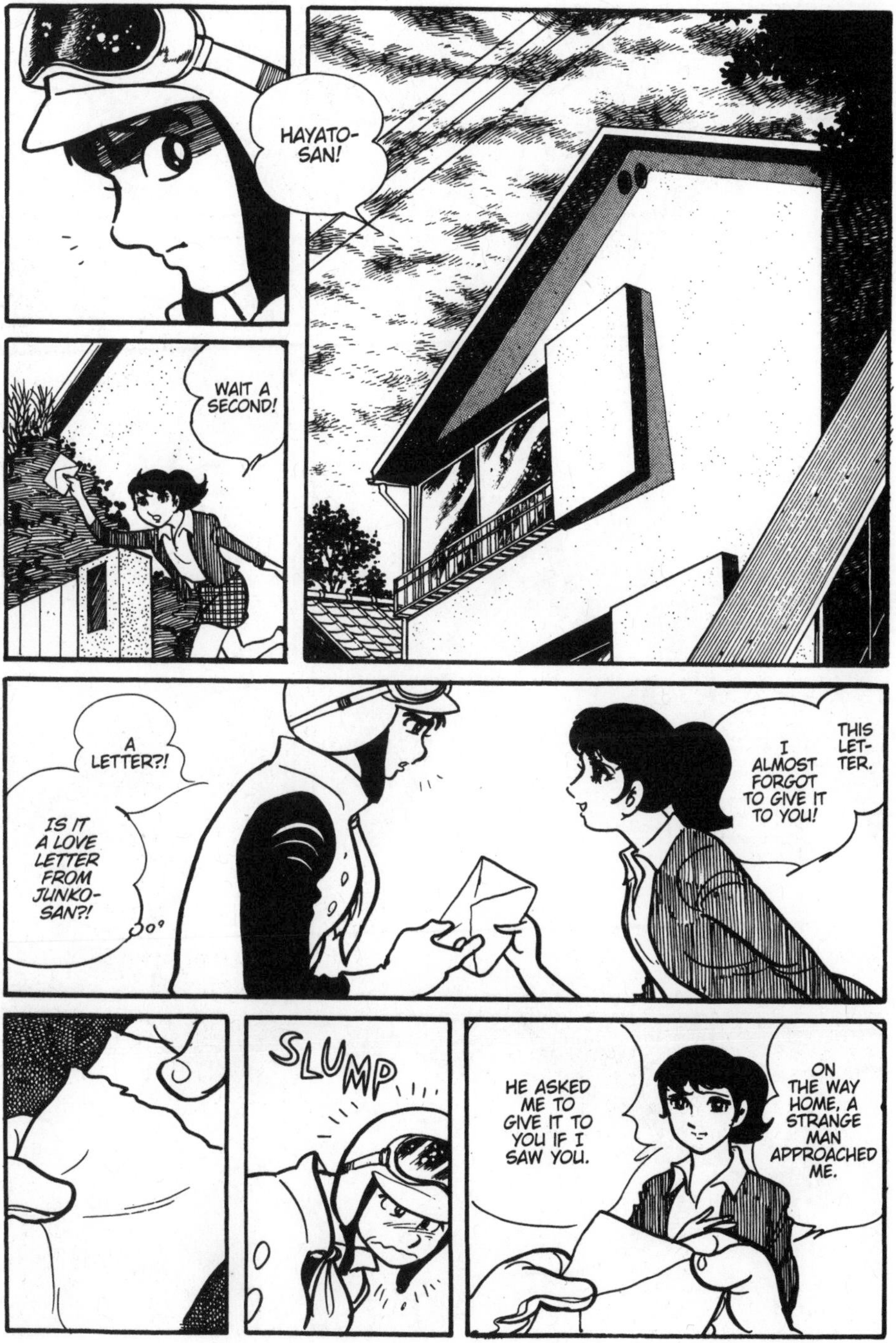
HAYATO-SAN!
WAIT A SECOND!
THIS LETTER. I ALMOST FORGOT TO GIVE IT TO YOU!
A LETTER?!
IS IT A LOVE LETTER FROM JUNKO-SAN?!
ON THE WAY HOME, A STRANGE MAN APPROACHED ME.
HE ASKED ME TO GIVE IT TO YOU IF I SAW YOU.
SLUMP

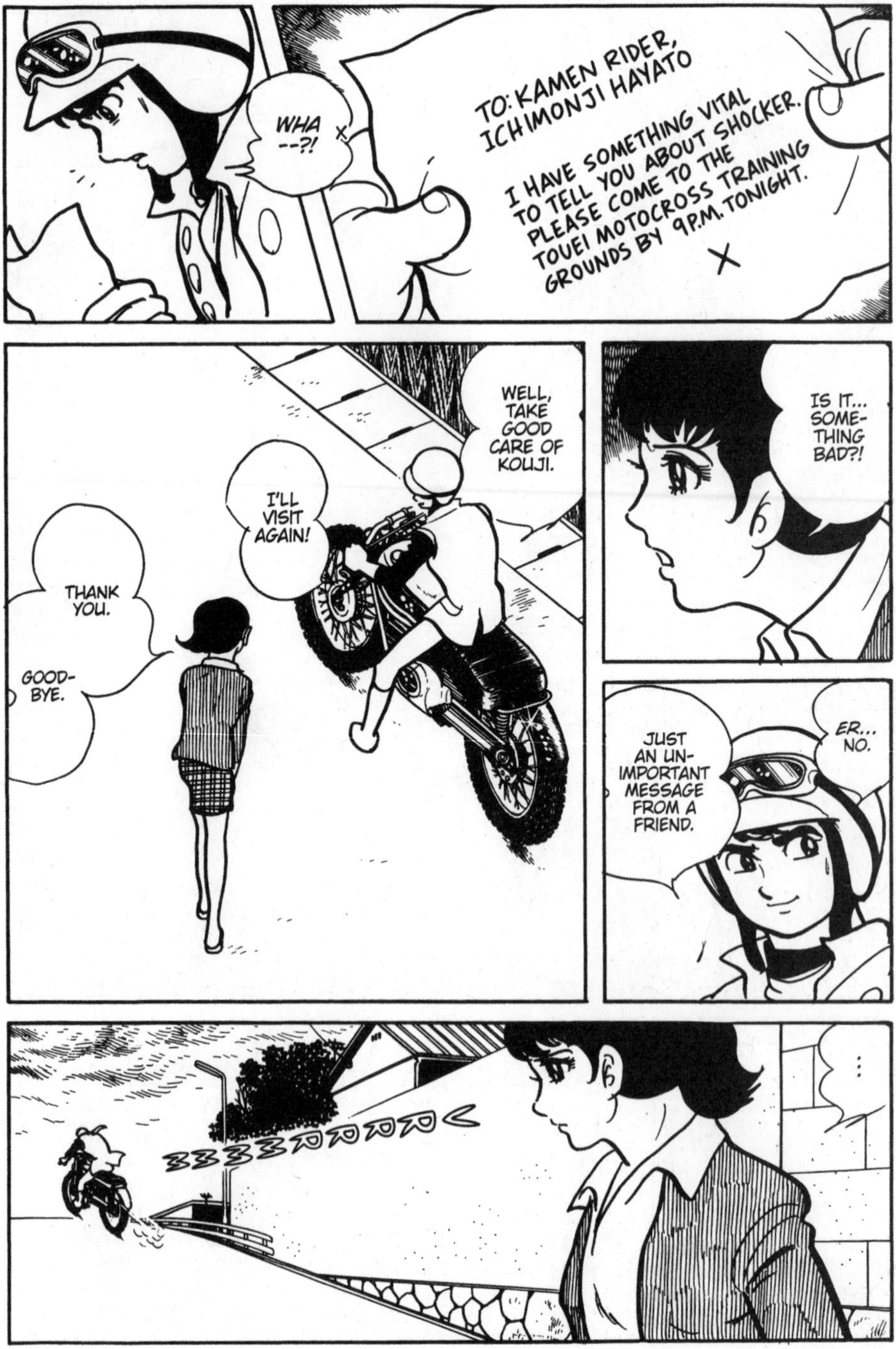
TO: KAMEN RIDER, ICHIMONJI HAYATO
I HAVE SOMETHING VITAL TO TELL YOU ABOUT SHOCKER. PLEASE COME TO THE TOUEI MOTOCROSS TRAINING GROUNDS BY 9P.M. TONIGHT.
WHA --?!
IS IT... SOME-THING BAD?!
ER... NO.
JUST AN UN-IMPORTANT MESSAGE FROM A FRIEND.
WELL, TAKE GOOD CARE OF KOUJI.
I'LL VISIT AGAIN!
THANK YOU.
GOOD-BYE.
...
BBBBRRRRRR

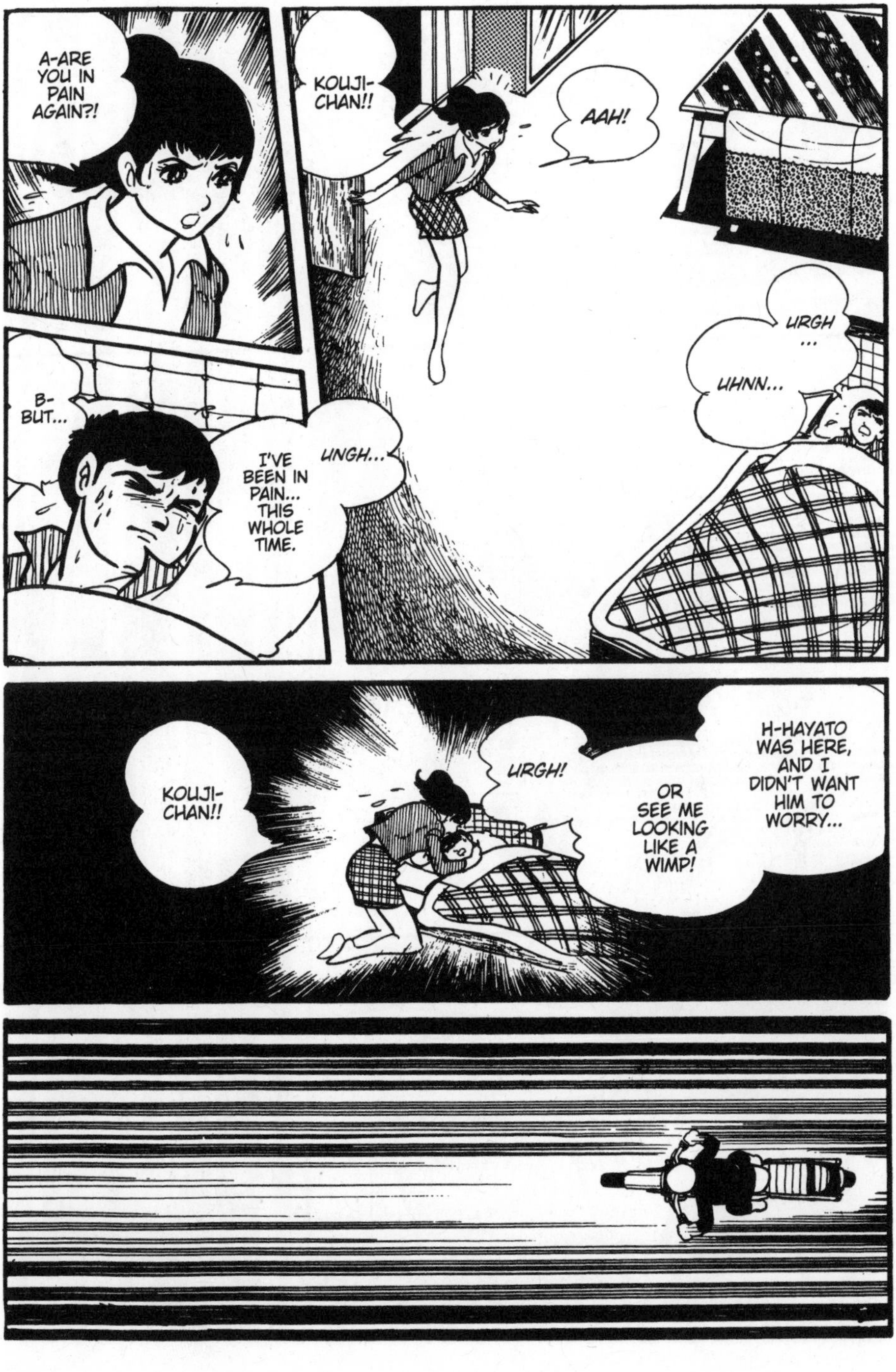
KOUJI-CHAN!!
AAH!
URGH ...
UHNN...
A-ARE YOU IN PAIN AGAIN?!
UNGH...
I'VE BEEN IN PAIN... THIS WHOLE TIME.
B-BUT...
H-HAYATO WAS HERE, AND I DIDN'T WANT HIM TO WORRY...
OR SEE ME LOOKING LIKE A WIMP!
URGH!
KOUJI-CHAN!!

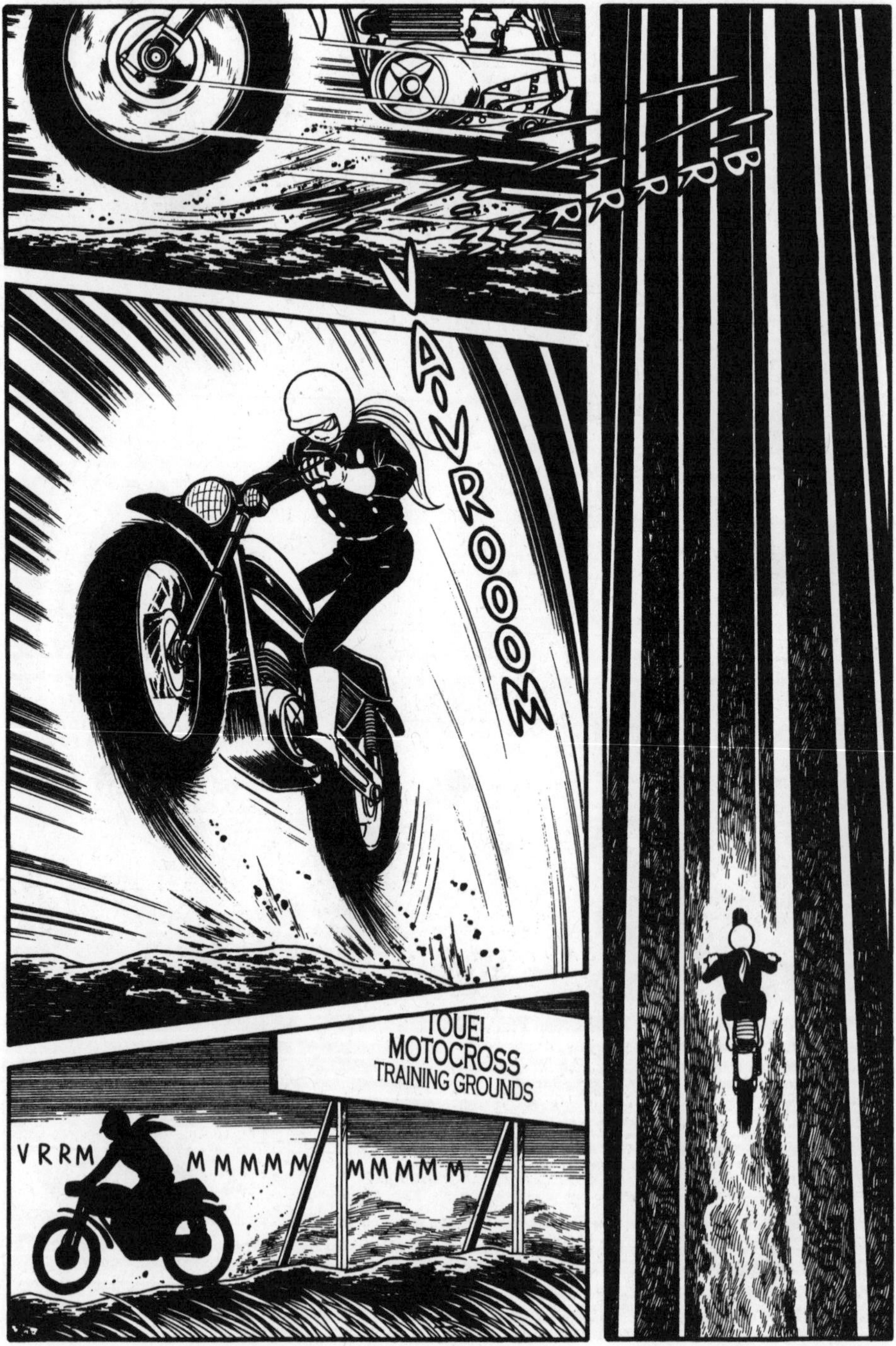
BRRRR
VAVROOOM
TOUEI
MOTOCROSS
TRAINING GROUNDS
VRRM MMMMM MMMMM

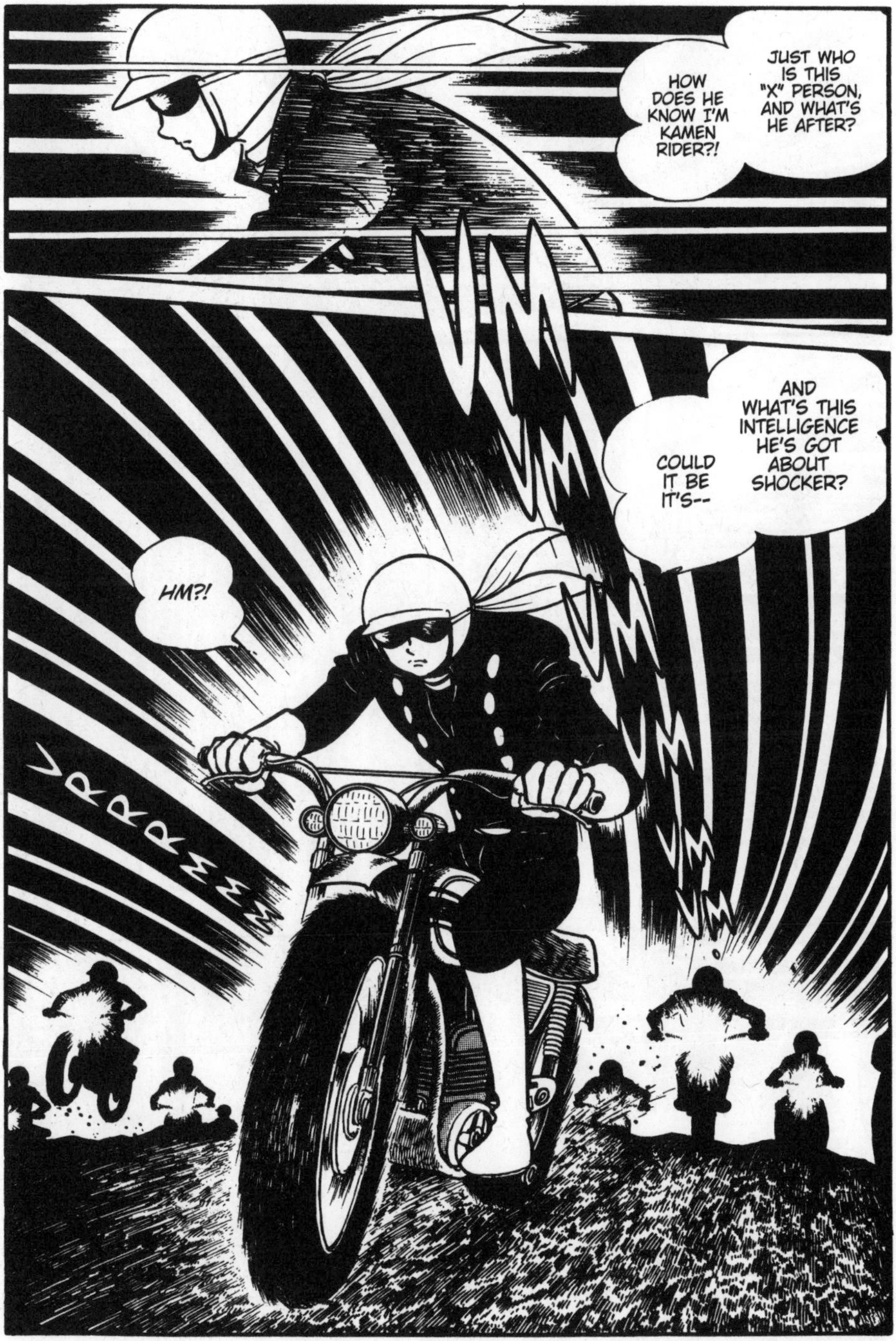
JUST WHO IS THIS "X" PERSON, AND WHAT'S HE AFTER?
HOW DOES HE KNOW I'M KAMEN RIDER?!
AND WHAT'S THIS INTELLIGENCE HE'S GOT ABOUT SHOCKER?
COULD IT BE IT'S--
HM?!
VRRRMMM

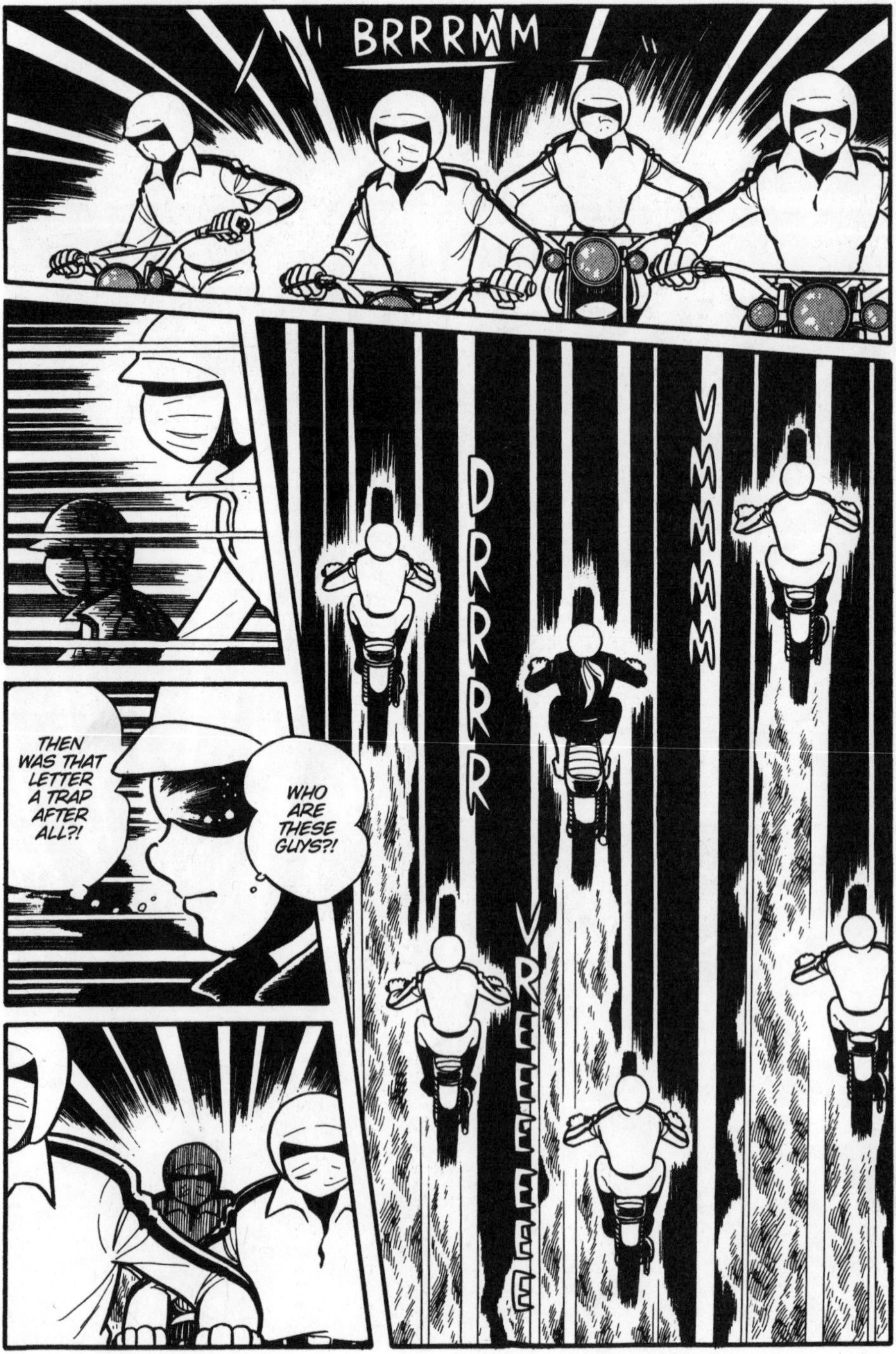
BRRRMM
VMMMMMM
DRRRRR
VREEEEEEEE
WHO ARE THESE GUYS?!
THEN WAS THAT LETTER A TRAP AFTER ALL?!

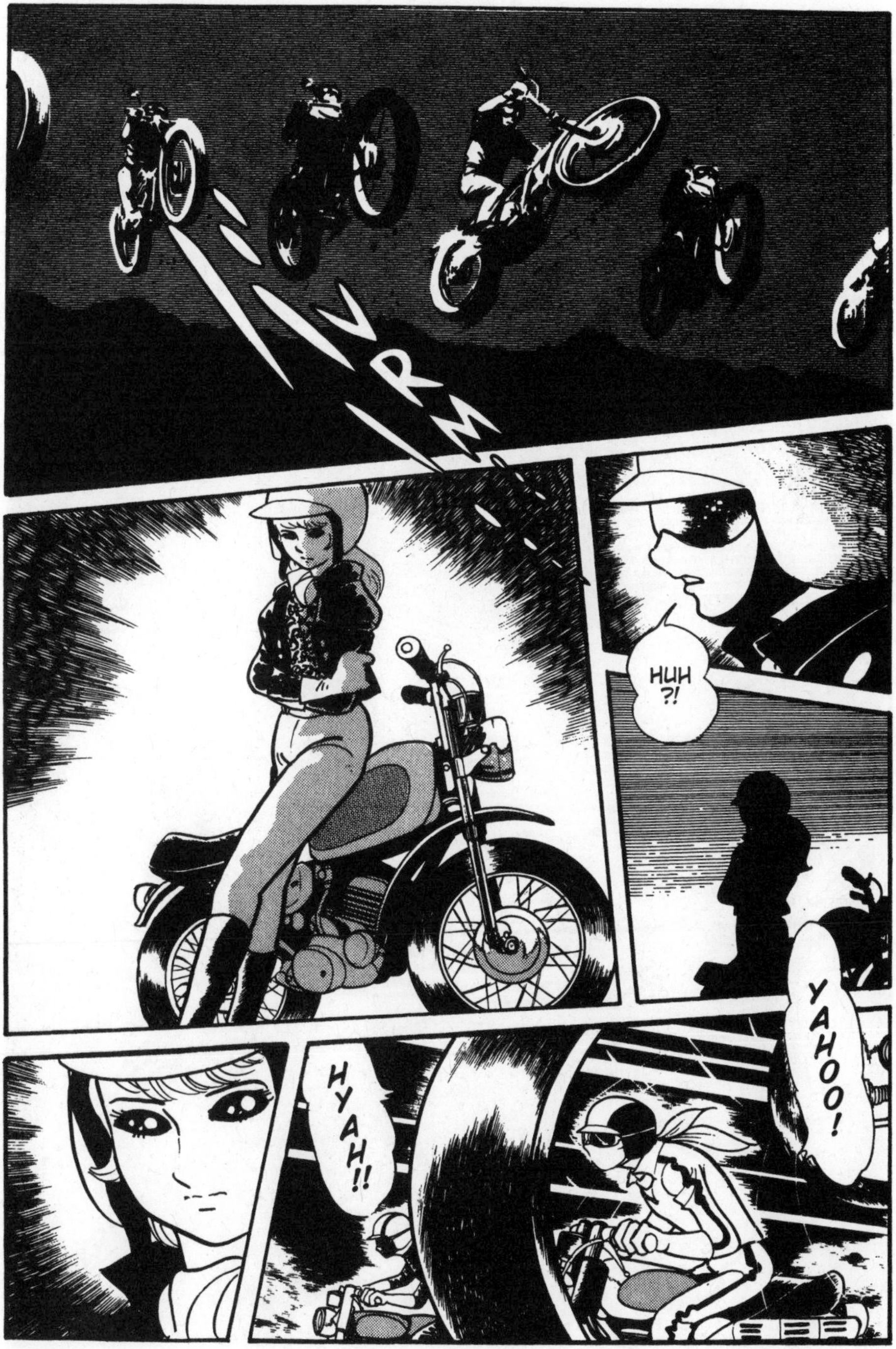
VRM
HUH?!
YAHOO!
HYAH!!

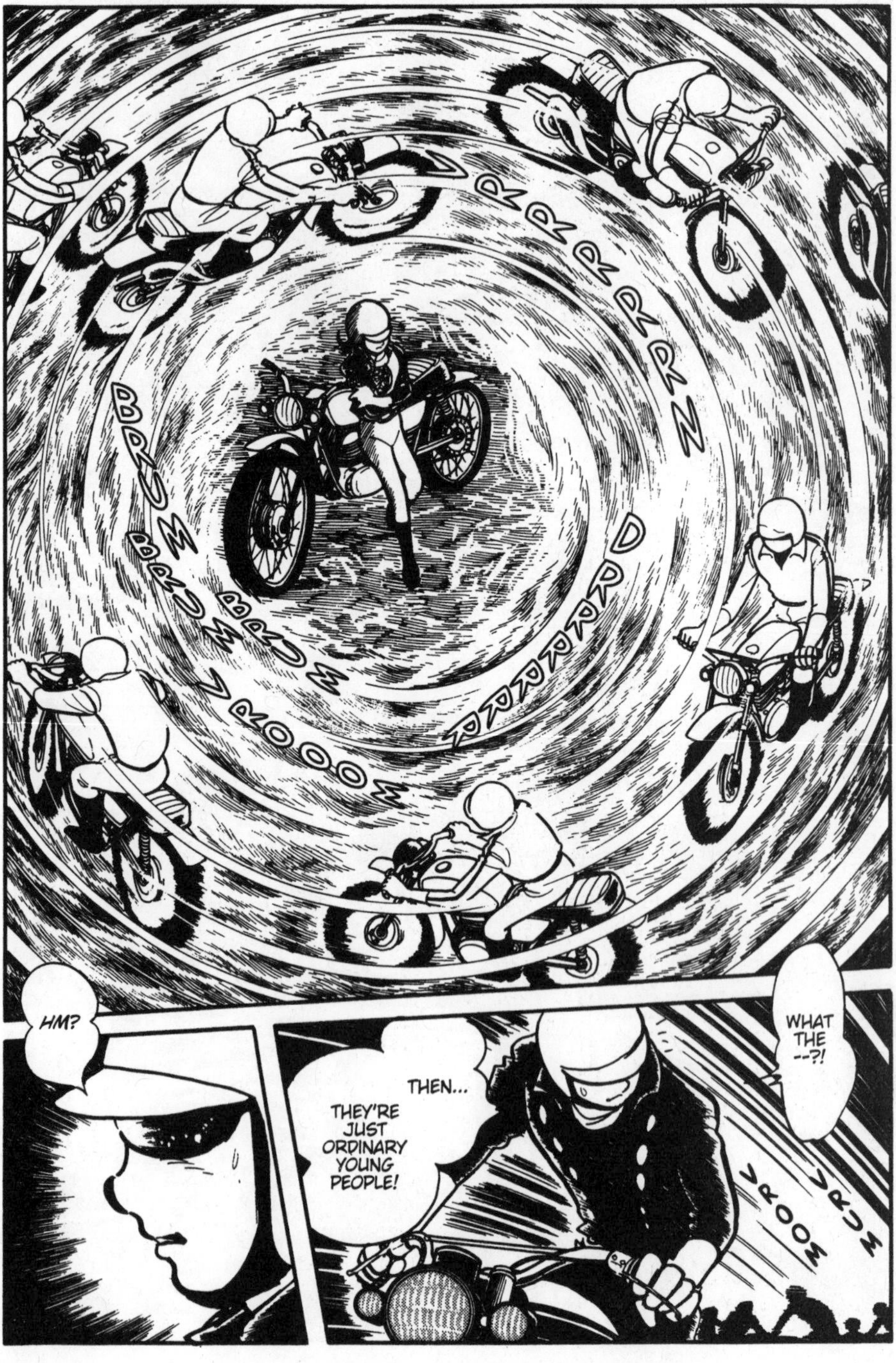
VRRRRRRN
DRRRRRRRR
BRUM
BRUM
BRUM
VROOOM
WHAT THE --?!
THEN...
THEY'RE JUST ORDINARY YOUNG PEOPLE!
VRUM
VROOM
HM?

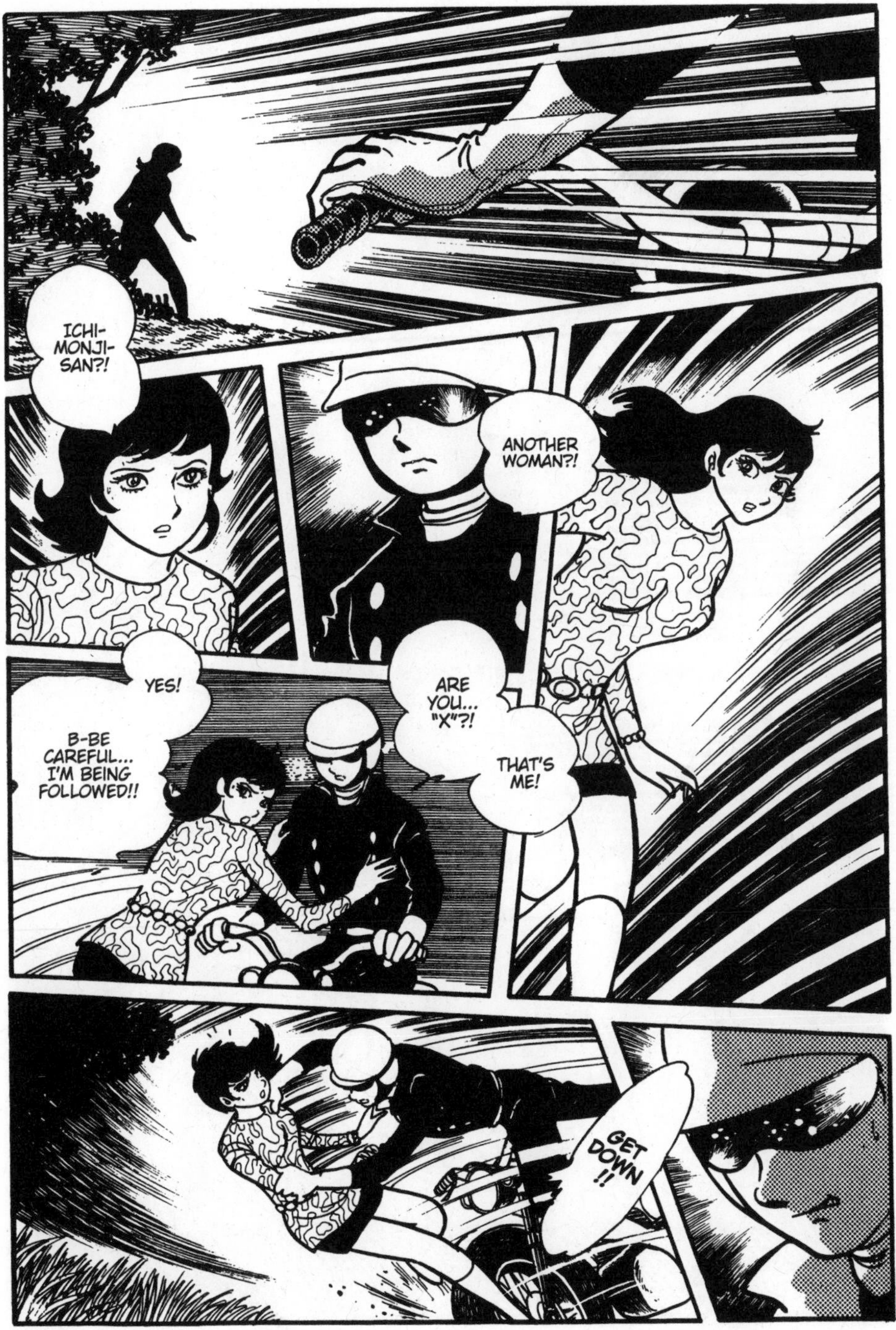

ANOTHER WOMAN?!
ICHI-MONJI-SAN?!
ARE YOU... "X"?!
THAT'S ME!
YES!
B-BE CAREFUL... I'M BEING FOLLOWED!!
GET DOWN!!

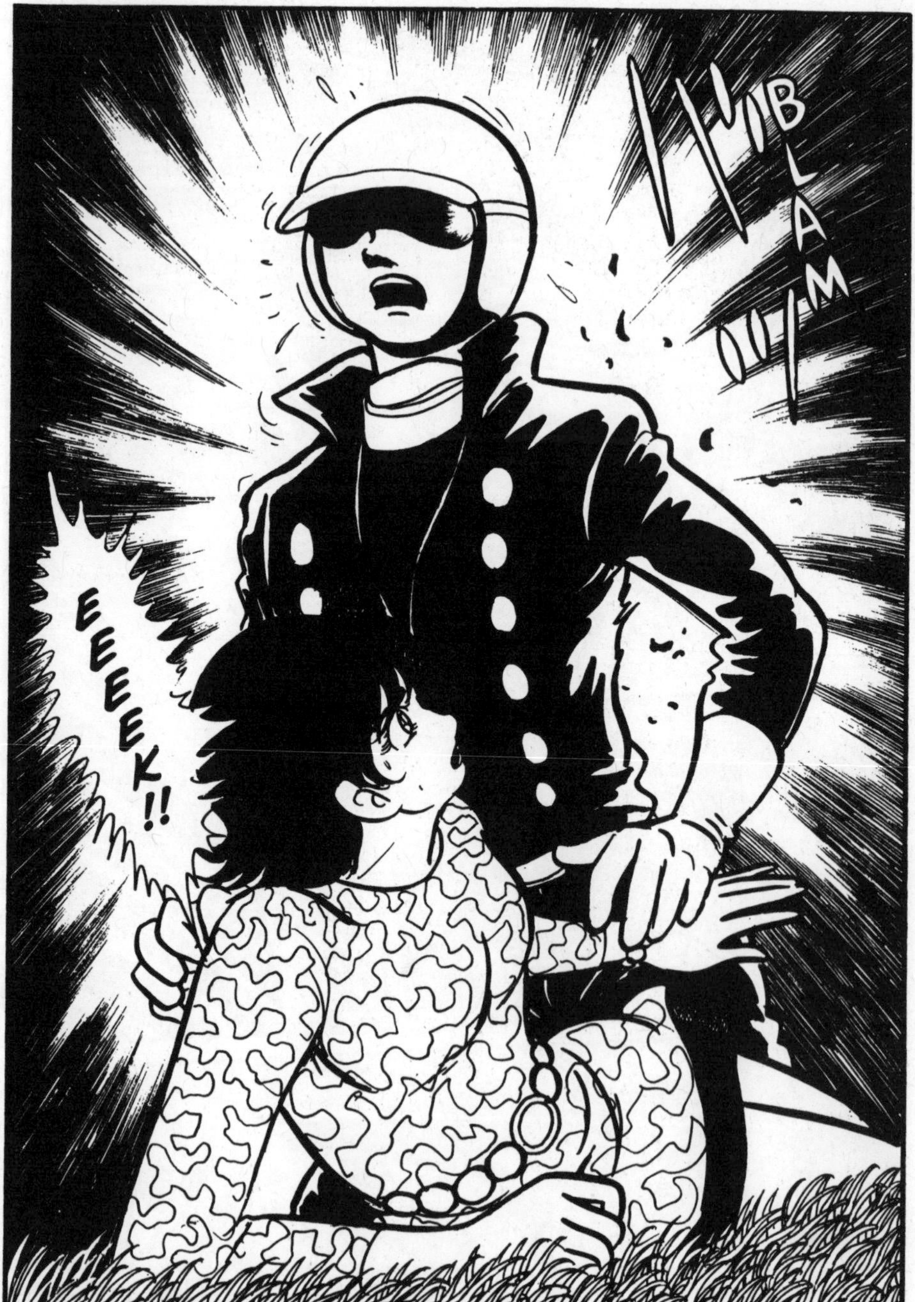
BLAM
EEEEK!!

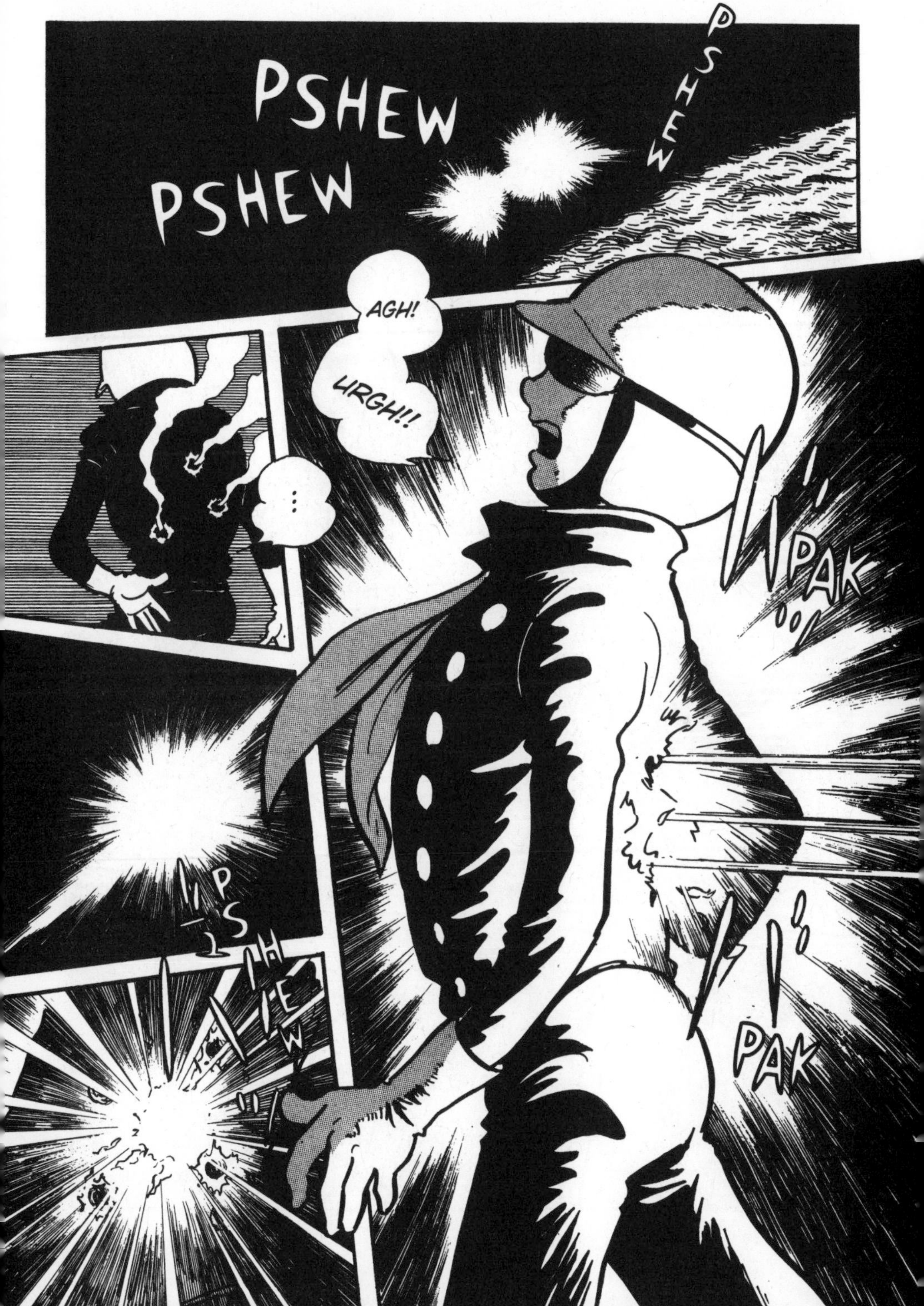
PSHEW
PSHEW
PSHEW
AGH!
URGH!!
PAK
PAK
...
PSHEW

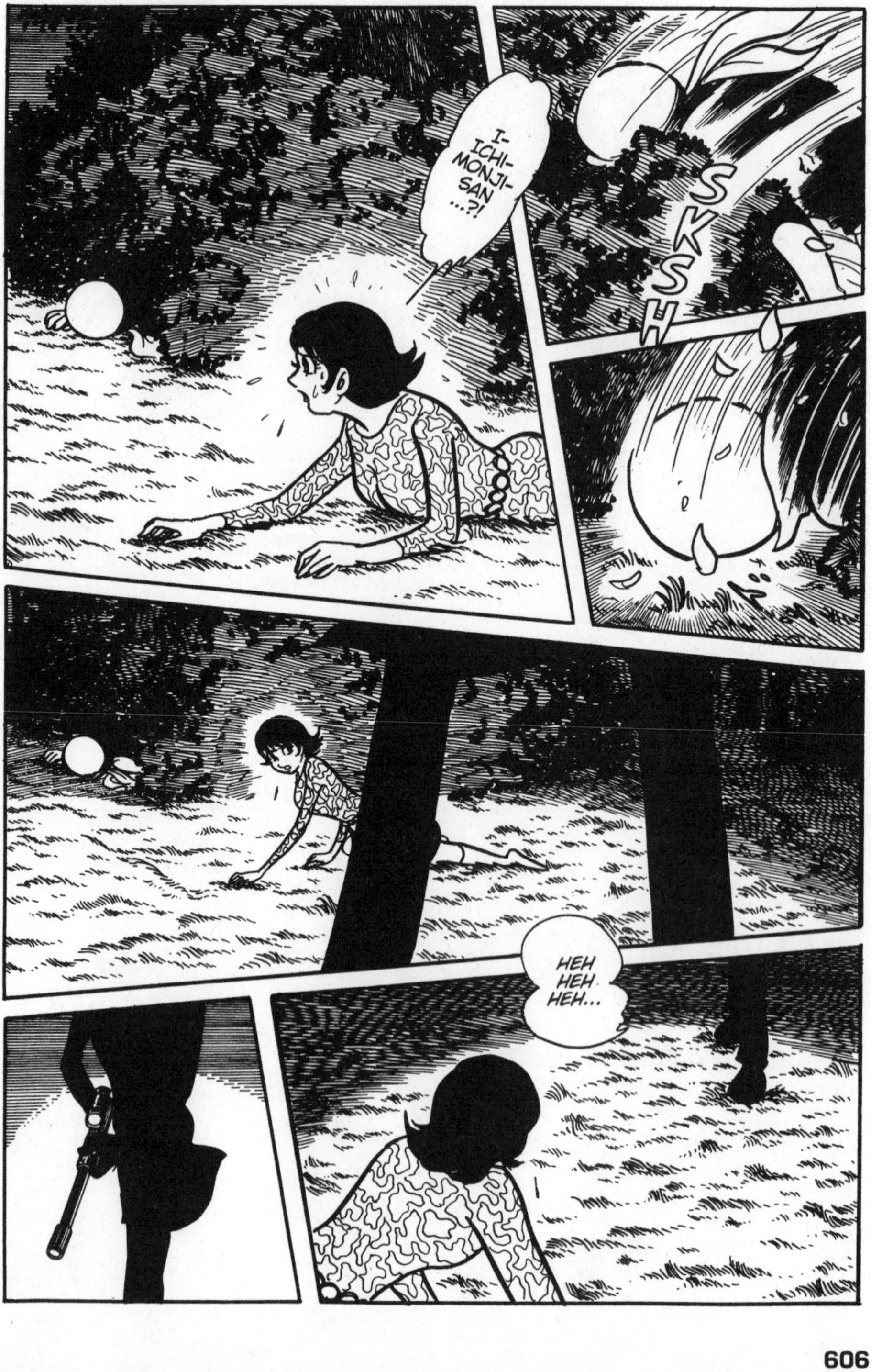
SKSH
I-ICHI-MONJI-SAN...?!
HEH HEH HEH...

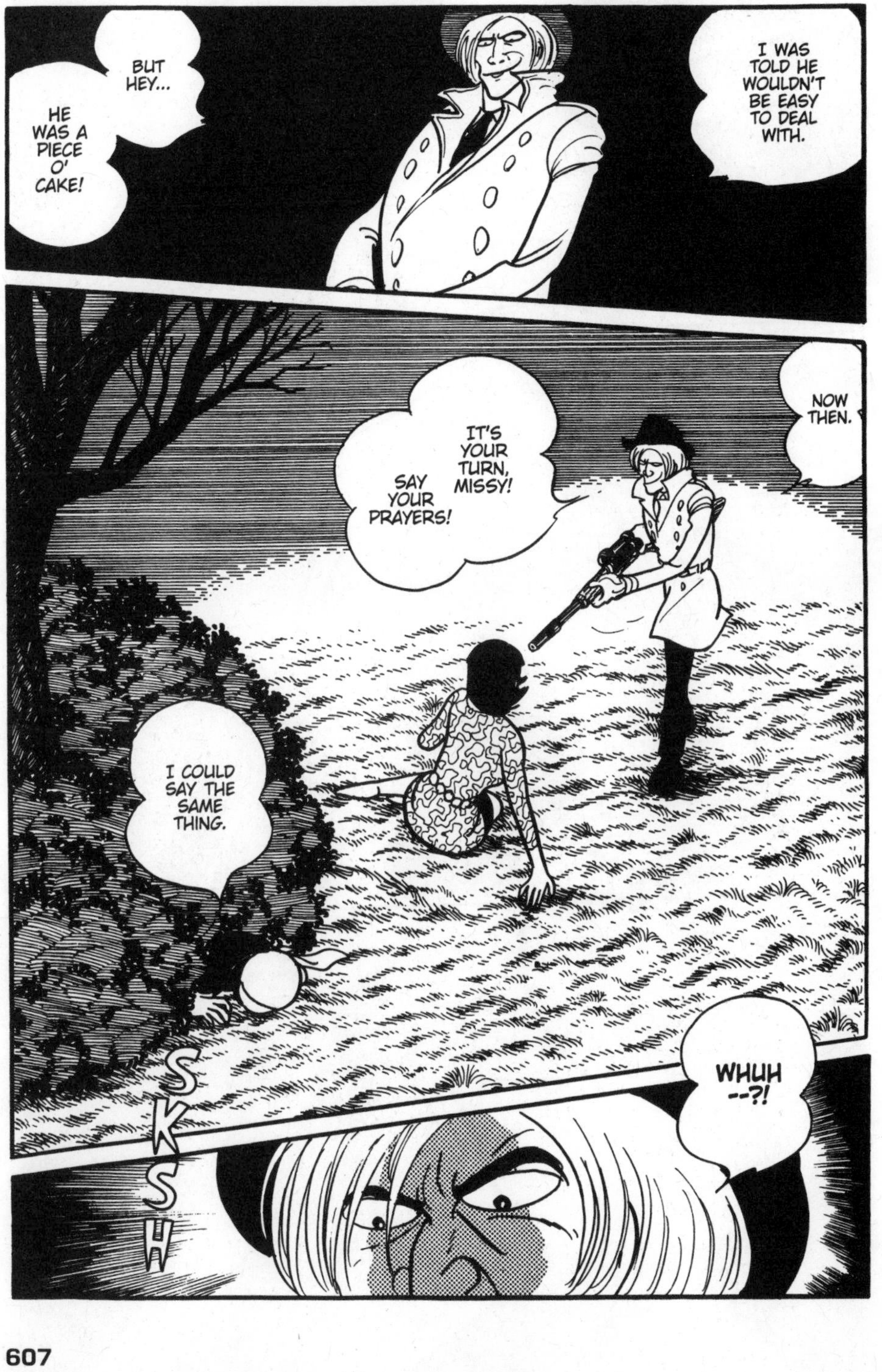
I WAS TOLD HE WOULDN'T BE EASY TO DEAL WITH.
BUT HEY...
HE WAS A PIECE O' CAKE!
NOW THEN.
IT'S YOUR TURN, MISSY!
SAY YOUR PRAYERS!
I COULD SAY THE SAME THING.
SKSH
WHUH --?!

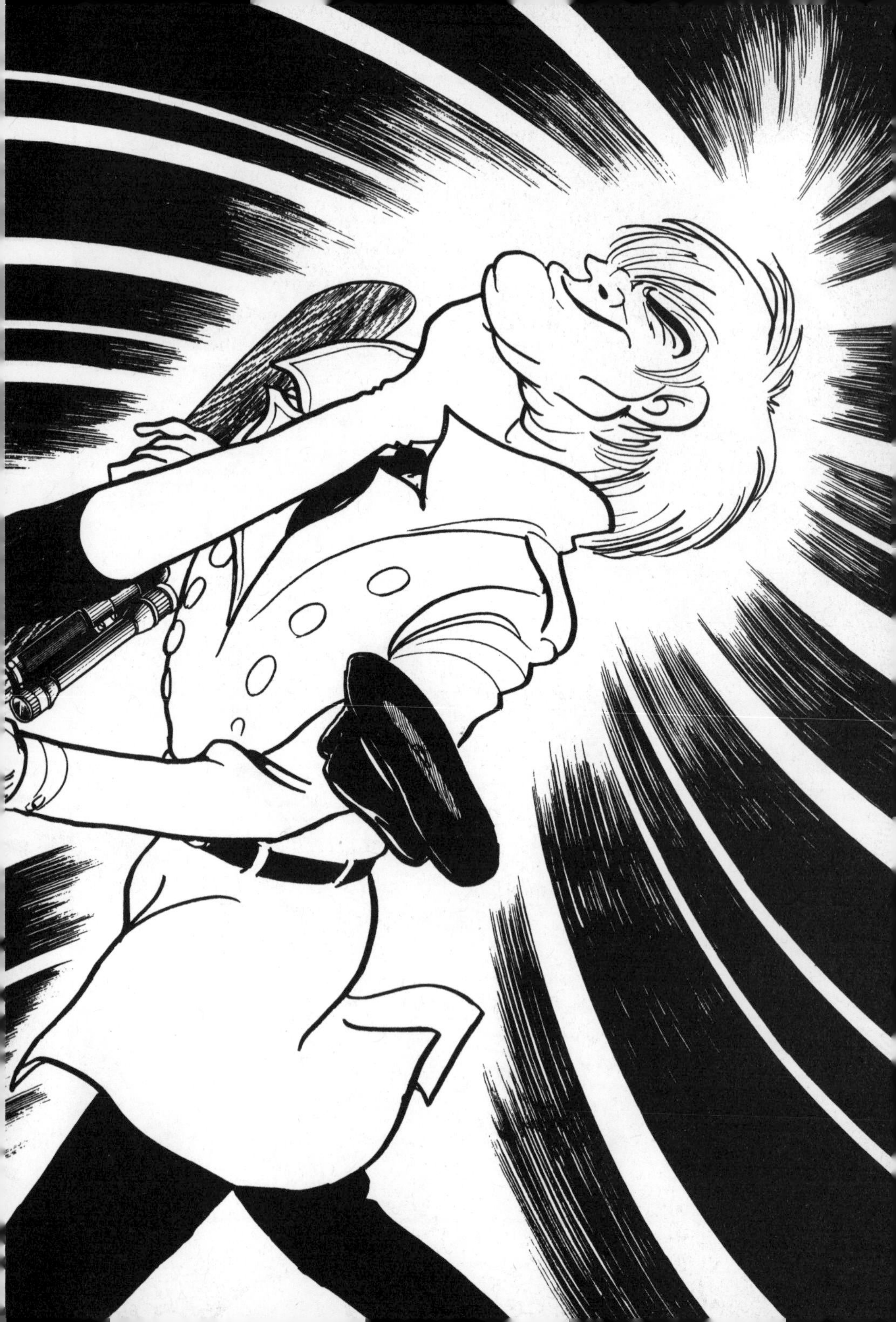

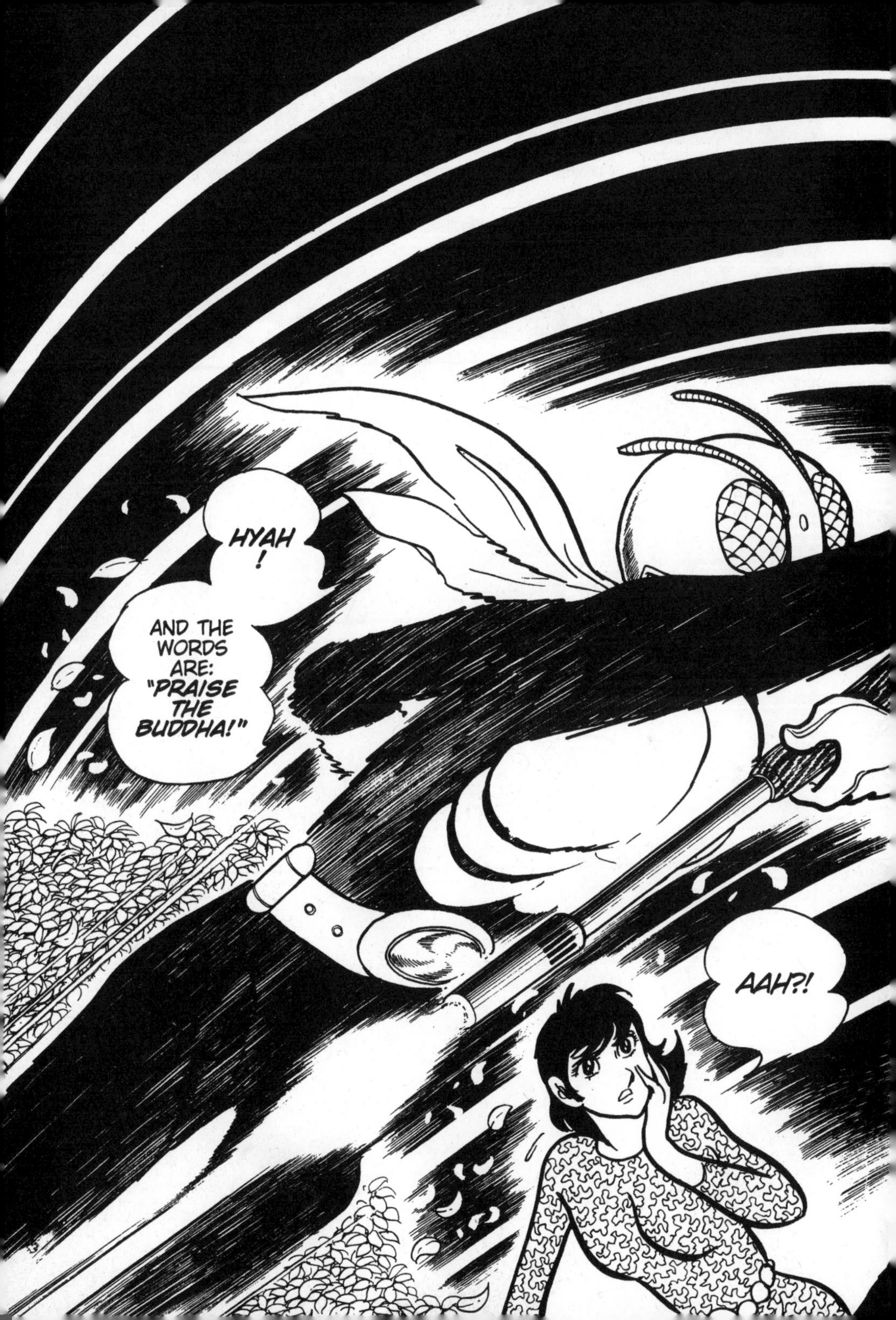
HYAH!
AND THE WORDS ARE: "PRAISE THE BUDDHA!"
AAH?!

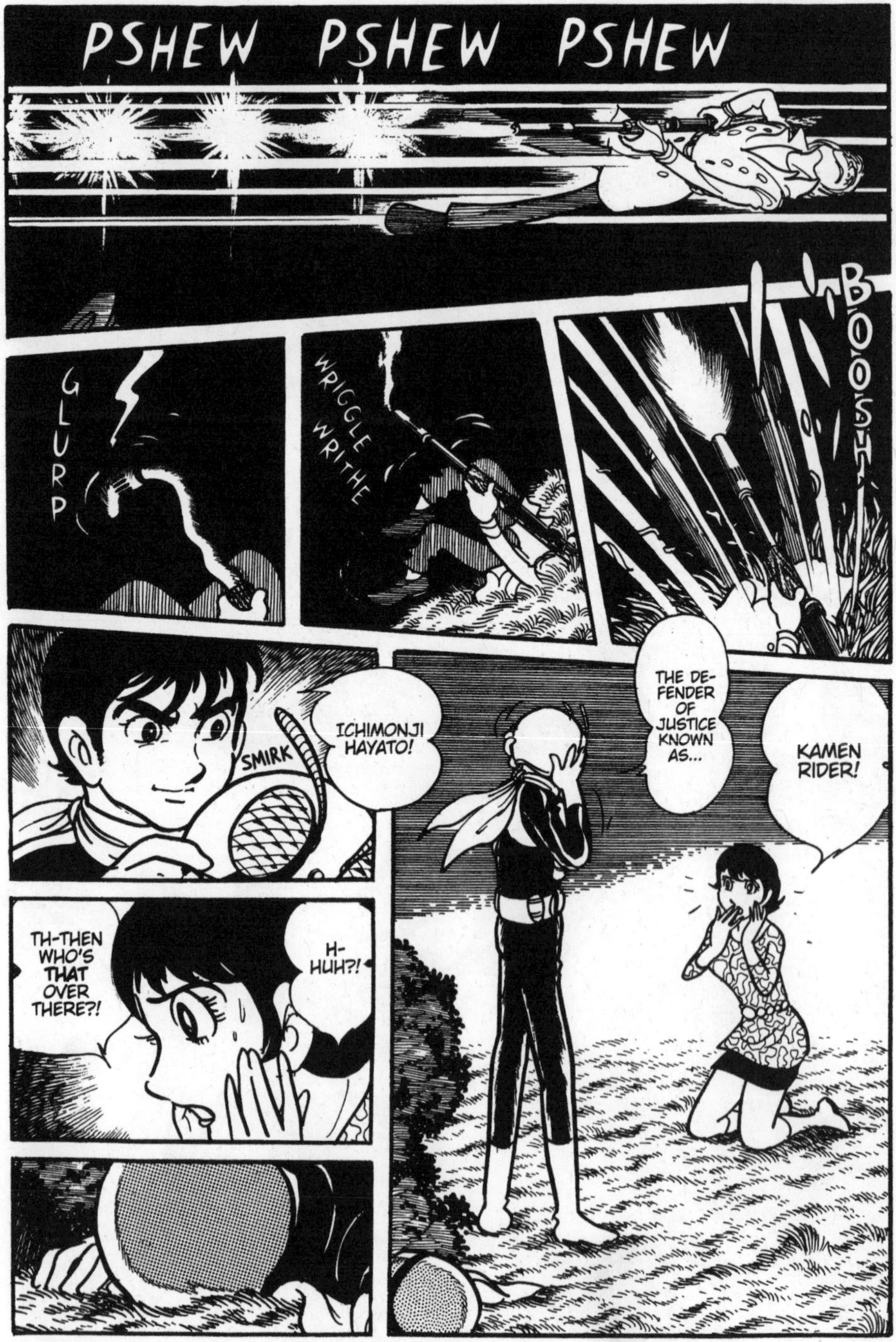
PSHEW PSHEW PSHEW
BOOOSH
WRIGGLE WRITHE
GLURP
THE DE-FENDER OF JUSTICE KNOWN AS...
KAMEN RIDER!
ICHIMONJI HAYATO!
SMIRK
H-HUH?!
TH-THEN WHO'S THAT OVER THERE?!

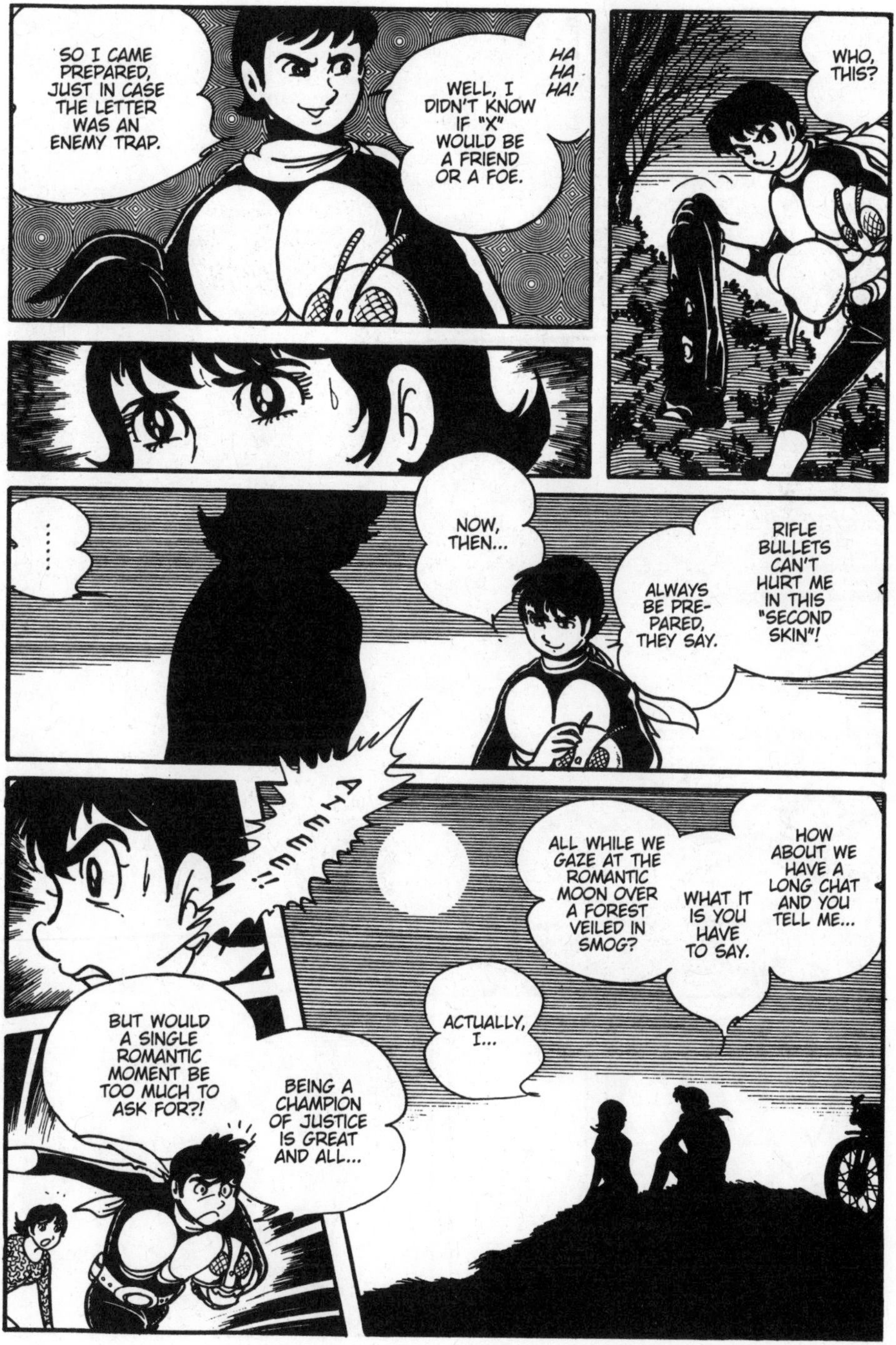
WHO, THIS?
HA HA HA!
WELL, I DIDN'T KNOW IF "X" WOULD BE A FRIEND OR A FOE.
SO I CAME PREPARED, JUST IN CASE THE LETTER WAS AN ENEMY TRAP.
RIFLE BULLETS CAN'T HURT ME IN THIS "SECOND SKIN"!
ALWAYS BE PRE-PARED, THEY SAY.
NOW, THEN...
......
HOW ABOUT WE HAVE A LONG CHAT AND YOU TELL ME...
WHAT IT IS YOU HAVE TO SAY.
ALL WHILE WE GAZE AT THE ROMANTIC MOON OVER A FOREST VEILED IN SMOG?
ACTUALLY, I...
AIEEE!!
BEING A CHAMPION OF JUSTICE IS GREAT AND ALL...
BUT WOULD A SINGLE ROMANTIC MOMENT BE TOO MUCH TO ASK FOR?!

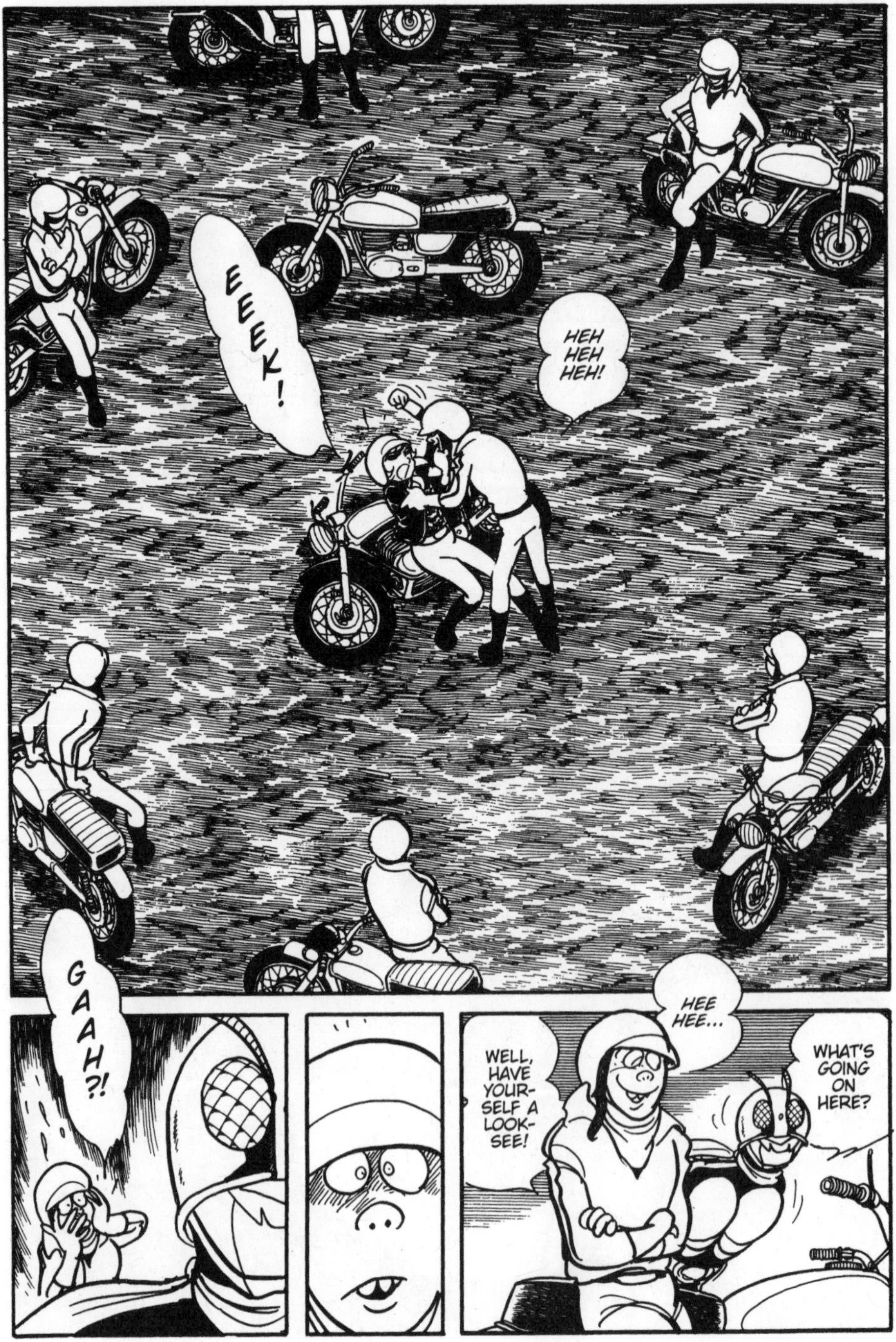
EEEK!
HEH HEH HEH!
WHAT'S GOING ON HERE?
HEE HEE...
WELL, HAVE YOURSELF A LOOK-SEE!
GAAH?!

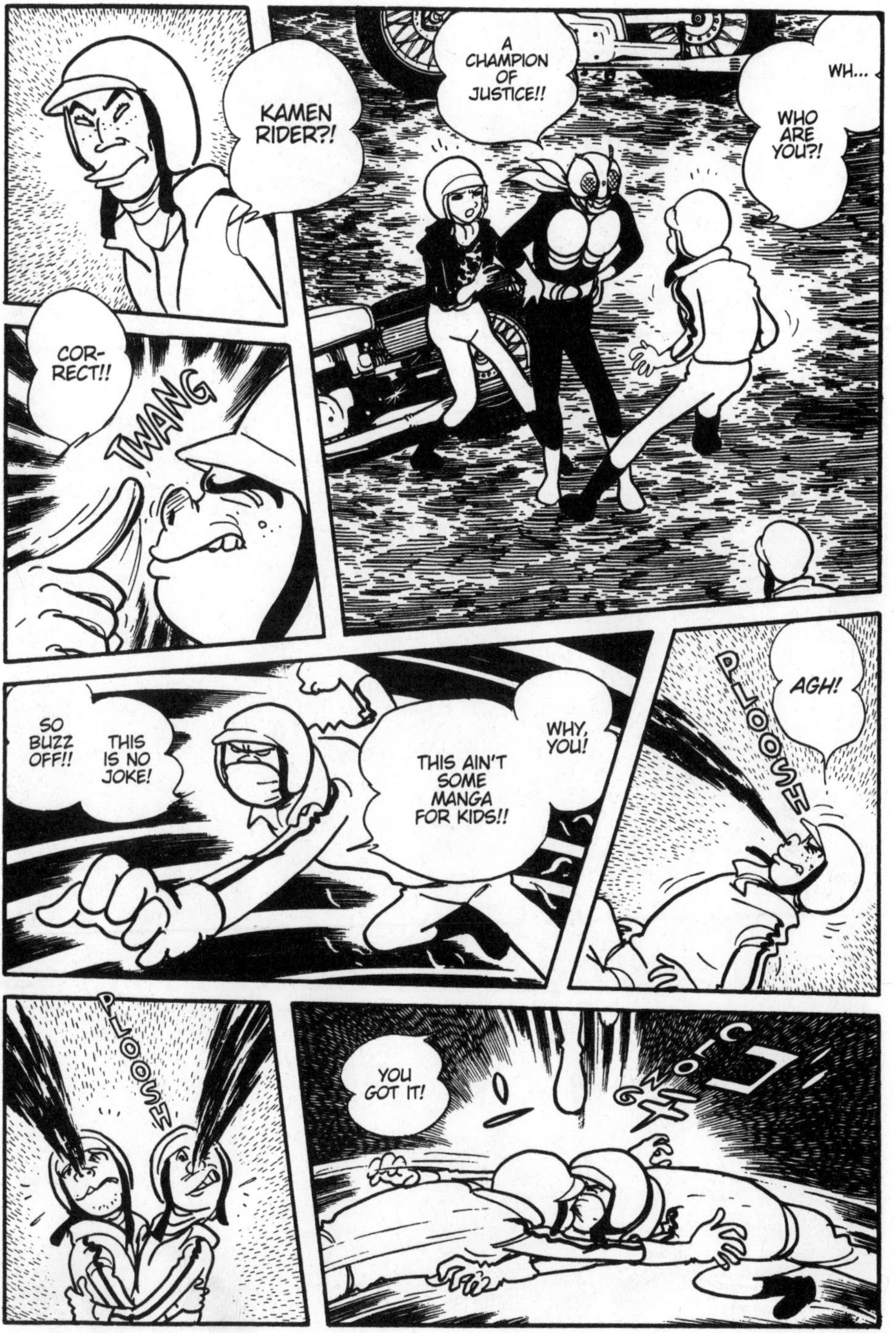
WH... WHO ARE YOU?!
A CHAMPION OF JUSTICE!!
KAMEN RIDER?!
COR-RECT!!
TWANG
AGH!
PLOOSH
WHY, YOU!
THIS AIN'T SOME MANGA FOR KIDS!!
THIS IS NO JOKE!
SO BUZZ OFF!!
CONG
YOU GOT IT!
PLOOSH

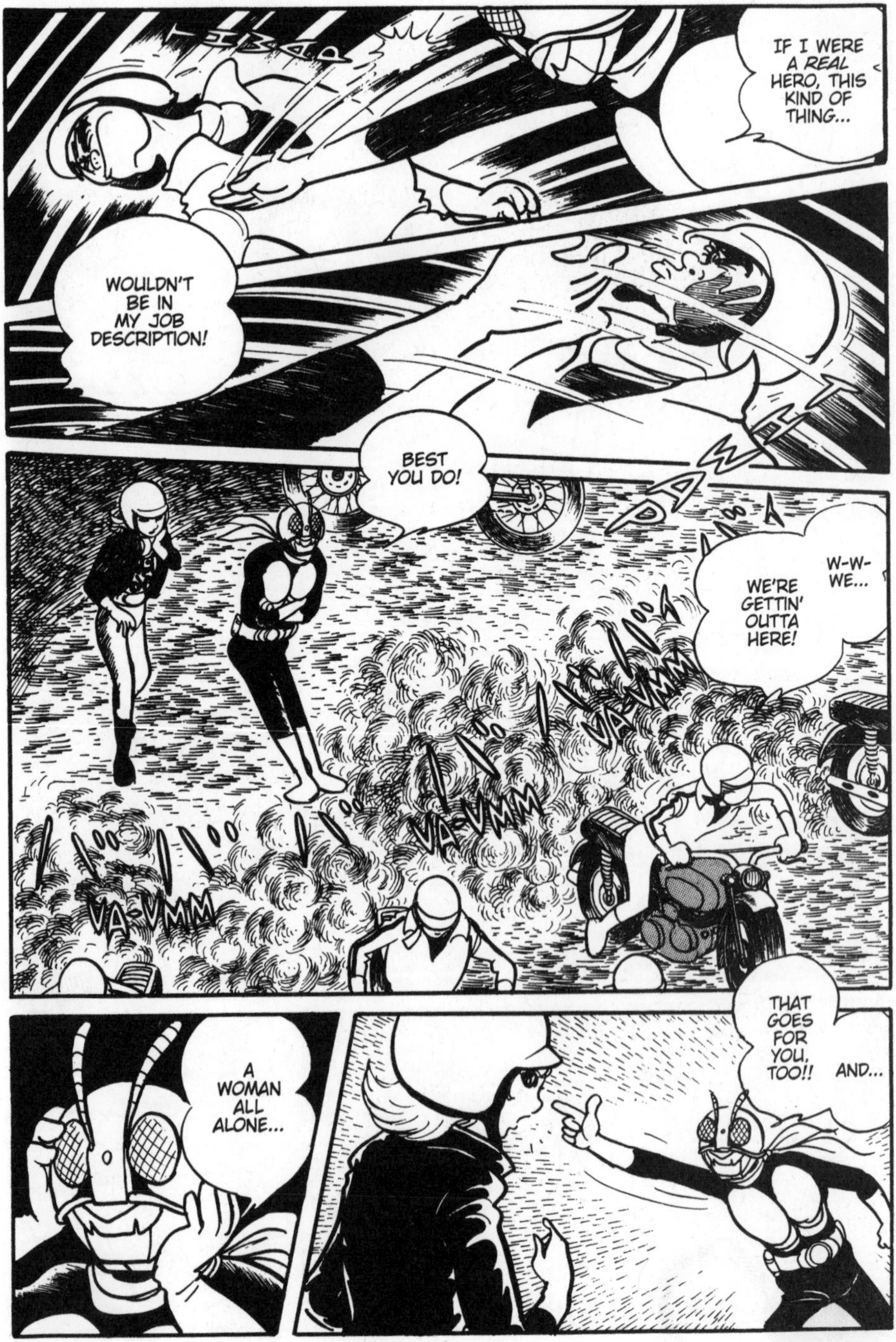
IF I WERE A *REAL* HERO, THIS KIND OF THING...
WOULDN'T BE IN MY JOB DESCRIPTION!
THWAP
BEST YOU DO!
W-W-WE...
WE'RE GETTIN' OUTTA HERE!
VA-VMM
VA-VMM
VA-VMM
THAT GOES FOR YOU, TOO!!
AND...
A WOMAN ALL ALONE...

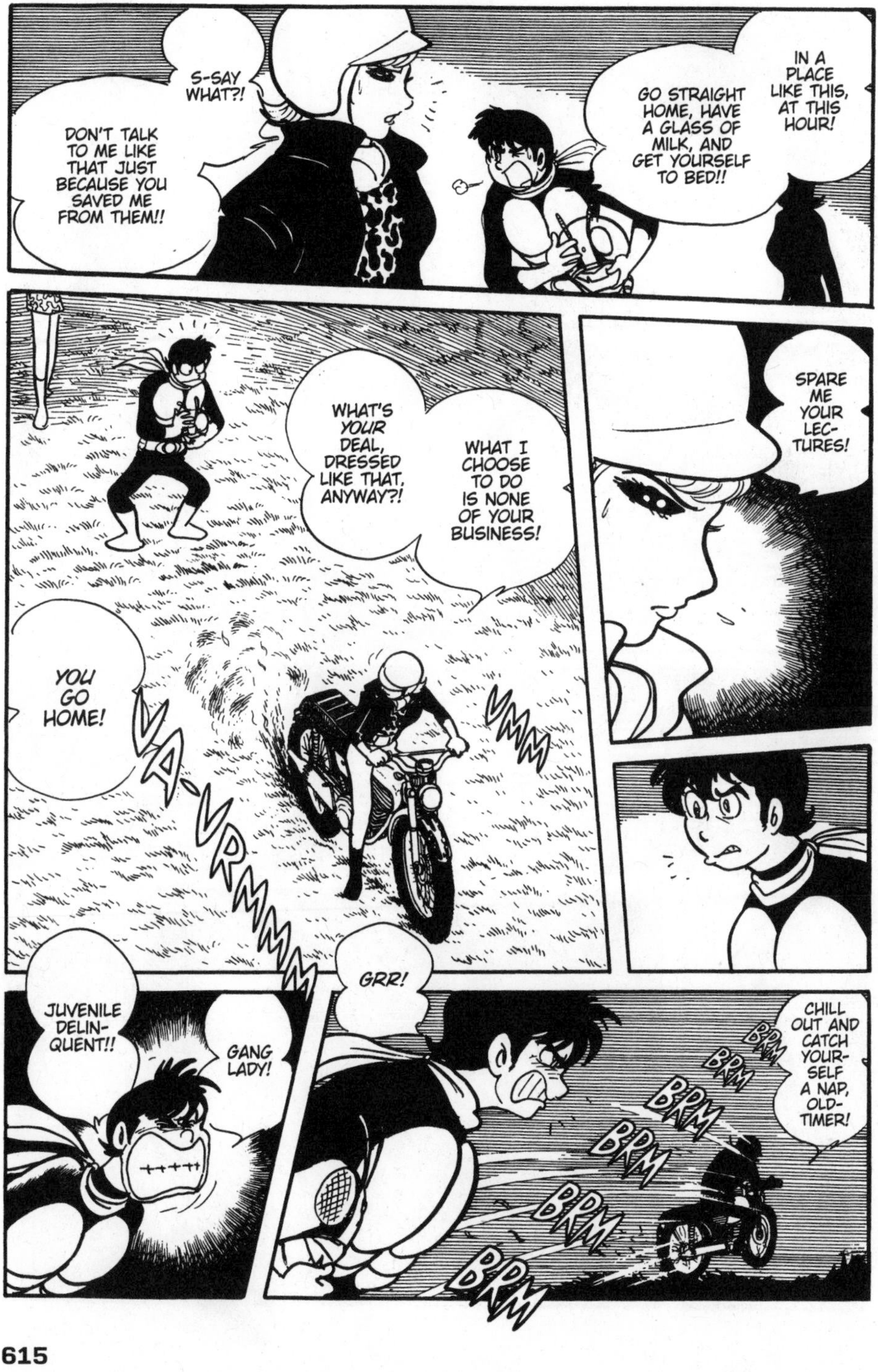
IN A PLACE LIKE THIS, AT THIS HOUR!
GO STRAIGHT HOME, HAVE A GLASS OF MILK, AND GET YOURSELF TO BED!!
S-SAY WHAT?!
DON'T TALK TO ME LIKE THAT JUST BECAUSE YOU SAVED ME FROM THEM!!
SPARE ME YOUR LEC-TURES!
WHAT I CHOOSE TO DO IS NONE OF YOUR BUSINESS!
WHAT'S *YOUR* DEAL, DRESSED LIKE THAT, ANYWAY?!
VMMM
VA-VRMMMMM
YOU GO HOME!
CHILL OUT AND CATCH YOURSELF A NAP, OLD-TIMER!
BRM
BRM
BRM
BRM
BRM
BRM
GRR!
GANG LADY!
JUVENILE DELIN-QUENT!!

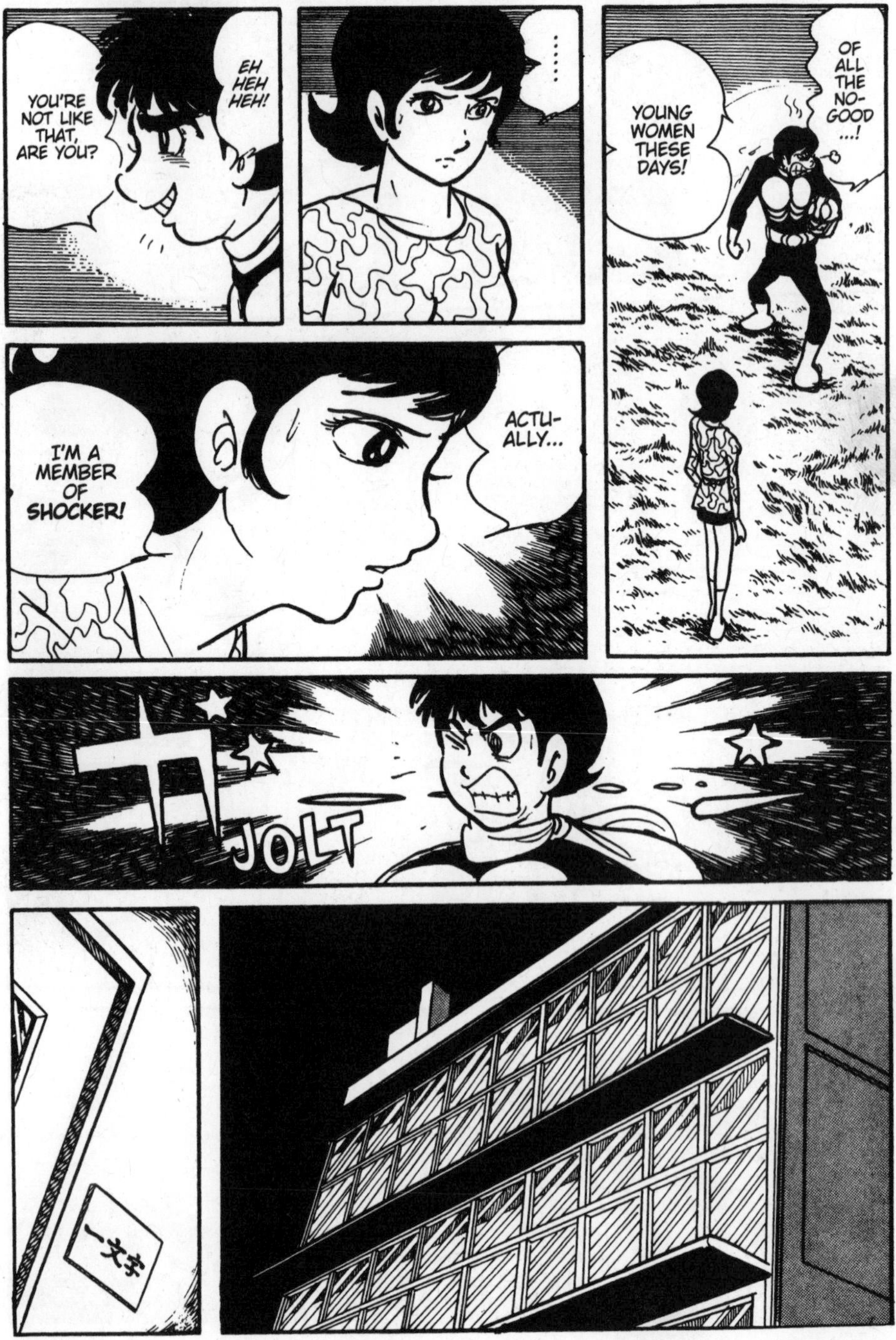
OF ALL THE NO-GOOD...!
YOUNG WOMEN THESE DAYS!
......
EH HEH HEH!
YOU'RE NOT LIKE THAT, ARE YOU?
ACTU-ALLY...
I'M A MEMBER OF SHOCKER!
JOLT
一文字

Sign: Ichimonji.

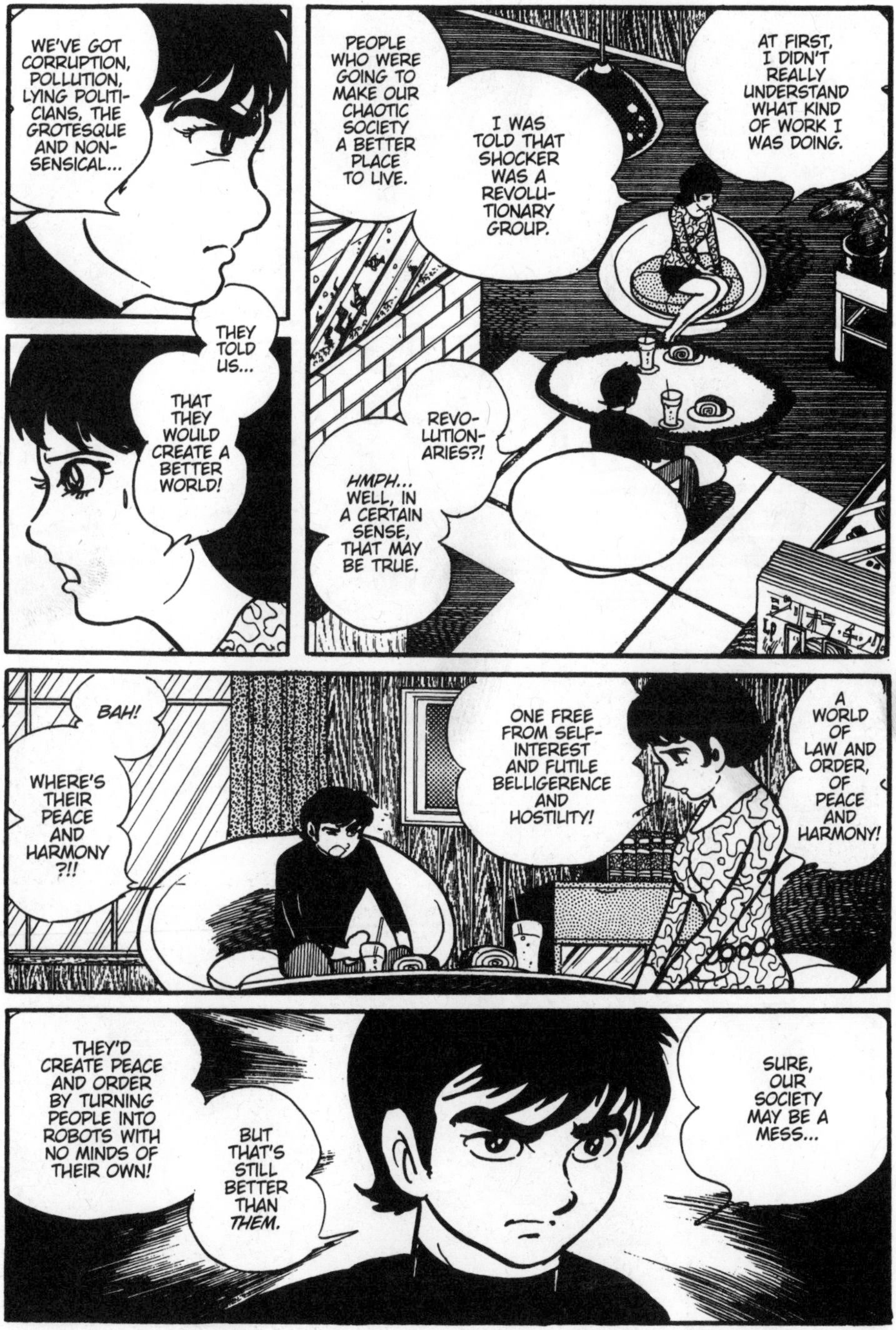
AT FIRST, I DIDN'T REALLY UNDERSTAND WHAT KIND OF WORK I WAS DOING.
I WAS TOLD THAT SHOCKER WAS A REVOLUTIONARY GROUP.
PEOPLE WHO WERE GOING TO MAKE OUR CHAOTIC SOCIETY A BETTER PLACE TO LIVE.
REVOLUTIONARIES?!
HMPH... WELL, IN A CERTAIN SENSE, THAT MAY BE TRUE.
WE'VE GOT CORRUPTION, POLLUTION, LYING POLITICIANS, THE GROTESQUE AND NONSENSICAL...
THEY TOLD US...
THAT THEY WOULD CREATE A BETTER WORLD!
A WORLD OF LAW AND ORDER, OF PEACE AND HARMONY!
ONE FREE FROM SELF-INTEREST AND FUTILE BELLIGERENCE AND HOSTILITY!
BAH!
WHERE'S THEIR PEACE AND HARMONY?!!
SURE, OUR SOCIETY MAY BE A MESS...
BUT THAT'S STILL BETTER THAN *THEM.*
THEY'D CREATE PEACE AND ORDER BY TURNING PEOPLE INTO ROBOTS WITH NO MINDS OF THEIR OWN!

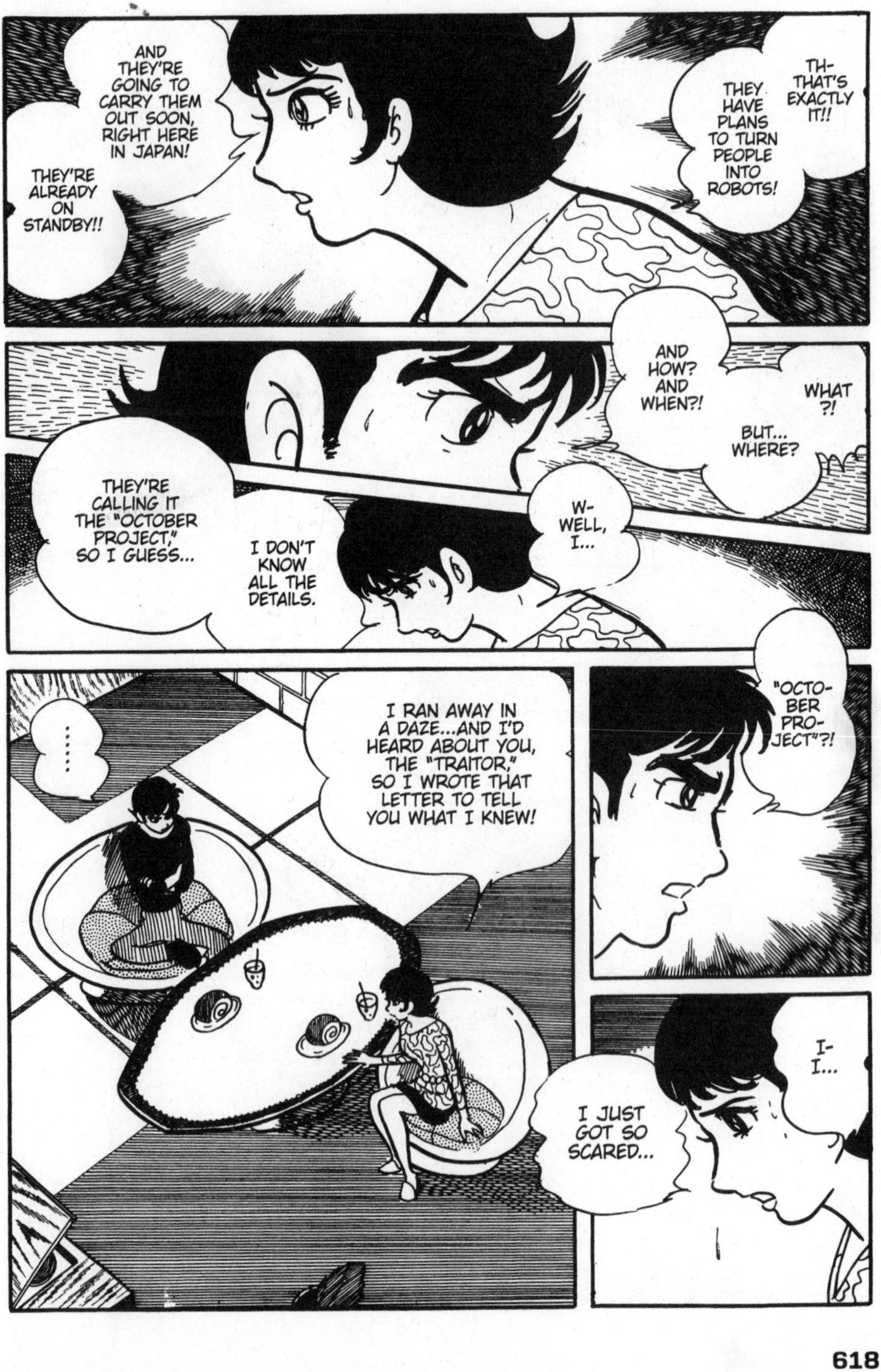
TH-THAT'S EXACTLY IT!!
THEY HAVE PLANS TO TURN PEOPLE INTO ROBOTS!
AND THEY'RE GOING TO CARRY THEM OUT SOON, RIGHT HERE IN JAPAN!
THEY'RE ALREADY ON STANDBY!!
WHAT?!
BUT... WHERE?
AND HOW? AND WHEN?!
W-WELL, I...
I DON'T KNOW ALL THE DETAILS.
THEY'RE CALLING IT THE "OCTOBER PROJECT," SO I GUESS...
"OCTOBER PROJECT"?!
I-I...
I JUST GOT SO SCARED...
I RAN AWAY IN A DAZE...AND I'D HEARD ABOUT YOU, THE "TRAITOR," SO I WROTE THAT LETTER TO TELL YOU WHAT I KNEW!
......

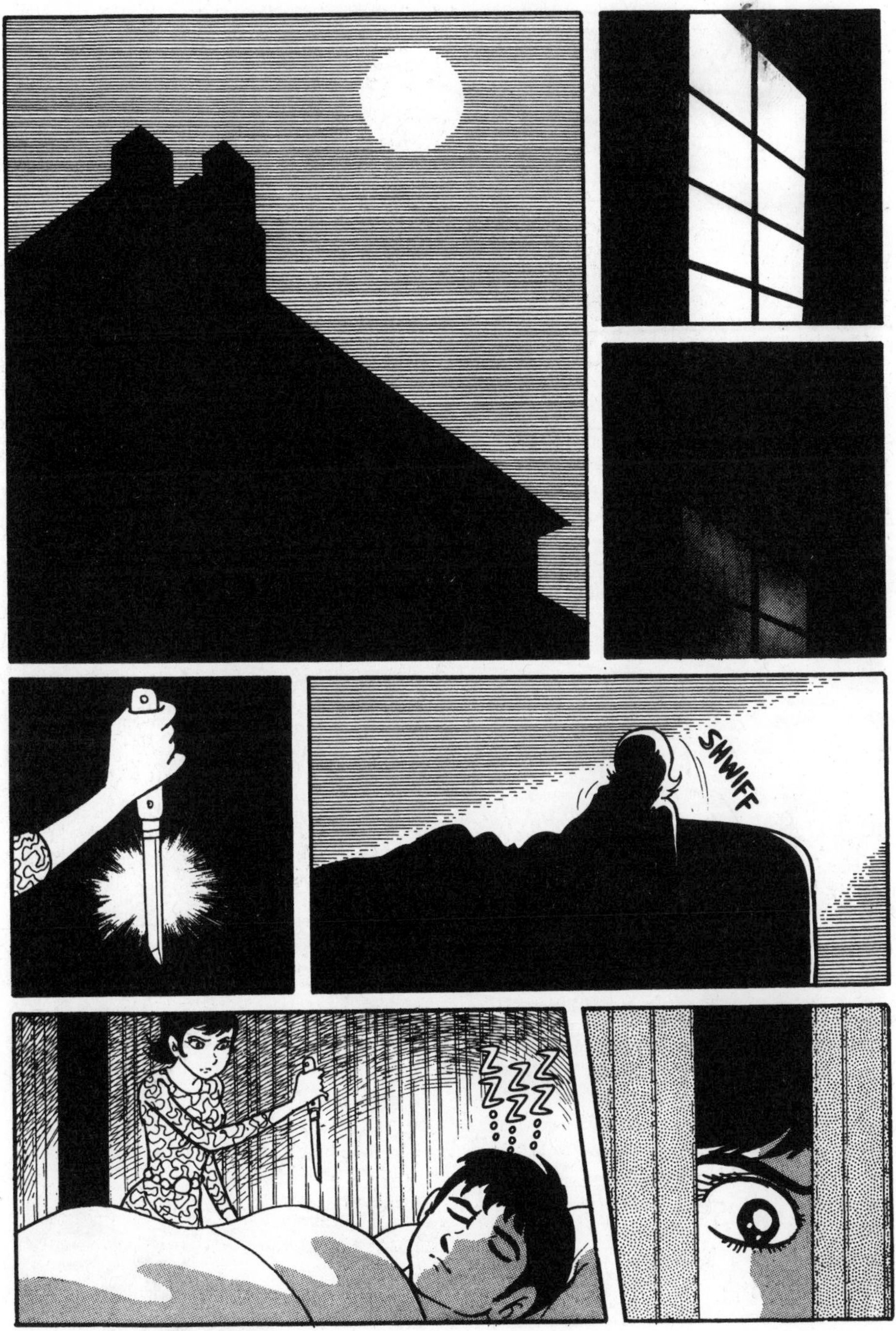
SHWIFF
ZZZ
ZZZ

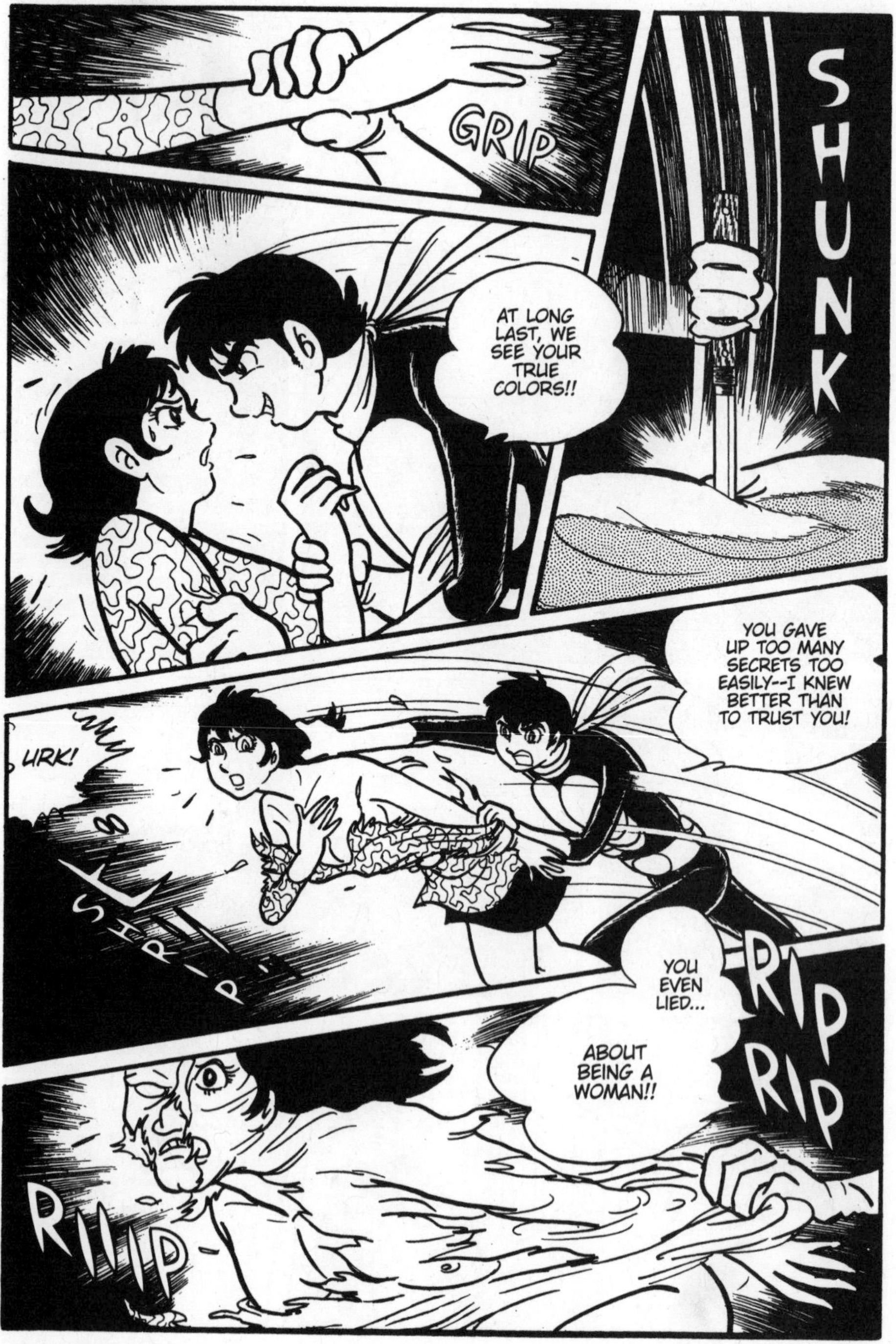
SHUNK
GRIP
AT LONG LAST, WE SEE YOUR TRUE COLORS!!
YOU GAVE UP TOO MANY SECRETS TOO EASILY--I KNEW BETTER THAN TO TRUST YOU!
URK!
SIRIP
RIP RIP
YOU EVEN LIED...
ABOUT BEING A WOMAN!!
RIIIP

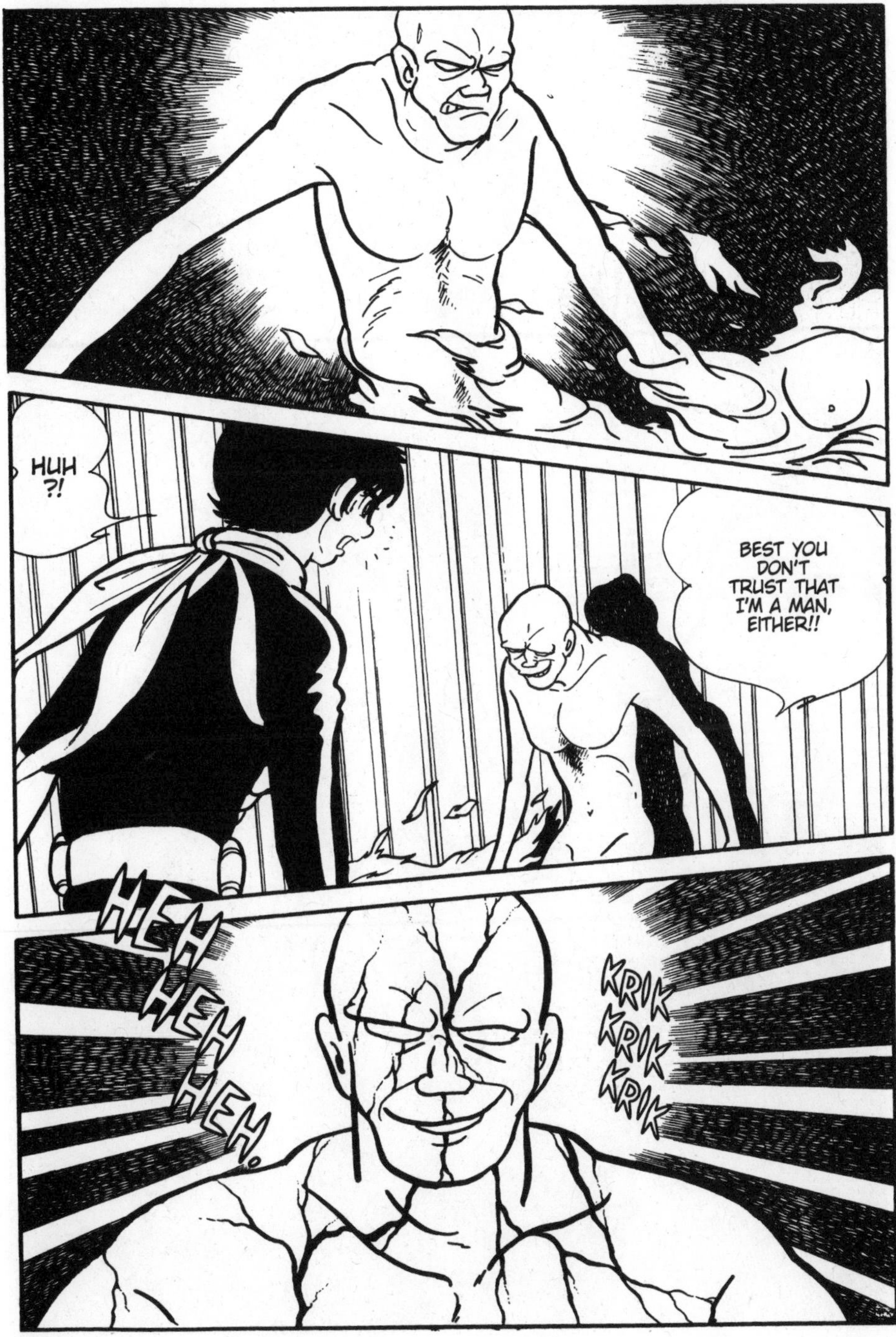
BEST YOU DON'T TRUST THAT I'M A MAN, EITHER!!
HUH ?!
KRIK KRIK KRIK
HEH HEH HEH HEH.

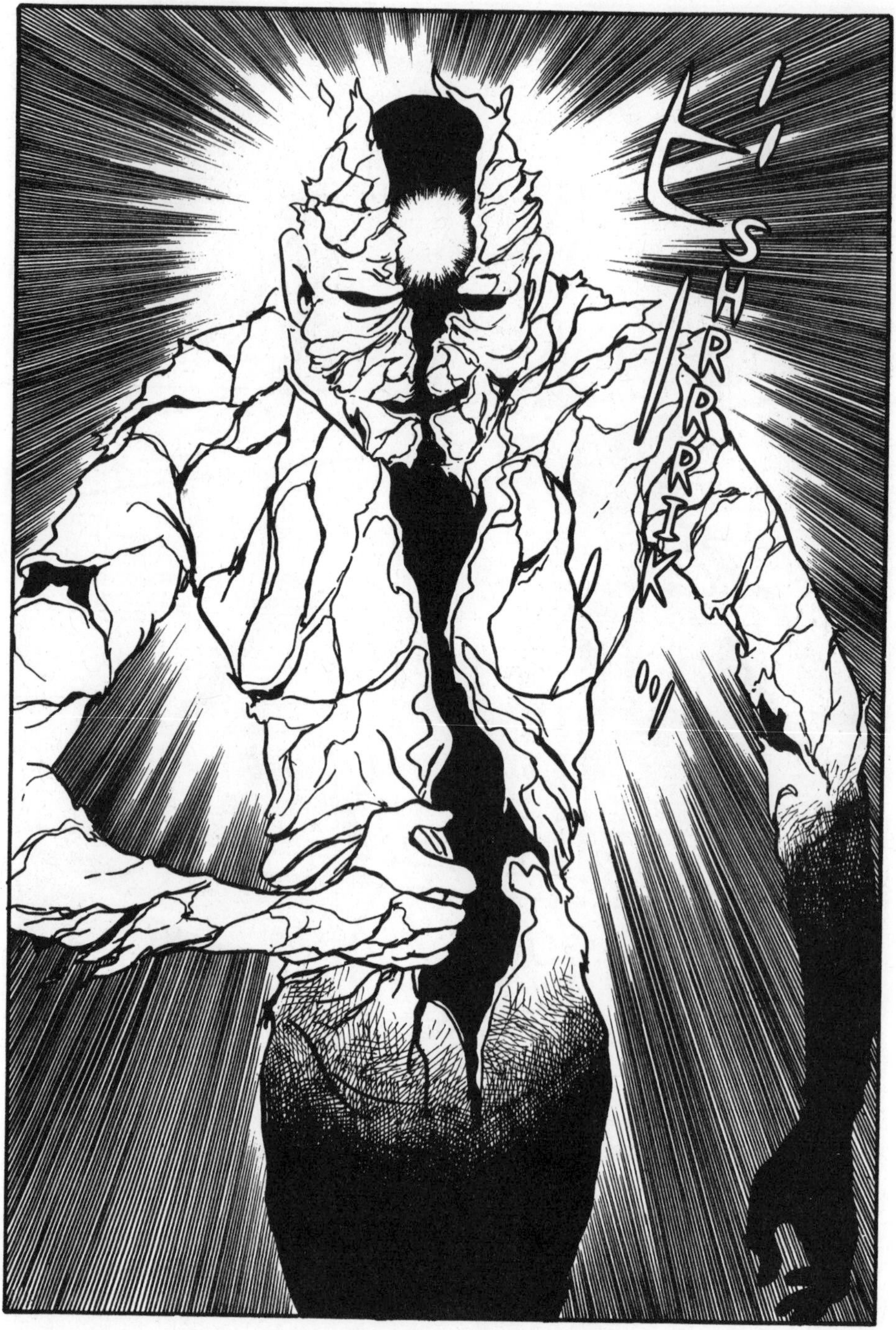
SHRRRRIK

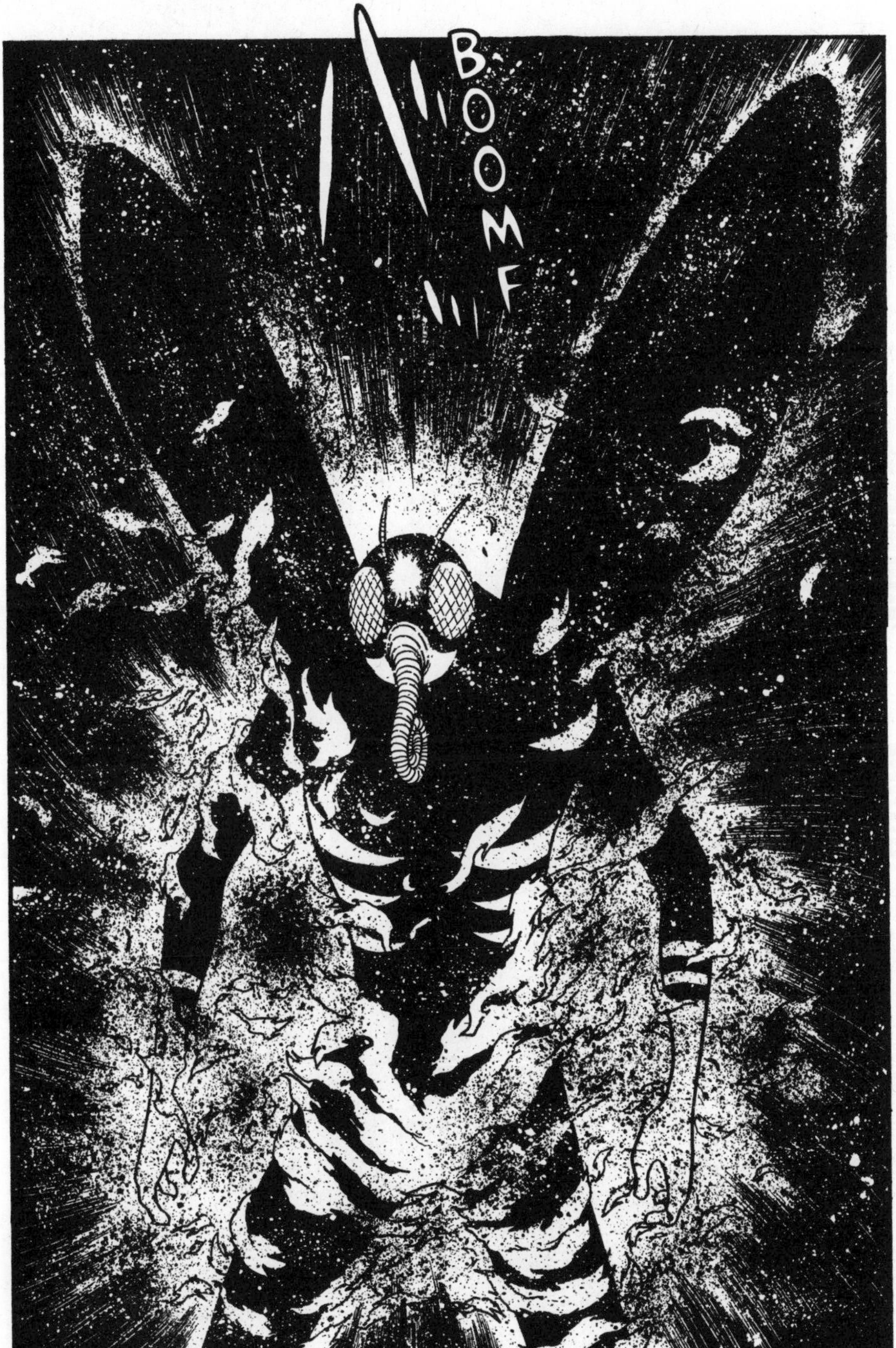
BOOMF

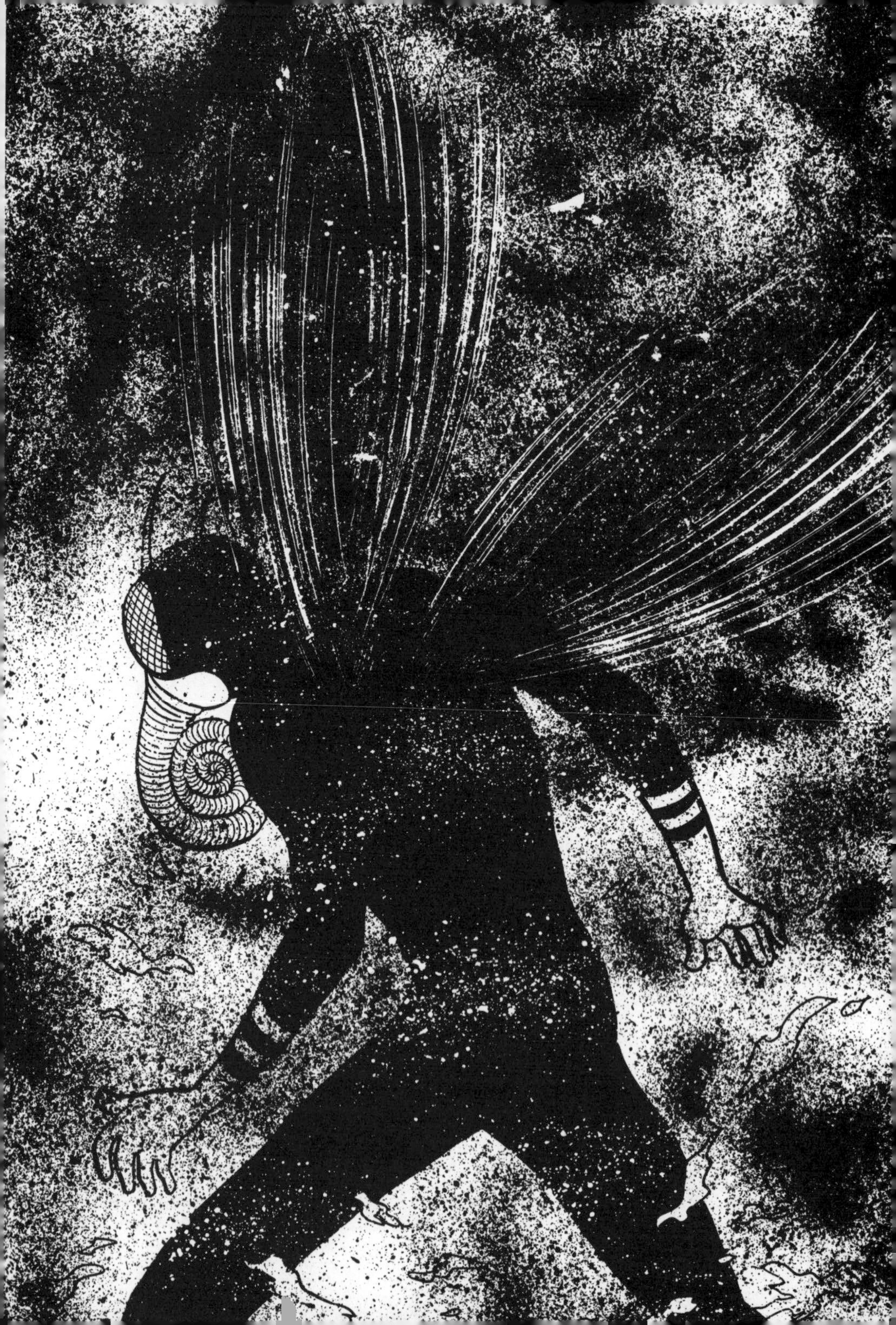

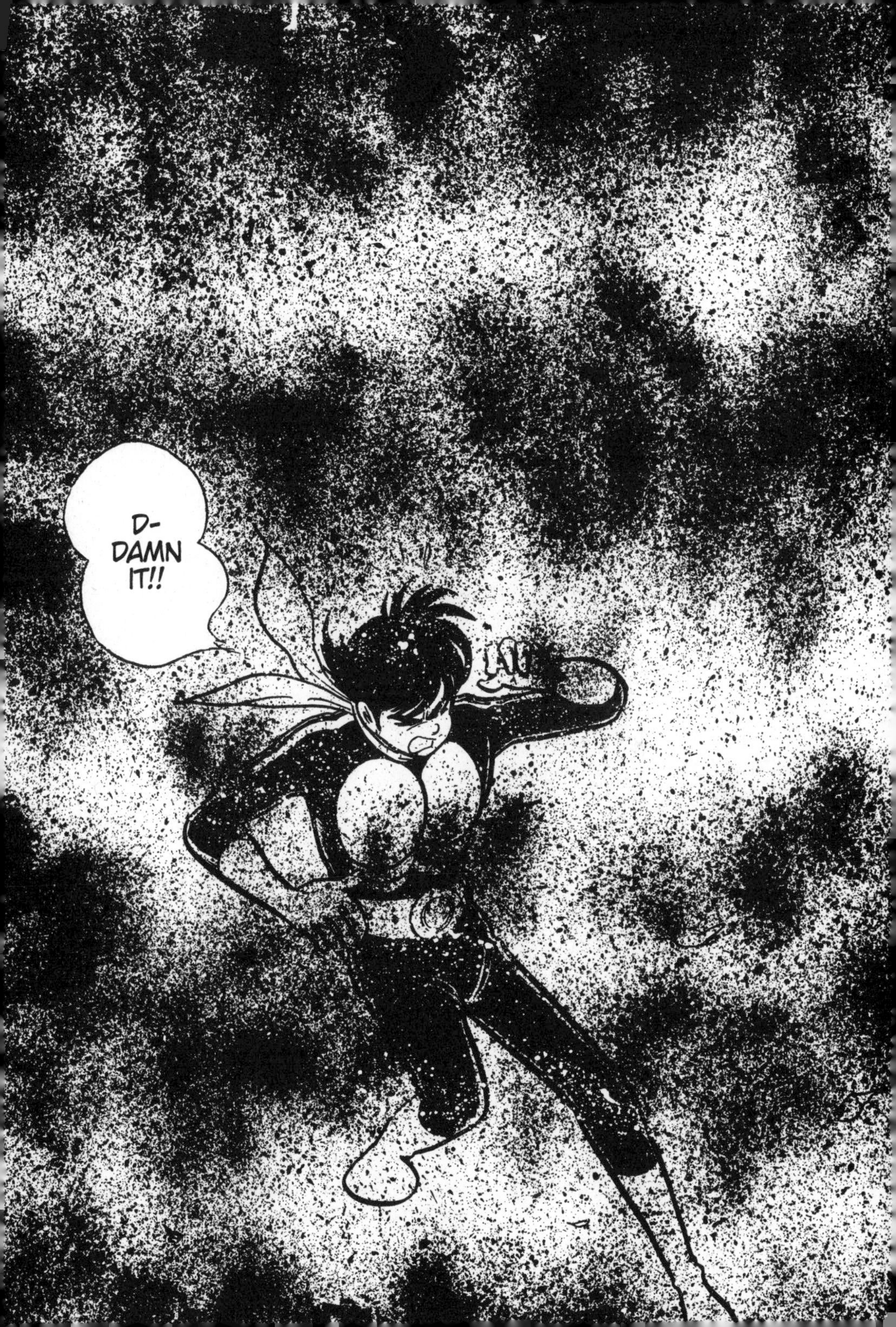
D-DAMN IT!!

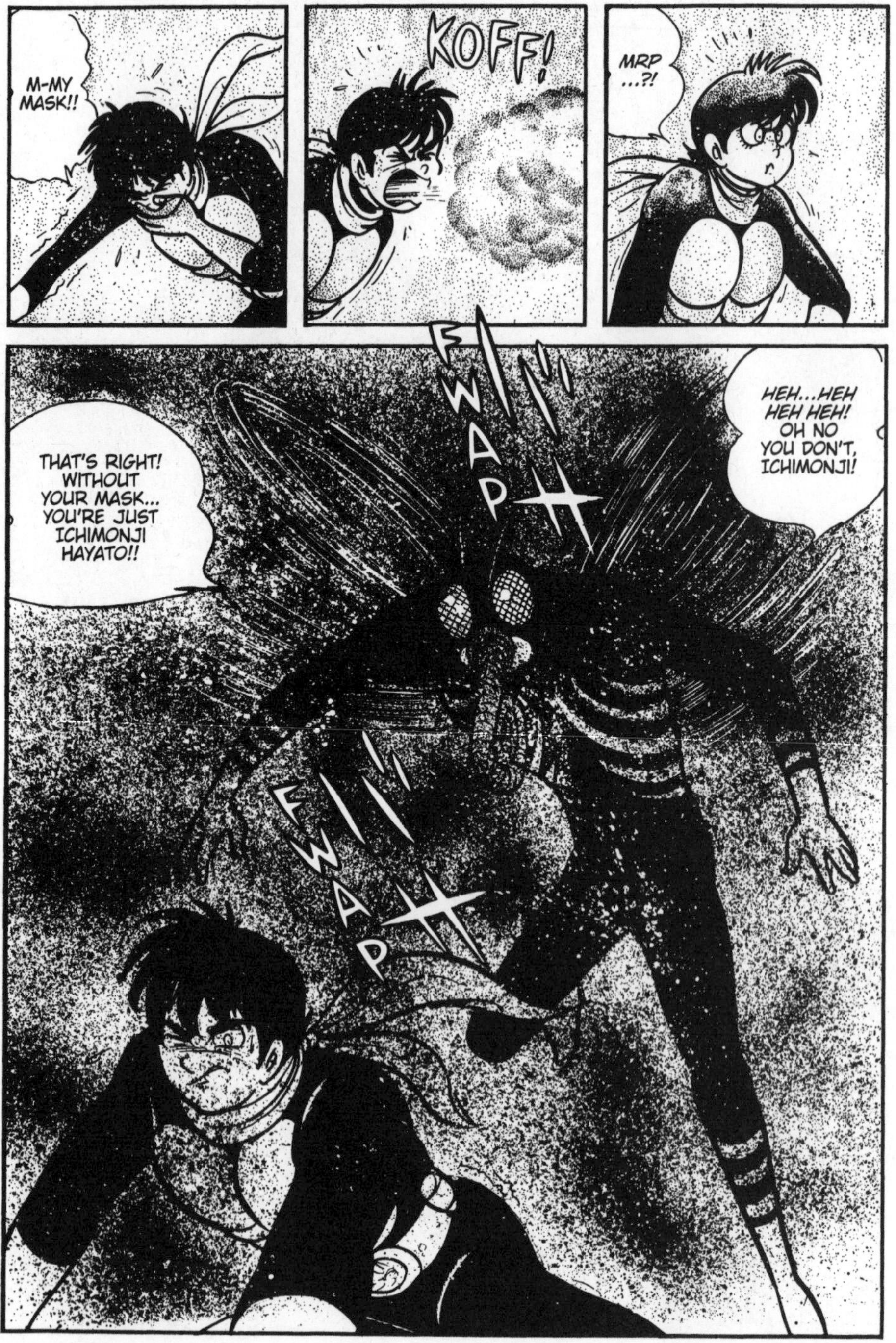
MRP ...?!
KOFF!
M-MY MASK!!
HEH...HEH HEH HEH! OH NO YOU DON'T, ICHIMONJI!
FWAP
THAT'S RIGHT! WITHOUT YOUR MASK... YOU'RE JUST ICHIMONJI HAYATO!!
FWAP

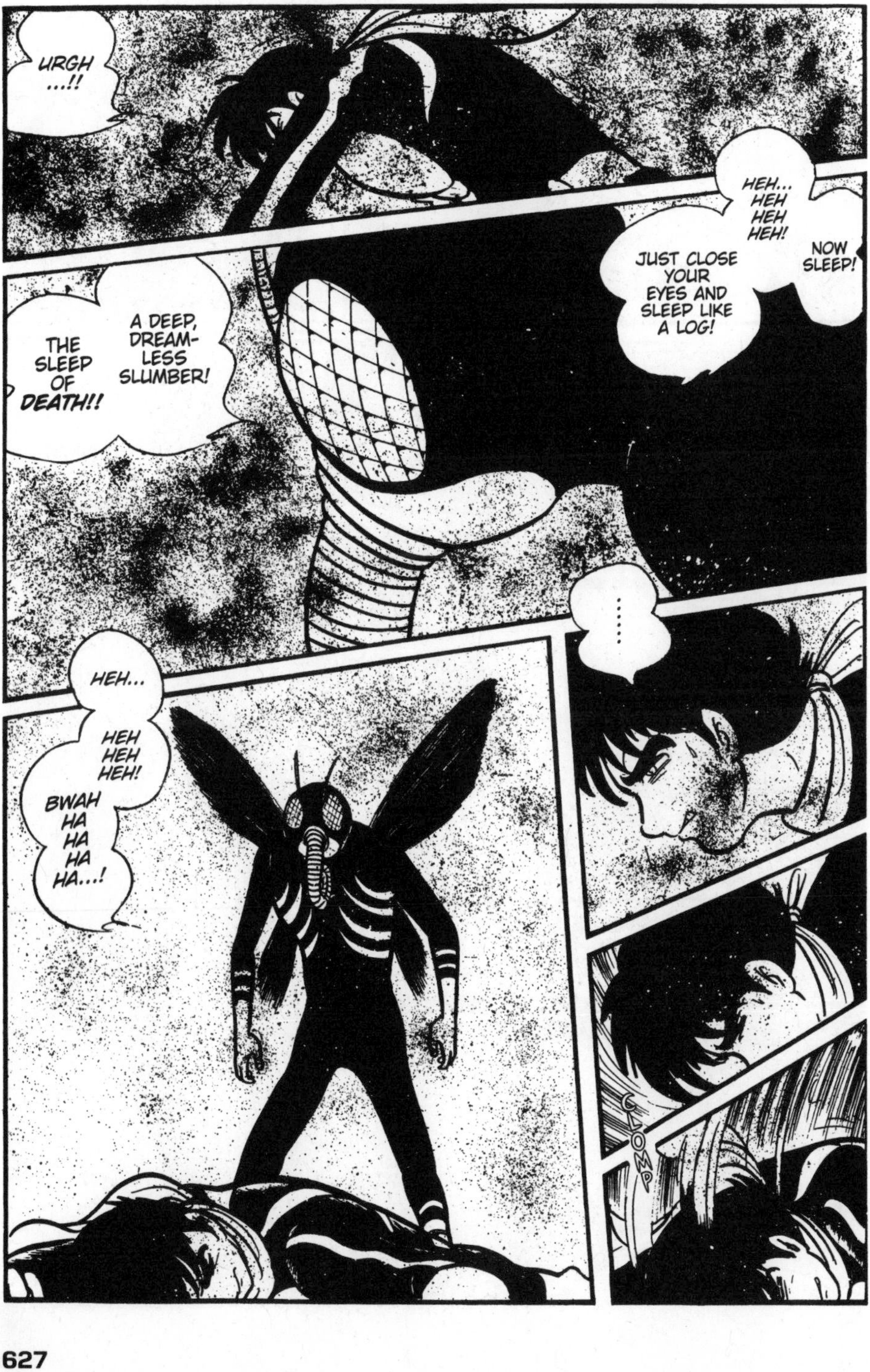
URGH ...!!
HEH... HEH HEH HEH!
NOW SLEEP!
JUST CLOSE YOUR EYES AND SLEEP LIKE A LOG!
A DEEP, DREAM-LESS SLUMBER!
THE SLEEP OF DEATH!!
......
CLOMP
HEH...
HEH HEH HEH!
BWAH HA HA HA HA...!

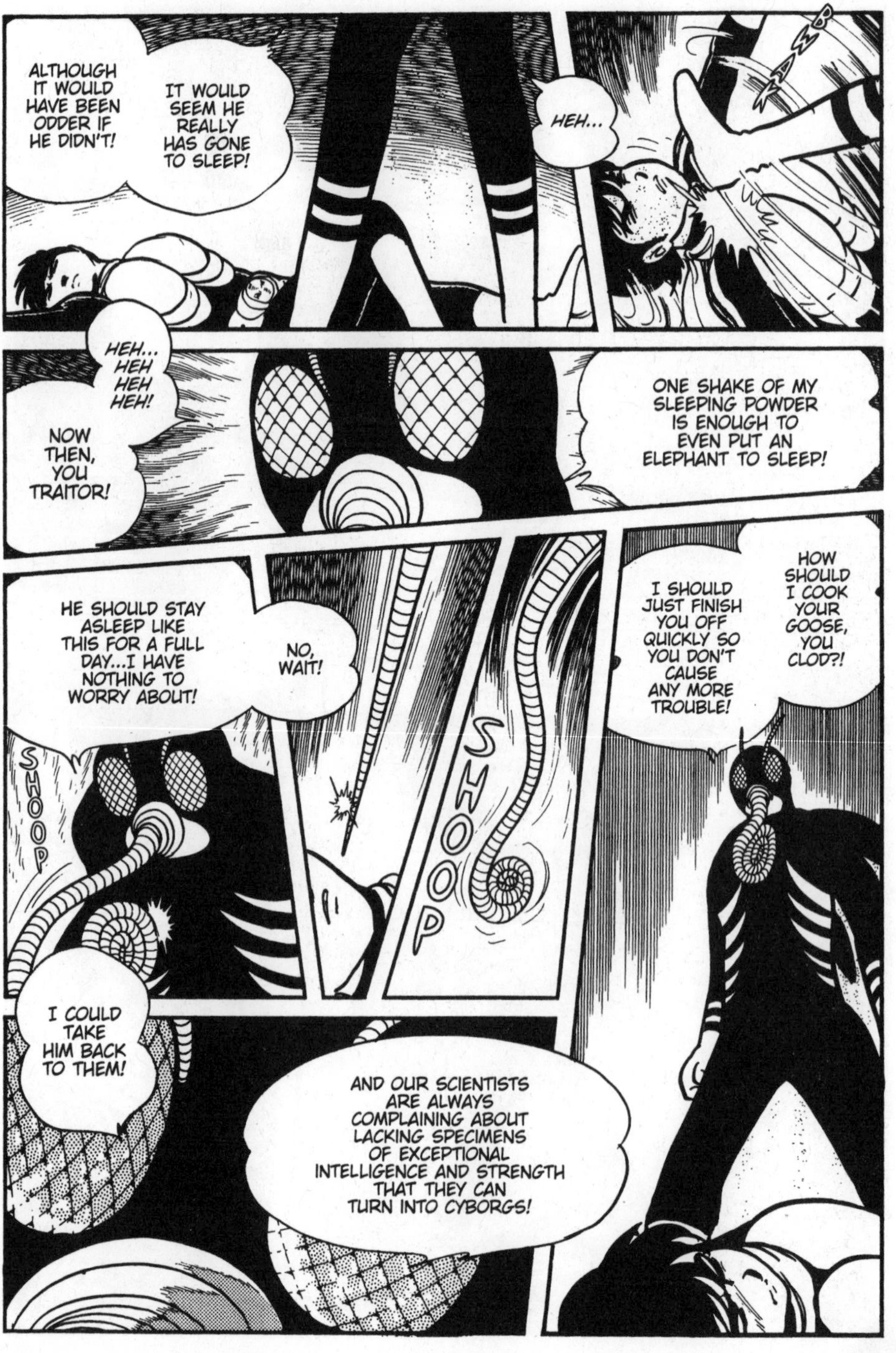
BWAK
HEH...
IT WOULD SEEM HE REALLY HAS GONE TO SLEEP!
ALTHOUGH IT WOULD HAVE BEEN ODDER IF HE DIDN'T!
ONE SHAKE OF MY SLEEPING POWDER IS ENOUGH TO EVEN PUT AN ELEPHANT TO SLEEP!
HEH... HEH HEH HEH!
NOW THEN, YOU TRAITOR!
HOW SHOULD I COOK YOUR GOOSE, YOU CLOD?!
I SHOULD JUST FINISH YOU OFF QUICKLY SO YOU DON'T CAUSE ANY MORE TROUBLE!
SHOOOP
NO, WAIT!
HE SHOULD STAY ASLEEP LIKE THIS FOR A FULL DAY...I HAVE NOTHING TO WORRY ABOUT!
SHOOP
I COULD TAKE HIM BACK TO THEM!
AND OUR SCIENTISTS ARE ALWAYS COMPLAINING ABOUT LACKING SPECIMENS OF EXCEPTIONAL INTELLIGENCE AND STRENGTH THAT THEY CAN TURN INTO CYBORGS!

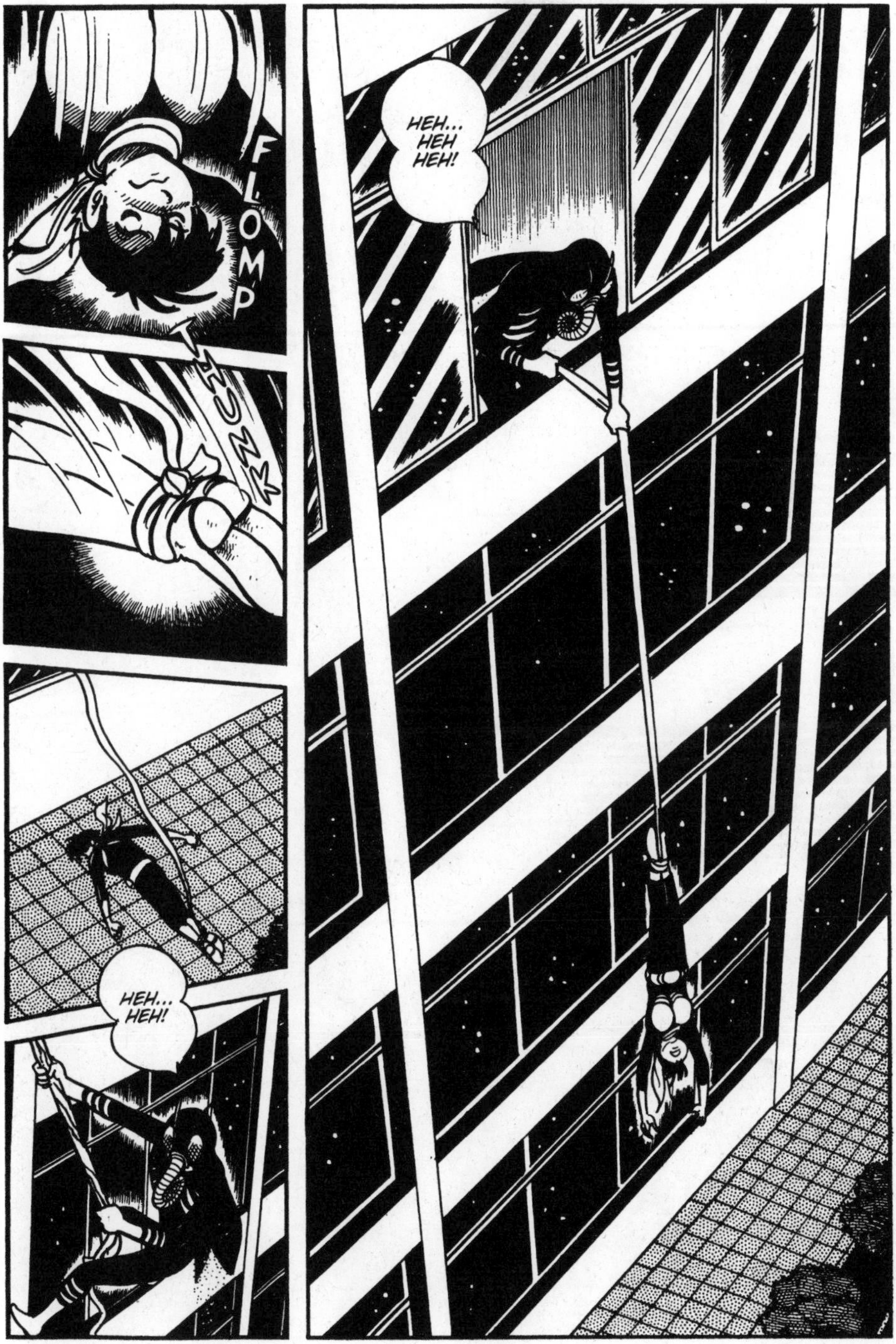
HEH... HEH HEH!
FLOMP
HUNK
HEH... HEH!

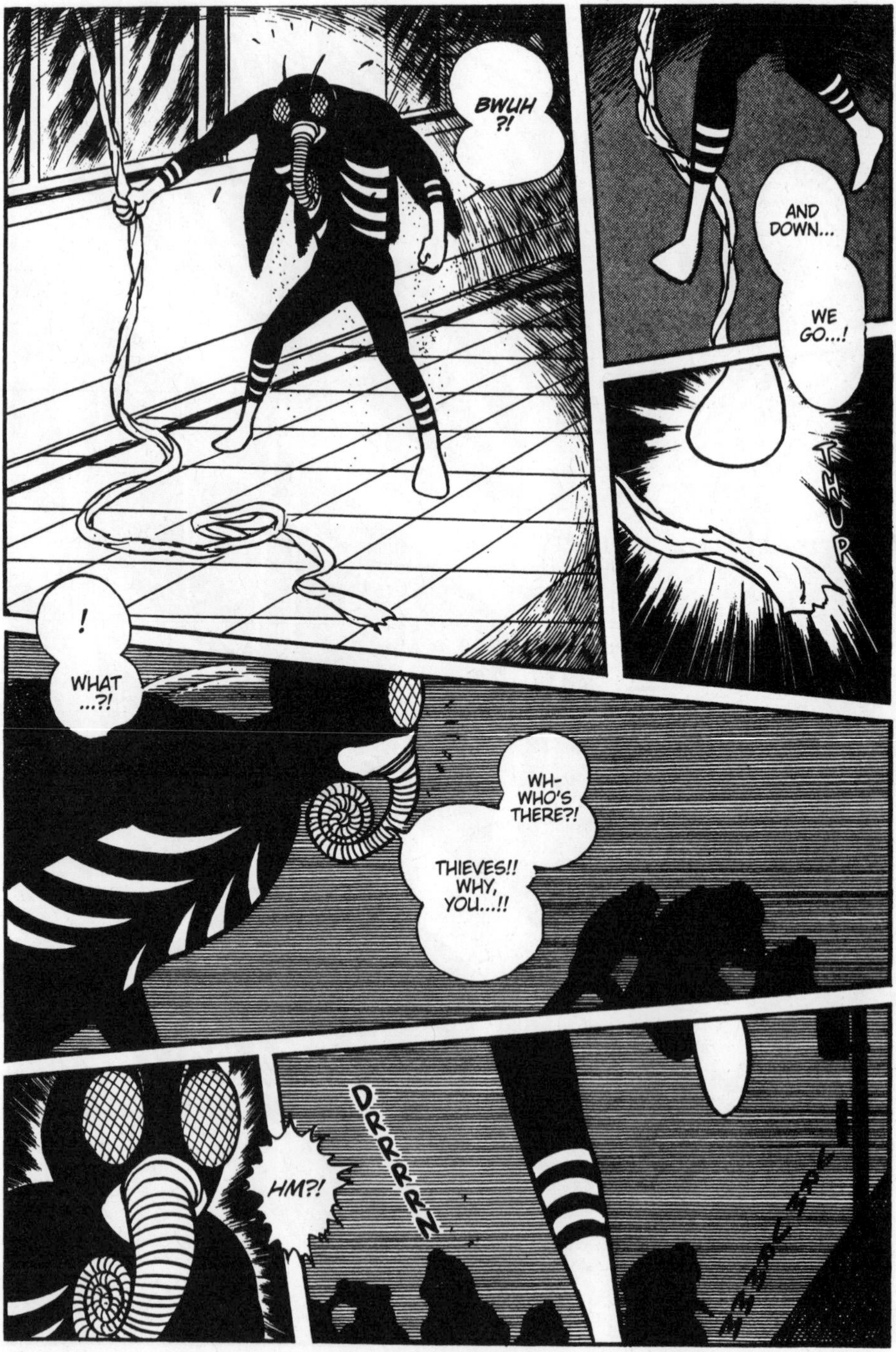
AND DOWN...
WE GO...!
THUP
BWUH ?!
!
WHAT ...?!
WH- WHO'S THERE?!
THIEVES!! WHY, YOU...!!
DRRRRRN
HM?!

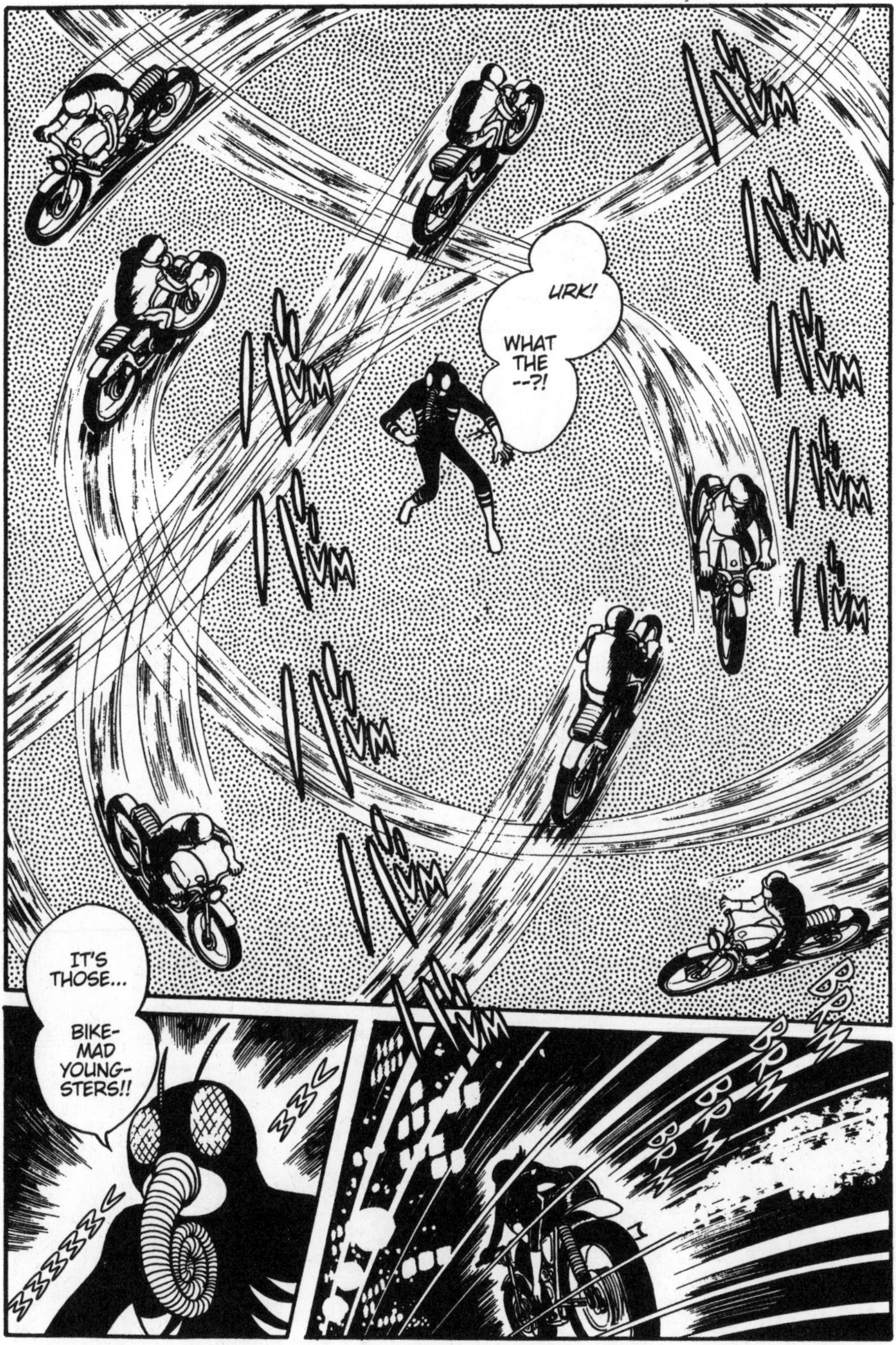
VVM
VVM
VVM
VVM
VVM
URK!
WHAT THE --?!
VVM
VVM
VVM
VVM
VVM
BRM BRM BRM BRM BRM
IT'S THOSE...
BIKE-MAD YOUNGSTERS!!

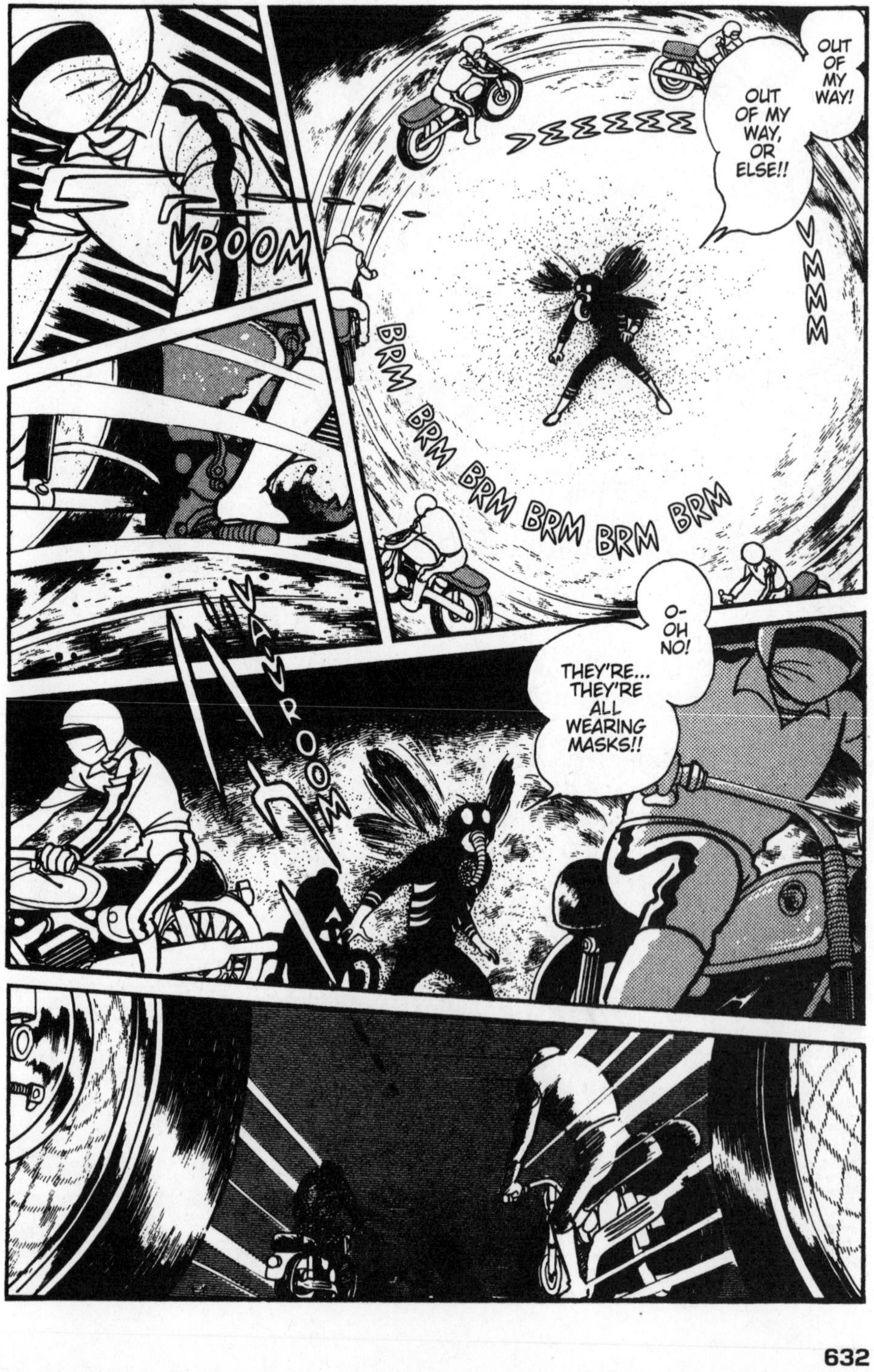
OUT OF MY WAY!
OUT OF MY WAY, OR ELSE!!
VMMM
BRM BRM BRM BRM BRM BRM
VROOM
O-OH NO!
THEY'RE... THEY'RE ALL WEARING MASKS!!
VAVROOOM

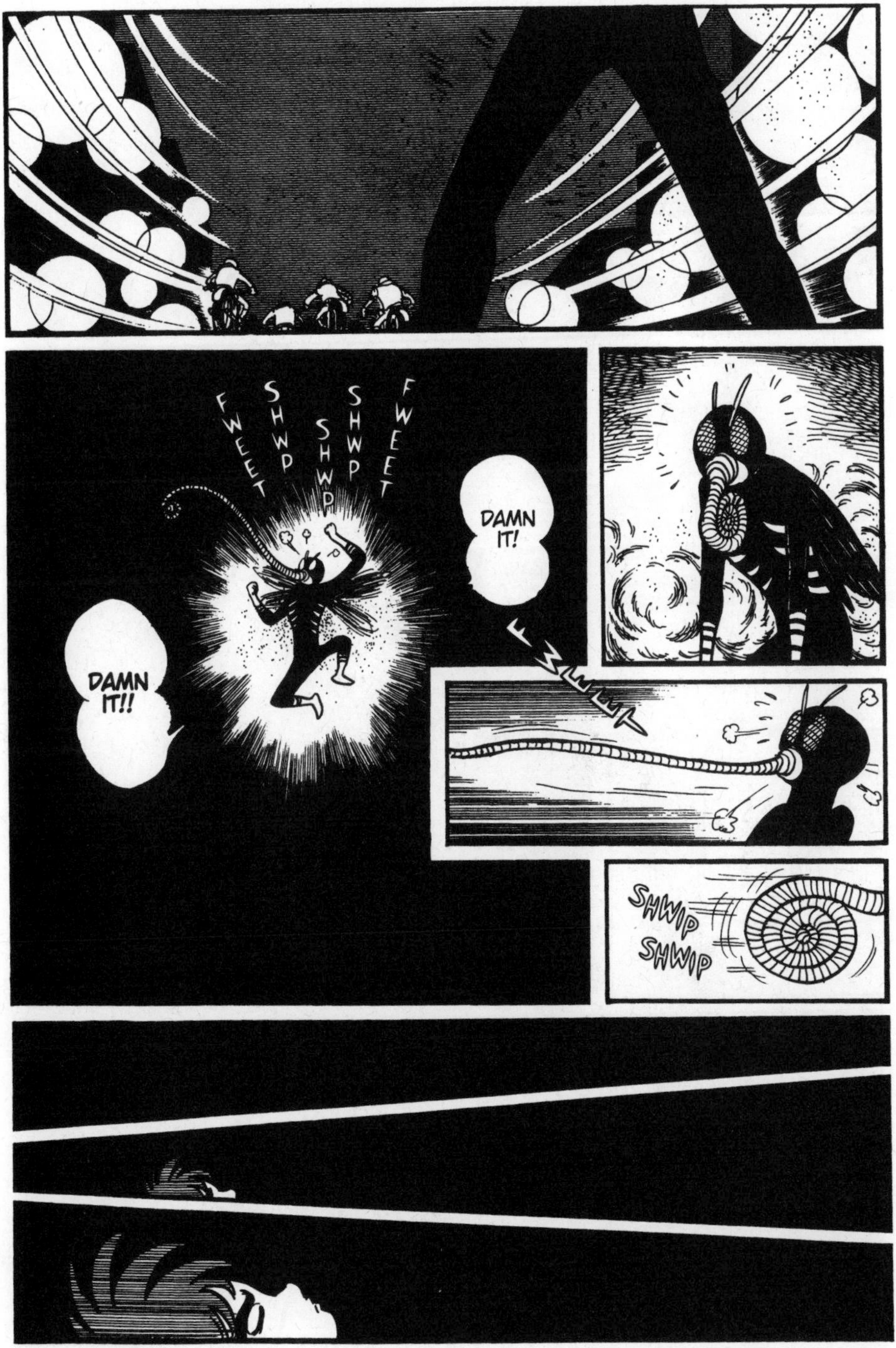
FWEEET
SHWIP
SHWIP
DAMN IT!
FWEET
SHWP
SHWP
SHWP
FWEET
DAMN IT!!

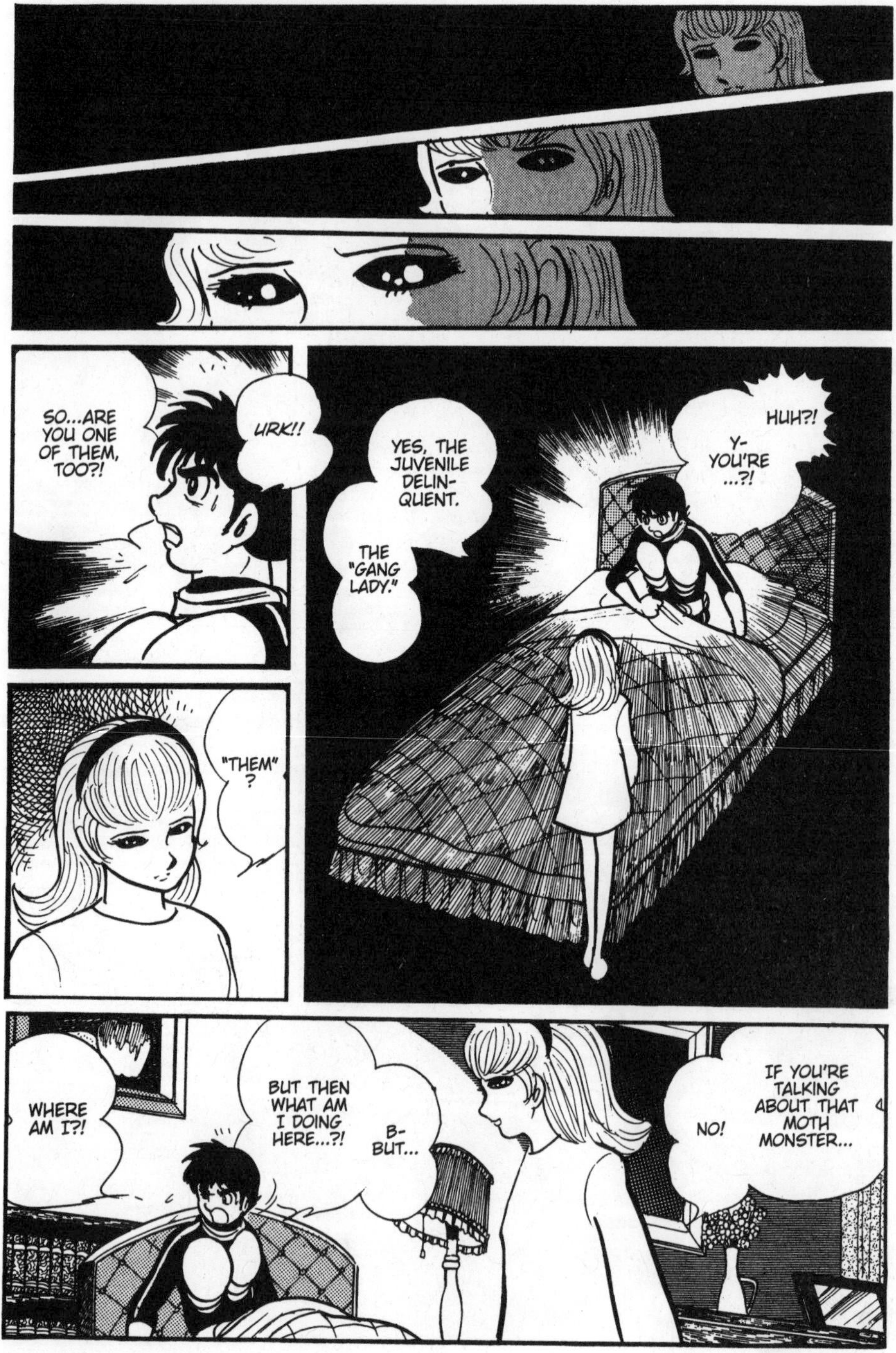
HUH?!
Y- YOU'RE ...?!
YES, THE JUVENILE DELIN-QUENT.
THE "GANG LADY."
URK!!
SO...ARE YOU ONE OF THEM, TOO?!
"THEM"?
IF YOU'RE TALKING ABOUT THAT MOTH MONSTER...
NO!
B- BUT...
BUT THEN WHAT AM I DOING HERE...?!
WHERE AM I?!

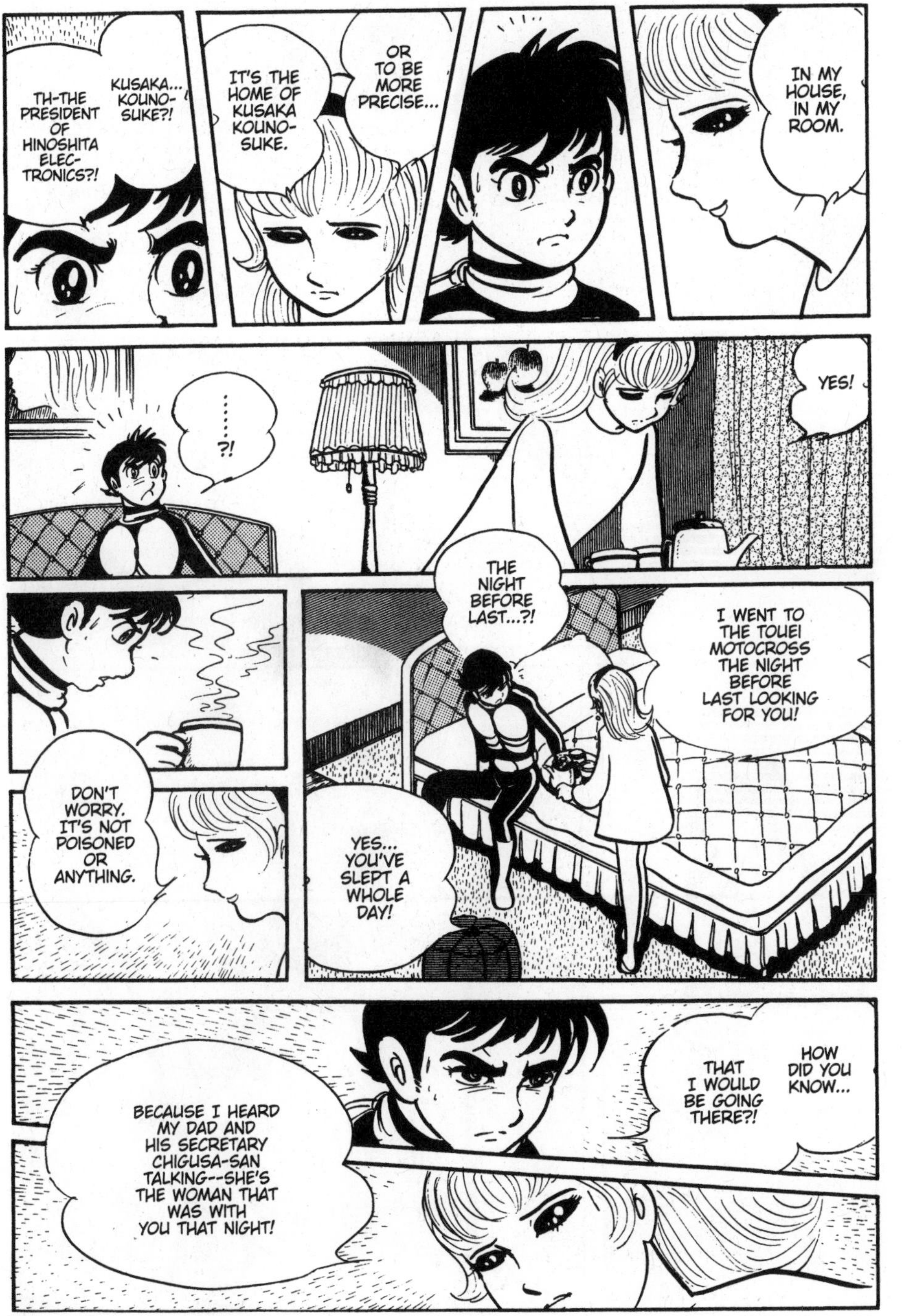
IN MY HOUSE, IN MY ROOM.
OR TO BE MORE PRECISE...
IT'S THE HOME OF KUSAKA KOUNO-SUKE.
KUSAKA... KOUNO-SUKE?!
TH-THE PRESIDENT OF HINOSHITA ELEC-TRONICS?!
YES!
......?!
I WENT TO THE TOUEI MOTOCROSS THE NIGHT BEFORE LAST LOOKING FOR YOU!
THE NIGHT BEFORE LAST...?!
YES... YOU'VE SLEPT A WHOLE DAY!
DON'T WORRY. IT'S NOT POISONED OR ANYTHING.
HOW DID YOU KNOW...
THAT I WOULD BE GOING THERE?!
BECAUSE I HEARD MY DAD AND HIS SECRETARY CHIGUSA-SAN TALKING--SHE'S THE WOMAN THAT WAS WITH YOU THAT NIGHT!

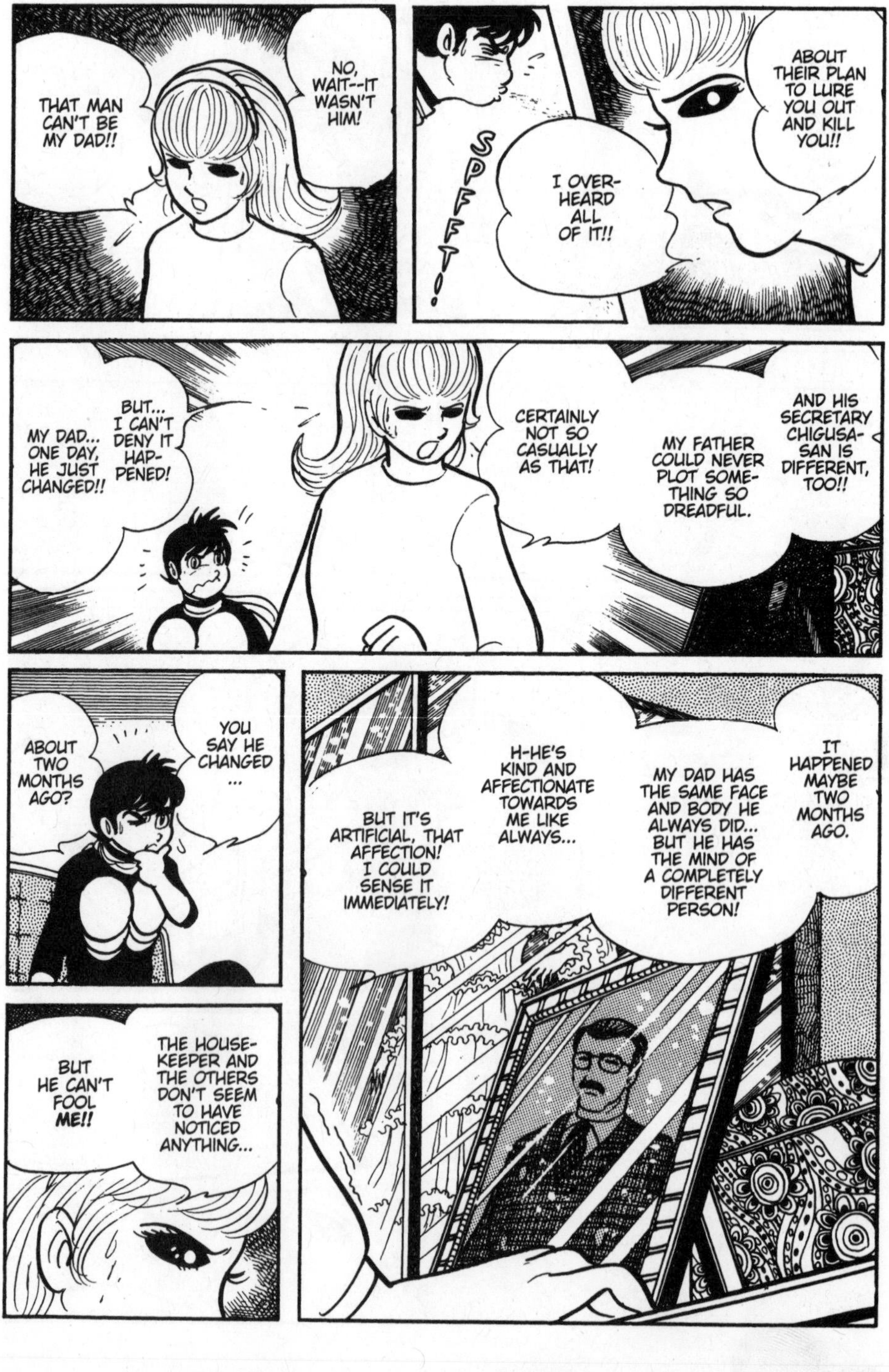
ABOUT THEIR PLAN TO LURE YOU OUT AND KILL YOU!!
I OVER-HEARD ALL OF IT!!
SPFFFT!!
NO, WAIT--IT WASN'T HIM!
THAT MAN CAN'T BE MY DAD!!
AND HIS SECRETARY CHIGUSA-SAN IS DIFFERENT, TOO!!
MY FATHER COULD NEVER PLOT SOME-THING SO DREADFUL.
CERTAINLY NOT SO CASUALLY AS THAT!
BUT... I CAN'T DENY IT HAP-PENED!
MY DAD... ONE DAY, HE JUST CHANGED!!
IT HAPPENED MAYBE TWO MONTHS AGO.
MY DAD HAS THE SAME FACE AND BODY HE ALWAYS DID... BUT HE HAS THE MIND OF A COMPLETELY DIFFERENT PERSON!
H-HE'S KIND AND AFFECTIONATE TOWARDS ME LIKE ALWAYS...
BUT IT'S ARTIFICIAL, THAT AFFECTION! I COULD SENSE IT IMMEDIATELY!
YOU SAY HE CHANGED ...
ABOUT TWO MONTHS AGO?
THE HOUSE-KEEPER AND THE OTHERS DON'T SEEM TO HAVE NOTICED ANYTHING...
BUT HE CAN'T FOOL ME!!

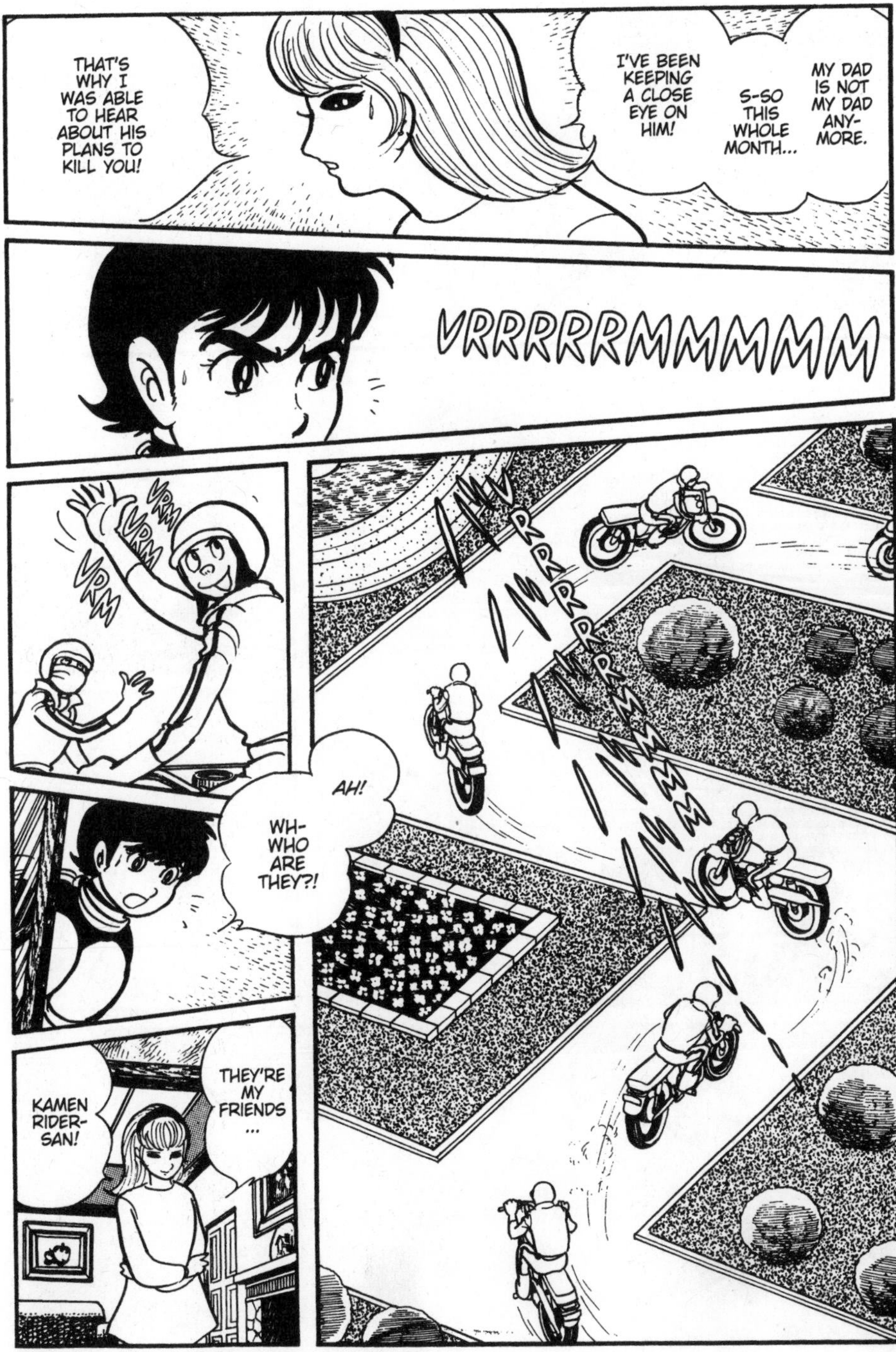
MY DAD IS NOT MY DAD ANYMORE.
S-SO THIS WHOLE MONTH...
I'VE BEEN KEEPING A CLOSE EYE ON HIM!
THAT'S WHY I WAS ABLE TO HEAR ABOUT HIS PLANS TO KILL YOU!
VRRRRRMMMMMM
VRRRRRMMMMM
VRM
VRM
VRM
AH!
WH-WHO ARE THEY?!
THEY'RE MY FRIENDS...
KAMEN RIDER-SAN!

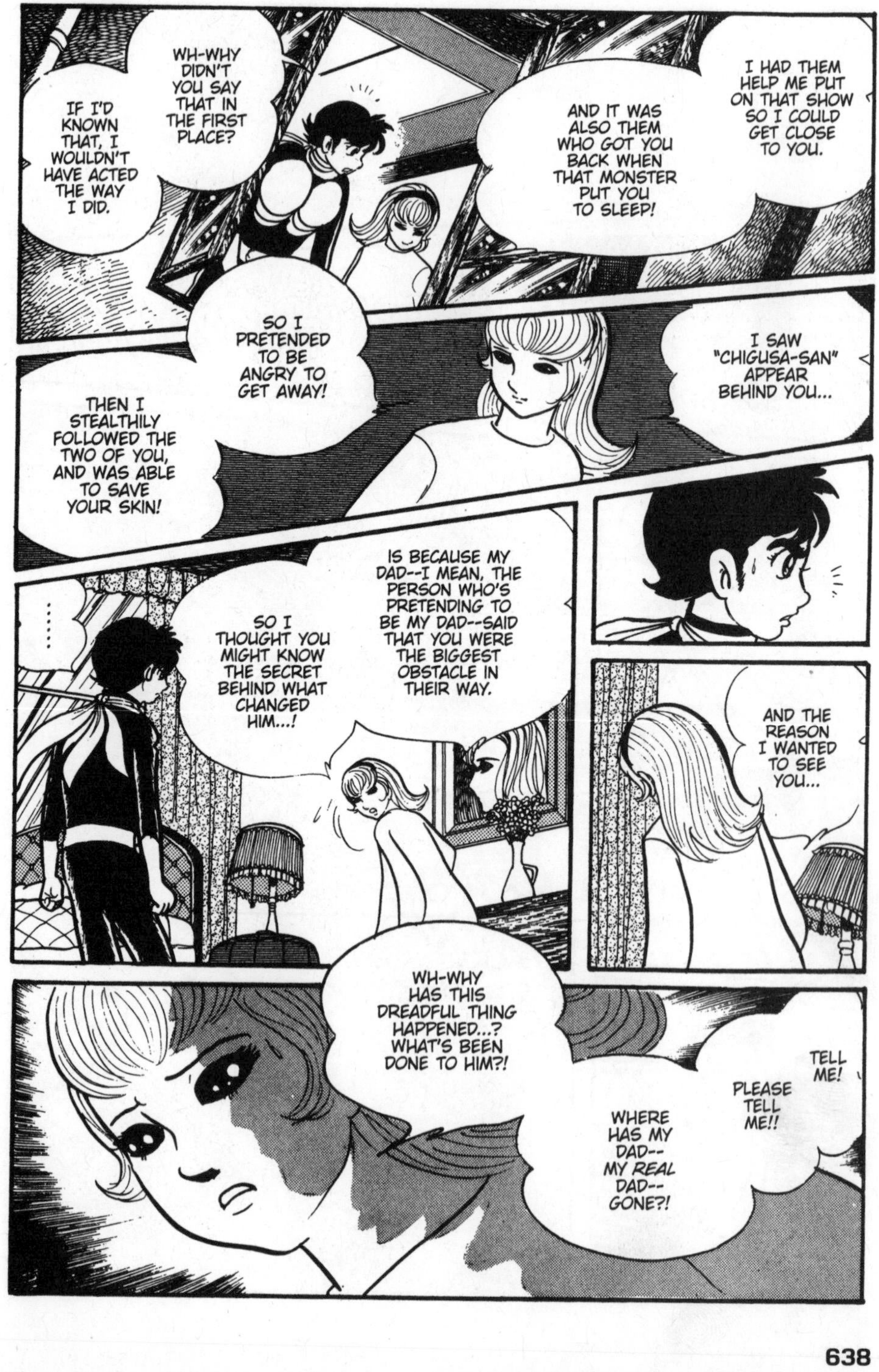
I HAD THEM HELP ME PUT ON THAT SHOW SO I COULD GET CLOSE TO YOU.
AND IT WAS ALSO THEM WHO GOT YOU BACK WHEN THAT MONSTER PUT YOU TO SLEEP!
WH-WHY DIDN'T YOU SAY THAT IN THE FIRST PLACE?
IF I'D KNOWN THAT, I WOULDN'T HAVE ACTED THE WAY I DID.
I SAW "CHIGUSA-SAN" APPEAR BEHIND YOU...
SO I PRETENDED TO BE ANGRY TO GET AWAY!
THEN I STEALTHILY FOLLOWED THE TWO OF YOU, AND WAS ABLE TO SAVE YOUR SKIN!
AND THE REASON I WANTED TO SEE YOU...
IS BECAUSE MY DAD--I MEAN, THE PERSON WHO'S PRETENDING TO BE MY DAD--SAID THAT YOU WERE THE BIGGEST OBSTACLE IN THEIR WAY.
SO I THOUGHT YOU MIGHT KNOW THE SECRET BEHIND WHAT CHANGED HIM...!
......
WH-WHY HAS THIS DREADFUL THING HAPPENED...? WHAT'S BEEN DONE TO HIM?!
TELL ME!
PLEASE TELL ME!!
WHERE HAS MY DAD-- MY REAL DAD-- GONE?!

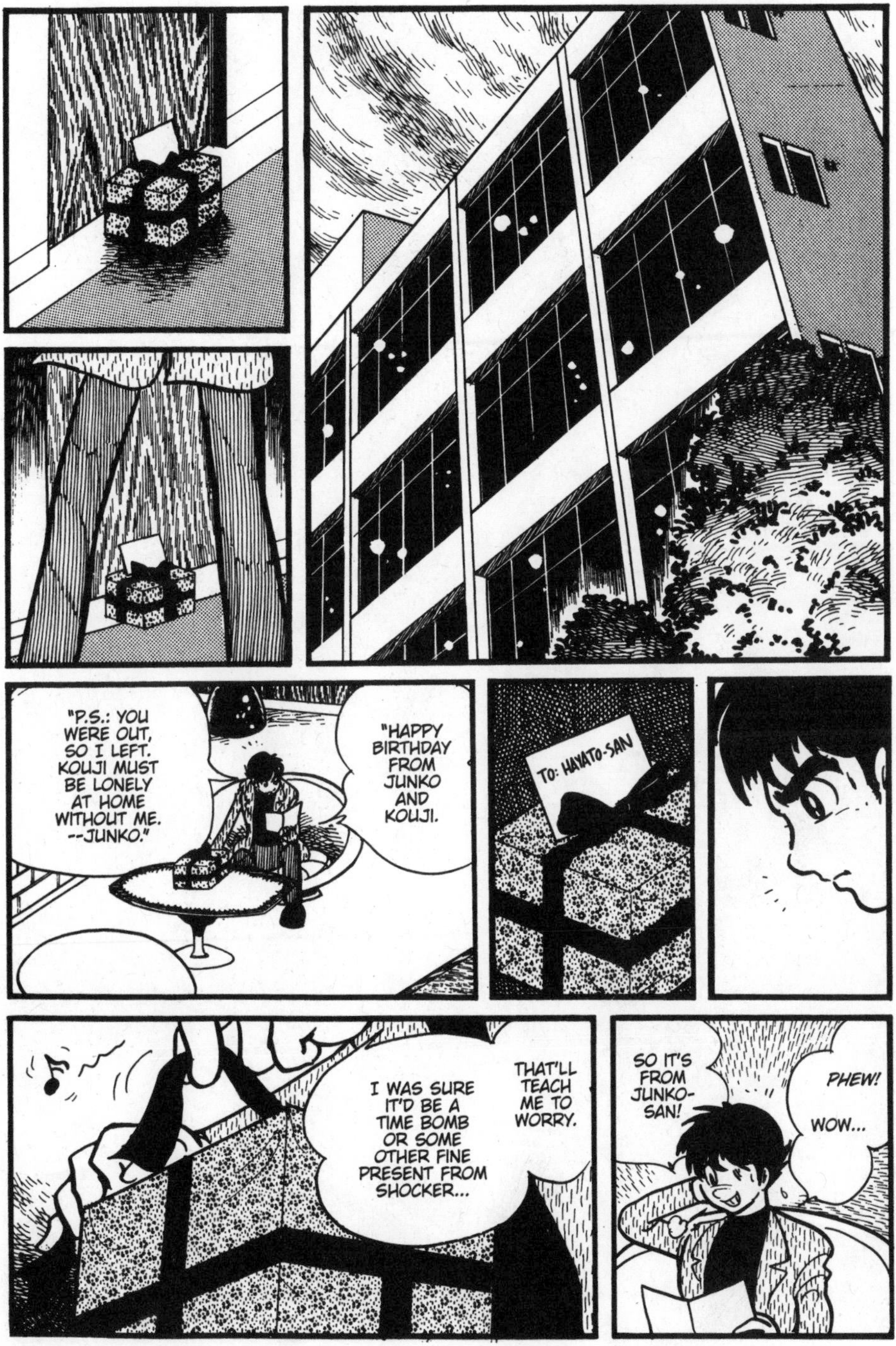
TO: HAYATO-SAN
"HAPPY BIRTHDAY FROM JUNKO AND KOUJI.
"P.S.: YOU WERE OUT, SO I LEFT. KOUJI MUST BE LONELY AT HOME WITHOUT ME. --JUNKO."
PHEW!
WOW...
SO IT'S FROM JUNKO-SAN!
THAT'LL TEACH ME TO WORRY.
I WAS SURE IT'D BE A TIME BOMB OR SOME OTHER FINE PRESENT FROM SHOCKER...

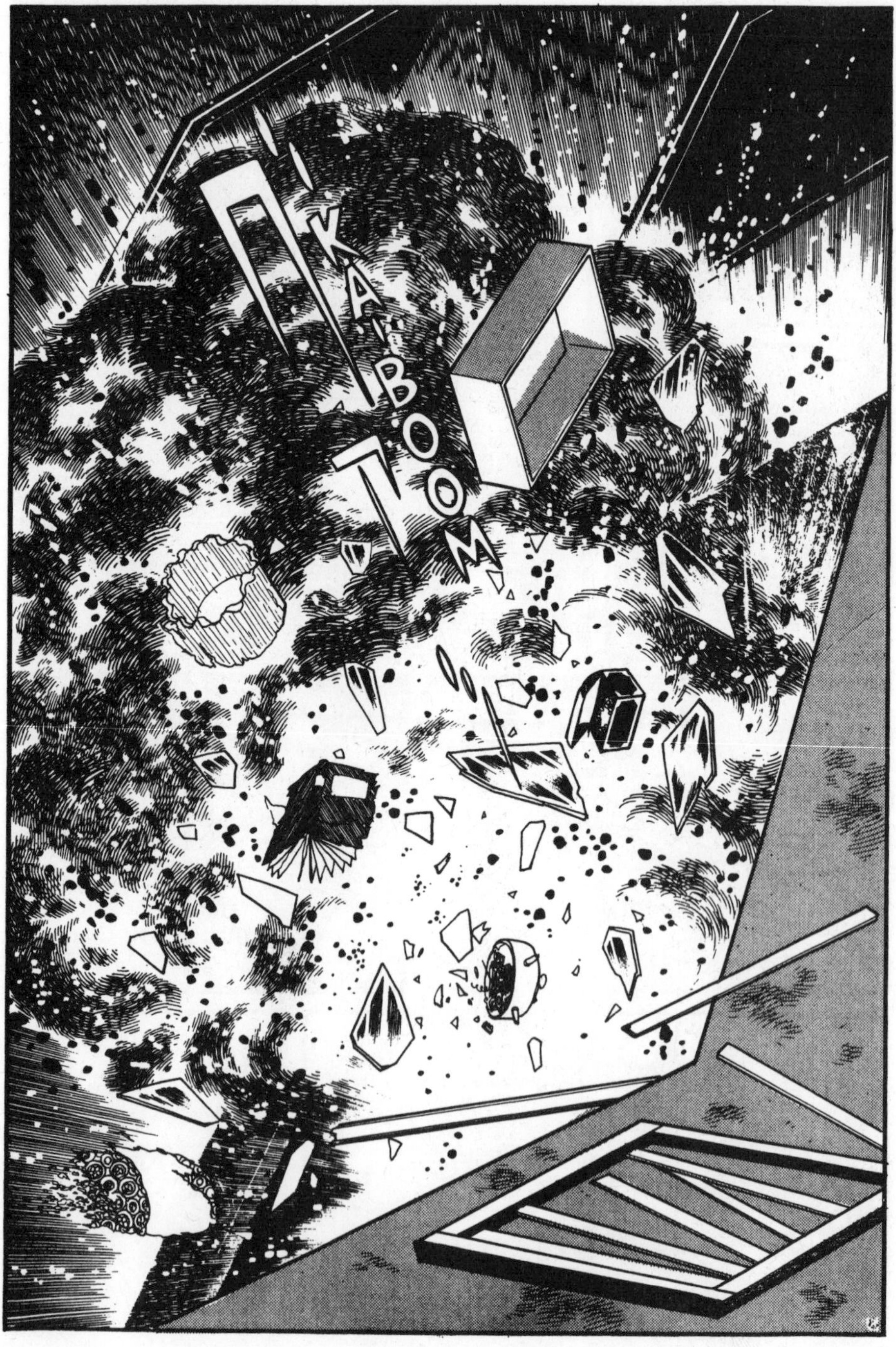
KA-BOOM

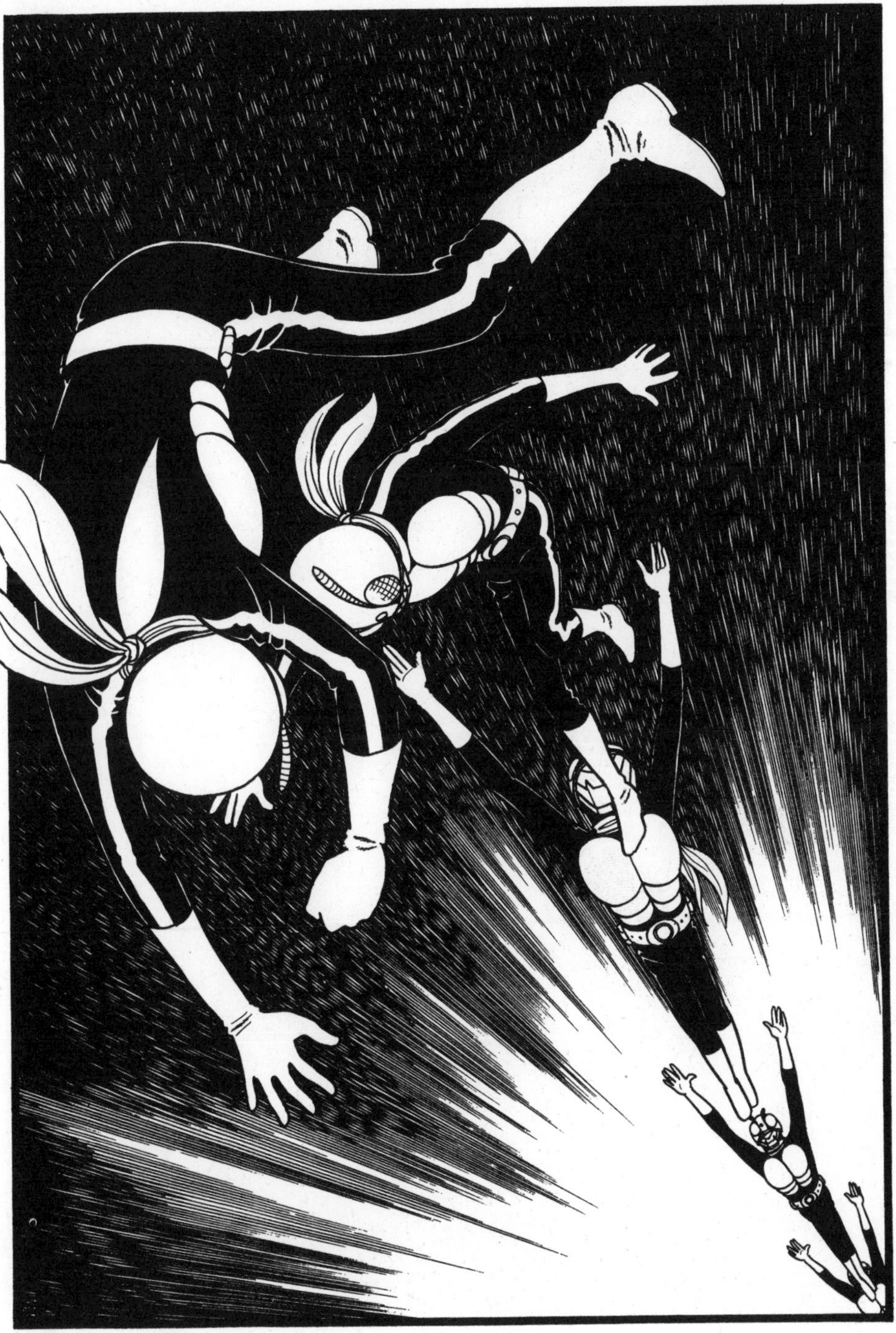

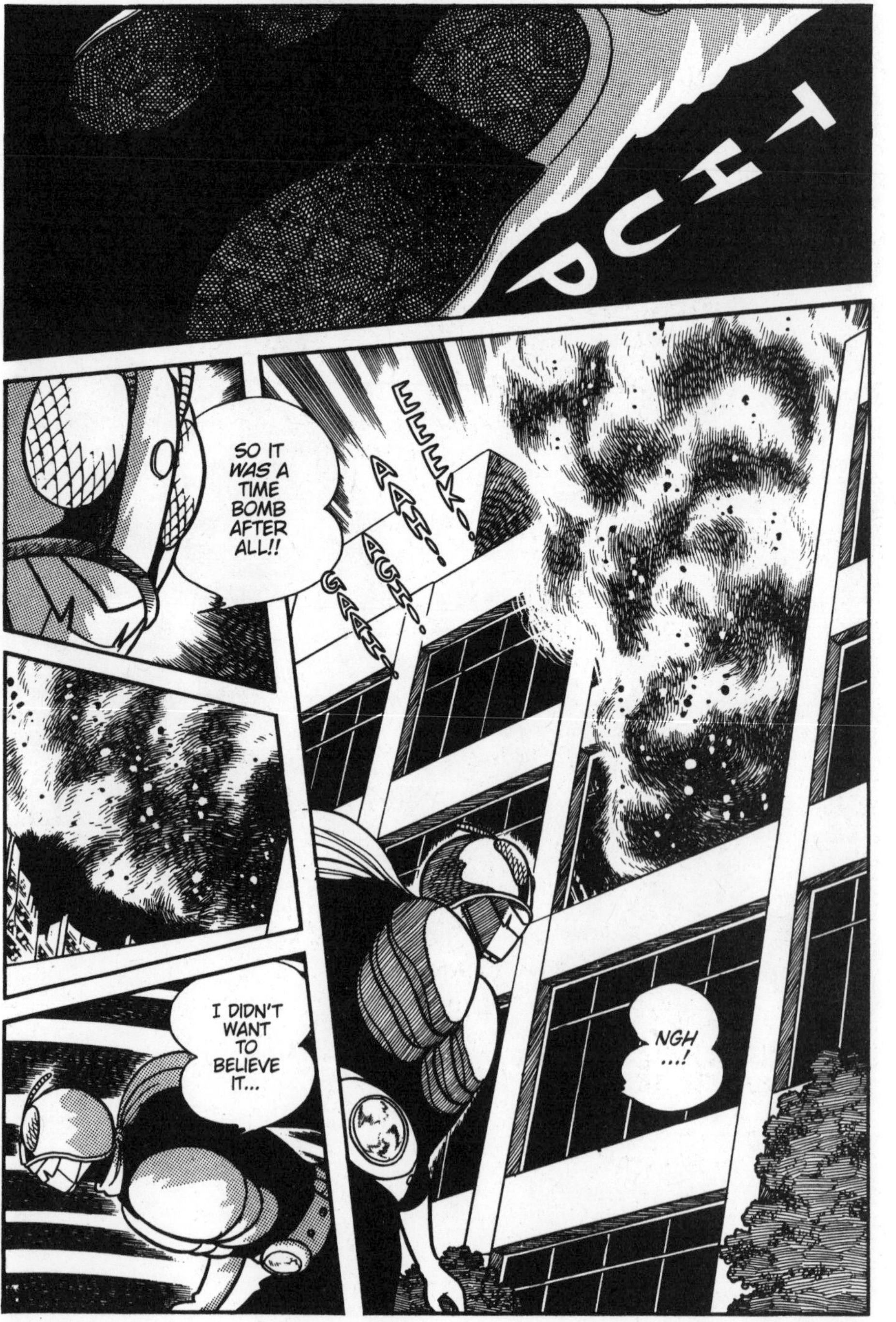
THUP
EEEEK!! AAH!! AGH!! GAAH!!
NGH ...!
SO IT WAS A TIME BOMB AFTER ALL!!
I DIDN'T WANT TO BELIEVE IT...

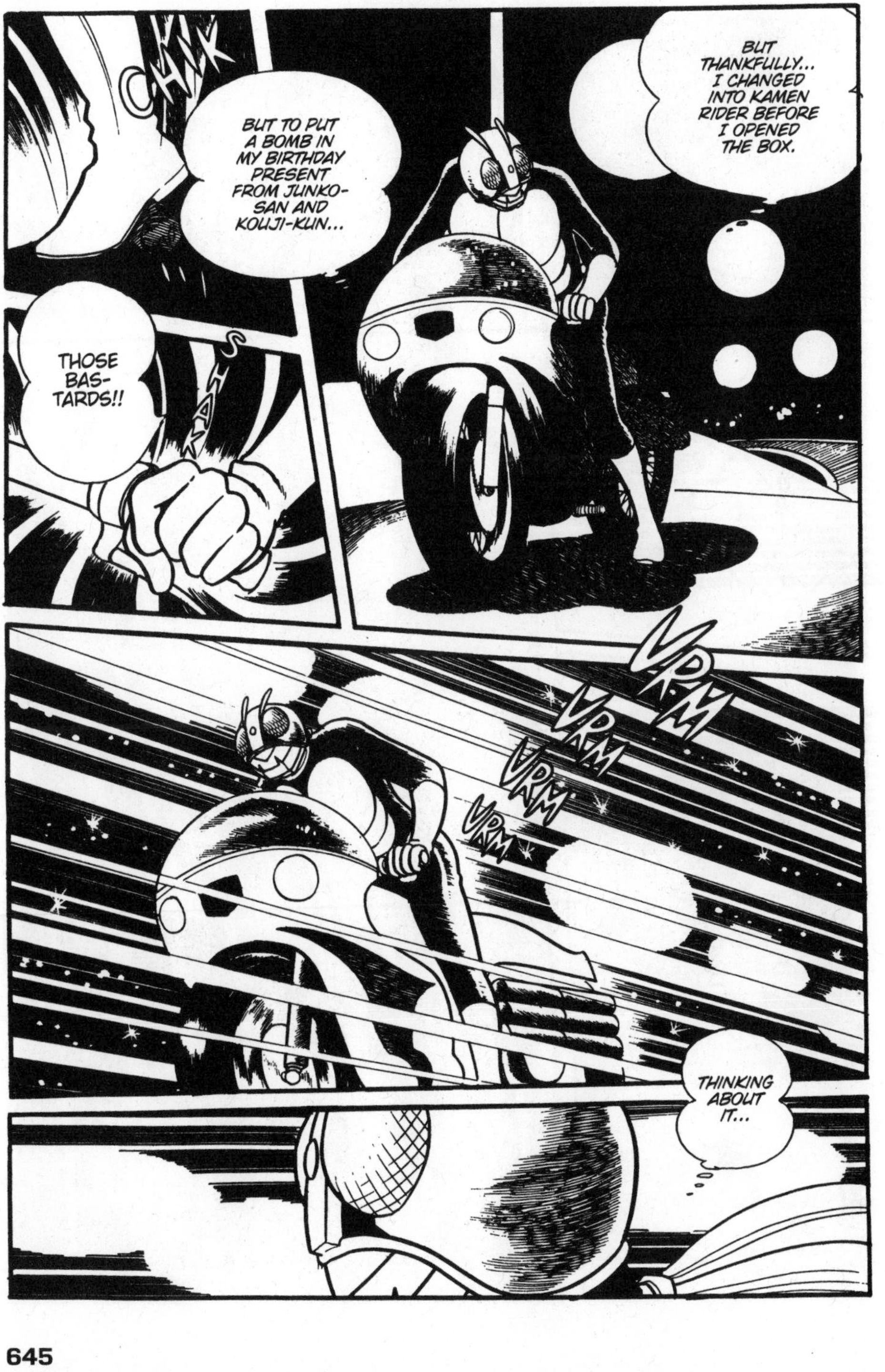
BUT THANKFULLY... I CHANGED INTO KAMEN RIDER BEFORE I OPENED THE BOX.
CHIK
BUT TO PUT A BOMB IN MY BIRTHDAY PRESENT FROM JUNKO-SAN AND KOUJI-KUN...
SHAK
THOSE BAS-TARDS!!
VRM VRM VRM VRM
THINKING ABOUT IT...

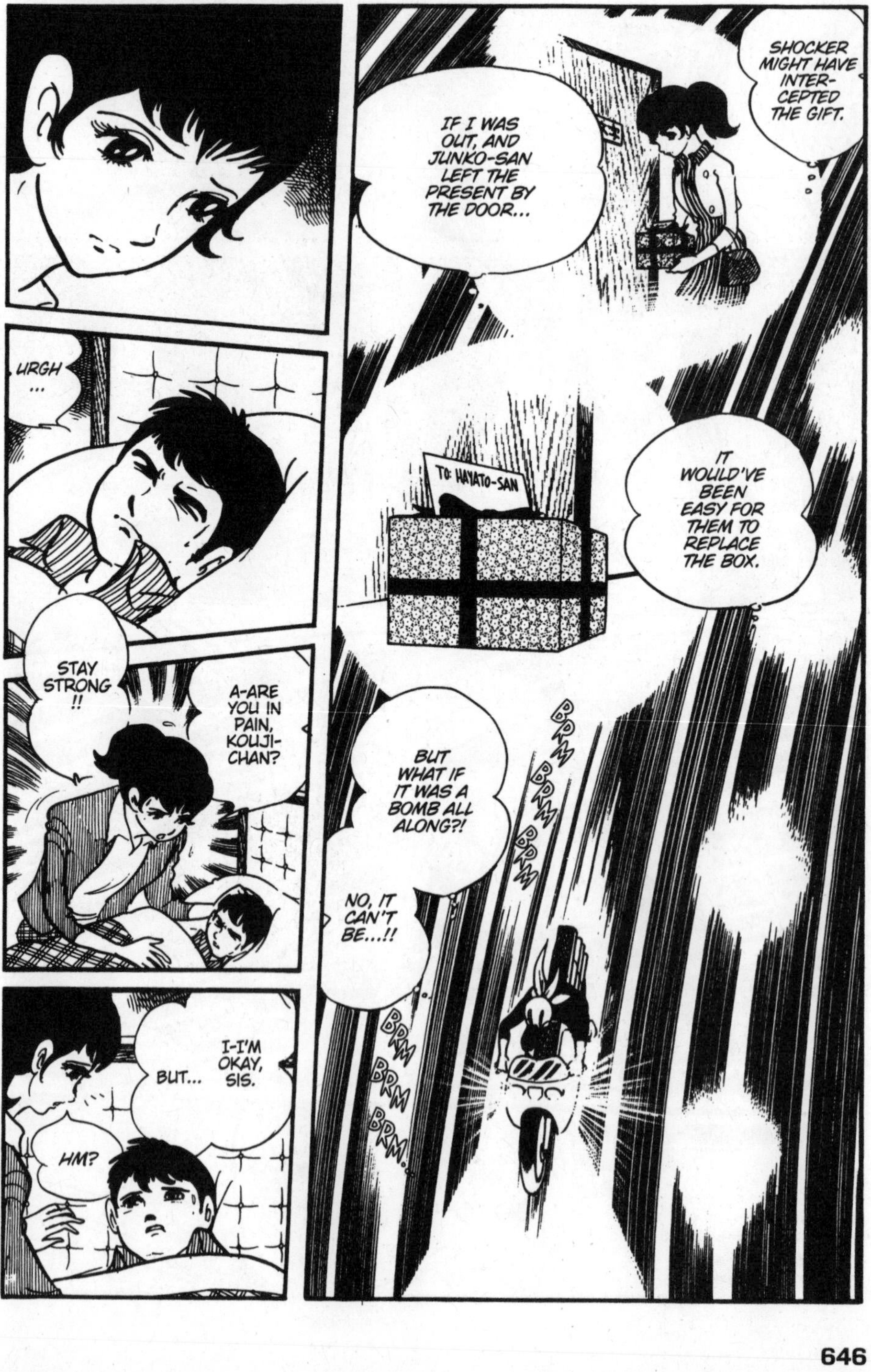
SHOCKER MIGHT HAVE INTER-CEPTED THE GIFT.
IF I WAS OUT, AND JUNKO-SAN LEFT THE PRESENT BY THE DOOR...
TO: HAYATO-SAN
IT WOULD'VE BEEN EASY FOR THEM TO REPLACE THE BOX.
BUT WHAT IF IT WAS A BOMB ALL ALONG?!
BRM BRM BRM BRM
NO, IT CAN'T BE...!!
BRM BRM BRM BRM..
URGH ...
A-ARE YOU IN PAIN, KOUJI-CHAN?
STAY STRONG !!
I-I'M OKAY, SIS.
BUT...
HM?

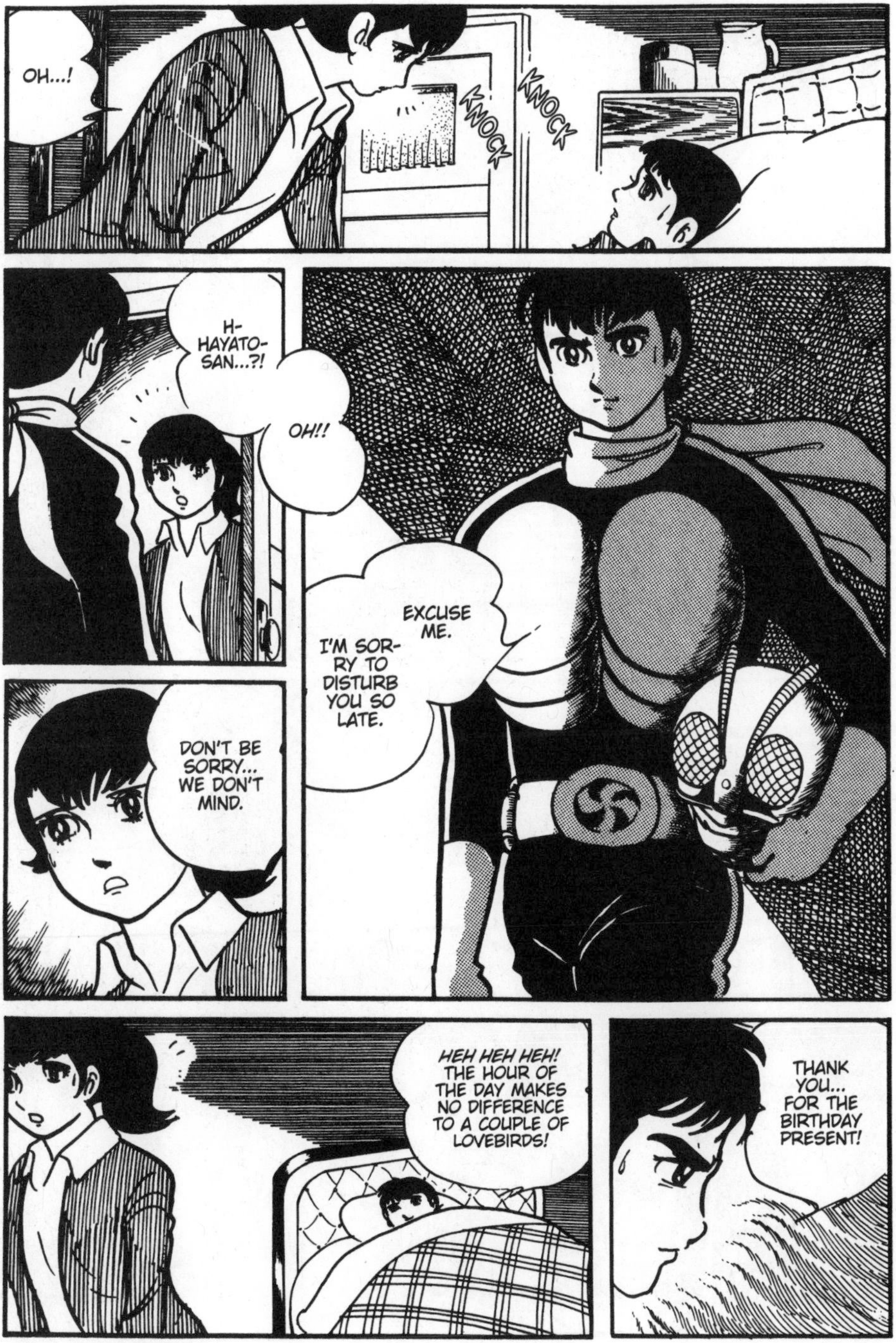
KNOCK
KNOCK
OH...!
EXCUSE ME.
I'M SORRY TO DISTURB YOU SO LATE.
H-HAYATO-SAN...?!
OH!!
DON'T BE SORRY... WE DON'T MIND.
THANK YOU... FOR THE BIRTHDAY PRESENT!
HEH HEH HEH! THE HOUR OF THE DAY MAKES NO DIFFERENCE TO A COUPLE OF LOVEBIRDS!

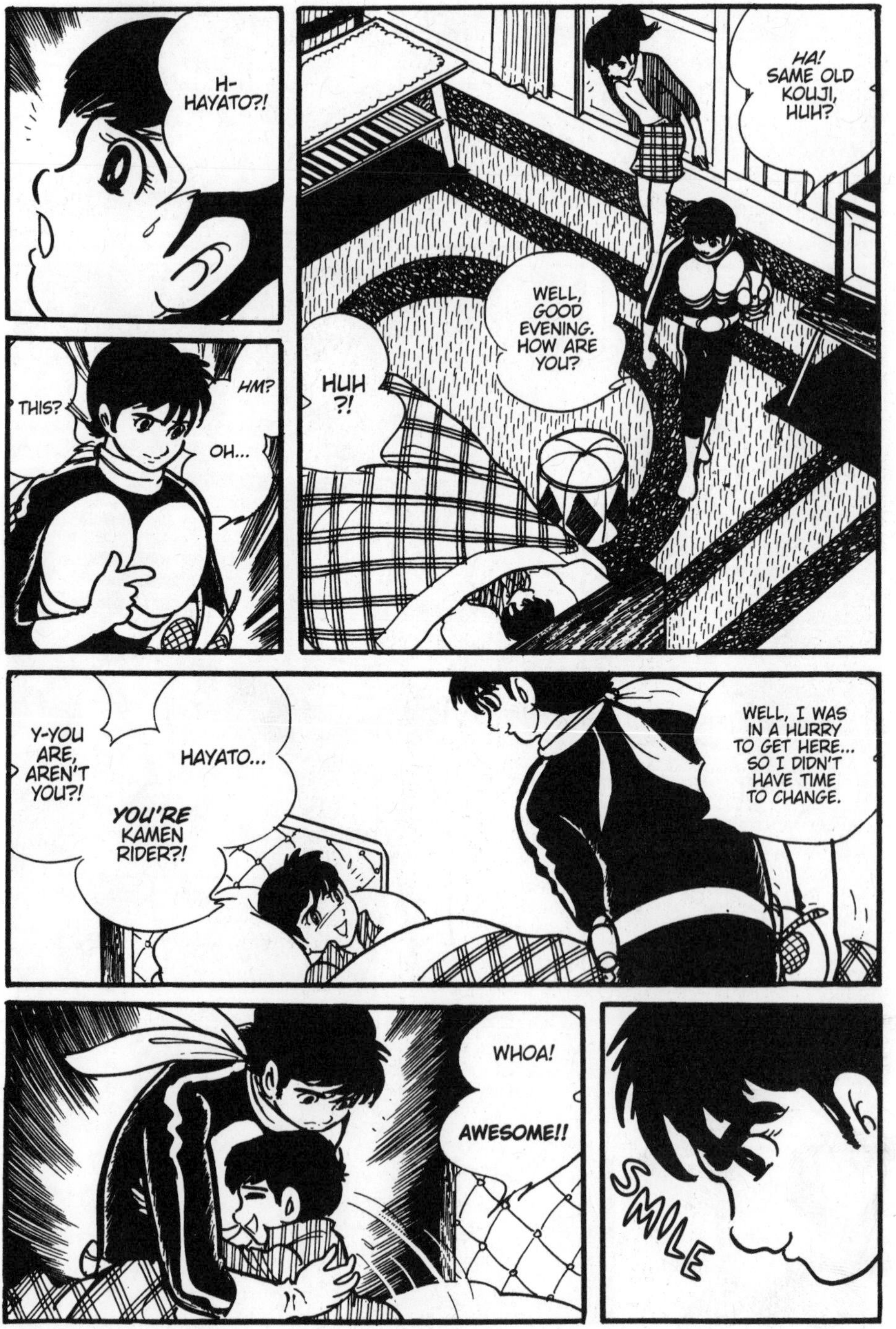

HA! SAME OLD KOUJI, HUH?
WELL, GOOD EVENING. HOW ARE YOU?
HUH ?!
H- HAYATO?!
HM?
THIS?
OH...
WELL, I WAS IN A HURRY TO GET HERE... SO I DIDN'T HAVE TIME TO CHANGE.
HAYATO...
YOU'RE KAMEN RIDER?!
Y-YOU ARE, AREN'T YOU?!
SMILE
WHOA!
AWESOME!!

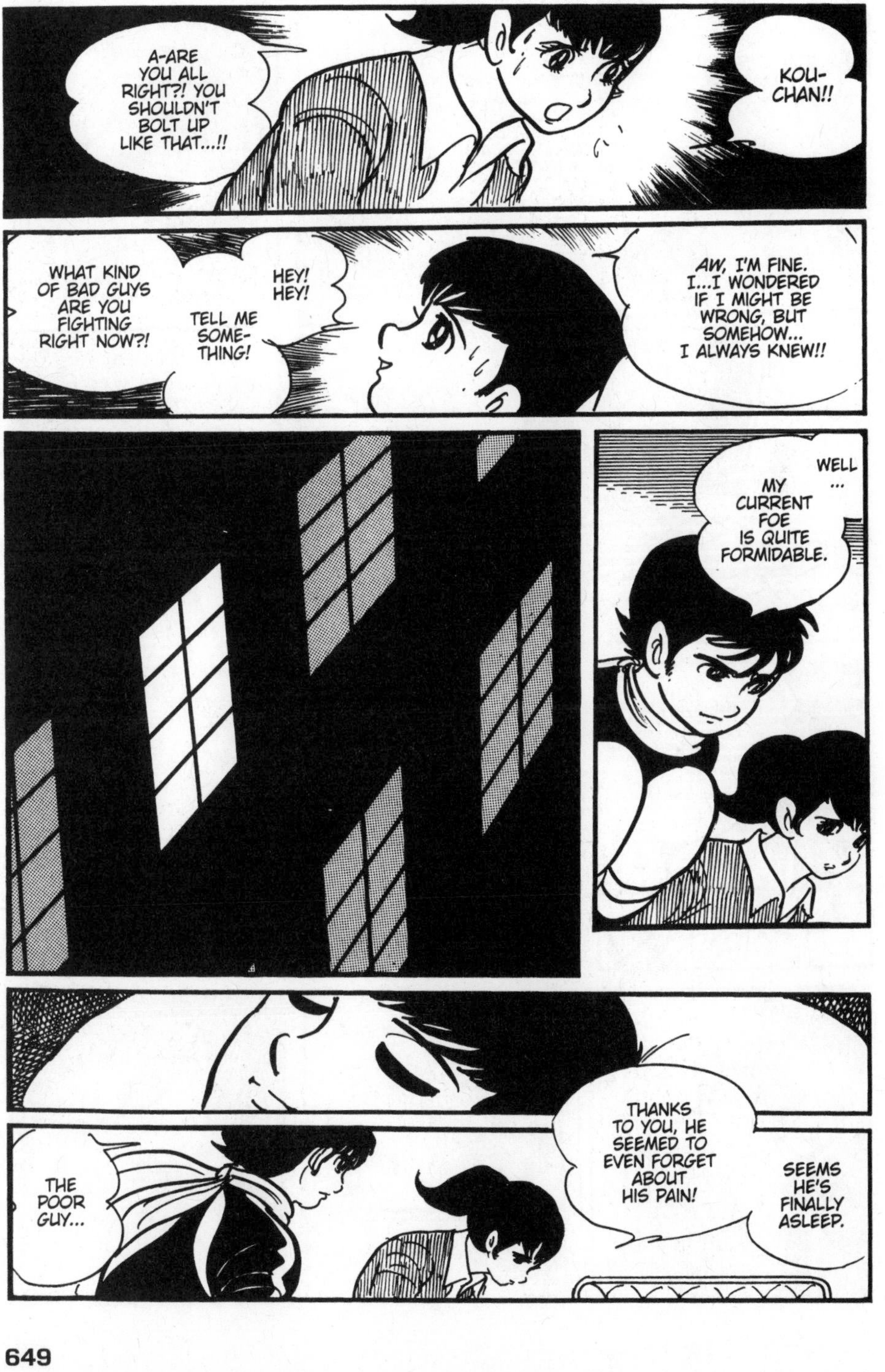

KOU-CHAN!!
A-ARE YOU ALL RIGHT?! YOU SHOULDN'T BOLT UP LIKE THAT...!!
AW, I'M FINE. I...I WONDERED IF I MIGHT BE WRONG, BUT SOMEHOW... I ALWAYS KNEW!!
HEY! HEY!
TELL ME SOME-THING!
WHAT KIND OF BAD GUYS ARE YOU FIGHTING RIGHT NOW?!
WELL ... MY CURRENT FOE IS QUITE FORMIDABLE.
SEEMS HE'S FINALLY ASLEEP.
THANKS TO YOU, HE SEEMED TO EVEN FORGET ABOUT HIS PAIN!
THE POOR GUY...

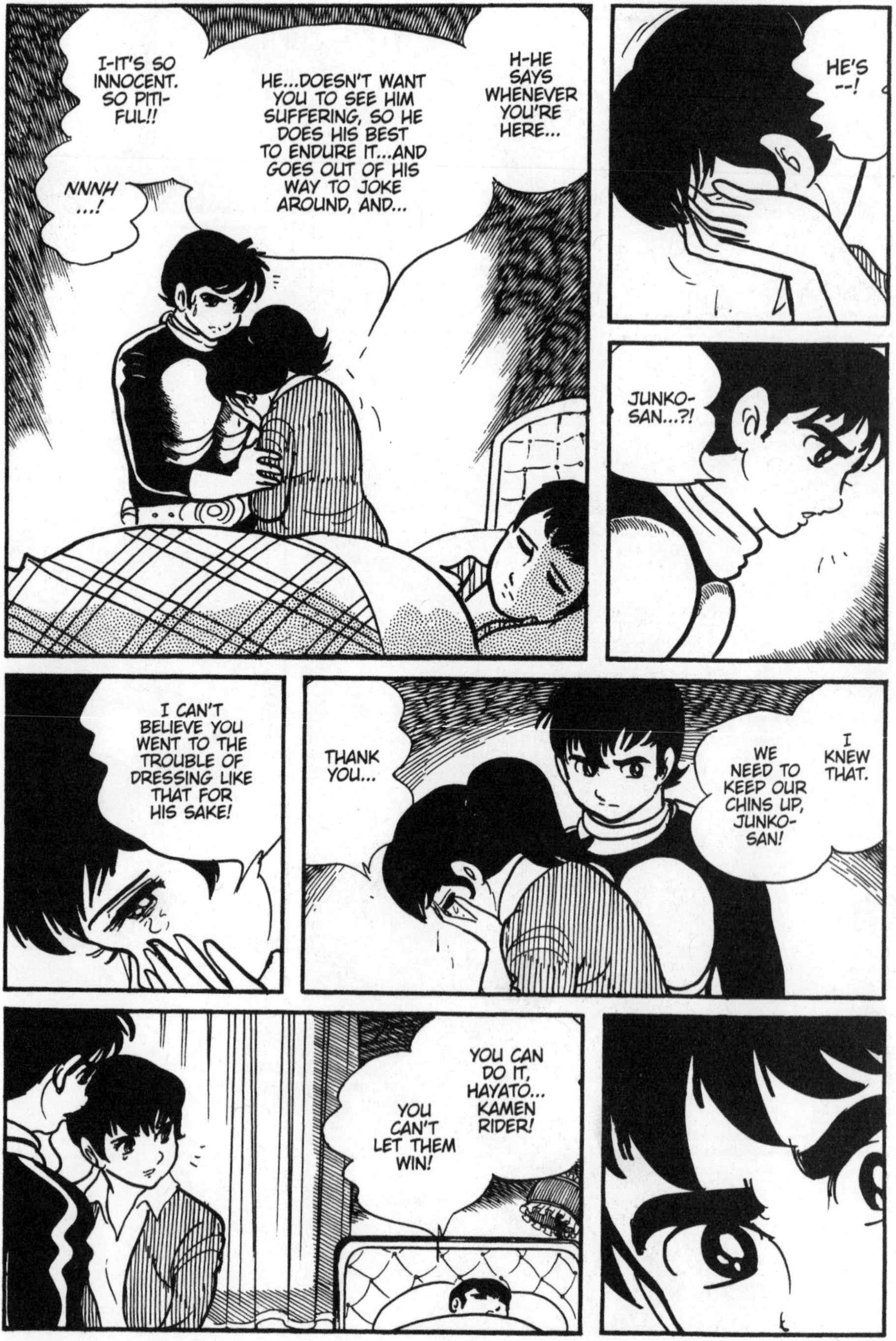
HE'S --!
JUNKO-SAN...?!
H-HE SAYS WHENEVER YOU'RE HERE...
HE...DOESN'T WANT YOU TO SEE HIM SUFFERING, SO HE DOES HIS BEST TO ENDURE IT...AND GOES OUT OF HIS WAY TO JOKE AROUND, AND...
I-IT'S SO INNOCENT. SO PITI-FUL!!
NNNH ...!
I KNEW THAT.
WE NEED TO KEEP OUR CHINS UP, JUNKO-SAN!
THANK YOU...
I CAN'T BELIEVE YOU WENT TO THE TROUBLE OF DRESSING LIKE THAT FOR HIS SAKE!
YOU CAN DO IT, HAYATO... KAMEN RIDER!
YOU CAN'T LET THEM WIN!

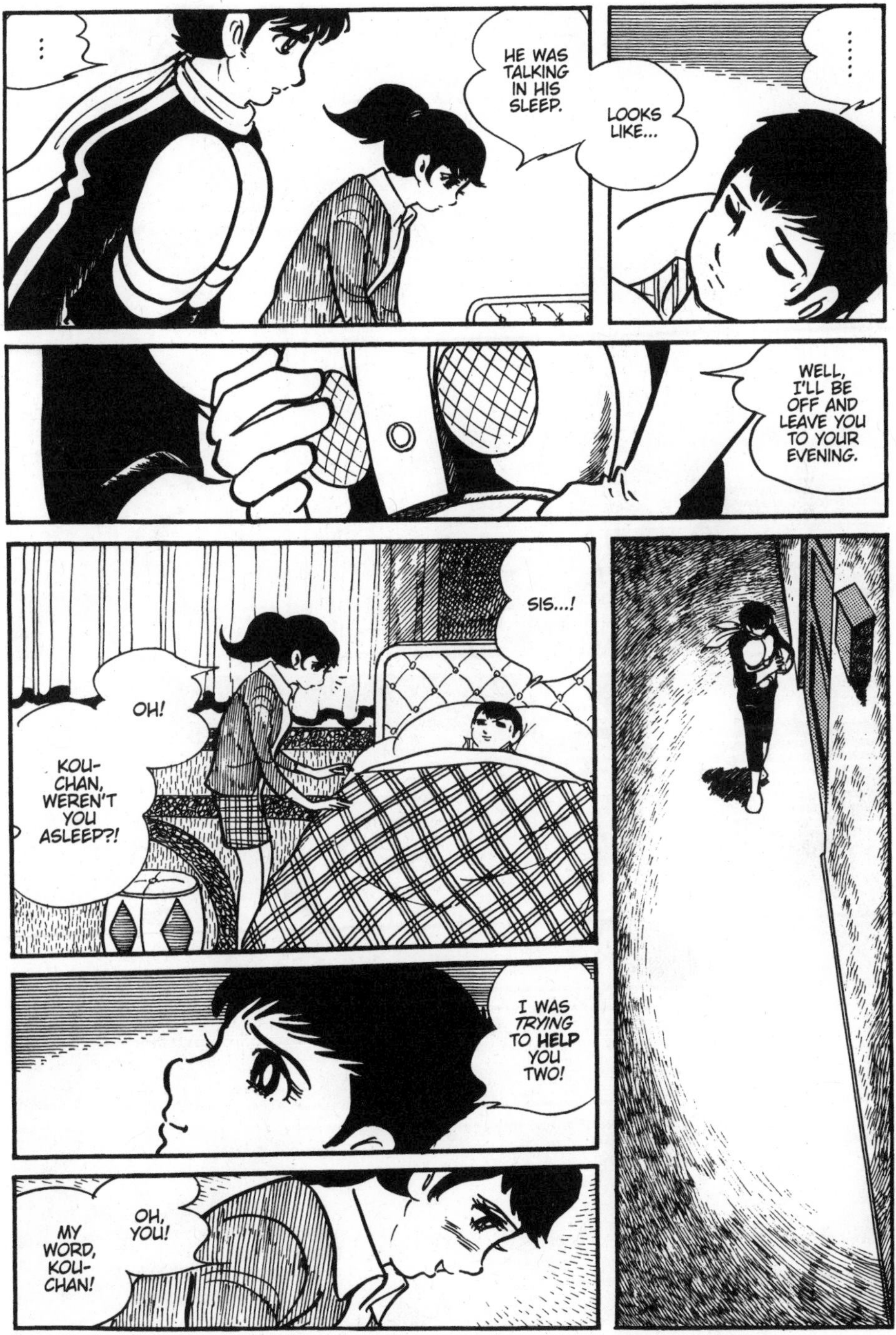
……
LOOKS LIKE...
HE WAS TALKING IN HIS SLEEP.
…
WELL, I'LL BE OFF AND LEAVE YOU TO YOUR EVENING.
SIS...!
OH!
KOU-CHAN, WEREN'T YOU ASLEEP?!
I WAS *TRYING* TO **HELP** YOU TWO!
OH, YOU!
MY WORD, KOU-CHAN!

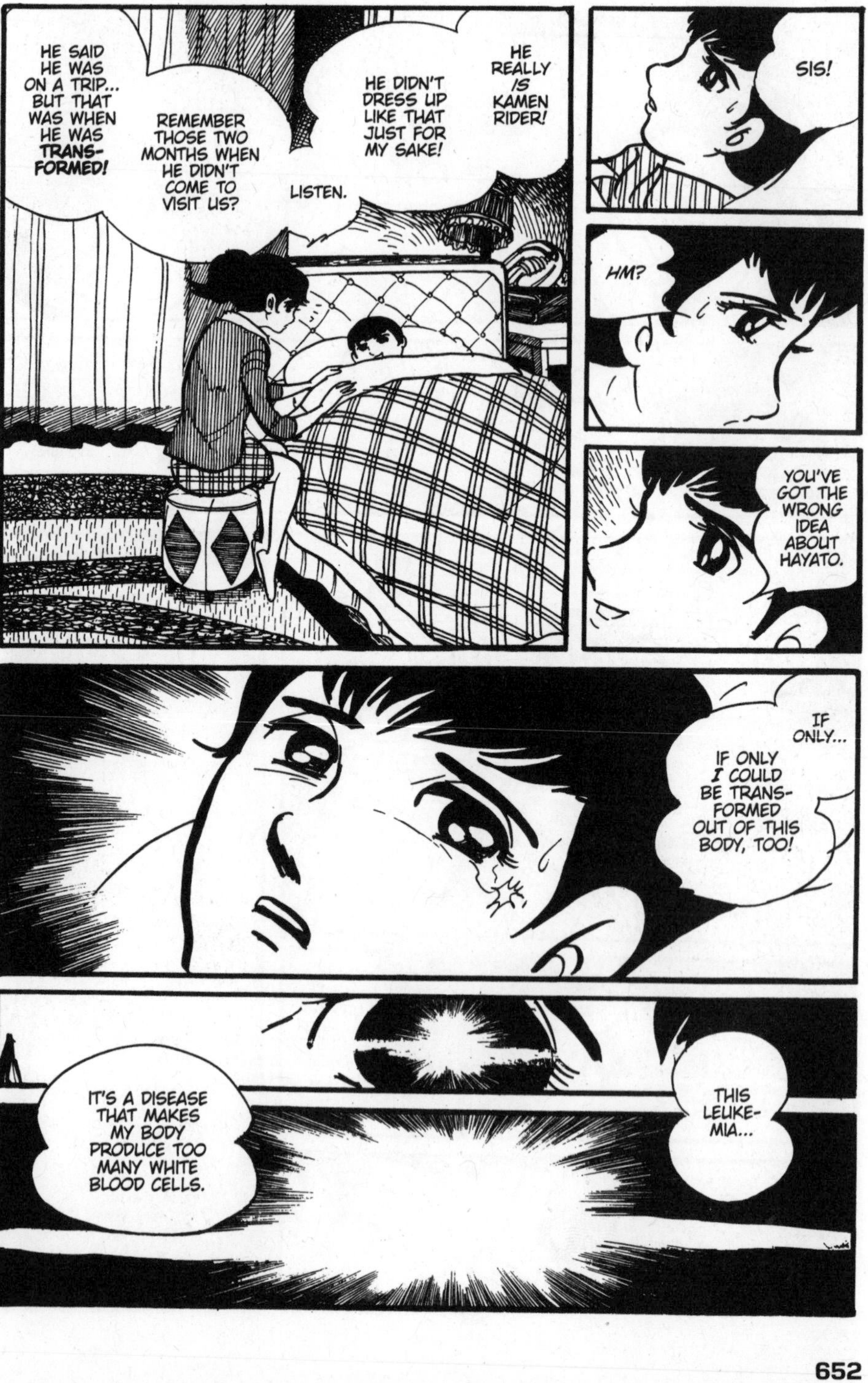
SIS!
HM?
YOU'VE GOT THE WRONG IDEA ABOUT HAYATO.
HE REALLY *IS* KAMEN RIDER!
HE DIDN'T DRESS UP LIKE THAT JUST FOR MY SAKE!
LISTEN.
REMEMBER THOSE TWO MONTHS WHEN HE DIDN'T COME TO VISIT US?
HE SAID HE WAS ON A TRIP... BUT THAT WAS WHEN HE WAS **TRANSFORMED!**
IF ONLY...
IF ONLY *I* COULD BE TRANSFORMED OUT OF THIS BODY, TOO!
THIS LEUKEMIA...
IT'S A DISEASE THAT MAKES MY BODY PRODUCE TOO MANY WHITE BLOOD CELLS.

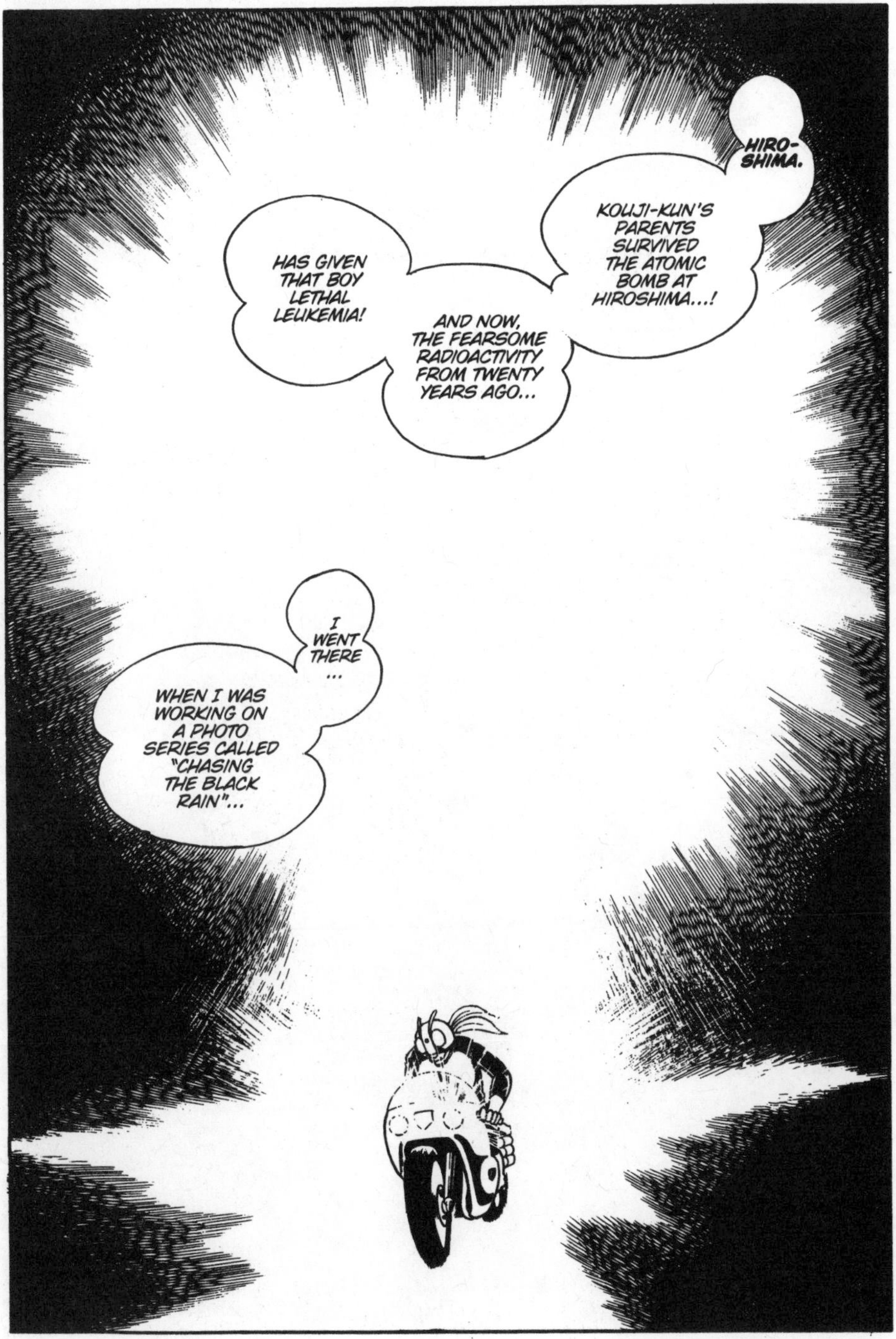
HIRO-SHIMA.
KOUJI-KUN'S PARENTS SURVIVED THE ATOMIC BOMB AT HIROSHIMA...!
AND NOW, THE FEARSOME RADIOACTIVITY FROM TWENTY YEARS AGO...
HAS GIVEN THAT BOY LETHAL LEUKEMIA!
I WENT THERE ...
WHEN I WAS WORKING ON A PHOTO SERIES CALLED "CHASING THE BLACK RAIN"...

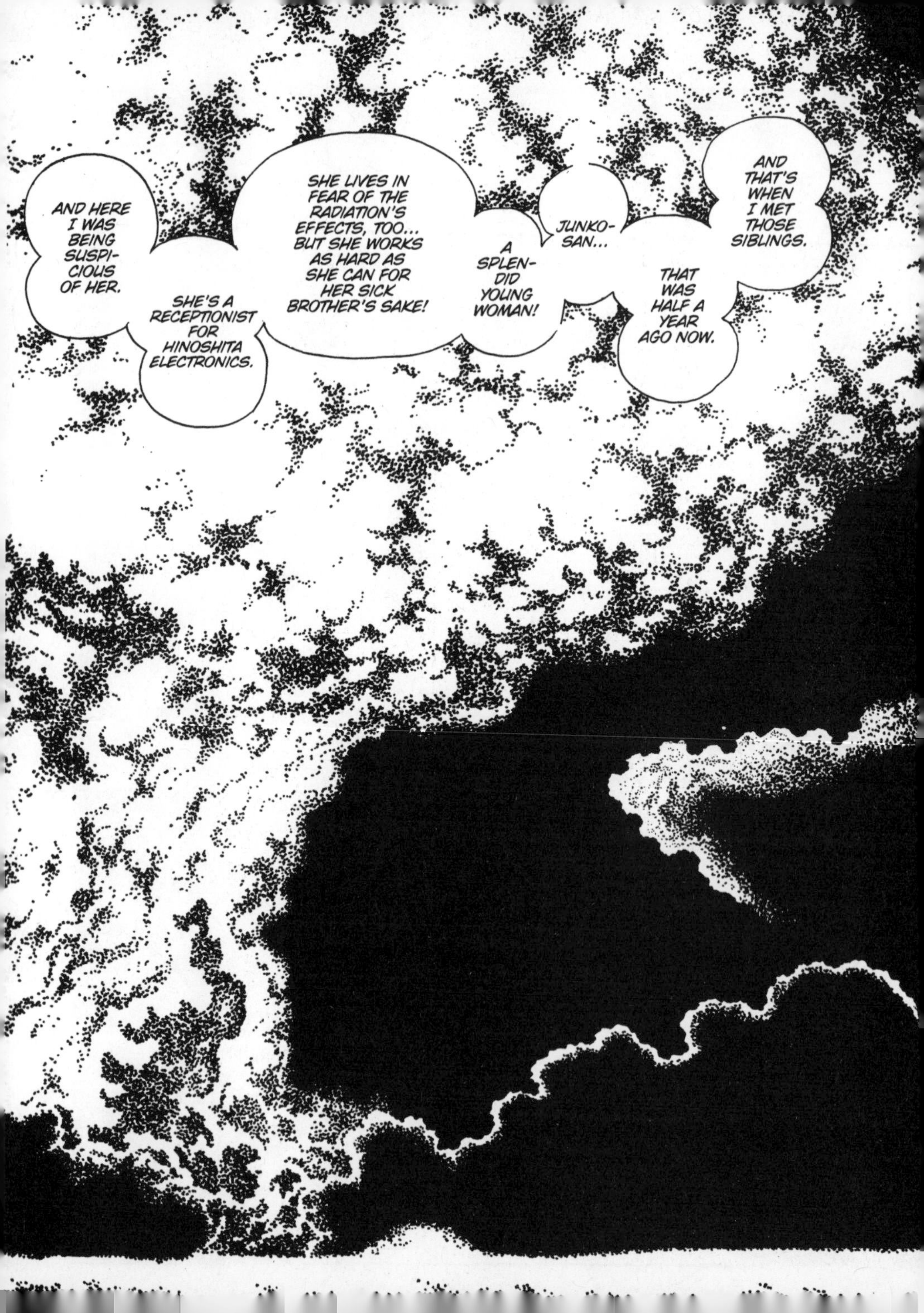
AND THAT'S WHEN I MET THOSE SIBLINGS.
THAT WAS HALF A YEAR AGO NOW.
JUNKO-SAN...
A SPLEN-DID YOUNG WOMAN!
SHE LIVES IN FEAR OF THE RADIATION'S EFFECTS, TOO... BUT SHE WORKS AS HARD AS SHE CAN FOR HER SICK BROTHER'S SAKE!
SHE'S A RECEPTIONIST FOR HINOSHITA ELECTRONICS.
AND HERE I WAS BEING SUSPI-CIOUS OF HER.

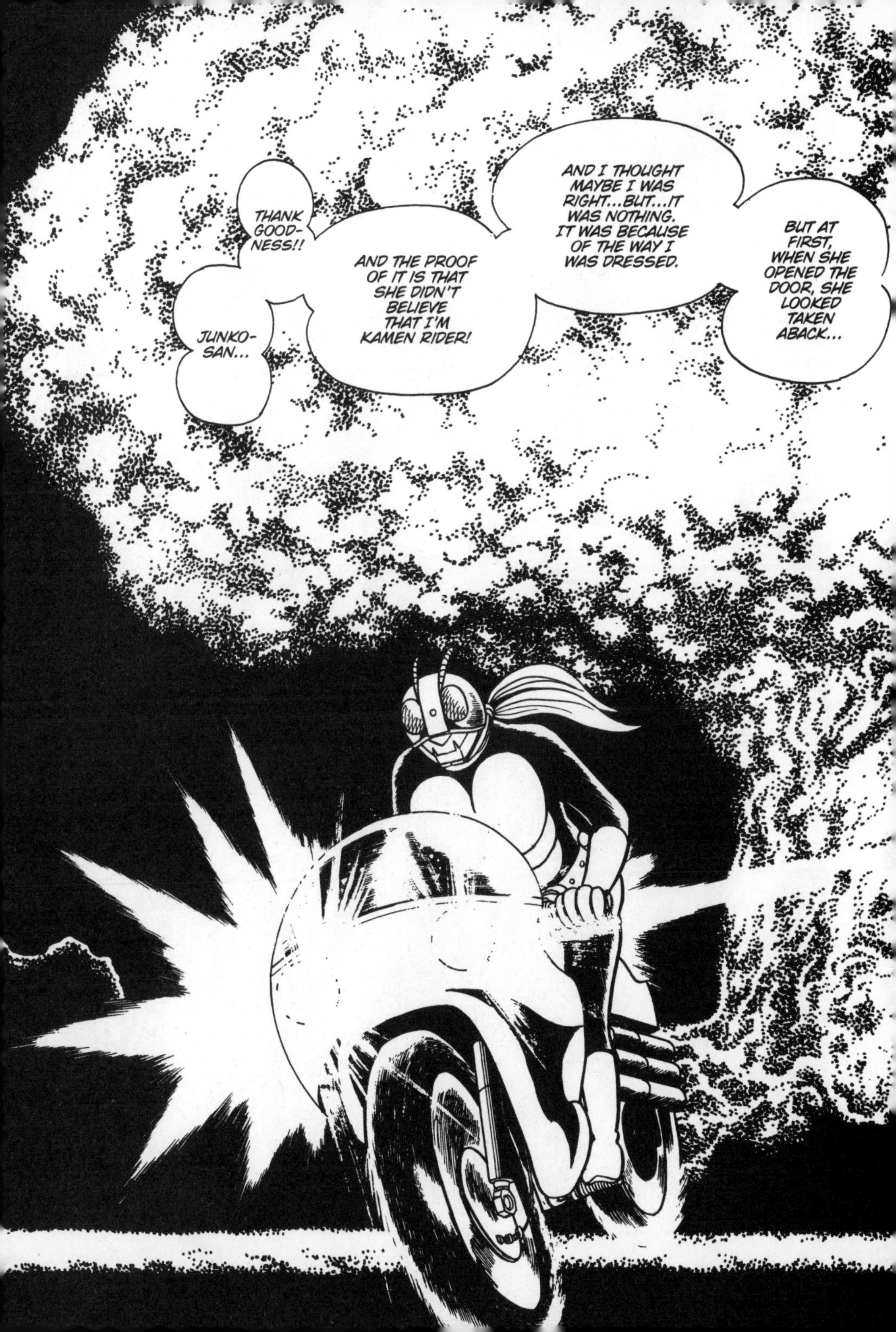
BUT AT FIRST, WHEN SHE OPENED THE DOOR, SHE LOOKED TAKEN ABACK...
AND I THOUGHT MAYBE I WAS RIGHT...BUT...IT WAS NOTHING. IT WAS BECAUSE OF THE WAY I WAS DRESSED.
AND THE PROOF OF IT IS THAT SHE DIDN'T BELIEVE THAT I'M KAMEN RIDER!
THANK GOOD-NESS!!
JUNKO-SAN...

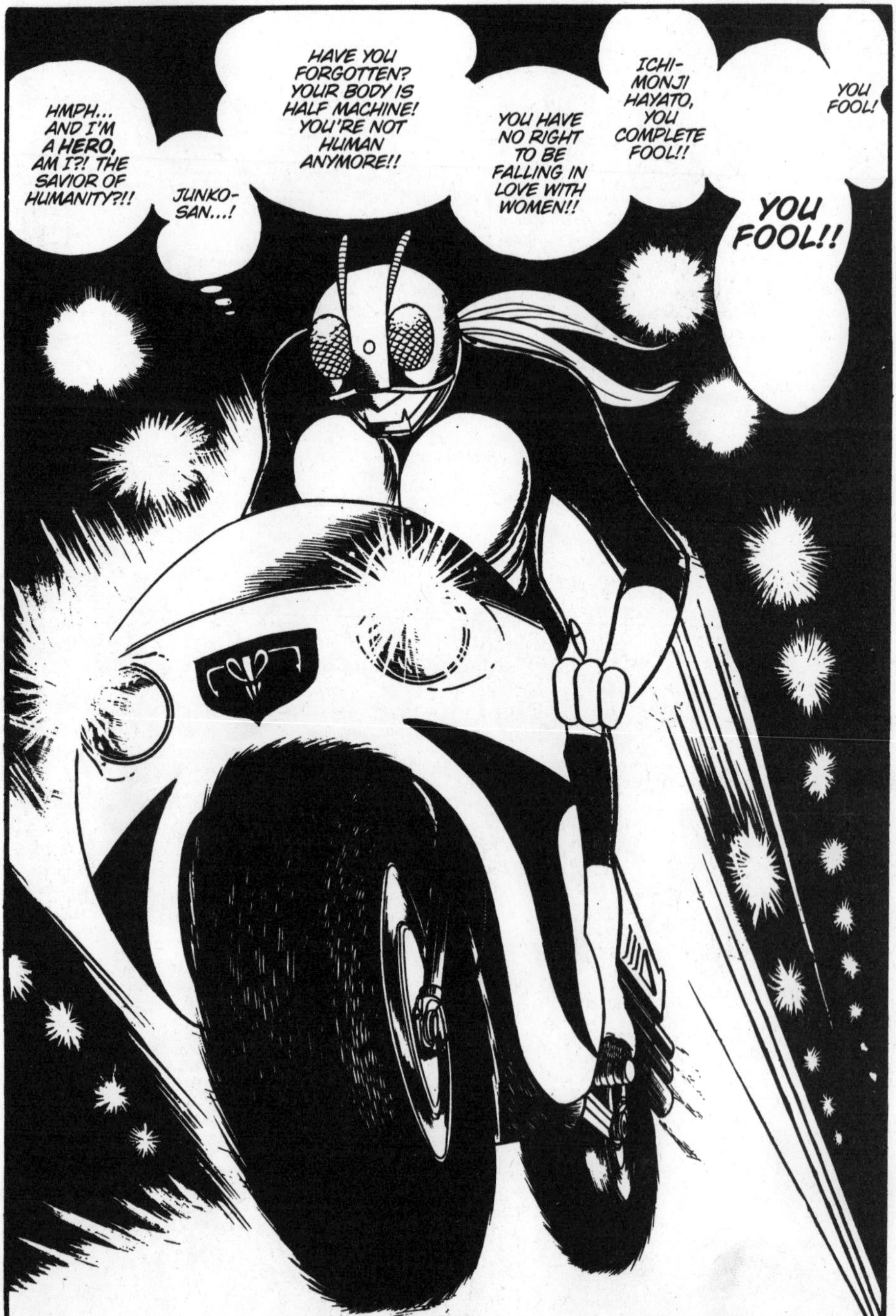
YOU FOOL!
YOU FOOL!!
ICHI-MONJI HAYATO, YOU COMPLETE FOOL!!
YOU HAVE NO RIGHT TO BE FALLING IN LOVE WITH WOMEN!!
HAVE YOU FORGOTTEN? YOUR BODY IS HALF MACHINE! YOU'RE NOT HUMAN ANYMORE!!
JUNKO-SAN...!
HMPH... AND I'M A HERO, AM I?! THE SAVIOR OF HUMANITY?!!

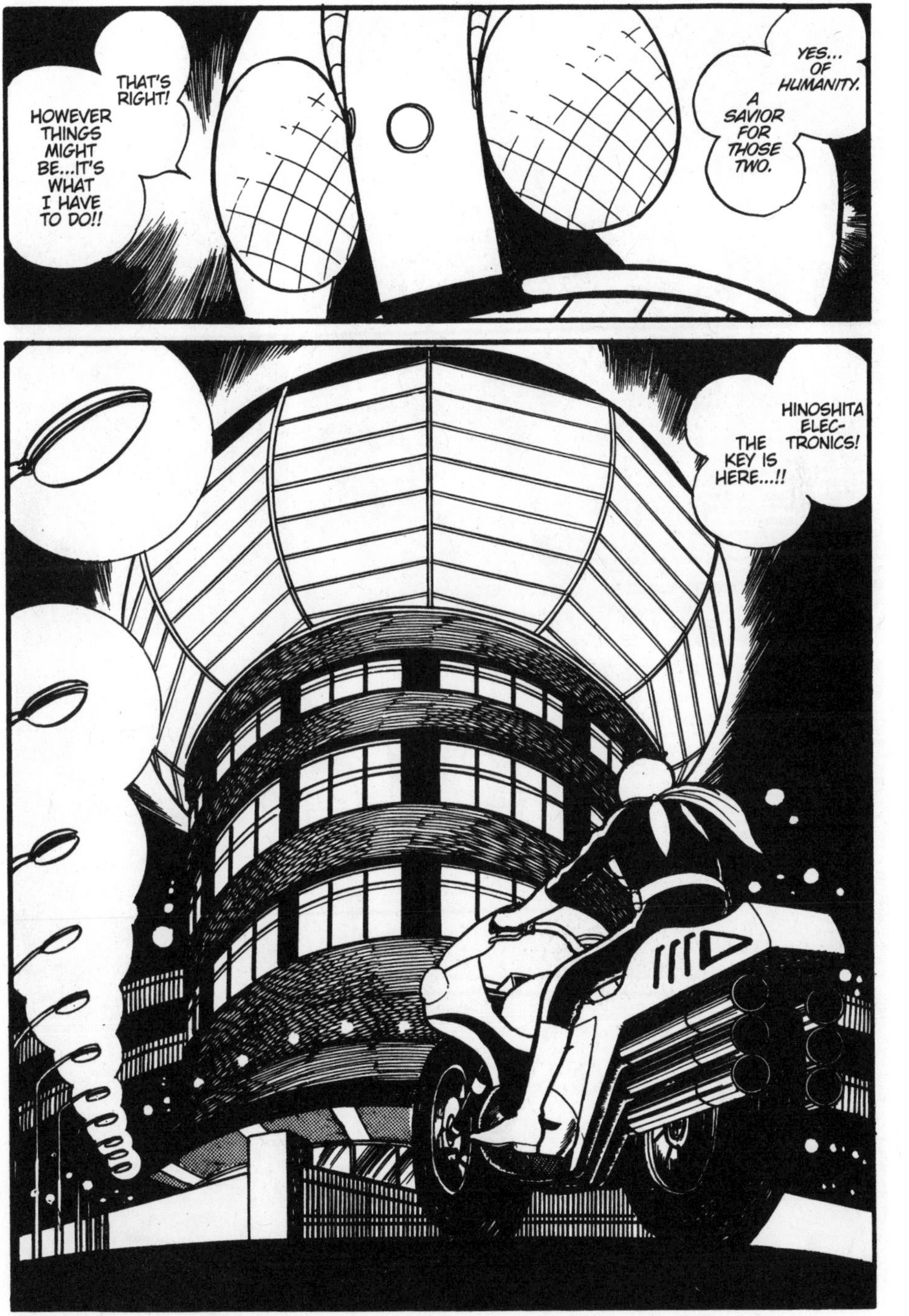
YES... OF HUMANITY.
A SAVIOR FOR THOSE TWO.
THAT'S RIGHT!
HOWEVER THINGS MIGHT BE...IT'S WHAT I HAVE TO DO!!
HINOSHITA ELEC-TRONICS!
THE KEY IS HERE...!!

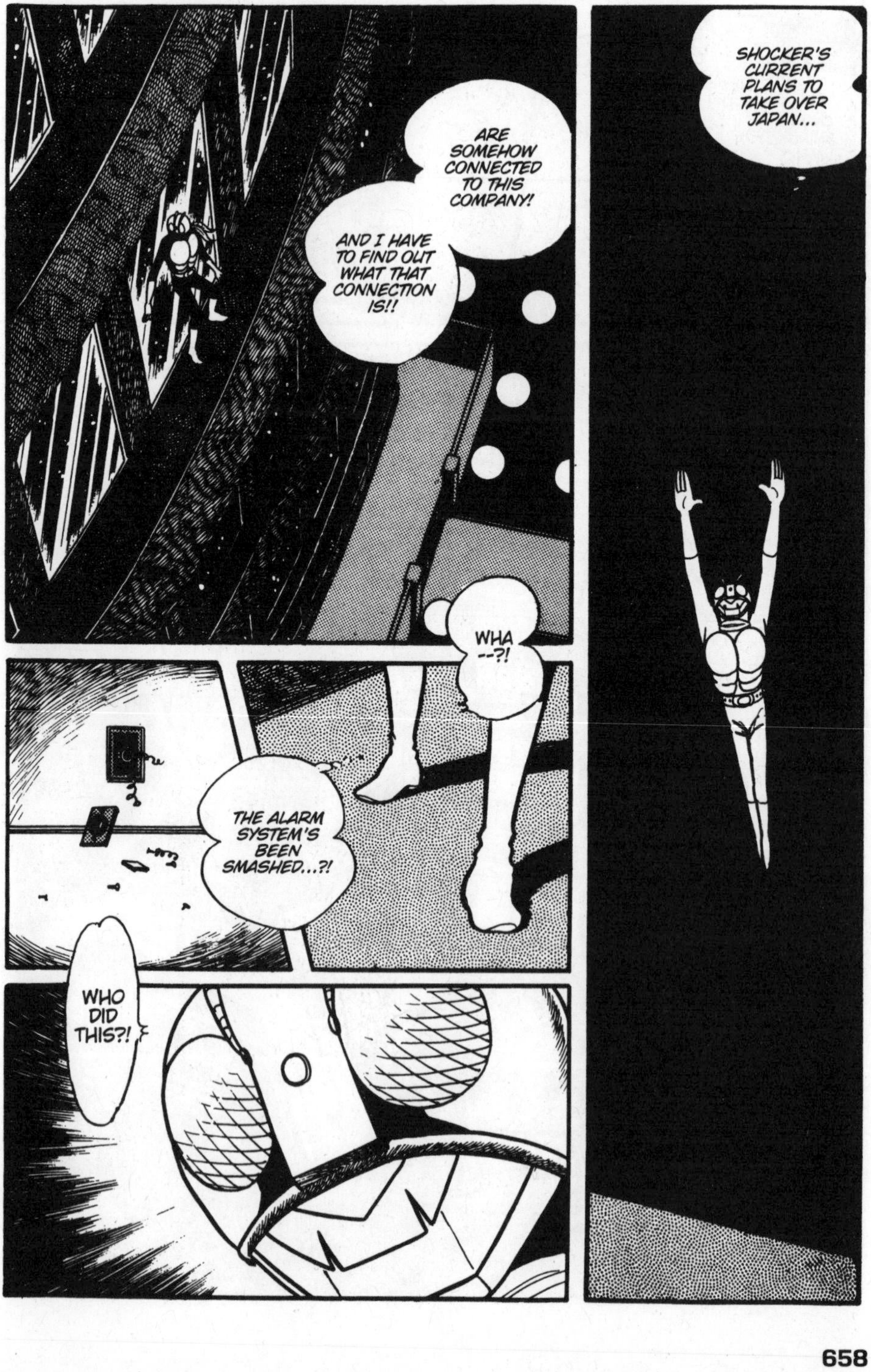
SHOCKER'S CURRENT PLANS TO TAKE OVER JAPAN...
ARE SOMEHOW CONNECTED TO THIS COMPANY!
AND I HAVE TO FIND OUT WHAT THAT CONNECTION IS!!
WHA --?!
THE ALARM SYSTEM'S BEEN SMASHED...?!
WHO DID THIS?!

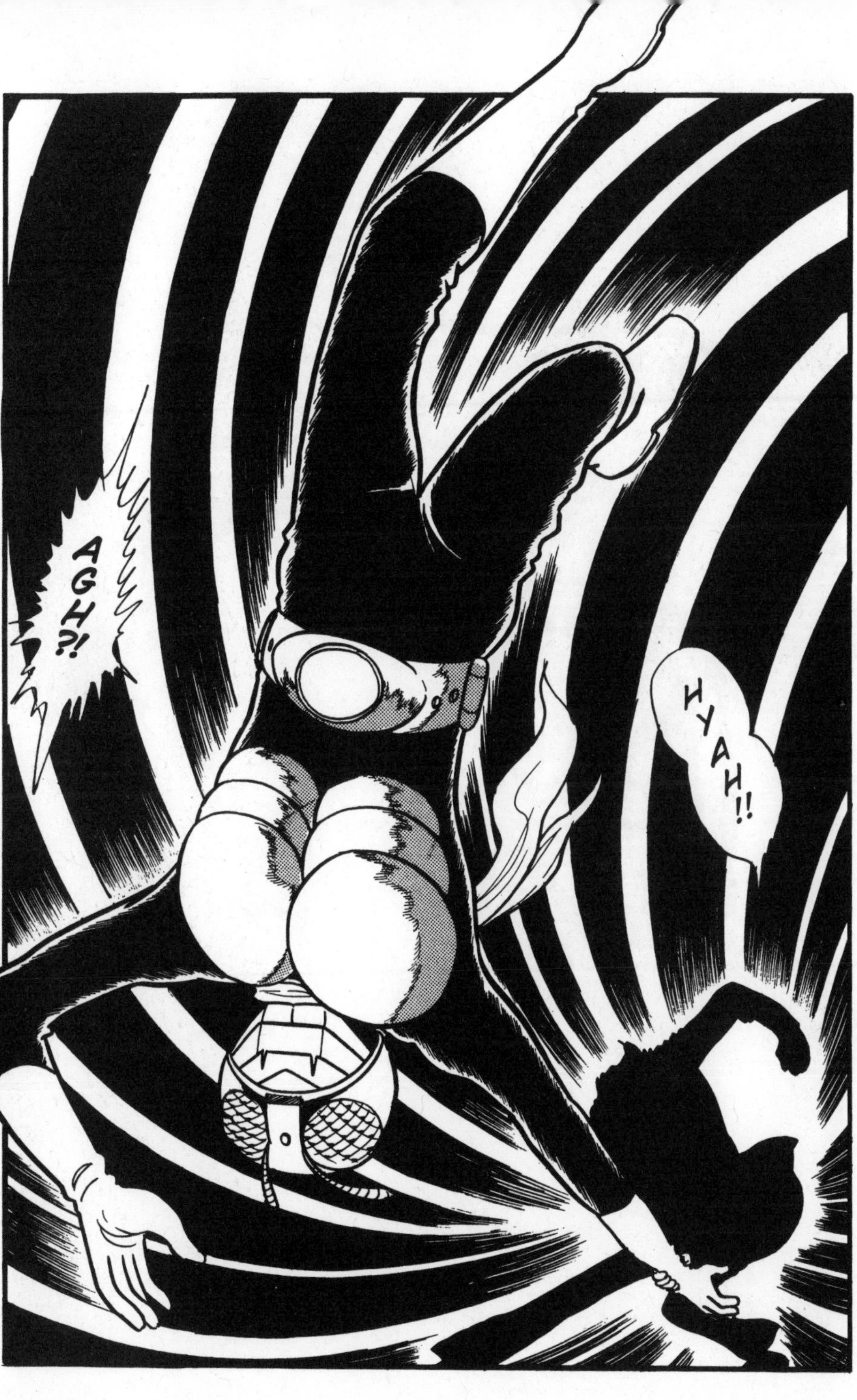
HYAH!!
AGH?!

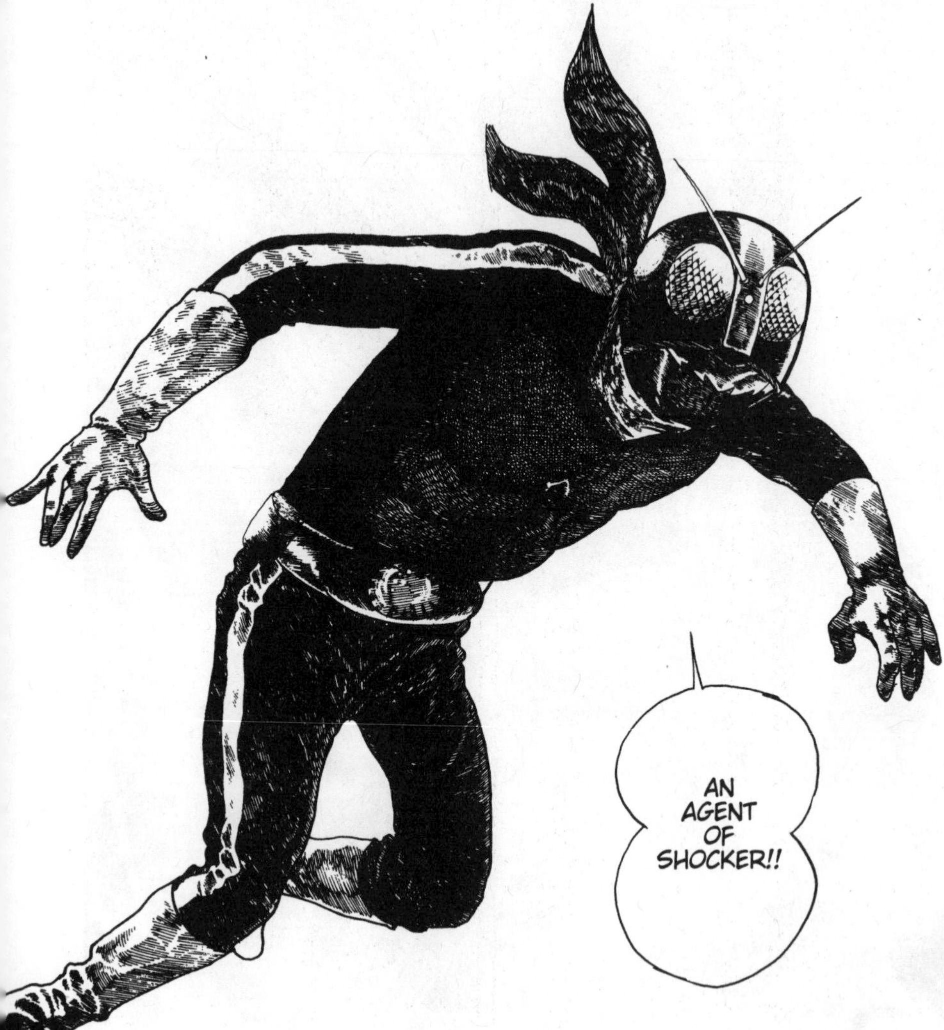
AN AGENT OF SHOCKER!!

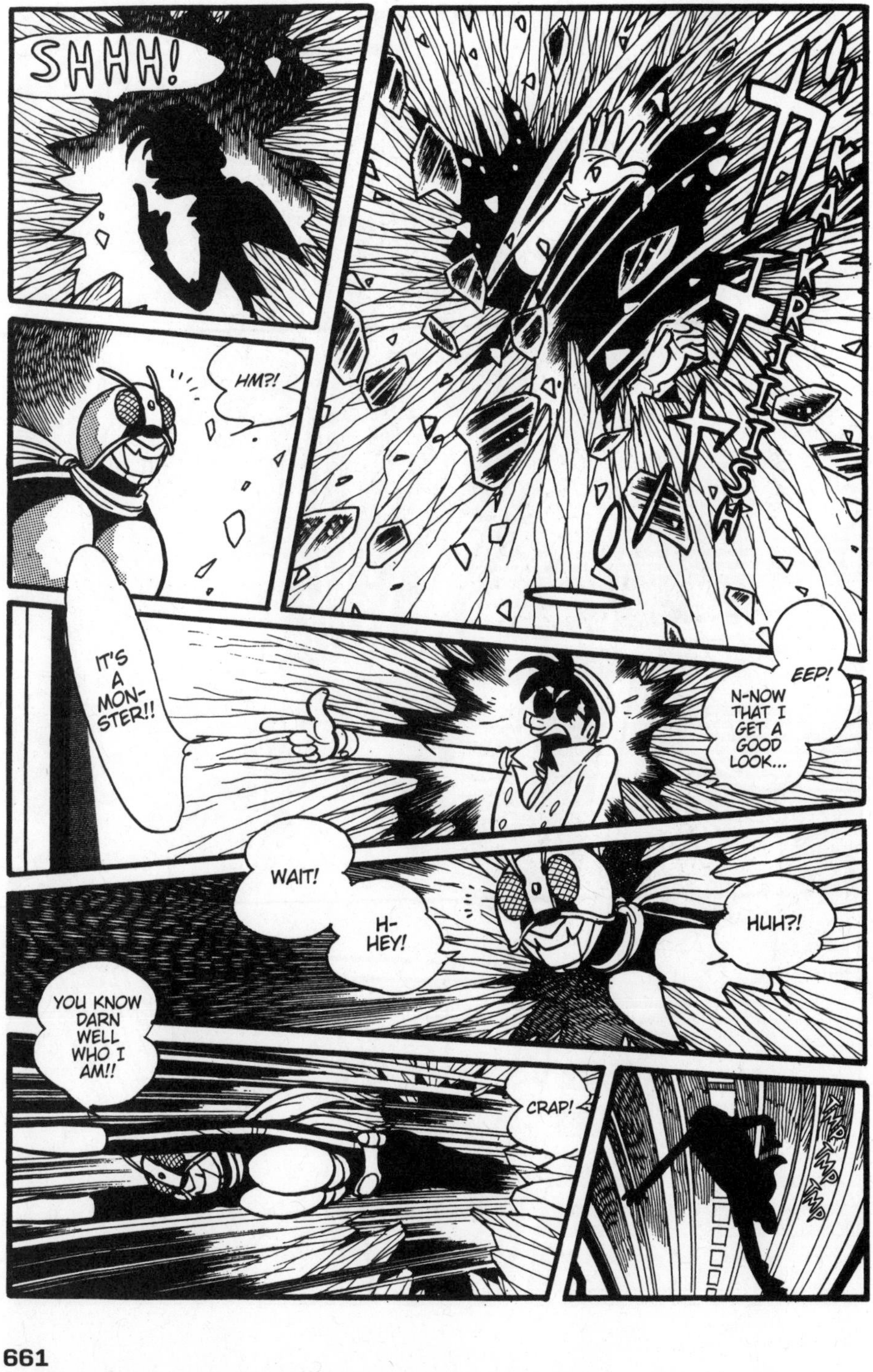
KRAKRIIISH
SHHH!
HM?!
EEP!
N-NOW THAT I GET A GOOD LOOK...
IT'S A MONSTER!!
HUH?!
H-HEY!
WAIT!
YOU KNOW DARN WELL WHO I AM!!
TMP TMP TMP
CRAP!

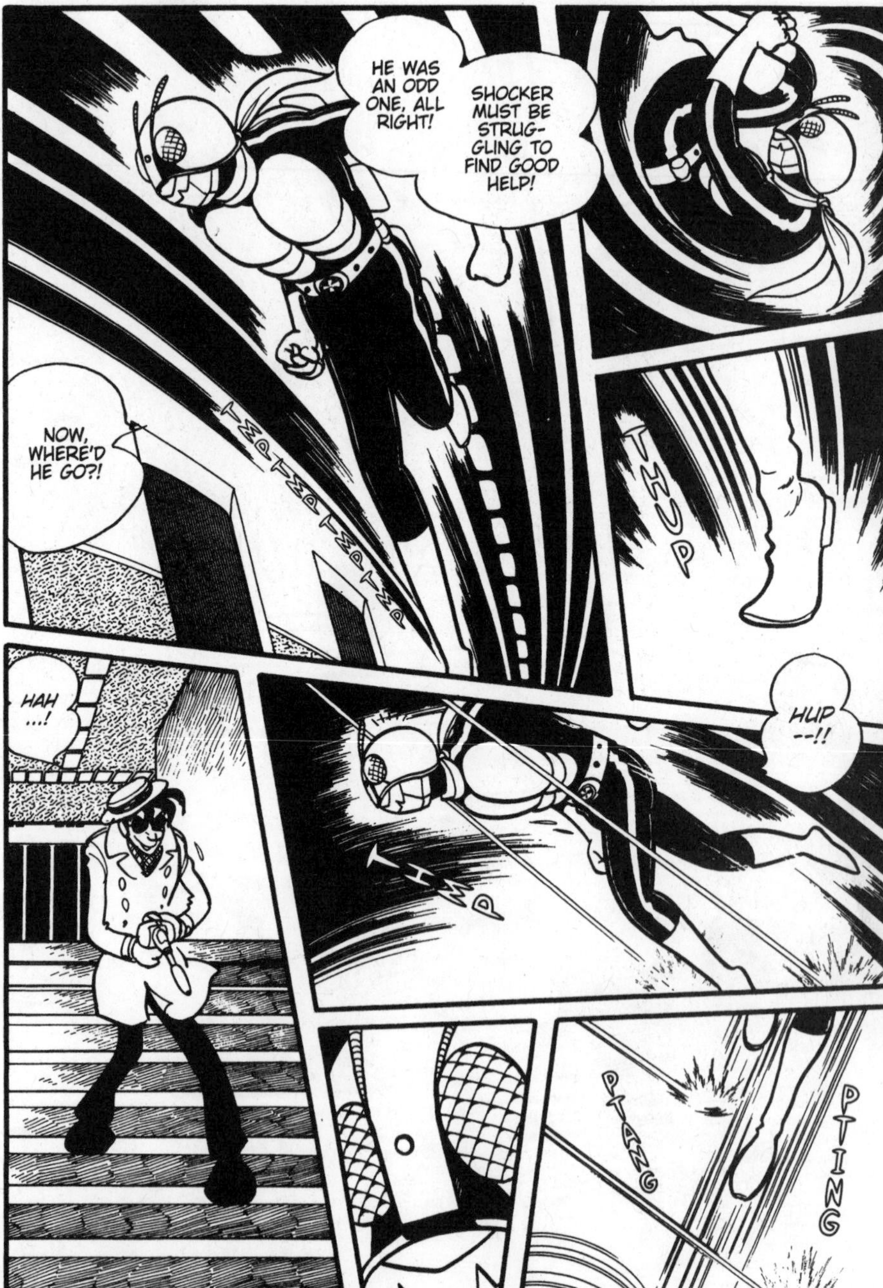
THUP
HE WAS AN ODD ONE, ALL RIGHT!
SHOCKER MUST BE STRUG-GLING TO FIND GOOD HELP!
NOW, WHERE'D HE GO?!
HUP --!!
THMP
PTING
PTANG
HAH ...!

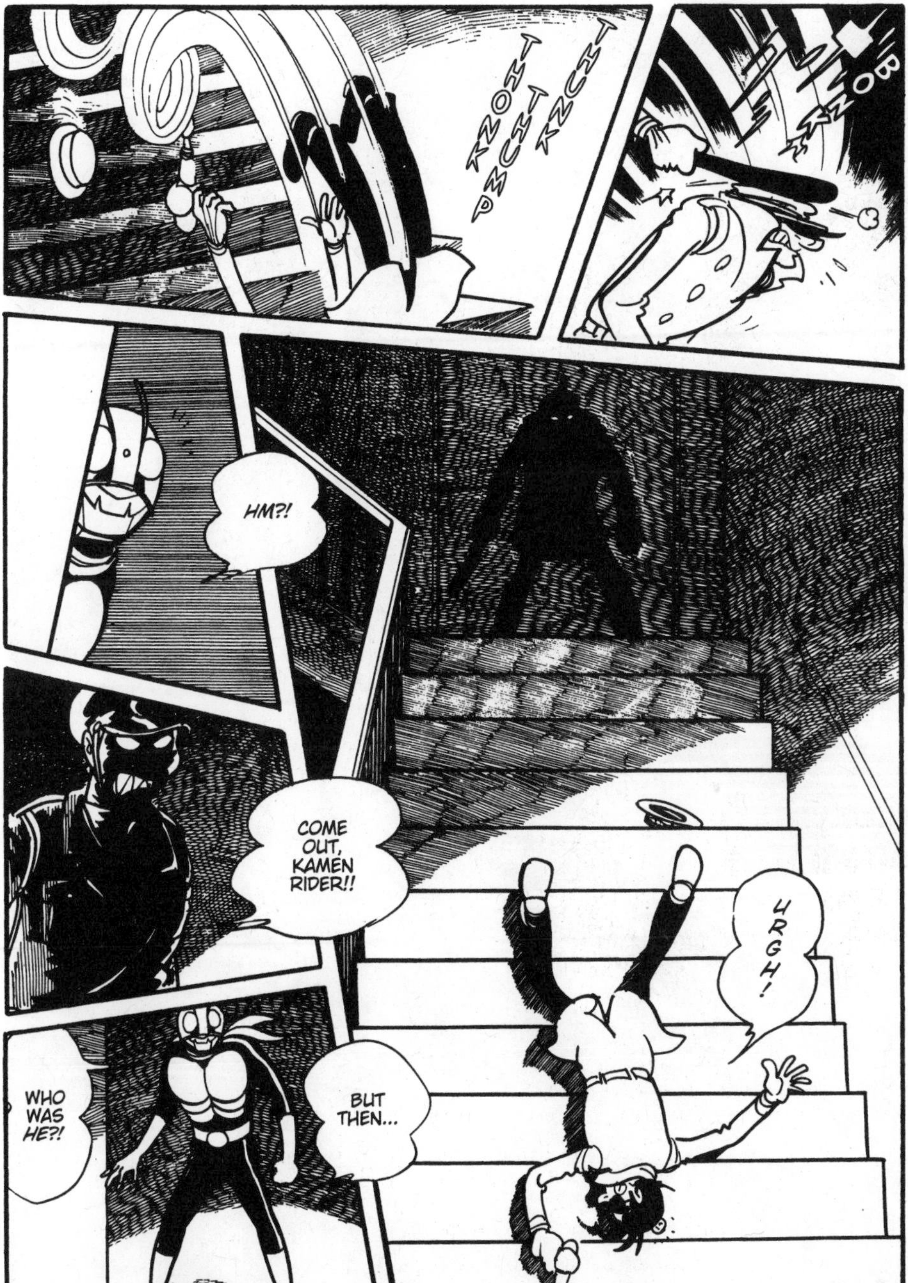
BONK
THUNK
THUMP
THONK
URGH!
HM?!
COME OUT, KAMEN RIDER!!
BUT THEN...
WHO WAS HE?!

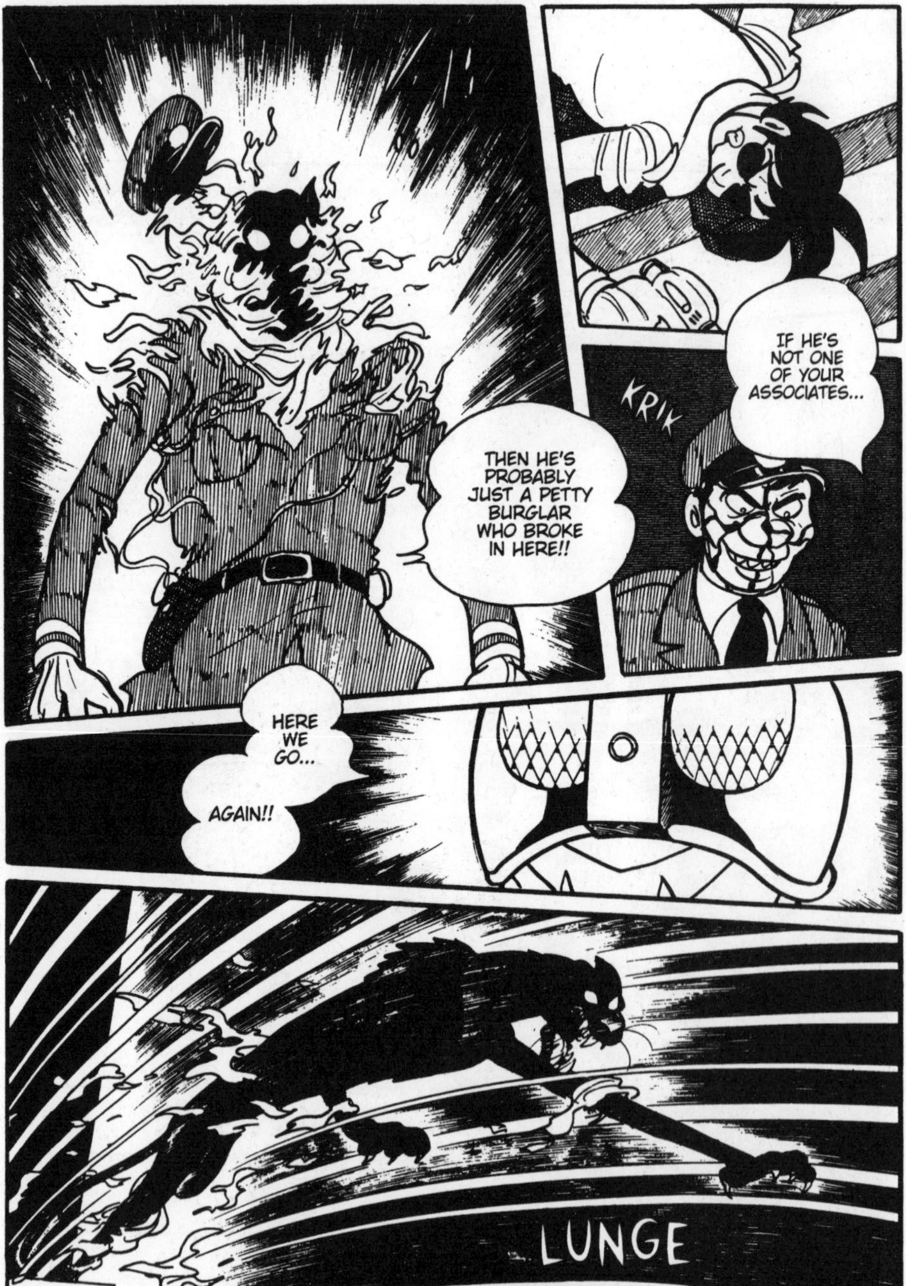
IF HE'S NOT ONE OF YOUR ASSOCIATES...
KRIK
THEN HE'S PROBABLY JUST A PETTY BURGLAR WHO BROKE IN HERE!!
HERE WE GO...
AGAIN!!
LUNGE

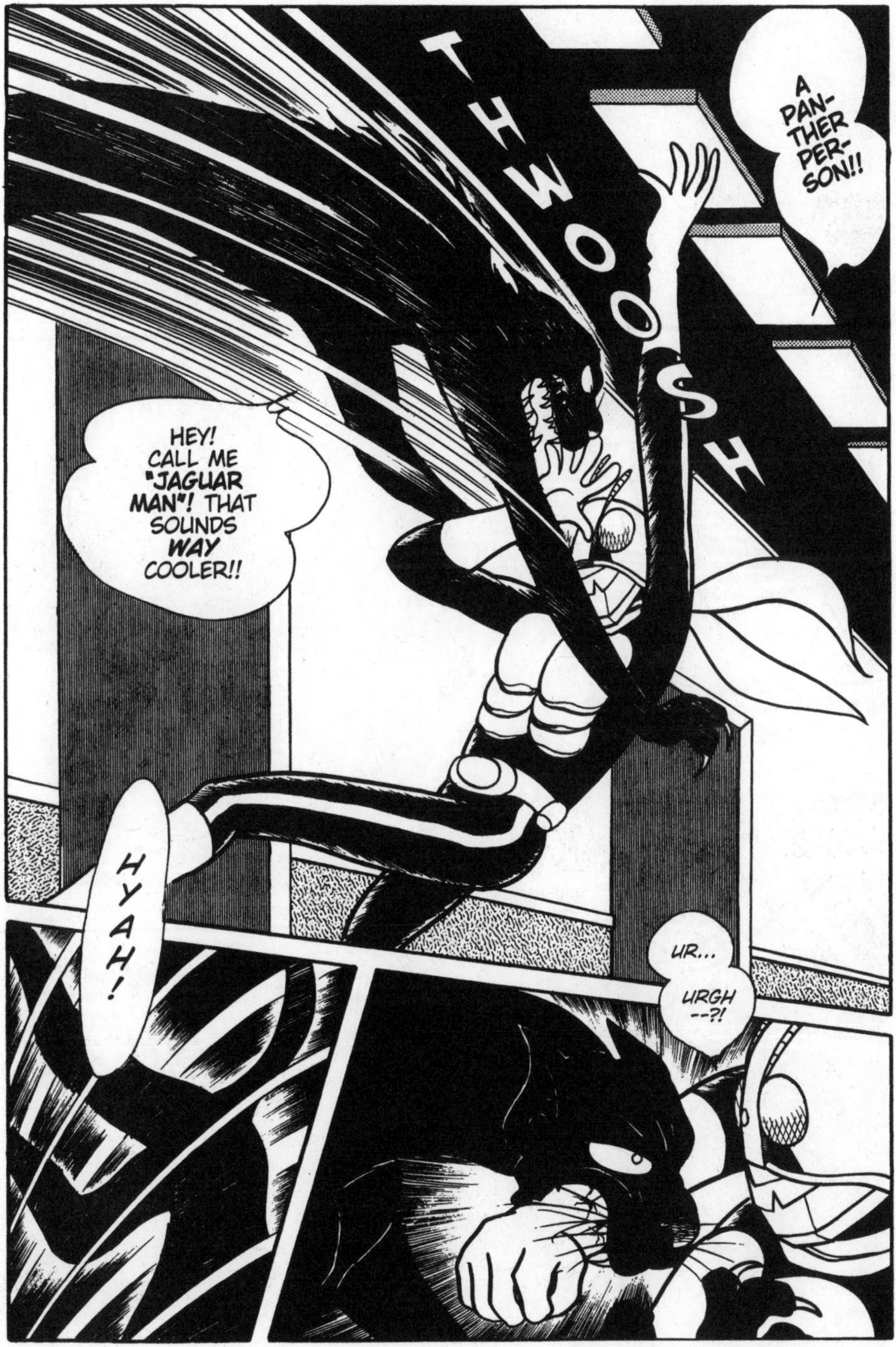
A PAN-
THER
PER-
SON!!
THWOOSH
HEY! CALL ME "JAGUAR MAN"! THAT SOUNDS WAY COOLER!!
HYAH!
UR...
URGH --?!

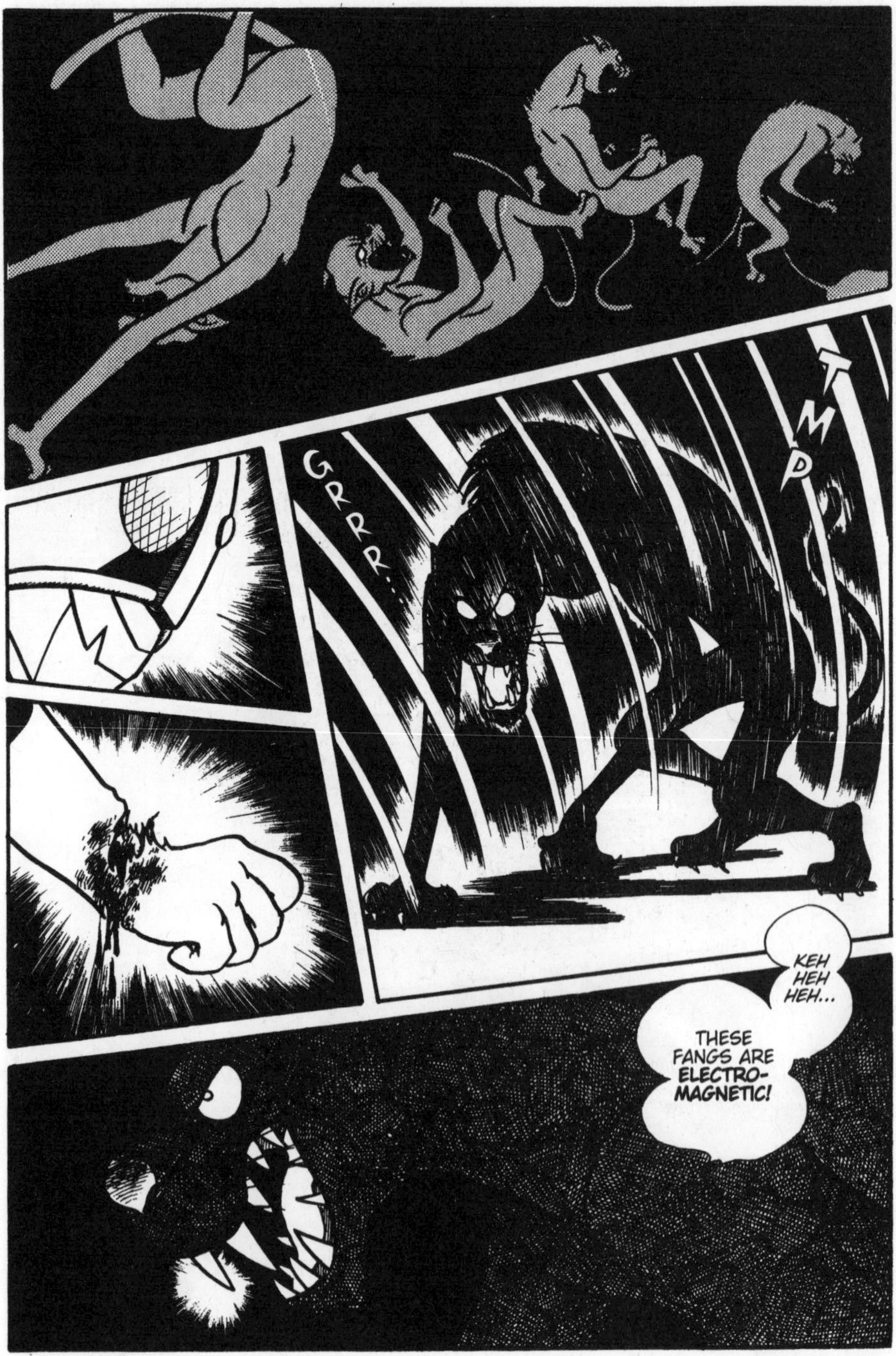
TMP
GRRR...
KEH HEH HEH...
THESE FANGS ARE ELECTRO-MAGNETIC!

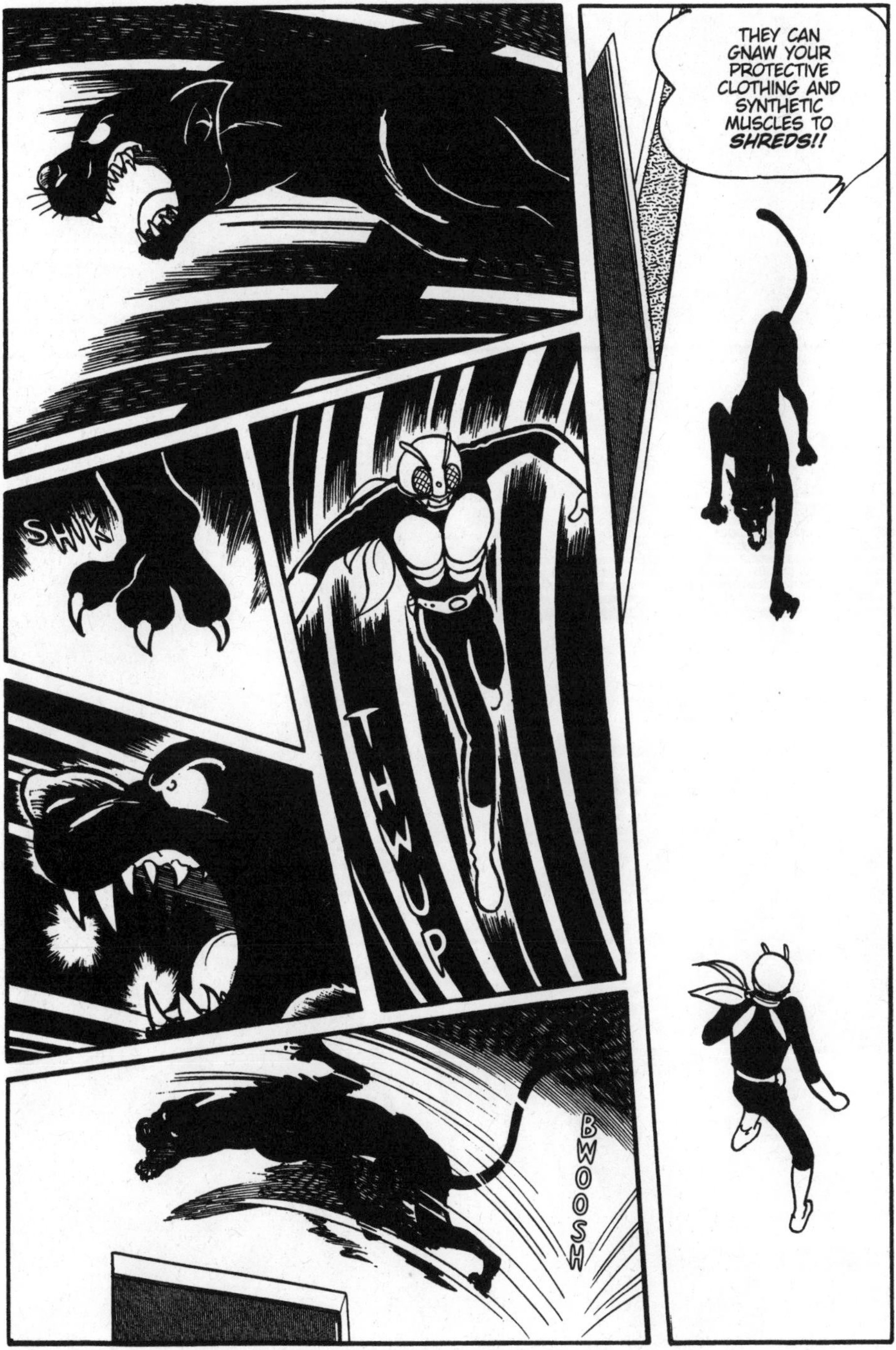
THEY CAN GNAW YOUR PROTECTIVE CLOTHING AND SYNTHETIC MUSCLES TO **SHREDS!!**
THWUP
SHIK
BWOOSH

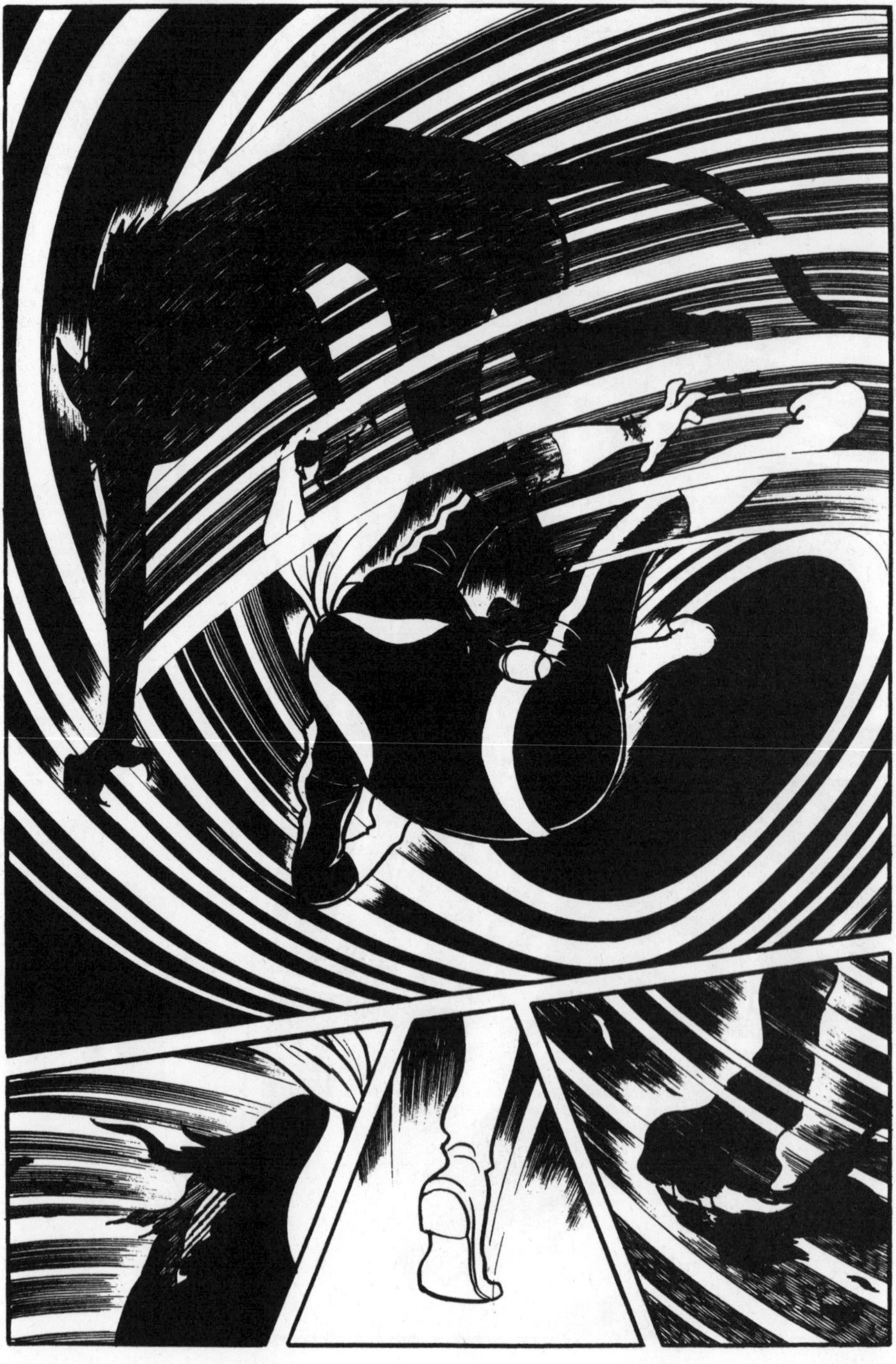

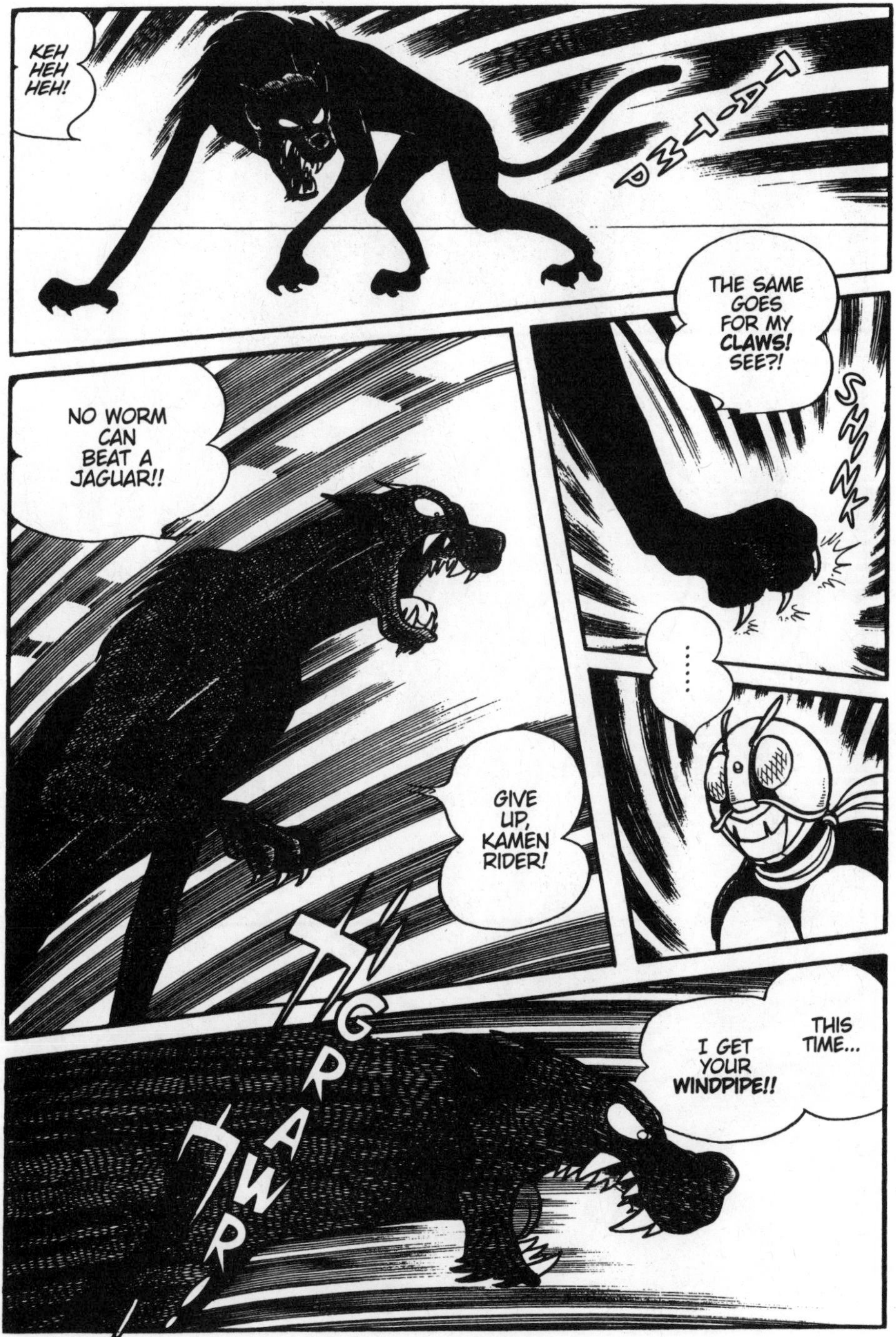
KEH HEH HEH!
TA-TAMP
THE SAME GOES FOR MY CLAWS! SEE?!
SHINK
......
NO WORM CAN BEAT A JAGUAR!!
GIVE UP, KAMEN RIDER!
THIS TIME...
I GET YOUR WINDPIPE!!
GRAWR!

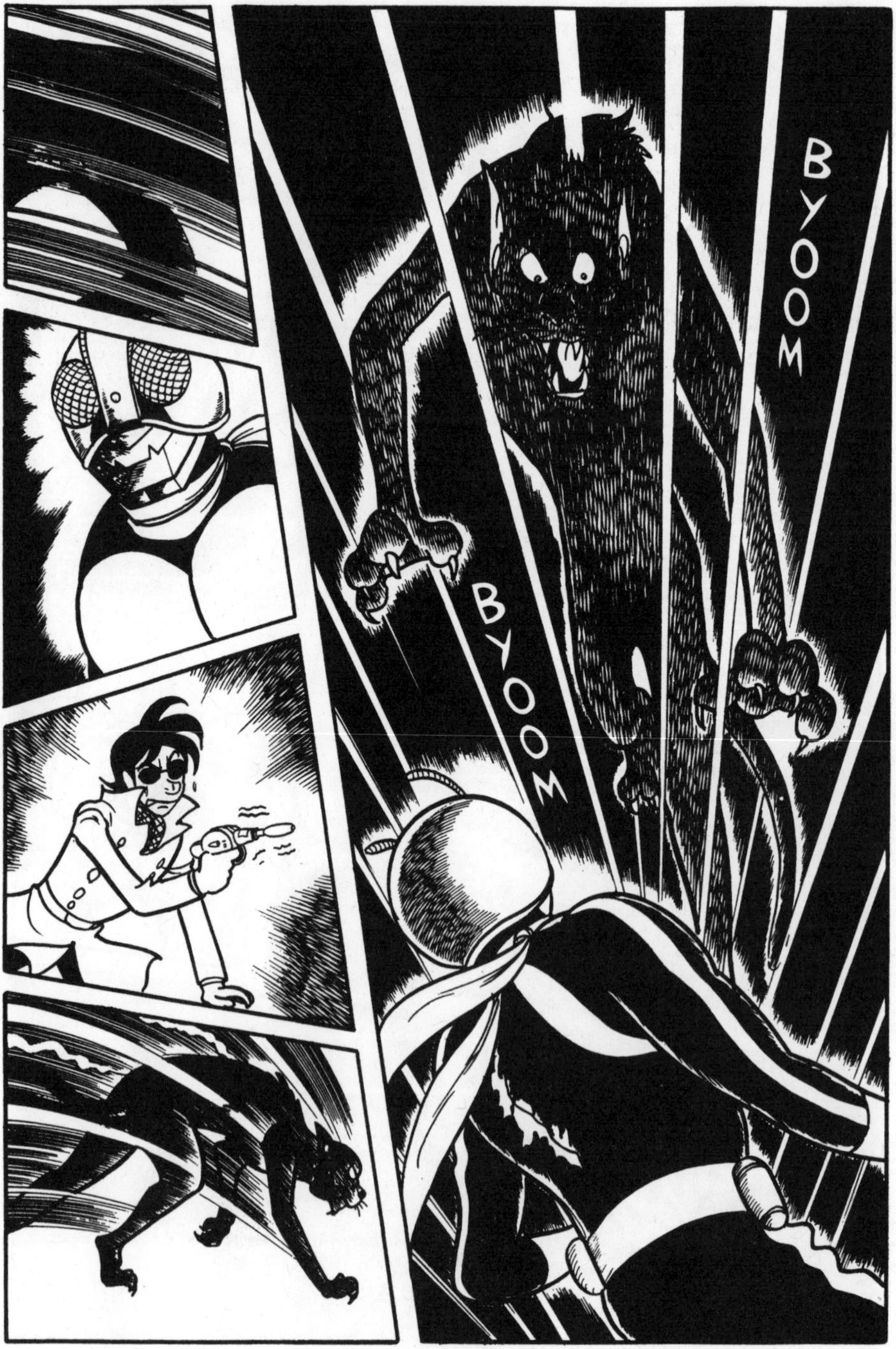
BYOOM
BYOOM

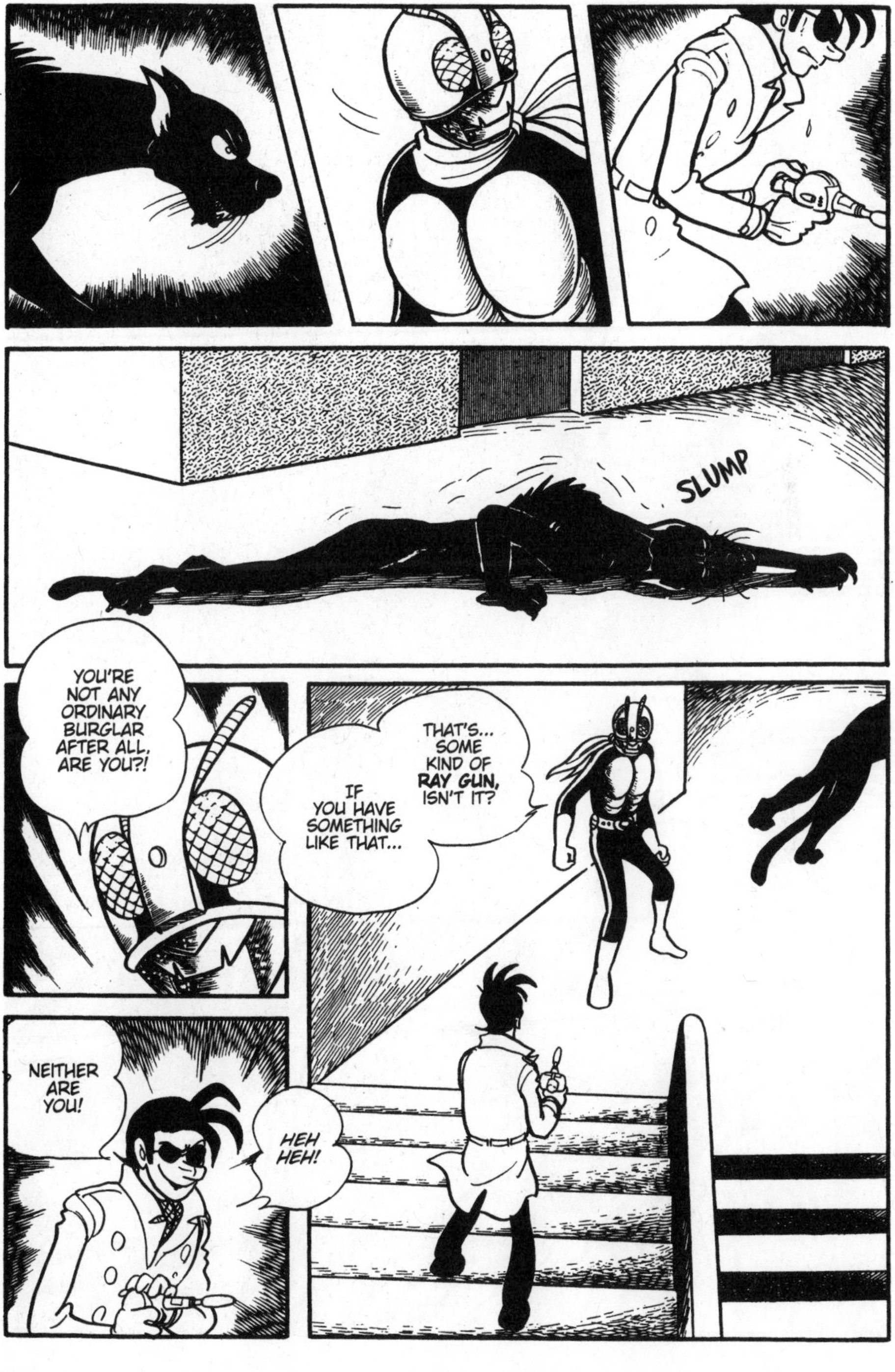
SLUMP
THAT'S... SOME KIND OF RAY GUN, ISN'T IT?
IF YOU HAVE SOMETHING LIKE THAT...
YOU'RE NOT ANY ORDINARY BURGLAR AFTER ALL, ARE YOU?!
NEITHER ARE YOU!
HEH HEH!

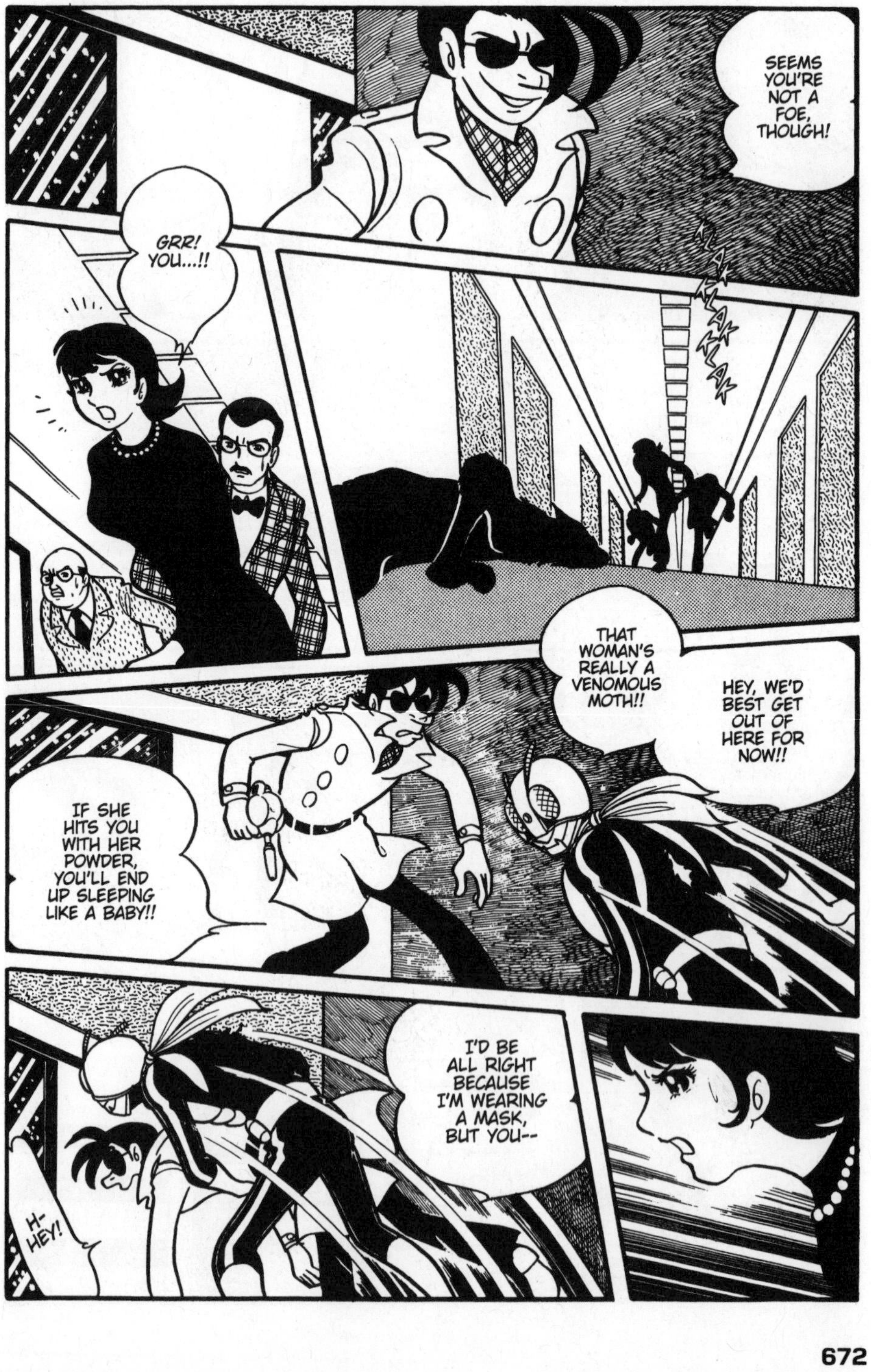
SEEMS YOU'RE NOT A FOE, THOUGH!
KLAK KLAK KLAK
GRR! YOU...!!
HEY, WE'D BEST GET OUT OF HERE FOR NOW!!
THAT WOMAN'S REALLY A VENOMOUS MOTH!!
IF SHE HITS YOU WITH HER POWDER, YOU'LL END UP SLEEPING LIKE A BABY!!
I'D BE ALL RIGHT BECAUSE I'M WEARING A MASK, BUT YOU--
H-HEY!

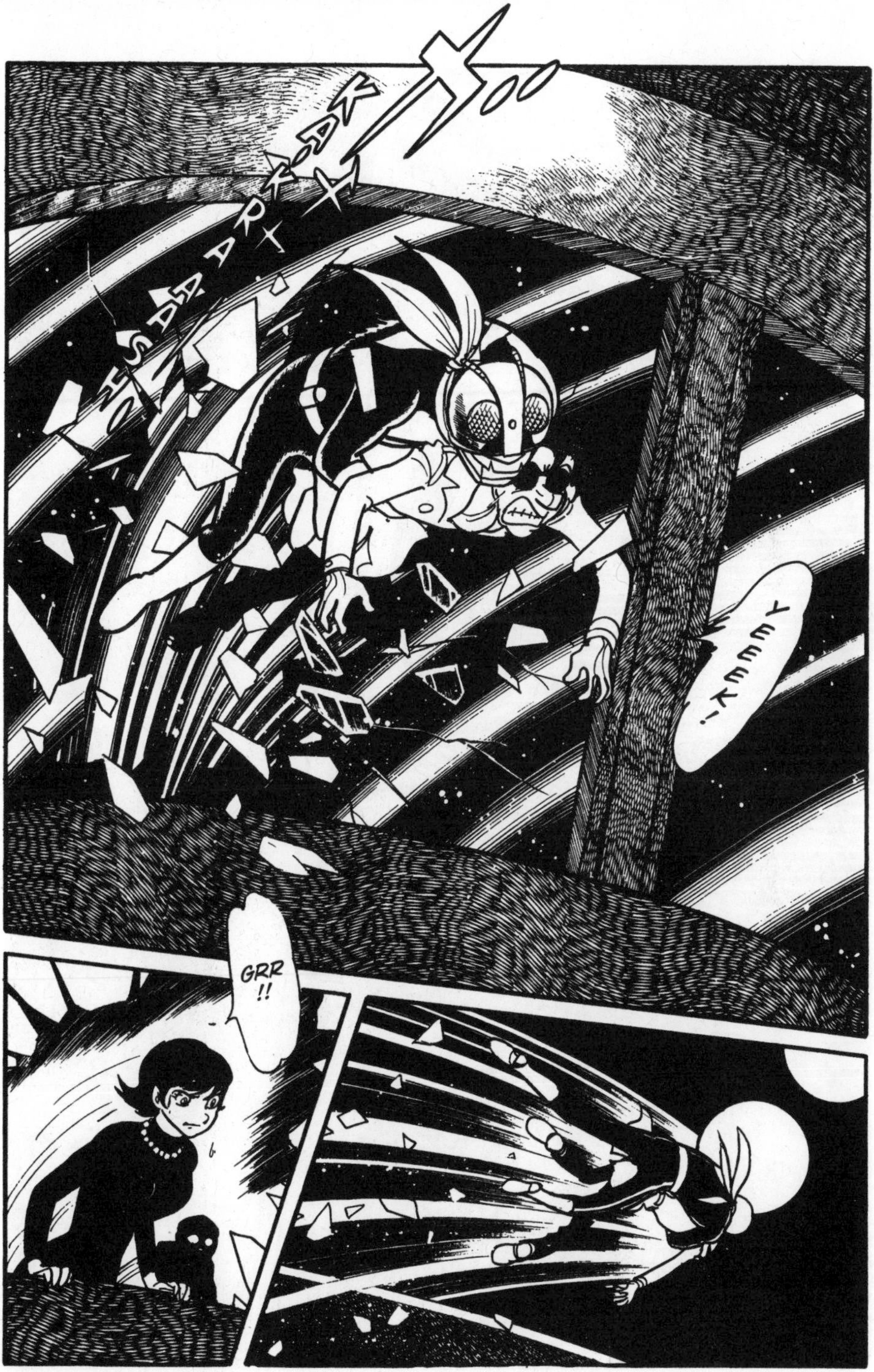
YEEEEK!
GRR !!

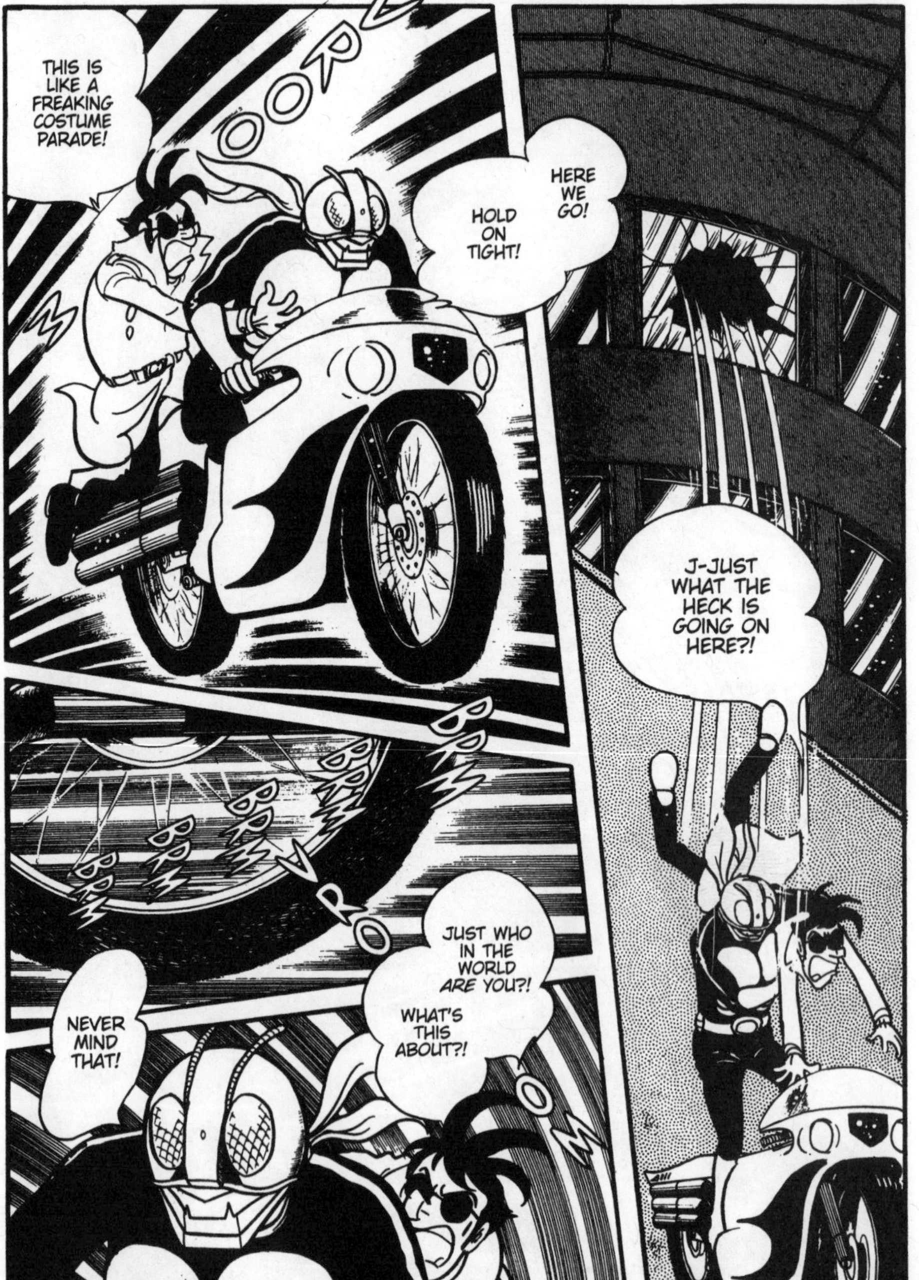
J-JUST WHAT THE HECK IS GOING ON HERE?!
HERE WE GO!
HOLD ON TIGHT!
VROOM
THIS IS LIKE A FREAKING COSTUME PARADE!
BRM BRM BRM BRM BRM
VROOM
JUST WHO IN THE WORLD *ARE* YOU?!
WHAT'S THIS ABOUT?!
NEVER MIND THAT!

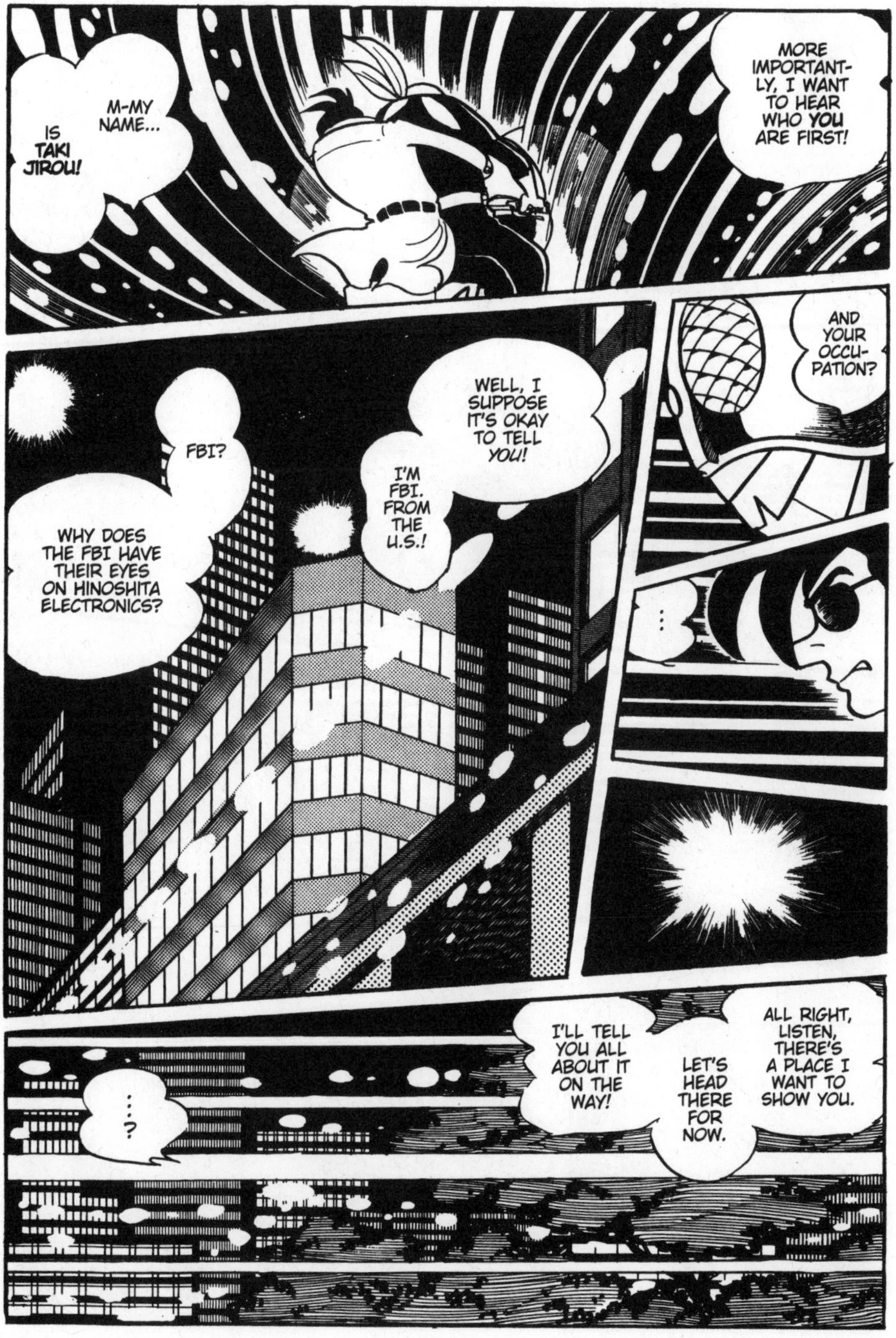
MORE IMPORTANTLY, I WANT TO HEAR WHO YOU ARE FIRST!
M-MY NAME...
IS TAKI JIROU!
AND YOUR OCCUPATION?
...
WELL, I SUPPOSE IT'S OKAY TO TELL YOU!
I'M FBI. FROM THE U.S.!
FBI?
WHY DOES THE FBI HAVE THEIR EYES ON HINOSHITA ELECTRONICS?
ALL RIGHT, LISTEN, THERE'S A PLACE I WANT TO SHOW YOU.
LET'S HEAD THERE FOR NOW.
I'LL TELL YOU ALL ABOUT IT ON THE WAY!
...?

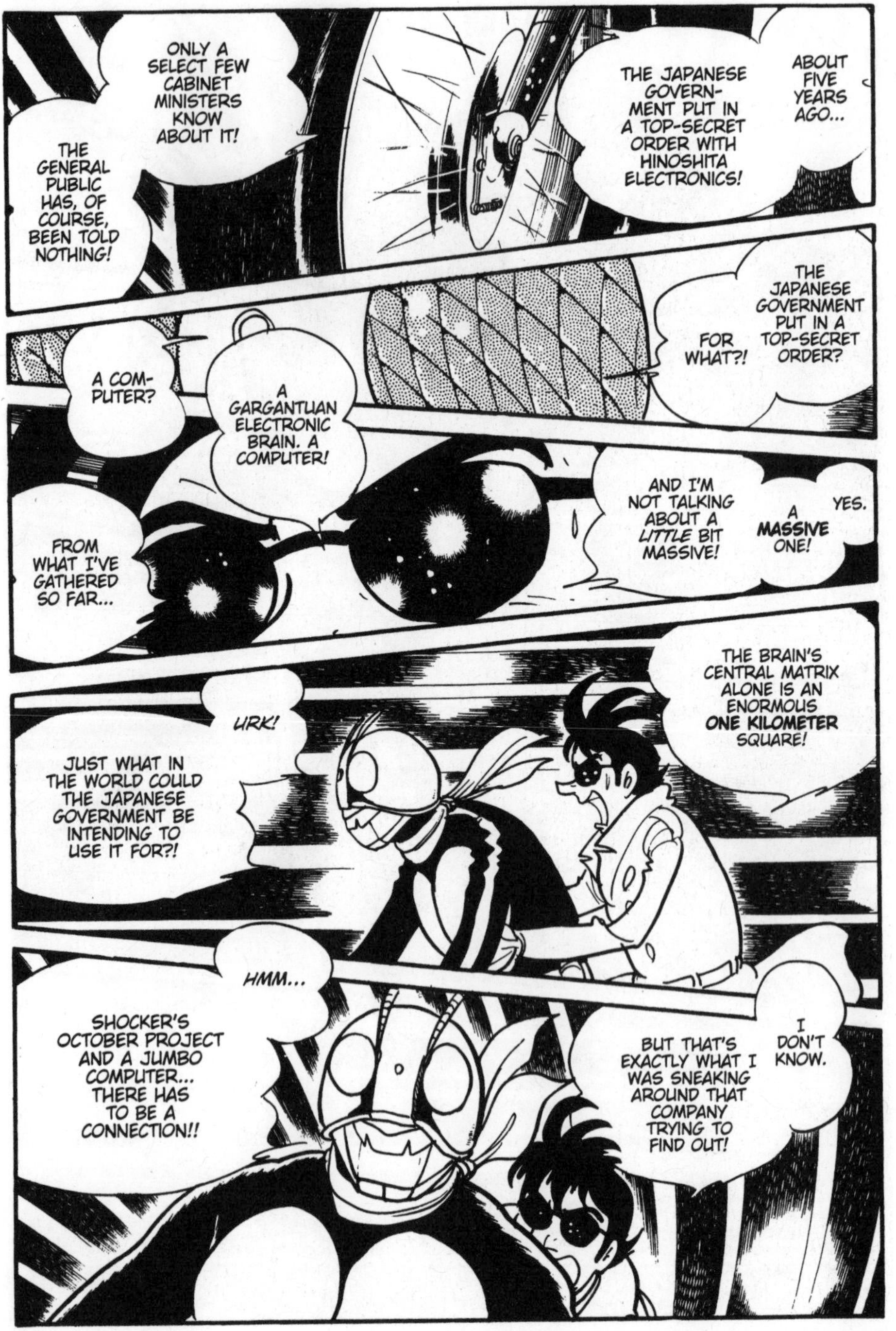
ABOUT FIVE YEARS AGO...
THE JAPANESE GOVERNMENT PUT IN A TOP-SECRET ORDER WITH HINOSHITA ELECTRONICS!
ONLY A SELECT FEW CABINET MINISTERS KNOW ABOUT IT!
THE GENERAL PUBLIC HAS, OF COURSE, BEEN TOLD NOTHING!
THE JAPANESE GOVERNMENT PUT IN A TOP-SECRET ORDER?
FOR WHAT?!
A GARGANTUAN ELECTRONIC BRAIN. A COMPUTER!
A COMPUTER?
YES.
A **MASSIVE** ONE!
AND I'M NOT TALKING ABOUT A *LITTLE* BIT MASSIVE!
FROM WHAT I'VE GATHERED SO FAR...
THE BRAIN'S CENTRAL MATRIX ALONE IS AN ENORMOUS **ONE KILOMETER** SQUARE!
URK!
JUST WHAT IN THE WORLD COULD THE JAPANESE GOVERNMENT BE INTENDING TO USE IT FOR?!
I DON'T KNOW.
BUT THAT'S EXACTLY WHAT I WAS SNEAKING AROUND THAT COMPANY TRYING TO FIND OUT!
HMM...
SHOCKER'S OCTOBER PROJECT AND A JUMBO COMPUTER... THERE HAS TO BE A CONNECTION!!

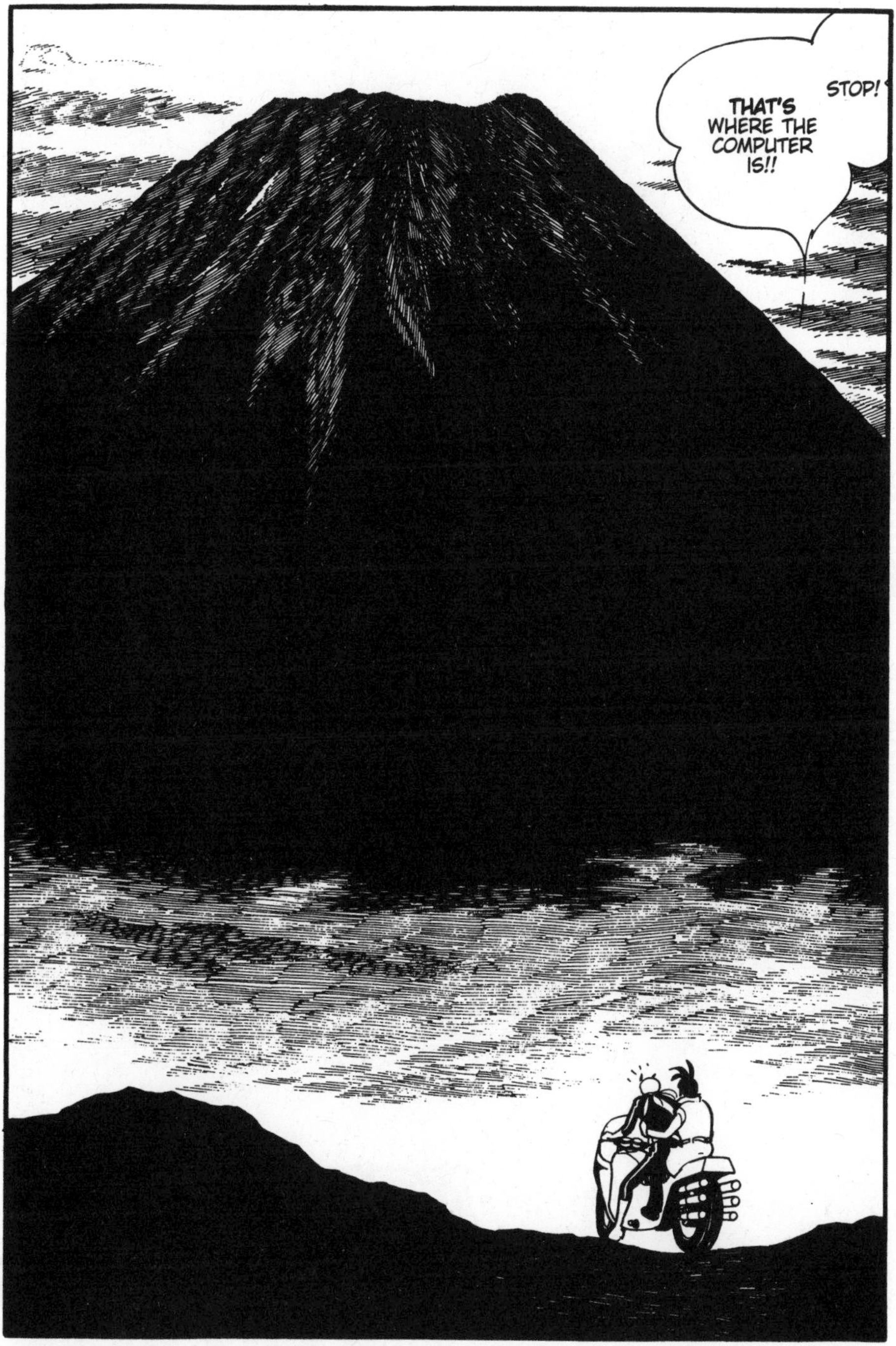
STOP!
THAT'S WHERE THE COMPUTER IS!!

KAMEN RIDER

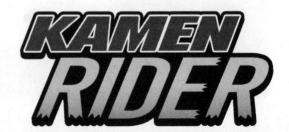

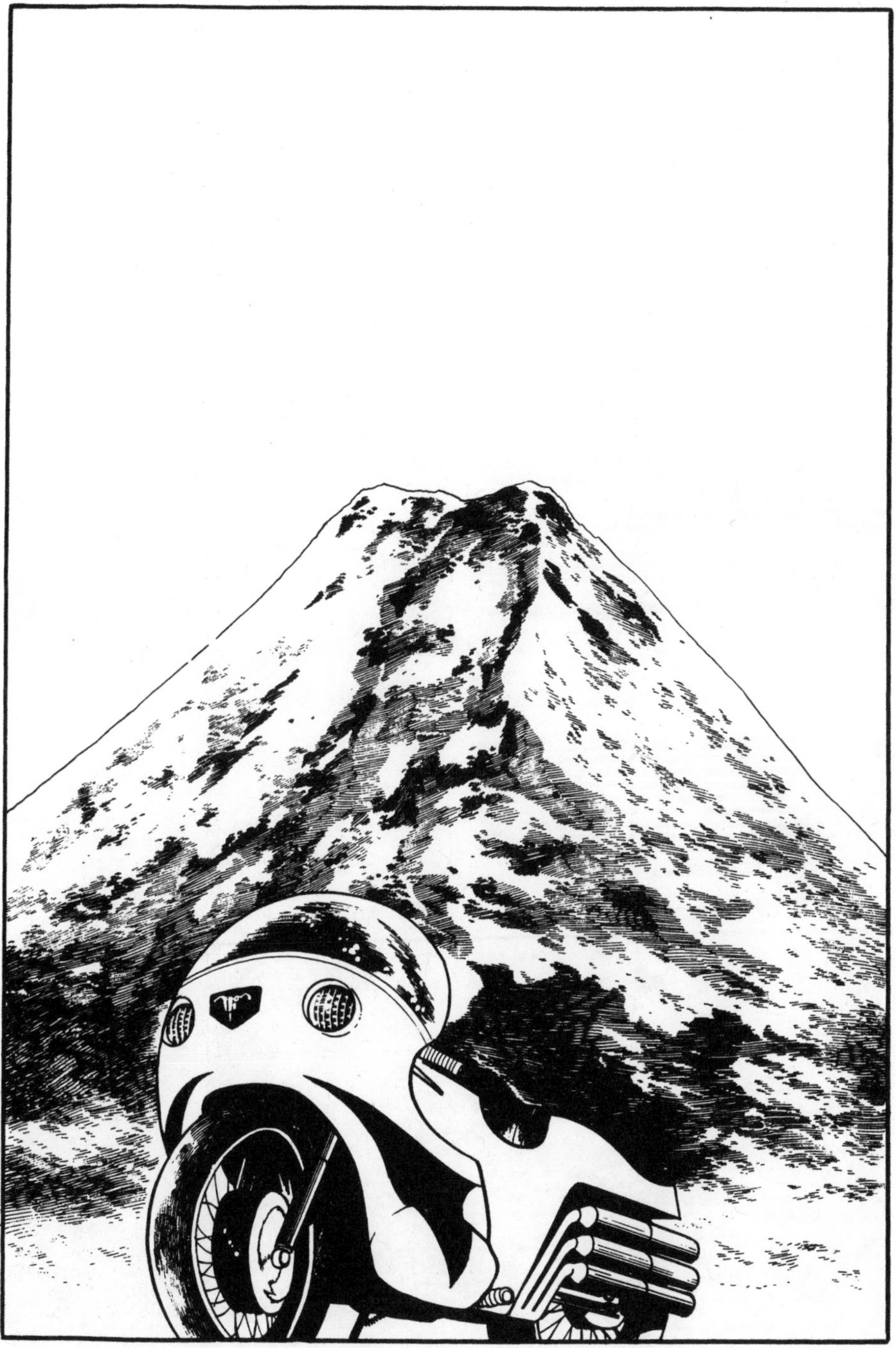

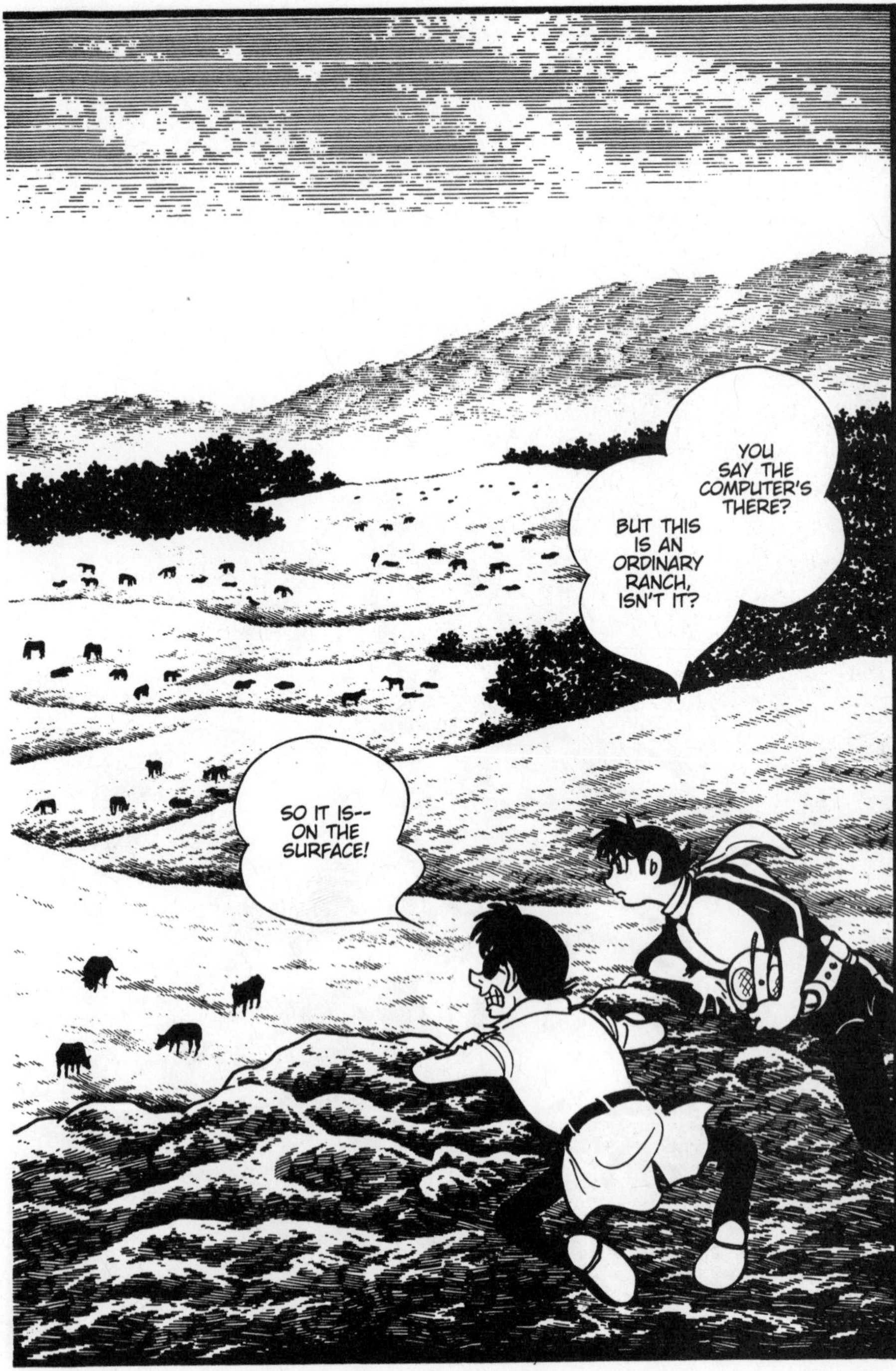
YOU SAY THE COMPUTER'S THERE?
BUT THIS IS AN ORDINARY RANCH, ISN'T IT?
SO IT IS-- ON THE SURFACE!

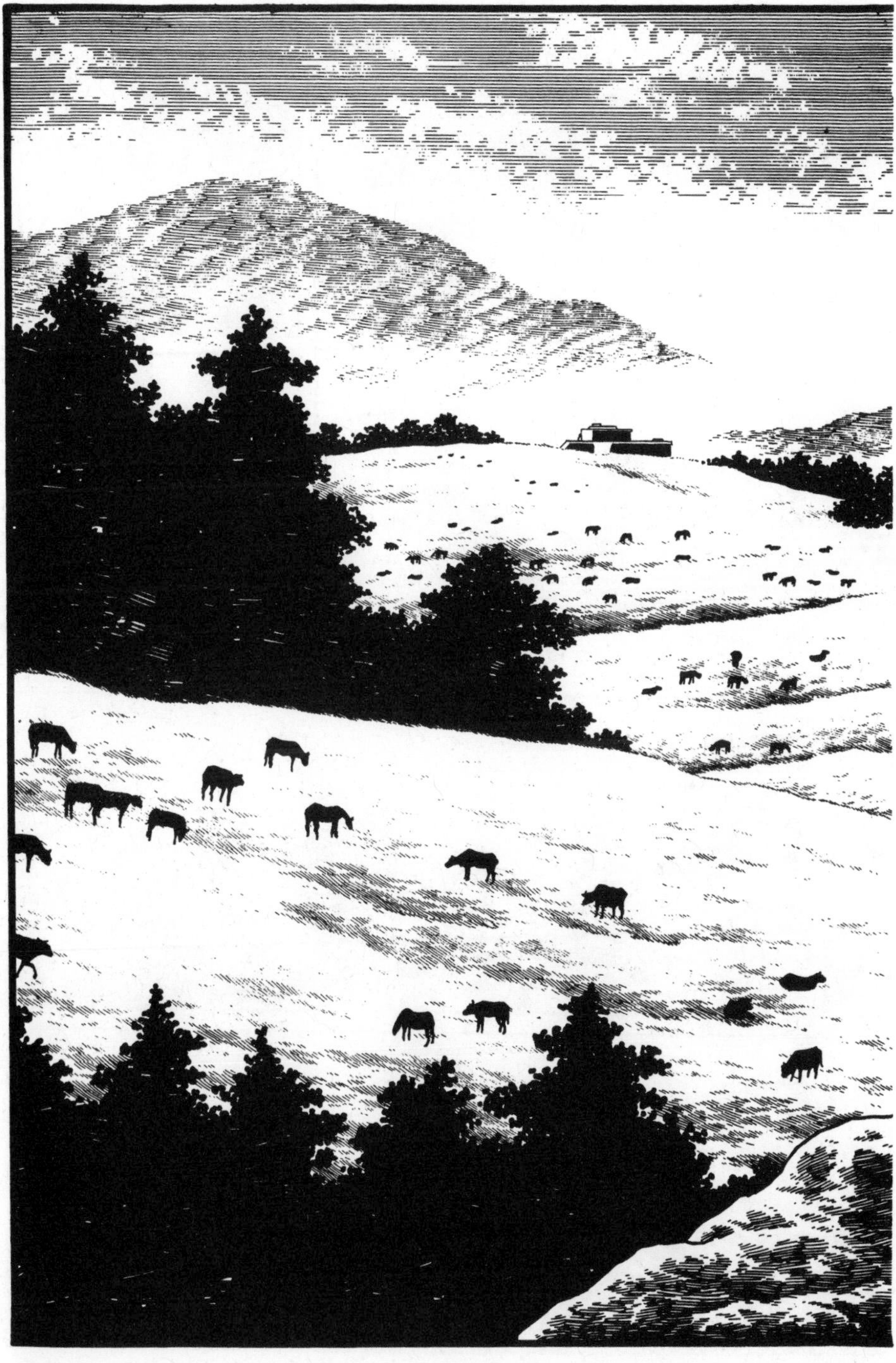

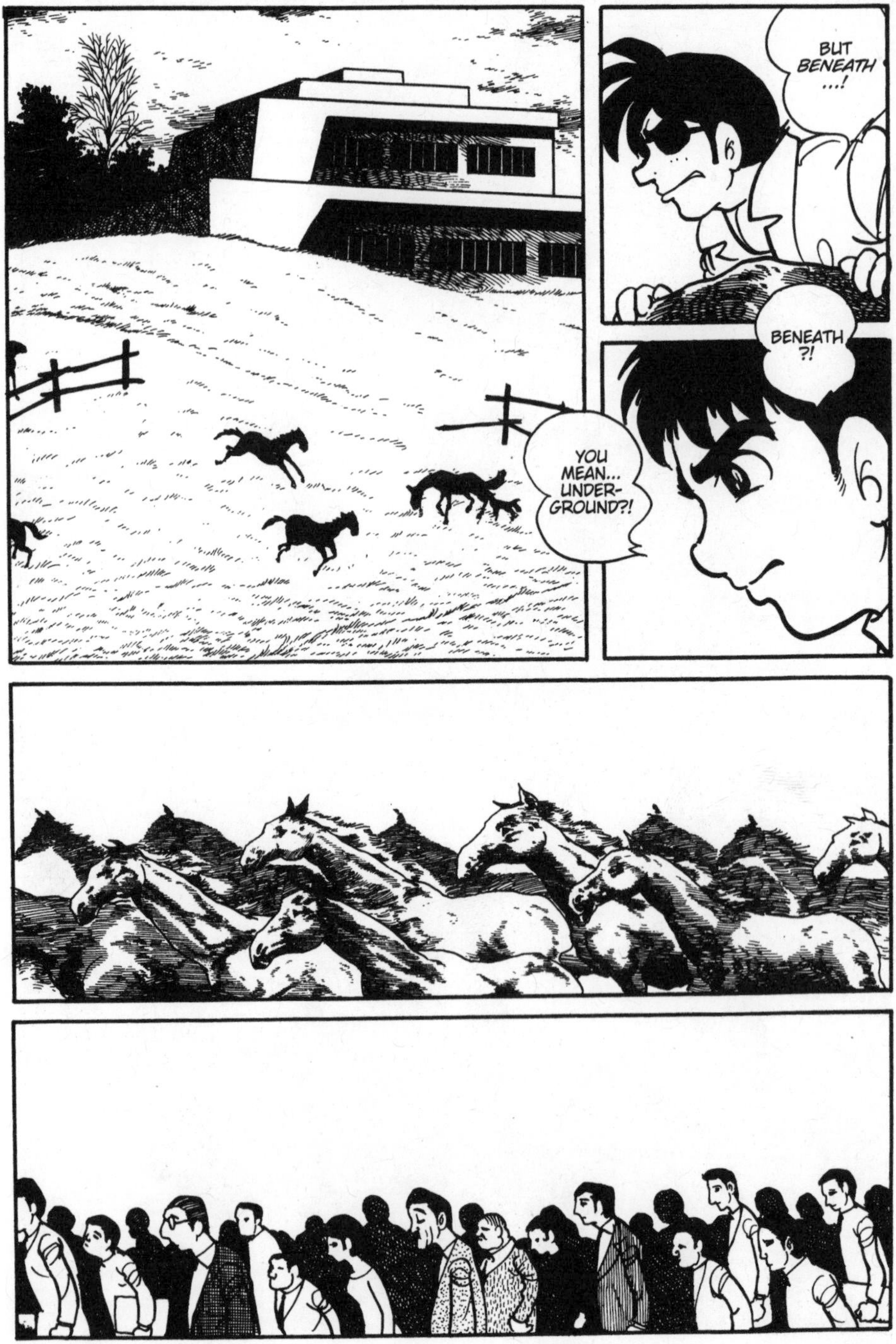
BUT BENEATH ...!
BENEATH ?!
YOU MEAN... UNDER-GROUND?!

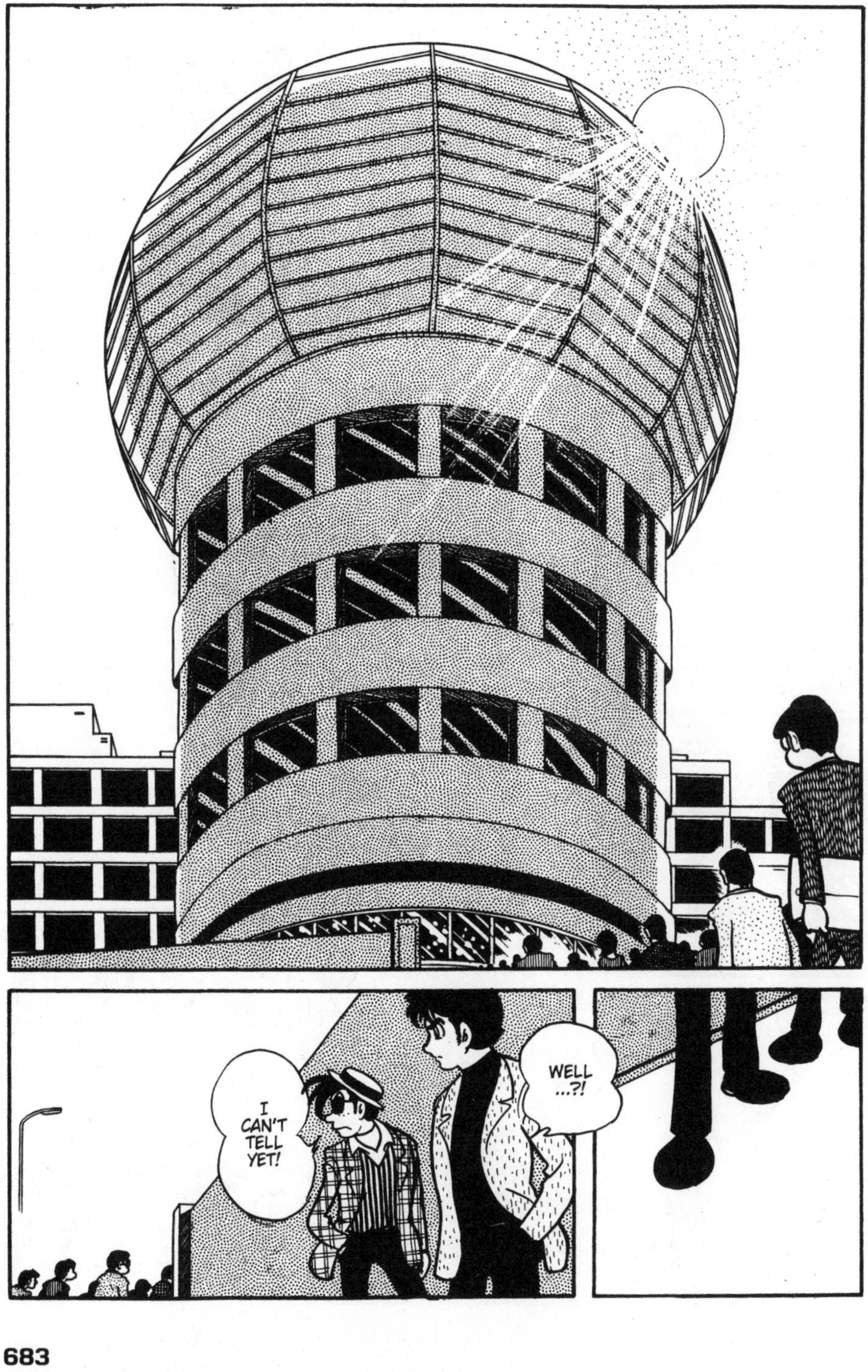
WELL ...?!
I CAN'T TELL YET!

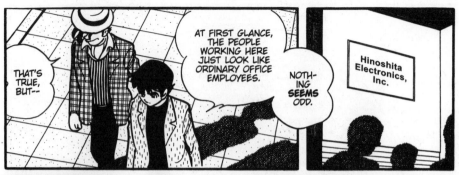

Hinoshita Electronics, Inc.
AT FIRST GLANCE, THE PEOPLE WORKING HERE JUST LOOK LIKE ORDINARY OFFICE EMPLOYEES.
NOTHING SEEMS ODD.
THAT'S TRUE, BUT--
I DO THINK IT'S POSSIBLE THAT EVERY EMPLOYEE IS BEING CONTROLLED!
IT MIGHT BE THAT ONLY PEOPLE VERY CLOSE TO THEM--LIKE THEIR CHILDREN, SIBLINGS, OR SPOUSES--ARE FINALLY NOTICING THE DIFFERENCES!
LIKE THE PRESIDENT'S DAUGHTER DID?!
Coffee
JUN
...

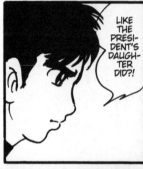

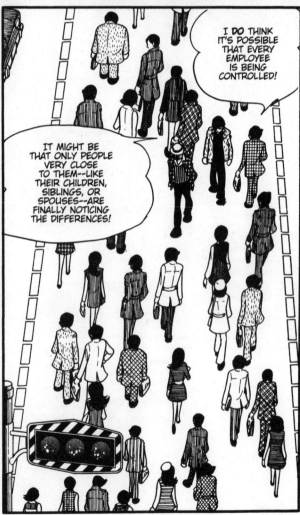

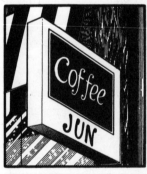

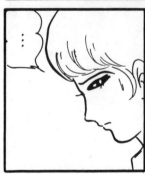

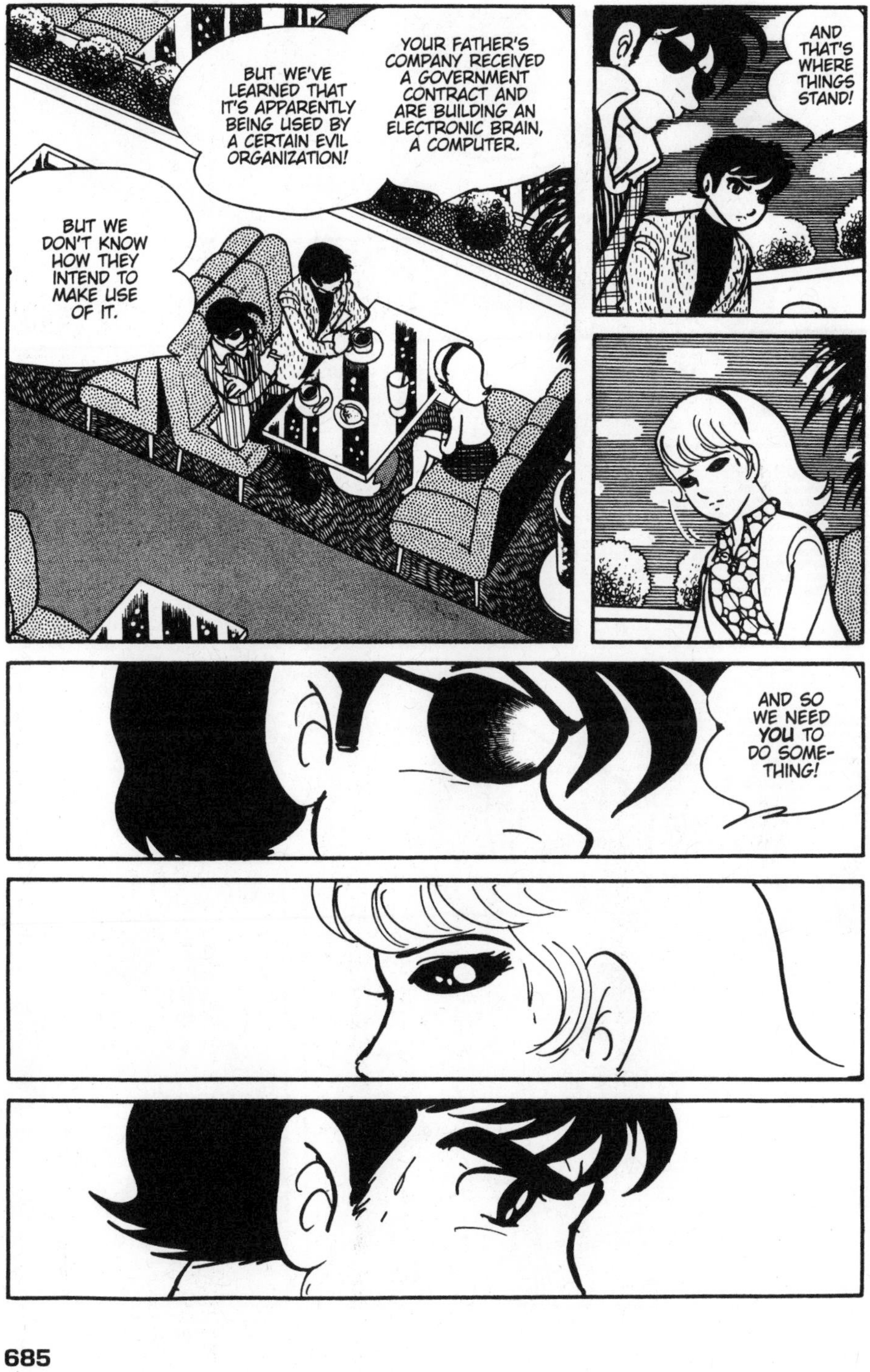
AND THAT'S WHERE THINGS STAND!
YOUR FATHER'S COMPANY RECEIVED A GOVERNMENT CONTRACT AND ARE BUILDING AN ELECTRONIC BRAIN, A COMPUTER.
BUT WE'VE LEARNED THAT IT'S APPARENTLY BEING USED BY A CERTAIN EVIL ORGANIZATION!
BUT WE DON'T KNOW HOW THEY INTEND TO MAKE USE OF IT.
AND SO WE NEED YOU TO DO SOME-THING!

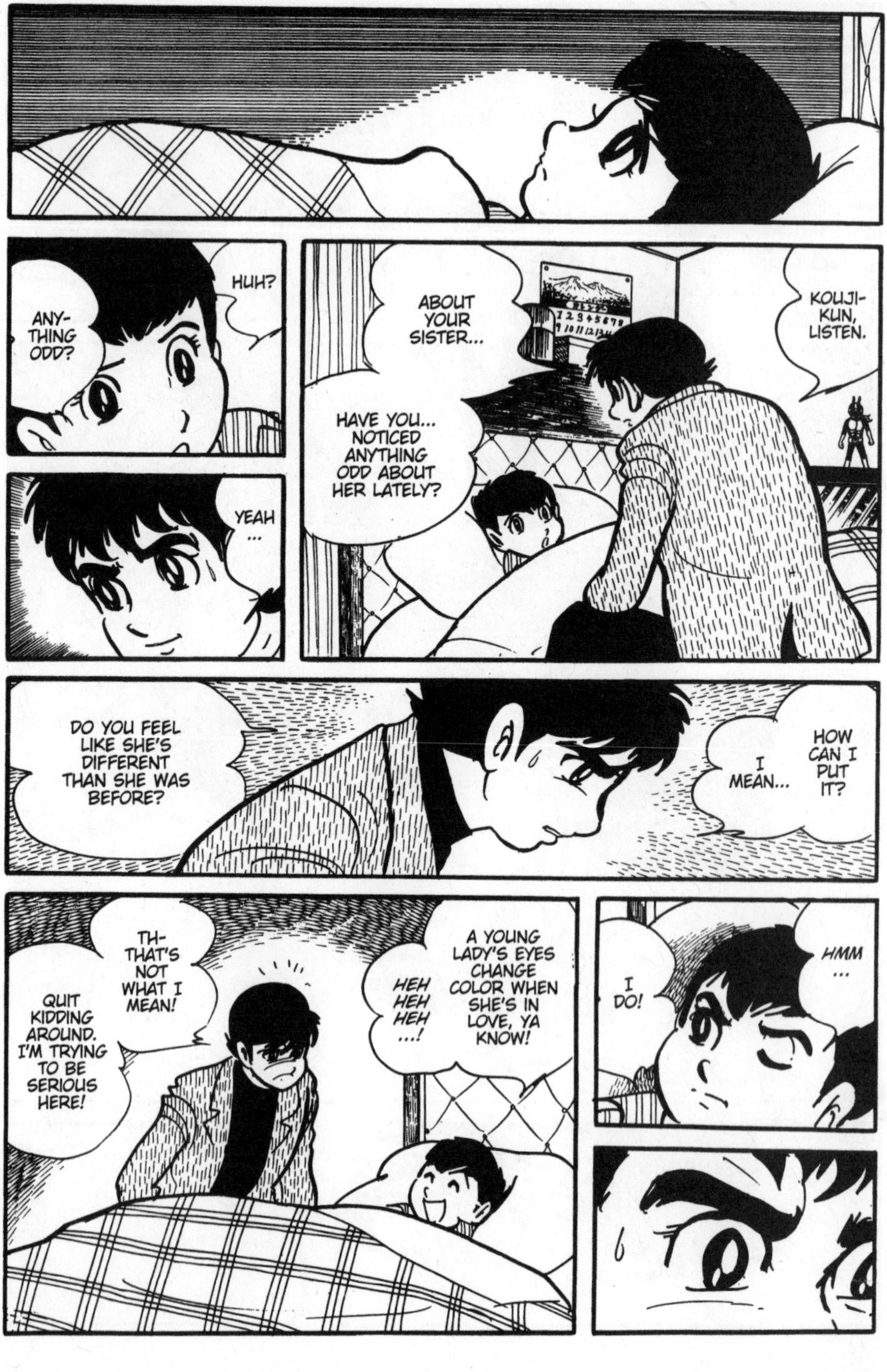
KOUJI-KUN, LISTEN.
ABOUT YOUR SISTER...
HAVE YOU... NOTICED ANYTHING ODD ABOUT HER LATELY?
HUH?
ANYTHING ODD?
YEAH ...
HOW CAN I PUT IT?
I MEAN...
DO YOU FEEL LIKE SHE'S DIFFERENT THAN SHE WAS BEFORE?
HMM ...
I DO!
A YOUNG LADY'S EYES CHANGE COLOR WHEN SHE'S IN LOVE, YA KNOW!
HEH HEH HEH ...!
TH-THAT'S NOT WHAT I MEAN!
QUIT KIDDING AROUND. I'M TRYING TO BE SERIOUS HERE!

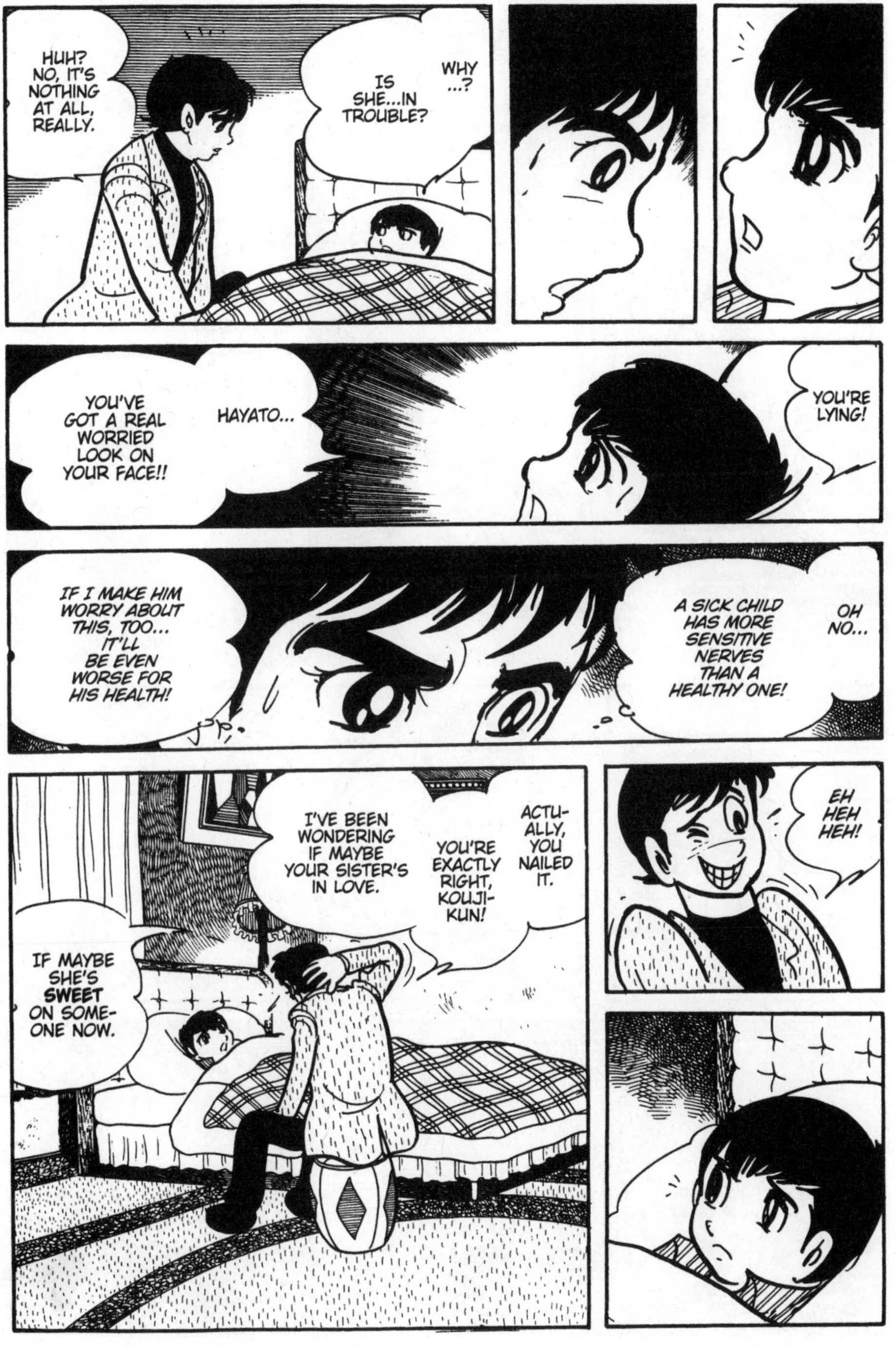
WHY ...?
IS SHE...IN TROUBLE?
HUH? NO, IT'S NOTHING AT ALL, REALLY.
YOU'RE LYING!
HAYATO...
YOU'VE GOT A REAL WORRIED LOOK ON YOUR FACE!!
OH NO...
A SICK CHILD HAS MORE SENSITIVE NERVES THAN A HEALTHY ONE!
IF I MAKE HIM WORRY ABOUT THIS, TOO... IT'LL BE EVEN WORSE FOR HIS HEALTH!
EH HEH HEH!
ACTU-ALLY, YOU NAILED IT.
YOU'RE EXACTLY RIGHT, KOUJI-KUN!
I'VE BEEN WONDERING IF MAYBE YOUR SISTER'S IN LOVE.
IF MAYBE SHE'S SWEET ON SOME-ONE NOW.

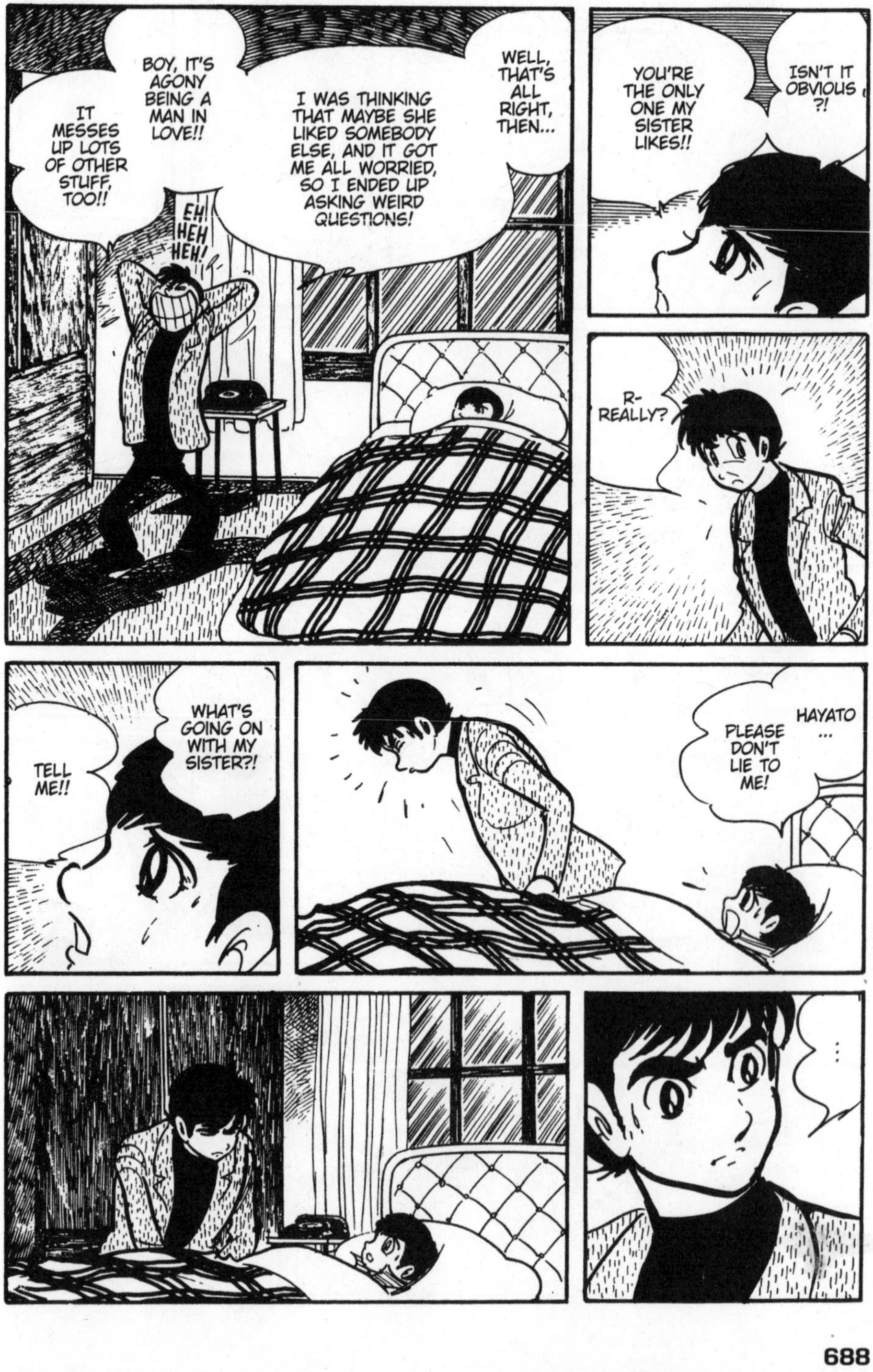
ISN'T IT OBVIOUS ?!
YOU'RE THE ONLY ONE MY SISTER LIKES!!
R-REALLY?
WELL, THAT'S ALL RIGHT, THEN...
I WAS THINKING THAT MAYBE SHE LIKED SOMEBODY ELSE, AND IT GOT ME ALL WORRIED, SO I ENDED UP ASKING WEIRD QUESTIONS!
BOY, IT'S AGONY BEING A MAN IN LOVE!!
IT MESSES UP LOTS OF OTHER STUFF, TOO!!
EH! HEH HEH!
HAYATO ...
PLEASE DON'T LIE TO ME!
WHAT'S GOING ON WITH MY SISTER?!
TELL ME!!
...

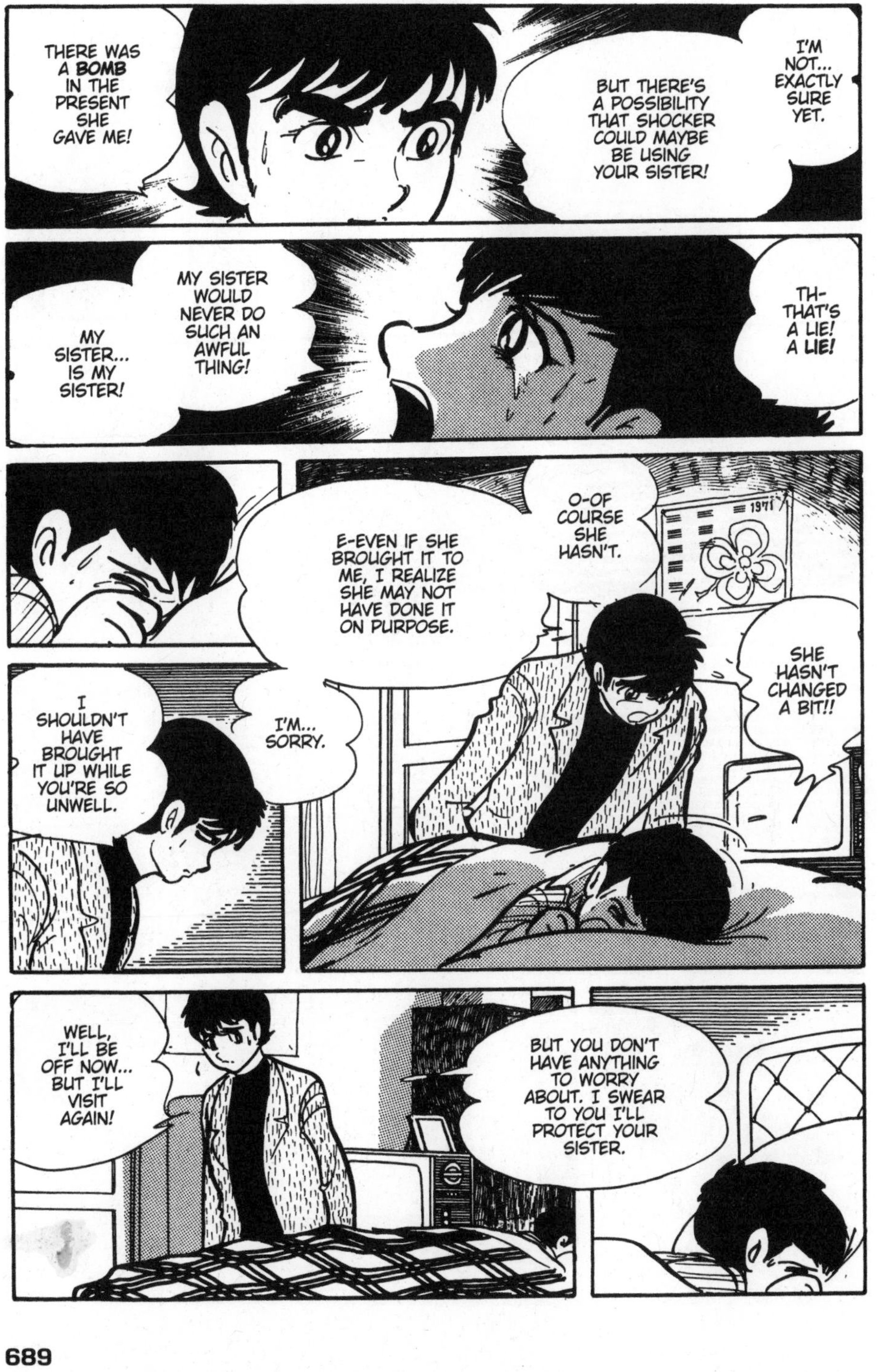
I'M NOT... EXACTLY SURE YET.
BUT THERE'S A POSSIBILITY THAT SHOCKER COULD MAYBE BE USING YOUR SISTER!
THERE WAS A **BOMB** IN THE PRESENT SHE GAVE ME!
TH- THAT'S A LIE! A **LIE!**
MY SISTER WOULD NEVER DO SUCH AN AWFUL THING!
MY SISTER... IS MY SISTER!
SHE HASN'T CHANGED A BIT!!
O-OF COURSE SHE HASN'T.
E-EVEN IF SHE BROUGHT IT TO ME, I REALIZE SHE MAY NOT HAVE DONE IT ON PURPOSE.
1971
I'M... SORRY.
I SHOULDN'T HAVE BROUGHT IT UP WHILE YOU'RE SO UNWELL.
BUT YOU DON'T HAVE ANYTHING TO WORRY ABOUT. I SWEAR TO YOU I'LL PROTECT YOUR SISTER.
WELL, I'LL BE OFF NOW... BUT I'LL VISIT AGAIN!

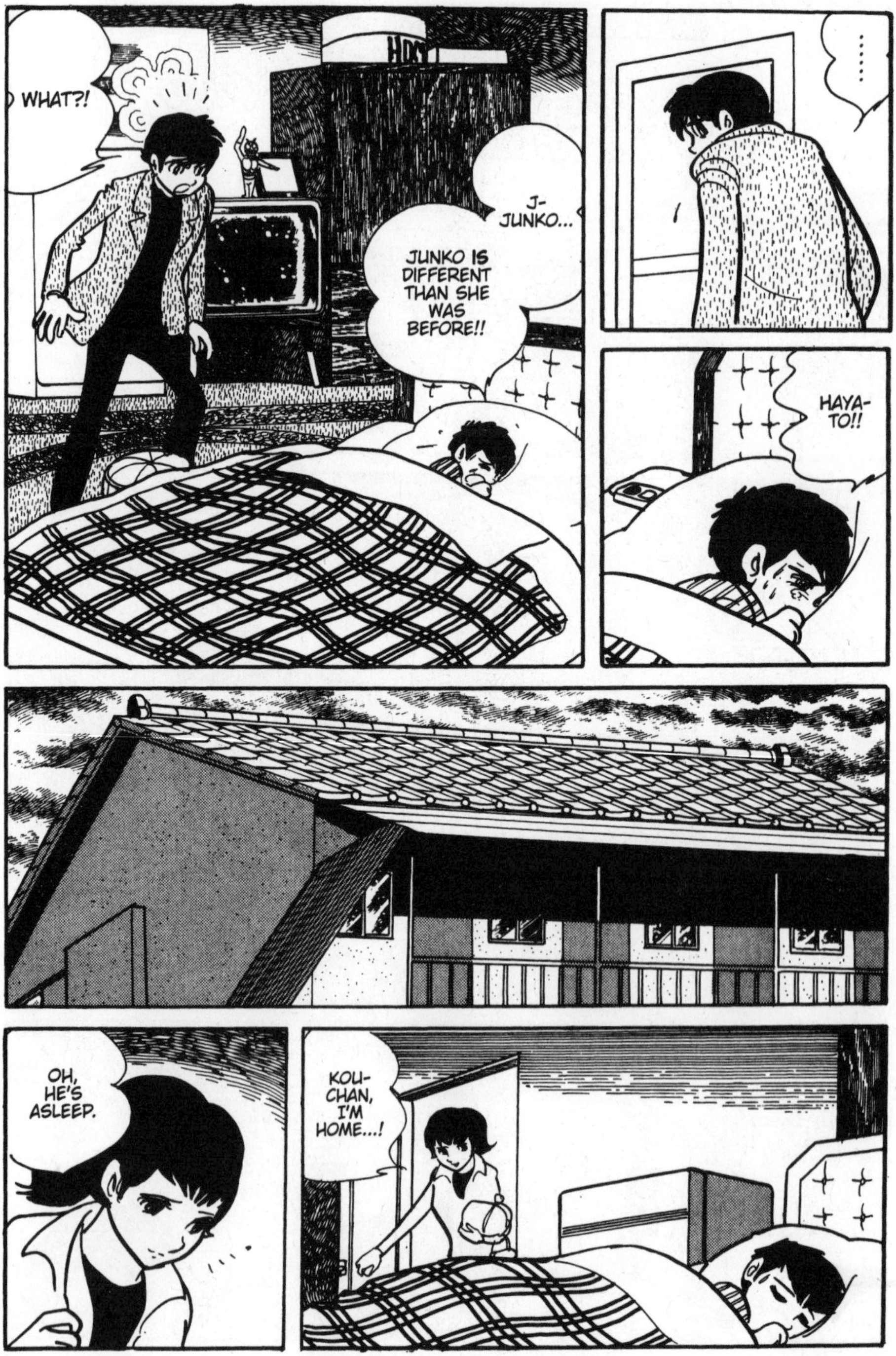
......
HAYATO!!
J-JUNKO...
JUNKO IS DIFFERENT THAN SHE WAS BEFORE!!
WHAT?!
KOU-CHAN, I'M HOME...!
OH, HE'S ASLEEP.

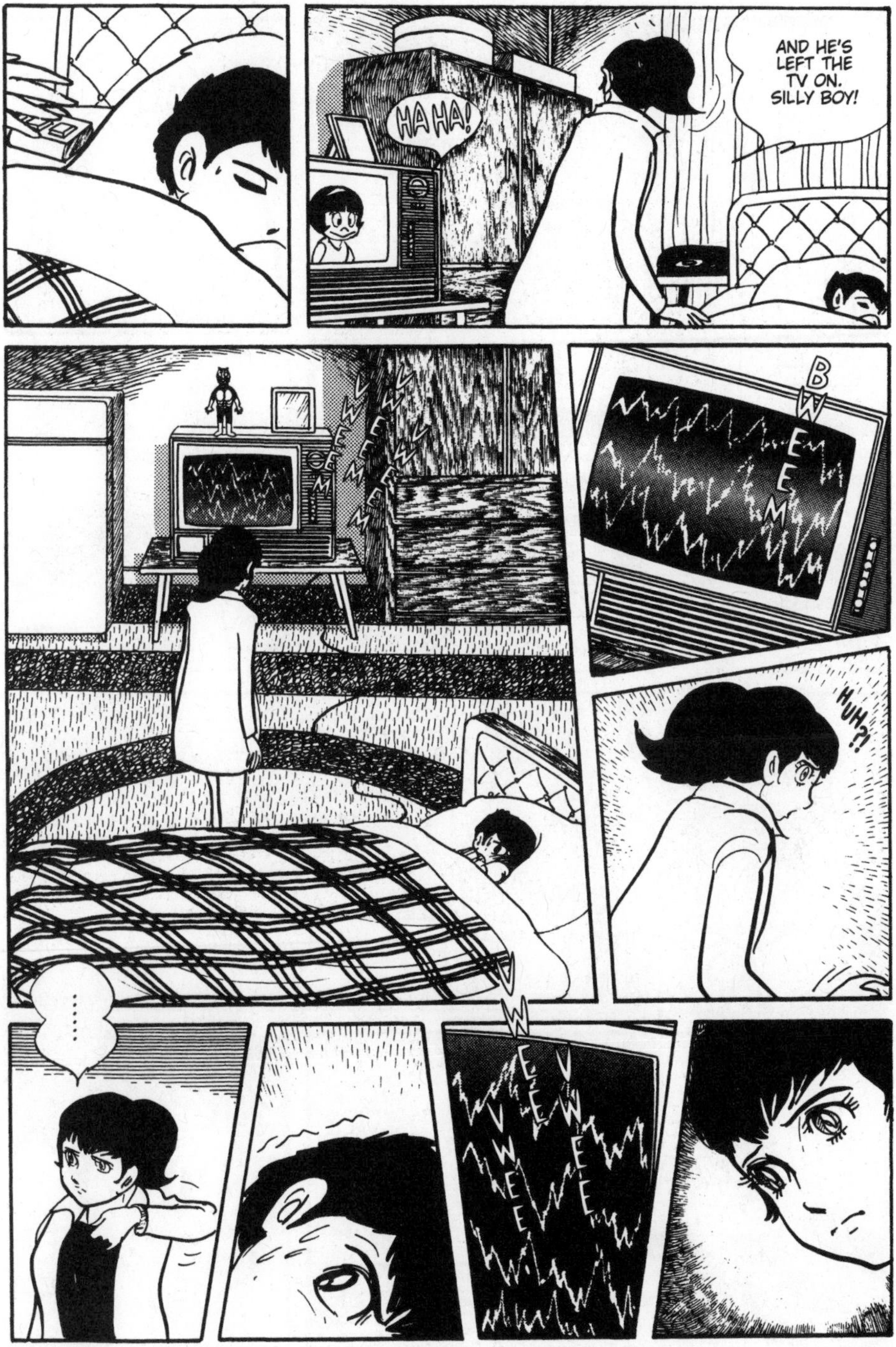
AND HE'S LEFT THE TV ON. SILLY BOY!
HA HA!
BWEEEM
HUH?!
......

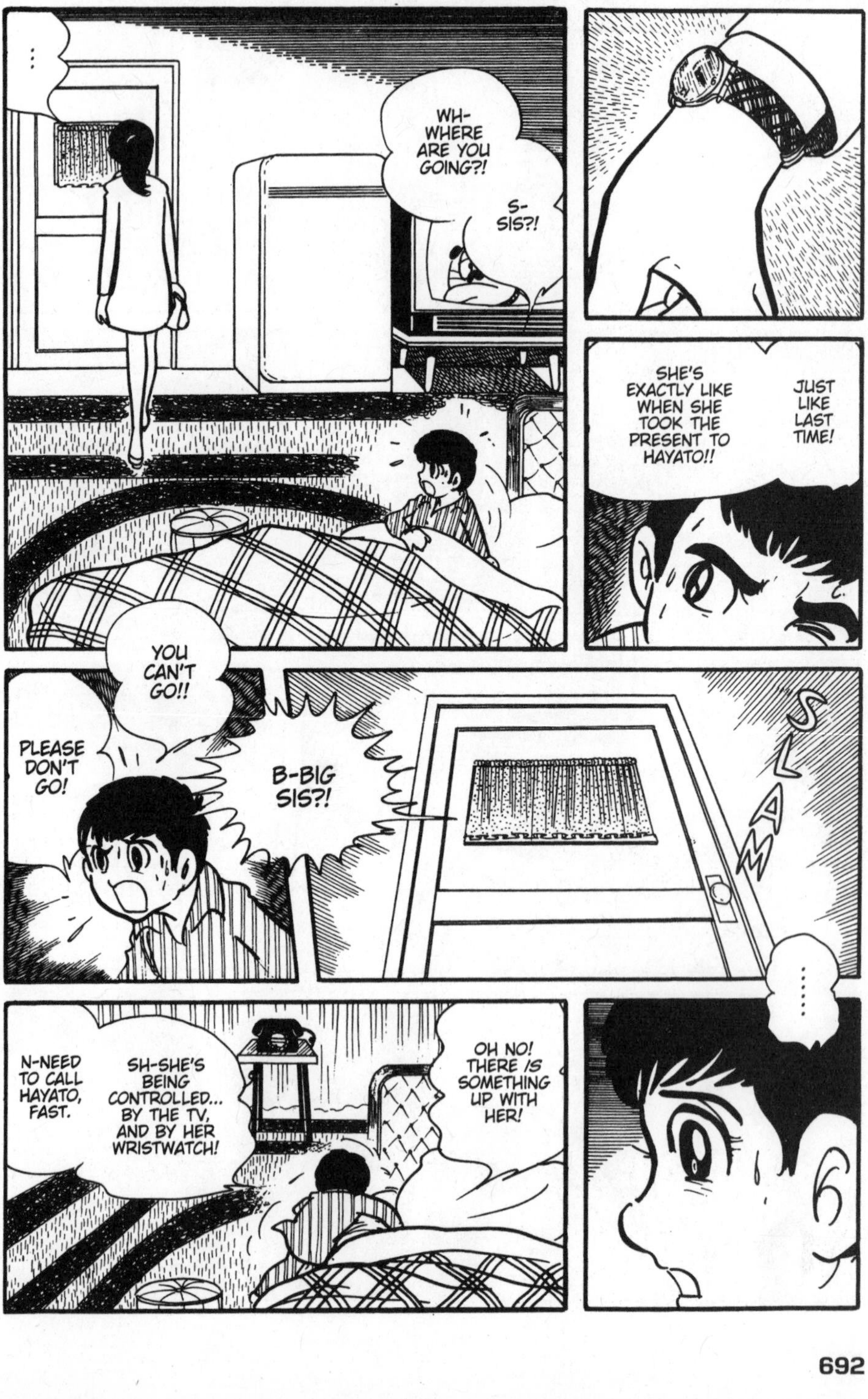
JUST LIKE LAST TIME!
SHE'S EXACTLY LIKE WHEN SHE TOOK THE PRESENT TO HAYATO!!
S-SIS?!
WH-WHERE ARE YOU GOING?!
...
SLAM
B-BIG SIS?!
YOU CAN'T GO!!
PLEASE DON'T GO!
......
OH NO! THERE IS SOMETHING UP WITH HER!
SH-SHE'S BEING CONTROLLED... BY THE TV, AND BY HER WRISTWATCH!
N-NEED TO CALL HAYATO, FAST.

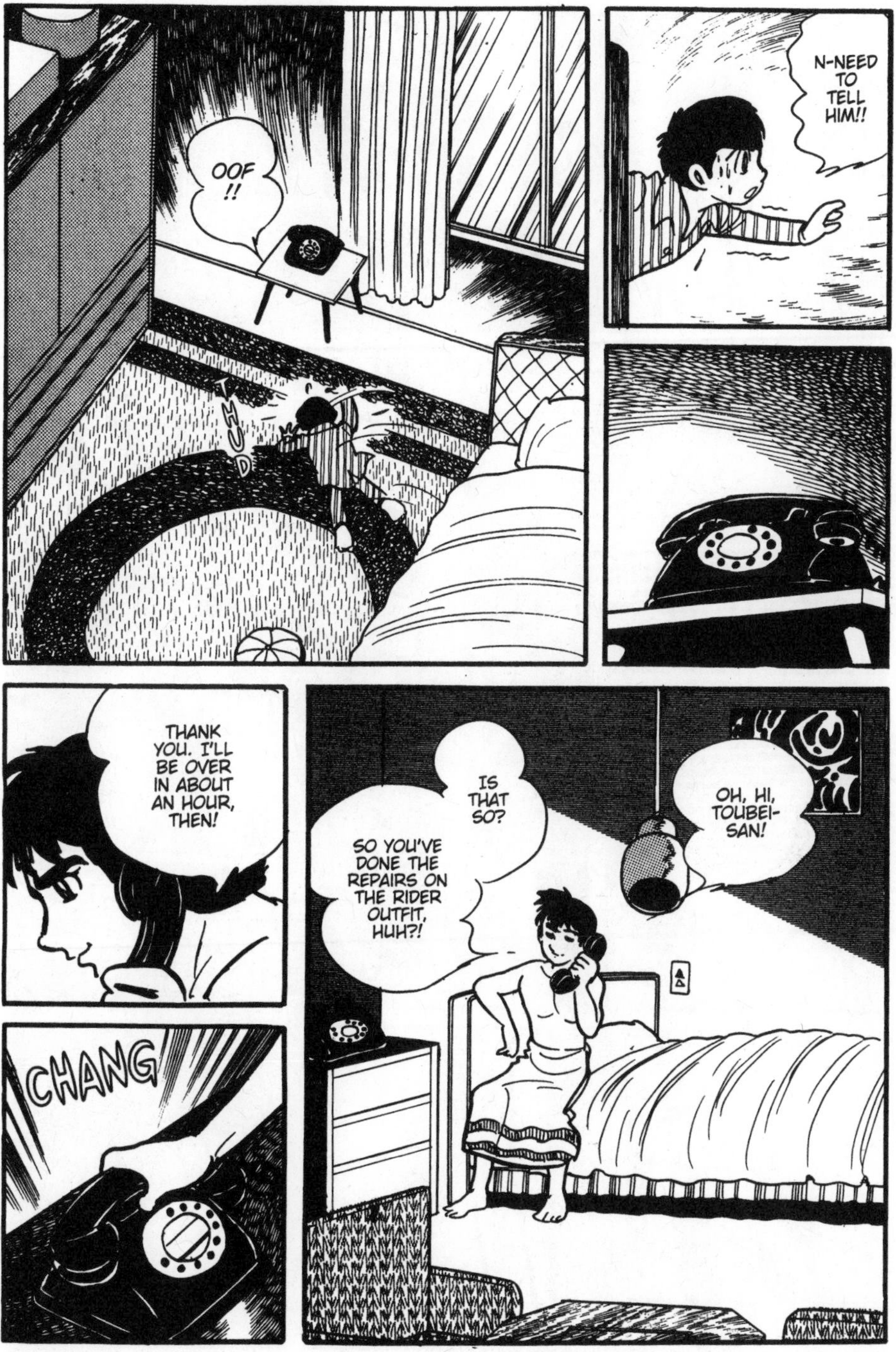
N-NEED TO TELL HIM!!
OOF !!
THUD
OH, HI, TOUBEI-SAN!
IS THAT SO?
SO YOU'VE DONE THE REPAIRS ON THE RIDER OUTFIT, HUH?!
THANK YOU. I'LL BE OVER IN ABOUT AN HOUR, THEN!
CHANG

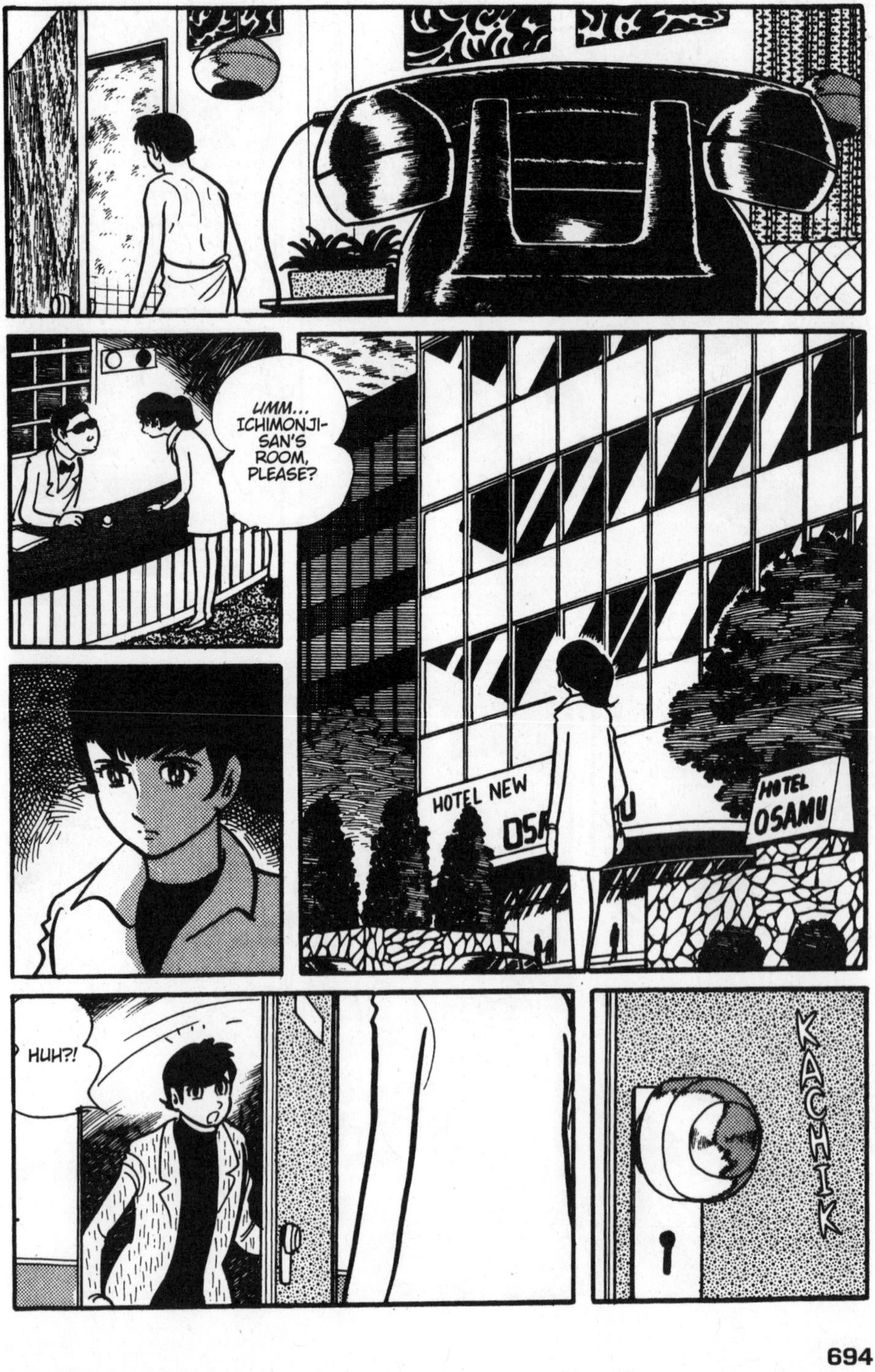
HOTEL NEW
HOTEL OSAMU
UMM... ICHIMONJI-SAN'S ROOM, PLEASE?
KACHIK
HUH?!

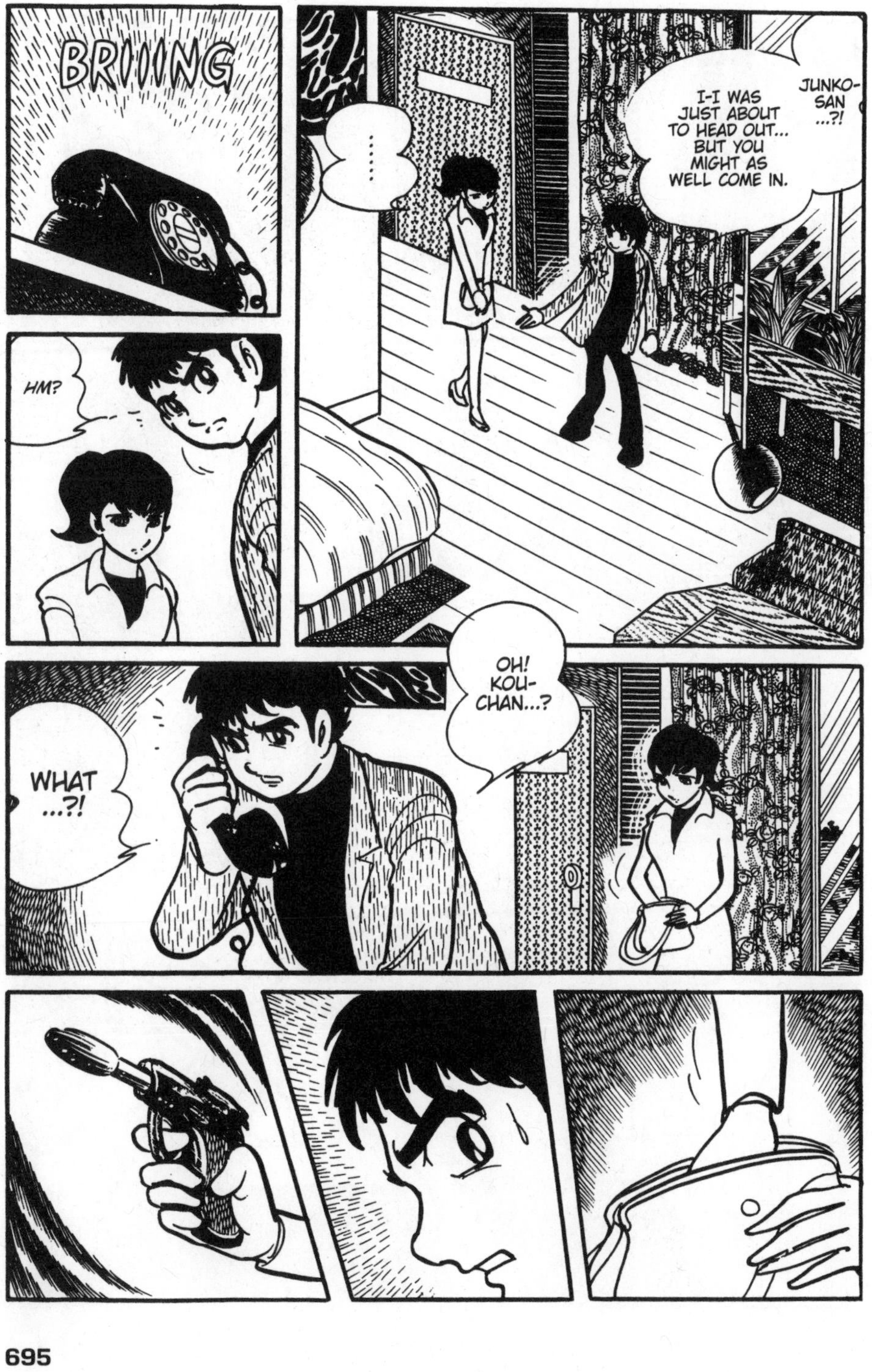
JUNKO-SAN ...?!
I-I WAS JUST ABOUT TO HEAD OUT... BUT YOU MIGHT AS WELL COME IN.
......
BRIIING
HM?
OH! KOU-CHAN...?
WHAT ...?!

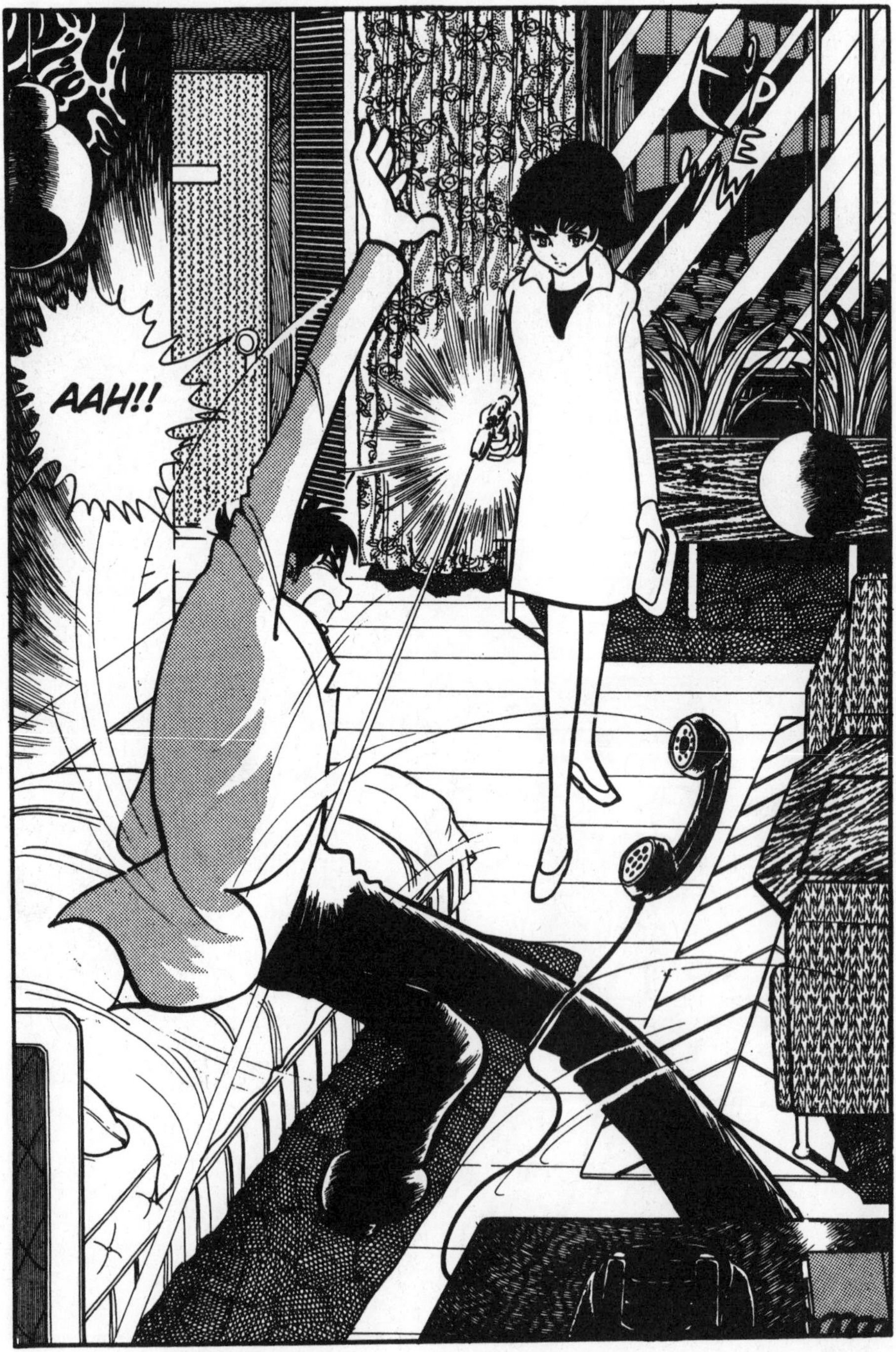
PEW
AAH!!

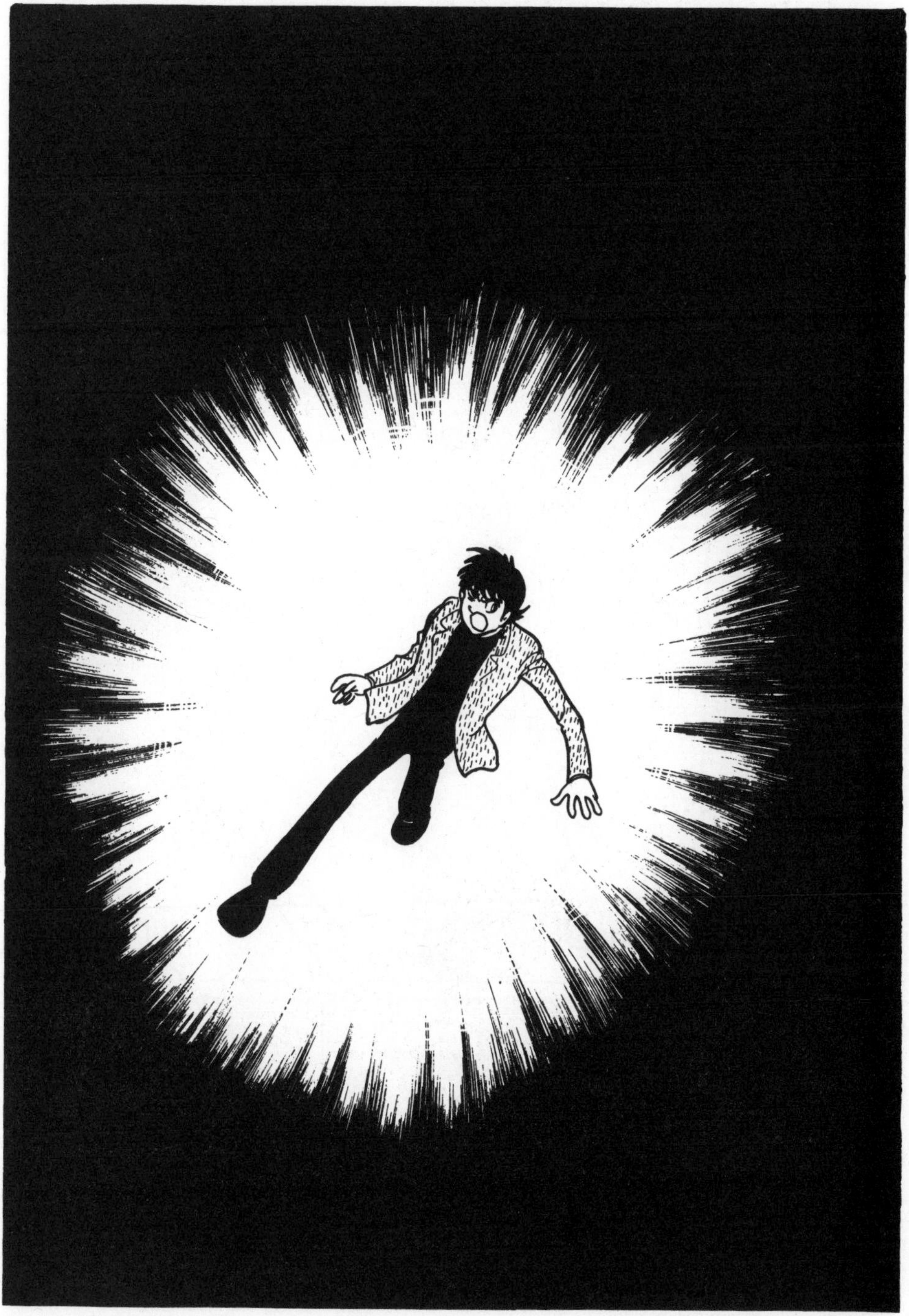

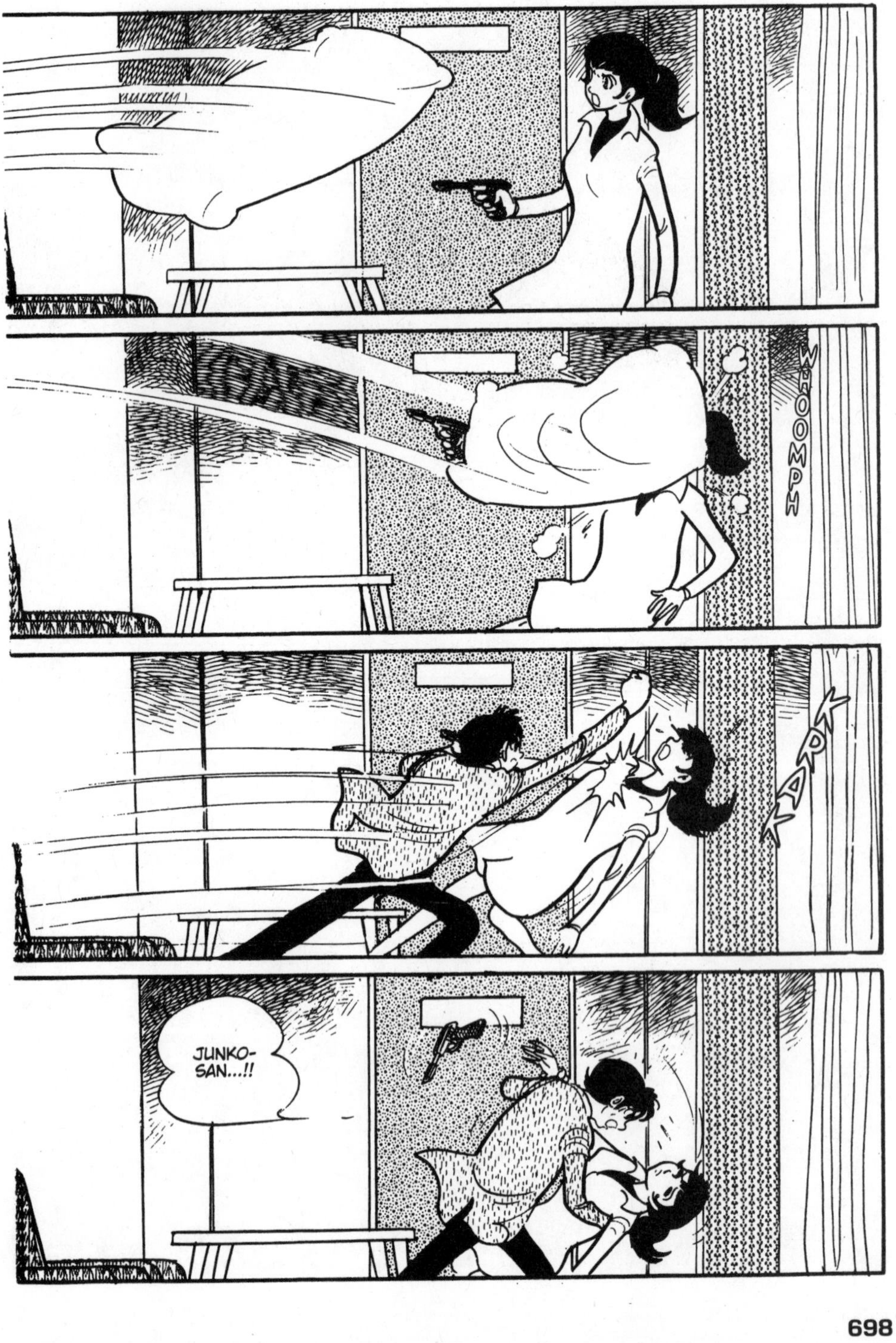
WHOOMPH
KRAK
JUNKO-SAN...!!

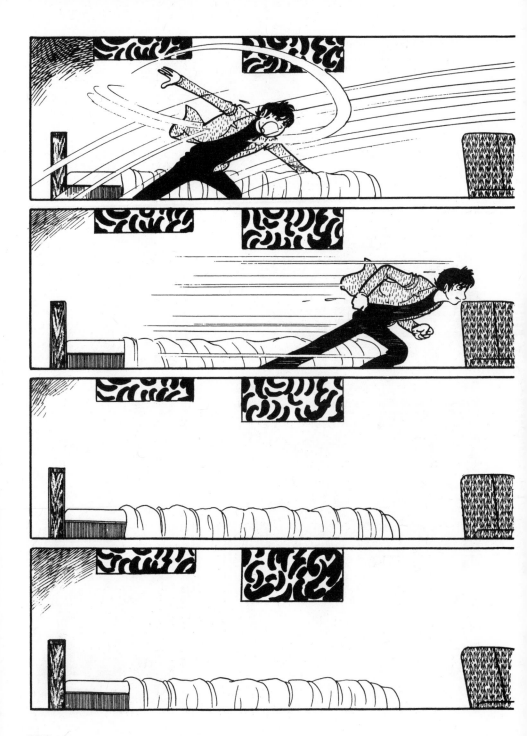

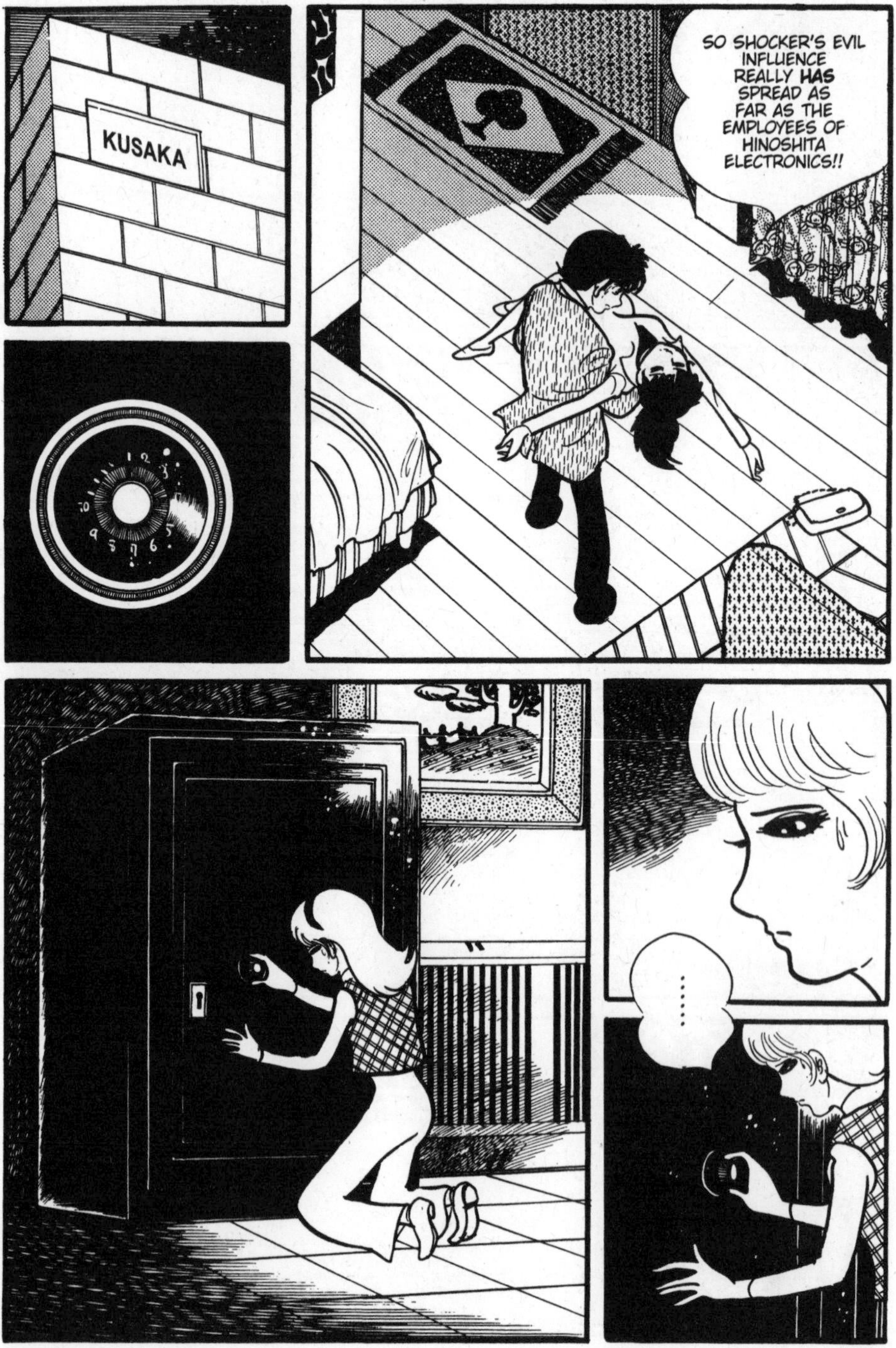

SO SHOCKER'S EVIL INFLUENCE REALLY **HAS** SPREAD AS FAR AS THE EMPLOYEES OF HINOSHITA ELECTRONICS!!
KUSAKA
......

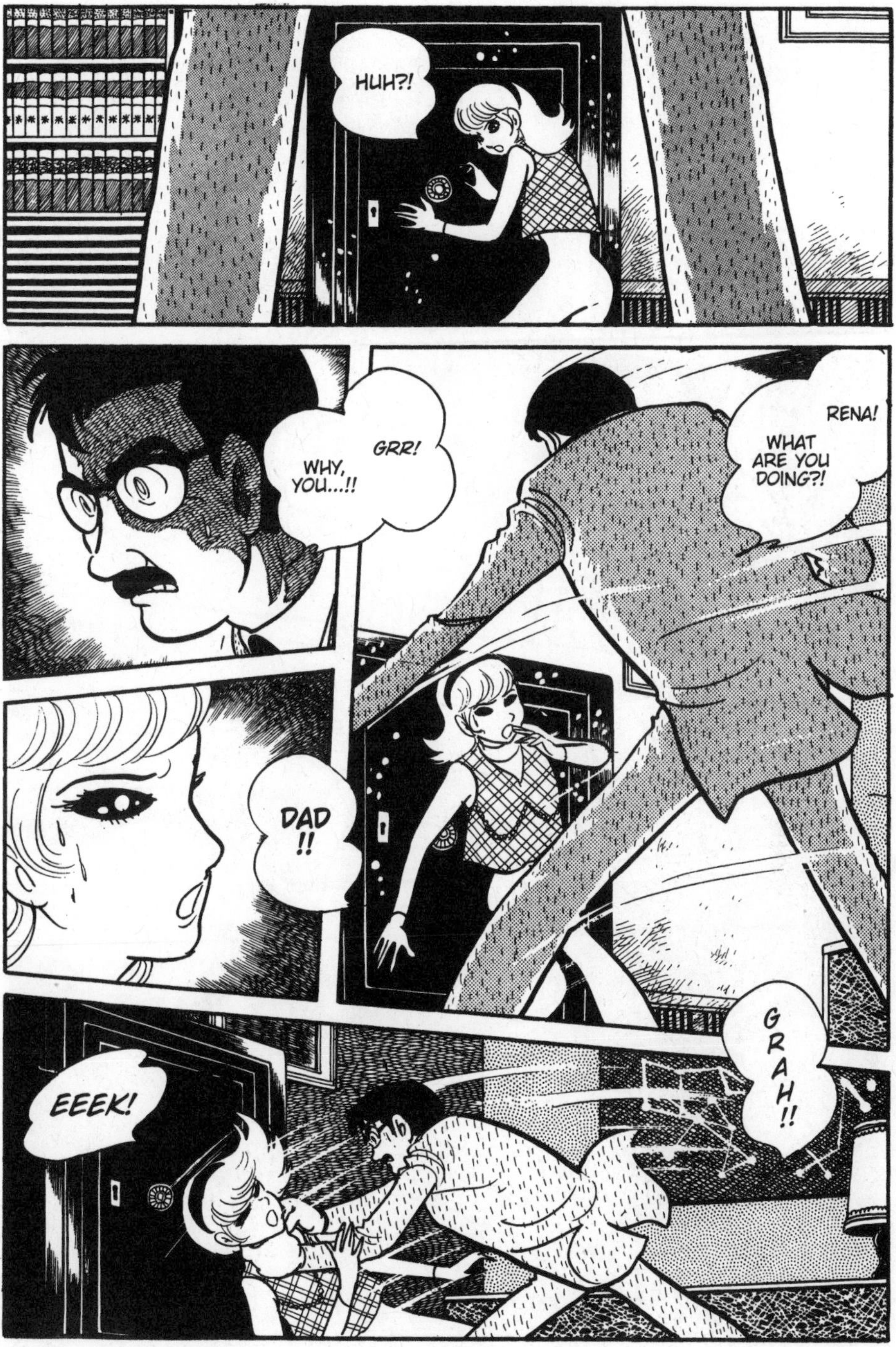
HUH?!
RENA! WHAT ARE YOU DOING?!
GRR! WHY, YOU...!!
DAD!!
GRAH!!
EEEK!

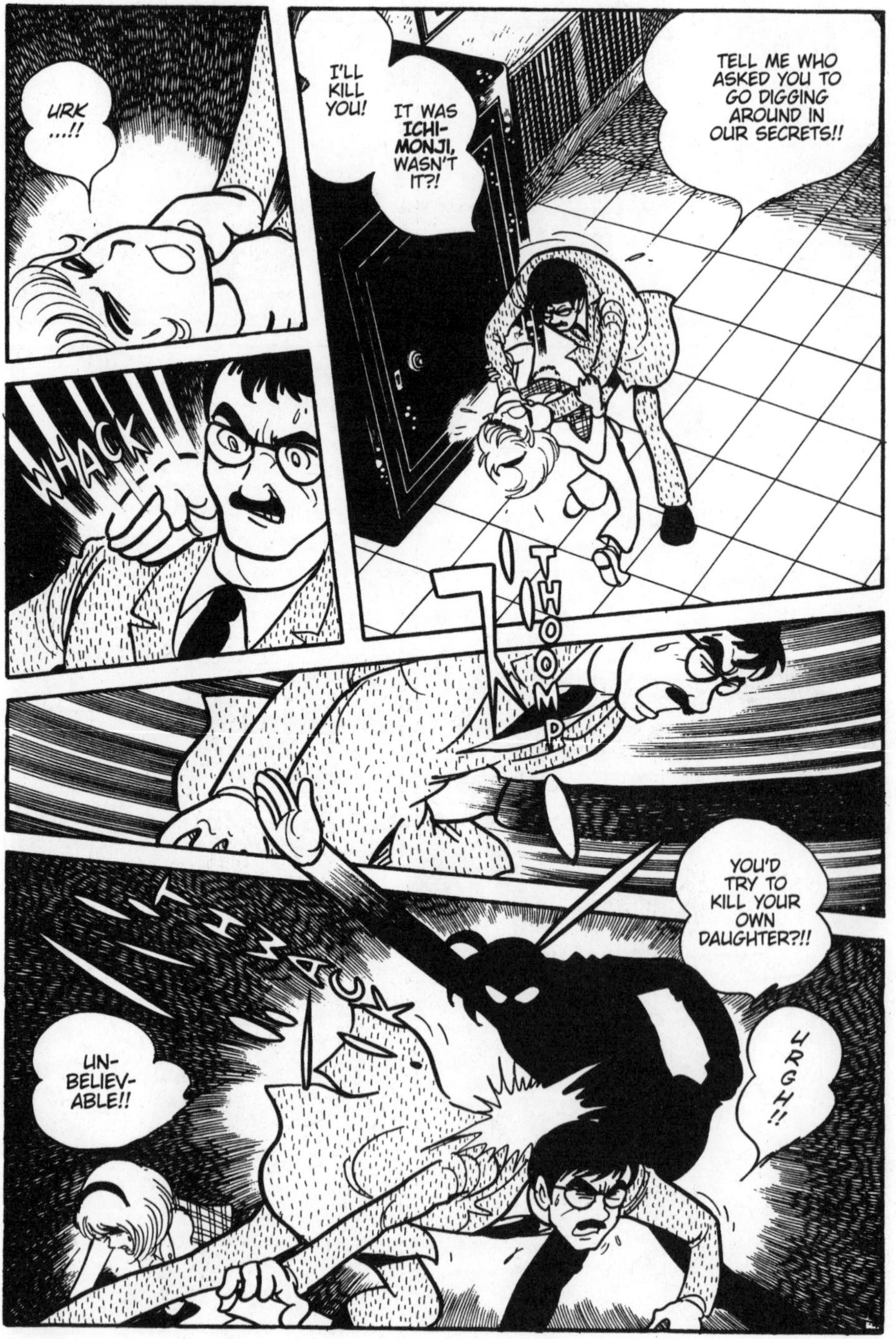
TELL ME WHO ASKED YOU TO GO DIGGING AROUND IN OUR SECRETS!!
IT WAS ICHIMONJI, WASN'T IT?!
I'LL KILL YOU!
URK ...!!
WHACK
THOOMP
YOU'D TRY TO KILL YOUR OWN DAUGHTER?!!
URGH!!
THWACK
UN-BELIEVABLE!!

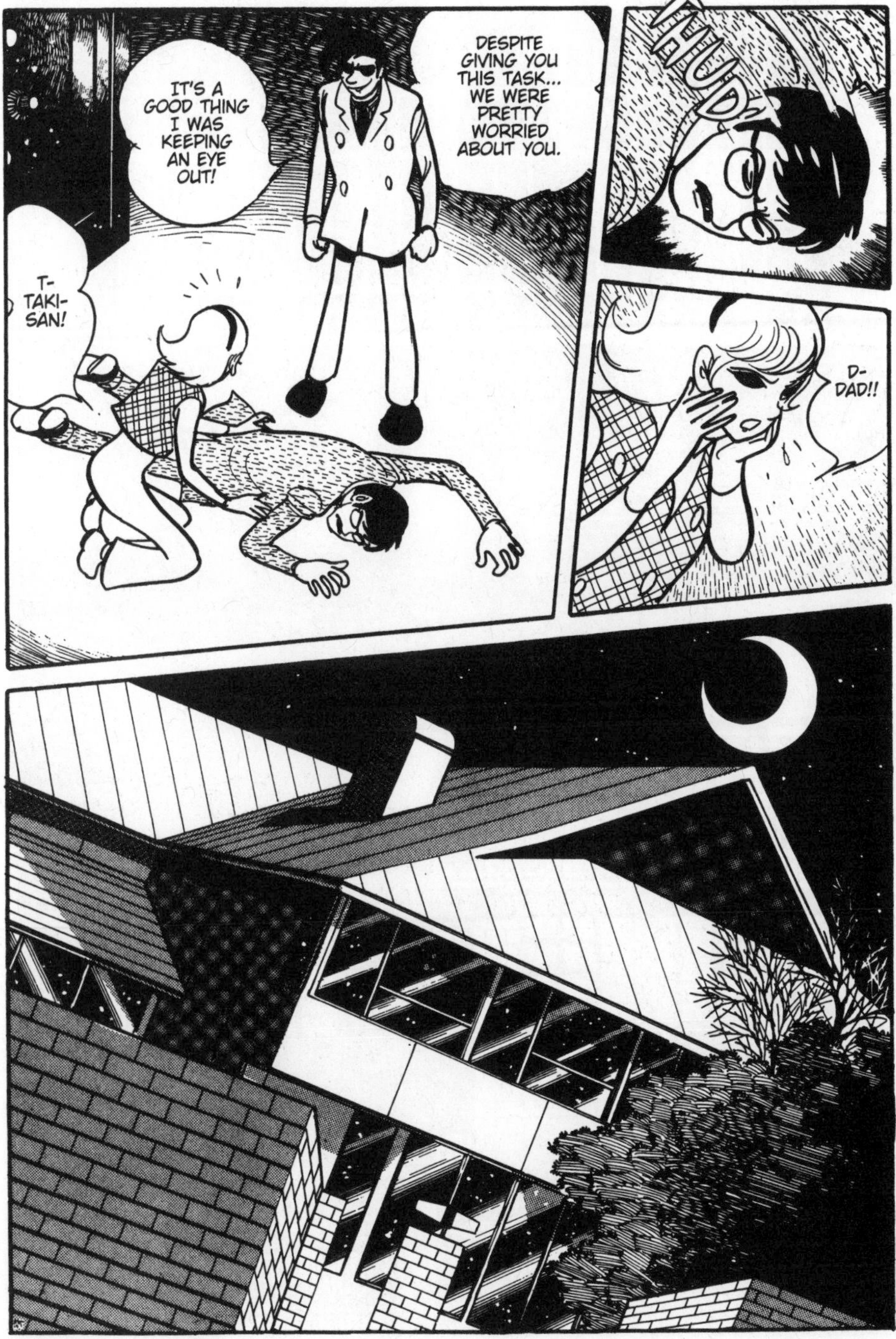
THUD
D-DAD!!
DESPITE GIVING YOU THIS TASK... WE WERE PRETTY WORRIED ABOUT YOU.
IT'S A GOOD THING I WAS KEEPING AN EYE OUT!
T-TAKI-SAN!

Sign: Hongou.

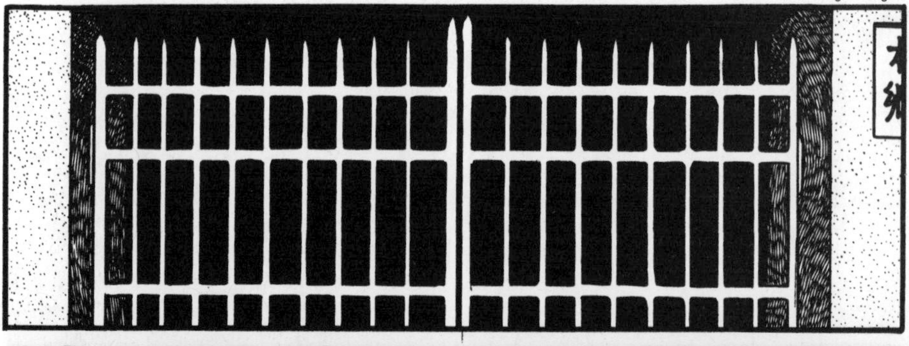

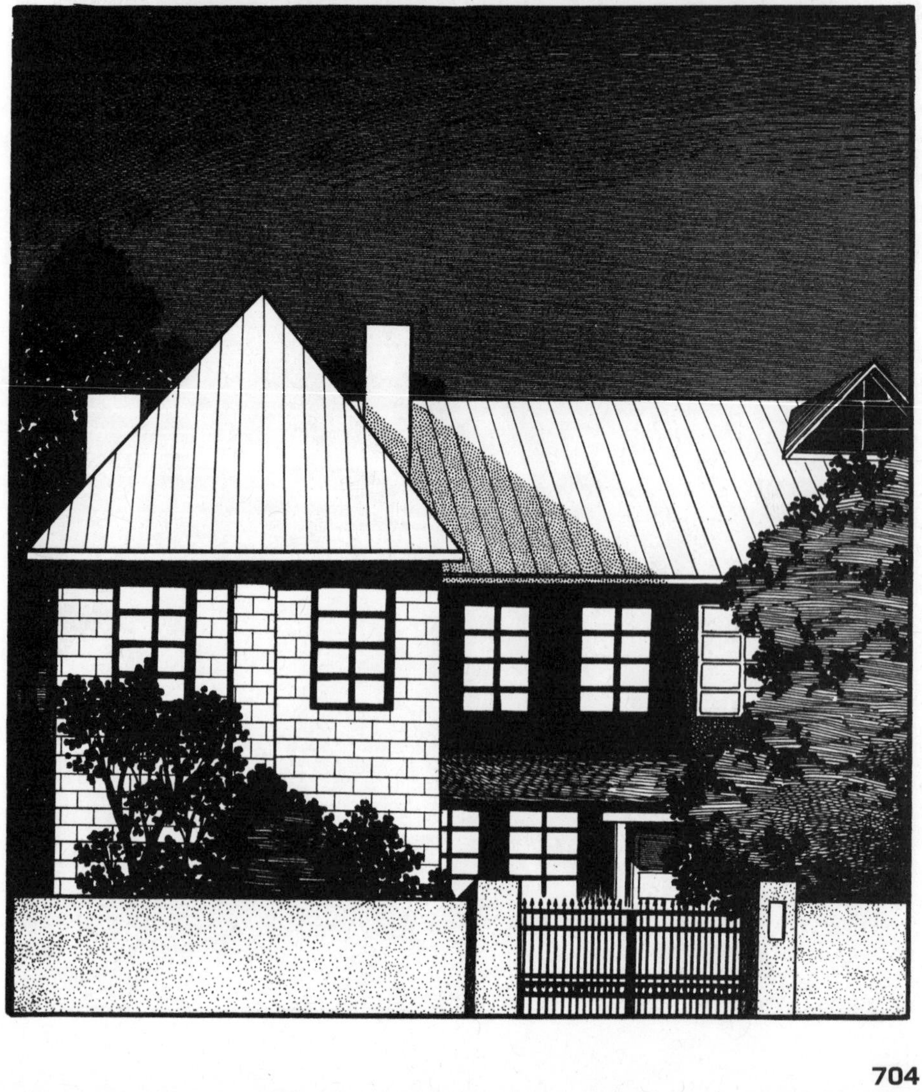

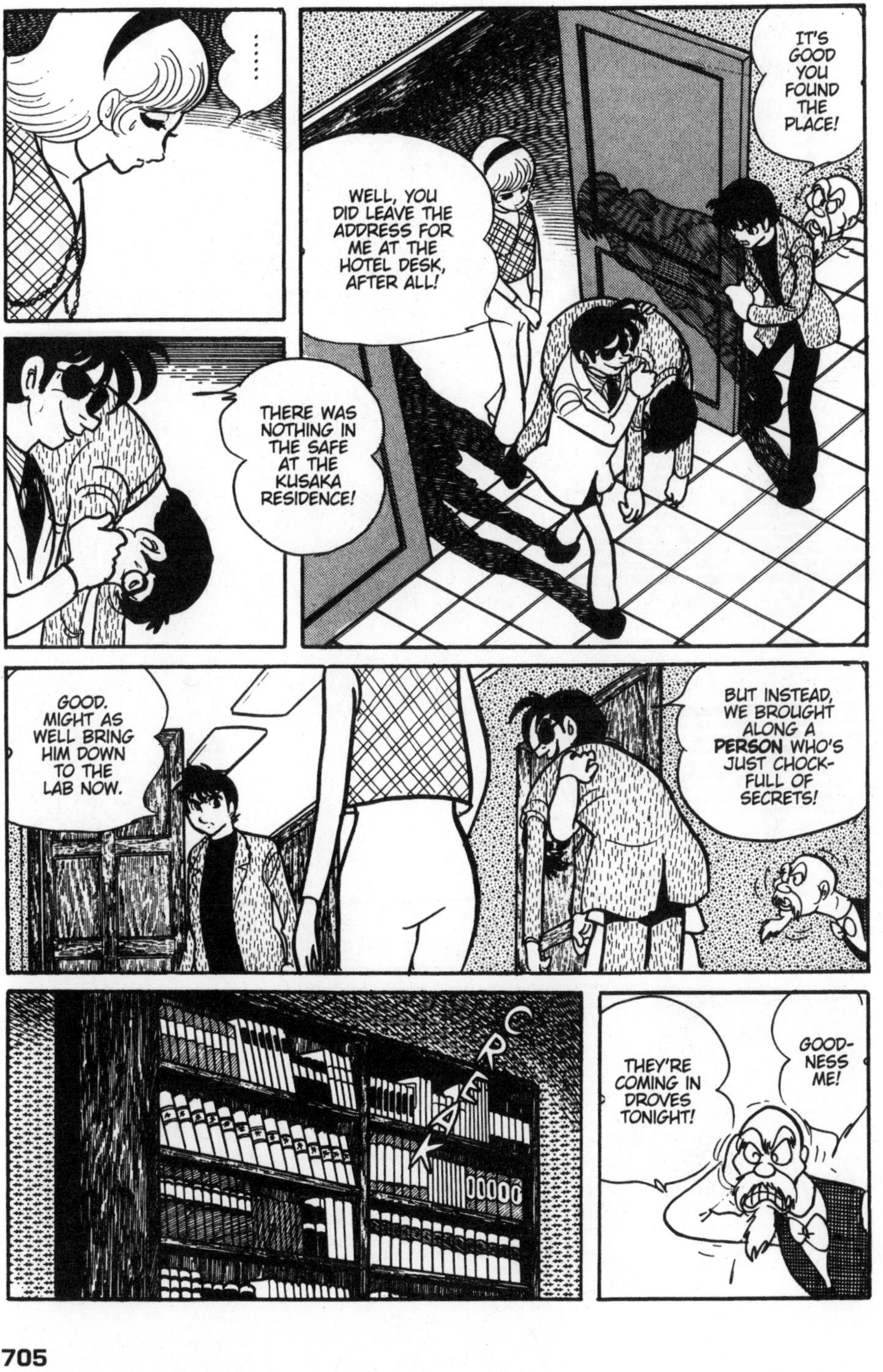
IT'S GOOD YOU FOUND THE PLACE!
WELL, YOU DID LEAVE THE ADDRESS FOR ME AT THE HOTEL DESK, AFTER ALL!
......
THERE WAS NOTHING IN THE SAFE AT THE KUSAKA RESIDENCE!
BUT INSTEAD, WE BROUGHT ALONG A **PERSON** WHO'S JUST CHOCK-FULL OF SECRETS!
GOOD. MIGHT AS WELL BRING HIM DOWN TO THE LAB NOW.
GOOD-NESS ME!
THEY'RE COMING IN DROVES TONIGHT!
CREAK

WHAT'S HAP-PENING OVER THERE?

WELL, KOUJI-KUN'S CONDITION WAS GETTING WORSE...

CLOMP CLOMP CLOMP CLOMP CLOMP CLOMP CLOMP

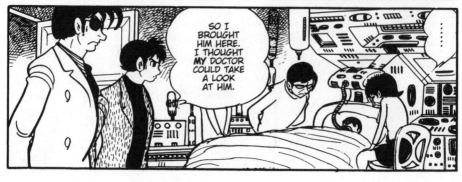

SO I BROUGHT HIM HERE. I THOUGHT MY DOCTOR COULD TAKE A LOOK AT HIM.

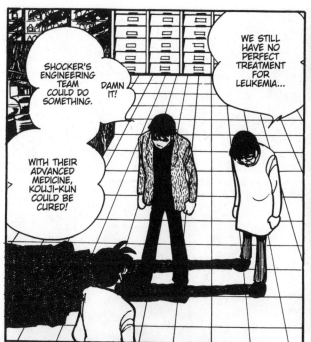

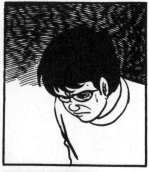

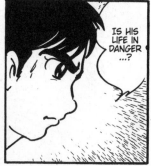

IS HIS LIFE IN DANGER ...?
WE STILL HAVE NO PERFECT TREATMENT FOR LEUKEMIA...
DAMN IT!
SHOCKER'S ENGINEERING TEAM COULD DO SOMETHING.
WITH THEIR ADVANCED MEDICINE, KOUJI-KUN COULD BE CURED!
LEUKEMIA IS A TYPE OF BLOOD CANCER!
THEY COULD COMPLETELY REPLACE THE BLOOD IN HIS BODY WITH THE TECHNOLOGY THEY USED TO TRANSFORM OURS!
SO HOW ABOUT WE SNATCH ONE OF THEM?
SZAP
HUH?!
I-I SEE...! SO WE SHOULD INFILTRATE THEIR FACILITY?!

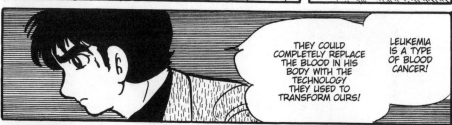

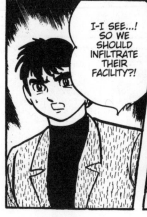

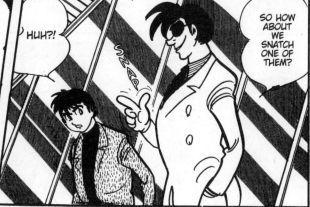

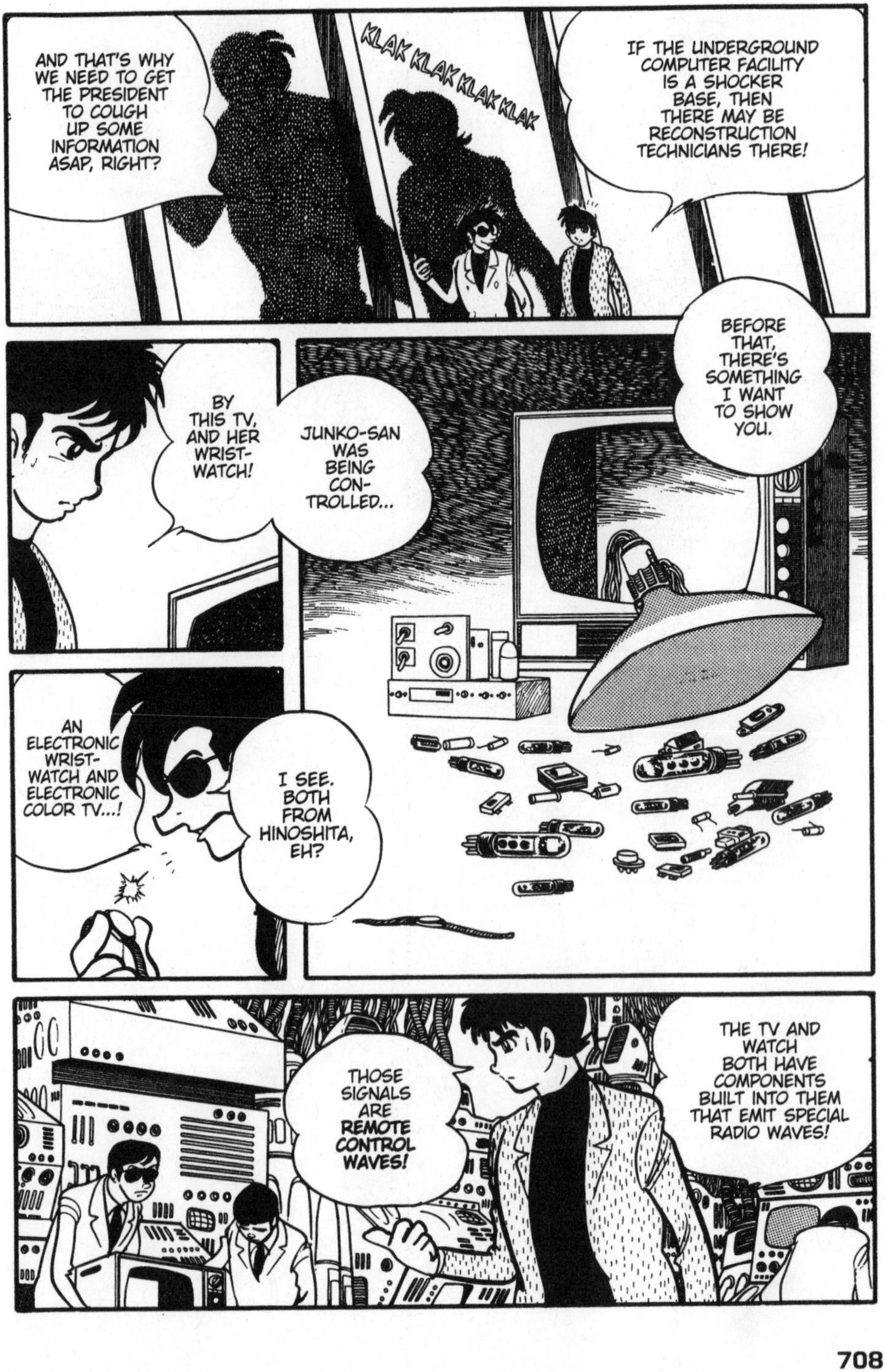
IF THE UNDERGROUND COMPUTER FACILITY IS A SHOCKER BASE, THEN THERE MAY BE RECONSTRUCTION TECHNICIANS THERE!
KLAK KLAK KLAK KLAK
AND THAT'S WHY WE NEED TO GET THE PRESIDENT TO COUGH UP SOME INFORMATION ASAP, RIGHT?
BEFORE THAT, THERE'S SOMETHING I WANT TO SHOW YOU.
JUNKO-SAN WAS BEING CON-TROLLED...
BY THIS TV, AND HER WRIST-WATCH!
I SEE. BOTH FROM HINOSHITA, EH?
AN ELECTRONIC WRIST-WATCH AND ELECTRONIC COLOR TV...!
THE TV AND WATCH BOTH HAVE COMPONENTS BUILT INTO THEM THAT EMIT SPECIAL RADIO WAVES!
THOSE SIGNALS ARE **REMOTE CONTROL WAVES!**

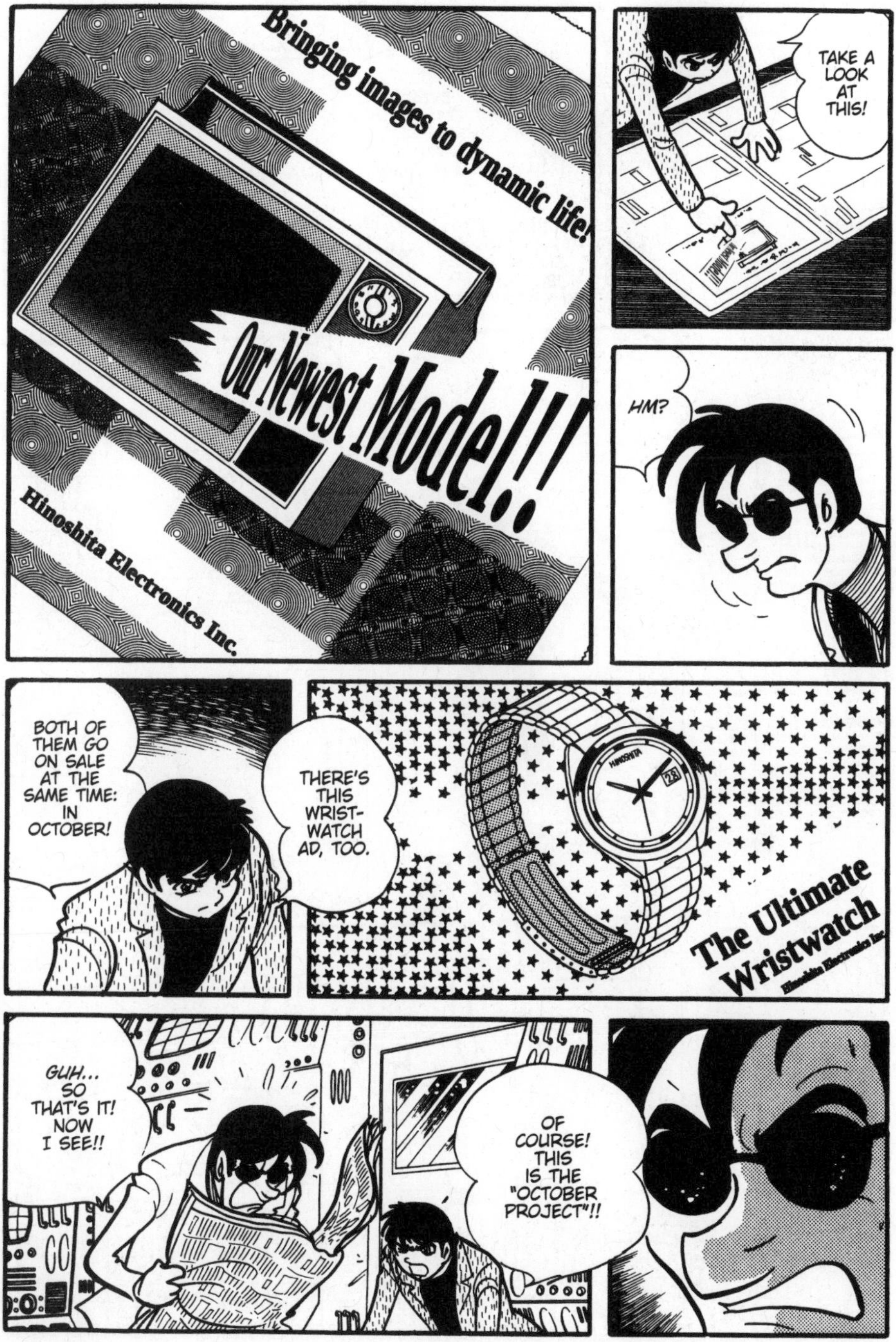
TAKE A LOOK AT THIS!
HM?
Bringing images to dynamic life!
Our Newest Model!!
Hinoshita Electronics Inc.
HINOSHITA
The Ultimate Wristwatch
Hinoshita Electronics Inc.
THERE'S THIS WRIST-WATCH AD, TOO.
BOTH OF THEM GO ON SALE AT THE SAME TIME: IN OCTOBER!
GUH... SO THAT'S IT! NOW I SEE!!
OF COURSE! THIS IS THE "OCTOBER PROJECT"!!

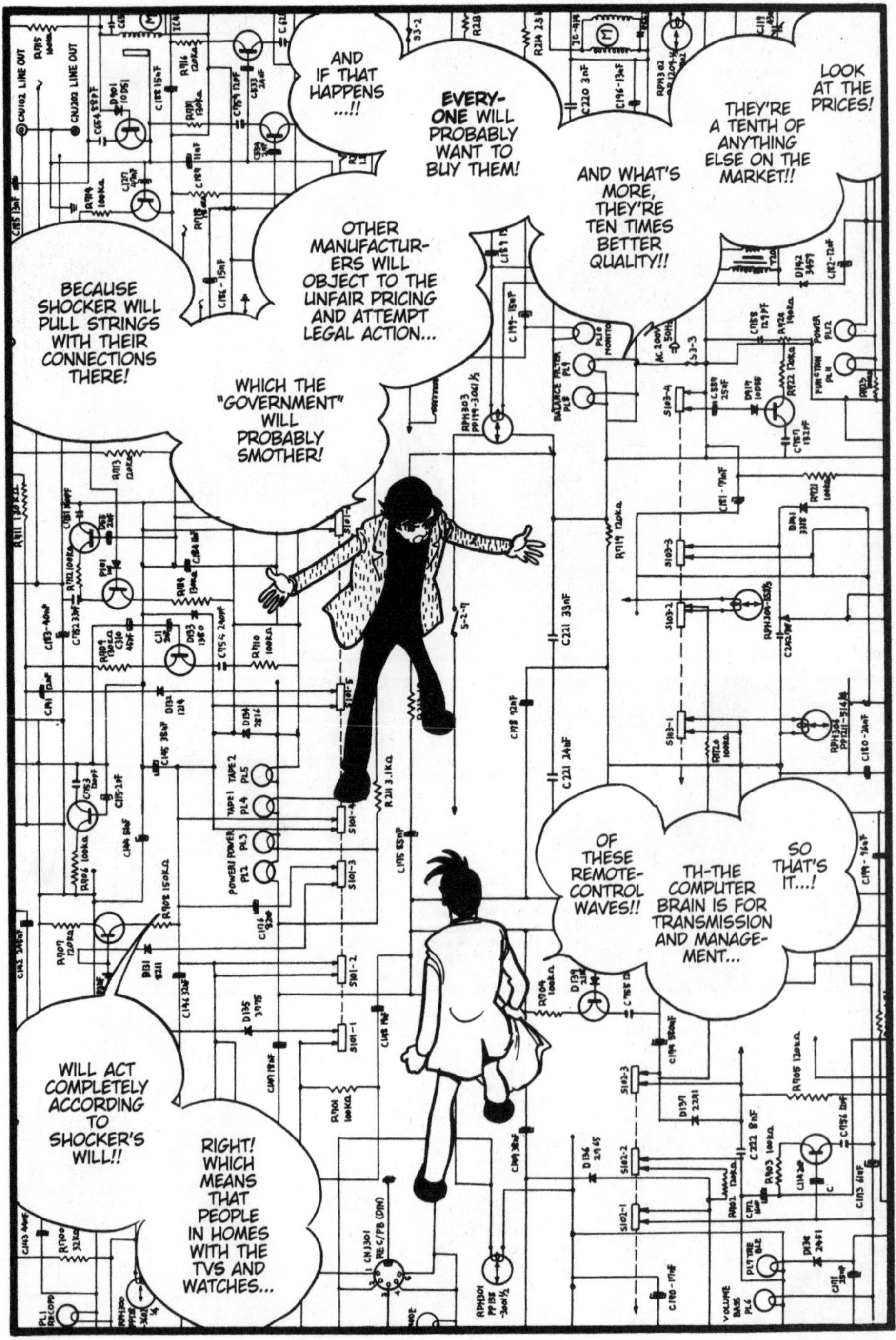
LOOK AT THE PRICES!
THEY'RE A TENTH OF ANYTHING ELSE ON THE MARKET!!
AND WHAT'S MORE, THEY'RE TEN TIMES BETTER QUALITY!!
EVERYONE WILL PROBABLY WANT TO BUY THEM!
AND IF THAT HAPPENS ...!!
OTHER MANUFACTURERS WILL OBJECT TO THE UNFAIR PRICING AND ATTEMPT LEGAL ACTION...
WHICH THE "GOVERNMENT" WILL PROBABLY SMOTHER!
BECAUSE SHOCKER WILL PULL STRINGS WITH THEIR CONNECTIONS THERE!
SO THAT'S IT...!
TH-THE COMPUTER BRAIN IS FOR TRANSMISSION AND MANAGEMENT...
OF THESE REMOTE-CONTROL WAVES!!
RIGHT! WHICH MEANS THAT PEOPLE IN HOMES WITH THE TVS AND WATCHES...
WILL ACT COMPLETELY ACCORDING TO SHOCKER'S WILL!!

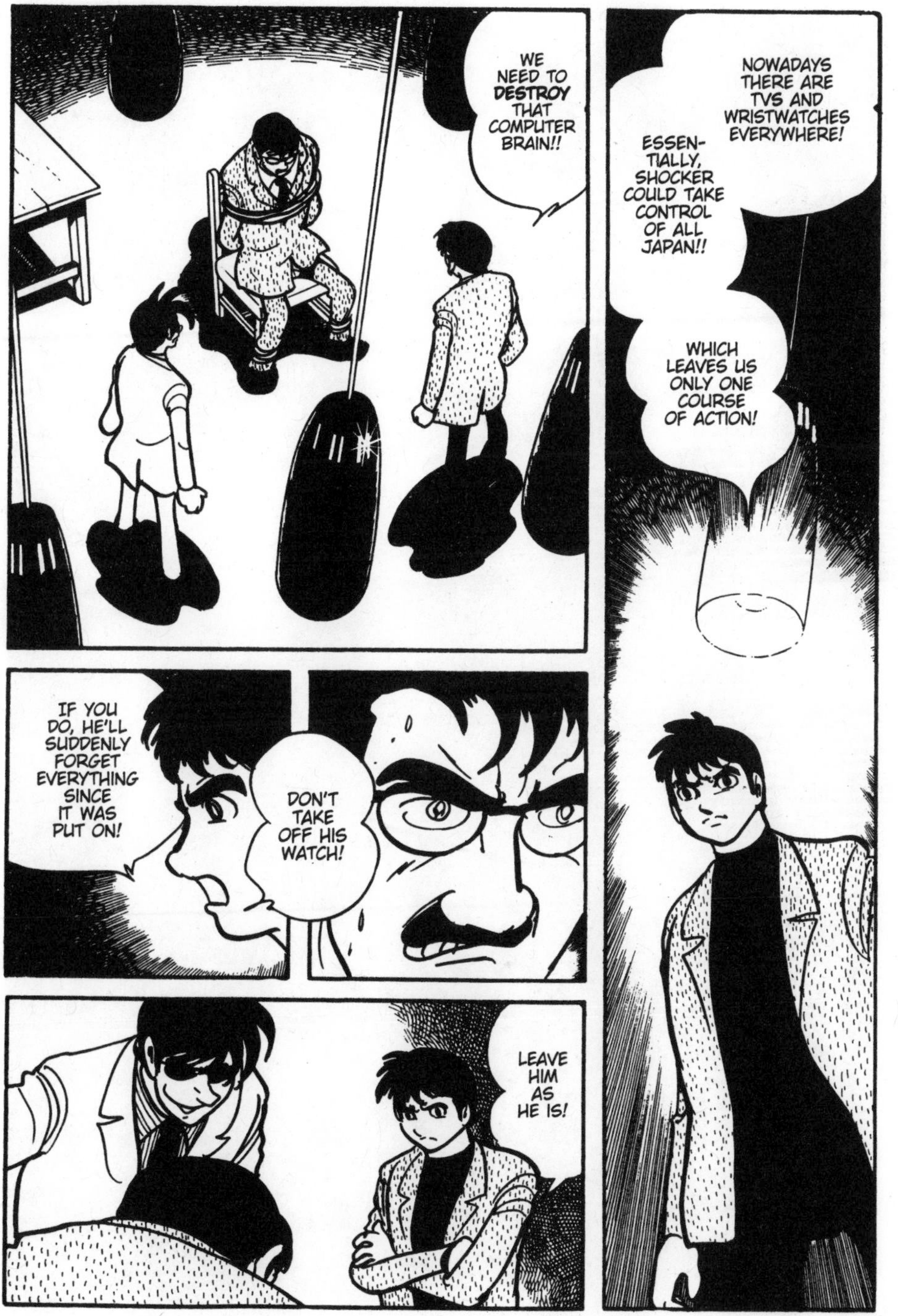
NOWADAYS THERE ARE TVS AND WRISTWATCHES EVERYWHERE!
ESSEN-TIALLY, SHOCKER COULD TAKE CONTROL OF ALL JAPAN!!
WHICH LEAVES US ONLY ONE COURSE OF ACTION!
WE NEED TO DESTROY THAT COMPUTER BRAIN!!
DON'T TAKE OFF HIS WATCH!
IF YOU DO, HE'LL SUDDENLY FORGET EVERYTHING SINCE IT WAS PUT ON!
LEAVE HIM AS HE IS!

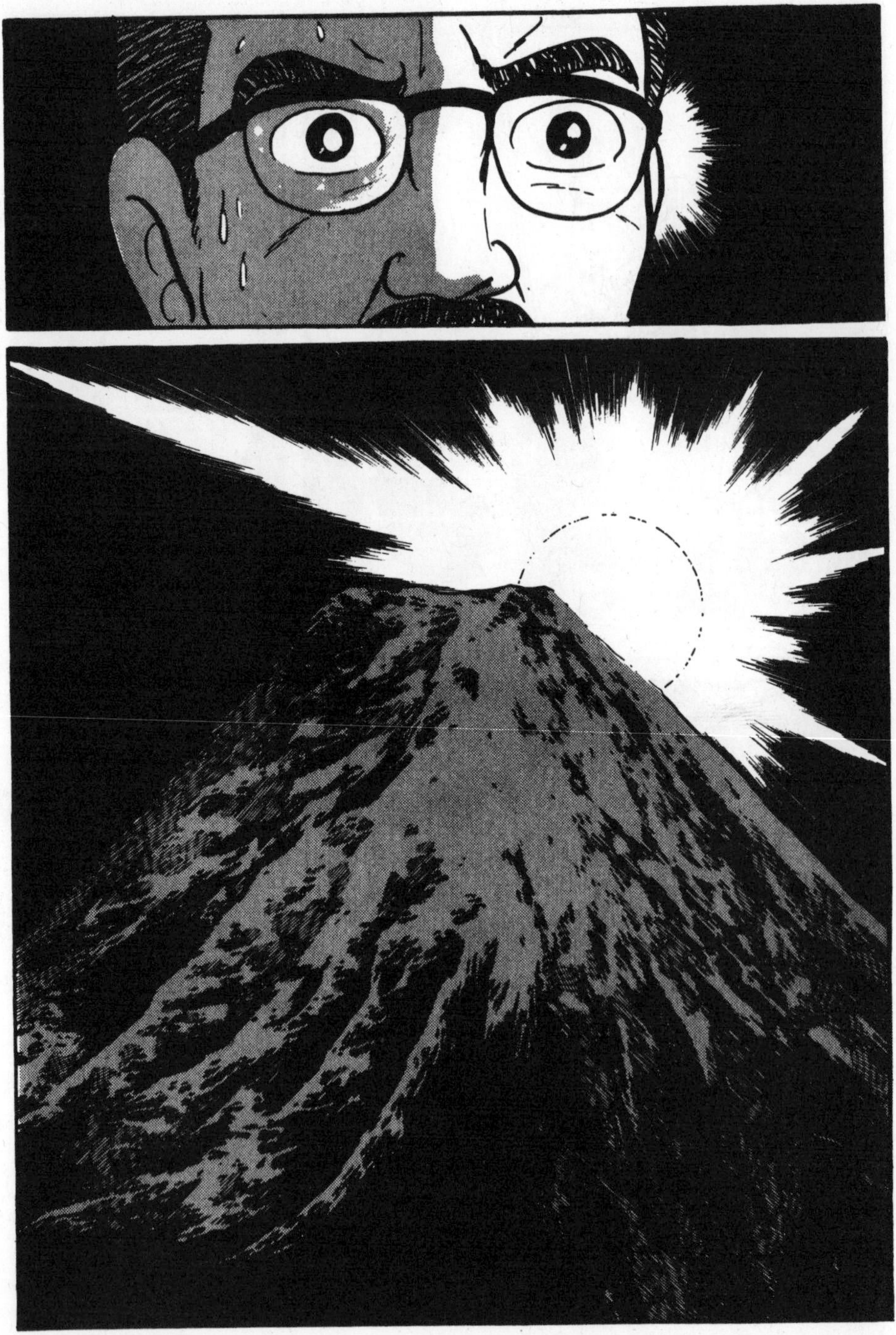

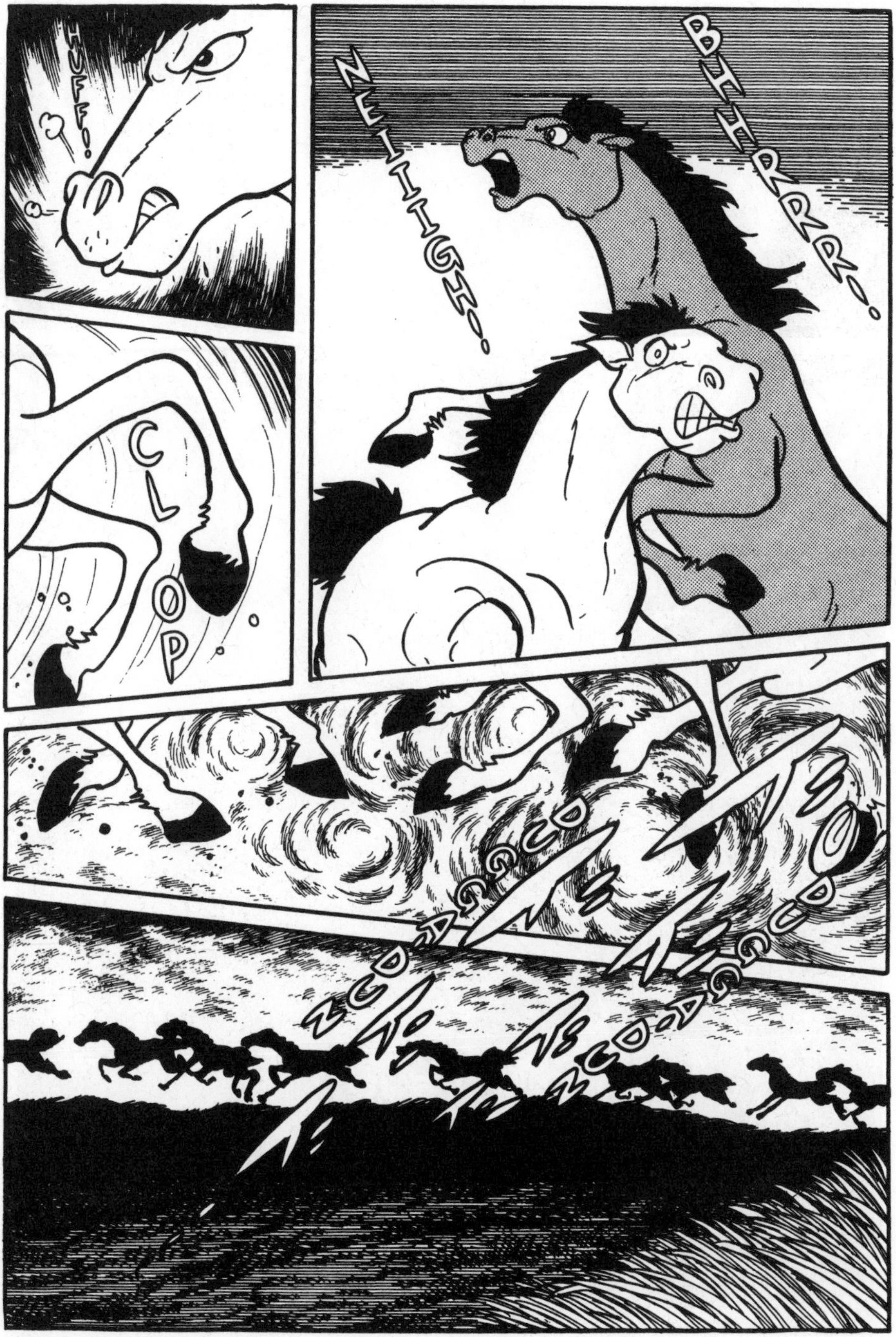
BHHRRRR!!
NEIIIGH!!
HUFF!
CLOP
DUGGADUN
DUGGADUN

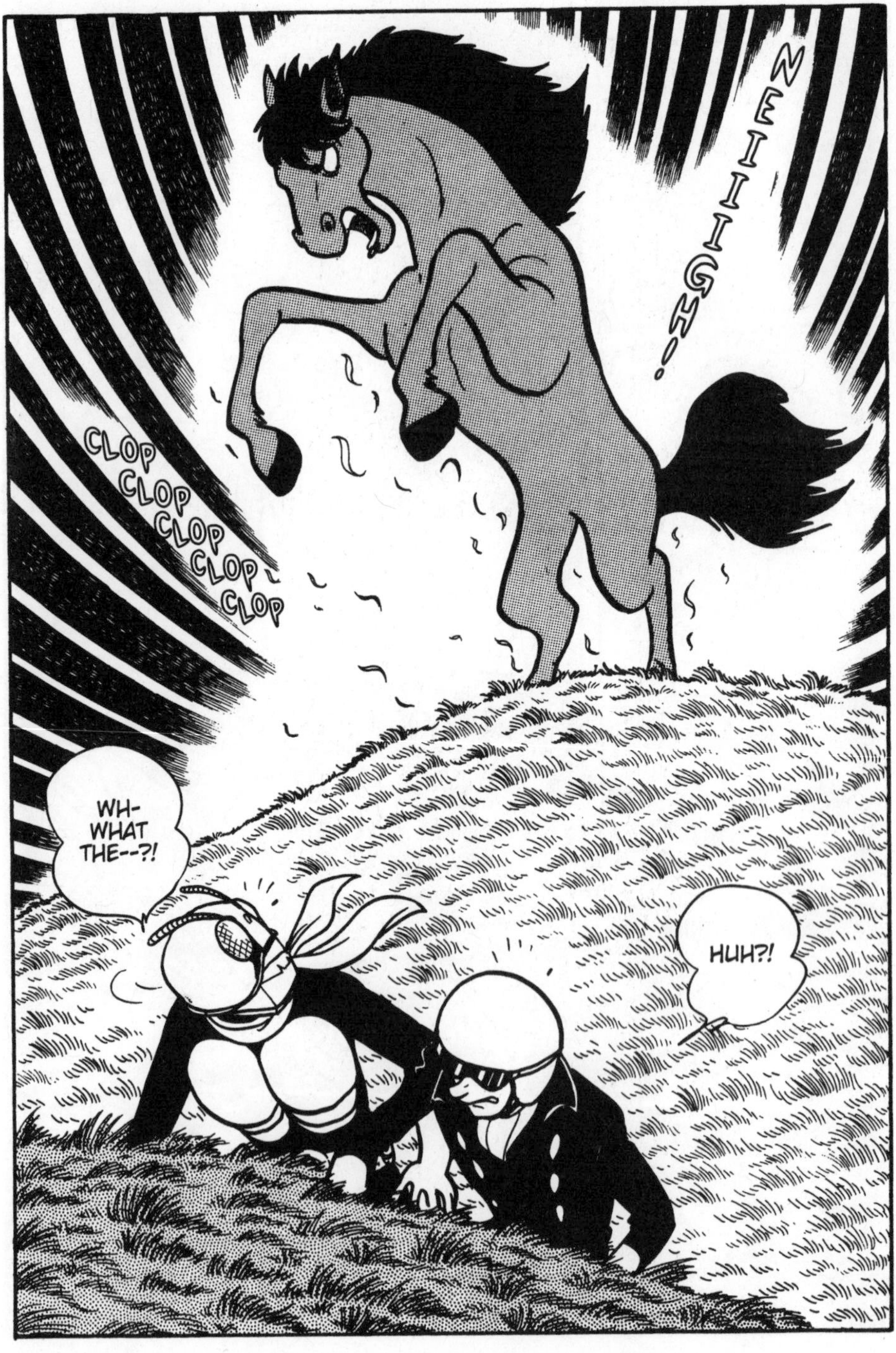
NEIIIIGH!!
CLOP CLOP CLOP CLOP CLOP
WH- WHAT THE--?!
HUH?!

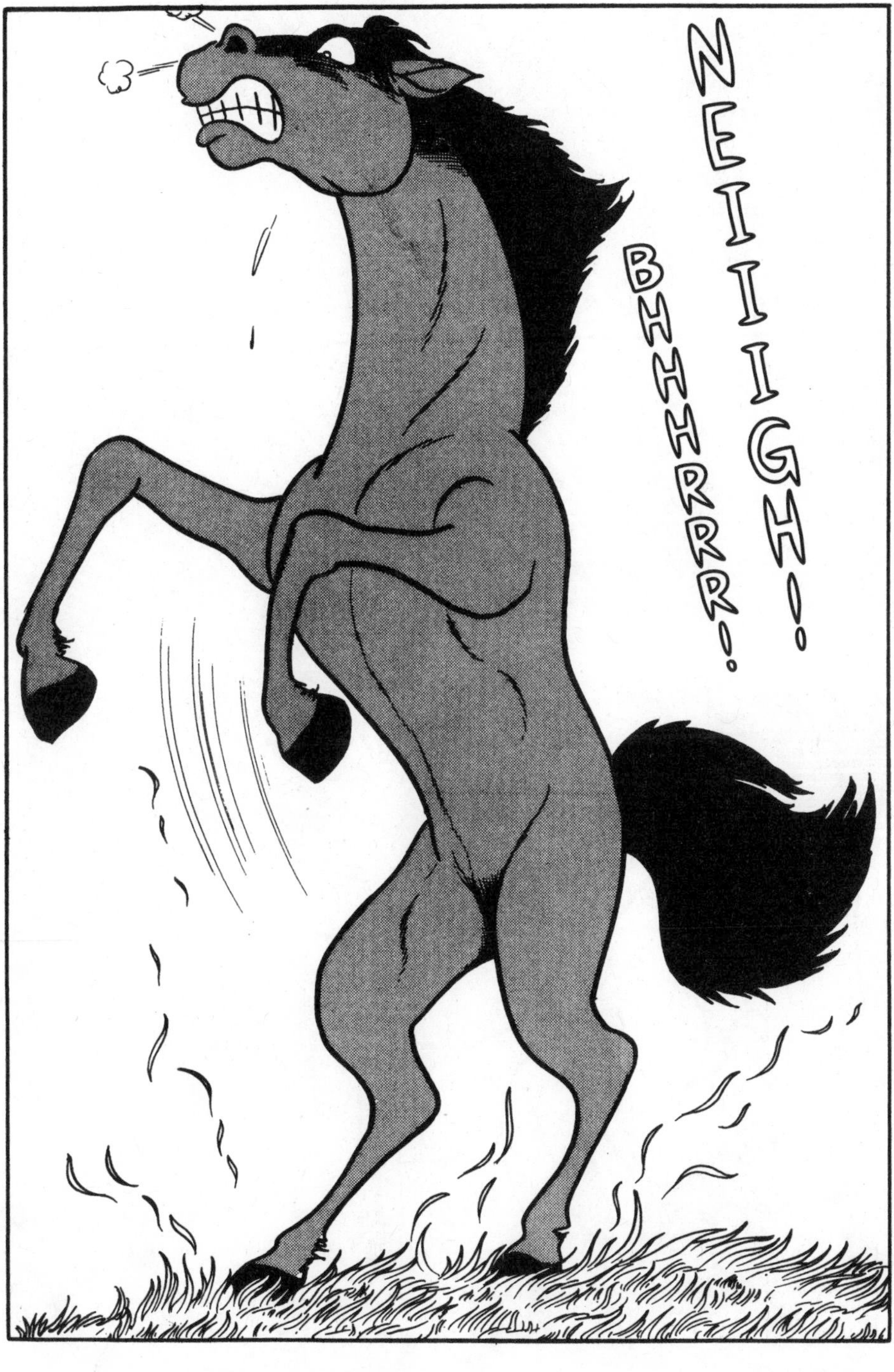
NEIIIGH!!
BHHHRRR!!

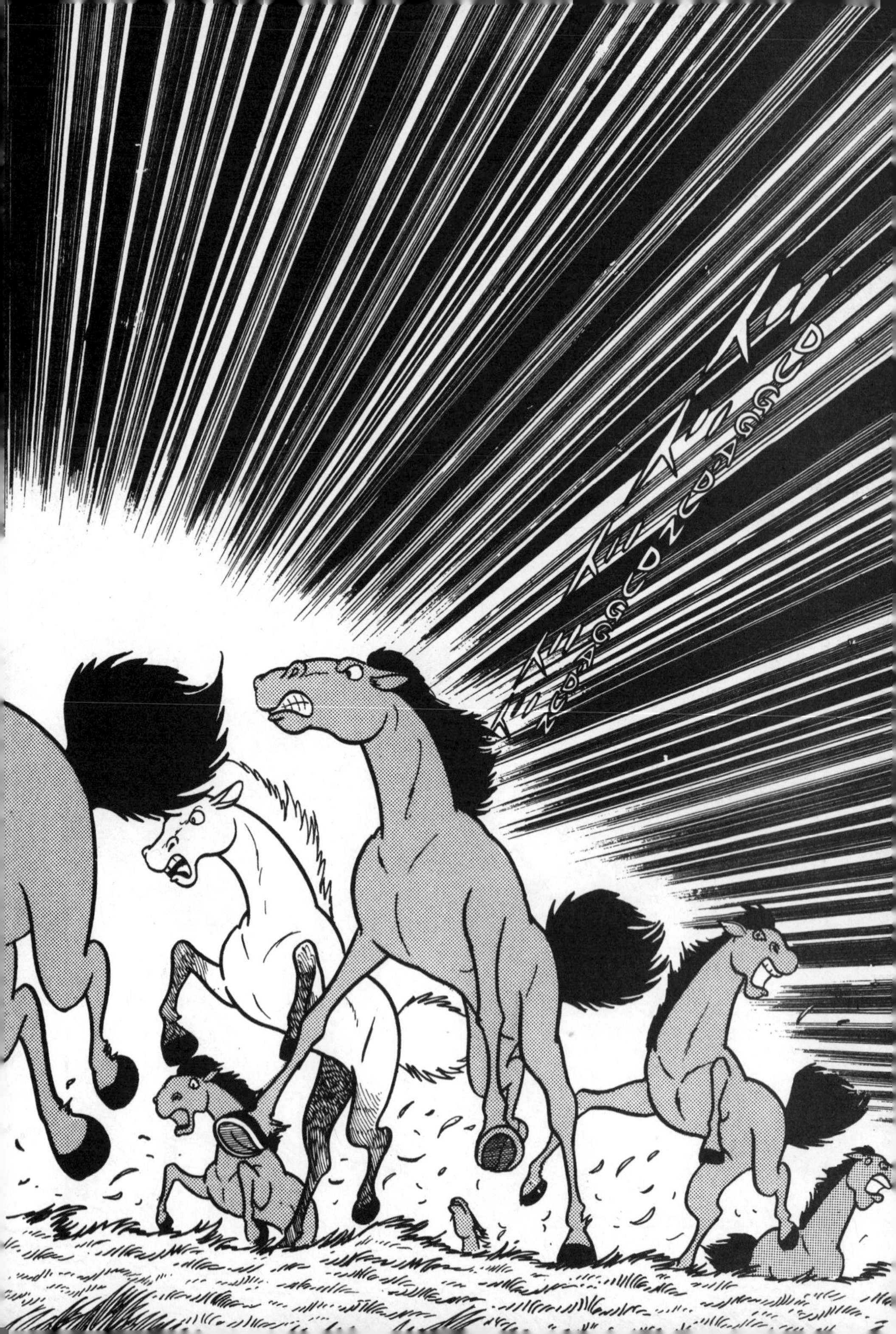

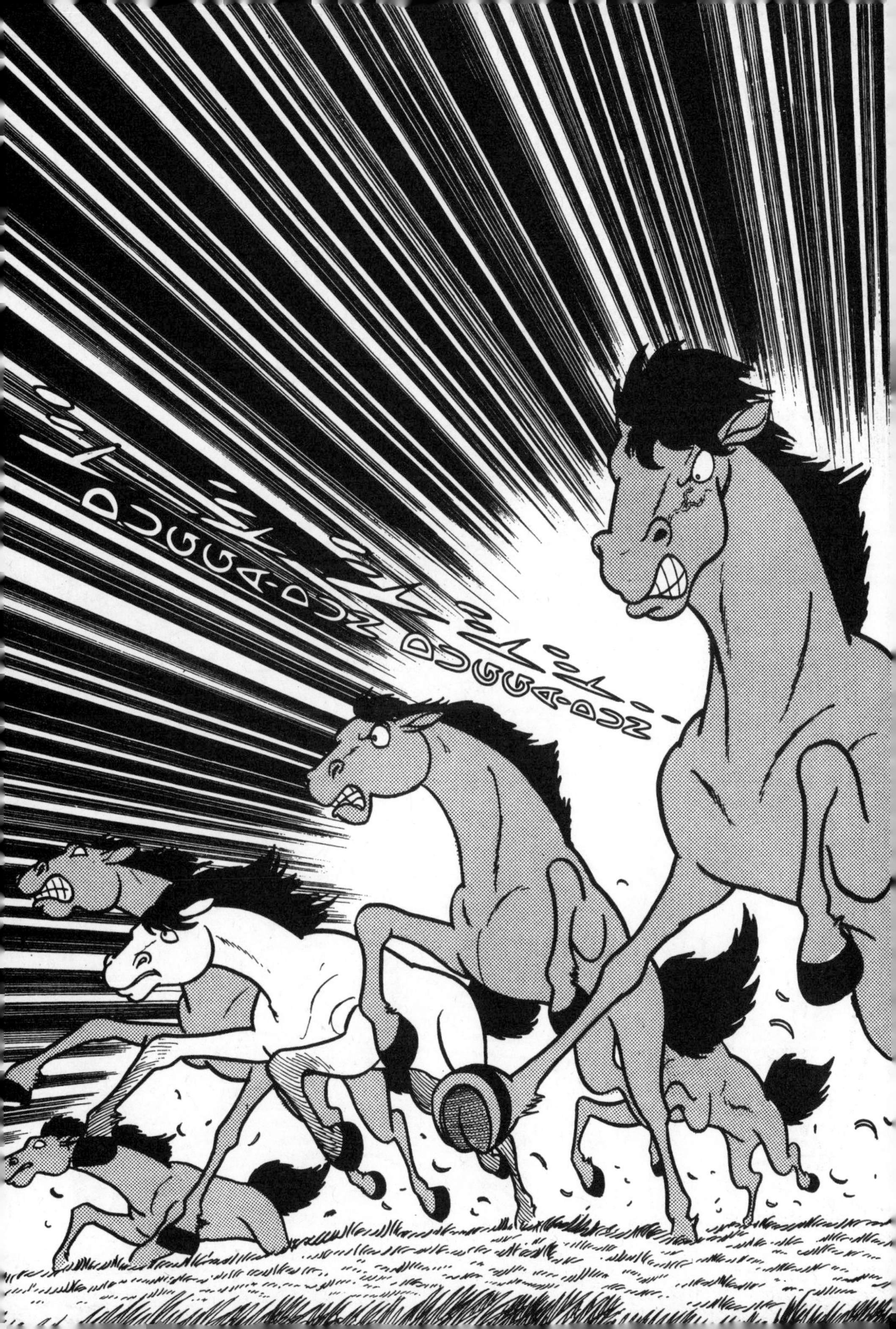
DUGGA-DUN
DUGGA-DUN

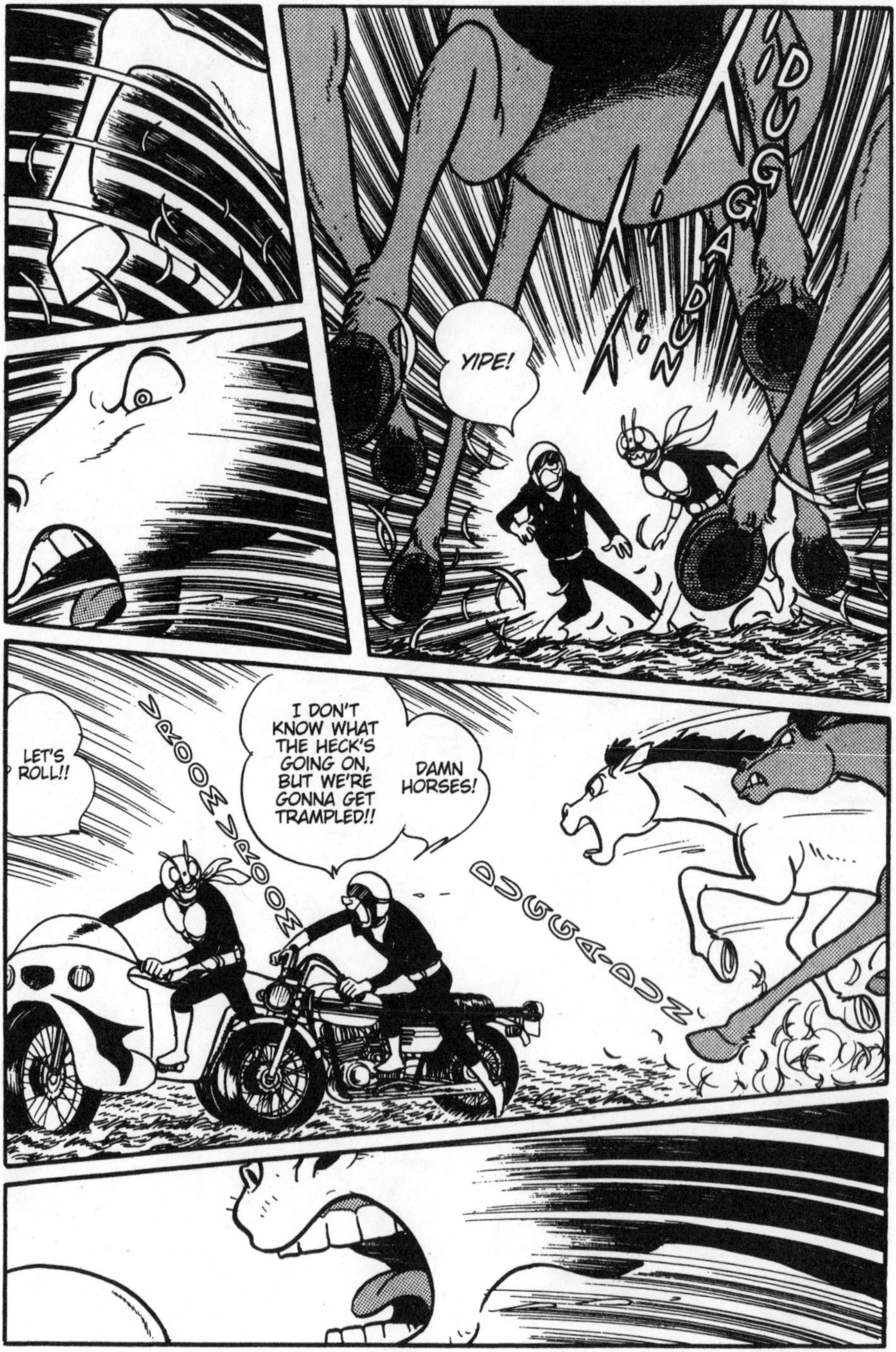
DUGGADUN!!
YIPE!
DUGGA-DUN
DAMN HORSES!
I DON'T KNOW WHAT THE HECK'S GOING ON, BUT WE'RE GONNA GET TRAMPLED!!
VROOM VROOM
LET'S ROLL!!

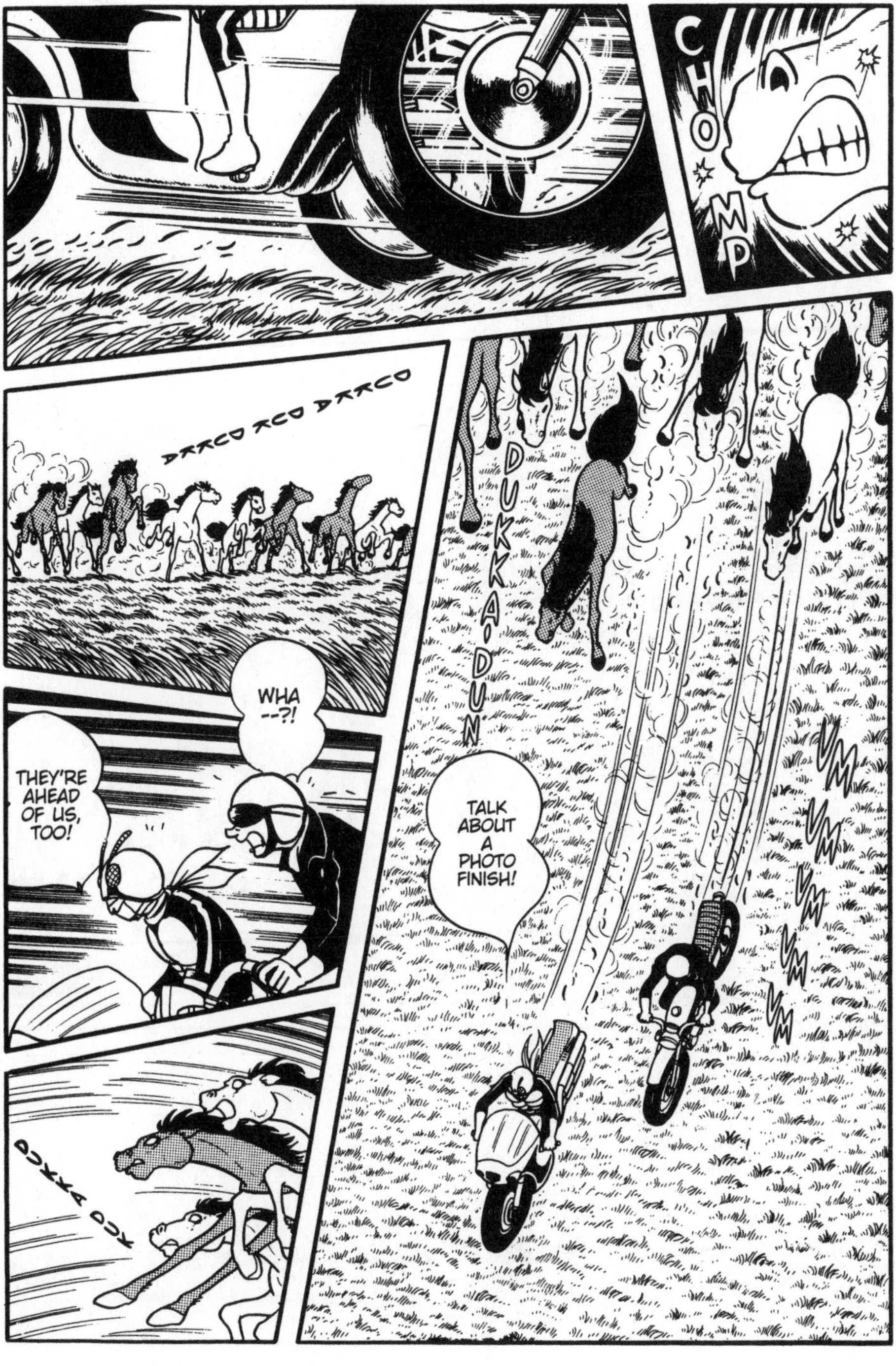
CHOMP
DUKKA-DUN
TALK ABOUT A PHOTO FINISH!
VM VM VM VM VM
DAKKA KA DAKKA
WHA--?!
THEY'RE AHEAD OF US, TOO!
DUKKA DUK

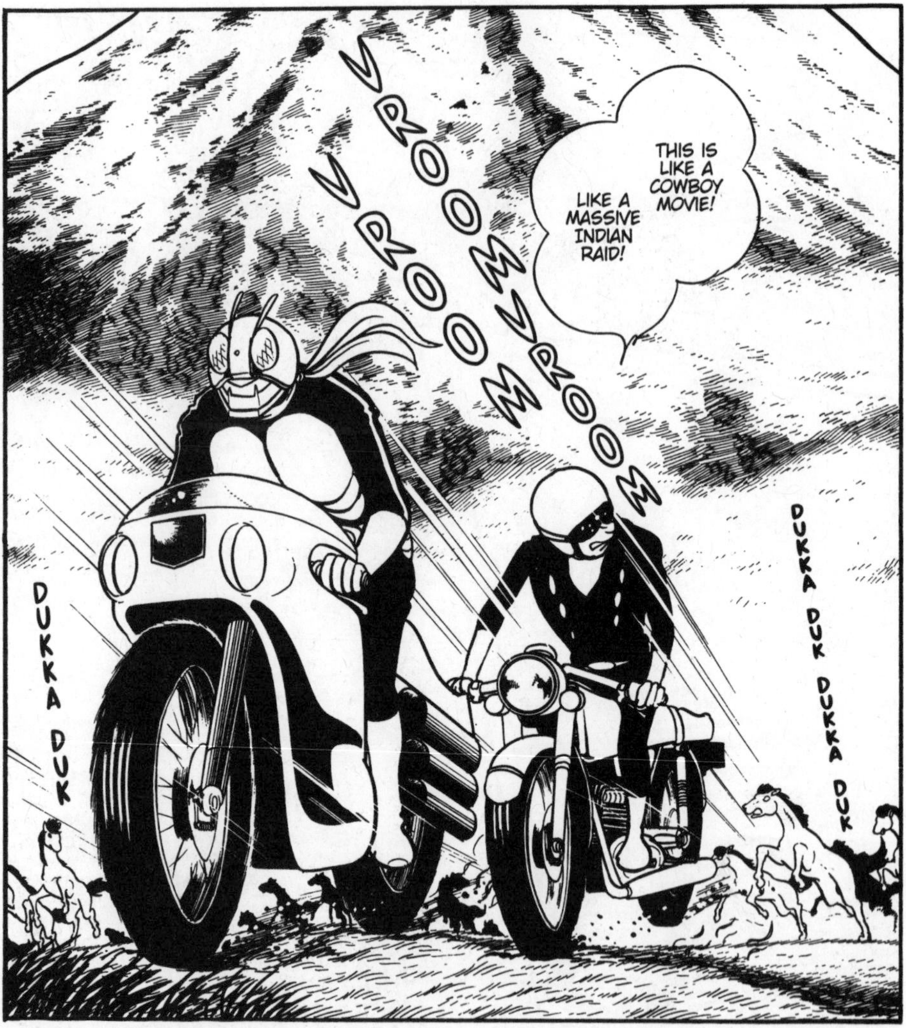
THIS IS LIKE A COWBOY MOVIE!
LIKE A MASSIVE INDIAN RAID!
VROOOM VROOOM
DUKKA DUK DUKKA DUKKA DUK
DUKKA DUK

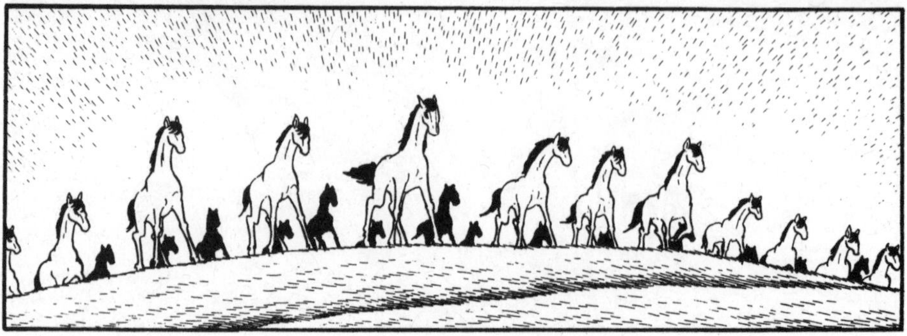

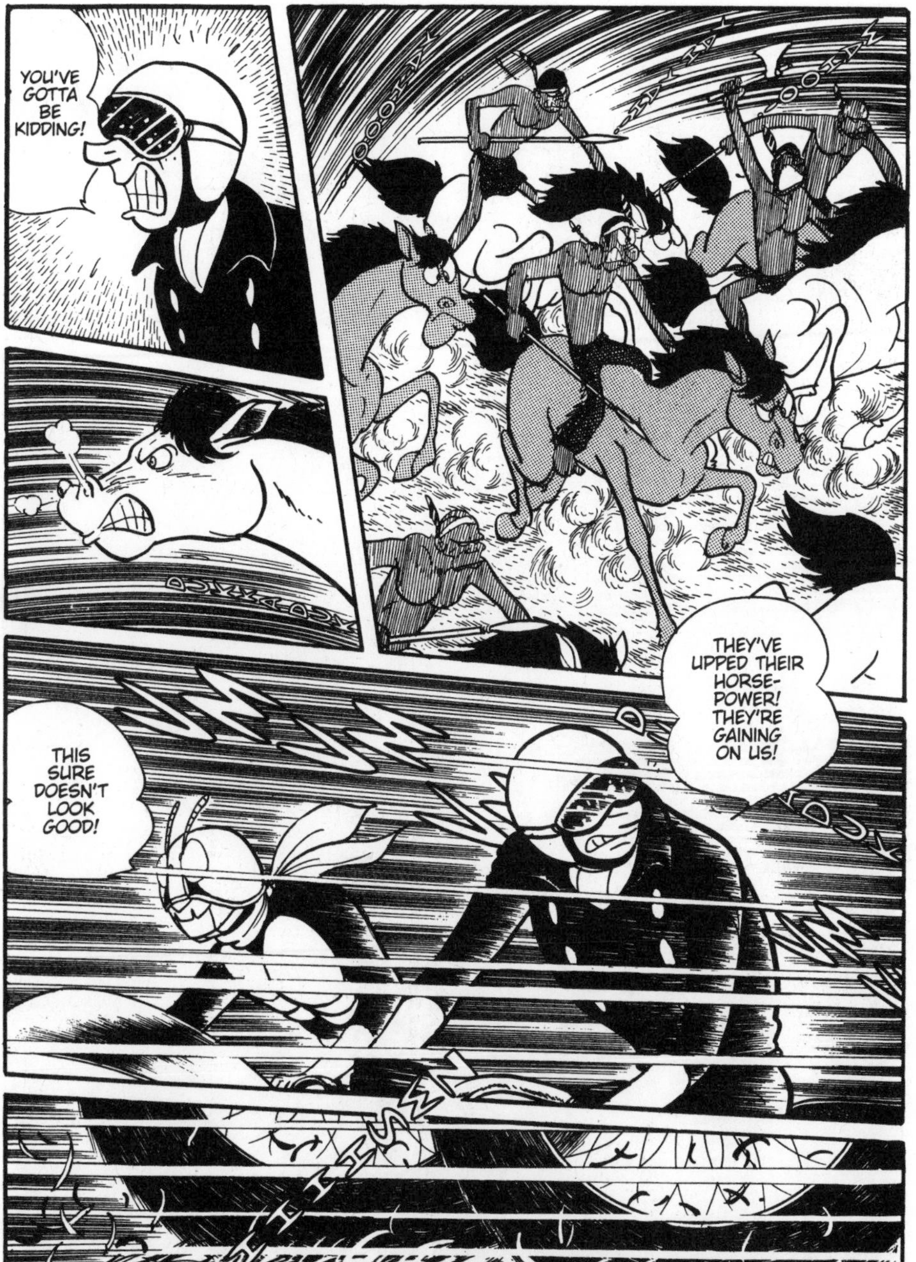

YOU'VE GOTTA BE KIDDING!
THEY'VE UPPED THEIR HORSE-POWER! THEY'RE GAINING ON US!
THIS SURE DOESN'T LOOK GOOD!

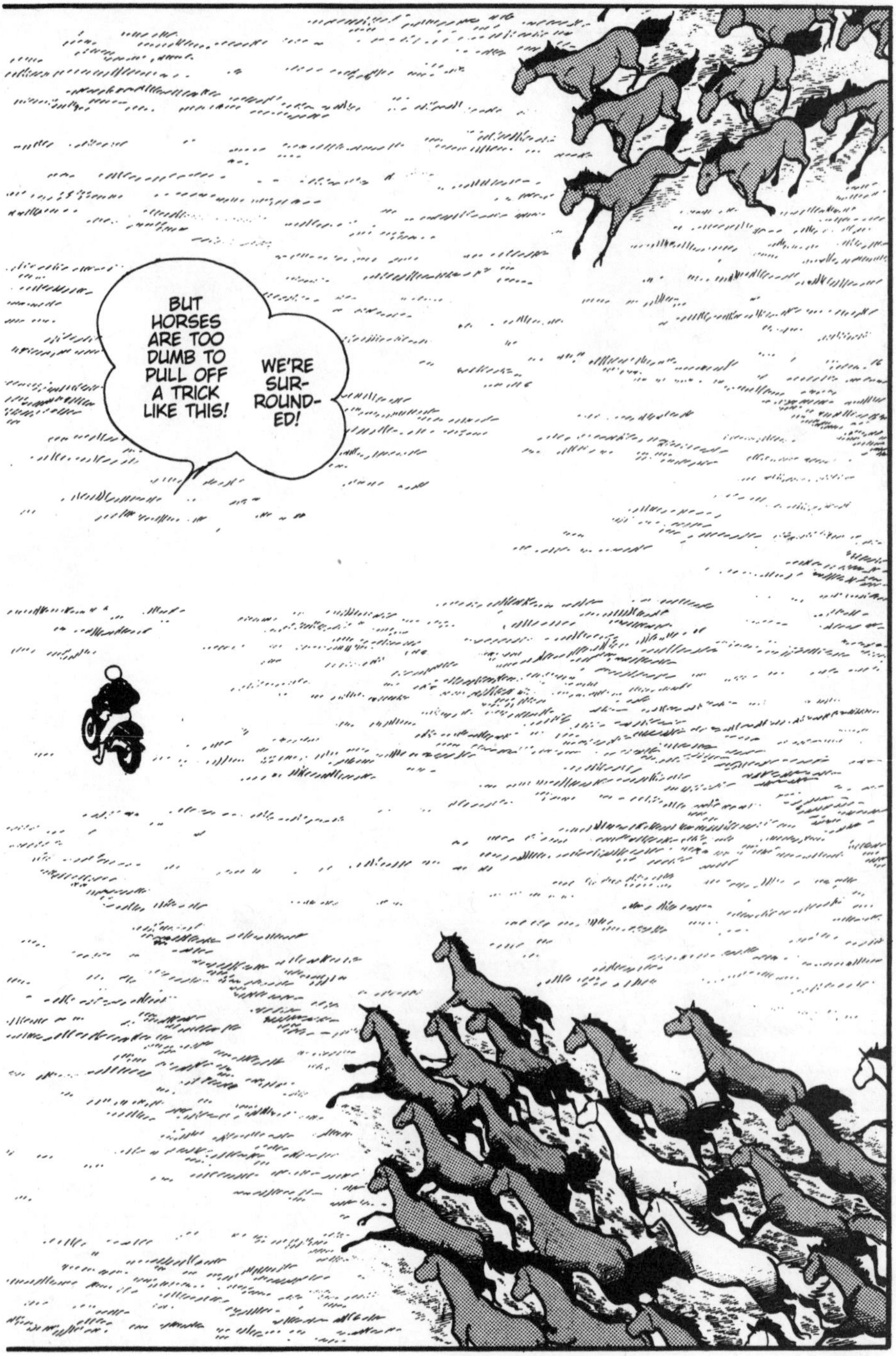
BUT HORSES ARE TOO DUMB TO PULL OFF A TRICK LIKE THIS!
WE'RE SUR-ROUND-ED!

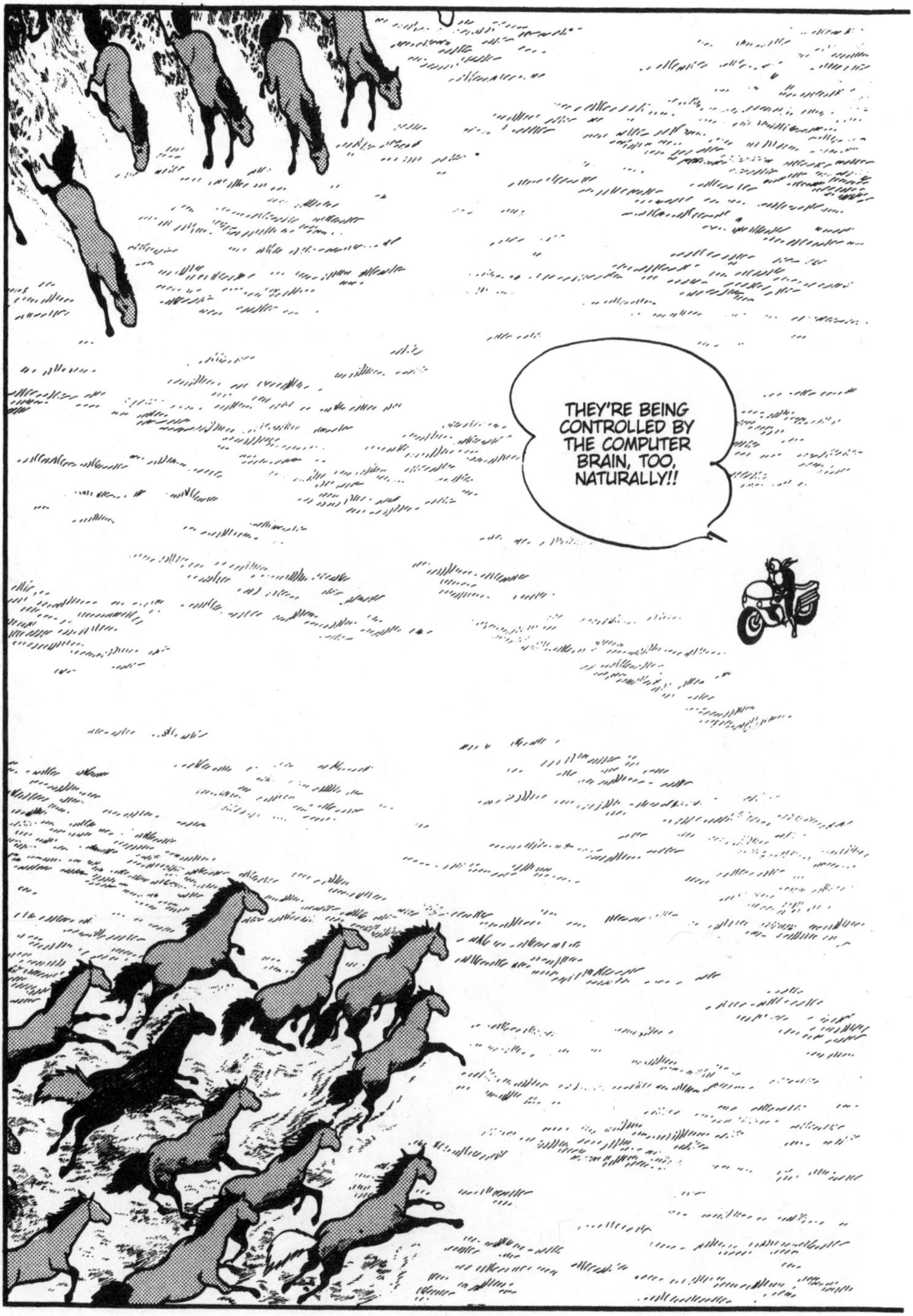
THEY'RE BEING CONTROLLED BY THE COMPUTER BRAIN, TOO, NATURALLY!!

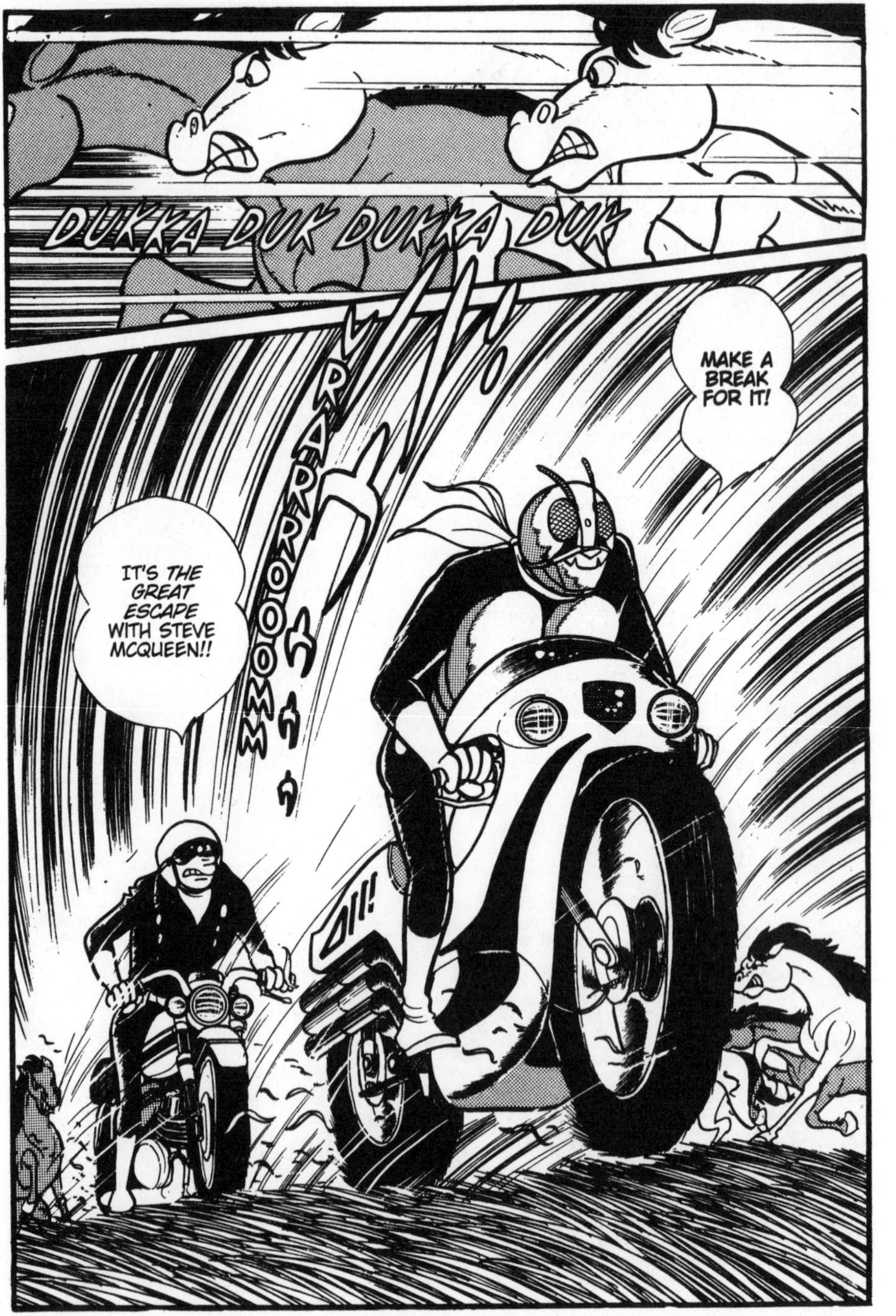
DUKKA DUK DUKKA DUK
MAKE A BREAK FOR IT!
VRARROOOOMM
IT'S THE GREAT ESCAPE WITH STEVE MCQUEEN!!

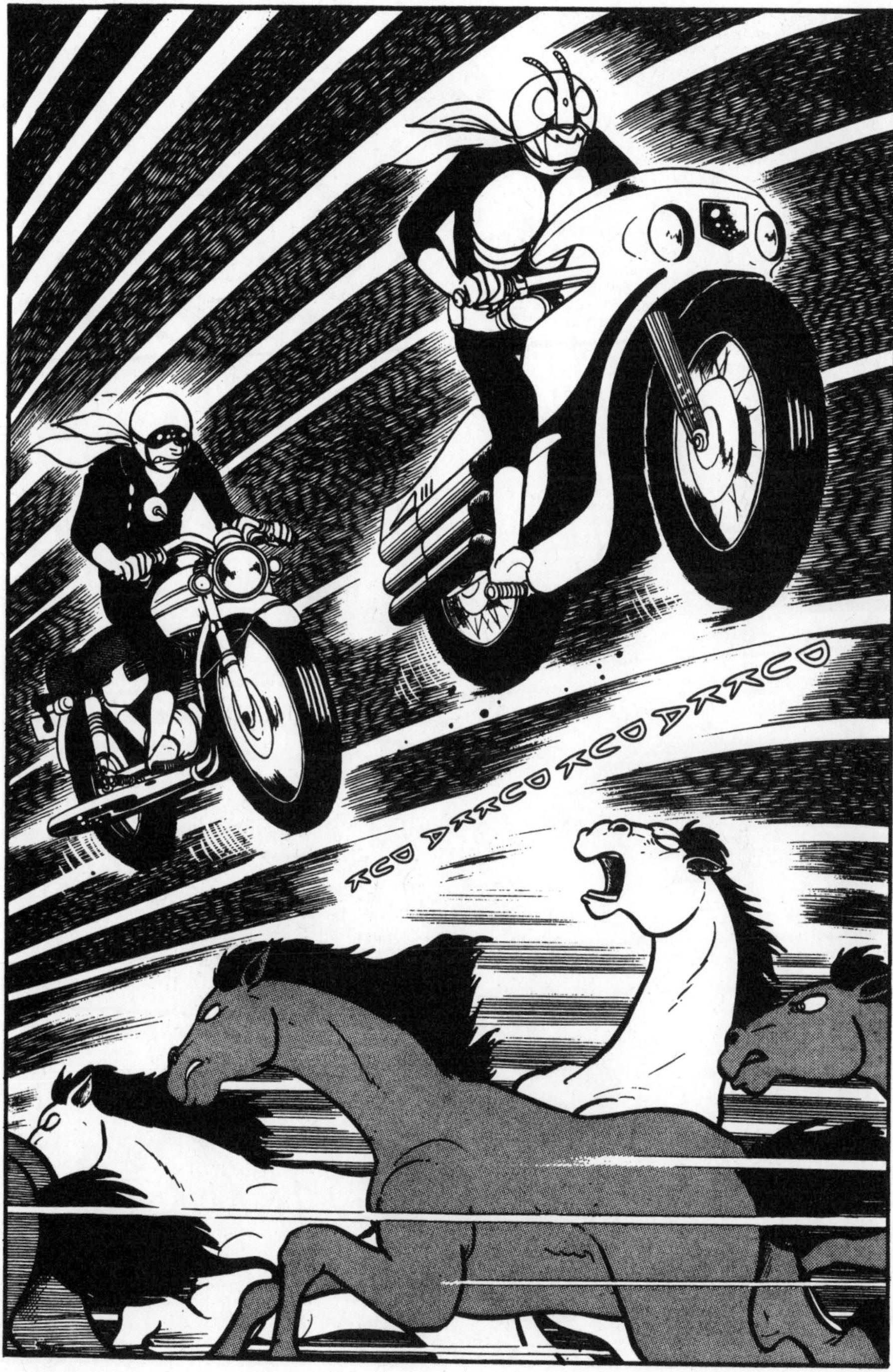

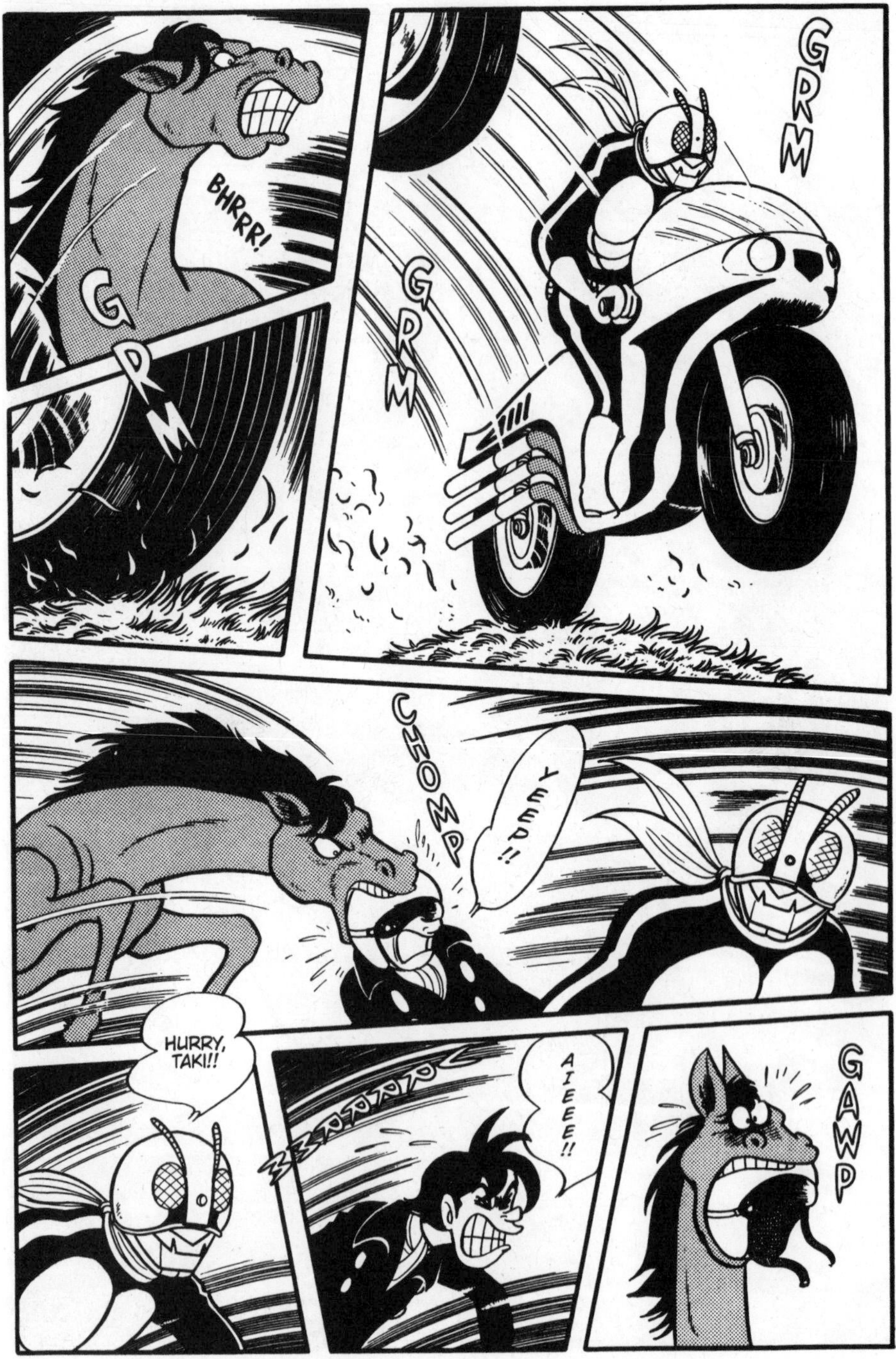
GRM
GRM
BHRRR!
GRM
CHOMP
YEEP!!
GAWP
AIEEEE!!
HURRY, TAKI!!

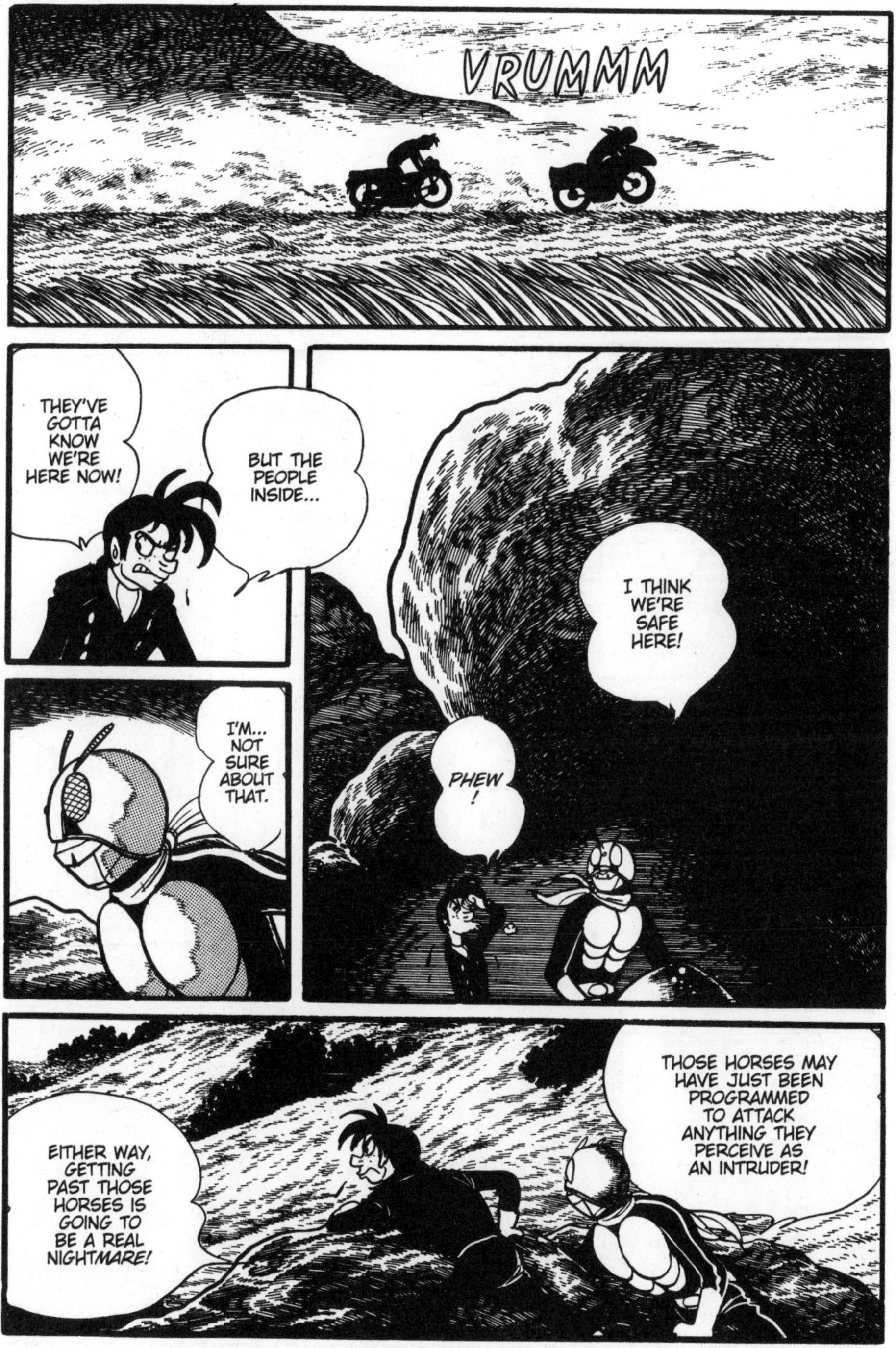
VRUMMM
I THINK WE'RE SAFE HERE!
PHEW!
THEY'VE GOTTA KNOW WE'RE HERE NOW!
BUT THE PEOPLE INSIDE...
I'M... NOT SURE ABOUT THAT.
THOSE HORSES MAY HAVE JUST BEEN PROGRAMMED TO ATTACK ANYTHING THEY PERCEIVE AS AN INTRUDER!
EITHER WAY, GETTING PAST THOSE HORSES IS GOING TO BE A REAL NIGHTMARE!

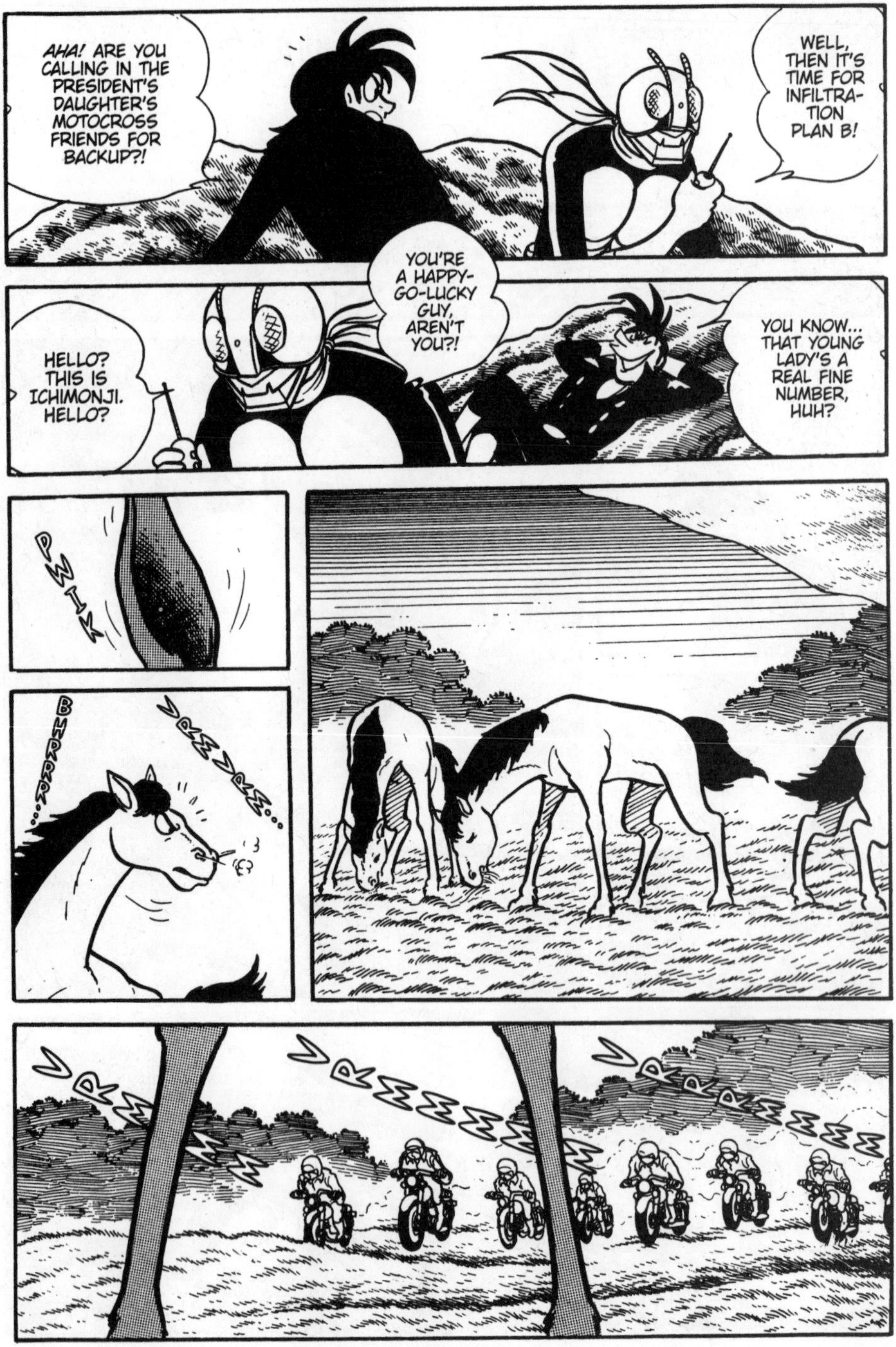
WELL, THEN IT'S TIME FOR INFILTRATION PLAN B!
AHA! ARE YOU CALLING IN THE PRESIDENT'S DAUGHTER'S MOTOCROSS FRIENDS FOR BACKUP?!
YOU KNOW... THAT YOUNG LADY'S A REAL FINE NUMBER, HUH?
YOU'RE A HAPPY-GO-LUCKY GUY, AREN'T YOU?!
HELLO? THIS IS ICHIMONJI. HELLO?
PWIK
VREVRE...
BHRRRR...
VRRREEEE
VREEEEMM
VRMMMM

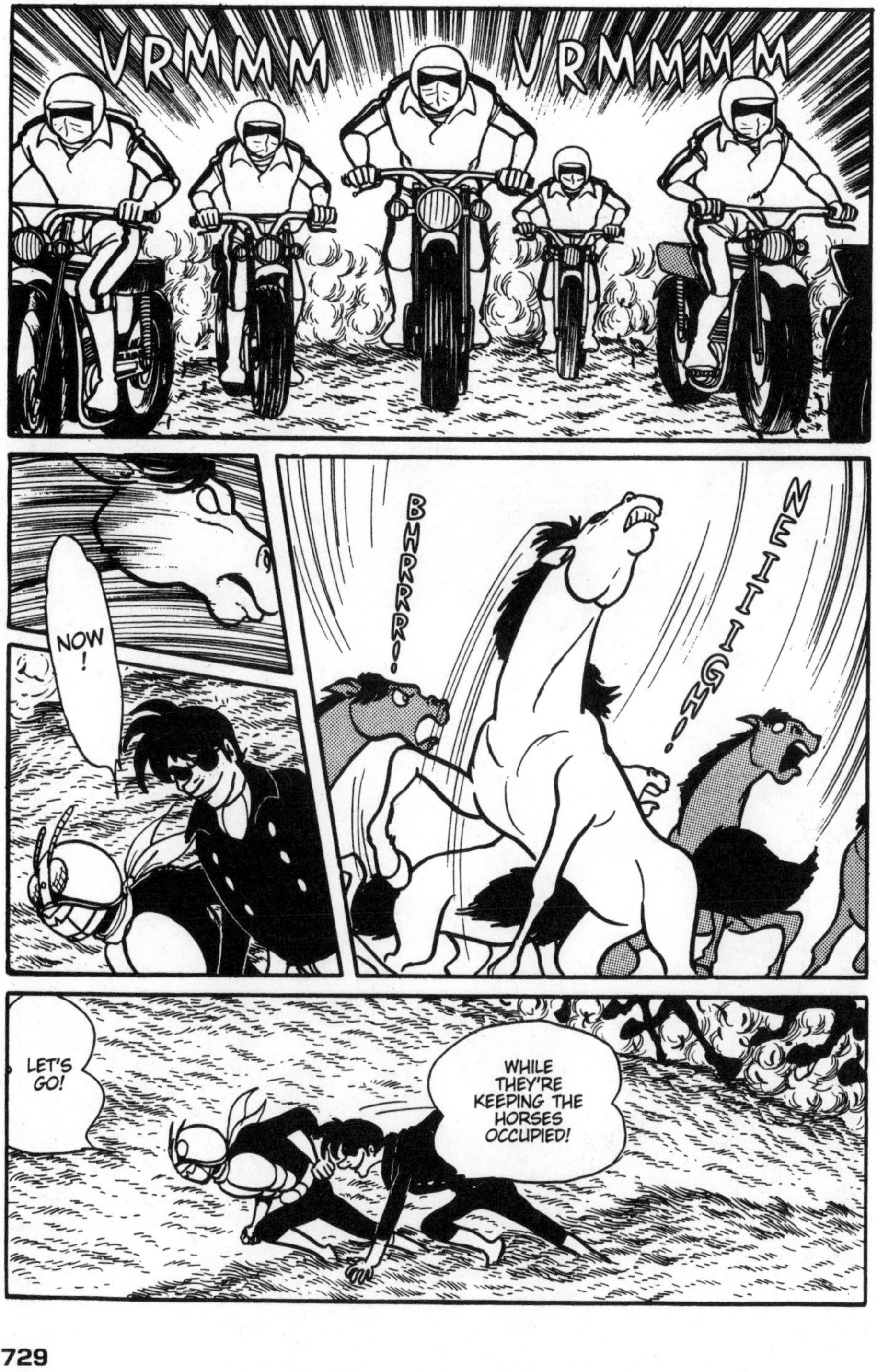

VRMMM VRMMMM
NEIIIGH!
BHRRRR!
NOW!
WHILE THEY'RE KEEPING THE HORSES OCCUPIED!
LET'S GO!

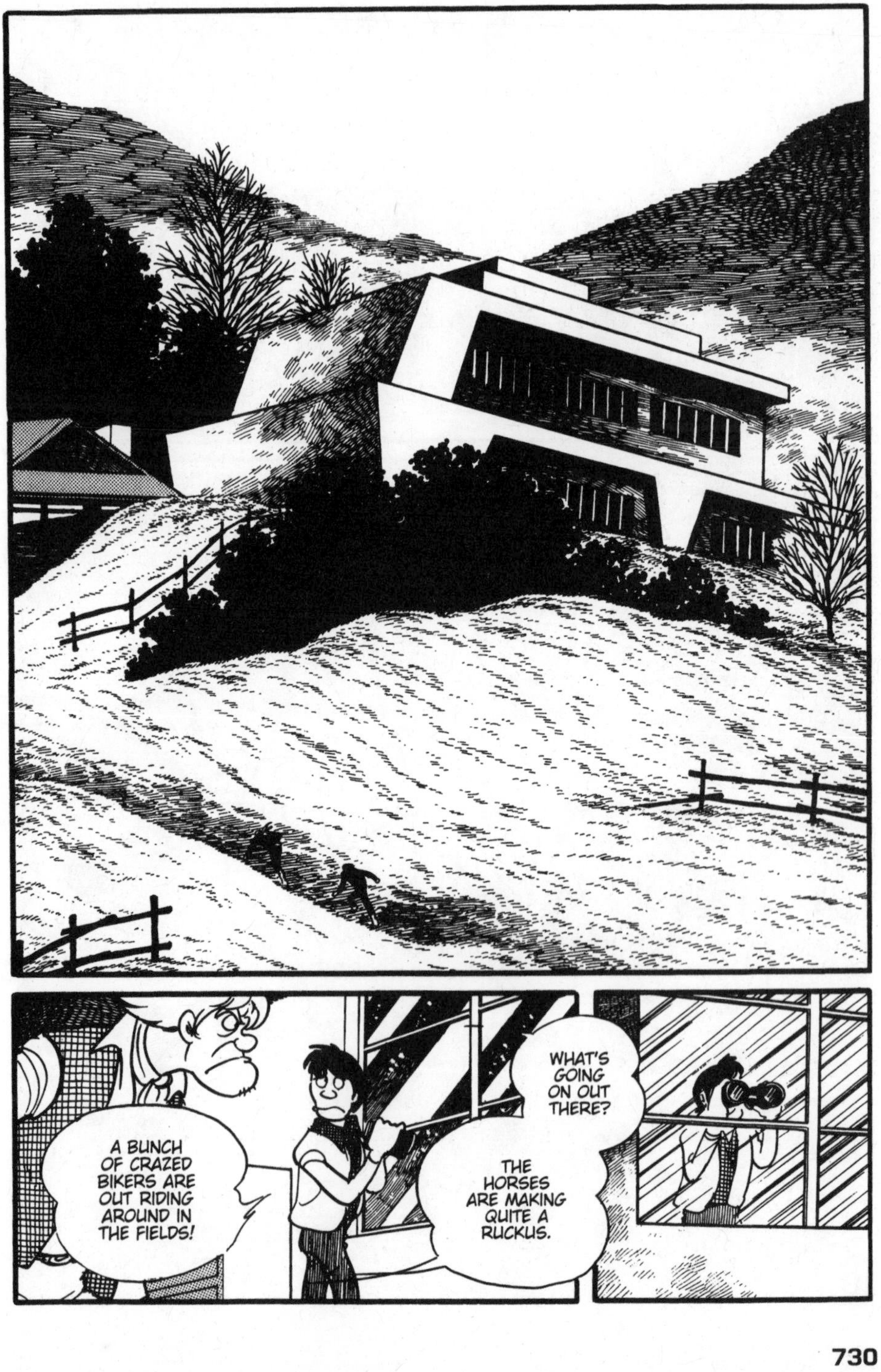
WHAT'S GOING ON OUT THERE?
THE HORSES ARE MAKING QUITE A RUCKUS.
A BUNCH OF CRAZED BIKERS ARE OUT RIDING AROUND IN THE FIELDS!

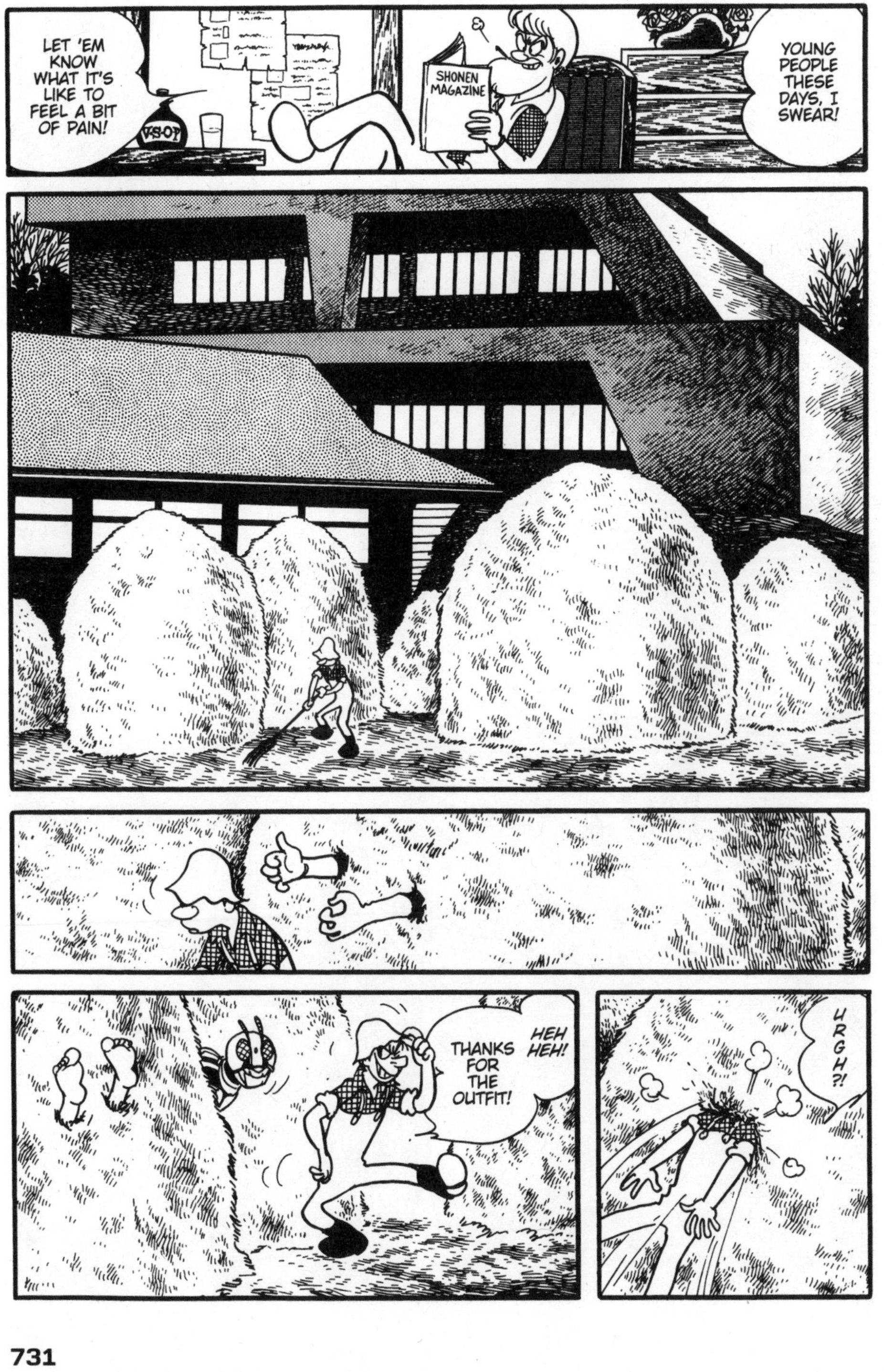
YOUNG PEOPLE THESE DAYS, I SWEAR!
SHONEN MAGAZINE
LET 'EM KNOW WHAT IT'S LIKE TO FEEL A BIT OF PAIN!
V.S.O.P.
URGH?!
HEH HEH!
THANKS FOR THE OUTFIT!

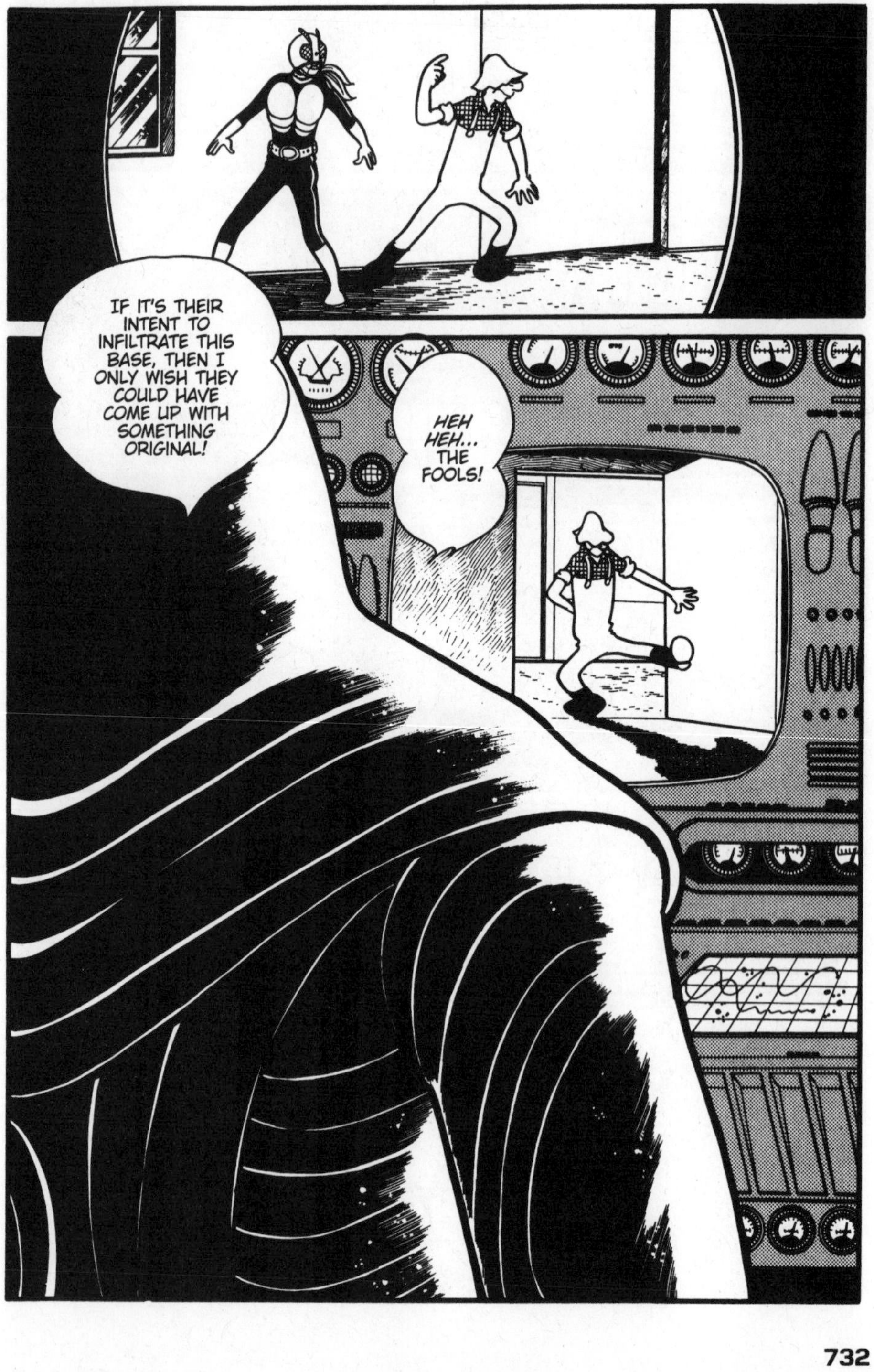
IF IT'S THEIR INTENT TO INFILTRATE THIS BASE, THEN I ONLY WISH THEY COULD HAVE COME UP WITH SOMETHING ORIGINAL!
HEH HEH... THE FOOLS!

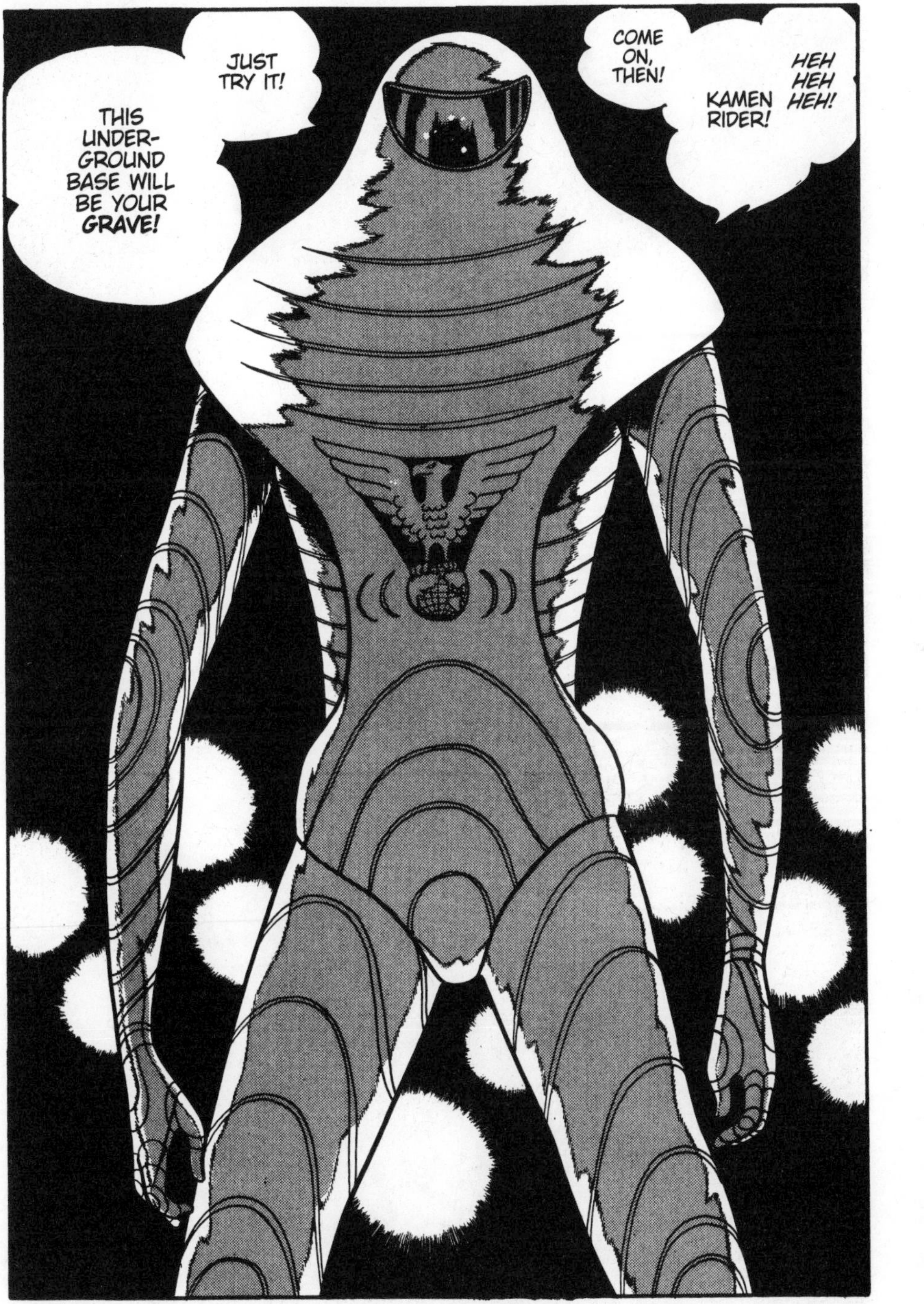
HEH HEH HEH!
KAMEN RIDER!
COME ON, THEN!
JUST TRY IT!
THIS UNDER-GROUND BASE WILL BE YOUR GRAVE!

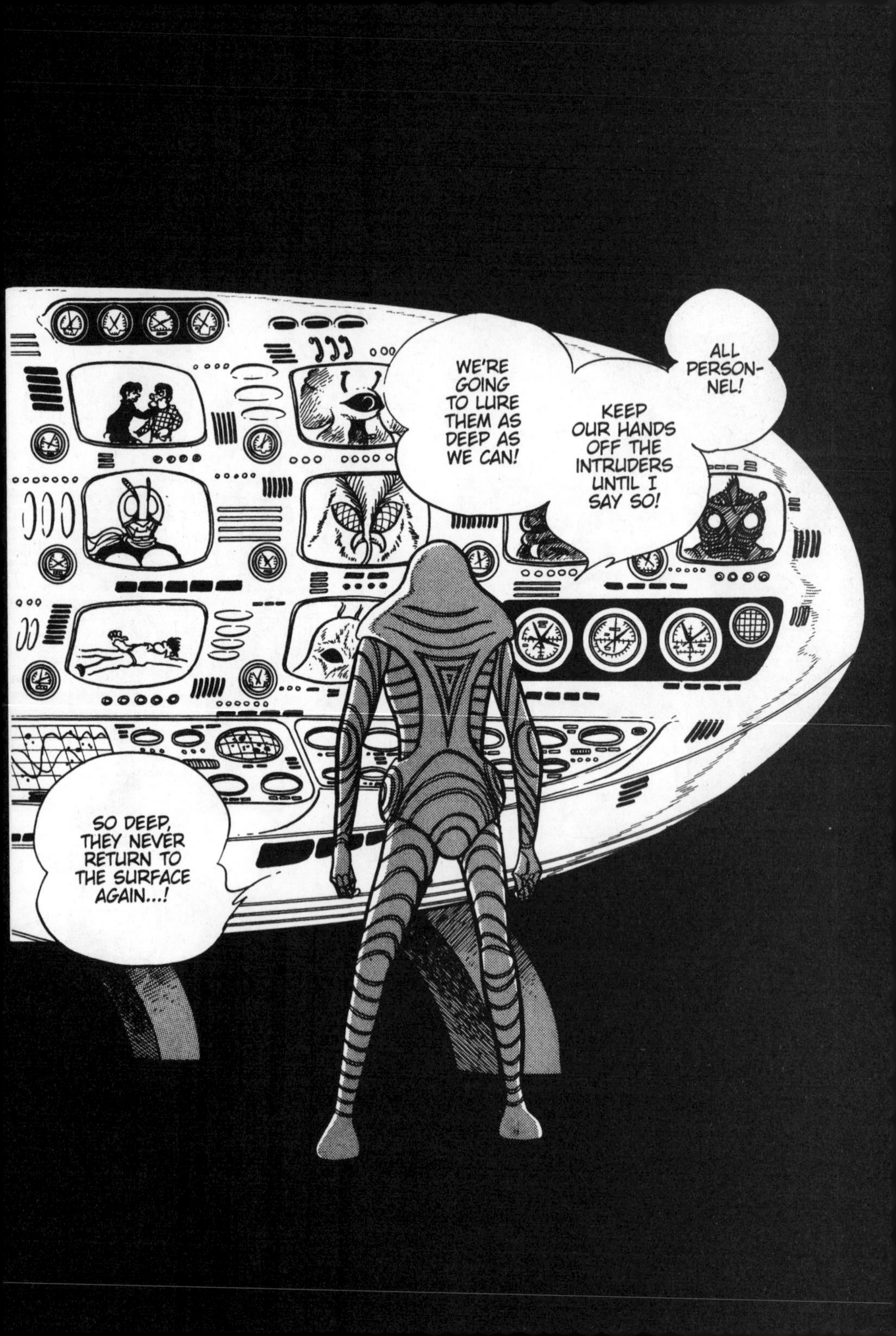
ALL PERSON-NEL!
KEEP OUR HANDS OFF THE INTRUDERS UNTIL I SAY SO!
WE'RE GOING TO LURE THEM AS DEEP AS WE CAN!
SO DEEP, THEY NEVER RETURN TO THE SURFACE AGAIN...!

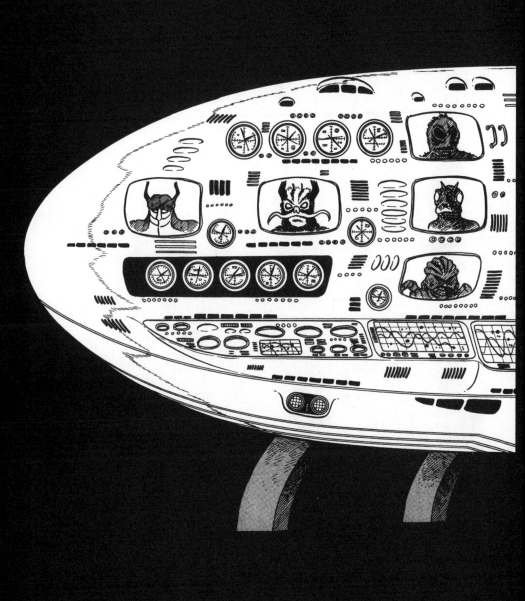

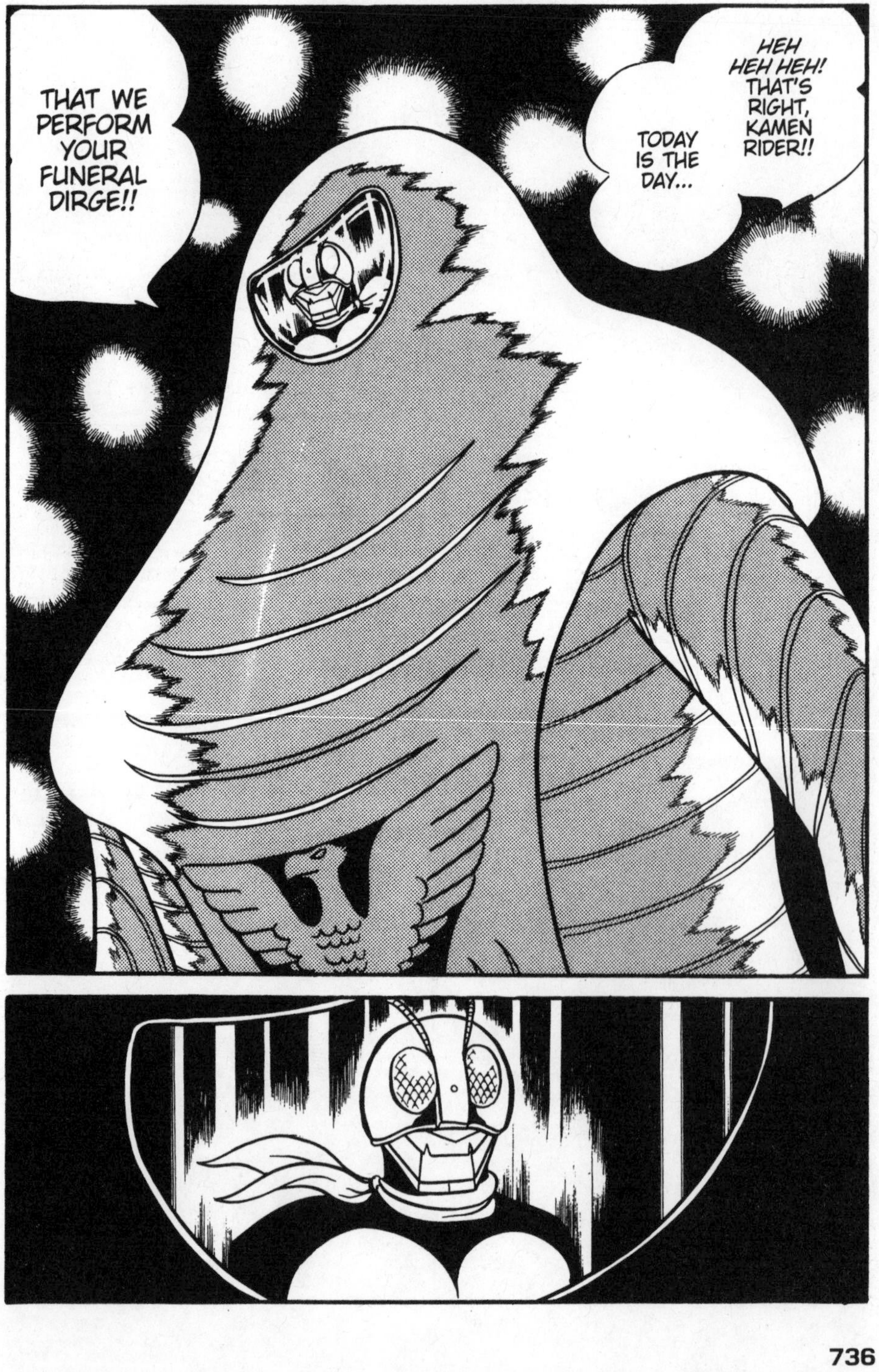
HEH HEH HEH! THAT'S RIGHT, KAMEN RIDER!!
TODAY IS THE DAY...
THAT WE PERFORM YOUR FUNERAL DIRGE!!

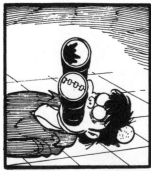

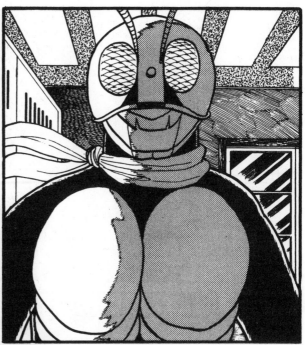

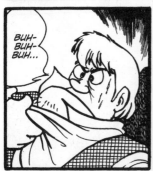

BUH-BUH-BUH...
TH-TH-THIS IS JUST A RANCH!
THERE AIN'T NO UNDER-GROUND ANYTHING!!
OH REALLY?
WHAP
WHAP

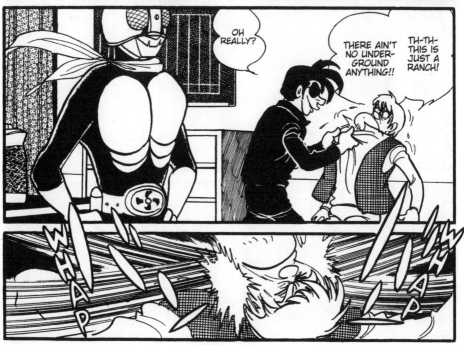

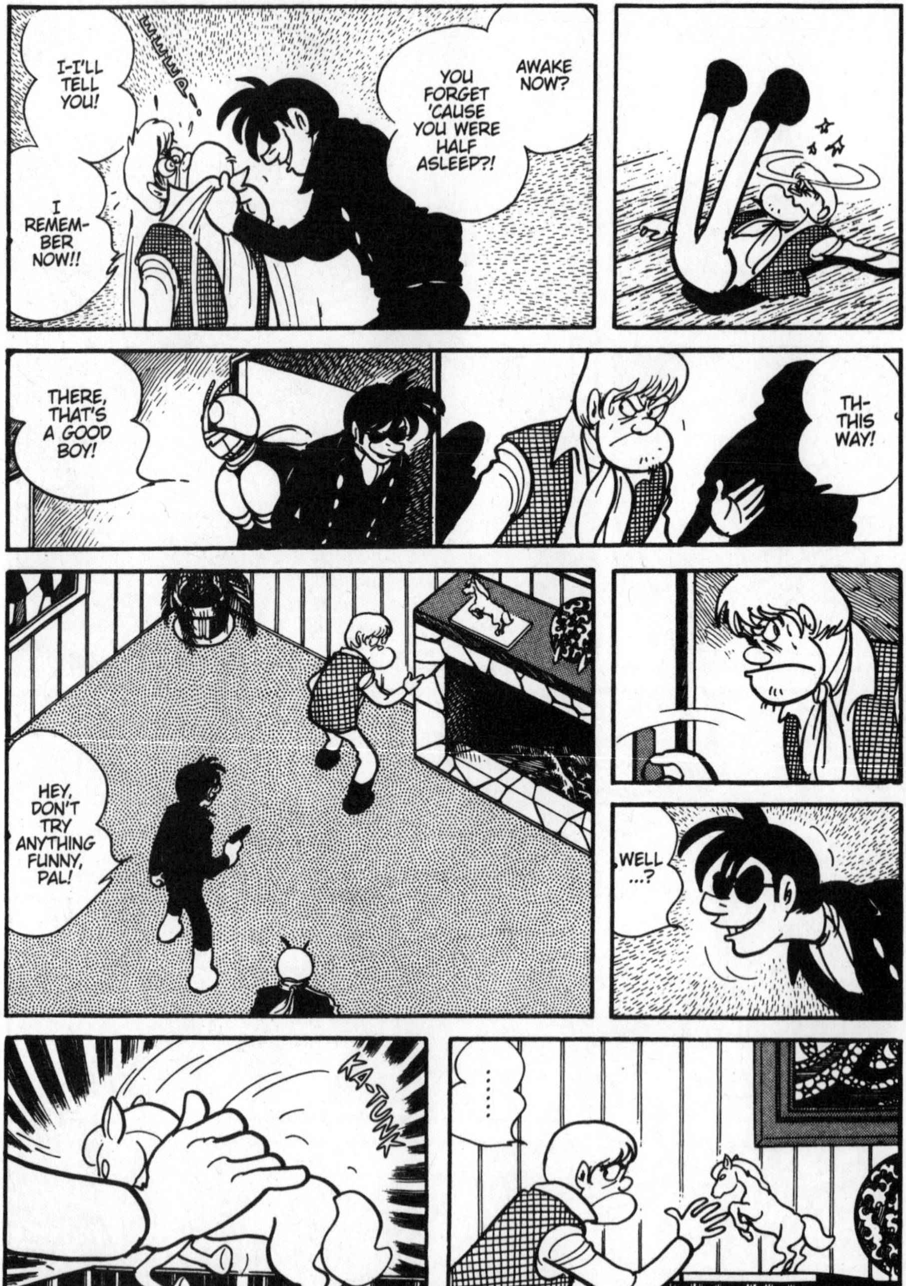
AWAKE NOW?
YOU FORGET 'CAUSE YOU WERE HALF ASLEEP?!
WWWWP!
I-I'LL TELL YOU!
I REMEMBER NOW!!
TH-THIS WAY!
THERE, THAT'S A GOOD BOY!
WELL ...?
HEY, DON'T TRY ANYTHING FUNNY, PAL!
......
KA-TUNK

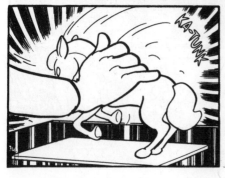

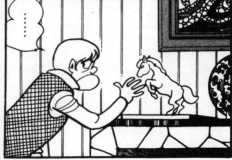

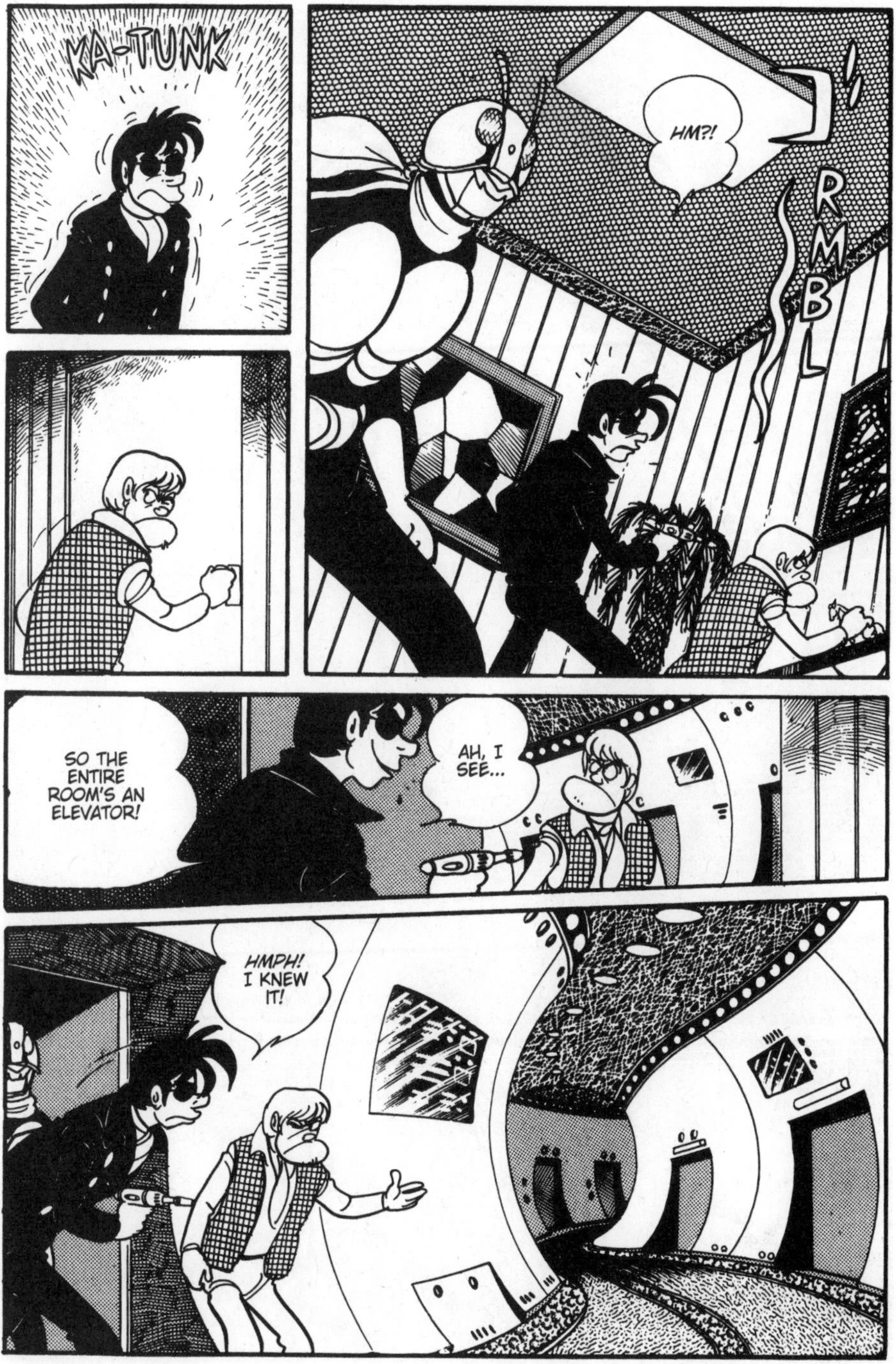
HM?!
RMBL
KA-TUNK
AH, I SEE...
SO THE ENTIRE ROOM'S AN ELEVATOR!
HMPH! I KNEW IT!

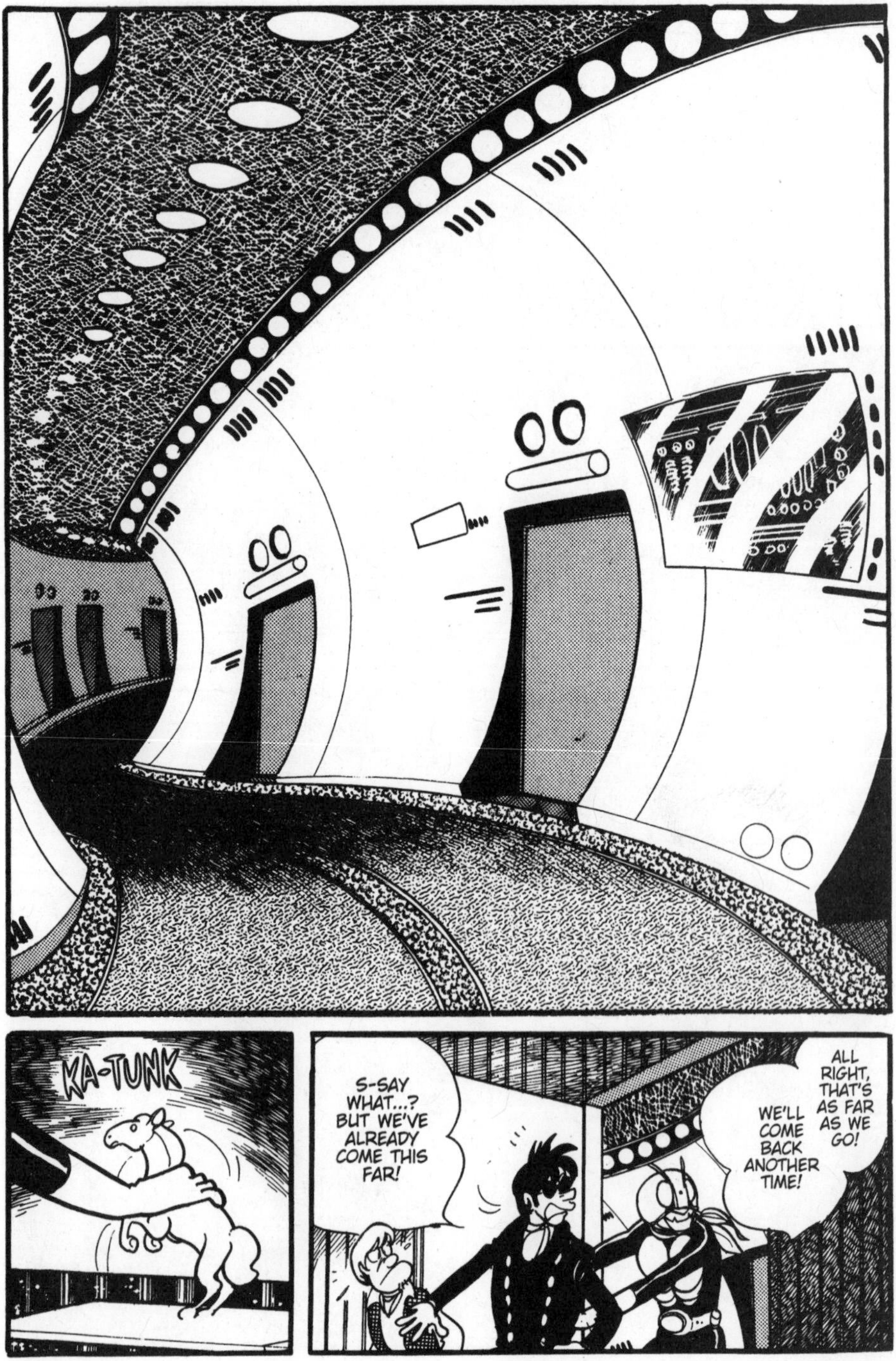
ALL RIGHT, THAT'S AS FAR AS WE GO!
WE'LL COME BACK ANOTHER TIME!
S-SAY WHAT...? BUT WE'VE ALREADY COME THIS FAR!
KA-TUNK

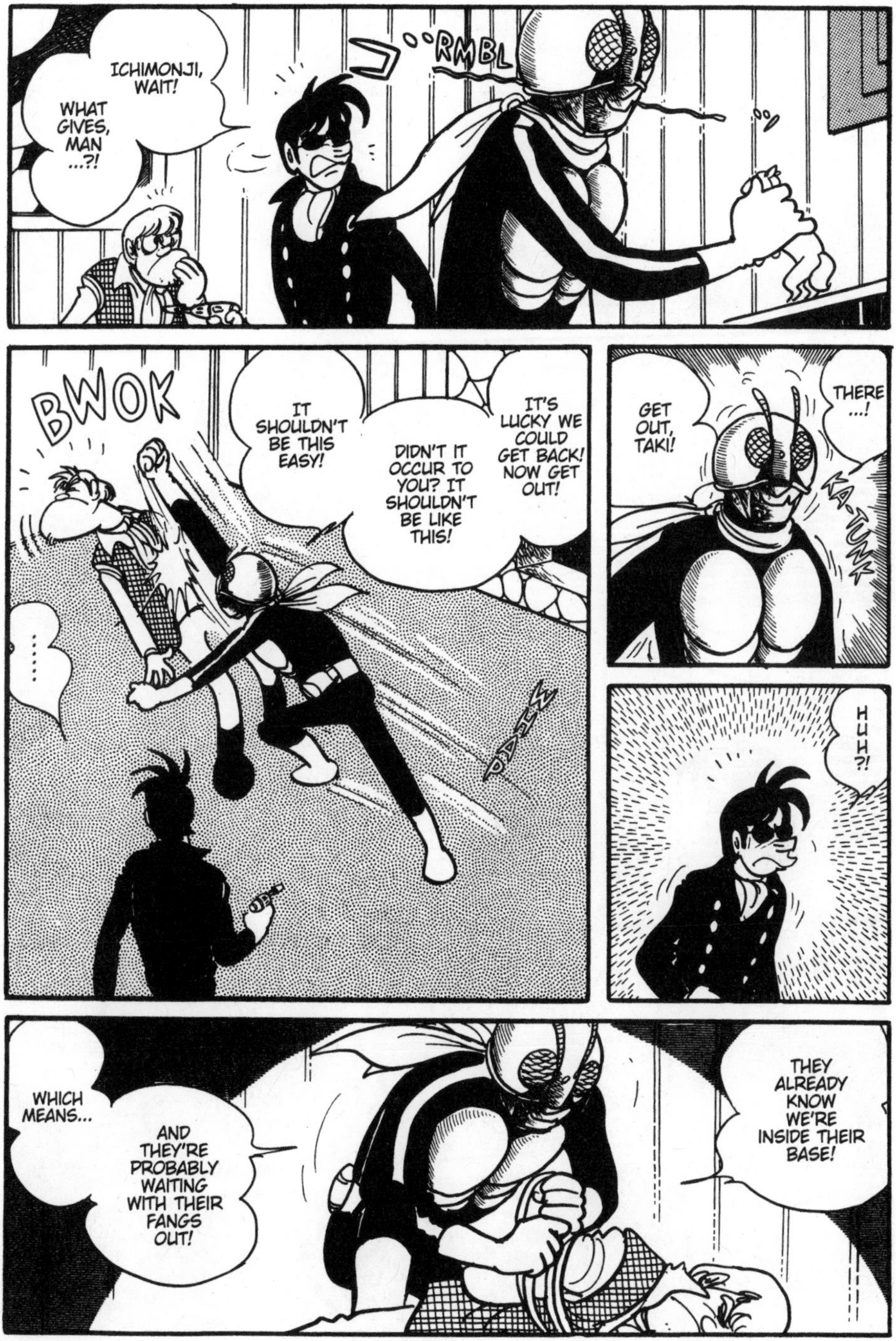
RMBL
ICHIMONJI, WAIT!
WHAT GIVES, MAN ...?!
THERE ...!
GET OUT, TAKI!
KA-TUNK
HUH?!
IT'S LUCKY WE COULD GET BACK! NOW GET OUT!
DIDN'T IT OCCUR TO YOU? IT SHOULDN'T BE LIKE THIS!
IT SHOULDN'T BE THIS EASY!
BWOK
WHAP
......
THEY ALREADY KNOW WE'RE INSIDE THEIR BASE!
AND THEY'RE PROBABLY WAITING WITH THEIR FANGS OUT!
WHICH MEANS...

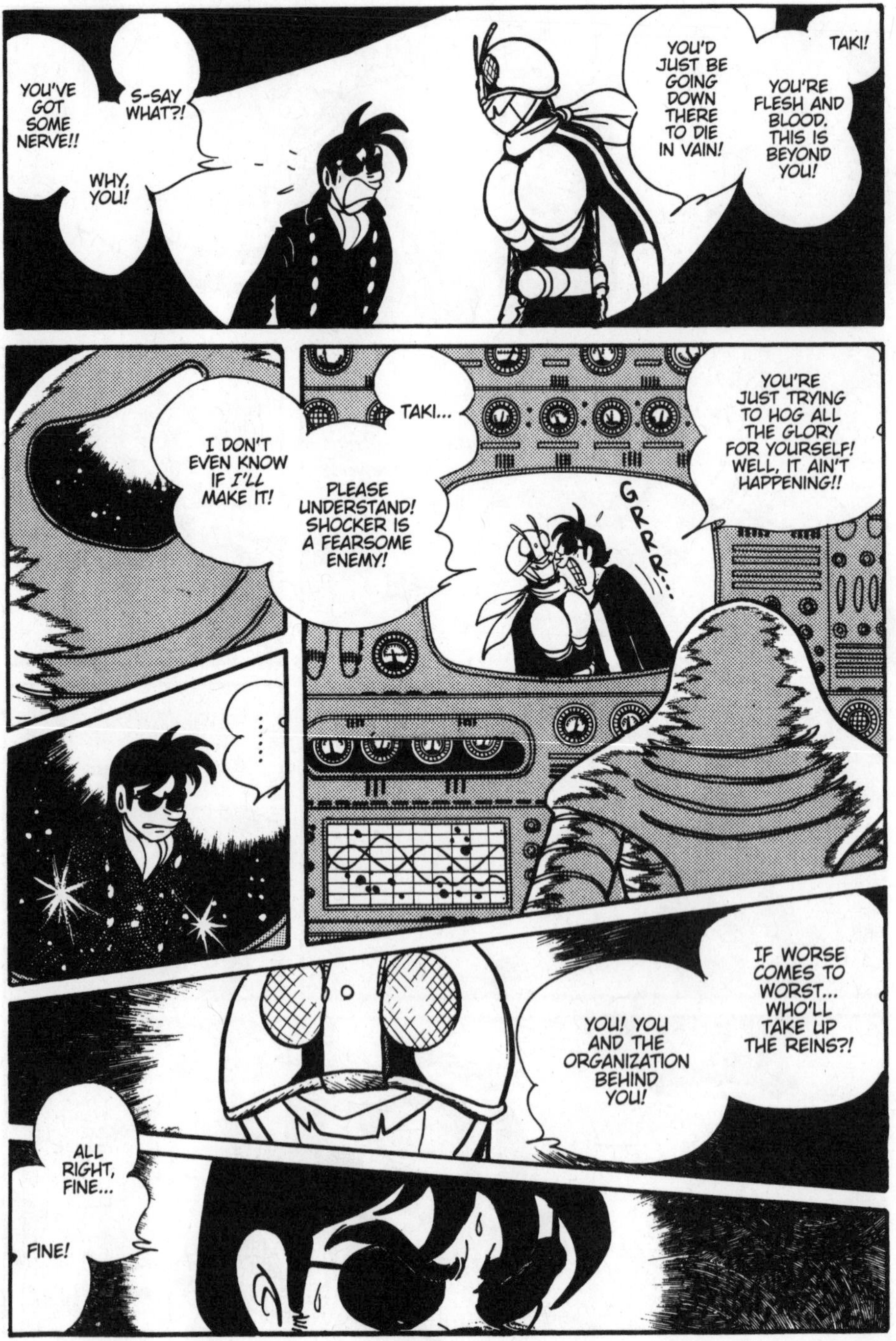

TAKI!
YOU'RE FLESH AND BLOOD. THIS IS BEYOND YOU!
YOU'D JUST BE GOING DOWN THERE TO DIE IN VAIN!
S-SAY WHAT?!
YOU'VE GOT SOME NERVE!!
WHY, YOU!
YOU'RE JUST TRYING TO HOG ALL THE GLORY FOR YOURSELF! WELL, IT AIN'T HAPPENING!!
GRRR...
TAKI...
PLEASE UNDERSTAND! SHOCKER IS A FEARSOME ENEMY!
I DON'T EVEN KNOW IF *I'LL* MAKE IT!
......
IF WORSE COMES TO WORST... WHO'LL TAKE UP THE REINS?!
YOU! YOU AND THE ORGANIZATION BEHIND YOU!
ALL RIGHT, FINE...
FINE!

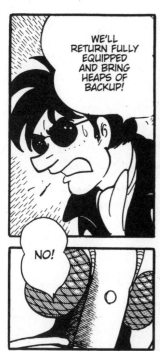

I'LL DO WHAT YOU SAY...
BUT I'VE GOT ONE REQUEST!
YOU LEAVE WITH ME!!
WE'LL RETURN FULLY EQUIPPED AND BRING HEAPS OF BACKUP!
NO!
WE PROBABLY WOULDN'T BE ABLE TO GET UNDERGROUND THAT WAY!
IT'S *BECAUSE* I'M ALONE THAT THEY'RE LETTING ME IN!
SO THEY CAN **KILL** ME!!
BUT...IF KAMEN RIDER IS GOING TO DIE, THEN THE OCTOBER PROJECT DIES WITH ME!!
WH-WHOA, ICHIMONJI! HOLD UP A SECOND!
SHOVE

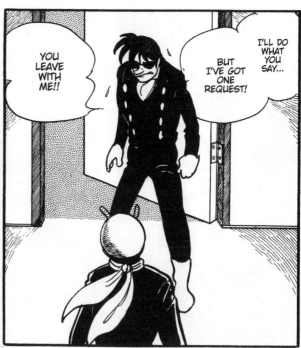

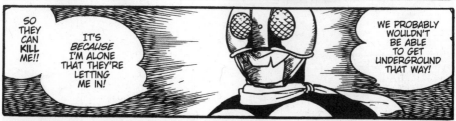

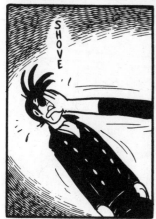

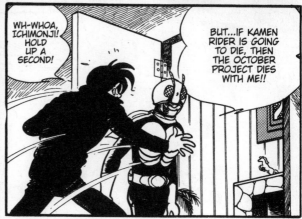

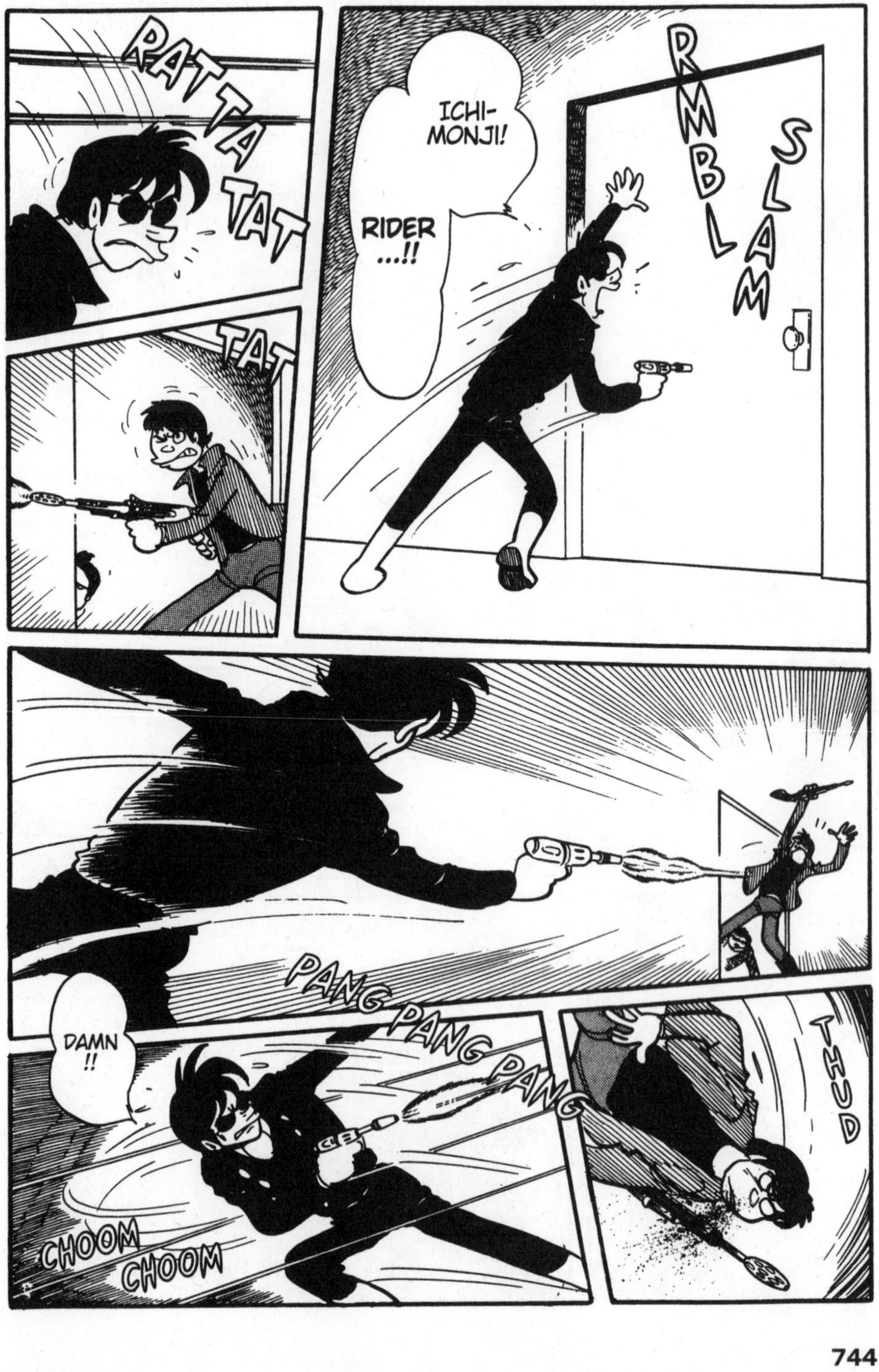
RMMBL
SLAM
ICHI-MONJI!
RIDER ...!!
RAT TA TAT
TAT
PANG PANG PANG
THUD
DAMN !!
CHOOM CHOOM

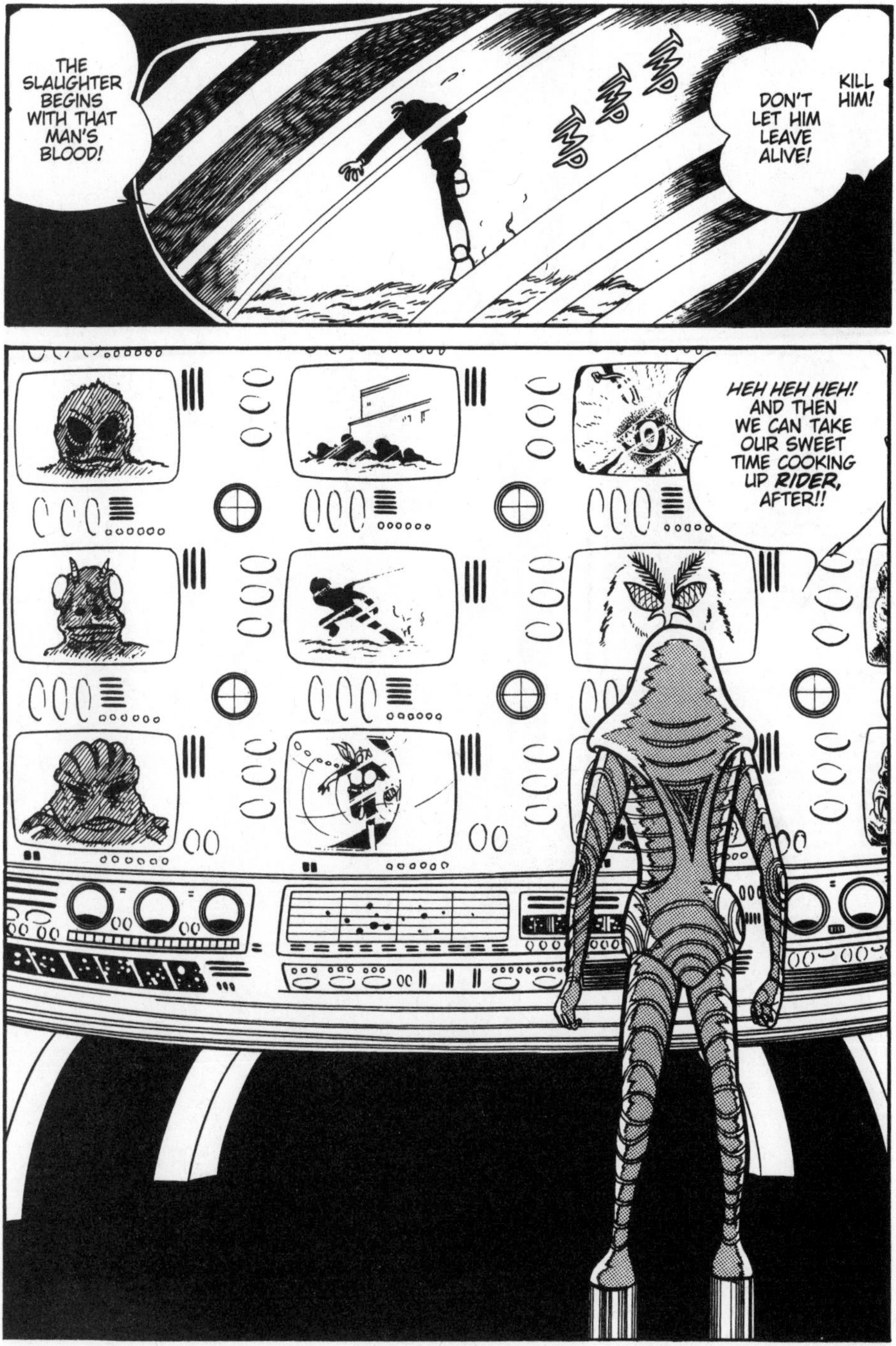
KILL HIM!
DON'T LET HIM LEAVE ALIVE!
THE SLAUGHTER BEGINS WITH THAT MAN'S BLOOD!
HEH HEH HEH! AND THEN WE CAN TAKE OUR SWEET TIME COOKING UP ***RIDER,*** AFTER!!

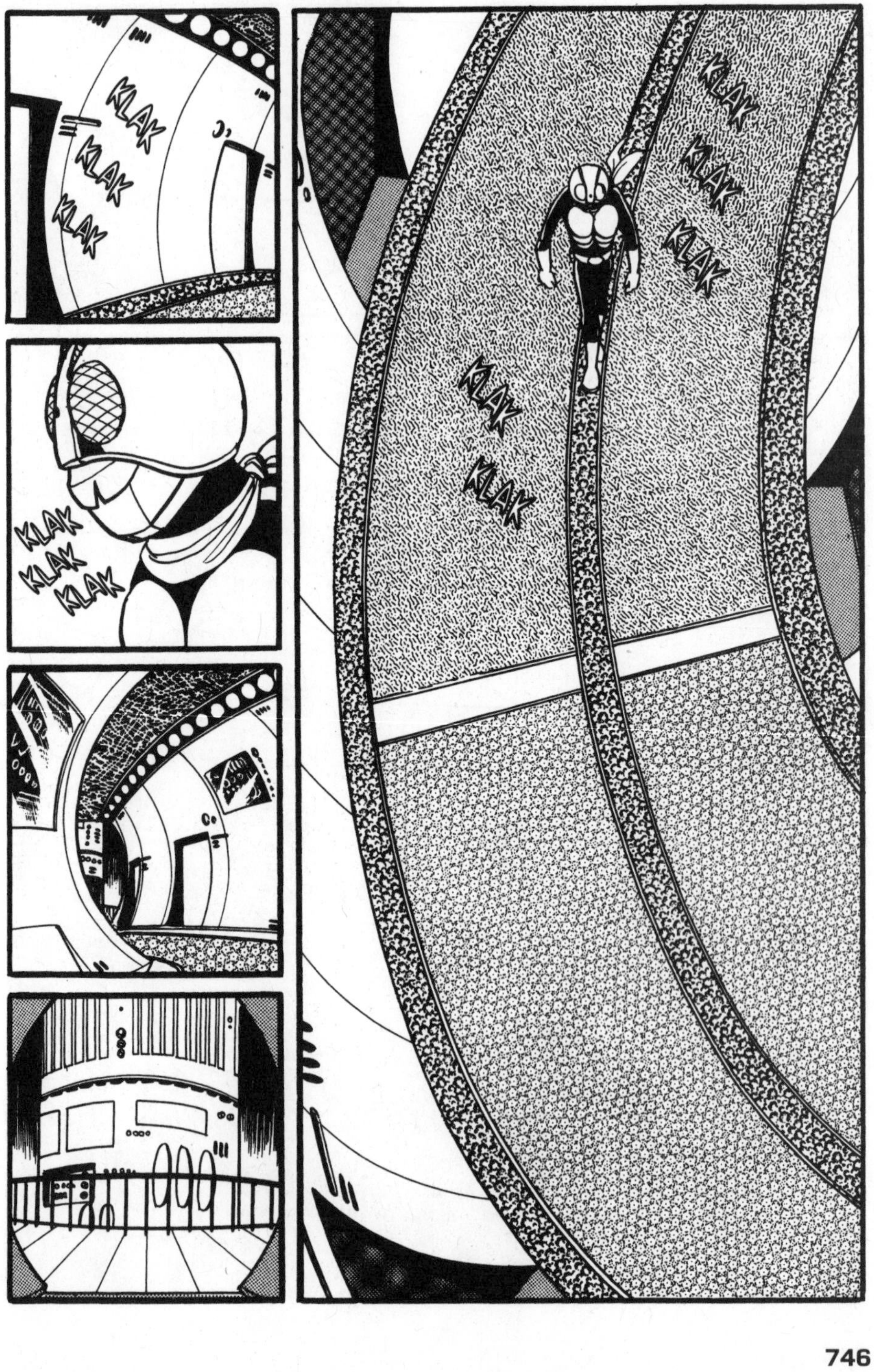
KLAK KLAK KLAK
KLAK KLAK
KLAK KLAK KLAK
KLAK KLAK KLAK

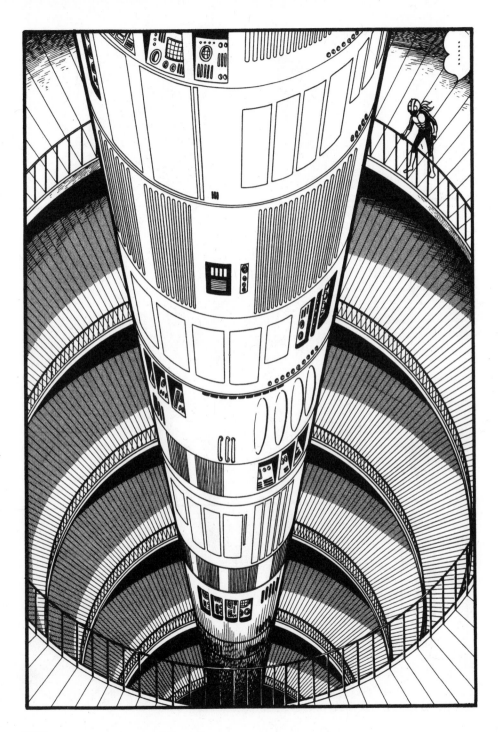

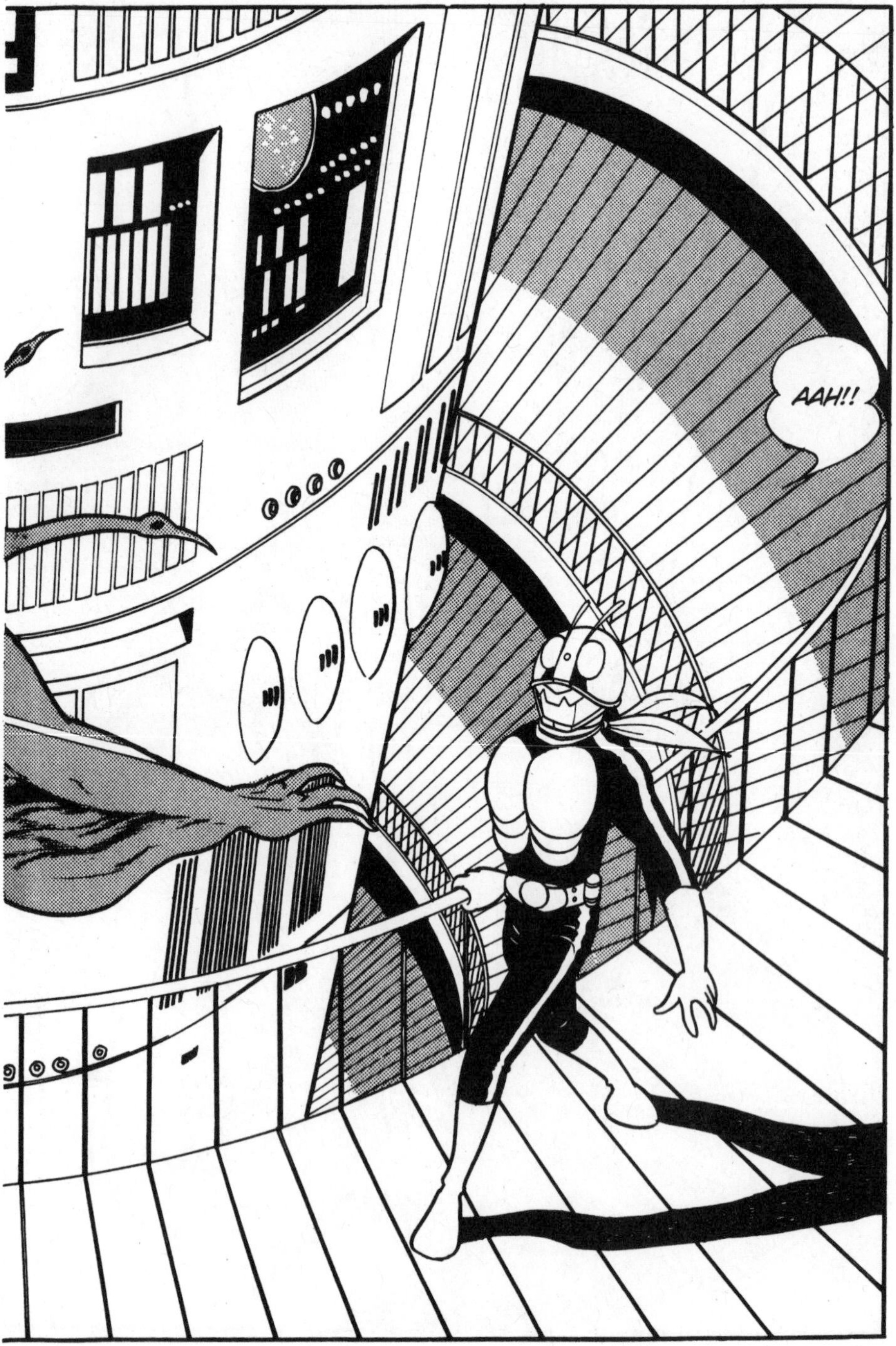
AAH!!

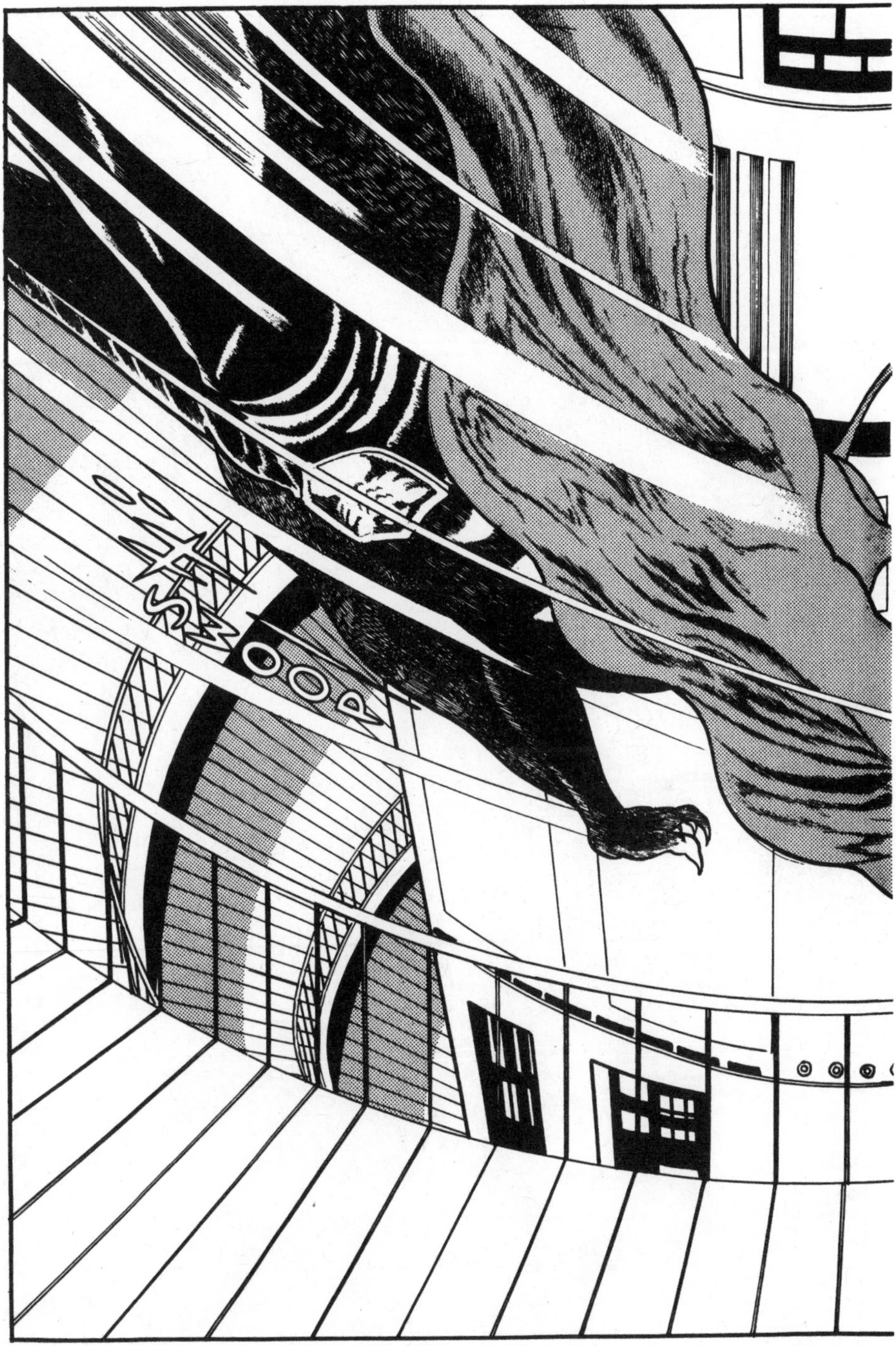
SWOOP

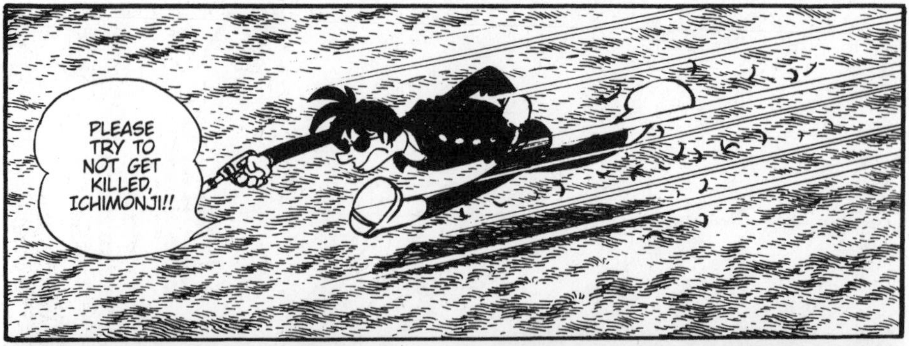
PLEASE TRY TO NOT GET KILLED, ICHIMONJI!!
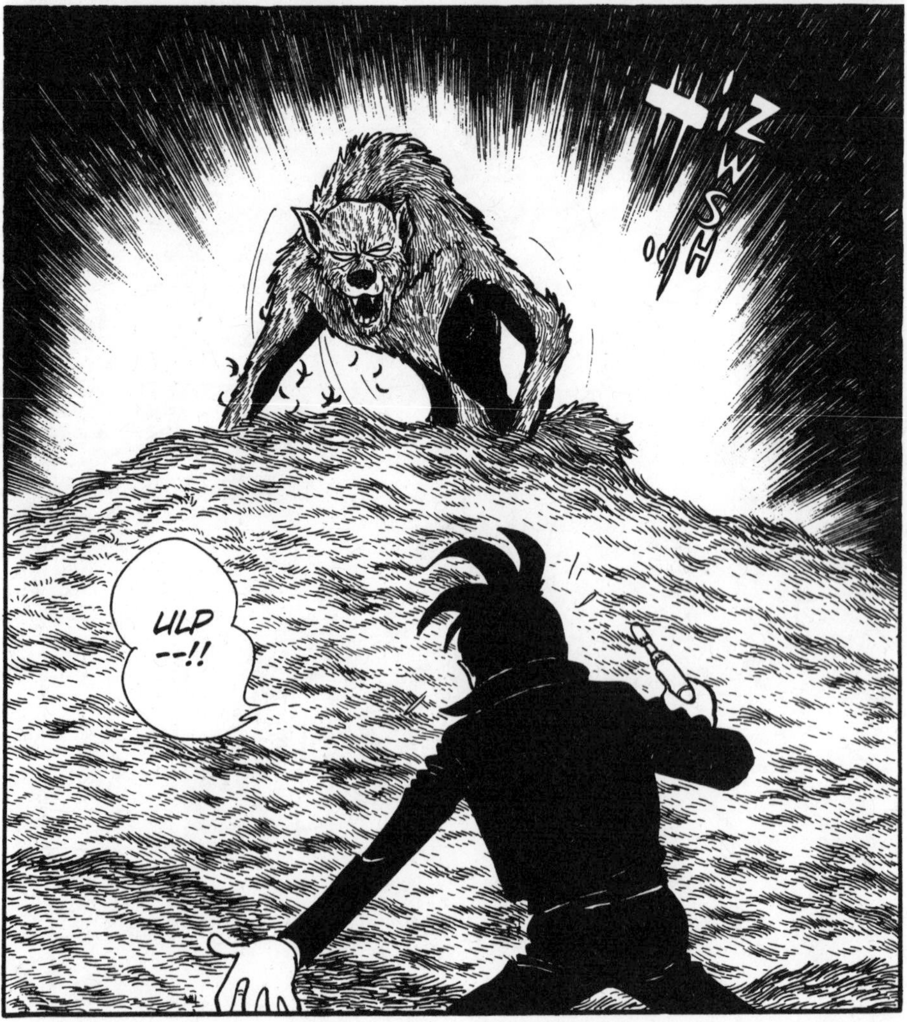
FWOOSH
ULP --!!

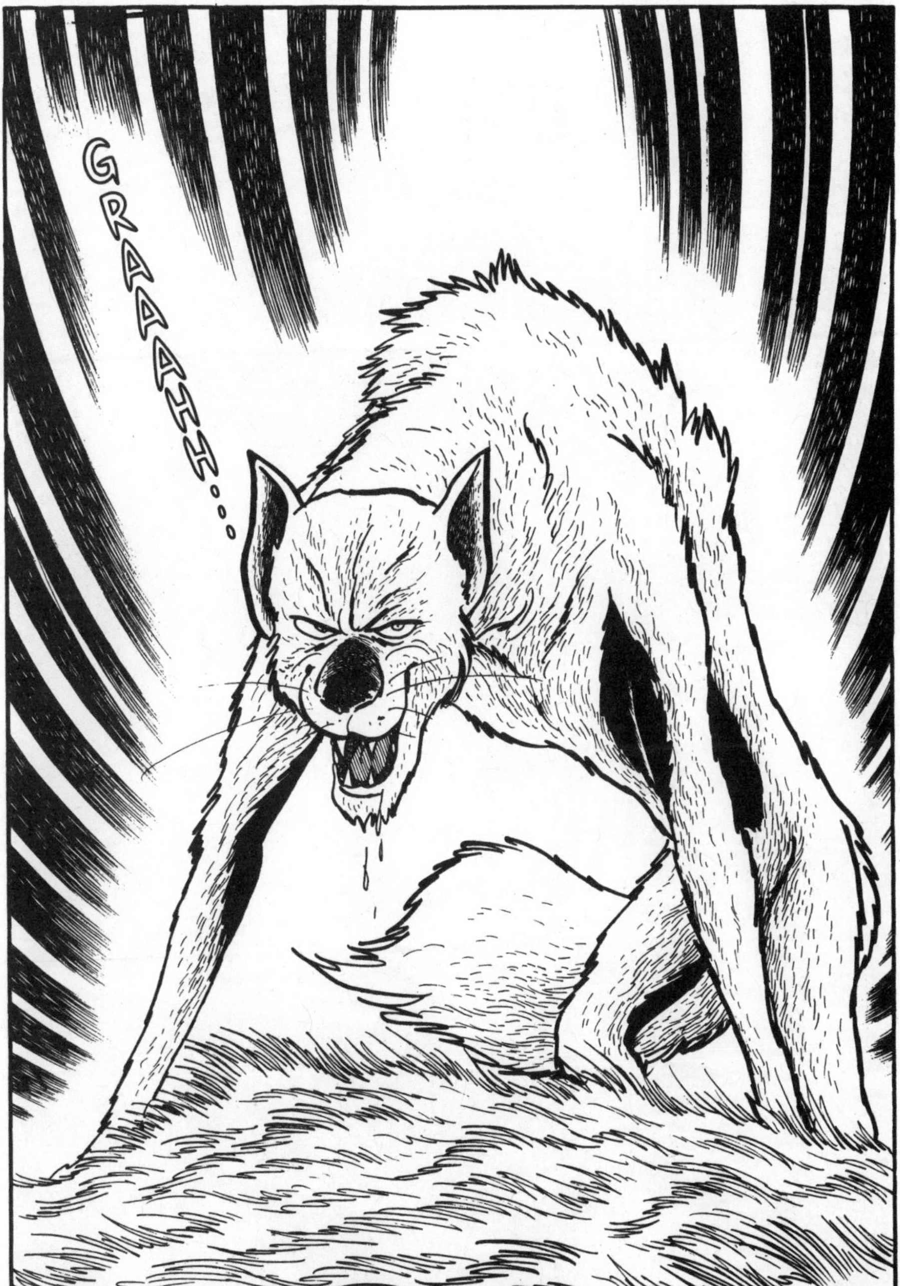
GRAAAAHH...

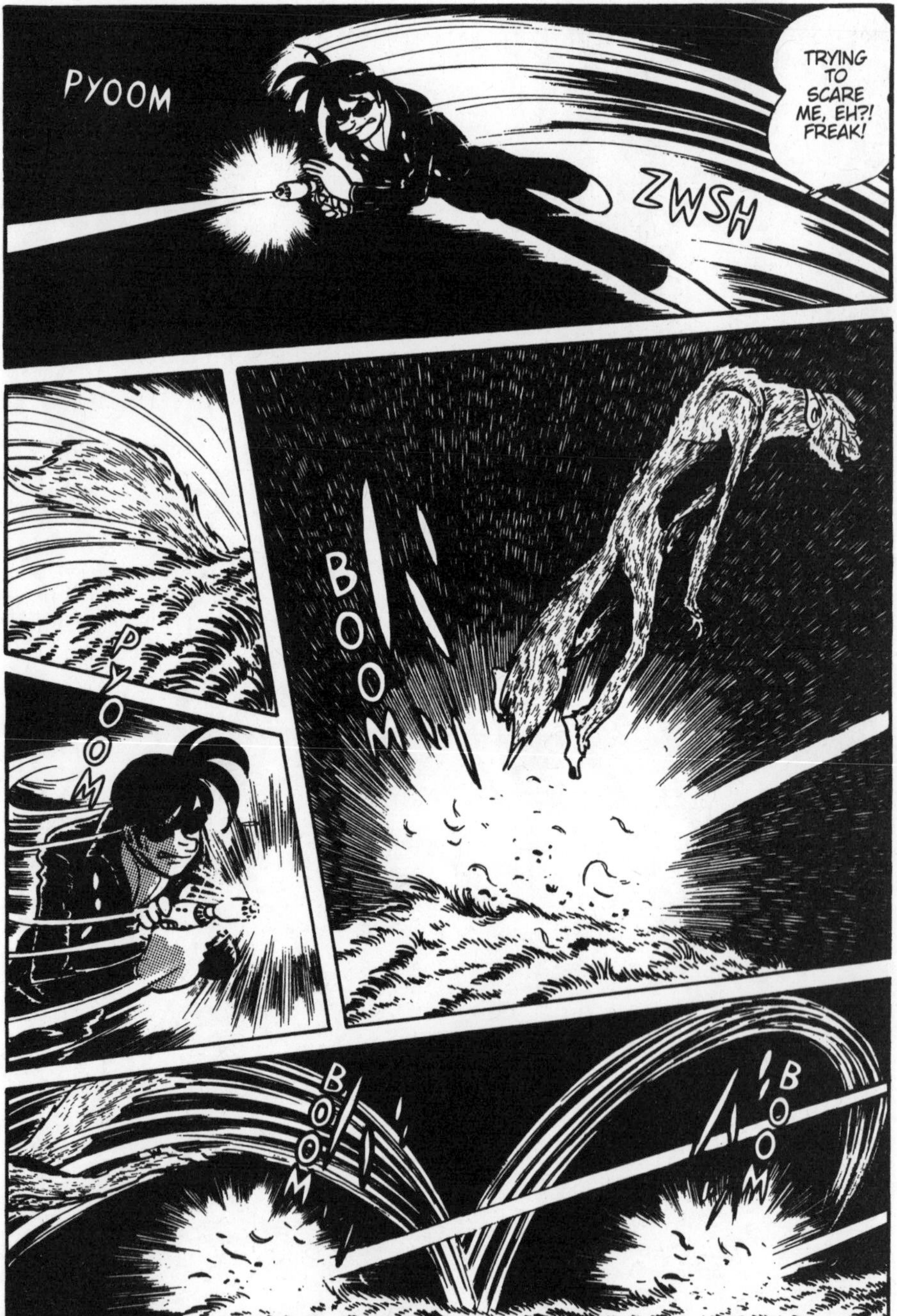

TRYING TO SCARE ME, EH?! FREAK!
ZWSH
PYOOM
BOOM
PYOOM
BOOM
BOOM

KEH HEH HEH!
GRRRRZ..
KSH KSH KSH KSH KSH
KSH KSH KSH
NNGH --!!
KSH KSH KSH KSH KSH

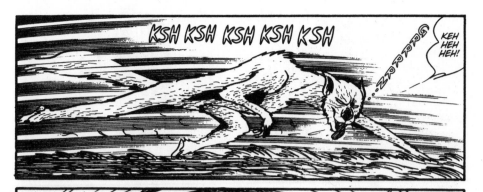

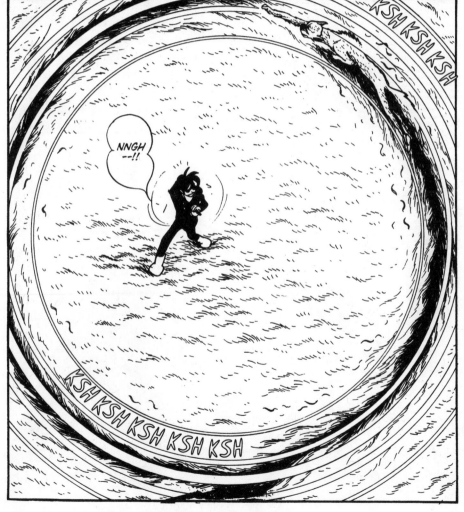

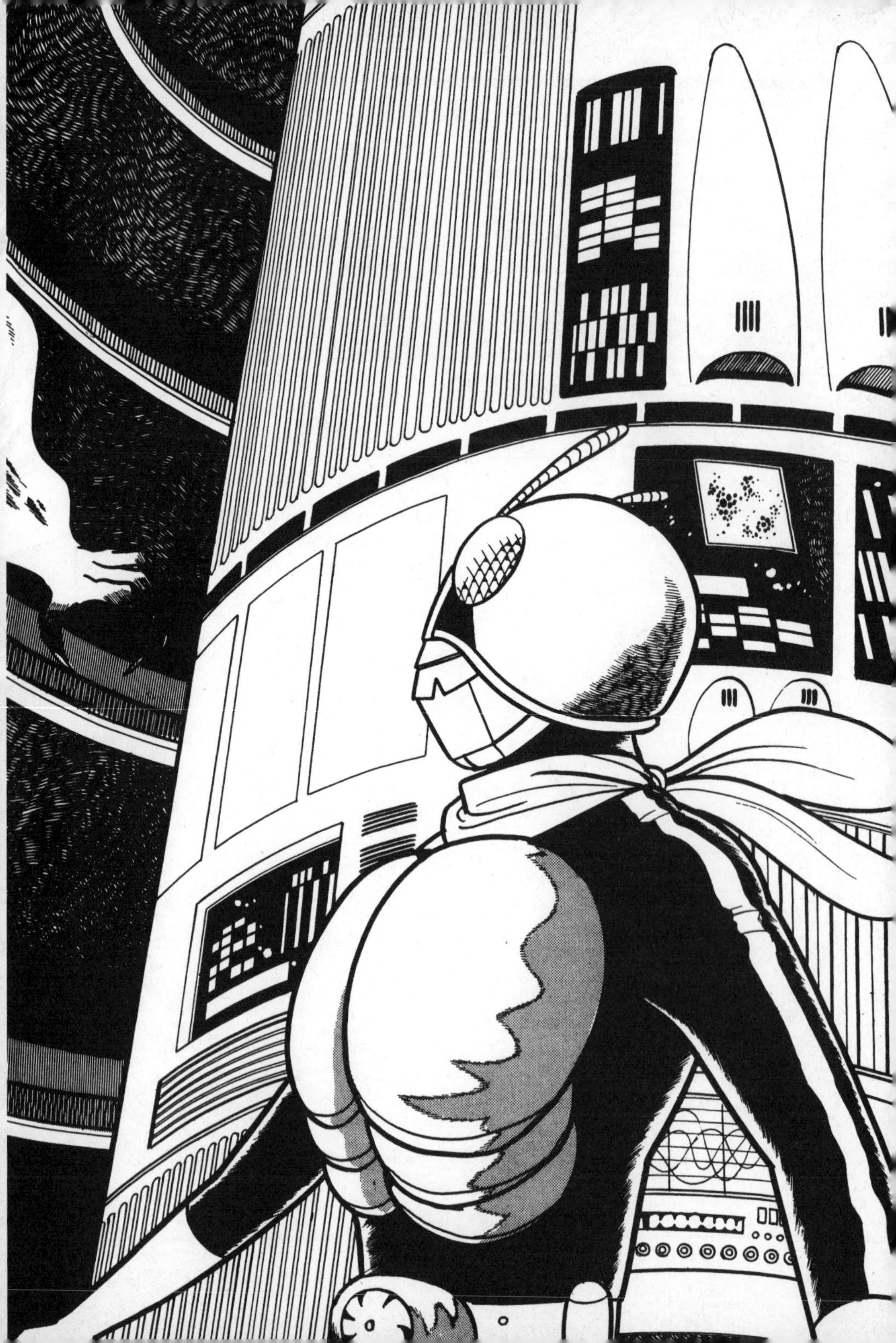

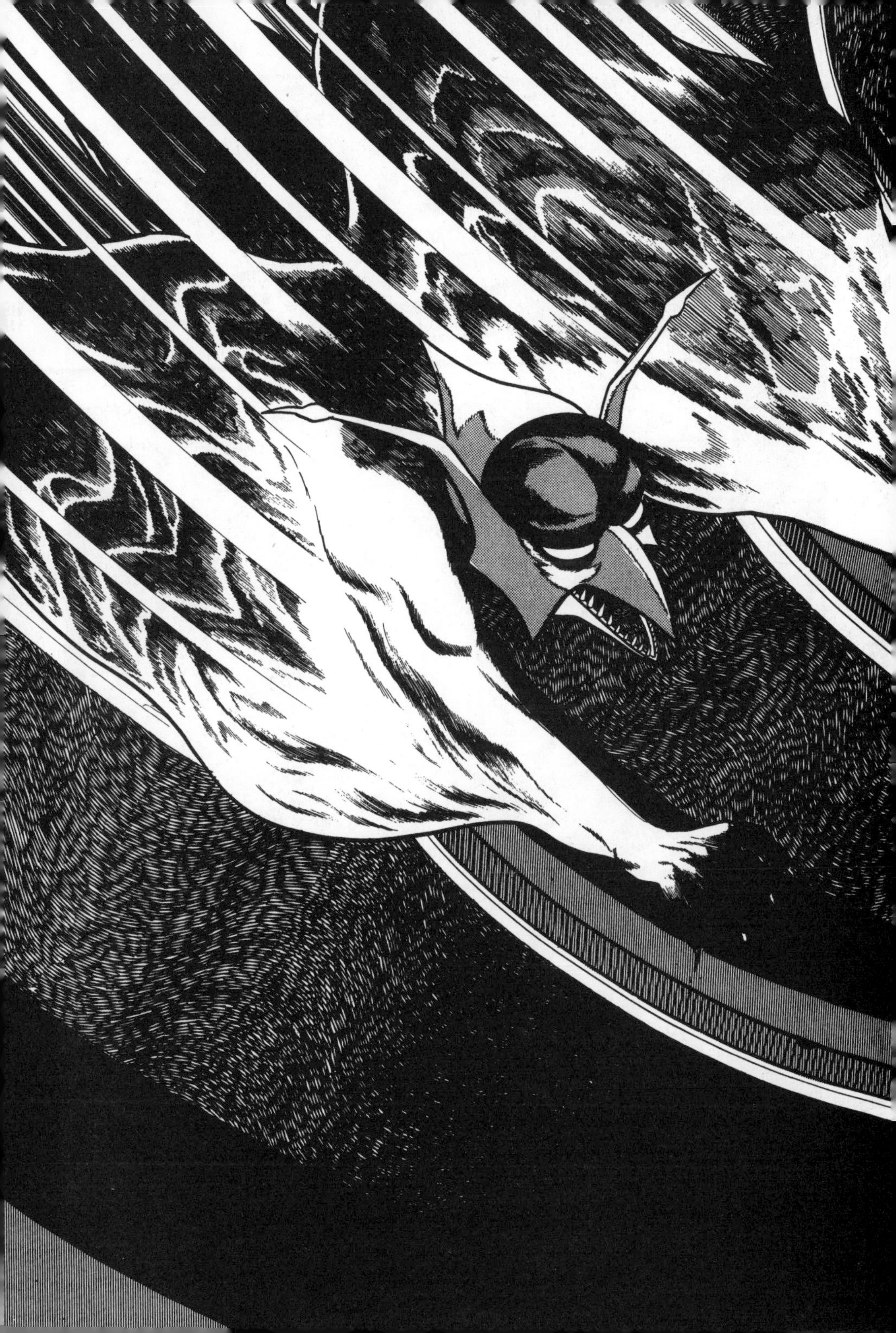

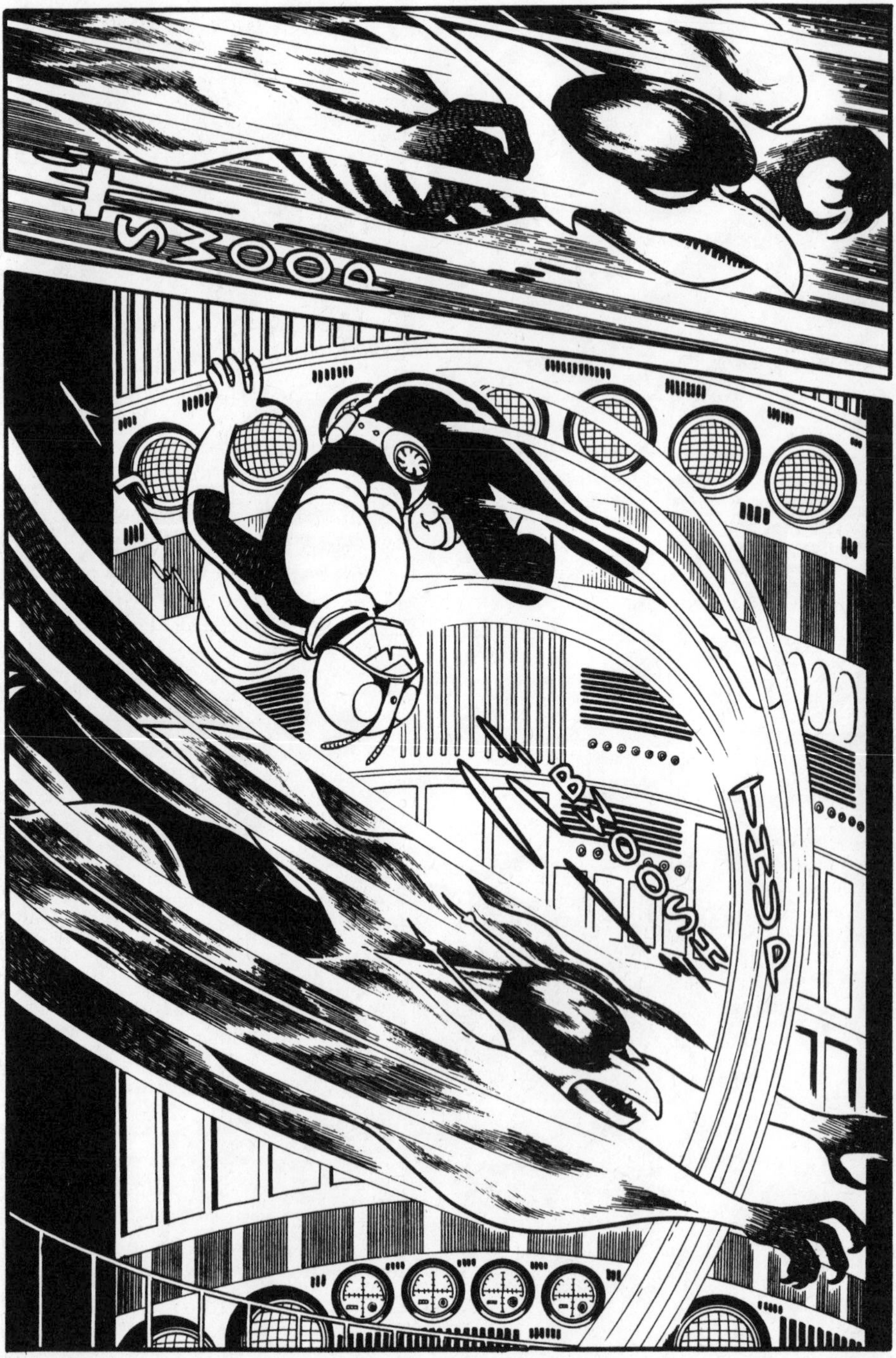
SWOOP
THUP
BWOOSH

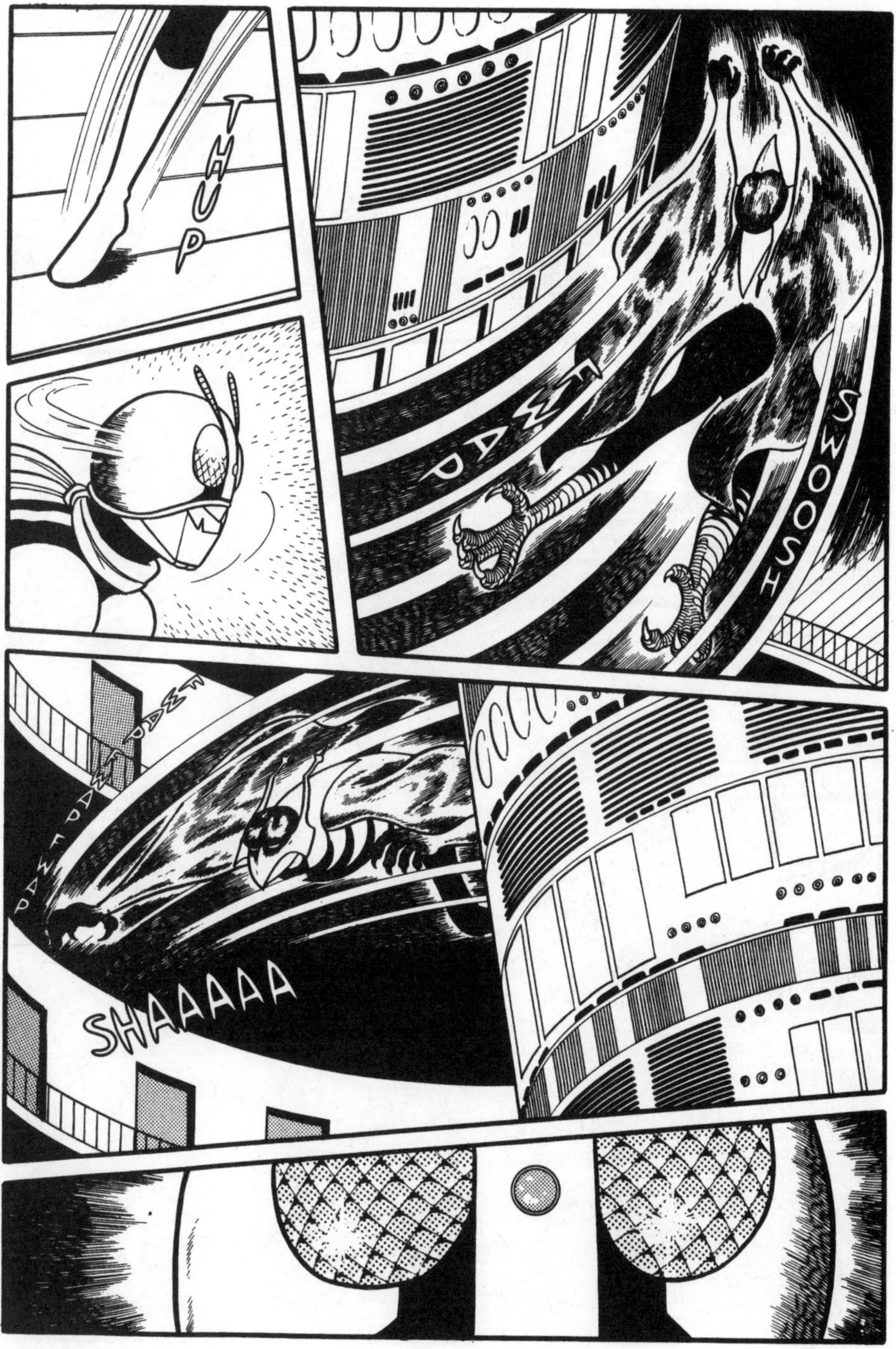
FWAP
SWOOSH
THUP
FWAPFWAPFWAP
SHAAAAA

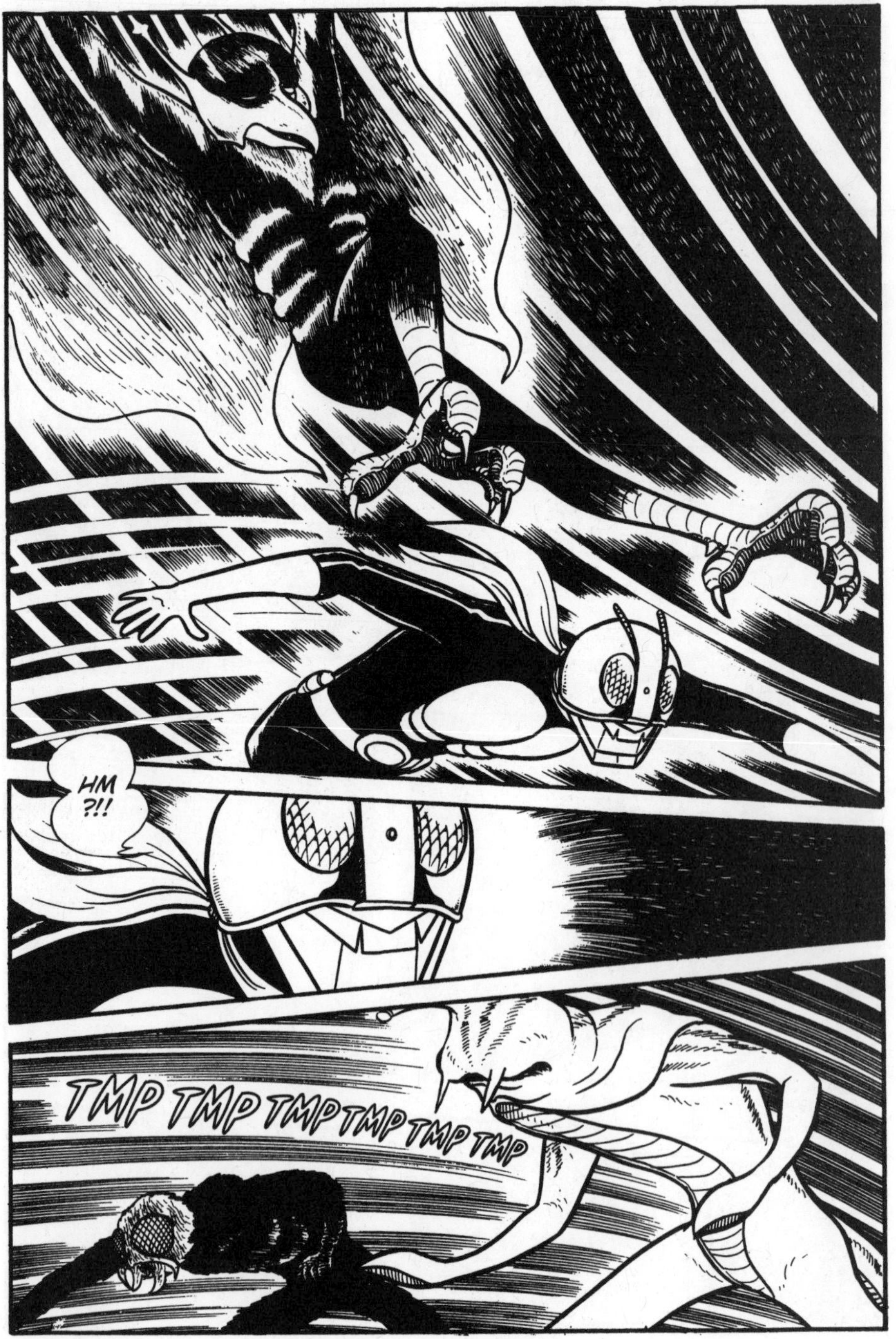
HM ?!!
TMP TMP TMP TMP TMP TMP TMP

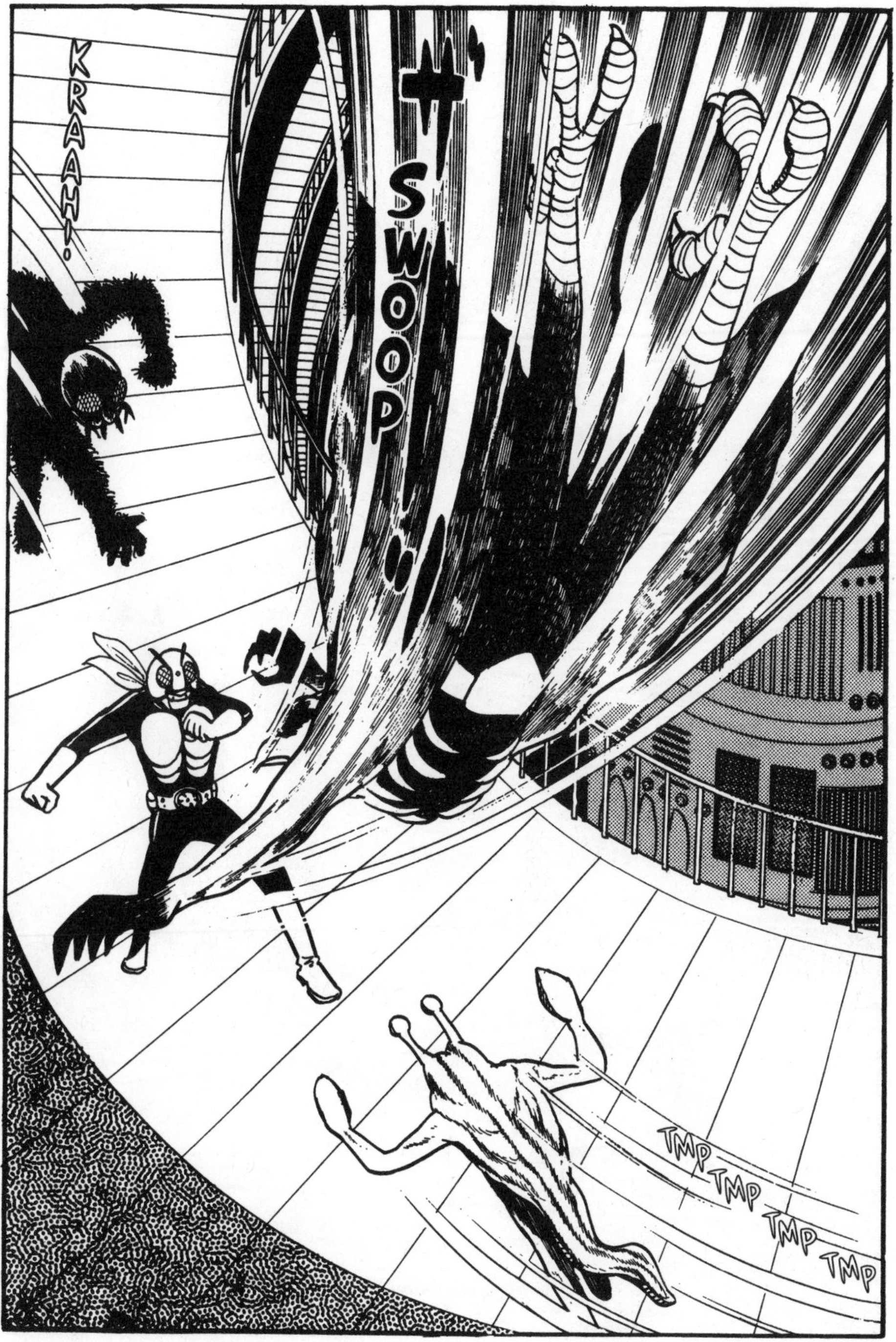
SWOOP
KRAAAH!
TMP TMP TMP TMP

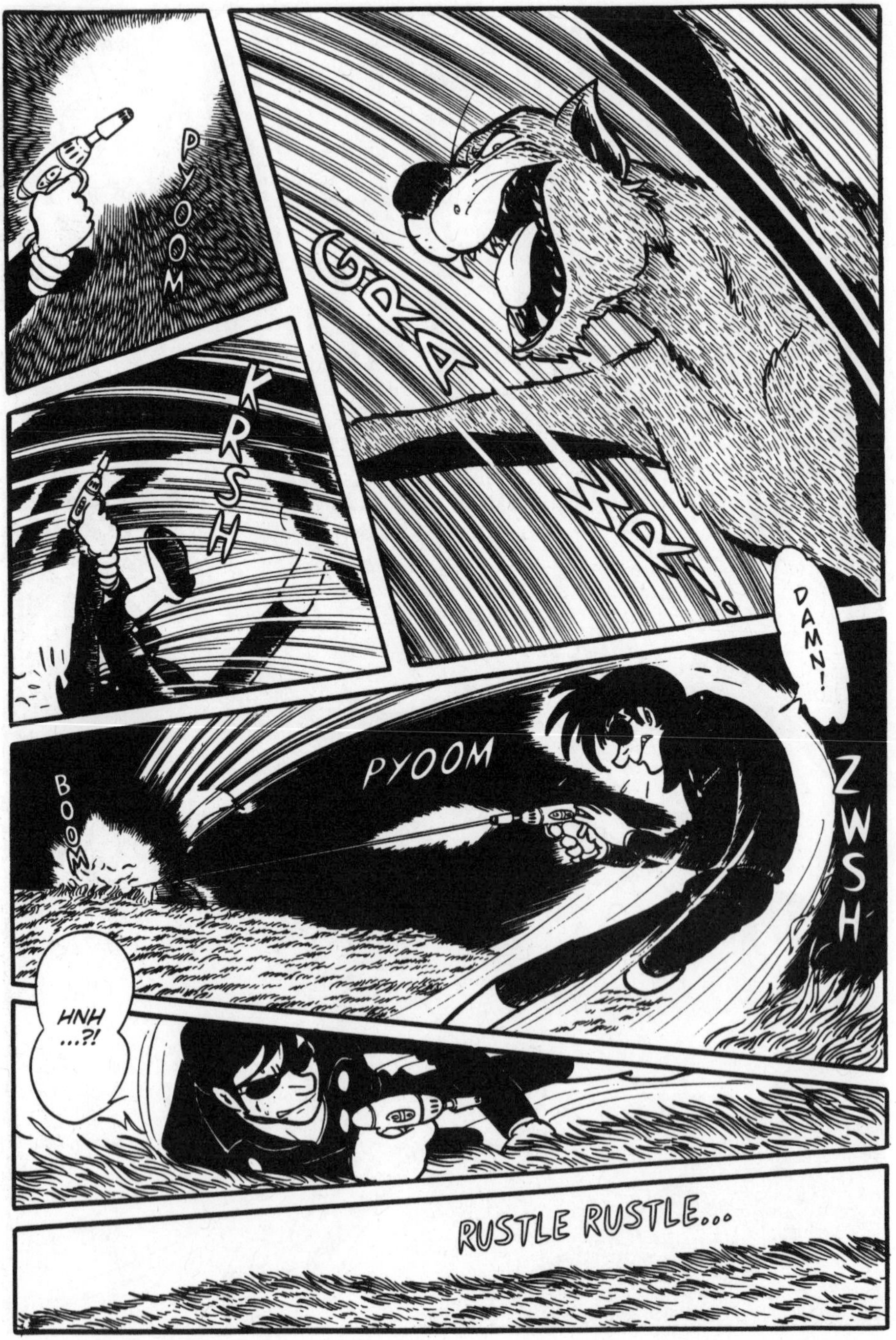
GRAA
WR!
PYOOM
KRSH
DAMN!
ZWSH
PYOOM
BOOM
HNH ...?!
RUSTLE RUSTLE...

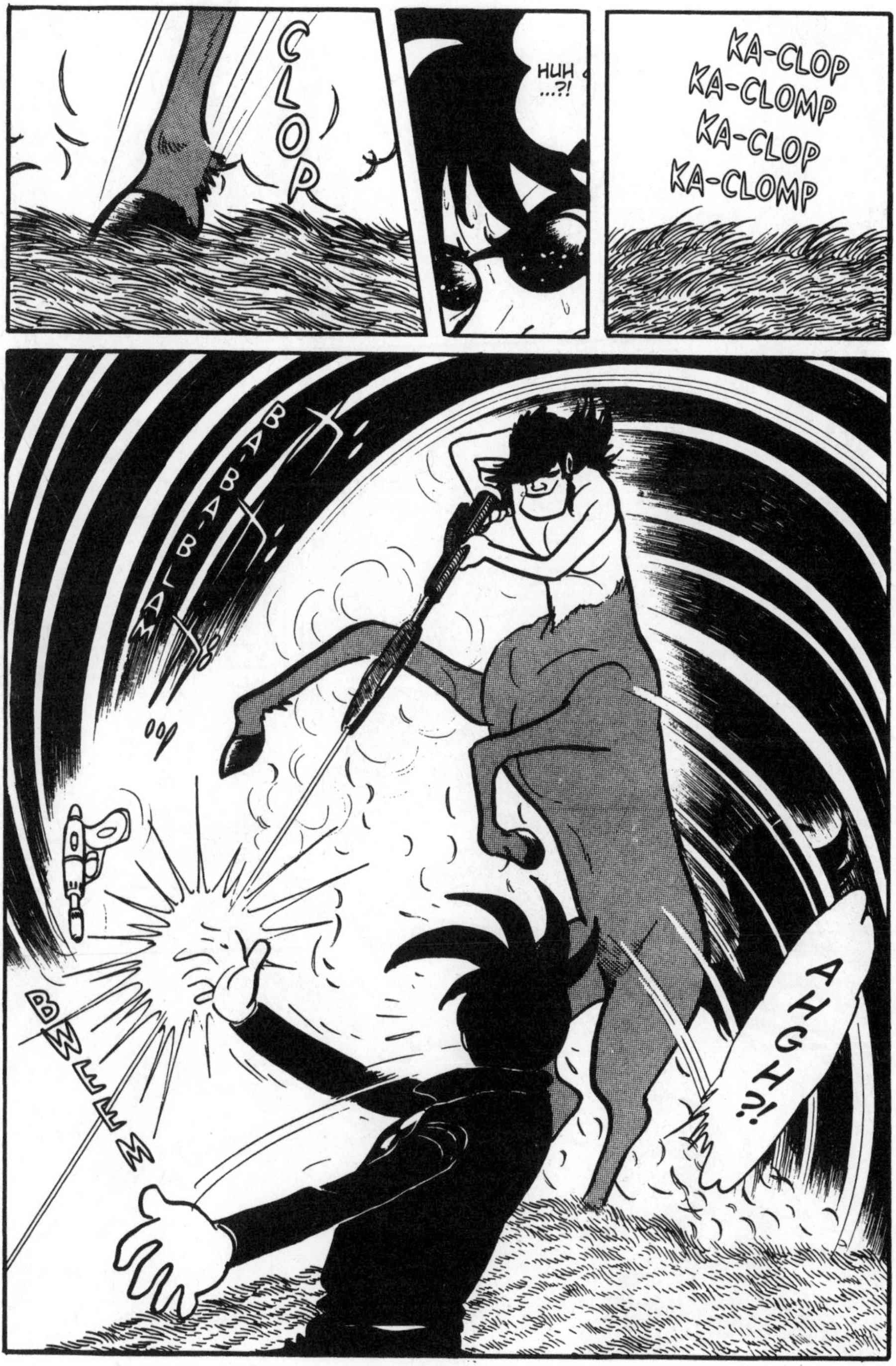
KA-CLOP
KA-CLOMP
KA-CLOP
KA-CLOMP
HUH ...?!
CLOP
AHGH?!
BA-BA-BLAM
BWEEEM

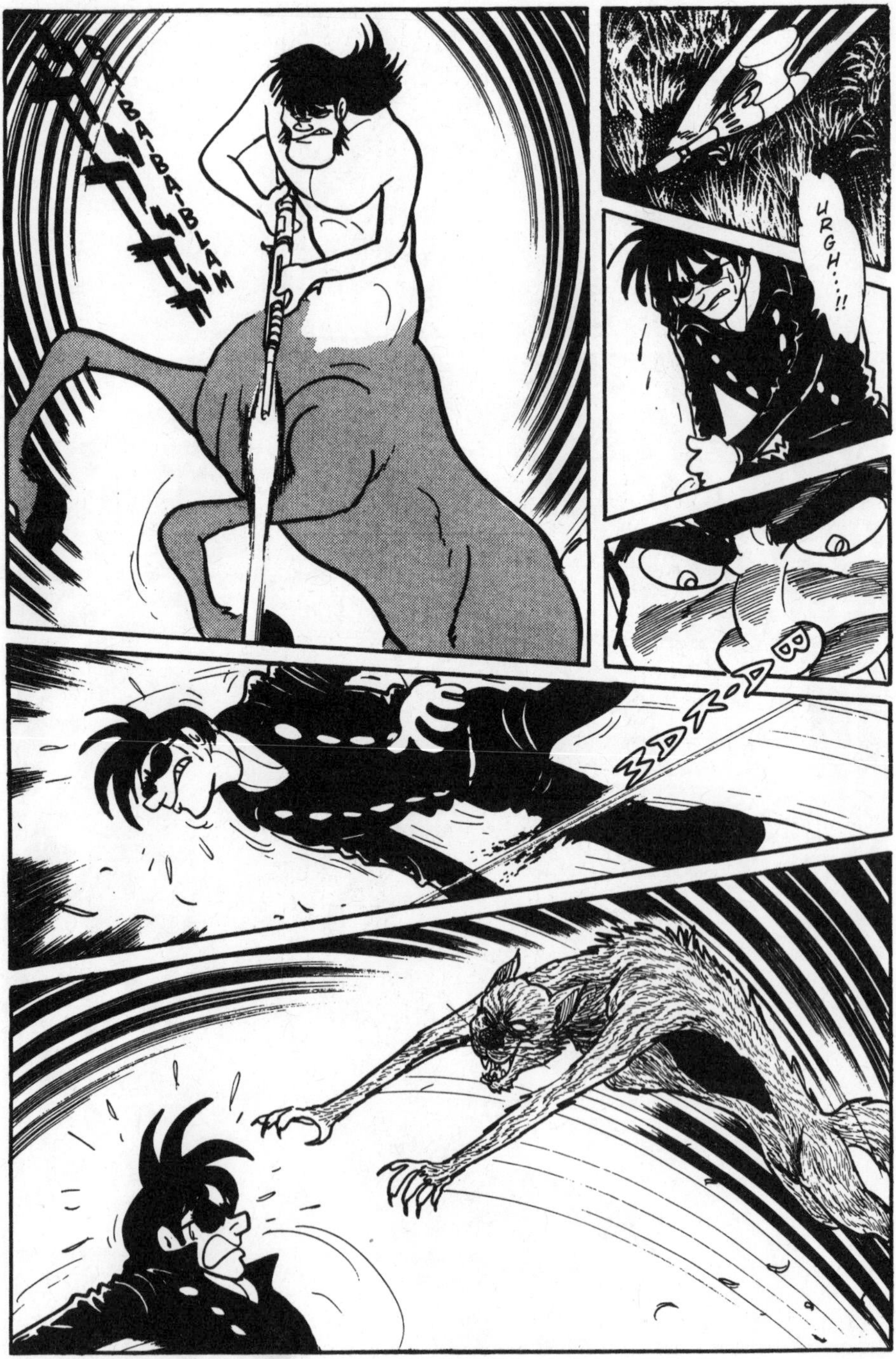

BLAM
BLAM
URGH...!!
BAM

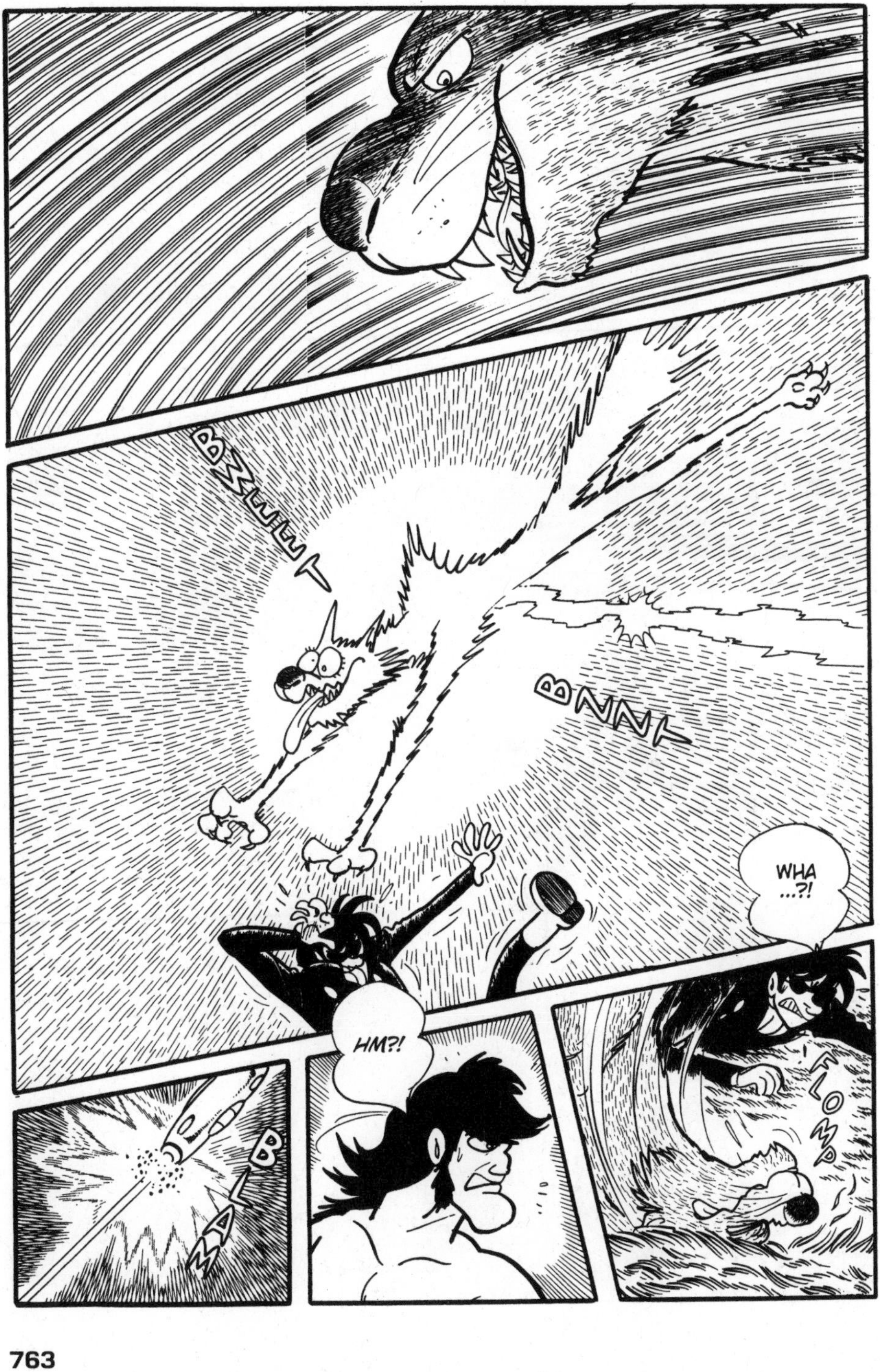
BZEEET
BNNNT
WHA ...?!
FLOMP
HM?!
BLAM

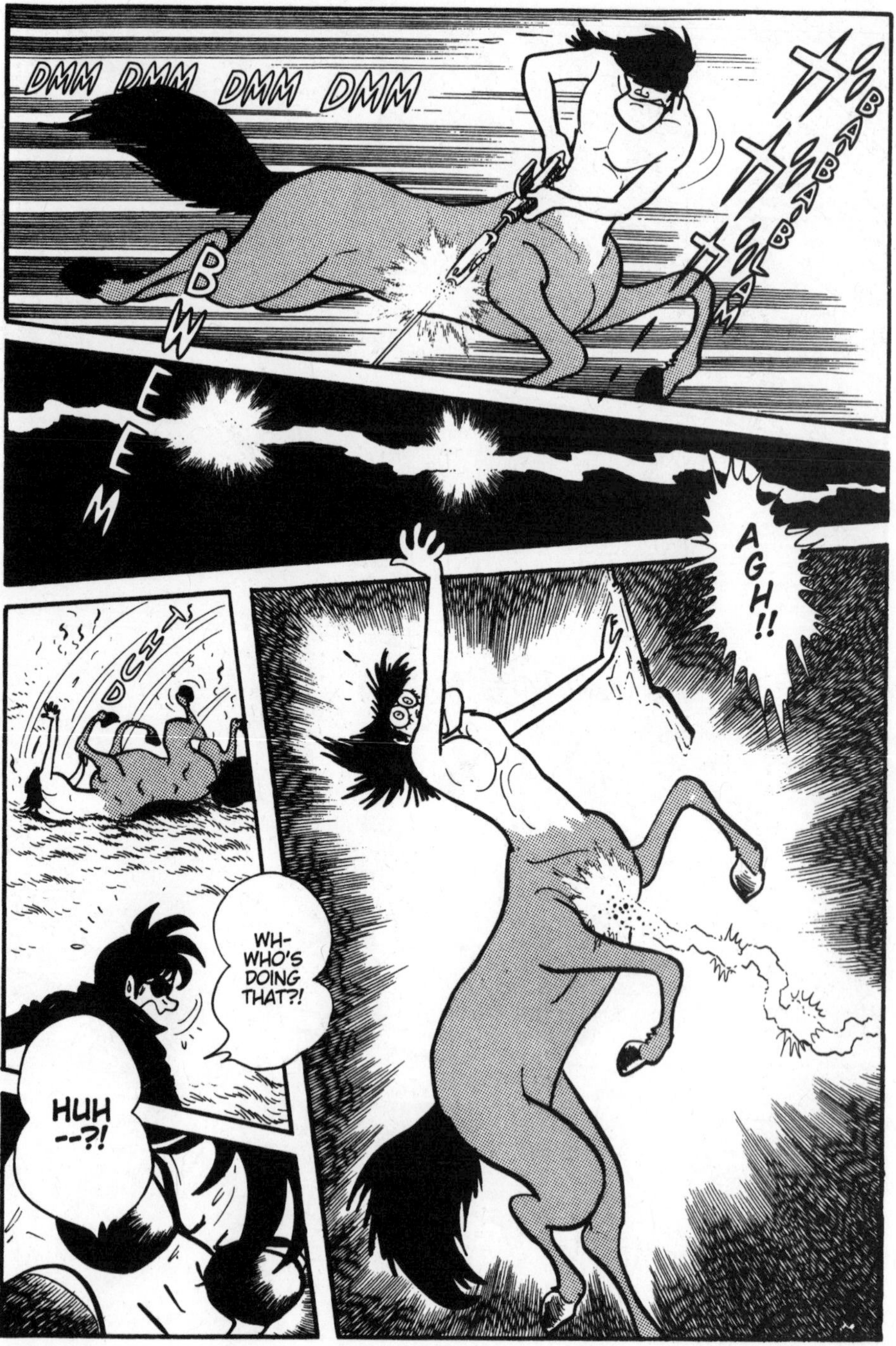

BA-BA-BA-BLAM
DMM DMM DMM DMM
BWEEEM
AGH!!
DCHT
WH-WHO'S DOING THAT?!
HUH --?!

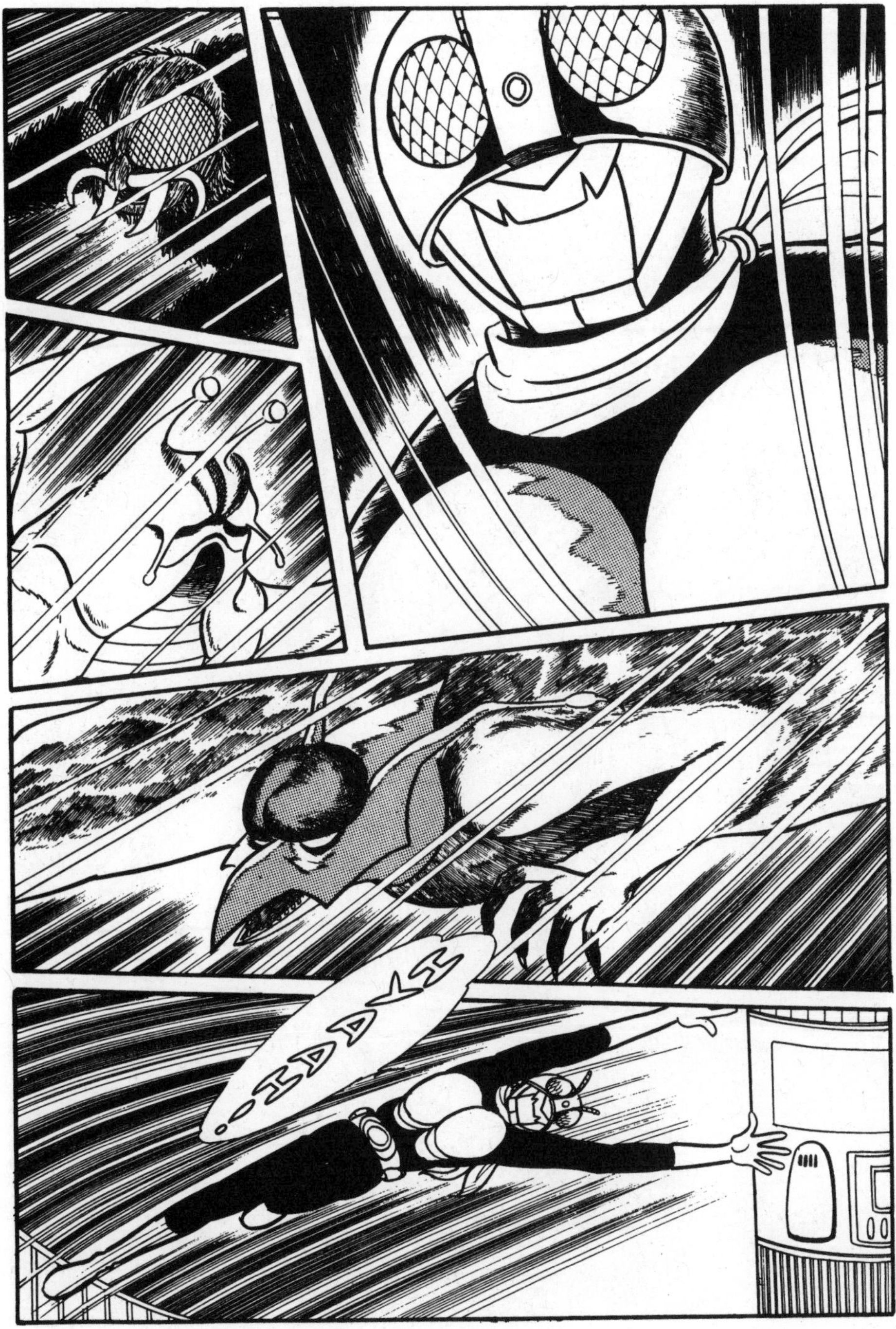
HYAAH-!

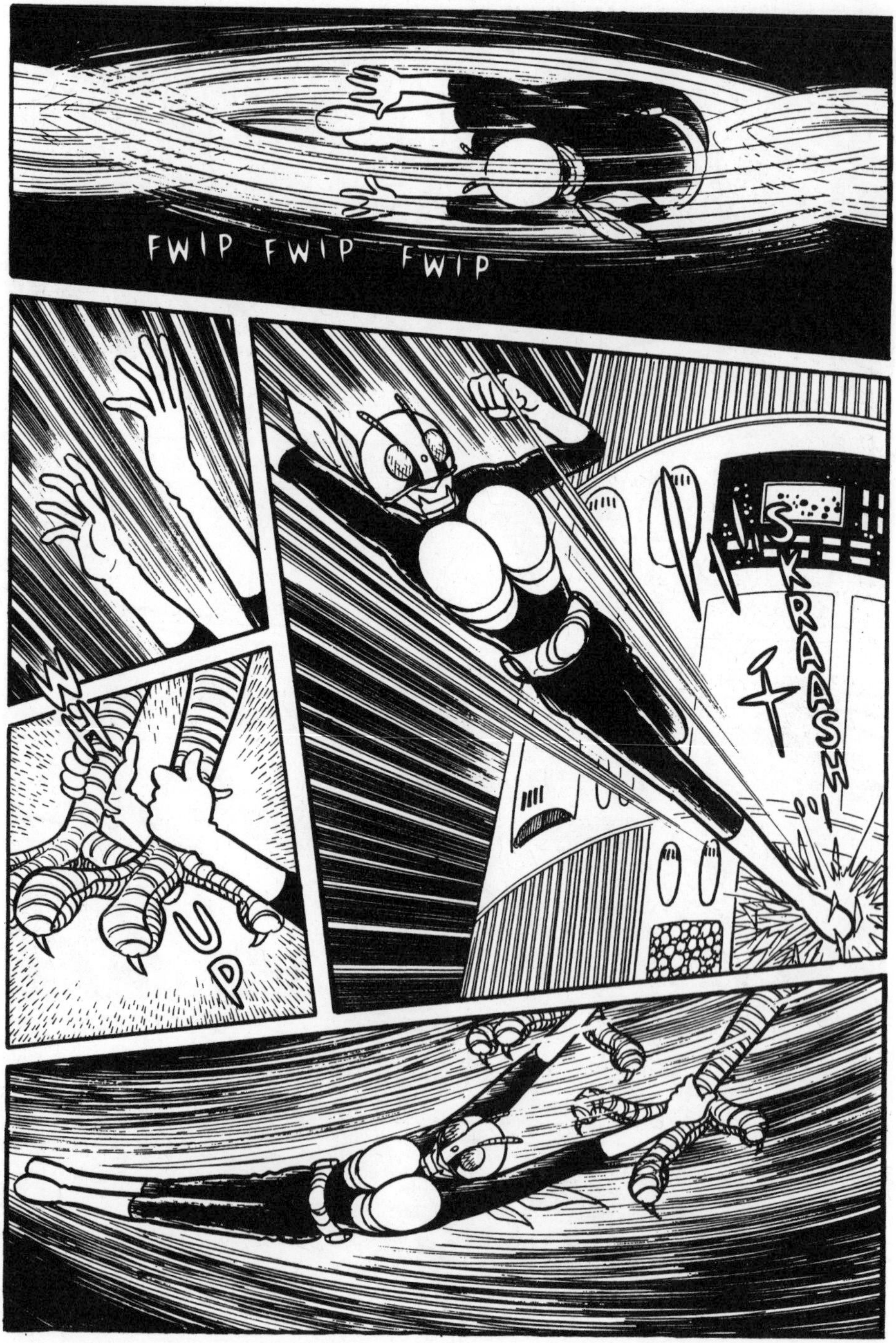
FWIP FWIP FWIP
SKRAASH!!
WHAUP

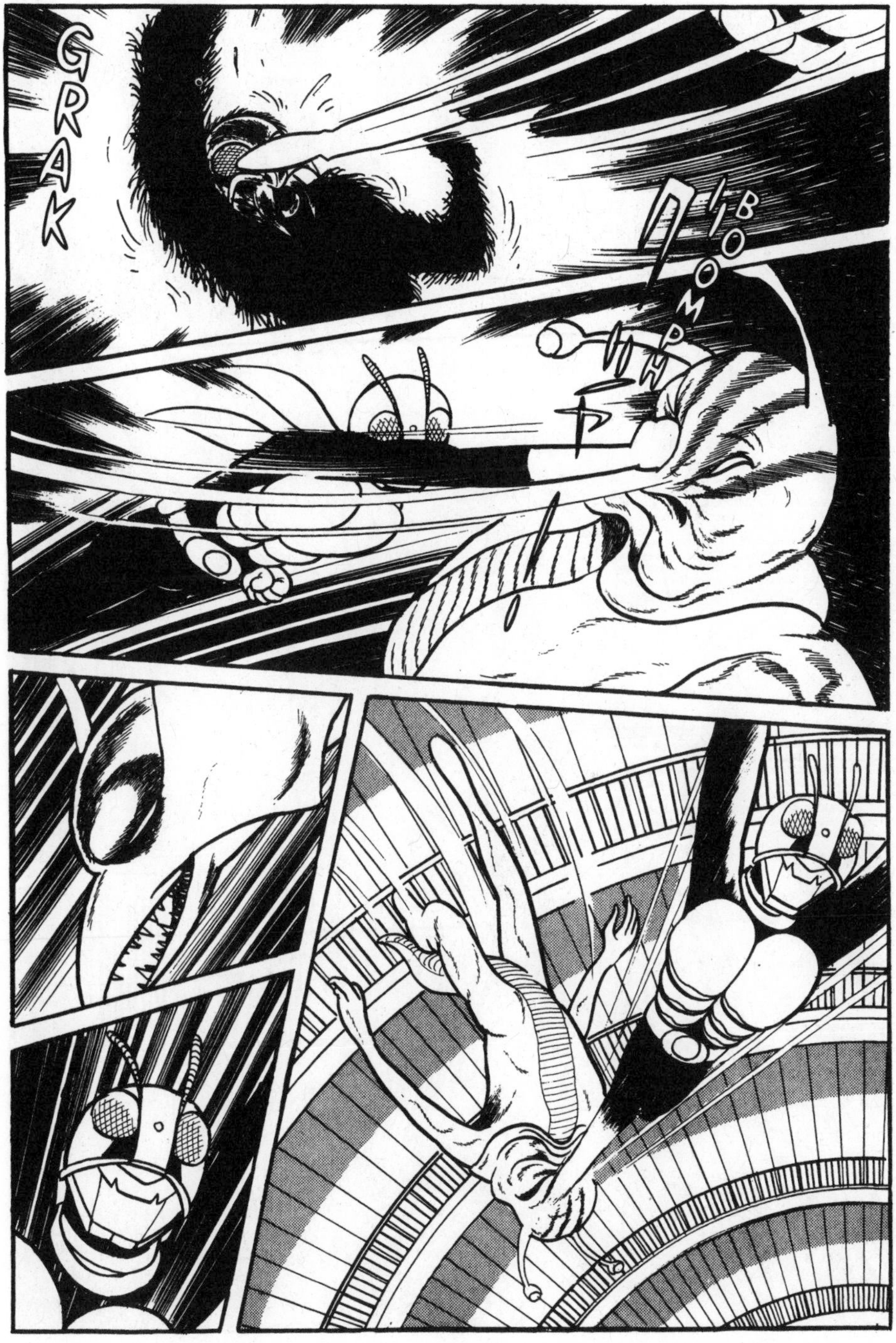
GRAK
BOOMPH

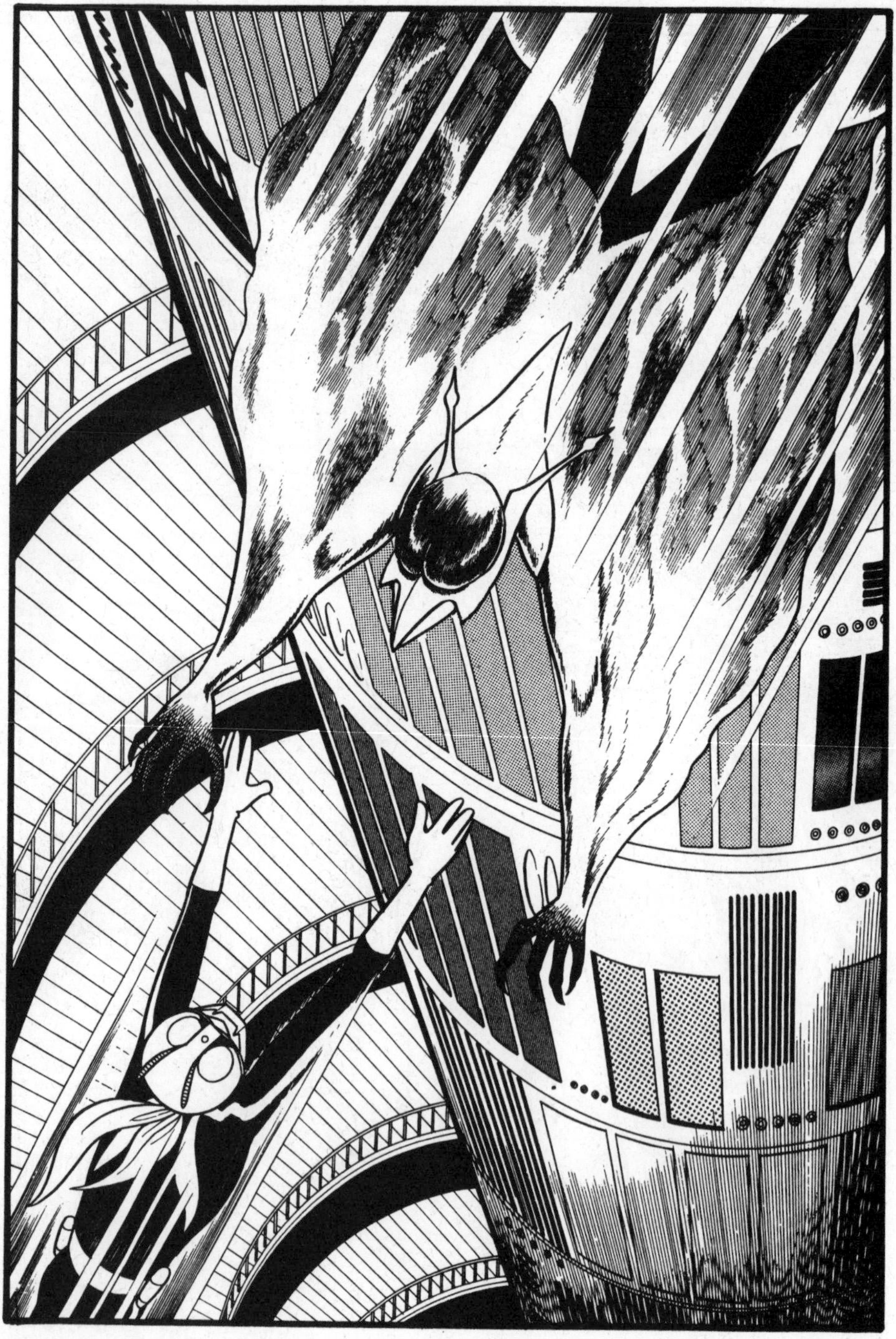

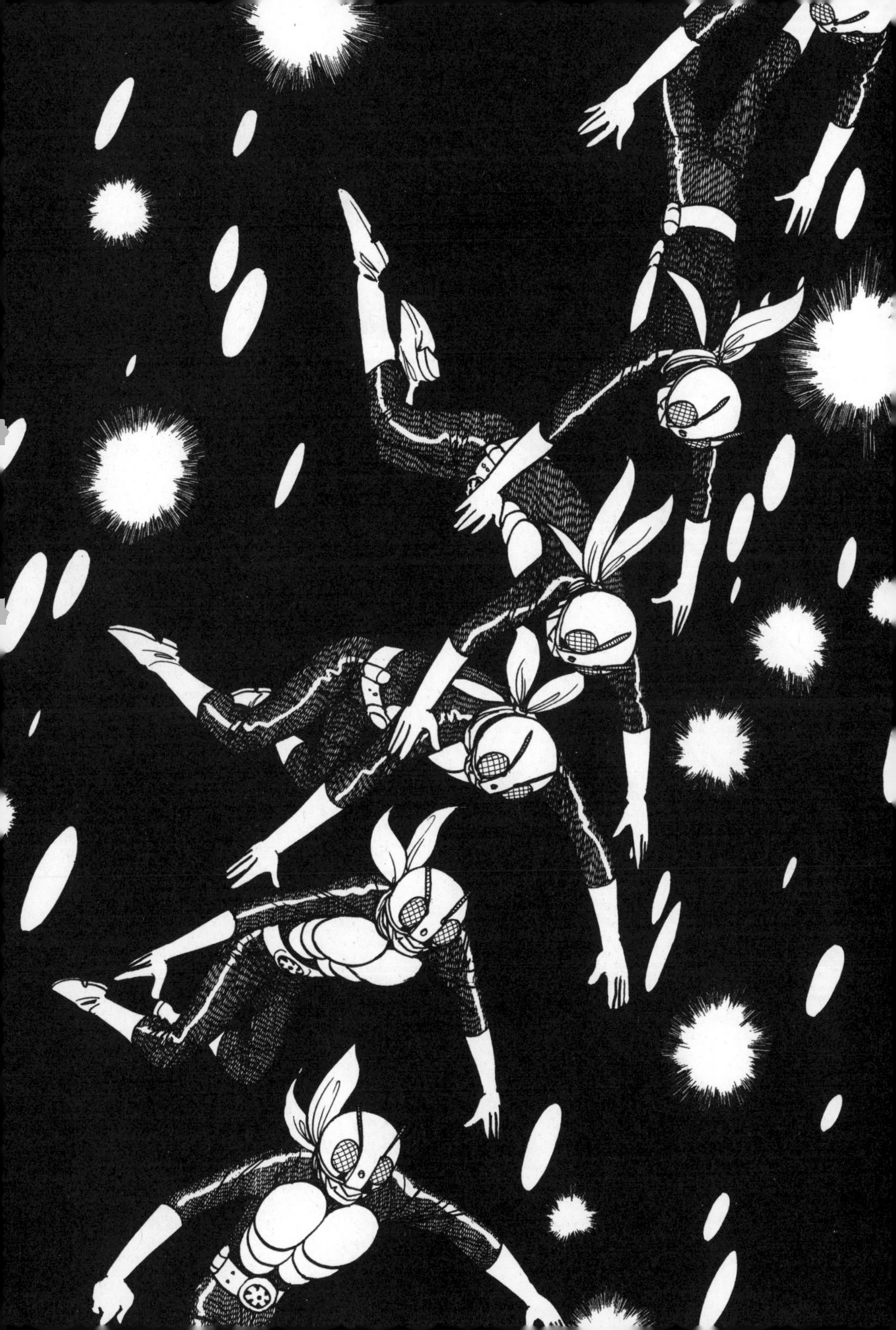

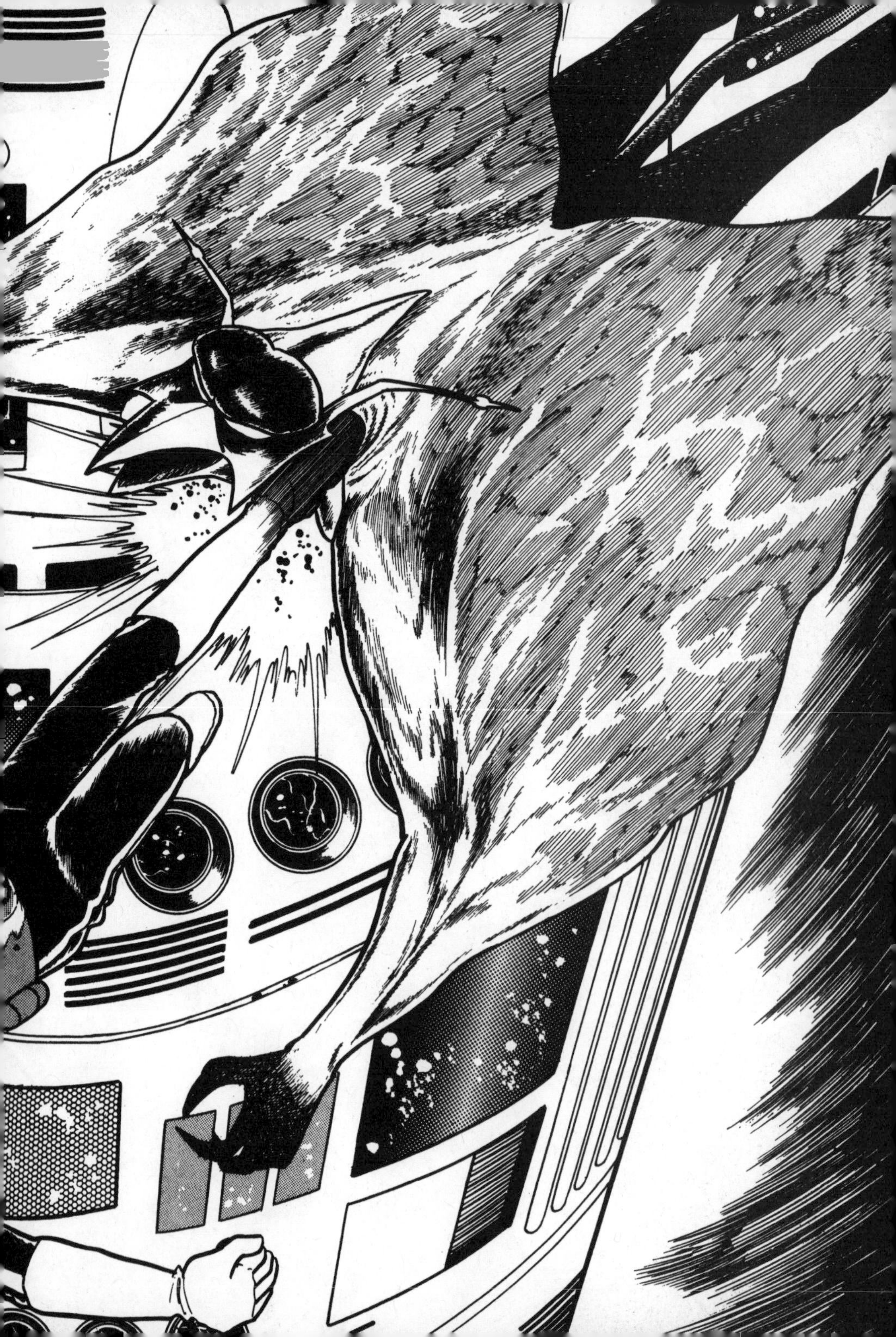

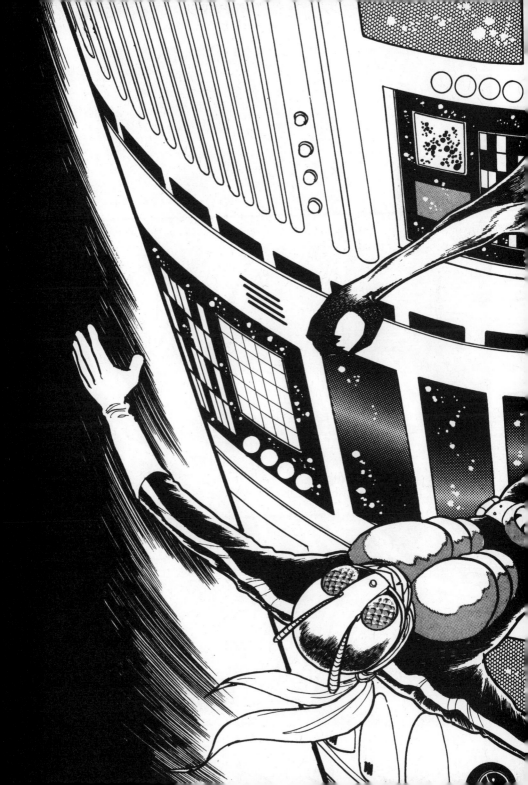

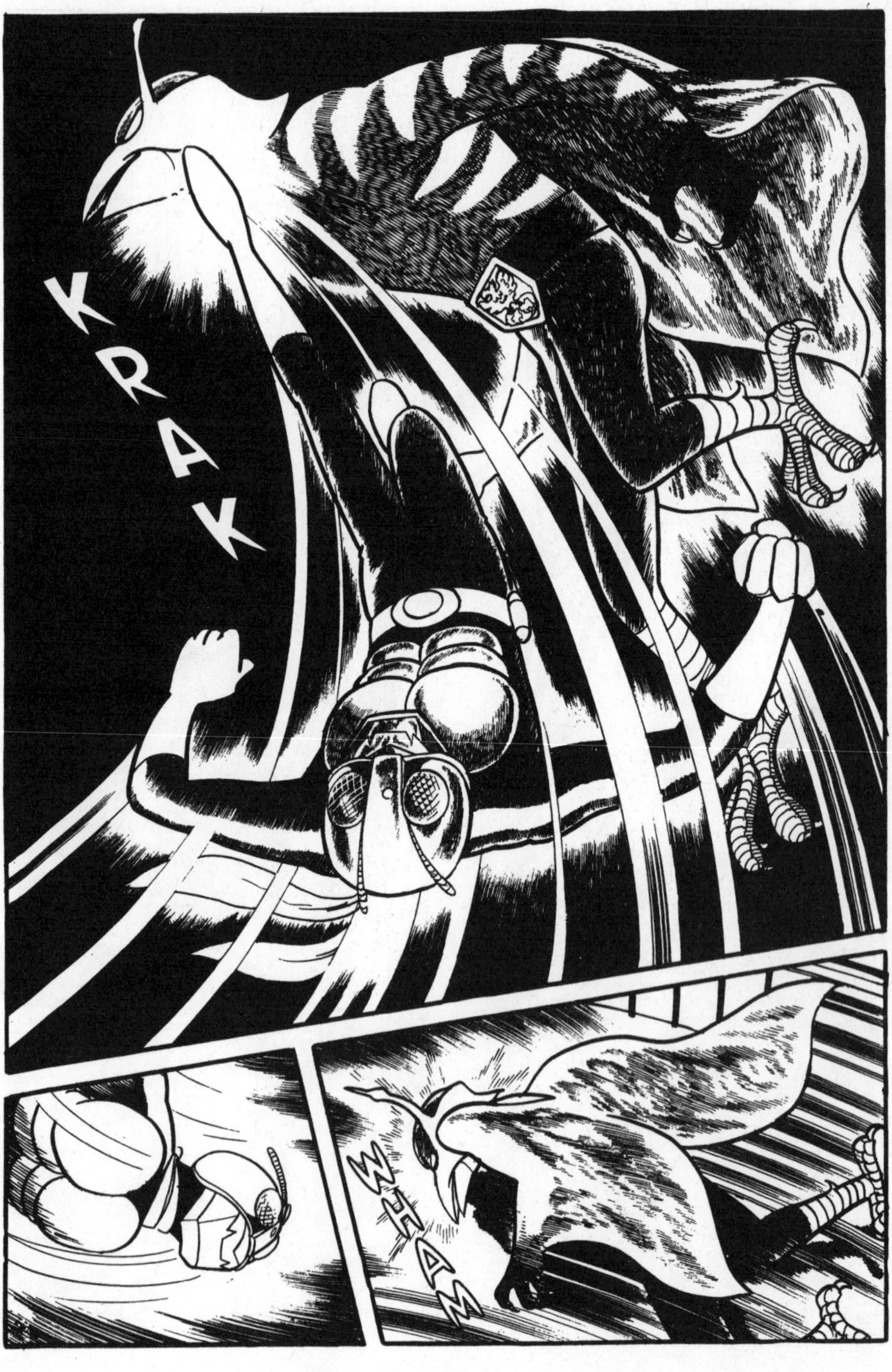
KRAK
WHAM

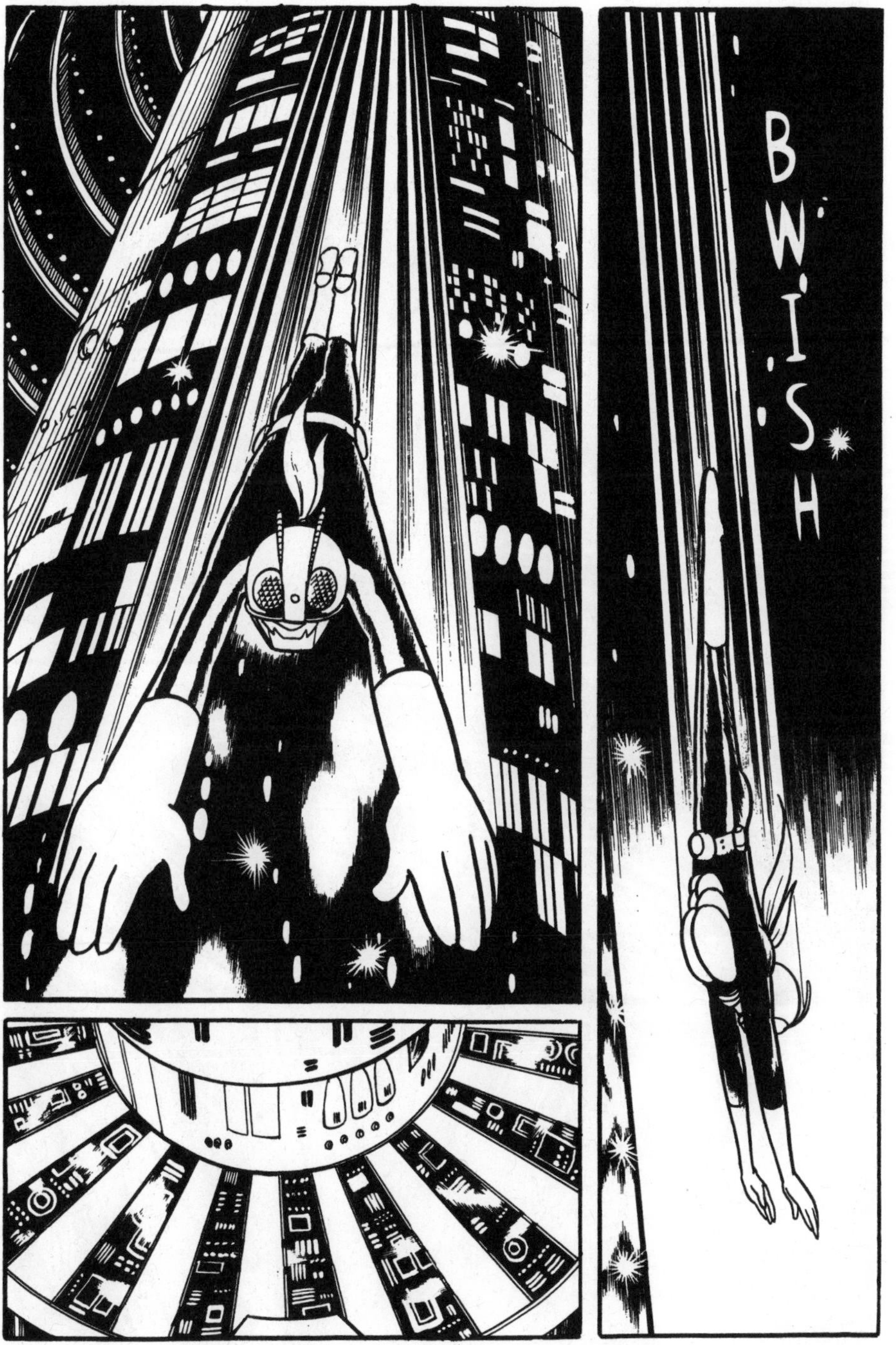
BWISH

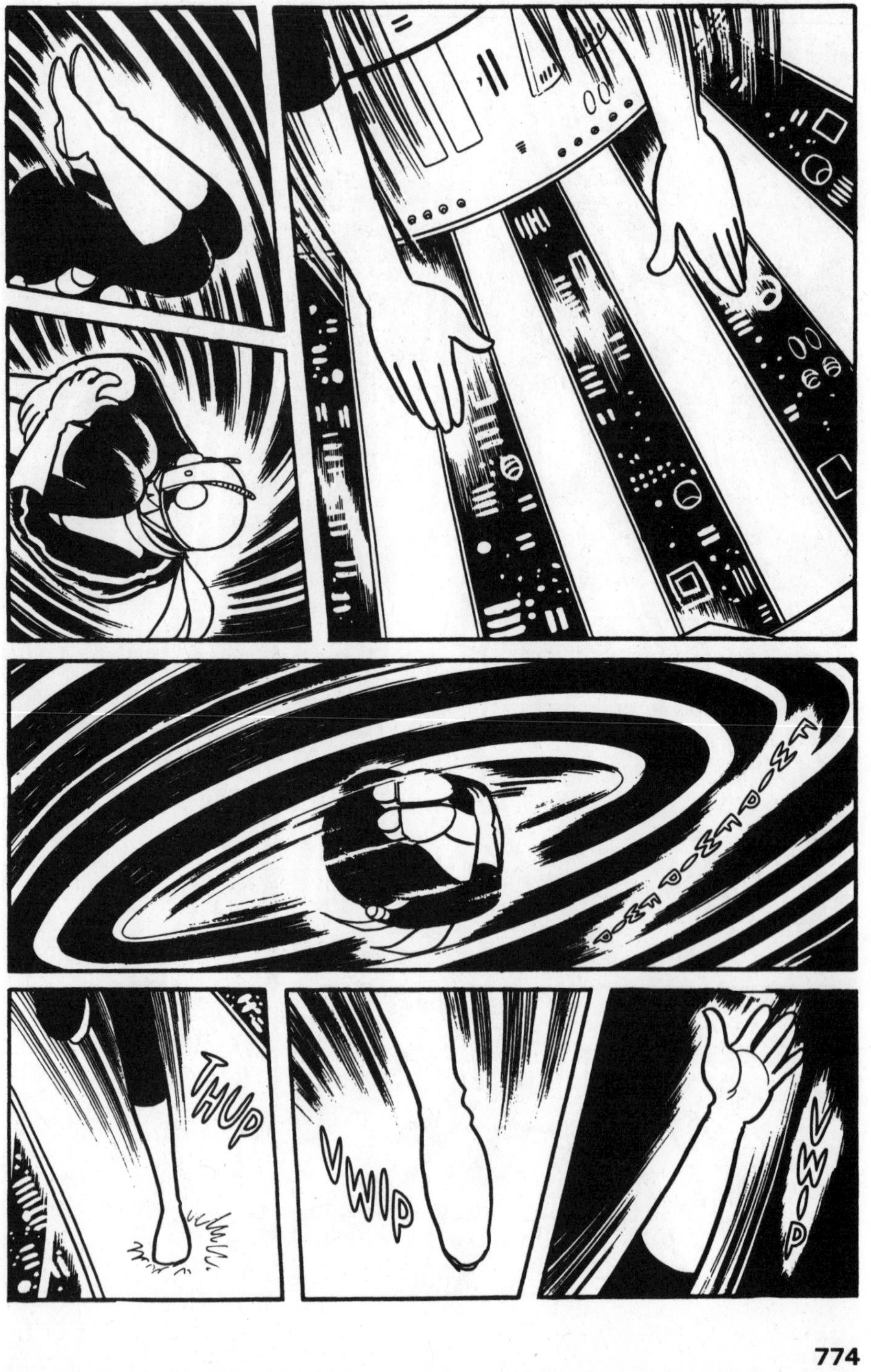
VWIP
VWIP
THUP

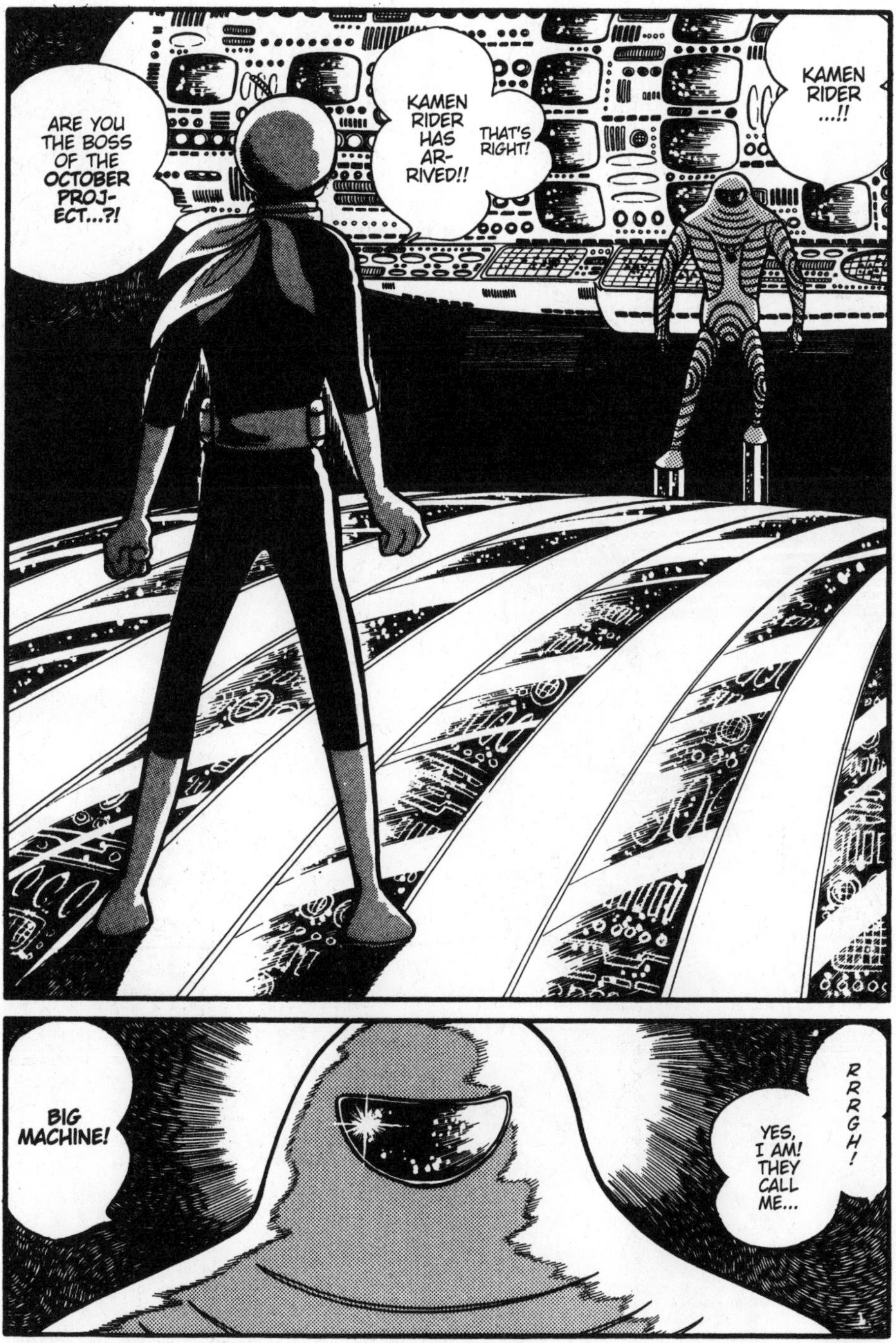
KAMEN RIDER ...!!
THAT'S RIGHT!
KAMEN RIDER HAS AR-RIVED!!
ARE YOU THE BOSS OF THE OCTOBER PROJ-ECT...?!
RRRGH!
YES, I AM! THEY CALL ME...
BIG MACHINE!

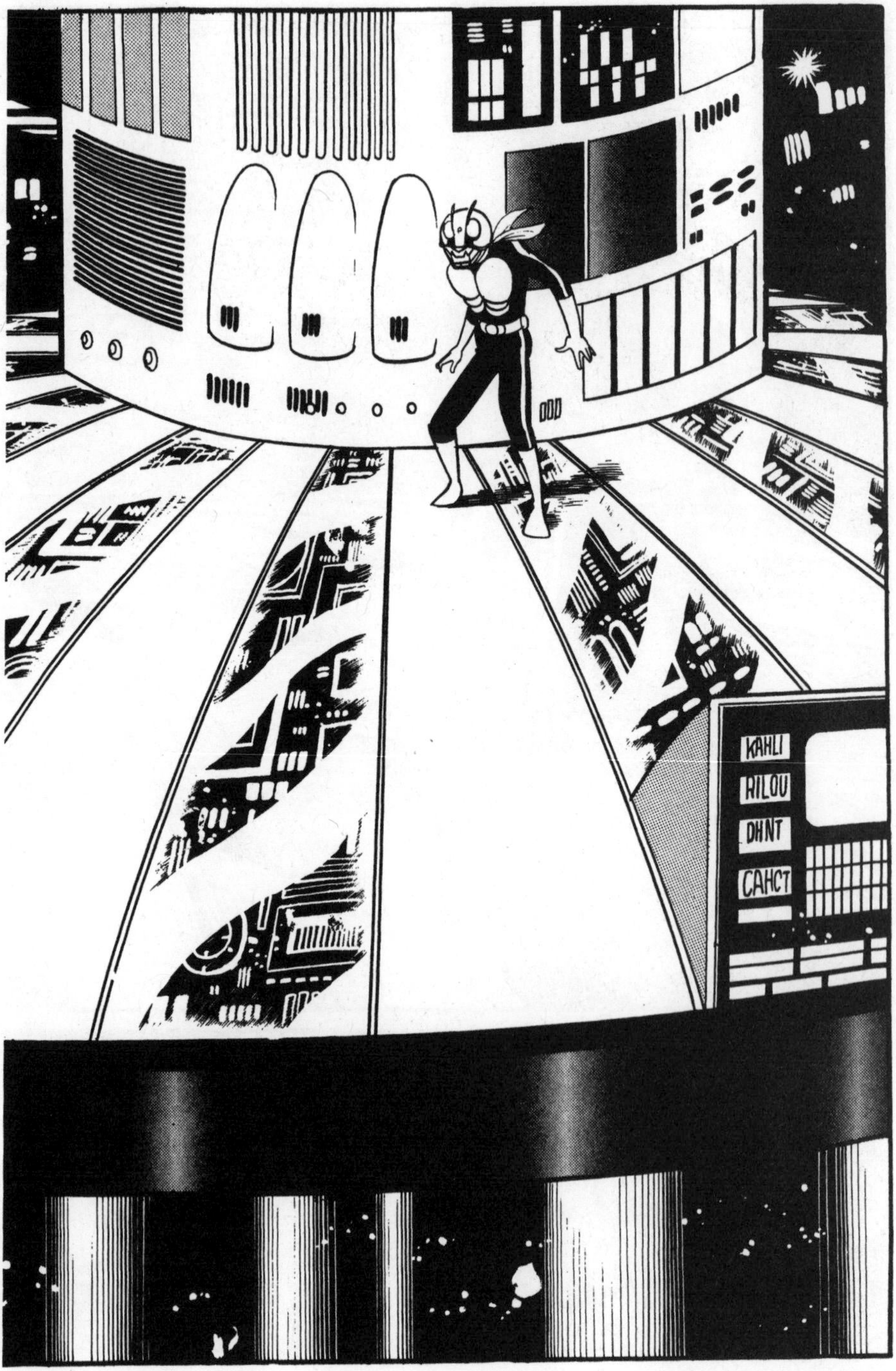
KAHLI
HILOU
DHNT
CAHCT

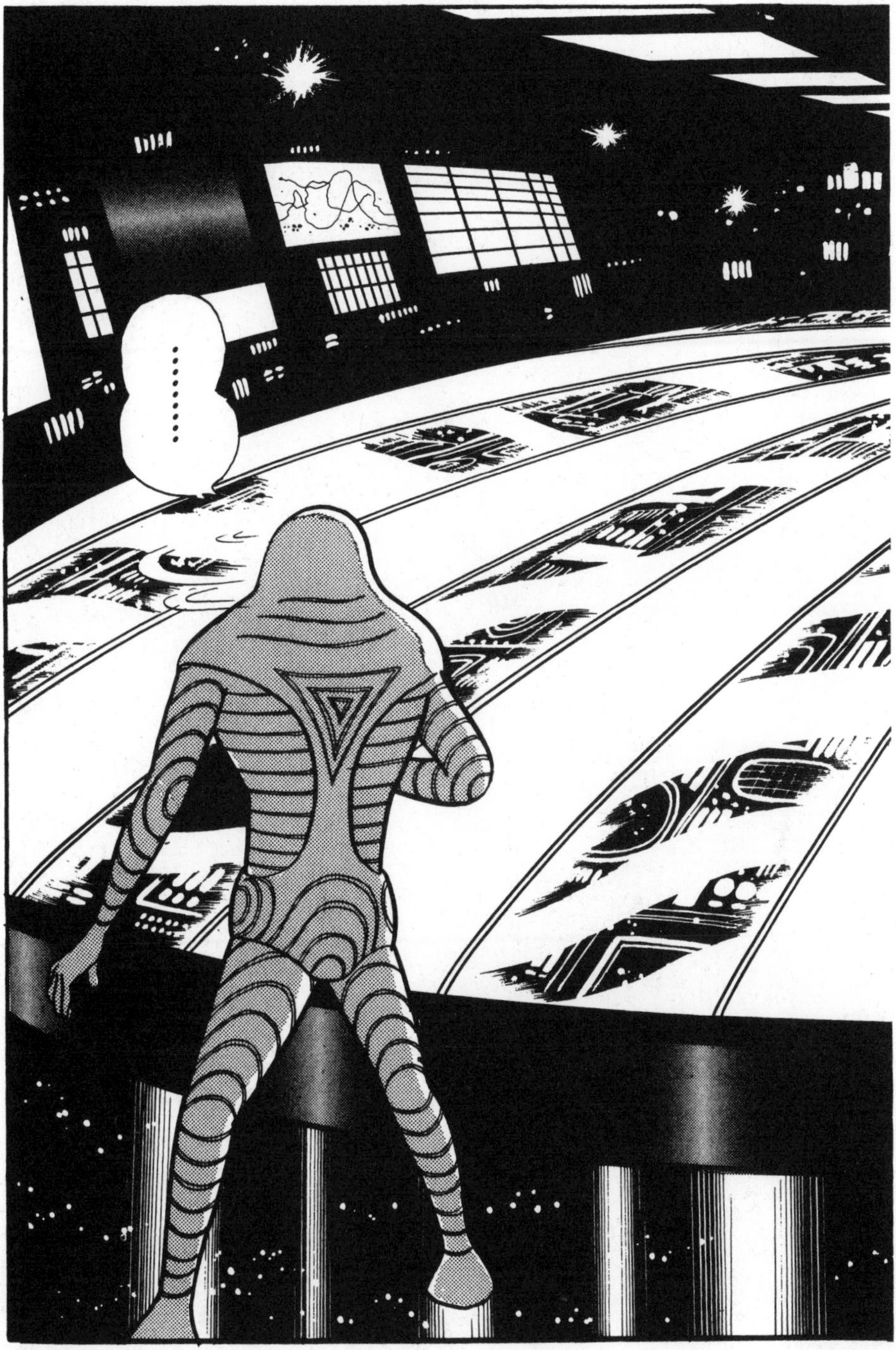
……

KAMEN RIDER

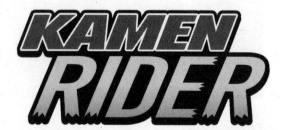

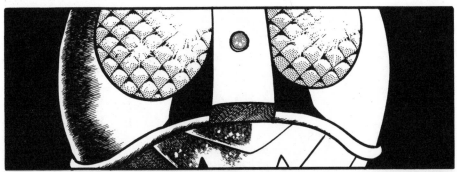

BIG MACHINE, JIG MACHINE, WHATEVER. DON'T CARE!

I'M HERE TO DESTROY THE COMPUTER BRAIN!!

IF YOU DON'T WANT TO GET SMASHED ALONG WITH IT, I RECOMMEND YOU COOPERATE!!

.....

THE VERY IDEA OF USING A COMPUTER...

TO TURN THE PEOPLE OF JAPAN INTO ROBOTS...!

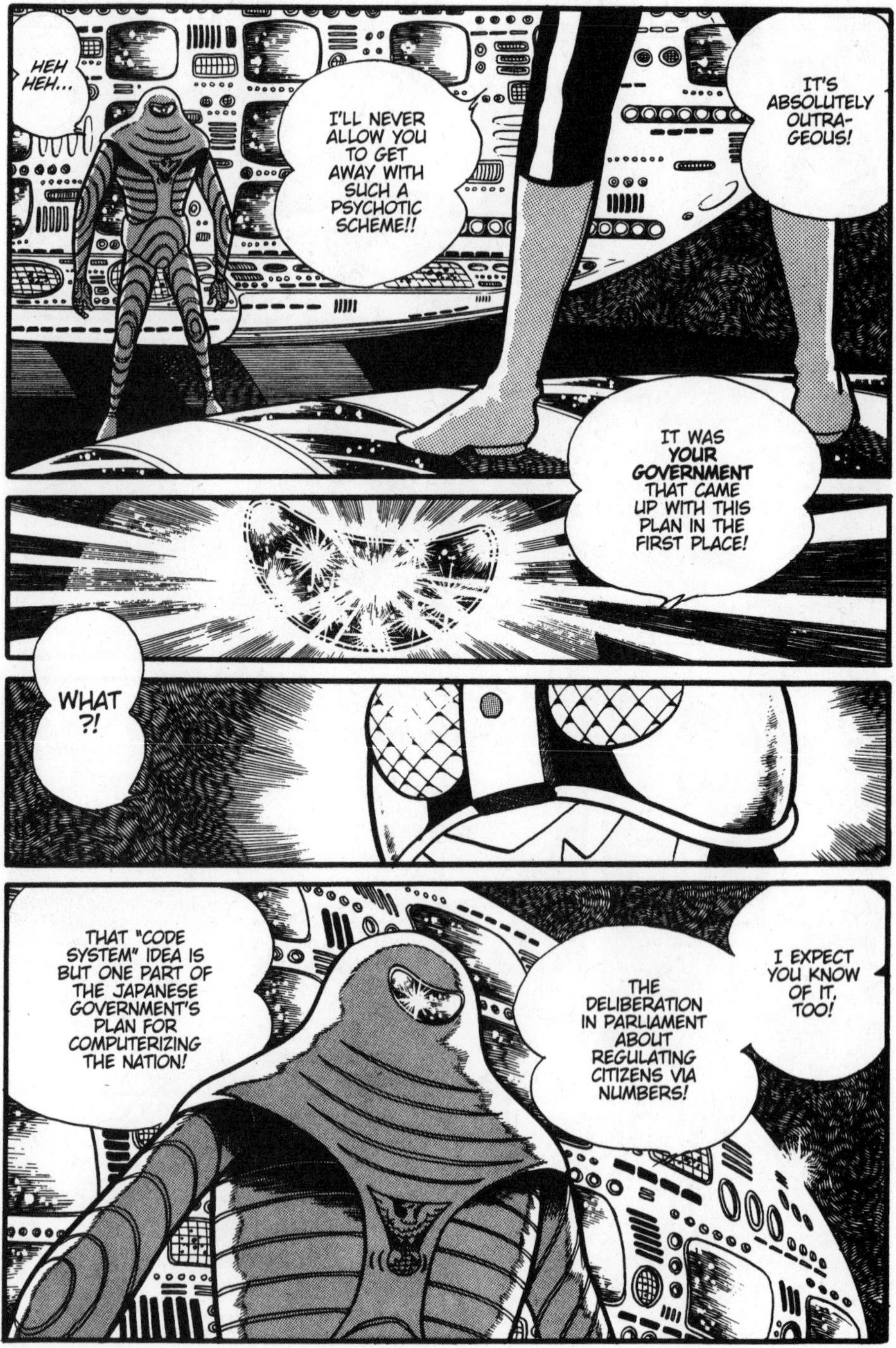
IT'S ABSOLUTELY OUTRAGEOUS!
I'LL NEVER ALLOW YOU TO GET AWAY WITH SUCH A PSYCHOTIC SCHEME!!
HEH HEH...
IT WAS YOUR GOVERNMENT THAT CAME UP WITH THIS PLAN IN THE FIRST PLACE!
WHAT ?!
I EXPECT YOU KNOW OF IT, TOO!
THE DELIBERATION IN PARLIAMENT ABOUT REGULATING CITIZENS VIA NUMBERS!
THAT "CODE SYSTEM" IDEA IS BUT ONE PART OF THE JAPANESE GOVERNMENT'S PLAN FOR COMPUTERIZING THE NATION!

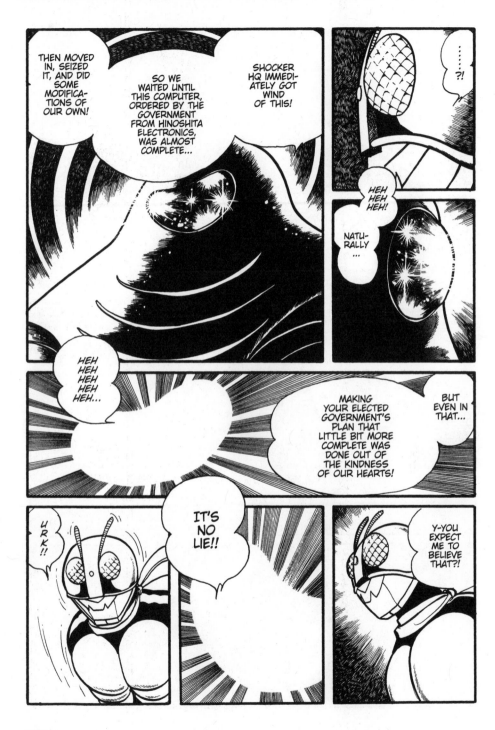

......?!
HEH HEH HEH!
NATURALLY...
SHOCKER HQ IMMEDIATELY GOT WIND OF THIS!
SO WE WAITED UNTIL THIS COMPUTER, ORDERED BY THE GOVERNMENT FROM HINOSHITA ELECTRONICS, WAS ALMOST COMPLETE...
THEN MOVED IN, SEIZED IT, AND DID SOME MODIFICATIONS OF OUR OWN!
HEH HEH HEH HEH HEH...
BUT EVEN IN THAT...
MAKING YOUR ELECTED GOVERNMENT'S PLAN THAT LITTLE BIT MORE COMPLETE WAS DONE OUT OF THE KINDNESS OF OUR HEARTS!
Y-YOU EXPECT ME TO BELIEVE THAT?!
IT'S NO LIE!!
URK!!

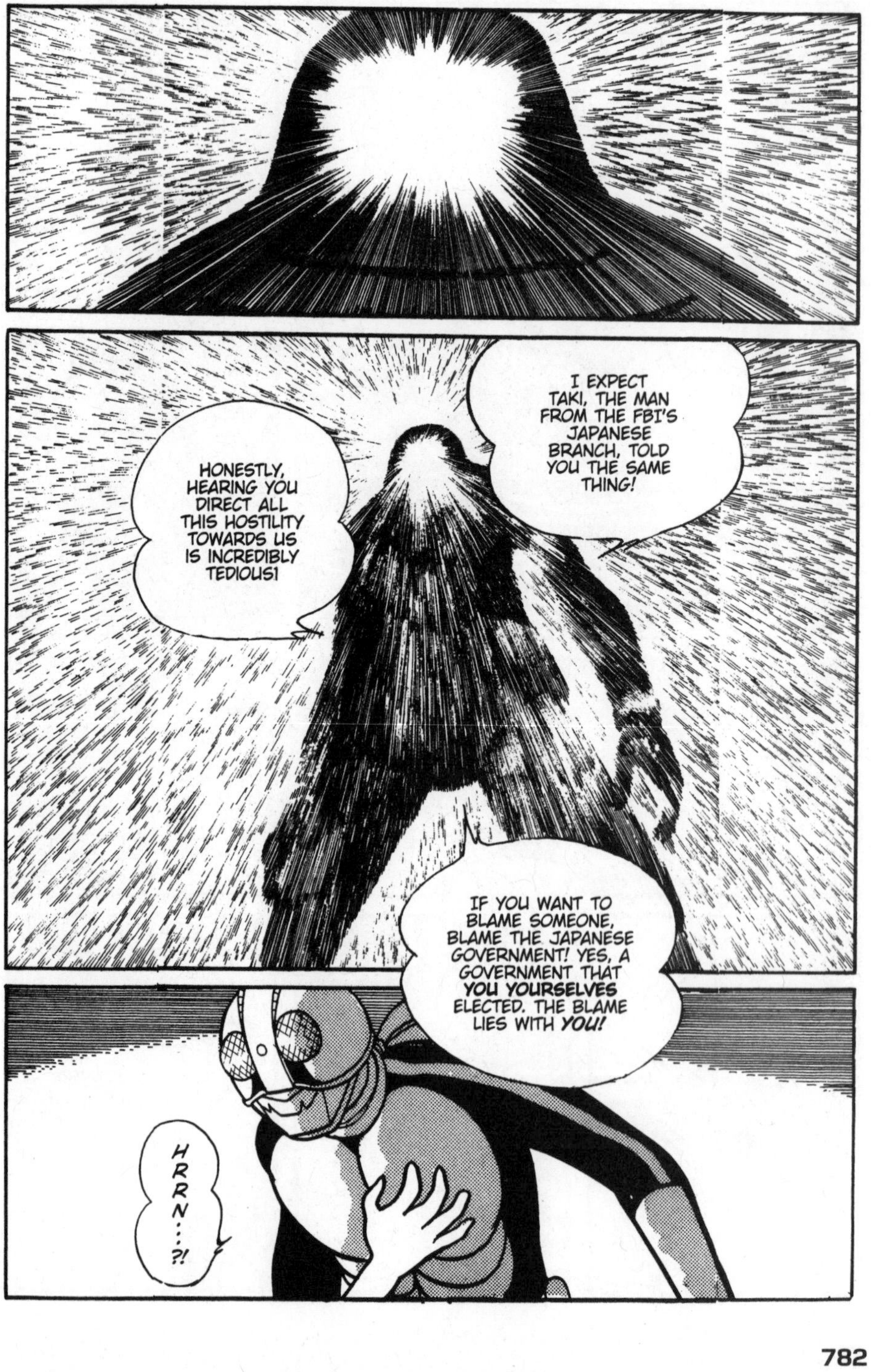
I EXPECT TAKI, THE MAN FROM THE FBI'S JAPANESE BRANCH, TOLD YOU THE SAME THING!
HONESTLY, HEARING YOU DIRECT ALL THIS HOSTILITY TOWARDS US IS INCREDIBLY TEDIOUS!
IF YOU WANT TO BLAME SOMEONE, BLAME THE JAPANESE GOVERNMENT! YES, A GOVERNMENT THAT **YOU YOURSELVES** ELECTED. THE BLAME LIES WITH ***YOU!***
HRRN...?!

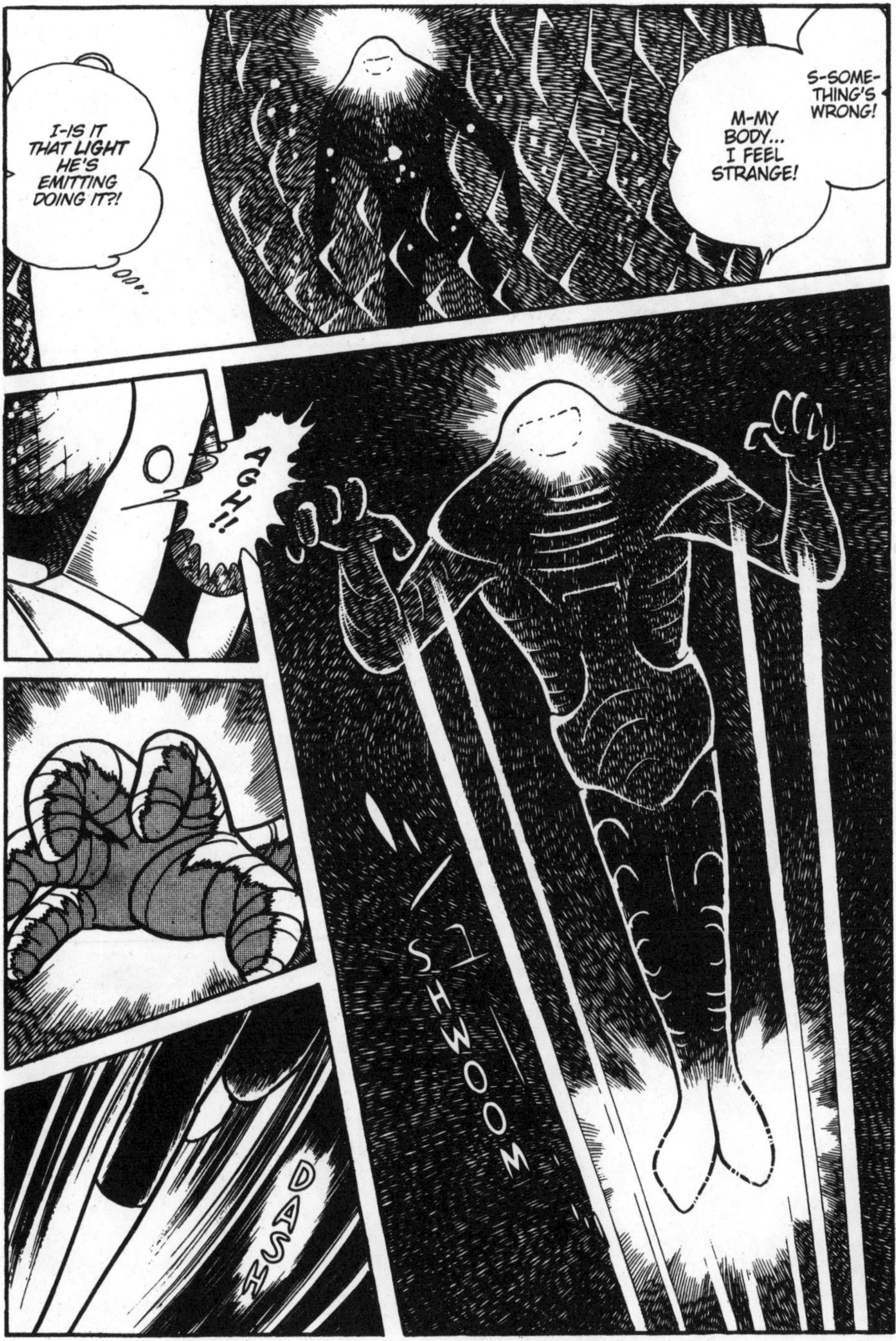
S-SOMETHING'S WRONG!
M-MY BODY... I FEEL STRANGE!
I-IS IT THAT LIGHT HE'S EMITTING DOING IT?!
SHWOOOM
AGH!!
DASH

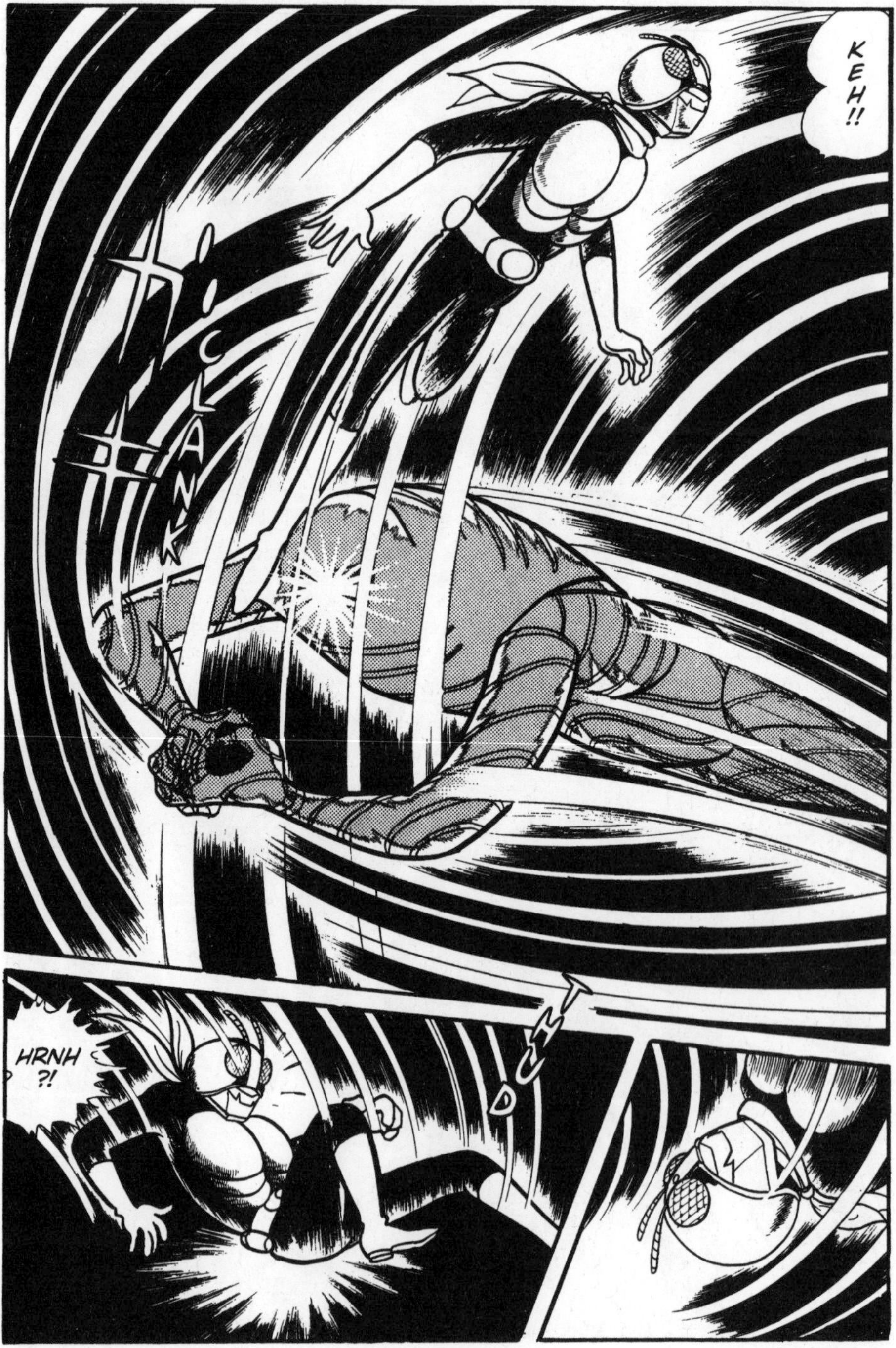
KEH!!
CLANK!
THUD
HRNH ?!

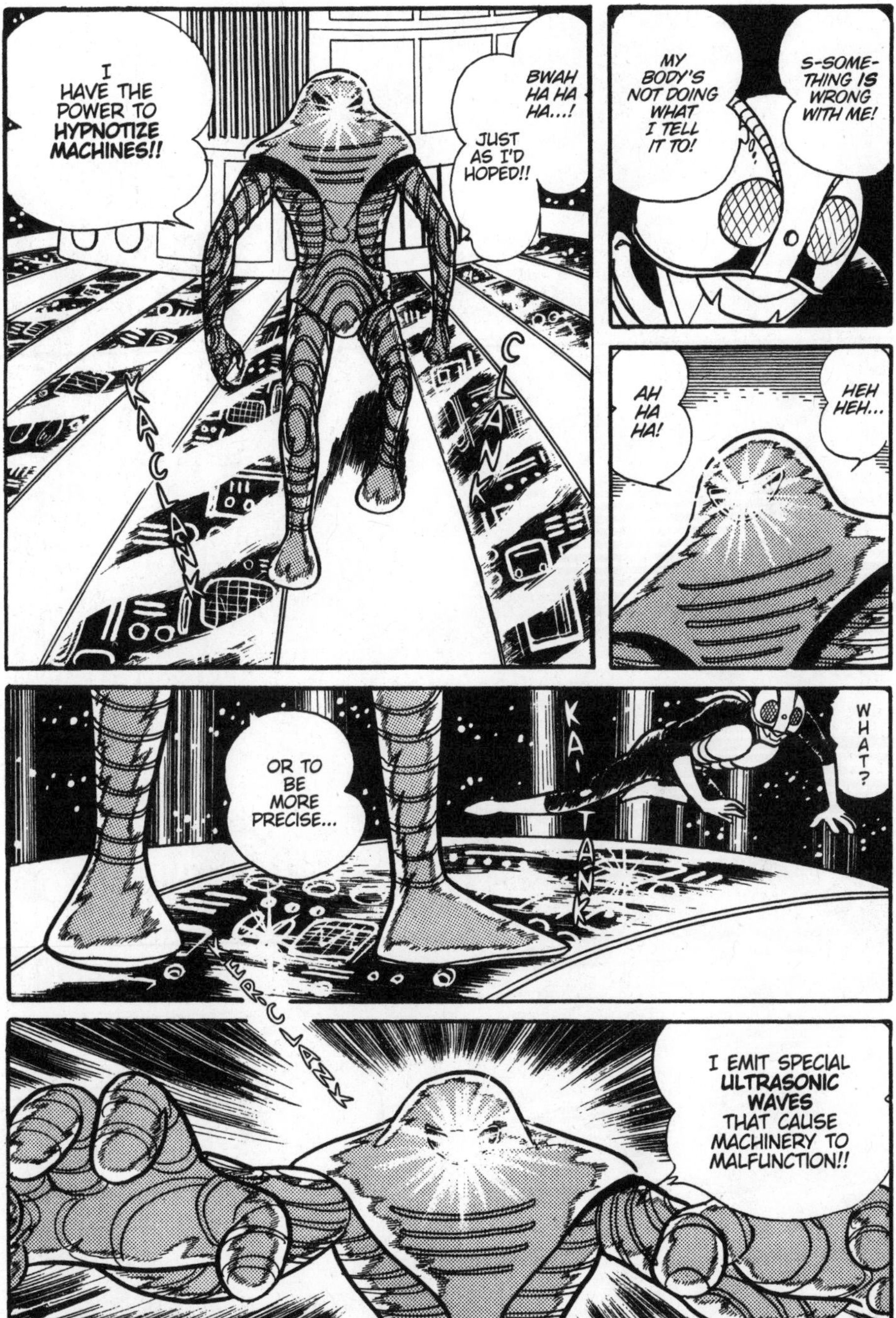
S-SOMETHING IS WRONG WITH ME!
MY BODY'S NOT DOING WHAT I TELL IT TO!
HEH HEH...
AH HA HA!
BWAH HA HA HA...!
JUST AS I'D HOPED!!
I HAVE THE POWER TO HYPNOTIZE MACHINES!!
CLANK
KA-CLANK
WHAT?
KA-TANK
OR TO BE MORE PRECISE...
KWR-CLAZZK
I EMIT SPECIAL ULTRASONIC WAVES THAT CAUSE MACHINERY TO MALFUNCTION!!

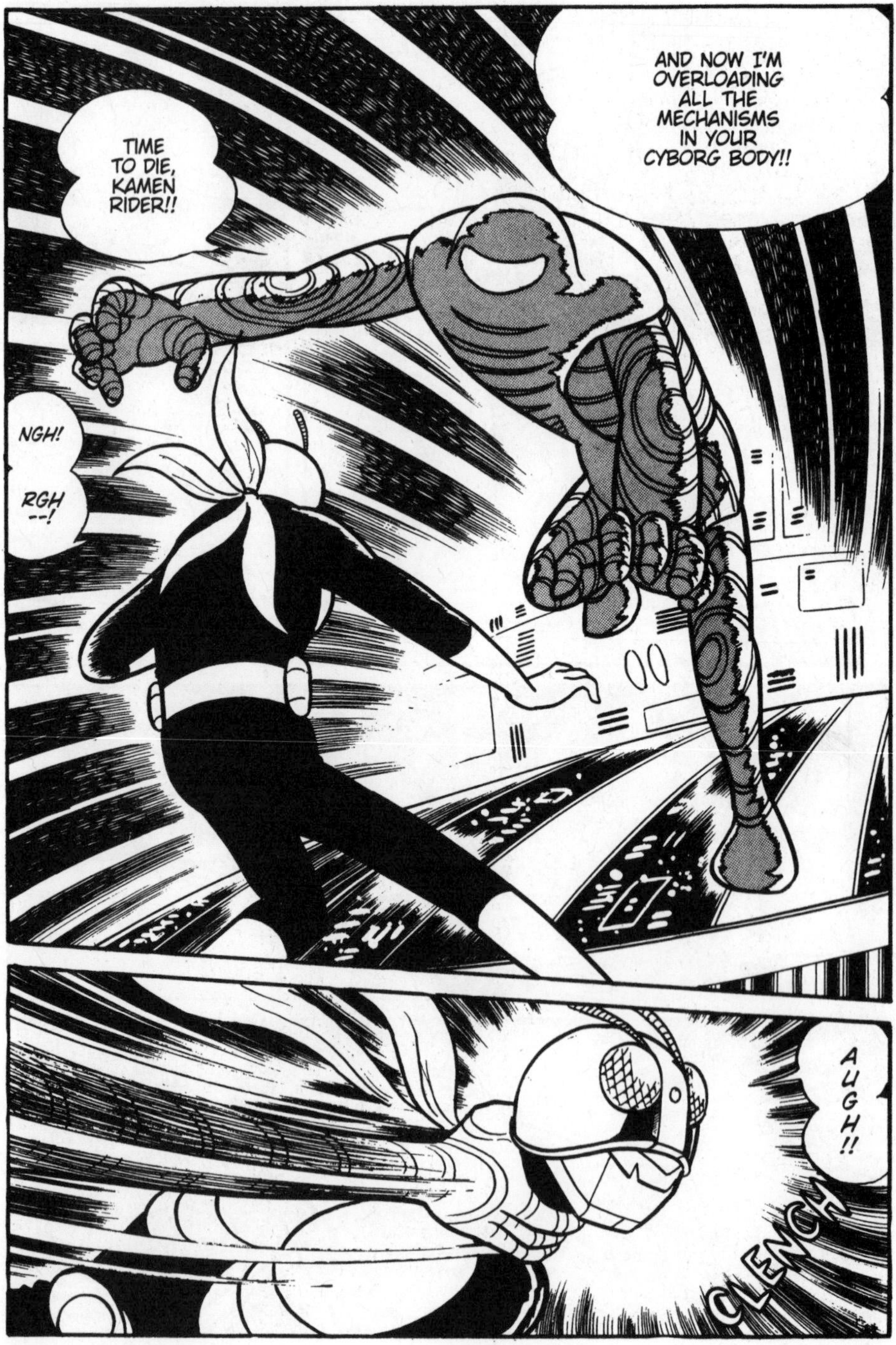
AND NOW I'M OVERLOADING ALL THE MECHANISMS IN YOUR CYBORG BODY!!
TIME TO DIE, KAMEN RIDER!!
NGH!
RGH --!
AUGH!!
CLENCH

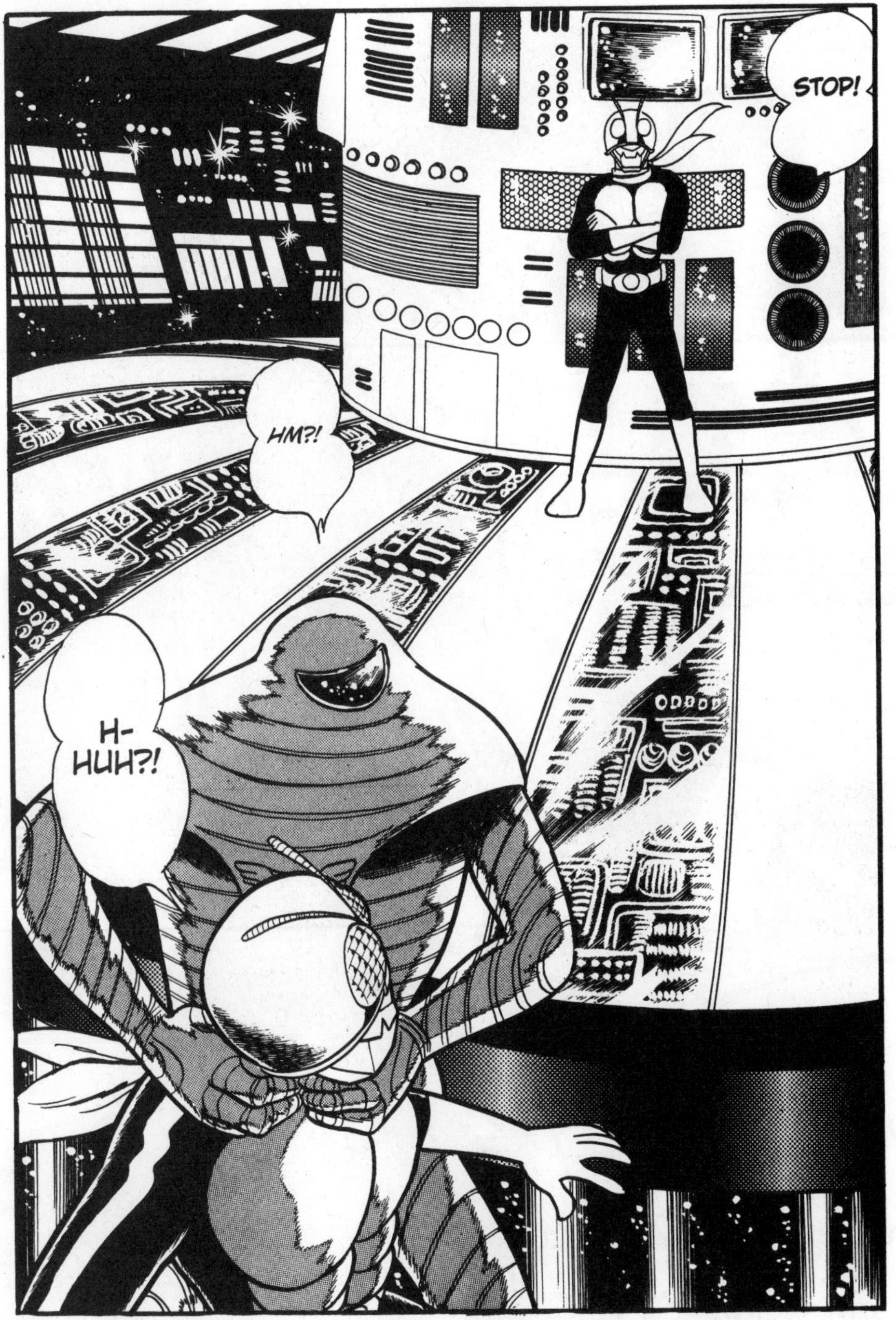
STOP!
HM?!
H-
HUH?!

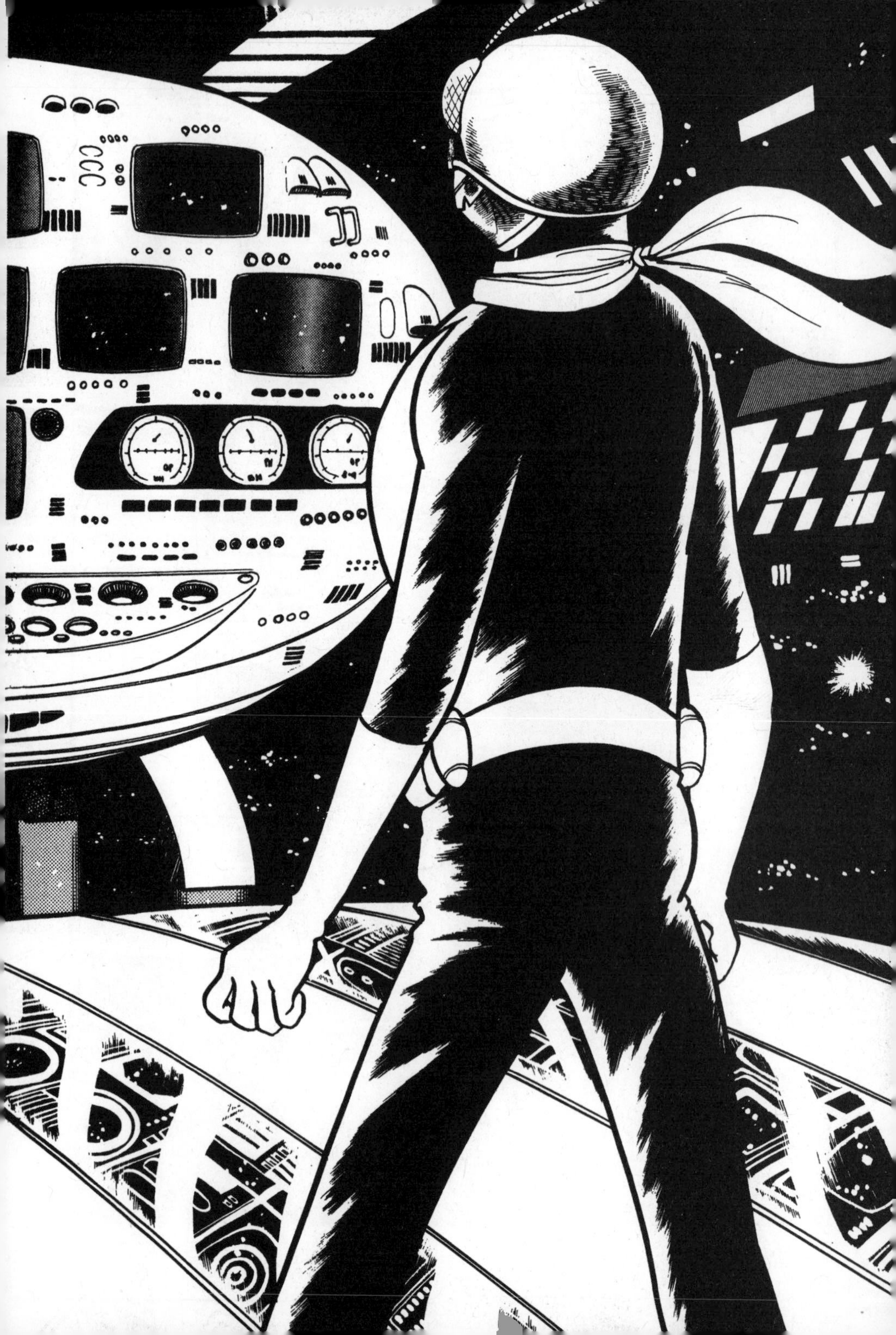

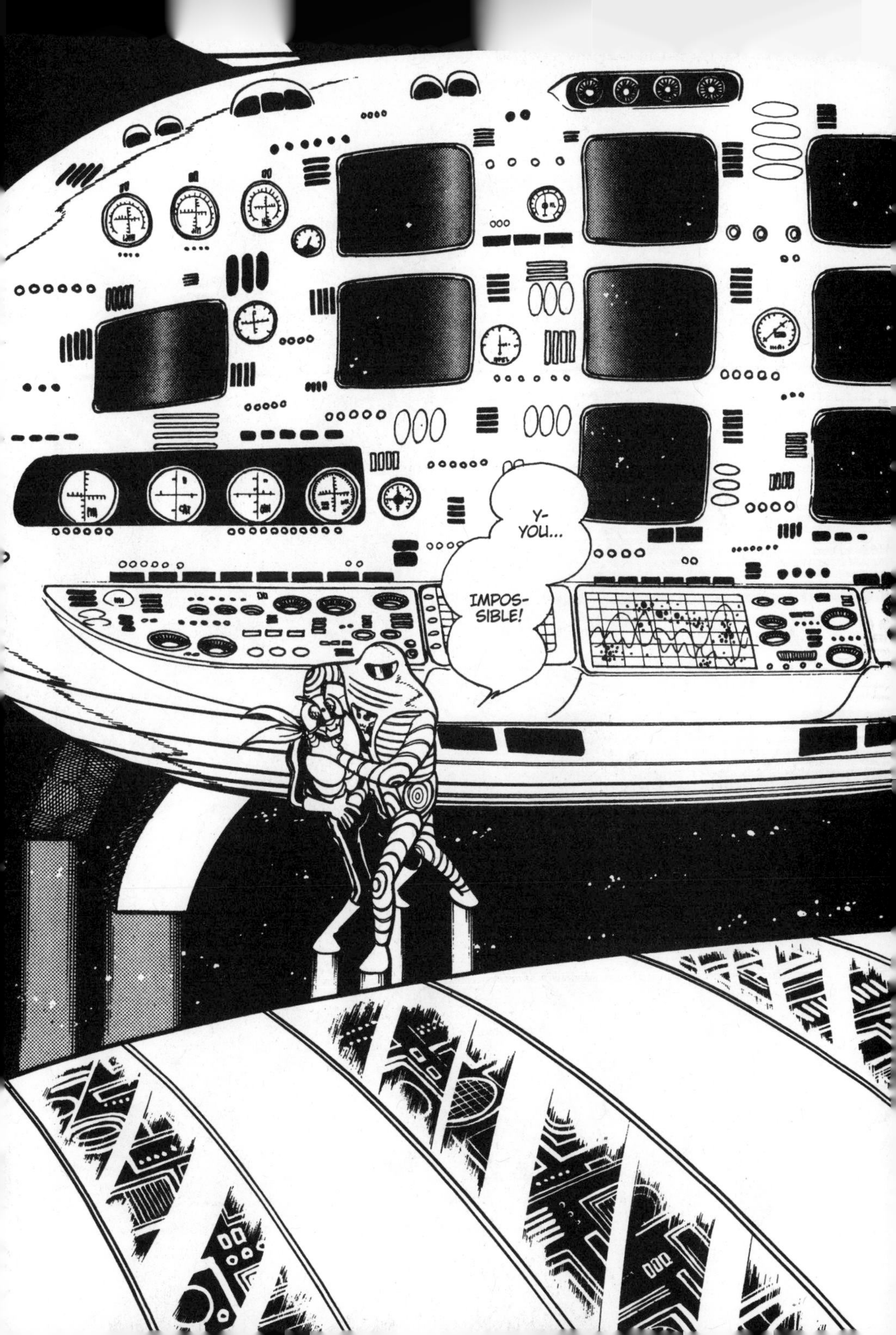
Y-
YOU...
IMPOS-
SIBLE!

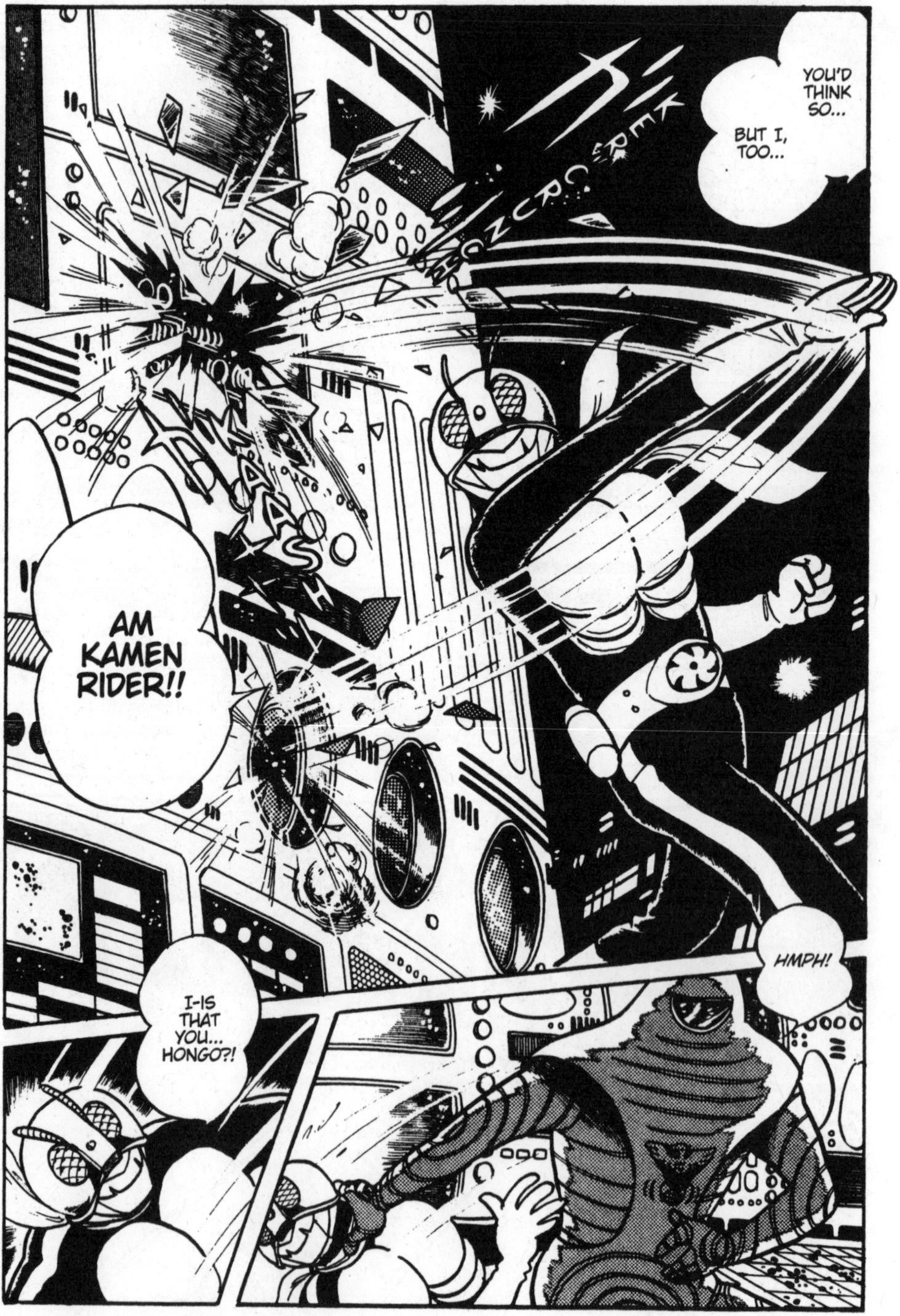
YOU'D THINK SO...
BUT I, TOO...
AM KAMEN RIDER!!
HMPH!
I-IS THAT YOU... HONGO?!

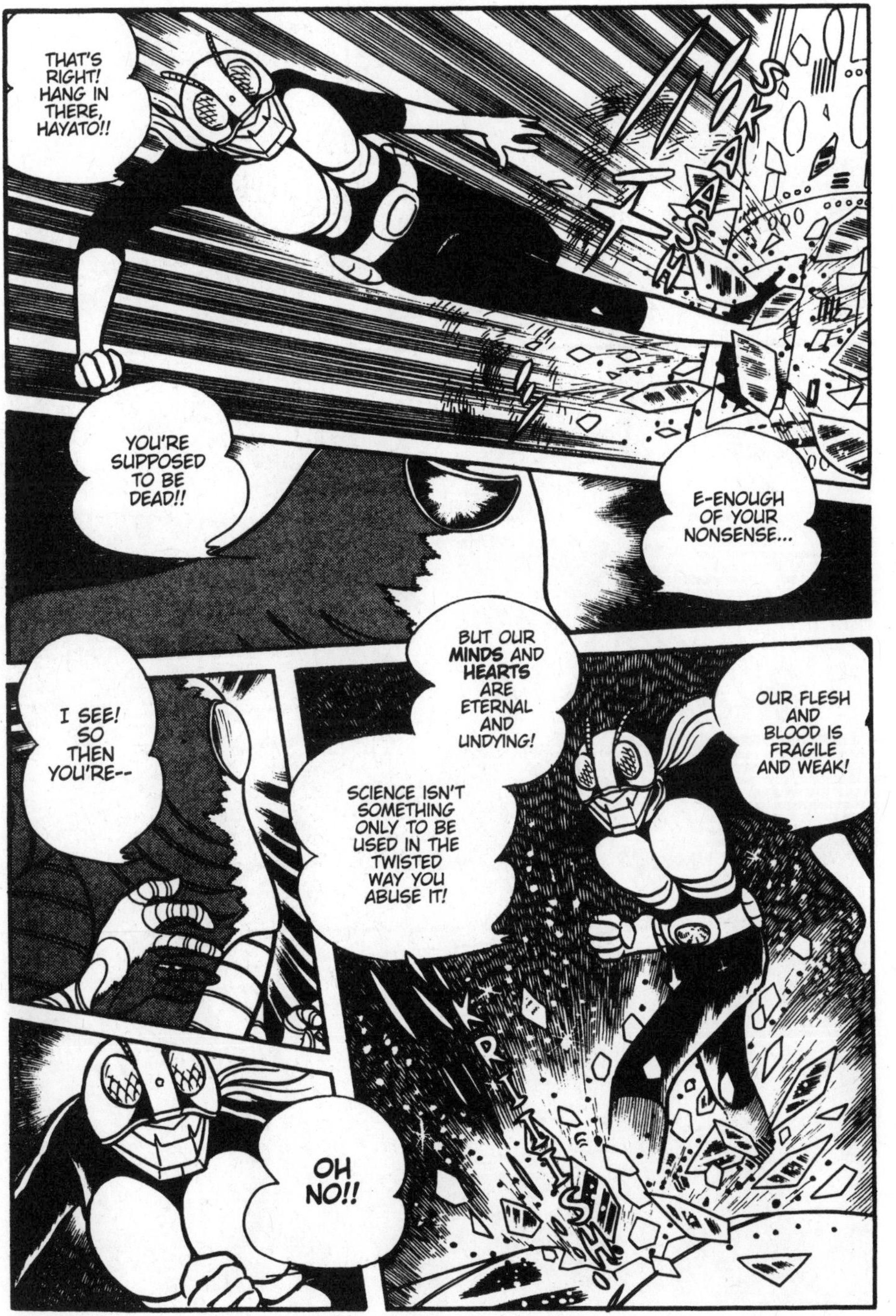
THAT'S RIGHT! HANG IN THERE, HAYATO!!
SKAASH
E-ENOUGH OF YOUR NONSENSE...
YOU'RE SUPPOSED TO BE DEAD!!
OUR FLESH AND BLOOD IS FRAGILE AND WEAK!
BUT OUR **MINDS** AND **HEARTS** ARE ETERNAL AND UNDYING!
SCIENCE ISN'T SOMETHING ONLY TO BE USED IN THE TWISTED WAY YOU ABUSE IT!
KRIIISH
I SEE! SO THEN YOU'RE--
OH NO!!

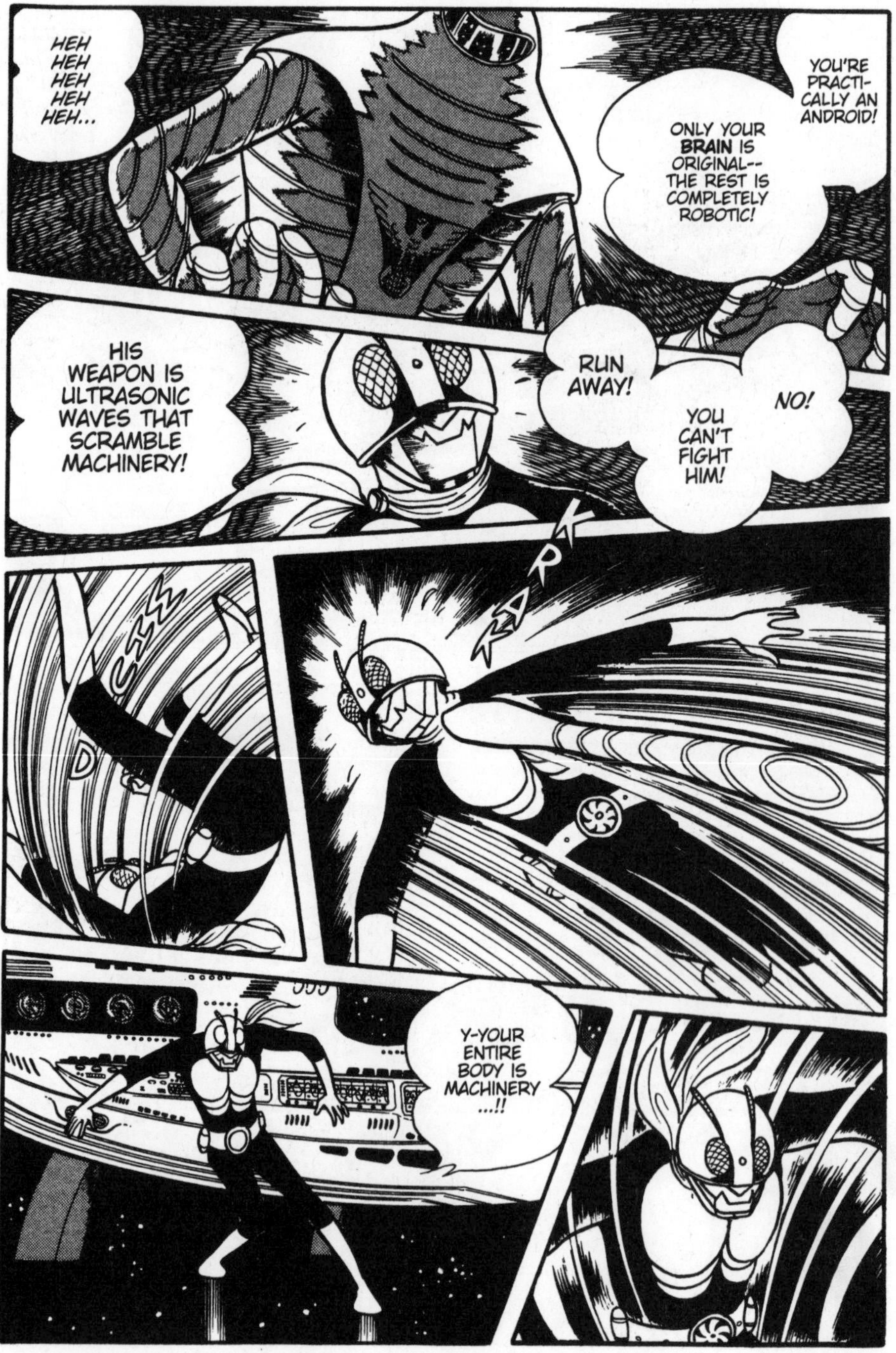
YOU'RE PRACTI-CALLY AN ANDROID!
ONLY YOUR **BRAIN** IS ORIGINAL-- THE REST IS COMPLETELY ROBOTIC!
HEH HEH HEH HEH HEH...
NO!
RUN AWAY!
YOU CAN'T FIGHT HIM!
HIS WEAPON IS ULTRASONIC WAVES THAT SCRAMBLE MACHINERY!
KRAK
Y-YOUR ENTIRE BODY IS MACHINERY ...!!

HEH HEH...
HEH HEH HEH!
YOU'RE MY PUPPET!
IT'S NO USE RUNNING!!
CHIK

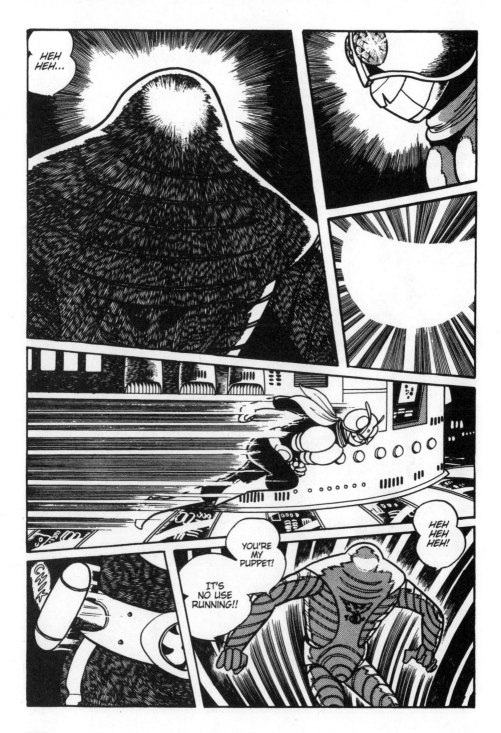

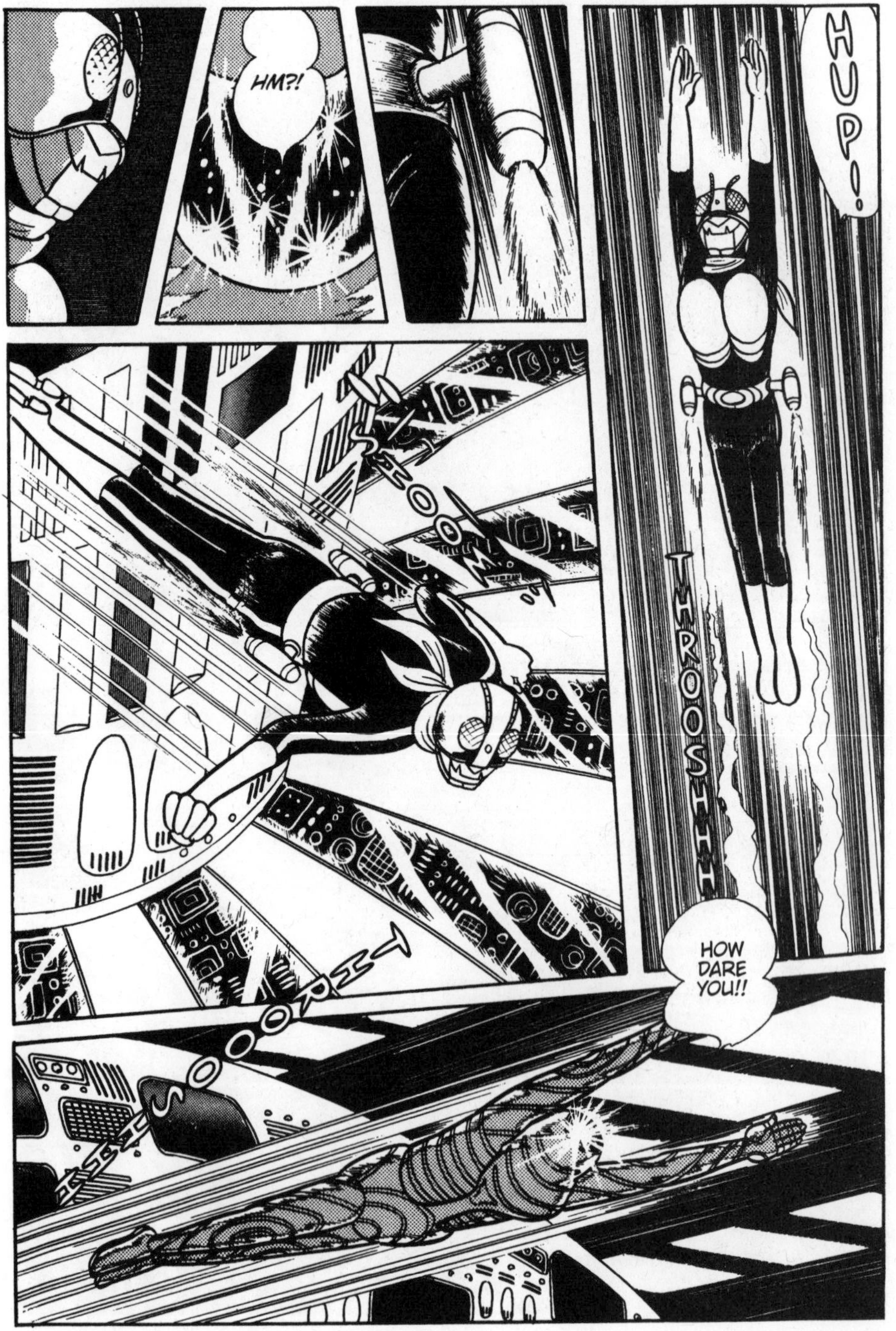
HUP!!
THROOSHHH
HM?!
SHOOOM
HOW DARE YOU!!
THROOOOSH

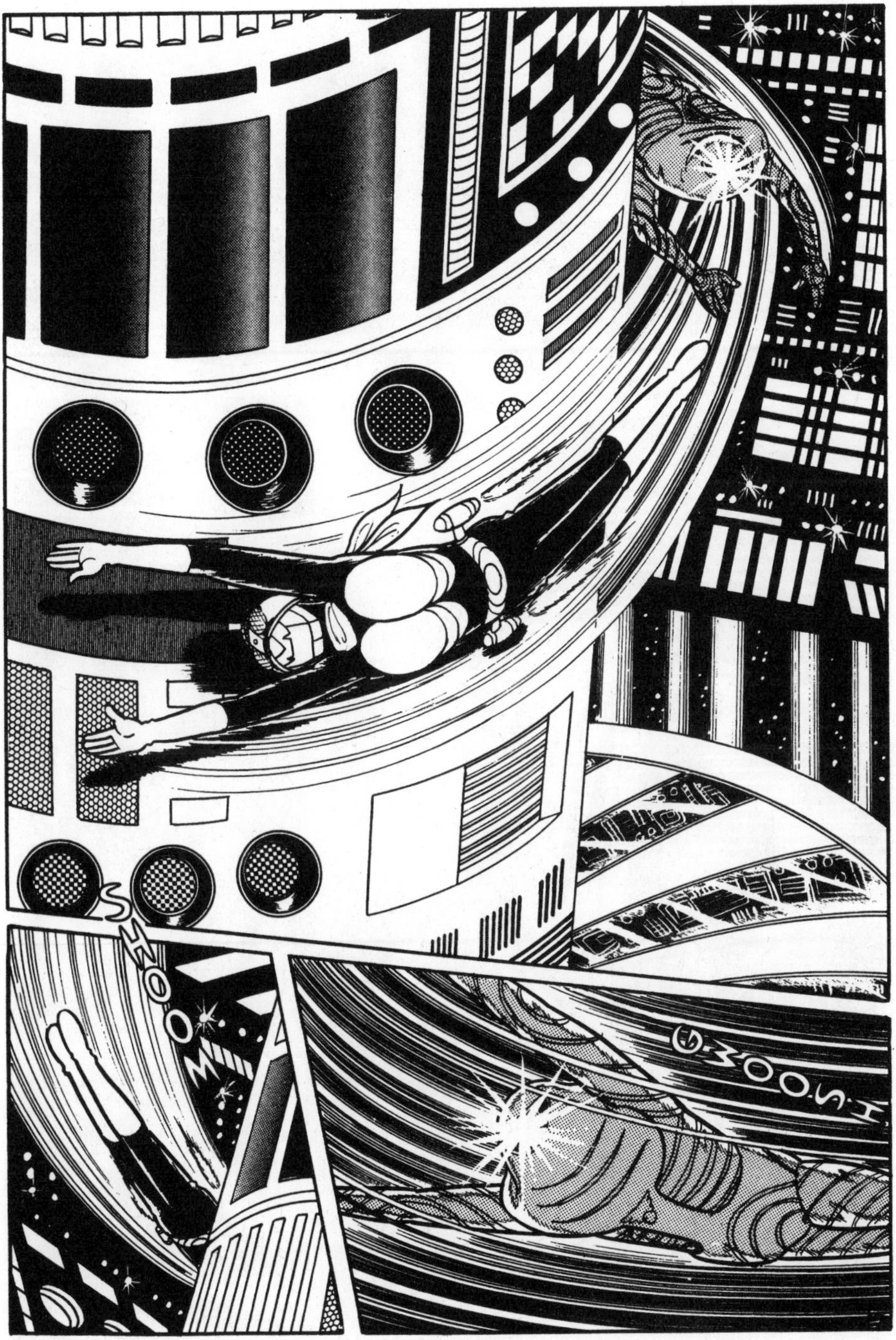
GZOOSH
SHOOOM

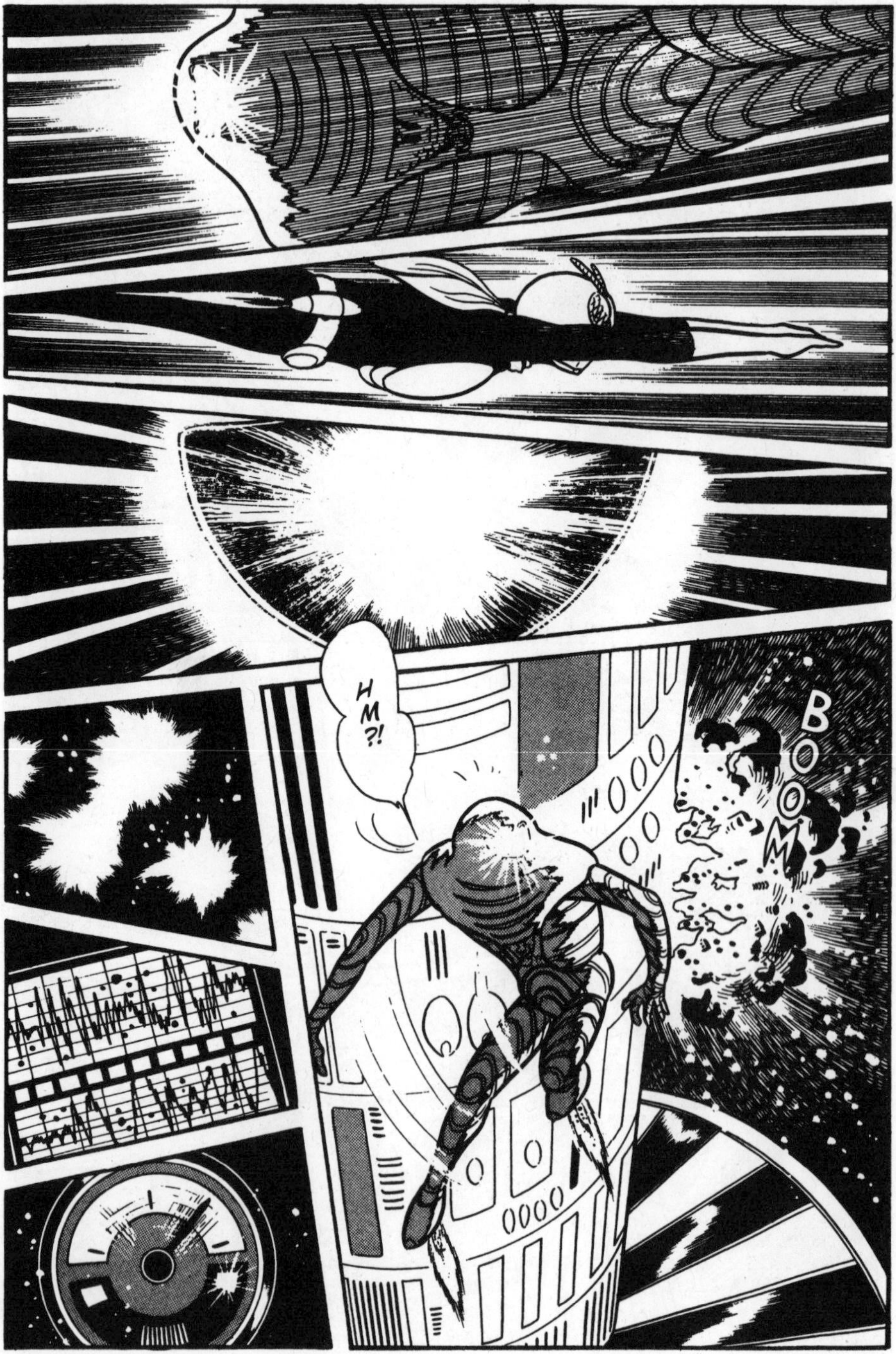
HM?!
BOOOM

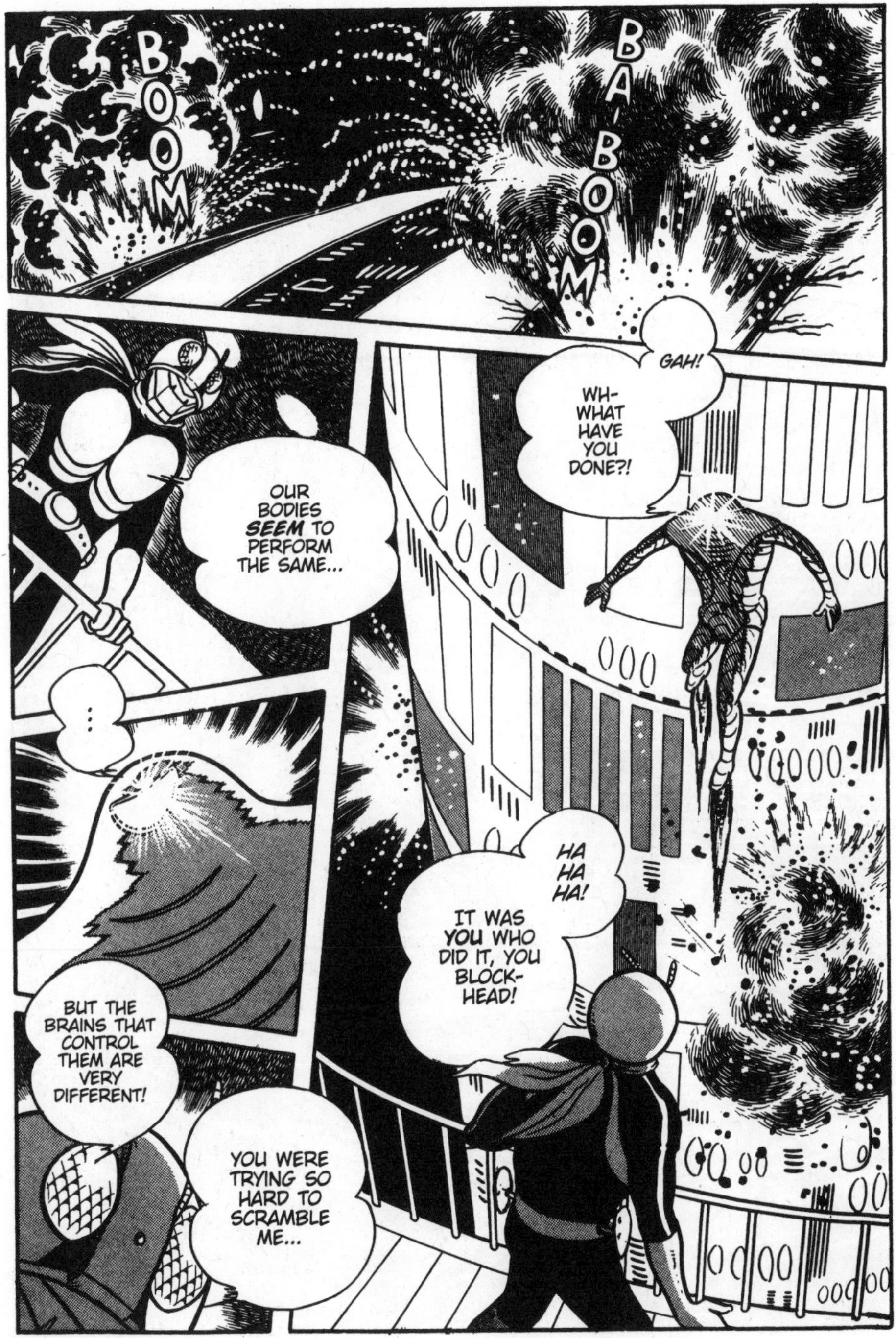
BA-BOOM
BOOM
GAH!
WH-WHAT HAVE YOU DONE?!
HA HA HA!
IT WAS YOU WHO DID IT, YOU BLOCK-HEAD!
OUR BODIES SEEM TO PERFORM THE SAME...
...
BUT THE BRAINS THAT CONTROL THEM ARE VERY DIFFERENT!
YOU WERE TRYING SO HARD TO SCRAMBLE ME...

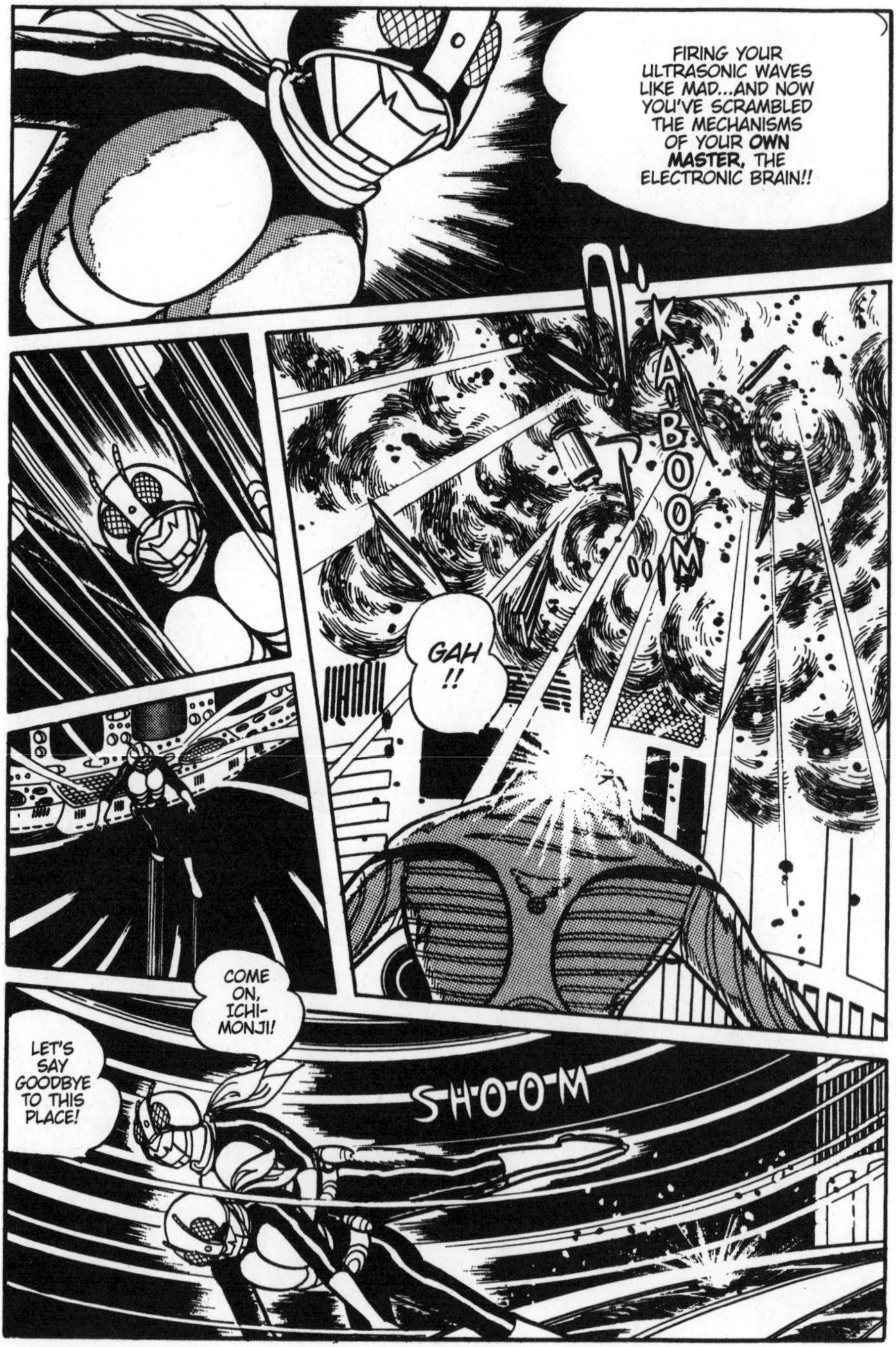
FIRING YOUR ULTRASONIC WAVES LIKE MAD...AND NOW YOU'VE SCRAMBLED THE MECHANISMS OF YOUR **OWN MASTER,** THE ELECTRONIC BRAIN!!
KABOOOM
GAH !!
COME ON, ICHI-MONJI!
LET'S SAY GOODBYE TO THIS PLACE!
SHOOM

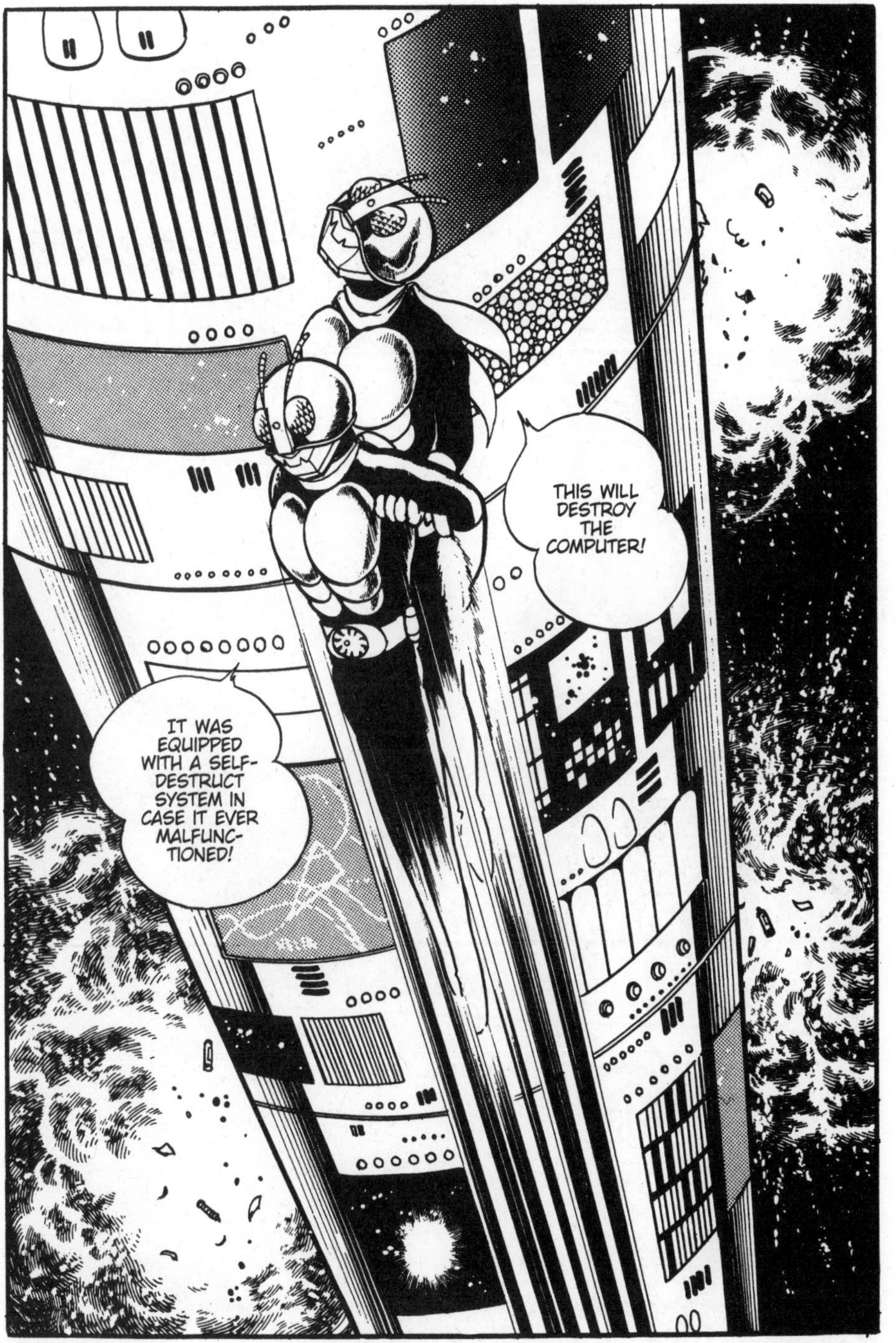
THIS WILL DESTROY THE COMPUTER!
IT WAS EQUIPPED WITH A SELF-DESTRUCT SYSTEM IN CASE IT EVER MALFUNCTIONED!

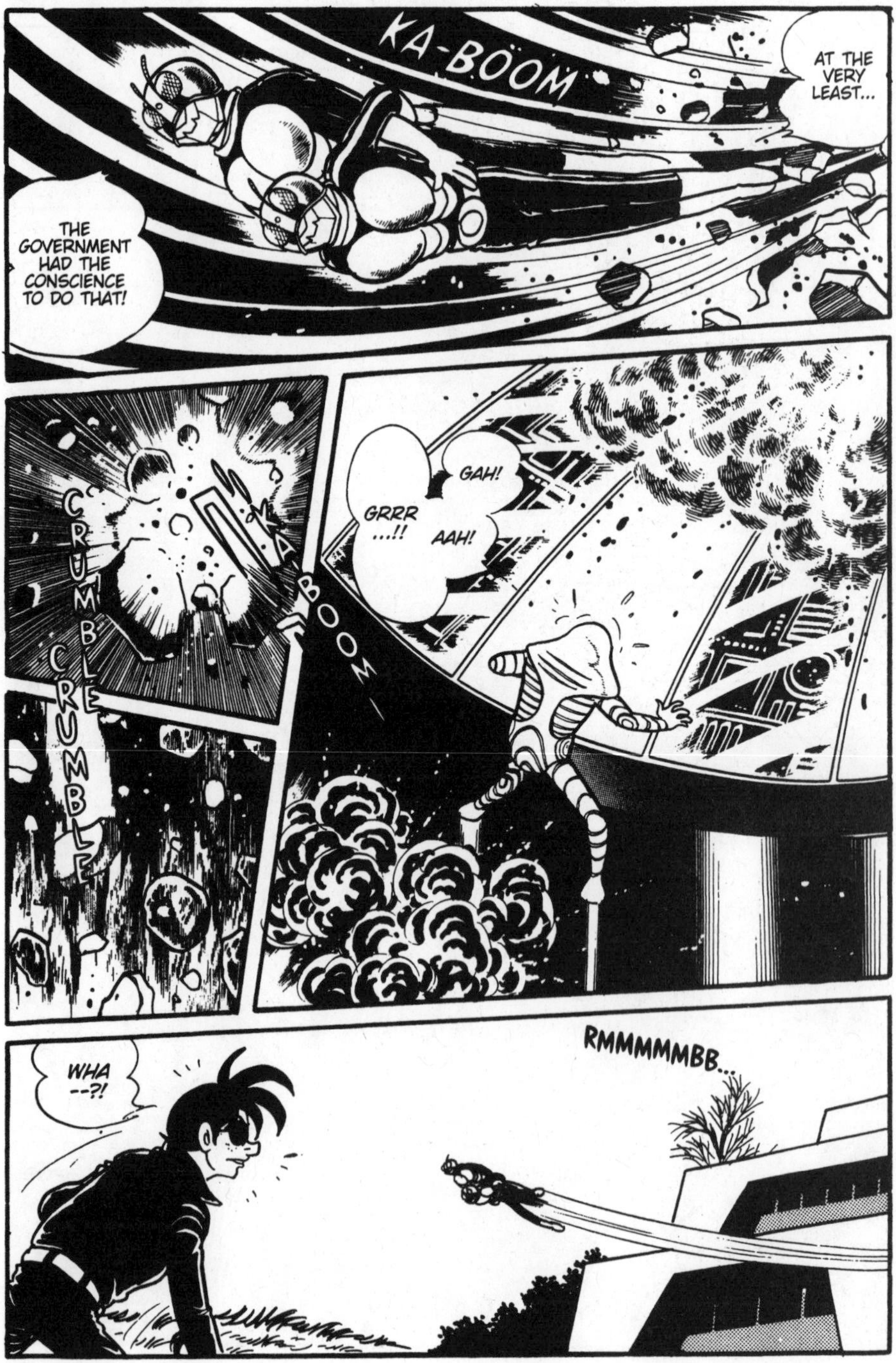
KA-BOOM
AT THE VERY LEAST...
THE GOVERNMENT HAD THE CONSCIENCE TO DO THAT!
GAH!
GRRR ...!!
AAH!
KA-BOOM
CRUMBLE
CRUMBLE
RMMMMMBB...
WHA --?!

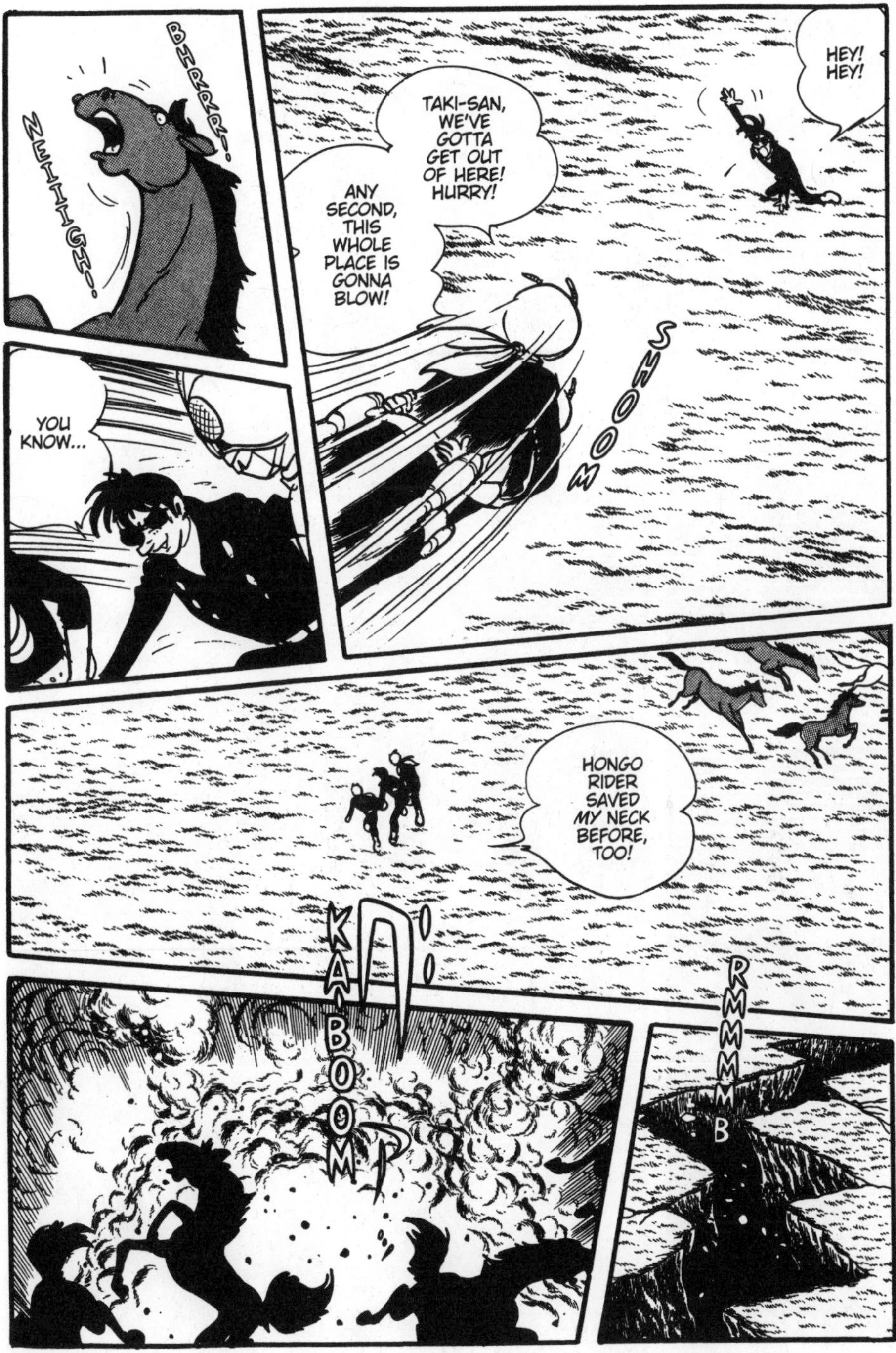
HEY! HEY!
TAKI-SAN, WE'VE GOTTA GET OUT OF HERE! HURRY!
ANY SECOND, THIS WHOLE PLACE IS GONNA BLOW!
SHOOOM
BHRRRR!
NEIIIGH!
YOU KNOW...
HONGO RIDER SAVED MY NECK BEFORE, TOO!
RMMMMB
KA-BOOM

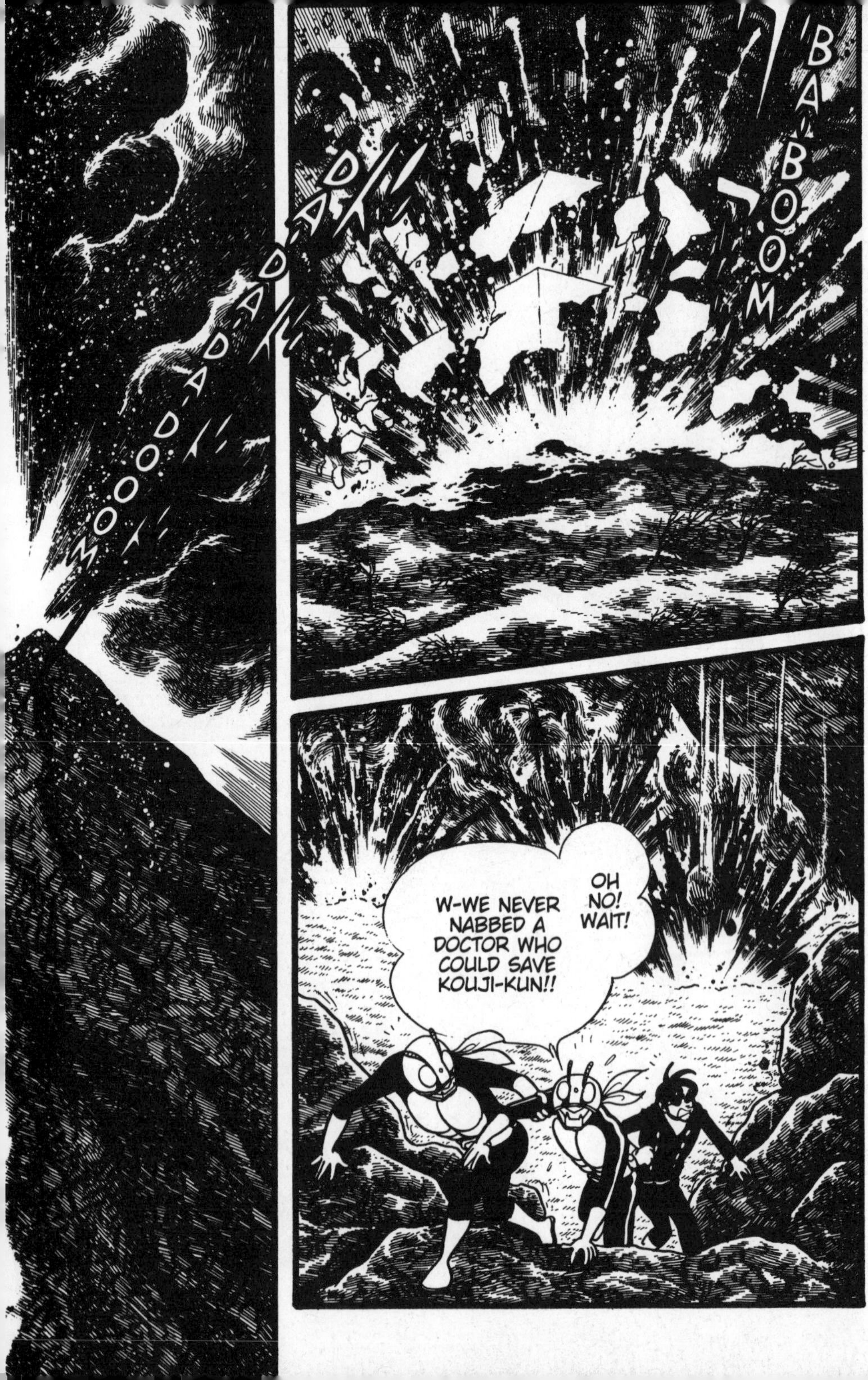
BA-BOOM
OH NO! WAIT!
W-WE NEVER NABBED A DOCTOR WHO COULD SAVE KOUJI-KUN!!
DA-DA-DA-DOOOM

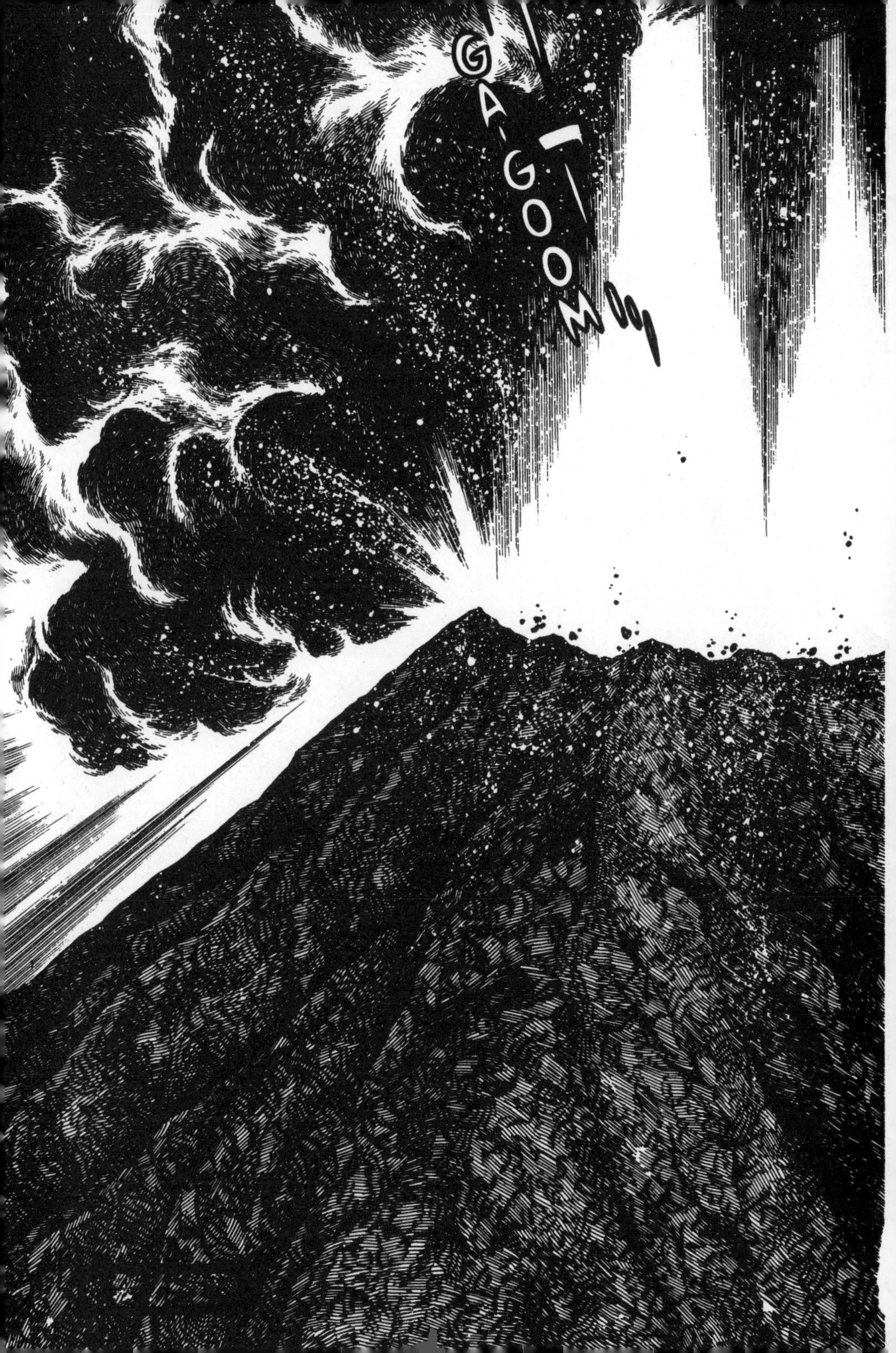
GA-GOOOM

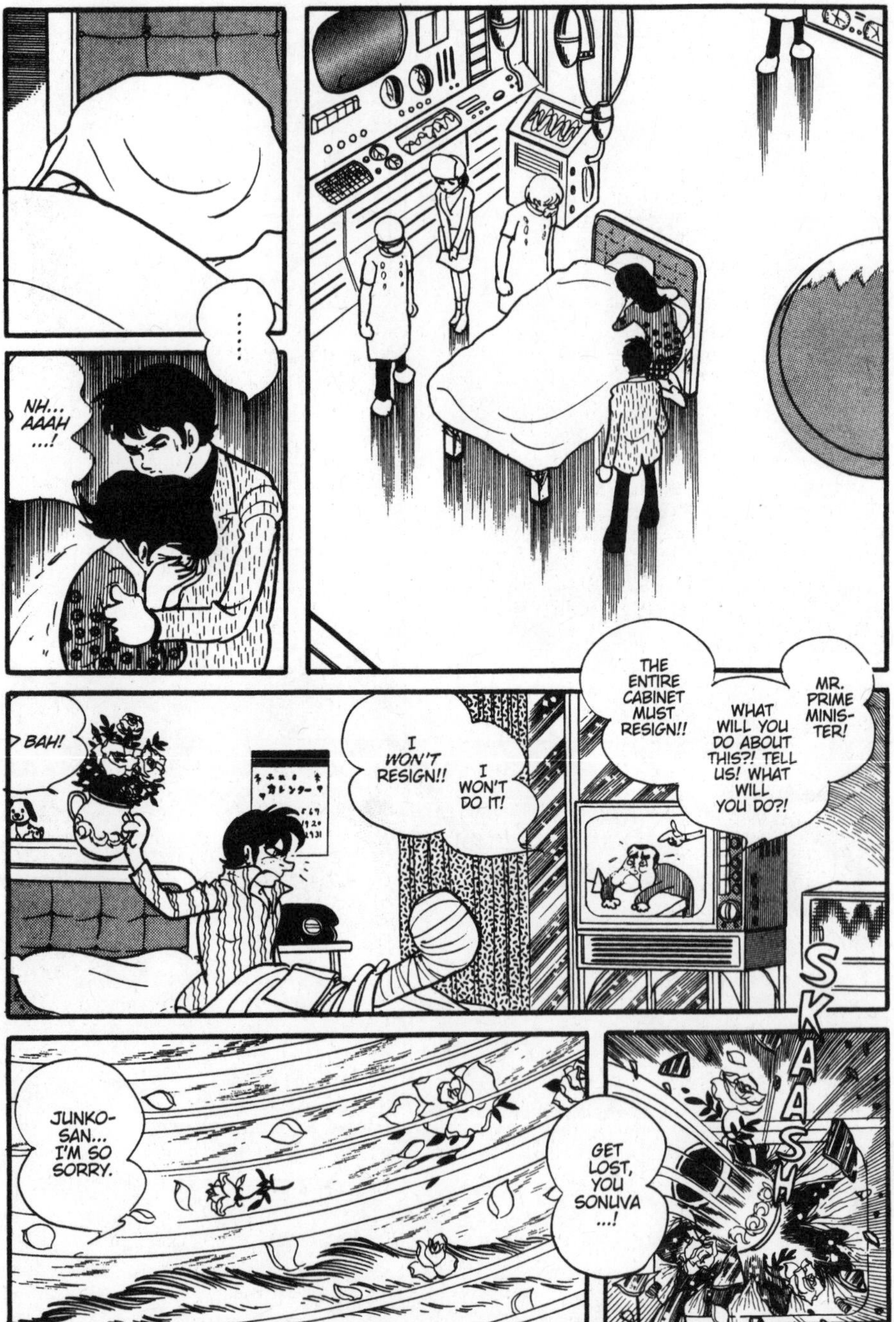
......
NH... AAAH ...!
MR. PRIME MINISTER!
WHAT WILL YOU DO ABOUT THIS?! TELL US! WHAT WILL YOU DO?!
THE ENTIRE CABINET MUST RESIGN!!
I WON'T DO IT!
I *WON'T* RESIGN!!
BAH!
SKAASH
GET LOST, YOU SONUVA ...!
JUNKO-SAN... I'M SO SORRY.

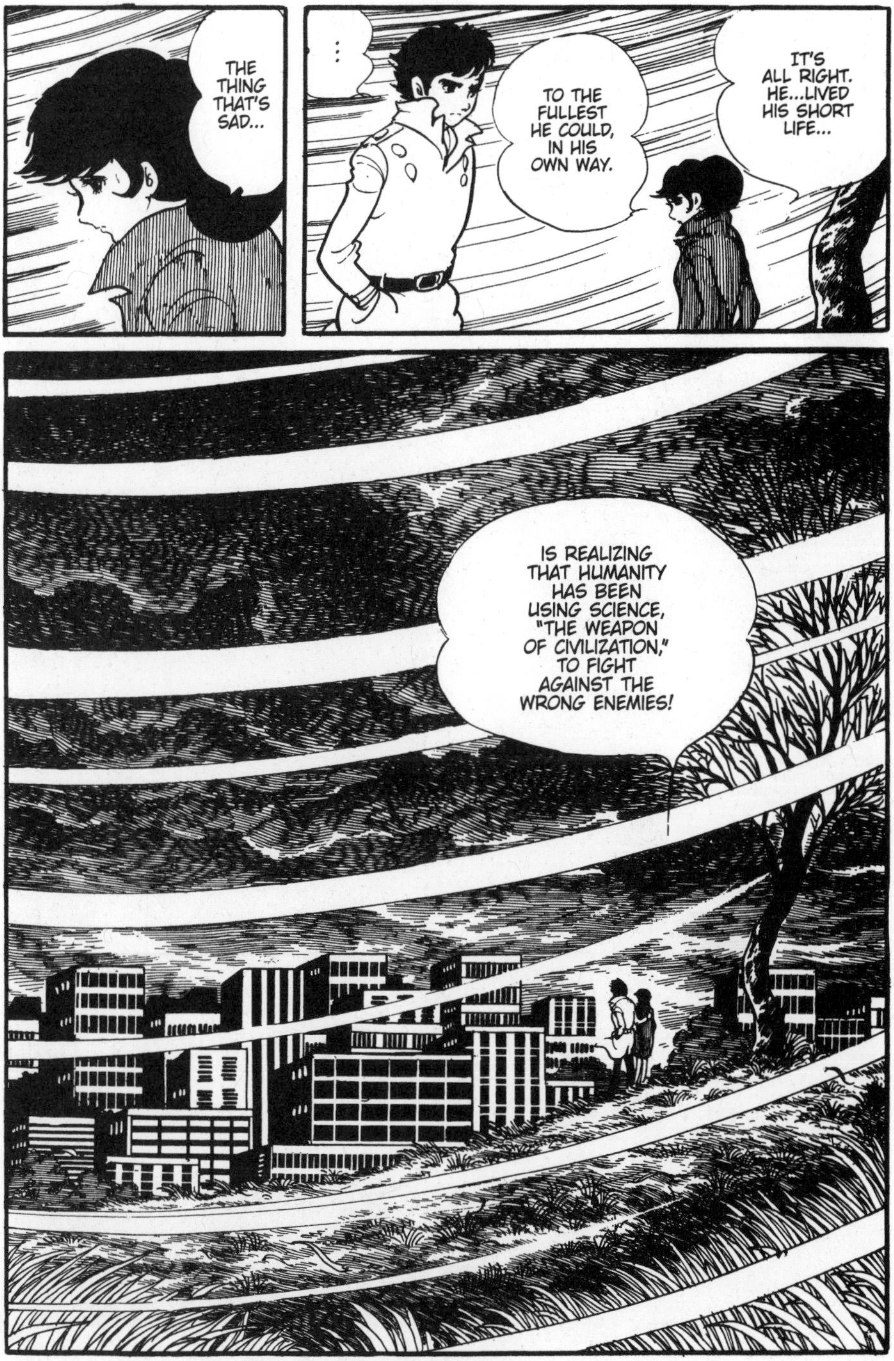
IT'S ALL RIGHT. HE...LIVED HIS SHORT LIFE...
TO THE FULLEST HE COULD, IN HIS OWN WAY.
...
THE THING THAT'S SAD...
IS REALIZING THAT HUMANITY HAS BEEN USING SCIENCE, "THE WEAPON OF CIVILIZATION," TO FIGHT AGAINST THE WRONG ENEMIES!

THE END

KAMEN RIDER

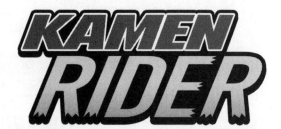

KAMEN RIDER
Illustration Collection

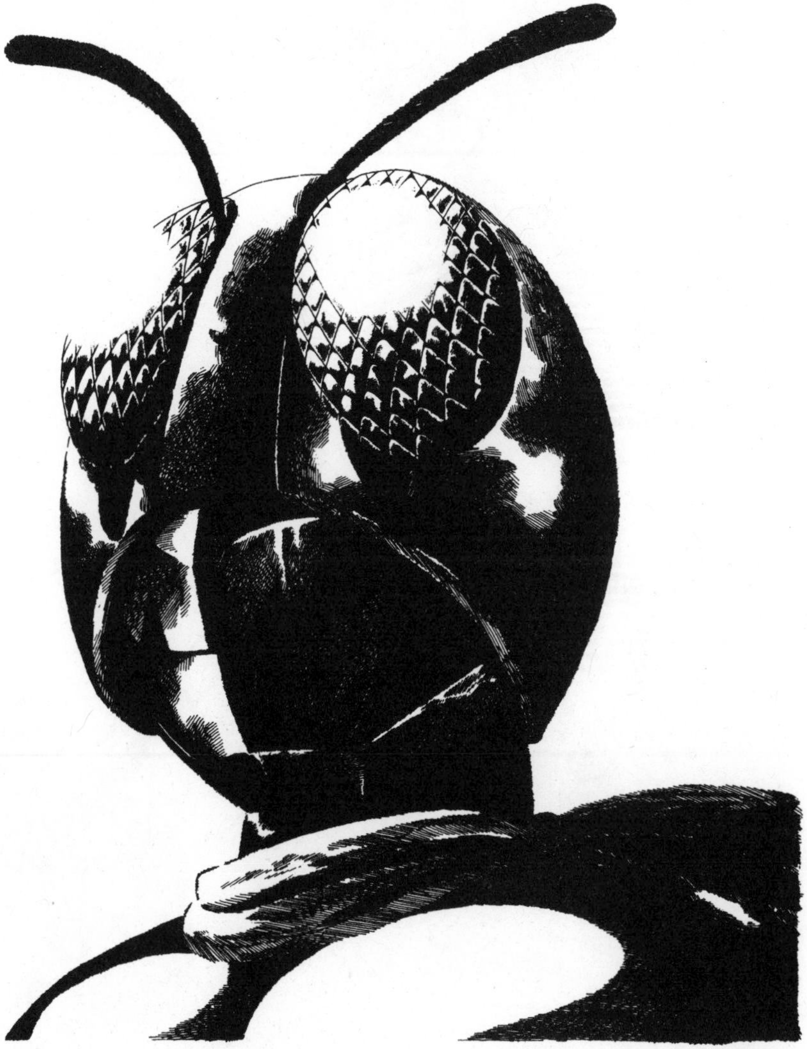

***Shuukan Bokura Magazine* 1971 Issue 16's cover illustration.**
This issue marked the first installment of *Kamen Rider*'s manga serialization.
The cover illustration made a powerful impression on readers.

Three cover illustrations done for the *Sun Comics* editions from Asahi Sonorama (1972). When this book went on sale, the “New No. 1” version of *Kamen Rider* was appearing on TV, so these cover illustrations depict the New No. 1 version which does not appear in the manga.

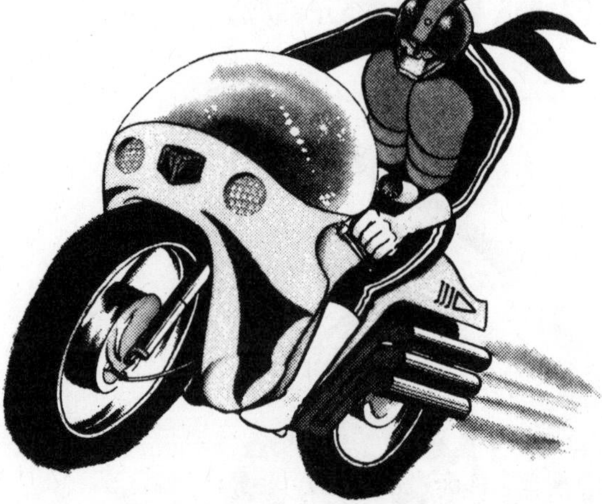

Second Volume Cover.

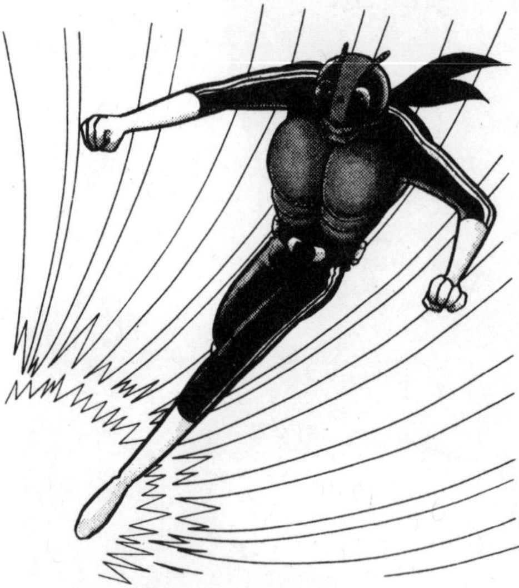

Third Volume Cover.

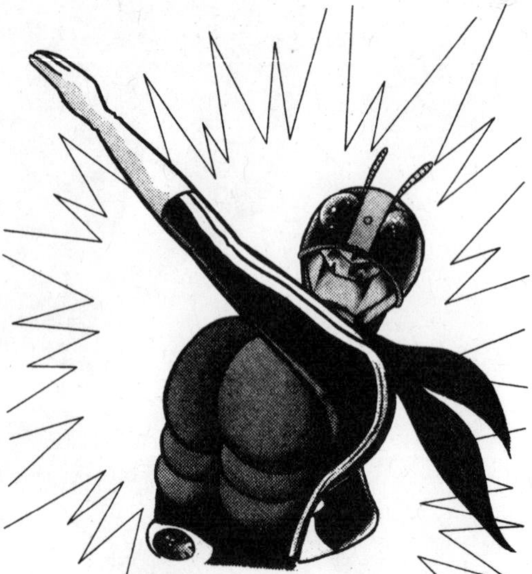

Fourth Volume Cover.

KAMEN RIDER

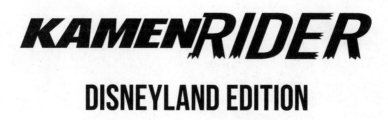

DISNEYLAND EDITION

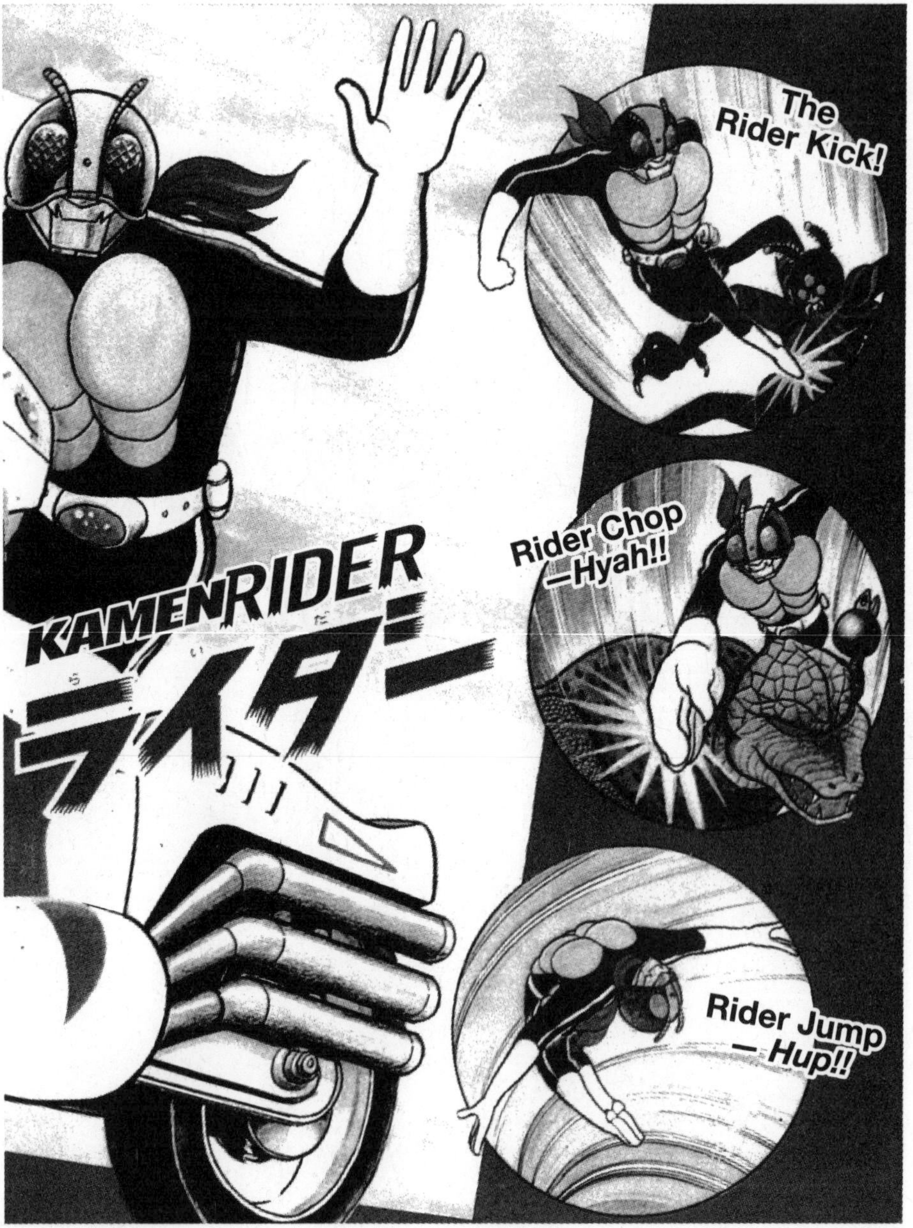
The Rider Kick!
Rider Chop —Hyah!!
Rider Jump — Hup!!
KAMENRIDER
ライダー

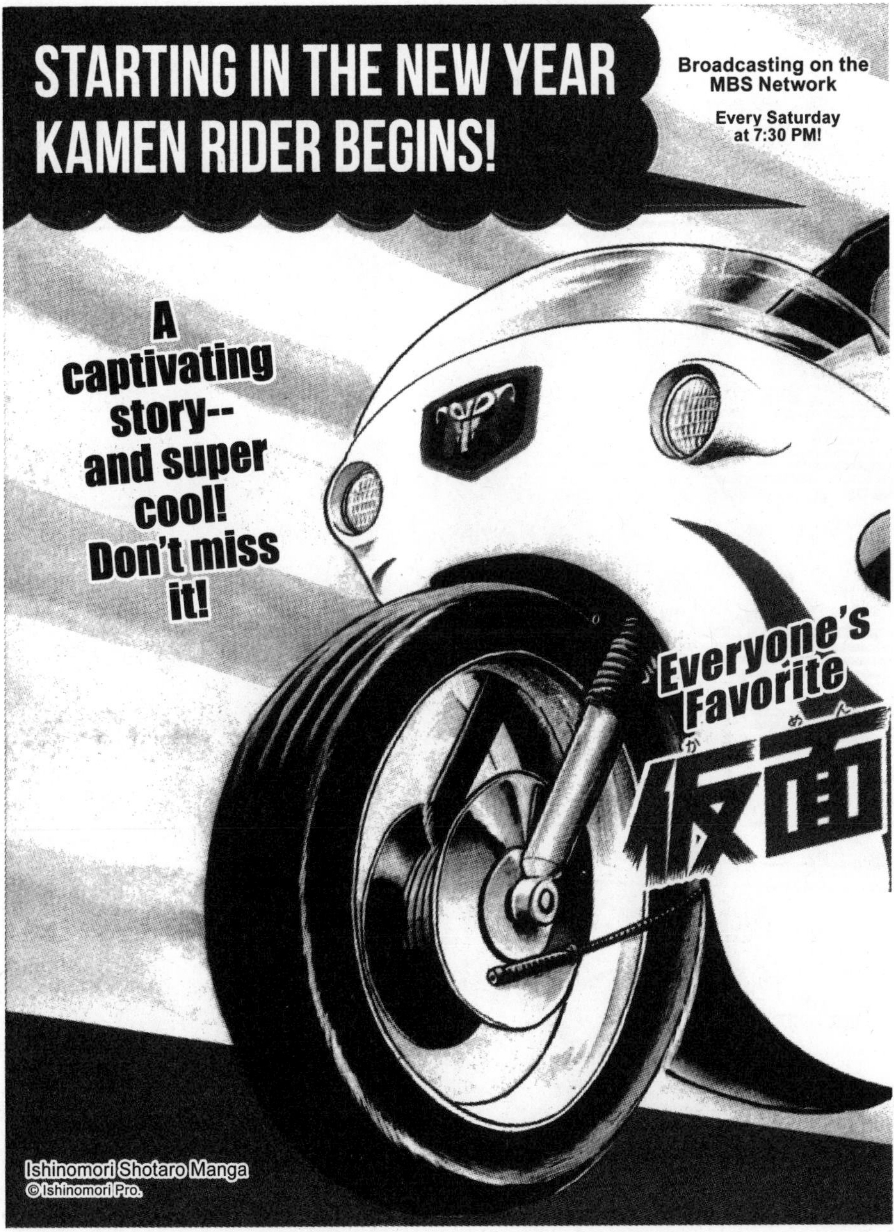
STARTING IN THE NEW YEAR
KAMEN RIDER BEGINS!
Broadcasting on the MBS Network
Every Saturday at 7:30 PM!
A captivating story-- and super cool! Don't miss it!
Everyone's Favorite
仮面
Ishinomori Shotaro Manga
© Ishinomori Pro.

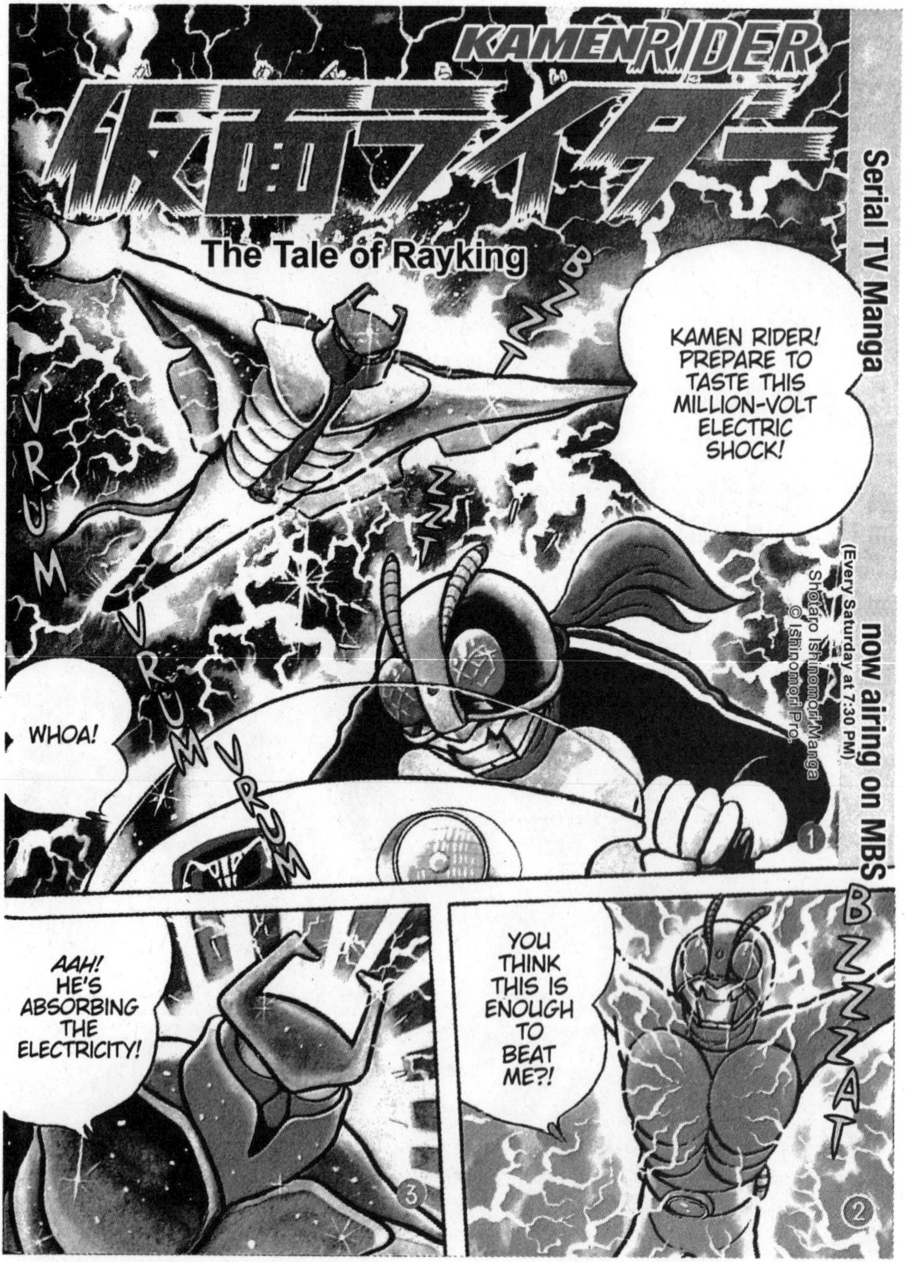
KAMEN RIDER
仮面ライダー
The Tale of Rayking
Serial TV Manga now airing on MBS
(Every Saturday at 7:30 PM)
Shotaro Ishinomori Manga
© Ishinomori Pro.
BZZZT
KAMEN RIDER! PREPARE TO TASTE THIS MILLION-VOLT ELECTRIC SHOCK!
ZZZT
VRUM
VRUM
VRUM
WHOA!
BZZZZAT
YOU THINK THIS IS ENOUGH TO BEAT ME?!
AAH! HE'S ABSORBING THE ELECTRICITY!

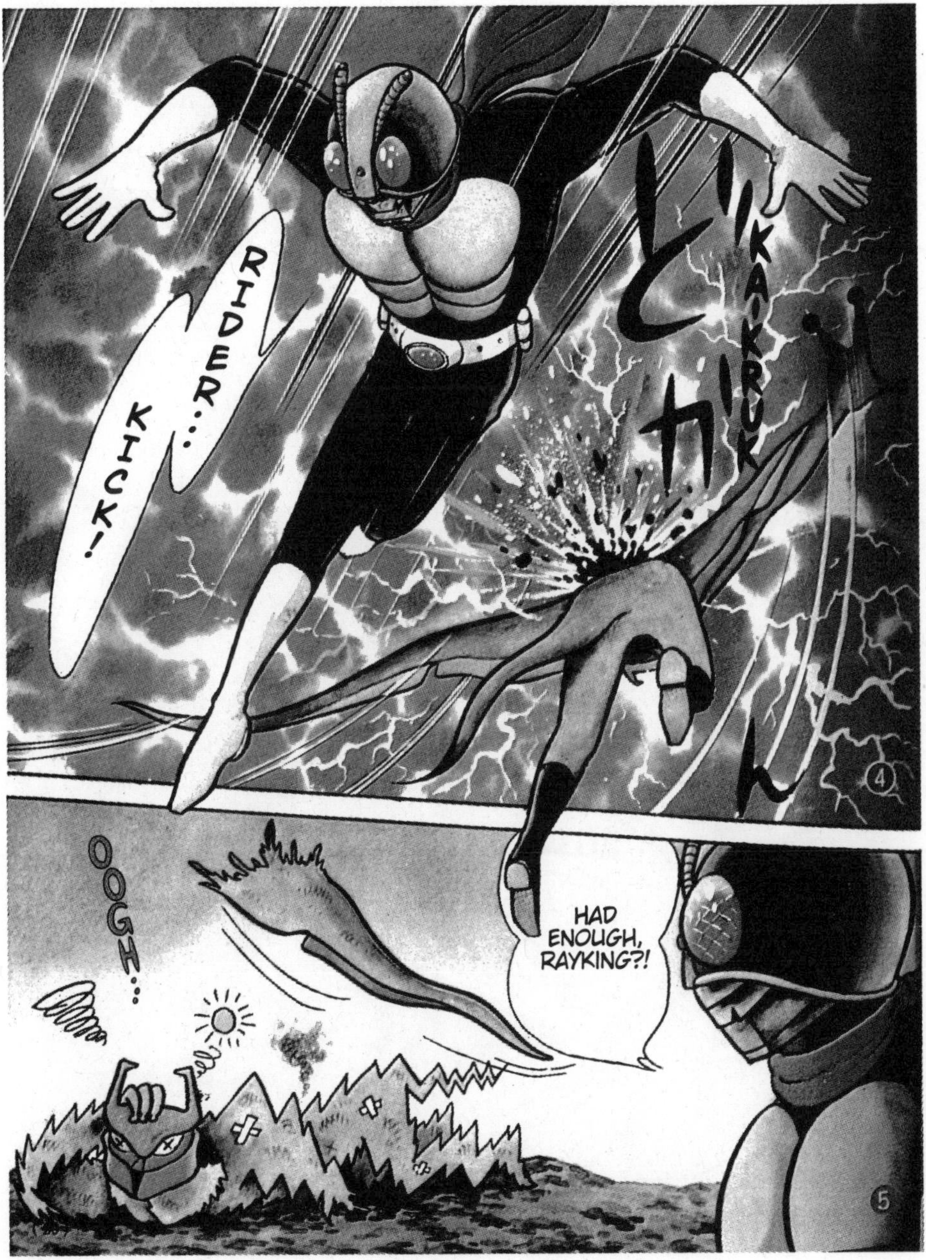
KAIKRUK
RIDER... KICK!
HAD ENOUGH, RAYKING?!
OOGH...

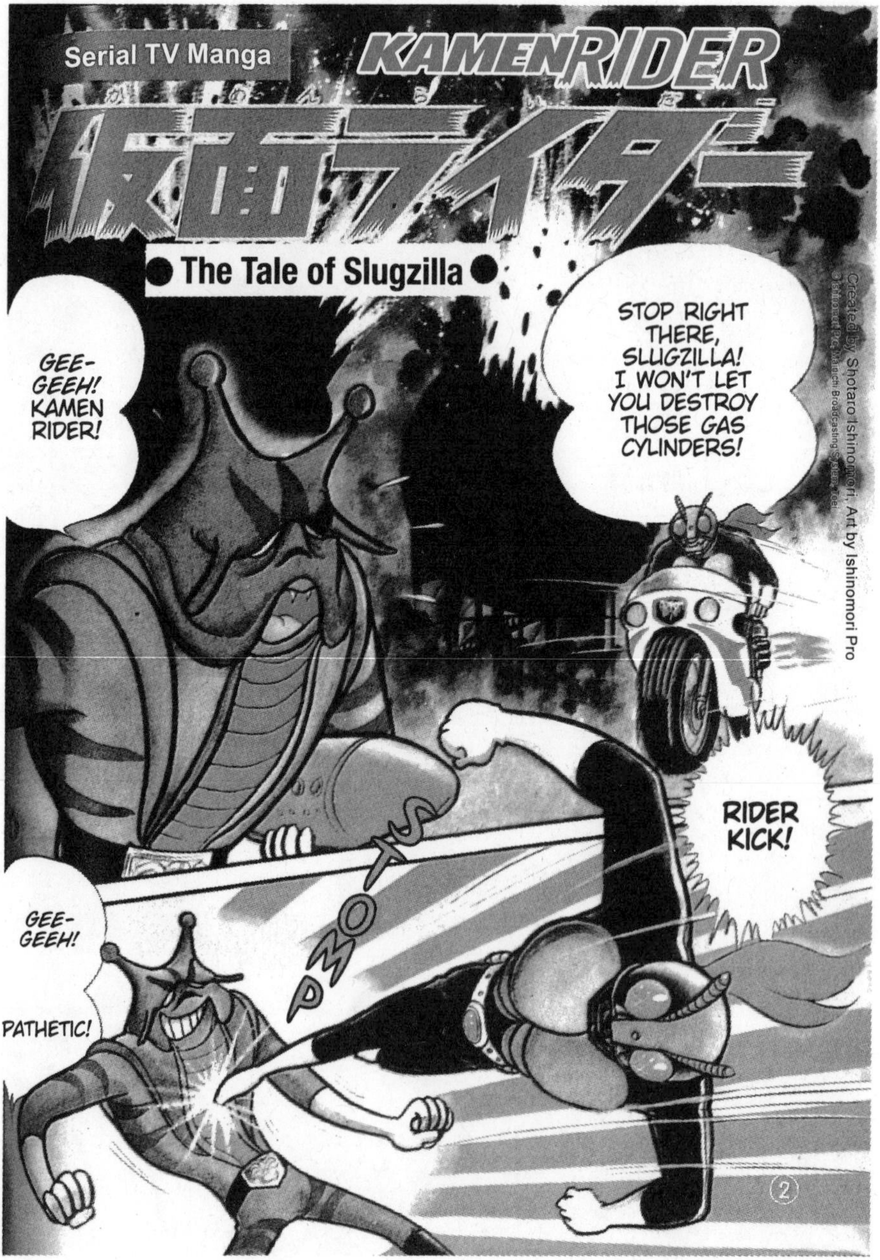
Serial TV Manga
KAMEN RIDER
仮面ライダー
● The Tale of Slugzilla ●
Created by Shotaro Ishinomori, Art by Ishinomori Pro
©Ishinomori Pro, Mainichi Broadcasting System, Toei
STOP RIGHT THERE, SLUGZILLA! I WON'T LET YOU DESTROY THOSE GAS CYLINDERS!
GEE-GEEH! KAMEN RIDER!
RIDER KICK!
STOMP
GEE-GEEH!
PATHETIC!
②

GLOOMP
I'LL LIQUIFY YOU WITH MY MONSTER ACID!
ACK!
NOT GOOD!
SALT
IN THAT CASE, I'LL JUST DISSOLVE *YOU* WITH **SALT!**
THOOSH
DEMONS OUT...
FORTUNE IN!
AAGH! I'M MELTING!

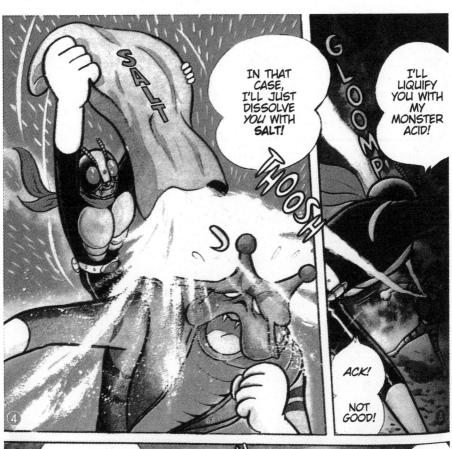

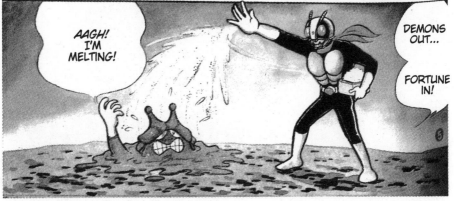

KAMEN RIDER

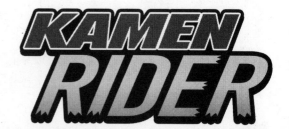

TANOSHII YOUCHIEN
(FUN KINDERGARTEN) EDITION

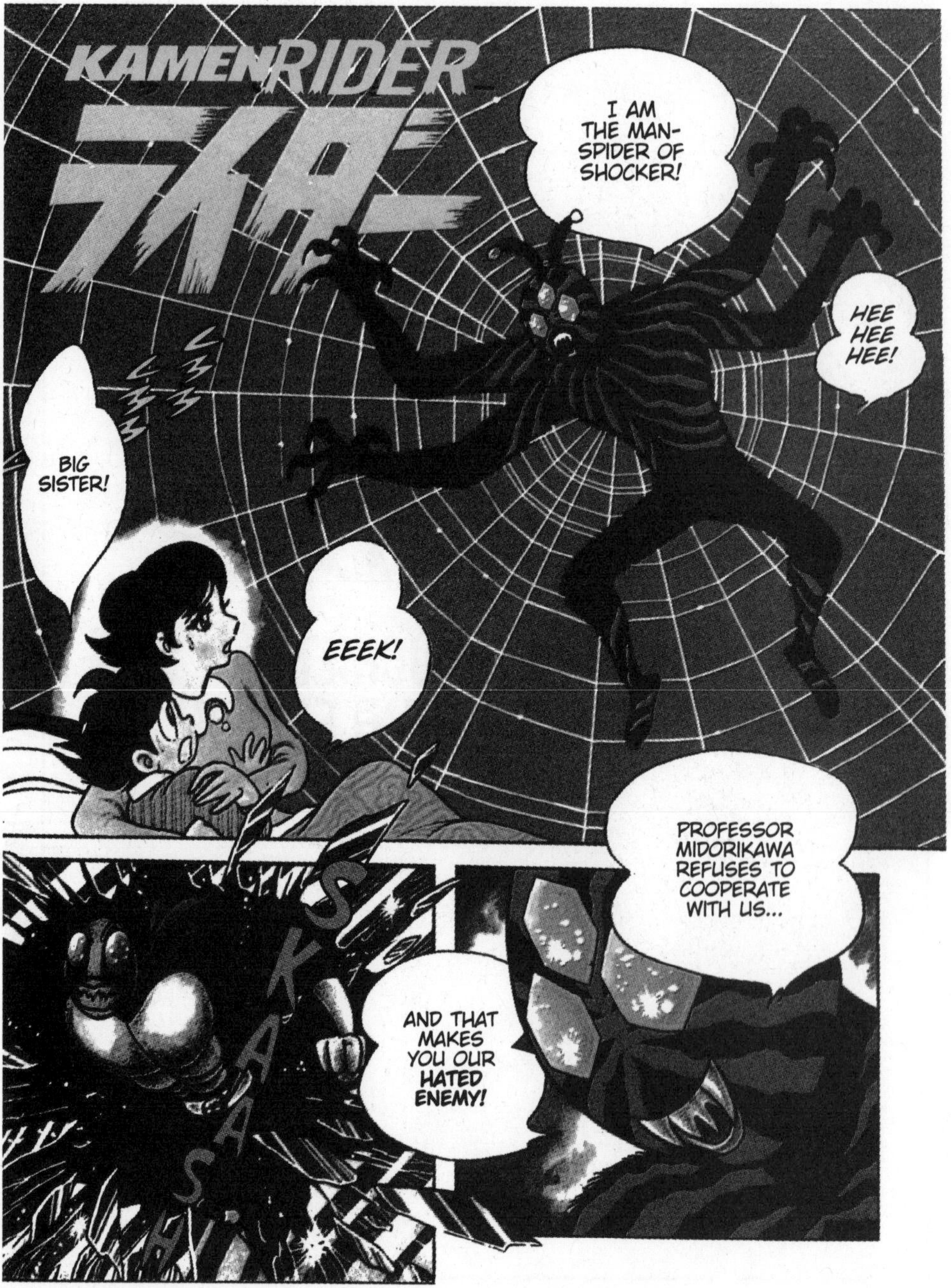
KAMEN RIDER
ライダー
I AM THE MAN-SPIDER OF SHOCKER!
HEE HEE HEE!
EEEK!
BIG SISTER!
PROFESSOR MIDORIKAWA REFUSES TO COOPERATE WITH US...
AND THAT MAKES YOU OUR HATED ENEMY!
SKAAASH

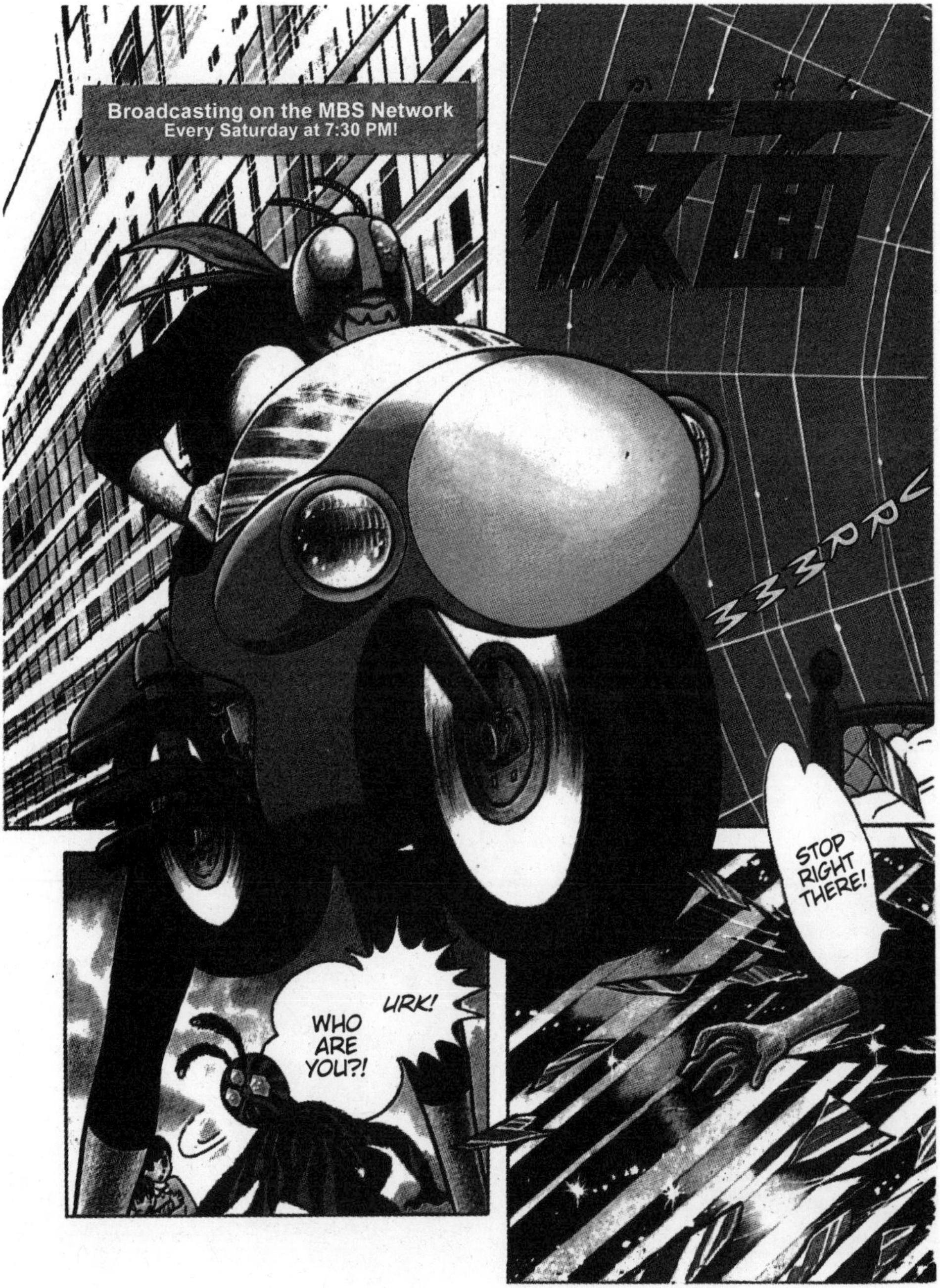
仮面
VRRRMMM
Broadcasting on the MBS Network
Every Saturday at 7:30 PM!
STOP RIGHT THERE!
URK!
WHO ARE YOU?!

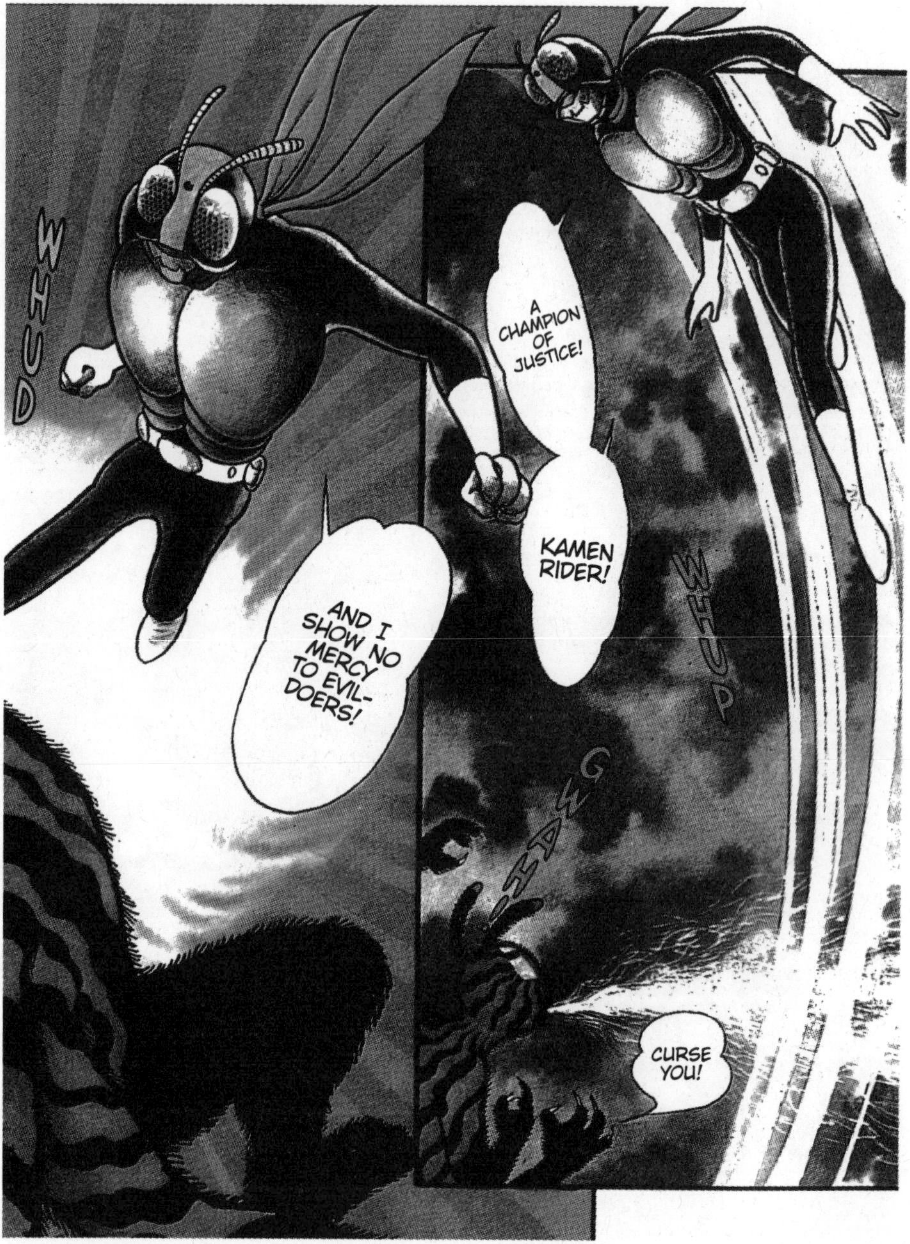
WHUP
A CHAMPION OF JUSTICE!
KAMEN RIDER!
GWAAH
CURSE YOU!
WHUD
AND I SHOW NO MERCY TO EVIL-DOERS!

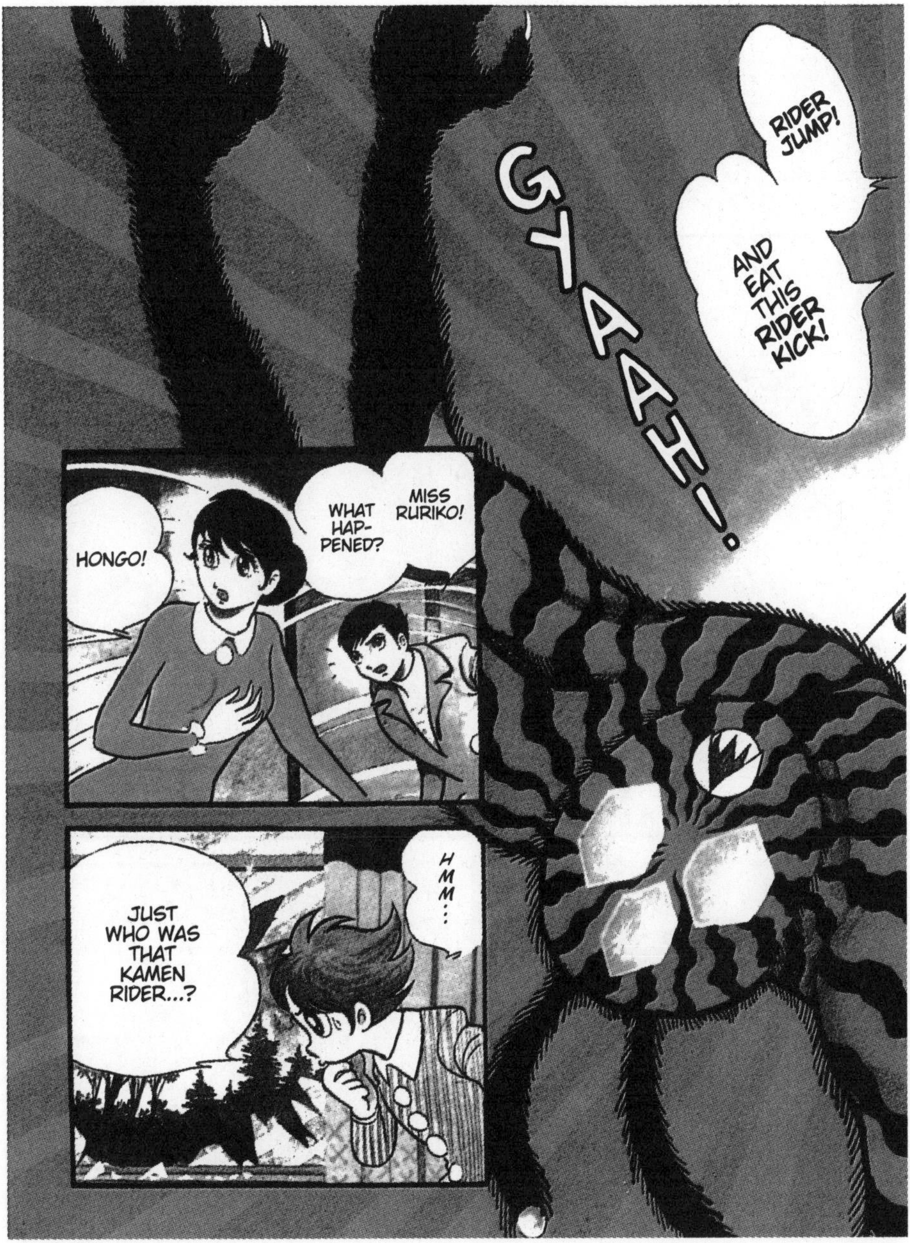
RIDER JUMP!
AND EAT THIS RIDER KICK!
GYAAH!!
MISS RURIKO!
WHAT HAP-PENED?
HONGO!
HMM...
JUST WHO WAS THAT KAMEN RIDER...?

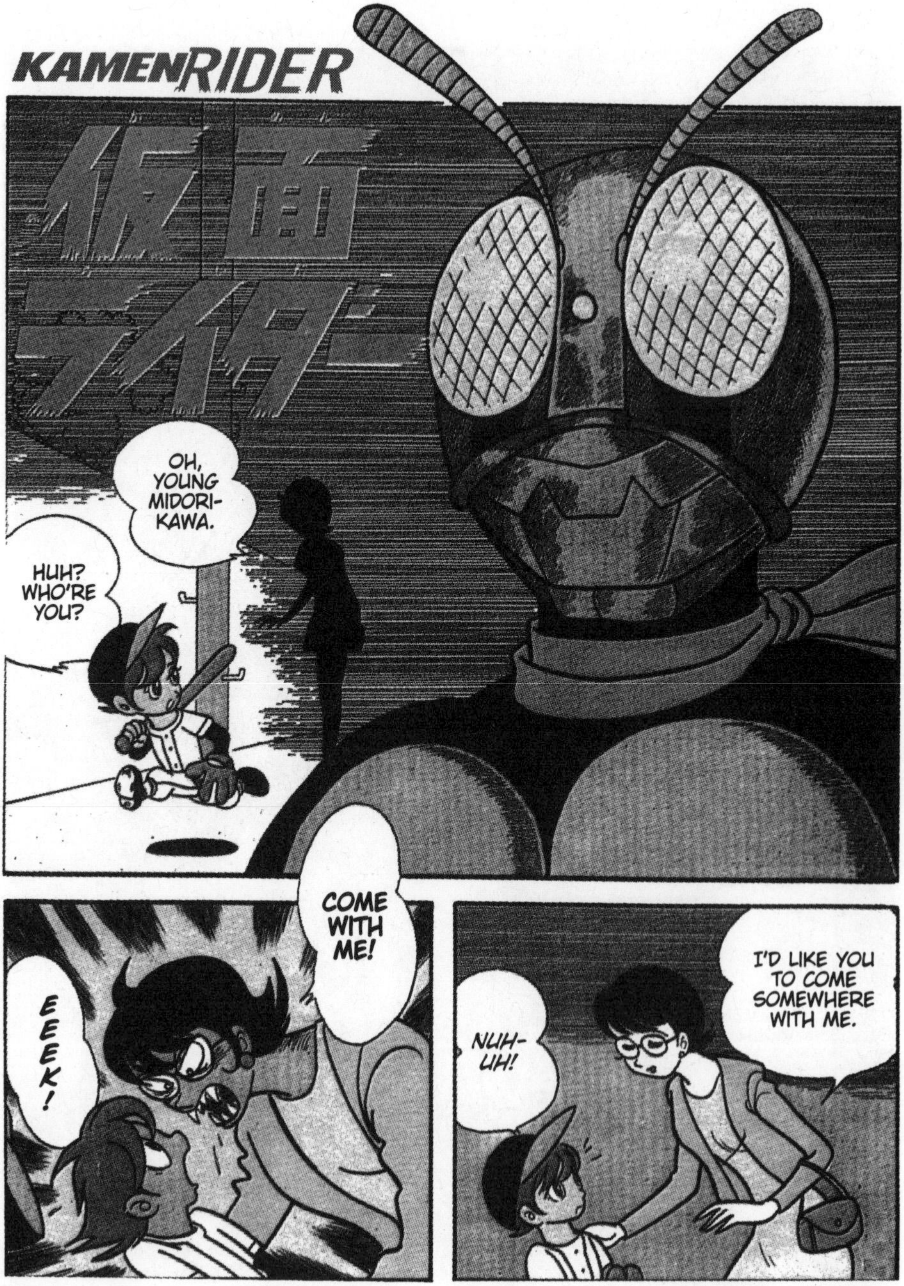
仮面ライダー
OH, YOUNG MIDORI-KAWA.
HUH? WHO'RE YOU?
I'D LIKE YOU TO COME SOMEWHERE WITH ME.
NUH-UH!
COME WITH ME!
EEEK!

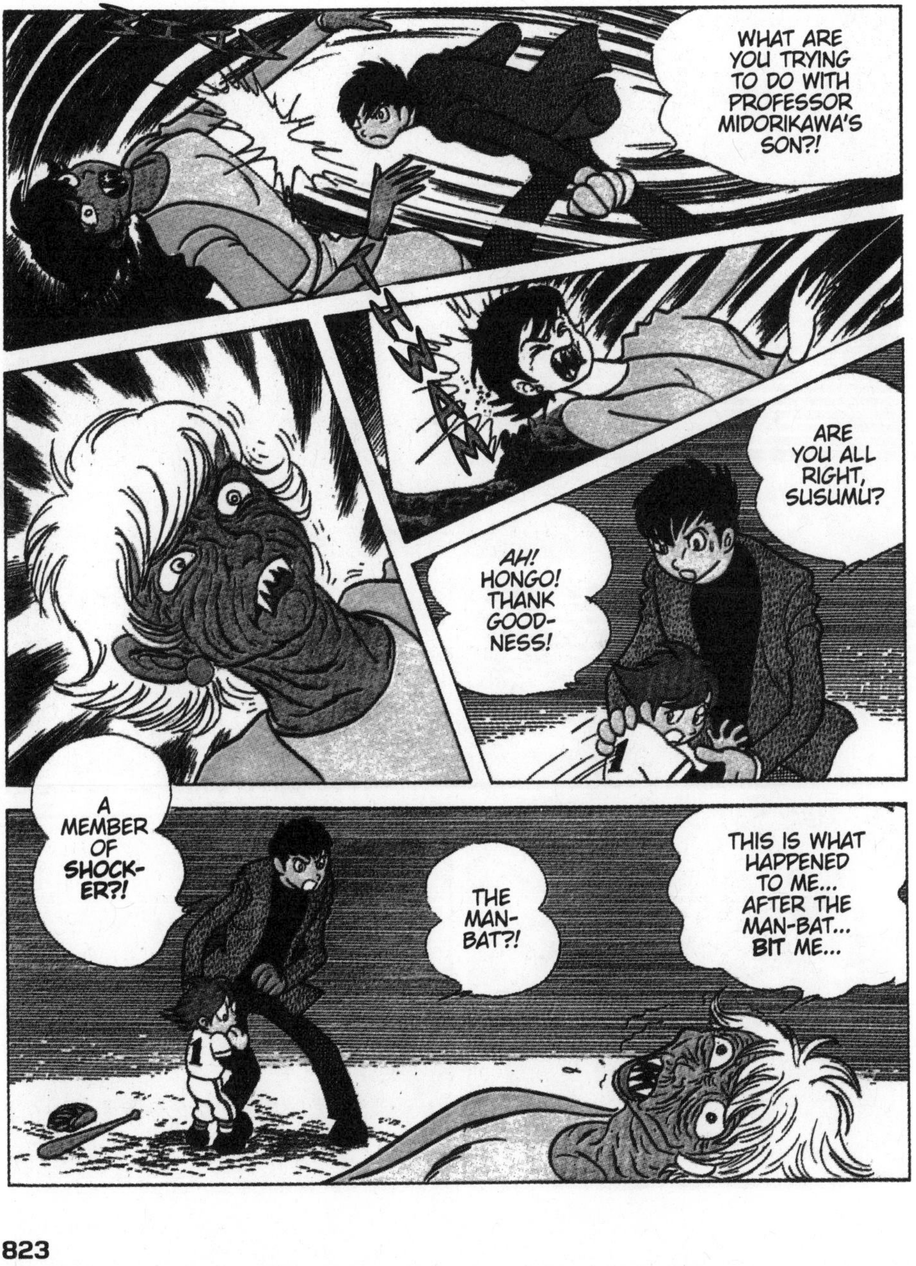
WHAT ARE YOU TRYING TO DO WITH PROFESSOR MIDORIKAWA'S SON?!
ARE YOU ALL RIGHT, SUSUMU?
AH! HONGO! THANK GOODNESS!
THIS IS WHAT HAPPENED TO ME... AFTER THE MAN-BAT... BIT ME...
THE MAN-BAT?!
A MEMBER OF SHOCKER?!

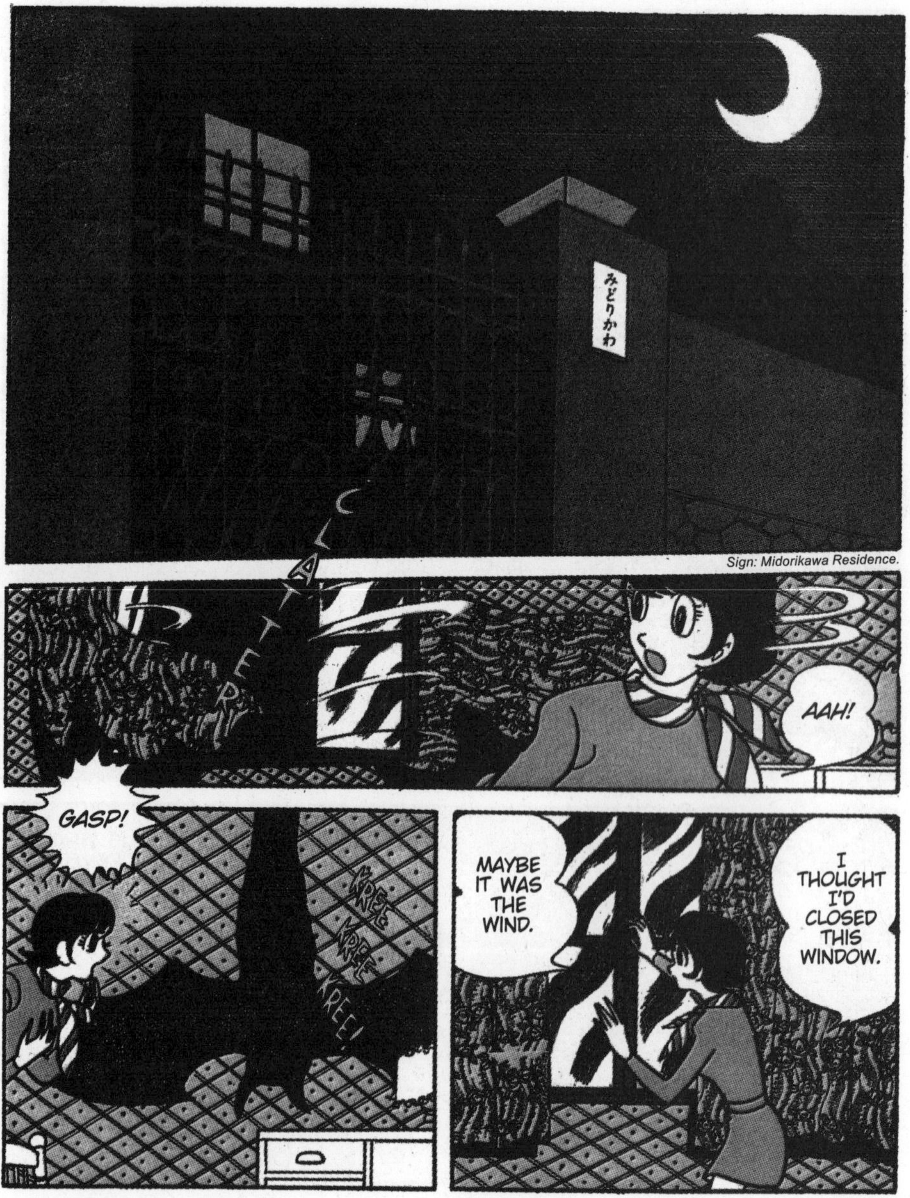
みどりかわ
CLATTER
AAH!
I THOUGHT I'D CLOSED THIS WINDOW.
MAYBE IT WAS THE WIND.
GASP!
KREE KREE KREE!
Sign: Midorikawa Residence.

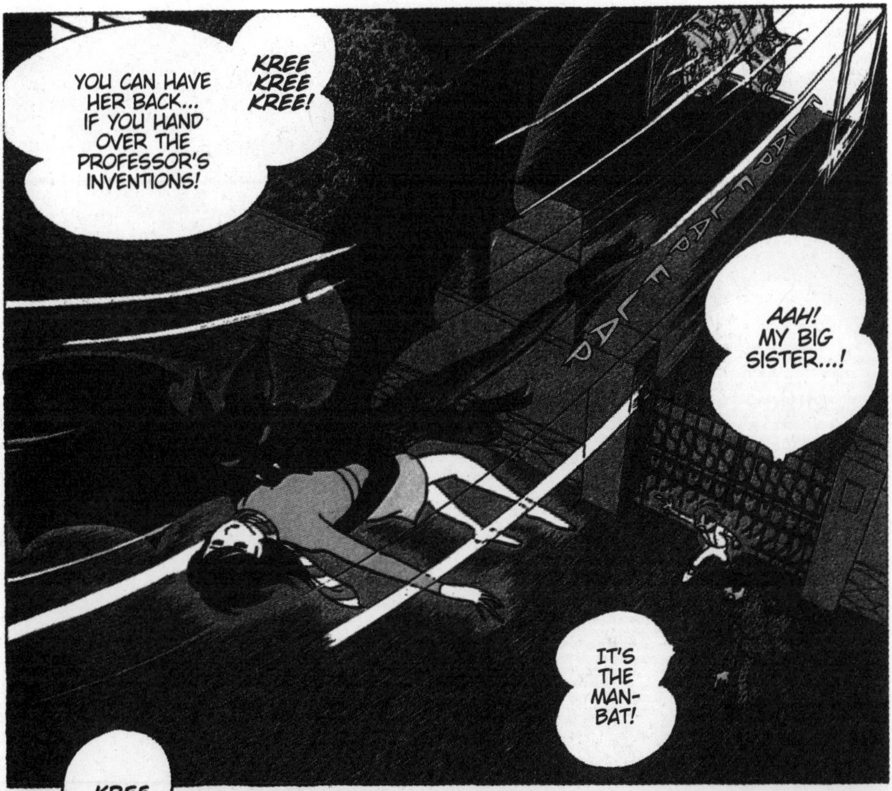
KREE KREE KREE!
YOU CAN HAVE HER BACK... IF YOU HAND OVER THE PROFESSOR'S INVENTIONS!
FLAP FLAP FLAP
AAH! MY BIG SISTER...!
IT'S THE MAN-BAT!
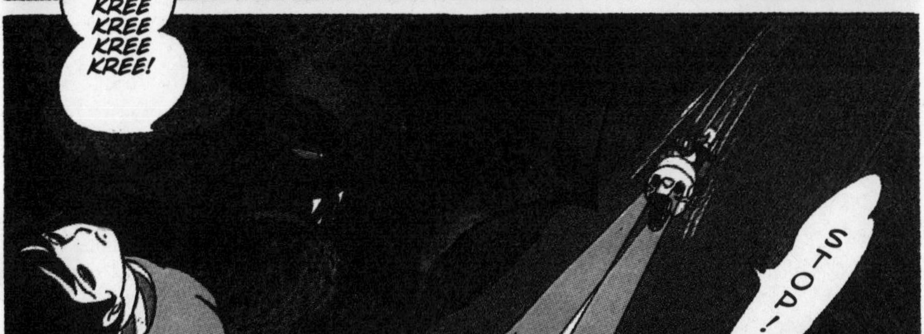
STOP!
KREE KREE KREE KREE!

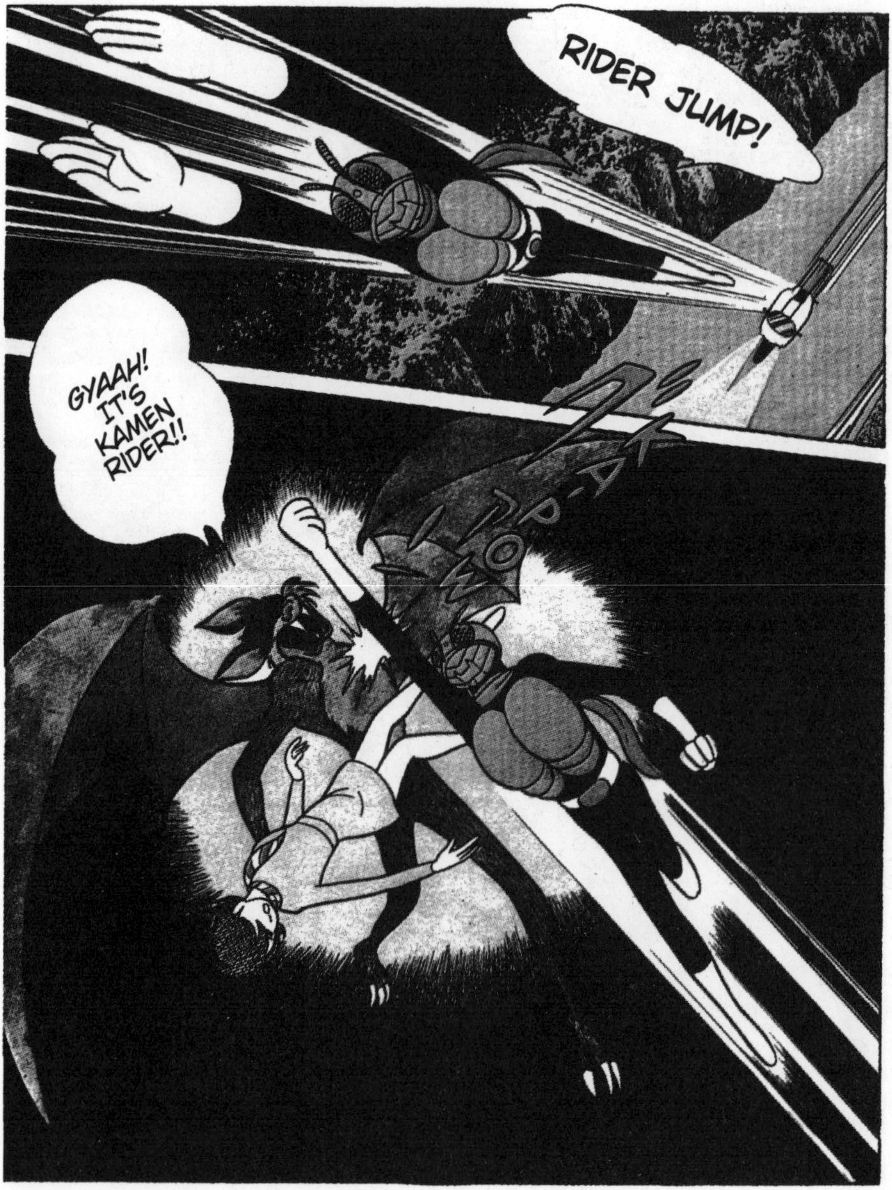
RIDER JUMP!
GYAAH! IT'S KAMEN RIDER!!
KA-POW

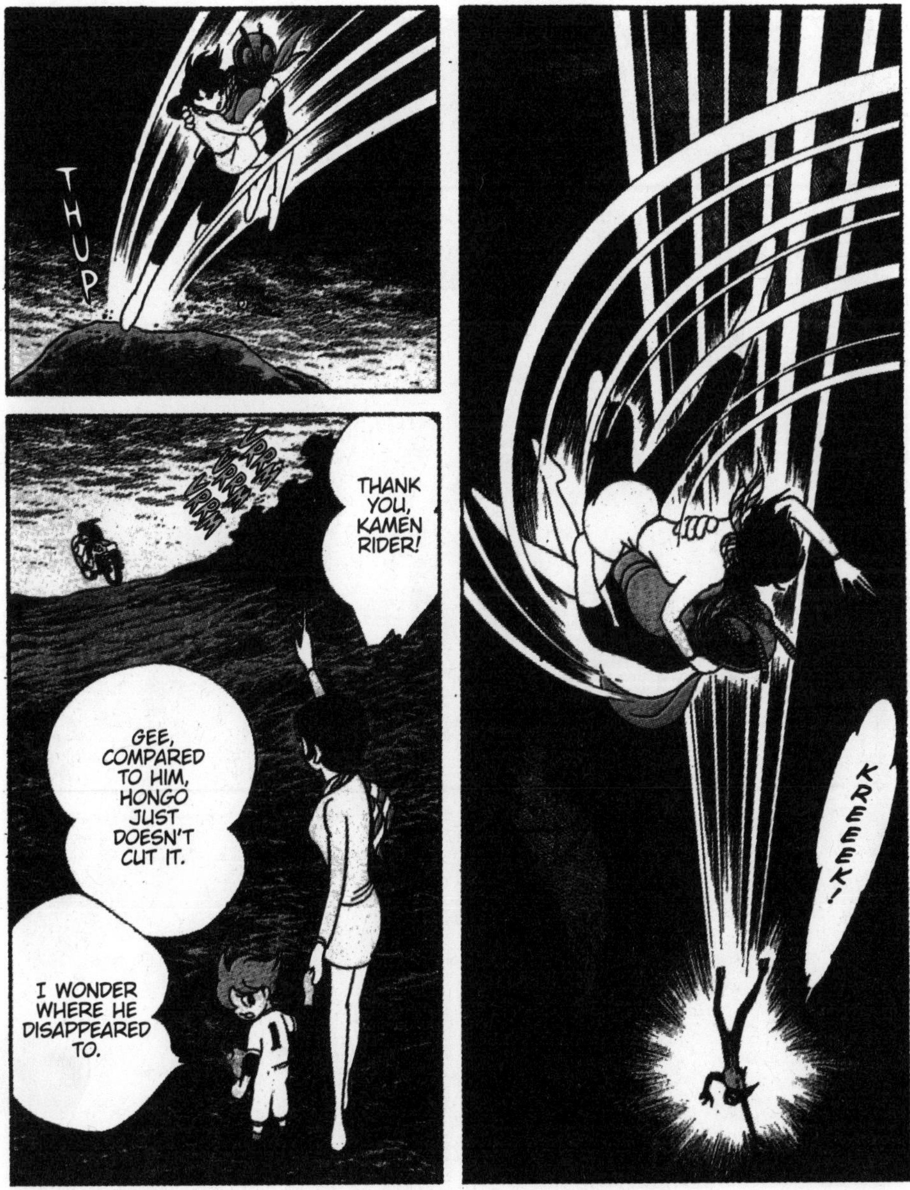
KREEEK!
THUP
VRRM VRRM VRRM
THANK YOU, KAMEN RIDER!
GEE, COMPARED TO HIM, HONGO JUST DOESN'T CUT IT.
I WONDER WHERE HE DISAPPEARED TO.

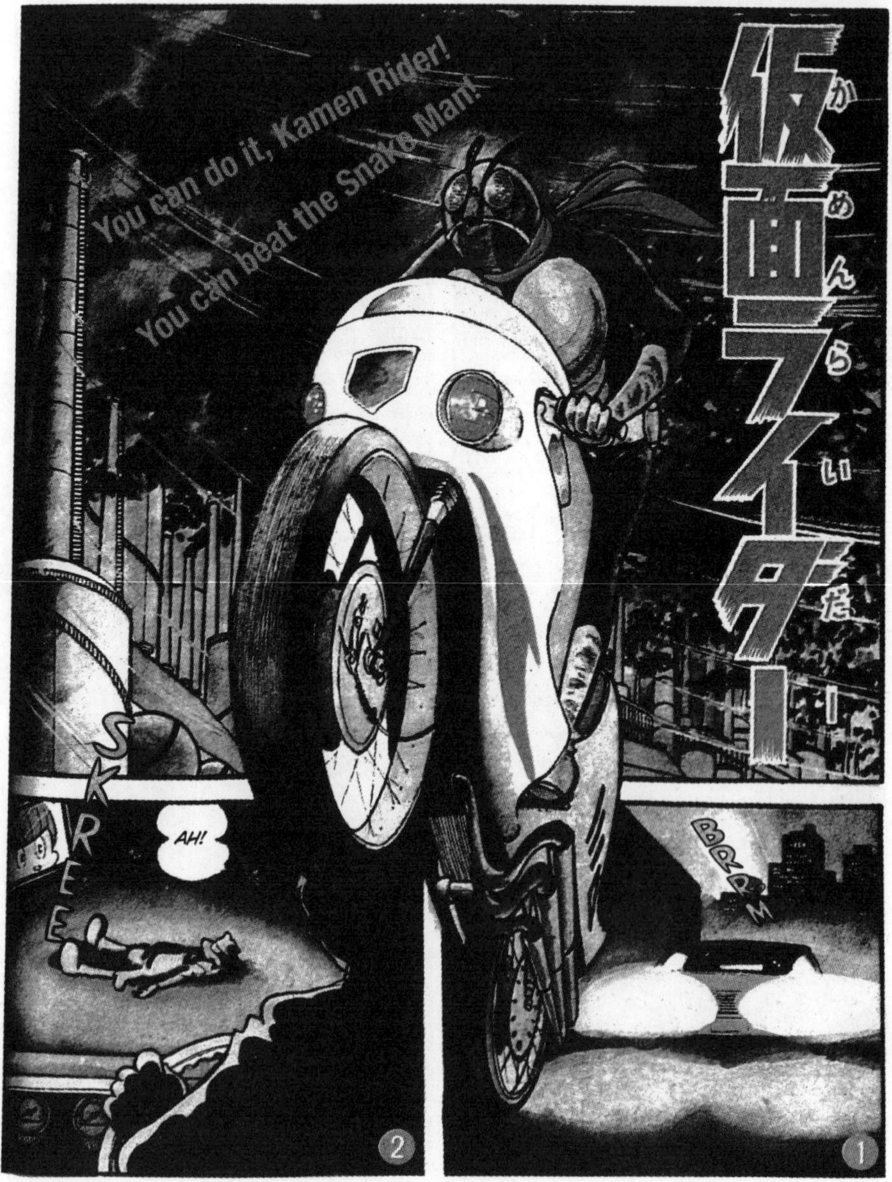
仮面ライダー
You can do it, Kamen Rider!
You can beat the Snake Man!
BRRRM
SKREEE
AH!

PRETTY DANGEROUS PLACE TO TAKE A NAP, ISN'T IT?
IS THIS GUY DRUNK?
AGH!
CHOMP
FWIP FWIP FWIP
A Shocker cyborg... Snake Man!

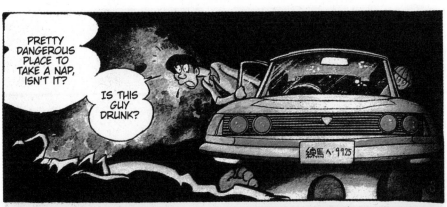

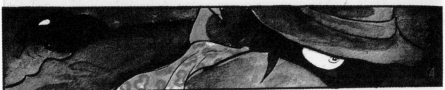

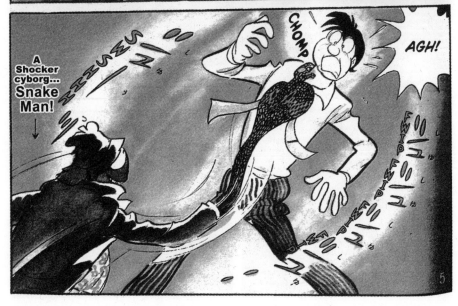

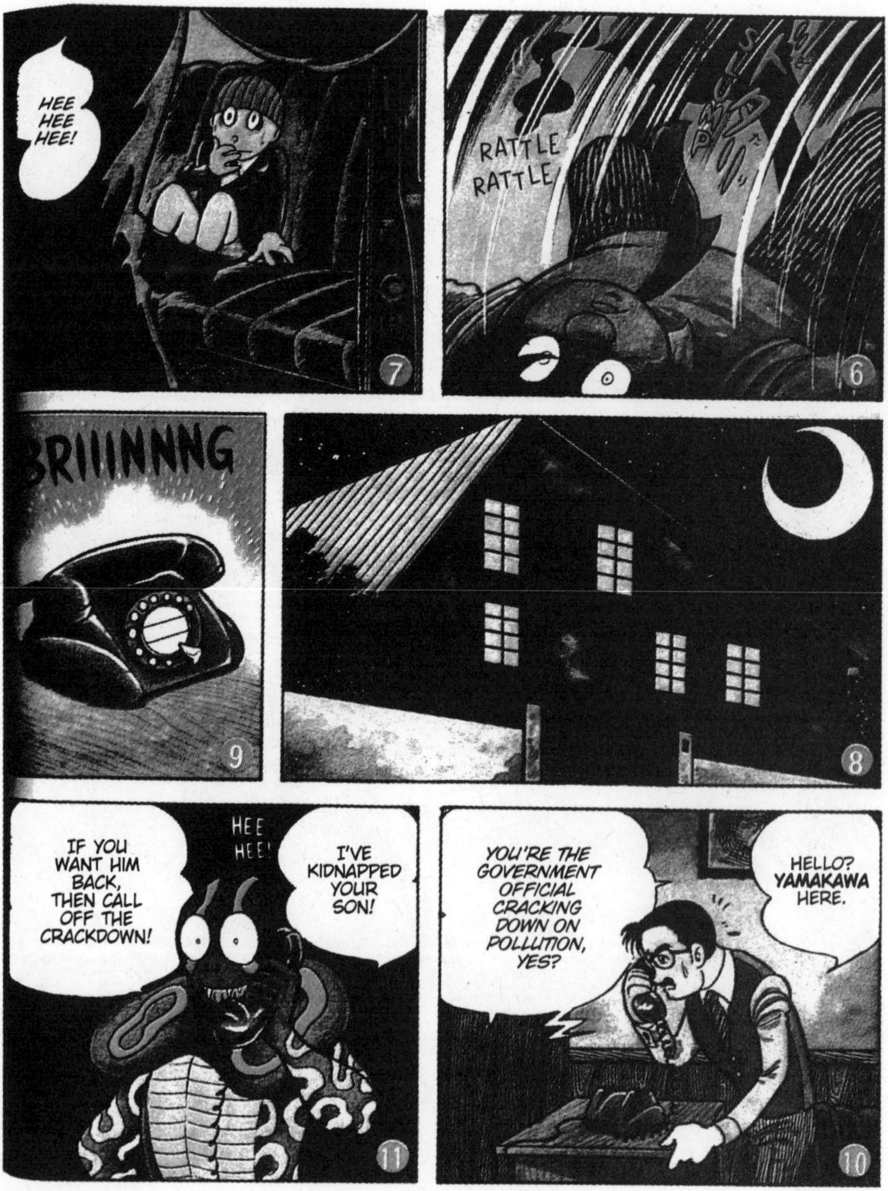
RATTLE RATTLE
HEE HEE HEE!
BRIIINNNG
HELLO? YAMAKAWA HERE.
YOU'RE THE GOVERNMENT OFFICIAL CRACKING DOWN ON POLLUTION, YES?
I'VE KIDNAPPED YOUR SON!
HEE HEE!
IF YOU WANT HIM BACK, THEN CALL OFF THE CRACKDOWN!

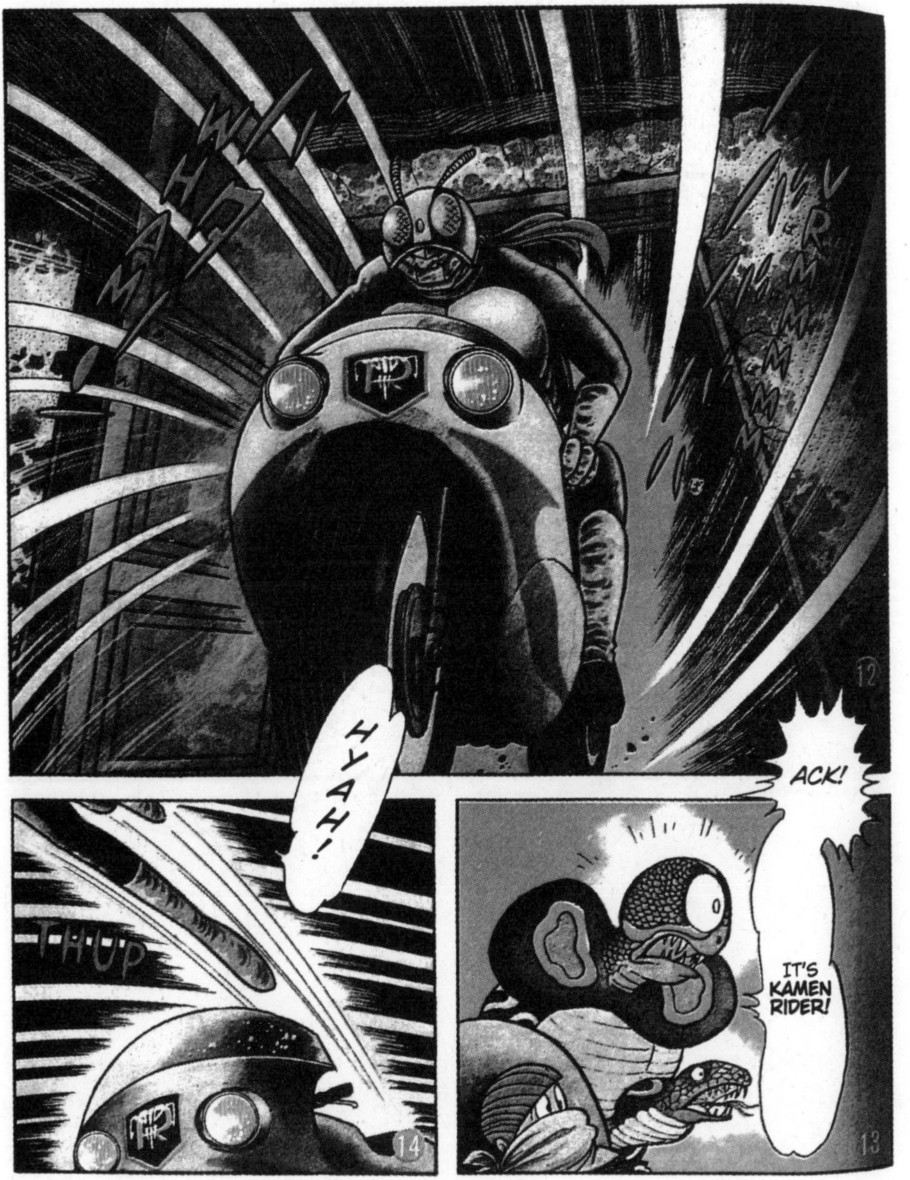
VRMMMMMM
WHHAM!
HYAH!
ACK!
IT'S KAMEN RIDER!
THUD

CURSE YOU!
SHAAH!
15
16
YOU THINK SHOCKER CAN BELCH OUT POLLUTION FOR FINANCIAL GAIN?!
I WON'T STAND FOR IT! TAKE THIS-- RIDER CHOP!
17

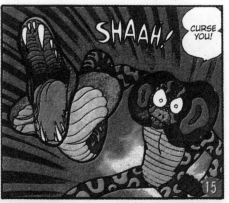

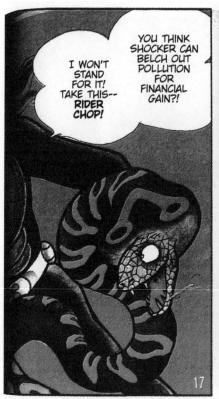

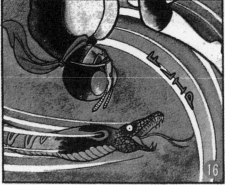

BIFFF
URGH! HE GOT ME!
GYAAH!
WHEEE!
HA HA HA!

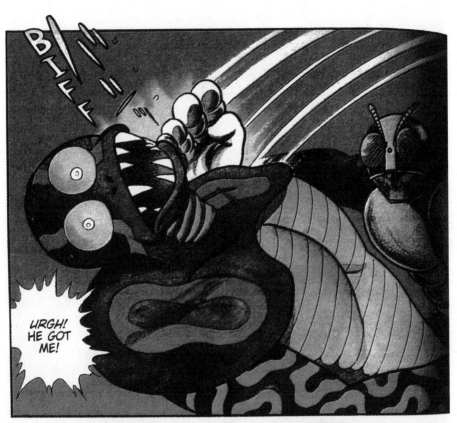

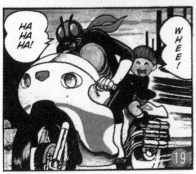

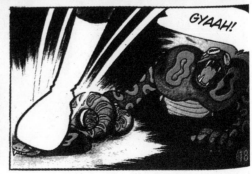

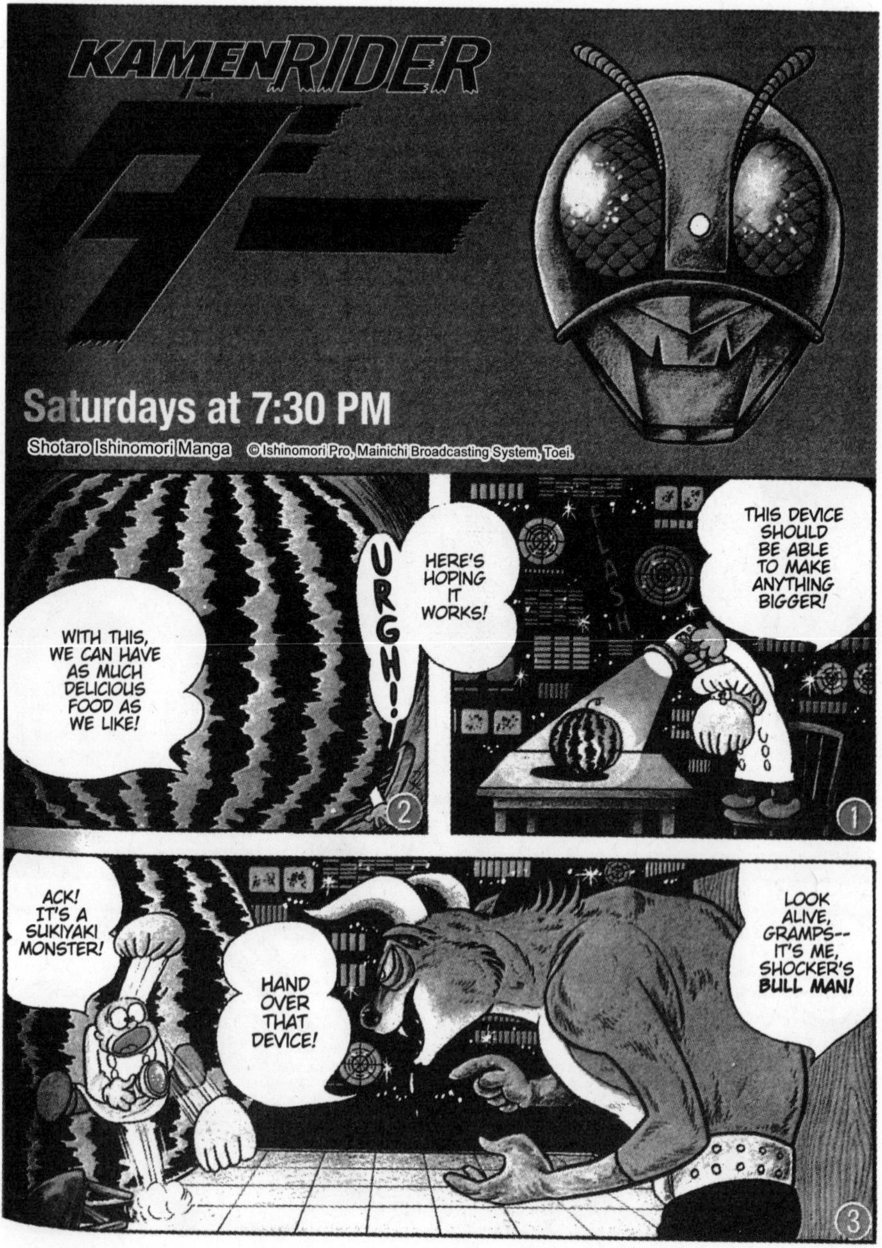
KAMEN RIDER
Saturdays at 7:30 PM
Shotaro Ishinomori Manga
© Ishinomori Pro, Mainichi Broadcasting System, Toei.
THIS DEVICE SHOULD BE ABLE TO MAKE ANYTHING BIGGER!
HERE'S HOPING IT WORKS!
URGH!
WITH THIS, WE CAN HAVE AS MUCH DELICIOUS FOOD AS WE LIKE!
LOOK ALIVE, GRAMPS-- IT'S ME, SHOCKER'S BULL MAN!
HAND OVER THAT DEVICE!
ACK! IT'S A SUKIYAKI MONSTER!

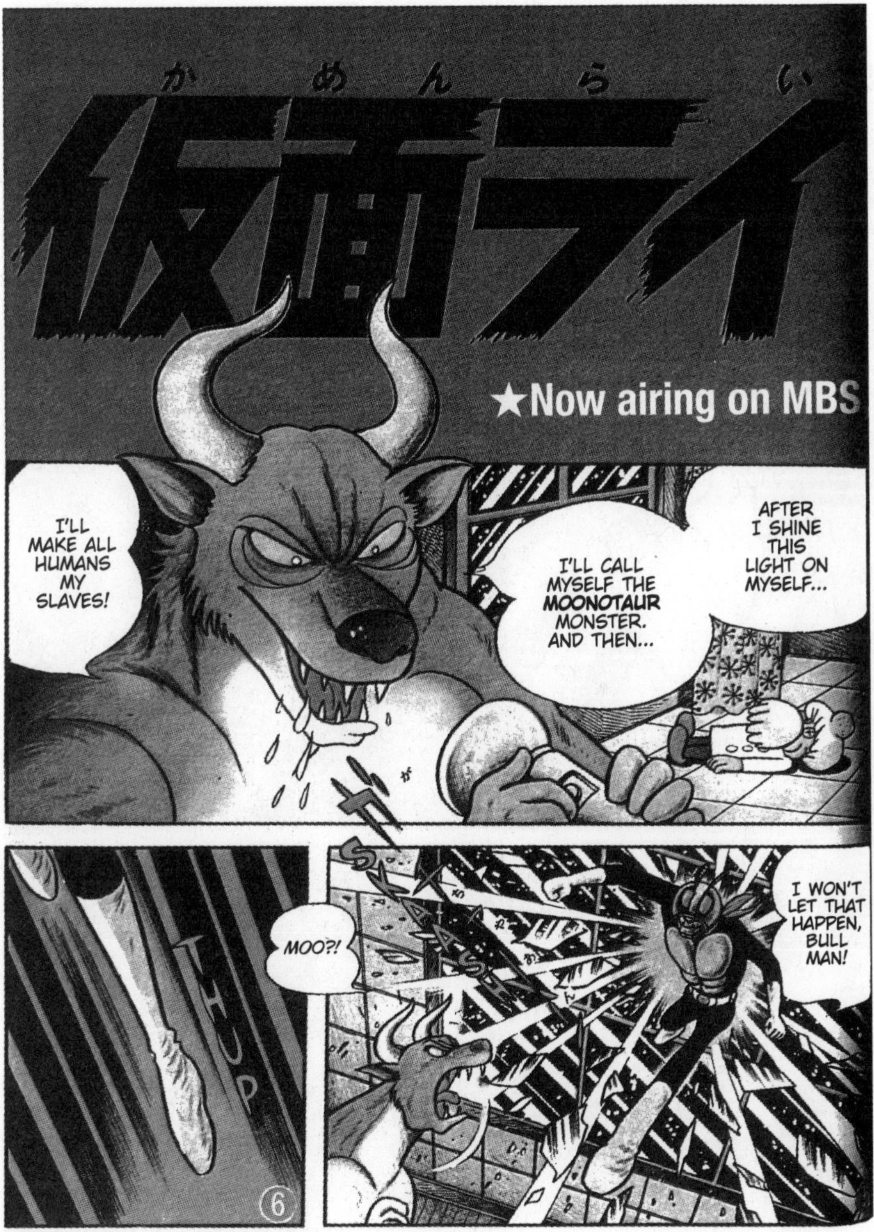
かめんらい
仮面ライ
★Now airing on MBS
AFTER I SHINE THIS LIGHT ON MYSELF...
I'LL CALL MYSELF THE **MOONOTAUR** MONSTER. AND THEN...
I'LL MAKE ALL HUMANS MY SLAVES!
I WON'T LET THAT HAPPEN, BULL MAN!
MOO?!
THUP
⑥

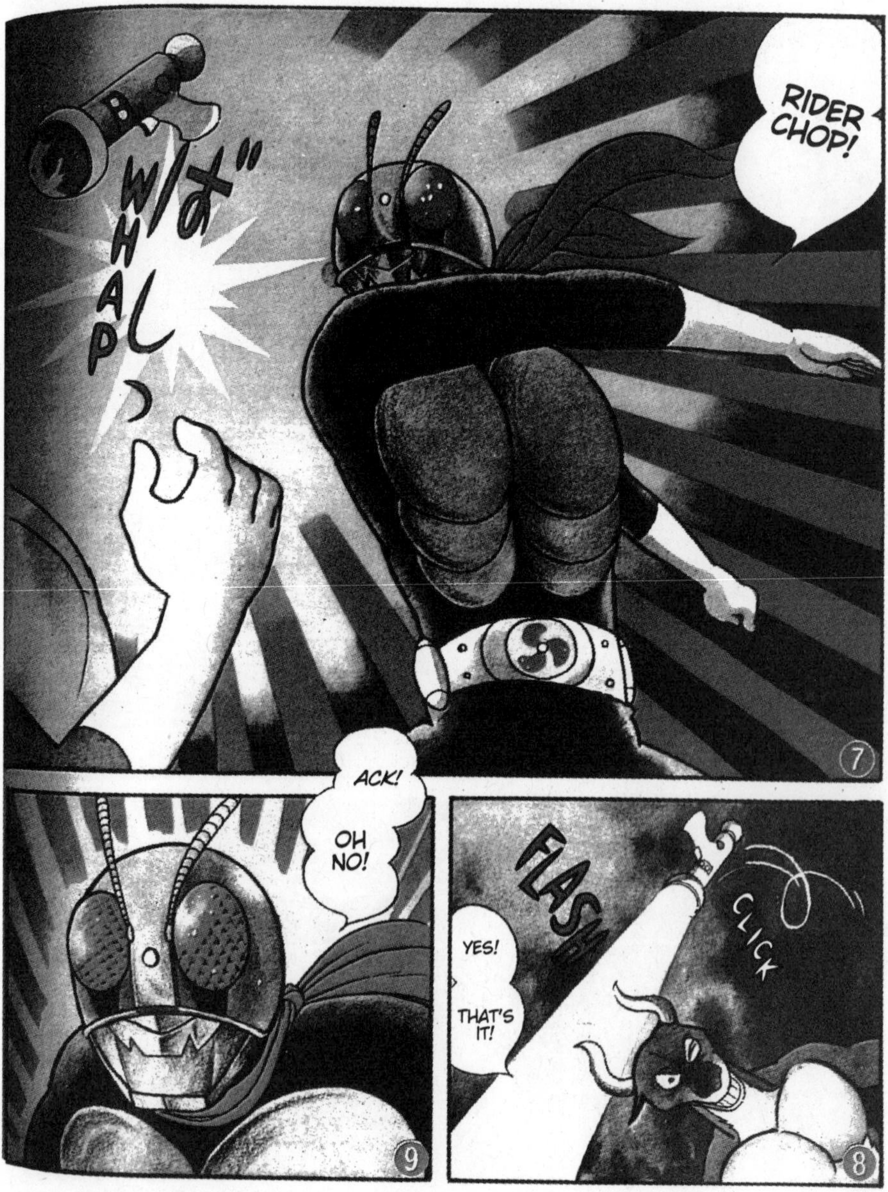
RIDER CHOP!
WHAP
ばしっ
FLASH
CLICK
YES!
THAT'S IT!
ACK!
OH NO!

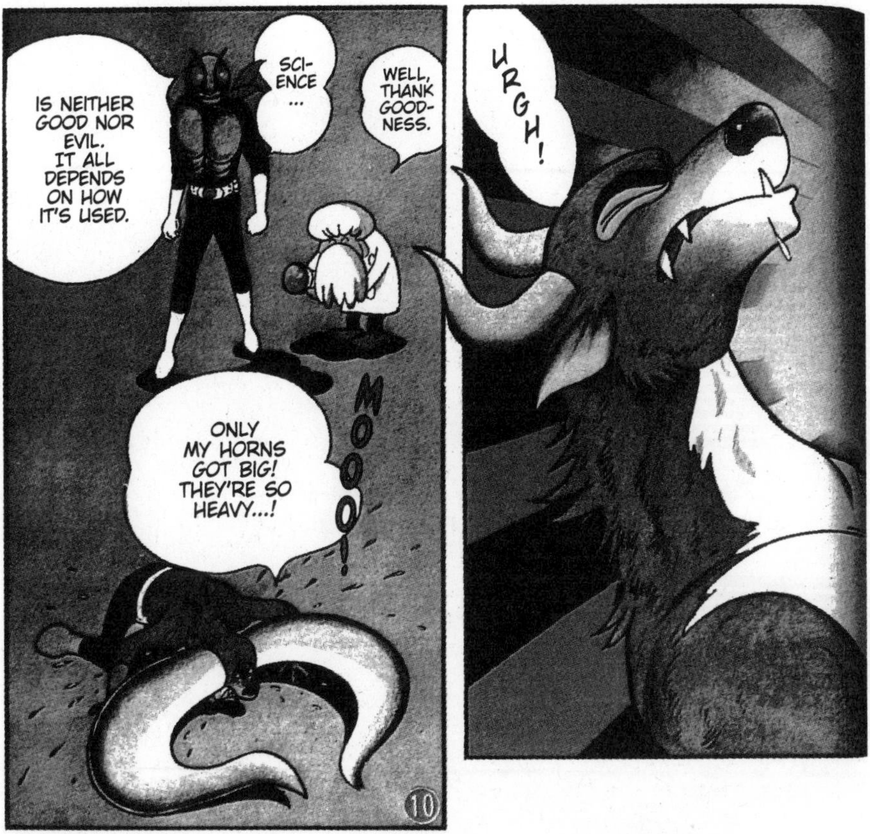
URGH!
WELL, THANK GOODNESS.
SCIENCE...
IS NEITHER GOOD NOR EVIL. IT ALL DEPENDS ON HOW IT'S USED.
MOOOOO!
ONLY MY HORNS GOT BIG! THEY'RE SO HEAVY...!
10

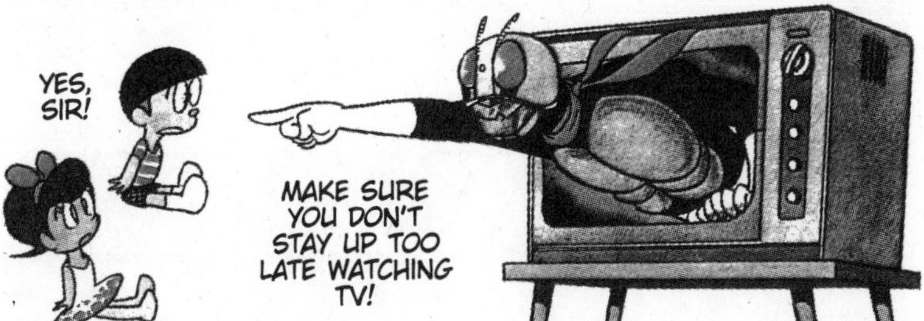
MAKE SURE YOU DON'T STAY UP TOO LATE WATCHING TV!
YES, SIR!

KAMEN RIDER

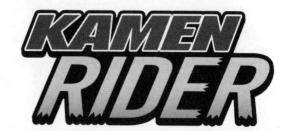

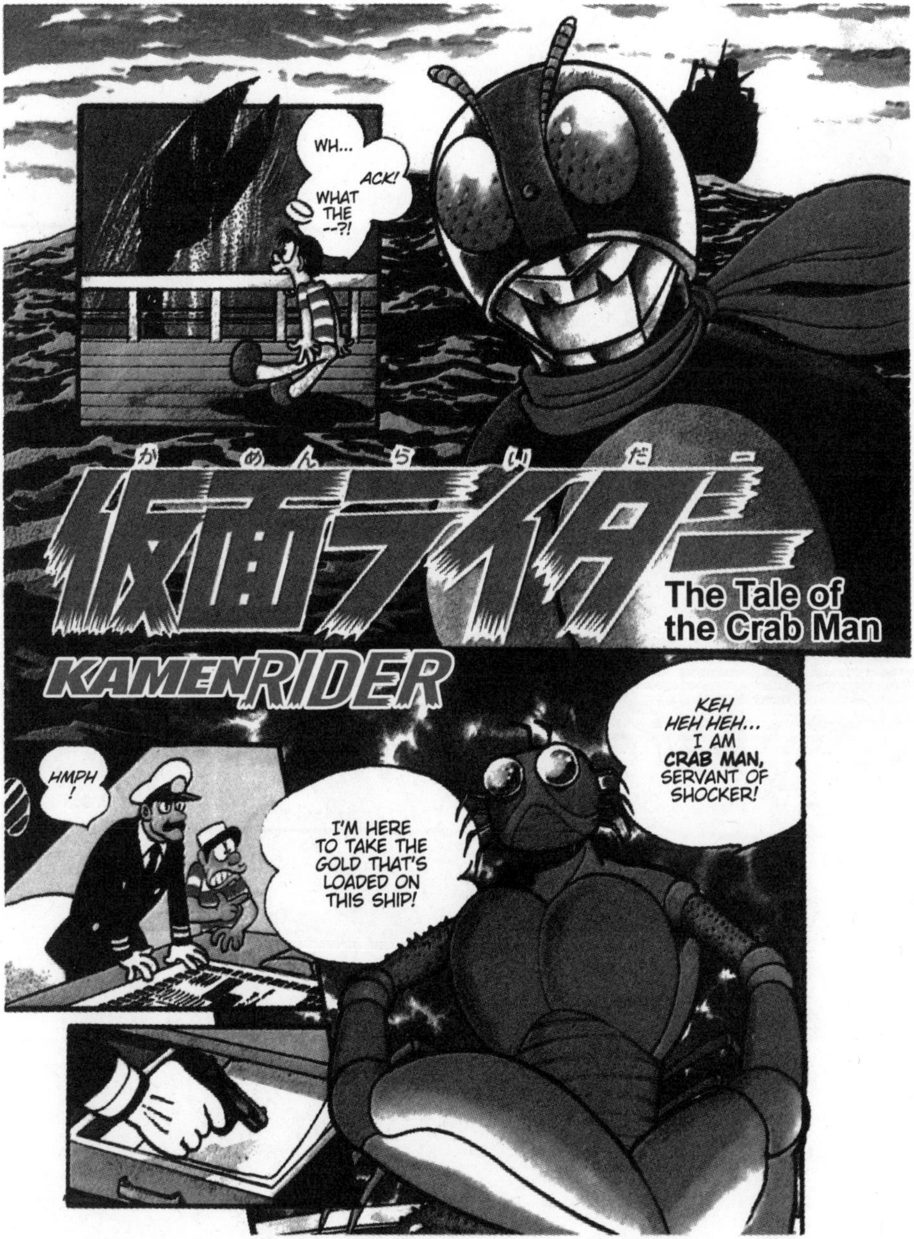
仮面ライダー
かめんらいだー
The Tale of the Crab Man
KAMEN RIDER
WH...
ACK!
WHAT THE --?!
KEH HEH HEH... I AM CRAB MAN, SERVANT OF SHOCKER!
I'M HERE TO TAKE THE GOLD THAT'S LOADED ON THIS SHIP!
HMPH!

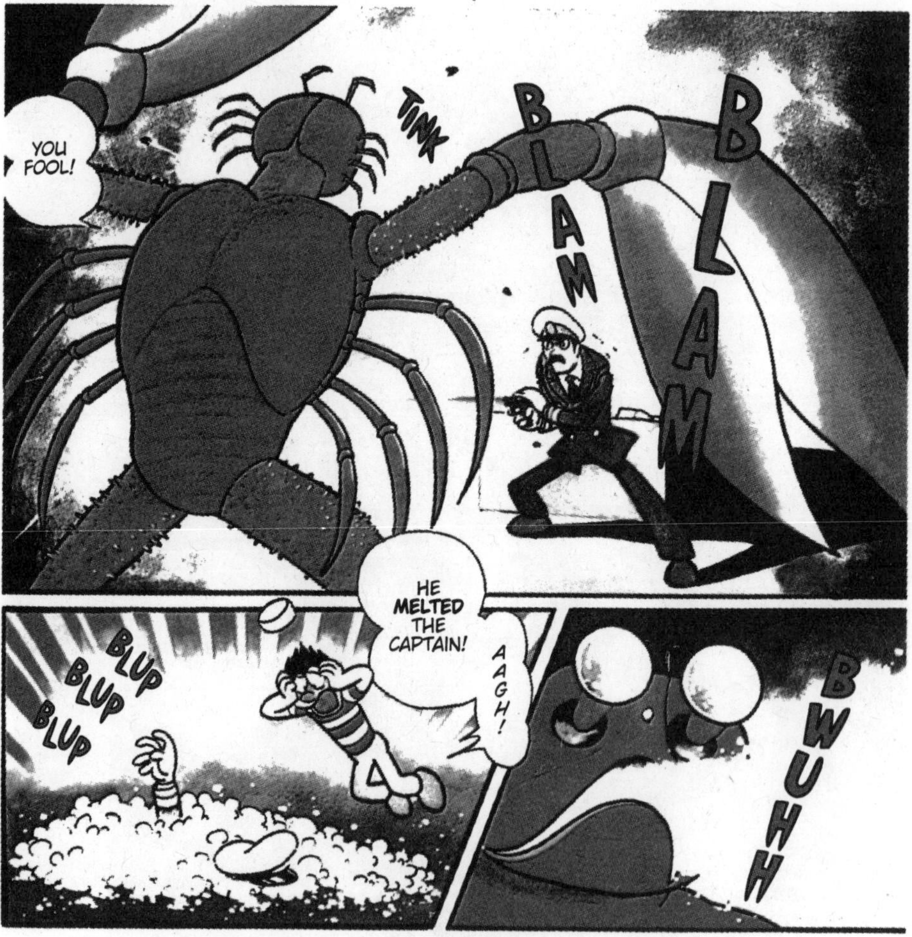
BLAM
BLAM
TINK
YOU FOOL!
BWUHH
HE MELTED THE CAPTAIN!
AAGH!
BLUP BLUP BLUP

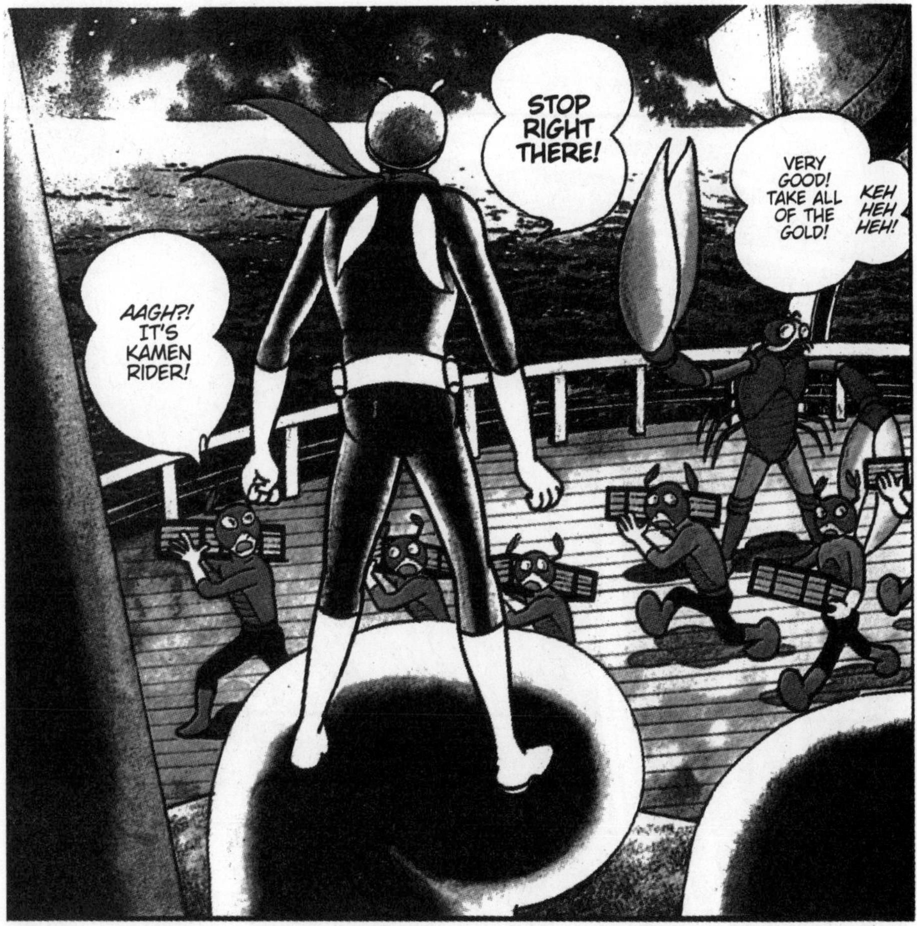
VERY GOOD! TAKE ALL OF THE GOLD!
KEH HEH HEH!
STOP RIGHT THERE!
AAGH?! IT'S KAMEN RIDER!

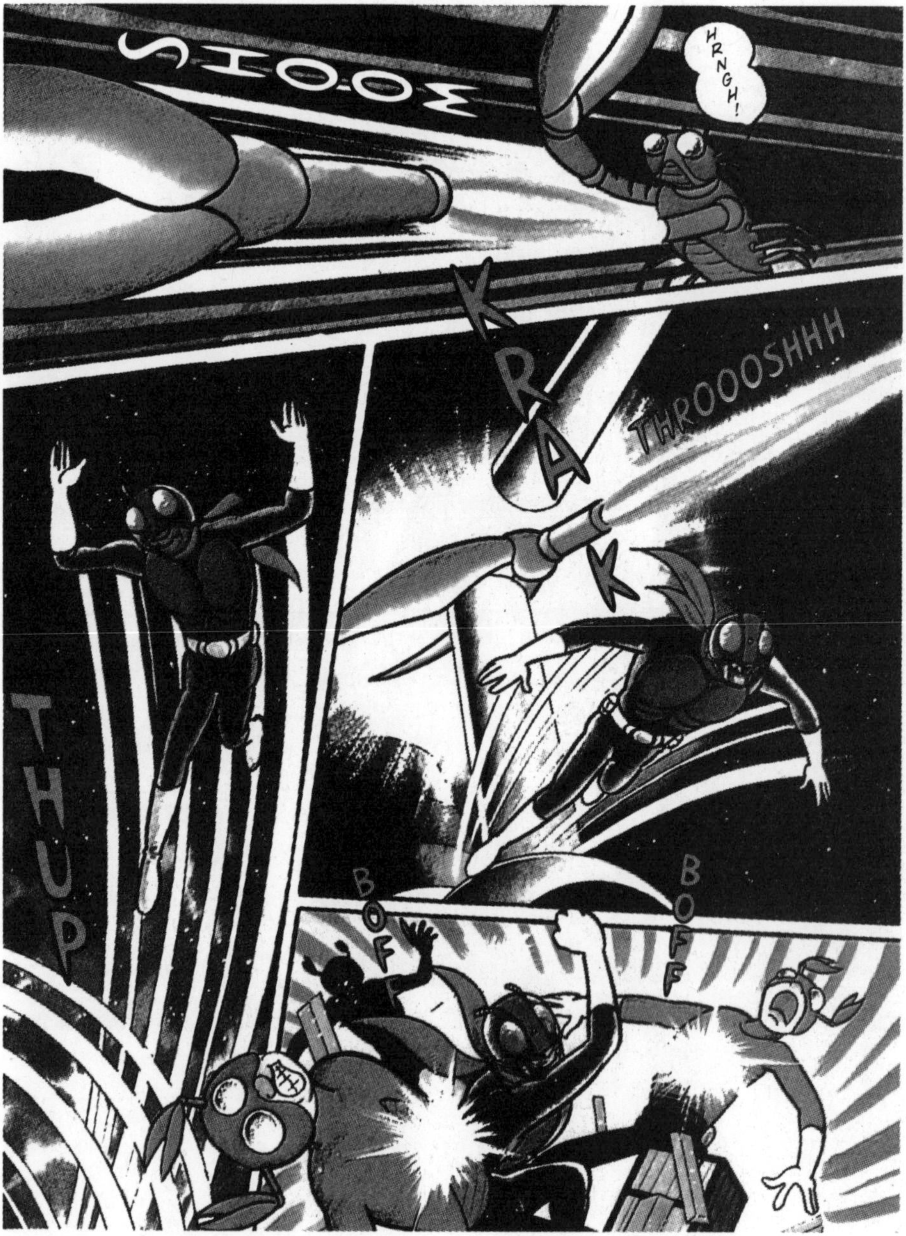
HRNGH!
WOOSH
KRAKK
THROOOSHHH
THUP
BOFF
BOFF

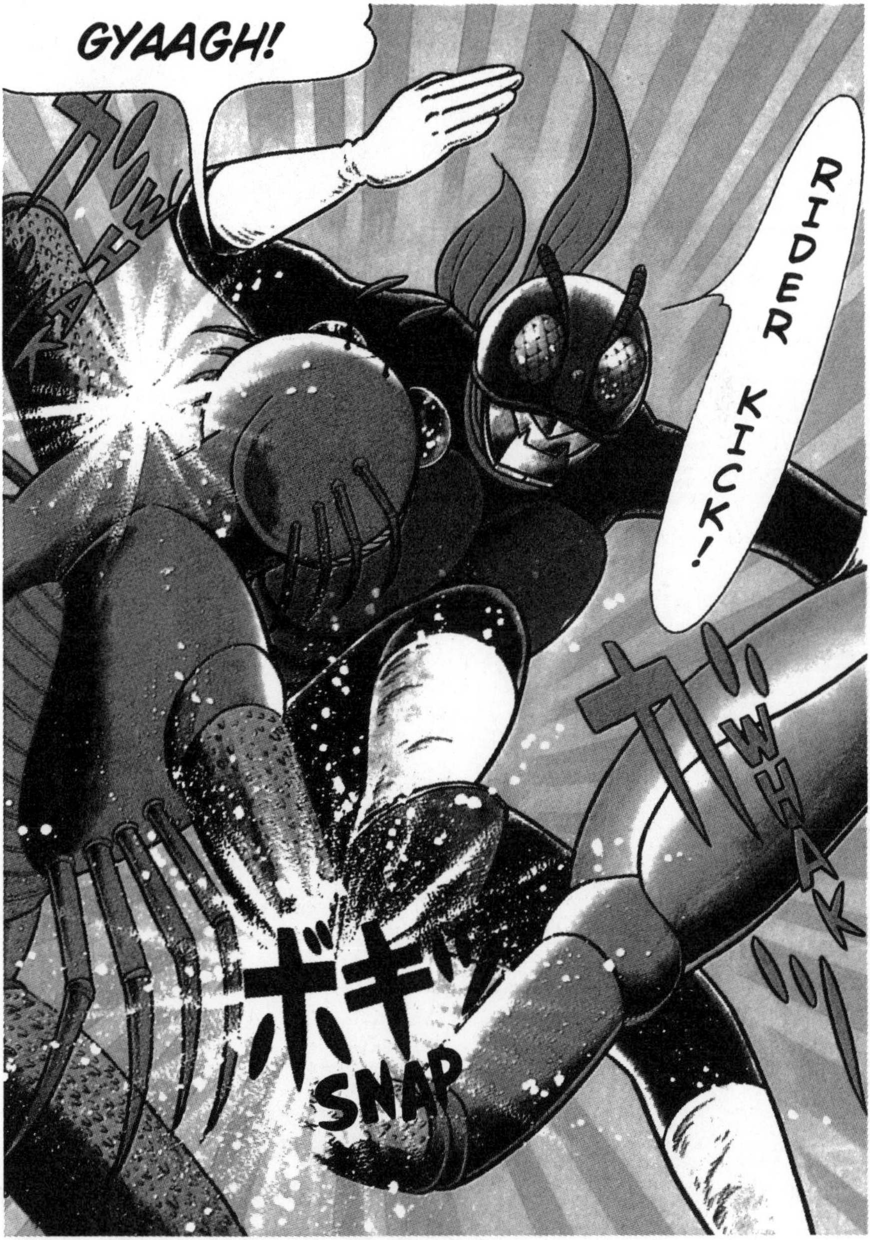
GYAAGH!
RIDER KICK!
WHAK
WHAK
SNAP

KAMEN RIDER

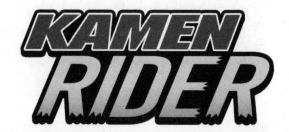

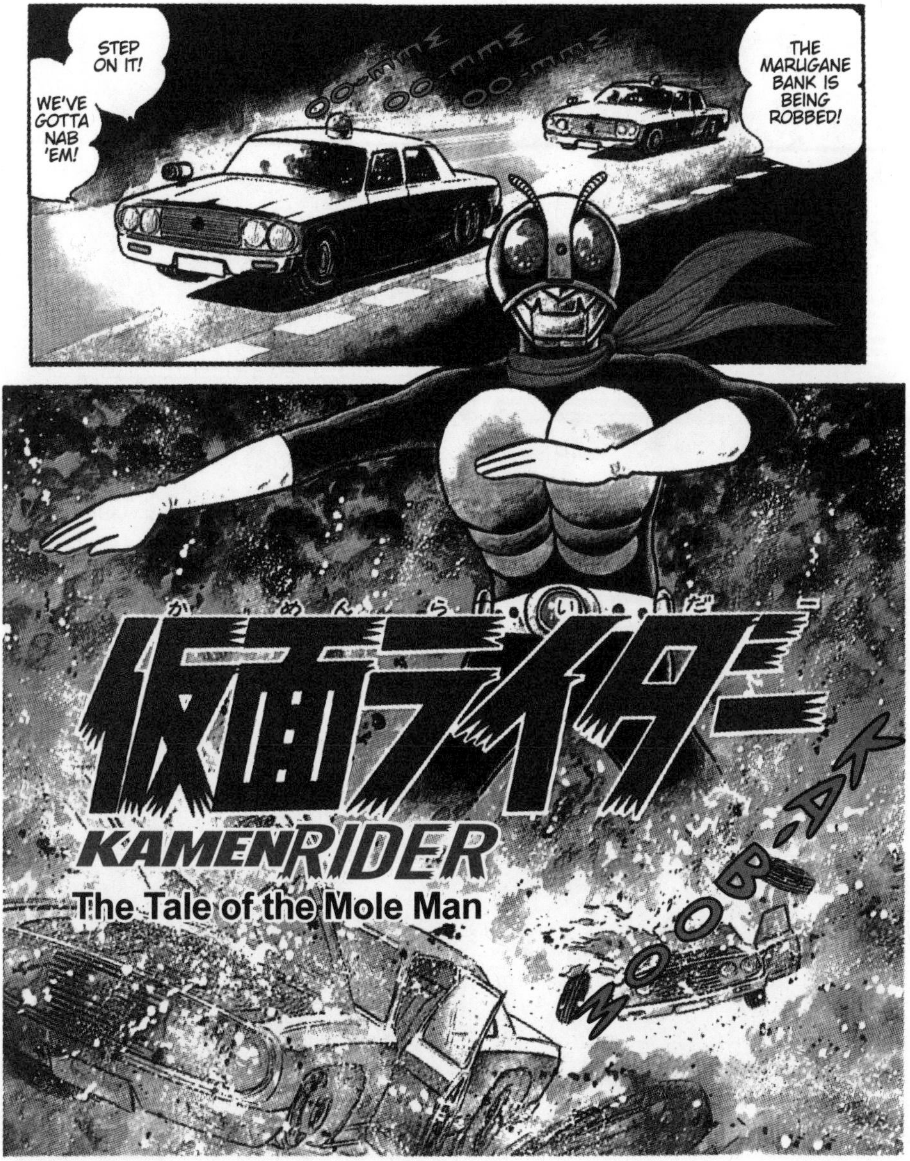
THE MARUGANE BANK IS BEING ROBBED!
STEP ON IT!
WE'VE GOTTA NAB 'EM!
かめんらいだー
仮面ライダー
KAMENRIDER
The Tale of the Mole Man
KA-BOOOM

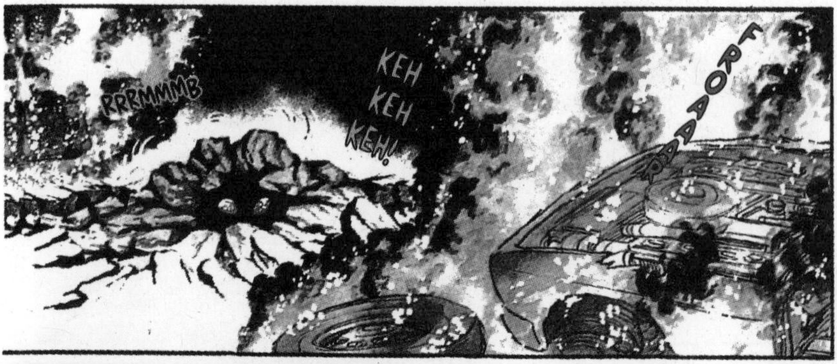
FROARR
KEH KEH KEH!
RRRMMMB

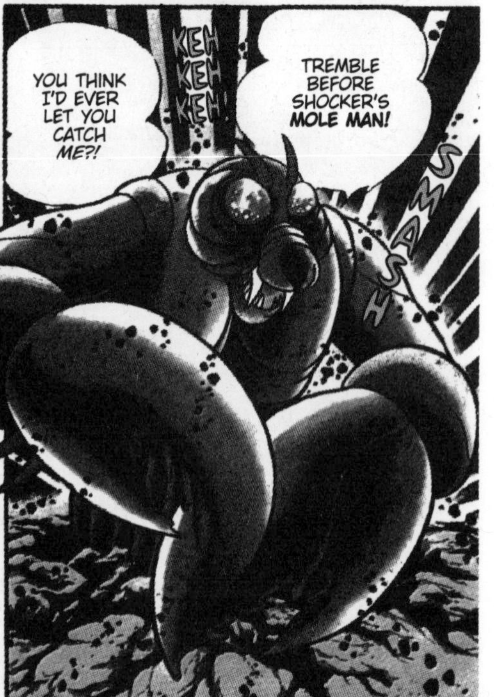
TREMBLE BEFORE SHOCKER'S **MOLE MAN!**
KEH KEH KEH
YOU THINK I'D EVER LET YOU CATCH *ME?!*
SMASH

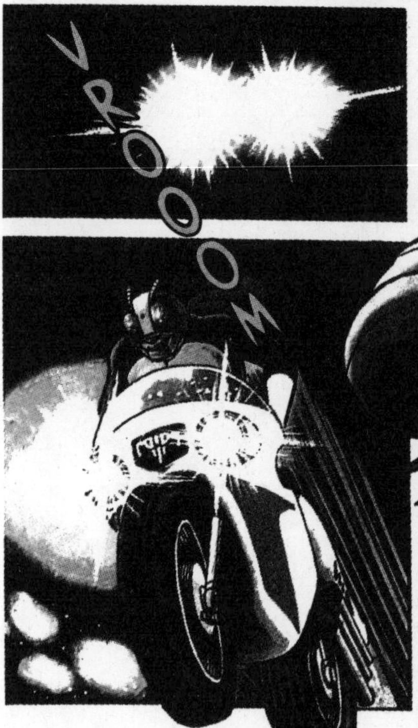
VROOOOM

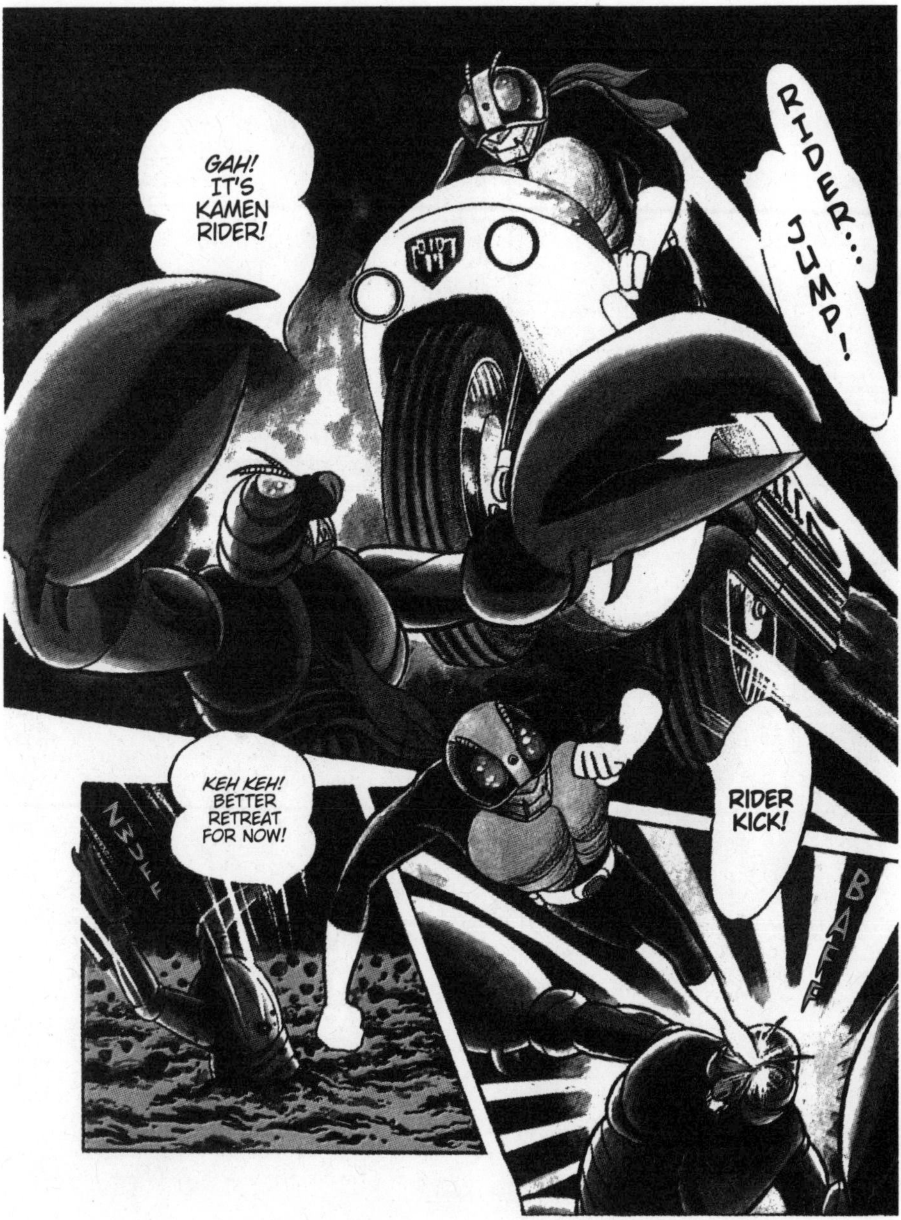
RIDER... JUMP!
GAH! IT'S KAMEN RIDER!
RIDER KICK!
BAFF
KEH KEH! BETTER RETREAT FOR NOW!
NWUFF

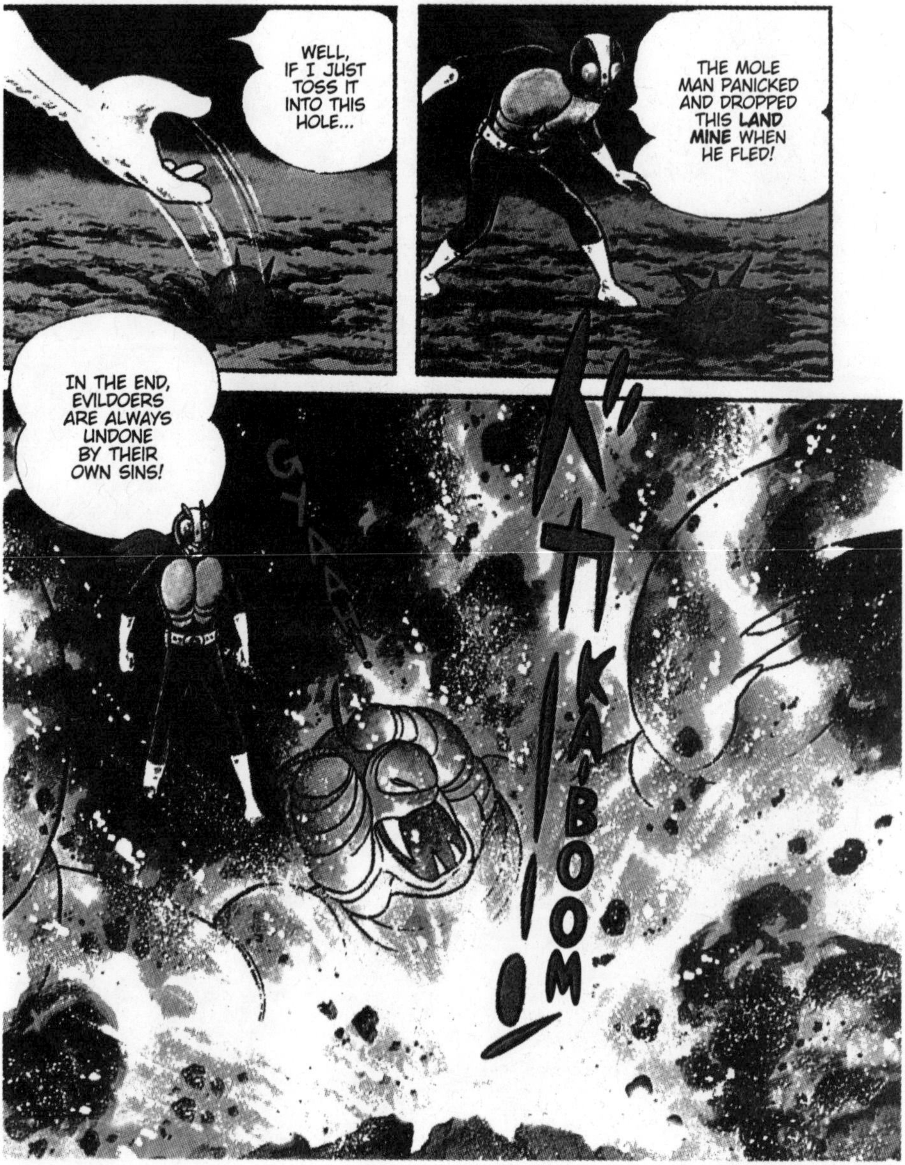
THE MOLE MAN PANICKED AND DROPPED THIS LAND MINE WHEN HE FLED!
WELL, IF I JUST TOSS IT INTO THIS HOLE...
KABOOM
GYAAAH!
IN THE END, EVILDOERS ARE ALWAYS UNDONE BY THEIR OWN SINS!

KAMEN
RIDER

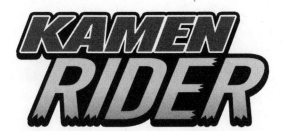

KAMEN RIDER

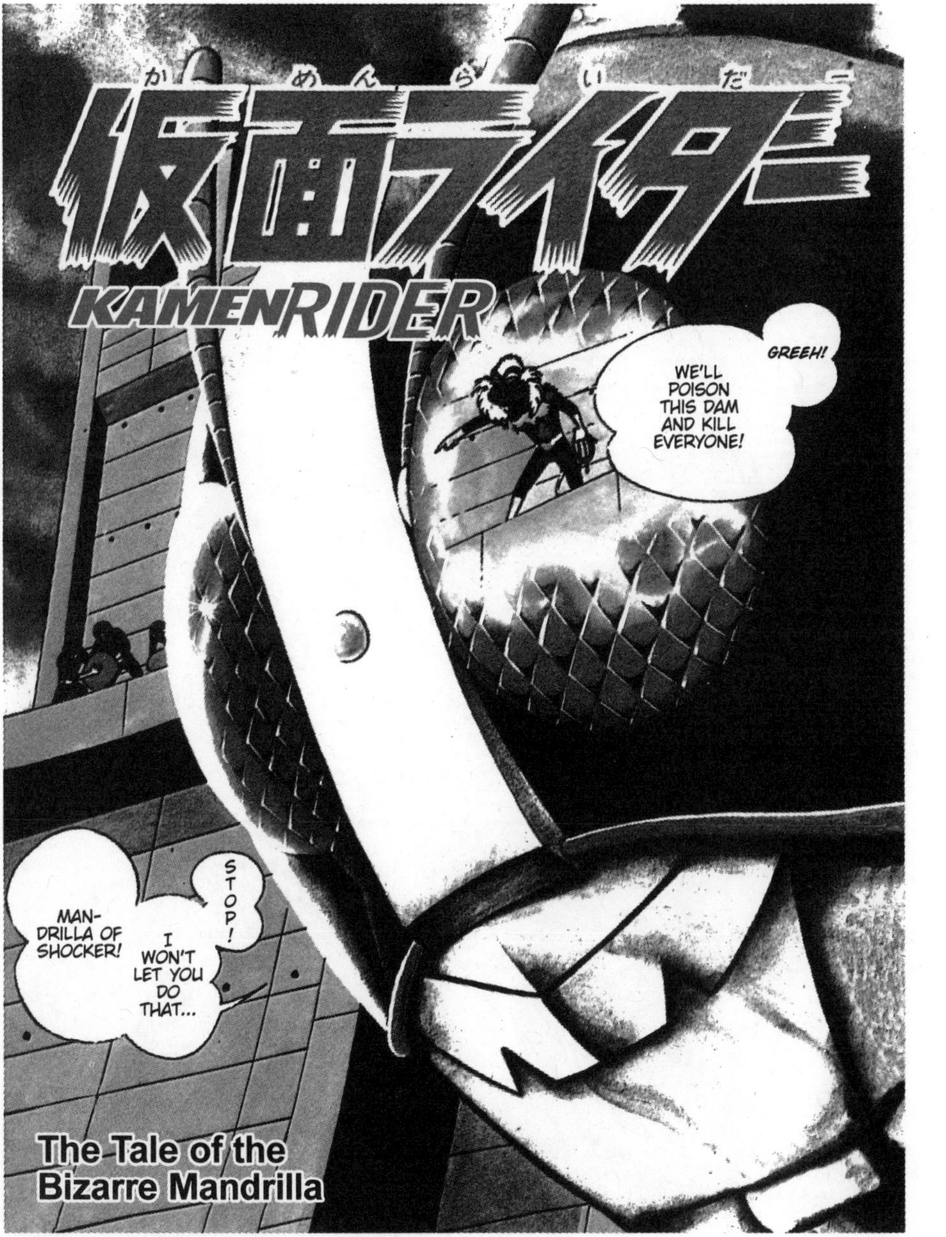
かめんらいだー
仮面ライダー
KAMEN RIDER
GREEH!
WE'LL POISON THIS DAM AND KILL EVERYONE!
STOP!
MAN-DRILLA OF SHOCKER!
I WON'T LET YOU DO THAT...
The Tale of the Bizarre Mandrilla

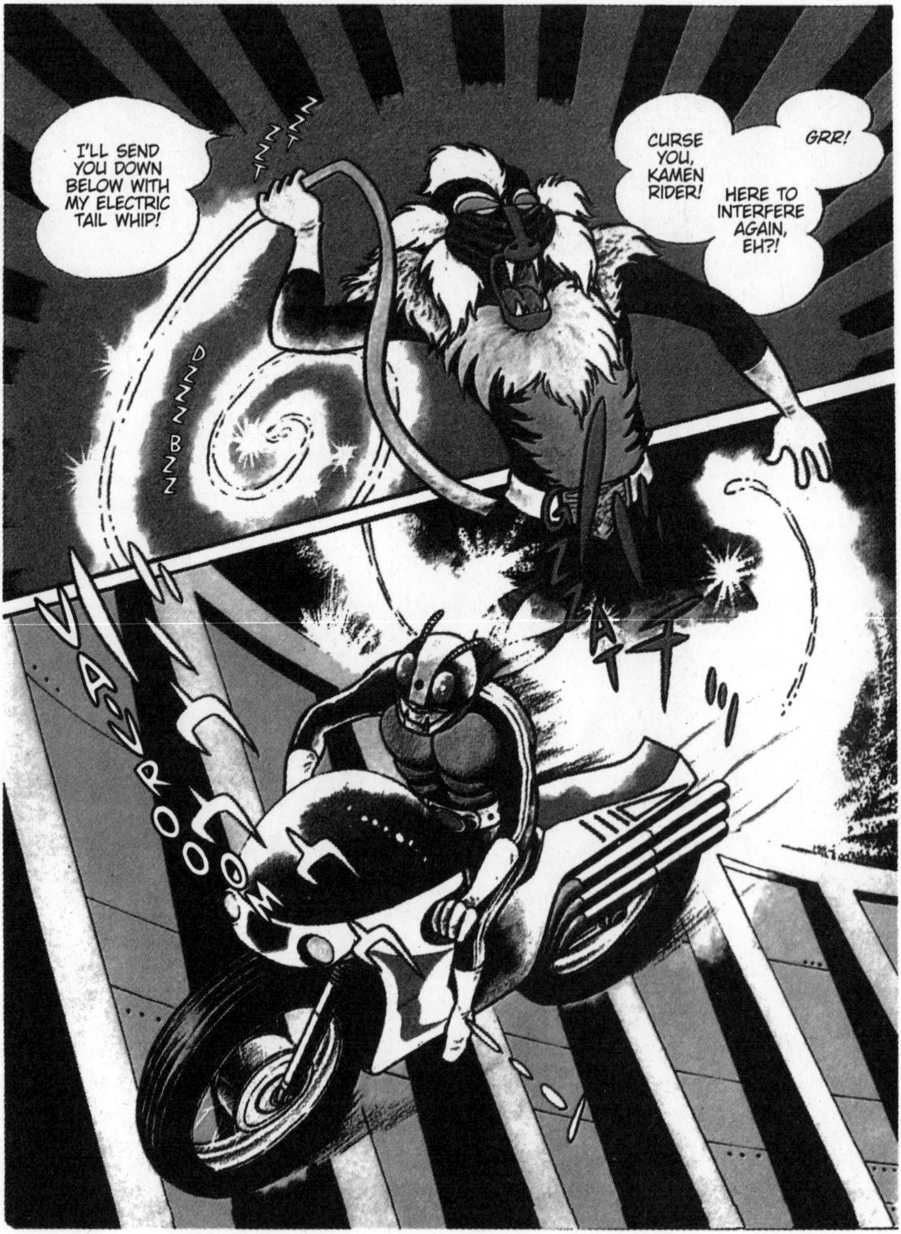
GRR!
CURSE YOU, KAMEN RIDER!
HERE TO INTERFERE AGAIN, EH?!
ZZZT ZZZT
I'LL SEND YOU DOWN BELOW WITH MY ELECTRIC TAIL WHIP!
DZZZZ BZZ
ZAT
VA-VROOOOM

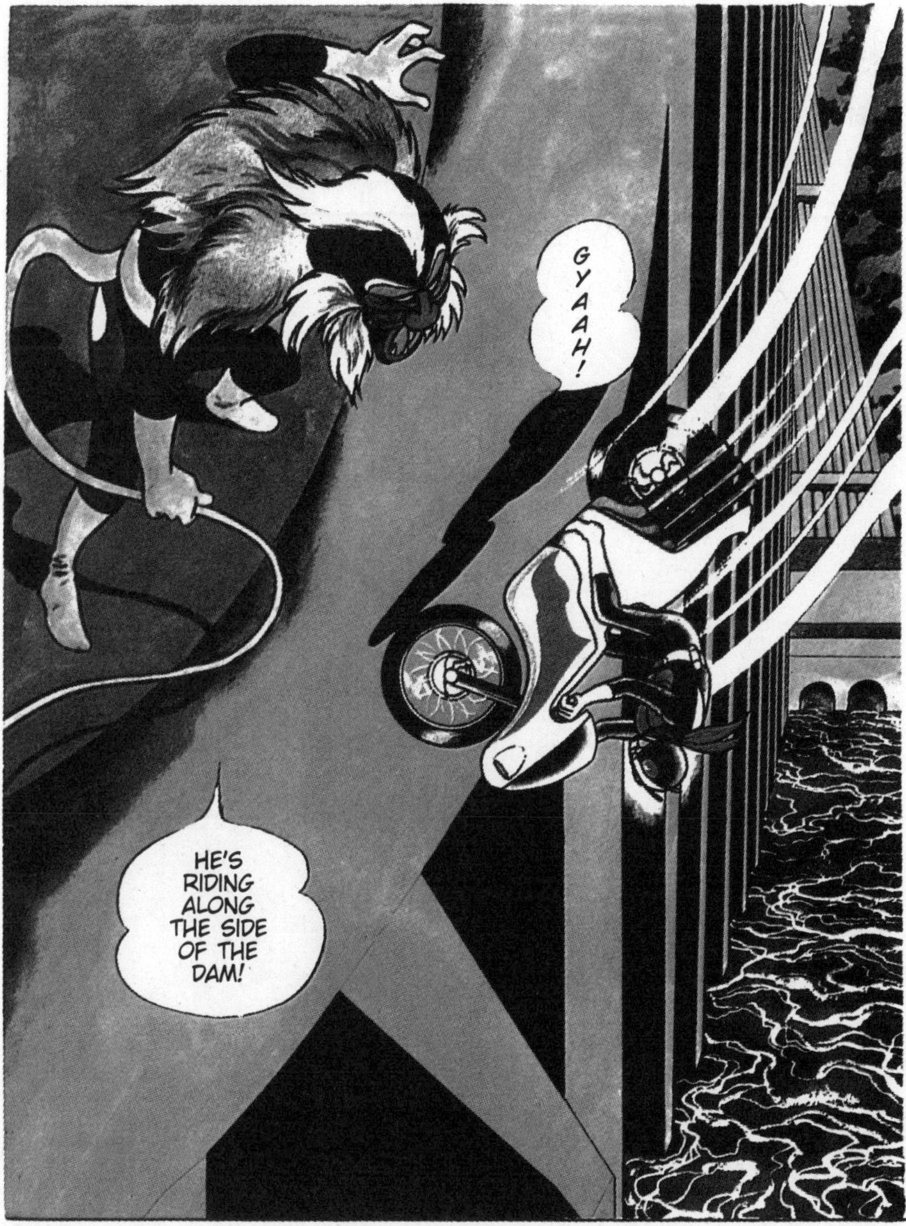
GYAAH!
HE'S RIDING ALONG THE SIDE OF THE DAM!

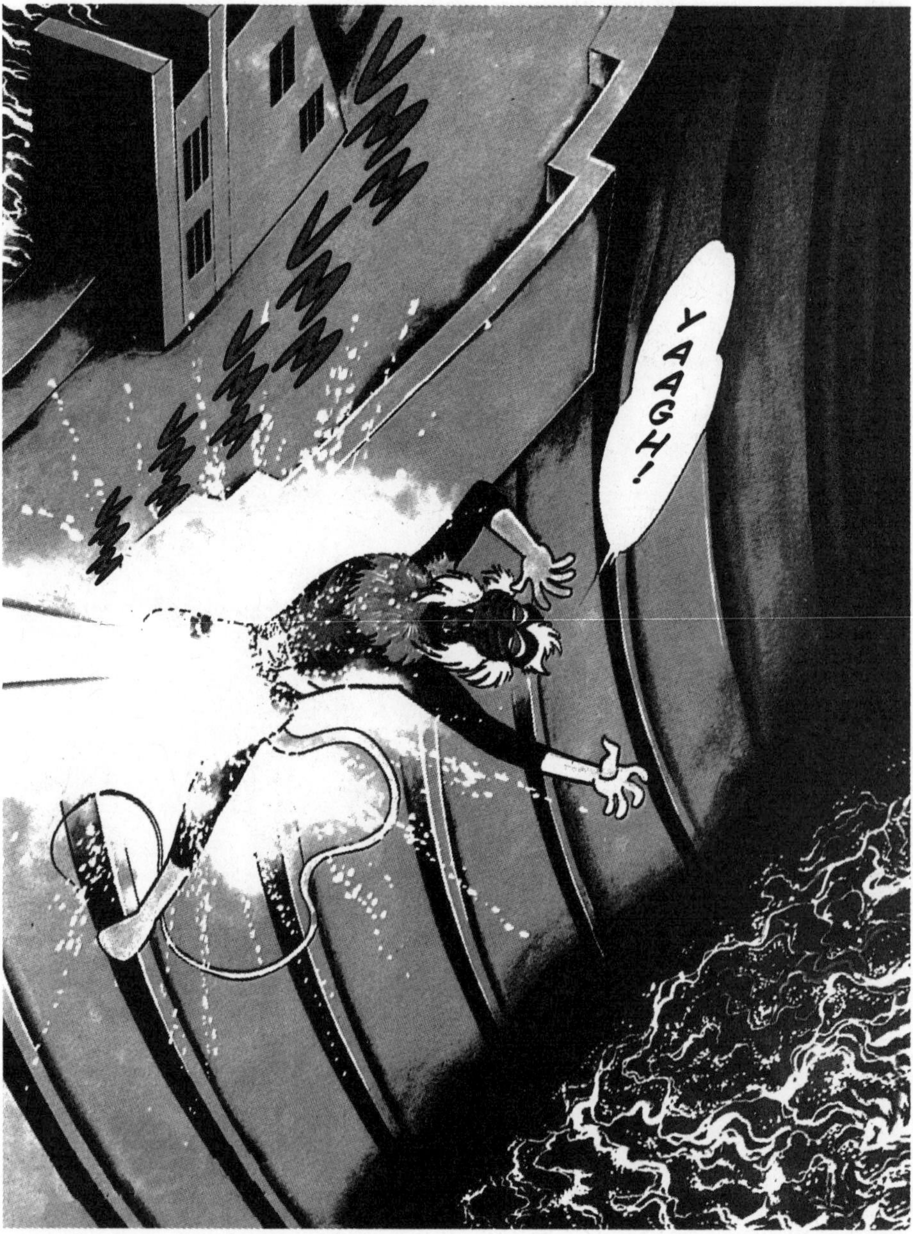
YAAGH!

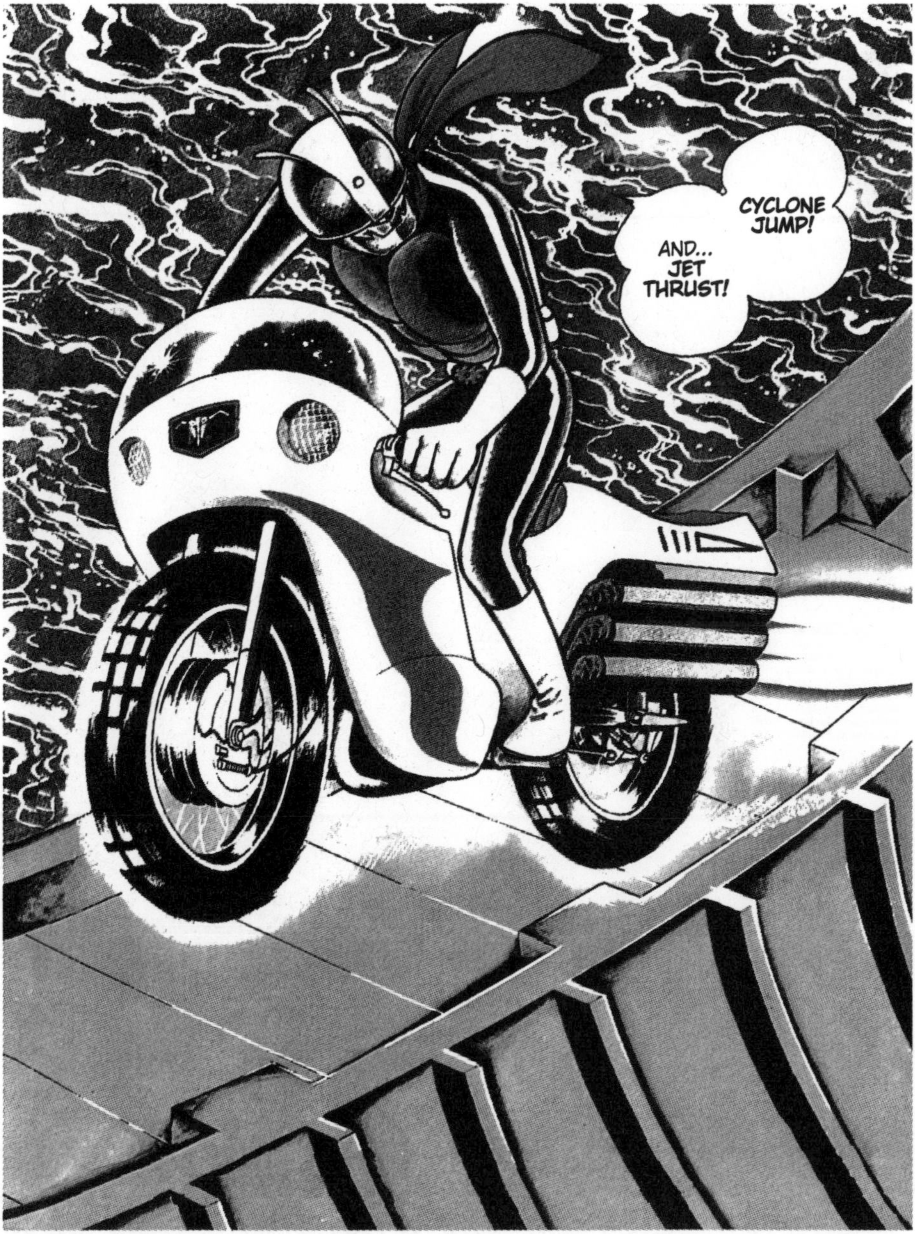
CYCLONE JUMP!
AND... JET THRUST!

KAMEN
RIDER

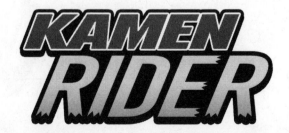

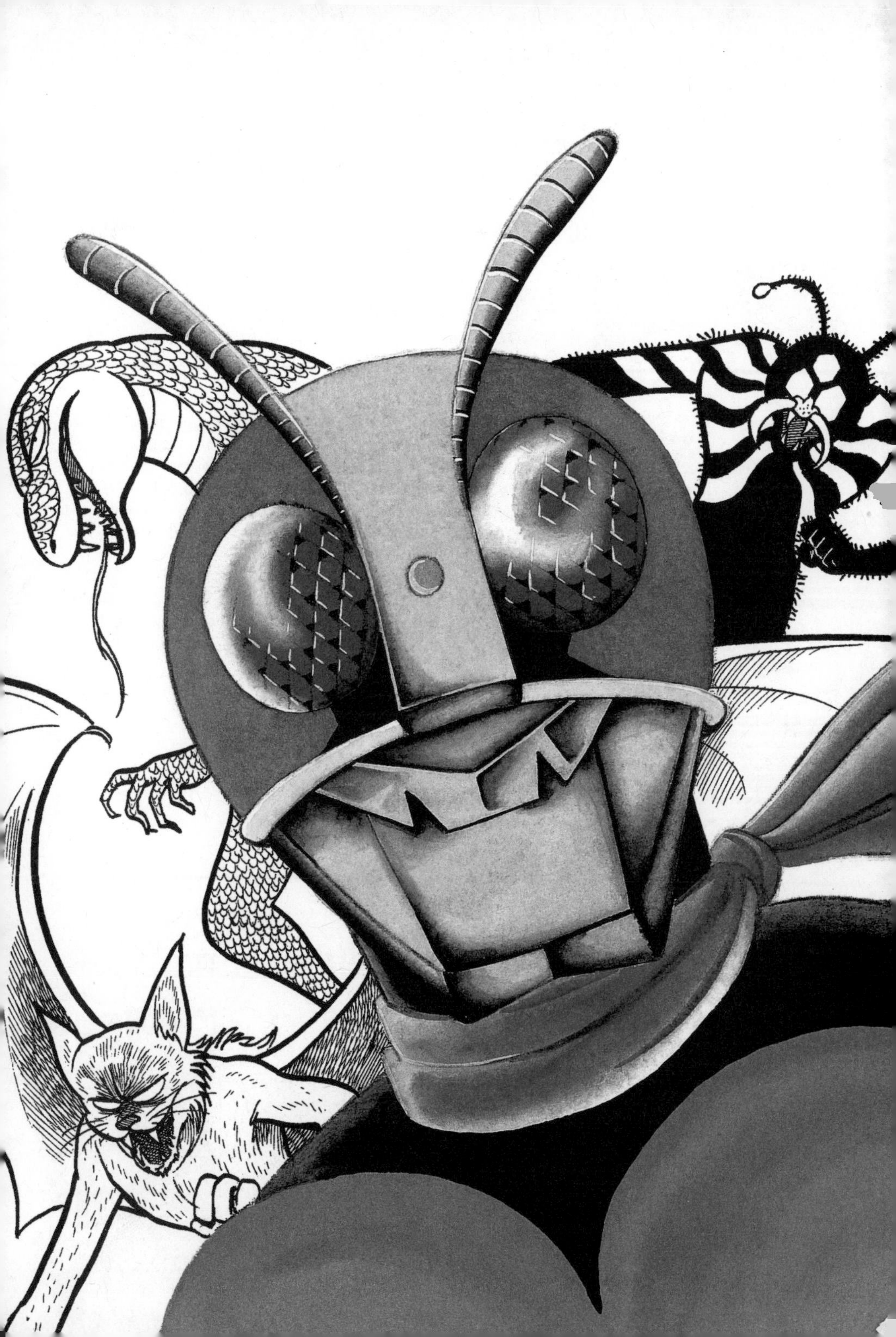

SEVEN SEAS ENTERTAINMENT PRESENTS

KAMEN RIDER

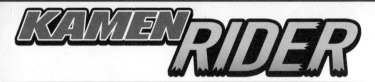

THE CLASSIC MANGA BY SHOTARO ISHI*NO*MORI

TRANSLATION
Kumar Sivasubramanian

LETTERING
Phil Christie

COVER DESIGN
Nicky Lim

LOGO DESIGN
George Panella

PROOFREADER
Brett Hallahan

COPY EDITOR
Dawn Davis

EDITOR
J.P. Sullivan

PRINT MANAGER
Rhiannon Rasmussen-Silverstein

PRODUCTION ASSOCIATE
Sandy Grayson

PRODUCTION MANAGER
Lissa Pattillo

MANAGING EDITOR
Julie Davis

ASSOCIATE PUBLISHER
Adam Arnold

PUBLISHER
Jason DeAngelis

Seven Seas press and purchase enquiries can be sent to Marketing Manager Lianne Sentar at press@gomanga.com. Information regarding the distribution and purchase of digital editions is available from Digital Manager CK Russell at digital@gomanga.com.

ISBN: 978-1-64505-942-4
Printed in Canada
First Printing: December 2021
10 9 8 7 6 5 4 3 2 1

READING DIRECTIONS

This book reads from *right to left*, Japanese style. If this is your first time reading manga, you start reading from the top right panel on each page and take it from there. If you get lost, just follow the numbered diagram here. It may seem backwards at first, but you'll get the hang of it! Have fun!!

1
2
3
4
5
6
7
8
9

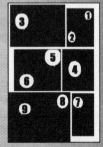

Follow us online: www.SevenSeasEntertainment.com